OLD ENGLISH GLOSSED PSALTERS PSALMS 1–50

Edited by Phillip Pulsiano

This book is the first volume of a complete edition of forty psalters written or owned in Anglo-Saxon England, half of which are glossed in Old English. An invaluable tool for comparative gloss scholarship, the study of the influence of vocabulary, the interpretation of glosses, the study of relations among psalters, and the study of the Latin text of the psalms in Anglo-Saxon England, the work also presents new insights on the development of centres of learning and the impact of the psalter on literary tradition. This volume addresses the first fifty psalms.

This landmark in Old English studies is the first attempt at a comprehensive edition. As an original and much-needed contribution to early medieval scholarship, it not only provides a standard edition of texts based on all known Anglo-Saxon psalters but also synthesizes many studies of psalter scholarship from the earliest times.

†PHILLIP PULSIANO was Professor of English at Villanova University and Executive Director of the International Society of Anglo-Saxonists.

til Kirsten og Anne

old english glossed psalters psalms 1–50

edited by
†PHILLIP PULSIANO

published in association with
The Centre for Medieval Studies,
University of Toronto,
by University of Toronto Press
Toronto Buffalo London

Toronto Buffalo London
Printed in Canada

ISBN 0-8020-4470-0

Printed on acid-free paper

Canadian Cataloguing in Publication Data

Main entry under title:
Old English glossed psalters pss 1–50

(Toronto Old English series ; 11)
ISBN 0-8020-4470-0 (v. 1)

1. Bible. O.T. Psalms. Latin. 2. English language – Old English, ca 450–1100. 3. Latin language, Medieval and modern – Glossaries, vocabularies, etc. 4. Manuscripts, Latin (Medieval and modern) – England. 5. Psalters – England – Texts. I. Pulsiano, Phillip, 1955–2000. II. Series.

BX2033.A2 2001 264'.028 C00-930742-7

University of Toronto Press acknowledges the financial assistance to its publishing program of the Canada Council and the Ontario Arts Council.

University of Toronto Press acknowledges the financial support for its publishing activities of the Government of Canada through the Book Publishing Industry Development Program (BPIDP).

contents

toronto old english series

1 *Computers and Old English Concordances* edited by Angus Cameron, Roberta Frank, and John Leyerle
2 *A Plan for the Dictionary of Old English* edited by Roberta Frank and Angus Cameron
3 *The Stowe Psalter* edited by Andrew C. Kimmens
4 *The Two Versions of Wærferth's Translation of Gregory's Dialogues: An Old English Thesaurus* David Yerkes
5 *Vercelli Homilies IX–XXIII* edited by Paul E. Szarmach
6 *The Dating of Beowulf* edited by Colin Chase
7 *Eleven Old English Rogationtide Homilies* edited by Joyce Bazire and James E. Cross
8 *Old English Word Studies: A Preliminary Author and Word Index* Angus Cameron, Allison Kingsmill, and Ashley Crandell Amos
9 *The Old English Life of Machutus* edited by David Yerkes
10 *Words and Works: Studies in Medieval English Language and Literature in Honour of Fred C. Robinson* edited by Peter S. Baker and Nicholas Howe
11 *Old English Glossed Psalters: Psalms 1–50* edited by Phillip Pulsiano

general editor's preface

Some forty psalters and fragments of psalters survive from Anglo-Saxon England. Of these, eleven contain continual interlinear glossing in Old English, one is partially glossed, two contain scattered glosses, two are binding strips from the same manuscript, and one contains King Alfred's prose translation of psalms 1–50 and a poetic translation of psalms 51–100. The present volume provides the first detailed collation of the Latin text and Old English glosses to the first fifty psalms. Its editor, Phillip Pulsiano, died of cancer on 23 August 2000, two weeks before his forty-fifth birthday, and before he could himself complete work on the remaining three volumes (see Acknowledgments below).

Psalter glosses provide a complicated map to the relations among the manuscripts, and serve as potential guides to their origin and provenance, to the links between centres, and to liturgical customs. They also provide important data for the lexicographer. Some glossed psalters would have been used and annotated for private reading; some would have served as textbooks in monastic and cathedral schools, as a way of teaching Latin and the liturgical texts that were to be learned by heart. The Old Testament *Book of Psalms,* usually called *Tehillim,* 'Praises,' in Hebrew, traditionally followed a fivefold or 'biblical' division; subsequent divisions include the eightfold or 'liturgical' system, a tenfold system, and the threefold or 'three fifties' division. The last was used by Augustine (whose commentary on the psalms was published as three hefty manuscript books) and by the present study.

Phillip Pulsiano's plans and rationale for this edition were announced in 1986 at an international conference on Anglo-Saxon glossography, just four years after he completed his doctoral dissertation on the *Blickling Psalter*. His ongoing investigations into the psalter manuscripts were summarized in his introductions and descriptions in two volumes of the *Anglo-Saxon Manuscripts in Microfiche Facsimile* project (II, IV), in his entry 'Psalter Glosses' in *The Blackwell Encyclopaedia of Anglo-Saxon England,* and in his chapter on 'Psalters' in *The Liturgical Books of Anglo-Saxon England.* Major articles by him on the individual psalters have appeared in *Anglo-Saxon England, Neuphilologische Mitteilungen, American Notes and Queries, Manuscripta, English Studies,* and *Traditio,* and in several essay collections.

Professor Pulsiano's scholarship reached beyond the psalters and Anglo-Saxon England—notably into Old Norse studies, Medieval Latin, hagiography, and bibliography, areas in which he was extraordinarily productive. The international community knew him as a generous and dedicated worker and colleague. He served, among other capacities, as the chair of his department at Villanova University, as series editor for *Studies in Anglo-Saxon Manuscripts and Culture,* as the Executive Director of the International Society of Anglo-Saxonists, and as compiler of the annual 'Research in Progress' report for the *Old English Newsletter.*

A valued friend to Anglo-Saxonists around the world, Phill is and will be much missed. The dominant note of the fifty psalms in this volume is that of suffering and pain, the agony and heroic struggle against injustice and death. But in the last ten, although suffering is still present, the darkness seems pierced by light, and a more unbreakable joy is foreseen.

As General Editor of the Toronto Old English Series, I here express my gratitude to Professor Joseph McGowan of the University of San Diego for his careful reading of the proofs. Thanks are (as ever) owed to Anna Burko of the Centre for Medieval Studies, Toronto, who copy-edited and formatted the complex text; her painstaking craftsmanship and linguistic expertise are visible on every page. I thank, too, the Editorial Board of this series and the University of Toronto Press for their continuing support.

Phill's dedication of this book to his wife Kirsten Wolf and their daughter Anne reflects another kind of debt, that of love.

R.F.
January 2001

acknowledgments

This project was first announced in 1986 at the International Conference on Glossography hosted by René Derolez at the Koninklijke Academie voor Wetenschappen, Letteren en Schone Kunsten van België in Brussels, and stems from a need for an accurate, collective edition of the Old English glossed psalters, accompanied by variants from all psalters known to have been written or owned in Anglo-Saxon England. The present volume stands as the first of three, each treating a set of fifty psalms. The introduction offered here merely guides the reader through the manuscripts and the use of the volume and its apparatus. A full critical introduction will comprise a fourth volume, which will also include an edition of the Latin commentary in the pre-Conquest glossed manuscripts.

I owe a debt of gratitude to the numerous libraries that have allowed me access to the manuscripts over the years, particularly the British Library, which holds the bulk of the manuscripts, and also Cambridge University Library, the Bodleian Library, Lambeth Palace Library, Salisbury Cathedral Library, Trinity College Library, Cambridge, The Pierpont Morgan Library, and the Bibliothèque Nationale, Paris. I would like to thank Timothy Graham for checking certain readings for me in the *Cambridge Psalter*. I would also like to thank both Herbert Pilch and Helmut Gneuss for making available to me proofs of their articles on the recently-discovered Sondershäuser Psalter fragment, and Christa Hirschler, Second Director of the Schloßmuseum, Sondershausen, for providing excellent colour photographs of the leaf. Anna Burko deserves more credit for the shape of the introduction and text than words can adequately express; her attention to detail in the copy-editing of the text, her professionalism, and her kindness throughout this project have made rewarding what could easily have become a contentious and dreary task. Finally, I am deeply grateful to Kirsten Wolf for reading the introduction to the edition and for her steadfast encouragement throughout this project.

P.P.
March 2000

abbreviations

ANQ	*American Notes and Queries*
ASE	*Anglo-Saxon England*
Bib. sac.	*Biblia sacra (see p. xx and n. 12)*
BL	British Library
BN	Bibliothèque Nationale
c.	century
ca	circa
cf.	compare
corr.	corrector, correction, corrected
diff.	different
ed(s)	editor(s), edition, edited (by)
eras.	erasure, erased
EETS	Early English Text Society
fol(s)	folio(s)
Ga.	Gallican
HBS	Henry Bradshaw Society
Hebr.	'Hebraic' (*see p. xx and n. 11*)
Hs.	Handschrift
interl.	interlinear, interlinearly
MS(S)	manuscript(s)
n(n)	note(s)
no(s)	number(s)
NQ	*Notes and Queries*
n.s.	new series
OE	Old English
om.	omission, omitted
orig.	original, originally
o.s.	original series
p(p)	page(s)
pl(s)	plate(s)
pt(s)	part(s)
punct.	punctuation
r	recto
repr.	reprint, reprinted
Ro.	Roman
s.v.	under the word
trans.	translator, translation, translated (by)
v	verso
vol(s)	volume(s)
vv	verses

bibliography

* Where multiple works by the same author or editor (or by authors/editors of the same name) are listed, an asterisk is used to identify the psalter edition or study cited (by author's or editor's name only) in the various note sections of the text.

Alexander, J.J.G. 1978. *A Survey of Manuscripts Illuminated in the British Isles,* vol. I: *Insular Manuscripts 6th to the 9th Century* (London)

Baker, Peter S. 1984. 'A Little-Known Variant Text of the Old English Metrical Psalms,' *Speculum* 59: 263–81

Barré, Henri. 1963. *Prières anciennes de l'occident à la mère du sauveur des origines à saint Anselme* (Paris)

Berghaus, Frank-Günter. 1979. *Die Verwandtschaftsverhältnisse der altenglischen Interlinearversionen des Psalters und der Cantica,* Palaestra 272 (Göttingen)

Biblia sacra. 1953. *Biblia sacra iuxta Latinam vulgatam versionem ad codicum fidem ... Liber psalmorum ex recensione Sancti Hieronymi cum praefationibus et epistula ad Sunniam et Fretelam* (Rome) [cited as *Bib. sac.*]

Brenner, Eduard, ed. 1908. *Der altenglische Junius-Psalter: Die Interlinear-Glosse der Handschrift Junius 27 der Bodleiana zu Oxford,* Anglistische Forschungen 23 (Heidelberg, repr. Amsterdam 1973)

Brock, E., ed. 1876. 'The Blickling Glosses' in *The Blickling Homilies,* ed. Richard Morris, vol. II, EETS o.s. 63 (London, repr. Millwood 1967): 251–63

*Campbell, A.P., ed. 1974. *The Tiberius Psalter, Edited from British Museum MS. Cotton Tiberius C vi,* Ottawa Mediaeval Texts and Studies 2 (Ottawa)

Campbell, Jackson J. 1963. 'Prayers from MS. Arundel 155,' *Anglia* 81: 82–117

Cockayne, Thomas Oswald, ed. and trans. 1864–6. *Leechdoms, Wortcunning, and Starcraft of Early England ...,* 3 vols, Rolls Series 35 (London; repr. London 1961, Wiesbaden 1965)

Colgrave, Bertram et al., eds. 1958. *The Paris Psalter, MS. Bibliothèque Nationale fonds latin 8824,* Early English Manuscripts in Facsimile 8 (Copenhagen)

Collins, Rowland L. 1963. 'A Reexamination of the Old English Glosses in the Blickling Psalter,' *Anglia* 81: 124–8

Cook, Albert S., ed. 1898. *Biblical Quotations in Old English Prose Writers, Edited with the Vulgate and Other Latin Originals, Introduction on Old English Biblical Versions, Index of Biblical Passages, and Index of Principal Words* (London and New York; repr. Folcroft 1971)

Crick, Julia. 1997. 'The Case for a West Saxon Minuscule,' *ASE* 26: 63–79

*Davey, William J. 1979. 'An Edition of the Regius Psalter and its Latin Commentary' (PhD diss. University of Ottawa)

———. 1987. 'The Commentary of the Regius Psalter: Its Main Source and Influence on the Old English Gloss,' *Mediaeval Studies* 49: 335–51

Derolez, Rene. 1972. 'A New Psalter Fragment with OE Glosses,' *English Studies* 53: 401–8

Deshman, Robert. 1997. 'The Galba Psalter: Pictures, Texts, and Contexts in an Early Medieval Prayerbook,' *ASE* 26: 109–38

Dewick, E[dward] S[amuel], ed. 1902. *Facsimiles of Horae de beata Maria virgine from English MSS of the Eleventh Century,* HBS 21 (London)

———. 1914. *The Leofric Collectar (Harl. MS. 2961) with an Appendix Containing a Litany and Prayers from Harl. MS. 863,* vol. I, HBS 45 (London)

Dietz, Klaus. 1968. 'Die ae. Psalterglossen der Hs. Cambridge, Pembroke College 312,' *Anglia* 86: 273–9

Dobbie, Elliott van Kirk, ed. 1942. *The Anglo-Saxon Minor Poems,* Anglo-Saxon Poetic Records 6 (New York and London)

Dodwell, C.R. 1990. 'The Final Copy of the Utrecht Psalter and its Relationship with the Utrecht and Eadwine Psalters (Paris, BN Lat. 8846, ca 1170–1190),' *Scriptorium* 44: 21–53 + pls

Dumville, D[avid] N. 1991. 'On the Dating of Some Late Anglo-Saxon Liturgical Manuscripts,' *Transactions of the Cambridge Bibliographical Society* 10: 40–57

———. 1992. *Liturgy and the Ecclesiastical History of Late Anglo-Saxon England: Four Studies,* Studies in Anglo-Saxon History (Woodbridge and Rochester)

Förster, Max. 1905. 'Ein altenglisches Prosa-Rätsel,' *Archiv* 115: 392–3

———. 1906. 'Die Lösung des ae. Prosarätsels,' *Archiv* 116: 367–71

———. 1912. 'Beiträge zur mittelalterlichen Volkskunde VIII,' *Archiv* 129: 16–49

———. 1914. 'Die altenglischen Beigaben des Lambeth-Psalters,' *Archiv* 132: 328–35

———. 1916. 'Nochmals ae. *fregen* "Frage",' *Archiv* 135: 399–401

———. 1925. 'Die Weltzeitalter bei den Angelsachsen' in *Neusprachliche Studien: Festgabe Karl Luick zu seinem sechzigsten Geburtstage, dargebracht von Freunden und Schülern* (Marburg): 183–203, at 192–3

———. 1929. 'Die altenglischen Verzeichnisse von Glücks- und Unglückstagen' in *Studies in English Philology: A Miscellany in Honor of Frederick Klaeber,* ed. Kemp Malone and Martin B. Ruud (Minneapolis): 258–77

Gibson, Margaret, T.A. Heslop, and Richard W. Pfaff, eds. 1992. *The Eadwine Psalter: Text, Image, and Monastic Culture in Twelfth-Century Canterbury,* Publications of the Modern Humanities Research Association 14 (London and University Park, Pennsylvania)

Gjerløw, Lilli. 1961. *Adoratio crucis: The Regularis concordia and the Decreta Lanfranci. Manuscript Studies in the Early Medieval Church of Norway* (Oslo)

Gneuss, Helmut. 1955. *Lehnbildungen und Lehnbedeutungen im Altenglischen* (Berlin)

———. 1981. 'A Preliminary List of Manuscripts Written or Owned in England up to 1100,' *ASE* 9: 1–60

———. 1998. 'A Newly-Found Fragment of an Anglo-Saxon Psalter,' *ASE* 27: 273–87

Hallander, Lars-G., ed. 1968. 'Two Old English Confessional Prayers,' *Stockholm Studies in Modern Philology* n.s. 3: 87–110

Hampson, R[obert] T[homas], ed. 1841. *Medii aevi Kalendarium, or Dates, Charters, and Customs of the Middle Ages ...* 2 vols (London, repr. New York 1978)

Hardwick, Charles, ed. 1858. *Historia monasterii S. Augustini Cantuariensis, by Thomas of Elham,* Rolls Series 8 (London)

Hargreaves, Henry, and Cecily Clark. 1965. 'An Unpublished Old English Psalter-Gloss Fragment,' *NQ* 210: 443–6

Harsley, Fred, ed. 1889. *Eadwine's Canterbury Psalter,* EETS o.s. 92 (London)

Heimann, Adelheid. 1975. 'The Last Copy of the Utrecht Psalter' in *The Year 1200: A Symposium* (New York): 313–38

Henel, Heinrich. 1934. *Studien zum altenglischen Computus,* Beiträge zur englischen Philologie 26 (Leipzig; repr. New York and London 1967)

———. 1934–5. 'Altenglischer Mönchsaberglaube,' *Englische Studien* 69: 329–49

Holthausen, F[erdinand]. 1899. 'Zu Sweet's *Oldest English Texts,*' *Anglia* 21: 231–44

———. 1941. 'Altenglische Interlinearversionen lateinischer Gebete und Beichten,' *Anglia* 65: 230–54

———. 1942–3. 'Eine altenglische Interlinearversion des athanasianischen Glaubensbekenntnisses,' *Englische Studien* 75: 6–8

Hughes, Dom Anselm, ed. 1958–60. *The Portiforium of Saint Wulfstan (Corpus Christi College, Cambridge, MS. 391),* 2 vols, HBS 89–90 (London)

James, M[ontague] R[hodes], ed. 1935. *The Canterbury Psalter* (London)

Ker, N[eil] R. 1957. *Catalogue of Manuscripts Containing Anglo-Saxon* (Oxford, repr. with supplement 1990)

Kimmens, Andrew C., ed. 1979. *The Stowe Psalter,* Toronto Old English Series 3 (Toronto)

Korhammer, P.M. 1973. 'The Origin of the Bosworth Psalter,' *ASE* 2: 173–87

Krapp, George P., ed. 1932. *The Paris Psalter and the Meters of Boethius,* Anglo-Saxon Poetic Records 5 (New York and London)

Kuhn, Sherman M., ed. 1965. *The Vespasian Psalter* (Ann Arbor)

Lapidge, Michael, ed. 1991. *Anglo-Saxon Litanies of the Saints,* HBS 106 (London)

———. 1992. 'Abbot Germanus, Winchcombe, Ramsey, and the Cambridge Psalter' in *Words, Texts, and Manuscripts: Studies in Anglo-Saxon Culture Presented to Helmut Gneuss on the Occasion of his Sixty-Fifth Birthday,* ed. Michael Korhammer (Cambridge): 99–129

Lindelöf, Uno. 1901. 'Die Handschrift Junius 27 der Bibliotheca Bodleiana,' *Mémoires de la Société néo-philologique à Helsingfors* 3: 3–73

———. 1904. *Studien zu altenglischen Psalterglossen,* Bonner Beiträge zur Anglistik 13 (Bonn)

*———, ed. 1909a. *Der Lambeth-Psalter: Eine altenglische Interlinearversion des Psalters in der Hs. 427 der erzbischöflichen Lambeth Palace Library,* vol. I: *Text und Glossar,* Acta Societatis scientiarum Fennicae 35.1 (Helsingfors)

*———. 1909b. 'Die altenglischen Glossen im Bosworth-Psalter (Brit. Mus. MS. Addit. 37517)' *Mémoires de la Société néo-philologique de Helsingfors* 5: 139–231 [cited as Lindelöf[2]]

———, ed. 1914. *Der Lambeth-Psalter,* vol. II: *Beschreibung und Geschichte der Handschriftverhältnis der Glosse zu anderen Psalterversionen ...,* Acta Societatis scientiarum Fennicae 43.3 (Helsingfors)

L'Isle, William, ed. 1630. *The Saxon-English psalter ... Out of Manuscripts most auntient remaining styll in the university library, & that of trinitye and Corpus Christi colledge in cambridge ...*

Logeman, H. 1889a. 'Anglo-Saxonica minora,' *Anglia* 11: 97–120

———. 1889b. 'Anglo-Saxonica minora,' *Anglia* 12: 497–518

Makothakat, John M. 1972. 'The Bosworth Psalter: A Critical Edition' (PhD diss. University of Ottawa)

Merritt, Herbert D. 1966. Review of *The Vespasian Psalter* ed. Sherman M. Kuhn, *Speculum* 41: 750–3

Morrell, Minnie Cate. 1965. *A Manual of Old English Biblical Materials* (Knoxville)

Napier, Arthur S., ed. 1883. *Wulfstan: Sammlung der ihm zugeschriebenen Homilien nebst Untersuchungen über ihre Echtheit,* Sammlung englischer Denkmäler 4 (Berlin)

New Palaeographical Society. 1912. *Facsimiles of Ancient Manuscripts, etc.,* series 1 (London)

Niver, Charles. 1939. 'The Psalter in the British Museum, Harley 2904' in

Medieval Studies in Memory of A. Kingsley Porter, ed. Wilhelm R.W. Koehler, 2 vols (Cambridge; repr. Freeport 1969): II, 667–87

Noel, William. 1995. *The Harley Psalter,* Cambridge Studies in Palaeography and Codicology 4 (Cambridge)

Nordenfalk, Carl. 1957. 'Book Illumination,' pt II of *Early Medieval Painting from the Fourth to the Eleventh Century,* trans. Stuart Gilbert, The Great Centuries of Painting (New York)

Ó Cróinín, Dáibhi. 1995. 'The Salaberga Psalter' in *From the Isles of the North: Early Medieval Art in Ireland and Britain. Proceedings of the Third International Conference on Insular Art Held in the Ulster Museum, Belfast, 7–11 April 1994,* ed. Cormac Bourke (Belfast): 127–35

Oess, Guido. 1908. *Untersuchungen zum altenglischen Arundel-Psalter,* Inaugural-Dissertation … der Ruprecht-Karls-Universität zu Heidelberg (Heidelberg)

*———, ed. 1910. *Der altenglische Arundel-Psalter: Eine Interlinearversion in der Handschrift Arundel 60 des Britischen Museums,* Anglistische Forschungen 30 (Heidelberg; repr. Amsterdam 1968)

O'Neill, Patrick P. 1986. 'A Lost Old-English Charter Rubric: The Evidence from the Regius Psalter,' *NQ* 231: 292–4

———. 1988. 'Another Fragment of the Metrical Psalms in the Eadwine Psalter,' *NQ* 233: 434–6

———. 1991. 'Latin Learning at Winchester in the Early Eleventh Century: The Evidence of the Lambeth Psalter,' *ASE* 20: 143–66

———. 1992. 'Syntactical Glosses in the Lambeth Psalter and the Reading of the Old English Interlinear Translation as Sentences,' *Scriptorium* 46: 250–6

*———. 1993. 'Further Old English Glosses and Corrections in the Lambeth Psalter,' *Anglia* 111: 82–93

Openshaw, Kathleen M.J. 1989. 'The Battle between Christ and Satan in the Tiberius Psalter,' *Journal of the Warburg and Courtauld Institutes* 52: 14–33 + pls

———. 1990. 'Images, Texts, and Contexts: The Iconography of the Tiberius Psalter, London, British Library, Cotton MS. Tiberius C. vi' (PhD diss. University of Toronto)

Orchard, Nicholas. 1995. 'The Bosworth Psalter and the St Augustine's Missal' in *Canterbury and the Norman Conquest: Churches, Saints, and Scholars 1066–1109,* ed. Richard Eales and Richard Sharpe (London and Rio Grande): 87–94

Pilch, Herbert. 1977. 'The Sondershäuser Psalter: A Newly Discovered Old English Interlinear Gloss' in *Germanic Studies in Honor of Anatoly Liberman,* ed. Martha Berryman et al., Nowele 31/32 (Odense): 313–23

Pulsiano, Phillip. 1982. 'Materials for an Edition of the Blickling Psalter' (PhD diss. State University of New York at Stony Brook)
———. 1983. 'A New Look at the Anglo-Saxon Glosses in the Blickling Psalter,' *Manuscripta* 27: 32–7
———. 1984. 'The Blickling Psalter: *aqua uel is,*' *NQ* n.s. 31.3: 553–4
———. 1985. 'The Latin and Old English Glosses in the "Blickling" and "Regius" Psalters,' *Traditio* 41: 79–115
———. 1989a. 'The Blickling Psalter: *gladii : sweord,*' *ANQ* n.s. 2.2: 43
———. 1989b. 'The Scribes and Old English Gloss of the *Eadwine's Canterbury Psalter,*' *Proceedings of the PMR Conference* 14: 223–60
———. 1993. 'New Old English Glosses in the Vitellius Psalter,' *ANQ* n.s. 6.4: 180–2
———. 1994a. *Anglo-Saxon Manuscripts in Microfiche Facsimile,* vol. II: *Psalters 1,* Medieval and Renaissance Texts and Studies 137 (Binghamton)
———. 1994b. 'New Old English Glosses in the Vitellius Psalter (II),' *ANQ* n.s. 7.1: 3–5
———. 1996. 'The Originality of the Old English Gloss of the Vespasian Psalter and its Relation to the Gloss of the Junius Psalter,' *ASE* 25: 37–62
———. 1998. 'The Prefatory Matter of the London, British Library, Cotton Vitellius E. xviii,' in *Anglo-Saxon Manuscripts and their Heritage,* ed. Pulsiano and Elaine M. Treharne (Aldershot): 85–118
———. Forthcoming. 'The Old English Gloss of the Eadwine Psalter' in *Into the Twelfth Century* ed. Mary Swan and Elaine M. Treharne (Cambridge)
Pulsiano, Phillip, and Joseph McGowan. 1994. 'Four Unedited Prayers in London, British Library, Cotton Tiberius A. iii,' *Mediaeval Studies* 56: 189–216
Roeder, Fritz, ed. 1904. *Der altenglische Regius-Psalter: Eine Interlinear-version in Hs. Royal 2. B. 5 des Brit. Mus.,* Studien zur englischen Philologie 18 (Halle)
Rosier, James L., ed. 1962. *The Vitellius Psalter, Edited from British Museum MS. Cotton Vitellius E. xviii,* Cornell Studies in English 42 (Ithaca)
Sainte-Marie, Dom Henri de, ed. 1954. *Sancti Hieronymi Psalterium ivxta Hebraeos,* Collectanea biblica Latina 11 (Rome and Vatican City)
Saunders, O. Elfrida. 1928. *English Illumination,* 2 vols (Florence)
Schlutter, Otto B. 1897. 'Zu Sweet's *Oldest English Texts,* II,' *Anglia* 19: 461–98
* Sisam, Celia, and Kenneth Sisam, eds. 1959. *The Salisbury Psalter, Edited from Salisbury Cathedral MS. 150,* EETS o.s. 242 (London; repr. 1969)
* Sisam, Celia.1964. Review of *The Vitellius Psalter* ed. James L. Rosier, *Review of English Studies* 15: 59–61 [cited as Sisam[2]]

Soeda, Afuri. 1997. 'The Blickling Psalter (The Pierpont Morgan Library, M. 776)' (PhD diss. Brown University)
Spelman, John, ed. 1640. *Psalterium Davidis Latino-Saxonicum vetus* (London)
Stevenson, J., ed. 1843. *Anglo-Saxon and Early English Psalter: Now First Printed from Manuscripts in the British Museum,* Surtees Society (London and Edinburgh)
Storms, G. 1948. *Anglo-Saxon Magic* (The Hague; repr. Folcroft 1975)
Sweet, Henry, ed. 1885. *The Oldest English Texts,* EETS o.s. 83 (London; repr. 1966)
Thorpe, Benjamin, ed. 1835. *Libri psalmorum versio antiqua Latina; cum paraphrasi Anglo-Saxonica ...* (Oxford)
Toswell, M.J. 1994. 'A Further Old English Gloss in Paris, Bibliothèque Nationale MS. lat. 8846,' *NQ* 239: 10–11
Turner, D.H., ed. 1962. *The Missal of the New Minster,* HBS 93 (London)
Vulgate: see *Biblia sacra*
Walters Art Gallery (Baltimore, Maryland). 1949. *Illuminated Books of the Middle Ages and Renaissance: An Exhibition Held at the Baltimore Museum of Art, January 27–March 13* (Baltimore)
Warren, F.E. 1885. 'An Anglo-Saxon Missal at Worcester,' *The Academy* 28: 394–5
Webber, Teresa. 1992. Ch. I.2, 'The Script' in *The Eadwine Psalter,* ed. Gibson et al. (see above): 13–24
Weber, Dom Robert, ed. 1953. *Le Psautier romain et les autres anciens psautiers latins,* Collectanea biblica Latina 10 (Rome and Vatican City)
Wieland, Gernot R., ed. 1982. *The Canterbury Hymnal, Edited from British Library MS. Additional 37517,* Toronto Medieval Latin Texts 12 (Toronto)
Wiesenekker, Evert. 1991. *Worde be Worde, Andgit of Andgite: Translation Performance in the Old English Interlinear Glosses of the Vespasian, Regius, and Lambeth Psalters* (Huizen)
*Wildhagen, Karl, ed. 1910. *Der Cambridger Psalter (Hs. Ff. 1. 23 University Libr. Cambridge) zum ersten Male herausgegeben, mit besonderer Berücksichtigung des lateinischen Textes,* vol. I: *Text mit Erklärungen,* Bibliothek der angelsächsichen Prosa 7 (Hamburg, repr. Darmstadt 1964)
———. 1913. 'Studien zum *Psalterium Romanum* in England und zu seinen Glossierungen' in *Festschrift für Lorenz Morsbach,* ed. F. Holthausen and H. Spies (Halle): 418–72
———. 1921. 'Das Kalendarium der Handschrift Vitellius E XVIII' in *Texte und Forschungen zur englischen Kulturgeschichte: Festgabe für Felix Liebermann zum 20. Juli 1921* (Halle): 68–118

Wilmart, A. 1930. 'The Prayers of the Bury Psalter,' *The Downside Review* 48: 118–216

Wormald, Francis, ed. 1934. *English Kalendars before AD 1100,* HBS 72 (London; repr. Woodbridge 1988)

———. 1946. 'The English Saints in the Litany in Arundel MS. 60' *Analecta Bollandiana* 64: 72–86

———. 1984a. 'An English Eleventh-Century Psalter with Pictures: British Library, Cotton MS. Tiberius C. vi' in *Francis Wormald: Collected Writings,* vol. I, *Studies in Medieval Art from the Sixth to the Twelfth Centuries,* ed. J.J.G. Alexander, T.J. Brown, and Joan Gibbs (London): 123–37, 180–1 + pls

———. 1984b. 'The "Winchester School" before St Ethelwold' in *Francis Wormald: Collected Writings:* I, 76–84, 177–8

Wright, David H., ed. 1967. *The Vespasian Psalter: British Museum Cotton Vespasian A. 1* (with a contribution by Alistair Campbell), Early English Manuscripts in Facsimile 14 (Copenhagen)

Zimmerman, E. Heinrich. 1916. *Vorkarolingische Miniaturen* (Berlin)

introduction

MANUSCRIPTS[1]

The sigla for the glossed psalters were first set forth in 1898 by Albert S. Cook, who discussed A–K and Paris, Bibliothèque Nationale, lat. 8824.[2] Uno Lindelöf designated London, British Library, Additional 37517 (the Bosworth Psalter) as L.[3] Helmut Gneuss called New York, Pierpont Morgan Library, M. 776 (the Blickling Psalter) the 'Lincoln Psalter,' and designated it as N (following the practice of Dom Robert Weber);[4] Karl Wildhagen had earlier called this psalter D^1.[5] Minnie Cate Morrell assigned it the siglum M, which is now accepted as standard.[6] Helmut Gneuss has designated Sondershausen, Schloßmuseum, Handschrift Br. 1 as N^s;[7] René Derolez has given the siglum N to both Cambridge, Pembroke College, 312, C. nos 1–2 and the Haarlem Stadsbibliotheek fragment. Although all three fragments (Sondershausen, Cambridge, and Haarlem) derive from the same manuscript, they are designated below as N^a, N^b, and N^c.[8]

In the case of E (the tripartite Eadwine Psalter), the siglum refers to the Roman version, which contains the Old English gloss. The Gallican version of E is designated ι in the second list of manuscripts. The treatment of O (Paris, BN, lat. 8846, a tripartite psalter copied from E) is more complex. As the Old English glosses number 26 words (glossing 22 lemmata of the Roman version), it seemed unnecessarily cumbersome to assign the siglum O to the entire text and thus record the variants, alterations, and erasures for the whole of the psalter in the apparatus to the glossed texts. The following system is thus adopted: the siglum O is used for only those sections in which the Old English gloss is found, τ* is used to designate the unglossed portions of the Latin text of the Roman version, and τ is used for the (unglossed) Latin text of the Gallican version.[9] For the Paris Psalter (Paris, BN, lat. 8824), see note 2 below.

1 See Bibliography for details on works referred to by author/editor only or by author/editor plus date of publication.

2 Cook: xxviii–xxx and xxiv ff. Anglo-Saxonists traditionally assign the siglum P to Paris, BN, lat. 8824. Since the MS contains not an interlinear gloss, but a prose translation of Pss 1–50 and a metrical translation of Pss 51–150, its OE text is excluded from this study, though variants from the Latin text (which is not the source for the OE translation) are included in the collation. The MS has thus been assigned the siglum ς, and is included in the second list of MSS below.

3 Lindelöf 1909b.

4 Gneuss 1955: 44.

5 Wildhagen 1913.

6 Morrell 1965.

7 Gneuss 1998; see also n. 79 below.

8 The designations N^1 and N^2 are not used, in order to avoid confusion with superscript numbers employed to designate different hands in the various MSS.

9 On the relationship between E and O, see Heimann, who posits an intermediary model linking the psalters. For discussions in favour of direct copying, however, see Dodwell, and Gibson et al. That O used E as a model seems certain.

Where appropriate in the descriptions of manuscripts, shelfmarks are followed by item numbers given in Ker's *Catalogue* and Gneuss's 'Preliminary List.'[10]

Since there exists no text of the 'Hebraic' psalter[11] glossed in Old English, and since this version was never used in the liturgy, the Hebraica contained in Florence, Biblioteca Medicea Laurenziana, Amiatino 1, Salisbury Cathedral 180 (double psalter), Cambridge, Trinity College, R. 17. 1 (987), and Paris, BN, lat. 8846 are omitted from this edition. While the *terminus* for texts included is the 11th century, an exception is made for two works from the 12th century, since they contain glosses in Old English: Cambridge, Trinity College, R. 17. 1 (987) and Paris, BN, lat. 8846. Only texts written or owned in England are included in the edition. Where appropriate, variants from other manuscripts are quoted from Weber's edition of the Roman version of the psalms and the 1953 edition of the Gallican version.[12]

Manuscripts written in England in the pre-Reform period are ABMβ; manuscripts written in the later 10th and 11th centuries are CDFGHIJKLλνξοϱσςυφ; 12th-century psalters containing glosses in Old English are E/ι and O/τ*/τ; psalters brought to England in the 10th and 11th centuries are δζϑμχψ; fragments containing the psalms are $N^{a}N^{b}N^{c}$αγηϰω; manuscripts containing important psalter components are επ. Psalters containing the Roman version are ABCDELMOαβγηλνςτ*; psalters containing the Gallican version are EFGHIJK$N^{a}N^{b}N^{c}$δεζϑιϰμξοπϱτφχψω.

10 Gneuss 1981. His item 150, Cambridge, St John's College, 82 (D. 7), is recorded as 'Psalter; Canticles,' but no psalms exist in this MS (Gneuss corrects the error in his unpublished revised draft of the handlist). The fragments record portions of *Cantemus domino* (vv 1–19) and *Quicumque vult* (vv 9–38). According to Dr Andrzej Piber, Curator in the MSS department of the Biblioteka Narodowa in Warsaw, Gneuss's item 942, to which he appends the note '?formerly Leningrad, Public Library, O. v. I. 45,' is not part of the Warsaw library's collection (personal correspondence 8 Sept. 1992). It was at one time in the Warsaw library created by the two bishops Jósef and Andrzej Zaluski in 1747, which was removed to St Petersburg after the collapse and division of the Polish kingdom in 1795. But according to the records of the Biblioteka Narodowa, when the MSS were returned to Warsaw after the reestablishment of the Polish state (many of them perished during World War II) MS O. v. I. 45 was not among them. Dr M.I. Demidov of M.E. Saltykov-Shchedrin State Public Library in St Petersburg, however, writes (pers. corresp. 18 Dec. 1992) that the MS 'should really have remained in the Public Library among the other manuscripts for which the library should have paid compensation to the Polish republic. But because this compensation was not paid, the manuscripts were returned to Warsaw. Manuscript Lat. O. v. I. 45 was among those returned manuscripts. Its further fate is not known.' In subsequent correspondence (pers. corresp. 7 July 1993), Prof. Gneuss informs me that Prof. Angus Cameron attempted to locate the MS in St Petersburg in 1974, but was not successful.

11 '*Psalterium iuxta Hebraeos*,' Jerome's translation into Latin from the Hebrew text. Ed. Sainte-Marie. Cited as 'Hebr.' in notes to the text.

12 Cited as Weber and *Biblia sacra* (*Bib. sac.*), respectively.

Manuscripts of Psalms with Old English Glosses

A London, BL, Cotton Vespasian A. 1 ['Vespasian Psalter'; Ker 203, Gneuss 381].[13] Roman. Written in 8th c., possibly of Canterbury origin. Identified with the psalter described by Thomas of Elmham as being kept on the high altar at St Augustine's.[14] Pss 2.4–150. Prefatory matter, canticles, and hymns (those on fols 155r–160v added in 11th c.). Continuous OE interlinear gloss of 9th c. to psalms, canticles, and hymns, with additions in 11th c., i.e. sporadic glosses to psalms and continuous gloss to fols 155r/1–20 *Hymnus ad matutinum diebus dominici* (*Te Deum laudamus*), and to 155r/21–156r/10 *Incipit fides catholici* (*Quicumque vult*).[15]

B Oxford, Bodleian Library, Junius 27 (5139) ['Junius Psalter'; Ker 335, Gneuss 641]. Roman. Written in 1st half of 10th c., Winchester.[16] Pss 2.4–46.4, 46.6–67.27, 68.7 *super*–144.6 *dicent*. Contains calendar (fols 2r–7v, which Wormald localizes to Winchester, but Dumville to Canterbury[17]) and computistical texts (12th-c.) on originally blank leaves (fols 8r–9r). Continuous OE interlinear gloss (10th c.) to the psalms.[18]

C Cambridge University Library, Ff. 1. 23 ['Cambridge Psalter' or 'Winchcombe Psalter'; Ker 13, Gneuss 4]. Roman. Written in mid 11th c. (Ker) or shortly after 1000 (Dumville 1991). Assigned by Ker to Winchcombe, but by both Dumville and Lapidge to St Augustine's, Canterbury.[19] Pss 1–150. Continuous OE interlinear gloss in red by original scribe in same size hand as main text.[20] Contains prayers (fols 4r, 276r–281v),[21] canticles (fols 251r–274r; ten of them are glossed), and litany (fols 274r–276r).[22]

D London, BL, Royal 2 B. v ['Regius Psalter'; Ker 249, Gneuss 451]. Roman.[23] Written in 10th c.; almost certainly from Winchester. Pss 1–150. Continuous

13 As stated earlier, Ker numbers are from his *Catalogue*, Gneuss numbers from his 1981 article.

14 For the account, see Hardwick: 98; see also facsimile ed. by Wright: 39–41.

15 Ed. Kuhn, facsimile ed. Wright. A brief description of the MS accompanied by a microfiche facsimile can also be found in Pulsiano 1994a: 43–49.

16 See Gneuss 1955: 43, Sisam and Sisam: 48.

17 Wormald 1984b, Dumville 1992: 1–38 (ch. 1, 'The Kalendar of the Junius Psalter'). Dumville assumes a direct relationship between the OE gloss of the Vespasian Psalter and that of the Junius Psalter; although such a relationship is intimated by Lindelöf 1901, with additional study by Brenner, the assumption (along with the view that the gloss to the Vespasian Psalter is original) cannot be sustained. See Pulsiano 1996.

18 Ed. Brenner.

19 Dumville 1991, Lapidge 1992.

20 Ed. Wildhagen 1910.

21 Ed. Barré: 131–2.

22 Ed. Lapidge 1991: 93–7.

23 For a brief description and microfiche facsimile see Pulsiano 1994a: 57–64.

OE interlinear gloss to the psalms and canticles,[24] with Latin scholia.[25] Contains an Office to the Virgin Mary (fols 1r–6r; mid 11th c.),[26] proverbs and maxims (fol. 6r),[27] added prayer in Old English (fol. 6v),[28] preface to the psalms (fol. 7rv), computistical texts (on ages of the world, measurements of Noah's ark, etc., fols 187r/6–190v/7) and a prognostication (fol. 190r/10–190v/7), followed by prayers (fols 190v/8–196v/9, 197r–198r/14),[29] a text that possibly functioned as a concluding section to the preceding prayer (fol. 198r/15–19),[30] and directions on days for fasting (fol. 196v/10–13).[31] A number of notes are added on fol. 198v.[32] Added texts are of different hands and dates: fol. 6rv, early 11th c.; fol. 6r/14–20, mid 11th c.; fols 190v/8–196v/9, 10th/11th c.; fol. 196v/10–13, early 11th c.; fols 197r– 198r/19, early 11th c.

E Cambridge, Trinity College, R. 17. 1 (987) ['Eadwine Psalter' or 'Eadwine's Canterbury Psalter' or 'Canterbury Psalter'; Ker 91]. Triple psalter, with Latin gloss to the Gallican version, Anglo-Norman gloss to the 'Hebraic' version, and OE gloss to the Roman version.[33] Written ca 1155–1160; Christ Church, Canterbury. Contains calendar (fols 2v–4r), psalm prefaces (fol. 5rv), canticles (fols 262v–281r), Ps 151 (fol. 281rv), notes on the Lord's Prayer and creeds (fols 281v–282r), chiromancy and onomancy (fol. 282rv), a portrait of the scribe Eadwine (fol. 283v), and two drawings of the waterworks of Canterbury Cathedral (fols 284v–285r, 286r).[34] Illustrated.[35] See ι below.

F London, BL, Stowe 2 ['Stowe Psalter' or 'Spelman Psalter'; Ker 271, Gneuss 499]. Gallican. Dated by Ker to mid 11th c., and by Sisam and Sisam to 1050–1075.[36] Assigned by Sisam and Sisam to southwestern England, but

24 Ed. Roeder, Davey 1979.
25 See Davey 1987.
26 Ed. Dewick; see also Barré: 142–3.
27 Printed by Roeder: xii; the proverbs are collated with those in London, BL, Cotton Faustina A. x, fol. 100v, by Dobbie 1942: 109.
28 Ed. Logeman 1889b: 499–501.
29 Ed. Logeman 1889b: 501–11 and 1889a: 112–15, Hallander.
30 Roeder: xii; see Pulsiano and McGowan.
31 Roeder: xii; see Henel 1934: 64.
32 See O'Neill 1986, Sisam and Sisam: 53, Logeman 1889b: 498.
33 Ed. Harsley, facsimile ed. James. See O'Neill 1988, Baker. For the 'Hebraic' psalter see p. xx and n. 11 above.
34 For the fullest and most recent discussion of the MS, see Gibson et al.
35 A picture cycle formerly prefaced the codex. The surviving leaves are London, Victoria and Albert Museum, 661 ['816–1894']; London, BL, Additional 37472 (1); and New York, Pierpont Morgan Library, M. 521 and M. 724.
36 Sisam and Sisam: 67.

by Turner to New Minster (Winchester).[37] Pss 1–105, 108–150. Continuous OE interlinear gloss to psalms and canticles (ending incomplete at fol. 180v).[38]

G London, BL, Cotton Vitellius E. xviii ['Vitellius Psalter'; Ker 224, Gneuss 407]. Gallican. Written ca 1060, Winchester, New Minster.[39] Pss 1–150. Calendar (fols 2r–7v),[40] computistical tables; notes on concurrents, epacts, and embolismic days; charms, prognostications, etc. (fols 8r–16v); added petitions to the Virgin Mary (fol. 17r/20a–17v), canticles (fols 131v/18–140v/16), prayers (fols 17r/1a–19a, 131v/10–17, 140v/17–141r/12, 143r/6–144r/19), litany (fols 141r/13–143r/6), and lections (fols 144v/1a–146r/32).[41] Continuous OE interlinear gloss to psalms and canticles.[42]

H London, BL, Cotton Tiberius C. vi ['Tiberius Psalter'; Ker 199, Gneuss 378]. Gallican. Dated by Ker to mid 11th c. and by Sisam and Sisam to 1050–1075.[43] Winchester, probably Old Minster. Pss 1–113.11. Continuous OE gloss to psalms.[44] Computistical tables (fols 2r–6r), illustrations (fols 6v– 19r),[45] extensive prefatory matter (fols 19r–30r) including a litany (fol. 23v)[46] and an OE translation of the homily *De septiformi spiritu* (fols 28r–30r).[47]

I London, Lambeth Palace, 427 ['Lambeth Psalter'; Ker 280, Gneuss 517]. Gallican. Written in 1st half of 11th c., Winchester. Pss 1–150. Continuous OE gloss to the psalms and canticles,[48] with Latin scholia. Contains psalm prefaces (fols 1r–2v), lunar prognostications and tables (fols 3r–4v), prayers with OE glosses (fols 141v–142r, 182v),[49] alliterative verse prayer in Old

37 Sisam and Sisam: 48, Turner: xi–xiii.

38 Ed. Kimmens. For a brief description of the MS and microfiche facsimile, see Pulsiano 1994a: 65–8.

39 On the date of the psalter see Pulsiano 1998. For a brief description of the MS and microfiche facsimile, see Pulsiano 1994a: 50–6.

40 Ed. Hampson: I, 421–33; Wormald 1934: 156–67. See Wildhagen 1921.

41 For the OE material, see Cockayne: I, 386, 388, 395, 396–7; Förster 1905, 1906, 1916, 1919; Henel 1934, 1934–5; Storms; also Förster 1929. A full listing of the MS contents, along with bibliography, can be found in Pulsiano 1998.

42 Ed. Rosier. See Pulsiano 1993, 1994b.

43 Sisam and Sisam: 48.

44 Ed. A.P. Campbell.

45 See Openshaw 1989, 1990. See also Wormald 1984a. For a brief description of the MS and microfiche facsimile, see Pulsiano 1994a: 38–42.

46 Ed. Lapidge 1991: 181

47 Collated by Napier, no. 7 for Latin, no. 8 for Old English. Ed. Logeman 1889a: 106–10; includes the antiquarian interlinear gloss.

48 Ed. Lindelöf 1909b, 1914. For corrections, see O'Neill 1993; see also O'Neill 1991, 1992.

49 Ed. Förster 1914.

English (fol. 183v),[50] litany (fol. 202v–204v),[51] prayers (fol. 205rv, 14th/15th c.), antiphons (fol. 209v, 15th c.), and fragments of a history of Kentish royal saints in Old English (fols 210r–211v, 2nd half of 11th c.).[52]

J London, BL, Arundel 60 ['Arundel Psalter'; Ker 134, Gneuss 304]. Gallican. Written in 2nd half of 11th c. (1073?), probably at Winchester (New Minster). Pss 1–150. Continuous OE gloss to the psalms and canticles.[53] Prefatory matter (fols 1r–12v) includes calendar (fols 2r–7v),[54] computistical texts and tables (fols 1rv, 8r–12r), and full-page illustration (fol. 12v). Fols 46v–52r contain a Latin paraphrase of Ps 50 (unglossed). Litany (fols 130r/19–132v).[55] Two added quires (2nd half of 12th c.) complete the litany and contain prayers (fols 133r–142v). Fols 143r–148v contain prayers,[56] followed by text on the age of the world in Old English (fol. 149r) and *Nomina episcoporum occidentalium saxonum* (fol. 149v).[57]

K Salisbury, Cathedral Library, 150 ['Salisbury Psalter'; Ker 379, Gneuss 740]. Gallican. Dated by Sisam and Sisam to ca 975; possibly written at Shaftesbury. Pss 1–50.12 *spiritum*, 53.3–99.4 *intro*[*ite*], 101.2 *orationem*–108.23 *sum*, 109.2 *dominare*–128.7 *qui*, 131.7 *pedes*–150. Continuous OE interlinear gloss (ca 1100) to psalms (wanting for Ps 151) and canticles.[58] Athanasian Creed, glossed by original scribe. Computistical matter and calendar (fols 1r–11r),[59] end-prayer (fol. 138r; OE gloss), and canticles (fols 138v–151v). Fols 152r–161r contain a litany (12th c.; original litany on fol. 151v erased),[60] and lessons from the Office of the Dead (12th/13th c.).

L London, BL, Additional 37517 ['Bosworth Psalter'; Ker 129, Gneuss 291]. Roman. Original text written in 2nd half of 10th c., with later additions

50 Ed. Logeman 1889a: 103, Dobbie: 94–6. The version here comprises 15 lines, while that in London, BL, Cotton Julius A. ii comprises 79 lines. Given the text's incompleteness and the fact that the following text, Ps 151, lacks a title, Dobbie (p. lxxxvi) suggests that one or more folios is missing. O'Neill 1991 (p. 145, n. 8) argues that, since fol. 182 is the last leaf of a perfect quire, Dobbie's view is doubtful.

51 Ed. Lapidge 1991: 215–18.

52 Ed. and trans. by Cockayne: III, 428–33; ed. Förster 1914: 332–5.

53 Ed. Oess 1910.

54 Ed. Wormald 1934: 142–53.

55 Ed. Lapidge 1991: 142–7. See Wormald 1946.

56 See Barré: 133–42, where he edits the prayer *Sancta et inmaculata dei genetrix uirgo Maria* on fols 145r–147v (with its later continuation on fol. 148r).

57 For the OE material, see Logeman 1889a and Förster 1925. For a brief description of the MS and microfiche facsimile, see Pulsiano 1994a: 13–18.

58 Ed. Sisam and Sisam.

59 Ed. Wormald 1934: 16–27.

60 Ed. Lapidge 1991: 283–7.

(10th/11th c. and 12th c.). Localized to either Christ Church Cathedral or St Augustine's Abbey, Canterbury.[61] Pss 1–150. The psalter proper (fols 4r–95r), Ps 151 (fol. 95v), canticles (fols 96r–104r), hymns (fols 105r–128r; 'Canterbury Hymnal'),[62] and monastic canticles (fols 129r–135r) were written 2nd half of 10th c.; the calendar (fols 2r–3r),[63] litany (fol. 104rv),[64] and texts and prayers of the Mass (fols 135v–139v) are somewhat later. A 12th-c. hand has added on fol. 64r/5–24 a series of incipits and rubrics to intercessory prayers and the psalm verses to be used with them. Continuous OE interlinear gloss to Pss 40.5, 50.4–21, 53.3–9, 63.2–11, 66.2–8, 68.2–37, 69.2–6, 70.1–24, 85.1–17, 101.2–29, 118.1–176, 119.1–7, 120.1–8, 121.1–9, 122.1–4, 123.1–8, 124.1–5, 125.1–6, 126.1–5, 127.1–6, 128.1–8, 129.1–8, 130.1–3, 131.1–18, 132.1–3, 133.1–3, 139.2, 139.9, 140.1–4, 142.1–12, and canticles on fols 101r–104r/4.[65] Extensive 12th-c. interlinear and marginal Latin commentary through Ps 39.7 *Holocaustum,* reduced to initial commentary on the psalms thereafter. Gallican alterations (with lapses) through Ps 39.7.[66]

M New York, Pierpont Morgan Library, M. 776 ['Blickling Psalter,' earlier called 'Lothian' or 'Morgan Psalter'; Ker 287, Gneuss 862]. Roman. Written in 8th c., with scattered OE glosses of early or mid 9th c. (26 glosses written in red ink) and 11th c., and Latin scholia of same dates.[67] Place of origin unknown, although assigned to Canterbury,[68] Lincoln,[69] Winchester,[70] Melrose,[71] southern England,[72] central or western England,[73] northern

61 Proponents of a Christ Church origin are Dumville 1992: 39–65 (esp. pp 50–51), and Korhammer. Korhammer (p. 186) also allows for the possibility of Winchester Abbey as place of origin. Wormald 1934 favours St Augustine's, a position reasserted most recently by Orchard.

62 Ed. Wieland.

63 Ed. Wormald 1934: 57–69.

64 Ed. Lapidge 1991: 138–9.

65 Ed. Lindelöf 1909b, Makothakat.

66 For a brief description and microfiche facsimile, see Pulsiano 1994a: 1–12.

67 First ed. Brock; the older stratum of glosses (the 'red' glosses) are set in boldface in his edition. Sweet (pp 122–3) reedited the older glosses. Wildhagen 1913 (p. 433n) offered corrections to Brock's and Sweet's texts; Collins also supplied corrections. 'Red' glosses also ed. Berghaus (pp 113–14). For further corrections and additional red glosses, see Pulsiano 1983, 1984, and 1989a. See also the comments on the glosses by Schlutter and by Holthausen 1899. For a list of psalm numbers at which the Latin glosses and the 'red' glosses can be found, see Crick: 76–8 'Appendix A: The Earliest Glosses in M. 776.'

68 New Palaeographical Society: I, pt x, pls 231 and 232; Nordenfalk: 125, Wright: 37–43.

69 Sweet: 122.

70 Crick: 73–4.

71 Soeda.

72 Walters Art Gallery: no. 1.

73 Alexander: 57.

England,[74] and Northumbria,[75] or an unknown area influenced by Northumbria and Canterbury.[76] Canterbury seems likely. Used probably as an oath-book by officials in Lincoln in the 16th and 17th c.[77] Associated with Royal 2. B. v in either Winchester or Canterbury.[78] Pss 9.9–9.30, 31.3–36.14, 36.39–50.19, 52.7–94.6 *deum*, 101.10–108.31, 111.5–150.6. Ps 9.9–9.30 misbound as fol. 64 (after Ps 115.15). Calendar (15th c.) and extracts from the four Gospels (15th c.).

N^{a} Sondershausen, Schloßmuseum, Hs. Br. 1 ['Sondershäuser Psalter']. Gallican. Continuously glossed fragment (one folio) containing Pss 6.9–7.9 *popul*[*os*].[79] Mid 11th c. Once part of N^{b} and N^{c}.

N^{b} Cambridge, Pembroke College, 312, C. nos 1 and 2 ['Cambridge fragments'; Ker 79, Gneuss 141]. Gallican. Binding strips, with continuous interlinear OE gloss, containing Pss 73.16 [*auror*](*am*)–23 *oder*(*u*)[*nt*], 74.2–3, 77.31 [*eoru*](*m*)–43 *po*(*s*)[*uit*].[80] Once part of N^{a} and N^{c}.

N^{c} Haarlem, Stadsbibliotheek, s.n. ['Haarlem fragments'; Ker Suppl. 79, see Gneuss 141]. Gallican. Binding strip containing Pss 119.4–5 *meus*, 120.4 *qui*–6 *luna*, 121.4 *tribus*–5, 122.2 *sicut*–end of verse. Continuous interlinear OE gloss.[81] Once part of N^{a} and N^{b}.

O Paris, BN, lat. 8846 [Ker Suppl. 419; called the 'Paris Psalter' by art historians]. Triple psalter, with Anglo-Norman interlinear gloss to the 'Hebraic' version[82] and Latin commentary to the Gallican. Written 1170–1200, Canterbury. Pss 1–98.6 *nomen*. Contains OE glosses to the Roman version at Pss 38.14 (fol. 69v) *amplius non ero*, 59.3 (fol. 103v) *deus–destruxisti*, 64.2 (fol. 109v) *Te–et*, 77.1 (fol. 135r) *populus–meam*, and 87.2 (fol. 154v) *deus–mee*.[83] A copy of Cambridge, Trinity College, R.17.1 (987). See τ* and τ below. The siglum O is used for those portions containing OE glosses, otherwise τ* is used for the text of the Roman version and τ for that of the Gallican.

74 Zimmermann: 273.
75 Saunders: I, 4.
76 According to the unpublished description prepared for The Pierpont Morgan Library.
77 See Pulsiano 1982: 12–13, Soeda: 375–8.
78 See Pulsiano 1985.
79 Ed. Pilch; a more accurate edition of the fragment is published by Gneuss 1998. I am grateful to Prof. Pilch for allowing me access to his article while still in proof and for sending me photocopies of the leaf along with his transcription notes, and to Prof. Gneuss for also providing me with a copy of his article in proof. I am grateful as well to Christa Hirschler, Second Director of the Schloßmuseum, Sondershausen, for providing colour photographs.
80 Ed. Dietz.
81 Ed. Derolez.
82 On the 'Hebraic' psalter see p. xx and n. 11 above.
83 Glosses to Pss 59, 64, 77, and 87 ed. Hargreaves and Clark, those to Ps 38 ed. Toswell.

Additional Manuscripts of the Psalms

α Basel, Universitätsbibliothek N. I. 2 [Gneuss 788]. Roman. Written in 8th c.; of unknown English origin. Single leaf. Pss 113.25(17)–115.16 *tuus* (2nd).

β Berlin, Staatsbibliothek Preussischer Kulturbesitz, Hamilton 353 ['Salaberga Psalter'; Gneuss 790]. Roman. Written in 8th c. in Northumbria; at the monastery of St John, Laon, according to a 12th-c. inventory (fol. 26v). Contains Apostles' Creed (fol. 1r), Pss 1–150 (fols 2ra–62ra), and canticles (fols 62rb–64v).[84]

γ Cambridge, University Library, Ff. 5. 27 [Gneuss 9]. Roman. Written in 7th/8th c., Jarrow or Wearmouth. A single leaf, severely damaged by water staining on the verso, containing Pss 90.7–92.5 *domine*.

δ Cambridge, Corpus Christi College, 272 ['Achadeus Psalter'; Gneuss 77]. Gallican. Written in the last quarter of 9th c., Rheims. Pss 1.1–*impiorum*, 2.2–25.5, 26.2 *ipsi*–36.22, 38.11 *amoue*–50.16, 52.1–79.15 *caelo*, 80.3–100.8, 101.12 *sicut*–150. Contains psalter prefaces (fols 1r–3r), litany (fols 151r–154r),[85] canticles (fols 155r–168r), and prayers (fols 168v–183v). Collects throughout psalms. Marginal commentary and glosses.

ε Cambridge, Corpus Christi College, 391 [Gneuss 104]. Gallican. The so-called 'Portiforium of Wulstan.'[86] Second half of 11th c., ca 1065, Worcester. The psalter proper comprises pp 25–200, followed by Ps 151 and canticles (pp 201–21).

ζ Cambridge, Corpus Christi College, 411 [Gneuss 106]. Gallican. Written early 10th c. Variously considered to be a continental production (Tours?) or from Canterbury (see prayer to St Augustine on fol. 140v). In England by ca 1000. Pss 1–150; wanting Pss 35.5 *omni*–36.14 *trucident*, 72.7–28. Contains prefatory matter, Ps 151 (fol. 123v–124r) canticles (fols 124r–137r), litany (fols 137r–138r),[87] prayers (fols 137r, 138v–140v), 2nd litany (fols 140rv),[88] and extracts from the Gospels (fols 141r–142v).

η Cambridge, Magdalene College, Pepys 2981 (3) [Gneuss 125]. Roman. Written in 9th c. (?); of unknown origin. Fragment containing Ps 37.20–21 *detra*[*hebant*].

ϑ Cambridge, St John's College, 59 (C. 9) ['Southampton Psalter'; Gneuss 148]. Gallican. Written in 10th c., Ireland. Pss 1–150. Canticle (*Audite cæli*), fols 99v–101r. Marginal commentary and glosses, Latin and Irish. Full-page illustrations.

84 For a recent discussion see Ó Cróinín.
85 Ed. Lapidge 1991: 110–14.
86 Ed. Hughes.
87 Ed. Lapidge 1991: 120–2.
88 Ibid.: 122–4.

ι Cambridge, Trinity College, R. 17. 1 (Gallican text).

ϰ Durham, Dean and Chapter Muniments, Misc. Charter 5670 [Gneuss 250]. Gallican. Written in middle of the 1st half of 11th c. Provenance uncertain. Pss 25.1 *domino*–26.4.

λ London, BL, Arundel 155 ['Eadui Psalter'; Ker 135, Gneuss 306]. Roman. Written in 1st half of 11th c., with 12th c. additions and alterations. Christ Church, Canterbury. Pss 1–150. Contains prayers, calendar,[89] computistical matter (fols 1r–10r), psalm preface and prayers (fol. 11rv), canticles (fols 133v–141r), litany (fols 141v–143r),[90] prayers and hymns (three groups: fols 143r–167r; prayers with responses fols 167r–170v; prayers, most with OE gloss, fols 171r–193v).[91] Original to the psalter are calendar (fols 2r–7v), preliminary matter (fols 8v–11r), psalms (fols 12r–132r), canticles (fols 133v–135r), collects (fol. 171r), and prayers and forms of confession glossed in Old English (fols 171r–191v). Fols 113–120 out of order. Fols 191v/19–193v written in different Latin hand, although OE gloss may be in same hand as that throughout glosses to prayers. Remainder in a 12th-c. hand, with added bifolium (fols 145r–146v) in another hand.[92]

μ London, BL, Cotton Galba A. xviii ['Athelstan Psalter'; Gneuss 334 (with Oxford, Bodleian Library, Rawlinson B. 484, fol. 85)]. Gallican. Written in 9th c., Liège region (?); later associated with Winchester (Old Minster).[93] Pss 1–150; wanting Ps 35.4 *noluit*–end and Ps 36.1–9. Contains calendar (fols 3r–14v),[94] and metrical verses (fols 14v–15v), computistical texts (fols 16r–17v), tables (fols 18v–20v), prayers (fols 22r–30r, 174v–177v), psalm prefaces and prayers (fols 30v–34v), Ps 151 (fols 162v–163r), canticles (fols 163r–174v), collects (fols 178r–199v), and transliterated Greek litany,[95] Pater noster, and Creed (fol. 200rv). Full-page illustrations.

ν London, BL, Harley 603 ['Harley Psalter'; Gneuss 422]. Roman, except for Pss 100–105.22, which are Gallican. Written in 1st quarter of 11th c., Christ Church, Canterbury. Pss 1–49.7 *testificabor*, 51.1 *qui potens*–61.12, 64–83.5 *saeculi*, 89.14 *et* (2nd)–97.9, 100–143.11 *alienorum*. Arranged in 3 columns. Numerous illustrations (wanting for Pss 67–99).[96] Smaller initials wanting for Pss 48–99.

89 Ed. Wormald 1934: 170–81.
90 Ed. Lapidge 1991: 148–52.
91 Ed. Logeman 1889a, Holthausen 1941, J.J. Campbell.
92 For a brief description and microfiche facsimile, see Pulsiano 1994a: 19–37.
93 For the most recent study of the psalter, see Deshman.
94 Ed. Hampson: I, 389–420. For a discussion of the calendar see Dumville 1992: 1–38.
95 Ed. Lapidge 1991: 172–3.
96 For the most recent discussion of the psalter see Noel.

ξ London, BL, Harley 863 [Gneuss 425]. Gallican. Written 1046 x 1072, Exeter. Pss 1–51.2, 51.3 *potens*–70.10 *unum*, 72.1–150. Contains calendar (fols 1r–6v), Ps 151 (fols 98v–99r), canticles (fols 99r–108v; *Quicumque vult* is glossed in Old English),[97] litany (fols 108v–111v),[98] petitions and prayers (fols 111v–117r),[99] and office (fols 117r–123v).

o London, BL, Harley 2904 ['Ramsey Psalter'; Gneuss 430]. Gallican. Written ca 975–1000. Origin uncertain, but associated with Winchester (Ramsey has also been suggested[100]). Pss 1–50.19 *contribulatus*, 51.4–150. Contains psalm preface and prayer (fols 1v–3r), Ps 151 (fol. 188rv), canticles (fols 188v– 208v), litany (fols 209r–213r),[101] and prayers (fols 213r–214v).

π London, BL, Royal 1. E. viii [Gneuss 449]. Bible. Gallican. Written in late 10th c., Christ Church, Canterbury. Prefaces (fols 8vb–9ra) and psalms (fols 9ra–31vb), including Ps 151. Fols 26r–30v supplied in a later hand.

ϱ Oxford, Bodleian Library, Douce 296 (21870) ['Crowland Psalter'; Gneuss 617]. Gallican. Written ca 1050, Crowland. Pss 1–9:37(16), 12.2–49.6, 50.12–100.8, 101.12–150. Contains calendar (fols 1r–6v),[102] computistical matter (fols 7r–8v), canticles (fols 106r–116v), litany (fols 117r–119r),[103] and prayers (fols 119v–130v).

σ Oxford, Bodleian Library, Laud lat. 81 (768) [Gneuss 655]. Gallican. Written in 2nd half of 11th c.; of unknown English origin. Pss 1–150. Contains canticles (fols 131v–144r), litany (fols 144v–146v),[104] and prayers (fols 147r–152r).

ς Paris, BN, lat. 8824 [called the 'Paris Psalter' by Anglo-Saxonists; Ker 367, Gneuss 891]. Roman. Written in mid 11th c.; of unknown English origin. Pss 1–20.6 *gloria*, 21–25.11 *sunt*, 26–26.4 *meae*, 26.5–37.23, 38.6 [*uani*]*tas*–50.10, 51.9 *adiutorem*–67.31 *que*, 68–79.20 *uirtutum*, 80.9 *Israhel*–96.1, 97.8 *manibus*–108.31, 109.6 *ruinas*–150.3 *lau*[*date*] (2nd). Contains canticles (fols 176r–183v), litany (fols 183v–184v),[105] and prayers (fols 185r–186r). Latin in left column, Old English in right (prose Pss 1–50, metrical Pss 51–150.3).[106] A few scattered illustrations.

τ* Paris, BN, lat. 8846 (Roman version). See MSS O and τ.

97 Ed. Holthausen 1942–3.
98 Ed. Lapidge 1991: 193–202.
99 Ed. Dewick 1914: 433–54.
100 See Niver.
101 Ed. Lapidge 1991: 203–9.
102 Ed. Wormald 1934: 254–65
103 Ed. Lapidge 1991: 235–9.
104 Ibid.: 240–3.
105 Ibid.: 250–3.
106 Ed. Thorpe, Krapp. Facsimile ed. Colgrave et al.

τ Paris, BN, lat. 8846 (Gallican text). See MSS O and τ*.

υ Rome, Vatican City, Bibliotheca Apostolica Vaticana, Reg. lat. 12 ['Bury Psalter'; Gneuss 912]. Gallican. Written in 2nd quarter of 11th c., Bury St Edmunds. Pss 1–50.14 *tuas*, 51–100, 101.12 *et*–150. Contains psalm prefaces and computistical matter (fols 1r–6v), calendar (fols 7r–12v),[107] additional computistical matter (fols 13r–20v), Ps 151 (fol. 146r), canticles (fols 146r–158v), litany (fols 159r–161r),[108] prayers (fols 145rv, 161v–181v),[109] and added text (fol. 182rv). Contains illustrations in the margins.

φ Rouen, Bibliothèque Municipale, 231 (A. 44) [Gneuss 920]. Gallican. Written in late 11th c.; possibly from St Augustine's, Canterbury. Pss 9.8 *parauit*–50.21 *obla*[*tiones*], 51.3 *qui*–100.7 *in,* 101.2 *ad*–150 (fols 1–114). Contains prayers (fols 114rv, 130v–131v, 198r–208r),[110] canticles (fols 115r–127r), litany (fols 127v–130r),[111] hymnal (fols 132r–197r), and extracts from the Gospels (fols 208v–210v).

χ Salisbury, Cathedral Library, 180 [Gneuss 754]. Written ca 900, Brittany; associated with Salisbury Cathedral in the later Middle Ages. Double psalter, containing Gallican version in left column and 'Hebraic' version[112] in right. Pss 2.2 *conuenerunt*–150. Contains psalm prefaces (fols 1r–18r), Ps 151 (fol. 164r), canticles (fols 164r–170v), litany (fols 170v–172r),[113] and prayers (fols 172r–173r).

ψ Utrecht, Universiteitsbibliotheek, 32 (Script. eccl. 484). ['Utrecht Psalter'; Gneuss 939]. Gallican. Written in 1st quarter of 9th c., Rheims (or Hautvillers?); later at Christ Church, Canterbury. Pss 1–150. Contains Ps 151 and canticles (fols 83v–91v). Numerous illustrations.[114]

ω Worcester, Cathedral Library, F. 173, fol. 1* [Gneuss 764]. Single leaf bound with a missal. Gallican. Dated to 10th c.;[115] of unknown English origin. Pss 33.20–34.7.

107 Ed. Wormald 1934: 240–51.
108 Ed. Lapidge 1991: 296–9.
109 Ed. Wilmart.
110 Ed. Gjerløw: 132–47.
111 Ed. Lapidge 1991: 265–9.
112 On the 'Hebraic' psalter see p. xx and n. 11 above.
113 Ibid.: 288–95.
114 For the relationship of this psalter to Cambridge, Trinity College, R. 17. 1 (987) and Paris, BN, lat. 8846, see Heimann, Dodwell. See, most importantly, Gibson et al.: 53–61, 186–92.
115 See Warren. I am grateful to Richard W. Pfaff for bringing this item to my attention.

PRESENTATION AND ARRANGEMENT OF MATERIAL

The material of this edition is presented one psalm-verse at a time, the Latin text arranged in a vertical list (one word per line) on the left side of the page, the Old English glosses and manuscript sigla set out in a horizontal list on the right side of the page, opposite each Latin lemma. Notes on both the Latin text and the glosses are presented at the end of each psalm-verse (see under Notes below).

Latin Text

The base text for the Latin is Dom Robert Weber's edition of the Roman psalter, with slight modifications: the initial word in each psalm-verse is capitalized (except where all manuscripts agree in recording a lowercase letter), while all other words, including proper names and terms for God, are lowercased; no indication of punctuation is given, for reasons made obvious by the arrangement of the material. When a Gallican word is not a variant of but an addition to the base text, the word is enclosed in parentheses and marked with an asterisk, e.g. Ps 4.8 '(et)'. Where a word in the Latin text of a glossed psalter does not belong to the mainstream tradition of either the Roman or the Gallican psalter, but is nevertheless glossed with an Old English word, the Latin lemma is enclosed in angled brackets, e.g. Ps 16.1 '⟨domine⟩.' An asterisk following a word indicates that a note on the Gallican version of the text is to be found in one or other of the note sections devoted to the Gallican variants.

Old English Glosses

With two general exceptions, abbreviated glosses are expanded and the expansions indicated by underlining (as opposed to italics). The two exceptions are *drihten* and *forþam/n*, which are presented exactly as they appear in manuscript. In rare instances of ambiguity as to the appropriate expansion, other glosses are recorded in their abbreviated forms as well, e.g. Ps 2.2 *ealdorm̄* C. Latin *uel* is recorded as *ł*. Accents are reproduced, but, again for reasons made obvious by the layout, punctuation is not indicated. A space enclosed in square brackets signals that part of the gloss is lost or unreadable (a common occurrence in the Vitellius Psalter [G]); no attempt is made to estimate the number of lost letters in such instances, although in most cases the reader will be able to reconstruct the gloss. Parentheses within glosses indicate that the enclosed letters are incomplete, e.g. Ps 4.3 *on (h)e[ ]rtun* A, where the ascender of *h* is lost as well as a letter (expected *o*) after *e*. These parentheses are only to alert the reader and should not be reproduced when the words are quoted in subsequent studies.

Word Order

The presence of a vertical bar (|) or a curly brace (}) just to the left of any string of Old English glosses is a signal to the reader to pay attention to word order. The vertical bar indicates that, in one or more manuscripts, the Old English gloss does not follow the word order of the Latin lemmata. For example, in the phrase *oculus meus* (Ps 6.7), a typical psalter gloss will have the order *ege min* (as in A); but the glossator of the Lambeth Psalter (I) adopts normal Old English word order: *min eage.* Thus, since the glosses are always recorded in the order in which they appear above the Latin in the manuscripts, *min* is listed as I's gloss for *oculus,* and *eage* for *meus.*

The curly brace points to a variation in Latin word order between the Roman and Gallican versions of a psalm-verse. For example, the Roman version of Ps 9.28(7) reads *Cuius os maledictione et amaritudine plenum est,* while the Gallican reads *Cuius maledictione os plenum est et amaritudine.* In such instances all the glosses for each lemma are presented together, and a curly brace is placed after the lemma. The assumption remains always that an Old English word is written above the corresponding lemma; if there is any departure in a particular manuscript, the exact order of the words is recorded in the notes on Gallican variants (sections GAg and GAu).

Multiple glosses, a common occurrence in the Lambeth Psalter (I), frequently repeat elements. For example, at Ps 4.2 *Cum inuocarem* is glossed *þa þa ic clypode ł þa þa ic gecigde.* There is no completely satisfactory method of recording the glosses in such a case, and the solution taken in this edition is to record the repeated elements as sparingly as possible (thus, at Ps 4.2 *þa þa* is recorded as the gloss for *cum* and *ic clypode ł þa þa ic gecigde* appears opposite *inuocarem*). In general, because of complications arising from word order and/or multiple glossing, the reader is reminded to look at the strings of glosses in context rather than in isolation.

Sigla

Sigla using letters of the Roman alphabet stand for glossed manuscripts of both Roman and Gallican psalters; unglossed manuscripts are represented by Greek sigla. A siglum followed by an asterisk indicates that the reader should refer to the notes for a detailed textual note on the Old English gloss. A siglum in italic script refers the reader to the notes for information on the Latin lemma and/or its variants. A siglum in parentheses indicates that, while there is no Old English gloss in that particular manuscript for the word under consideration, there is nevertheless a relevant note under either the OE or the LT registers or both.

Hands

The question of scribal hands presents certain difficulties. The practice adopted here is to assign a superscript number after the siglum to indicate the hand, in those instances where a distinct hand can be seen. In the Stowe Psalter (F), the hand of a 16th-century corrector can be clearly distinguished from all the other hands in the manuscript and is represented here as F^2. For example, at Ps 2.13 *ira* is glossed by *graman,* with the *g* written on an erasure by the 16th-century corrector. The gloss is thus recorded as 'graman F/F^2' (with an asterisk added to draw the reader's attention to the note supplied in the OE section). In most instances, however, the hands of the various correctors cannot be distinguished, and so the generic term 'corrector' (*corr.*) is used in the notes.

The Lambeth, Vitellius, and Eadwine Psalters present more complex circumstances. The Lambeth Psalter contains a large number of glosses in what Lindelöf calls the 'darker hand,' but these glosses may well have been added by the original glossator at a later time. A recent study by Wiesenekker arrives at the same conclusion, based on an analysis of translation practice.[116] Accordingly, no distinction is made here among the hands in this psalter (a list of the darker glosses can be found in Lindelöf 1909a). The Vitellius Psalter presents an analogous situation. A number of its glosses (though considerably fewer than in the Lambeth Psalter) were added either in the main hand or in the hand of a corrector. In his edition Rosier enclosed these glosses in parentheses, but was unable to determine which hand was responsible for which. In the present edition I make no attempt to distinguish the hands by the use of superscripts, but do draw attention to these glosses in the notes. The Eadwine Psalter exhibits eight main glossing hands.[117] While the sections of the psalms for which each hand was responsible can be determined, it is impossible (or at least not feasible here) to determine the hand of each individual gloss. Main hands are identified by a superscript number (E^1, E^2, etc.); the hand of a corrector is identified simply by a superscript 'x' (e.g. E^x), without indication of which corrector is at work, even though the corrector in particular instances may be one of the main

116 'The majority of [the glosses in the "darker" hand] stem from the hand of the main glossator, or they were inserted by one or more people who had so thoroughly acquainted themselves with the contents and translation methods of their model as to produce similar results, which is hardly imaginable. It is more likely that the main glossator himself subjected his own work to a series of thorough revisions and corrections, which he carried out in his own spirit' (Wiesenekker: 334).

117 See Webber; also Pulsiano 1989b. I have revised my assessment of the relationship of the *Eadwine* gloss to that of the D-type and A-type traditions in my forthcoming article, 'The Old English Gloss of the Eadwine Psalter.'

hands returning to the work at a later time. I equivocate on this point in Pss 1–10, as it is often difficult to distinguish between corrector and main hand, which may be the same in the majority of cases; the notes, however, will always indicate the alterations and erasures. Glosses that are combinations of original gloss and correction are represented by a superscript number and 'x,' separated by a virgule (e.g. $E^{2/x}$). The determination of each hand of the correctors requires a separate extended study (beyond that of Berghaus 1979), the undertaking of which may outweigh its fruitfulness.

No attempt has been made to ascertain individual hands for the group of manuscripts that do not contain Old English glosses (i.e. those assigned Greek sigla).

Notes

The notes following each psalm-verse comprise six sections. The first records both Latin and Old English readings in this edition that diverge from the readings published by previous editors; the second provides textual notes on the Old English glosses; the third and fourth give textual notes on Latin lemmata in, respectively, the glossed and unglossed manuscripts. The last two sections record Gallican variants in glossed and unglossed manuscripts. Not all psalm-verses require notes in every section; when a section is blank, it is omitted.

Ordinal numbers, used to identify lemmata and/or glosses when there are multiple occurrences of the same spelling in the same verse, are case-specific for both Latin and Old English. For example, if two occurrences of *et* follow one of *Et,* they are counted as first and second rather than as second and third.[118]

Notes on Editorial Variants (ED)

Unpublished dissertations are omitted, as are editions that have been superseded or contain such errors as to be of minimal value to the present work. The latter include L'Isle's unprinted 1630 edition of E, Spelman's 1640 edition of F, Stevenson's 1843 edition of A, Sweet's 1885 edition of A, Lindelöf's 1904 study, and Oess's 1908 partial edition of J. Also omitted, since the present edition treats the glossed psalters, are Thorpe's 1835 edition of the Paris Psalter (P) and Krapp's edition of its Old English text (this psalter is here classed among those assigned Greek sigla).

I have not recorded instances where previous editors have ignored *u/v* distinctions in the Latin or have not followed the manuscripts precisely in the use

118 Note, however, that in Appendix 2, where references are to the Latin text in specific manuscripts, which may or may not reflect the version of the text and the capitalization used in the present edition, it has not been practical to make case a factor in the counting of identical occurrences.

of capital letters in initial words or display lines, e.g. Ps 11.2 SALuum (B)] Salvum *Brenner;* SALVVM (C)] SALUUM *Wildhagen.* Ps 17.2 DILIgam (D)] Diligam *Roeder.* Ps 43.1 D̅S̅ (BD)] Deus *Brenner, Roeder;* DEVS (E)] Deus *Harsley;* AURIBVS (C)] AVRIBVS *Wildhagen;* Audiuimus (BE)] audivimus *Brenner, Harsley;* Annuntiauerunt (BE)] annuntiaverunt *Brenner, Harsley.* Such notes would have only limited value and would detract attention from substantive departures.

Details of all editions, articles, and reviews that are cited (by author/editor) in this section will be found in the Bibliography on pp xi–xviii .

Notes on Old English Glosses (OE)

This section supplies textual notes on the glosses; the presence of a note here is usually signalled by the addition of an asterisk to a manuscript siglum. The siglum alone, without reference to hand or corrector, is what counts to identify multiple occurrences of the same spelling of a gloss in the same verse; thus *his* '($E^{2/x}$)' following *his* '(E^{1})' is still the '*(2nd)*' example of *his* in the relevant verse in E.

Notes on Latin Text (LTg *and* LTu)

In these sections, in addition to supplying variant spellings for the lemmata, I have recorded the use of manuscript capitals (primary rather than secondary) in display lines.[119] As in the lists of glosses, square brackets around a blank space indicate that part of a lemma has been lost or is unreadable, and parentheses surround letters that are only partially visible. For the lemmata in glossed manuscripts, all accents are recorded and detailed textual notes are supplied.

For the lemmata in unglossed manuscripts, accents are not recorded, and it was deemed unnecessary to clutter the notes with detailed comments on erasures. Interlinear additions are briefly noted, however, since they may well have importance for tracing a particular path in the transmission of the psalter texts, and other textual notes are occasionally provided on matters of interest or where there is need for clarification.

119 Compare, for example, the record of capitals for L at Ps 38.2. L uses large initials for *Dixi* through *custodiam* (comprising one MS line) and secondary initials for *ut* through *mea* (comprising one MS line); the rest of the psalm continues in the regular script. In this MS, the display line marks the psalm as of special significance. Capitals elsewhere in the MS also claim significance, as with those to Ps 20, since this is the first psalm of the Matins for Sunday, or those to Ps 32, the first psalm at Matins for Monday. Other indications of monastic use are found throughout. The record of capitals in the display lines thus cannot be ignored.

Notes on Gallican Variants (GAg *and* GAu)

The variants have been checked against Weber's edition of the Roman psalter (listed as *Ga.* in his notes) and the 1953 edition of the Gallican psalter; comparative readings from continental psalters included in these two editions but not included in the present edition are indicated in the notes. In certain instances, readings from Dom Henri de Sainte-Marie's edition of the 'Hebraic' psalter[120] are recorded in the notes in order to clarify particular variants. Except in rare instances, textual notes are not provided and accents are not recorded under GAu.

Editorial Principles

The present edition is based upon conservative principles, favouring empiricism over speculation. No emendations are made in this edition, and no presumptions are made about a reading. Reconstructions of glosses and lemmata are strictly avoided. It is an easy matter to read Ps 2.12 *g[ ]gripað ge* G and reconstruct the gloss as *gegripað ge;* but there is a hole in the leaf in this instance, and it would be misrepresentative to attempt any reconstruction, no matter how obvious. The concern here is to strip away vestiges of editorial intervention and to establish what can be seen in the various texts; emendation remains the prerogative of the user. In a number of instances, Lindelöf was able to read more letters in the Lambeth Psalter than are visible today. The reason is that the manuscript was rebound sometime in the last decade, and so certain glosses are, in a sense, 'lost' to the gutter of a tight binding. In other instances, however, a wealth of new glosses have been recovered, as in the case of the Vitellius Psalter, whose leaves, owing to the Ashburnham House fire of 1731, are now mounted in paper frames but can be profitably studied with the aid of fibre-optic light.

In the preparation of the present edition and collation, the original manuscripts were used for all psalters containing Old English glosses, except for N^a and N^c, since these are binding strips (along with N^b *membra disjecta* of the same manuscript); for these, suitable photographs have been relied upon. The unglossed psalters (those assigned Greek sigla) have been checked against microfilm copies and photographs.

120 On this psalter see p. xx and n. 11 above.

appendix 1

THE BLICKLING PSALTER (M) GLOSSES

The *Blicking Psalter* (New York, Pierpont Morgan Library, M. 776, assigned the siglum M) contains 26 of the oldest psalter glosses, written in red ink as both interlinear and marginal glosses in a hand of the late 8th or early 9th century. The glosses were first printed by Brock in 1876, followed by Sweet in 1885, with corrections and an additional gloss (no. 10) by Collins in 1963 and corrections by Pulsiano in 1983. Wildhagen also offered a number of corrections in his 1913 study. Berghaus recorded 23 of the glosses in 1979. Additional glosses were recorded by Pulsiano in 1983 and 1989 (nos 9 and 26).

Sweet's record of the glosses (in his pp 122–3) is confusing, conflating lemmata from the psalms with those written as part of the gloss by the 'red' hand, or in other cases omitting the referent in the gloss. Thus for no. 3 he reads 'tetenderunt arcum : tinde bogan'; no. 4 'plagae vestigia cicatrices : dolgsuaþhe'; no. 6 'cataracte forsceta'; no. 13 'inseparunt : þem ascadendu*m*'; no. 15 'obdormiet : onhrernisse'; 16–17 torrens in austro: suþrador australis : smoltregn' (with a note 'Preceded by toris [=torrens?]'); 24 'promptuaria : hordern'; no. 25 'fecundae : berende'. His criticism of Brock's alphabetical arrangement ('He has thrown them into alphabetical order') should be weighed against his own adoption of the same arrangement ('For the sake of convenience'), but omitting psalm and verse numbers. Brock records the lemma for no. 13 as 'cum carbonibus' (from the psalm-verse); for no. 15 'obdormiet.' Berghaus (pp 113–14) supplies lemmata from the psalm-verses, omitting those that accompany the glosses, thus adding another layer of confusion. He also omits prepositions and Latin glosses, and overlooks nos 9, 10, and 26 and the second gloss in no. 3 'arcum : bogan').

A complete list of the 'red' Old English glosses is presented below. Notes are keyed to the numbers assigned to the glosses. To the left of the colon are given the lemmata from the psalms, to the right the glosses (which at times contain their own lemmata).

1. 9.10 in oportunitatibus : on geherlicnissum (*fol. 64r, right margin*)
2. 34.14 conplacebam : quemde (*fol. 4r, right margin*)
3. 36.14 tetenderunt arcum : tetendit. tinde bogan (*fol. 5v, right margin*)
4. 37.6 cicatrices : plagę uestigia dolgsuaþhe (*fol. 6r, right margin*)

1. geherlicnissum] r *possibly to be read as* p; geheplicnissum *Sweet, Collins, Berghaus.*
4. cicatrices] *orig.* cycatrices: y *deleted,* i *interl.* plagę] plagæ *Brock.*

5.	37.9	rugiebam : granode ł asten (*fol. 6r, left margin*)
6.	41.8	cataractarum : cataracte forsceta catarecte aqua*m* concludunt (*fol. 9v, right margin*)
7.	106.29	in auram : in wedr (*fol. 59r, interl.*)
8.	106.34	in salsilaginem : on saltne mersc (*fol. 59r, interl.*)
9.	108.29	diploide : sciccing tuif[e]al[dum] (*fol. 61v, interl.*)
10.	111.10	fremet : grimmeþ (*fol. 62r, right margin*)
11.	117.13	Inpulsus : ascoben (*fol. 65v, interl.*)
12.	117.13	uersatus sum : afeoll (*fol. 65v, interl.*)
13.	119.4	desolatoriis : þem ascadendu*m*. quia carbones inseparunt scoria de ferro (*fol. 73v, right margin*)
14.	119.5	incolatus meus : min wrecscype (*fol. 73v, interl.*)
15.	120.3	commotionem : onhrernisse (*fol. 74r, interl.*)
16–17.	125.4	torrens in austro: suþrador australis toris smolt regn (*fol. 75v, right margin*)
18–19.	127.3	nouella oliuarum : þa gingan eletriow qui fructifere*n*s [es]t (*fol. 76r, right margin*)
20.	128.4	concidet : sliet (*fol. 76v, interl.*)
21.	130.2	ablactatus : from milcum adoen (*fol. 77r, interl.*)
22.	134.13	memoriale : gemyndelic (*fol. 78v, interl.*)
23.	136.2	In salicibus : on welgum (*fol. 80r, interl.*)
24.	143.13	Promptuaria : cellaria uini. i*d est* hordern (f*ol. 85r, left margin*)
25.	143.13	foetosae : fecundae berende (*fol. 85r, interl.*)
26.	149.6	gladii : sueord (*fol. 88r, interl.*)

8. saltne] a *faint;* s[a]ltne *Brock;* s[ ]ltne *Berghaus.*

9. diploide] *1st* i *on eras.* tuif[e]al[dum]] tuif alþ *MS: reconstruction assumes reading of* d *for* ð (*transcribed as* þ), *and necessary emendation of* e *and* um.

12. afeoll] *although written above* uersatus sum, *properly glosses* caderem (*later in verse*), *as recorded by Berghaus.*

13. desolatoriis] *1st* i *written in red and retraced in brown ink.*

15. onhrernisse] *like* berende (*no. 25*), *final* e *has prolonged tongue, with bottom of letter looping upwards;* onhrernisset *Brock;* on hrernisse *Wildhagen.*

16–17. smolt regn] *taken by Sweet as compound, rejected by all others.*

18–19. eletriow] o *interl. in red;* eletri[o]w *Sweet, Collins.* fructiferens [es]t] *conflated as* fructiferenst: *2nd* f *questionable, may be* u.

23. salicibus] sallicibus *Berghaus.*

24. Promptuaria] *altered by corr. from* Prumptuaria. cellaria] celluria (?).

25. foetosae] fetose *Berghaus.* berende] berendet *Brock.*

26. sueord] *following* ancipites *glossed* ut f[:::] parte acutum.

appendix 2

FOLIO REFERENCES FOR PSALM VERSES

For the convenience of readers wishing to consult manuscripts, the lists below match psalm verses in psalters ABCDEFGHIJKLM with their manuscript folio numbers. Psalm titles are not included in the disposition of the verses, nor is the numbering of occurrences of identical words case-sensitive.

A London, BL, Cotton Vespasian A. 1 (Vespasian Psalter)

12r 2.4–3.2 me (*2nd*)
12v 3.3–4.5 cor(dibus)
13r 4.5 (cor)dibus–5.8 tuae
13v 5.8 introibo–6.3 sunt
14r 6.3 omnia–7.3 redimat
14v 7.3 neque–13 con(uertamini)
15r 7.13 (con)uertamini–8.4
15v 8.5–9.6 sęculi
16r 9.7 Inimici–16 eorum
16v 9.17–26 tempore
17r 9.26 Auferuntur–35 enim
17v 35 derelictus–10.6
18r 10.7 Pluet–11.7
18v 11.8 Tu–12.6
19r 13.1–6 consilium
19v 13.6 inopis–15.2 tu
20r 15.2 quoniam–10
20v 15.11–16.8 me
21r 16.9–15
21v 17.2–8 sunt
22r 17.8 et (*4th*)–17
22v 17.18–28
23r 17.29–38
23v 17.39–49 me (*2nd*)
24r 17.49 a–18.8 fidele
24v 18.8 ientiam–19.4
25r 19.5–20.5
25v 20.6–21.3 meus
26r 21.3 clamabo–21.15 mea
26v 21.15 Factum–21.24
27r 21.25–22.2 conlocauit
27v 22.2 super–23.4
28r 23.5–24.6 domine
28v 24.6 et–24.16
29r 24.17–25.5
29v 25.6–11
31r 26.1–7
31v 26.8–27.3 me (*2nd*)
32r 27.3 cum (*3rd*)–28.3 aquas
32v 28.3 deus–29.6
33r 29.7–30.4 tu
33v 30.4 et (*2nd*)–12 meis (*2nd*)
34r 30.12 Qui–21
34v 30.22–31.5 operui
35r 31.5 Dixi–32.4
35v 32.5–17 autem
36r 32.17 uirtutis–33.9
36v 33.10–23 suorum
37r 33.23 et–34.10 tibi
37v 34.10 eripens–20 loquebantur
38r 34.20 et–35.3 inueniret
38v 35.3 iniquitatem–13
39r 36.1–11
39v 36.12–23
40r 36.24–34
40v 36.35–37.6 meae (*1st*)
41r 37.6 a–15
41v 37.16–23
42r 38.2–8
42v 38.9–39.4 nostro
43r 39.4 uidebunt–12 tua (*2nd*)
43v 39.12 semper–40.2
44r 40.3–11
44v 40.12–41.7 iordanis
45r 41.7 et (*2nd*)–42.2
45v 42.3–43.5

46r	43.6–16
46v	43.17–26
47r	44.2–10 tuo
47v	44.10 Adstitit– 45.3 contur(babitur)
48r	45.3 (contur)babitur– 46.3 terribilis
48v	46.3 rex–47.8 uehe(menti)
49r	47.8 (uehe)menti–48.4
49v	48.5–14 post
50r	48.14 ea–49.1
50v	49.2–13 taurorum
51r	49.13 aut–23
51v	50.3–10
52r	50.11–21

B Oxford, Bodleian Library, Junius 27 (Junius Psalter)

10r	2.4–13
10v	3.2–4.2
11r	4.3–5.4
11v	5.5–12 æternum
12r	5.12 exultabunt–6.9
12v	6.10–7.6
13r	7.7–15
13v	7.16–8.6
14r	8.7–9.7 destruxisti
14v	9.7 Perit–16
15r	9.17–26 eius (*1st*)
15v	9.26 polluuntur–33
16r	9.34–10.4
16v	10.5–11.6 pauperum
17r	11.6 nunc–12.5
17v	12.6–13.4 nonne
18r	13.4 cognoscent–14.4 magnificat
18v	14.4 Qui–15.7
19r	15.8–16.4
19v	16.5–14 eos
20r	16.14 et–17.6
20v	17.7–15
21r	17.16–25 meam
21v	17.25 et (*2nd*)–35 proelium
22r	17.35 et–44
22v	17.45–18.3
23r	18.4–11
23v	18.12–19.6
24r	19.7–20.5
24v	20.6–14
25r	21.2–11
25v	21.12–20 me
26r	21.20 ad–28 patriæ
26v	21.28 gentium–22.4
27r	22.5–23.5 domino
27v	23.5 et–24.5
28r	24.6–14
28v	24.15–25.2
29r	25.3–12
29v	26.1–6 immolabo
30r	26.6 in (*2nd*)–14
30v	27.1–7
31r	27.8–28.8 solitudinem
31v	28.8 et–29.7 habundantia
32r	29.7 non–30.2
32v	30.3–10 meus
33r	30.10 anima–16
33v	30.17–23 meæ
34r	30.23 dum–31.6 tempore
34v	31.6 oportuno–32.2 cythara
35r	32.2 in (*2nd*)–11
35v	32.12–22
36r	33.2–10
36v	33.11–21
37r	33.22–34.6
37v	34.7–15 conuenerunt
38r	34.15 congregauerunt– 25 nostræ
38v	34.25 ne–35.6 tua
39r	35.6 et–13

39v	36.1–9
40r	36.10–20 peribunt
40v	36.20 Inimici–28
41r	36.29–38
41v	36.39–37.8
42r	37.9–17
42v	37.18–23
43r	38.2–8
43v	38.9–39.3 dixerit
44r	39.3 gressus–11 dixi
44v	39.11 Non–17 dominus
45r	39.17 qui–40.7 est
45v	40.7 cor–14
46r	41.2–9 suam
46v	41.9 et–42.3 aduxerunt
47r	42.3 in (*1st*)–43.5
47v	43.6–15
48r	43.16–24
48v	43.25–44.14 intus
49v	44.14 In–45.6 commouebitur
50r	45.6 Adiuuabit–46.4 nobis
50v	46.4 et–47.8
51r	47.9–48.3
51v	48.4–13 intellexit
52r	48.13 comparatus–21 intellexit
52v	48.21 comparatus–49.9 uitulos
53r	49.9 neque–18
53v	49.19–50.5 agnosco
54r	50.5 et–14
54v	50.15–21

C Cambridge, University Library Ff. 1. 23 (Cambridge Psalter)

5r	1.1
5v	1.2–6
6r	2.1–7 meus
6v	2.7 es–13
7r	3.2–7 domine
7v	3.7 saluum–4.4 quoniam
8r	4.4 magnificauit–8
8v	4.9–5.6 malignus
9r	5.6 neque–9
9v	5.10–13 benedices
10r	5.13 iustum–6.5
10v	6.6–10
11r	6.11–7.6 ini(micis)
11v	7.6 (ini)micis–9 domine (*2nd*)
12r	7.9 Secundum–14 ipso
12v	7.14 parauit–8.2 dominus
13r	8.2 noster–5
13v	8.6–9.2 tibi
14r	9.2 domine–7 eorum
14v	9.7 destruxisti–12 psallite
15r	9.12 domino–16
15v	9.17–21
16r	9.22–26 suorum
16v	9.26 dominabitur–31 suo
17r	9.31 humiliauit–35 enim
17v	9.35 derelictus–10.2 confido
18r	10.2 quomodo–6 diligit
18v	10.6 iniquitatem–11.3
19r	11.4–8
19v	11.9–12.4
20r	12.5–13.1 bonum
20v	13.1 non (*3rd*)–3 sanguinem
21r	13.3 Contrito–7 suę
21v	13.7 Lętetur–14.4 non
22r	14.4 décipit–15.4 accelerauerunt
22v	15.4 Non–8 dominus
23r	15.8 ne–16.1 meae
23v	16.1 Auribus–6 me
24r	16.6 deus–11
24v	16.12–15 dum
25r	16.15 manifestabitur–17.6 laquei
25v	17.6 mortis–10
26r	17.11–16 aquarum
26v	17.16 et–20
27r	17.21–26 cum

27v 17.26 uiro–31
28r 17.32–36
28v 17.37–42 nec (*2nd*)
29r 17.42 exaudiuit–47
29v 17.48–18.2 manuum
30r 18.2 eius–7 usque
30v 18.7 ad–11 pretiosum
31r 18.11 multum–15
31v 19.2–7 peti(tiones)
32r 19.7 (peti)tiones–20.2 super
32v 20.2 salutare–7 benedic(tione)
33r 20.7 (benedic)tione–12 te
33v 20.12 mala–21.3 non
34r 21.3 ad–9 uult
34v 21.9 eum–15 mea
35r 21.15 Et–19 mea
35v 21.19 et–21.25 preces
36r 21.25 pauperum–29 regnum
36v 21.29 et–22.2 educa(uit)
37r 22.2 (educa)uit–6 domini
37v 22.6 in–23.5 benedictionem
38r 23.5 a–9 gloriae
38v 23.9 Quis–24.5 sustinui
39r 24.5 tota–10 miseri(cordia)
39v 24.10 (miseri)cordia–15 dominum
40r 24.15 quoniam–20 confundar
40v 24.20 quoniam–25.3 com(placui)
41r 25.3 (com)placui–8
41v 25.9–26.1 timebo
42r 26.1 Dominus (*2nd*)–4 domini
42v 26.4 et–8 tuum
43r 26.8 domine–12 testes
43v 26.12 iniqui–27.2
44r 27.3–6 dominus
44v 27.6 quoniam–28.1 filios
45r 28.1 aríetum–6
45v 28.6–29.2 meos
46r 29.2 super–7
46v 29.8–11
47r 29.12–30.3 protectorem
47v 30.3 et–8 tua
48r 30.8 misericordia–11
48v 30.12–16 mea
49r 30.16 Libera–20 sperantibus
49v 30.20 in (*1st*)–24 sancti
50r 30.24 eius–31.3 clamarem
50v 31.3 tota–6 multarum
51r 31.6 ad–11
51v 32.1–6
52r 32.7–11 cogitationes
52v 32.11 cordis–16 multitudine
53r 32.16 fortitudinis–22 sperauimus
53v 32.22 in–33.6
54r 33.7–11
54v 33.12–18 dominus
55r 33.18 exaudiuit–23 non
55v 33.23 derelinquet–34.4 michi
56r 34.4 mala–9 delectabitur
56v 34.9 super–13 con(uertetur)
57r 34.13 (con)uertetur–17
57v 34.18–23 dominus
58r 34.23 meus (*2nd*)–27 dominus
58v 34.27 qui–35.5 bonę
59r 35.5 maliciam–10
59v 35.11–36.2 arescent
60r 36.2 et–7 faciente
60v 36.7 iniquitatem–12 den(tibus)
61r 36.12 (den)tibus–17 confirmat
61v 36.17 autem–22 male(dicentes)
62r 36.22 (male)dicentes–27
62v 36.28–33 derelin(quet)
63r 36.33 (derelin)quet–37
63v 36.38–37.3 infixę
64r 37.3 sunt–7 ingredi(ebar)
64v 37.7 (ingredi)ebar–12 appropiauerunt
65r 37.12 et (*2nd*)–16
65v 37.17–21 mihi
66r 37.21 quoniam–38.4 intra
66v 38.4 me–7 ignorat
67r 38.7 cui–12 eius

67v	38.12 Veruntamen– 39.3 deprecationem
68r	39.3 mean–6 est
68v	39.6 quis–10 ecce
69r	39.10 labia–13 comprehederunt
69v	39.13 me–16
70r	39.17–40.3 in (*1st*)
70v	40.3 terra–7 lo(quebantur)
71r	40.7 (lo)quebantur–12 inimi(cus)
71v	40.12 (inimi)cus–41.3
72r	41.4–7 meus
72v	41.7 A–10 ini(micus)
73r	41.10 (ini)micus–42.1
73v	42.2–5 confi(tebor)
74r	42.5 (confi)tebor–43.4 multus
74v	43.4 tui–10 con(fudisti)
75r	43.10 (con)fudisti– 15 commutationem
75v	43.15 capitis–21 nostri
76r	43.21 et–25
76v	43.26–44.5 procede
77r	44.5 et (*2nd*)–8
77v	44.9–13 deprecabuntur
78r	44.13 omnes–18 progenie
78v	44.18 Propterea– 45.5 sanctificauit
79r	45.5 tabernaculum–10
79v	45.11–46.6 et
80r	46.6 dominus–47.2
80v	47.3–9 uidi(mus)
81r	47.9 (uidi)mus–14 eius
81v	47.14 et–48.5 in
82r	48.5 psalterio–11 et (*1st*)
82v	48.11 stultus–15 eos
83r	48.15 Et (*2nd*)–19
83v	48.20–49.3 ardebit
84r	49.3 et (*2nd*)–8 sunt
84v	49.8 semper–14 lau(dis)
85r	49.14 (lau)dis–19
85v	49.20–49.23
86r	50.3–6 iustificeris
86v	50.6 in–11
87r	50.12–17
87v	50.18–21

D London, BL, Royal 2 B. v (Regius Psalter)

8r	1.1–5 neque
8v	1.5 peccatores– 2.6
9r	2.7–3.3
9v	3.3–4.2 tribu(latione)
10r	4.2 (tribu)latione–9 et
10v	4.9 requiescam–5.8 ado(rabo)
11r	5.8 (ado)rabo–13
11v	6.2–9 omnes
12r	6.9 qui–7.6 inimicus
12v	7.6 animam–13 conuer(tamini)
13r	7.13 (conuer)tamini 8.3 laudem
13v	8.3 Propter–10
14r	9.2–9 cum
14v	9.9 iustitia–16
15r	9.17–24 peccator
15v	9.24 in–30 leo
16r	9.30 in (*2nd*)–36 peccatoris
16v	9.36 et–10.5 cælo
17r	10.5 sedes–11.4
17v	11.5–12.3 Vsquequo
18r	12.3 exaltabitur–13.1
18v	13.2–5 illic
19r	13.5 trepidauerunt–14.4 nihilum
19v	14.4 deductus–15.4 nominum
20r	15.4 illorum–11 adimple(bis)
20v	15.11 (adimple)bis–16.6 deus
21r	16.6 inclina–16.13 meam
21v	16.13 ab–17.4 dominum
22r	17.4 et–9
22v	17.10–16 in(spiratione)
23r	17.16 (in)spiratione–23
23v	17.24–31

24r	17.32–40 et	44v	34.26 qui (*2nd*)–35.6 et
24v	17.40 precincxisti–47	45r	35.6 ueritas–13
25r	17.48–18.4 sermones	45v	36.1–8 et
25v	18.4 quorum–10	46r	36.8 derelinque–15
26r	18.11–19.2	46v	36.16–24 contur(babitur)
26v	19.3–10	47r	36.24 (contur)babitur–32 et
27r	20.2–8	47v	36.32 querit–40
27v	20.9–14	48r	37.2–7
28r	21.2–10 uentre	48v	37.8–14 mutus
28v	21.10 spés–17 me	49r	37.14 qui–22 meus
29r	21.17 Foderunt–25 neque	49v	37.22 ne–38.6 uanitas
29v	21.25 auertit–31	50r	38.6 omnis–13 percipe
30r	21.32–22.5	50v	38.13 lacrimas–39.6 fecisti
30v	22.6–23.6	51r	39.6 tu–12 mise(ricordias)
31r	23.7–24.4	51v	39.12 (mise)ricordias–17
31v	24.5–12 dominum	52r	39.18–40.6
32r	24.12 legem–20	52v	40.7–13 con(firmasti)
32v	24.21–25.6	53r	40.13 (con)firmasti–41.6 me
33r	25.7–26.1	53v	41.6 spera–11
33v	26.2–6 eius	54r	41.12–42.5 mea
34r	26.6 hostiam–12 per(sequentium)	54v	42.5 et–43.6 uentilabimus
34v	26.12 (per)sequentium–27.3	55r	43.6 et–14 qui
35r	27.4–9 ex	55v	43.14 in (*2nd*)–22 cordis
35v	27.9 tolle–28.7 commouebit	56r	43.22 Quoniam–44.3 tuis
36r	28.7 dominus–29.6 eius	56v	44.3 Propterea–10 regina
36v	29.6 Ad–13 conpungar	57r	44.10 a–18 erunt
37r	29.13 Domine–30.7 superuacue	57v	44.18 nominis–45.7 sunt
37v	30.7 Ego–13 corde	58r	45.7 gentes–46.3
38r	30.13 et–19 iniquitatem	58v	46.4–47.3
38v	30.19 in–24 retri(buet)	59r	47.4–12 propter
39r	30.24 (retri)buet–31.5 operui	59v	47.12 iudicia–48.6 timebo
39v	31.5 Dixi–10 spe(rantes)	60r	48.6 in–13 intellexit
40r	31.10 (spe)rantes–32.7	60v	48.13conparatus–19 con(fitebitur)
40v	32.8–15 intel(legit)		
41r	32.15 (intel)legit–33.2 tempore	61r	48.19 (con)fitebitur–49.5
41v	33.2 semper–10	61v	49.6–14
42r	33.11–20 et	62r	49.15–22 quando
42v	33.20 de–34.4 erubescant	62v	49.22 rapiat–50.7 me
43r	34.4 qui (*2nd*)–12 retri(buebant)	63r	50.7 mater–16
43v	34.12 (retri)buebant–18 populo	63v	50.17–21
44r	34.18 graui–26 reuerentia		

E Cambridge, Trinity College R. 17. 1 (Eadwine Psalter)

6r	1.1–3 omnia
6v	1.3 quęcunque–6
7r	2.1–6 p̄di(cans)
7v	2.6 (p̄di)cans–13
8r	3.2–5 mea
8v	3.5 ad–9
9r	4.2–5 peccare
9v	4.5 quę–10
10r	5.2–6 iniusti
10v	5.6 ante–11 dolose
11r	5.11 agebant–13
11v	6.2–5 eripe
12r	6.5 animam–11 auer(tantur)
12v	6.11 (auer)tantur–uelociter
13r	7.2–7 domine
13v	7.7 in–13 nisi
14r	7.13 conuertamini–18
14v	8.2–5 Quid
15r	8.5 est–10
15v	9.2–5 causam
16r	9.5 meam–11 non
16v	9.11 derelinques–17 iudicia
17r	9.17 faciens–24 lau(datur)
17v	9.24 (lau)datur–29 inno(centum)
18r	9.29 (inno)centum–35 con(sideras)
18v	9.35 (con)sideras–39
19r	10.2–5 suo
19v	10.5 dominus–8
20r	11.2–4 dominus
20v	11.4 uniuersa–9
21r	12.1–3 inimicus
21v	12.3 meus–6
22r	13.1–3 declinauerunt
22v	13.3 simul–5 deum
23r	13.5 non–7
23v	14.1–5 non
24r	14.5 accepit–15.1 domine
24v	15.1 quoniam–7 tribuit
25r	15.7 intellectum–11
25v	16.1–3 uisitasti
26r	16.3 nocte–9 impiorum
26v	16.9 qui–14 uenter
27r	16.14 eorum–15
27v	17.2–3 salutis
28r	17.3 meę–8 quoniam
28v	17.8 iratus–15 dissipa(uit)
29r	17.15 (dissipa)uit–20 quoniam
29v	17.20 uoluit–27 electus
30r	17.27 eris–33
30v	17.34–39 pedes
31r	17.39 meos–46 claudi(cauerunt)
31v	17.46 (claudi)cauerunt–51
32r	18.2–5 In
32v	18.5 omnem–10 sanctus
33r	18.10 permanet–15 semper
33v	18.15 Domine–19.2 tribulationis
34r	19.2 protegat–8 domini
34v	19.8 dei–10
35r	20.2–6
35v	20.7–12 po(tuerunt)
36r	20.12 (po)tuerunt–14
36v	21.2–4 habitas
37r	21.4 laus–11 deus
37v	21.11 meus–16
38r	21.17–22 humilitatem
38v	21.22 meam–27 Viuet
39r	21.27 cor–32
39v	22.1–4 mecum
40r	22.4 es–10
40v	23.1–4 mundo
41r	23.4 corde–10 uirtutum
41v	23.10 ipse–24.1 animam
42r	24.1 meam–7 boni(tatem)
42v	24.7 (boni)tatem–14 manifestetur

43r 24.14 illis–22 isrł
43v 24.22 ex–25.2 me (*2nd*)
44r 25.2 ure–10 manibus
44v 25.10 iniquitates–12
45r 26.1–5 Quoniam
45v 26.5 abscondit–9 me (*2nd*)
46r 26.9 neque–14
46v 27.1–3 cum (*2nd*)
47r 27.3 operantibus–7 refloruit
47v 27.7 caro–9
48r 28.1–7 domini
48v 28.7 intercidentis–11
49r 29.2–5
49v 29.6–11 ad(iutor)
50r 29.11 (ad)iutor–13
50v 30.2–7 super(uacue)
51r 30.7 (super)uacue–12 obprobrium
51v 30.12 uincis–17
52r 30.18 tua–22 miri(ficauit)
52v 30.22 (miri)ficauit–25
53r 31.1–3
53v 31.4–7
54r 31.8–11
54v 32.1–5 mi(sericordia)
55r 32.5 (mi)sericordia–11 sęculum
55v 32.11 sęculi–18 in
56r 32.18 misericordia–22
56v 33.2–5 In(quisiui)
57r 33.5 (In)quisiui–11 egerunt
57v 33.11 et–18 tribu(lationibus)
58r 33.18 (tribu)lationibus–23
58v 34.1–4 meam
59r 34.4 Auertantur–10 domine
59v 34.10 quis–15 igno(rauerunt)
60r 34.15 (igno)rauerunt–21 Dila(tauerunt)
60v 34.21 (Dila)tauerunt–27 qui
61r 34.27 uolunt–28
61v 35.2–7 multa
62r 35.7 Homines–13
62v 36.1–2
63r 36.3–9 dominum
63v 36.9 ipsi–15
64r 36.16–22 maledicentes
64v 36.22 autem–29 uero
65r 36.29 hęreditate–35
65v 36.36–40
66r 37.2–5 superposuerunt
66v 37.5 caput–11 oculorum
67r 37.11 meorum–17 Quia
67v 37.17 dixi–23 meum
68r 37.23 domine–meę
68v 38.2–6 posuisti
69r 38.6 dies–12 corripuisti
69v 38.12 hominem–14
70r 39.2–4 nostro
70v 39.4 Videbunt–9 tuam
71r 39.9 in–13 uiderem
71v 39.13 Multiplicati–18 et (*1st*)
72r 39.18 pauper–tradeueris
72v 40.2–4
73r 40.5–10 sperabam
73v 40.10 qui–14
74r 41.2–6 uultus
74v 41.6 mei–11 me
75r 41.11 dum–12
75v 42.1–5
76r 43.1–2
76v 43.3–8 affli(gentibus)
77r 43.8 (affli)gentibus–14 circuitu
77v 43.14 nostro–21 expandimus
78r 43.21 manus–26
78v 44.2–3 Propterea
79r 44.3 benedixit–9 gradibus
79v 44.9 eburneis–15 eam
80r 44.15 proxime–18
80v 45.2–4 con(turbati)
81r 45.4 (con)turbati–11 uidete
81v 45.11 quoniam–46.2 Omnes
82r 46.2 gentes–10 uenerunt
82v 46.10 cum–sunt
83r 47.2–8 naues

83v 47.8 tharsis–15 ęternum
84r 47.15 et (*1st*)–scła
84v 48.2–7
85r 48.8–13 comparatus
85v 48.13 est–18 descendit
86r 48.18 cum–21
86v 49.1–4 sursum
87r 49.4 et–11 uo(latilia)
87v 49.11 (uo)latilia–18 furem
88r 49.18 simul–23
88v 50.3–3 secundum
89r 50.3 magnam–8 tuę
89v 50.8 manifestasti–15 te
90r 50.15 conuertentur–21 holocausta
90v 50.21 tunc–uitulos

F London, BL, Stowe 2 (Stowe Psalter)

1r 1.1–2
1v 1.3–2.2 conue(nerunt)
2r 2.2 (con)uenerunt–11
2v 2.12–3.5
3r 3.6–4.3 quid
3v 4.3 diligitis–10
4r 5.2–11 eorum
4v 5.11 linguis–6.3 sum
5r 6.3 sana–11
5v 7.2–7 meorum
6r 7.7 Et–16
6v 7.17–8.4
7r 8.5–9.3
7v 9.4–13 eorum
8r 9.13 recordatus–22 despicis
8v 9.22 in (*1st*)–30 leo
9r 9.30 in (*3rd*)–38
9v 9.39–10.4
10r 10.5–11.3 proximum
10v 11.3 suum–9
11r 12.1–6
11v 13.1–3 eorum (*3rd*)
12r 13.3 ad–7
12v 14.1–5
13r 15.1–8 semper
13v 15.8 quoniam–16.2
14r 16.3–11
14v 16.12–17.3 meum (*1st*)
15r 17.3 et (*1st*)–10 calígo
15v 17.10 sub–18
16r 17.19–28
16v 17.29–37 me
17r 17.37 et–47 meus
17v 17.47 et (*2nd*)–18.4 quorum
18r 18.4 non–12
18v 18.13–19.4
19r 19.5–10
19v 20.2–10 tempore
20r 20.10 uultus–21.2
20v 21.3–12
21r 21.13–21 manu
21v 21.21 canis–29
22r 21.30–22.4 umbre
22v 22.4 mortis–6
23r 23.1–10 uirtutum
23v 23.10 ipse–24.7 meas
24r 24.7 ne–16 quia
24v 24.16 unicus–25.1
25r 25.2–11
25v 25.12–26.4
26r 26.5–11
26v 26.12–27.3 peccatoribus
27r 27.3 et–9 eos
27v 27.9 et (*3rd*)–28.6 uitulum
28r 28.6 libani–29.2
28v 29.3–10
29r 29.11–30.3
29v 30.4–11
30r 30.12–19
30v 30.20–25

31r	31.1–6 sanctus
31v	31.6 in (*1st*)–11
32r	32.1–10 reprobat
32v	32.10 autem–18
33r	32.19–33.2
33v	33.3–11
34r	33.12–21
34v	33.22–34.3
35r	34.4–10
35v	34.11–18 magna
36r	34.18 in (*2nd*)–26
36v	34.27–35.3
37r	35.4–12 manus
37v	35.12 peccatoris–36.6 tuam
38r	36.6 et (*2nd*)–14 inopem
38v	36.14 ut (*2nd*)–23
39r	36.24–34 eius
39v	36.34 et (*2nd*)–37.2 me (*1st*)
40r	37.2 neque–11
40v	37.12–20 sunt
41r	37.20 qui–38.3
41v	38.4–12 defeci
42r	38.12 in–39.3 fecis
42v	39.3 Et (*4th*)–11 meo
43r	39.11 ueritatem–17 te (*2nd*)
43v	39.17 et (*2nd*)–40.3
44r	40.4–12
44v	40.13–41.5 confessionis
45r	41.5 sonus–12 me
45v	41.12 Spera–42.4 meam
46r	42.4 Confitebor–43.4
46v	43.5–14
47r	43.15–23
47v	43.24–44.3
48r	44.4–11
48v	44.12–18
49r	45.2–10
49v	45.11–46.6
50r	46.7–47.3
50v	47.4–14 eius
51r	47.14 et–48.5 meam (*1st*)
51v	48.5 aperiam–13 in(tellexit)
52r	48.13 (in)tellexit–20 uidebit
52v	48.20 lumen–49.3 noster
53r	49.3 et (*1st*)–12 est
53v	49.12 enim–50.21 similis
54r	49.21 arguam–50.3 miserationum
54v	50.3 tuarum–12
55r	50.13–21

G London, BL, Cotton Vitellius E. xviii (Vitellius Psalter)

18r	1.1–5
18v	1.6–2.11 [ei]
19r	2.11 in (*2nd*)–4.2 michi
19v	4.2 Mis[er]ere–5.5
20r	5.6–6.2
20v	6.3–7.2 per(sequentibus)
21r	7.2 (per)sequentibus–12
21v	7.13–8.7 [eum]
22r	8.7 super–9.10 pauperi
22v	9.10 adiutor–20
23r	9.21–30 rape[re]
23v	9.30 pauperem–10.2 montem
24r	10.2 sicut–11.5 sunt
24v	11.5 quis–12.6 cantabo
25r	12.6 domino–13.5 trepida(uerunt)
25v	13.5 (trepida)uerunt–15.2 meus
26r	15.2 es–11
26v	16.1–10
27r	16.11–17.7 clamaui
27v	17.7 [E]t (*2nd*)–17 assumpsit
28r	17.17 me (*2nd*)–28
28v	17.29–39
29r	17.40–51
29v	18.2–11
30r	18.12–19.7

30v	19.8–20.9 oderunt (*1st*)
31r	20.9 oderunt (*2nd*)–21.8 me (*2nd*)
31v	21.8 locuti–18 mea
32r	21.18 [I]psi–28 terrę
32v	21.28 Et (*2nd*)–22.5 me
33r	22.5 [Inpin]guasti–23.9 uestras
33v	23.9 et (*1st*)–24.9 docebit
34r	24.9 mites–21
34v	24.22 [Li]bera–25.12 ęcclesis
35r	25.12 benedicam–26.7
35v	26.8–27.2
36r	27.3–28.1 domino (*2nd*)
36v	28.1 [filios]–29.2 delectast[i]
37r	29.2 inimicos–12 circum(dedisti)
37v	29.12 (circum)dedisti– 30.10 meus (*1st*)
38r	30.10 anima–19 iustum
38v	30.19 [i]niquitat[e]m– 31.2 dominus
39r	31.2 pecc[atu]m– 31.10 sperantem
39v	31.10 autem–32.10 popul[orum]
40r	32.10 et–22 [n]os
40v	32.22 [quemad]modum– 33.13 diligit
41r	33.13 dies–34.1
41v	34.2–11 ignorabam
42r	34.11 interrogabant–20 terrę
42v	34.20 [l]oque[n]tes–35.3 eius

43r	35.3 [ut]–13 iniquitat[em]
43v	35.3 [expuls]i–36.10
44r	36.11–21
44v	36.22–33 eum (*2nd*)
45r	36.33 cum–37.5 sunt
45v	37.5 caput–15
46r	37.16–38.3 silui
46v	38.3 a–12 uane
47r	38.12 [con]turbatur–39.6
47v	39.7–14
48r	39.15–40.4
48v	40.5–14
49r	41.2–8
49v	41.9–42.4 deum
50r	42.4 [q]ui–43.8 nos (*2nd*)
50v	43.8 et–19
51r	43.20–44.3
51v	44.4–13 tuum
52r	44.13 [de]pręcabuntur– 45.5 [dei]
52v	45.5 [sanc]tificauit–46.5
53r	46.6–47.9 ciuita[te]
53v	47.9 [d]omini–48.6 iniquitas
54r	48.6 calcanei–16 animam
54v	48.16 [meam]–49.5 ordin[ant]
55r	49.5 testamentum–17 proiecisti
55v	49.17 sermones–50.6 tuis
56r	50.6 et (*2nd*)–19 contribulatus
56v	50.19 cor–21

H London, BL, Cotton Tiberius C. vi (Tiberius Psalter)

31r	1.1–1 impiorum
31v	1.1 et (*1st*)–2.3
32r	2.4–3.3
32v	3.4–4.5
33r	4.6–5.8
33v	5.9–6.5
34r	6.6–7.6 compre(hendat)
34v	7.6 (compre)hendat–18
35r	8.2–10

35v	9.2–14
36r	9.15–26
36v	9.27–38 preparati(onem)
37r	9.38 (preparati)onem– 10.8 ęquitatem
37v	10.8 uidit–11.9
38r	12.1–6
38v	13.1–7
39r	14.1–5

39v	15.1–11
40r	16.1–10
40v	16.11–17.4 meis
41r	17.4 saluus–15 eos
41v	17.15 fúlgura–28 oculos
42r	17.28 superborum–40 supplan(tasti)
42v	17.40 (supplan)tasti–51
43r	18.2–11 dulciora
43v	18.11 super–19.7 suum
44r	19.7 Exaudiet–20.7
44v	20.8–21.5 te
45r	21.5 sperauerunt–17 me (*2nd*)
45v	21.17 Foderunt–28 terrę
46r	21.28 Et–22.5 me
46v	22.5 Inpinguasti–23.5
47r	23.6–24.6
47v	24.7–18
48r	24.19–25.9
48v	25.10–26.3 hoc
49r	26.3 ego–12 me (*3rd*)
49v	26.12 testes–27.5 opera
50r	27.5 manuum–28.4
50v	28.5–29.5
51r	29.6–30.2
51v	30.3–12 meis
52r	30.12 Qui–22 ciuitate
52v	30.22 munita–31.4
53r	31.5–11
53v	32.1–14
54r	32.15–22
54v	33.2–16
55r	33.17–34.3 animę
55v	34.3 męę–14 compla(cebam)
56r	34.14 (compla)cebam–26 gratu(lantur)
56v	34.26 (gratu)lantur–35.5
57r	35.6–36.2
57v	36.3–14
58r	36.15–27 in
58v	36.27 seculum–38
59r	36.39–37.9 rugie(bam)
59v	37.9 (rugie)bam–20 confirmati
60r	37.20 sunt (*1st*)–38.5 meum
60v	38.5 Et–14 priusquam
61r	38.14 abeam–39.8 uenio
61v	39.8 In–17 que(rentes)
62r	39.17 (que)rentes–40.7 loque(batur)
62v	40.7 (loque)batur–41.3
63r	41.4–12 me
63v	41.12 Spera–42.5
64r	43.2–11 nostros
64v	43.11 et–22 die
65r	43.22 ęstimati–44.4
65v	44.5–15 proxi(mę)
66r	44.15 (proxi)mę–45.7 sunt (*2nd*)
66v	45.7 regna–46.7
67r	46.8–47.9
67v	47.10–48.5
68r	48.6–16
68v	48.17–49.4 discernere
69r	49.4 populum–17 proiecisti
69v	49.17 sermones–50.3 miserationum
70r	50.3 tuarum–15 con(uertentur)
70v	50.15 (con)uertentur–21

I London, Lambeth Palace, 427 (Lambeth Psalter)

5v	1.2–6
6r	2.1–7
6v	2.8–13
7r	3.2–8 causa
7v	3.8 dentes–4.5 quę
8r	4.5 dicitis–5.2 domine
8v	5.2 intellige–8 tue
9r	5.8 Introibo–12 eis

9v	5.12 Et (*3rd*)–6.7 per
10r	6.7 singulas–7.2 persequentibus
10v	7.2 me (*2nd*)–8 te
11r	7.8 Et (*3rd*)–15 iniustitiam
11v	7.15 concepit–8.4 digitto(rum)
12r	8.4 (digitto)rum–9.1
12v	9.2 –9 aequita(te)
13r	9.9 (aequita)te–16 fecerunt
13v	9.16 In (*3rd*)–23 pauper
14r	9.23 comprehenduntur–29
14v	9.30–34
15r	9.35–10.2 in (*2nd*)
15v	10.2 montem–7
16r	10.8–11.6 fiducialiter
16v	11.6 agam–12.4 meus
17r	12.4 Illumina–13.2 deum
17v	13.2 Omnes–5 timore
18r	13.5 ubi–14.4 conspectu
18v	14.4 eius–15.4
19r	15.5–11 delec(tationes)
19v	15.11 (delec)tationes–16.5
20r	16.6–12
20v	16.13–17.2 refu(gium)
21r	17.2 (refu)gium–17.8 sunt (*1st*)
21v	17.8 et (*2nd*)–15 multi(plicauit)
22r	17.15 (multi)plicauit–21 puritatem
22v	17.21 manuum–28 facies
23r	17.28 et–35 proelium
23v	17.35 Et–41
24r	17.42–48
24v	17.49–18.4
25r	18.5–10 saeculi
25v	18.10 iudicia–15
26r	19.2–7 nomine
26v	19.7 domini–20.5 ei
27r	20.5 longitudinem–11
27v	20.12–21.5 libe(rasti)
28r	21.5 (libe)rasti–13 multi
28v	21.13 tauri–19 mea
29r	21.19 et–21
30r	21.32–22.5 me
30v	21.5 Impinguasti–23.4
31r	23.5–24.2
31v	24.3–7
32r	24.8–15
32v	24.16–25.1 domino [fol. 32 doubled]
32ra	25.1 sperans–10 sunt
32vb	25.10 dextera–26.3
33r	26.4–8
33v	26.9–27.1 me (*1st*)
34r	27.1 nequando–5
34v	27.6–28.2 honorem
35r	28.2 afferte–9
35v	28.10–29.6 fletus
36r	29.6 et (*2nd*)–13 tibi
36v	29.13 gloria–30.7 superuacuae
37r	30.7 Ego–13 datus
37v	30.13 sum–19 iustum
38r	30.19 iniquitatem–24 quoniam
38v	30.24 ueritatem–31.5 abscondi
39r	31.5 Dixi–9 eorum
39v	31.9 constringe–32.5 iudicium
40r	32.5 misericordia–12 eius
40v	32.12 populus–19
41r	32.20–33.5 me (*2nd*)
41v	33.5 Accedite–14 et
42r	33.14 labia–21
42v	33.22–34.5 faciem
43r	34.5 uenti–12
43v	34.13–19 aduersantur
44r	34.19 mihi–26 reuerentia
44v	34.26 qui–35.5
45r	35.6–12 non
45v	35.12 moueat–36.7 eum
46r	36.7 Noli–14 suum
46v	36.14 ut–20
47r	36.21–28
47v	36.29–36
48r	36.37–37.4 meis
48v	37.4 a (*2nd*)–11

49r 37.12–17
49v 37.18–38.2 consis(teret)
50r 38.2 (consis)teret–7
50v 38.8–13
51r 38.14–39.6 tibi
51v 39.6 Annuntiaui–11
52r 39.12–16
52v 39.17–40.5 ani(mam)
53r 40.5 (ani)mam–11 re(suscita)
53v 40.11 (re)suscita–41.4 mihi (*2nd*)
54r 41.4 cotidie–9 mandauit
54v 41.9 dominus–42.1 homine
55r 42.1 iniquo–43.2 nobis
55v 43.2 Opus–8
56r 43.9–16 est
56v 43.16 et–22
57r 43.23–44.3
57v 44.4–9 quibus
58r 44.9 delectauerunt–17 filii
58v 44.17 constitues–45.6 commouebitur
59r 45.6 adiuuabit–46.3 magnus
59v 46.3 super–47.2
60r 47.3–11 fines
60v 47.11 terrae–48.4 me(ditatio)
61r 48.4 (me)ditatio–12 ęternum
61v 48.12 Tabernacula–18 omnia
62r 48.18 neque–49.3
62v 49.4–11
63r 49.12–19 lin(gua)
63v 49.19 (lin)gua–50.3 tuam
64r 50.3 et–10 lętitiam
64v 50.10 et–18 dedis(sem)
65r 50.18 (dedis)sem–21

J London, BL, Arundel 60 (Arundel Psalter)

13r 1.1–1 abiit
13v 1.1 in–2.6 sion
14r 2.6 montem–3.7
14v 3.8–5.3
15r 5.4–13
15v 6.2–7.3 dum
16r 7.3 non–15
16v 7.16–8.10
17r 9.2–14 de
17v 9.14 inimicis–26 tempore
18r 9.26 Auferuntur–36 queretur
18v 9.36 peccatum–10.8
19r 11.2–12.4 meus
19v 12.4 Inlumina–13.4 iniquitatem
20r 13.4 qui–15.2 bonorum
20v 15.2 meorum–16.1 meam (*2nd*)
21r 16.1 Auribus–13
21v 16.14–17.8
22r 17.9–21 secundum (*2nd*)
22v 17.21 puritatem–35
23r 17.36–46
23v 17.47–18.8
24r 18.9–19.6
24v 19.7–20.9 tuis
25r 20.9 dextera–21.9
25v 21.10–22 unicornium
26r 21.22 humilitatem–32
26v 22.1–23.4
27r 23.5–24.7 memineris
27v 24.7 Secundum–20 erubescam
28r 24.20 quoniam–25.12
28v 26.1–8
29r 26.9–27.4
29v 27.5–28.8
30r 28.9–29.11 est (*2nd*)
30v 29.11 adiutor–30.10 est
31r 30.10 in–20
31v 30.21–31.5
32r 31.6–32.6
32v 32.7.–20 pro(tector)
33r 32.20 (pro)tector–33.13 dies
33v 33.13 uidere–34.4 meam

34r 34.4 Auertantur–14
34v 34.15–26 meis
35r 34.26 Induantur–35.9
35v 35.10–36.9 susti(nentes)
36r 36.9 (susti)nentes–21
36v 36.22–35 sicut
37r 36.35 cedros–37.8 et
37v 37.8 non–20 sunt (*1st*)
38r 37.20 super–38.7
38v 38.8–39.4
39r 39.5–13
39v 39.14–40.6 quando
40r 40.6 morietur–41.4 nocte
40v 41.4 dum–12 me
41r 41.12 Spera–43.4 terram
41v 43.4 et (*1st*)–16 et
42r 43.16 confusio–44.2 regi
42v 44.2 Lingua–13 depreca(buntur)
43r 44.13 (depreca)buntur–45.7 regna
43v 45.7 dedit–47.2 ciuitate
44r 47.2 dei–48.2
44v 48.3–15 matutino
45r 48.15 et (*2nd*)–49.6
45v 49.7–21 te
46r 49.21 et–50.12
46v 50.13–21

K Salisbury, Cathedral Library 150 (Salisbury Psalter)

12r 2.2 [aduer]sus–12
12v 2.13–3.9
13r 4.2–9
13v 4.10–5.9
14r 5.10–6.4
14v 6.5–7.3 redimat
15r 7.3 neque–12 patiens
15v 7.12 numquid–8.3 des(truas)
16r 8.3 (des)truas–9.5 causam
16v 9.5 meam–14
17r 9.15–23
17v 9.24–32 deus
18r 9.32 auertit–10.2
18v 10.3–11.3 unusquisque
19r 11.3 ad–12.2
19v 12.3–13–3 eorum
20r 13.3 linguis–14.1
20v 14.2–15.4 eorum
21r 15.4 de–11
21v 16.1–16.9 adflixerunt
22r 16.9 Inimici–17.3 re(fugium)
22v 17.3 (re)fugium–10 descendit
23r 17.10 et (*2nd*)–18 me (*2nd*)
23v 17.18 quoniam–28 superborum
24r 17.28 humiliabis–38 donec
24v 17.38 deficiant–48
25r 17.49–18.7
25v 18.8–15 semper
26r 18.15 Domine–19.9
26v 19.10–20.8
27r 20.9–21.4
27v 21.5–15 cera
28r 21.15 liquescens–25 depre(cationem)
28v 21.25 (depre)cationem–32 cæli
29r 21.32 iustitiam–22.6
29v 23.1–9
30r 23.10–24.8
30v 24.9–18
31r 24.19–25.7 enarrem
31v 25.7 uniuersa–26.3 meum
32r 26.3 Si (*2nd*)–10 dere(liquerunt)
32v 26.10 (dere)liquerunt–27.3
33r 27.4–9
33v 28.1–10
34r 28.11–29.8
34v 29.9–30.4
35r 30.5–13 tamquam

35v	30.13 mortuus–21	46r	39.13 mei–40.3 non
36r	30.22–31.5 impie(tatem)	46v	40.3 tradat–11
36v	31.5 (impie)tatem–32.3 bene	47r	40.12–41.6 ad(huc)
37r	32.3 psallite–13	47v	41.6 (ad)huc–12
37v	32.14–33.3	48r	42.1–43.2
38r	33.4–14	48v	43.3–14 subsannati(onem)
38v	33.15–34.2 scutum	49r	43.14 (subsannati)onem–24
39r	34.2 et (*2nd*)–11 ignora(bam)	49v	43.25–44.7
39v	34.11 (ignora)bam–19 oderunt	50r	44.8–18 gene(ratione)
40r	34.19 me–28	50v	44.18 (gene)ratione–45.9
40v	35.2–11 scien(tibus)	51r	45.10–46.9
41r	35.11 (scien)tibus–36.7	51v	46.10–47.10
41v	36.8–18 et	52r	47.11–48.6
42r	36.18 hereditas–28 dere(linquet)	52v	48.7–15 uete(rascet)
42v	36.28 (dere)linquet–37	53r	48.15 (uete)rascet–49.3 exardescet
43r	36.38–37.8 illusionibus		
43v	37.8 et–17 supergaudeant	53v	49.3 et (*2nd*)–15 tribulationis
44r	37.17 mihi–38.4 in	54r	49.15 et (*2nd*)–23
44v	38.4 meditatione–12	54v	50.3–12 [rest of psalm wanting]
45r	38.13–39.6 tibi		
45v	39.6 Adnuntiaui–13 capitis		

L London, BL, Additional 37517 (Bosworth Psalter)

4r	1.1–2	12r	17.36–51
4v	1.3–2.12 dominus	12v	18.2–15 semper
5r	2.12 et–4.7 [4.7 Dedisti…meo from fol. 5v repeated on fol. 5r]	13r	18.15 Domine–20.5
		13v	20.6–21.7
5v	4.7 Dedisti–5.12	14r	21.8–23
6r	6.2–7.7 tuorum	14v	21.24–22.4
6v	7.7 Exurge–8.6 honore	15r	22.5–24.3
7r	8.6 coronasti–9.15 ad(nuntiem)	15v	24.4–20
7v	9.15 (ad)nuntiem–30 sua	16r	24.21–26.1 timebo
8r	9.30 Insidiatur–10.6 iniquita(tem)	16v	26.1 Dominus–12 me (*1st*)
8v	10.6 (iniquita)tem–12.4 meus	17r	26.12 quoniam–27.9 heredi(tati)
9r	12.4 Inlumina–13.6	17v	27.9 (heredi)tati–29.5
9v	13.7–15.5 qui	18r	29.6–30.5 mihi
10r	15.5 restituisti–16.6	18v	30.5 quoniam–16
10v	16.7–17.5 iniquitatis	19r	30.17–31.2
11r	17.5 conturbauerunt–18 qui	19v	31.3–11
11v	17.18 oderunt–35	20r	32.1–15

20v 32.16–33.8
21r 33.9–34.2
21v 34.2–14 conplacebam
22r 34.14 tamquam–26
22v 34.27–35.12
23r 35.13–36.12 eum
23v 36.12 dentibus–25
24r 36.26–37.2 furore
24v 37.2 tuo–14
25r 37.15–38.7 quamquam
25v 37.7 in–39.5 respixit
26r 39.6 in (*1st*)–15
26v 39.16–40.11
27r 40.12–41.10
27v 41.11–43.3
28r 43.4–16 confusio
28v 43.16 uultus–44.4 accingere
29r 44.4 gladio–17
29v 44.18–45.12
30r 46.2–47.9 uirtutum
30v 47.9 in (*2nd*)–48.11 sapientes
31r 48.11 morientes–49.2
31v 49.3–20 aduersus (*2nd*)
32r 49.20 filium–50.12
32v 50.13–21

M New York, Pierpont Morgan Library M. 776 (Blickling Psalter)

64r 9.9–21 eos
64v 9.21 ut–30 pauperem
[9.30 respiciunt–31.3 mea wanting]
1r 31.3 dum–11
1v 32.1–12 populus
2r 32.12 quem–33.2
2v 33.3–15
3r 33.16–34.3
3v 34.4–13 ieiunio
4r 34.13 animam–23 meum
4v 34.23 deus–35.6 tua
5r 35.6 et–36.3 in (*1st*)
5v 36.3 habita–15
[36.16–38 wanting]
6r 36.39–37.10
6v 37.11–20 me (*1st*)
7r 37.20 et (*2nd*)–38.7
7v 38.8–39.4 nostro
8r 39.4 Uidebunt–13 uiderem
8v 39.13 Multiplicati–40.4
9r 40.5–14
9v 41.2–10 es
10r 41.10 Quare–42.5
10v 43.2–11 nostris
11r 43.11 et–22 die
11v 43.22 aestimati–44.5
12r 44.6–17 filii
12v 44.17 constitues–45.9 posuit
13r 45.9 prodigia–46.9
13v 46.10–47.12 filiae
14r 47.12 iudae–48.10
14v 48.11–19 benedicetur
15r 48.19 et–49.8 holocausta
15v 49.8 autem–19
16r 49.20–50.7
16v 50.8–19 spernit
[rest of psalm wanting]

psalms 1–50

PSALM 1

1

Beatus	eadig *CDGF^{2}*H*, eadi *J*, Æði *E^{1}** (*IL*)
uir	wer C*DF^{2}GJ*, se wcrc *E^{1}** (*HIL*)
qui	se C, se þe D*J*, se ðe *G*, se (ð)e F*, þe E^{1} (*HIL*)
non	ne CE^{1}F*GJ*, na D (*HIL*)
abiit	gewat C*G*, eode D*E^{1}*, ferde F*J* (*HIL*)
in	in C, on DE^{1}FG (*HIL*)
consilio	geþeahte CFG, geþeahte D, ðere rede ł þæhte E$^{1/x}$* (*HIL*)
impiorum	arleasra CDF, arleasre E^{x}*, arleas G (*HL*)
et	⁊ CE^{1}F^{2}GH (*L*)
in	on CE^{1}DF^{2}GH (*L*)
uia	wege CF^{2}GH, wege D, þan wege E^{1} (*L*)
peccatorum	synfulra CDF^{2}G, synfulr H, of þan sunfullan E^{1} (*L*)
non	na CDF^{2}H, ne GE^{1} (*L*)
stetit	stod CDE^{1}F^{2}H, gestod G (*L*)
et	⁊ CDE^{1}F^{2}GH (*L*)
in	on CDE^{1}F^{2}GH (*L*)
cathedra	þrymsetle C, þrysetle F^{2}, heahsetle DG, heahse[ ]le H*, þan setele E^{1} (*L*)
pestilentiae	cwyldes *C*, cwyldes ł wawan *DH*, wolberendra *G*, of þan quulmere *E^{x}** (F**IJL*)
non	na CF^{2}H, ne E^{1}G (*L*)
sedit	sæt CDF^{2}H, set E^{1}, siteð G (*L*)

ED: se (ð)e (F)] se ðe *Kimmens*. abíít (E)] abiit *Harsley*. pestilentiæ (D)] pestilentiae *Roeder*. pestilentię (E)] pestilentiae *Harsley*.

OE: F: *except for* se (ð)e…arleasra, *all glosses to Ps 1 written in 16th-c. hand on eras.* Æði (E^{1})] *possibly by corr.* se were (E^{1})] *possibly by corr.* se (ð)e (F)] *cross-stroke of* ð *not visible*. ðere rede ł þæhte (E$^{1/x}$)] ede ł þæhte *on eras. by corr.* arleasre (E^{x})] *on eras.* heahse[ ]le (H)] *letter lost due to tear in leaf.* pestilentiae (F)] *gloss eras.* of þan quulmere (E^{x})] *on eras.*

LTg: Beatus] BEATVS CDEFGHIJL. uir] VIR CEFGHIL; UIR J. qui] QVI GHIJL. non (*1st*)] NON GHIJL. abiit] abíít E; ABIIT GHJ; HABIIT L. in (*1st*)] IN HL. consilio] CONSILIO HL. abiit in consilio] ABiit in consilio I: *later hand has written* non abiit in consilio *again, with each letter beside or within corresponding letter in main hand.* impiorum] IMPIORVM HL. et (*1st*)] ET L. in (*2nd*)] IN L. uia] VIA L. peccatorum] PECCATORVM L. non (*2nd*)] NON L. stetit] STETIT L. et (*2nd*)] ET L. in (*3rd*)] IN L. cathedra] CATHEDRA L. pestilentiae] pestilentie CJ, I: *eras. after 2nd* i;

pestilentiæ D; pestilentię GH, E: *on eras.;* PESTILENTIE L. non *(3rd)*] NON L. sedit] SEDIT L.

LTu: Beatus] BEA[ ] ς; BEATVS VIR ζι; BEATUS VIR τ*τ; BEATVS VIR QVI ν; BEATUS VIR QVI NON ABIIT ε; BEATVS VIR QVI…IMPIORUM λ; BEATVS VIR…HABIIT IMPIORUM μ; BEATUS VIR…HABIIT…IMPIORUM υ; BEATUS…HABIIT…IMPIOrum ξ; BEATVS VIR QVI…IMPIORVM ο; BEATUS VIR QVI…IMPIORVM…VIA PECCATORVM δ: *wanting vv 2–end;* BEATUS UIR…SEDIT β; BEATVS VIR QVI…SEDIT π; BEATVS VIR …PECCATORVM…SEDIT ϱ; BEATVS…QVI…HABIIT…VIA…PESTILENTIE…SEDIT σ. abiit] habiit ζϑνς. et (*1st*)] Et ϑ. et (*2nd*)] Et ϑ. pestilentiae] pestilentie ιςτ*τ; pestilentię εϑξο.

2

Sed		ac CDE^{1}F^{2}GHI*J (*L*)
in		on CDE^{1}F^{2}HIJ, in G (*L*)
lege		æ CE^{x}*F^{2}GHIJ, ę D (*L*)
domini		drihnys C, drihtnes F^{2}I*, drihtenes J, drihn̄ G, driht́ H, of þan lauorde E^{1} (*D*L*)
fuit*		wæs C, wes *E^{1}*
uoluntas	|	willa C*D*E^{1}**GH, willan F^{2}J, his I (*L*)
eius	|	hys C, his D*E^{1}**F^{2}GH, is J, willa I (*L*)
et		⁊ CD*E^{1}**F^{2}GHIJ (*L*)
in		on CDE^{1}F^{2}GHIJ (*L*)
lege	|	æ CE^{1}F^{2}GHJ, ǽ D, his I (*L*)
eius	|	hys C*, his DE^{1}F^{2}GHJ, æ I (*L*)
meditabitur		byð smead C, bið ł smead F^{2}, smeaþ J, s[ ]að G, smeað ł foreþæncð D, smeað ł foreþænð H, he smeaþ ł foreþenceþ I*, sceal smægan ł þencean E$^{1/x}$* (*L*)
die		dagys C*, dæges DGHIJ, dagis F^{2}, bi deige E^{1} (*L*)
ac		⁊ CD*E^{1}F^{2}*GHIJ (*L*)
nocte		nihtes CDF^{2}GHIJ, bi nihte E^{1} (*L*)

ED: bið ł smead (F)] biðsmead *Kimmens.*

OE: ac (I)] s. fuit : wæs *interlin. after word.* æ (E^{x}) (*1st*)] *on eras.* domíní (D)] *gloss* (?) *eras.* drihtnes (I)] e *slightly obscured by stain.* willa (C)] *2nd* l *and perhaps* a *retraced in red crayon.* willa (E^{1})] *on eras. from Lat. line below.* his (E^{1}) (*1st*)] *on eras. from Lat. line below.* ⁊ (E^{1})] *on eras. from Lat. line below.* hys (C) (*2nd*)] *leg of* h *retraced in red crayon.* he smeaþ ł foreþenceþ (I)] þenc *slightly obscured by stain.* sceal smægan ł þencean (E$^{1/x}$)] smægan *added on eras. by corr. from Lat. line above,* ł *added in next line in left margin.* dagys (C)] *retraced in red crayon.*

LTg: Sed…nocte] SED…VOLVNTAS EIVS…EIVS MEDITABITVR…NOC[ ] L. domini] domíní D: *on eras.; written by same corr. who wrote* qu *of 2nd* quod, *2nd* Et, defluet, *and* fatiet *in Ps 1.3,* eius *in Ps 2.6,* o *of* eo *in Ps 2.13, and 1st* l *of* maliloquam *and 2nd* e (*retouched*) *of* felaspeculan *in Ps 11.4.* fuit] *on eras.* E; *lost* D: *perhaps due to eras. of previous word;* FVIT L: *eras. but visible: see GAg.* uoluntas] *on eras.* E. eius (*1st*)] *on eras.* E. et] E: *partly on eras., added in right margin.* ac] F^{2}: *written in 16th-c. hand over another word* (*2 letters*); ác E. nocte] NOC[ ] L: *remainder wanting.*

LTu: δ: *remainder of psalm* (*vv 2–end*) *wanting.* die] dię ε.

GAg: fuit] *om.* FGHIJ; for DL *see LTg.*

GAu: fuit] *om.* εζθιλμξοπϱστυψ

3

Et		⁊ CE^{1}F^{2}GHIJ
erit		bið CDF^{2}*GJ*, biþ *H,* he bið I, sceal beon E^{1}
tamquam		swa swa *C*DF^{2}*H*I, swa *G*J, alswea *E^{1}*
lignum		treow CDE^{1}F^{2}HI, þæt treow GJ
quod		þæt CGHJ, þæt D, ðæt F^{2}, þet E^{1}, þe I
plantatum	|	geplantud C*, geplantad *G*, geplantod J, plantud DF^{2}H, geplantod is þæt ðe geset I, is *E^{1}*
est	|	ys C, is DF^{2}HIJ, bið G, geset E^{1}
secus		neh C*F^{2}, wið DHI, be GJ, bi E^{1}
decursus		ryne C*DF^{2}H, ða rynas E^{1}, rynas I, þam rynum G, þam rinum J
aquarum		wætera CF^{2}GHIJ, wætra D, of þa wæteras E^{1}*
quod		þæt *C*GHJ, þæt F^{2}, þet *E^{1}*, þæt þe I (*DL*)
fructum	|	wæstm C*DF^{2}HJ, westm I, his E^{1} (*G*)
suum	|	hys C, his DF^{2}HIJ, wæstm ł blæd E$^{1/x}$*
dabit		sylyð C*, sylð F^{2}, syleð G, syleþ J, selð DH, selð ł forgifð I, sceal giuan E^{1}
in		on CDE^{1}F^{2}GHIJ
tempore	|	tide C*DF^{2}HJ, tíde G, his E^{1}I
suo	|	his CDGHJ, hys F^{2}, tide I, timan *E^{1}*
Et		⁊ *CE^{1}*F^{2}*G*HIJ (*DL*)
folium	|	leaf CDF^{2}HI, leafa GJ, his E^{1}
eius	|	his CDF^{2}GHIJ, læf E^{1}
non		ne CE^{1}F^{2}GIJ, na DH
decidet*		gefeallað *C**, fylð F^{2}, feallað G, fealleþ J, tofleuwð I, sceal tofallan E^{1}* (*D*L*)
et		⁊ C*E^{1}F^{2}GHIJ
omnia		eall CF^{2}, ealle D*G*HJ, ealle þingc I, alle þa þing E^{1}

quaecumque	swa hwæt swa *C*GIJ*, swa hwelce swa *D*, swa hwylce swa *F²*, swa hwilc swa *H*, þa hit æure *E¹* (*L*)
fecerit*	deð CG, deþ J, he deð F²I, he deþ H, doth E¹ (*D*L*)
prosperabuntur	beoð gesundfullude C, beoð gesundfullude D, beoþ gesundfullude H, beoð gesunfullude F², beoð gespedde ł beoð gesundfullode I, gesundfulliað *G*, gesundfulliaþ J, beoð sundfullede E¹*

ED: ęrit (G)] erit *Rosier.* tanquam (C)] ta[m]quam *Wildhagen.* alswea (E)] al swea *Harsley.* swa swa (I)] swaswa *Lindelöf.* geplantod is þæt ðe geset (I)] geplantod is ł þæt ðe geset *Lindelöf.* défluet (GH)] defluet *Rosier, Campbell.* quęcunque (CE)] quęcu[m]que *Wildhagen;* quaecunque *Harsley.*

OE: geplantud (C)] ge *retraced in red crayon.* neh (C)] *eras. before word.* ryne (C)] yn *retraced in pencil.* of þa wæteras (E¹)] *eras.* (*1 letter?*) *after* þa. wæstm (C)] wæ *retraced in pencil.* wæstm ł blæd (E¹/ˣ)] wæstm ł *added by corr.* sylyð (C)] l *and* ð *retraced in pencil.* tide (C)] *top of* t *retraced in red crayon.* defluet (D)] *gloss* (?) *eras. above word.* gefeallað (C)] fealla *retraced in red crayon, 2nd* a *may orig. have been another letter.* sceal tofallan (E¹)] *letter eras. before* f. ⁊ (C) (*3rd*)] *retraced in red crayon.* swa hwæt swa (C)] hw *and 2nd* swa *retraced in red crayon,* æ *may orig. have been* e. fatiet (D)] *eras.* (*of gloss?*) *above word.* beoð sundfullede (E¹)] *1st* d *retraced, possibly on eras., right leg of* n *possibly retraced.*

LTg: erit] ęrit GH. tamquam] tanquam CEH: *orig.* tamquam: *left leg of 1st* m *eras. to form* n, G: *orig.* tamquam: *right leg of 1st* m *eras. to form* n. plantatum] E: plan *on eras.;* plan[ ] G. quod (*2nd*)] D: q *and 1st leg of* u *on eras.: see LTg note to v. 2* domini; Quod CE, L: *eras. after* Q, *with traces of orange ink visible.* fructum] *lost* G. suo] E: *following punct. on eras.* Et (*2nd*)] D: *on eras.: see LTg note to v. 2* domíní; [ ]t G: *initial* E *lost;* et CEL. decidet] C: *orig.* dicidet: *1st* i *altered to* e, L: id *eras. but visible;* defluet D: *on eras.: see GAg.* omnia] omni[ ] G. quaecumque] quecumque DJL; quęcumque FGI; quęcunque E, C: *orig.* quęcumque: *left leg of* m *eras. to form* n; quecunque H: *orig.* quecumque: *right leg of* m *eras. to form* n. fecerit] L: *underlined and* faciet *interl. by corr.;* fatiet D: *on eras.: see GAg.* prosperabuntur] prosperabuntu[ ] G.

LTu: tamquam] tanquam ζϑιλϱτ*τ. quod (*2nd*)] Quod βνςτ*. Et (*2nd*)] et βνςτ*. decidet] decidit β. quaecumque] quęcumque μνοϱ; quęcunque εζϑι; quecumque ξσς; quecunque τ*τ.

GAg: decidet] defluet FIJ, D: *see OE, see also LTg note to v. 2* domíní; défluet GH. fecerit] faciet FGHIJ, L: *see LTg;* fatiet D: *see OE, see also LTg note to v. 2* domíní.

GAu: decidet] defluet εζϑιλμξοπϱστυψ. fecerit] faciet εζϑιλμξοπϱστυψ.

4

Non — nalys C, nalǽs G, nalæs J, na F^{2}H, Na E^1*, ne I*

sic — swa CDE^1*F^{2}HIJ, swá G

impii — þa arleasan CIJ, þa árleasan G, þa arleas F^2, arlease DH, arleasa *E^1**

non — nalys C, nalæs GJ, na E^1*HI

sic — swa C*D*E^{1}GHIJ, sy F*

sed — ac CF^{2}GHIJ, ah E^1

tamquam — swa swa *C*DF^2*GH*IJ, swa *E^1*

puluis — dust CDF^{2}HI, mil ł dust J, þet dust E^1* (*G*)

quem — þæt CDF^2*, þæt GHJ, þet E^1

proicit | awearp *C*, awyrpð *D*, awea[ ]pð *F^2**, aweorpeð G, awurpeð J, wyrpþ H, se wind E^1 (I*)

uentus | wind CDF^{2}GHI*J*, aworpet E^1

a — from CF^2, fram GJ, fram I, from of *E^1*, of DH

facie — ansyne C*D*F^2*GHI*, ansine *E^1*J (*L*)

terrae — eorðan *CDF^{2}HJ*, eorþan *E^1*I, eorþa[ ] *G* (*L*)

ED: impíí (E)] impii *Harsley*. tanquam (C)] ta[m]quam *Wildhagen*. swa swa (GIJ)] swaswa *Rosier, Lindelöf, Oess*. pro[ ]cit (F)] proicit *Kimmens*. awea[ ]pð (F)] awearpð *Kimmens*. á (E)] a *Harsley*. facię (E)] faciae *Harsley*. terrę (E)] terrae *Harsley*. eorþan (I)] eorþa *Lindelöf* (*but correct in appendix, p. 323*).

OE: Na (E^1)] *orig*. Ne: e *altered to* a *by corr.* ne (I)] synt. s. sunt *interl. after* ne. swa (E^1)] *eras. after word extending to following* arleasa. arleasa (E^1)] *eras. after word.* na (E^1)] *orig*. ne: e *altered to* a *by corr.* sy (F)] *orig. gloss, incompletely eras.; letter fragments visible before this word, above* non. þet dust (E^1)] *eras. after* þet, *trace of* d *visible* (dust *written on next line*). þæt (F^2)] *part of orig. gloss, mistakenly to* quem, *visible through eras. after* þæt: *2 descenders visible, followed by ascender and cross-stroke of* ð; *Kimmens reads* rpð. awea[ ]pð (F^2)] *letter fragment visible after 2nd* a; *Kimmens reads* awearpð: *'r barely visible around hole in MS.'* proicit (I)] *gloss eras. above word.*

LTg: sic (*2nd*)] síc D. impii] impíí E. tamquam] tanquam E, C: *orig*. tamquam: *left leg of 1st* m *eras. to form* n, GH: *orig*. tamquam: *right leg of 1st* m *eras. to form* n. puluis] *lost* G. proicit] proícít C; proıecıt D; pro[ ]cit F: *letter lost due to hole in leaf.* uentus] uentos J. a] á E. facie] facię DEGL; faciae I. terrae] terrę CDEFHJL; terr[ ] G.

LTu: tamquam] tanquam εζϑιλϱτ*τ. proicit] proiecit βϑ; proiciet ς. uentus] uentos ς. facie] facię ενξυ; faciae λψ. facie terrae] faci&errae μ. terrae] terrę ιξ; terre σςτ*τ; terræ ϑ.

5

Ideo	forþon CF^{2}J, forðon D, f[ ]rþon *G**, forþan H, Forðan E^{1}, forþi I
non	ne CE^{1}F^{2}GI, na DH, nan J
resurgunt	arisað CDG, arisaþ *E*^{1}*HIJ, ar[ ]sað F^{2}*
impii	arlease *C*DH, ða arlease F^{2}, þa arleasan GIJ, þa arlesan *E*^{1}
in	on CDE^{1}*F^{2}GHIJ
iudicio	dome CDE^{1}F^{2}*G*HIJ
neque	ne CE^{1}F^{2}I, na J, ⁊ ne DH (*G*)
peccatores	þa synfullan C*IJ, þa sinfullan F^{2}, synfulle DH, þa firen ł synfullan E$^{1/x}$* (*G*)
in	on CDE^{1}F^{2}GIJ
consilio	geþeahte CF^{2}GIJ, <u>ge</u>þeahte D, geþeahte ł rede E$^{1/x}$*
iustorum	rihtwisra CE^{x}*F^{2}I, ryhtwisra D, soðfæstra GJ

ED: f[ ]rþon (G)] forþon *Rosier.* impíí (E)] impii *Harsley.* [ ]res G] *peccatores Rosier.*

OE: f[ ]rþon (G)] *letter lost due to hole in leaf.* arisaþ (E^{1})] *eras. after word.* ar[ ]sað (F^{2})] *letter lost due to hole in leaf.* on (E^{1}) (*1st*)] *eras. after word.* þa synfullan (C)] *right leg of 1st* n, f, *and* u *retraced in pencil.* þa firen ł synfullan (E$^{1/x}$)] *orig.* þa firenfullan: ł syn *interl. by corr.* geþeahte ł rede (E$^{1/x}$)] ł rede *on eras. by corr.* rihtwisra (E^{x})] *on eras. by corr.*

LTg: Ideo] [ ]deo G: *initial* I *lost.* resurgunt] E: *scraping above and below word.* impii] ímpii C; impíí E. iudicio] iudici[ ] G. neque] *lost* G. peccatores] [ ]res G.

LTu: consilio] concilio ζλμπ, ϱ: *orig.* consilio: s *deleted,* c *interl.*

6

Quoniam	forþon C, forðon DJ, forðon ðe F^{2}, Forðan þe E^{1}, forþan þe I (*G*)
nouit	| w(a)t C*, wat IJ, wiste D, wyste F^{2}, dryhten E^{1}
dominus	| drihtyn C, drihten F^{2}GI, driħt J, cneow E^{1}*
uiam	weg CDF^{2}GIJ, weig E^{1} (*H*)
iustorum	rihtwisra CF^{2}IJ, soðfæstra G, þara soþfestra E^{1}
et	⁊ CE^{1}F^{2}GIJ
iter	siðfæt C*F^{2}GI, siþfæt DJ, siþfet E^{1}
impiorum	arleasra F^{2}IJ, þara arleasra E^{1}, arleas[ ] *G**
peribit	forweorðyð C, forweorðeð G, forwurðeþ J, forwurþað E^{1}*, forwyrð D, forwyrð ł losaþ I, loseað ł forwyrþaþ F^{2}

ED: w(a)t (C)] wat *Wildhagen.* arleas[ ] (G)] ar[ ] *Rosier.*

OE: w(a)t (C)] at *faint, back of* a *not visible.* cneow (E^{1})] *eras.* (*2 letters*) *before* *word.* arleas[ ] (G)] s *cropped.* siðfæt (C)] fæt *retraced in pencil.* forwurþað (E^1)] *eras. before word.*

LTg: Quoniam] [ ]m G. uiam] uia H. impiorum] im[ ] G.

LTu: peribit] ξ: *lost to damage.*

PSALM 2

1

Quare	forhwon *C*F^2, forhwan *E*^{2}, forhwi GI, hwy *D*, hwi H, forþan J
fremuerunt	grymetydon *C**, grymetedon DGI, grymmetedon *E*^{2}*, grimetedon H, gnornode J (F*)
gentes	þeoda *C**D*G*HIJ, ðeoda F^2, þeode E^2
et	⁊ CF^{2}GHIJE^2
populi	folc CDF^{2}GHIJE^2*
meditati	smeagynde C, smeagende J, s(m)[ ](g)ende G*, smeadon DHI, hi smeadon F^2, smeagdon E^2*
sunt	synt C, synd GJ
inania	in idelnnysse *C**, idelnessa I, idelnesse E^2, unnyttu ł idelu D*, unnite ł idele H, on idle G, on idel J (F*)

ED: forhwan (E)] Forhwan *Harsley.* fremuérunt (E)] fremuerunt *Harsley.* s(m)[ ](g)ende (G)] sm[ ]gende *Rosier.* in idelnnysse (C)] in idelnysse *Wildhagen.*

OE: F: *except for illegible gloss to* inania (*v. 1*), be *of* becomon (*v. 2*), ge *of* gegripað (*v. 12*), of (*v. 12*), r *of* rihtan (*v. 12*), aman *of* graman (*v. 13*), hys (*v. 13*), *and* ealle (*v. 13*), *all glosses to Ps 2 written in 16th-c. hand on eras.* grymetydon (C)] do *retraced in pencil.* grymmetedon (E^2)] don *on eras.* fremuerunt (F)] *gloss eras.* þeoda (C)] od *retraced in pencil.* folc (E^2)] *eras. before word.* s(m)[ ](g)ende (G)] *right leg of* m *lost, top of* g *lost due to hole.* smeagdon (E^2)] don *on eras., eras. after word.* in idelnnysse (C)] *2nd* n *in* idelnnysse *interl.* unnyttu ł idelu (D)] e *interl.* inania (F)] *part of orig. gloss visible: ascender followed by 3–4 illegible letters and* yt.

LTg: Quare] QUARE C; QVAre D; QVARE E. fremuerunt] FREMUÉRUNT C; fremuérunt E. gentes] GENTES C; g[ ] G. inania] inánia C.

LTu: δ: *v. 1 wanting,* χ: *vv 1–2* principes *wanting.* Quare] QUare β; QVARE ιξτ*τ; QUARE FREMUERUNT μ; QUARE FREMUErunt ψ; QUARE...GENTES λϱ. sunt inania] ξ: *lost due to damage.*

2

Adstiterunt	ætstodon *CDF*^{2}*HI*, etstoden *E*^{2}, æt gestodan GJ
reges	cyningas CDF^{2}GH, kyningas I, kyniges J, eorðan E^2

terrae | eorðan *C*DGIJ,* eorþan *F^{2}H,* cyninges *E^2* (*L*)
et ⁊ CF^{2}GHJE^{2}*
principes ealdorm̄ C, ealdormenn D, ealdormen HJ, ealdermen E^2, [ ]ldorm[ ] *G,* ealdras F^{2}I
conuenerunt gesomnedun *C,* becomon DF/F^2*H, becomen E^x*, eftcomon G, eftcomon ł samod comon J, ⁊ samod comon I
in on C*F^{2}GIJ
unum annysse C*, toso m̲ne D, tosomne E^x*H, an F^{2}GIJ
aduersus wið CG, ongean DE^x*HJ, togeanes F^{2}I
dominum drihten C*F^2, dryhten E^x*, drihtne GIJ, driħt H
et ⁊ CF^{2}GHIJE^x*
aduersus wið CG, togeanes F^{2}I, ongean E^x*HJ (*K*)
christum | criste C*E^2*F^2*GJ, crist DH, his criste ł his gecorenum̲ I*
eius | hys C*, his E^{2}F^{2}GHJ (*K*)

ED: Astitérunt (C)] A[d]stitérunt *Wildhagen.* etstoden (E)] Et stoden *Harsley.* terrę (CE)] terre *Wildhagen;* terrae *Harsley.* ealdorm̄ (C)] ealdorm*enn Wildhagen.* [ ]ldorm[ ] (G)] [ ]m[ ] *Rosier.* eftcomon (J)] eft comon *Oess.*

OE: eorðan (C)] an *retraced in pencil.* ⁊ (E^2) *(1st)*] *eras. after word.* becomon (F/F^2)] *see OE note to F at v. 1.* becomen (E^x)] *on eras.* on (C)] n *retraced in pencil.* annysse (C)] annyss *retraced in pencil.* tosomne (E^x)] *on eras.* ongean (E^x) (*1st*)] *on eras.* drihten (C)] ri *and* en *retraced in pencil.* dryhten (E^x)] *on eras.,* y *interl.* ⁊ (E^x) (*2nd*)] *on eras.* ongean (E^x) (*2nd*)] *on eras.* criste (C)] c *and* s *retraced in pencil.* his criste ł his gecorenum̲ (I)] *eye of 2nd* e *in* gecorenum̲ *partly obscured.* hys (C)] *retraced in pencil.*

LTg: Adstiterunt] F: A *possibly supplied later;* Astitérunt C: *letter eras. after* A; Astiterunt E, H: A *partly lost due to burning from ink, letter* (?) *eras. after* A; Asstiterunt I. terrae] terrę CDFGHJL, E: *2nd* r *in left margin* (ter/rę). principes] G: c *partly cropped due to hole in leaf.* conuenerunt] conuenérunt C. aduersus] [ ]sus K: *text begins here.* christum] cristum F. eius] eíus K.

LTu: Adstiterunt] Asstiterunt δ; Astiterunt εζιλξοπστ*τυ; Asteterunt βϑ; Adstixerunt μ. terrae] terrę ειν; terre ξοσςτ*τ; terræ ϑ. aduersus] adusus ϑ: *no expansion indicated.*

3

Disrumpamus tosliten we *C,* we tosliten *D*F^2*E^x*,* we tosliton G*HK,* uton toslitan J, uton tobrecan *I*
uincula | bendas CDF^{2}GJK, bændas H, heora E^{2}I
eorum | hyra CD, heora F^{2}GHJK, bendas E^{2}I
et ⁊ CE^{2}F^{2}GHIJK
proiciamus aworpyn we *C*,* aweorpan we E^2, aweorpen F^2, awurpen J,

	utun awyrpan DH, onweg awurpon G, uton aweg awerpan I, utawurpan K
a	from C, fram DGHJK, fram F²I (*E*)
nobis	I us CF²GHIJK, ús D, heora E²
iugum	I ioc C, geoc DE²F²GHJK, heora I
ipsorum	I heora CDF²GHJK, ioc I, from us E²

ED: Dirumpámus (C)] Di[s]rumpámus *Wildhagen.* Dirumpamus (D)] Disrumpamus *Roeder.* á (E)] a *Harsley.*

OE: we tosliten (Eˣ)] *on eras.* aworpyn we (C)] py *retraced in pencil.*

LTg: Disrumpamus] Dirumpámus C: *eras after* i; Dirumpamus E, D: s (*partly visible*) *eras. after* i, HIK: *eras. after* i. proiciamus] próiciámus C. a] á E.

LTu: Disrumpamus] Dirumpamus εζιλξπϱστ*τχ.

4

Qui	se *AB*CGJ, se þe DH, Se þe E², se ðe F²I, þa K
habitat	eardað ABC*F²GH*K*, eardaþ DIJ, eardeð E²
in	in AB, on CDE²F²GHIJK
caelis	heofenum A*E²I*, heofenum *G*, heofonum *BDH*J, heofonum *F²*, hefynum *C*, heofenan *K* (*L*)
inridebit	bismerad A*, bysmerað *F²*, bismrað *BG*, bysmrað *C**, bysmraþ *J*, gebismeraþ ł hyscð *I*, hyscþ D, hiscð *H*, hyspð *K*, ispeð ł hyscþ *Eˣ**
eos	hie ABCG, hy D*F², hi HK, hig IJ, hio E²
et	⁊ A*B*CE²F²GHIJK
dominus	dryhten B, drihten E²F²GIK, driht̄ A, drih̄t C*HJ
subsannabit	hyspeð *A*BDF²G*K*, hyspyð *C*, hyspeþ H, hyspeð ł holeð E²/ˣ*, ahiscð J, tælð I
eos	hie ABC*E²G, hi F²HIK, hig J

ED: cælis (D)] caelis *Roeder.* cęlis (EI)] caelis *Harsley, Lindelöf.* bismerad (A)] bismerað *Sisam²: see OE; Sisam² also notes eras. of ca 3 letters before* hie.

OE: eardað (C)] að *retraced in pencil.* bismerad (A)] *faint stroke perhaps visible on right side of* d, *at intersection of bowl and ascender* (*typical placement for* ð), *thus giving* bismerað. bysmrað (C)] *stem of* y *and* r *retraced in pencil.* ispeð ł hyscþ (Eˣ)] *added by corr.* hy (D)] *another* hy *written above and to left of gloss, apparently added after Lat. gloss in right margin* (*cf. Roeder: 'vielleicht da das untere* hy *mit der lat. Randglo. zu nahe aneinander kam und undeutlich wurde'*). drih̄t (C)] h̄t *retraced in pencil.* hyspeð ł holeð (E²/ˣ)] hyspeð ł *added by corr.* hie (C) (*2nd*)] ie *retraced in pencil.*

LTg: Qui] AB: *Ps 2 begins here.* habitat] abitat K. caelis] cælis BDK; celis C; cęlis EGHIL; coelis F: o *in 16th-c. hand on eras.* (*Kimmens:* 'co *gone over by s. xvi glossator*'). inridebit] B: *descender of* r *eras.;* irridebit CEFGIJ, H: *1st* r *on eras.*, K: *orig.* inridebit: n *altered to* r. et] Et B. subsannabit] A: *2nd* b *on eras.*, K: *orig.* subsanabit: *macron added above 1st* a *by corr.;* subsannábit C.

LTu: in] *om.* β. caelis] cęlis ειξοχ; celis σςτ*τυ; cælis ϑ; *om.* β. inridebit] irridebit εζϑιλνξοπϱστ*τυχ.

5

Tunc — ðonne A, þonne BE^{2}F^{2}GHIJK, þonne CD
loquetur — spriceð *A*B, sprecyð he C*, sprecð he E^{2}, he spycð DK, he spycþ H, he sprycð F^{2}, he sprycþ G, he sprecð IJ
ad — to ABCDE^{2}F^{2}GHIJK
eos — him ABCGH, him DF^{2}, heom IJK, hem E^{2}
in — in AB, on CDE^{2}F^{2}GHIJK
ira | eorre AB, yrre C*F^{2}GK, irre J, his DE^{2}HI
sua | his ABGJK, hys C*F^{2}, eorre D, yrre H, irre E^{2}, graman I
et — ⁊ *AB*CE^{2}F^{2}GHIJ, ⁊ ⁊ K
in — in AB, on CDE^{2}F^{2}GHIJK
furore | hatheortnisse AD, hatheortnysse *C**F^{2}, hatheortnesse BGHJK, his E^{2}I
suo | his ABC*DF^{2}GJK, hatheortnesse I, wylme ł hatheortnysse E$^{2/x*}$
conturbabit — gedroefeð A, gedrefeð BG, he gedrefyð C*, gedrefð DF^{2}*H,* he gedrefð E^{2}I, he gedrefeþ J, gedrefde K*
eos — hie ABCG, heo E^{2}, hy F^{2}, hi H, hig IJ, his K

OE: sprecyð he (C)] yð *and cross-stroke of final* e *retraced in pencil.* yrre (C)] e *retraced in pencil.* hys (C)] *retraced in pencil.* hatheortnysse (C)] rtnyss *retraced in pencil.* his (C)] *retraced in pencil.* wylme ł hatheortnysse (E$^{2/x}$)] ł hatheortnysse *added by corr.* he gedrefyð (C)] he, ge, y, *and cross-stroke of* ð *retraced in pencil.* gedrefde (K)] *otiose stroke before word* (*Sisam notes* '? c *begun*').

LTg: loquetur] A: e *on eras.* et] Et AB. furore] furóre C. conturbabit] H: *2nd* b *on eras.*

LTu: loquetur] loquitur β. in (*1st*)] *lost* ξ. conturbabit] conturbauit ς.

6

Ego — ic ABCF^{2}*G*HIJK, Ic E^{2}
autem — soðlice ABCE^{2}GI, soþlice DF^{2}HJ, witodlice K
constitutus | geseted AB*G*H, gesetyd C, gesetet D, geset F^{2}I*K, wæs geset J, heom E^{2}
sum | ic eam A, ic eom BC, eom DF^{2}GHIK, heom J, geseted E^{2}

rex — cyning ABCF^{2}G, cyncg H, kyning IJ, cining E^{2}K
ab — from ABC*, From E^2, fram DF^{2}GHJ, fram I, of K
eo — him ABE^{2}F^{2}GHI, him *C**DJ, heo K
super — ofer ABC*DF^{2}GHIJK, ofor E^2
sion — sion ABF^{2}HJ, syon *C*E^2*, seon G, sceawere *I*
montem | mont A, munt BCDF^{2}GHJK, his E^{2}I
sanctum | ðone halgan A, þone halgan BCGJ, haligne DE^{2}H, haline K, haligan F^2, halga I
eius | his ABCF^{2}GHJ*K*, dune E^{2}I
praedicans — bodiende A*BDH*, bodiynde *C**, bodigende *F^{2}GIJK*, ⁊ lerende *E^2* (*L*)
praeceptum | bibod A, bebod *BCDF^{2}GHJ*, beboda *K*, drihtnes E^2, his I (*L*)
domini* | dryhtnes B, dryhƚ A, drihnes C*, his F^{2}GHJK, bebod *E^2*, bebod ł lare I (*D*)

ED: soðlice (E)] soþlice *Harsley*. From (E)] fro*m Harsley*. sion (Lat.) (K)] Sion *Sisam*. syon (C)] s[i]on *Wildhagen*. p̄dicans (D)] praedicans *Roeder*. p̄ceptum (D)] praeceptum *Roeder*.

OE: geset (I)] *top of* s *faint*. from (C)] *retraced in pencil*. him (C)] *retraced in pencil*. ofer (C)] o *interl*., fer *retraced in pencil*. syon (C)] s *retraced in pencil*. bodiynde (C)] de *retraced by corr. in light brown ink*. drihnes (C)] *retraced by corr. in light brown ink*.

LTg: Ego] G: g *cropped at bottom by tear in leaf*. constitutus] G: *1st* tu *interl*. eo] éo C. sion] syon EI, C: y *on eras. by corr*. eius] eíus K. praedicans] predicans CFGHJL, B: ns *eras*. (*presumably in preparation for Lat. commentary in right margin*) *but visible;* prędicans K; p̄dicans DE. praeceptum] pręceptum B; preceptum CFGHJL; p̄ceptum DE; præceptum K. domini] E: *eras. after word;* eius D: *on eras.: see LTg note to Ps 1.2* domíní, *see also GAg*.

LTu: constitutus] constitus ζ. sion] syon ειστ*τ. montem] in montem υ. praedicans] prędicans βελμνυ; predicans ζϑξπςτ*τ; p̄dicans ιοχ. praeceptum] pręceptum ενυ; preceptum ζϑξοςτ*τ; p̄ceptum ιπσμχ. domini] ipsius ϑ: *cf. Weber MSS* moz^c.

GAg: domini] eius GHIJ, F: *top of ascender of* s *eras*., D: *see LTg;* eíus K.

GAu: domini] eius δεζιλμξοπρστυχψ.

7

Dominus — drihten E^{2}F^2, dryhƚ AB, driћt CGH, drihƚ J
dixit — cwæð ABCDG, cweð E^2, cwæþ HJK, sæde F^{2}I
ad — to ABCE^{2}F^{2}GIJK
me — me ABCE^{2}F^{2}GIJK
filius | sunu ABC*DF^{2}HIK, cild G, bearn J, min E^2*

meus	I	min ABCF^{2}GHIJK, sunu E^{2}
es	I	eart CDE^{2}*F*^{2}HJK, ðu A, þu BGI
tu	I	þu CHJK, ðu D*E*^{2}F^{2}, earð A, eart BGI
ego		ic A*B*CDE^{2}F^{2}GHIJK
hodie		todege A, todæge BCJ, todæg DE^{2}F^{2}HIK, [ ]dæge *G*
genui	I	ic cende AB, cende CDF^{2}K, cænde H, acende G, acænde J, gestrynde I, þe E^{2}
te	I	ðec A, ðe *B,* þe CF^{2}GHIJ*K,* acende *E*^{2}

ED: tú (E)] tu *Harsley.* todege (A)] to dege *Kuhn.* todæge (BC)] to dæge *Brenner, Wildhagen.* todæg (DI)] to dæg *Roeder, Lindelöf.* té (EK)] te *Harsley, Sisam.*

OE: sunu (C)] u *(both) retraced by corr. in light brown ink.* min (E^{2})] *eras. before word.*

LTg: Dominus] [ ]us G. es] és F. tu] tú E. ego] Ego B. hodie] [ ]die G. te] té BE, K: *accent added by glossator.*

LTu: meus] *om.* υ.

8

Postula		bide AB*C*IK, bide þu J, gyrn DE^{x}*H, girn þu F^{2}, [ ] þu *G*
a		from A, from C, fram B, fram DF^{2}GHJ, to E^{2}, æt I, et K
me		me ABC*DE^{2}F^{2}GHIJK
et		⁊ ABC*DE^{2}F^{2}GHIJK
dabo	I	ic sellu A, ic selle BD, ic sylle C*GI, ic sille F^{2}H, sille J, ic gife K, ic þe E^{2}
tibi	I	ðe ABF^{2}, þe CGHIJK, selle E^{2}
gentes		ðeode A, þeode BE^{2}, þeoda CDGHJK, ðeoda F^{2}I
hereditatem		erfeweardnisse AD, erfeweardn[ ] *B**, yrfeweardnysse *C,* yrfewerdnisse F^{2}, yrfeweardnisse H, yrfwerdnysse I, yrfeweardnesse *E*^{2}J, erfwerdnesse K, yrfewerd[ ] *G*
tuam		ðine AF^{2}, þine C*DE^{2}GHIJK (*B*)
et		⁊ A*B*CE^{2}F^{2}GHIJK
possessionem	I	onæhte ABC, æhte F^{2}I, æhta HJK, æht G, anwaldnesse D^{2}*, þine E^{2}
tuam	I	ðine AF^{2}, þine BC*DGHIJK, anwældnesse E^{x}*
terminos	I	gemæru ABC*I, gemæro DF^{2}HJK, eorðan E^{2}* (*G*)
terrae	I	eorðan *ABCDGH*I, eorþan *JK,* eordan *F*^{2}, gemerum *E*^{2} (*L*)

ED: gyrn (E)] Gyrn *Harsley.* heredi[ ]tem (G)] hered*itatem* *Rosier.* hęreditatem (E)] haereditatem *Harsley.* onæhte (AB)] on æhte *Kuhn, Brenner.* [ ]nos (G)] *terminos* *Rosier.* terrę (CEG)] terre *Wildhagen, Rosier;* terrae *Harsley.*

OE: gyrn (E^{x})] *on eras.* me (C)] *retraced in red crayon.* ⁊ (C) (*1st*)] *retraced in red* *crayon.* ic sylle (C)] ic s *retraced in red crayon.* erfeweardn[ ] (B)] *end of word eras. by corr., presumably to make room for Lat. commentary in right margin.* þine (C) (*1st*)] *retraced in pencil, except stem of* þ. anwaldnesse (D^{2})] *orig. gloss to* possessionem *eras.,* anwaldnesse *written in 12th-c. hand: cf. Pss 21.30* falleð, *28.1–2* Afferte *and* afferte, *28.6* comminuet eas *and* dilectus, *29.2* delectasti, *38.13* et deprecationem meam, *38.14* refrigerer, *49.23* godes, *57.5* deafe. þine (C) (*2nd*)] ine *retraced in pencil.* anwældnesse (E^{x})] *on eras.* gemæru (C)] emæ *retraced in pencil.* eorðan (E^{2})] *eras. before word.*

LTg: Postula] Póstula C; [ ]la G. hereditatem] hęreditatem CE; heredit[ ] B: *end of word eras. by corr., presumably to make room for Lat. commentary in right margin;* heredi[ ]tem G. tuam (*1st*)] B: *eras. by corr., presumably to make room for Lat. commentary in right margin.* et (*2nd*)] Et B. terminos] [ ]nos G. terrae] terrę ACEFGHJKL; terræ B; terre D.

LTu: Postula] Postola ψ. hereditatem] hęreditatem ειϱ. possessionem] possesionem ϑν; possessionem ς: ses *interl.* tuam] β: u *interl.* terrae] terrę ειπσ; terre ξςτ*τ; terræ ϑ.

9

Reges		ðu reces A, þu recest BF^{2}, þu recyst C*, ðu gereccest D, þu geræcest H, þu gereccest K, þu gewissast I, þu wissast ł þu reccest J*, þu scęlt stieren E^{x}* (*G*)
eos		hie ABCE^{2}G, hy D, hi F^{2}HK, hig IJ
in		in AB, on CDE^{2}F^{2}GHIJK
uirga	I	gerde A, girde BH, gyrde C*DF^{2}GIK, girda J, isenre E^{2}
ferrea	I	iserre A, iserne B, isynre C, isernre DH, isenre *F*^{2}I, issene K, yrenre G, irenre J, gerde E^{2}
et*		⁊ A*B*CDE^{2}*G*I (*HK*)
tamquam		swe swe A, swa swa B*CDE*^{2}F^{2}*GH*IJ, swa K
uas	I	fęt AD, fæt BC*F^{2}HIJK, fæ[ ] G, tygelwyrhten E^{2}*
figuli	I	lames AB, lamys C, lame J, crocwirhtan ł tygelwirhtan I, tigelwyrhtan *D*H, tigolwyrhtan K, tigelen F^{2}, [ ]es *G,* fct E^{2}
confringes	I	ðu gebrices A, þu gebricest B, ðu gebrycst C, þu gebrycest G, ðu brecest D, þu bricst F^{2}, þu brytst K, þu tobrecest H, þu tobrytst I, þu tobritest J, þu heo E^{2}
eos	I	hie ABCG, hy D, hi F^{2}HK, hig IJ, gebrecest E^{2}

ED: eos (G) (*1st*)] *eos Rosier.* isernre (H)] insernre *Campbell.* tanquam (C)] ta[m]quam *Wildhagen.* swa swa (BGIJ)] swaswa *Brenner, Rosier, Lindelöf, Oess.* [ ]es (G)] *no gloss Rosier.*

OE: þu recyst (C)] u *and* recyst *retraced in pencil.* þu wissast ł þu reccest (J)] reccest *extends above following* hig. þu scęlt stieren (E^{x})] *on eras.* gyrde (C)] *retraced in pencil.* fæt (C)] æt *retraced in red crayon.* tygelwyrhten (E^{2})] h *interl.*

LTg: Reges] *lost* G. ferrea] ferea F. et] G: *added by later hand,* H: *added interl.* (*by glossator?*), K: *added later: see GAg;* Et B. tamquam] tanquam CEGH: *orig.* tamquam: *right leg of* m *eras. to form* n. figuli] D: *orig.* uguli: *left stroke of* u *used as ascender of* f; *lost* G.

LTu: et] *interl.* χ. tamquam] tanquam εζϑιλϱτ*τ.

GAg: et] *om.* F; *eras.* J; *for* GHK *see LTg.*

GAu: et] *om.* δεζϑιλμοπστψ.

10

Et — ٦ ABCE^2F^2HIJK (*G*)
nunc — nu ABCDE^2*F^2HIK*, na J (*G*)
reges — cyningas ABC*DF^2GJ, cynincgas H, ciningas K, kyníges E^2*, þa kyningas I
intellegite — ongeotað A*B*, ongytað *C**DF^2*H*, ongeteð *E^2*, ongitað *G*, ongitaþ *IJ*, ongytaþ K (*L*)
erudimini — bioð gelærde A*, beoð gelærde *B*, beoð gelærede CD, bioð geláérede E^2, beoð gelærede HIK, beoþ gelærede F^2, ge beoð gelærede GJ
omnes* — alle A, ealle BCE^2 (*L*)
qui | ða ðe A, þa ðe B, þa þe CE^2, ge þe DGJ, ge ðe F^2I, þa K
iudicatis | doemað A, demað BCDK, demaþ F^2IJ, ge demað E^2H (*G*)
terram — eordan A, eorðan BCDF^2GJ, eorþan HK, eorðan ł rica I, on eorðan E^2

ED: [ ]tis (G)] *iudicat*is *Rosier.* ge demað (E)] gedemað *Harsley.*

OE: nu (K)] na *eras. before word* (*Sisam reads* n·). nu (E^2)] *eras. after word.* cyningas (C)] ni *retraced in pencil.* kyniges (E^2)] *eras. after word.* ongytað (C)] ta *retraced in pencil,* g *and* y *show traces of pencil.* bioð gelærde (A)] o *interl.*

LTg: Et] *lost* G. nunc] *lost* G. intellegite] intelligite BCEFHIJL; intellígite G: *2nd* i *on eras. of* e. erudimini] Erudimini B. omnes] *eras.* L: *see GAg.* iudicatis] [ ]tis G.

LTu: intellegite] intelligite δεζϑιλξοπστ*τυχ, ϱ: *orig.* intellegite: *2nd* e *deleted,* i *interl.* erudimini] herudimini ψ.

GAg: omnes] *om.* FGHIJK, L: *see LTg.*

GAu: omnes] *om.* δεζϑιλμξοπϱστυχψ.

11

Seruite — ðeowiað AC, þeowiað BDF^2HK, þeowiaþ J, þeowiæþ E^2, ðeowiaþ ł hyrsumiaþ I (*G*)
domino — dryhtne AB, drihtne C*F^2G*IJ, drihten E^2K, drih̄t H

in	in AB, on C*DE^{2}*F^{2}GHIJK
timore	ege ABC*DE^{2}F^{2}GHIJK
et	⁊ A*B*CE^{2}F^{2}GHIJK
exultate	wynsumiað ABC*G*, g̲e̲blissiað D, geblissiað F^{2}H, geblissiaþ *K*, geblissieð E^{2}, blissiað J, blissað ł gefeagaþ I
ei	him ABE^{2}F^{2}IJ, hi̲m̲ CDK, hi H (*G**)
cum*	mid AC*DE^{2}IJ*K*, on F^{2}GH, mid cw[ ] B*
tremore	cwaecunge ł byfunge A/A^{2}*, cwacunge C, fyrhto DE^{2}F^{2}HK, fyrhtu GJ, ogan ł mid fyrhtu I (*B*)

ED: exultat[ ] (G)] exult*ate Rosier.* ei (G)] *Rosier records* h[ ] *as gloss, but only ascender visible.*

OE: drihtne (C)] *retraced in pencil.* drihtne (G)] i *partly lost due to small hole in leaf.* on (C)] *retraced in pencil.* on (E^{2})] *eras. after word.* ege (C)] *retraced in pencil.* ei (G)] *ascender* (*of* h? *see ED*) *visible in initial position.* mid (C)] *interl. above following* cw. mid cw[ ] (B)] *end of 2nd word eras. by corr., presumably to make room for Lat. commentary in right margin.* cwaecunge ł byfunge (A/A^{2})] ł byfunge *added above* cwæcunge *probably in same hand as that of fols 155–60* (*11th-c.*).

LTg: Seruite] *lost* G. et] Et B. exultate] K: *orig.* exaltate: *1st* a *altered to* u; exultat[ ] G. ei] *lost* G. cum] K: *on eras. by corr.: see GAg.* tremore] B: *eras. by corr., presumably to make room for Lat. commentary in right margin.*

LTu: in] cum ο: *altered from* in.

GAg: cum] in FG; *for* K *see LTg.*

GAu: cum] in μοψ, ϱ: ł cum *interl.*

12

Adprehendite	gegripað *ABC***F/F*^{2}**HJ*, g̲e̲gripað *D*, gegrypað *E*^{2}*, gegripaþ K, g[ ]gripað ge *G**, underfoð ł gegripað *I* (*L*)
disciplinam	styre A^{2}*, steore J, steore ł lare I, lare DF^{2}GHK, lare oððe stiernesse E^{2}, þeodscipe B, ðeodscipe C*
nequando	ðylęs hwonne A, þylæs hwonne B*DH, ðylæs hwanne C, þiles hwonne E^{2}, ðilæs hwonne F^{2}, þelæs ahwanne I, þalæs hwon K, þylæs G, þilæs J
irascatur	eorsie A, yrsige CF^{2}K, yrsig̲e̲ ł eorsig̲e̲ D, yrsie E^{2}*, yrsyge G, yrsig̲e̲ H, irsige J, yrsige ł þæt ne yrsige I (*B*)
dominus	dryhten B, drihten E^{2}GIK, dryht̄ A, driħt CF^{2}J, driħ H
et	⁊ A*B*CE^{2}F^{2}GHIJK
pereatis	ge forweorðen AB, ge forweorðan F^{2}, ge forweorþen G, ge forweorðen H, g̲e̲ forwyrðen D, ge forwyrðen E^{2}*, ge forwyrþan K, ge forwurðaþ IJ, forwurðyn C*

de		of ABCDE^{2}F*GHIJK
uia	|	wege ABC*F^{2}GJK, wege D, geweyge E^2, þam rihtan H, rihtum I
iusta	|	ðæm ryhtan B, rihtwise C*, ryhtum D, rihtum E^2, rihtum K, rihtan F/F^2*J, [ ]ihtan G, wege HI

ED: Apprehendite (C)] A[d]prehendite *Wildhagen.* Adp̄hendite (D)] Adprehendite *Roeder.* [ ]pprehendite (G)] Apprehendite *Rosier.* nequando (CDEFJK)] ne quando *Wildhagen, Roeder, Harsley, Kimmens, Oess, Sisam.* ðylęs hwonne (A)] ðy lęs hwonne *Kuhn.* þylæs hwonne (B)] þy læs hwonne *Brenner.* ðylæs hwanne (C)] ðy læs hwanne *Wildhagen* (*as* ðylæs hwanne *in corrigenda*). yrsie (E)] yrhe *Harsley.* [ ]ihtan (G)] rihtan *Rosier.*

OE: gegripað (C)] g *and* ð *retraced in pencil.* gegrypað (E^2)] *eras.* (*ca 13 mm*) *after word.* gegripað (F/F^2)] *see OE note to F at v. 1.* g[ ]gripað (G)] *hole in leaf after 1st* g. styre (A^2)] *added probably in same hand as that of fols 155–60* (*11th-c.*). ðeodscipe (C)] pe *retraced in pencil.* þylæs hwonne (B)] y *faint but visible, eras. after word* (*presumably of gloss*) *to make room for Lat. commentary in right margin.* yrsie (E^2)] s *malformed.* forwurðyn (C)] forwu *and* ð *retraced in pencil, 2nd* r *interl.* ge forwyrðen (E^2)] ð *interl.* of (F)] *see OE note to F at v. 1.* wege (C)] ge *retraced in pencil.* rihtwise (C)] riht *retraced in pencil.* rihtan (F/F^2)] *see OE note to F at v. 1.*

LTg: Adprehendite] Adpraehendite A; Adp̄hendite D; Adpprehendite L; Apprehendite EFHIJ, C: *eras. after* A, *1st* p *added interl. by corr.;* [ ]pprehendite G: *initial* A *lost.* irascatur] B: *eras. by corr. presumably to make room for Lat. commentary in right margin.* et] Et B.

LTu: Adprehendite] Adpręhendite β; Adpraehendite μψ; Apprehendite ζιλξϱστ*τυ, δ: *orig.* Adprehendite: *1st* p *interl. above* d, *but without deleting mark;* Appraehendite ο; Apprehenditae π; Apphendite εχ. pereatis] β: *2nd* e *interl.;* periatis ϑ. de] di ϑ.

13

Cum		ðonne AF^2, þonne BHI, þonne CDJ, þonne *G,* þone K, Myd þe E^2
exarserit		beorneð AB, byrnyþ *C,* byrneð D, byrneþ F^{2}HK, abyrneð G, þe onberneð E^2, he onbærneþ J, bið onæled I
in		in ABE^2, on C*F^{2}GJ*K*
breui		scortnisse AB, sceortnysse C*, scortnysse F^2, scortnesse E^{2}K, scortan J, anunga ł in sceortnisse D, annunga H, hrædnesse G, hrædlice I
ira	|	eorre ABD*, yrre C*GHK, yrra I, irra J, graman F/F^2*, hys E^2
eius	|	his ABCDGHIJ*K*, hys F*, yrres E^2

beati — eadge AB, eadige C*GIJ, eadige D, eadig H, edige K, eadige bioþ E^{2}, eadige beoþ F^{2}
omnes — alle A, ealle BC*DE^{2}F*GHIJK
qui — ða ðe A, þa ðe BK, þa þe C*GHIJ, ða þe F^{2}, þæ þe E^{2}, þe D
confidunt | getreowað AB, getreowað D, getruwað C, getreowiað E^{2}, getrywiað G*, truwiaþ K, getripaþ J, truwiaþ ł þa þe gelyfað ł gehihtaþ I, on F^{2}H
in | in AB, on CD*E*^{2}GIJK, hine F^{2}H
eum* | hine ABCDE^{2}, him GI*J*, him K, treowiað F^{2}, getriwað H (*D*)

OE: on (C) (*1st*)] n *retraced in pencil.* sceortnysse (C)] *retraced in pencil.* eorre (D)] *gloss extends above following* his. yrre (C)] y *retraced in pencil.* graman (F/F^{2})] *see OE note to F at v. 1.* hys (F)] *see OE note to F at v. 1.* eadige (C)] ge *retraced in pencil.* ealle (C)] alle *retraced in pencil.* ealle (F)] *see OE note to F at v. 1.* þa þe (C)] þe *retraced in pencil.* getrywiað (G)] i *interl.*

LTg: Cum] [ ]um G: *initial* C *lost.* exarserit] exárserit C. in (*1st*)] im K. eius] eíus K. in (*2nd*)] E: n *on eras.* eum] eo D: *orig.* eum: u *eras.*, o *in dark ink with orig. macron visible above, written by same corr. of fols 8r–9r and 29v* (*see LTg note to Ps 1.2* domini): *see GAg.*

GAg: eum] eo FGHIK, D: *see LTg;* ea J.

GAu: eum] eo δεζϑιλμξοπϱστυχψ.

PSALM 3

2

Domine — eala drih́t *C**, eala ðu drih́t F, drihten E^{2}, dryht̄ *A*, drih́t G, la drih́t J (*BDIKL*)
quid — hwet A, hwæt B*C**, tohwy DF, tohwi E^{2}HIK, tohwon GJ
multiplicati — gemonigfaldade A, gemonigfealdade B, gemonigfealdode C*, gemonigfealdode G, gemænigfylde D, gemanifalde E^{2}, gemænigfylde HI, gemænigfylde F*, gemanifealde K, gemonige ł hwæt gemonigfilde J*
sunt — sindun A, sindon BJ, syndon CG, synd DFK, sind H, synt E^{2}I
qui — ða ðe AB, þa ðe DFH, þa þe CE^{2}GIJ, þa K
tribulant — swencað ACDK, swenceað BG, swæncað H, swæncaþ J, tregiað oððe swencað E^{2}, swencaþ ł gedrefaþ I, drefað F
me — mec *A*, me BCE^{2}FGHJK
multi — monge *A*, monige BCGJ, mænige DH, manie E^{2}, manige FK, manege I

insurgunt		arisað ABC*K, onarisað DGH, onarisaþ FJ, onariseð E^2, onarisað ł wiðstandaþ I
aduersum		wið AC*, wiþ B, angean DE^2, ongean HIK, togeanes FGJ
me		me ABC*E^{2}FGHJK

ED: tohwy (DF)] to hwy *Roeder, Kimmens.* tohwi (EIK)] to hwi *Harsley, Lindelöf, Sisam.* onariseð (E)] on ariseð *Harsley.*

OE: eala drih̄t (C)] s. o *written before* eala, *2nd* a *and* drih̄t *retraced in pencil.* hwæt (C)] wæt *retraced in pencil.* g̲e̲monigfealdode (C)] *initial* g, *1st* o, *and final* e *retraced in pencil, final* e *obscured.* gemænigfylde (F)] *orig.* gemægnigfylde: *2nd* g *eras.* gemonige ł hwæt g̲e̲monigfilde (J)] g̲e̲monigfilde *orig.* g̲e̲monigefilde: *middle* e *eras., word extends above following* sindon. arisað (C)] a (*both*) *retraced in pencil.* wið (C)] *retraced in pencil.* me (C) (*2nd*)] *retraced in pencil.*

LTg: Domine] I: s. o *written above word;* DOMINE C; DN̄E ABDK; DN̄e L. quid] C: i *interl.* me (*1st*)] A: *added by corr. in right margin.* multi] A: *preceded by eras.*

LTu: Domine] DN̄E ιτ*τυ; DN̄e β; DOMINE QUID ς; DN̄E QUID MULTIPLIcati μ; DN̄E...QVID MVLtiplicati ξ; DN̄E QUID MULTIplicati νψ; DN̄E...MULTIPLICATI ϱ; DN̄E...TRIbulant π; DN̄E...SUNT λ. aduersum] β: *orig.* aduersus: *final* s *crossed through,* m *interl.;* aduersus ϑ.

3

Multi		monge *A*, monige *BC*GJ, mánie *E^2*, manige FK (*DL*)
dicunt		cweoðað AB, cweðað C, cweðaþ F, cweþaþ K, cwædon G, cweþað ł secgað D, cweðæt ł seggeð E^2, cweþað ł secað H, secgað I, secað J
animae		salwle A, sawle B*CHIJK*, saule *DE^{2}FG* (*L*)
meae		minre ABC*DE2FHIJ*K, mire *G** (*L*)
non	|	nis AB, nys F, nis nan E^2, nis na I, ne CG, na JK
est	|	ys C, is GJK
salus		haelu A*, hælo BDFHIJ, hæle ł o G*, hæle E^2, hæl CK
illi*		hire AB*D*E^2*GJ, hyre F, him CIK (*L*)
in		in AB, on CDE^2*FGHIJK
deo		gode BCDE^2*FGHIJK, d̲e̲o A
eius		hire ABGI, híre E^2*, his ł hire D, his ł hyre H, hys C, his FJ*K*

ED: meæ (D)] meae *Roeder.* meę (E)] meae *Harsley.* híre (E)] hire *Harsley.*

OE: mire (G)] *orig.* mine (?)*: descender added to* n *to form* r. haelu (A)] h *altered from* s. hæle ł o (G)] ł o *written above* e *in* hæle (= ł hælo). hire (E^2)] *retraced in darker ink.* on (E^2)] *retraced in darker ink.* gode (E^2)] *in lighter ink by main hand.* híre (E^2)] *in lighter ink by main hand, perhaps with traces of eras. after* í.

LTg: Multi] multi ABCE, D: m *eras. but visible under ultraviolet*, L: *ligature added by corr., connecting base of 1st 2 legs of* m, *3rd leg extended below line to create majuscule.* animae] animę CDGHL; anime EFIJK. meae] meæ D; meę EFGHJL; mee I: *letter eras. after 1st* e. illi] D: *eras.*, L: *altered to* ipsi *by corr.: see GAg.* eius] eíus K.

LTu: Multi] *lost due to damage* ξ; multi βνςτ*. animae] anime ιξπσςτ*τυ; animę ελνχ; animæ ϑ. meae] meę ιλνξ; meæ ϑμ; mee σςτ*τ.

GAg: illi] ipsi FGHIJK, L: *see LTg.*

GAu: illi] ipsi δεζϑιλμξοπϱσυτχψ.

4

Tu		ðu AF, þu BC*E^2*G*IJK
autem		soðlice ABCE^{2}I, soþlice FJ, cuðlice G, witodlice K
domine		drihtyn C*, dryhten E^2, dryht̄ AB, driȟt FGJ (*I*)
susceptor	I	ondfenge AB, andfange C*, andfengend GJ*, anfeng K, anfoend D, onfoend H, anfenge ł underfond I, underfang F, min E^2
meus	I	min ABCFGIJK, onfeng E^2*
es		earð A, eart BCIJ*K*, ært *E*^{2}, ðu eart F, ⁊ þu eart G (*D*)
gloria	I	wuldur AD, wuldor BC*GHIJK, wulder F, ⁊ mine E^2
mea	I	min ABCFGHIJK, wuldor E^2
et		⁊ ABCE^{2}FGHIJK
exaltans	I	uphebbende ABDFH, uppahebbende G, upahebbende IJ, uphebbend K, ahebbynde C, mines E^2
caput	I	heafud AC*, heafod BDF*GH*IJ, hæfod K, hefdes E^2 (*L*)
meum	I	min ABC*FGIJK, uphebbende E^2

ED: és (E)] es *Harsley.* et (B)] Et *Brenner.*

OE: þu (C)] þ *retraced in pencil.* drihtyn (C)] rihtyn *retraced in pencil.* andfange (C)] fange *retraced in pencil.* andfengend (J)] *1st* d *interl.* onfeng (E^2)] *eras. after word.* wuldor (C)] *retraced in pencil.* heafud (C)] h *retraced in pencil.* min (C) (*2nd*)] in *retraced in pencil.*

LTg: Tu] [ ]u G: *initial* T *lost.* domine] I: o *written above word.* es] és DEK. caput] H: t *on eras.;* capud GL.

LTu. Tu autem] *lost to damage* ξ. caput] capud ξ; cap̄ χ. meum] mevm χ.

5

Uoce	I	mid id stefne A, mid stefne *B*, stefne C*DFGH*, stæfne J, stefn K, mine *E*^{2}, mid minre I (*L*)
mea	I	minre ABCDGH, mine FJ, min K, stefne *E*^{2}I

ad   to ABCE^{2}FGIJK
dominum   drihtne CFIJ, drihten E^{2}, drihtene K, dryht̄ AB, driħt G
clamaui   is cleopede A, ic cleopode BDH, ic clypude FK, ic clypode GI, ic clipode J, ic cleopige C, ic cige ł cleowede E^{2}
et   ⁊ A*B*CE^{2}FGHIJK
exaudiuit | geherde A, gehierde B, he gehyrde CDFGHIJK, he me E^{2}
me | mec A, me BC*D*FGHJK, gehirde E^{2}
de   of ABCDE^{2}*FGHIJK
monte | munte ABCFGJK, his DE^{2}HI
sancto | ðæm halgan AB, þam halgan CDH, þære halgæn E^{2}, halgan FI, haligan G*, halian K, halgum J
suo | his ABCGJK, hys F, munte DH, dune ł munte E^{2}, dune I

ED: [ ]oce (H)] Voce *Campbell.* mine (E)] Mine *Harsley.* mea (C)] méa *Wildhagen.* ic cige ł cleowede (E)] ic cige ł cleopede *Harsley* (*emended*).

OE: of (E^{2})] f *altered from another letter.* haligan (G)] i *interl.*

LTg: Uoce] Voce BDEFGL; [ ]oce] H: *initial* V *lost.* mea] E: m *malformed.* et] Et B. me] mé D.

LTu: Uoce] Voce ζινοπϱσςυχ.

6
Ego   ic ABCD*FGHIJK, Ic E^{2}
dormiui   hneappade A, hnappade B, hnæppode F, slep *C*DE^{2}*HIK, slepte G, slæpte J
et   ⁊ ABCE^{2}FGIJK
somnum* | slepan A, slapan B, slæp ic ongan G, slæpingan J, hnappunge C, swefne *E*^{2}, ic swodrode F, swefnode K, ic eom I (*D*L*)
cepi* | ongon *AB,* ic onfeng *CE*^{2}, ic eom J, geswefod I (*D*L*)
et   ⁊ ABCE^{2}FGIJK
resurrexi*   ic eft aras ABG*J,* ic aras CDE^{2}FK, ic uparas I (*HL*)
quoniam*   forðon A*D,* forþon BCGJ, forðæn þe E^{2}, forþon þe F, forþan I, forþā K (*L*)
dominus   dryhten B, drihten E^{2}FIK, dryht̄ A, driħt C, driht̄ J, driħ G
suscepit | onfeng ABCFGH, anfeng DK, onfenc J, þe underfengc I, me E^{2}
me | mec AB, me CFGHJK, onfeng E^{2} (*D*)

ED: ic (D) (*1st*)] *no gloss Roeder.* cępi (E)] coepi *Harsley.* et (B) (*2nd*)] Et *Brenner.* ic eft aras (A)] ic eftaras *Kuhn.* forðon (A)] for ðon *Kuhn.*

OE: ic (D) (*1st*)] *eras.* slep (E^{2})] *eras. after word.* somnum coepi (D)] *gloss eras.; under ultraviolet, only a few letters visible:* sw[ ]þe (?), *followed by ca 8 illegible letters.*

LTg: dormiui] dormíui C. somnum cepi] somnum coepi ABC, D: *eras. but visible under ultraviolet,* L: soporatus sum *added above* coepi: *see GAg;* sompnum cępi E. resurrexi] L: ex *added above* re *by corr.,* x *orig. added interl. between* e *and* s *but eras.: see GAg.* quoniam] D: *eras. but visible* (qm̄), L: quia *added interl. by corr.: see GAg.* me] mé D.

LTu: somnum] sompnum τ*. cepi] coepi βν. suscepit] suscipiet ϑ.

GAg: somnum cepi] soporatus sum FGHIJK, L: *see LTg.* resurrexi] exsurrexi FIK, J: s *interl.,* L: *see LTg;* exurrexi G, H: *eras. after 1st* x. quoniam] quia FGHIJK, L: *see LTg.*

GAu: somnum cepi] soporatus sum δεζϑιλμοπρστυχψ; soporatu[ ] ξ. resurrexi] exurrexi ειλπυτχ, ρ: *orig.* exsurrexi: s *deleted; exsurrexi* ζϑμξοσψ, δ: *orig.* exurrexi: s *interl.* quoniam] quia δεζϑιλμξοπρστυχψ.

7

Non	I	ne ABCF*G*J, Ne E^2, na K, ic ne DHI
timebo	I	ondredu ic A, ondrædo ic B, ondræde ic C, ondræde DHI, ic ondræde F, ic adræde K, ondrede ic me E^2, ondræde ic me GJ
milia		ðusend A, þusend BE^2GJ, þusynd C, þusendu DH, ðusenda F, þusenda IK
populi		folces ABDE^2FGHIJK, folcys C
circumdantis	I	ymsellendes A, ymbsellendes *B,* ymbsyllyndys *C**, ymbsyllende F*G,* ymbsillende *J,* ymbesyllende K, ymbsellende ł ymbtrymmende *DH,* ymbtrymmende(s) I*, me *E^2*
me	I	me ABC*F*G*JK, ymbsellendræ E^2
exsurge		aris *AC**DF*GH*I*J*K, arís *B,* ac arís *E^2** (*L*)
domine		dryhten B, drihtyn C*, drihten F, min drihten E^2, dryhī A, driħt GJ (*I*)
saluum	I	halne ABCDG*H*JK, gehæl FI, gedo E^2
me		me ABCDE^2FGHIJK
fac	I	doa A, dó BD, do GHJK, gedo C, halne E^2*
deus		god ABCE^2FGIJK
meus		min ABCE^2FIJK, m[ ] *G*

ED: circundantis (C)] circu[m]dantis *Wildhagen.* circundanti[ ] (G)] circumdant*is Rosier.* ymbtrymmende(s) (I)] ymbtrymmendes *Lindelöf.* meus] D *records* i*d* e*st* pater mi *interl., where* mi, *as vocative form of* meus, *is clearly part of Lat. gloss, being written on same line as 1st part of gloss and followed, as is typical, by a punctus. Roeder rightly omits gloss, Campbell includes it but without comment; cf. ÆGram 110.17:* o pater mi…eala ðu fæder min.

OE: ymbsyllyndys (C)] *2nd and 3rd* y *and final* s *retraced in pencil.* ymbtrymmende(s) (I)] *descender and part of shoulder of* s *lost.* me (C) (*1st*)] *retraced in pencil.* aris

(C)] ri *retraced in pencil.* ac arís (E^2)] *eras. after* c *and* s. drihtyn (C)] drihty *retraced in pencil.* halne (E^2)] *eras. after word.*

LTg: Non] [ ]on G: *initial* G *lost.* circumdantis] B: *somewhat large initial* c *but not to be taken as majuscule* (*see also* conteruisti *v. 8*), J: *2nd* i *on eras.;* circumdantes D: es *eras. but visible under ultraviolet;* circundantis E, C: *orig.* circumdantis: n *added after* u, *macron eras.* (*smudge remains*), H: *orig.* circumdantis: *right leg of* m *eras.;* circundanti[ ] G: *orig.* circumdanti[ ]: *right leg of* m *eras.* me (*1st*)] *lost* G. exsurge] Exsurge B; exurge AEGHJL, C: *eras. after* x. domine] I: s. o *written above word.* saluum] H: *eras. before word.* meus] m[ ] G.

LTu: circumdantis] circundantis ειλϱτ*τ; crcumdantis ϑ; circūdantis σχψ; ci[ ]undantis ξ. exsurge] exurge δειλξπϱςτ*τυχ. saluum] psaluum ξ.

8

Quoniam		forðon ABD, forþon C*FH, Forðæn E^2, forþā þe G, forðan þe I, forþon þe J, forþan K
tu		ðu A, þu BCE^{2}FGHIJK
percussisti		sloge ABC*, ofsloge D, ofsloge FGHIJK, ofsloge ł smite E^2
omnes		alle A, ealle BCDE^2*FGHIJK
aduersantes		wiðerbrocan A, wiðyrbrocan C*, wiþerbrecan B, wiþergende DH, wiðergiende E^2, þa wiðrigendan I, ða wiðriende F, þa wiðerwerda[ ] G*, þa wiðerweardan J, wiþerwyrde K
mihi		me AB*CE*^{2}FHI*J*K (*G*)
sine		butan ABC*E^{2}GIK, buton FJ
causa		intingan ABCDFGHIJ, intyngan E^2, intinga K
dentes	|	toeð AB, teð CK, teþ DFHI, toðes G, toþas ł teþ J, ⁊ þæra synfulra E^2
peccatorum	|	synfulra ABC*DFIJK, syn(f)ullra G*, synfulfra H, tęð E^2
conteruisti*		ðu forðræstes A, þu forþræstes *B,* þu forþræstyst C*, þu forbryttest DH, þu forbrytest K, þu abrutedest E^2*, ðu tobryttest F, þu geþreadest G, þu geþreadest ł tobrittest J, þu forgnide ł þu tobryttest I (*L*)

ED: forðon (A)] for ðon *Kuhn.* þa wiðerwerda[ ] (G)] þa wiðerwerdan *Rosier.* syn(f)ullra (G)] synfullra *Rosier.*

OE: forþon (C)] þon *retraced in pencil.* sloge (C)] slo *retraced in pencil, eras.* (?) *after word, crude* n *in pencil apparently written after* e. ealle (E^2)] *gloss eras. after word,* s *visible in final position.* wiðyrbrocan (C)] roc *retraced in pencil.* þa wiðerwerda[ ] (G)] *right leg of final letter* (n?) *lost.* butan (C)] an *retraced in pencil.* synfulra (C)] y, *left leg of* n, *and* fulra *retraced in pencil.* syn(f)ullra (G)] *descender of* f *lost.* þu forþræstyst (C)] u *and* orþr *retraced in pencil.* þu abrutedest (E^2)] *on eras.*

LTg: mihi] *lost* G; michi EJ, C: *orig.* mihi: *small* c *interl. by corr.* conteruisti] B: c *somewhat large but not majuscule* (*see also v. 7* circumdantis); contruisti L: *letter eras. after 1st* t; contriuisti E: *cf. Weber MSS* med, *see GAg*.
LTu: percussisti] percusisti ϑ. mihi] michi ιλξϱςτ*τ. conteruisti] contriuisti ντ*: *cf. Weber MSS* med, *see GAg*.

GAg: conteruisti] contriuisti FGHIJK, E: *see LTg*.

GAu: conteruisti] contriuisti δεζϑιλμξοπϱστυχψ, ντ*: *see LTg*.

9

Domini		dryhtnes ABD, drihtnes E^{2}I, drihtyn C*, drihtne F, drihten K, drih̄t GH, driht̄ J
est		is ABC*DE^2*FGIJ*K*, is is H
salus		haelu ABC, hælo DGHJ, hęlo E^2, hæl FIK
et		⁊ ABCDE^{2}FGHIJK
super		ofer ABDE^{2}FGHJK, ofyr C, ofor I
populum	I	folc ABCDGHIJ, folce F, fol K, þin E^2
tuum	I	ðin A, þin BCGHI*JK, ðine F, folc E^2
benedictio	I	bledsung ABD, bletsung CFGJK, bletsuncg H, þin E^{2}I
tua	I	ðin ABF, þin CDGH*J*K, bletsung E^{2}I

ED: drihtnes (E)] Drihtnes *Harsley*. et (B)] Et *Brenner*.

OE: drihtyn (C)] drihty *retraced in pencil*. is (C)] *retraced in pencil*. is (E^2)] *eras. after word*. haelu (C)] ælu *retraced in pencil*. þin (I) (*1st*)] s. & sit : ⁊ si *written after* þin.

LTg: est] ést K. tua] J: *orig.* tuo: o *altered to* a.

PSALM 4

2

Cum	mid ðy *A*, mid þy C, mid þy þe G, mid þi þe J, þonne *D*, þonne *K*, þanne E^2, þa þa I (*B*F**H*)
inuocarem	ic gecede A, ic gecegde B, ic gecigde CD, ic gecigede E^2*, ic þe gecigde GJ, ic clypige K, ic clypodę ł þa þa ic gecigde I (F*)
te*	ðe ABE^2, þe C (*DL*)
exaudisti*	ðu geherdes AB, þu gehyrdest C, þu gehyrdest *D*GK, þu geherdest E^2, þu gehirdest J, gehyrde F^2*, geherde I (*L*)
me	me ABCE^{2}F^2*GJ*K* (*D*)
deus	god ABCE^{2}F^2**G*IJK

iustitiae	rehtwisnisse *A,* ryhtwisnesse *BD,* rihtwisnysse *C*F,* rihtwisnesse *E^{2}GIJK* (*L*)
meae	minre A*BCFGIJK*, mire *DE^{2}* (*HL*)
in	in ABG, on CDE^{2}FIJK
tribulatione	geswencednisse A*, geswencednesse B, geswince C*DE^{2} GJK*, gedrefednysse F, gedrefednesse ł on gedeorfe I
dilatasti	ðu gebrꝺddes A, þu gebræddes B, þu tobræddyst C, þu tobreddest DE^{2}, ðu tobreddest F, ðu tobrædest K, þu tobræddest J, [ ]ræddest *G,* þu tobræddest ł þu gerymdest I*
me*	me ABCE^{2}FGIJK (*DL*)
Miserere	mildsa AK, miltsa B, myltsa *C,* Miltse E^{2}, gemiltsa DFI, miltsa ðu *G,* mildsa þu J
mihi*	me AB*CDE^{2}*GJK, min *F*I (*L*)
domine*	drihtyn C, drihtæn E^{2}, dryhī AB (*DL*)
et	⁊ ABCE^{2}FGIJK
exaudi	geher AB, gehyr CDFGIK, gehir J, gehire E^{2}
orationem	I gebed AC*DFK, ge(b)ed B*, bene GJ, mine E^{2}, min I
meam	I min ABCFK*, mine GJ, gebed E^{2}I

ED: mid þy (C)] midþy *Wildhagen.* þa þa (I) (*1st*)] þaþa *Lindelöf.* þa þa (I) (*2nd*)] þaþa *Lindelöf.* ðu geherdes (B)] þu geherdes *Brenner.* mé (K) (*Lat.*)] me *Sisam.* iustitię (E)] iustitiae *Harsley.* meę (E)] meae *Harsley.* mire (E)] mi[n]re *Harsley.* Mis[ ]ere (G)] Miserere *Rosier.* Miserere (H)] Misere *Campbell.* miltsa ðu (G)] mil[ ]a *Rosier.* mihi domine (D)] *supplied Roeder.* [ ]ei (G)] mei *Rosier.* et (B)] Et *Brenner.* ge(b)ed (B)] gebed *Brenner.*

OE: Cum inuocarem (F)] *gloss eras.* (*by 16th-c. corr.*). ic gecigede (E^{2})] þe *eras. after* ic. gehyrde me god (F^{2})] *written in 16th-c. hand.* rihtwisnysse (C)] ht *retraced in pencil.* geswencednisse (A)] ge *interl.* geswince (C)] ince *retraced in pencil.* geswince (K)] *letter eras. after* w (*Sisam reads* ?e). þu tobræddest ł þu gerymdest (I)] gerymdest *divided to allow alignment of following* me *with* mihi, *thus* ge me rymdest; *subscript marks indicate order of elements.* gebed (C)] *1st* e *retraced in pencil.* ge(b)ed (B)] *bowl of* b *lost.* min (K)] *on eras.*

LTg: H: *vv 1–5 unglossed, v. 6 begins on fol. 33r.* Cum] CUm A; CVM BDFK; CUM C. inuocarem] L: *2 letters eras. after word,* e *visible.* te] *om.* L (*see previous note*): *see GAg.* te exaudisti me] D: *eras., apparently done after OE gloss was written.* exaudisti] exaudiuit L: *orig.* exaudisti: st *altered to* u, t *added above final* i: *see GAg.* me (*1st*)] mé K. deus] de[ ] G: *left leg of* u (?) *visible.* iustitiae] iustitię ADEGJKL; iustitiæ B; iustitie F; iustiae C. meae] meæ BK; meę DEFGHL. dilatasti] dil[ ]ti G. me (*2nd*)] *eras.* D; mihi (m^{1}) L: *orig.* me: e *eras. but visible,* i *added interl.: see GAg.* Miserere] Miserére C; Mis[ ]ere G. mihi] D: *eras. but visible under ultraviolet;* michi C: *orig.*

mihi: *small* c *interl. by corr.*, E: *as* m^1 *in MS but expanded to* michi *elsewhere, eras. after word* (*1 letter?*); *mei* L: *orig.* mihi: *1st* i *altered to* e, h *eras.: see GAg.* domine] D: *eras. but visible under ultraviolet* (dñe), L: *underlined to signal deletion: see GAg.*

LTu: Cum] CUm β; Cvm ι; CVM τ*τ; CVM INuocarem ξ; CUM INUOCAREM μψ; CUM…TE ν; CUM…EXAUDIUIT ϱ; CUM…ME λ; CUM…DEUS π. iustitiae] iustitiæ ϑχ; iustitię ιξο; iustitie σςυ; iusticiae ϱ: *orig.* iustitiae: *2nd* t *deleted*, c *interl.;* iusticie τ*τ. meae] meæ ϑ; meę ζινχ; męę ς; mee στ*τ. Miserere] misserere ϑ. mihi] michi ς.

GAg: te] *om.* FGHIJK; *for* DL *see LTg.* exaudisti] exaudiuit FGHIJK, L: *see LTg.* me (*2nd*)] mihi FIJK, L: *see LTg;* michi GH. mihi] mei FHIJK, L: *see LTg;* [ ]ei G: *right leg of* m (?) *visible.* domine] *om.* FGHIJK; *for* DL *see LTg.*

GAu: te] *om.* δεζϑιλμξοπϱστυχψ. exaudisti] exaudiuit δεζιλμξοπϱστυχψ. me (*2nd*)] mihi δεζϑμξοπυχψ; michi ιλϱστ. mihi] mei δεζϑιλμξοπϱστυχψ. domine] *om.* δεζϑιλμξοπϱστυχψ.

3

Filii	|	bearn AB*CD*GJK, eala bearn I*, sunu F, Monna *E*^{2}
hominum	|	monnan A, monna BCG, manna DFIJK, bearna E^2
usquequo		hu longe A*C*, hu lange BDE^2*FGJK, la hu lange I*
graues*		hwefie *A*, hefige B*CDF*GJK, swǽre ł heuie E^2*, þwere ł sware I (*L*)
corde		on (h)e[ ]rtan A*, on heortan BIJ, on heort[ ]n G, of heortan D, of heorten E^2*, heortan *CFK*
ut	|	tohwon ABCDE^2**F*, tohwan GJ, tohwi IK
quid	|	(*J*)
diligitis		lufiað ge ABCE^2*F, lufiað ge D, lufige ge I, lufigeað G, lufiaþ J, lufast þu K
uanitatem		idelnisse A, idelnesse BDE^2*GJ, idelnysse C*F, idelnessa I, idelnese K
et		⁊ ABCDE^{2}FGIJK
quaeritis		soecað *A*, soeceað *B*, secað *CDE*^{2}**F*, ge seceað *G*, ge secaþ I*J*, secest *K* (*HL*)
mendacium		leasunge ABG, leasunge D, leasunga CFIJ, leasungæ E^2, læsunga K

ED: Filíí (E)] Filii *Harsley.* hominum (G)] hom*i*num *Rosier.* monna (G)] ma[ ]a *Rosier.* usquequo (BEH)] usque quo *Brenner, Harsley, Campbell.* graues (CD)] grau[i]s *Wildhagen;* grau[ ] *Roeder.* on (h)e[ ]rtan (A)] on heortan *Kuhn.* on heort[ ]n (G)] on heort[ ] *Rosier.* tohwon (ABCDEF)] to hwon *Kuhn, Brenner, Wildhagen, Roeder, Harsley, Kimmens.* tohwi (IK)] to hwi *Lindelöf, Sisam.* ge seceað (G)] geseceað *Rosier.* ge secaþ (J)] gesecaþ *Oess.*

OE: eala bearn (I)] s. o *written before* eala. hu lange (E^{2})] *on eras.* la hu lange (I)] s. estis : synt ge *written after* lange. swǽre ł heuie (E^{2})] *on eras.* on (h)e[ ]rtan (A)] *ascender of* h *lost, letter lost after* e. of heorten (E^{2})] *on eras.* tohwon (E^{2})] *on eras.* lufiað ge (E^{2})] *on eras.* idelnysse (C)] idel *retraced in pencil.* idelnesse (E^{2})] *on eras.* secað (E^{2})] *eras. before word* (2 *letters*), *with traces of initial* g *visible; Harsley reads* ge (?).

LTg: Filii] D: *otiose stroke above* ii; Fílii C; Filíí E. usquequo] úsquequo C. graues] A: *orig.* graui: i *altered to* e, s *interl.*, C: *orig.* grauis: i *altered to* e, D: es *eras. but visible,* L: e *altered to* i, *final letter eras.;* graui BF: *cf. Weber MSS* Xδ*σ, *see GAg.* graui corde ut (F)] *Kimmens: 'gone over in a textura-like hand because of extensive rubbing at bottom of f. 3r.'* quid] J: i *eras. after* d. quaeritis] quęritis FG; queritis ABCDEHJKL.

LTu: graues] grauis πς. diligitis] dilegitis β. quaeritis] queritis ζιξσςτ*τυψ; quęritis βελμνϱ; q̄ritis ϑχ.

GAg: graues] graui GHIJK, F: *see LTg; for* ABL *see LTg.*

GAu: graues] graui δεζϑιλμξοϱσςτυχψ.

4

(Et)*		⁊ FGIJK
Scitote		weotað A, witað B*CDF,* witaþ *K,* Witoð E^{2}, witað ge *G,* witaþ ge *J,* wite ge *I* (*HL*)
quoniam		ðætte A, þætte BC, þætte D, þæt ðe F, þæt ge G, þæt I, þeðte E^{x}*, forðon J, forþā K
magnificauit*	ǀ	gemiclað ABC, gemiclade D, gemiclade G, gemycelade F, gemyclude K, gemærsode I, gemiclode ł gemærsode J, drihten E^{2}*
dominus	ǀ	dryhten B, drihten IK*, dryhī A, drih̄t CFGJ, gemiclædæ E^{2}
sanctum	ǀ	ðone halgan A, þone halgan B, halgan þone C, haligne DGJ, his þone F, his E^{2}*I (*K*)
suum	ǀ	his ABDGJK, halgan FI, hæligne E^{2}*
dominus		dryhten AB, drihtyn C, drihtæn E^{2}, drih̄t FGJ, dominus K
exaudiuit*		gehereð *A,* gehiereð B, gehyrð CI, gehirð J, gehyrde *D,* gehirde E^{2}, gehyrde FGK (*L*)
me		me *A*BCE^{2}FGJK
dum*		ðonne *A,* þonne BFI, þonne *CD,* þone K, þanne E^{2}, mid þy þe G, mid þy J
clamarem*		ic cleopiu *A,* ic cleopige *B,* ic clypige C*D*IK, ic clipige J, ic clypede E^{2}*, ic clypode F, ic clipode G (*L*)
ad		to ABCDE^{2}FGIJ*K*
eum		him ABCE^{2}*FGIJ, him DK

OE: þeðte (E[x])] *on eras.* drihten (E[2])] *eras. before word.* drihten (K)] æfter *eras. after* drihten *as gloss to* sanctum (sc̄m *misread as* secundum). his (E[2])] s *in darker ink, eras. after word.* hæligne (E[2])] i *interl., word retraced in darker ink.* ic clypede (E[2])] cly *on eras.* him (E[2])] *on eras.*

LTg: Scitote] C: et *added before word by same hand that added interl.* c *above* mihi (*e.g. in v.* 2); Sscitote L: *eras. after* S; scitote FGHIJK. sanctum] K: *see OE note to* drihten. exaudiuit] A: *orig.* exaudiet: *2nd* e *deleted by subscript dot,* ui *interl.;* exaudi D: *orig.* exaudiuit: uit *eras. but visible under ultraviolet;* exaudiet B, L: *orig.* exaudiuit: *2nd* u *altered to* e *and followed by eras.: cf. Weber MSS* αγδσ moz med, *see GAg.* me] A: e *obscured by stain.* dum] A: d *obscured by stain*, D: d *eras. but visible under ultraviolet*, L: cum *written above* me *by corr.: see GAg.* clamarem] A: *orig.* clamauero: ue *and* o *deleted by subscript dots,* em *interl.*, D: rem *eras. but visible under ultraviolet;* clamaro L: o *altered from another letter and followed by eras.;* clamauero B: *cf. Weber MSS* M[2]TPQUVXαγδσ moz med, *see GAg.* ad] ád K.

LTu: Scitote] scitote δεζϑιλμξοπρστυχψ. exaudiuit] exaudiet ς: *see GAu.*

GAg: Scitote] Et scitote FGHIJK; et Scitote C: *see LTg.* magnificauit] mirificauit GHIK, F: *late accents added* (= míríffcauít); mirrificauit J: *1st* r *interl.* exaudiuit] exaudiet FGHIJK; *for* ABL *see LTg.* dum] cum FGHIJK, L: *see LTg.* clamarem] clamauero FGHIJK; *for* AB *see LTg.*

GAu: Scitote] Et scitote δεζϑιλμξοπρστυχψ. magnificauit] mirificauit δεζϑιλμξοπρστυχψ. exaudiuit] exaudiet δεζιλμξοπρστυχψ, ς: *see LTu;* exaudiat ϑ. dum clamarem] cum clamauero δεζϑιλμξοπρστυχψ.

5

Irascimini		eorsiað ABD*F*, yrsiað CIK, yrsyað E[2]*, irsiaþ J, iersiað ge G
et		⁊ ABCE[2]*F*GIJK
nolite		nyllað AB, nellað *C*, nellen ge D, nellen ge E[2]*, nellan ge G, nylle ge *F*, nelle ge I, nelle ge na K, nellan J
peccare		syngian AB*C*DGIJ, singian F, sengien E[2], synnian K
quae		ða ðe *A*, þa þe *BCE[2]GK*, þa ðe *D*, þa ðe *F*, þe *J*, þa þing þe *I* (*HL*)
dicitis		cweoðað A, cweðað BC*G, cweðaþ J, cweþað K, ge cweþað D, ge cweðað *F*, ge cweðæþ E[2], ge secgaþ I
in		in AB, on CDE[2]FGIJK
cordibus	|	heortum ABF, heortum D, heortan CGJK, ewræn E[2], eowrum I
uestris	|	eowrum AB*F*G, eowrum CDJ, eowre K, heortum E[2]I
et		⁊ ABCE[2]*F*GJ (*HIK*)
in		in A, on BC*DE[2]*F*GIJK
cubilibus	|	bedcleofum AB, incleofum DG, inclyfum C**F*, incleofan K,

	incofum J, diglum ł on incofan ł on eowrum clyfum I, ewrum E^{2}
uestris |	eowrum ABFG, eowrum C*J, eowre K, bedcliofum *E*^{2}
conpungimini	bioð geinbryrde A, beoð geinbryrde B*C*, onbryrdaþ D, onbryrdað *F*, onbrydaþ K, ge beoð onbryrde G, ge beoð onbrirde J, bemænaþ ł behreowsiaþ *I*, wesæþ onbryrdað ł reowsiað *E*$^{2/x}$*

ED: quæ (D)] quae *Roeder*. quę (E)] quae *Harsley*. ge cweðæþ (E)] gecweðæþ *Harsley*. on (G) (*1st*)] *no gloss Rosier*. et (B) (*2nd*)] Et *Brenner*. compungimini (C)] co[n]pungimini *Wildhagen*. onbryrdað (F)] obryrdað *Kimmens*.

OE: yrsyað (E^{2})] *eras. before word*. nellen ge (E^{2})] *in darker ink*. cweðað (C)] að *retraced in pencil*. on (C) (*2nd*)] *retraced in pencil*. inclyfum (C)] c *and* yfu *retraced in pencil*. eowrum (C) (*2nd*)] ru *retraced in pencil*. wesæþ onbryrdað ł reowsiað (E$^{2/x}$)] onbryrdað ł reowsiað *written by corr.* (*except* on?), yrd *and* ł reowsiað *on eras*.

LTg: Irascimini] F: ra *added on eras., late accents added* (= Irascímíní). et (*1st*)] F: & *added on eras*. nolite] nolíte C, F: *accent added late*. peccare] peccáre C. quae] quæ D; quę CEFGHIL; que JK; qui AB. dicitis] F: *late accents added* (= dícítís). uestris (*1st*)] F: *late accent added* (= uestrís). et (*2nd*)] FK: *added by corr. on eras*., H: *on eras.; om*. I. in (*2nd*)] F: *late accent added* (= ín). cubilibus] F: *late accents added* (= cubílíbus). uestris (*2nd*)] E: ri *retouched in darker ink*. conpungimini] F: *late accent added* (= conpungímini); compungimini I: *orig*. conpungimini: *1st* n *deleted by subscript dots, macron added above* o; compungimini E, C: *orig*. conpungimini: *left leg added to* n *to form* m, *eras. after following* n.

LTu: quae] quæ μσχ; quę εζιξϱ; que ϑσςτ*τ. et (*2nd*)] *om*. κιλμοπϱσυ; *interl*. δ. in (*2nd*)] In π. conpungimini] conpungemini ϑ; compungimini ιλπτ, οϱ: *orig*. conpungimini: *1st* n *deleted*, m *interl.;* cōpungimini στ*υχ.

6

Sacrificate	onsecgað AC**F*, onsecgeað B, onsecgaþ D, Onseagæð E^{2}, onsægeað G, onseccað H, offriaþ I, offriað J, ofriaþ K
sacrificium	onsegdnisse A, onsægdnesse BDI, onsægdnysse C*, onsægednysse F, onsægednesse GJ, onsægðnesse H, þa onsegdnesse. ał geoffrieð offrunge E^{2}*, ofrunga K
iustitiae	rehtwisnisse A, ryhtwisnesse B*D*, rihtwisnysse C*F*, rihtwisnesse *HIJ*, of rihtwisnesse *E2**, rihtwisnes *K*, soðfæstnesse *G* (*L*)
et	⁊ ABCE^{2}FGHIJK
sperate	gehyhtað AB, gehihtað C*, gehyhten ge D, gehihte ge H, hihtað ge *G*, hihtað J, hihtaþ K, gewenæþ E^{2}, hopiað FI

in		in AB, on C*DE^{2}FGIJK
domino		drihtne C*FI, dryhtne D, drihten E^{2}K, dryhꞇ̄ AB, driht̄ G, drihꞇ̄ J
multi		monge *A*, monige *BCD*GHJ, Monige *E*^{2}, manige FK, manege I (*L*)
dicunt		cweoðað AB, cweðað C*FG, cweðaþ DJ, cweþað H, cweþaþ K, cweðæþ E^2*, secgaþ I
quis		hwelc AB, hwylc C*FGHK, hwylce D, hwilc E^{2}J, la hwilc I
ostendit		oteaweð A, æteaweð B, ætywyð C, ætæweð E^2*, æteowað F, ætieweð G, æteowð J, ætywð IK, oðeowð D, þeowð H
nobis		us ABC*DE^2*FGHIJK
bona		god AC*DK, gód BH, gode E^2*, godu GI, gódu FJ

ED: iustitię (E)] iustitiae *Harsley.* us (G)] *no gloss Rosier.* gód (H)] god *Campbell.*

OE: onsecgað (C)] g *written below line,* cað *retraced in pencil.* onsægdnysse (C)] on *and* ægdny *retraced in pencil.* þa onsegdnesse. ał geoffrieð offrunge (E^2)] dnesse. ał geoffrieð offrunge *written in lighter ink by main hand.* of rihtwisnesse (E^2)] of rihtwis *written in lighter ink by main hand.* gehihtað (C)] h, ht, *and* ð *retraced in pencil.* on (C)] *retraced in pencil.* drihtne (C)] rihtne *retraced in pencil.* cweðað (C)] ða *retraced in pencil.* cweðæþ (E^2)] *eras. before word.* hwylc (C)] h *and* ylc *retraced in pencil.* ætæweð (E^2)] *on eras.* us (C)] *retraced in pencil.* us (E^2)] *on eras.* god (C)] *retraced in pencil.* gode (E^2)] *on eras.*

LTg: Sacrificate] F: cr *added on eras.* iustitiae] iustitię DEFGHJL; iustitiæ K. sperate] spęrate G. multi] Multi ABCEL, D: M *eras. but visible.*

LTu: iustitiae] iustitię ιξχ; iustitiæ ϑμ; iusticiae ϱ: *orig.* iustitiae: *2nd* t *deleted,* c *interl.;* iustitie σς; iusticie τ*τ. multi] Multi βνςτ*. ostendit] ostendet ϑ.

7

Signatum		getacnad *A*, getacnod *BE*^{2}FHJ, getacnud *C**, getacnad G, tacnod *D*K, getacnod ł gemearcod I (*L*)
est		is ABE^{2}FGHIJ*K*, ys C*
super		ofer ABCFGHJK, ófer E^2*, ofor I
nos		us ACE^{2}FGIJ*K*, ús B
lumen	|	loht A, leoht BC*DFGHIJK, drihten E^2
uultus	|	ondwlitan ABD, andwlitan C*FGHIJ, ansyne K, þet lioht E^2
tui		ðines ADF, þines BGHIJ, þinys C, þinnes E^2, þine K
domine	|	drihtyn C, dryhꞇ̄ AB, driht̄ FGJ, onwlitan E^2* (*I*)
dedisti		ðu saldes *A*, ðu sealdes *B*, þu sealdes *D*, þu sealdyst *C**, ðu sealdest F, þu sealdest *E*^{2}GHI, sealdest J, ðu geafe K (*L*)
laetitiam		blisse A*BCDE*^{2}*FGH*I*JK* (*L*)

in	in AB, on CDE^{2}F*GHIJK (*L*)
corde	| heortan ABCDFGHJK, herte E^{2}, minre I (*L*)
meo	| minre ABCE^{2}FGHK, mynre J, mine D, heortan I (*L*)

ED: lętitiam (E)] laetitiam *Harsley.* lęticiam (C)] lęti[t]iam *Wildhagen.*

OE: getacnud (C)] *orig. seems to have read* getacmud; *hand responsible for retracing in pencil retraced* tac, *altered* m *to* n, *using right leg of orig.* m *to form left leg of* u (*but not erasing right leg of* u, *which now takes on appearance of* i: -tacmud > -tacnu(i)d); *as orig. reading is obscured, that of corr. is taken here, although orig. right leg of* u *is not recorded as* i. ys (C)] *retraced in pencil.* ófer (E^{2})] *ligature connecting* fe *eras.* leoht (C)] *retraced in pencil.* andwlitan (C)] and *retraced in pencil.* onwlitan (E^{2})] *on eras.* þu sealdyst (C)] st *retraced in pencil.* on (F)] *orig.* an: a *altered to* o.

LTg: Signatum] signatum ABCEL, D: s *eras. but visible.* est] ést K. nos] nós K: *accent added by corr.* domine] I: s. o *written above word.* dedisti] Dedisti ABCEL, D: *initial letter eras. but visible.* laetitiam] lætitiam B; lętitiam EFG; lęticiam C: *eras. above* c, *possibly altered from orig.* t; letitiam DHJKL. *Fol. 5v in* L *begins* Dedisti letitiam in corde meo, *in hand of main scribe, but another hand* (L^{2}) *has added* dedisti leticiam in corde meo *at end of final line of fol. 5r;* L *thus has 2 diff. readings for* dedisti laetitiam.

LTu: Signatum] signatum βνςτ*. dedisti] Dedisti βνςτ*. laetitiam] lætitiam ϑ; lętitiam ειλξϱχ; letitiam σςυ; leticiam τ*τ.

8

A	from *AC,* from *B,* fram FI, fram GJ, of *DE^{2}*K (*L*)
tempore*	tide AC*D*E^{2}, tíde B, wæstme FGIJ, wæsman K
frumenti	hwętes A, hwætes BDE^{2}FGHIJ, hwætys C, hwætes ⁊ *K*
(et)*	⁊ FGJ
uini	wines ABDE^{2}FG*I*JK, wínes *H,* winys C
et	⁊ ABCE^{2}FGHIJK
olei	eles ADFGHI*K,* oeles B, elys *C**, éles E^{2}, elas J
sui	his ABDE^{2}FGHIJK, hys C (*L*)
multiplicati	| gemonigfaldade A*, gemonigfealdode BG, gemonifealdude C*, gemonigefealdode J, gemænigfylde I, hi gemænigfilde F, gemyclude *K,* hy synd D, hi sind H, hy send E^{2}
sunt	| sindun A, sindan B, syndon CGJ, synd F, synde K, hi synt I, gemænigfyld DH, gemanifæld E^{2}

ED: á (E)] a *Harsley.* wínes (H)] wines *Campbell.* ólei (C)] olei *Wildhagen.*

OE: elys (C)] s *retraced in pencil.* gemonigfaldade (A)] *orig.* gemongefaldade: i *written below* n, *2nd* e *eras.* gemonifealdude (C)] i, de, *and perhaps* g *retraced in pencil.*

LTg: A] a ABCL, D: *eras. but visible;* á E. tempore] D: *eras. but visible.* frumenti] K: et *eras. after word.* uini] H: *eras. before word,* I: *eras. before and after word, with possible eras. of gloss before word.* olei] K: *eras. after word;* ólei C. sui] L: *added by corr., although* sui *appears in hand of main scribe in line below.* multiplicati] K: *eras. (5–7 letters) before word.*

LTu: A] a βνςτ*.

GAg: tempore] fructu FGHIJK. frumenti] frumenti et FGJ; *for* HIK *see LTg notes to* frumenti *and* uini.

GAu: tempore] fructu δεζϑιλμξοπϱτυχψ; ffructu σ. frumenti] frumenti et ϑμοϱψ.

9

In	in AB*G*, on CDE²FHIJK
pace	sibbe ABE²FGHIJK, sybbe CD
in	in ABC, on DE²FGHIJK
idipsum	ða ilcan A, þa ilcan BC, þære ilcan G, þare ilcan J, þæt selfe DE², ðæt sylfe F, þæt sylfe HK, him sylfum I
obdormiam*	ic neapiu A, ic hnappige B, ic hnappige C, ic hnæppie F, ic slape *D*HK, ic slæpe E²*I, ic slepte G, ic slæpte J
et	⁊ ABCE²FGHIJK
requiescam	gerestu A, gereste BC, ic gereste I, reste DHK, réste E², ic reste FGJ

ED: idipsum (ABCE)] id ipsum *Kuhn, Brenner, Wildhagen, Harsley.* obdormiam (B)] obdormian *Brenner.*

OE: ic slæpe (E²)] *small eras. after* e.

LTg: In] *lost* G. obdormiam] D: ob *eras. but visible: see GAg.*

LTu: In] in ϑ. idipsum] idipso ψ.

GAg: obdormiam] dormiam FGHIJK, D: *see LTg.*

GAu: obdormiam] dormiam δεζϑιλμξοπϱστυχψ.

10

Quoniam	forðon *AB*J, forþon *CE²*, forðan F, [ ]þā þe *G*, forðan þe I (*DI.*)
tu	ðu AB, þu CE²FGIJK
domine	dryhten B, drihten C, drihcten E²*, dryhꞇ̄ AB, driht́ FGJ, eala þu dr̄ I
singulariter	synderlice ABCDE²*F*GHIJK
in	in AB, on CDE²FGHIJK
spe	hyhte A*B*DE²F, hihte CGHIJK

constituisti — gesettes AB, gesettyst C, þu g̲esettest D, ðu gesettest F, þu gesettest E²JK, þu gesetest H, þu gesettestð G, gesettest I
me — me ABCE²FGHIJK, mec D

ED: forðon (A)] for ðon *Kuhn.* [ ]þā þe (G)] [ ]þam þe *Rosier.* eala þu dr̄ (I)] eala þu d*rihten Lindelöf.* me (G)] m[ ] *Rosier.*

OE: drihcten (E²)] c *interl.*

LTg: Quoniam] *lost* G; quoniam ABCEL; [ ]m̄ D: *initial letter* (q?) *eras.* singulariter] F: *followed by late, illegible addition.* spe] spé B.

LTu: Quoniam] quoniam βδνςτ*χ.

PSALM 5

2

Uerba | word A*CDFGHJK,* Mine *E²**, mine *I*
mea | min ABCFJ, mina D, mine GHK, word E²I
auribus | mid earum ABFGIJ, earum CH, earum̲ D, earan K, drihten E²
percipe | onfoh ABCDGHIJ, underfoh F, opena K, earum E²
domine | dryhten B, drihtyn C, drihten FK, dryħt A, driħt G, driht̄ J, eala þu dr̄ I*, ænfoh *E²*
intellege — onget A, ongit B*K,* ongyt CD*HI*, ongiet *E²**, ongyte ðu *F,* ongyt ðu *G,* ongit þu J (*L*)
clamorem | cleopunge AB, clypunge CDFH, clypunga GJK, mine clipunge E², mine I
meum | mine ABCDE²*FGHJK, clypunge I

ED: dryħt (A)] dryht̄ *Kuhn.* eala þu dr̄ (I)] eala þu d*rihten Lindelöf.*

OE: Mine (E²)] e *interl.* eala þu dr̄ (I)] s. o *written before* eala. ongiet (E²)] *eras.* (*2 letters*) *after word,* ł *visible in initial position.* mine (E²)] *on eras.*

LTg: Uerba] UERBA CE; UErba K; Verba DHIJ; [ ]rba G: *initial* V *partly visible.* domine] E: *eras. after word.* intellege] intellige EGI, F: *orig.* intellege: *2nd* e *deleted by subscript dot,* i *interl.*, H: *2nd* i *on eras.*, KL: *orig.* intellege: *2nd* e *altered to* i.

LTu: Uerba] Verba δζοπσχ; UERba β; VERba υ; UERBA ιτ*τ; VERBA MEA ς; VERBA MEA AURIBUS μ; VERBA MEA AVRIBVS ξ; VERBA MEA AURIbus ψ; VERBA MEA AURIBUS PERCIPE λϱ. intellege] intellige εζϑιλξοπστ*τυχ, ϱ: *orig.* intellege: *2nd* e *deleted by subscript dot,* i *interl.*

3

Intende — behald *A,* beheald *BC,* beeald J, begym *DE²**HIK, begim F, [ ]d *G* (*L*)

uoci		stefne ABCDE^{2}*GK, stæfne HJ, to stefne I, stemne F
orationis	|	gespreces AB, gesprecys C, g̲ebedes D, gebedes E^{2}GHJK, gebede F, mines I
meae	|	mines A*BDE*^{2}**FGHJ*K, minys *C*, gebedes I (*L*)
rex	|	cynin A, cynin[ ] B*, cining CK, cyning DFH, cýning G, kyning E^{2}*J, min I*
meus	|	min ABCDE^{2}FGHJK, kyning I
et		⁊ ABCDE^{2}FGHIJK
deus	|	god ABCFGHJK, godd D, min E^{2}I
meus	|	min ABCFGHJK, god E^{2}I

ED: intende (B)] Intende *Brenner*. [ ]nde (G)] *Intende Rosier.* [ ]d (G)] *no gloss Rosier.* meæ (D)] meae *Roeder.* meę (E)] meae *Harsley.* cynin[ ] (B)] cyning *Brenner.* min (G) (*2nd*)] mi[ ] *Rosier.*

OE: begym (E^{2})] m *on eras.* stefne (E^{2})] *on eras.* min (I) (*1st*)] s. tu es : þu eart *written before word.* cynin[ ] (B)] in *faintly visible, expected final* g *not visible except for possible fragment of descender.* kyning (E^{2})] *right leg of 2nd* n *on eras.*

LTg: Intende] intende ABCDEL; [ ]nde G. meae] meæ BD; meę CEFGHL; mee J.

LTu: Intende] INtende χ; intende βϑνςτ*. meae] meæ ϑμ; meę βζιλνξςχ; mee στ*τ.

4

Quoniam		forðon AD, forþon BCHJ, Forðæn E^{2}, forþan ðe F, forþan þe I (*G*)
ad	|	to ABCDFGHIJ*K*, drihten *E*^{2}
te	|	ðe AB*FG, þe CDHIJK, ic E^{2}
orabo	|	ic gebidu A, ic gebidde BCDFGHIK, ic bidde J, to þe E^{2}
domine	|	drihten F, dryht̄ AB, drih̄t CGJ, hlaford K, gebidde *E*^{2} (*I*)
mane		on marne AB, on morgyne C, on mergen D*HJ*, on morgen E^{2}K, on ærnemergen FGI
et*		⁊ ABCDE^{2}J
exaudies		ðu geheres A, þu gehieres B, þu g̲ehyrst C, ðu gehyrst D, þu gehérst E^{2}, ⁊ þu gehyrst F, ⁊ þe gehyrst H*, ⁊ þu gehyrdest G, þu gehyrst I, þu gehyrdest JK
uocem	|	stefne *A*BCDE^{2}K, stæfne HJ, [ ]tefne G, stemne F, mine I
meam	|	mine *A*BCDE^{2}FGJK, minre H, stefne I

ED: [ ]m (G)] *Quoniam Rosier.* forðon (A)] for ðon *Kuhn.* to (G)] *no gloss Rosier.* ðe (G)] [ ]e *Rosier.* on ærnemergen (FI)] on ærne mergen *Kimmens, Lindelöf.* uocem (G)] *uocem Rosier.* [ ]tefne (G)] [ ]tef:[ ] *Rosier.*

OE: ðe (B)] *faint but visible.* ⁊ þe gehyrst (H)] ⁊ *partly eras.*

LTg: Quoniam] [ ]m G. ad] E: *eras. above word;* ád K. domine] I: s. o *written above word,* E: *eras. after word.* mane] H: *eras. after word.* uocem] A: m *added by corr.* meam] me[ ] A: *added by corr., remainder of word lost due to trimming of leaf.*

GAg: et] *om.* FGHIK.

GAu: et] *om.* δεζιλξοπϱστυχψ.

5

Mane		on marne AB, on morgene C, on morgen DK, on mergen HJ, On mergen E^2, on ærnemergen F, [ ]gan *G**
adstabo	I	ic ætstondu A, ic ætstande B*C*DFG*HIJ*, ic þe *E^2* (*K*)
tibi	I	ðe AB, þe CDFHIJK, (þ)e G*, et stande E^2*
et		⁊ ABCDE^2FGHIJK
uidebo		gesio A, geseo C, ic geseo BFHIJK, ic g̲eseo D, ic gesyo E^2, ic geseo þe G
quoniam		forðon AJ, forþon BC, forðan ðe F, forðan þe I, forðæn E^2, forðan G, forðam K, þæ̲tte DH
non	I	ne AB, na DFGHIJK, nes C, þu eart E^2*
uolens*	} I	wellende A, willende BDHIJ, willynde C, wyllende FK, na willende *E^2*, [ ]ende G
deus*	}	god ABCE^2*FGIJK
iniquitatem		unrehtwisnisse A, unrihtwisnysse C, unryhtwisnesse BD, onrihtwisnysse F, unrihtwisnesse *E^2*GIJK, unrihtwise H
tu	I	ðu AB, þu CFGIJ
es	I	earð A, eart BCFGIJ

ED: [ ]e (G)] *Mane Rosier.* on ærnemergen (F)] on ærne mergen *Kimmens.* astabo (C)] a[d]stabo *Wildhagen.* [ ]gan (G)] *no gloss Rosier.* ic ætstande (G)] *no gloss Rosier.* (þ)e (G)] þe *Rosier.* forðon (A)] for ðon *Kuhn.* [ ]olens (G)] *uolens Rosier.* [ ]e̲u̲s (G)] deus *Rosier.* tú (E)] tu *Harsley.* és (E)] es *Harsley.*

OE: [ ]gan (G)] *letter* (r?) *visible before* g, a *questionable.* (þ)e (G)] *ascender of* þ *visible,* e *obscured.* et stande (E^2)] a *malformed* (?), *but see v. 6* awirged. þu eart (E^2)] *eras.* (*1–2 letters*) *after* eart; *gloss to end of verse is in following order:* þu eart god na willende unrihtwisnesse. god (E^2)] *eras. after word* (*above* uo *in* uo/lens).

LTg: Mane] [ ]e G. adstabo] astabo E, C: *letter eras. after 1st* a, H: *1st* a *on eras.;* ástabo K: *letter eras. after* á; asstabo I. tu] tú E. es] és E.

LTu: adstabo] astabo εζιλμξπστ*τυχ, ϱ: *orig.* adstabo: d *deleted by subscript dot;* asstabo o.

GAg: uolens deus] deus uolens EFHIJK; [ ]olens [ ]e̲u̲s G: *bowl of* d *lost,* s *partly cropped at bottom.*

GAu: uolens deus] deus uolens δεζιλμξοπστ*τυχψ.

6

Non*	ne AB, Ne E^{2}, na C, ne ne FIJ, ⁊ na HK, [ ]e G
habitabit	eardað *A*BCGH, eardiað D, eardaþ FJK, eardæþ E^{2}, eardaþ ł wunað I
iuxta	neh AB, nieh C, neah E^{2}GJK, wið DFHI
te	ðe AF*B*, þe CD*E*^{2}GHIJ*K*
malignus	awerged AB, awyrgyd C, awyrged DFGHK, awirged E^{2}*J, se awergeda I
neque	ne ABE^{2}, ny ne C, ne ne FIJ, ⁊ na HK
permanebunt	ðorhwuniað A, þurhwuniað BCGH, ðurhwuniað F, þurhwuniaþ IJ, þuhwunað K, þurþwuniæþ *E*^{2}
iniusti	ða unrehtwisan A, ða unryhtwisan B, þa unrihtwisan CGI*J*, unrihtwise FHK, unsoðfestæn E^{2}
ante	biforan A, beforan BCE^{2}GJK, ongean DH, ætforan FI
oculos	| egum A, eagum BC, eagan DFGH, eagon J, egan K, þine E^{2}, þinum I
tuos	| ðinum A, þinum CJ, þine DH, ðine F, þinan G, þinnan K, minum B, eagum E^{2}I

ED: Neque (G)] *Neque Rosier.* [ ]e (G)] *no gloss Rosier.* té (K)] te *Sisam.*

OE: awirged (E^{2})] ed *on eras.*, a *resembles that of v. 5* etstande.

LTg: habitabit] A: *2nd* h *altered from another letter.* te] E: *eras. above word;* té B, K: *accent added by corr.* permanebunt] E: *eras. above* bunt (permane/bunt). iniusti] J: *eras.* (?) *after final* i.

LTu: iniusti] μ: in *interl.*

GAg: Non] Neque FGHIJK.

GAu: Non] Neque δεζϑιλμξοπϱστυχψ.

7

Odisti	ðu fedest A, þu feodust C, þu feodest G, þu feodes B, ðu hat̄ ł ðu feodest D, atedest ł þu feodest H, þu hatest ł feodest E^{2}*, ðu hutudest F, þu hatodest I, ðu hatodest K, þu ascunodest J (*L*)
domine*	dryhten B, drihten E^{2}, dryht̄ A, driħt C
omnes	alle A, ealle BCDE^{2}FGHIJK
qui	ða ðe A*F, þa þe BCE^{2}GI, þa ðe J, þe DH, þa K
operantur	wircað AF, wircaþ J, wyrcað CDHK, wyrcaþ I, wyrceað BG, wurceþ E^{2}
iniquitatem	unrehtwisnisse A, unrihtwisnysse CF, unryhtwisnesse D*, unrihtwisnesse E^{2}GHIJ, unryhtwisnessa B, unrihwisnesse K

perdes	ðu forspildes *A,* þu forspildes B, þu forspildyst C, þu forspillest DE^{2}GHJ, ðu forspillest F, þu forspilst ł þu amyrst I, forsplst K
eos*	hie ABC, þa DE^2, ealle FGIJK
qui	ða ða A, þa ðe BK, þa þe CGIJ, ða þe F, þe DE^{2}H
loquuntur	spreocað A, sprecað B*CD*E^{2}F*GHIJ*, specað K (*L*)
mendacium	leasunge ABDE^{2}GH, leasunga CFIJ, leassungan *K*
Uirum	wer A*BDFGH*J, wera *C*K, wére *E*^{2}*,* þæne wer þe is *I* (*L*)
sanguinum	bloda ABDGH*J,* blod CFK, blode E^2, blodgita ł geotende ł wer bloda I
et	⁊ ABCE^{2}FGHIJK
dolosum	ðone fæcnan A, þone fæcnan B, facenfullne D*, facenfulne HI, fakenfulne E^2, facnfulne F, facenfulle GJ, facnfulle K, sar C
abominabitur	onscunað *AB*C*H*, onscuniað *DF**, onscuniaþ *J*K, onsceonað *G,* gehiscð ł onscunaþ *I,* amanseð ł onscuniað *E*$^{2/x}$* (*L*)
dominus	dryhten B, drihten E^2*FK, dryht̄ A, driħt CGJ

ED: ðu hat̄ ł ðu feodest (D)] ðu hat<u>est</u> ł ðu feodest *Rosier.* þu hatest ł feodest (E)] þu hatest ł feoðest *Harsley.* ðu hutudest (F)] ðu hatudest *Kimmens.*

OE: þu hatest ł feodest (E^2)] *on eras.,* de *in ligature.* ða ðe (A)] *small pen slip at base of* e, *making it seem altered from another letter.* unryhtwisnesse (D)] *otiose mark* (*in shape of macron?*) *above* t. facenfullne (D)] *2nd* n *interl.* onscuniað (F)] *bowl of* ð *cropped.* amanseð ł onscuniað (E$^{2/x}$)] ł onscuniað *added by corr.* drihten (E^2) (*2nd*)] ten *on eras.*

LTg: Odisti] L: *eras.* (*3 letters*) *after word: see GAg.* perdes] A: *2nd* e *on eras.* loquuntur] loquntur DH, G: *orig.* locuntur: c *altered to* q, *2nd* u *interl.;* locuntur CIJL, K: c *on eras. by corr.* mendacium] K: *eras. above* u, m *added later in main hand.* Uirum] Virum BCDEFHIL; [ ]irum G: *initial* V *lost.* sanguinum] J: *2nd* u *on eras.* (?). abominabitur] A: *eras. after 1st* b; abhominabitvr D; ab'-ominabitur F: *spiritus asper* (ˈ-) *added above line;* abhominabit[ ] G; abhominabitur EIJL, C: *orig.* abominabitur: h *interl. in hand that added small superscript* c *to* mihi (*e.g. Ps 4.2*) *and* et *before* Scitote (*Ps 4.4*).

LTu: loquuntur] locuntur βδεζμνοπσςυχ. mendacium] β: *orig.* mendacum: i *interl.* Uirum] Virum εινξοϱστ*τυ. sanguinum] sanguinem β. abominabitur] abhominabitur βδζϑιμξϱτ*τυ, σ: h *interl.*

GAg: domine] *om.* FGHIJK, L: *see LTg note to* Odisti. eos] omnes FGHIJK.

GAu: domine] *om.* δεζϑιλμξοπϱστυχψ. eos] omnes δεζϑιλμξοπϱστυχψ.

8

Ego	ic ABCD*FGHIJK,* Ic E^2
autem	soðlice ACE^{2}GI, soþlice BDFHJ, witodlice K
in	in ABG, on CDE^{2}FHIJK

multitudine		mengu A, menigeo BG, mænigeo C, menego D, mengeo H, manege E^2, mycel(ny)sse F*, mycelnysse I, mænigfealdnesse J, manifealde *K* (*L*)
misericordiae	I	mildheortnisse A, mildheortnysse *CF,* mildheortnesse B*GHJ,* mildheortnes *D*, mildheornese *K,* þinre *E*²I (*L*)
tuae	I	ðinre A, þinre B*CDHJK,* ðine *F,* þire G, mildheortnesse *E²I* (*L*)
introibo		ic inga AD*HK,* ic ingá BC, ic ingange *GIJ,* ic ingonge E^2*, ic infare *F*
domine*		dryhten B, drihtyn C, drihten E^2, dryhꞇ̄ A
in		in AB, on CDE^2FGHIJK
domum	I	hus ABCDGHJK, huse F, þin E^2, þinum I
tuam	I	ðin A, þin BCDGHJK, ðinum F, hus E^2, huswiste ł into þinum huse I
⟨et⟩		⁊ *C* (*G*)
adorabo		ic gebidda A, ic gebidde B*C*E^2*F*G*HIJ*K,* ic gebidde D
ad		to ABCDE^2FGHIJ*K*
templum	I	temple ABCDFGHJK, þinum E^2*, þinum I
sanctum	I	ðæm halgan A, þam halgan B, halgan CE^2, halgum D, halgum FGHI, haligum J, halian K
tuum	I	ðinum AF, þinum BCGHJ, þinum D, þinan K, temple E^2I
in		in AB, on CDE^2FGHIJK
timore	I	ege ABCDFGHJK, þinum E^2I
tuo	I	ðinum ABF, þinum CJ, þinum DGH, þinre K, ege E^2I

ED: multitudiné (K)] multitudine *Sisam.* mycel(ny)sse (F)] mycelnysse *Kimmens.* misericordię (E)] misericordiae *Harsley.* misericordíæ (K)] misericordiæ *Sisam.* tuę (E)] tuae *Harsley.*

OE: mycel(ny)sse (F)] ny *obscured.* ic ingonge (E^2)] *interl. letter after 1st* n *eras.* ic gebidde (E^2)] *eras. before and after word.* þinum (E^2)] *eras.* (*2 letters*) *before word.*

LTg: Ego] ego FGHIJK. multitudine] L: *right 2 legs of* m *on eras.* (?); multitudiné K: *accent added by corr.* misericordiae] misericordie D; misericordię CEFGHJL; misericordíæ K. tuae] tuę CDEFJK; tuæ L; tue I: *orig.* tuae: a *eras.* introibo] Introibo FGHIJK. adorabo] K: *letter eras. after* d, *initial* a *perhaps altered from false start of ampersand;* et adorabo C; et adhorabo G: et (&) *interl.* ad] ád K.

LTu: Ego] ego δεζϑιλμξοπϱστυχψ. misericordiae] misericordię ιοχ; misericordie ξσςτ*τ; missericordiæ ϑ. tuae] tuę ιξουχ; tue σςτ*τ; tuæ ϑ. introibo] Introibo δεζϑιμξοπϱστυχψ.

GAg: domine] *om.* FGHIJK.

GAu: domine] *om.* δεζϑιλμξοπϱστυχψ.

9

Deduc* } gelæd ABCDFGHIJ, geled E^2, læd K
me* } me ABCDE^{2}FGHIJK
domine* } drihten E^2, dryht̄ AB, driħt CGHJ, eala ðu drħt F (*I*)
in in AB, on CE^{2}FGHIJK
tua* } ðine AF, þine BE^{2}G, þinre CHIJK, þire D
iustitia* } rehtwisnisse A, ryhtwisnesse BD, rihtwisnysse CF, rihtwisnesse E^2*GHIJK
propter fore ABCDE^{2}H, for GIJK, forðam F
inimicos | feondum ABFGHIJ, feondum CD, feonda K, minum E^2
meos | minum ABFGI, minum CDHJ, minra K, fiondum E^2
dirige gerece A*BE^{2}FHK, gerece CD, gerece ðu G, gewissa IJ
in in AB, on CDE^{2}FGHIJK
conspectu | gesihðe ABFGIJ, gesihðe CD, gesihþe H, gesyhðe K, þinre E^2
tuo* | ðinre A, þinre BCDHJ, ðine F, þinum G, minre *I*, gesihðæ E^2
uiam | weg ABCDFGHJK, mine E^2, þinne I
meam* | minne ABCDFGHJK, weg E^2*I*

ED: iustitiam tuam (G)] iustitia tua *Rosier.*

OE: rihtwisnesse (E^2)] wisnesse *on eras.*, n *altered from* r. gerece (A)] *1st* e *lacks cross-stroke.*

LTg: domine] I: s. o *written above word.* tuo] I: *written on eras. by later hand in lighter brown ink.* meam] I: *written on eras. by later hand in lighter brown ink.*

LTu: iustitia] iusticia ϱτ*τ. dirige] direge β. tuo] [ ]o ε.

GAg: Deduc me domine] Domine deduc me FGHIJK. tua iustitia] iustitia tua FHIJK; iustitiam tuam G.

GAu: Deduc me domine] Domine deduc me δεζϑιλμξοπϱστυχψ. tua iustitia] iustitia tua δεζιλμξοπσυχψ; iusticia tua τ, ϱ: *orig.* iustitia tua: *2nd* t *deleted by subscript dot,* c *interl.* tuo] meo δμοψ, χ: *deleted and* tuo *interl. in late hand.* meam] tuam δμοψ, χ: *deleted and* meam *interl. in late hand.*

10

Quoniam forðon ABD, forþon CGHJ, Forðæn E^2, forðạn F, forþan þe I
non | nis ABDE^{2}FHI, ne CG, na JK
est | ys C, is GJ*K*
in in AB, on CDE^{2}FGHIJK
ore | muðe ABCGJ, muþe DFHIK, hiræ E^2
eorum | heara A, heora DFGHIJK, hira B, hyra C, muðe E^2
ueritas soðfestnis A, soþfæstnis D, soðfæstnys CF, soþfæstnys H, soðfæstnes BGI, soþfæstnes K, soþfæstnesse J, sodfestnesse E^2

cor — heorte ABCDFHIJK, heort[ ] G, ⁊ heortæ E^2*
eorum — heara A, heora FGHIJK, hira B, hyra C, here E^2
uanum — idel ABDFGHIJK, ydyl C, ydel E^2
est — is ABDE^{2}FGHIJ*K*, ys C

ED: forðon (A)] for ðon *Kuhn.*

OE: ⁊ heortæ (E^2)] *letter* (n?) *eras. after* heortæ.

LTg: Quoniam] [ ]uoniam G: *initial* Q *lost.* est (*1st*)] ést K. est (*2nd*)] ést K.

11

Sepulchrum — byrgen ABFGI, byrgyn C, byrigen DHK, berien E^2*, birge J
patens — open ABI, opyn C, opengende D, openende E^2*, opnigende FJ, openiende G, onpengende H, opigende K
est — is ABE^2*FGHIJ*K*, ys C
guttur | hraece A, hrace BDHK, hraca CG, brace F, hrace ł þrotu I, þrota J, heore E^2*
eorum | heara A, heora CDFGHIJK, hira B, hrache E^2
linguis | tungum ABDH, tungan C, tunge K, mid tungan FJ, hioræ E^2, mid heora G, on heora I
suis | heara A, heora CDFHJK, hira B, tungæn E^2, tungum G, tungum I
dolose — faccenlice A, facenlicc B, facynlice C, facenfullice DFJ, fakenfullice I, facenfulliche E^2, facenfulle GH, facn K
agebant — dydun A, dydon BCDFGH, didon J, dydan K, hi dydun I, deoden E^2
iudica — doem AB, dém D, dem CHIK, deme E^2, dem ðu F, de þu GJ
illos — hie ABCG, hy DK, hi E^2*HI, hig J, heom F
deus — god ABCE^{2}FHIJK

Decidant | gefallen *A*, gefeallen B, gefeallyn C, gefellaþ F, gefeallað G, hi feollan J, hy ahreosen D, hi areosen H, ahresan K, feallan hi ł gehreosan hi I, Fræm E^2
a | from A, from C, fram B*D*GJK, fram FHI, hieræ *E*^{2}
cogitationibus — geðohtum A, geþohtum BCFHJ, geþohtum D, goðohtum GK, geþohtum I, geþohtum *E*^{2}
suis | heara A, heora CDFGHIJK, hira B, hie afeallæd E^2
secundum — efter AE^2, efter D, æfter BFGHI, æfter J, æftyr C, neah K
multitudinem — mengu A, mengo B, menego D, mænigeo C, mænigo F, mænego HK, micelnesse GJ, mænigfyldnysse *I*, felefaldnesse E^2*
impietatum — arleasnissa A, arleasnessa BD*I*K, arleasnysse C,

	arleasnyssa F, arleasnesse *E*²*G*HJ
eorum	heara A, heora DE²FGHIJK, hira B, hyra C
expelle	onweg adrif ABC, adręf D, adref E², adræf HK, utadræf *F,* utadrif ðu J, utad[ ] *G,* afyrsa ł utadræf I
eos	hie ABCG, hy DE²F, hi HIK, hig J
quoniam	forðon ABCJ, forþan FI, forðæn E², forþam G, forðā K
exacerbauerunt*	onscunedon *A*B, hi onscunydon C, hy gremedvn *D*,* hy gremeden E², hy gremedon F, hi gegremedon I, hig gremedon J, hi gremodan K, hie agrimsedon G
te	ðe A*B*FG, þe CE²IJK
domine	dryhten B, drihtyn C, drihten E²FG, dryhī A, driht J (*HI*)

ED: á (E)] a *Harsley.* onweg adrif (AB)] on weg adrif *Kuhn, Brenner.* utadræf (F)] ut adræf *Kimmens.* forðon (A)] for ðon *Kuhn.* hy gremedvn (D)] hy gremedun *Roeder.* té (B)] te *Brenner.*

OE: berien (E²)] *on eras.* openende (E²)] *on eras.* is (E²)] i *on eras.* heore (E²)] *letter eras. before word.* hi (E²)] *eras. after word.* felefaldnesse (E²)] *on eras.; after 2nd* l *scribe began* n (*left leg*), *but altered to* d. hy gremedvn (D)] *orig.* hy gremedon: o *deleted by subscript dot,* v *interl.*

LTg: est] ést K. Decidant] A: i *on eras.* a] D: *otiose strokes on right side of back;* á E. cogitationibus] cogitatibus E. multitudinem] multitudinēm I. impietatum] E: pietatum *crossed through with blunt point,* G: u *on eras., eras.* (*of cauda?*) *below* e; impietatem I. expelle] Eexpelle F; ex[ ] G. exacerbauerunt] exaceruauerunt A, D: *1st* u *altered from* b. te] té B. domine] I: s. o *written above word;* domin[ ] H: *hole in leaf.*

LTu: Sepulchrum] [ ]epulchrum τ. patens] ψ: s *interl.* agebant] aiebant ζ. cogitationibus] ι: *2nd* o *altered from* b.

GAg: exacerbauerunt] irritauerunt FGHIJ, K: nt *ligature made by corr., adding ascender and cross-stroke to right leg of* n (N), *eras. between legs of* n *at top.*

GAu: exacerbauerunt] irritauerunt δεζιλξοπϱστυχ, ϑ: *1st* r *interl.;* inritauerunt μψ.

12

Et	⁊ ABCDE²*FGHIJK
laetentur	blissien A, blissigen *B,* blissiyn *C,* blissian *JK,* blissiað *G,* geblissigen *D,* geblissigen *E²*H,* geblissian *FI* (*L*)
omnes	alle A, ealle BCFGIJ, eale K, ælle E²
qui	ða A, þa BC, ða þe F, þa þe E²GIJ, þa K
sperant	gehyhtað AB, gehihtað GJ, gehihton C, hyhtað D, hihtað HK, hihtaþ I, hyhteð E², hopiaþ F
in	in AB, on C*E*²FGIJK
te	ðe *AB*FG, þe CE²IJK

in		in *A*B, on CDE^{2}FGHIJK
aeternum		ecnisse *A,* ecnysse *CFI,* ecnesse *BDE^{2}*GHK,* écnesse *J* (*L*)
exultabunt		gefioð A, gefeoð B, hi gefeoð C, hy ahebbað DF, hi ahebbað H, wynsumiað G, hi gefeagaþ I, hyo fagniæð E^{2}*, blissiaþ J
et		⁊ ABCE^{2}FGHIJK
inhabitabis*	|	ðu ineardas A, þu ineardas C, þu ineardast B, ðu oneardast D, þu oneardast H, þu ineard[ ] G, þu eardast JK, þu geeardast I*, þu onwunast F, þu on E^{2}*
in	|	in ABC, on DFHIJK, him E^{2}* (*G*)
eis	|	him ABCJK, hi<u>m</u> DH, heom F, heo<u>m</u> I, eærdæst E^{2} (*G*)
et		⁊ ABCDE^{2}*FGHIJK*
gloriabuntur		wuldriað ABCG, wuldriaþ J, wyldriað K, hy wuldriað DF, hie wuldrieð E^{2}*, hi wuldrian H, gewuldriaþ I
in		in ABG, on CDE^{2}FHIJK
te		ðe ADE^{2}FG, þe BCHIJK
omnes		alle A, ealle BCDE^{2}*FGHIJ, eale K
qui		ða ðe A, þa þe BCFGIJ, þæ þe E^{2}, þa K
diligunt		lufiað ACDHJK, lufiaþ FI, lufigeað B, lufiæd E^{2}, lufi[ ] *G*
nomen	|	noman AB, naman CDFGHJK, þíne E^{2}, þinne I
tuum	|	ðinne AF, þinne BCGHJK, nomæn E^{2}, naman I

ED: lętentur (CE)] letentur *Wildhagen;* laetentur *Harsley.* æternum (D)] aeternum *Roeder.* ęternum (E)] aeternum *Harsley.* habitabi[ ] (G)] habitab*is Rosier.*

OE: ⁊ (E^{2})] *on eras.* geblissigen (E^{2})] *on eras.;* æll (?) *eras. before word: cf. following gloss* (*to* omnes). ecnesse (E^{2})] *small eras. after word.* hyo fagniæð (E^{2})] fagniæð *on eras.* þu geeardast (I)] t *faint but visible.* þu on (E^{2})] on *on eras.* (?). him (E^{2})] *on eras.* (?). hie wuldrieð (E^{2})] wuldrieð *on eras.* ealle (E^{2})] *on eras.*

LTg: laetentur] lætentur B; letentur DHJKL; lętentur CEFGI. in (*1st*)] E: *right leg of orig. minuscule* n *eras., new right leg added to form majuscule* n (N) *to fill line.* te (*1st*)] A: *eras. after word;* té B. in (*2nd*)] A: *added in left margin by corr.* aeternum] æternum BDK, A: *æ added in left margin by corr.;* ęternum CEGIL; eternum FJ, H: *eras. after word.* in (*3rd*)] *lost* G. eis] *lost* G. et (*2nd*)] Et FHIJK; [ ]t G: *initial* E *lost.* diligunt] dilig[ ] G.

LTu: laetentur] lętentur ειλν; letentur ξυςι*τυψ; lætentur ϑ. in te (*1st*)] υ: *interl.,* β: *written in left margin.* aeternum] ętemum ιμνξ; eternum σςτ*τ; æternum ϑ. exultabunt] exsultabunt ϑ. inhabitabis] habitabunt υ. et (*2nd*)] Et δεζϑιλμξοπϱστυχψ. diligunt] dilegunt β. nomen] β: no *interl.*

GAg. inhabitabis] habitabis FHIJK; habitabi[ ] G.

GAu: inhabitabis] habitabis δεζϑιλμξοπϱστχψ.

13

Quoniam — forðon A*J*, forþon BC*G*, Forðæn E^2, forðan *F*, forþan *I* (*HK*)

tu — ðu A, þu BCE^{2}FGIJK (*L*)

domine* — drihtyn C, drihten E^2, dryht̄ AB (*L*)

benedices — ðu bledsas *A*, þu bletsas B, bletsast CDFGJK, bletsæst E^2*, gebletsast I

iustum* — ðone rehtwisan A, þone ryhtwisan B, þone rihtwisan C, þane rihtwisan I, þa rihtwisan J, þane rihtwisne E^2*, rihtwisne DF, rihtwise K, r[ ] G

domine — drihten E^2, dryht̄ AB, drih́t C*FJ*, drih́ *G* (*HIK*)

ut — swe swe A, swa swa BC, swa DE^2*FGHIJK

scuto — mid scelde AI, mid scilde BJ, mid scylde CG, of scylde DE^2*H, of scilde F, scyld K

bonae | godes AB*DE*^{2}**FGJ*, gódes *H*, godys *C*, god *K*, mid *I* (*L*)

uoluntatis | willan ABCDFGHJK, willen E^2*, þinum godan I

tuae | dines A, þines B*DE*^{2}**H*, þinys *C*, þinne *J*, willan *I* (*FGKL*)

coronasti | ðu gebegades A, þu gebeagades B, þu gebiegodyst C*, þu gebeagadest G, þu gewuldorbeagodest IJ, ðu gehelmvdest D*, þu gehelmodest F, þu gehelmedest HK, þu us E^2 (*L*)

nos | usic A, ús B, us CDFGHIJK, gehelmedest E^2*

ED: forðon (A)] for ðon *Kuhn*. iu(s)to (G)] iusto *Rosier*. bonę (G)] bone *Rosier*. gódes (H)] godes *Campbell*. tuę (I)] tuae *Lindelöf*. tuę (E)] tuae *Harsley*. coronasti nos (I)] *to be read as coming after* tuę, *though written after* iusto *in MS* (*in typical scribal practice of completing a line by writing it at end of line above*); *but Lindelöf prints* tu benedices iusto coronasti nos Domine ut scuto bone uoluntatis tuae. ðu gehelmvdest (D)] ðu gehelmudest *Roeder*.

OE: bletsæst (E^2)] *small eras. after word.* þane rihtwisne (E^2)] *on eras.* swa (E^2)] *on eras.* of scylde (E^2)] *on eras.* godes (E^2)] *on eras.* willen (E^2)] *on eras.* þines (E^2)] *gloss eras. after word, descender visible in initial position,* s (*long*) *visible in final position.* þu gebiegodyst (C)] *2nd* e *interl.* ðu gehelmvdest (D)] *orig.* ðu gehelmedest: v *written above 3rd* e, *but without subscript deleting dot.* gehelmedest (E^2)] *eras. before* h.

LTg: Quoniam] quoniam FGHIJK. tu] L: *eras. after word: see GAg.* benedices] A: *orig.* benedicis: *2nd* i *altered to* e. iustum] E: *final* u (ū) *on eras. by corr.;* iusto L: *see GAg.* domine (*2nd*)] Domine FGHK, I: s.o *written above word;* Qomine (Qn̄e) J. bonae] bone DEIJKL; bonę CFGH. tuae] tuę CDEHIJ, F: *added interl.*, K: *added by corr. on eras.;* tue G; tuæ L. coronasti] L: a *obscured by stain.*

LTu: Quoniam] quoniam δεζθιλμοπϱστυχ. benedices] benedicis β. domine (*2nd*)] Domine δεζιλμξοπϱστυχψ. bonae] bone βδιλσςτ*τυψ; bonȩ εμνξοπϱ; bonæ ζθ. tuae] tuȩ ζιλ, ξϱχ: *interl.;* tuæ θ; tue σςτ*τ, δ: *interl.; om.* εμοπυψ.

GAg: domine (*1st*)] *om.* FGHIJK, L: *see LTg note to* tu. iustum] iusto FHIJK, L: *see LTg.;* iu(s)to G: *tear in leaf, ascender of* s *partly visible.*

GAu: domine (*1st*)] *om.* δεζιλμξοπϱστυχψ. iustum] iusto δεζθιλμνξοπϱστυχψ.

PSALM 6

2

Domine		dryhten *A*, drihten G*E*^{2}, driħt *C*J, eala þu drihten F (*BD*H**IK*)
ne	|	nales AB, nalys C, na DFJK, ne GI
in	|	in ABCG, on DE^2*FIJK
ira*	}|	eorre AB, yrre CDK, irre J, hætheortnysse F, hatheortnes I, þinum *E*^{2}*, þinum G
tua*	}|	ðinum A, þinum BCDJ, þine F, þinre I, þire K, yrre E^{2}G
arguas		ðu dreast A, þu þreast B*C*, þu ðreage D, ne þrægæ þu E^2*, ne þrea ðu F, ne þrea þu J, þrea ðu I, ðrea ð[ ] *G*, þrea K*
me		me ABCE^{2}FJK (*G*)
neque		ne ABCE^{2}GJ, ne ne F, ⁊ na DIK
in		in ABC, on DE^{2}FGHI, on on J
furore*	}|	hatheortnisse AD, hatheortnesse B, hatheortnysse C, graman FJ, yrre H, wræþe K, þinre G, þinum E^{2}I
tuo*	}|	ðinre A, þinre BCDK, ðinum F, þinum HJ, wylme E^2, hatheortnesse G, yrre I
corripias		ðu ðreast ł cid A/A^2*, þu þreast B, þu ðreast C, þu ðrea ł cide D, þu þrea ł cide H, cid K, ne ðrea þu F, ne þrea þu *J,* ne gegrip þu E^2, gewemmest G, styr þu I
me		me ABCE^{2}FGHIJK

ED: ðrea ð[ ] (G)] ðreað[ ] *Rosier.* me (D) (*2nd Lat.*) *no gloss*] *Roeder records gloss* me.

OE: H: *interl. eras. extends from* Domine *to* neque; *letter fragments are visible* (*but illegible*), *suggesting that a gloss was originally inserted.* on þinum (E^2)] *eras. above words.* ne þrægæ þu (E^2)] g *altered from another letter.* þrea (K)] ðu þe *eras. before word* (*Sisam records* ðu þ?e). ðu ðreast ł cid (A/A^2)] ł cid *added in later hand but not, according to Kuhn, that of fols 155–60* (*11th-c.*).

LTg: Domine] I: s. o *written in bowl of* D; DÑE ABDEK; DOMINE C. (*1st*) in] *on eras.* E. ira] *on eras.* E. arguas] C: *initial* a *altered from* t, *with top stroke added by glossator;* arg[ ] G. me (*1st*)] *lost* G. corripias] corripies J.

LTu. Domine] DOMINE ιλμςτ; DN̄E βνξϱςυτ*χψ. ne] NE λμνξϱςψ. in (*1st*)] IN λμνξϱψ. ira] IRA ν. arguas] ARGVAS λ; Arguas ξ.

GAg. ira tua…furore tuo] furore tuo…ira tua FGHIJK.

GAu. ira] furore δεζϑιοπστυχ; FVRORE λξ; FURORE μϱ; FUROre ψ. tua] tuo δεζϑιμοπστυχψ; TUO λϱ; TVO ξ. furore tuo] ira tua δεζϑιλμξοπϱστυχψ.

3

Miserere — mildsa *A*K, miltsa CD, Miltsa E^{2}, miltsa (ð)u G*, miltse þu J, gemiltsa BI, gemltsa F (H*)

mihi* — me AB*C*D*E*^{2}GJK, min F*I (H*)

domine — drihtyn C, drihten E^{2}F, dryht̄ AB, drih̄t GJ

quoniam — forðon ABCJ, forðan FI, forðæn E^{2}, forðā G

infirmus | untrum ABCDFI, untrum̲ HK*, ic untrum J, ic untru[ ] G, ic eom E^{2}

sum | ic eam A, ic eom BCFHIK, ic eom̲ D, eom J, seac ł untrum E^{2}

sana — hael A, hæl BK, hæle DH, gehæl CFI, gehele E^{2}, hæl þu GJ

me — me ABCE^{2}FGHIJK

domine — drihtyn C, dryhten D, drihten E^{2}I, dryht̄ AB, drih̄t FGJ

quoniam — forðon ABJ, forþon C, forðan FI, forðæn þe E^{2}, forðan þe G

conturbata — gedroefed A, gedrefyde C, ge̲drefede D, gedrefede E^{2}GHJK, gedrefde BF, gedrefede þe I

sunt — sindun A, sindon B, syndon CDGHJ, synd FK, synt I, beoð ł sinden E^{2}* (*L*)

omnia* — all A, ealle BCDJ, eallæ E^{2} (*F*)

ossa | ban ADFHJK, bán B, bane G, lymu C, mine E^{2}I

mea | min AB, mine CDFGHJK, bæn E^{2}, ban I

ED: Miserere (G)] *M*iserere *Rosier.* miltsa (ð)u (G)] *no gloss Rosier.* forðon (A) (*1st*)] for ðon *Kuhn.* sum (G)] *sum Rosier.* sana (G)] sane *Rosier.* forðon (A) (*2nd*)] for ðon *Kuhn.*

OE: Miserere mei (H)] *eras. above words, most likely of gloss.* miltsa (ð)u (G)] *cross-stroke of* ð *not visible.* min (F)] *eras.* (?) *after* i. untrum̲ (K)] in *eras. before* un, *eras.* (*4 letters?*) *after* un. beoð ł sinden (E^{2})] d *altered from* t.

LTg: Miserere] A: *orig.* Miserire, *2nd* i *altered to* e. mihi] michi E, C: *orig.* mihi, *small* c *added interl. by corr.* sunt] L: *eras. after word.* omnia] F: *added above line between* sunt ossa *in later hand: see GAg.*

LTu: Miserere] Misserere θ. mihi] michi ςτ*. conturbata] β: ta *interl.*

GAg: mihi] mei FGHIJK. omnia] *om.* GHIK; *for* F *see LTg.*

GAu. mihi] mei δεζϑιλμξοπϱστυχψ. omnia] *om.* δεζϑιλμξοπϱστυχψ.

4

Et ⁊ *ABCDE^{2}*FGHIJK (*L*)
anima | sawl A*BCF, saul DH, sauwl G, sawle IJ, sawel K, min E^{2}*
mea | min ABCDFGHIJK, sæwle E^{2}
turbata | gedroefed A, gedrefyd C, gedrefed D, gedrefed FHIJK, gedrefedu BG, is E^{2}*
est | is ABFGHIJ*K*, ys C, swiðe E^{2}
ualde | swiðe ACE^{2}GIJ, swiþe BDH, swyðe K, ðearle F, gedrefed E^{2}*
et ⁊ *ABCDE^{2}*FGHIJK (*L*)
tu ðu ABF, þu CDE^{2}GHIJK
domine drihten E^{2}FI, dryht̄ AB, drih̄t CGJ, drih̄ H
usquequo hu longe AB, hu lange CE^{x}*FHIJK, hu lange D, hwonne hugu G

ED: usquequo (BCE)] usque quo *Brenner, Wildhagen, Harsley.*

OE: sawl (A)] *letter* (?) *eras. after* l. min (E^{2})] *eras.* (*1 letter*) *after word.* is (E^{2})] s *on eras.* gedrefed (E^{2})] *punct. on eras. after word.* hu lange (E^{x})] *on eras.*

LTg: Et] et ABCDEL. est] ést K. et] Et ABCDEL.

LTu: Et] et βνςτ*. et] Et βνςτ*.

5

Conuertere gecer *AB,* gecyr FI, gecyrr *C,* gecyr ðu *G,* beo gecyrred *D,* beo gecyrred *E^{x}**HK, gehwirf J (*L*)
(domine)* drihten FK, drih̄t GHJ
et ⁊ ABCE^{2}FGHIJ (*K*)
eripe genere ABCE^{2}G, genera FIJ, nere DH , nera K
animam | sawle ABCFHJK, saule DG, mine E^{2}I
meam | mine ABCDFGHJK, sæwle E^{2}, sawle I
saluum halne AB*C*DE^{x}*G*HJ*, gehæl FI, hal *K*
me me ABCDE^{x}*FGHIJK
fac do AE^{x}*GJK, dó BD, gedo CH
propter fore AB*CE^{2}*H, for DGIJK, forþan F
misericordiam | mildheortnisse A, mildheortnysse CF, mildheortnesse BGHIJK, miltse D, þinre E^{2}
tuam | ðine A, þinre BCDFGHIJK, mildheortnesse E^{2}

OE: beo gecyrred (E^{x})] *on eras.* halne (E^{x})] *on eras.* me (E^{x})] *on eras. by corr.* do (E^{x})] *on eras.*

LTg: Conuertere] conuertere ABCDEL; [ ]onuertere G: *initial* C *only partly visible.* et] ⁊ K: *added by corr.* saluum] H: *eras. before word;* Saluum K (*not indicating new verse*); salfum C. propter] proter C.

LTu: Conuertere] conuertere βνςτ*. et] *interl.* δ; *om.* ψ. saluum] π: *orig.* psaluum: p *eras.* me] *interl.* ε. misericordiam] missericordiam ϑ.

GAg: Conuertere] Conuertere domine FHJK, I: s. o *written above* domine; [ ]onuertere domine G.

GAu: Conuertere] Conuertere domine δεζϑιλμξοπϱστυχψ.

6

Quoniam		forðon A, forþon BC, forðan K, forðæn þe E^{2}, forþan þe FI, forðon þe G, forþon þe J
non	I	nis ABFI, ne CE^{2}GJ, na K
est	I	is E^{2}GJ*K*, ys C
in		in AB, on CDE^{2}FGHIJK
morte		ðeaðe A, deaðe BCFGHJK, deaþe DE^{2}, deaþe ł on deaðscufan I*
qui		se *A*B, se ðe F, se þe GJ, þe CI, þa K, hwylc þe E^{2}
memor	I	gemyndig AB*C*DFGHI, gemindig J, gemyndi K, þines E^{2}
sit	I	sie AB*DG, si H, sy CIJ, beo K, gemundige E^{2}*
tui	I	ðin AF, þin BCDGHIJK, syo E^{2}*
in		in ABGJ, on CDE^{2}FHIK
inferno		helle ABCDE^{2}FGHIK, on helle J
autem		soðlice ABCE^{2}FGHI, soþlice J, witolice K
quis		hwelc ABD, hwylc CE^{2}FGHK, hwilc J, la hwa I
confitebitur		ondetteð AB, ondeteð E^{2}, andetteð G, andettaþ J, andyttyð C, geandettað D, geandetteð H, geandetteþ FI, andet K*
tibi		ðæ A, þe BCDE^{2}GHIJK, ðe F

ED: forðon (A)] for ðon *Kuhn.* forðæn þe (E)] Forðæn þe *Harsley.* þe (G)] þ[ ] *Rosier.*

OE: deaþe ł on deaðscufan (I)] *1st* e *blotted.* sie (B)] *word stained, but visible.* gemundige (E^{2})] *written in lighter brown ink.* syo (E^{2})] *written in lighter brown ink.* andet (K)] *stroke after* t (*false start?*).

LTg. est] ést K. qui] A: *followed by eras.* memor] mémor C.

LTu. qui] δ: ł quis *interl.* in (*2nd*)] β: *interl.*

7

Laboraui		ic won A, ic wan BG, ic wonn C, ic wan ł ic swanc J, ic swanc DFIK, Ic swanc E^{2}*, is swang H
in		in AB, on CDE^{2}FGHIJK
gemitu	I	geamrunge A, geomrunge B, geomrunge C, geomrunga DH, geomerunga *F*, iumerunge G, gemerunge J, geomerunge K, minre E^{2}I

meo | minre ABCDFGHJK, geomrunge E^{2}I
lauabo ic ðwea AF, ic þwea BCJ, ic hwea G, ic ðwea ł ic swilige I, ic swylige ł þwea D, ic swylige HK, ic wessce E^2*
per ðorh A, þurh BCDE^{2}GHIJK, ðurh F
singulas syndrie A, syndrige BCGI, syndriga DH*K*, sindrige *J*, sindræ E^2, ænlipie F (*L*)
noctes nęht A, nihta BD*F*HIK, nihte CGJ, niehtæ E^2
lectum | bed AK, bedd BCDFH, bed ł reste J, reste G, min E^{2}I
meum | min ABCFHJK, mín D, minre G, bed E^{2}I
lacrimis | mid tearum AB, mid tearum *E^2**, of tearum D, of tearum *FH*, tearum *GJ*, tearas C, tæran *K*, mid minum *I*
⟨meis⟩ | minum F, minum J, min̄ G, minan K, tearum I
stratum strene AB, stræle D*F**H, strelum *E^2**, stræte C, strewene G, strecednysse I, beddincge J
meum mine ABCDH, minum F, minum *E^2**, minre J, min̄ G, mine ł mine beddinge I
rigabo ic wetu A, ic wæte BCK, ic wete E^2, ic lecce ł wæte DF, ic łecce ł wæte H, ic læcce G, ic beþwea ł ic gelecce I, ic geanlæte J

ED: ic þwea (B)] io þwea *Brenner.*

OE: Ic swanc (E^2)] anc *on eras.* ic wessce (E^2)] w *on eras.* mid tearum (E^2)] *eras. after word.* stræle (F)] ræ *partly obscured.* strelum (E^2)] *written in lighter brown ink.* minum (E^2)] *written in lighter brown ink.* ic łecce ł wæte (H)] ic lecce ł wæte *Campbell.*

LTg. gemitu] F: *orig.* gemito, o *altered to* u. singulas] L: a *formed from another letter,* K: *orig.* singulos: o *altered to* a *by corr.;* singulos J. noctes] F: e *formed from another letter, eras. before* s. lacrimis] E: cri *retraced in darker ink,* mis *on eras.;* lacrimis meis FGHIJK: *cf. Weber MSS* Mβσ^2. stratum] E: stra *retraced in darker ink,* F: stra *added later on eras.,* st *formed from other letters in ligature.* meum] E: ū *retraced in darker ink.*

LTu: gemitu] gemito ε. singulas] singulos ς. lacrimis] lacrimis meis δεζιλμξοπϱστυχψ: *cf. Weber MSS* Mβσ^2.

8
Turbatus gedroefed A, gedrefed BDE^{2}FGHIJK, gedrefyd C
est is ABDE^{2}FGHIJ*K*, ys C
prae* | fore AB, for *CD*GJ, fram F, fram IK, min *E^2** (*L*)
ira* | eorre ABD, yrre CGK, irre J, hatheortnysse F, hatheortnesse I, eægæ E^2

oculus	|	ege A, eage B, eage D, eahge H, eagan CFG, eagon J, egan K, min I, for þinum E^2
meus	|	min ABDFHJ, mine CGK, eage I, yrrum E^2
inueteraui		ic aldade A, ic ealdade B, ic ealdode CDFHJK, ic ealdig[ ] *G*, ⁊ ic eælddige E^2, ic forealdode I
inter		betwih A, betwyh C, betweoh BE^2GJ, betweox DFH, betwux I, betwyx K
omnes		alle A, ealle BDGH, eallum FI, eallum CJ, eællum E^2, eallan K
inimicos	|	feond A, fiend B, fynd H, feondum CFIJ, feondan K, in sibbum G, mine D, minum E^2
meos	|	mine ABH, minum CF, minum GIJ, minan K, fynd D, fiondum E^2

ED: Turbatus (G)] *T*urbatus *Rosier.* prę (E)] prae *Harsley.* eællum (E)] eallu*m* *Harsley.*

OE: min (E^2)] *eras.* (*1 letter*) *after word.*

LTg: est] ést K. prae] pre CDL; prę E. inueteraui] inuet[ ]raui G.

LTu: prae] prę ν; pre ςτ*. oculus] oculos ε. meus] meos ε.

GAg: prae] a FGHIJK. ira] furore FGHIJK.

GAu: prae] a δεζθιλμξοπρστυχψ. ira] furore δεζθιλμξοπρστυχψ.

9

Discedite		gewitað ABCDHN^a, gewítað F, gewitaþ IK, gewítæð E^2, onweg gewitað G, onweg gewitaþ J
a		from A, From E^2, from BCG, fram DHJ, fram FIKN^a
me		me ABCDE^2FGHIJKN^a
omnes		alle A, ealle BCDFGHIJKN^a, eælle E^2
qui		ða A, þa K, þe BCDH, þa þe FGJ, þæ þe E^2, ge þe I (*N^a*)
operamini	|	wircað A, wyrcað DI, wyrcaþ *F*HK, wircaþ J, wyrceað BCG, unriht E^2 (*N^a*)
iniquitatem	|	unrehtwisnisse A, unryhtwisnesse BD, unrihtwisnysse CF, unrihtwisnesse GIJKN^a, unrihtwisnessa H, wirchað E^2
quoniam		forðon ADJ, forþon BCN^a, forðan H, forðam G, forðā K, forþæn þe E^2, forðan ðe F, forþan þe I
exaudiuit	|	geherde A, gehirde BJ, gehyrde CDFGHIK, g[ ] *N^a*, drihten E^2
dominus	|	dryhten B, drihten IKN^a, dryht̄ A, drih̄t CFH, driht̄ J, drih̄ G, geherde E^2*
uocem		stefne ABCDGIK, steefne N^a*, stæfne E^2HJ, stemne F

fletus	wopes ABDF*G*HIJN^{a}, wopys C, weopes E$^{2/x}$*, wopa K
mei	mines *A*BDE$^{2/x}$*FGHIJ, minys C, minre K, m[ ] *N^{a}**

ED: From (E)] from *Harsley.* a me (N^{a})] ame *Pilch.* fram me (N^{a})] fromme *Pilch.* unrihtwisnesse (N^{a})] unriht wisnesse *Pilch.* forðon (A)] for ðon *Kuhn.* forþon (N^{a})] for þon *Pilch.* flętus (G)] fletus *Rosier.*

OE: geherde (E^{2})] erde *on eras.* steefne (N^{a})] *2nd* e *seems inserted in smaller hand.* weopes (E$^{2/x}$)] *eras. before word,* es *added by corr.* mines (E$^{2/x}$)] es *added by corr.* m[ ] (N^{a})] *right leg of* m *lost.*

LTg: qui] q[ ] N^{a}. operamini] F: *orig.* operantur: *deleting dots below* ntur, mini *added later interl.: cf. Weber MS group* σ; *lost* N^{a}. exaudiuit] ę[ ] N^{a}. fletus] flętus G. mei] A: *added in later hand: see LTg note to v. 10* Exaudiuit; m[ ] N^{a}: *right leg of* m *lost.*

10

Exaudiuit	geherde *A*, gehirde B*J, gehyrde *CDE^{2}**FHIKN^{a}, hyrde *G* (*L*)
dominus	dryhten B, drihten C*E^{2}IKN^{a}, dryht̄ A, drih̄t FGJ, drih̄ H
deprecationem I	boene AB, bene *CD*E^{2}FGHJ, ben[ ] *N^{a}*, gebed K, mine I
meam I	mine ABCDE^{2}FGJ, minre H, min K, bene I (*N^{a}*)
dominus	dryhten B, drihtyn C, drihten FN^{a}, dryht̄ A, drih̄t J, [ ]ih̄t *G*, ⁊ drihten E^{2}
orationem	gebed ABCDFGIJN^{a}, gebedd H, bene E^{2}K
meam	min ABCFGIJN^{a}, mine E^{2}K
adsumpsit*	genom AB, genam *C*, onfeng *D*G, onfengc J, anfeng K, o[ ] N^{a}, he underfeng F, underfeng *E^{x}**I

ED: dep̄cationem (D)] deprecationem *Roeder.* ben[ ] (N^{a})] bene *Pilch.* [ ]ih̄t (G)] [ ]rih̄ *Rosier.*

OE: gehirde (B)] dryhten *eras. after word (separate from following* dryhten) *in order to align gloss and lemma.* gehyrde (E^{2})] *on eras.* drihten (C)] r *faint but visible.* underfeng (E^{x})] erfeng *on eras.*

LTg: Exaudiuit] exaudiuit CDEL, A: *eras.* (*3 letters?*) *before word,* m *faintly visible in initial position, perhaps orig.* mei: *see LTg note to v. 9* mei; [ ]xaudiuit G. deprecationem] C: r *interl. by corr.;* dep̄cationem D; depr(e)[ ] N^{a}. meam (*1st*)] *lost* N^{a}. dominus (*2nd*)] [ ]minus G. adsumpsit] assumpsit DE, C: *eras. after* a, *1st* s *added by corr.*

LTu. Exaudiuit] exaudiuit νςτ*, β: ui *interl.* deprecationem] depraecationem δ. adsumpsit] assumpsit τ*, ν: *orig.* adsumpsit, *1st* s *interl.*

GAg. adsumpsit] suscepit FHIJK; suscępit G; su[ ] N^{a}.

GAu. adsumpsit] suscepit δεζϑιλμξοπϱστυχψ.

11

Erubescant	scomien A, scamigen B, scamigyn C, scamian F, sceamian K, scamiaþ J, [ ]miað *G**, gescæmie E^{2}, ablysigen ł scamien DH, ablysian hi ł scamian I, ablysigen ł scamiað N^{a}
et	⁊ ABCDE^{2}FGHIJKN^{a}
conturbentur	sien gedroefde A, sin gedrefde B, syn gedrefyde C, sien gedrefede E^{2}G*, sind gedrefede J, syn gedrefede K, syn drefed DH, syn gedrefed *N*^{a}, aðracian F, syn hi geunrotsode ł gedrefede I (*L*)
(uehementer)*	þearle N^{a}, ð[ ]rle F*, swiðe G, swiþe J, swyþe K, swiðlic ł swiðe I
omnes	alle A, ealle BCDFGHIJKN^{a}, eælle E^{2}
inimici	| feond AB*, fynd CDFGHIJK, find *N*^{a}, mine E^{2}
mei	| mine ABCDFGHIJK, fiend E^{2} (*N*^{a})
auertantur*	sien forcerred A, sien forcirrede B, syn forcyrred C, sýn gecerred D, syn gecyrred FHN^{a}, sin gecyrred K, syon gecerred E^{2}, sien gecyrrede G, syn gecyrrede I, sýn gecirrede J (*L*)
retrorsum*	on bec A, on bæc BC, on hinder DE^{2}
et	⁊ ABCDE^{2}FGHIJKN^{a}
erubescant	scomien A, scamigen B, scomigyn C, scamiaþ J, scamie E^{2}, sceamian heom F, scomiað hiora *G*, aswarnien D, aswarnigen H, aswarnian K, aswarnian hi ł gesceamige heom I, aswarnien ł *N*^{a}
ualde	swiðe ABCE^{2}GJN^{a}, swiþe DH, swyðe F, swyþe K, þearle I
uelociter	hreðlice A, hrædlice BCFGKN^{a}, hredlice E^{2}, rædlice J, hrędlice ł anunga D, hrædlice ł onunga H, hredlice ł swiftlice I

ED: conturbentur uehementer (H)] conturbentur *Campbell.* syn gedrefed (N^{a})] synge drefed *Pilch.* ð[ ]rle (F)] ðearle *Kimmens.* omnes (G)] *omnes Rosier.* ealle (G)] [ ]lle *Rosier.* inimici (G)] *ini*mici *Rosier.* syn gecyrred (N^{a})] synge cyrred *Pilch.* ęrubescant (G)] erubescant *Rosier.* aswarnien ł (N^{a})] aswar[c]nien *vel Pilch.*

OE: [ ]miað (G)] co (?) *visible before* m. sien gedrefede (G)] n *interl.* ð[ ]rle (F)] *medial letters obscured and illegible.* feond (B)] *letter eras.* (*incomplete* f ?) *before word.*

LTg: Erubescant] [ ]ubescant G. conturbentur] L: uehementer *added above word by corr.: see GAg;* conturbe[ ] N^{a}. inimici] inim[ ] N^{a}. mei] *lost* N^{a}. auertantur] L: *2nd* r *obscured by stain from fol. 5v* domum. erubescant] ęrubescant G; erube[ ] N^{a}.

GAg. conturbentur] conturbentur uehementer FHIJK, L: *see LTg;* conturbentur uehemen[ ] G; conturbe[ ] uehementer N^{a}. auertantur] conuertantur FGHIJKN^{a}. retrorsum] *om.* FGHIJKN^{a}.

GAu: conturbentur] conturbentur uehementer δεζιλμξοπρστυχψ; conturbentur uechimenter ϑ. auertantur] conuertantur δεζιλμξοπρστυχψ; conuertentur ϑ. retrorsum] *om.* δεζϑιλμξοπρστυχψ.

PSALM 7

2

Domine	I	eala drihten I*, drihten N^a, dryht̄ *A,* driht̄ *C,* drih̄t FJ, drih̄ *G,* Min E^2 (*DK*)
deus	I	god ABCFGJKN^a, drihten E^2, min I
meus	I	min ABCFGJKN^a, god E^2I
in		in AB, on CDE^2FGHIJK (*N^a*)
te		ðe ABDG, þe CE^2FHIJK (*N^a*)
speraui		ic gehyhte AB, ic gehihte CGH, ic gehyhte D, ic hihte JK, ic gehihte ł ic hopode I, ic hopie F, ic gehopede $E^{2/x}$* (*N^a*)
libera*		gefrea A, gefreo B, alys D, [ ]lys C*, gehæl F, gehel I, halne GJN^a, hal K, gefriolsa ł alys $E^{2/x}$* (*L*)
me		me ABCDE^2FGIJKN^a
(fac)*		do GJKN^a
ab*		from ABCG, fram ł of J, of FIKN^a, ⁊ genere me from E^2
omnibus		allum AD, eallum BCFI, eallum GJ, eællum E^2, eallan K (*N^a*)
persequentibus		ochtendum A, ehtendum BE^2FHJN^a, ehtendum D, iehtyndum C, æhtendum I, ehtend G, ehtende K
me		me ABCE^2FGJK, minra *N^a*
et		⁊ ABCDE^2FGIJKN^a
eripe*		genere ABCE^2GN^a, genere D, alis F, alys I, ales J
me		me *A*BCE^2FGJN^a (*L*)

ED: speraui (G)] sper*aui Rosier.* saluum (G)] *s*aluum *Rosier.* [ ]lys (C)] alys *Wildhagen.* gchel (I)] gehæl *Lindelöf.* me fac (N^a)] mefac *Pilch.* ex o[ ] (N^a)] exo[mnibus] *Pilch.* minra (N^a)] *me Pilch.* genere me (N^a)] genereme *Pilch.*

OE: eala drihten (I)] s. o *written before* eala. ic gehopede ($E^{2/x}$)] hopede *on eras. by corr.* [ ]lys (C)] *initial letter not visible.* gefriolsa ł alys ($E^{2/x}$)] ł alys *added by corr.*

LTg: Domine] DN̄E ADEK; DOMINE C; [ ]omine G. in] *lost* N^a. te] *lost* N^a. speraui] *lost* N^a. libera] L: Saluum me fac ex *added above* libera me *by corr.: see GAg.* omnibus] o[ ] N^a. me (*2nd*)] N^a: *right leg of* m *lost.* me (*3rd*)] L: *added by corr.;* m A: *written by corr. in right margin, with* e (?) *lost due to trimming of leaf* (*another* me *added in later hand in bottom margin of fol. 14r*).

LTu. Domine] DN̄E βιλμνρςτ*τυχψ. deus] DEUS λμνρςψ. meus] MEUS λμνρψ. in] IN λμρψ. te] TE λμρ. speraui] SPERAUI λρ.

GAg: libera me ab] saluum me fac ex FGHIJKN^{a}; *for* L *see LTg.* eripe] libera FGHIJKN^{a}.

GAu: libera me ab] saluum me fac ex δζϑιμορστυχψ, ε: me *interl.;* salvvum me fac ex λπ; psaluum me fac ex ξ. eripe] libera δεζϑιλμξοπρστυχψ.

3

Nequando — ðyles æfre A, þylæs æfre B, þelæs æfre C, þylæs hwonne D*G*, þyles hwonne E^{2}*, ðilæs hwonne H, þilæs hwonne JN^{a}, ðilæs ahwænne F, þæt he ne ahwanne I, þalæs K

rapiat — geslæcce A*, gereafige BJ, reafige C, gegripe ł reafie D, gegripe ł reafige H, gegripe *FK*N^{a}, gerefne G, gelęcce ł þe læs þe he gripe I*, gegripæð E^{2}

ut — swe swe A, swa swa BC*DFGHIJN^{a}, swa K, swæ E^{2}

leo — lea A, leo BCDFGHIJKN^{a}, se leo E^{2}

animam | sawle ABCFJK, saule DGH, mine E^{2}I (*N^{a}*)

meam | mine ABCDFGHJK, saule E^{2}, sawle I (*N^{a}*)

dum — ðonne AF, þonne BGHIJK, þonne CDN^{a}, þanne E^{2}*

non | nis ABDE^{2}*FHI, nys C, ne GJN^{a}, na K

est | is G*K*, biþ J, byð N^{a}

qui — se ðe ABG, se þe CE^{2}*FIJN^{a}, þa K

redimat — alese A, aliese B, alyse CDHKN^{a}, alise E^{2}J, alyseþ F, ne aliese G, generie I

neque — ne ABE^{2}*GIJ, ny C, ⁊ na DHK, ne ne F (*N^{a}*)

qui — se ðe AF, se þe BCI, se se G, þe DE^{2}*H, þe þe J, þa K, þæ N^{a}

saluum — hie hale *AB,* hie halne G, hi hale CJ, halne DH*N^{a},* hælne E^{2}*, gehalne F, gehæle I, hal K

faciat — gedoe A, gedó B, gedo *C*E^{2}*F, gedeð G, gedeþ J, dó D, do HKN^{a}

ED: Nequando (CDEFJKN^{a})] Ne quando *Wildhagen, Roeder, Harsley, Kimmens, Oess, Sisam, Pilch.* ðyles æfre (A)] ðy les æfre *Kuhn.* þylæs æfre (B)] þy læs æfre *Brenner.* þelæs æfre (C)] þe læs æfre *Wildhagen* (*as* þelæs æfre *in corrigenda*). swa swa (BGIJ)] swaswa *Brenner, Rosier, Lindelöf, Oess.* byð (N^{a})] bjð *Pilch.* se þe (N^{a})] seþe *Pilch.* qui sal(u)[ ] (N^{a})] quisalu[m] *Pilch.* þæ (N^{a})] þœ *Pilch.*

OE: þyles hwonne (E^{2})] hwonne *on eras. by corr.* (?). geslæcce (A)] cce *written in diff., probably contemporaneous, hand: see Merritt p. 752 and Kuhn p. 161, where* gelæcce *is suggested as correct form,* s *overlooked by corr.* gelęcce ł þe læs þe he gripe (I)] ł þe læs þe he gripe *written in blank space to right of line above and signalled to follow* gelęcce. swa swa (C)] *2nd* a *obscured by show-through from fol. 11v.* þanne (E^{2})] *on eras.* (*by corr.?*). nis (E^{2})] *eras. before word.* se þe (E^{2})] þe *on* *eras.* (*by corr.?*). ne (E^2)] *on eras.* (*by corr.?*). þe (E^2)] *on eras.* (*by corr.?*). hælne (E^2)] ne *on eras.* (*by corr.?*). gedo (E^2)] *small eras. after word.*

LTg: Nequando] Nęquando G. rapiat] [ ]apiat F: *initial letter eras.;* rapiad K. animam] a[ ] N^a: *back of* a *lost.* meam] *lost* N^a. est] ést K. neque] n[ ] N^a: *right leg of* n *lost.* saluum] saluam B, A: *orig.* saluum: *2nd* u *deleted by dot,* a *interl.;* sal(u)[ ] N^a: *right minim of* u *lost due to tear in leaf.* faciat (C)] *2nd* a *on eras. by corr.*

LTu: Nequando] nequando ϑ. redimat] redimet ϑ.

4

Domine	I	drihten F, dryht̄ AB, driht̄ C, drih̄t J, drih̄ G, hlaford K, Min E^2 (*IN^a*)
deus	I	god ABCFGJK, drihten E^2, min I (*N^a*)
meus	I	min ABCFGJKN^a, god E^{2}I
si		gif ABDE^{2}GIJKN^a, gef C, gyf FH
feci	I	ic dyde ABCDHIKN^a, ic dide F, ic þas *G*J, ic þis E^2*
istud	I	ðis AD, þis BC*HIK, þys F, ðys *N^a*, dyde E^{2}GJ
si		gif ABDGHIJKN^a, gef C, gyf F, ⁊ gif E^2
est		is ABDE^{2}FGHIJ*K*N^a, ys C
iniquitas		unrehtwisnis A, unryhtwisnes BD, unrihtwisnys CF, unrihtwisnes HIJK, unrihtw[ ]nes G*, unryhtwisnesse E^2, [ ]s *N^a*
in		in AB, on CDE^{2}FGHIJ*K*N^a
manibus		hondum A, hondum G, handum BCD, handum FHIJN^a, handen E^2, handan K
meis		minum AFIJN^a, minum BCDH, mine E^2, min G, minan K

ED: Domine (G)] *D*omine *Rosier.* si est (N^a)] siest *Pilch.* gif is (N^a)] gifis *Pilch.* unrihtw[ ]nes (G)] unrihtw[ ] *Rosier.* [ ]s (N^a)] [unrihtwisnes] *Pilch.* on handum (N^a)] onhandum *Pilch.*

OE: ic þis (E^2)] *eras. after* þis. þis (C)] *bowl of* þ *faint but visible.* unrihtw[ ]nes (G)] w *cropped at top.*

LTg: Domine] I: s. o *written above word; lost* N^a. deus] [ ]us N^a. feci] fęci G. istud] is[ ]ud N^a: *medial letter obscured by taped crease.* est] ést K. iniquitas] *lost* N^a. in] K: *scribe orig. wrote* im, *then eras. ligature connecting 3rd leg of* m, *using it as 1st leg of* m *in following* manibus.

5

Si	gif ABD*G*IJK, Gif E^2, gef C, gyf FH (*N^a*)
reddidi	ic agald A, ic ageald B*C*DE^{2}FGHJ, ic agvlde K, ic forgeald I (*N^a*)

retribuentibus	ðaem geldendum A, þæm geldendum B, þam gyldendum C, gyldendum DK, gyldendum F, gildendum H, geldendum E^2, [ ]yldendum *N^a*, þam æftergyldendum *G*, þam æftergildendum J, forgyldendum I
mihi	me AB*CDE*^{2}FGHI*J*K*N^a*
mala	yfel ABK, yfyl C, yfelu DFGHIN^a, yfela E^2, yfele J
decidam	ic gefallu A, ic gefalle B, ic gefealle CGJ, fealla ic I, ic ahreose DE^2, ic areose F*H* (*KN^a*)
merito	bi gewyrhtum A, be gewyrhtum BF, by gewyrhtum C, be gewyrhtum DE^2*, be gewyrhtum GH, be gewyrhtan K, [ ]e gewyrhtum N^a, be geearnunge I, be gearnunga J*
ab	from A, from BC, fram DGJK, fram E^2FHIN^a
inimicis	feondum ABFHIJN^a, feondum CD, fiondum E^2, feondon K, freondum G
meis	minum ABE^2FIJN^a, minum CDGH, minan K
inanis	idelhende AB, idylhende C, idel D*H*, on idel E^2FK, in idlum G, on idlum I, on idelnesse J (*N^a*)

ED: michi (N^a)] mihi *Pilch.* décidam (H)] decidam *Campbell.* ab inimicis (N^a)] abinimicis *Pilch.* inánis (H)] inanis *Campbell.*

OE: be gewyrhtum (E^2)] r *altered from* w. be gearnunga (J)] *orig.* bea-: *1st* g *written over* a.

LTg: Si] [ ]i G: *initial* S *lost, outline visible; lost* N^a. reddidi] réddidi C; *lost* N^a. retribuentibus] rętribuentibus G; [ ]ribuentibus N^a. mihi] michi EJN^a, C: *orig.* mihi: *small* c *added interl. by corr.* decidam] K: *written at end of line above but repeated in left margin by corr.* (decidam); décidam H; *lost* N^a. inanis] inánis H; *lost* N^a.

LTu: reddidi] ϑ: *final* di *interl.* mihi] michi ιλϛτ*τ, πϙ: *orig.* mihi: c *added interl.*

6

Persequatur	oehteð AB, ehte DHK, ehteð FG, ehteþ J, á iehtyð C, sy ehtende ł ehte I, fulfylgæt E^2* (*N^a*)
inimicus	se feond ABC, feond DFGHIJKN^a, fynd E^2
animam	| sawle ABCFJKN^a, saule DGH, minre *E^2*, mine I
meam	| mine ABCDFGHJKN^a, saule E^2, sawle I
et	⁊ ABCDE^2*FGHIJK (*N^a*)
conprehendat	gegripeð *A**B*G*, gegripyð *C*, gegripeþ F, gegripað *J*, gegripe *D*K, gegripæ *E^2**, gripe *H*, gehæftnige hi ł gegripe hi *I* (*N^a*)
eam*	hie ABCE^2*, hy D

et   ꝛ ABCDE^{2}FGHIJKN^a
conculcet   fortrideð AB, fortredyð C, fortredeþ D, fortredeð FH, fortredað GN^a, fortredaþ J, fortredeæþ E^2, he fortrede I, fortredde K
in | in A*B, on CDFGHIJKN^a, min E^2
terra | eorðan ABCD*F*GHIKN^a, eorþan J, lif E^2
uitam | lif ABCDFGHJK, min I, on E^2 (*N^a*)
meam | min ABCFGH*J*K, (m)in N^a*, lif I, eorðæn E^2
et   ꝛ ABCE^{2}FGHIJKN^a
gloriam | wuldur AC, wuldor BDFGHJKN^a, min E^2*I
meam | min ABCDFGHJK*N^a*, wuldor E^{2}I
in   in AB, on CDE^2*FGHIJK (*N^a*)
puluerem   dust A*B*CDFH, duste IK, dúste E^2*, myll G, mill ł on dust J (*N*)
deducat   gelaedeð A, gelædeð BGN^a, gelædyð C, gelædeþ FJ, gelede he D, gelede he E^2*, gelæde he H, gelæde I, lædeð K

ED: fulfylgæt (E)] Fulfylgæt *Harsley.* et (B) (*1st*)] Et *Brenner.* comprehendat (C)] co[n]prehendat *Wildhagen.* conp̄hendat (D)] conprehendat *Roeder.* et (B) (*2nd*)] Et *Brenner.* in terra (N^a)] interra *Pilch.* on eorðan (N^a)] oneorðan *Pilch.* et (B) (*3rd*)] Et *Brenner.* min (N^a)] *no gloss Pilch.*

OE: fulfylgæt (E^2)] *on eras.* ꝛ (E^2)] *eras. after word.* gegripeð (A)] *2nd* g *slightly above line.* gegripæ (E^2)] *eras. before and after word; Harsley reads* hie *before and* þ (?) *after.* hie (E^2)] ꝛ *eras. before word.* in (A) (*1st*)] i *malformed.* (m)in (N^a)] *right minim of* m *visible.* min (E^2)] *eras. before word.* on (E^2)] *on eras.* (*by corr.?*). dúste (E^2)] *eras.* (*25 mm*) *after word.* gelede he (E^2)] *on eras.* (*by corr.?*).

LTg. Persequatur] [ ]ur N^a. animam] E: *eras. above* ani(/mam). et (*1st*)] *lost* N^a. conprehendat] conpraehendat A; conp̄hendat D; comprehendat GI, C: *orig.* conprehendat: *right leg added to 1st* n *by corr. to form* m, H: *orig.* conprehendat: *middle leg added to 1st* n *to form* m; cōprehendat E; comp̄hendat J; [ ](r)ehendat N^a: r *fragmentary.* terra] terram F: *cf. Weber MSS* Kσ*. uitam] *lost* N^a. meam (*2nd*)] mea J. meam (*3rd*)] N^a: *1st 2 legs of initial* m *lost.* in (*2nd*)] *lost* N^a. puluerem] [ ]rem N^a.

LTu: conprehendat] conpraehendat β; comprehendat δζιτ*τ, ϱ: *orig.* conprehendat: *1st* n *deleted by subscript dot,* m *interl.;* conprehandat ν; cōp̄hendat εϑοσυχ; cōprehendat λ: *eras. after* ō; conp̄hendat μ; comprẹhendat ξ. terra] terram ψ.

GAg: eam] *om.* FGHIJKN^a.

GAu: eam] *om.* δεζϑιλμξοπϱστυχψ.

7

Exsurge		aris *ABCDFHIJK*, Aris *E^2*, aris þu *G* (*LN^a*)
domine		dryhten B, drihtyn C, drihten E^{2}N^a, dryht̄ A, driħt GJ, drħt F, hlaford K (*I*)
in		in AB, on CDE^{2}FGHIJKN^a
ira	|	eorre ABDHN^a, yrre CK, erra E^2, irre J, graman F, þynum G, þinum I
tua	|	ðinum A, ðinum B, þinum CDHJ, þinum E^{2}FN^a, þinre K, yrre G, graman I
et*		⁊ ABCE^{2}GJN^a (*I*)
exaltare		hefe up A*B, uppahefe C, upahefe DFHKN^a, upaheue E^2, upahefe ðu G, upahefe þu J, si ðu upahafen I
in		in ABDG, on CE^{2}FHIJK (*N^a*)
finibus		endum ABFH, endum CD, ende E^{2}K, gemærum I, gemæru J, gem[ ]u G (*N^a*)
inimicorum	|	feonda ABCDFG*H*JKN^a, fyonde E^2, minra I
tuorum*	|	ðinra A, þinra BCD, þinre E^2, minra FGK, minre J, myra N^a, sceaþana ł feonda I (*L*)
(Et)*		⁊ FGI
Exsurge		aris *ACFGJK**, áríś B, Aris *E^2*, uparis *I* (*HL*)
domine		dryhten B, drihten E^2*N^a, dryht̄ A, driht̄ C, driħt FGJ (*I*)
deus		god ABCE^{2}FGJKN^a
meus		min ABCE^2*FG*JKN^a
in		in ABG, on CDE^{2}FHIJK (*N^a*)
praecepto		bebode A*BCDE^{2}FHJK*, bebod *G*, beboda *I* (*LN^a*)
quod		ðæt A, þæt BC, þæt GJ, þæt þe I, þet E^2, þe DFH, ðe N^a, þa K
mandasti		ðu bibude A, þu bebude BCE^{2}FGHIJKN^a, ðu bebude D

ED: Exurge (C) (*1st*)] Ex[s]urge *Wildhagen.* drħt (F)] drihten *Kimmens.* on eorre (N^a)] oneorre *Pilch.* et (B) (*1st*)] Et *Brenner.* et (I)] *Lindelöf reads the gloss* ⁊: *see LTg.* [ ](u)s (N^a)] [finib]us *Pilch.* Exurge (C) (*2nd*)] Ex[s]urge *Wildhagen.* Exsurge (N^a) *no gloss*] aris *Pilch.* p̄cepto (D)] praecepto *Roeder.* ðe þu bebude (N^a)] ðeþu bebude *Pilch.*

OE: hefe up (A)] *eras. before* up. aris (K)] ⁊ *eras. before word.* drihten (E^2) (*2nd*)] *small eras. after word and above* urge *in* Exurge. min (E^2)] *on eras.* min (G)] n *on eras.*

LTg: Exsurge (*1st*)] Exurge AEGHJL, C: *letter eras. after* x, K: *eras.* (*2 letters?*) *after* x; *Sisam reads late* te *eras. in margin; lost* N^a. domine (*1st*)] I: s. o *written above word.* et] I: & *added later* (*by glossator?*) *above* e *of following* exaltare; *a mark similar to those used to indicate word order in MS is written above added* & (*or below* et *directly above in preceding line: v. 6* et gloriam), *but this is not, as Lindelöf takes it,* *a tironian* et. in (*2nd*)] *lost* N^{a}. finibus] [ ]us N^{a}: *left minim of* u *lost*. inimicorum] H: rum *partly obscured by hole in leaf.* tuorum] L: meorum *added above word by corr.: see GAg.* Exsurge (*2nd*)] Exurge AEJL, C: *letter eras. after* x, H: *eras. after* E; exsurge FI, K: Et *eras. before word;* exurge G; [ ]ge N^{a}. domine (*2nd*)] I: s. o *written above word.* in (*3rd*)] *lost* N^{a}. praecepto] præcepto B; precepto CEFHIJKL; precępto G; p̄ccpto D; [ ]pto N^{a}.

LTu: Exsurge (*1st*)] Exurge διλνξπϱστ*τχψ, ε: *orig*. Exsurge: s *eras*. et] *interl*. δξ. Exsurge (*2nd*)] Exurge ντ*; exurge διλνξπϱσυψ; exsurge εζϑο. praecepto] precepto ζιπϛτ*τ; pręcepto λνξϱ; præcepto μ; p̄cepto εϑοσχ.

GAg: et] *om*. FHKN^{a}. tuorum] meorum FGHIJKN^{a}, L: *see LTg*. Exsurge (*2nd*)] Et exsurge FI; [ ]t exurge G: *initial* E *lost; for* K *see LTg*.

GAu: et] *om*. μοχψ; *for* δξ *see LTu*. tuorum] meorum δεζϑιλμξοπϱστυχψ. Exsurge (*2nd*)] Et exurge διλξπϱστυψ, ε: *orig*. Exsurge: s *eras*.; Et exsurge ζμο.

8

Et	⁊ *ABCE²FGHIJK* (*DN^{a}*)
synagoga	gesomnunge A*H*, g̲esomnunge *C*, gesomnunga F, gesomnung BD, gesamnunga I, sio gesomnung *G*, seo gesomnung J, somnung *K*, [ ]nung N^{a}, g̲esomnung̲e ł motstowe E^{2}* (*L*)
populorum	folca ABCDFG*HIJKN^{a}, þinra folcæ E^{2}
circumdabit	ymbscleð AB, ymbsylyð *C*, ymbselleð D*E^{2}**, ymbsylleð *H*, ymbesealde K, utan ymbseteð G, uton ymbsetteþ J, ymbtrymdon F, ymbtrymð ł ymbhwyrfeþ I, ymb[ ] *N^{a}*
te	ðe AF, þe CDE^{2}GHIJK*N^{a}* (*B*)
et	⁊ *ABCE²FGHIJK* (*DLN^{a}*)
propter	fore ABDH, for CE^{2}*FGIJK (*N^{a}*)
hanc	ðissum A, þissum B, þyssum̲ C, ðyssum G, ðisum F, þisum J, [ ]um ł þas N^{a}, þas DE^{2}*H*K, þissere intingan I
in	in AB, on CDE^{2}FGHIJKN^{a}
altum	heanisse A, heanesse BG, heanysse C, heannesse D*N^{a}*, heahnesse H*IK, heachnesse E^{2}, heannyssum F, heannessum̲ J
regredere	gaa eft A, gá eft B, gáá C, gehwyrf DIK, gehwyrfþ H, gehwyrf ðu N^{a}, gehwyrfdum F, gang ðu G, gang þu J, agen gechere E^{2}

ED: et (B)] Et *Brenner.* ymb[ ] þe (N^{a})] ymb [setteð þe] *Pilch.* [ ]e (N^{a})] *om. Pilch.* altu(m) (N^{a})] altum *Pilch.* on heannesse (N^{a})] on heannese *Pilch.* regredere (N^{a})] ingredere *Pilch.*

OE: gesomnunge ł motstowe (E^2)] *all except initial* g *on eras.* folca (G)] o *on eras.* (?). ymbselleð (E^2)] *on eras., with eras. above* (circun/)dabit *in next line.* for (E^2)] *eras. after word.* heahnesse (H)] *orig.* heohnesse: a *written above* o, *but without subscript deleting dot.*

LTg: Et] et ABCDEFGHIJKL; *lost* N^a. synagoga] sinagoga CGHJKL; [ ]oga N^a. circumdabit] circundabit E, H: n *interl., macron* (?) *above* u *eras.;* circúndabit C: *eras. to left of* n, *perhaps of leg;* circum[ ] N^a. te] té B; [ ]e N^a. et] Et ABCDEFGHIJKL; *lost* N^a. propter] [ ]ter N^a. hanc] H: n *interl.* altum] altu(m) N^a: *middle leg of* m *lost due to tear in leaf.*

LTu: Et] et βδεζϑιλμνξοπϱσςτ*τυχψ. synagoga] β: *orig.* sinagoga: y *interl.;* sinagoga ζϑντ*τψ. circumdabit] circundabit ϑιλτ*, ε: n *altered from* m; circūdabit ζστ. et] Et βδεζϑιλμνξοπϱσςτ*τυχψ. regredere] β: *orig.* regredire (*with* i *on eras.?*): e *interl.;* regredire ϑ.

9

Domine*		dryhten *B*, drihten *C*GIK, drichten *E*^{2}, dryht̄ *A*, drih́t FJ, drih́ H (*DL*)
iudica*		doem AB, dem CDE^2*K, dem H, demð I, dem ðu FGN^a, dem þu J
populos		folc ABDGK, folcc H; folce CFJ*N*^{a}, folcæ E^2, folctruman I
iudica		doem AB, dem CDE^2**FHIJK*, dem ðu *G*
me		mec A, me BCDE^{2}FGHJK
domine		dryhten B, drihtyn C, drihten E^2, dryht̄ A, drih́t GJ, drh́t F (*I*)
Secundum		efter A, æfter BD*FGHI*, æfter *J*, æftyr C, Efter E^2, neah *K*
iustitiam	I	rehtwisnisse A, ryhtwisnesse BD, rihtwisnysse *C*F, rihtwisnesse HJK, rihtwisnes[ ] G*, minre E^{2}I
meam	I	minre ABCFGJK, rihtwisnesse I, soðfestnesse E^2
et		⁊ ABCE^{2}FGIJK
secundum		efter A, æfter BFGI, æfter JK*, æftyr C, efter E^2
innocentiam	I	unsceðfulnisse A, unsceðfulnesse B, unsceðfulnysse C, unsceaðfulnesse G, unscæþfulnesse J, unscyldignisse D*, unscyldignysse F, unscyldignesse H, unscyldinesse K, minræ unscyldinesse E^2*, minre I
manuum*		honda A, handa BC*D*, handum E^2
mearum*	I	minra ABCD, minre FGJK, minum E^2, unscildignesse ł unscæðdinesse I
super		ofer ABE^{2}FGJK, ofyr C, ofor I
me		me ABCE^{2}FGJK

ED: [ ](u)s (N^{a})] [domi]nus *Pilch.* Iudica (G)] *I*udica *Rosier.* meam (G) (*2nd*)] mea*m* *Rosier.* unscildignesse ł unscæðdinesse (I)] unscildignesse ł unscæððinesse *Lindelöf.*

OE: dem (E^{2}) (*1st*)] *eras. after word.* dem (E^{2}) (*2nd*)] *eras. before and after word.* rihtwisnes[ ] (G)] *top of ascender of* s (?) *visible after 2nd* s. æfter (K)] *scribe began* e, *then altered letter to* æ. unscyldignisse (D)] *orig.* unscyldignesse: *1st* e *deleted by subscript mark,* i *interl.* minræ unscyldinesse (E^{2})] scyl *on eras.*

LTg: Domine] domine ABCDEL. iudica (*2nd*)] Iudica FGHIJK. populos] popul[ ] N^{a}. domine] I: s. o *written above word.* Secundum] secundum FGHIJK. iustitiam] iustiam C. manuum] manuum D: *2nd* u *indicated by superscript mark in shape of small* c *tilted to left.*

LTu: Domine] domine βνςτ*. iudica (*2nd*)] Iudica δεζϑιλμξοπρστυχψ. Secundum] secundum δεζϑιλμνξοπρστυχψ. iustitiam] iusticiam τ*τ, ϱ: *orig.* iustitiam: *2nd* t *deleted by subscript dot,* c *interl.* manuum] β: *orig.* manum: *2nd* u *interl.*

GAg: Domine] dominus FGHIJK; [ ](u)s N^{a}: *left minim of* u *lost.* iudica (*1st*)] iudicat FGHIJKN^{a}. manuum] *om.* FGHIJK. mearum] meam FGHIJK.

GAu: Domine] dominus δεζϑιλμξοπρστυχψ. iudica (*1st*)] iudicat δεζϑιλμξοπρστυχψ. manuum] *om.* δεζϑιλμξοπρστυχψ. mearum] meam δεζϑιλμξοπρστυχψ.

10

Consummetur	sie fornumen *A*BG,* sy fornumen C*F,* si fornumen J, si fornumen ł si geendod *I,* sie geendud D, si geændad H, si geendod *K,* bio geendod E^{2}*
nequitia	nið AB*C*DGH, nyð J, niþ K, man ł nið F, man ł niðscipe I, þæ heteniþæs E^{2}
peccatorum	ðeara synfulra A, þara synfulra B, synfulra CDFGHIJK, þæræ fyranfulræ E^{2}
et	⁊ ABCE^{2}FGHIJK
dirige*	gerece ABCD*H*K**, gereche E^{2}, gereceþ G*, gerece þu F, gerece þu ł rihtlæce J, gewissa I
iustum	ðone rehtwisan A, ðone ryhtwisan B, þane rihtwisen E^{2}, þane rihtwisan I, rihtwisne CDFJ, rihtwisne G, rihtwise *K,* riht *H* (*I*)
(et)*	⁊ F
scrutans	smegende A, smeagende BFIJ, smeagynde C*, smægende E^{2}, smeagend G, scrudniende DH, scrudnigende K
corda	heortan ABCDE^{2}FGHIJK
et	⁊ ABCDE^{2}FGHIJK
renes	eðre A, ædre B, æddran CH, edran D, ædran K, syna ł ædran

	lændenu I*, lændenu F, lendena G, lændena J, lendan ł lundlagan E[2]*
deus	god ABCE[2]FIJK, go(d) G*

ED: gereceþ (G)] ger[ ]ceþ *Rosier.* syna ł ædran lændenu (I)] syna ł ædran ł lændenu *Lindelöf* (*see p. 8, n. 1*). go(d) (G)] god *Rosier.*

OE: sie fornumen (A)] i *added below line.* bio geendod (E[2])] *letter eras. after 1st* o *and 2nd* d. gerece (H)] *eras. after 1st* e, *small eras. after 2nd* e. gerece (K)] di *eras. before word.* gereceþ (G)] *see note to Ps 8.3.* smeagynde (C)] s. est : ys *written in left margin before word.* syna ł ædran lændenu] syna ł ædran *written in right margin after* et; lændenu *written on next line.* lendan ł lundlagan (E[2])] lendan *on eras.* go(d) (G)] *ascender of* d *cropped.*

LTg: Consummetur] A: *orig.* Consumetur: *1st* m *added interl. in another hand,* K: *1st* m *on eras. by corr.;* Consumetur BFI; [ ]onsumetur G: *initial* C *lost, outline visible: cf. Weber MSS* PQRUXδσ med. nequitia] C: *eras.* (*of* s?) *after* a. dirige] HK: *eras. after word: see GAg.* iustum] HK: *eras after word,* I: *while flanking signs* ÷ *and* : *appear after this word, it is difficult* (*given that this is hair side of leaf*) *to confirm eras. of orig.* et, *although this is most likely the case.*

LTu: Consummetur] δ: sumetur *interl.* (> Consumetur) *as alternate reading;* Consumetur εζλοπστ*υ, λξ: *eras. after* u. dirige] direge β.

GAg: dirige] diriges FGJ; *for* HK *see LTg.* iustum] iustum et F.

GAu: dirige] diriges δεϑιλξοπϱστυψ. iustum] iustum et δμοψ.

11

Iustum	rehtwisne A, ryhtwisne B, rihtwisne FGJ, rihtwis CE[2]*I, ryht D, riht HK
adiutorium	fultum ABCE[2]FGIJ, fultum DH*K*
meum	minne ABFJ, min CDE[2]GIK (*H*)
a	from ABCG, fram FJ, fram *E*[2]IK
domino*	drihtne FG*I*, drihtny C, dryht̄ AB, driht̄ E[2], driht J (*K*)
qui	se ABCDE[2]H, se þe FGIJ, þa K
saluos	hale ABCDE[2]HK, gehæle F, halige G, gehælð I, halne J
facit	gedoeð AB, gedeð CF, gedeþ J, deþ DE[2]H, deð G, dæþ K
rectos	| ða rehtan AB, þa rihtan C, ryhtwise D, rihtwise E[2]HJ, rihte FK, þa rihtwisan G, þa rihtgeþancodon I
corde	| on heortan AB, heortan CFGJK, heorten E[2], on heorte DH

ED: á (E)] a *Harsley.*

OE: rihtwis (E^{2})] *eras. after word.*

LTg: adiutorium] ádiutorium K. meum] H: *eras. above word, perhaps of gloss.* a] á E. domino] I: *right leg of* n *eras.*, K: n̄ *on eras. by corr.* (domino).

LTu: domino] δχ: *orig.* deo: n *added interl. to form* domino.

GAu: domino] deo ζιλμπτ, σ: *orig.* domino.

12

Deus	god ABCE^{2}FGJK (I*)
iudex	doema AB, dema CFGHIJK, deme DE^{2}
iustus	rehtwis A, ryhtwis BD, rihtwis CE^{2}FGHIJ*K**
(et)*	⁊ *F*GI
fortis	strong ABCG, strang DE^{2}*F*HIJK
et	⁊ ABCE^{2}FGHIJK
longanimis*	longmod A*C*, langmod BDG, langmodi E^{2}, geþyldig FIJ, geþyldi K
numquid	ah AB, ah ł hu ne *C*, cwist hu D, cwist þu *E^{2}**, cwyst þu *H*, cwyðst þu K, cwystu ł a F*, cweðsþu la I, cwyst þu la J, ac ne G
irascitur	eorsað ABD, eorseð *E^{2}H*, yrsað *CF*, yrsaþ *K*, yrsað he *GI*, irsaþ he *J* (*L*)
per	ðorh A, þurh BCDE^{2}GHJK, geond F, iand I
singulos	syndrie A, syndrige BCDGK, sindrige HJ, sendrie E^{2}, ænlipie FI
dies	dægas A, dagas BCDFGHIJK, daǵes E^{2}

ED: nunquid (C)] nu[m]quid *Wildhagen.* ah ł hu ne (C)] ah ł hune *Wildhagen* (*as* ah ł hu ne *in corrigenda*). cwist hu (D)] cwisthu *Roeder.* cwist þu (E)] cwistþu *Harsley.* cwystu ł a (F)] cwys tu la *Kimmens.* daǵes (E)] dages *Harsley.*

OE: Deus (I)] est : is *written in bowl of* D. rihtwis (K)] t *interl.* cwystu ł a (F)] *perhaps* cwystu ła, *with mistaken cross-stroke through* l. cwist þu (E^{2})] *all but* c *on eras.*

LTg: iustus] K: *eras. after word.* et fortis] F: et for *added later on eras.* longanimis] C: a *malformed.* numquid] nunquid E, C: *orig.* numquid: *left leg of* m *eras. to form* n, H: *2nd* n *interl., macron* (?) *eras. above* u. irascitur] H: *2nd* i *on eras.*, I: *2nd* i *formed from another letter;* irascetur CEFJL, K: *orig.* irascitur: *2nd* i *altered to* e; [ ]rascetur G: *cf. Weber MSS* HKT*βγδ.

LTu: numquid] numquit β; nunquid εζιλ. irascitur] irascitur χ: *orig.* irascetur: e *deleted by subscript dot and partly eras.*, i *interl.;* irascetur βϑμνοϱτ*ψ, δ: ł i *added interl.* (> irascitur).

GAg: iustus] iustus et G, F: et *added later on eras.* (*see LTg*), I: *partly eras.; for* K *see LTg.* longanimis] patiens FGIJK, H: *eras. above word, perhaps of gloss.*

GAu: iustus] iustus et δϑμοψ. longanimis] patiens δεζϑιλμξοπϱστυχψ.

13

Nisi		nemne *AB*, nymðe *CD*I, nimþe *H*, nynðe G, buton F, butan K, bute *E*^{2}, buta J (*L*)
conuertamini*	|	ge sien gecerde *AB*, ge̲ syn gecyrrede *C*, ge sien G, ge ge̲cyrren D, ge gecyrrede F, gecyrrede ge I, gecirrede J, gecyrande K, ge gecherren E^2
(fueritis)*	|	beoð F, beon K, sind J, gecyrde G, wesan ł butan ge gecyrran I
gladium	|	sweord ABDE^{2}FGHJ, swurd CK, his I
suum	|	his ABCDE^{2}FGHJK, swurd I
uibrauit*		cweceð *A*B, cwecyð brogdetteð ł bliccetteð *C*, ascęcþ *D*, ascæcð FH, ascæhð K, seceþ J, [ ]cæceþ G, ascæcð ł cwahte *E*^{2}*, he acwecð ł asceacð I (*L*)
arcum	|	bogan *ABCD*FGHJK, bogen *E*^{2}, his I (*L*)
suum	|	his ABCDEFGHJK, bogan I
tetendit		ðeneð A, þeneð B, aþenyð C, aþeneð G, aþeneþ J, he aþenede DE^{2}FH*I*, he þenan K
et		⁊ ABCE^{2}FGHIJK
parauit		gearwað AB, ge̲gearwað C, gegearwað G, gegearwaþ J, gyrede DH, gýrede E^2*, gegyrede F, he gearcode I, he gearcaþ K
illum		ðone A, þone BC, hine DE^{2}FGHIJK

ED: Nisi (G)] *N*isi *Rosier.* nymðe (C)] nymþe *Wildhagen.* nynðe (G)] [ ]:e *Rosier.* ge sien (G)] gesien *Rosier.* [ ]cæceþ (G)] *no gloss Rosier.*

OE: ascæcð ł cwahte (E^2)] æcð ł *on eras.* gýrede (E^2)] ý *on eras.*

LTg: Nisi] H: N *faded but visible;* nisi ABCDEL. conuertamini] A: ue *on eras.* (*before gloss was added*); conuertimini BC. uibrauit] uibrabit CDEL, A: *2nd* b *on eras.: cf. Weber MSS* S^{2}TPQβδ moz med, *see GAg.* arcum] Arcum ABCDEL. tetendit] tendit I: *eras. before word.*

LTu. Nisi] nisi βνςτ*. conuertamini] conuertimini ς. gladium] glaudium β. uibrauit] uibrabit ντ*: *cf. Weber MSS* S^{2}TPQβδ moz med, *see GAu.* arcum] Arcum βνςτ*. tetendit] detendit ϑ.

GAg: conuertamini] conuersi fueritis FHIJK; conuersi fuęritis G. uibrauit] uibrabit FHI, GK: *orig.* uibrauit: *2nd* u *altered to* b; *for* ACDEL *see LTg.*

GAu: conuertamini] conuersi fueritis δεζϑιλμξοπϱστυχψ. uibrauit] uibrabit εζιξοπϱτχψ, υ: b *altered from* u; *for* ντ* *see LTu.*

14

Et	⁊ *ABCE*^{2}FGIJK (*DL*)
in	in AB, on CDE^{2}FGIJK
ipso*	him ABCE^{2}FIK, him D, ðæm G, þam J
parauit	gearwað AB, gerwaþ K, gegearwað C, gegearwað G, gegearwaþ J, gearcode F, he gegyrede I, gérede E^2
uasa	featu A, fatu BCDE^{2}HI, fæt FG, fata JK
mortis	deaðes ABGH, deaðys C, deaþes DE^{2}FJK, þeades I
sagittas	strelas A, strælas BGIJ, flana CDE^{2}FHK
suas	his ABDE^{2}FGHIJK, hys C
ardentibus	beornedvm A*, birnendum B, byrnendum DH*J*, byrnendum E^{2}FG, bernynde C, byrnende K, byrnen I
effecit	gefremede ABDE^{2}FH, gefremyde *C,* gefremde K, he gefremode I, gefremeð *G,* gefremeþ J

ED: et (B)] Et *Brenner.* sagittas (B)] Sagittas *Brenner.*

OE: beornedvm (A)] *orig.* beornedem: v *written above 3rd* e, *but without deleting dot.*

LTg: Et] et ABCDEL; [ ]t G: *letter fragment visible in initial position.* ardentibus] ardentes J: *cf. Weber MSS* β moz. effecit] effécit C; effęcit G.

LTu: Et] et βνςτ*. parauit] *om.* ς. uasa] β: *orig.* uassa: *1st* s *crossed through;* uassa ϑ.

GAg: ipso] eo FGHIJK.

GAu: ipso] eo δεζϑιλμξοπϱστυχψ.

15

Ecce	sehðe AB, on gesihðe D, on gesyhþe H, efnenu CI, efne FGJK, eællengæ E^2
parturiit	cenneð A*B*, cennyð *C*, cænneþ *J*, he geeacnað *DFH*, he geæcnað *E*^{2}, he ge(e)acnaþ *K**, geeacnode *I*, gebyreð *G*
iniustitiam	unrehtwisnisse A, unryhtwisnesse BD, unryhtwisnesse E^2*, unrihtwisnesse HI*K*, unrihtwisnysse F, on unrihtwisnysse *C,* on unrihtwisnesse J, on rihtwisnesse G
(et)*	⁊ FJ
concepit	geecnað A, geeacnað B, geiecnað C, geeacnaþ J, ⁊ geeacnað *G*, he onfeng DE^{2}F*H*, ⁊ he feng K, gecende I (*L*)
dolorem	sar ACDE^{2}HJK, sár BFG, sarnessa I
et	⁊ ABCDE^{2}FGH*I*JK

peperit	cenneð AB, cennyð C, gecenð G, gecænþ J, he cende D*E*²FH, cende K, gehrifede ł acende I
iniquitatem	unrehtwisnisse A, unryhtwisnesse BD, unrihtwisnysse CF, unrihtwisnesse HIJK, unrihcwisnesse E², unriht G

ED: on gesyhþe (H)] ongesyhþe *Campbell.* he ge(e)acnaþ (K)] he geeacnaþ *Sisam.* iniusticiam (C)] iniusti[t]iam *Wildhagen.* peperíít (E)] peperiit *Harsley.*

OE: he ge(e)acnaþ (K)] *only lower curl of 2nd* e *visible, small eras.* (?) *to right,* c *malformed, as though scribe began 1st leg of* n *but altered to* c. unryhtwisnesse (E²)] y *altered from* i, t *altered from* c, sse *on eras. from* parturit *above.*

LTg: Ecce] [ ]cce G: *fragments of initial* E *visible.* parturiit] parturit BCDFGHIJK, E: i *retraced,* t *on eras.: cf. Weber MSS* MS²KT*Uδσ² moz. iniustitiam] K: et *eras. after word;* iniusticiam C: *orig.* iniustitiam: *cross-stroke of 2nd* t *eras. to form* c, *small eras. before and after 2nd* i. concepit] G: *eras before word;* concępit HL. et] I: *small eras. before word, perhaps of punct.* peperit] peperíít E.

LTu. parturiit] ο: *2nd* i *interl.;* parturit δζϑιμπστ*τψ, β: *2nd* t *interl.* iniustitiam] iniusticiam τ*τ, ϱ: *orig.* iniustitiam: *2nd* t *deleted by subscript dot,* c *interl.* concepit] concoepit β; concępit υ. iniquitatem] inęquitatem ε.

GAg: iniustitiam] iniustitiam et FJ; *for* GK *see LTg notes to* iniustitiam *and* concepit.

GAu: iniustitiam] iniustitiam et ϑμοπ, δ: et *added interl.*

16

Lacum	seað ABCDFI, Seað E², seaþ *H*JK
aperuit	ontynde ABC, openude DH, openede E², he openode FK, he geopnode I, he geopede J, bið gecyrred G
et	⁊ ABCDE²FGHIJK
effodit	dalf A, dealf B*C*, he dealf K, adealf DE²F*H,* adylfð G, adilf J, he underdealf I
eum	ðone A, þone C, þæne I, hine BDE²FGHJK
et	⁊ ABCE²FGHIJK
incidit	ingefeol A*, gefeoll B*C,* gefealleð G, gefealleþ J, he onbefeol I, he feol K, hreas D*H,* he hreas F, onhreas E²
in	in AB, on CDE²FGHIJK
foueam	seað AB*C*DE²GH, seaþ J, seað ł on pit F, þam seaþe I, pytt K
quam	ðone ðe A, þone þe BC, þone̲ DE²H, þone FG, þe IJ, þa K
fecit	he dyde AB, he worhte CDFH, he wrohte E², he geworhte IJ, he gewyrceð *G,* he macode K

ED: effódit (H)] effodit *Campbell.* íncidit (H)] incidit *Campbell.*

OE: ingefeol (A)] o *interl.*

LTg: Lacum] H: L *faint but visible.* effodit] effódit CH. incidit] íncidit CH. foueam] fóueam C: *eras. after* ó. fecit] fęcit G.

LTu: Lacum] LAcum β.

17

Conuertetur		sie gecerred A, sie gecirred B, sy gecyrred *C*I, bið gecyrred D, bið gecyrred E^{2}, bið gecyrred F*G,* byþ gecyrred H, biþ gecirred J, biþ gecyrred K
dolor	|	sar ABCDE^{2}GHJK, sár F, his I
eius	|	his ABCDE^{2}FGHJ*K,* sar I
in		in AB, on CDE^{2}FGHIJK
capite*	|	heafde ABDH, heafud *C,* heafod FGJK, heauode *E*^{2}*, his I (*L*)
eius	|	his ABCDE^{2}FGHJ*K,* heafde I
et		⁊ ABCE^{2}FGHIJK
in		in AB, on CDE^{2}FGHIJK
uertice*	|	hnolle AB*CE*^{2}, hnol *D*FHJK, hnifel ł hnoll G, his I (*L*)
eius*	|	his ABCE^{2}FGJK, hnolle I
iniquitas	|	unrehtwisnis A, unryhtwisnes BD, unrihtwisnes H*K,* unrihtwisnysse CF, unrihtwisnesse E^{2}*, unriht GJ, his I
eius	|	his ABCE^{2}FGJ*K,* unrihtwisnes I (*D*)
descendet		astigeð *AB,* astah *DE*^{2}FH*K,* nyðerafylð C, ofdune astigeð G, ofdune astigeþ J, becume I (*L*)

OE: heauode (E^{2})] *2nd* e *on eras. from* capite *below.* unrihtwisnesse (E^{2})] *on eras.,* t *altered from* c.

LTg: Conuertetur] Conuertétur C; Conuertętur G. capite] E: te *on eras.;* caput CL: *cf. Weber MSS* αγδ moz^{c} med, *see GAg.* eius (*1st*)] eíus K: et *eras. after word.* eius (*2nd*)] eíus K. uertice] uerticem DEL; uérticem C: *cf. Weber MSS* Μαγ moz^{c}, *see GAg.* iniquitas] K: ini *on eras. by corr.* eius (*4th*)] D: *eras. after word* (ei<u>us</u>); eíus K (*where it is 3rd occ.*). descendet] K: et *on eras. by corr.,* L: et *on eras.* (?); descendit BD, A: *1st* i *altered to* e, E: *orig.* discendit: *2nd* i *on eras.: cf. Weber MSS* HMSKδσ^{2} moz^{x}.

LTu: Conuertetur] Conuertetur et ϑ. in capite eius] in caput eius μ: *interl.* capite] caput ν: *cf. Weber MSS* αγδ moz^{c} med, *see GAu* uertice] uerticem νςτ*: *cf. Weber MS* Μαγ moz^{c}, *see GAu.* eius (*3rd*)] ipsius νςτ*: *cf. Weber MSS* β moz, *see GAu.* descendet] discendit β; discendet ϑ; descendit ς.

GAg: capite] caput FGIJK, H: *eras. after* t, *perhaps back of* d *to form* t, CL: *see LTg.* uertice] uerticem FGHIJK, DEL: *see LTg; for* C *see LTg.* eius (*3rd*)] ipsius FGHIJK.

GAu: capite] caput δεζιλμνξοπϱστυχψ, ν: *see LTu;* capud ϑ. uertice] uerticem δεζϑιλμξοπϱστυχψ, νςτ*: *see LTu.* eius (*3rd*)] ipsius δεζϑιλμξοπϱστυχψ, νςτ*: *see LTu.*

18

Confitebor		ic ondettu A, ic ondetto B, ic ondette D, ic andette CE^2*FGHIJK
domino		dryhtne ABD, drihtne CGI, drihtene E^{2}H, drihten K, drhtne F, driħt J
secundum		efter AE^2, æfter BCFGK, æfter IJ
iustitiam	|	rehtwisnisse A, ryhtwisnesse BD, rihtwisnysse *C*F, rihtwisnesse GHIJK, his E^2
eius	|	his ABCDFGHIJ*K*, rihtwisnesse E^2*
et		⁊ ABCDE^{2}FGHIJK
psallam		ic singu A, ic singe BCE^{2}FHI*K*, ic synge D, singe *G*J
nomini	|	noman ABD, naman CFGHIJK, drihtnes E^2
domini	|	dryhtnes B, drihtnys C, drihtnes FI, dritnes G, dryht̄ A, driħt J, namen E^2
altissimi		ðæs hestan *A*, þæs heahstan CI, ðæs hyhstan D, þæs hihstæn E^2*, þæs hihstan HJ, þæs hyhstan K, þæm heahstan B, þam hehstan F, þam heahstan G

ED: iusticiam (C)] iusti[t]iam *Wildhagen.*

OE: ic andette (E^2)] *2nd* t *interl.* drihtene (E^2)] *eras.* (*1 letter*) *after word.* rihtwisnesse (E^2)] *on eras.* þæs hihstæn (E^2)] *1st* s *on eras., formed from another letter.*

LTg: iustitiam] iusticiam C: *orig.* iustitiam: *cross-stroke of 2nd* t *eras. to form* c. eius] eíus K. psallam] G: p *altered from* s; sallam K. altissimi] A: *orig. final letter eras. to form* i.

LTu: iustitiam] iusticiam τ*τ, ϱ: *orig.* iustitiam: *2nd* t *deleted by subscript dot,* c *interl.*

PSALM 8

2

Domine		drihtyn *C*, drihten F, Drichten *E^2*, dryht̄ *A*, driħt GJ, eala drihten I* (*BDK*)
dominus	|	dryhten B, drihten G, dryht̄ A, driħt *C*FJ, god E^2, ure I (*K*)
noster	|	ur A, ure BCDE^{2}FGHJ, drihten I (*K*)
quam		hu ABCDE^{2}H, la hu I, eala ðu swyðe F, eala hu swiðe GJ (*K*)
admirabile		wundurlic *A*CH, wundorlic B*D*GJK, wuldorlic F, wunderlich E^2, egesful ł hu wundorlic *I*
est		is ABE^{2}FGHIJ*K*, ys C
nomen	|	noma ABD, nama CGHK, name E^2*, naman FJ, þin I
tuum	|	ðin AF, þin BCE^{2}GHJK, nama I
in		in AB, on CDE^{2}FGHJK, ofor I

uniuersa	alre A, ealre BCDE^{2}FGH, ealra JK, ealle I
terra	eorðan ABCDFGHIJ, eorþan K, eorðen E^2
Quoniam	forðon A, forþon BCJ, forþon E^2, forðan F, forþam *G,* forþan þe I
eleuata	upahefen A, upahæfen B, upahafyn C, upahafen DFGIJ, upahauen E^{2}H, ahafen K
est	is ABE^{2}FGHIJ*K,* ys C
magnificentia	micelnis A, micelnes BG, micylnys C, micelnesse J, g̲e̲miclung ł mærð D, gemiclung ł mærð H, gemyclung ł merð E^2*, mærþ K, gemærsod F, þin I
tua	ðin AF, þin BCDE^{2}HJK, þine G, mycelnys *I*
super	ofer ABE^{2}FGJK, ofyr C, ofor I
caelos	heofenas A*GHK,* heofonas B*DFIJ,* hefynas *C,* heofones *E^2* *(L)*
⟨deus⟩	god *C*

ED: forðon (A)] for ðon *Kuhn.* forþon (E)] Forþon *Harsley.* cælos (D)] caelos *Roeder.* cęlos (E)] caelos *Harsley.*

OE: eala drihten (I)] s. *written before* eala, þe eart *written in left margin and signaled for inclusion after* drihten. name (E^2)] þi *eras. on next line above* (no/)men: *cf. following* þin. gemyclung ł merð (E^2)] y *altered from* u.

LTg: Domine] DOMINE C; DÑE ABDEK. dominus] DOMINUS C, DÑS K. noster] ÑR K. quam] QUAM K. admirabile] ammirabile ADI. est (*1st*)] ést K. Quoniam] [ ]oniam G. est (*2nd*)] ést K. tua] I: *eras. after word.* caelos] cælos DK; cęlos EFGJL; celos deus C.

LTu: Domine] DOMINE ς; DÑE βιλμνϱτ*τυχψ. dominus] DOMINUS λμνϱψ; DOMInus ς. noster] NOSTER λμνϱψ. quam] QUAM λϱ. admirabile] ADMIrabile λ; ammirabile ευ, β: *orig.* admirabile: *1st* m *interl.,* ο: *orig.* admirabile: d *deleted by subscript dot,* m *interl.* tuum] tuu υ: *macron wanting.* caelos] cælos ϑχ; cęlos ιμξπυ; celos λσςτ*τ.

3

Ex	of *ABCDE^2*FHIJK (*L*)
ore	muðe ABCDE^{2}G, muþe FHIJK
infantium	cilda ABC, cildra DFHIK, childra E^2, on cilda GJ
et	⁊ ABCDE^{2}FGHIJK
lactantium	milcdeondra *A*, meolcteondra B, meolciyndra *C,* meolciendra *G,* meolccigendra J, sucendra D*FIK,* succendra *H,* sukendre *E^2*
perfecisti	ðu gefremedes A, þu gefremedes B, þu gefremydyst C, þu gefremedest G, þu gefremodest J, þu fulfremedest DE^{2}HI, ðu fulfremodest F, fulfremedest K
laudem	lof AB*C*DE^{2}GHIJK, laf F

propter — fore *ABDE*^{2}H, for *C*FGIJK (*L*)
inimicos | feondum ABCGHJ, feondum D, fiondum E^2, feondun F, feondan K, þinum I
tuos | ðinum AF, þinum B*H*, þinum CDE^{2}J, ðinum G, þinan *K*, feondum I
ut — ðæt A, þæt B, þæt CDFHIJK, þet E^2, þætte G
destruas — ðu toweorpe ADI, þu toweorpe B*HJ*, þu toworpe C, þu towurpe F, þu towerpe E^{2}K, þu toweorp[ ] G
inimicum — feond *A*BCDE^{2}FHI, fynd JK, [ ]d G*
et — ⁊ ABCDE^{2}FGJ
defensorem* — gescildend A*B, gescyldend CDE^{2}F, þone gescildend J, þone gescyldend ł þone forhoredan G*, wrecend ł ⁊ scildend I

ED: ex (B)] Ex *Brenner.* lactæntium (H)] lactentium *Campbell.* meolcteondra (B)] meolc teondra *Brenner.* meolccigendra (J)] meolc cigendra *Oess.* fore (E)] Fore *Harsley.* destruas (G)] destrua*s Rosier.* déstruas (H)] destruas *Campbell.* þone gescyldend ł þone forhoredan (G)] þone gescyldend ł þone forhosedan *Rosier: see his note and Sisam*^{2} *p. 61.*

OE: [ ]d (G)] *Rosier writes: 'A small, mismounted fragment covers part of the gloss to* diriges [7.10]; *the fragment, with the gloss letters* -:yn-, *may belong to the gloss to* inimicorum *in v. 3, i.e.,* (f)ynd.' gescildend (A)] *orig.* gesceldend: *2nd* e *deleted by subscript dot,* i *interl.* þone gescyldend ł þone forhoredan (G)] ł þone forhoredan *added in diff.* (?) *hand.*

LTg: Ex] ex ABCDEL. lactantium] A: m *added by corr.;* lactentium GI, C: *orig.* lactantium: *2nd* a *altered to* e *by corr.,* E: e *altered from another letter, minim eras. after* i, F: *orig.* lactantium: *2nd* a *deleted by subscript dot,* e *interl.;* lactentivm K: e *on eras. by corr.,* v̄ *interl.;* lactæntium H: *orig.* lactantium: *2nd* a *altered to* æ. laudem] C: *eras. after* l, a *altered from* d. propter] Propter ABCDEL. tuos] H: os *interl. in main hand,* K: *small eras. after word.* destruas] déstruas H. inimicum] A: *2nd* m *added by corr.*

LTu: Ex] ex βνςτ*. lactantium] lactentium εζιλξοπτ*τυχ, δ: *orig.* lactantium: e *interl. by corr.,* ϱ: *orig.* lactantium: *2nd* a *deleted by subscript dot,* e *interl.* propter] Propter βνςτ*. destruas] distruas ϑ; destruam ς.

GAg: defensorem] ultorem FGHIJK.

GAu: defensorem] ultorem δεζϑιλμξοπϱστυχψ.

4

Quoniam — forðon AJ, forþon BCGH, Forðan E^2, forðan F, forþan þe I
uidebo — ic gesie A, ic geseo BCDE^{2}FGHIJ*K*
caelos — heofenas A*G*, heofonas B*DFHIJ*, hefynas *C*, heofenes *E*^{2}, heofe *K** (*L*)

(tuos)*		ðine F, þine GIJ
opera		werc A, weorc BCDE²FGHIJK
digitorum	|	fingra ABCDFG*HJK, fingre E², þinra I
tuorum	|	ðinra AF, þinra BCDE²G*HJK, fingrena I
lunam		monan ABCDE²GIJK, monam H, mona F
et		⁊ ABCDE²FGHIJ
stellas		steorran ABCDFGHIJ, steorren E²
quas*		ða AF, þa BCDE²GJK, þe I, hwylc *H**
tu		ðu AB, þu CE²FGHIJK
fundasti		gesteaðulades A, gestaðolades B, gestaðolodyst C, gestaþelodest DF, gestaþeladest G, gestaþolodest HK, gestaðelodest E²IJ

ED: forðon (A)] for ðon *Kuhn.* cælos (D)] caelos *Roeder.* cęlos (E)] caelos *Harsley.* þinra (G)] *no gloss Rosier.* quę (I)] quae *Lindelöf.*

OE: heofe (K)] *tall* s *of lemma and interl.* os *of following* tuos *left little space to complete gloss.* fingra (G)] a *slightly cropped at bottom.* þinra (G)] *top of gloss cropped.* hwylc (H)] *in lighter ink and perhaps in diff. hand.*

LTg: uidebo] K: ui *on eras. in main hand.* caelos] cælos D; cęlos CGHJL, K: s *on eras. in main hand,* E: *orig.* cęlos tuos: tuos *deleted by subscript dots: see GAg;* celos I. quas] H: *on eras. in lighter ink,* K: *orig.* que: *on eras. by corr.,* e *deleted by subscript dot,* as *interl.: see GAg.*

LTu: caelos] cælos ϑχ; cęlos ιξο; celos σςτ*τυ. quas] *interl.* χ.

GAg: caelos] caelos tuos F; cęlos tuos GHJ, K: *2nd* os *interl.;* celos tuos I; *for* E *see LTg.* quas] quę GIJ, F: ę *eras. but legible,* a *and descender* (*of* s?) *written above line; for* K *see LTg.*

GAu: caelos] caelos tuos δεζλμπρψ; cælos tuos ϑχ; cęlos tuos ιξο; celos tuos στυ. quas] quae δεμπρυψ; quę ζϑιλξο; que στ.

5

Quid		hwet AE², hwæt BCDFHK, la hwæt I, forðon *GJ**
est		is ABDE²FGHIJ*K*, ys C
homo		mon ABD, man HK, mann C, se mæn E², se mann F, se mon G, se man IJ
quod		ðæt A, þæt BHI, þæt CDE²FGJK
memor	|	gemyndig ABDI, gemindig FH, gemyndi K, gemendig E²*, ðu his gemyndig G, þu is gemindig J, sy *C*
es	|	ðu sie A*B*, sy *FJ*, sie *G,* eart D*H*K*, ert E²*, þu eart I, gemyndig C
eius	|	his ABDE²*FHI*K*, hys C

aut		oððe ACFGHIJ, oþþe BE^2, oþðe DK (*L*)
filius	I	sunu ABCDFGH, bearn JK, monnes E^2, mannes I
hominis	I	monnes ABG, monnys C, mannes DFH, manna JK, sunu E^2, bearn I
quoniam		forðon ABG, forþon CJ, forðan þe F, forþan þe I, forðæn þæt E^2, þæt D, þæt H, þa K
uisitas		ðu neosas A, þu neosas B, þu neosast *C*E^2*H, ðu neosast D, þu geneosast FGIJ, þu geneosodest K
eum		hine ABCDE^2FGHIJK

ED: és (G)] es *Rosier.* forðon (A)] for ðon *Kuhn.*

OE: forðon (J)] *perhaps reading gloss to* Quoniam *in v. 4.* gemendig (E^2)] *orig.* gemindig: *1st* i *altered to* e. eart (D)] a *interl.* ert (E^2)] t *on eras. in lighter brown ink.* his (E^2)] hi *on eras. in lighter brown ink.* þu neosast (E^2)] *eras.* (*15 mm*) *after* þu, neosast *on eras. in lighter brown ink.*

LTg: Quid] [ ]uid G: *initial* Q *lost.* est] ést K. memor] mémor C. es] és BFG, K: *on eras. by corr.* eius] eíus K. aut] L: *ligature added connecting* au. uisitas] uísitas C: *eras. after* a.

LTu: quoniam] quod ϑ. uisitas] uissitas ϑ.

6

Minuisti	ðu gewonedes A, þu gewonodes B, þu gewanudyst C*, þu wanodest DHK, ðu wanodest F, þu wanedest E^2*, þu gewanodest ł þu gelitludest I, ðu lytledost G, þu litlodest J
eum	hine ABCDE^2*FGHIJK
paulo	hwoene A, hwene BC, hwæne *J,* hwe[ ] G*, lytle DFHK, litle E^2*, lythwon ł hwæne I
minus	laessan A, læssan B*C*, læs DE^2*FG*H*IJ*K*
ab	from AE^2, from B, fram CDGHJK, fram FI
angelis	englum ABFHIJ, englum CDG*, éanglan E^2*, englan K
gloria	mid wuldre ABCGIJ, of wuldre DFHK, of wuldor E^2
et	⁊ ABCE^2FGHIJK
honore	mid are *A*BCG, mid hare J, arweorðunga DH, arweorðunge E^2, weorðmynt F, wyrðmynte I, wyrðmynt *K*
coronasti	ðu gebegades A, þu gebeagades B, þu gebiegodyst C, ðu gebeag[ ]dest *G,* þu gewuldorbeagodest FI, þu wuldorbeagodest J, ðu gehelmudest D, þu gehelmvdest H*, þu gehelmedest E^2*, þu gehelmodest K
eum	hine ABCDE^2*FGHIJK

ED: hwe[ ] (G)] hwene *Rosier.* pauló minus (J)] paulóminus *Oess.* mínus (H)] minus *Campbell.* þu gehelmvdest (H)] þu gehelmudest *Campbell.*

OE: þu gewanudyst (C)] s *interl.* þu wanedest (E^2)] *on eras. in lighter brown ink.* hine (E^2) (*1st*)] *on eras. in lighter brown ink.* hwe[ ] (G)] *letter fragments visible after* e. litle (E^2)] *on eras. in lighter brown ink and retraced in darker ink.* læs (E^2)] *on eras. in lighter brown ink.* englum (G)] *bottom of* g *cropped.* éanglan (E^2)] *on eras.* þu gehelmvdest (H)] *orig.* þu gehelmedest: v *written above 3rd* e, *but without deletion mark.* þu gehelmedest (E^2)] helmedest *on eras.* hine (E^2) (*2nd*)] *orig.* him: *right leg of* m *used to form back of* e.

LTg: paulo] pauló J. minus] C: m *altered from* o; mínus HK. honore] K: h *interl.,* A: *orig.* honorem: m *eras.* coronasti] corona[ ]ti G.

LTu: eum] eum domine ς.

7

Et		⁊ *ABCDE^{2}FGHIJK* (*L*)
constituisti		gesettes ABE^2*, gesettest D, gesettest K, gesetst H, þu gesettyst C, þu gesettest FIJ, þu gese[ ]test *G**
eum		hine ABCE^{2}FHIJK (*G*)
super		ofer ABCDE^2*FGHJK, ofor I
opera		werc A, weorc BCDFGHJK, wiorc E^2, geweorc I
manuum	|	honda A, handa BC*D*FGHJK, handæ E^2*, þinra *I*
tuarum	|	ðinra AF, þinra BCDGHJK, þinræ E^2*, handa I

ED: et (B)] Et *Brenner.* þu gese[ ]test (G)] þu gesettest *Rosier.*

OE: gesettes (E^2)] *eras. after word until following* hine. þu gese[ ]test (G)] *letter lost due to hole.* ofer (E^2)] *orig. glosses to* super opera *eras.,* ofer wiorc *begins above* a *in* opera. handæ þinræ (E^2)] *in MS as* þinræ handæ *but marked for transposition.*

LTg: Et] et ABCDEFGHIJKL. constituisti] constituist[ ] G. eum] *lost* G. manuum] D: *1st* u *interl.,* I: *eras. above word* (þinra *begins above* um).

LTu: Et] et βδεζϑιλμνξοπϱσςτ*τυχψ. manuum] manum βεζ.

8

Omnia	all A, ealle BCGJ, eal þing DH, Eælle þing E^2*, ealle þing FIK
subiecisti	ðu underdeodes A, þu underþeddes B, þu underþeoddyst C*, ðu underþeoddest D, þu underþeodest F, þu underþeoddest HJ, þu underþiedest E^2, ðu underðiedest *G,* þu underðeoddest I, underþeoddest K
sub	under ABDE^2*FGHI*J*K, undyr C

pedibus	I	fotum ABE^{2}FGHJ, fotum CD, fotan K, his I
eius	I	his ABE^{2}FGHJ*K*, hys C, fotum I
oues		scep ABC, sceap DE^{2}FGHIJ, scæp K
et		⁊ ABCE^{2}FGHIJK
boues		oxan ABCDFGHIJ, oxæn E^2, oxsan K
uniuersa*		all A, eall B, ealle *C*DFGH*I*JK, eællæ E^2*
insuper	I	ec ðon A, eac ðon B, iec þon ma *C,* ⁊ ufonon þæt DE^2*H**, onufan þæt G, onufon F, onufan J, ⁊ onufan K, þær to eacan I
et	I	⁊ ABCFGHIJK
pecora		netenu AB, nytynu C, nytenu F, nytena GI*K*, nitena *J,* neat *D*E^2*H*
campi		feldes ABDE^{2}GHIJ, feldys C, ðæs feldes F, fellda K

ED: ðu underðiedest (G)] þu underðiedest *Rosier.* ínsuper (H)] insuper *Campbell.* uniuersas (C)] uniuersa *Wildhagen.* eac ðon (B)] eacðon *Brenner.* onufon (F)] on ufon *Kimmens.* onufan þæt (G)] on ufan þæt *Rosier.* ⁊ ufonon þæt (H)] ⁊ ufon on þæt *Campbell.* ⁊ onufan (K)] ⁊ on ufan *Sisam.*

OE: Eælle þing (E^2)] þing *on eras.* þu underþeoddyst (C)] r *interl.* under (E^2)] *eras. (5 mm) after word.* eællæ (E^2)] ⁊ *eras. before word.* ⁊ ufonon þæt (H)] on þæt *written above following* ⁊.

LTg: subiecisti] subięcisti G. sub] sup J. eius] eíus K. uniuersa] I: *eras. after word;* uniuersas C: *orig.* uniuersa: *2nd* s *added interl. by corr.: cf. Weber MSS* TPQUVXαγ moz^c, *see GAg.* insuper] ínsuper CH. pecora] HK: *letter eras. after* e; peccora DJ.

LTu: sub pedibus] suppedibus δ. uniuersa] ϱ: *orig.* uniuersas: *2nd* s *eras.* pecora] peccora ϑχ.

GAg: uniuersa] uniuersas FGHJ, K: *eras. after word, final* s *interl.,* C: *see LTg.*

GAu: uniuersa] uniuersas δειλμξοπστυχ.

9

Uolucres	I	fuglas *ABC,* fugelas D, fugelas *FGHIJK,* heofæne *E*^{2}* (*L*)
caeli	I	heofenes A, heofones B*D,* hefenys *C,* heofenæs *G,* heofonas *H,* heofonas *J,* heofonan F*I,* heofena *K,* fuglæs *E*^{2} (*L*)
et		⁊ ABCE^{2}FGHIJK
pisces		fiscas AB, fihsas C, fixas DFGHIJ, fixsa K, sefysces E^2*
maris		saes A, sæs BDGHJ, sæys C, sǽ F, sæ IK
qui		ða AH, þa BCDE^{2}K, ða ðe FG, þa þe I, þa ðe J

perambulant — geondgað AB, þurhgað *C*F, ðurhgað D, þurhgaþ HK, þurchgangeð E^2*, þurhgangað G, þurhgangeþ J, iandfarað I
semitas — stige AGJ, stiga BDE^2*H, stig C, weg stiga K, paðas FI
maris — saes A, sǽs B, sæs DE^2*FGHJK, sæys C, sæ I

ED: cæli (D)] caeli *Roeder.* cęli (E)] caeli *Harsley.*

OE: heofæne (E^2)] *final* e *added later* (?). sefysces (E^2)] *eras.* (*5 mm*) *after word, extending above following* maris. þurchgangeð (E^2)] þurch *on eras.* stiga (E^2)] *eras. before word.* sæs (E^2)] *on eras.*

LTg: Uolucres] A: *although questionable,* h *appears to be inscribed* (*drypoint*) *to left of* U, *and* b *inscribed below that;* Volucres BCEFHIKL, G: *eras. after* u. caeli] cæli DK; cęli CEGHJL; celi I: *orig.* caeli: a *eras.* perambulant] C: bu *interl.*

LTu: Uolucres] Volucres εινξοστ*τυ. caeli] cęli ειξουχ; cæli ϑμ; celi σςτ*τ.

10

Domine — Drichten E^2, dryht̄ AB, drih̄t CF*G*HJ, eala drihten I* (D*K*)
dominus — | drihten F, dryht̄ AB, drih̄t CGHJ, ure I, godd E^2
noster — | ur A, ure BCE^{2}FGHJ, drihten I
quam — hu ABCE^{2}H, la hu I, eala þu swyðc F, eala hu swiðe GJ
admirabile — wundurlic *A*C, wundorlic BE^{2}FGH*J*, egesful is ł hu wundorlic *I* (*DK*)
est — is ABE^{2}FGHIJ, ys C (*K*)
nomen — | noma *A*B, nama CGH, naman FJ, þin E^{2}I
tuum — | ðin AF, þín B, þin CGHJ, nomæ E^2, nama I
in — in AB, on CE^{2}FGHIJ
uniuersa — alre A, ealre BCFGIJ, eælre E^2, ealrae H
terra — eorðan ABCG, eorþan FHIJ, eorðæn E^2

ED: admirabiłe (J)] admirabile *Oess.*

OE: DK: *verse unglossed, presumably because v. 10 repeats v. 2.* eala drihten (I)] s, o *written before* eala.

LTg: Domine] [ ]omine G: *initial* D *lost.* admirabile] ádmirabile K; admirabiłe J; ammirabile ADI. est] ést K. nomen] A: *final* n *added by corr.*

LTu: admirabile] ammirabile ευ, ο: *orig.* admirabile: d *deleted by subscript dot,* m *interl.*

PSALM 9

2

Confitebor — ic ondetto *A*, ic ondette *BD*, Ic ondette E^{2}*, ic andette *CFGH* I*J*K*
tibi — ðe AF, þe B*C*DE^{2}GHIJK
domine — dryhten AB, drihtyn C, drihten E^{2}, driħt FH, driħ GJ, driht̄ I
in — in AB, on CDE^{2}FGHIJK
toto — alre A, ealre BCDFGHIJK, eællre E^{2}
corde | heortan ABCDFGHK, eortan J, minre E^{2}I
meo | minre ABCDFGHK, minre J, heortæn E^{2}, heortan I
narrabo — ic secgo A, ic secge BCG, ic secge ł rece H, ic secge ł ic recce J*, ic recce F, ic cyþe DK, ic cyþe ł secge E^{2}, ic recce ł ic gecyþe I
omnia — all A, ealle BCDFGHIJK, eælle E^{2}*
mirabilia | wundur A, wundru BCD, wundra FJK, wundre *E*^{2}, wuldra G, wuldor H, þine I
tua | ðin A, þine BCDE^{2}GHJK, ðine F, wundra I

OE: I: *psalm-title* in finem pro occultis filiis psalmus dauid *is glossed as follows:* for diglum bearn sealm. Ic ondette (E^{2})] *eras. after* Ic. ic secge ł ic recce (J)] *1st* c *in* recce *on eras.* eælle (E^{2})] *eras. after word.*

LTg: Confitebor] H: *initial* C *nearly completely faded;* CONfitebor ABD; CONFITEBOR CE; COnfitebor K. tibi] TIBI C. mirabilia] E: *eras. above* (mira/)bilia.

LTu: Confitebor] COnfitebor β; CONFITEBOR ιλμνϱτψ; CONFITEbor ς; CONFItebor τ*; CONfitebor χ. tibi] TIBI λμϱψ. domine] DOMINE λϱ. in] IN λ. toto] TOTO λ.

3

Laetabor — ic biom geblissad A, ic beo geblissod *C*, ic blissige *BDGHK*, Ic blissige *E*$^{2/x}$*, ic blissie *FJ*, ic geblissige I (*L*)
et — ⁊ ABCDE^{2}FGHIJK
exultabo — ic gefie *A*, ic gefeo BC, ic gefægnie D, ic gefagenie E^{x}*, ic gefægnige I, fægnige K, ic upahebbe F, ic wynsumige G, ic wunsumige H, ic winsumige J
in — in AB, on CE^{2}FGHIJK
te — ðe A*B*FG, þe CE^{2}HIJK
et* — ⁊ ABCE^{2}*
psallam — singu A, singe D, singe E^{2}*K*, ic singe BCFI, ⁊ singe HJ, ⁊ ic singe G
nomini | noman ABD, naman CFGHJK, þinum E^{2}I

tuo	I	ðinum AF, þinum B, þinum CD, þinne GHJK, naman I, þæm hihstæn E^2
altissime	I	ðu hehsta A, þu hehsta B, þu heahsta C, eala ðu hehsta D, þam hehstan F, þam heahstan G, þam hihstan *H*, þam hihstan J, ðone hyhstan K, eala þu se hexta I*, namæn E^2

ED: Lętabor (EG)] Laetabor *Harsley;* Letabor *Rosier.*

OE: Ic blissige (E$^{2/x}$)] sige *on eras.*, g *altered from* e. ic gefagenie (E^x)] *on eras.* ⁊ (E^2) (*2nd*)] ic *eras. after word.* eala þu se hexta (I)] s. o *written before* eala.

LTg: Laetabor] Lætabor BK; Letabor DJL; Lętabor CEFGH. exultabo] A: *letter eras. after* o. te] té B. psallam] sallam K. altissime] H: *eras. after* m.

LTu: Laetabor] LAetabor β; Lętabor ει; Lætabor ϑ; Letabor υτ*τ. et (*2nd*)] *om.* ς: *cf. Weber MSS* S*K*T*αγδσ* moz^c. altissime] β: *1st* s *interl.*

GAg: et (*2nd*)] *om.* FGHIJK.

GAu: et (*2nd*)] *om.* δεζιλμξοπϱσςτυχψ.

4

In		in ABC*G*HJ, on DIK, On E^x*
conuertendo		forcerringe A, forcirringe B, forcyrringe C, gecyrringe D, gecyrringe E^x*K, gecyrrincge I, ic gecyrre F, togecyrrenne GH, togecirrende J
inimicum	I	fienda A, feond BCDF*GI, feondum HJ, feonda K*, mine E^2
meum	I	min A, minne BCDFI, mine G, minum HJ, minan K, fiend E^2
retrorsum		on bec *A*, on bæc BCGHK, on bæcc J, under bæc F, on bæcling I, on bęclincg ł hinder E^2, on hinder D
infirmabuntur		bioð geuntrumad A, beoð geuntrumod GH, beoþ geuntromod J, beoð geuntrumade B, beoð geuntrumude C, hy geuntrumiað D, hy geuntrumiað E^2, hi geuntrumiaþ F, hi geuntrumian K, syn hi geuntrumode I
et		⁊ ABCDE^{2}FGHIJK
perient*		forweordað A, forweorðað BGH, forweorðaþ D, forweorþaþ J, forweorþeð E^2, forwurðað C, forwurðon I, forwyrðan K, losiað F
a		from A*E^2,* from B, fram CDF, fram I, on GHJ, of K
facie	I	onsiene *A,* onsine B, ansyne CF*G*K, ansine J, gesihðe D, ðynre H, þinre E^{2}I
tua	I	ðinre AF, þinre BCJK, þynre G, ansyne HI, onsine ł sihthe E^2*

ED: á (E)] a *Harsley.*

OE: On (Ex)] *on eras.* gecyrringe (Ex)] *on eras.* feond (F)] n *interl.* feonda (K)] *preceded by partial gloss* feo *and and eras. minim; Sisam reads* feon. onsine ł sihthe (E^2)] ł sihthe *slightly above line, possibly added later by main hand.*

LTg: In] [ ]n G. retrorsum] A: m *added by corr.* a] á E. facie] A: *eras. after* i; facię G.

LTu: facie] ζ: e *interl.;* faciae εψ; facię ξ.

GAg: perient] peribunt FGHIJK.

GAu: perient] peribunt δεζθιλμξοπρστυχψ.

5

Quoniam		forðon ABG*H,* forþon CIJ, forðæn þe E^2, forðan þe F
fecisti		ðu dydest A, þu dydyst C, þu didest I, þu dydes B, ðu gedydest G, þu gedydest H, þu gedidest J, ðu worhtes D, þu worhtest F, þu worhttest K, þu geworhtes E^2
iudicium	|	dom ACDFGHJK, dóm B, minne E^{2}I
meum	|	minne ABCDFGHJK, dom E^{2}I
et		⁊ ABCE^{2}FGHIJK
causam	|	intingan ACDFGHJ, intingbn B, intinge K, minne E^{2}I
meam	|	minne *A*BCFJ, minne G, mine H, intingæn E^2, intingan I
sedes*		ðu sites *A,* þu sites B, þu sityst C, þu sitst D*I**, ðu sitst F*K,* þu sits E^2, þu sittest J, ðu si[ ]est *G**, þu siest *H*
super		ofer ABCFGHIJK, ouer E^x*
thronum		ðrymseld A, þrymseld B, þrymsetl CK, þrymsetl DG, ðrymsetl FI, þrimsetl J, þrymstel H, heæhsętle ł þrimsetle E^2*
qui		ðu A, þu B, þu þe CE^{2}GHIJ, ðu þe D, ðu ðe F, þe K
iudicas		doemes AB, demst CDFI, demest E^{2}GH, demast J, demes K
aequitatem*		efennisse *AD,* efnesse B, efennysse *C,* euennesse ł enlicnesse *E^2,* rihtwisnysse F, rihtwisnesse GHIJK (*L*)

ED: forðon (A)] for ðon *Kuhn.* forðæn þe (E)] Forðæn þe *Harsley.* intingbn (B)] intingan *Brenner* (*emended*). þu sitst (I)] þu sæt *Lindelöf: see OE.* ðu si[ ]est (G)] ðu siest *Rosier.* ęquitatem (CE)] equitatem *Wildhagen;* aequitatem *Harsley.*

OE: þu sitst (I)] *orig.* þu siti: *eras. evident around* iti, tst *written by glossator in left margin, thus* siti > sitst. ðu si[ ]est (G)] *letter eras. due to alterations to lemma; fragment visible.* ouer (E^x)] *on eras. in lighter brown ink.* heæhsętle ł þrimsetle (E^2)] ł þrim *written above* setle. euennesse ł enlicnesse (E^2)] en *in* enlicnesse *written in left margin.*

LTg: Quoniam] H: *initial* Q *faded but visible.* meam] A: *final* m *added by corr.*

sedes] A: *orig.* sedis: i *altered to* e, H: es *on eras.*, I: *orig.* sedis: i *altered to* e, *eras. after word,* K: es *on eras. by corr.;* sedis G: *2 letters eras. after word: cf. Weber MSS* H^{2}γ, *see GAg.* aequitatem] A: m *added by corr.;* ęquitatem CDE; æquitatem L.

LTu: sedes] υ: *eras. after final* s, *2nd* e *altered from* i; sedis β: *orig.* sedes: i *interl.*, ϱ: *orig.* sedisti: ti *eras.*, *1st* i *deleted by subscript dot,* e *interl.* iudicas] β: *initial* i *interl.* aequitatem] ęquitatem β; equitatem τ*.

GAg: sedes] sedisti FJ; *for* GHIK *see LTg.* aequitatem] iustitiam FGHIJ, K: *partly written around rough section of vellum (leaving division between* i *and* a), a *somewhat poorly formed at top left.*

GAu: sedes] sedisti δϑμοψ. aequitatem] iustitiam δεζϑιλμξοπσυχψ; iusticiam τ, ϱ: *orig.* iustitiam: *2nd* t *deleted by subscript dot,* c *interl.*

6

Increpasti — ðu ðreades A, ðu þreades B, þu ðreadyst C, þu ðreadest DGI, ðu þreadest F, þu þreadest HJ, þu þrædest K, þu ðreadest ł ciddest E$^{2/x*}$

gentes — ðeode A, þeoda BCDHIJK, ðeoda FG, þiode E^{x*}

et — ⁊ ABCDE^{x*}FGHIJK

periit — forweorðed *A,* forweorðeð *B,* forwurðyð *C,* forweorðað FGH, forweorþeð J, forwearð DI, forwarð E^{x*}, forwurdan K

impius — se arleasa ABCDFI, se arlease E^{x*}, arlease K, þa árleasan G, þa arleasan H*J

nomen | noman ABD, naman CGIJK, nama FH, ⁊ hioræ E^2

eorum | heara A, hira B, hyra C, heora DFGHIJK, nomæn E^2

delisti — ðu adilgades *A,* ðu adiligades *B,* þu adilgodes *E^2,* þu adilgodyst *C,* ðu adylgadest *G,* þu adilegadest *HJ,* þu adilgodest *I,* ðu dilgodest *D,* ðu dylegodest *F,* adylegudest *K* (*L*)

in — in A, on BCDE^{2}FGHIJK

aeternum — ecnisse A, ecnesse *BDE^{2}GHJK,* ecnysse *CFI* (*L*)

et — ⁊ ABCDE^{2}FGHIJK

in — in ABC, on DE^{2}FGHIJK

saeculum — weoruld A, weorold *B,* woruld *CDG,* worold *E^2,* weorulde *F,* worlde *I,* worlda *HJ,* worolde *K* (*L*)

saeculi — weorulde *AF,* weoroldc *D,* worulde *CDE^2,* worold *K,* world *HJ,* [ ]uld *G**, word *I* (*L*)

ED: Increpasti (B)] increpasti *Brenner.* æternum (D)] aeternum *Roeder.* ęternum (E)] aeternum *Harsley.* sæculum (D)] saeculum *Roeder.* sclm (EIJ)] saeculm *Lindelöf;* seculum *Harsley, Oess.* sæculi (D)] saeculi *Roeder.* scli (FIJ)] seculi *Kimmens;* saeculi *Lindelöf;* seculi *Harsley, Oess.* [ ]uld (G)] woruld *Rosier.*

OE: þu ðreadest ł ciddest ($E^{2/x}$)] ðreadest ł ciddest *on eras. in lighter brown ink.* þiode (E^{x})] *on eras. in lighter brown ink.* ⁊ (E^{x}) (*1st*)] *on eras. in lighter brown ink.* forwarð (E^{x})] *on eras. in lighter brown ink.* se arlease (E^{x})] *on eras. in lighter brown ink.* þa arleasan (H)] *2nd* a *malformed, perhaps formed from another letter.* [ ]uld (G)] *letter fragments visible before* u, *but obscured by tear in leaf.*

LTg: Increpasti] Incrępasti G. periit] périit C; periet AB. delisti] delesti BCDEFGHIJKL, A: *2nd* e *obscured, possibly altered from another letter: cf. Weber MSS* $M^{1}\alpha\beta\delta^{2}$. aeternum] æternum BDK; ęternum CEFGHIL; eternum J. saeculum] sæculum BD; seculum CFGHKL; sclm EIJ. saeculi] sęculi AL; seculi CGHK; sæculi D; scłi EFIJ.

LTu: periit] μ: *2nd* i *interl.*, χ: *1st* i *interl.;* perit βϑ. delisti] delesti δεζιλμνξοπϱσςτ*τυ, χ: *orig.* delisti: *1st* i *altered to* e. aeternum] ęternum βειμ; æternum ϑ; eternum λξσςτ*τ. saeculum] sęculum ειν; seculum ςτ; scłm βζϑλμξοπστ*υχ. saeculi] sęculi ειν; scłi βζϑλμξοπστ*τυχ.

7

Inimici		feond A, fiend BE^{2}*, fynd CDF*G*HJK, fynd ł sceaþan I
defecerun		asprungun A*C*, asprungon B, geteorodon D, geteorodon *F*GHJ, getyorodon E^{x}*, ateorodun I, ateorodan K
framea		mid sweorde AB, mid swurde *C,* of sweorde D*E*^{x}**F,* of swyrde *K,* fram sweordtige *I,* cocor *GH*J
in		in AB, on CE^{x}*FGHIJK, [ ]n D*
finem		ende ABCDE^{2}FGIJK, ænde H
et		⁊ ABCE^{2}FGHJK
ciuitates	|	cestre A, ceastru B, cestra C, ceastra DI*K, ceaster FH, ceastera G, ceastre J, hiræ E^{x}*
eorum*	|	heara A, hira B, heora CDFJK, hyora G, ceæstræ E^{2} (*HI*)
destruxisti		ðu towurpe AG, þu towurpe BCHJ, þu tobræce DK, ⁊ þu tobræce I, þu towurpe ł bræce $E^{2/x}$*, ðu tobræce ł towurpe F
Periit	|	forwearð *AB*CDI, forwearþ K, forweorðeð *GH,* forweorþeð J, losað F, hieræ *E*^{2}
memoria		gemynd ABCFGHIK, gemynd D, gemind E^{2}, gemindig *J*
eorum	|	heara A, hira B, heora CDFHIJK, hyora G, forweorþ E^{2}
cum		mid ABCDE^{x}*FGHIJK
sonitu		swoege A, swege B*C*FGHIJ, hlynne D, hlydne $E^{2/x}$*, hlyde K

ED: [ ]nimici (G)] Inimici *Rosier.* defecęrunt (G)] defecerunt *Rosier.* framéa (C)] frámea *Wildhagen.* [ ]n (D)] on *Roeder.* Perÿít (E)] Periit *Harsley.* Pęriit (G)] Periit *Rosier.*

OE: fiend (E^{2})] *eras. before word.* getyorodon (E^{x})] *on eras. in lighter brown ink.*

of sweorde (E^{x})] *on eras. in lighter brown ink.* on (E^{x})] *on eras. in lighter brown ink.* [ ]n (D)] *initial letter eras., with only fragment visible.* ceastra (I)] [ ]or<u>um</u> : [ ]eora *written in left margin by glossator; Lindelöf reads* eorum : heora, *but initial letters are now lost due to rebinding.* hiræ (E^{x})] ræ *on eras.* þu towurpe ł bræce ($E^{2/x}$)] ł bræce *in slightly lighter brown ink,* a *of* æ *altered from* e. mid (E^{x})] *on eras. in lighter brown ink.* hlydne ($E^{2/x}$)] h *on eras. in lighter brown ink.*

LTg: Inimici] [ ]nimici G. defecerunt] defecérunt C; defecęrunt G. framea] E: *final* a *on eras. in darker ink;* framéa C: *final* a *altered by corr. from another letter;* frameę FH, K: ę *on eras. by corr.;* framéę G; frameae I. eorum (*1st*)] H: *on eras.,* I: *orig. om.: see OE note to* ceastra. Periit] H: P *faint but visible;* Períít E; Pęriit G; Perit AB: *cf. Weber MSS* Hβδ. memoria] J: m *eras. before word.* sonitu] sónitu C.

LTu: defecerunt] deferunt ζ. framea] frameę ειλξ; frameæ ζμ; frameae οπϱυχψ; framee στ. ciuitates eorum] σ: tates eorum *written by corr.* eorum] *added* ε; *interl.* χ. destruxisti] distruxisti ϑ. Periit] Perit βϑ.

GAg: eorum (*1st*)] I: *orig. om.: see OE note to* ceastra.

GAu: eorum (*1st*)] *om.* δζϑιλμξοπϱτυψ.

8

Et	⁊ *ABCDE^{x}*FGHJK* (*IL*)
dominus̩	drihtyn C, drihten DE^{x}*FIK, dryhт̄ AB, driħt GH, driħ J
in	in A, on BCDE^{x}*FGHIJK
aeternum	ecnesse A*BGHIJK,* ecnysse *CF,* ecnisse *D,* æcnesse *E^{x}** (*L*)
permanet	ðorhwunað A, þurhwunað BCDGH, ðurhwunað FK, þurhwunaþ J, þurhwuneð E^{x}*, ⁊ þurhwunað I
parauit	gearwade *AB,* gearwude *C,* gearwode *K,* he gearwade *D,* he geærwæde *E$^{2/x}$*,* he gegearwode *FI,* gegearwod *HJ,* gegearwað *G* (*L*)
in	in AB, on CDE^{2}FGHIJK
iudicio	dome ABCDFGHIJK, þæm dome E^{2}
sedem*	| seld AB, setl CDGJK, stel H, ðrymsetl F, his E^{2}I
suam*	| his ABCDFGHK, heora J, setle E^{2}, ðrymsetl I

ED: et (B)] Et *Brenner.* driħ (J)] driht*en Oess.* æternum (D)] aeternum *Roeder.* eternum (C)] ęternum *Wildhagen.* ęternum (E)] aeternum *Harsley.* ⁊ þurhwunað (I)] þurhwunað *Lindelöf.*

OE: ⁊ (E^{x})] *on eras. in lighter brown ink.* drihten (E^{x})] *on eras. in lighter brown ink.* on (E^{x}) (*1st*)] *on eras. in lighter brown ink.* æcnesse (E^{x})] *on eras. in lighter brown ink.* þurhwuneð (E^{x})] *on eras. in lighter brown ink.* he geærwæde ($E^{2/x}$)] de *on eras. in lighter brown ink.*

LTg: Et] et ABCDEFGHIJKL. aeternum] æternum BDK; eternum CJL; ęternum EFGH. parauit] Parauit ABCDEFGHIJK; Parabit L.

LTu: Et] et βδεζϑιλμνξοπϱσςτ*τυχψ. aeternum] ęternum ειvξ; æternum ϑ; eternum λσςτ*τ. parauit] Parauit βδζϑιλμξοπϱσςτ*τυχ, ψ: *Ps 9 begins here;* Parabit ν, ε: b *altered from* u.

GAg: sedem suam] thronum suum FGHIJK.

GAg^2: sedem suam] thronum suum δεζϑιλμξοπϱστυφχψ.

9

Et — ⁊ *ABCDE^{2}FGHIJK* (*L*)
ipse — he ABCDE^2*FIK, he sylf G, he silf J, sylf H
iudicabit — doemeð *A,* demeð BE^2, demeþ D, demð CFHI, demþ J, he demð G, demde K
orbem | ymbhwyrft ABCDFHI, ymbhwirft J, ymbhwyrht G, ymbehwyrf K, eorðæn E^2
terrae | earðan A, eorþan *BJK,* eorðan *CDFGH*I, ymbhwyrft *E^2** (*L*)
in — in AB, on *CDE^x**FGHIJK
aequitate — efennisse A*D,* efnesse *BG*I, efynnysse *C,* efennysse *E^x**, emnysse *F,* emnesse *HJ,* unrihtwisnesse *K** (*L*)
iudicabit — doemeð *A,* demeð *B*K, demyð *C,* he demeð *DE^x**, he demð GH, he demþ IJ, he demd F (*LM*)
populos — folc ABCDE^x*K, folce F, folcum GHJ, folctruman I (*M*)
cum* — mid ABCDE^x*G, mid ł on H, on FIJK
iustitia — rehtwisnisse A, ryhtwisnesse BD, rihtwisnysse C*F, ryhtwisnesse E^x*, rihtwisnesse GIJK, rihtwysnesse H

ED: terræ (D)] terrae *Roeder.* terrę (E)] terrae *Harsley.* ęquitate (E)] aequitate *Harsley.*

OE: he (E^2)] *orig.* hi: i *altered to* e. ymbhwyrft (E^2)] *letter eras. after* b (*cross-stroke of* e? *visible*), *2 letters eras. after* t, *2nd of which is* s (*long*). on (E^x)] *written in lighter brown ink below eras. gloss.* efennysse (E^x)] *written in lighter brown ink below eras. gloss.* unrihtwisnesse (K)] *lemma misread as* inæquitate. he demeð (E^x)] demeð *on eras. in lighter brown ink.* folc (E^x)] *on eras. in lighter brown ink.* mid (E^x)] *on eras. in lighter brown ink.* rihtwisnysse (C)] nysse *written above* twis. ryhtwisnesse (E^x)] *on eras. in lighter brown ink.*

LTg: Et] et ABCDEFGHIJKL. iudicabit (*1st*)] A: b *altered from another letter.* terrae] terrę BCEFGHJKL; terræ D. in] D: *eras. after word.* aequitate] æquitate BK; ęquitate CDEFGHJL. iudicabit (*2nd*)] Iudicabit BCDEL, A: b *altered from another letter*, M: b *on eras.; Ps 9 begins here in* M *at fol. 64r.* populos] M: *2nd* o *on eras.* iustitia] M: *eras. after* a.

LTu: Et] et βδεζϑιλμνξοπϱσςτ*τυφχψ. iudicabit (*1st*)] iudicauit ϑ. terrae] terrę ειvξoπφ; terre ζστ*τ; terræ ϑμ. in aequitate] in æquitate μ, β: *orig*. iniquitate: æ *interl. above 2nd* i, ϑ: æ *inter.;* in ęquitate ειλvφ; in ęquitate ęquitatę ξ; in equitate σςτ*τυ. iudicabit (*2nd*)] Iudicabit βvςτ*; iudicauit ϑ. iustitia] iusticia τ*τφ, ϱ: *orig*. iustitia: *2nd* t *deleted by subscript dot,* c *interl.*

GAg: cum] in FGHIJK.

GAu: cum] in δεζϑιλμξoπϱστυφχψ.

10

Et	⁊ *ABCE*^{2}*FG*HIJK (*DLM*)
factus	geworden ABDFGHIJ, gewordyn C, geworðen E^{x}*, gedon K
est	is ABE^{x}*FGHIJ*K,* ys C
dominus	dryhten B, drihtyn C, drihten E^{x}*K, dryhт̄ A, drih̄t FGHJ
refugium	geberg A, gebeorg B, gebeorh CGHJ, rotsung ł frofr D, scyld ł rotsung ł frofer E^{x}*, frofer K, gener F, ner ł rotnes I
pauperum*	ðearfena AF, þearfena B, þearfyna C, þearfana DE^{x}*, þearfan GHJ, þærfan K, þam þearfan I
adiutor	fultum *AB,* fultum *C,* to fultume F, fultumend *E*^{2}*, fultumiend GI*, gefultumend H, gefultumiend J*, gefylsta *D,* fylstend *K* (*LM*)
in	in AB, on CDE^{2}FGHIJM*
oportunitatibus	gelimplicnissum A, gelimplicnessum B, gelimplicnyssum C, gerecum D, g[ ]recum F*, gehyþelicnessum ł on gerecvm *E*$^{2/x}$*, gehyðelicnesse G, gehiðlicnesse ł þæslicnesse *H,* gehiþlicnesse ł þæslicnesse J*, gedafenlicnessum I, geherlicnissum M* (*K*)
in	in AB, on CDFGHIJK, ⁊ on E^{2}
tribulatione	geswencednisse A, geswencednesse B, geswencednysse C, geswince D*G*HJK, gedrefednysse FI*, eærfoðnesse ł swince E$^{2/x}$*

ED: et (B)] Et *Brenner*. adiutor (G)] audiutor *Rosier.* fultumiend (G)] [ ]tumiend *Rosier.* g[ ]recum (F)] gerecum *Kimmens*. gehiðlicnesse ł þæslicnesse (H)] gehiðlicnesse ł þæs licnesse *Campbell*. on geherlicnissum (M)] on geheplicnissum *Brock;* geheplicnissum *Berghaus*. tribula[ ]o[ ] (G)] tribulatione *Rosier*. geswince (G)] gesw[ ] *Rosier.*

OE: geworðen (E^{x})] *on eras. in lighter brown ink.* is (E^{x})] *on eras. in lighter brown ink.* drihten (E^{x})] *on eras. in lighter brown ink.* scyld ł rotsung ł frofer (E^{x})] *on eras. in lighter brown ink,* ł rotsung *written above* ł frofer. þearfana (E^{x})] *on eras. in lighter brown ink.* fultumend (E^{2})] ⁊ *eras. before word.* fultumiend (I)] ÷ : he (> est : he [is]) *written in right margin*, is *most likely lost due to trimming of leaf.* gefultumiend (J)] i *interl.* g[ ]recum (F)] *letter fragments visible after* g, rec *obscured but visible.*

gehyþelicnessum ł on gerecvm̲ (E$^{2/x}$)] ł on gerecvm̲ *added by corr.* gehiþlicnesse ł þæslicnesse (J)] ł þæslicnesse *interl. above* on gehiþlicnesse. on geherlicnissum (M)] *written in red in blank space toward right margin, above* tribulatione. gedrefednysse (I)] *2nd* d *altered from* n. eærfoðnesse ł swince (E$^{2/x}$)] ł swince *written in slightly lighter brown ink.*

LTg: Et] [ ]t G: *initial* E *lost;* et ABCDELM. est] ést K. adiutor] ádiutor K; Adiutor ABCDELM. oportunitatibus] opportunitatibus EH: *1st* p *interl.*, K: *1st* p *interl. by corr.* tribulatione] tribula[ ]o[ ] G.

LTu: Et] et βνςτ*. est] es ε: *added.* dominus] domine ε: e *altered from another letter.* adiutor] Adiutor βνςτ*. oportunitatibus] opportunitatibus ιλφ, ξπ: *1st* p *interl.*

GAg: pauperum] pauperi FGHIJK.

GAu: pauperum] pauperi δεζθιλμξοπϱστυφχψ.

11

Et		⁊ *ABCDE*^{2}FG*H*IJK (*LM*)
sperent		gehtað A, gehyhtað B, gehihtað C, hyhten D, hihten H, hihtan K, wenen ł hyhten E^{x}*, gehihtende GJ, opiað F, hopiaþ I
in		in A, on BCE^{x}*FGHIJK
te		ðe ABFG, þe CE^{x}*HIJK (*M*)
omnes*		alle A, ealle BCDE^{x}*
qui		ða A, þa BK, þa þe CE^{x}*I, ða ðe F, ealle þa ðe G, þa ðe ealle J
nouerunt		cunnun ABC, cuþon ł wiston D, cuðon ł wiston F, cuþon HI, wistan K, cuðen ł cniewen E^{x}*, witon G, witon ł cunnon J (*M*)
nomen	|	noman *A*B, naman CFGJK, þinne E^{2}I (*M*)
tuum	|	ðinne *A*F, þinne BCJK, þ[ ]nne G*, nomæn E^{2}, naman I
quoniam	|	forðon *AB,* forþon *C,* Forðæn *E*^{2}*, forðam K, forðan ðe F, forþan þe I, forðon þe J, forðon þu ðe G (*DLM*)
non	|	ðu ne A, þu ne BCFI, þu na DH, þu no J, ne GE^{2}, na K
derelinques*	|	forletes A, forlætes B, forlætst CDF, forlæst H, forlætest GJ, forletst þu E$^{2/x}$*, forlete I, þu forlete K
quaerentes		ða soecendan A*B,* þa secendan *C,* ða secendan *F,* þa secenden *I,* secende *DE*^{x}**GHJK* (*L*)
te		ðe A*B*F, þe CE^{x}*HIK, te G, þu J (*M*)
domine		dryhten B, drihten E^{x}*, dryht̄ A, driħt CFHJ, driħ G (*I*)

ED: þ[ ]nne (G)] þinne *Rosier.* forðon (A)] for ðon *Kuhn.* té (B)] te *Brenner.*

OE: wenen ł hyhten (E^{x})] *written on eras. in lighter brown ink.* on (E^{x})] *written on* *eras. in lighter brown ink.* þe (E^x)] *written on eras. in lighter brown ink.* ealle (E^x)] *written on eras. in lighter brown ink.* þa þe (E^x)] *written on eras. in lighter brown ink.* cuðen ł cniewen (E^x)] *written on eras. in lighter brown ink.* þ[ ]nne (G)] *letter lost due to hole.* Forðæn (E^2)] *eras.* (þe?) *after word.* forletst þu ($E^{2/x}$)] *eras. before* forletst, þu *on eras.* secende (E^x)] *on eras. in lighter brown ink.* þe (E^x)] *on eras. in lighter brown ink.* drihten (E^x)] *on eras. in lighter brown ink.*

LTg: Et] H: *initial* E *faint but visible;* et BCDE, A: *added by corr. in left margin,* M: *added interl. by glossator,* L: *added interl. by corr.* te (*1st*)] tê M. nouerunt] nouérunt M. nomen] A: *final* n *interl. by corr.;* nômen M. tuum] A: uu *in ligature,* m *added by corr.* quoniam] Quoniam ABCDELM. quaerentes] querentes BCDEHJKL; quęrentes FGI. te (*2nd*)] té B; tê M. domine] I: s. o *written above word.*

LTu: Et] et βνςτ*. quoniam] Quoniam βνςτ*. derelinques] derelinquis ε. quaerentes] quęrentes βελνουφ; querentes ζιξϱσςτ*τ; q̄rentes ϑ; quærentes μ.

GAg: omnes] *om.* FGHIJK. derelinques] dereliquisti FGHIJ, K: sti *on eras. by corr.*

GAu: omnes] *om.* δεζϑιλμξοπϱστυφχψ. derelinques] dereliquisti δζϑιλμξοπϱτυφχψ; derelinquisti σ.

12

Psallite	singað *ABCD,* singæþ E^2, syngað F, singaþ HIK, singað ge *G,* singan ge J (*LM*)
domino	drihtne CE^2FGHIJ, drihtene K, dryhť AB
qui	se ABCGJ, se þe F, se ðe I, ðe DE^x*, þe H*, þa K (*M*)
habitat	eardað ABCFGK, eardaþ DHJ, eærdæþ E^2, wunaþ I
in	in AB, on $CDE^2FGHIJK$
sion	sion ABJ*C,* syon ł on besceawodnesse $E^{2/x}$*, sion ł on besceawodnysse F, besceawodnisse DH, ðe G, þæm munte I
adnuntiate	secgað *A,* secgeað *B,* secað *C,* Secgæþ ł bodieð $E^{2/x}$*, bodiað *DFH,* bodiaþ J, bodigeað ge *G,* cyþað ł bodiað *I,* ⁊ bodiaþ *K* (*LM*)
inter	betwih AC, betweoh B, betweox DFH, betweoxe E^x*, betwux I, betweon G, betweonu͟m J, betwynan K
gentes	ðeode A, þeode C, þyode E^2*, þeoda BDGH, ðeodum F, þeodum I, þeodu͟m J, þeodan K
mirabilia	| wundur A, wundru BCDG, wundra JE^2*, bigenga F, his gecneordnyssa ł his ymbhoga I (*L*)
eius	| his $ABCE^2FGJ$*K*

ED: sion (K)] Sion *Sisam.* Annuntiate (C)] A[d]nuntiate *Wildhagen.* wundra (E)] wundora *Harsley.*

OE: ðe (E^x)] *on eras.* þe (H)] *eras. before word.* syon ł on besceawodnesse ($E^{2/x}$)]

initial s *altered from* y, n ł on besceawodnesse *on eras.* (?), on bescea *written above* wodnesse. Secgæþ ł bodieð (E$^{2/x}$)] þ ł bodieð *on eras.* betweoxe (E^{x})] *on eras.* þyode (E^{2})] *on eras.* wundra (E^{2})] *orig.* wundor: o *deleted by subscript dot,* a *added.*

LTg: Psallite] [ ]sallite G: *initial* P *lost;* psallite ABCDEL; psállite M. qui] quî M. sion] syon E, C: *orig.* sion: i *deleted by subscript dot,* y *interl. by corr.* adnuntiate] Adnuntiate ABDL; Adnuntiâte M; Annuntiate E, C: *1st* n *on eras. by corr., eras. after* i; annuntiate IK, G: *1st* n *altered from another letter,* H: *1st* n *on eras.* mirabilia] L: Studia *added above word by corr.: see GAg.* eius] eíus K.

LTu: Psallite] psallite βνςτ*. sion] syon ειστ*τυφ. adnuntiate] Adnuntiate βνς; Annuntiate τ*; annuntiate εζιλξπρστυφχ, ο: *orig.* adnuntiate: d *deleted by subscript dot,* n *interl.*

GAg: mirabilia] studia FGHIJK; *for* L *see LTg.*

GAu: mirabilia] studia δεζϑιλμξοπρστυφχψ.

13

Quoniam		forðon *A,* forþon *BC,* forðæn *E*^{2}*, forðan ðe *F,* forþan þe I, forðon þe GJ (*DLM*)
requirens		soecende *A*B, secynde C, secende DE^{2}F*H*IK, he secende J, he seceð G
sanguinem	I	blod ABCDFGHIJK, hieræ E^{2}
eorum	I	heara A, hira B, hyra C, heora DFHIJK, hiora G, blod E^{2}
memoratus*	I	gemynd AB, gemynde I, he gemunde D, he munde K, gemyndig C, gemindig F, he gemyndig G, he gemindig J, he is E^{2}
est	I	is ABFGJ, he is I, he ys C*, gemyndi E^{2} (*K*)
et*		⁊ ABCDE^{2}
non	I	nis ABE^{2}, na CJK, ne G, he na DH, he ne F, he nis I
est	I	is GJ*K*, ys C
oblitus	I	ofergeotol AB, ofergyttul C, ofergytol G, ofergitol J, ofergeat DH, ofergitende E^{2}, forgeat F, forgytol I, forgyten K (*M*)
orationem*	I	gebed AB*C,* gebedu *D,* gebeda G, clypunge FI, clypunga JK, þeærfne E^{2}* (*LM*)
pauperum	I	ðearfena AF, þearfena BDGHIJ, þearfyna C, þearfan K*, gebede E^{2}*

ED: forðon (A)] for ðon *Kuhn.* forðon þe (G)] forðan þe *Rosier.* requírens (H)] requirens *Campbell.*

OE: secende (E^{2})] he :s *eras. before word.* he ys (C)] he *written in left margin.* þeærfne (E^{2})] *orig.* þeærfnes: s *eras.* þearfan (K)] þeaf *eras. before word.* gebede (E^{2})] *letter eras. after 2nd* e.

LTg: Quoniam] F: Q *faint but visible;* quoniam ABCDELM. requirens] A: ens *on eras. by corr.;* requírens H. est (*1st*)] ést K. est (*2nd*)] ést K. oblitus] oblîtus M. orationem] orationes CDL, M: *orig.* oratiônem: m *deleted by subscript dot,* ł s *interl. in later hand: cf. Weber MSS* T^{1}PQUVX moz.

LTu: Quoniam] quoniam βνςτ*. orationem] orationes ν: *cf. Weber MSS* T^{1}PQUVX moz.

GAg: memoratus] recordatus FGIJK, H: *eras. above word, perhaps of gloss.* et] *om.* FGHIJK. orationem] clamorem FGHIJK.

GAu: memoratus] recordatus δεζθιλμξοπρστυφχψ. et] *om.* δεζθιλμξοπρστυφχψ. orationem] clamorem δεζθιλμξοπρστυφχψ.

14

Miserere		mildsa *A*BH*K, miltsa J, gemyltsa C, gemiltsa DFI, geMiltse $E^{2/x}$*, gemiltsa ðu G (*M*)
mihi*		me AB*CDE*^{2}GHJK, min FI
domine		drihten E^{2}J, dryht̄ AB, driht CFG, eala þu drihten I*
et*		⁊ ABCE^{2}
uide		geseh A, geseoh BCDFHIK, gesioh E^{2}, ⁊ geseoh GJ
humilitatem		eaðmodnisse A*, eaðmodnesse BH, eaþmodnesse D, eadmodnysse CF, eædmodnesse E^{2}*, eadmodnesse GIJK (*M*)
meam		mine ABCDE^{x}*FGHIJK
de		of ABCFGJ, fram E^{2}, be I
inimicis	ǀ	fiendum A, feondum BFH, feondum CDJK, fyondum E^{2}, minum GI (*M*)
meis	ǀ	minum ABFHJ, minum CDE^{2}K*, feondum GI

OE: mildsa (H)] sa *obscured by stain.* geMiltse ($E^{2/x}$)] ge *added in left margin.* eala þu drihten (I)] s. o *written before* eala. eaðmodnisse (A)] dn *obscured by stain.* eædmodnesse (E^{2})] *eras. after word (4 letters),* mi *visible in initial position.* mine (E^{x})] *on eras., eras. before word, traces of ascender visible.* meis (K)] ⁊ beode *incised with blunt point in large clumsy hand at bottom of fol. 16v (where* mei *is last word on leaf).*

LTg: Miserere] A: *orig.* Miserire: *2nd* i *altered to* e; Miserêre M. mihi] michi E, C: *orig.* mihi: c *interl. by corr.* humilitatem] humilitâtem M. inimicis] inimícis M.

LTu: Miserere] Misserere ϑ. mihi] michi τ*.

GAg: mihi] mei FGHIJK. et] *om.* FGHIJK.

GAu: mihi] mei δεζθιλμξοπρστυφχψ. et] *om.* δεζθιλμξοπρστυφχψ.

15

Qui	ǀ	ðu *A,* þu *BC,* þu ðe *D,* þu þe *E*^{2}GHIJK, ðu þe F (*LM*)
exaltas	ǀ	uphest A, uphefest B, upphefst C, upahefest GJ, upahefst I, ahefst DE^{x}*FHK

me mec A, me BCDE^{x}*FGHIJK
de of ABCDE^{x}*FH*IJK, æt G
portis | geatum AI, geatum BC, gatum D, gatum E^{x}*F, geate J, gatan K, gum H*, deaðes G
mortis | deaðes ABFK, deaðys C, deaþes J, þeaþes I, deofles D, deofleos H, deofles ł deoðes E^{x}*, geate G
ut ðæt A, þæt BFK, þæt CDE^{2}GHIJ
adnuntiem ic secge *ABC,* ic bodige D*E^{2}*F*GH**J, ic bodege *K,* ic bodige ł þæt ic kyþe *I*
omnes all A, ealle BCDFGHIJK, ælle E^{2}
laudes* lofu ABCDHJ, lufu G, lofe *E^{2}*, lofa K, herunga F, herunga ł lofunga I
tuas ðin A, þin BG, þine CE^{2}IK, ðine F, þina DH, þines J
in in AB, on CDE^{2}FGHIJK
portis geatum ABIJ, geatum CG, gatum DE^{2}, gatum FH, gatan K
filiae doehter A, dohter *E^{2}*, dohtor B, dohtvr *D**, dohtur *H,* dohtra *CFGJK,* dehter ł dohtra *I* (*LM*)
sion sine A, sione BGJ, syon *E^{2}*, syonys *C,* siones F, þæs muntes I

ED: filiæ (D)] filiae *Roeder.* filię (E)] filiae *Harsley.* dohtvr (D)] dohtur *Roeder.* sion (K)] Sion *Sisam.*

OE: ahefst (E^{x})] *on eras.,* a *and ascender eras. before word.* me (E^{x})] *on eras.* of (E^{x})] *on eras.* of (H)] *on eras.* (?). gatum (E^{x})] *on eras.* gum (H)] *on eras* (?). deofles ł deoðes (E^{x})] *on eras.* ic bodige (H)] g *obscured by stain.* dohtvr (D)] *orig.* dohtor: v *written above* o, *but without subscript deleting dot.*

LTg: Qui] qui ABCDELM. adnuntiem] annuntiem AEI, C: *orig.* adnuntiem: d *deleted by subscript dot, 1st* n *interl. by corr.,* G: *left leg of 1st* n *on eras.* (?), H: *1st* n *on eras.,* K: *1st* n *on eras. by corr., 2nd* n *altered by main hand from another letter.* laudes] E: ł laudes *added interl. by corr., followed by eras.: see GAg.* filiae] filiæ D; filię CEFGHKLM; filie J, I: *eras. after 2nd* i. sion] syon E, C: *orig.* sion: i *deleted by subscript dot,* y *interl. by corr.*

LTu: Qui] qui βνςτ*. de] *interl.* ε. ut] Ut ς. adnuntiem] annuntiem εζιλξπϱσςτ*τυφχ, β: *orig.* adnuntiem: *1st* n *interl.,* o: *orig.* adnuntiem: d *deleted by subscript dot,* n *interl.;* adnuntiam ϑ. filiae] filię βζιλμνξπφχ; filiæ ϑ; filie στ*τυ. sion] syon ειλξστ*τυφ.

GAg: laudes] laudationes FGHIJK, E: *see LTg.*

GAu: laudes] laudationes δεζιλμξοπϱστ*τυφχψ.

16

Exultabo ic gefio A, ic gefeo B*C,* ic blissige DHIK, ic blissie F, Ic blissige ł winsumie $E^{2/x}$*, ic wynsumige G, ic winsumige J (*M*)

in	in AB, on CDE²FGHIJK
salutari	| haelu A, hælo BCDGH, halo F, hæle JK, halwendum I, þinre E²
tuo	| ðinre AF, þinre BCDGHJK, þine I, helo E²
infixae	gefestnade A, gefæstnade *B,* gefæstnode *D,* gefæstnode *FGK,* gefestnode *H,* ongefæstnode *C,* ongefæstnod *J**, onafæstnode *I,* onfestnode *E²* (*L*)
sunt	sindon AB, syndon G, synt CD, sint E², synd FHIJK (*L*)
gentes	ðeode A, þeode C, ðeoda BF, þeoda DHIJK, þiodæ E², þ[ ] G
in	in AB, on CDE²FGHIJK
interitu	forwyrd *AB*CK, forwyrde DE²*FGHI*J* (*M*)
quem	ða A, þa BCK, þe DH, þæ E², ða ðe F, þa ðe G, þa þe J, þæt þe I
fecerunt	dydun A, dydon C, dydon dydon B, hy worhton D, hi worhton FHK, geworhton *G*J, hie geworhten E², hi geworhtun I (*M*)
in	in AB, on CDE²*FGHIJK*
laqueo	| grin A, grine BFHIK, gryne CD, þis gegrine G, gegrinum E², þisum J
isto	| ðissum A, þissum BI, þissum DE², ðyssum F, þyssum H, þisse C, þyson G, þyssan K, grine J
quem	ða A, þa BCK, þe DHI, þæ *E²,* ða ðe FG, þa þe J
occultauerunt*	gedegladon *A*, gedegledon B, gediglydon C, hy digledon D, hie digledon E²/x*, hi digledon H, hi dilogodon K, hi bediglodon ł behiddon F, hig bedygledon ł behyddun I, hi ær digle dydon GJ (*M*)
mihi*	me *C* (*ABDEM*)
conprehensus	gegripen *ABE²**F*GHJK,* gegripen D, gegripun *C,* gehæft ł gelæht I (*M*)
est	is *A*BDE²*FHK, ys C, bið G, biþ J
pes	| fot *A*BDFGHJK, fet C, hieræ E², heora I (*M*)
eorum	| heara *A,* hira B, hyra C, heora DFGHJ*K,* fot E²I

ED: infixæ (D)] infixae *Roeder.* infixę (E)] infixae *Harsley.* gentes (G)] gentes *Rosier.* compréhensus (C)] co[n]prehensus *Wildhagen.*

OE: Ic blissige ł winsumie (E²/x)] ł *written in left margin.* ongefæstnod (J)] *letter* (e?) *eras. after* d. forwyrde (E²)] *orig.* forwyrðe: ð *altered to* d, *eras. after word.* hie digledon (E²/x)] *eras. after* hie, digledon *on eras.* (*an* e *is visible after and slightly below* hie, *added by glossator to clarify* quem *below*). gegripen (E²)] ⁊ *eras. before word.* is (E²)] *eras. before word.*

LTg: Exultabo] Exultábo C; Exultâbo M: *eras. after* x. infixae] infixę BCEFGHL;

infixæ D; infixe IJK. sunt] *om.* L. interitu] intéritu M; interritu J: *small eras. after 1st* i, *perhaps shoulder of* n, *right leg of which then forms left leg of following* n; interitum AB: *cf. Weber MSS* H²Mβγ moz^c. fecerunt] fecęrunt G; fecérunt M. in (*3rd*)] In FGHIJK. quem (*2nd*)] E: e *added interl. by corr.* (q̲u̲em). occultauerunt] A: *eras. after word* (*3–4 letters*); occultauérunt M: *eras. after word: see GAg note to* mihi. mihi] michi C: *orig.* mihi: c (*malformed*) *interl. by corr.*, E: *word crossed through; om.* BD; *eras.* AM: *cf. Weber MSS* SKαβγδ moz med, *see GAg.* conprehensus] M: conpre *on eras.*; conpraehensus A; compréhensus C: *orig.* conpréhensus: *right leg added to 1st* n *by corr. to form* m; comprehensus EG, H: *orig.* conprehensus: *middle leg added to 1st* n *to form* m; compræhensus K. est] A: *written by corr.* pes] A: *written by corr.*; pés M. eorum] A: *written by corr.*, K: *on eras.*

LTu: Exultabo] Et exsultabo ϑ. infixae] infixę βειλμνοπϱφ; infixe δζξσςτ*τυ; infixæ ϑ. interitu] interitum β: *orig.* interitu: m *interl.* in (*3rd*)] In δεζϑιλμξοπϱστυφχ. conprehensus] conpraehensus βψ; comp̄hensus ζ, ε: m *altered from* n; comprehensus ιξπτ*τ, ϱ: *orig.* conprehensus: *1st* n *deleted by subscript dot,* m *interl.*; cōprehensus λφ; conpræhensus μ; conpręhensus ν; co̲m̲pręhensus ο: *orig.* conpręhensus: *1st* n *deleted by subscript dot, macron added above* o; cōp̄hensus σχ; compraehensus υ.

GAg: occultauerunt] absconderunt FGHIJK. mihi] *om.* FGHIJK; *for* ABDEM *see LTg notes to* mihi *and* occultauerunt.

GAu: occultauerunt] absconderunt δεζϑιλμξοπϱστυφχψ. mihi] *om.* δεζϑιλμξοπϱστ*τυφχψ.

17

Cognoscitur	I	oncnaweð A, oncnaweð B, oncnawyð *C,* bið oncnawen *DFK,* byð oncnawen *H,* biþ oncnawon ł ongiton *I,* oncnawen *G,* oncnawan *J,* drihtnes *E²* (*LM*)
dominus	I	dryhten B, drihtyn C, drihten K, drih̄t FGJ, dryht̄ dryht A, domes E²
iudicia	I	domas ABDFGHIJK, dom C, bið oncneæwen E²
faciens		donde ABCGJK, fre̲m̲mende DH, wyrcende FI
in		in AB, on CDE^x*FGHIJK
operibus		wercum A, weorcum BCFGI, weorcu̲m̲ DHJK, worcu̲m̲ E^x*
manuum	I	honda AB, handa CDFGHJK, hiere E², his I
suarum	I	his ADHJK, hira B, heora CF, hieora G, hændæ E², handa I
conprehensus	I	bifongen *A,* befongen B, befongyn *C,* g̲e̲gripen D, gegripen *E²***FGHJ,* gripen *K,* is *I* (*LM*)
est	I	bið ABG, byð C, is DE²*FHJ*K,* gehæft I
peccator		se synfulla ABCDHI, se synfullæ E^x*, synfulra F, synful K, gesyngad G, gesingod J (*M*)

ED: oncnawen (G)] cnawen *Rosier.* comprehensus (C)] co[n]prehensus *Wildhagen.*

OE: on (E^{x})] *on eras. in slightly lighter brown ink.* worcum (E^{x})] *on eras. in slightly lighter brown ink.* gegripen (E^{2})] *eras. before word, traces of 5 letters visible, last 2 of which are* ed. is (E^{2})] *eras. before word (3 letters?).* se synfullæ (E^{x})] *on eras.*

LTg: A: *top line of fol. 16v eras.: see LTg notes to v. 16* est pes eorum. Cognoscitur] D: *orig.* Cognoscetur: i *written over* e, E: i *on eras.;* Cognoscetur CFIJKL, H: *initial* C *faded but legible;* Cognoscêtur M: *orig.* Cognoscitur: i *altered to* ê; [ ]ognoscȩtur G: *initial* C *lost.* conprehensus] L: *small eras.* (?) *after 1st* n; conpraehensus AM; comprehensus EGIJ, C: *orig.* conprehensus: *right leg added to 1st* n *to form* m, H: *orig.* conprehensus: *middle leg added to 1st* n *to form* m; comprȩhensus K. est] ést K. peccator] peccâtor M.

LTu: Cognoscitur] Cognoscetur εζϑιλμνξοπϱσςτυφψ, χ: *orig.* Cognoscitur: i *altered to* e. conprehensus] conprȩhensus βν; conp̄hensus ϑ; conpræhensus μ; comp̄hensus υ, ε: m *altered from* n; comprehensus ζιξοτ*τ, λ: *orig.* conprehensus: *1st* n *eras., macron added,* π: *orig.* conprehensus: *1st* n *altered to* m, ϱ: *orig.* conprehensus: *1st* n *deleted by subscript dot,* m *interl.;* cōp̄hensus σχ; cōprehȩnsus φ; conpraehensus ψ.

18

Conuertantur	bioð gecerde A, beoð gecerde B, beoð gecyrryde C, beoð gecyrrede G, beoþ gecirrede J, syn gecyrred D, sin gecyrred HK, syn gecirred F, syn gecyrrede I, gewirfede ł gecherred bioð E^{2}
peccatores	ða synfullan ADF, þa synfullan BCGHIJ, þæ senfullan E^{2}*, synfulle K
in	in ABJ, on CDFGHK, to I, into E^{2}*
infernum	helle ABCDE^{2}FGHIK, on helle J (*M*)
omnes	alle A, ealle BDFGHIJK, eælle E^{2}, eallum C
gentes	ðeode A, þeoda BCDGHIJK, ðeoda F, ðioda E^{2}
quae	ða ðe *A,* þa ðe *BFJ*, þa þe *CGI,* þe *DH,* þa *K,* þæ E^{2} (*LM*)
obliuiscuntur	ofergeoteliað A, ofergeteliað B, ofergytoliað C, ofergytað DGH, ofergitað F, ofergitaþ J, bioþ ofergitende E^{2}, forgitaþ I, forgytað K (*M*)
dominum*	dryhten AB, drihtyn C, drihten E^{2}K, god FGIJ

ED: Conuertantur (G)] *Con*uertantur *Rosier.* ealle (G)] *no gloss Rosier.* quȩ (E)] quae *Harsley.*

OE: þæ senfullan (E^{2})] *eras. after* þæ (*long* s *followed by* e?), s *altered from another letter.* into (E^{2})] *letter eras. after word.*

LTg: infernum] inférnum M. quae] M: ae *on eras.;* quȩ DGL, A: ȩ *altered from* *another letter,* E: *written as* q *with cauda,* H: ę *on eras.,* F: *orig.* qui: i *altered to* ę; que K: e *on eras. by corr.;* qui BI: *cf. Weber MSS* Vαβγ moz. obliuiscuntur] obliuiscúntur M.

LTu: Conuertantur] Conuertentur ς. quae] quę βινοϱφχ; que ϑξστ*τ; quæ μ; qui ες.

GAg: dominum] deum FGHIJK.

GAu: dominum] deum δεζϑιλμξοπϱστυφχψ.

19

Quoniam	. forðon AB, forþon CJ, Forðæn E^{2}, forðan ðe F, forþan þe I, forþam G
non	nales AB, nalæs GJ, na CE^{x}*FK, ne I
in	in AB, on DE^{2}FGHIJK
finem	ende ABCDE^{2}FGHIJK (*M*)
obliuio	| ofergeotulnis A, ofergetelnes B, ofergetelnis E^{x}*, ofyrgytolnys C, ofergittolnis D, ofergitulnis H, ofergitol F, forgitelnes I, forgiten K, ne bið GJ
erit	| bið ABCK, ne bið F, byð I, ofergyttoll G*, ofergitol J
pauperum*	ðearfena *A*F, þearfena BGHJ, þearfana D, þærfena E^{x}*, þearfan CK*, þes þearfan I*
patientia	geðyld ABFGI, geþyld CDHK, geþild E^{x}*J
pauperum	ðearfena A, þearfena BGIJ, þearfyna C, ðearfana D, þearfana H, þeærfæna E^{2}*, ðearfa F, þearfan K*
non	ne ABCE^{2}GIJ, na DFHK
peribit	forweorðeð AB, forwurðyð *C,* forweorðaþ D, forweorðað F, forweorðeð GH, forwurðaþ J, forwyrð E^{2}IK (*M*)
in	in A, on BCDE^{2}FGHIJK
finem	ende ABCDE^{2}FGHIJK (*M*)

ED: forðon (A)] for ðon *Kuhn.* pauperum (G)] paupe*r*um *Rosier.* þearfena (G)] þearfen[ ] *Rosier.*

OE: na (E^{x})] *on eras.* ofergetelnis (E^{x})] *on eras.* ofergyttoll (G)] *1st* t *altered from another letter* (?). þærfena (E^{x})] *on eras.* þearfan (K)] *2 letters eras. before word, 1st of which is* p; *Sisam reads* ?pa. þes þearfan (I)] r *blotted.* geþild (E^{x})] *on eras.* þeærfæna (E^{2})] *eras. before word.*

LTg: finem (*1st*)] fînem M. pauperum (*1st*)] A: m *added by corr., trace of macron* (?) *above* u; pauperis L: *cf. Weber MSS* moz, *see GAg.* peribit] perîbit C; perîbit M. finem (*2nd*)] fînem M.

LTu: pauperum (*1st*)] pauperis ς: *cf. Weber MSS* moz, *see GAu.*

GAg: pauperum (*1st*)] pauperis FGHIJK, L: *see LTg.*

GAu: pauperum (*1st*)] pauperis δεζϑιλμξοπϱστυφχψ, ς: *see LTu.*

20

Exsurge		aris *A*B*C*DF*HJ*K, Aris *E*^{2}*, aris þu *G* (*LM*)
domine		drihtyn C, drihten E^{2}, dryht̄ AB, driħt FGHJ (*I*)
non		ne ABCE^{2}FGI, na J
praeualeat*		meg A, mæg *BC*, framige *D*, bið gestrangod FJ, swiþie ł framie E$^{2/x}$*, swiðað ne fremiað G, sy gestrangod I (*L*)
homo		mon ABDE^{2}, man FGHIJK, mann C
iudicentur		sien doemed A, sien doemde B, syn demyde C, syn demed DH, sind demed K*, syn gedemed F, syn gedemde I, bið demende G, beoð gedemed E^{x}*, beoð gedemede J
gentes		ðeode A, þeoda BCD*G*HIJK, ðeoda F, þiode E^{x}*
in		in A, on BCDE^{2}FGHIJK
conspectu	|	gesihðe ABCGH, gesihþe J, gesyhðe DF, gesyhþe K, þinre E^{2}I
tuo	|	ðinre ABF, þinre CDGHJK, gesihþe E^{2}, gesihðe I

ED: ne (G)] n[ ] *Rosier.* swiðað ne fremiað (G)] swiðað ł ne fremiað *Rosier.* þeoda (G)] þeod[ ] *Rosier.*

OE: Aris (E^{2})] *letter eras. after word.* swiþie ł framie (E$^{2/x}$)] ł *written in left margin,* se *eras. after* framie. sind demed (K)] e (?) *eras. after* d *in* sind. beoð gedemed (E^{x})] *on eras.* þiode (E^{x})] *on eras.*

LTg: Exsurge] M: s *on eras.;* Exurge AEHJL; [ ]xurge G: *initial* E *lost;* Exurde C. domine] I: s. o *written above word.* praeualeat] preualeat BDL; prȩualeat C; p̄ualeat E. gentes] gent[ ]s G.

LTu: Exsurge] EXsurge β; Exurge δειλνξπρσςτ*τυχψ; EXVRGE φ. praeualeat] prȩualeat ν; preualeat ςτ*.

GAg: praeualeat] confortetur FGHIJK.

GAu: praeualeat] confortetur δεζθιλμξοπρστυφχψ.

21

Constitue		gesete ABCFHIK, g̲esete D, Gesete þu E^{2}, gesete þu GJ
domine		drihten E^{2}G, dryht̄ AB, driħt CJ, drħt F (*I*)
legislatorem		aeeladtow A, ǽlatteow B, æelatteow C, æs lædend DE^{x}*H, ǽlædende F, ælædende K, ælædend GJ, æsellend I (*M*)
super		ofer ABE^{2}FGHJK, ofyr C, ofor I
eos		hie ABE^{2}G, hi CK, hy DH, hig FIJ
ut*		ðæt A, þæt B, þæ̲t̲ CD, þet E^{2}
sciant	|	witen ABDHK, wityn C, þæ̲t̲ witan FI, þæ̲t̲ hie witon G, þæ̲t̲ hi witon J, þiodæ E^{2}
gentes	|	ðeode A, þeoda BCDGHIJ, ðeoda F, þeda K, wytæn E^{2}

quoniam | ðette A, þætte B, þæt DI, þæt H, forþon C, forþan ðe F, forðon þe hie G, forðon hi J, þeð hyo E^{x}*
homines | men ABDE^{2}*GH*JK, menn CF, hi menn I
sunt | hie sindun A, hi syndon C, sindon B, syndon G, synt DI, sint E^{2}, synd FHJ, synd synd K

ED: legislatorem (G)] legislatorum *Rosier.* æelatteow (C)] æe latteow *Wildhagen.* ælædend (J)] æ lædend *Oess.*

OE: æs lædend (E^{x})] *added by corr. in dull black ink,* lædend *on eras.* þeð hyo (E^{x})] *on eras.* men (E^{2})] *gloss eras. before word.* men (H)] *eras.* (*of gloss?*) *after word.*

LTg: domine] I: s. o *written above word.* legislatorem] lêgislatôrem M.

LTu: Constitue] Constituae δψ; Constituę ε; Constituæ ϑ.

GAg: ut] *om.* FGHIJK.

GAu: ut] *om.* δεζϑιλμξοπϱστυφχ.

22 (1)

Ut | tohwon A*BCGJ,* Tohwæn *E^{2},* tohwy *DFH,* tohwi *IK*
quid | (*K*)
domine | drihten E^{2}, dryht̄ AB, drih́t CFGJ
recessisti | gewite ðu ABH, gewite þu CIK, gewit ðu D, gewít þu *F,* gewito þu E^{2}*, þu gewite GJ (*M*)
longe | feor ABDF*H*IJK*, feorr CG, fyor E^{2}
despicis | ðu forsist A, þu forsihst BJ, þu forsyhst *C*E^{2}*GH*, ðu forsyhst D, ðu forsihst F, þu forsixst I, þu forsyxst K (*M*)
in | in AB, on CDFGH*IJK, ob E^{2}
oportunitatibus | gemalicnissum A, gemalicnessum B, ungedafenlicnyssum C, gerecum D, gerecum F*H,* gehydelicnesse G, gehídlicnesse J, gedafenlicnessum ł on neadþearfnessum I, weorccum *K,* hiræ gehyþnesse ł on gerecvm *E^{2}*
in | in ABC, on DE^{2}FGHIJK
tribulatione | geswencednisse A, geswencednesse B, geswencydnysse C, geswince D, geswince GHIJK, gedrefednysse F, eærfodnesse E^{2} (*M*)

ED: tohwon (ABC)] to hwon *Kuhn, Brenner, Wildhagen.* Tohwæn (E)] To hwæn *Harsley.* tohwy (DF)] to hwy *Roeder, Kimmens.* tohwi (IK)] to hwi *Lindelöf, Sisam.*

OE: gewito þu (E^{2})] n *eras. after* gewito, fyo *eras. after* þu. feor (K)] fo *eras. before word.* þu forsyhst (E^{2})] u *and* syh *on eras.* þu forsyhst (H)] *small eras. before* þu. on (H) (*1st*)] *preceded by* id est. gemalicnissum (A)] *lemma misread as* in(o)portunitatibus; *see also* BC.

LTg: Ut] Vt BCDEFGHIJK. quid] K: d *altered from* t. recessisti] M: *1st* s *on eras.;* recesisti F. longe] H: *small eras. after word.* despicis] déspicis CM. oportunitatibus] opportunitatibus E, H: *1st* p *interl.*, K: *1st* p *interl. by corr.* tribulatione] tribulatiône M.

LTu: Ut] Vt ινορσφ; Et τ*τφ. recessisti] ε: *1st* s *interl.;* recensisti ζ; requisisti ϑ. despicis] dispicis βϑ. oportunitatibus] opportunitatibus ζιλφ, ξπ: *1st* p *interl.*

23 (2)

Dum	ðonne AF, þonne BGIK, þonne CDE^{x}*HJ
superbit	oferhygdgað AB, oferhydgað CG, oferhídgaþ J, ofermodgað DFK, ofermodgaþ H, ofermodgeð E^{x}*, ofermodigaþ I
impius	se arleasa AB*C*FI, se arlease E^{x}*, þe arleasa DH, arleas GJ, arleasse K
incenditur	bið inæled A*, bið onæled BDFG, bið onælyd C, byþ onæled I, biþ onæled JK*, bið anæled H, bioð onǽled E^{x}*
pauper	ðearfa AF, þearfa BCDHJ, þærfa K, þearf[ ] *G,* þarfa E^{x}*, se þearfa I
conprehenduntur	bioð bifongne *A,* beoð bifongne B, beoð befongynne *C,* hy beoð gegripene D, hi beoð gegripene F, hy biþ gegrypæne *$E^{2/x}$*,* hi beoþ gegripen *K,* hig beoð gegripene ł gelæhte *I,* beoð gegripene *GH,* beoþ gegripene *J* (*M*)
in	in AB, on CDE^{2}FGHIJK
cogitationibus* |	geðohtum AB, geþohtum CH, geþohtum D, geþeahtum FI, geþeahte K, heora G, heore J, hiræ E^{2} (*LM*)
suis* |	heara A, hira B, heora CD, geþohtum E^{2}, geþohtum G, gaþeahtum J
quas*	ða AB, þa C, þam ðe DE^{x}*, ða þe F, þa þe GJ
cogitant	hie dencað A, hie ðencað B, hi þenceað *C,* hy þohton DE^{x}*, hie þohton G, hi þohtan H, hig þohton J, ðohton F

ED: comprehenduntur (C)] co[n]prehenduntur *Wildhagen.* cōp̄henduntur (E)] comprehenduntur *Harsley.* conp̄henduntur (K)] conprehenduntur *Sisam.*

OE: þonne (E^{x})] *on eras.* ofermodgeð (E^{x})] *on eras.* se arlease (E^{x})] *on eras.* bið inæled (A)] *orig.* bið inælled: *deleting dots above and below 2nd* l. biþ onæled (K)] *letter eras. after* onæled. bioð onǽled (E^{x})] *on eras.* þarfa (E^{x})] *on eras.* hy biþ gegrypæne ($E^{2/x}$)] hy *on eras.,* ⁊ *eras. before word, with traces of letters before* (*ascender and 1 letter*) *and after* (*2 descenders*) hy. þam ðe (E^{x})] *on eras.* hy þohton (E^{x})] hy *on eras.*

LTg: impius] ímpius C. pauper] paup[ ] G. conprehenduntur] M: *orig.* conpraehenduntur: a *deleted by red deleting dot within lobe;* conpraehenduntur A; comprehenduntur GIJ, C: *orig.* conprehenduntur: *right leg added to 1st* n *by corr. to form* m, H: *orig.*

conprehenduntur: *middle leg added to 1st* n *to form* m; cōp̄henduntur E; conp̄henduntur K. cogitationibus] L: i. consiliis *and* Quibus *added above word by corr.: see GAg;* cogitatiônibus M: bus *on eras.* cogitant] cógitant C.

LTu: Dum] Cum τ*τ. conprehenduntur] β: tur *interl.;* comprehenduntur ιπτ, λ: *orig.* conprehenduntur: *1st* n *eras., macron added,* ϱ: *orig.* conprehenduntur: *1st* n *deleted by subscript dot,* m *interl.;* conpraehenduntur μψ; conprȩhenduntur νξ; cōp̄henduntur οτ*χ; cōprȩhenduntur σ; conp̄henduntur υ; comp̄henduntur φ; conp̄hendantur ϑ.

GAg: cogitationibus suis quas] consiliis quibus FGHIJK; *for* L *see LTg note to* cogitationibus.

GAu: cogitationibus suis quas] consiliis quibus δεζιλμξοπϱστυφχψ; consilis quibus ϑ.

24 (3)

Quoniam	forðon AB, forþon C, Forðæn E^2, forðan ðe F, forðam þe G, forðan þe I, forþon þe J
laudatur	bið hered ABDH, bið heryd C, bið herod *K,* bið geherod FIJ, bið gehered *E^2*, beoð gehered G (*M*)
peccator	se synfulla ABCDFHI, se synfulle E^2, synfulla K, synfulle G, synful J
in	in AB, on CDE^2FGHIJK
desideriis	lustum ABC, gewilnungum DHJ, gewylnungum F, gewilnunge G*E^2**, gewilnunga K, gewilnungum I (*M*)
animae	| sawle A*BCFIJK,* saul *D,* saule *GH,* his *E^2** (*LM*)
suae	| his AB*DFGHIJK,* hys *C,* sæule *E^2* (*L*)
et	⁊ A*B*CE^2FGIJK
qui*	se AB, se þe CDE^x*
iniqua*	ða unrehtan A, ða unryhtan B, unriht *C,* unryhtu D, unrihttu K, unrihte E^x*, se ðe unriht G, se unrihtwisa F, unrihtwis J, se unrihtdæda I
gerit*	doeð A, deð BE^x*, deþ *C*D
benedicitur	bið bið bledsad A, bið bletsad B, byð bletsod *C,* he bið gebletsod DF*H,* he byð gebletsod *E^x**, he bið gebletson K, bið gebletsad G, biþ gebletsod J, ⁊ bið gebletsod I (*LM*)

ED: forðon (A)] for ðon *Kuhn.* desiderííś (E)] desideriis *Harsley.* animæ (D)] animae *Roeder.* animȩ (E)] animae *Harsley.* suæ (D)] suae *Roeder.* suȩ (E)] suae *Harsley.* sue (I)] suae *Lindelöf.*

OE: gewilnunge (E^2)] *eras. before word from Lat. line above, Insular* g *altered to Caroline* g. his (E^2)] *eras. before and after word.* se þe (E^x)] *on eras.* unrihte (E^x)] *on eras.* deð (E^x)] *on eras.* he byð gebletsod (E^x)] *on eras.*

LTg: laudatur] E: *2nd* u *and stem of* r *on eras.,* K: *2nd* u *on eras. by corr.;* laudâtur M.

desideriis] desidériis M; desiderííś E. animae] animę BCEGHJLM; animæ D; anime FK, I: *eras. after* m. suae] suę CEFGHJKL; suæ D; sue I: *orig.* suae: a *eras.* et] Et B, *but not indicating new verse.* iniqua] C: *initial* i *interl.* gerit] gérit C. benedicitur] H: *2nd* i *on eras.;* benedicétur C; benedicetur DL, E: *orig.* benedicitur: *2nd* i *altered to* e; benedícetur M.

LTu: desideriis] desideris ϑ. animae] anime δσςτ*τ; animę εζιμνξοπϱφ; animæ ϑ. suae] suę ειvξοϱφ; suæ ϑ; sue σςτ*τ. et] ut τ*. iniqua gerit] iniqua agerit ς. benedicitur] benedicetur νςχψ.

GAg: qui] *om.* FGHIJK. iniqua] iniquus FGHIK; iniquis J. gerit] *om.* FGHIJK.

GAu: qui] *om.* δεζϑιλμξοπϱστυφχψ. iniqua] iniquus δεζιλμξοπϱστυφχψ; inicus ϑ. gerit] *om.* δεζϑιλμξοϱστυφχψ.

25 (4)

Inritauit*		bismerað *A*, bismrað *B*, bysmrað G, gebysmrað J, bysmryde *C*, hyspeð DK, geabylgode F, gremedæ E^{x}*, gehypste ł gremede I (*LM*)
dominum		drihten JK, drihcten E^{x}*, dryhτ̄ AB, driħt CG, drħt F
peccator		se synfulla ABCDFHIK, se synfullæ E^{2}*, synfull G, sinfulle J
secundum		efter A, æfter BDFGIK, æfter HJ, æftyr C, efter E^{2}
multitudinem		mengu AB, mænigeo C, menigeo G, mænigo J, mænigfaldnisse D, mænifyldnysse F, mænigfealdnisse H, manifealdnesse K, mycelnes I, micelnesse ł mænigfeldnisse E^{2}*
irae	I	eare A, yrre *CK*, eorres B, yrres *G*, graman *F*, his *D*E^{2}*HIJ* (*L*)
suae	I	his AB*FGK*, hys *C*, yrres *D*E^{2}, irres *J*, yrre *H*, yrscipes *I* (*L*)
non	I	he ne AB*C*I, ne DE^{2}FGHJ, na K (*M*)
inquiret*	I	soeceð *A*B, secyð C, secð DFHI, seceð GK, seceþ J, onsecð $E^{2/x}$* (*M*)

ED: Irritabit (C)] I[n]ritabit *Wildhagen.* irę (E)] irae *Harsley.* suæ (D)] suae *Roeder* suę (E)] suae *Harsley.* sue (I)] suae *Lindelöf.* queret (I)] quaeret *Lindelöf.* q:ret (J)] quaeret *Oess.*

OE: gremedæ (E^{x})] *on eras.* drihcten (E^{x})] *on eras.* se synfullæ (E^{2})] se *and* u *on eras., letter eras. after* synfullæ. micelnesse ł mænigfeldnisse (E^{2})] *eras.* (*ca 12 mm*) *before* micelnesse. onsecð ($E^{2/x}$)] on *on eras., letter eras. after word.*

LTg: Inritauit] Inritâbit M: *orig.* Inritâuit: u *deleted,* b *interl.;* Irritauit AB, E: u *altered from another letter;* Irritabit L, C: *orig.* Inritabit: n *altered to* r. irae] irę CDEFGHIL; ire JK. suae] suę CEFGHL; suæ D; sue JK, I: *orig.* suae: a *eras.* non] C: *interl.*, M: *written in right margin and indicated for inclusion after* suae. inquiret] A: *orig.* inquirit: *3rd* i *altered to* e; inquîret M.

LTu: Inritauit] Irritabit νς, β: *orig.* Inritabit: *1st* r *interl.;* Irritauit τ*. dominum] dominus ς. secundum] sæcundum ϑ. irae] ire εσςτ*τ; iræ ϑ; irę ιvξυφ. suae] suę βιvξυφ; suæ ϑμ; sue σςτ*τ. non] *interl.* β.

GAg: Inritauit] Exacerbauit FGIJK, H: *orig.* Exaceruauit: *1st* u *altered to* b. inquiret] quęret FG; queret HK, I: *orig.* quaeret: a *eras.;* q:ret J.

GAu: Inritauit] Exacerbauit δεζιλμξοπϱστυφχ; Exaceruauit ϑψ. inquiret] queret δεζιλξστψ; quaeret μυχ; quęret οπϱφ; q̄ret ϑ.

26 (5)

Non	I	nis ABDFHI, nys C, ne G, Ne E^{2}, na JK
est	I	is E^{2}*GJ*K*
deus		god ABCE^{2}FGIJK
in		in AB, on CDE^{x}*FGHIJK
conspectu	I	gesihðe ABE^{2}FGJ, gesihþe C, gesyhðe D, gesihþe H, ansyne K, his I
eius	I	his ABDE^{2}*FG*K,* hys C, is J, gesihðe I
polluuntur*	I	bioð bismiten A, beoð besmitene B*D,* beoð besmityne *C,* beoþ besmitene J, besmitene FG, [ ]esmitene I*, his E^{2} (*LM*)
(sunt)*	I	synd FJ, synt I, wégæs E^{2}, bioð G
uiae	I	wegas A*BCDFGHIJK*, bioð *E^{2}* (*L*)
eius*	I	his ABFGIJK, hys C, besmitene E^{2}
in		in AB, on CDE^{2}FGHIJK
omni		alle A, ealle CGJ, eallan K, ealre BF, ælcere DH, ælcre I, ęghwylce E^{2}
tempore		tid A, tide BCDFGHIJ, tyde E^{2}, tidan K (*M*)
Auferuntur		bioð afirred A, beoð afyrryd C, beoð afyrred DHK, bioð afyrred E$^{2/x}$*, bið afirde B, bioð afýrrede *G,* beoþ afirrede J, beoð ofyrsede F, syn afyrsude I (*M*)
iudicia		domas ABCD*G*HIJK, domæs E^{2}*, dom F
tua		ðine A, þine BCDGHIJK, þíne E^{x}*, ðin F
a		from A, from BC, fram FGJK, fram I, of DE^{2}*, on H (*M*)
facie		onsiene *A*B, ansyne *C*DE^{x}*GHIK, ansine FJ
eius		his ABE^{x}*FGIJ*K,* hys C
omnium		allra A, eallra C, ealra BDFGHIJ, ælre E^{2}, eallan K
inimicorum	I	fienda A, feonda BCDFHIJ, feonde E^{2}, feondan K, his G (*M*)
suorum	I	his ADE^{2}HI, hys C, hira B, heora FJK, feonda G (*M*)
dominabitur		waldeð AB, wealdyð C, he wylt D, be wylt H, he wælt E^{2}, he gewylt I, anweald F, ongewealde G, gewildeþ J, he rixsað K (*M*)

ED: inquintae (I)] inquinatae *Lindelöf.* [ ]esmitene (I)] besmitene *Lindelöf.* uiæ (D)] uiae *Roeder.* uię (E)] uiae *Harsley.* uie (I)] uiae *Lindelöf.* bioð afýrrede (G)] bioð afyrrede *Rosier.* dominabitur (C)] domínabitur *Wildhagen.* be wylt (H)] bewylt *Campbell.*

OE: is (E?)] *eras. after word.* on (Ex) (*1st*)] *on eras.* his (E2) (*1st*)] *eras. after word.* [ ]esmitene (I)] *initial letter obscured by eras. from line above: ascender visible.* bioð afyrred (E2/x)] oð *on eras.* domæs (E2)] s *on eras.* þíne (Ex)] *on eras.* of (E2)] *on eras.* ansyne (Ex)] *on eras.* his (Ex) (*3rd*)] *on eras.*

LTg: est] ést K. eius (*1st*)] eíus K. polluuntur] D: *orig.* pulluuntur: *1st* u *eras.*, o *written on eras.*; pullúuntur M: *1st* u *on eras.*; pulluuntur C; pulluntur L. uiae] uiæ BD; uię CEFGHJKL; uie I: *orig.* uiae: a *eras.* tempore] témpore M. Auferuntur] G: *left leg of* A *cropped,* M: *eras. after word.* iudicia] G: *orig.* iudicie, *with* e *interl.*: e *altered to* a *by later hand.* a] á M. facie] A: *eras. after* i; facię C. eius (*3rd*) (*2nd in Ga. MSS*)] eíus K. inimicorum] inimicôrum M. suorum] suôrum M. dominabitur] dominábitur M.

LTu: polluuntur] pulluuntur ς, ν: *2nd* l *interl.*, β: *orig.* polluuntur: *1st* u *interl.* uiae] uiæ ϑ; uię ιvξφ; uie σςτ*τ. tempore] temporę ξ. Auferuntur] Auferentur ϑ. omnium] Domnium τ*: *cf. LTu note to v. 27* Dixit. facie] faciae ψ.

GAg: polluuntur] inquinatę sunt GH; inquintae sunt I: *orig.* inquinatae sunt: *1st* a *eras.*; inquinate sunt J, F: *letter eras. after 2nd* i, K: *letter eras. after 1st* n. eius (*2nd*)] illius FGHIJK.

GAu: polluuntur] inquinatae sunt δχψ; inquinatę sunt εζιλοϱφ; inquinnatæ sunt ϑ; inquinatæ sunt μ; inquinate sunt ξπστυ. eius (*2nd*)] illius δεζϑιλμξοπϱστυφχψ.

27 (6)

Dixit	cweð A, cwæð BCG, cwæþ K, he cwæð DE2H, he cwæþ J, sæde F, he sæde I
enim	soðlice ABCFGI, soþlice DHJ, sodliche E2, witodlice K
in	in AB, on CDE2FGHIJK
corde	heortan ABCDGHIJK, heorten E2, heorte F
suo	his ABE2FGIJK, hys C
non	I ne ABCGJ, ic ne DE2FHI (*K*)
mouebor	I biom ic onstyred A, beom ic onstyred B, beôm ic onstyryd C, beom astired DE2*, beo astyrod F*, beo astyred H, beo astyrod ł awænd I, beoð onstyred G, beoð onstired J, ic na beo astyrud K* (*M*)
de*	of ABCDE2GHJ, fram FI, on K
generatione	cneorisse ABDGHJ, cneorysse C, cynrine F, cynrene K, gecynde E2*, mægðe I (*M*)

in	in ABC, on DFGHIJ, into E^2
generationem	cneorisse *ABD*GH*J*, cneorysse C, cynrine F, gecyonde *E^2**, mægðe I (*M*)
sine	butan ABCDGHI, bvtan K, buton E^{2}FJ
malo	yfle ABCI, yfele DE^2*G*HJK, yfelum F

OE: beom astired (E^2)] o *interl.* beo astyrod (F)] *orig.* be ostyred: *scribe added small* o *after* e *and altered orig.* o *to* a. ic na beo astyrud (K)] na *eras. before* ic. gecynde (E^2)] y *on eras.* gecyonde (E^2)] y *on eras., small eras. at bottom of 1st* e.

LTg: corde] cordę (?) G: *Ps 13.2* de *has similar cauda.* non] K: *eras. above word: see OE note to* ic na beo astyrud. mouebor] mouêbor M. generatione] generatiône M. generationem] A: (*deleting?*) *dot above* m; generatiône<u>m</u> M: *macron added by corr.* (?); generatione DJ, E: *orig.* generationem: m *deleted by subscript dots: cf. Weber MSS* MSKPXαγ moz^x. malo] ma[ ] G.

LTu: Dixit] ixit τ*τ: *cf. LTu note to v. 26* omnium. generationem] generatione τ*.

GAg: de] a FGHIJK.

GAu: de] a δεζθιλμξοπϱστυφχψ.

28 (7)

Cuius	ðes A, þæs BCDE^{2}GHIJK, ðæs F
os*	} muð *ABCE^2*FGH, muþ IJK (*DM*)
maledictione*	} awergednisse A, awergednesse B, awyrgednysse C, mid awyrgednesse I, of wyrgnisse DE^2, of wirignysse F, of wirignesse H, of wyrgednesse K, wyrgcwedolnesse G, wirigcwedolnesse J (*M*)
et*	} ⁊ ABCE^{2}FGIJK
amaritudine*	} bitternisse A, bityrnysse C, biternisse D, biternysse FI, biternesse BE^{2}GHJ, biternes K (*M*)
plenum*	} ful AJK, full BCDE^{2}FGHI
est*	} is ABE^{2}FGHIJK, ys C
et	⁊ ABCE^{2}FGHIJK
dolo	facne ABCI, facn FJ, facen G, of facne DE^2*H,* facnful K (*M*)
sub	under *ABD*FGHIJK, undyr *C,* Vnder *E^2* (*LM*)
lingua	tungan ABCDFGIJK, tungen E^2
eius	his ABDE^{2}FGHIJ*K,* hys C
labor	gewin ABJ, gewinn CG, geswinc DE^{2}HIK, geswingc F
et	⁊ ABCE^{2}FGHIJK
dolor	sar ACDE^{2}FHJK, sár BG, sarnes I

ED: ós (CE)] [h]ós *Wildhagen;* os *Harsley.* ős (A)] os *Kuhn.*

LTg: os] ős A; ós BDEM, C: *orig.* hós: h *eras.* maledictione] maledictiône M. amaritudine] ámaritudine M. dolo] H: *followed by small eras.;* dólo M. sub] Sub ABCDELM. eius] eíus K.

LTu: Cuius] Quius τ. os] *interl.* β. sub] Sub βνςτ*. eius] ęius ξ.

GAg: os maledictione et amaritudine plenum est] maledictione os plenum est et amaritudine FGHIJ; maledictione ós plenum est et amaritudine K: est *on eras. of orig. punct.*

GAu: os maledictione et amaritudine plenum est] maledictione os plenum est et amaritudine δεζϑιλμξοπρστυφχψ.

29 (8)

Sedet	siteð *AB*G, sityð *C,* sitteþ JK, he siteð *DE*^{2}H, he sittet F*, he sit I (*LM*)
in	in AB, on CDE^{2}FGHJK, mid I
insidiis	searwum AB*E*^{2}F, searwum C*D*K, searwvm H, searwungum I, sirwungum J, settungum G
cum	mid ABCDE^2*FGHIJ*K*
diuitibus	ðæm weoligum A, þæm welgum B, þam welegum C, welegum DK, welegum E^{2}G, weligum F, weligum ł ricum I, welum HJ (*M*)
in	in AB, on CDE^{2}FGHIJK
occultis	degulnissum A, deagelnessum B, digolnysse C, digelnissum DH, digelnyssum F, digolnessum J, digelnesse E^{2}G, diglum I, digole K
ut	det A, þæt CDHI, þæt FK, þætte B, þætte G, þæt þe J, þeð E^2
interficiat	he ofsle A, he ofslea BCDE^2*F*HI, ofslea *K,* ofslyhð G, ofslihþ *J*
innocentem	ðone unscyldgan A, þone unscyldgan B, þone unscyldigan C, unscyldigne DE^{2}FGH, unscildigne J, unscyldige K, þane unscildigne I

ED: sidiis (D)] (in)sidiis *Roeder* insidíís (E)] insidiis *Harsley.* searwvm (H)] searwum *Campbell.* diuitibus (BE)] dıVıtıbus *Brenner, Harsley.*

OE: he sittet (F)] *as* he sitt& (*& influenced by lemma?*). mid (E^2)] *orig.* mið: ð *altered to* d.

LTg: Sedet] sedet BCDELM, A: *orig.* sedit: i *altered to* e. insidiis] insidíís E; sidiis D. cum] K: m *on eras. by corr.* diuitibus] diuítibus M. interficiat] FJ: at *on eras.,* K: *2nd* t *altered from* d *by corr.*

LTu: Sedet] sedet βντ*; *om.* ς. insidiis] insedis ϑ. in (*2nd*)] *eras.* δ: *cf. Weber MS* M. occultis] ε: *1st* c *interl.;* ocultis ϑς.

30 (9)

Oculi	egan AH, eagan BCDFGI, Eagan E^2, eagon J, gan K
eius	his AB*C*E^{2}FGHIJ*K*
in	in AB, on CDE^{2}FGHIJK
pauperem	ðearfan AFI, þearfan BCDGHJK, þærfen E^2
respiciunt	gelociað ABC, lociað G, lociaþ J, beseoþ D, beseoð E^{2}HK, beseoh F, beseoð ł behealdaþ I
insidiatur	setað A, sætað B, settað C, he syrwð DE^{2}FHK, he syrwaþ I, serwaþ J, syrwað ł sætað G* (*M*)
in	in AB, on CDE^{2}FGIJK
occulto*	degulnisse A, deagolnesse B, digylnysse *C,* dygelnisse D, digelnisse *E^2**, digelnysse F, dygelnesse I, digolnesse K, diglum GJ (*L*)
sicut*	swe swe A, swa swa BCDE^{2}FJ, swa G, swylce I, ealswa K
leo	lea A, leo BDE^{2}FGIJK, lyo *C*
in	in AB, on CDE^{2}FGIJK
cubili*	| bedcleofan AB, incleofe DE^2, scræfe FK*, resthuse G, his CIJ
suo*	| his A*BE^{2}GK, hyre F, gebedclyfan C, resthuse J, scræfe I (*L*)
Insidiatur	setað A, sætað B, settað C, he syrwð DE^{2}FHK, he syrwað I, sirwað J, syrwað ł sætað G
ut	þæt AGH, þæt CDE^{2}FIJK, þætte B
rapiat	he geræafie A, he gereafige B, he gereafige C, he reafige G*K,* he reafaþ J, he gripe DF, he grípe E^2, gripe H, he gelæcce I
pauperem	ðearfan ABD, þearfan FHJK, ðearfen E^2*, [ ]earfan G*, þone þearfan C, þane þearfan ł wreccan I (*M*)
rapere	gereafian ABC, gegripan D, gegripan FH, gegripen E^2, to gegrip[ ] I*, gripe K, strude *G,* strúde J
pauperem	ðearfan A, þearfan BCDGHIJK, þearfen E^2, ðeafan F
dum	ðonne AF, þonne BG, þonne CDHJK, þanne E^2, þænne I (*L*)
abstrahit*	he atið *A,* he atihð *B,* he atygð *C,* he atyhð K, he hine framatyhð *D**, he hine fram tyþ H, he hine framatyht *E^2,* he framatihð F*, tihð G, tihþ J, he wiðtihð I (*L*)
eum	hine ABCDE^{2}FGHIJK

ED: swa swa (J)] swaswa *Oess.* syrwað ł sætað (G) (*2nd*)] syrwað ł sæteð *Rosier.* [ ]earfan (G)] þearfan *Rosier.* strude (G)] scrud[ ] *Rosier.* þearfan (G)] þearf[ ] *Rosier.* attrahit (C)] a[d]trahit *Wildhagen.* he hine fra<u>m</u>atyhð (D)] *see Sisam §109.* he hine framatyht (E)] he hine fram atyht *Harsley.*

OE: syrwað ł sætað (G) (*1st*)] ł sætað *added in diff.* (?) *hand.* digelnisse (E2)] digel *on eras. from Lat. line below.* scræfe (K)] r *interl.* his (A)] i *written below* h. ðearfen (E2)] *eras. before word.* [ ]earfan (G)] *ascender visible in initial position.* to gegrip[ ] (I)] *Lindelöf notes hole in leaf after* p; *MS too tightly bound to confirm.* he framatihð (F)] *eras. after* he.

LTg: eius] eíus K; eus C. insidiatur (*1st*)] insidiâtur M. occulto] E: oc *on eras.*, L: abscondito *added above word by corr.: see GAg;* occultis C: *cf. Weber MSS* moz^x med. leo] léo C. suo] sua L: *orig.* suo: o *altered to* a *by corr.: see GAg.* rapiat] rapiad K. rapere] rape[ ] G. pauperem (*2nd*)] *Ps 9 ends here in* M. dum] L: *eras. after word.* abstrahit] abstrahet B, A: *orig.* abstrahit: i *altered to* e; adtrahit D; attrahit L, C: *1st* t *on eras. by corr.*, E: ł abstrahet *written by corr. to right of column and signaled for notice: cf. Weber MSS* α*δ med moz^c, *see GAg.*

LTu: occulto] oculto ς. abstrahit] β: *orig.* adstrahit: b *interl.;* attrahit ντ*; adtrahit ς: *cf. Weber MSS* α*δ med moz^c.

GAg: occulto] abscondito FGHIJK, L: *see LTg.* sicut] quasi FGHIJK. cubili] spelunca FGHIJK. suo] sua FGHIJK, L: *see LTg.* abstrahit] áttrahit G; attrahit IK, H: *1st* t *on eras.;* attrait J: *see LTg.*

GAu: occulto] abscondito δεζϑιλμξοπϱτυφχψ, σ: *written by corr. along with preceding* in. sicut] quasi δεζϑιλμξοπϱστυφχψ. cubili] spelunca δεζιλμξοπϱστυφχψ; speloncа ϑ. suo] sua δεζϑιλμξοπϱστυφχψ. abstrahit] attrahit ιλξπϱστυφχ, ε: h (?) *interl.*, ο: *1st* t *altered from* d; attragit ζ; atrachit ϑ; adtrahit δμψ.

31 (10)

In	in *AB*, on *CDE*2FGHIJK̇ (*L*)
laqueo	ǀ gerene A, gryne BCF, grine GIJK, grene E2, his DH
suo	ǀ his ABE2FGIJK, hys C, grine D, grine his H
humiliabit	geeaðmodað *ABC*, he geeadmet I, eadmedde *K*, g̲enyþrað D, genyþrað E2, genyþerað F, geniþrað H, gehyneð G, gehineþ J
eum	hine ABĊDE2FGHIJK
inclinabit	onhęldeð *A*, onhyldyð *C*, onhyldeð G, onhildeþ J, inheldeð B, he onhyldeð DFK, he onhildeþ *H*, he onheldeð E2, he ahyldeð I
se	hine A*B*DE2FGIJK, hyne C
et	⁊ ABCDE2FGHIJK

cadet — falleð AB, feallyð C, fealleð GK, fealleþ J, he fylð I*, gehreoseþ D, gehreoseð E^2, gehreowseþ H, gereoseð F
dum* — ðonne A, þonne BFK, þonne CD*E*^{2}H*J*, þone G, þænne I
dominabitur* — he waldeð AB, he waldyð C, he wealdeþ D, he wealdeð E^{2}FK, anwaldað G, anwealdaþ J, wyldende I
(fuerit)* — bið G, biþ J, he bið I
pauperi* — ðearfan A, þearfan BC, þam ðearfan D, þam ðearfen E^2, þam þearfan GJK, ða ðearfan F, þane ðearfan I

ED: grine (G)] grin[ ] *Rosier.* humiliauit (B)] humiliavit *Brenner.* inclinabit (C)] inclina[u]it *Wildhagen.* hine (G) (*2nd*)] h[ ]ne *Rosier.*

OE: he fylð (I)] he *on eras.*

LTg: In] in ABCDEL. humiliabit] A: b *on eras.*, K: *traces of eras. evident at bottom of bowl of* b; humiliauit BC. inclinabit] A: b *on eras.*, C: *orig.* inclinauit: u *altered to* b *by corr.*, H: *orig.* inclinauit: u *altered to* b. se] sé B. dum] E: d *on eras.*, J: *orig.* cum: c *altered to* d: *see GAg.*

LTu: In] in βντ*. humiliabit] humiliauit σς. inclinabit] inclinauit ς.

GAg: dum] cum FGHIK; *for* J *see LTg.* dominabitur] dominatus fuerit FHIJK; dominatus fuęrit G. pauperi] pauperum FGHIJK.

GAu: dum] cum δεζιλμξοπρστυφχψ. dominabitur] dominatus fuerit δεζϑιλμξοπρστυφχψ. pauperi] pauperum δεζϑιλμξοπρστυφχψ.

32 (11)

Dixit — cweð A, cwæð BC*G*, he cwæð DE^{2}H, he cwæþ JK, sæde F, he sæde I
enim — soðlice ABCE^{2}FGHI, soþlice J, witodlice K
in — in AB, on CDE^{2}FGHIJK
corde | heortan BCDFGHIJK, heorten E^2, his A
suo | his BE^{2}FGHIJK, hys C, heortan A
oblitus — ofergeotul A, ofergitul B*, ofyrgyttul *C*, ofergitol FJ, ofergytol G, oferget DH, ofergeten E^2, forgiten I, forgyten K
est — is ABE^{2}FGIJ*K*, ys C
deus — god ABCE^{2}FGIJK (*H*)
auertit — forcerreð A, forcirreð B, he fromcyrryð C, he acyrde DE^{2}FH*K*, he acyrð I, onweg acyrreð G, aweg cirreð J
faciem | onsiene A, onsine B, ansyne CDE^2*FHK, ansine J, his GI
suam | his ABFJK, hys C, hise E^2, ansyne GI
ne | ðæt he ne A, þæt he ne B, þæt he ne CI, na K, þylæs DG, þiles E^2, þelæs F, þilæs HJ

uideat	I gese A, geseo BIK, ge̲seo C, he geseo DE^{2}FGHJ
usque*	oð ABC, oþ D, oðð E^{2}
in	on DE^{2}FIK, oð GH, oþ J
finem	ende ABCDE^{2}FGHIJK

ED: [ ]ixit (G)] *Dixit Rosier.*

OE: ofergitul (B)] er *obscured by stain but visible.* ansyne (E^{2})] a *malformed, possibly altered from* o.

LTg: Dixit] [ ]ixit G: *initial* D *lost.* oblitus] oblítus C. est] ést K. deus] H: *followed by small eras.* auertit] K: a *written in left margin by main hand.*

LTu: uideat] uidiat ϑ.

GAg: usque] *om.* FGHIJK.

GAu: usque] *om.* δεζϑιλμξοπϱστυφχψ.

33 (12)

Exsurge	aris *A*B*C*F*G*I*J*K, Aris *E*^{2} (*HL*)
domine	dryhten B, drihtyn C, drihten E^{2}K, dryht̄ A, drih́t FGJ (*I*)
deus	god ABCE^{2}FGJK
meus*	min ABCE^{2}
et*	⁊ ABCE^{2}J
exaltetur	sie upahefen A, sie upahæfen B, sy uppahafyn C, sy upahefen DH, sy upahauen E^{2}, sy upahafen FIJ, sie upahafen G, si ahafen K
manus	hond AB, hand CDE^{2}FHK, handa GJ, hand ł miht I
tua	ðin AF, þin BCE^{2}IJK, þine G
ne	ne ABCDE^{2}*FHI, na K, þylæs G, þilæs J
obliuiscaris	ofergeotela ðu A*, ofergeotola ðu B, ofergytola þu C, ofergyt þu D, ofergyt ðu H, ofergit þu E^{2}, ofergit ðu F, ðu ofergytelice G, þu ofergitol si J*, forgit ðu I, forgyt *K*
pauperum	ðearfena A, þearfena BGIJ, þeaŕfana DH, þærfene E^{2}, þearfan CFK
in*	in AB, on CDE^{2}
finem*	ende ABCDE^{2}

ED: ðu ofergytelice (G)] þu ofergytelice *Rosier.*

OE: ne (E^{2})] *small eras. before word.* ofergeotela ðu (A)] t *malformed.* þu ofergitol si (J)] t *altered from* l.

LTg: Exsurge] Exurge AEGHJL, C: *bowl of* g *slightly malformed.* domine] I: s. o *written above word.* obliuiscaris] K: a *on eras.*

LTu: Exsurge] Exurge βδειvξπρσςτ*τυφχ. deus] ϑ: *interl.* in finem] σ: *underdotted to indicate deletion: see GAu.*

GAg: meus] *om.* FGHIJK. et] *om.* FGHIK. in finem] *om.* FGHIJK.

GAu: meus] *om.* δεζϑιλμξοπρστυφχ. et] *om.* δζιλμξοπρστυφχψ. in finem] *om.* δεζϑιλμξοπρτυφχψ, σ: *see LTu.*

34 (13)

Propter		forðon ABG, forþon CJ, forðan F, fore DH, Fore E^2*, for K, forhwan I
quid		hwæt CDGHK, hwet E^2*
inritauit		bismirað *A,* bismrað *B,* bysmrað *CG,* bismraþ *J,* bysmrade D*H,* bismrade *E^2,* bysmarade *F,* bysmrede *K,* gremede *I* (*L*)
impius		se arleasa ABCDHI, se árleasa F, se arlease E^2*, ðe arleasa K, arleas GJ (*L*)
dominum*		dryhten AB, drihtyn C, drihtne *E^2**, drihte K, driħt J, god FGI
dixit		cwæð AB, cwæþ CJ, cwyþ DK, cwyð H, cweð E^2, he cwæð I, sæde FG
enim		soðlice ABCE^{2}FGI, soþlice DHJ, witodlice K
in		in AB, on CDE^{2}FGHIJK
corde	|	heortan ABCDFGHJK, his E^{2}I
suo	|	his ABCDGHJK, hys F, heortæn E^2, heortan I
non	|	ne ABCE^{2}FGJ, na K, he ne I
requiret	|	soeceð *A*B, secyð C, secaþ F, seceð G, seceþ J, secð K, secð ł myngað DH, secð ł myngeð E^2, gesecð I
deus*		god ABCE^2

ED: forðon (A)] for ðon *Kuhn.*

OE: Fore (E^2)] e *on eras.* hwet (E^2)] hw *on eras.* se arlease (E^2)] *on eras.* drihtne (E^2)] t *interl.*

LTg: inritauit] irritauit ABGHIJKL, E: uit *on eras. by corr.,* F: *1st* r *slightly malformed, perhaps by eras.;* irritabit C. impius] inpius L. dominum] E: n *on eras.* requiret] A: *orig.* requirit: *2nd* i *altered from* e.

LTu: inritauit] irritauit δεζιλvξοπρσςτ*τυφχψ, ϑ: *1st* r *interl.* requiret] requirit β.

GAg: dominum] deum FGIJK, H: *followed by eras., new punct. on eras.* deus] *om.* FGHIJK.

GAu: dominum] deum δεζϑιλμξπρστυφχψ. deus] *om.* δεζϑιλμξοπρστυφχψ.

35 (14)

Uides	ðu gesist A, þu gesihst *B*H, ðu gesyhst C*D*, þu gesyhst *E^x**, þu gesyhsð *G,* þu gesyxt K, gesyhst *F*, geseah *J,* þu gesihst ł geseoh þu *I*
quoniam	ðætte A, þætte B, þæt DH, þeð E^2, forþon C, forðon GJ, forðan IK, forþon þe F
tu	ðu ABD, þu CE^2FHK
laborem	gewin ABJ, gewinn CG, geswinc DE^x*FHIK
et	⁊ ABCDE^x*FGHIJK
dolorem	sar ACDE^x*GHJK, sár BF, sarnessa I
consideras	ðu sceawas A, þu sceawas BJ, þu sceawast CG, besceawast DH, besceawest E^x*, beceawast F, bescæwast K, þu besceawast I
ut	ðæt A, þæt B, þæt CDE^x*FGHIJK
tradas	ðu selle ADE^x*, þu selle B, þu sylle CFHK, þu sylest G, þu sillest J, þu belæwst I
eos	hie ABCG, hy DE^x*FH, hi IK, his J
in	in AB, on CDE^x*FGHIJK
manibus*	honda *AB,* handa CK, hondum D, handum FGH, handum E^x*J, handan I (*L*)
tuis*	ðine *A,* þine *B*C, þinum D*E^x*J,* ðinum F, þinum GHI, þinan K (*L*)
Tibi	ðe *AB*FG, þe *CDE^x**HIJK (*L*)
enim*	soðlice ABCE^x*
derclictus	forlen A, forlæten BGJ, forlætyn C, læfed DE^x*FH*K,* gelæfed ł forlæten I*
est	is ABE^x*FGHIJ*K,* ys C
pauper	ðearfa A, þearfa BCDFGHJ, se þearfa I, þearfene E^x*, þeafan K
pupillo*	feadurleasum A, fæderleasum BC, steopcilde DE^x*FI, steopcild K, steopcildum G, steopcildum J
tu	ðu AG, þu BCDE^2FHIJK
eris	bist ABDE^2GJ, byst HI*K,* bitst F, eart C
adiutor	fultum ABCF, fultum ł gefylsta I*, gefylsta DH, gefylst *K,* fultumiende E^2, gefultumiend GJ

ED: steopcilde (E)] steopcild*e Harsley.*

OE: þu gesyhst (E^x)] *on eras.* geswinc (E^x)] *on eras.* ⁊ (E^x)] *on eras.* sar (E^x)] *on eras.* besceawest (E^x)] *on eras.* þæt (E^x)] *on eras.* ðu selle (E^x)] *on eras.* hy (E^x)]

on eras. on (E^{x})] *on eras.* handum (E^{x})] *on eras.* þinum (E^{x})] *on eras.* þe (E^{x})] *on eras.* soðlice (E^{x})] *on eras. by corr.* læfed (E^{x})] *on eras.* gelæfed ł forlæten (I)] ł forlæten *added in right margin by glossator.* is (E^{x})] *on eras.* þearfene (E^{x})] *on eras.* steopcilde (E^{x})] *on eras., orig.* steopcildum: um *eras.*, e *added in ligature with* d. fultum ł gefylsta (I)] e *in* gefylsta *'squeezed in' between* gf.

LTg: Uides] Vides BDEIJ; [ ]ides G: *initial* V *lost;* vides F: *orig.* Tides: *minuscule* v *written after* T *in another hand.* manibus] L: manus *added above word by corr.*, E: ł nus *added interl. by corr. above* (ma/)nibus; manus AB: *cf. Weber MSS* αβ med, *see GAg.* tuis] L: tuas *added above word by corr.;* tuas AB, E: *orig.* tuis: i *deleted by 2 light strokes on either side,* a *interl.: cf. Weber MSS* αβ med, *see GAg;* suas J. Tibi] tibi ABCDEL. derelictus] K: *eras. after word.* est] ést K. eris] K: i *altered from another letter* (e?). adiutor] ádiutor K.

LTu: Uides] Vides ινορστ*τυφ; Uidens β. dolorem] dolorum ς. tuis] tuas β: *orig.* tuis: a *interl.* Tibi] tibi βνςτ*; Tibi domine ρ. eris] eras θμ.

GAg: manibus] manus FGHIJK, ABEL: *see LTg.* tuis] tuas FGHIK, ABEL: *see LTg.* enim] *om.* FGHIJK. pupillo] orphano FGHIJ; orfano K.

GAu: manibus tuis] manus tuas δεζθιλμξοπρστυφχψ. enim] *om.* δεζθιλμξοπρστυφχψ. pupillo] orfano δζθμοπρχψ; orphano ειλξστυφ.

36 (15)

Contere		forðræst A, forþræst B*CJ*, þu forþræstest G, þu forbrytest *DE*^{2}***H*K, þu forbryt F, forbrec ł tobryt I*
brachium	|	earm *A*BCDFGHJK, earm ł anweald I, þes firenfullæs E^{2}*
peccatoris	|	ðes synfullan A, þæs synfullan BCI, synfulles DFH*JK,* synfulra G, eærm E^{2}
et		⁊ ABCE^{2}FGHIJK
maligni		ðes awergdan A, þæs awergdan B, þæs awyrgydon C, þæs awirgedan I, awyrgedes DE^{2}*GK, awyrgydes H, awirigdes J, awirgedan F
requiretur*		bið soht ABDE^{2}HK, biþ soht J, byð asoht C, byþ gesoht F, bið gesoht G, byð gesoht I (*L*)
delictum*		scyld ABCDG, scild E^{x}*J, synne F, syn I, synfulles K (*L*)
eius*		his ABCDE^{x}*GIJK, hys F
(et)*		⁊ FGHIJK
nec*	|	ne ABCDE^{x}*GJ, na FHK, he ne I
inuenietur	|	bið gemoeted A, bið gemeted B*G,* bið gemetyd *C,* biþ gemeted J, he met bið D, he meted biþ *H,* gemet biþ F, byð gemet I, bið funden K, onfunden bioð E^{x}**

ED: Cóntere (H)] Contere *Campbell.*

OE: þu forbrytest (E^{2})] *on eras.* (?). forbrec ł tobryt (I)] forbrec ł *added in left margin by glossator.* þes firenfullæs (E^{2})] s *on eras.* awyrgedes (E^{2})] y *altered from* r, des *on eras.* scild (E^{x})] *on eras.* his (E^{x})] *on eras.* ne (E^{x})] *on eras.* onfunden bioð (E^{x})] *on eras.*

LTg: Contere] Cóntere CH; [ ]ontere J: *initial letter wanting;* Conteris D, E: is *on eras. by corr.* brachium] A: *eras. after* a. peccatoris] J: i *on eras.,* K: *orig.* peccatores: *2nd* e *altered to* i. requiretur] requeretur L: *orig.* requiretur: i *altered to* e *by corr.* delictum] L: peccatum *added above word by corr.: see GAg.* inuenietur] inueniétur C; inuenięţur H; inuenięţ[ ] G.

LTu: Contere] Conteris τ*.

GAg: requiretur] quęretur FG; queretur HJK; quaeretur I. delictum] peccatum FGHIJK, L: *see LTg.* eius] illius et FGHIK; illis et J: s *altered from another letter, eras. after* illis. nec] non FGHIJK.

GAu: requiretur] queretur ζιξστ; quaeretur δεπυψ; quęretur λμορφ; q̄retur ϑ; quæretur χ. delictum] peccatum δεζϑιλμξοπρστυφχψ. eius] illius et δεζϑιλμξοπρστυφχψ. nec] non δεζϑιλμξοπρστυφχψ.

37 (16)

Regnauit*	} |	ricsað *AB*C*G*, ryhsað *D*F, rixað HI, rixaþ J, rixsaþ K, drihten *E*^{2} (*L*)
dominus*	} |	dryhten B, drihtyn C, dryh̄t A, driht̄ FG, drih̄ J, rixæþ E^{2}
in		in AB, on CDE^{2}FGHIJK
aeternum		ecnisse A*B,* ecnysse *CFI,* ecnesse *DGHJK,* eþcnesse *E*^{2} (*L*)
et		⁊ ABCE^{2}FGIJK
in		in AB, on CE^{2}FGIJK
saeculum		weoruld A, weorold *B,* woruld *C,* worulde *F,* worulda *G**, worlda *J,* worlde *I,* worolde *K,* worldæ *E*^{2} (*DHL*)
saeculi		weorulde *A,* weorolde *B,* worulde *C,* aworuld *F,* woruld *G,* world *J,* worlde *E*^{2}I* (*DHKL*)
peribitis	|	forweorðað AB, forweorðeð G, forwurðaþ *C,* forwurðeþ J, forwyrþað K, forweorðaþ ge D, forweorðað ge H, ge forweorðaþ F, ge forwurðaþ I, þiodæ E^{2}
gentes	|	ðeode A, þeoda BCDFGHJK, ðeoda *I,* forweorðæþ E^{2}
de		of ABCDE^{2}*FHIK, on GJ
terra	|	eorðan ABCDHIJ, eorþan FK, his E^{2}G
eius*	|	his ABDFIJK, hys C, eorþæn E^{2}, eorðan G (*L*)

ED: [ ]ominus (G)] *Dominus Rosier.* in : in (A)] *Kuhn prints text and gloss twice.*

æternum (D)] aeternum *Roeder.* ęternum (E)] aeternum *Harsley.* eternum (I)] aeternum *Lindelöf.* sęculum (G)] seculum *Rosier.* sclm (DEFIJK)] saeculum *Roeder, Lindelöf;* seculum *Harsley, Kimmens;* seculum *Oess;* sæculum *Sisam.* scli (DFIJK)] saeculi *Roeder, Lindelöf;* seculi *Kimmens, Oess;* sæculi *Sisam.* worulda woruld (G)] woruld woruld *Rosier.*

OE: worulda (G)] a *written on next line before* woruld. worlde (I) (*2nd*)] e *somewhat faint.* of (E^{2})] f *on eras., eras. after word.*

LTg: Regnauit] L: Dominus regnabit *added above by corr.: see GAg;* Regnabit CDE, A: b *on eras.* aeternum] æternum BDK; ęternum CEFGHL; eternum J, I: *orig.* aeternum: a *partly eras.* saeculum] sæculum B; seculum CH; sęculum G; sclm DEFIJKL. saeculi] sęculi A; sæculi B; seculi CG, E: *eras. above* (secu/)li; scli DFHIJKL. peribitis] perîbitis C. gentes] I: s. o *written above word.* eius] L: illius *added above wórd by corr.: see GAg.*

LTu: Regnauit] REgnauit β; Regnabit νςτ*. aeternum] ęternum ειν ξφ; æternum ϑ; eternum σςτ*τ. saeculum] seculum βςτ; sæculum ϑ; sęculum ιν; sclm εζλμξοπϱστ*υφχ. saeculi] seculi βζπςτ; sęculi ειν ϱ; scli ϑλμξοστ*υφχ.

GAg: Regnauit dominus] Dominus regnabit FHIJK, L: *see LTg;* [ ]ominus regnabit G. eius] illius FGHIJK, L: *see LTg.*

GAu: Regnauit dominus] Dominus regnabit δεζϑιλμξοπϱτυφχψ; Dominus regnauit σ. eius] illius δεζϑιλμξοπϱστυφχψ.

38 (17)

Desiderium — lust AB, lust oððe g̲ewilnung C, gyrninge DFH, girninge K, willum GJ, gewilnunga I, Gewillung ł gyrnigge E$^{2/x*}$

pauperum — ðearfena A, þearfena BGI, þearfyna C, þearfana DH, ðearfana F, þeærfenæ E^{2}, þearfa J, þearfan K

exaudiuit — geherde A, gehirde B, gehyrde CDFHI, gyehirde E^{2}*, gehyrende G, gehyrrende J, gehyrð K

dominus — dryhten B, drihtyn C, drihten E^{x}*K, dryht̄ A, driħt FJ, driħ G

desideria* — lustas ABC, gyrnenga D, gearcunge FGJ, gearcunga ł gegearwungnessa I , gearwunga K, gewilnunge ł gyrnenga E$^{2/x*}$ (*L*)

cordis — heortan ABCDE^{x}*FGHIJK

eorum — heara A, hira B, hyra C, heora DFGHIJK, heore E^{x}*

exaudiuit* — geherde AB, gehyrde CDFGHIK, gehirde E^{2}*J (*L*)

auris — I eare ABCDFHIJ, eara G, earan K, þin E^{2}*

tua — I ðin AF, þin BCDHIJ, þine GK, eæræ E^{2}

ED: eara (G)] ear[ ] *Rosier.* þine (G)] [ ]ne *Rosier.*

OE: Gewillung ł gyrnigge ($E^{2/x}$)] ł *written in left margin.* gyehirde (E^{2})] y *altered from* i, *eras. before word, letter eras. after* r. drihten (E^{x})] *on eras.* gewilnunge ł gyrnenga ($E^{2/x}$)] ł *written in left margin,* y *altered from* i, gyrnenga *on eras.* heortan (E^{x})] *on eras.* heore (E^{x})] *on eras.* gehirde (E^{2})] he (?) *eras. before word,* de *on eras.* þin (E^{2})] þ *altered from* h, n *altered from another letter (traces of descender and ascender visible on left leg).*

LTg: desideria] L: Preparationem *added above word by corr.: see GAg.* exaudiuit (*2nd*)] L: ex *underlined to indicate deletion: see GAg;* exaudíuit C.

LTu: ϱ: *wanting Pss 9.38–12.1.*

GAg: desideria] preparationem FHJK; (p)reparationem G: *descender of initial* p *lost;* praeparationem I; *for* L *see LTg.* exaudiuit (*2nd*)] audiuit FGHIJK, L: *see LTg.*

GAu: desideria] praeparationem δεμπυψ; preparationem ζστ; p̄parationem ϑιλοφχ; prȩparationem ξ. exaudiuit (*2nd*)] audiuit δεζϑιλμξοπστυφχψ.

39 (18)

Iudicare		doem AB, dem C, deman DG*H*JK, To demene $E^{2/x*}$, to demen F^{2*}, gedem I
pupillo		ðæm freondleasan A, þam freodleasan C, steopbearne B, steopcilde $DE^{x*}F^{2}$HI, steopcild GJ, steopcildan K
et		⁊ $ABCDE^{x*}F^{2}$GHIJK
humili		ðæm heanan A, ðæm eaðmodan B, þam eadmodum G, þan eadmcdan *C,* þam eadmodan J, eaðmodum DH, eadmodum $E^{x*}F^{2}$, eadmodan K, eaðmedum I*
ut		ðætte A, þætte B, þætte CDE^{2}H, þæt F^{2}GIJ, ⁊ K
non	|	no AC, nó B, na $DE^{2}F^{2}$HK, ne I, he ne GJ
adponat	|	tosette AB*CGJ,* geteohige ł togesette D, geteohige ł togesette E^{2*}, getiohige ł togesette *H,* togeset *K,* gesette *F^{2},* gedyrstlæce *I**
ultra		mae A, máa B, ma C, ofer þæt DF^{2}HK, ofer þet E^{2}, ofor ðæt ł [ ]ononforð I*, ofer þam G, ofer þam J
magnificare		gemicla A*C,* gemiclian BDF^{2}H, gemyclian K, gemiclien *E^{2*},* gemicclian GJ, gemiclian ł mærsian I*
se		hine $ABCDE^{2}F^{2}$GHIJK
homo		mon $ABE^{2}F^{2}$G, monn C, man JK, mann I
super		ofer $ABDE^{2}F^{2}$GHJK, ofyr C, ofor I
terram		eorðan $ABDF^{2}$GIJ, eorþan HK, eorðæn E^{2}, eordan C

ED: [ ]vdicare (H)] *Campbell writes that initial* I *is covered with tape; rather, the letter was orig. in green ink and has burned away.* eaðmedum (I)] *Lindelöf does not* *record added gloss* ⁊ ðam eadmod: *see OE.* ofor ðæt ł [ ]ononforð (I)] ofor ðæt ł heononforð *Lindelöf.* gemiclian (H)] gumiclian *Campbell.*

OE: F: *Gloss to v. 39 written in 16th-c. hand on eras.* To demene (E$^{2/x}$)] mene *on eras.* steopcilde (E^{x})] *on eras.* ⁊ (E^{x})] *on eras.* eadmodum (E^{x})] *on eras.* eaðmedum (I)] um *on eras.* (?); *at bottom of fol. 15r* ⁊ ðam eadmod (> eadmod[an]) *is written by cruder hand in light brown ink.* geteohige ł togesette (E^{2})] *2nd* g *altered from* e. gedyrstlæce (I)] *eras.* (*of gloss?*) *in right margin following word.* ofor ðæt ł [ ]ononforð (I)] ł [ ]ononforð *written in left margin; initial letters lost due to tight binding.* gemiclien (E^{2})] ⁊ *eras. before word.* gemiclian ł mærsian (I)] sian *written in right margin and indicated for inclusion.*

LTg: Iudicare] [ ]vdicare H: *initial* I *lost.* humili] húmili C. adponat] apponat FGIJK, H: *1st* p *on eras.;* appónat C. magnificare] E: *gloss eras. above* magnifi(/care); magnificáre C.

LTu: non] *interl.* σ. adponat] apponat δεζιλμνξοπστ*τυφχψ.

PSALM 10

2

In	in *AB*, on *C*DE^{2}F^{2}**G*HI*J*K*
domino	dryhtne A*B*D, drihtne *C*F^{2}HI, drihten E^{2}K, drih̄t GJ
confido	ic getreowu A, ic getreowe B, ic getruwie *C,* ic getrywe DHK, ic getryowe E^{x}*, ic getrúwie F^{2}, ic getreowige I, ic getriwe J, ic trywe G
quomodo	hu ABCE^{2}GJ, humeta DF^{2}HK, la humeta I
dicitis	cweaðað ge A, Cweðað ge B, cweðað ge CG, cweðaþ ge J, cweþe ge E^{2}, ge cweðaþ F^{2}, secgað D, segaþ K, secgað ge H, segge ge I
animae	saule *D*H,* sawle *F^{2}JK,* to sawle *BCI,* to saule *G,* to minre A, minre *E^{2}* (*L*)
meae	minre *BCDF^{2}GHI*J, mine *K,* sawle A, sæule E^{2}* (*L*)
transmigra	fer AC, feor B, aleor D*H,* aleor ł flygan E^{x}*, oferfare F^{2}, ic lære J, [ ]c lære *G,* gewit ł far I*, gewit K
in	in AB, on CDF^{2}GHIJK, ouer E^{x}*
montem	mont A, munt BCDF^{2}GHJK, munte I, dune E^{2}*
sicut	swe swe A, swa swa BCF^{2}HIJ, swa GK, swæ E^{2}
passer	spearwa ABCDF^{2}GHIJ, spearwe K, se spearwe E^{2}

ED: Cweðað ge (B)] cweðað ge *Brenner.* animę (E)] animae *Harsley.* anime (I)] animae *Lindelöf.* meæ (D)] meae *Roeder.* meę (E)] meae *Harsley.* mee (I)] meae *Lindelöf.* transmígra (H)] transmigra *Campbell.* swa swa (IJ)] swaswa *Lindelöf, Oess.*

OE: F: *gloss to Ps 10 written in 16th-c. hand on eras.* I: *psalm-title* In finem psalmus dauid *glossed as follows:* on ende sealm dauides. ic getryowe (E^{x})] *on eras.* saule (D)] u *on eras., perhaps formed from another letter.* sæule (E^{2})] *eras. after word,* s *visible initially, followed by 2 illegible letters.* aleor ł flygan (E^{x})] *on eras.* gewit ł far (I)] ł far *written in bottom margin below lemma.* ouer (E^{x})] *on eras.* dune (E^{2})] *on eras.*

LTg: In] IN ABCK; [ ]n G: *initial* I *lost.* domino] Domino B; DOMINO C. confido] CONFIDO C: *orig.* COFÍDO: n *interl. by corr.* animae] animę CDEFH; animæ BL; anime GJK, I: *orig.* animae: *2nd* a *eras.* meae] meæ BDKL; meę EF; mee G: *2nd* e *obscured by mount,* I: *orig.* meae: a *eras.;* męę H. transmigra] transmígra H; [ ]smigra G.

LTu: ϱ: *Ps 10 wanting.* In] IN βϑιλμνςτ*τφχψ. domino] DOMINO λμνςφχψ. confido] CONFIDO λμνψ; COnfido ς; CONfido χ. animae] animę εϑιμνσφ; anime ζξπςτ*τυ. meae] meę ϑινξσυφ; mee ςτ*τ; meæ χ.

3

Quoniam	forðon ABDHJ, forþon CG, forþon þe F^{2}*, Forðæn þe *E*^{2}, forðan þe I
ecce	sehde A, sehðe B, gesihðe C, on gesihðe D, on gesyhðe H, efne F^{2}GIJK, ællungæ *E*^{2}
peccatores	ða synfullan AB, þa synfullan CGI, þa sinfullan J, synfulle DK, sinfulle H, synfull F^{2}, þæ firenfullæn *E*^{2}*
tetenderunt*	ðenedon A, þenedon B, þenydon *C*, ðenydon F^{2}, aðenedon D, aþenedon GHK, aþenodon J, aþenedun ł bændon I, æþeniæþ *E*^{2} (*L*)
arcum	bogan *A*BCDF^{2}GHIJK, heræ bogæn E^{2}*
parauerunt	gearwadon A, gearwodon BGJ, gearwydon C, hy gyredon DH*, hi gyredon K, hy gyrdon F^{2}, geærwiæþ E^{2}, hi gærcodon I
sagittas	| strelas A, strælas BCGJ, flana DF^{2}HIK, hieræ E^{2}
suas	| heara A, hira B, hyra C, heora DF^{2}HIK, his GJ, flanc E^{x}*
in	in AB, on CDE^{2}F^{2}GHIJK
faretra	cocere A*E*^{x}*F^{2}, cocore BD*GHJ*, kokere *I*, coxre ł on earhfære *C*, cere *K*
ut	ðæt A, þæt BI, þæt CDF^{2}HK, þæt þe GJ, þettę E^{2}
sagittent	hie scotedon A*, hie scotoden B, hig scotodon G, hi scotodon J, hy scotigen D, hi scotigen H, hi scotien E^{2}, hy scotien F^{2}, hi sceotigen I, hi scotigent K, hi gesceotydon C
in	in AB, on CDE^{2}F^{2}GHIJK
obscuro	degelnisse A, deagolnesse B, digulnysse C, digolnysse ł on forsworcennesse I*, ðystrum D, þystrum H, þystrum K, þisternesse E^{2}, ðysternesse F^{2}, hyolstre G, heolstre J

rectos	ða rehtan A, þa ryhtan B, þa rihtan C, ryhtwise D, rihtwise HK, riht F^{2}*, on rihte I, þa rihtwisan GJ, þæ rihtæn E^{2}
corde	on heortan ADH, heortan BCF^{2}GJK, heortæn E^{2}, heortan ł ða rihtgeþancedon I

ED: forðon (A)] for ðon *Kuhn*. on g̲esyhðe (H)] ong̲esyhðe *Campbell*.

OE: forþon þe (F^{2})] *ascender of* þ *in* forþon *carries a cross-stroke.* þæ firenfullæn (E^{2})] *eras. marks* (?) *below gloss.* heræ bogæn (E^{2})] *orig.* hiræ bogæn: i *altered to* e. hy gyredon (H)] *eras. before* hy, *perhaps of punct. extending from Lat. text.* flane (E^{x})] *on eras. in lighter brown ink.* cocere (E^{x})] *on eras. in lighter brown ink.* hie scoteden (A)] d *altered from leg of* n. digolnysse ł on forsworcennesse (I)] nesse *of* forsworcennesse *written in left margin and signaled for inclusion.* riht (F^{2})] *2 descenders of original gloss visible after word.*

LTg: Quoniam] E: *on eras. in dark ink.* ecce] E: *on eras. in dark ink.* peccatores] E: *on eras. in dark ink.* tetenderunt] E: *on eras. in dark ink,* L: in *added interl. by corr.: see GAg;* tetendérunt C. arcum] A: m *added by corr.* faretra] pharetra EGIJK, H: *punct. on eras. after word;* pháretra C: *cf. Weber MSS* H* med.

LTu: Quoniam] quoniam ϑ. faretra] pharetra δεζιλμνξοπσςτ*τυφψ; fharetra β: *orig.* pharetra: p *deleted,* f *interl.*

GAg: tetenderunt] intenderunt FGHIJK, L: *see LTg.*

GAu: tetenderunt] intenderunt δεζϑιλμξοπστυφχψ.

4

Quoniam	forðon ABGJ, Forðon E^{2}, forþon C, forþon þe *F*^{2}I, forþam K
quae	ða A, þa *BCHK*, ða þe *D*, þa þe *F*^{2}*GJ*, þæ ðe *E*^{2}*, þa þingc þe I (*L*)
perfecisti	ðu gefredes A, þu gefremedes B, þu gefremydyst C, ðu dydest D, þu dydest HK, þu fulfremodost E^{2}, þu fulfremadest F^{2}, þu fulfremedyst I, þu gefremodest *G*J
destruxerunt	hie towurpun A, hie towurpon B, hi towurpon CI, towurpon *G*J, hy tobrecon DF^{2}, hy tobræcon H, hie tebrecon E^{2}, hi tobræce K
iustus	| se rehtwisa AB, se ryhtwisa D, se rihtwisa HI, se rihtwise F^{2}, rihtwis C, rihwis K, rihtwisness̲e G, rihtwisnesse J, eællungæ E^{2}
autem	| soðlice ABCGI, soþlice F^{2}J, witodlice K, se soðfestæn E$^{2/x}$*
quid	hwęt A, hwæt BCDF^{2}GHIJK, wet E^{x}*
fecit	dyde he ABCD, dydo he E^{2}, he dyde F^{2}H, dyde *G*IJK

ED: forðon (A)] for ðon *Kuhn*. quæ (D)] quae *Roeder.* quę (E)] quae *Harsley.*

que (I)] quae *Lindelöf.*

OE: þæ ðe (E^{2})] ðe *interl.* se soðfestæn (E$^{2/x}$)] se *on eras.* wet (E^{x})] *on eras., eras. after word.*

LTg: Quoniam] F: Q *faded but visible.* quae] quæ BD; quę CEGHL; quc JK, F: *orig.* quç (?): *cauda eras. by* F^{2}, I: *orig.* quae: a *eras.* perfecisti] perfęcisti G. destruxerunt] destruxęrunt G. fecit] fęcit G.

LTu: quae] quę ενξοσχ; que ιςτ*τ; quæ μ; quę tu ϑ; quęm ζ; quem λφ. destruxerunt] distruxerunt ϑμ.

5

Dominus		dryhten B, drihtyn C, drihten E^{2}K, dryht̄ A, driħt F^{2}*G*J (I*)
in		in AB, on CDE^{2}F^{2}GHIJK
templo	|	temple ABDF^{2}GHIJK, temple C, his E^{2}
sancto		ðæm halgan A, þam halgan B, þan halgan C, þæm hælgæn E^{2}, halgum D, halgum H, halgan F^{2}GI, haligan K*, haligum J
suo	|	his ABDF^{2}GHIJ, hys C, temple E^{2}
dominus		drihten E^{2}IK, dryht̄ AB, driħt CF^{2}GJ
in		in AB, on CE^{2}F^{2}GIJK
caelo		heofene A, heofone *BE^{x}*F^{2}*, heofen̄ *G*, heofunne *C*, heofonum *IJ*, heofenan *K* (*DHL*)
sedis		seld AB, setl *CDGHIJK*, setle *E^{x}*F^{2}* (*L*)
eius		his ABDE^{x}**F*^{2}GHIJ*K*, hys C
Oculi		egan AHK, eagan BCDGI, egæn E^{2}*, eagen F^{2}, eagon J
eius		his ABE^{2}*F*^{2}GIJ*K*, hys C
in		in AB, on CDE^{x}*F^{2}GHIJK
pauperem		ðearfan A, þearfan BCDGHJK, þearfena F^{2}*, þarfena E^{x}*, þone þearfan I
respiciunt		gelociað AB, gelocigeað C, lociað G, lociaþ J, bescoð DE^{x}*F^{2}H, beseoþ K, beseoþ ł behealdað I
palpebrae		bregas A, bræwas *BCF^{2}GHIJK*, brewas *D*, bræwes *E^{x}** (*L*)
eius		his ABF^{2}GIJ*K*, hys C, hise E^{x}*
interrogant		frignað *A*B, frinað C, ahsiað DE^{x}*, acxiað G, acsiað H, axsiað *K*, axiaþ J, axiaþ ł befrinaþ I, alisiaþ F^{2}
filios	|	bearn ABCDGHIJK, mænne E^{2}, sunu F^{2}
hominum	|	monna *A*B, manna CDGHIJK, mænna F^{2}*, sunu ł bearn E^{2}

ED: cælo (D)] caelo *Roeder.* cęlo (E)] caelo *Harsley.* palpebrę (E)] palpebrae *Harsley.* pálpebrę (H)] palpebrę *Campbell.*

OE: Dominus] I: est : is *written in left margin.* haligan (K)] *eras.* (*ca 15 mm*) *after word.*

heofone (E^{x})] *on eras.*, fo *interl.* setle (E^{x})] *on eras.* his (E^{x}) (*2nd*)] *on eras.* egæn (E^{2})] *eras. before and after word.* on (E^{x}) (*2nd*)] *on eras.* þearfena (F^{2})] *orig.* þearfana: a *altered to* e. þarfena (E^{x})] *on eras.* beseoð (E^{x})] *on eras.* bræwes (E^{x})] *on eras.* hise (E^{x})] *on eras.* ahsiað (E^{x})] *on eras.* mænna (F^{2})] *orig.* mænne: e *altered to* a.

LTg: Dominus] [ ]ominus G: *initial* D *lost.* caelo] cælo BDK; cęlo CEFGHIL. sedis] sedes CDEFGHIJL, K: *2nd* e *on eras.*: *cf. Weber MSS* M^{2}αβδ moz med. eius (*1st*)] F: *top of ascender of* s *eras. due to eras. of orig. gloss;* eíus K. eius (*2nd*)] F: *top of ascender of* s *eras. due to eras. of orig. gloss;* eíus K. palpebrae] palpebræ BK; palpebrę CDEFGJL; pálpebrę H. eius (*3rd*)] eíus K. interrogant] A: *orig.* interrogat: *2nd* n *interl. by corr.*, K: nt (*in ligature*) *on eras. by corr.* hominum] A: *final* m *added by corr.*

LTu: caelo] cęlo εζιλξοπσυφ; cælo ϑμ; celo ςτ*τ. sedis] δ: *orig.* sedes: *2nd* e *deleted,* i *interl.;* sedes εζιλμνξοπσςτ*τυφ, χ: *2nd* e *altered from* i. Oculi] culi τ*τ. palpebrae] palpebrę ενξπυφ; palpebre ζισςτ*τ; palpebræ ϑ.

6

<table>
<tr><td>Dominus</td><td></td><td>dryhten B, drihtyn C, Drihten E^{2}, drihten I, dryht̄ A, drih́t F^{2}GJ</td></tr>
<tr><td>interrogat</td><td></td><td>frigneð AB, frinyð C, frineð G, freniaþ J, ahsað D, acsað H, axæþ E^{2}, axsað K, axsað ł befrinð I, alisiaþ F^{2}</td></tr>
<tr><td>iustum</td><td></td><td>ðone rehtwisan A, þone ryhtwisan B, ryhtwisne D, rihtwisne CF^{2}HI, rihtwise K, rihtwisnesse GJ, þæ soþfestæn E^{2}</td></tr>
<tr><td>et</td><td></td><td>⁊ ABC$E^{2}F^{2}$GHIJK</td></tr>
<tr><td>impium</td><td></td><td>ðone arleasan A, þone arleasan B, þone arleasne I*, þæ ærleæsæn E^{2}, arleasne CDF^{2}H, arlease K, arleasnesse GJ</td></tr>
<tr><td>qui</td><td>|</td><td>se ACI, sé B, ðe D, þe HK, ð F^{2}*, se þe G, þe ðe J, soþlice E^{2}</td></tr>
<tr><td>autem</td><td>|</td><td>soðlice AB, soþlice CF^{2}HK, soþlice D, soðlice þe I, ðonne soðlice G, þonne soþlice J, þa þe E^{2}*</td></tr>
<tr><td>diligit</td><td></td><td>lufað ABCDGK, lufaþ F^{2}HIJ, lufigæþ E^{2}</td></tr>
<tr><td>iniquitatem</td><td></td><td>unrehtwisnisse A, unryhtwisnesse BD, unrihtwisnysse CI, unrihtwisnesse H, unrihtwisnes K, unrihtwisne F^{2}, unrihtnesse E^{2}, unriht GJ</td></tr>
<tr><td>odit</td><td></td><td>fiað A, feoð BC, he fioþ ł hatað $E^{2/x}$*, he hatað D, he hataþ F^{2}, he hatat H, hatað GI, hataþ J, hat K</td></tr>
<tr><td>animam</td><td>|</td><td>sawle ABCDF^{2}IJK, saule GH, his E^{2}</td></tr>
<tr><td>suam</td><td>|</td><td>his ABDF^{2}GHIJK, hys C, sæwle E^{2}</td></tr>
</table>

ED: ð (F)] ðæt *Kimmens.* ðonne soðlice (G)] þonne soðlice *Rosier.*

OE: þone arleasne (I)] þone *written above* arleasne. ð (F^{2})] *no mark to indicate expansion.* þa þe (E^{2})] *orig.* þæ þe: æ *altered to* a. he fioþ ł hatað ($E^{2/x}$)] hatað *on eras.*

LTg: odit] K: o *altered from* d. animam] A: *final* m *added by corr.* suam] A: *added by corr.*

LTu: diligit] dilegit β. odit] hodit ς.

7

Pluit*	rineð *AB*, rinyð *C*, rineþ I, rinð K, he rinð DH, He rinþ E^{2}*, he rynde F^{2}, hit rinð G, hit rinþ *J*
super	ofer ABDE^{2}F^{2}GHI*JK, ofyr C
peccatores	ða synfullan AI*, þa synfullan BCGJ, synfullan F^{2}, synfulle DHK, ðæ firen ł senfullæn E^{2}*
laqueos	giren A, gryn C*D*, grin BF^{2}HJK, grinu I, gegrine E^{2}*, gegrin G
ignis	fyres ABDF^{2}GHJK, fyr I, fyryn C, swæ fires E^{2}*
(et)*	⁊ *AJ*
sulphur	swefelrec *A*, swefles réc B, sweflenrec G, sweflenréc J, sweflðrosm DE$^{2/x}$*F^{2}, sweflþrosm H, ⁊ swefl C, ⁊ swefel I**K*
et	⁊ *A*BCE^{x}*F^{2}GHIJK
spiritus	gast ABCDF^{2}GHIJK, gæst E^{2}
procellarum	ysta ABCDH, ysta ł storm E^{2}, yst(a) ł storma I*, storm F^{2}, storma GJ
pars	dael A, dæl B*C*DE^{2}F^{2}GHIJK
calicis	calices AB, calicys *C*, calicis F^{2}, cælcis *H*, cęlos D, ceolos E^{2}, þrowung GJ, drencfætes I
eorum	heara A, hira B, hyra C, heora DF^{2}GHK, here E^{2}, heora ł heora calices I*

ED: ofer (I)] ofor *Lindelöf.* ignis (I)] ignis et *Lindelöf.* yst(a) ł storma (I)] ysta ł storma *Lindelöf.* cálicis (H)] calicis *Campbell.*

OE: He rinþ (E^{2})] e *on eras.* ofer (I)] *orig.* ofor: *2nd* o *altered to* e. ða synfullan (I)] *1st* a *interl.* ðæ firen ł senfullæn (E^{2})] ł sen *interl.* gegrine (E^{2})] *eras. before word.* swæ fires (E^{2})] *eras. after final* s. sweflðrosm (E$^{2/x}$)] ðrosm *on eras.* ⁊ swefel (I)] est : is *written in left margin.* ⁊ (E^{x})] *on eras.* yst(a) ł storma (I)] *back of 1st* a *not visible.* drencfætes heora ł heora calices (I)] ł heora calices *written in bottom margin below Lat.* calicis.

LTg: Pluit] Fluit J; Pluet ABC: *cf. Weber MSS* αβγ, *see GAg.* laqueos] laqueus D: *cf. Weber MSS* moz^{x}. ignis] ignis et A: et *added interl. by corr.: cf. Weber MSS* MKαβγδζ moz^{c}, *see GAg.* sulphur] A: phur *added by corr.*, K: et *eras. before word.* et] A: *written by corr. on eras.*, ph *eras. but visible before word* (*cf.* sulphur *above*). pars] párs C. calicis] cálicis CH.

LTu: Pluit] χ: *orig.* Pluet: et *deleted by subscript dot,* it *interl.* ignis] ignis et β: *cf. Weber MSS* MKαβγδζ moz^{c}. sulphur et] χ: et *interl.*, βμ: et *om.*: *cf. Weber MSS* KT*ζ. calicis] calices π.

GAg: Pluit] Pluet I: ł it [= Pluit] *interl.*, GK: *orig.* Pluit: i *altered to* e, ABC: *see LTg.* ignis] ignis et J, A: *see LTg.*

GAu: Pluit] Pluet ελξοπσφ. ignis] ignis et δϑοψ, β: *see LTu.* sulphur] solfur ϑ.

8

Quoniam		forðon ABJ, forþon CG, forðan I, Forþon þe E^{2}, forðon þe F^{2}
iustus		rehtwis A, ryhtwis BDE^{x}*, rihtwis C*F*^{2}GHJK, se rihtwisa I
dominus		drihten E^{x}*K, dryht̄ AB, driħt CF^{2}GJ, driht̄ I
(et)*		⁊ *ABCE*^{2}GHJ (*DL*)
iustitiam*		rehtwisnisse A, ryhtwisnesse BD, rihtwisnysse C, rihtwisnesse E^{x}*F^{2}GH*J*K, rihtwisnyssa I
dilexit		lufað ABGK, lufaþ J, lufude C, he lufode DE^{x}*F^{2}, he lufude H, þe lufode I
aequitatem		rehtwisnesse A, efnesse B*GJ,* efennessa *D,* efennesse *E*^{x}**H,* efennysse *CF*^{2}*,* efnesse *K,* emnesse *I* (*L*)
uidit		gesið A, gesihð B*D*J, gesyhð GH, geseah *C*F^{2}IK, gesioþ E^{2} (*L*)
uultus	I	ondwleota A, ondwlita BD, andwlita H, ⁊wlitan C, andwlitan GJ, anwlita I, wlite F^{2}, ansyne *K,* his E^{2}
eius	I	his ABCDF^{2}GHIJK, onsiene ł andwlite E^{2}

ED: forðon (A)] for ðon *Kuhn.* ęquitatem (E)] aequitatem *Harsley.* equitatem (I)] aequitatem *Lindelöf.*

OE: ryhtwis (E^{x})] *on eras.* drihten (E^{x})] *on eras.* rihtwisnesse (E^{x})] *on eras.,* n *altered from* s. he lufode (E^{x})] *on eras.* efennesse (E^{x})] *on eras.*

LTg: iustus] F: *ligature of* st *obscured by eras. at top.* dominus] dominus et BCDEL, A: et *interl. by corr.*: *cf. Weber MSS* SKαβγδη moz, *see GAg.* iustitiam] iustitia J. aequitatem] equitatem DG, I: *orig.* aequitatem: *initial* a *eras.;* ęquitatem CEFHJL; æquitatem K. uidit] uidet CDL: *cf. Weber MSS* ζ moz^{e}. eius] eíus K.

LTu: Quoniam] quoniam ϑ. dominus] dominus et νςτ*: *cf. Weber MSS* SKαβγδη moz, *see GAu.* iustitiam] iusticiam τ*. aequitatem] ęquitatem εινφ; equitatem ζξσςτ*τ; æquitatem ϑμ. uidit] uidet ντ*: *cf. Weber MSS* ζ moz^{e}.

GAg: dominus] dominus et GHJ, I: et *added interl.*, K: et *on eras. by corr.; for* ABCDEL *see LTg.* iustitiam] iustitias GHIK, F: *ligature of* st *obscured by eras. at top.*

GAu: dominus] dominus et ζϑιλξστφ, επχ: et *interl.; for* νςτ* *see LTu.* iustitiam] iustitias δεζιλμξπσυχψ, ο: *orig.* iustias: ti *added interl. by corr.;* iusticias τφ.

PSALM 11

2

Saluum	halne *ABC*DGHJK, gehæl F^2*I, hælne E^2
me	me AB*C*E^{2}F^{2}GIJK
fac	doo A, do E^{2}F^{2}GJK, gedó B*, gedo *C*
domine	drihten E^2, dryhт̄ AB, driћt CF^{2}GJ
quoniam	forðon ABF^{2}GJ, forþon C, forðan K, forðan þe I, forðon þe E^2
defecit	asprong ABC, teorode DH, ateorede E^x*, ateorode F^{2}I, ateorod K, geswiþraþ J, geswi(ð)[ ] *G**
sanctus	se halga ABCI, se hæli E^2*, halig DF^{2}HJ, hali K, haligne G
quoniam	forðon ABDE^{2}F^{2}GH, forþon CJ, forðan K, forðan ðe I
deminutae	gewonade *A,* gewonode *B,* gewonude *C,* gewanode *DG*K,* gewænede *E^2*, gewanede *H,* gewænede *F^2*, gewunode *J,* gelytlode *I* (*L*)
sunt	sind AF^2, sint BE^2, synt DI, synd *C*HK, syndon GJ
ueritates	soðfestnisse A, soðfæstnessa BGH, soðfæstnysse *C*F^2, soþfæstnissa D, soþfestnesse E^2, soðfæstnyssa I, soþfæstnesse J, soðfestnessa K
a	from A*E^2*, fro<u>m</u> BCD, fra<u>m</u> F^{2}GHJ, fram IK
filiis	| bearnum A, bearnu<u>m</u> BCDF^{2}GHI, bearn J, bearna K, mænnæ *E^2*
hominum	| monna AB, manna DF^{2}GHIJK, mannum C, beærnum E^2

ED: forðon (A) (*1st*)] for ðon *Kuhn.* defęc[ ] (G)] defęci*t Rosier.* geswi(ð)[ ] (G)] geswiðrað *Rosier.* forðon (A) (*2nd*)] for ðon *Kuhn.* diminutę (E)] diminutae *Harsley.* ueritates (C)] ueritat[i]s *Wildhagen.* á (E)] a *Harsley.* filíís (E)] filiis *Harsley.*

OE: F: *gloss to Ps 11.1–3* proximum *written in 16th-c. hand on eras.* gedó (B)] *tail of* g *slightly obscured by stain.* ateorede (E^x)] *on eras.* geswi(ð)[ ] (G)] *ascender and cross-stroke of* ð *visible, letter fragments visible.* se hæli (E^2)] i *on eras., eras. after word.* gewanode (G)] *scribble in light ink after word*: sals[ ] se (?).

LTg: Saluum] SALuum AB; SALVVM C. me] ME C. fac] FAC C. defecit] defęc[ ] G. deminutae] deminutę BD; diminutę CEFHL, A: ę *on eras.;* diminutae I; diminute G, K: *1st* i *altered from another letter*, J: *orig.* diminuti: *final* i *altered to* e. ueritates] C: *orig.* ueritatis: *2nd* i *altered to* e. sunt] súnt C. a] á E. filiis] filíís E.

LTu: ϱ: *Ps 11 wanting.* Saluum] SALUUM λμνςτ*; SALVVM ιτφ. me] ME λμνς. fac] FAC λμν. domine] DN̄E λμ. quoniam] QM̄ λ. deminutae] diminutę δεινξοπυφ; diminute ζσςτ*τ; diminutæ ϑ; diminutae χ. filiis] filis ϑ.

3

Uana	ða idlan A, þa idlan *BC,* idelu *DH,* ydel *F^2,* idel *GJ,* idele *K,* Idelnesse *E^2,* unnyttu ł idelnyssa *I* (*L*)
locuti	spreocende *A,* sprecende BGJ, sprecynde C, hy spræcon D, hy spræcan E^2, hi spræcon F^2*H,* spræcon I, specaþ K
sunt	is *A,* sint B, synt C, wæron GJ
unusquisque	anra gehwelc AB, anra gehwylc CDG, anra gehwilc F^2HIJ, anre gewylc E^x*, æghwylc K
ad	to ABCDE^2F^2GHIJK
proximum	| ðæm nestan A, þæm nehstan B, þam neahstan C, þam nihstan G, nehstan D*E^2, nyhstan F^2H, nihstan J, nyxtan K, heora I
suum	| his ABE^x*FGJK, hys C, nyxtan I
labia	welure A*, weolure B, welere *DE^2*GH, welyras *C,* weleras FIJK
dolosa	faecne A, fæcne B*C,* facne *E^2,* facenfulle FGJ, facnfulra K, facenfullum H, ðurh fakenfulle I* (*DL*)
in	in AB, on CDE^2FGHIJK
corde	heortan ABCDFGHI, heorten E^2, eortan J, heorttan K
et	⁊ ABCDE^2FGHIJ
corde	heortan ABCIJ, of heortan DFH, of heorten E^2, on heortan G
locuti	spreocende A, sprecende BGJ, sprecynde C, specende K, hy spræcon D*H,* hi spræcon FI, hyo spręcon E^x*
sunt	sindun A, sindon B, synd CK, wæron GJ
mala*	ða yflan A, þa yflan BC, yfelu D, yfele E^2 (*I**)

ED: unusquisque (B)] unus quisque *Brenner.*

OE: anre gewylc (E^x)] *on eras.* nehstan (D)] s *interl.* his (E^x)] *on eras.* welure (A)] *1st* e *and* l *overlap.* ðurh fakenfulle (I)] ðurh *written in right margin and signaled for inclusion.* hyo spręcon (E^x)] *on eras.* mala (I)] s. mala. yfel *written to right of* sunt *and below* dolosa.

LTg: Uana] [ ]ana G: *initial* V *lost,* B: *initial letter* (V?) *eras., traces of yellow visible;* Vana CDEFHIJKL. locuti (*1st*)] loquti H: *orig.* locuti: c *altered to* q; locutus A: *cf. Weber MSS* αβ moz^c. sunt (*1st*)] est A: *cf. Weber MSS* αβ moz^c. labia] E: ł o *interl.* (> labio); labio CD. dolosa] E: ł o *interl.* (> doloso), L: *orig.* doloso: *3rd* o *altered to* a; doloso CD. locuti (*2nd*)] loquti H: *orig.* locuti: c *altered to* q. mala] I: *see OE.*

LTu: Uana] Vana εζινξσςτ*τφ. unusquisque] unusquiquę ζ. labia] labio ν. dolosa] doloso ν.

GAg: mala] I: *orig. om., added by glossator: see OE; om.* FGHJK.

GAu: mala] *om.* δεζθιλμξοπστυφχψ.

4

Disperdat | tostrigdeð A, tostregdyð C, tostregd tostæncð I*, tostencð F, tostencað G, tostæncaþ J, forspildeð B, forspille DHK, Drihten E^2
dominus | dryhten A, drihten IK, dryht̄ B, drih́t CFGJ, forspille E^2*
uniuersa alle A, ealle BCDFGHIJ, eale K, eælle E^2
labia | weolure A, weoloras B, welyras C, welras D*, weleras FGHIJK, inwiddæn ł facne E^2
dolosa | faecne A, fæcne CD*H, facenfulle BGJ, facnfulle FK, ða fakenfulle I, weleræs E^2
et* ⁊ ABCE^{2}GIJK (*H*)
linguam | tungan ABCDFGHJK, tunga I, þæ yfelcweþenden E^2
maliloquam* | yfel spreocende A, yfel sprecende B, yfyl sprecynde C, ifel sprecende GJ, ða felaspeculan *D**, þa felaspeculan H, ða felaspecolan F, fælaspecelan K, micelsprecende ł ⁊ ða swyðsprecelan tunga I, tungæn E^2

ED: tostregd tostæncð (I)] tostregd ł tostæncð *Lindelöf.* yfel sprecende (B)] yfelsprecende *Brenner.* ða felaspeculan (D)] ða fela speculan *Roeder.*

OE: tostregd tostæncð (I)] tostæncð *written in left margin; Lindelöf's* ł *not visible, but may be lost due to tight binding.* forspille (E^2)] *2nd* l *on eras.* welras fæcne (D)] þæt sint þa ðe willað oþer cweþan oðer ðencan *written in right margin as translation of Lat. marginal gloss below it:* hi sunt qui uolunt aliud loqui aliud cogitare. ða felaspeculan (D)] *2nd* e *retouched by corr.: see LTg note to Ps 1.2; OE gloss is followed by* ł maliloquam *in hand of glossator* (*see Roeder p. 17n*).

LTg: et] H: *ampersand added interl., possibly by glossator.* maliloquam] D: *eras. of 2 letters after 1st* a, *1st* l *written by corr.: see LTg note to Ps 1.2, see also GAg;* malíloquam C.

LTu: Disperdat] Dissperdat ν. et] *added* δ.

GAg: et] *om.* F. maliloquam] magniloquam FGHIJ, K: gni *on eras., eras. after word; for* D *see LTg.*

GAu: et] *om.* ειλμπστψ; *eras.* ζ. maliloquam] magniloquam δεζθιλμνξοπστυφχψ.

5

Qui ða A, þa BCDHK, þa ðe F, þa þe GJ, þa þe I, þæ E^2
dixerunt cwedun A, cwædon BCDFH, cwædun I, cwædan K, cweþæþ E^2, cweðað *G,* cweþað J
linguam | tungan ABCDFGH*IJK, ure E^2
nostram | ure ABCDFGHIJK, tungæn E^2*
magnificabimus we micliað AB, we gemicliað D*H,* we gemycliað K,

		ðe gemiclað F, we micliæþ E^2, we miclydon *C*, gemicclian we GJ, uton gemiclian ł we mærsiað ł we gemicliaþ I
labia	I	weolre A*, weoloras B, welyras C, weleras DFGHIJK, ure E^2*
nostra	I	ure ABCDFGHIJK, weleræs E^2
a		from A*E*^{2}, fro̲m̲ BC, fram FI, fra̲m̲ GJ, of DHK
nobis		us ABCDE^{2}FHIJK
sunt		sindun A, syndun C, syndon GIJ, sint BE^2, synd DFHK
quis		hwelc AB, hwylc CDFGHK, hwilc E^{2}J, la hwa I
noster	I	ur A, ure BCDFGHIJK, is E^2
est*	}I	is ABDF*GHIJK*, ys C, ure E^2
dominus*	}	dryhten B, drihten E^{2}F*G*IK, dryht̄ A, driħt CJ, driħ H

ED: dixęrunt (G)] dixerunt *Rosier.* á (E)] a *Harsley.* is (H)] *no gloss Campbell.* drihten (G)] driħt *Rosier.*

OE: tungan (H)] *letter eras before word.* tungæn (E^2)] þæ *eras. after word: cf.* þæ *2 lines above in MS.* ure (E^2) (*2nd*)] *eras. before word.* weolre (A)] l *malformed.*

LTg: dixerunt] dixęrunt G. magnificabimus] H: *small eras. after word, perhaps of punct.;* magnificábimus C. a] á E. est] H: *small eras. after word, perhaps of punct.;* ést K. dominus] domi[ ]us G.

GAg: est dominus] dominus est FHIJ; domi[ ]us est G; dominus ést K.

GAu: est dominus] dominus est δεζθιλμξοπστυφχψ.

6

Propter		fore ABDH, for *C*FGIJK, For E^2
miseriam		ermðe AB, yrmðe *C*DFK, yrmþe E^2*HI, yrmðum G, yrmþum J
inopum		weðlena A, wædlena B, wædlyna C, [ ]ædlena *G,* wædlum J*, on wædlan K, wædlena ł hæfenleasra I*, unspedigra DH, unspedigra ł wedlum E^2*, unspedig F
et		⁊ ABCE^{2}FGHIJK
gemitum		geamrunge A, geomrunge BCDFI, geomrumge H, geomerunge G, geomrunga J, gemerunga K, giomrungu̲m̲ E^2*
pauperum		ðearfena A, þearfena BFGIJ, þearfyna C, ðearfana D, þearfana H, þeærfnæ E^2, ðearfan K
nunc	I	nu ABCDGHJK, nu ða FI, drihten E^2
exsurgam	I	ic arisu *A,* ic arise B*CDFGHIJ,* ic [ ]rise *K**, cweþ *E*^{2} (*L*)
dicit	I	cwið AB, cwyþ D, cwæð CGHK, cwæþ J, cweð F, cwęð ł sæde I, nu E^2
dominus	I	dryhten B, drihtyn C, drihten IK, dryht̄ A, driħt FHJ, driħ G, ic arise E^2

Ponam ic setto AB, ic sette CF*G*IK, ic asette DH, Ic asette E^{x}*, ic sece J

super* ofer ABCDE^{x}*, on HIK, in mine *G*, mine J (*L*)

salutare* hęlu *A*, hælo BFGJ, hæle CK, help ł halwendnesse DE^{x}*, hælo ł on halwendnesse H, hælo ł on ðam halwendum I* (*L*)

meum* mine ABDE^{x}*, minre C (*L*)

fiducialiter getrewlice A, getreowlice B, getrywlice *C*, getreowfullice DE^{x}*H, getréowfullice F, getrywlice ł baldlice I, bealdlice GJ*, geleaflice K

agam ic dom A, ic dem DH, ic deme F, ic dó B, ic do CE^{x}*GIJ

in in AB, on CDE^{x}*FGHIJ

eo hine AB, him G, him IJ, hyne C, ðæm D, þæm H, ðam F, ðæm E^{x}*

ED: Propter (B)] propter *Brenner.* exurgam (C)] ex[s]urgam *Wildhagen.* [ ]onam (G)] Ponam *Rosier.* in (*OE*) (G)] *no gloss Rosier.* ðæm (E^{x})] ðæms *Harsley.*

OE: yrmþe (E^{2})] e *on eras.* wædlum (J)] w *altered from* r. wædlena ł hæfenleasra (I)] asra *written in right margin.* unspedigra ł wedlum (E^{2})] un *on eras.* giomrungum (E^{2})] *eras. after word extending rest of line, 3 dots written on eras. direct reader to 3 dots above* þeærfnæ *on next line.* ic [ ]rise (K)] ara *eras. after* ic. Ic asette (E^{x})] *on eras. in lighter brown ink.* ofer (E^{x})] *on eras. in lighter brown ink.* help ł halwendnesse (E^{x})] *on eras., with* help ł halwend *in lighter brown ink, 1st* l *interl.* hælo ł on ðam halwendum (I)] dum *written in right margin.* mine (E^{x})] *on eras.* getreowfullice (E^{x})] *on eras.* bealdlice (J)] *eras. before word.* ic do (E^{x})] *on eras.* on (E^{x})] *on eras.* ðæm (E^{x})] *on eras.*

LTg: Propter] C: e *interl.* miseriam] misériam C. inopum] [ ]nopum G. exsurgam] exurgam AEJKL, CH: *eras. after* x. Ponam] [ ]onam G: *initial* P *lost.* super] L: in *written above word by corr.: see GAg.* salutare] A: m *eras. after* e, L: e *deleted by subscript dot,* i *interl. by corr.: see GAg.* meum] L: *underlined by corr. to indicate deletion: see GAg.* fiducialiter] fiduciáliter C.

LTu: miseriam] misseriam ϑ. exsurgam] exurgam βδειλνξπστ*τυφχψ. Ponam] [ ]onam τ*τ: *initial letter wanting.* meum] meo ϑ. fiducialiter] uiducialiter β.

GAg: super] in FHIJK, G: *written by corr. on eras.,* L: *see LTg.* salutare] salutari FGIJK, H: *punct. on eras. after word,* L: *see LTg.* meum] *om.* FGHIJK, L: *see LTg.*

GAu: super] in δεζϑιλμξοπστυφχψ. salutare] salutari δεζϑιλμξοπστυφχψ. meum] *om.* δεζιλμξοπστυφχψ.

7

Eloquia gesprec *ABC*, gesprecu G, gespreca J, spreca D, spræca FH, spræcu I*, sprece E^{x}*, spæce K

domini	dryhtnes AB, drihtnys C, drihtnes FGI, drihtenes K, drihnes E^{x}*, driħt J
eloquia	gesprec AB*C*, gesprecu G, gespreca J, spreca D, spræca FH, spræcu I, spæc K, sprecha E^{x}*
casta	clæne ABCFIJ, clene G, syfra DE^{x}*H, syfre K
argentum	seolfur A, seolfor BDE^{x}*FGHIJ, sylfur C, seolfer K
igne	fyre ABC, of fyre DFHK, on fyre E^{x}*, mid fyre GIJ
examinatum	amearad A, amered BD*E^{x}**FGHJ, ameryd C, amerod IK (*L*)
(probatum)*	afandod F, bið gehlutrudu G, biþ gefandod J, gefandod I, fandad K*
terrae	earðan A, eorðan *BCDF*I, eorþan *H*, eorðen *E^{2}**, eorþe *GJK* (*L*)
purgatum	geclasnad A, geclænsud C, ⁊ geclænsað G, ⁊ geclænsod J, aclensod DE^{2}, aclænsod FHK, afeormod I
septuplum	seofenfaldlice A, sufunfealdlice *C**, sefonfealdlice D, seofonfaldlice E^{2}, seofonfealdlice FGIJ, seofanfealdlice H, seofenfealde K

ED: gesprecu (G) (*1st*)] gespreca *Rosier.* drihnes (E)] drih[t]nes *Harsley.* syfra (E)] sysra *Harsley.*

OE: spræcu (I) (*1st*)] s. sunt : sint *written above and to left of gloss.* sprece (E^{x})] *on eras.* drihnes (E^{x})] *on eras.* sprecha (E^{x})] *on eras.* syfra (E^{x})] *on eras.* seolfor (E^{x})] *on eras.* on fyre (E^{x})] *on eras.* amered (E^{x})] *on eras.* fandad (K)] od *eras. after word.* eorðen (E^{2})] ðen *on eras.* sufunfealdlice (C)] a *interl.*

LTg: eloquia] C: i *interl.* examinatum] E: *final* m *on eras.*, L: probatum *written below and to right by corr.: see GAg.* terrae] terræ BL; terrę CEFGHK; terre DJ. septuplum] séptuplum C.

LTu: Eloquia] Ęloquia ξ. eloquia] ęloquia ε. examinatum] examinatvm τ*; examinatum probatum ς: *cf. Weber MSS* η moz^{x} med. terrae] terrę εζιλμνοφ; terræ ϑ; terre ξσςτ*τ. septuplum] septiplum ϑ.

GAg: examinatum] examinatum probatum FGHIJ, L: *see LTg,* K: ł minatum *interl.*

GAu: examinatum] examinatum probatum δεζϑιλμξοπστυφχψ, ς: *see LTu.*

8

Tu	ðu AD, þu BCE^{2}FG*H*IJK
domine	drihten E^{2}*F, dryhten B, dryht̄ A, driħt CGJ, o. eala dr̄ I, hlaford K
seruabis	aldes A, healdes B, healdyst *C,* gehealdst D*FH, geheældest E^{2}, gehealdest GJK, gehealtst I*

nos	usic A, us BCDE^2FGHIJK
et	⁊ ABCDE^2*FGHIJK
custodies	gehaldes A, gehealdes *B,* gehealdyst C, þu gehealdest G*J, beweardast DH*K, bewéardast F, beweardest E^x*, gescildst I
nos	usic A, us BCDE^x*FHIJK (G*)
a	from AB, fro<u>m</u> C, fra<u>m</u> DHJK, fram *E^x**FI (G*)
generatione	cneorisse ABHJ, cnerisse D, cnyorisse E^x*, cneornesse K, cneorisse ł mægðe I, cynne C, cynryne F, [ ]sse G*
hac	ðisse *A,* þisse BC, þysse K, ðisre DE^x*, þysre HI, oð F
in	in A, on BCDE^x*FGHJK, symle oððe æfre ł on I
aeternum	ecnisse *ADH**, ecnysse *C,* écnysse *F,* ecnesse *BE^2GIJK* (*L*)

ED: nos (G) (*2nd*)] *Rosier reads gloss as* [ ]s: *see OE.* á (E)] a *Harsley.* æternum (D)] aeternum *Roeder.* ęternum (E)] aeternum *Harsley.*

OE: drihten (E^2)] *eras. after word.* gehealdst (D)] *eras.* (us?) *after word.* gehealtst (I)] *letter eras. after* t. ⁊ (E^2)] *eras. after word.* þu gehealdest (G)] þu *interl.* beweardast (H)] *orig.* beweardest: a *written above 2nd* e, *but without subscript deleting dot.* beweardest (E^x)] *on eras.* nos (G) (*2nd*)] *top of ascender of* s (?) *of gloss visible.* us (E^x)] *on eras.* fram (E^x)] *on eras.* a (G)] *gloss eras.* cnyorisse (E^x)] *on eras.* [ ]sse (G)] *eras. before 1st* s. ðisre (E^x)] *on eras.* on (E^x)] *on eras.* ecnisse (H)] *orig.* ecnesse: *2nd* e *deleted by subscript dot,* i *written above.*

LTg: Tu] H: *initial letter faint but visible.* seruabis] seruábis C. custodies] custodias B. a] á E. hac] A: *small eras. after word.* aeternum] æternum BDK; ęternum CEFHL; eternum GJ.

LTu: Tu] TU β. hac] hanc β. aeternum] ęternum ειvξφ; æternum ϑ; ẹternum σςτ*τ.

9

In	in AB, on CDFGHI*JK, On E^2
circuitu	ymbhwyrfte ABCE^2*F, ymbehwyrfte *K,* embhwyrfte ł eall abutan I*, trundulnisse D, trundelnesse *H,* ymbgan(g)e G*, ymbgange J
impii	ða arleasan A, þa arleasan BI*J, þara arleasra C, þæ ærleæsæ E^2, þa a[ ] G*, arleasæ DFK, arleasæ H*
ambulant	gongað AB, gangað DFHK, gængæð E^2, gangeþ J, hi gondgað C*, [ ]að G*, gað oððe faraþ I*
secundum	efter AE^2K, æfter BDFGI, æft<u>er</u> HJ, æftyr C
altitudinem	| hehnisse A, heahnesse DHK, heahnysse F, heahnysse ł heannysse I*, heanisse B, heanysse C, heanesse GJ, þinre E^2
tuam	| ðinre AD, þinre B*C*FG*HIJ, þine K, heahnesse E^x*

multiplicasti ðu gemonigfaldades A, þu gemonigfaldades B, þu gemonigfealdodyst C, ðu gemonigfyldest D, þu gemonigfyldes E^{2}, ðu gemænigfyldest F, þu gemænigfyldest HIJ, gemænifylde K, micel monigfealdodest G
filios | bearn ABCDGHJK, bearn ł suna I, sunu F, monnæ E^{2}
hominum | monna AB, manna CDFG*HIJK, beærn E^{2}

ED: ymbgan(g)e (G)] ymbgange *Rosier.*

OE: on embhwyrfte ł eall abutan (I)] on emb *written in left margin,* ł *above line.* ymbhwyrfte (E^{2})] b *altered from* d. ymbgan(g)e (G)] *2nd* g *fragmentary.* þa arleasan (I)] *orig.* þa arleasen: *2nd* e *altered to* a, a *then deleted by subscript dot and* an *written interl. in very light ink.* þa a[ ] (G)] *eras. after 2nd* a. arleasæ (H)] æ *partly effaced, perhaps to form* e. hi gondgað (C)] n *malformed.* [ ]að (G)] *eras. before* a. gað oððe faraþ (I)] *eras. (3 letters) before* gað. heahnysse ł heannysse (I)] *2nd* h *interl.* þinre (G)] *touched up in late (16th-c.?) hand.* heahnesse (E^{x})] *on eras.* manna (G)] *touched up in a late (16th-c.?) hand.*

LTg: circuitu] K: *2nd* i *on eras.;* circum̲itu H: *macron above 1st* u, *not in usual 'straight-bar' style of hand of Lat. text.* tuam] C: *eras. after word.*

LTu: circuitu] β: r *interl.* ambulant] ambulabunt ϑ: *cf. Weber MSS* αδη moz.

PSALM 12

1
Usquequo hu longe *ABCD,* hu lange *E^{2}FHI*JK, hu lang *G*
domine drihtyn *C,* drihten E^{2}, dri(h)ten G*, dryht̄ AB, drih̄t FHJ, o. eala dr̄ I
obliuisceris ofergeotulas ðu A, ofergeotulast ðu B, ofyrgytyst þu *C**, ofergytst ðu D, ofergyst þu *H,* ofergyts ðu F, ofergietst þu E^{2}*, ofergtalast þu J*, [ ]fergytelast [ ]u G*, forgitst ðu *I**, forgitst þu K
me mec A, me B*C*E^{2}FGHIJ
in in AB, on CDE^{2}*FHJK, (o)n G*, of I
finem ende ABCDE^{2}FGIJK, ænde H
quousque* hu longe *A*BC, hu lange FI, oþ hwæt D, oþ hwet *E$^{2/x}$**, oð hwæt H, oð þæt J, oð [ ]æt G* (*L*)
auertis acerres ðu A, acerrest ðu B, acyrryst þu C, acyrrest ðu DE^{2}*, acyrrest þu *H,* þu oncyrrest GJ, cyrst K, awens ðu F, awendst þu *I**
faciem onsiene AB, onsyne D, onsine E^{2}, ansyne CFGHIK, ansine J

tuam ðine A, þine BDE^{2}GHIJK, þinre C, ðin F
a from ABC, fram DGHJK, fram *E*^{2}FI
me me ABCDE^{2}FHIJK, [ ]e G*

ED: USquequo (BE)] Usque quo *Brenner, Harsley*. VSQVEQVO (C)] VSQVE QVO *Wildhagen*. dri(h)ten (G)] drihten *Rosier*. obliuiscéris (I)] obliuiscеris *Lindelöf*. ofergeotulast ðu (B)] ofergeotulas ðu *Brenner*. [ ]fergytelast [ ]u (G)] ofergytelast þu *Rosier*. (o)n (G)] on *Rosier*. oð [ ]æt (G)] oð þæt *Rosier*. á (E)] a *Harsley*. [ ]e (G)] me *Rosier*.

OE: dri(h)ten (G)] *ascender of* h *lost*. ofyrgytyst þu (C)] r *interl*. ofergietst þu (E^{2})] *eras. (7 mm) before word, all except* er *on eras*. ofergtalast þu (J)] ta *on eras., hole in leaf after 1st* a. [ ]fergytelast[ ]u (G)] *letter fragments visible before* f *and* u. forgitst ðu (I)] g *slightly malformed*. on (E^{2})] *eras. before word*. (o)n (G)] *right side of* o *visible*. oþ hwet (E$^{2/x}$)] hwet *on eras*. oð [ ]æt (G)] *bowl of* ð (?) *visible before* æ, *ascender and cross-stroke lost*. acyrrest ðu (E^{2})] acyrrest *on eras*. awendst þu (I)] d *interl*. [ ]e (G)] *letter fragments, most likely of* m, *visible in initial position: minim and shoulder followed by 2 fragmentary minims*.

LTg: Usquequo] USquequo ABE; VSQVEQVO C; Vsquequo DFGI; [ ]squequo H: *initial letter lost, faint traces of blue ink visible*. domine] DN̄E C. obliuisceris] H: *small eras. above 2nd* i; obliuísceris C; obliuiscéris I. me (*1st*)] mé C. quousque] A: quo *on eras.*, E: *on eras. by corr. in black ink,* que *retraced in brown ink,* L: quo *underlined by corr. to indicate deletion, another* quo *added after* usque: *see GAg*. auertis] HI: i *altered from another letter*. a] á E.

LTu: ϱ: *wanting v. 1*. Usquequo] USquequo β; Vsquequo δεζϑξοπχψ; VSQUEQVO ιλφ; VSQUEQUO μτ*; USQUEQUO ντ; VSQEQuo ς. domine] DN̄E λμν. obliuisceris] OBLIUISCERIS λ. auertis] ο: ł e *interl.;* auertes ϑ.

GAg: quousque] usquequo FGHIJK, L: *see LTg*.

GAu: quousque] usquequo δεζϑιλμξοπϱστυφχψ.

2

Quamdiu hu longe *A*BCDE$^{2/x}$*, hv longe K, hu lange FH*I*J, (h)u lange G*
ponam sette ic ABDE^{2}HK, ic sette FGJ, ic gesette C, gesette ic I
consilium* geðaeht A, geðeaht B, geþeaht CDFGHJK, geþeæhtunge E^{2}, geþeahtunga geþeaht I*
in in AB, on CDE^{2}FGHIJK
animam* | saule AGH, sawle B*CD*FIJK, mine E^{2} (*L*)
meam* | mine AB*C*G, minre *D*FHIJK, sæule E^{2} (*L*)
dolorem | sar ABCGHIJ*K*, sár DF, on E^{x}*

in	I	in AB, on CDFGHIJK, minre E^{2}
corde	I	heortan ABCDFGHIJK, heortæn E^{2}
meo	I	minre ABCGIJK, mine D, min H, sær E^{2}*
per		ðorh A, þurh BCDE^{x}*FGHIJ, ðuh K
diem		deg A, dæg BCDE^{x}*FG*H*JK, dæg ł iand dæ[ ] I*

ED: Quamdiu (BE)] quam diu *Brenner;* Quam diu *Harsley.* (h)u lange (G)] hu lange *Rosier.* geþeahtunga geþeaht (I)] geþeahtunga ł geþeaht *Lindelöf.* dæg ł iand dæ[ ] (I)] dæg ł iand dæg *Lindelöf.*

OE: hu longe ($E^{2/x}$)] hu *on eras.*, h *altered from another letter, eras. after* longe. (h)u lange (G)] *ascender of* h *lost.* geþeahtunga geþeaht (I)] geþeaht *added in left margin.* on (E^{x}) (*2nd*)] *on eras.* sær (E^{2})] *eras. after word.* þurh (E^{x})] *on eras.* dæg (E^{x})] *on eras.*, d *altered from* ð. dæg ł iand dæ[ ] (I)] *final letter lost due to tight binding, fragment only visible.*

LTg: Quamdiu] A: diu *on eras.*, I: Q *faint but visible.* animam meam] D: *orig.* anima mea: *macrons added by another hand above final* a *in both words* (= animam meam), *cf. v. 4* mortem *below;* anima mea CL: *cf. Weber MSS* βηTQX moz^{c} med, *see GAg.* dolorem] K: *eras. above 2nd* o. diem] H: *eras. after punct. following word.*

LTu: Quamdiu] Quandiu ϑ. animam meam] anima mea v: *cf. Weber MSS* TQXβη moz^{c} med, *see GAu.*

GAg: consilium] consilia FGHIK, J: *orig.* consilio: *2nd* o *altered to* a. animam meam] anima mea FGHIJK, CL: *see LTg.*

GAu: consilium] consilia δεζϑιλμξοπϱστυφχψ. animam meam] anima mea δεζϑιλμξοπϱστυφχψ, v: *see LTu.*

3

Usquequo		hu longe A*BCK,* hu lange *FGIJ,* Oþ wænne *$E^{2/x}$** (*DHL*)
exaltabitur		bið upahefen A, bið upahæfen B, bið upahafyn C, bið upahafen DE^{x}*H, byþ upahafen F, beoð upahafen G, beoþ upahafen J, byð upahafen I, beoð ahafen K
inimicus	I	se feond AB, feond CDFHI, fynd GJK, min E^{2}
meus	I	min AB*C*FI, mine GJK, fyond E^{2}
super		ofer ABE^{x}*FGJK, ofyr C, ofor I
me		mec A, me BCE^{x}*FGIJK

ED: Usquequo (C)] Usque quo *Wildhagen.* Vsquequo (BDEJ)] Usque quo *Brenner;* Usquequo *Roeder, Oess;* Vsque quo *Harsley.* me (G)] [ ] *Rosier.*

OE: Oþ wænne ($E^{2/x}$)] wænne *on eras.* bið upahafen (E^{x})] *all except* n *on eras.*, f *altered from another letter.* ofer (E^{x})] *on eras.* me (E^{x})] *on eras.*

LTg: Usquequo] Vsquequo BDEFHJKL, I: V *faint but visible;* [ ]squequo G: *initial* V *lost.* meus] C: u *on eras.*

LTu: Usquequo] Vsquequo νϱστ*τυφ.

4

Respice | geloca _ABCGJ,_ beseoh _DFH*IK,_ min _E^{x}*_ (_L_)
et | ⁊ ABCDFGHIJK, drihten E^{x}*
exaudi | geher ABI, gehyr CDFGHJK, god E^{2}
me | me ABCFGHIJK, lócæ E^{2}*
domine | drihten F, dryht̄ AB, driħt CGJ, s. o driht̄ I, hlafor K, on E^{x}*
deus | god ABCFGIJK, me E^{x}*
meus | min ABCFGIJK, ⁊ gehire me E$^{2/x}$*
inlumina inliht _A,_ inleht _B,_ onlyht _CDFK,_ Ọnliht _E^{x}*_, onliht _HI,_ onliht þu _J_ (_GL_)
oculos | egan AK, eagan BCDFGHI, eagon J, mine E^{x}*
meos | min A, mine BCFGH*IJ_K,_ eægæn E^{x}*
ne | ne A, þylæs BCFGH, þyles D, þiles E^{x}*, þilæs J, þæt IK
umquam | æfre AB_CDF_G_HJ_, nefre E^{2}, næfre K, ic æfre ne I
obdormiam | ic aslepe A, ic aslape C, ic aslæpæ E^{2}*, ic slape BDFHJK, ic slafe G, slape I
in in AB, on CDE^{2}FGHIJ*K
mortem deaðc A_BCGHI,_ deaþe _DFJK,_ deæþe E^{2} (_L_)

ED: Illumina (C)] I[n]lumina *Wildhagen.* [ ]umina (G)] Illumina *Rosier.* þylæs (C)] þy læs *Wildhagen.* unquam (C)] u[m]quam *Wildhagen.*

OE: beseoh (H)] *orig.* beseah: o *written above* a, *but without subscript deleting dot; eras. before* b. min (E^{x})] *on eras.* drihten (E^{x})] *on eras.* lócæ (E^{2})] æ *on eras.* on (E^{x})] *on eras.* me (E^{x})] *on eras.* ⁊ gehire me (E$^{2/x}$)] hire me *on eras.* Onliht (E^{x})] *on eras.* mine (E^{x})] *on eras.* mine (H)] *small eras. before* m. eægæn (E^{x})] *on eras.* þiles (E^{x})] *eras. after word.* ic aslæpæ (E^{2})] *letter eras. after* aslæpæ. on (J)] *eras. after word.*

LTg: Respice] respice ABCDEFGHIJKL. inlumina] Inlumina ABDFJL; Illumina EHIK, C: *1st* l *formed from another letter;* [ ]umina G: *lower portions of 1st 3 lost letters visible.* meos] K: *eras. after word.* umquam] unquam C: *eras. after* u, GH. *orig.* umquam: *right leg of 1st* m *eras. to form* n. mortem] D: *orig.* morte: *macron added by another hand above* e (= morte<u>m</u>: *cf. v. 2* anima<u>m</u> mea<u>m</u>); morte BCFGIJKL: *cf. Weber MSS* S^{2}βγ moz med.

LTu: Respice] respice βδεζιλμνξοπϱσςτ*τυφχψ. inlumina] Inlumina βδμνςψ: Illumina εζιλξοπϱστ*τυφχ. ne] Ne ϑ. umquam] unquam ελτφ. mortem] morte βδζϑλμνοπϱσςυψ: *cf. Weber MSS* S^{2}βγ moz med.

5

Nequando		ne æfre AC, þylæs æfre B, þilæs æfre *J,* þeð nefre ne E$^{2/x}$*, ðules hwonne D, þulæs hwonne *H,* þylæs hwænne *FG,* þalæs hwonne *K,* ahwanne þæt ne *I*
dicat		cweðe ABCDE^{2}G, cweþe HJK, cweðen F, secge ł cweðe I
inimicus	|	feond ABCDFIK, fynd G, find J, min E^{2}
meus	|	min ABCFIK, mine GJ, fiond E^{2}
praeualui		ic strongade A, ic strongode B, ic gestrangude *C,* ic magude *DH,* ic macude *F**, ic magode *K,* ic magude ł swiþige *E$^{2/x}$**, ic swiðige *G,* ic swigige *J,* ic oforswiðrode ł swað I* (*L*)
aduersus		wið ABG, wið oððe ongen C, wiþ ł ongean J, ongean DE^{x}*H, agen ł ongen I, togeanes F*K*
eum		him ABE^{2}, him K*, hyne C, hine DFGHIJ
Qui		ða A, þa BCK, þa ðe D, ða þe F, þa þe GHIJ, þæ þe E^{2}
tribulant	|	swencað ABCDH, swenceað G, swæncaþ J, swencton K, drefað F, gedrefaþ I, me E^{2}
me	|	me ABCDFGHIJK, eærfoþigæþ ł swencað E^{2}*
exultabunt		gefiað A, gefeoð BC, hy blissiað D, hi blissiaþ F, blissiað K, hie hyhtaþ ł blyssieð E^{2}, gladiað ł blissiað I, wynsumiað G, winsumiaþ J
si		gif ABE^{2}GHIJK, gef C, gyf F, ges D
motus	|	onstyred ABC, astirod I, ic gedrefed DHK, ic beo FJ, ic bio E^{2}, ic beo [ ] G*
fuero	|	ic beam A, ic beom BC, ic beo I, beo DK, onstyred E^{2}, astired J, ged(re)fed F*

ED: Nequando (CDE)] Ne quando *Wildhagen, Roeder, Harsley.* nequando (FJK)] ne quando *Kimmens, Oess, Sisam.* ic beo ged(re)fed (F)] ic beo gedrefed *Kimmens.* fuero (G)] *fu*ero *Rosier.*

OE: þeð nefre ne (E$^{2/x}$)] þeð nefre *on eras.* ic macude (F)] mac *partly obscured.* ic magude ł swiþige (E$^{2/x}$)] ic magude *on eras.* oforswiðrode ł swað (I)] ł swað *added in right margin.* ongean (E^{x})] an *on eras.* him (K)] *written as* hï. eærfoþigæþ ł swencað (E^{2})] g *interl.* ic beo [ ] (G)] *only cropped letter fragments visible after* beo. ged(re)fed (F)] *descender and fragment of right shoulder of* r *visible, left and bottom portion of* e *visible.*

LTg: Nequando] nequando FGHIJK. praeualui] preualui DEFGHJL; pręualui CK. aduersus] áduersus K.

LTu: Nequando] nequando βδεζϑιλμξοπϱστυφχψ; [ ]equando ς. praeualui] pręualui ελνξϱφ; preualui ζϑιπςτ*τ; p̄ualui οσχ. exultabunt] exsultabunt ϑ.

6

Ego		ic *ABCDE^{2}FGHIJK* (*L*)
autem		soðlice ABCGHI, soþlice E^{2}FJ, witodlice K
in		in ABC, on DE^{2}FGIJK
tua*	}|	ðinrc A, þinre BCGK, ðine D, þine *E^{2}*, mildheortnysse F, mildheortnesse HJ, mildheortnysse I
misericordia*	}|	mildhertnisse A, mildheortnesse BD*E^{2}*, mildheortnysse *C*, mildheortnesse G, mildheortnes K, þinre FIJ, þine H
sperabo*		ic gehyhtu A, ic gehihte GJ, gehyhte BE$^{2/x}$*, hihtað C, hyhte DH, ic hihte K, ic gehihte ł hopode I, ic hopude F (*L*)
exultabit	|	gefið *A*, gefihð *B*, gefihþ *C*, blissað *DFHI*, blissiað *K*, wynsumiað *G*, wynsumiaþ *J*, Min *E^{2}* (*L*)
cor	|	heorte ABCDFGHIJK, heortæ E^{2}
meum	|	min ABCDFGHIJK, winsumaþ ł blisseð E$^{2/x}$*
in		in AB, on CE^{2}FGIJK
salutari	|	haelu A, hælo BCDFHI, hæle GJK, þine E^{2}
tuo	|	ðinre A, þinre BCDFGHJK, þinre ł on ðinu halwendan I, helo E^{2}
Cantabo		ic singu *A*, ic singe *BCE^{2}GHIJK*, ic synge *DF* (*L*)
domino		dryhtne ABD, drihtny C, drihtne E^{2}FI, drihtene HK, driħt G, driħ J
qui		se ABCE^{2}, se ðe FG, se þe J, þe DH, þa K, þam þe I
bona	|	god ABDHK, gód J, goód C, gode þyngc F, goda I, me E^{2}
tribuit	|	selð AB, sylyð C, syleþ G, sylleþ J*, sealde DFHIK, selde E^{2}*
mihi	|	me ABCDFGHI*J*K, góde *E^{2}*
et		⁊ ABCDE^{2}FGHIJK
psallam		ic singu A, ic singe BCE^{2}*HIJ*K, ic singe̲ D, ic sínge F, ic sin[ ] *G*
nomini	|	noman ABD, naman CFGHIJK, þinum E^{2}
tuo*	|	ðinum A, þinu̲m̲ B, nomæn *E^{2}**, drihtnys *C*, dryhtnes *D*, drihtnes FHI, driħt J, driħ G (*L*)
altissime*		ðu hehsta A, þu hehsta̲ B*C*, ðæs heahstan *D*, þæs heahstan I, ðæs hyhstan F, þæs hystan H, þæs hyhstan K, þæm hihstæn *E^{2}*, þa̲m̲ hyhstan G, þa̲m̲ hihstan J (*L*)

ED: ego (I)] Ego *Lindelöf.* ic (G) (*1st*)] [ ] *Rosier.* spęraui (G)] speraui *Rosier.* Exultauit (C)] Exulta[b]it *Wildhagen.* [ ]xultabit (G)] *E*xultabit *Rosier.* gode þyngc (F)] gode þynge *Kimmens.* ⁊ (H)] *no gloss Campbell.* ic sin[ ] (G)] ic sing[ ] *Rosier.*

OE: gehyhte (E^2/x)] hyhte *on eras.* winsumaþ ł blisseð (E^2/x)] isseð *on eras.* sylleþ (J)] lleþ *on eras.* selde (E²)] de *on eras.* nomæn (E²)] o *on eras. due to eras. in Lat. line below, eras.* (*ca 16 mm*) *after word.*

LTg: Ego] ego ABCDEFGHIJKL. tua misericordia] E: *written as* misericordia tua, *but with the letter* .a. *above* tua *and* .b. *above* misericordia *to indicate transposition.* misericordia] C: *word eras. after* a. sperabo] L: ui *added by corr. above* o: *see GAg.* exultabit] Exultabit BDEFHJK, A: b *on eras.;* [ ]xultabit G; Exultauit L, CI: *2nd* u *on eras.* Cantabo] cantabo ABCDEFGHIJKL. mihi] michi EJ. psallam] G: p *added later,* H: p *added interl.,* J: p *added interl. by glossator.* tuo (*2nd*)] E: *on eras., 18 mm space between* uo; domini CDL: *cf. Weber MS* K, *see GAg.* altissime] E: *orig.* altissimi: *final* i *altered to* e; altissimi CDL: *cf. Weber MS* K, *see GAg.*

LTu: Ego] ego βδεζϑιλμνξοπϱσςτ*τυφχψ. tua misericordia] misericordia tua τ*: *see GAu.* exultabit] Exultabit βδεμνοπϱςτ*υφχψ; Exultauit ζιλξστ; Exsultabit ϑ. Cantabo] cantabo βδεζϑιλμνξοπϱσςτ*τυφχψ. mihi] michi ιλξςτ*τ, ϱ: *small* c *interl.* tuo (*2nd*)] domini νς: *cf. Weber MS* K, *see GAu.* altissime] altissimi βνς: *cf. Weber MS* K, *see GAu.*

GAg: tua misericordia] misericordia tua FGHIJK: *see text above for order of glosses.* sperabo] speraui FHIJK, L: *see LTg;* spęraui G. tuo (*2nd*)] domini FGHIJK, CDL: *see LTg.* altissime] altissimi FGHIJK, CDL: *see LTg.*

GAu: tua misericordia] misericordia tua δεζιλμξοπϱστυφχψ, τ*: *see LTu;* missericordia tua ϑ. sperabo] speraui δεζϑιλμξοπϱστφχψ. tuo (*2nd*)] domini δεζϑιλμξοπϱστυφχψ, νς: *see LTu.* altissime] altissimi δεζϑιλμξοπϱστυφχψ, βνς: *see LTu.*

PSALM 13

1

Dixit		cweð *A*, cwæð *CDE²GHK*, cwæþ J, sæde F, sæde ł cwæð I* (*B*)
insipiens		se unwisa AB*C*DF, unwis GHJ, unwisse K, se unwise ł unsnotræ E²*, se unsnotera ł se unwita I*
in		in AB, on CDE^x*FGHIJK
corde	|	heortan BCDFGHIJK, herte E^x*, his A
suo	|	his BCDE^x*FGHIJ, heora K, heortan A
non	|	nis ABE^x*F, nys CI, ne G, na HJK
est	|	is GHJ*K*
deus		god ABCE^x*FGHIJK
Corrupti		gewemde *AB*G, gewe<u>mm</u>yde *C,* gewemmede K, hy <u>ge</u>wemmede *D,* hy gewemmede *E^x**, hi gewemmede F, gewemmede I, gewænde HJ (*L*)

sunt		sindun A, sindon B, syndon CGHJ, hi syndon I, synt DE^{x}*, synd FK
et		⁊ ABCDE^{x}*FGHJK
abominabiles		onscuniendlic A, onscuniendlice B*F,* onscuniyndlice *C,* onsceongenlice *D**, onscunigenlice E^{x}*, onscunigendlic *GHJK,* asceonigendlic ł gehyspendlic *I* (*L*)
facti	|	gewordne A, gewordene BFGHIJ, gewordyne C, hy gewordene D, gedone K, hie sint ł byoð E^{2}
sunt	|	sind A, sint B, synt D, synd FK, syndon GHJ, hi synt C, ⁊ hi synt I, gewordene E^{2}*
in		in AB, on CDE^{2}FGHIJK
uoluntatibus*	|	lustum AC, lustum BG, lustum J, willum D, biggenon F, ymbhigdinyssum I, hieræ E^{2}, heora H (*L*)
suis	|	heara A, hira B, hyra C, heora DFGJK, sinum I, willæn E^{2}, lustum H
Non	|	nis ABD*F,* Nis E^{2}, nys C, nys na *I**, ne *GH,* na *JK*
est	|	is GHJK
qui		se ðe AB*F*G, se þe CE^{2}HIJ, þe D, þa K
faciat		doe A, dó BCD, do E^{2}FGHJ*K,* do ł gefremme I
bonum		god ACE^{2}FGHIK, gód BJ
non	|	nis ABE^{2}*F, nys C, nys na I, ne GH, na JK
est	|	is GHJ
usque		oð ABCDFGHI, oþ JK, se oðð E$^{2/x}$*
ad		on DE^{2}K, to I
unum		enne A, ænne BE^{2}*G, anne DK, anum FI, ende CHJ

OE: sæde ł cwæð (I)] sæde *written in bowl of* D *in* Dixit. se unwise ł unsnotræ (E^{2})] unwise ł *added later by main hand.* se unsnotera ł se unwita (I)] se unwita *written in right margin.* on (E^{x}) (*1st*)] *on eras.* herte (E^{x})] *on eras.* his (E^{x})] *on eras.* nis (E^{x}) (*1st*)] *on eras.* god (E^{x}) (*1st*)] *on eras.* hy gewemmede (E^{x})] *on eras.* synt (E^{x})] *on eras.* ⁊ (E^{x})] *on eras.* onsceongenlice (D)] *3rd* n *interl.* onscunigenlice (E^{x})] *on eras.* gewordene (E^{2})] *eras. before word.* nys na (I)] *right leg of 2nd* n *partly obscured.* nis (E^{2}) (*2nd*)] *eras. before word.* se oðð (E$^{2/x}$)] se *on eras.* ænne (E^{2})] *eras. before word.*

LTg: Dixit] DIxit A; DIXIT BCE; DIXit D; DIXIt K; [ ]ixit G: *initial* D *lost.* insipiens] INSIPIENS C. est (*1st*)] ést K. Corrupti] corrupti ABCDEL. abominabiles] I: *letter eras. after 1st* b, K: omina *on eras.;* abhominabiles CDFGJL. uoluntatibus] L: studiis *added by corr. in right margin: see GAg.* Non] non FGHIJK. qui] F: *eras. after word.* faciat] faciad K.

LTu: Dixit] DIXIT ιλμνϱςτφ. insipiens] INSIPIENS λμϱ; INSIPIens ν; INsipiens ς.

in (*1st*)] IN λϱ. corde] CORDE λϱ. suo] svo ε. Corrupti] corrupti βϑνςτ*; Corupti ε. abominabiles] abhominabiles βδμξσςτ*υφ; habominabiles ν. Non] non δεζϑιλμξοπϱστυφχψ.

GAg: uoluntatibus] studiis FGHIJK, L: *see LTg*.

GAu: uoluntatibus] studiis δεζιλμξοπϱστυφχψ; studis ϑ.

2

Dominus		drihten K, Drihten E^{2}, dryht̄ AB, driħt CFGHJ
de		of ABCDE^{2}F*G*IJK, on H
caelo		heofene A, hefune *C*, heofone *DE^{2}*, heofena *K*, heofonum *BFHJ*, heofonum I, heofenum *G* (*L*)
prospexit		forðlocað ABC, forðlocade G, forðlocode H, forþlocade J, gelocode D, gelocede E^{2}, beheold *F*, beseah I, besceawaþ K
super		ofer ABDE^{2}FGHJK, ofyr C, ofor I
filios	|	bearn ABCDGHIJ, bear K, sunu F, mannæ E^{2}
hominum	|	monna AB, manna CDFGHIJK*, beærn E^{2}
ut		ðæt A, þæt BIJ, þæt CDFGHK, þet E^{2}
uideat		he gese A, he gesie B, he geseo CDFIJ, he gesio E^{2}, geseo *K*, he gesyhð GH
si		hweðer A, hwæðer B, hwæðyr C, gif DE^{2}IK, gyf F, hwæt GHJ
est		sie AB, sy GHJ, sy ł is I*, is CDE^{2}FK
intellegens		ongeotende A, ongietende B, ongetynde *C*, ongytende DG, ongitende F*HJ*, ænig andgitel ł undergytende *I**, ongetende ł understandende *E^{x}**, ynderstandende K
aut		oððe ABCFGH, oþðe *D*K, oþþe E^{2}IJ
requirens		soecende AB, secynde C, secende DE^{2}FG*H*IJK
deum		god ABCFGHIJ, gode E^{2}*, drihten K

ED: cęlo (E)] caelo *Harsley*. forðlocode (H)] forð locode *Campbell*. ongetende ł understandende (E)] ongetende ł understa*n*d*e*nd*e* *Harsley*. requírens (H)] requirens *Campbell*.

OE: manna (K)] *letter eras. after 1st* n, *Sisam reads* e *eras.* sy ł is (I)] ł is *written in bottom margin below lemma.* ænig andgitel ł undergytende (I)] ł undergytende *written in bottom margin below lemma.* ongetende ł understandende (E^{x})] *on eras., 3rd and final* de *in ligature.* gode (E^{2})] e *perhaps added later by main hand: slightly below line and in slightly darker ink.*

LTg: de] dę (?) G: *Ps 9.27* corde *has similar cauda.* caelo] cælo B; cęlo CEFGHKL; celo DJ. prospexit] F: *cross-stroke through descender of 1st* p (= pro) *eras.* uideat] uidead K. intellegens] intelligens CEI, H: *2nd* i *on eras.* aut] D: au *on eras.* requirens] requírens H.

LTu: caelo] celo εξσςτ*τ; cęlo ζινουφχ; cælo ϑμ. intellegens] intelligens εζϑιλξπσ τ*τυφ, ο: *orig.* intellegens: *2nd* e *deleted by subscript dot,* i *interl.*

3

Omnes   alle A, ealle BCDFGHIJK, Eælle E^{2}
declinauerunt   onhaeldon A, onheldon B, onhyldon C, framahyldon D, framahyldan K, framahyldæþ E^{2}, hi ahyldon F, ahyldon GH, ahildon J, hi ahyldon ł framgewendon I
simul   somud A, somod BG, samod CFHIJ, somed E^{2}, ætsomne D, ætgædere K
inutiles   unnytte ABCDI, unnyt K, onnitte F, on unnytte GHJ, ⁊ on unnytenesse E^{2}
facti | gewordne A, gewordene BDFGHJ, gewordyne C, gewurdene I, gedone K, sindon E^{2}
sunt | werun *A*, wæron B, synd CJK, synt DF, syndon H, s[ ]ndon G, hi syndon I, gewordene E^{2}
non | nis ABE^{2}F, nys C, nys na I, ne GH, na JK
est | is GHJ*K*
qui   se ðe ABCFG, se þe E^{2}HIJ, ðe D, þa K
faciat   doe A, dó BCD, do E^{2}FGHIJK
bonum   god AE^{2}FGHIK, gód BCJ
non | nis ABF, nys C, nys na I, ne E^{2}GH, na JK
est | is E^{2}GHJ*K*
usque   oð ABCFGHIJ, oþ K, odð E^{x}*
ad   to E^{2}I, on *K*
unum   enne *A*, ænne BG, æne E^{2}*, anum FI, anum K, ende CHJ

Sepulchrum | byrgen ABDF*G*HIJ, byrgyn C, byrigen K*, Openende E$^{2/x}$*
patens | open ABI, opyn C, opengende DK, opniende F, openigende G, opnigende J, opnigen H, is E^{2}
est | is ABFGHIJ*K*, ys C, byrgen E^{2}*
guttur   hraecae A, hrace BD, hraca CG, raca HJ, raca ł þrotu ł I*, in(no)ð F*, celo K, ciolæn ł hracen E^{2}*
eorum   heara A, heora BDFGHIJK, hyra C, hioræ E^{2}
linguis   tungum A, tungum B, tungan CDGHJ, tungæn E^{2}, tangan F, tunge K, on tungum I
suis   heara A, hira B, hyra C, heora DFGHIJK, heore E^{x}*
dolose   faecenlice A, facenlice B, facynlice C, facenfullice DE^{x}*, facenfullice GHIJ, facnfullice F, facnfule K
agebant   dydun A, dydon B, hi dydon C, hy dydon DF, hy deodon E^{x}*, hi dydan K, hi dedun I, doð GH, doþ J

uenenum		atur AD, ater B, attor *C*FGHJ, átter E^{2}, atter I* (*K*)
aspidum		nedrena *A*, nædrena BFG, nædryna C, nedrana D, nedrana E^{x}*, næddrena *HJ*, deafra næddran ł nædryna I, nædran K
sub	|	under ABCDE^{2}*FIJK, under G, tungan H
labiis	|	weolerum A, weolerum B, welerum DG, welerum E^{2}FI, welyre C, tungan J, lippan K, under H
eorum		heara A, hira B, heora CDFGHIJ*K, heore E^{2}

Quorum		ðeara A, þara BCGHIJK, ðara DF, þæræ E^{2}
os		muð *A*CE^{2}GH, múð B, muþ FIJK (*D*)
maledictione		awergednisse A, awergednesse B, awyrgednysse F, of awyrgednisse D, of awyrgednes K, of awargednesse E^{x}*, mid awyrgednysse I, awyrgydlice C, wyrigcwydolnesse G, wirigcwedolnesse HJ
et		┐ ABCDE^{2}FGHIJK
amaritudine		bitternisse A, biternesse BGHJ, biternysse C, bitternysse I, of biternisse D, of biternesse E^{2}, (of)erbyternysse F*, bite[ ] *K**
plenum		ful ADE^{x}*K, full BCFGHIJ
est		bið AB*, ys byð C, is DE^{2}*FHIJ*K*
ueloces	|	hreðe A, hræde BC, hrade DF, hraðe *G*H, hraþe K, raþe J, swifte ł hræde I, ┐ hiræ E^{2}
pedes		foet A, fóet B, fet CDE^{2}GHIJ*K*, fot F
eorum	|	heara A, hira B, hyra C, heora DFHI*J, hieora G, hræþe ł snelle E^{2}* (*K*)
ad		to ABCDE^{2}FGHIK, ┐ *J*
effundendum		ageotenne ADFGH, ageotanne BI, ageotynne C, to ageotende J, geotende K, ægiotænæ ł to scedende E^{2}*
sanguinem		blod ABCDE^{2}*FGHIJK

Contritio		forðrȩstednis A, forðræstednes B, forþræstydnys C, forðræstness G, forðræstnes H, forþræstnes J, forbrytednis D, forbrytednys F, Forbrytednesse *E*^{x}*, forbrytnes K, tobrytednys ł forgnidennys I*
et		┐ ABCDE^{2}FGHIJK
infelicitas		ungeselignis A, ungesælignes BHJ, ongesælignys C, ungesælignis D, ungeselignes E^{2}, ungesæligness *G*, ungesælignys I, ungesælines K, on ungesælignys F
in		in AB, on CDE^{2}FGHIJK
uiis	|	wegum ABFGI, wegum CDHJ, wege K, hieræ *E*^{2}
eorum	|	heara A, hira B, heora CFGHIJK, wegum E^{2}
et		┐ ABCE^{2}FGHI*JK
uiam	|	weg ABCDFGHIJ, wegg K, sibbe E^{2}

pacis	I	sibbe ABCFGI*JK, sybbe DH, weg E^{2}
non	I	ne ABC, hy na D, hy ne G, hie ne E^{2}, he ne F, hig ne H, na JK, ⁊ hi ne I
cognouerunt	I	oncneowun A, oncneowon BDE^{2}F, oncnewun C, hig oncnewon J, ongeaton GH, angetun ł ne oncneowon I, gecneowan K
Non	I	nis ABD*FI*, nys C, ne *GH*, Ne E^{2}, na *JK*
est	I	is E^{2}GHJ*K*
timor	I	ege ABCDFGHIJK, godes E^{2}
dei	I	godes ABDFG*H*IJK, godys C, ege E^{2}
ante		biforan A, beforan BCDGHIJK, ætforan F, beforen E^{2}*
oculos	I	egum A, eagum I, eagan BCDFGH, eagon J, egan K*, hieræ E^{2}
eorum	I	heara A, hira B, hyra C, heora DFGHIJK, eægum E^{2}*

ED: framahyldæþ (E)] fram ahyldæþ *Harsley.* dó (B)] ðó *Brenner.* in(no)ð (F)] innoð *Kimmens.* áspidum (H)] aspidum *Campbell.* under (E)] under *Harsley.* under (J)] unde. *Oess.* heora (D) (*3rd*)] ðara *Roeder.* ós (A)] os *Kuhn.* a[ ]ne (K)] am[ ]ne *Sisam.* (of)erbyternysse (F)] oferbyternysse *Kimmens.* uíís (E)] viis *Harsley.* ⁊ (I) (*3rd*)] *no gloss Lindelöf.*

OE: odð (E^{x})] *on eras.* æne (E^{2})] *eras. before word.* byrigen (K)] *otiose stroke (false start?) after word.* Openende (E$^{2/x}$)] nende *on eras.* byrgen (E^{2})] y *on eras.* raca ł þrotu ł (I)] *no 3rd gloss follows.* in(no)ð (F)] *2nd* n *obscured by eras., lower part of* o *visible,* ð *partly obscured.* ciolæn ł hracen (E^{2})] h *'squeezed in' below* p *in* patens *above.* heore (E^{x})] *on eras.* facenfullice (E^{x})] *on eras.* hy deodon (E^{x})] *on eras.* atter (I)] est : is *written in right margin after word.* nedrana (E^{x})] *on eras.* under (E^{2})] de *in ligature.* heora (J) (*3rd*)] a *partly obscured.* of awargednesse (E^{x})] *on eras.* (of)erbyternysse (F)] *partly eras.: fragment of* o *and stem of* f *visible,* e *obscured but visible.* bite[ ] (K)] *partly lost due to MS damage: see* uenenum *in LTg.* ful (E^{x})] *on eras.* bið (B)] is *eras. before word.* is (E^{2}) (*3rd*)] hiræ *eras. after word.* heora (I) (*4th*)] s. sunt : synt *written in right margin after word.* hræþe ł snelle (E^{2})] ł snelle *added by main hand.* ægiotænæ ł to scedende (E^{2})] ł to scedende *added by main hand.* blod (E^{2})] *gloss eras. before word.* Forbrytednesse (E^{x})] *on eras.* tobrytednys ł forgnidennys (I)] tobrytednys *written in left margin,* est : is *written in bowl of* C *in* Contritio. ⁊ (I) (*3rd*)] *top of* ⁊ *eras.* sibbe (I)] we *eras. before word.* beforen (E^{2})] be *on eras.* egan (K)] *small eras. before word.* eægum (E^{2})] *gloss eras. after word.*

LTg: sunt] A: *orig.* st (*no macron visible*): t *altered to* u, nt *added.* est (*1st*)] ést K. est (*2nd*)] ést K. ad (*1st*)] ád K. unum] A: m *added by corr.* Sepulchrum] Sępulchrum G: *initial letter faint but visible.* est (*3rd*)] ést K. uenenum] K: *lost due to MS damage: initial letter excised from fol. 21v, but cut extends through fol. 20, hence* *damage to this leaf;* uenénum C. aspidum] A: m *added by corr.;* áspidum H. os] ós AD. amaritudine] a[ ]ne K: *medial letters lost to MS damage, 2 minims visible after* a: *see note to* uenenum *above.* est (*4th*)] ést K. ueloces] uęloces G. pedes] pede[ ] K: *final letter lost due to MS damage: see* uenenum *above.* eorum (*3rd*)] K: *lost due to MS damage: see* uenenum. ad (*2nd*)] et J: *on eras.* Contritio] Contricio E. infelicitas] infęlicitas G. uiis] uíís E. Non] non FGHIJK. est (*5th*)] ést K. dei] H: d *possibly on eras.*

LTu: guttur] guttor β; gutur ϑ. dolose] dolosae π. uenenum] ueninum ϑ. labiis] labis βϑ. ueloces] et uelociter ς. effundendum] ν: *1st* n *interl.;* effundum ϑ. Contritio] Contricio ιτ*τψ. uiis] uis ϑ. Non] non δεζϑιλμξοπϱστυφχψ; [ ]on τ*: *initial letter wanting.*

4

Nonne	|	ah ne *AB,* hu ne *CD,* la hu ne *I**, hie ne *E*^{2}, hi ne F, ac hi ne *G,* ac hig ne HJ, na ne K (*L*)
cognoscent	|	oncnawað ABDF, oncnæwað C, oncnewon E^{2}, oncneowon GHJ, angeatun ł oncnawað I*, cnawað K
omnes		alle A, ealle BCDFGHIJK, eælle E^{2}
qui		ða ða A, þa þe BC*E*^{2}*FGI, þa ðe DHJ, þa K
operantur		wircað A, wyrcað DF, wyrceað BCG, wircæþ E^{2}, weorcað H, wyrcaþ I, wircaþ J, wyrcað K
iniquitatem		unrehtwisnisse *A,* unryhtwisnesse B, unrihtwisnysse CFI, unrihtwisnesse K, unryht D, unriht GHJ, unrihtnesse E^{2}
qui		ða *A,* þa *BC*K, þa ðe *DF*, þa þe *E*^{2}*I, ge þe GHJ (*L*)
deuorant		forswelgad A, forswelgað BCDFK, forswelgæþ E^{2}, forswelgaþ I, fræton G*HJ*
plebem	|	folc ABCDFGHIJK, min E^{2}
meam	|	min ABCDFGHIJK, folc E^{2}
sicut		swe A, swa BCK, swæ E^{2}, swa swa FGHIJ
escam		mete ABCDFG*H*IJ, méte E^{2}, mettas K
panis		hlafes *A*BDE^{2}FGHIJ, hlafys C, breades K

ED: [ ]onne (G)] Nonne *Rosier.* hu ne (CD)] hune *Wildhagen, Roeder.* þa ðe (H)] þa þe *Campbell.* Qui (B)] qui *Brenner.* Qvi (E)] qui *Harsley.* déuorant (H)] deuorant *Campbell.* swa swa (GIJ)] swaswa *Rosier, Lindelöf, Oess.*

OE: la hu ne (I)] *crudely-formed* ł (?), *similar to that before* oncnawað, *written in left margin.* angeatun ł oncnawað (I)] ł oncnawað *written in right margin.* þa þe (E^{2}) (*both*)] *orig.* þæ þe: æ *altered to* a.

LTg: Nonne] I: N *faint but visible;* [ ]onne G: *initial letter only partly visible;* nonne ABCDE, L: N *written above* n *by corr.* qui (*1st*)] Qvi E: *not indicating verse division.*

iniquitatem] A: m *added by corr., eras.* (*of macron*) *above* e. qui (*2nd*)] Qui ABCDEL. deuorant] déuorant H. escam] H: *eye of* e *effaced.* panis] A: s *'squeezed in.'*

LTu: Nonne] ε: nc *interl.;* nonne βνςτ*. qui (*1st*)] qvi τ*. qui (*2nd*)] Qui βνςτ*. escam] ęscam εν.

5

Deum* god *ABC,* gode E^{x}*, drihten GK, driħt HJ, driht̄ I, drħt F (*DL*)
non | ne ABGHJ, na K, hi ne CI, hie ne E^{2}, hi na F
inuocauerunt | gecedun A, gecegdun B, gecigdon CGHJ, gecygdon DF, gecygden E^{2}, cigdon ł hi na ne cleopedon I, hi clypedon K
illic der A, þær BCGHI, ðær DE^{x}*F, þar JK
trepidauerunt forhtaðum A, forhtodun B, forhtodon GHJ, hi forhtodon C, hy forhtodon D, hie forhtodon E^{2}, hi forhtudon F, hi forhtedun I, hi forhtodan K
timore mid ege ABGHIJ, ege CDF*K**
ubi ðer A, þer E^{2}, þær BCDGK, ðær F, þar HJ, þær þær I
non | ne ABCJ, na DFK, ne nes $E^{2/x}$*, næs I, se ne H, ege G
erat | wes A, wæs BDFHJK, bið C, ne G, næn E^{2}
timor | ege ABCDE^{2}FH*K, ege ł egsa I, se ege J, wæs G

ED: [ ]ominum (G)] Dominum *Rosier.* ubi (G)] ub*i Rosier.*

OE: gode (E^{x})] *on eras.* ðær (E^{x})] *on eras.* cgc (K) (*1st*)] *otiose stroke* (*false start?*) *or small* c *before word.* ne nes ($E^{2/x}$)] *on eras.* ege (H)] *2nd* e *partly obscured.*

LTg: Deum] deum ABCDEL. timore] K: *small eras. after word.*

LTu: Deum] deum βνςτ*. trepidauerunt] tripidauerunt ϑ.

GAg: Deum] Dominum FHIJK; [ ]ominum G: *initial letter only partly visible.*

GAu: Deum] Dominum δεζϑιλμξοπϱστυφχψ.

6

Quoniam forðon ABDE^{2}*H, forþon CFGJ, forðon þe I, forðam K
deus god ABCE^{2}, drihten *G,* driħt *FJ,* driht̄ *I* (*HK*)
in in ABH, on CDE^{2}*FGIJK
generatione cneorisse ABDJK, cneorysse C, cneorisne GH, cneowrisse E^{2}, cynryne F, cnosle ł mægðe I
iusta ðere rehtan A, þære ryhtan B, þære rihtan *C,* ryhtwisre D, rihtwisre F, on rihtwisre I, rihtwisne E^{2}, rihtwis G*H*JK
est is ABE^{2}FGHIJK, ys C
consilium geðaeht A, geðeaht *B*F, geþeaht CDIK, þæt geþeaht GH*J, geþeahtunge E^{2}

inopis	weðlan A, wædlan B*C*F, wedlan D, wedlon E^{x}, wædlena GH, wændlena J, ðæs hæfenleasan ł wædlan I*, on wædlan K
confudisti*	ðu gescendes *A*, þu gescendes B, þu gescyndyst *C*, ðu gedrefdest DE^{x}*, þu gedrefdest K, ðu gedrǽf[ ]est F*, þu togute GHJ, ge forsawon ł ge gescendon I*
quoniam	forðon *ABD*FJ, forþon *C*H, forðan *E^{x}**, forðan þe I, forþā (þ)[ ] *G**, forðam K (*L*)
deus*	god ABCE^{x}*, drihten G, driht́ FHJ, drihƚ̄ I (*L*)
spes	| hyht ABDF, hiht CGIJK, hihte E^{x}*, his H
eius	| his ABDE^{x}*FGIJ*K*, hys C, hiht H
est	is ABE^{x}*FGHIJ*K*, ys C

ED: forðon (A) (*1st*)] for ðon *Kuhn.* forðon (E)] Forðon *Harsley.* in (G)] *in Rosier.* on (G)] [ ]n *Rosier.* iusta (E)] justa *Harsley.* inopis (G)] in*o*pis *Rosier.* wædlena (G)] wæd[ ]a *Rosier.* confudistis (C)] confudisti *Wildhagen.* ðu gedrǽf[ ]est (F)] ðu gedrǽfdest *Kimmens.* forðon (A) (*2nd*)] for ðon *Kuhn.* forþā (þ)[ ] (G)] forþ[ ] *Rosier.* est (G) (*2nd*)] *est Rosier.* is (G) (*2nd*)] *no gloss Rosier.*

OE: forðon (E^{2})] *eras. after word.* on (E^{2})] his *eras. after word.* þæt geþeaht (H)] *2nd* e *partly obscured.* ðæs hæfenleasan ł wædlan (I)] ðæs hæfenleasan *written in left margin.* ðu gedrefdest (E^{x})] *on eras. by corr.* ðu gedrǽf[ ]est (F)] *partly obscured by eras., letter fragment visible after* f. ge forsawon ł ge gescendon (I)] ł ge gescendon *written in right margin and signaled for inclusion.* forðan (E^{x})] *on eras. by corr.* forþā (þ)[ ] (G)] *descender of 2nd* þ *lost.* god (E^{x}) (*2nd*)] *on eras. by corr.* hihte (E^{x})] *on eras. by corr.* his (E^{x})] *on eras. by corr.* is (E^{x}) (*2nd*)] *on eras. by corr.*

LTg: deus (*1st*)] dominus FGHIJK: *cf. Weber MSS* γ moz, *Bib. sac. MSS* $Q^{2}\Phi^{p}$VDΩ, *etc.* iusta] C: *orig.* iuxta: x *deleted by subscript dot,* s *interl.,* H: s *on eras.* consilium] B: *somewhat large* C, *although not marking verse division.* inopis] ínopis C. confudisti] confudistis AC: *final* s *added interl. by corr.: cf. Weber MSS* KTPQUδ moz^{c}, *see GAg.* quoniam] *lost* G, *although part of* q *and top of* u (?) *visible;* E: ł quia *interl. by glossator;* quia ABCDL: *cf. Weber MSS* HM^{2}KT*. deus (*2nd*)] L: dominus *written interl. above* deus *by corr.: see GAg.* eius] eíus K. est (*2nd*)] ést K.

LTu: deus (*1st*)] dominus δεζιλξοπϱστυφχ: *cf. Weber MSS* γ moz, *Bib. sac. MSS* $Q^{2}\Phi^{p}$VDΩ, *etc.* iusta] β: *orig.* ista: *crude* u *interl.;* iuxta ς. quoniam] quia βνς: *cf. Weber MSS* HM^{2}KT*.

GAg: confudisti] confudistis FGHIJK, AC: *see LTg.* deus (*2nd*)] dominus FGHIJK, L: *see LTg.*

GAu:] confudisti] confudistis δεζθιλμξοπϱστφχψ. deus (*2nd*)] dominus δεζθιλμξοπϱστυφχψ.

7

Quis		hwelc ABD, hwylc CF*G*HK, hwilc E^2J, la hwa I
dabit		seleð ABE^2*, sylyð C, selð D, sylð FK, syleð GH, sileþ J, forgyfð I
ex		ofer AB, ofyr C, of *E^2*FI, on G (*J*)
sion		sion AB*C*F, seone *G*, syon *E^2*, ansyne H, ansine *J*, heofenum I
salutare		haelu A, hælo BDFH, hæle CGJK, helo E^2, þone halwendan ł hælo I
israhel		israel A, ysrahelys C, isræhelæ *E^2*, israhele FG, israelo H*J*, ða getreowfullan *D* (*IK*)
dum*		ðonne AF, þonne B, þonne CHJ, þone IK, þanne E^2 (*G*)
auertit*		forcerreð A, forcirreð B, forcyrryð *C*, acyrreð DE^2, acyrreþ K*, aweg acyrreð G, aweg cirreþ H, aweg ceorrat J, awænt F, awent I
dominus		dryhten AB, drihten E^2GI, driht CHJ, driht F, drihte *K*
captiuitatem		heftned A, hæftned BD, hæftnyd CGHJ, heftnieþ E^2, hæftnede I, hæftnunge F, hæftlingas K
plebis	|	folces ABDFI, folcys C, folcces K, folc HJ, his E^2G
suae	|	his *ABDFHIJK*, hys *C*, folces *E^2G* (*L*)
⟨et⟩		⁊ K
Laetetur*	|	blissað A*B*C*F*G, blissiað H, blissiaþ J, geblissaþ I, blissie *D*, blissige K, Iacob *E^2* (*L*)
iacob	|	iacob CGHJ, iaco F, n K*, blissæþ E^2
et		⁊ ABCDEFGHIJK
exultet*		gefið A, gefihð B, gefyhð C, gefeoge D, gehyht E^2, fægnað F, fægnaþ I, fægnigen K, wynsumað G, wunsumiað H, wynsumiaþ J (*L*)
israhel		israhela F, israhel CH*J*, ysrahel E^2*, folc israhel G, geseonde god *I*, geleaffule K

ED: sion (K)] Sion *Sisam.* isrł (DEIJK) (*1st*)] israel *Roeder, Harsley, Lindelöf, Oess;* Israhel *Sisam.* þonne (C)] þonne *Wildhagen.* suę (E)] suae *Harsley.* iacob (K)] Iacob *Sisam.* isrł (IJ) (*2nd*)] israel *Lindelöf;* israhel *Oess.* israhel (K)] Israhel *Sisam.*

OE: seleð (E^2)] ð *altered from* n. acyrreþ (K)] reþ *on eras.* n (K)] *for* nomen. ysrahel (E^2)] on *eras. before word.*

LTg: Quis] [ ]uis G: *initial* Q *lost.* ex sion] exion EJ. sion] syon G, C: *orig.* sion: i *deleted by subscript dot,* y *interl.* israhel (*1st*)] isrł DEIJK. auertit] auerterit C: *cf. Weber MS* S, *see GAg.* dominus] K: *on eras. by corr.* suae] suę ACDEFGHIJL; suæ B; suę et K: *eras. after* suę. Laetetur] Lætetur B; Letetur D; Lętetur CE, L: exultabit *written interl. by corr.: see GAg.* exultet] L: letabitur *written interl. by corr.: see GAg.* israhel (*2nd*)] isrł IJ.

LTu: ex sion] σ: si *interl.;* ex syon ετ*τφ; exion διυ. israhel (*1st*)] israel ενς; isrł ιλξπρστ*τυφ. auertit] auerterit νς: *see GAu.* captiuitatem] captitatem β; captiuitate υ. suae] suę ειν ξυφ; sue ζςτ*τ; suæ ϑμ. Laetetur] Letetur ςτ*. israhel (*2nd*)] isr̄l β; israel ειvς; isrł ξοπστ*τυφ.

GAg: dum] cum FHIJ, K: c *altered from another letter;* c[ ] G: *letter fragment visible after* c. auertit] auerterit FGHIJL, K: *2nd* e *altered from* i, rit *on eras.*, C: *see LTg.* Laetetur] exultabit FGHIK, L: *see LTg;* exultauit J. exultet] lętabitur F; laetabitur I; letabitur GHJK, L: *see LTg.*

GAu: dum] cum δεζϑιλμξοπρστυφχψ. auertit] auerterit δεζϑιλμξοπρστυφχψ, νς: *see LTu.* Laetetur] exultabit δεζιλμξοπρστυφχψ; exultauit ϑ. exultet] laetabitur δζμπψ; lętabitur ειορφ; letabitur ϑλξστυ; lætabitur χ.

PSALM 14

1

Domine		dryhten A*, Drihten E^{2}, drih̄t FJ, drih̄ G, s. o eala drih̄t *C*, eala þ(u) o. drihten I* (*BK*)
quis		hwelc ABDH, hwylc *C*FGK, hwilc IJ, wylc E^{2}
habitabit		eardað *ABC*FGHK, eardaþ DJ, eærdæþ E^{2}, sceal geeardian ł hwa wunað I*
in		in AB, on CDE^{2}FGHIJK
tabernaculo	|	selegescote AB, sielegesceote C, eardungstowe DH, gesele ł eardungstowe ł teld E$^{2/x}$*, eardungstowe ł getelde I, getelde FJ, earddunga K, þinum G
tuo	|	ðinum AF, þinum BI, þinum CJ, þinre DK, getelde G
aut		oððe ABCFGHIJ, oþðe DK, oþðæ E^{2}
quis		hwelc ABDH, hwylc CFK, hwilc GIJ, wylc E^{2}
requiescet		geresteð *A*BDFGH, gerestyð C, gersteþ J, gerest I, resteþ E^{2}, resteð K
in	|	in ABG, on CDE^{2}FHIJK
monte	|	munte ABCFIJK, ðinum D, þinum G, þinum H, þinre E^{2}
sancto	|	ðæm halgan A, þæm halgan B, ðam haligan D, þam halgan GH, þan halgan C, hælgæn E^{2}, halgum FJ, halgum I, halian K
tuo	|	ðinum A*, þinum CIJ, þinum F, þinan K, his B, munte DH, munte þinan G, dune ł munte E^{2}*

ED: requiescet (G)] requiescat *Rosier.* in (OE) (G)] on *Rosier.*

OE: dryhten (A)] h *interl.* eala þ(u) o. drihten (I)] eala þ(u) *written in left margin,* *right side of* u *lost.* sceal geeardian ł hwa wunað (I)] ł hwa wunað *written in right margin.* gesele ł eardungstowe ł teld ($E^{2/x}$)] ł eardungstowe ł teld *on eras.* ðinum (A) (*2nd*)] i *written below line.* dune ł munte (E^2)] ł munte *added later by main hand.*

LTg: Domine] DÑE BK; DOMINE C. quis (*1st*)] QVIS C. habitabit] A: *2nd* b *on eras.;* HABITAbit C; habitauit B. requiescet] A: *orig.* requiescit: *2nd* i *altered to* e.

LTu: Domine] DÑE βλμνορστφ; DÑe ϑχ; DOMINE ς. quis] QUIS λμνρ. habitabit] HABITABIT λρ; HABITAbit μν; habitauit ς. in (*1st*)] IN λρ. tabernaculo] TABERnaculo λ; TAbernaculo ρ. requiescet] requiescit β.

2

Qui	se ABC, Se E^2, ðe D, þe H, se ðe F, se þe GIJ (*K*)
ingreditur	ingęð A, ingæð BCDH, ingeþ E^2, ingangeð G, ingangeþ J, infærð F, infærþ I (*K*)
sine	butan ABDGHIK, buton CFJ, butæn E^2
macula	womme ABCGI*K, wemme DE^2, wæmme *F*J, wæmme H
et	⁊ ABCDE^2*FGHI*JK
operatur	wirceð A, wyrceð B, wyrceað C, wyrcð DFH*K*, wyrcþ E^2, wyrcð ł ⁊ byþ wyrcende I*, gewyrceað G, geweorcaþ J
iustitiam	rehtwisnisse A, ryhtwisnesse BD, rihtwisnysse *C*FI, rihtwisnesse E^x*GHJK

ED: Qui (B)] qui *Brenner.*

OE: ingeþ (E^2)] i *on eras., word written in slightly darker ink.* womme (I)] est : hi[ ] *written in right margin across from gloss and partly lost due to trimmed leaf.* ⁊ (E^2)] *eras. after word.* ⁊ wyrcð ł ⁊ byþ wyrcende (I)] ⁊ wyrcð *written in left margin.* rihtwisnesse (E^x)] *on eras. by corr., traces of orig. gloss visible before word.*

LTg: Qui] K: *lost due to MS damage: initial letter excised from fol. 21v, but cut extends through fol. 20, hence damage to this leaf.* ingreditur] [ ](d)itur K: d *cropped on left: see* Qui *above.* macula] F: *eras. before* l. operatur] ope[ ] K: *partly lost due to MS damage: see* Qui. iustitiam] iusticiam C: *orig.* iustitiam: *2nd* t *deleted by subscript dot,* c *interl.*

LTu: iustitiam] iusticiam τ*τφ.

3

Qui	se ABC, se ðe F, Se þe E^2*, se þe GIJ (*K*)
loquitur	spriceð AB, sprecyð C, sprycð DF, spryceþ E^2, sprycþ H, sprecð GI, sprecþ J (*K*)
ueritatem	soðfestnisse A, soðfæstnesse B, soðfæstnysse CI, soþfæstnisse D, soþfestnesse E^2, soþfæstnysse F, soðfæstnesse G, soþfæstnesse HJ, soþfæstnes K
in	in AB, on CDE^2FGHIJK

corde	I	heortan ABCDFHIJK, his E^{2}G
suo	I	his ABDFHIJK, hys C, heortæn E^{2}, heortan G
et*		⁊ ABCDE^{2}, se þe F, se ðe I, þe G, ꝥ J (*L*)
non		nis A, nys C, ne BDE^{2}FGHIJ (*K*)
egit		dyde BDF*H*, deð *G*, deþ E^{2}JK, worhte se ðe ne dyde I*
dolum		facæn A, facen BG, facyn C, facn DFHJK, faken I, inwyd ł facn E$^{2/x}$*
in		in AB, on CDE^{2}FGHIJK
lingua	I	tungan ABCDFHJK, his E^{2}GI
sua	I	his ABCFJK, tungan GI, tungæn E^{2}
Nec		ne ABCGJ, Ne E^{2}, ne ne DF*H*I (*K*)
fecit		he dyde ABC, dyde DE^{x}*FHI, deð G, deþ J (*K*)
proximo	I	ðæm nestan A, þæm nihstan B, þam nehstan C, þæm nixtan I, þam nihstan J, nehstan D, nextan F, nyhstan H, his *E*^{2}GK
suo	I	his ABCFIJ, þam nyhstan G, niextæn E^{2}*, nyxtan *K*
malum		yfel ABDE^{2}FGHIJK, yfyl C
et		⁊ ABCE^{2}FGHJK
obprobrium		edwit *AB*C, edwit ł hosp E^{x}*, hosp DF*G*JK, osp *H**, bysmerunga ł hosp *I*
non		ne ABCDE^{2}FGHJ, na K, ⁊ ne I
accepit		onfeng ABCF, anfeng DE^{2}*H, onfehð *G*J, underfengc I, feng K
aduersus		wið ABCG, wiþ ł ongean J, ongean DE^{2}*, angean H, togeanes FIK
proximum*	I	ðæm nestan A, þæm nihstan B, þam nehstan C, þam nyhstan J, þa nyxtan I, neahstan D, nehstan F, nyhstan H, nyxtan K, his E^{2}*G (*L*)
suum*	I	his ABDFHIJK, hys C, niextæn E^{2}, þa nyhstan G (*L*)

ED: ꝥ (J)] þ*e Oess.* worhte se ðe ne dyde (I)] worhte ł se ðe ne dyde *Lindelöf.* ne ne (D)] nene *Roeder.* opprobrium (C)] o[b]probrium *Wildhagen.* obprobriu[ ] (G)] obprobri*um Rosier.*

OE: Se þe (E^{2})] Se *written in left margin.* worhte se ðe ne dyde (I)] se ðe ne dyde *written in left margin.* inwyd ł facn (E$^{2/x}$)] ł facn *added later* (*by corr.?*) *in slightly darker ink.* dyde (E^{x})] *on eras.* niextæn (E^{2}) (*1st*)] *eras. before word.* edwit ł hosp (E^{x})] *on eras.* osp (H)] *small eras.* (?) *after* p. anfeng (E^{2})] a *altered from* o, g *on eras., 2nd* n *altered from* h. ongean (E^{2})] *on eras.* his (E^{2}) (*4th*)] *on eras.*

LTg: Qui] K: *lost due to MS damage: see note to v. 2* Qui. loquitur] [ ]tur K: *partly lost due to MS damage: see v. 2* Qui. et (*1st*)] L: t *crossed through by corr.,* qui *inserted* *before word: see GAg.* non (*1st*)] K: *lost due to MS damage, right leg of 2nd* n *visible: see v. 2* Qui. egit] ęgit GH. Nec] K: *lost due to MS damage, fragment* (*lower portion*) *of* N *visible: see v. 2* Qui; Nęc H. ſecit] [ ]cit K: *partly lost due to MS damage, fragments* (*lower portions*) *of* f *and* e *visible: see v. 2* Qui. proximo] E: mo *on eras.* suo] K: *added interl. by corr.* obprobrium] obprobriu[ ] G; opprobrium AHI, C: *orig.* obprobrium: b *altered to* p. accepit] accępit G. proximum] L: *final* m *deleted by superscript dot,* os *written interl. by corr.: see GAg.* suum] L: *final* m *deleted by superscript dot,* os *written interl. by corr.: see GAg.*

LTu: egit] ęgit ε. Nec] Nęc ξ. fecit] fęcit ξ. malum] mala ς. obprobrium] opproprium β: *orig.* obproprium: b *crossed through,* p *interl.;* opprobrium εϑλοπφχ. accepit] acepit ϑ.

GAg: et (*1st*)] qui FGHIJ, L: *see LTg,* K: *lost to MS damage: see note to v. 2* Qui. proximum suum] proximos suos FGHIJK, L: *see LTg.*

GAu: et (*1st*)] qui δεζϑιλμξοπϱστυφχψ. proximum suum] proximos suos δεζϑιλμξοπϱ στυφχψ.

4

Ad		to ABCDFGHIJK, To E^2
nihilum		nowihte AB*C*, ealles nahte D*H*, nahte F*GIJK*, næhte *E*^{2}
deductus	|	gelaeded A, gelæded BGJ, gelædyd C, gelæd bið ł geteald D, gelæd bið ł geteald H, geteald biþ ł læd F, gelæd IK, biþ E^2
est	|	bið ABCDG, biþ H, is FIJ*K*, geled E^2*
in		in AB, on CDE^2FGHIJK
conspectu	|	gesihðe ABFI, gesyhðe CD, gesihþe HJ, ansyne K, his E^2G
eius	|	his ABFIJK, hys C, gesihþe E^2*G*
malignus		se awergda AB, se awyrgyda C, se awyrgeda DFHK, se æwyrgedæ E^2*, se awyrgeda ł yfelcunda I, awyrged G, awirged J
timentes	|	ondredende A, ondrædende BG, ondrædynde C, ondrædenne J, adrædende K, ða ondrædendan D, þa ondrædendan FHI*, soðlice E^2
autem	|	soðlice ABCFGI, soþlice J, witodlice K, þæ þe drihten E^2
dominum	|	dryten A, dryhten D, drihten GK, dryht B, drih̄t CFJ, drih̄t I, ondredæþ E^2
magnificat*		gemiclað ABC, he gemiclað DF, gemicliað G, gemiccliaþ J, he gewuldraþ I, bið gewuldrud K, he hig̃ gemuclað E^x*
Qui		se ABC, Se þe E^2, se ðe F, se þe *G*IJ, þe K
iurat		swereð ABH, sweryð C, sweræþ E^2, swerað FGIK, sweraþ J, swereð ł ryhtgehet D

proximo	I	ðæm nestan A, þæm nihstan B, þam nehstan C, þæm nextan I, þam nihstan J, nehstan DF, nyhstan H, nyxtan K, his E^{2}*G
suo	I	his ABDFHIJK, hys C, þam nyhstan G, niextæn E^{2}
et		⁊ ABCFHIK, ⁊ hiene E^{2}, ⁊ hine GJ
non		ne ABCDE^{2}GHJ, na FIK
decipit		bswac *A*, beswac *BC*, beswicð DE^{x}*G*K*, beswycð H, beswicþ J, swicð F, bepæcð ł ⁊ hine na beswiceþ I
eum*		hine ABC (*L*)

ED: [ ]ui (G)] Qui *Rosier.* swerað (I)] sweraþ *Lindelöf.*

OE: geled (E^{2}) *eras.* (*1–2 letters*) *after word.* se æwyrgedæ (E^{2})] *2nd* e *interl.* þa ondrædendan (I)] þa *interl.* he hig̃ gemuclað (E^{x})] gemuclað *added* (?) *in slightly darker ink.* his (E^{2}) (*2nd*)] *eras. after word.* beswicð (E^{x})] *on eras.*

LTg: nihilum] nichilum CEGHJK. est] ést K. eius] eiu[ ] G. Qui] [ ]ui G: *initial* Q *lost.* decipit] K: *orig.* decepit: *2nd* e *altered to* i; décipit C; decepit AB: *cf. Weber MSS* M*SKδζ. eum] L: *indicated for deletion by underlining in hand of corr.: see GAg.*

LTu: nihilum] nihielum ϑ; nichilum ιλξσςτ*τφ, ϱ: c *interl.* dominum] i: ł nus *interl.* decipit] decoepit β; decepit ϑχ.

GAg: magnificat] glorificat FGHIJK. eum] *om.* FGHIJK, L: *see LTg.*

GAu: magnificat] glorificat δεζιλμξοπϱστυφχψ. eum] *om.* δεζϑιλμξοπϱστυφχψ.

5

Qui		se *ACI,* sé *B,* se ðe *FG,* se þe *JK* (*DEHL*)
pecuniam	I	feh A, feoh B*CDFH*IJK, his G, ⁊ his E^{2}
suam	I	his ABCDFHIJK, fioh E^{2}, feoh G
non		ne ABCDE^{2}FGHJ, na K, þe ne I
dedit		salde AB, sealde CDFHI, seleþ E^{2}, syleð G, syleþ J, geaf K
ad		to ABCDE^{2}FGHI*J*K
usuram		westemscette A, wæstmscette BC, gytsunge ł to hyre D/D^{3}*, gytsunge ł gestreone H*, gytsunge F, westme oðð to hýre E^{2}*, eacan GJ, gafole IK
et		⁊ ABCE^{2}FGHJK
munera		gefe AB, gyfe C, medsceattas D, metsceattas F, metsceattes H, lac GJK, lac ł sceattas I, his læc E^{2}
super	I	ofer ABD^{3}*FGHIJ, ofyr C, of K, ne E^{2}
innocentem*	I	ðone unsceðfullan A, þone unsceðfullan BC, þone unscyldigan D, þone unscildigan F, unscyldigan H, unscyldigne *G*J, þa unscildigne ł ofer ða unscæððigan I*, ynscyldigan *K,* onfehþ E^{2}

non | ne ABCGHK, na DJ, he ne F, ⁊ ne I, ofer E^{2}
accepit | onfeng AB*C*D, anfeng HK, onfengc FI, onfehð *G*, onfehþ J, ðone unscyldygen E$^{2/x}$*

Qui se ACK, sé B, se þe D^{3}*FGIJ, Se þe E^{2}
facit | doeð AB, deþ CDFHIJK, deð G, þæs E^{2}
haec | ðas A*D*, þas *BCFHK*, þas þonne *G*, þas þonne *J*, þas þingc I, deþ *E*^{2} (*L*)
non ne ABCE^{2}FGH*I*J, na K
commouebitur* bið he onstyred AB, bið he onstyryd C, bið he onstyred G, biþ he unstired J, bið gedrefed ł astyred D, bið gedrefed ł astyred H, bið he astyred ł gedrefed E^{2}*, byð astyrod ł ne bið awend I, beoð astyrurd K, biþ gedræfed F (*L*)
in in AB, on CDE^{2}FGHIJK
aeternum ecnisse A*D*, ecnysse *CH*, écnysse *F*, ecnesse *BE*^{2}*GIJK* (*L*)

ED: usuram (G)] usurum *Rosier.* hæc (D)] haec *Roeder.* hęc (E)] haec *Harsley.* Non (I)] non *Lindelöf.* æternum (D)] aeternum *Roeder.* ęternum (E)] aeternum *Harsley.*

OE: gytsunge ł to hyre (D/D^{3})] ł to hyre *added in another (contemporaneous?) hand.* gytsunge ł gestreone (H)] streone *written above following gloss.* westme oðð to hýre (E^{2})] r *of* hýre *inserted,* e *interl.* ofer (D^{3})] *added in another (contemporaneous?) hand.* þa unscildigne ł ofer ða unscæððigan (I)] ł ofer ða unscæððigan *written toward right margin after* accepit. ðone unscyldygen (E$^{2/x}$)] ldygen *by corr., with* yld *on eras.* se þe (D^{3})] *added in another (contemporaneous?) hand.* bið he astyred ł gedrefed (E^{2})] astyred ł ge *on eras.,* y *interl.*

LTg: Qui (*1st*)] qui ABCDEFGHIJKL. pecuniam] pecúniam C; peccuniam H, D: *1st* c *interl.* ad] J: *on eras.* innocentem] G: *eras. after final* e (-em), K: *2nd* e (-em) *altered from another letter, followed by eras.* accepit] accépit C; accępit G. haec] hæc BDL; hec C; hęc EFGHJ; hǽc K. non (*3rd*)] Non I. commouebitur] L: com *indicated for deletion by underlining in hand of corr.: see GAg.* aeternum] æternum BD; ęternum CEFGHKL; eternum J, I: *orig.* aeternum: a *eras.*

LTu: Qui (*1st*)] qui βδεζϑιλμνξοπϱσςτ*τυφχψ. et] Et ϑ innocentem] innocentes ς: *see GAu.* haec] hęc ειvξυφ; hæc ϑ; hec σςτ*τ. aeternum] ęternum βειvξπφ; æternum ϑ; eternum σςτ*τ.

GAg: innocentem] innocentes FJ. commouebitur] mouebitur FGHIJK, L: *see LTg.*

GAu: innocentem] innocentes δεζϑμοπϱυψ, ς: *see LTu.* commouebitur] mouebitur δεζϑλμξοπϱστυφχψ.

PSALM 15

1

Conserua — gehald *AB*, geheald *CE*²FHI*K*, geheald D, geheald þu GJ
me — me AB*C*E²F*G*IJK
domine — dryhten E², drihten G, dryht̄ AB, driħt CF, driħ J, driht̄ I*, hlaford K
quoniam — forðon ABE²FG, forþon *C*J, forðan DH, forþā K, forðan þe I
in* } in A*G*, on *B*CDE²*FH*IJ*K* (*L*)
te* } de A, ðe *B*D*F*I, þe C*E*²*GH*J*K* (*L*)
speraui* } ic gehyhte A*BG*, ic gehihte C, ic gehihte IJ, ic hyhte D, ic hihte *HK*, ic gewene ł hihte E²*, ic hopude *F** (*L*)

ED: me (G) (*OE*)] m[ ] *Rosier.* forðon (A)] for ðon *Kuhn.* i[ ] (G) (*Lat.*)] *in Rosier.* ic gehyhte (G)] ic gehyht[ ] *Rosier.*

OE: driht̄ (I)] s. o. *written before word, slightly below line.* ic gewene ł hihte (E²)] ł hihte *written above* ic gewene. ic hopude (F)] h *interl.*

LTg: Conserua] CONserua AB; CONSERVA C; Conserva E; COnserua K. me] MÉ C; [ ]e G: *initial letter only partly visible.* quoniam] C: o *malformed, scribe began to write* n. in te speraui] L: speraui in te *written above by corr.;* speraui in te FHK; speraui in té B; speraui i[ ] [ ]e G: *with order* in þe ic gehyhte *for gloss; cf. Hebr. Ps 16.1* speraui in te. te] E: m *eras. after word.*

LTu: Conserua] COnserua βχ; CONSERUA λμνϱς; CONSERVA φ. me] ME λμνϱ. domine] DN̄E λμνϱ. quoniam] QUONIAM λϱ. in te speraui] speraui in te δεζιμξoπστυφχ; SPERAVI in te λ; SPERAui in te ϱ.

2

Dixi — ic cweð *A*, ic cwæð *BG*, ic cwæþ *IJ*, ic cwiþe *E*², ic sæde *CFHK*, ic segde *D* (*L*)
domino | to dryhtne B, to drihtne GI*, to dryht̄ A, drihtne DFH, drihten K, driħt C, driħ J, min E²
deus | god ABCFGHIJK, drihten E²
meus | min ABCDFGHIJK, god E²
es | eart CFJ, ear K, ðu A, þu BGI*E*²
tu | ðu F, þu CJK, earð A, eart BGI, eært *E*²
quoniam — forðon ABDHJ, forþon C, forðæn E², forðon ðe F, forðan þe I, for(ð)am G*, forðam K
bonorum | goda ABDFGHIK, góda CJ, minræ E²
meorum | minra ABCDFGHIJK, góde E²

non	|	ðu ne AI, þu ne BCFGJ, þu na DHE2*, na þu na K
indiges*	|	biðearft A, beþearft BHJ, beðearft DF, beðærft E2*, be[ ]earft G*, beþearfst CI, beþearf K

ED: dixi (I)] Dixi *Lindelöf.* to drihtne (I)] drihtne *Lindelöf.* forðon (A)] for ðon *Kuhn.* for(ð)am (G)] forðam *Rosier.*

OE: to drihtne (I)] to *written in left margin to left of initial* C *in* Conserua. for(ð)am (G)] *cross-stroke of* ð *not visible.* þu na (E2)] u *on eras.*, a *altered from* æ *and followed by eras.* (*1–2 letters*). beðærft (E2)] *on eras.* be[ ]earft (G)] *bowl of* ð (?) *visible after 1st* e.

LTg: Dixi] dixi ABCDEFGHIJKL. es] és E. tu] tú E. indiges] C: *orig.* indies: g *added interl. by corr. in light brown ink.*

LTu: Dixi] dixi βδεζϑιλμνξοπϱσςτ*τυφχψ. bonorum] ψ: *majuscule* D *written in left margin before word.* meorum] eorum ε. indiges] indies ς.

GAg: indiges] eges FIJK; ęges GH.

GAu: indiges] eges δεζϑιλμξοπϱστυφχψ.

3

Sancti*		halge *A*, halige *C*GJ, halgum *BD*H, halgum I, halgan F, þæ hælgæn *E2* (*L*)
qui		ða A, þa BK, þe CE2HI, ðe DF, þá þe G, þa þe J
in*	}	in A, on BCDE2FGHIJK (*L*)
terra*	}|	eorðan ABCDI, eorþan HJK, eorða[ ] G*, lande F, his E2* (*L*)
sunt*	}|	sindun A, sindon B, syndon CI, synt D, synd FGHJK, eorðæn E2* (*L*)
eius	|	his ABFGHJ*K*, hys C, his ł on his lande I*, beoð E2*
mirificauit		gewundrade AB, gewundrude C, he gewundrudude H, he wundrude D, he wundrade F, wundrude K, gewundriað G, gewundriaþ J, hie wundriæþ *E2*, he gemærsode I
omnes		alle A, ealle BCFGHIJK, eælle E2
uoluntates	|	willan ABCDFGHIJK, mines E2
meas	|	mine ABCDFHI, minne GJ, mines K, wyllæn E2
inter*		bitwih A, betwih BC, betweox D, betweoh J, betwion E2*, betwe(o)[ ] G*, on FIK (*L*)
illos*		hie ABCE, hy D, heom F, him K, [ ]e *G*, þam (*L*)

ED: eorða[ ] (G)] eorðan *Rosier.* betwe(o)[ ] (G)] betweo[ ] *Rosier.*

OE: eorða[ ] (G)] *left leg of final letter visible.* his (E2)] *on eras.* eorðæn (E2)] *eras.*

(*2 letters?*) *before word.* his ł on his lande (I)] ł on his lande *written in left margin.* beoð (E^2)] *on eras.* betwion (E^2)] *orig.* betwioh: h *altered to* n. betwe(o)[ ] (G)] o *cropped on right side.*

LTg: Sancti] Sanctos A: *orig.* Sancti: o *added below line,* s *added interl.;* Sanctis BCDEL: *cf. Weber MSS* K^{2}αβγη moz med, *see GAg.* in terra sunt] L: sunt in terra *written above by corr.: see GAg.* eius] eíus K. mirificauit] mirificabit E: ł uit *interl.* inter illos] L: in eis *written above by corr.: see GAg.*

LTu: Sancti] Sc̄i β; Sanctis νϛτ*: *cf. Weber MSS* K^{2}αβγη moz med, *see GAu.* mirificauit] mirificabit μ; mirificauit mihi ϑ.

GAg: Sancti] Sanctis FHIJK, BCDEL: *see LTg;* [ ]anctis G: *initial* S *lost.* in terra sunt] sunt in terra FGHIJK, L: *see LTg.* inter illos] in eis FHIJK, L: *see LTg;* in ei[ ] G.

GAu: Sancti] Sanctis δεζϑιλμξοπϱστυφχψ, νϛτ*: *see LTu.* in terra sunt] sunt in terra δεζϑιλμξοπϱστυφχψ. inter illos] in eis δεζϑιλμξοπϱστυφχ.

4

Multiplicatae		gemonigfaldade *AB,* gemonigfealdude *C,* Gemonigfealdode *E^2,* gemonigfealdode *G,* gemonigfealde *J,* gemenigfylde *DH,* gemænigfylde *F*I, gemyclude *K* (*L*)
sunt		sindun A, sindon B, syndun C, syndon DI, sint E^2, synd FGHK, wæron J
enim*		soðlice ABC, soþlice E^2*
infirmitates	|	medtrymnisse *A,* mettrymnessa B, mettrymnysse C, untrumnessa DJ, untrumnessa H, untrumnyssa I, untrumnesse K, on untrumnyssa F, hire E^2, hyra G
eorum	|	heara A, hira B, hyra C, heora DFHIJK, untrumnesse E^2, untrumnesse G
postea		efter ðon A, æfter þon B, æfter þon J, æft̄ þam C*, æfter þam G, efter þon þe E^2, æfter þan ł syððan I*, siþðan D, siðþan F, siþþan H, syþan K*
adcelerauerunt		hreaðedon *A,* hreaðydon *C,* hradedon *B,* hy efston D*FH,* hig efston *GJ,* hie efston *E^2,* efston *K,* hi genealæhton ł efstun *I* (*L*)
Non	|	ne ABCFGJ, na IK, Ic ne E^2
congregabo	|	gesomniu ic A, gesomnige ic BGJ, gesomnige ic *C,* ic gesomnige H, ic somnige D, gesomnige E^2, ic ne gæderige F, ic gegadrige I, ic gaderige K
conuenticula	|	gesomnunge ABC, gesamnunga I, gemetinga DF, gemetinge GK, gemettinga H, gemittinge J, hieræ E^2

eorum	I	heara A, hira B, hyra CG, heora DFHIJK, gemetinga ł somnunge E^{2}*
de		of ABCDE^{2}*FGHIJK
sanguinibus		blodum AB*C*FH, blodum̲ DE^{2}, blodum ł of blodwitum I, blode GJK
nec		ne ABCDE^{2}FG*H*IJ, na K
memor	I	gemyndig ABC, ic gemyndig DFH, ic gemyndi K, ic ne gemyndig I, ic ne bio E^{2}*, beo GJ
ero	I	ic biom A, ic beom BC, beo DFHI, gemindig E^{2}, gemyndig G, ic gemindig J (*K*)
nominum	I	nomena AB, namana DI*K*, namena G, naman CFJ, naman[ ] H*, hioræ E^{2}
illorum*	I	heara A, hira B, heora CDFHIJK, hyra G, nómæn *E*^{2}*
per		ðorh A, þurh BCE^{2}GHIJK, ðurh DF
labia	I	weolure A, weolore B, welcras CDFHIJ, welera GK, mine E^{2}
mea	I	mine ABCDFGIJ*K*, mines H, weleræs E^{2}*

ED: Multiplicaticatæ (B)] Multiplicaticatae *Brenner.* Multiplicatę (C)] Multiplicat[i] *Wildhagen.* æft̄ þam (C)] æft*yr* þam *Wildhagen.* gesomnige ic (G)] gesomnige *Rosier.* naman[ ] (H)] namana *Campbell.*

OE: soþlice (E^{2})] soþ *on eras., retraced in darker ink.* æft̄ þam (C)] *cf., e.g., Ps 5.11* secundum : æftyr *against Ps 8.18* secundum : æfter. æfter þan ł syððan (I)] ł syððan *written in left margin.* syþan (K)] s[ ]sy *eras. before word,* w *or* y *eras. after 1st* s. gemetinga ł somnunge (E^{2})] *on eras.* of (E^{2})] *on eras., with eras. before and after.* ic ne bio (E^{2})] *eras. after* bio. naman[ ] (H)] *only letter fragment visible in final position, due to hole in leaf caused by ink of initial on fol. 39r.* nómæn (E^{2})] ó *on eras., word on eras. from Lat. line below.* weleræs (E^{2})] *part of* æ *and* s *on eras. from Lat. line above.*

LTg: Multiplicatae] Multiplicatę DFGHL, A: ę *on eras.*, C: *orig.* Multiplicati: *final* i *altered to* ę; Multiplicate E, J: *orig.* Multiplicati: *final* i *altered to* e, K: ca *on eras. by main hand;* Multiplicaticatæ B. infirmitates] A: in *eras. before word.* adcelerauerunt] accelerauerunt ABCEFGIJKL, H: *2nd* r *obscured by hole in leaf.* congregabo] congregábo C. sanguinibus] C: *1st* i *interl.* nec] nęc H. ero] K: *lost* (*along with gloss, although letter fragment visible*), *due to excision of initial on fol. 21v.* nominum] [ ]minum K: *partly lost due to excision of initial on fol. 21v.* illorum] E: *on eras.* mea] me[ ] K: *partly lost due to excision of initial on fol. 21v, fragment of* a *visible.*

LTu: Multiplicatae] Multiplicatæ β: *orig.* Multiplicati: æ *interl.;* Multiplicatę δεζϑλνξοπρφ; Multiplicate ιστ*τυ; Multiplicati ς. adcelerauerunt] accelerauerunt δεζιλμνξοπρστ*τυφχψ. de] ψ: *majuscule* D *in left margin.* ero] *om.* ς. nominum] nomium ϑ.

GAg: enim] *om.* FGHIJK. illorum] eorum FGHIJK.

GAu: enim] *om.* δεζθιλμξοπϱστυφχψ. illorum] eorum δεζθιλμξοπϱστυφχψ.

5

Dominus		drihten E^{2}**G*I*K, dryht̄ AB, driħt CF, driħ J
pars		dael A, dæl BFGHIK, dǽl D, del E^{2}, dælþ J, dælnymynd C
hereditatis	I	erfewordnisse A, erfeweardnesse *D*, yrfeweardnesse BJ, yrfeweardnysse *C*I, yrfwerdnysse F, yrfewerdnisse H, erfwerdnes K, yrfes G, minre *E*^{2}
meae	I	minre A*BCFHIK*, mines *G*, mine *J*, erfeweardnesse *E*^{2}* (*DL*)
et		⁊ ABCE^{2}*FGIJ, (⁊) *K**
calicis		celces A, calices BE^{2}*F, calicys C, cælicis *D*, calicis H, þrowunge GJ, drencfætes I (*K*)
mei		mines ABDE^{2}*F*H**I, minys *C*, minre G, mine JK
tu		ðu ADF, þu BCE^{2}*GHIJK
es		earð A, eart BCDFGHIJK, eært E^{2}
qui	I	ðe D, þe E^{2}FHK, þu þe G, ðu þe I, þa ðe J
restituisti*	I	ðu gesettes A, þu gesettes B, þu gesettyst C, gesettes H, gesettest ł ageafe D, ageafe K, gesettest F, eft gesettest GJ, geedlæsast ł þu ðe geedstaþolo[ ] I*, me E^{2} (*L*)
mihi*	}I	me AB*C*DFGIJK, gesettest ł agefe *E*^{2}* (*L*)
hereditatem*		erfeweardnisse A, yrfeweardnesse BDJ, yrfeweardnysse *C*I, yrfeweardnisse H, yrfeweærdnesse *E*^{2}, yrfwerdnysse F, yrfe G, erfw[ ] *K**
meam*		mine ABCE^{2}*FIJK, min G (*L*)

ED: hęreditatis (E)] haereditatis *Harsley.* meæ (D)] meae *Roeder.* meę (E)] meæ *Harsley.* (⁊) (K)] ⁊ *Sisam.* minre (G)] mine *Rosier.* geedstaþolo[ ] (I)] *O'Neill p. 93 reads* geedstaþole 〈...〉; *if final letter is* e *it lacks a tongue.* mi (E)] michi *Harsley.* hęreditatem (E)] haereditatem *Harsley.*

OE: drihten (E^{2})] *bowl of* d *partly on eras.* drihten (I)] ÷ : is *written in left margin.* erfeweardnesse (E^{2})] *on eras.* ⁊ (E^{2})] *on eras.* (⁊) (K)] *only top-stroke visible.* calices (E^{2})] *on eras.* mines (E^{2})] *on eras.* mines (H)] *descender of* s *slightly effaced due to eras. in Lat. line below.* þu (E^{2})] *eras. (15 mm) before word.* geedlæsast ł þu ðe geedstaþolo[ ] (I)] ł þu ðe geedstaþolo[ ] *written in right margin and signaled for inclusion; final word cropped, leaving last letter partly formed.* gesettest ł agefe (E^{2})] ettest ł agefe *on eras.* erfw[ ] (K)] *partly lost due to excision of initial on fol. 21v, letter fragment visible after* w. mine (E^{2})] *on eras.*

LTg: Dominus] [ ]ominus G: *initial* D *lost.* hereditatis] hęreditatis CE; hereditates D: *cf. Weber MS* δ. meae] meæ BDKL; meę EFGJ; męę H. et] e[ ] K: *partly lost due to excision of initial on fol. 21v.* calicis] calices D, K: *lost due to excision of initial on fol. 21v.* mei] C: *eras. after word,* H: *punct. written on eras. after word.* restituisti] L: *final* ti *underlined to indicate deletion, 2nd* i *altered to* e: *see GAg.* mihi] L: *underlined to indicate deletion: see GAg;* michi C: *orig.* mihi: c *added interl. in light brown ink;* mi E (mihi/michi). hereditatem] hęreditatem CE; her[ ] K: *partly lost due to excision of initial on fol. 21v.* meam] L: *underlined to indicate deletion,* michi *written above by corr.: see GAg.*

LTu: Dominus] DN̄s β. hereditatis] hęreditatis ειϱυφ; ˡ-ereditas ν: *spiritus asper* (ˡ-) *interl.* meae] meę εζιξσφχ; meæ ϑμ; mee ϛτ*τ. mei] meis ϛ. mihi] michi ιλξϛτ*τφ. hereditatem] hęreditatem εϱ.

GAg: restituisti] restitues FGHJK, L: *see LTg.* mihi hereditatem meam] hereditatem meam mihi FGI; her[ ] meam mihi K; hereditatem meam michi HJ, L: *see LTg notes to* mihi *and* meam.

GAu: restituisti] restitues δεζϑιλμξοπϱστυφχψ. mihi hereditatem meam] hereditatem meam mihi δζϑμοσυχψ; hęreditatem meam mihi ε; hereditatem meam michi ιλξτ, π: c *interl.;* hęreditatem meam michi φ, ϱ: c *interl.*

6

Funes — rapas ABCDFGHI*JK, Rapes E^2
ceciderunt | gefeollun AC, gefeollon BDGHJ, gefellon F, feollun I, feollan *K*, me E^2
mihi | me AB*C*DFGHI*JK*, gefeollon *E*^{2}
in — in AB, on CDE^{2}FGHI*JK
praeclaris — berhtnisse A, beorhtnesse *B*, beorhtnysse *C*, beorhtnese *K*, beorhtum *DJ*, beorhtum *FGH*, bryhtum *E*^{2}, þurhbe[ ] I* (*L*)
etenim — ⁊ soðlice AB*C*G, ⁊ soþlice E^{2}J, witedlice F, witodlice I, ⁊ witodlice K
hereditas — erfeweardnis A, yrfeweardnysse *C*, yrfeweardnis DH, yrfewardnes *E*^{2}, yrfweardnes BI, yrfwerdnys F, erfwerdnes K, yrfes GJ
mea — min ABE^{2}FIK, mine C, mines GJ
praeclara — berht A*B*, beorht *CFGK*, beorhtu *DH*, bryhte *E*^{2}*, þurhscinendlic ł þurhbeorht I*, þurhbeorht *J* (*L*)
est — is ABE^{2}FGHIK, ys C, wæs J
mihi — me AB*CE*^{2}FG*HIJ* (*K*)

ED: pręclaris (E)] praeclaris *Harsley.* etenim (BE)] et enim *Brenner, Harsley.* hęreditas (E)] haereditas *Harsley.* p̄clara (K)] præclara *Sisam.* m^i (K)] mihi *Sisam.*

OE: rapas (I)] A.(?) S.D. *written in left margin, and* stafas *written below.* on (I)] *written in right margin.* þurhbe[ ] (I)] *written in right margin and cropped; orig. gloss above* praeclaris *eras.* bryhte (E^2)] y *malformed* (*false start?*). þurhscinendlic ł þurhbeorht (I)] ł þurhbeorht *written in right margin.*

LTg: ceciderunt] cæciderunt K. mihi (*1st*)] michi EJK, C: *orig.* mihi: c *added interl. in light brown ink.* praeclaris] preclaris BDFGHJL; præclaris K; pręclaris CE. etenim] C: *eras.* (*2 letters?*) *after word.* hereditas] hęreditas CE. praeclara] præclara B; pręclara C; preclara DEFGHJL; p̄clara K. mihi (*2nd*)] michi EHJ, C: *orig.* mihi: c *added interl. in light brown ink;* mi K (mihi/michi).

LTu: mihi (*1st*)] michi ιλξςτ*τ, ϱ: c *interl.* praeclaris] pręclaris ελνξϱ; p̄claris ζσφχ; preclaris ϑιπςτ*τ. hereditas] hęreditas ειϱφ. praeclara] pręclara ζλνξφ; preclara ϑιπςτ*τ; p̄clara οσ. mihi (*2nd*)] michi ιλξςτ*τφ, πϱ: c *interl.*

7

Benedicam		ic bledsiu A, ic bletsige BDHIJK, ic bledsige C, Ic bletsie E^2, ic bletsie F, gebletsige G
dominum*		drihten E^2, dryht̄ AB, driħt CFH, driħ GJ (*I*)
qui		se AC, sé B, se ðe F, se þe IJ, þa þe G, þe E^2, þa K
mihi*	}	me AB*CE*^{2}FGHIJK (*L*)
tribuit*	}	seleð AB, sylyð C, syllað G, silleþ J, salde DE^2, sealde FHIK (*L*)
intellectum		ondget *A,* andgit BIJ, andgyt CDE^{2}FGHK
insuper		ec ðon AB, iec þon ma C, ofer þæt DE^{2}J, ofer þæt FG*H,* ofer K, onufan þæt ł þær toeacan I*
et		⁊ ABCE^{2}FGH*J**K
usque		oð ABCGI*J, oðð DE^{2}HK, oððe F
ad		on D, to FK
noctem		nęht A, niht BGHJK, nyht D, nihte CI, nyhte E^{2}F
increpauerunt		ðreadun A, þreadun C, þreadon BDJ, ðreadon *F**, þréadon G, þrædon *K**, ⁊ ðreaddon I, onhreadan *H,* begripen E^2*
me		me ACE^2*FGIJK, mec B (*L*)
renes		eðre A, ædra C, edran D, ædran BFK, æddran H, æddran ł lendenu I, lendene E^2*, lendena G, lændena J
mei		mine ABCDE^{2}FGHIJK

ED: ínsuper (H)] insuper *Campbell.* ec ðon (B)] ecðon *Brenner.* ofer þæt (H)] oferþæt *Campbell.* onufan þæt ł þær toeacan (I)] onufan þæt ł þær to eacan *Lindelöf.* þréadon (G)] þ́readon *Rosier.*

OE: onufan þæt ł þær toeacan (I)] ł þær toeacan *written in right margin, eras. after* ł. ⁊ (J)] *interl.* oð (I)] *eras. after word.* ðreadon (F)] *obscured by eras., but legible.*

þrædon (K)] *gloss eras. before word.* begripen (E^{2})] *on eras.* me (E^{2}) (*2nd*)] *on eras.* lendene (E^{2})] *on eras.*

LTg: dominum] I: ł o (= domino) *interl.* mihi] L: *underlined to indicate deletion: see GAg;* michi E, C: *orig.* mihi: c *added interl. in light brown ink.* tribuit] L: michi *written interl. after word by corr.: see GAg.* intellectum] A: *orig.* intellectum: *macron eras.,* m *added by corr.* insuper] ínsuper H. et] *interl.* J. increpauerunt] H: a *interl.,* K: *1st* u *on eras. by main hand, followed by eras. of letter;* increpuerunt F: *cf. Weber MS* med. me] L: m *and* e *partly on eras., possibly altered from* re (*see following* renes).

LTu: mihi] michi ιξςτ*τ, πϱ: c *interl.* increpauerunt] increpuerunt ζιλ: *cf. Weber MS* med.

GAg: dominum] domino I (*alternate reading*): *see LTg.* mihi tribuit] tribuit mihi FGHIK; tribuit michi J, L: *see LTg notes to* mihi *and* tribuit.

GAu: dominum] domino μ. mihi tribuit] tribuit mihi δεζμοπσυφχ; tribuit michi ιλξτ, πϱ: c *interl.*

8

Prouidebam	I	ic foresaeh A, foreseah BC, ic forseo GJ, ic foresceawode D, ic foresceawade H, ic forsceawode F, ic forescæwode K, ic foresceawige I, Drihten E^{2}
dominum	I	drihtyn C, drihten I, drih̄t FH, dryht̄ AB, drih̄ GJ, ic foresceawode E$^{2/x}$*
in		in AB, on CDE^{2}FGHIJK
conspectu	I	gesihðe ABCFGHIJ, gesyhðe DK, minre E^{2}
meo	I	minre ABCDFGHIJK, gesihþe E^{2}
semper		aa A, simle BE^{2}J, symble CFH, symle DGI, æfre K
quoniam		forðon ABFHJ, forþon C, forðæn E^{2}, forðan þe I, forðam þe G
a		to ABDE^{2}F*HK*, æt G, on *CI* (*J*)
dextris		ðere swiðra A, ðære swiðran B, þære swiðran C, ðæm swiðran DE^{2}*, þam swyþran K, ða swiðran H, swyðran FG, swiðran I*J*
est		is ABFHIJ*K*, ys C, he is DE^{2}*, his G
mihi		me AB*CDE*^{2}**F*GIJK
⟨dominus⟩		drih̄t *C*
ne	I	ne A*BCDFGHJ*, na *K*, þæt ic *E*^{2}*, þæt ic ne *I* (*L*)
commouear	I	biom ic onstyred A, beom ic onstyryd C, beo ic onstyred B, ic astyred beo ł drefed D, ic astyred beo ł gedrefed H, ic astyred beo *F*, ic astyrud beo K, astyred ne beo E^{2}*, beo astyrod ł þæt ic ne beo awend I, beo ic onwended G, beo ic onwændeþ *J*

ED: forðon (A)] for ðon *Kuhn.*

OE: ic foresceawode (E$^{2/x}$)] sceawode *in lighter brown ink by corr., but not on eras.* ðæm swiðran (E^{2})] swiðran *on eras.* (?). he is (E^{2})] *on eras.* me (E^{2})] *on eras.* þæt ic (E^{2})] *on eras.* astyred ne beo (E^{2})] *on eras.*, e *in* beo *altered from* i.

LTg: a] C: *orig.* ad: d *eras.*, H: *eras. after word,* K: *added by corr., letter eras. after word.* a dextris] dextris J: *eras. before word.* est] ést K. mihi] F: hi *eras. but visible;* michi EJ; michi dominus C: *orig.* mihi dominus: c *added interl. in light brown ink.* ne] J: *on eras.*, K: *letter eras. after word,* L: *orig.* nec: c *deleted by subscript dot;* nę F: *cauda added in another hand: cf., e.g., Pss 16.8* protegę, *24.4* edocę, *24.5* docę, *24.7* nę, *24.17* eruę, *24.20* eruę; nec BDEGI. commouear] J: c *on eras.;* commuear F: *eras. after 2nd* m.

LTu: a] ad ςυψ. mihi] michi ιλξςτ*τ, ϱ: c *interl.;* mihi dominus ν. ne] λϱ: *orig.* nec: c *deleted;* nec βϑινσςτ*χ.

9

Propter		fore ABC, for DE^{2}F*G*HIJ, forþā K
hoc		ðissum A, þissum BC, ðisum D, ðysum F, þysum H, þisum J, þyssum G, þyssum þingum I, þis E^{2}*
delectatum*		gelustfullad *A*BG, gelustfullud CK, gelustfullod FJ, gelustfullude D, gelustfullede E^{2}*, gelustfullode H, geblissod I (*L*)
est		is ABFHIJ*K*, ys C, wæs G
cor	|	heorte ABCDFGIJ, heortan H, heort K, min E^{2}
meum	|	min ABCDFGIJK, mine H, heorte E^{2}
et		⁊ ABCDE^{2}FGH*IJK
exultauit		gefiht A, gefihð B, gefyhð C, gefiehde D, gefihde H, gefeade ł blissade I, upahefþ *F*, wynsumigeað G, winsumiaþ J, gefagenede E^{2}*, fægnaþ *K*
lingua		tunge ABCDE^{2}*GIJK, tunga F, tungan H
mea		min ABCGIK, mine E^{2}FHJ
insuper		ec ðon A, eac ðon B, iec þon ma C, ofer þæt E^{2}*, ⁊ ofer *H*, ⁊ onufon þæt F, onúfan þæt G, onufan þæt J, toeacan I
et		⁊ ABCE^{2}FGHJK (I*)
caro	|	flęsc AD, flæsc BCFGHI, flæs J, flæcs K, min E^{2}
mea	|	min ABCFGHIJK, flesc E^{2} (*D*)
requiescet		gerësteð *A*G, gerestyð C, geresteþ J, ⁊ geresteþ I, resteð B*D*FH, rest *E*^{2}K
in		in AB, on CDE^{2}FGHIJK
spe		hyhte A*BD*E^{2}F, hihte CGHIJK

ED: ínsuper (H)] insuper *Campbell.* eac ðon (B)] eacðon *Brenner.* onufon þæt (F)] on ufon þæt *Kimmens.* onúfan þæt (G)] on úfan þæt *Rosier.* onufan þæt (J)] on ufan þæt *Oess.* toeacan (I)] to eacan *Lindelöf.*

OE: þis (E^2)] *eras. after word (20 mm) extending to end of line.* gelustfullede (E^2)] *2nd* e *on eras.* ⁊ (H) (*1st*)] *written below* n *of preceding* mine. gefagenede (E^2)] *on eras.* tunge (E^2)] *eras.* (*17 mm*) *before word.* ofer þæt (E^2)] ofer *on eras.* et (I) (*2nd*)] ⁊ *eras.*

LTg: Propter] G: *initial letter partly lost.* delectatum] A: *orig.* dilectatum: i *altered to* e, L: de *underlined to indicate deletion,* c *deleted by subscript dot.* est] ést K. exultauit] F: *orig.* exultabit: b *deleted by subscript dot, 2nd* u *interl.,* K: *2nd* u *on eras. by corr.* insuper] ínsuper H. mea (*2nd*)] meo D. requiescet] A: *orig.* requiescit: *2nd* i *altered to* e; requiescit D, E: *2nd* i *on eras.*: *cf. Weber MSS* MSKβγδ moz^c. spe] spé BD.

LTu: Propter] PROPTER β. exultauit] exsultauit ϑ; exultabit βμν. requiescet] requiescit β.

GAg: delectatum] lętatum FGIJ; letatum HK, L: *see LTg.*

GAu: delectatum] laetatum δζμοπϱχψ; lętatum εϑιφ; letatum λξστυ.

10

Quoniam — forðon ABE^2, forþon CFH, forðon þe J, forðan þe I, forðam þe G
non | ne ABC, na HK, þu ne E^{2}FGIJ*
derelinques | forletesde A, forlætest DGHJK, forlætst I, forletest E^{2}F, forlætes ðu B, forlætyst þu C
animam | sawle ABC, saule DGHK, sawle FIJ, mine E^2
meam | mine ABCFGHIJK, sæwle E^2
in — in AB, on CDE^{2}FGHIJK
inferno — helle ABCDE^{2}FGHIJ*K*
nec | ne ABCD*E*^{2}F*GH*IJ, na K
dabis | ðu seles AB, þu sylyst C, ðu selst D, þu sylst H, þu sillest J, þu ne selest E^2, ðu ne selst F, þu ne sylest G, þu ne sylst I, sylst K
sanctum | ðone halgan A, þone halgan BCG, þone halgan J, halgan I, haligne DFH, halgum K, þinne E^2*
tuum | ðinne ADF, þinne BCGHJ, þine I*, þinum K, hæligne E^2
uidere — gesean A, geseon BCDFGHIJK, to gesionne E^2
corruptionem — gebrosnunge *A*BCDGHJ, gebrosnunga FK, gegrip ł brosnunge E^2, forrotodnesse ł awemmendnysse ł gebrosnunge I*

ED: forðon (A)] for ðon *Kuhn.* forðon (E)] Forðon *Harsley.* mine (A)] min *Kuhn.*

OE: þu ne (J)] ne *interl. by another hand in lighter ink.* þinne (E^2)] *eras. after word.* þine (I)] *letter eras. after* n. gegrip ł brosnunge (E^2)] ł brosnunge *added later* (?) *by main hand.* forrotodnesse ł awemmendnysse ł gebrosnunge (I)] nesse *on eras.*, ł awemmendnysse ł gebrosnunge *written in right margin.*

LTg: inferno] K: o *altered from another letter.* nec] E: *eras. above word;* nęc GH. corruptionem] A: m *added by corr.*

LTu: derelinques] σ: e *interl.;* derelinquis β; relinques π. inferno] infernum ς. nec] nęc ξ.

11

Notas		cuðe ABCDFH, cuþe *G*IJ, cyþ K, Cuþe þu E^2
mihi		me AB*CDE*^{2}FGHI*J*K
fecisti		ðu dydest ADFH, þu dydest I*K, þu dydes B, þu gedydyst C, þu gedydest *G,* þu gedidest J, dydest E^2
uias	I	wegas ABCDFGHIJK, liues *E*^{2}
uitae	I	lifes A*BDFGHIJK,* lifys *C,* wegæs *E*^{2} (*L*)
adimplebis	I	ðu gefylles A, þu gefylles B, þu gefyllyst C, ðu gefyllest D, þu gefyllest IK, ðu gefullest F, þa gefyllest H, to gefyllenne G, to gefillenne J, ⁊ þu me *E*^{2}
me	I	me ABCDFGHJK, gefillest E^2
laetitia		blisse A*BCK,* of blisse *DE*^{2}**FH,* mid blisse *G*I*J* (*L*)
cum		mid ABCDE^x*FGHIJK
uultu		ondwleotan A, ondwlitan B, andwlitan CDFGHJ, andwliten E^x*, anwlitan I, ansyne K
tuo		ðinum AF, þinum BCDJ, þinum HI, þine E^x*, þinre GK
delectationes		gelustfullunge AB, gelustfullunge C, lustfullunga GJ, gelustfulnessa DH, gelustfulnyssa FI*, gelustfulnesse E^x*, gelustfulnes K
in		in A, on BCDE^{2}FGHIJK
dextera	I	ðere swiðran, A, þære swiðran BC, swiðran FGI, swiþran J, swyðre K, ðinre D, þinre H, þine E^2*
tua	I	ðinre AFJ, þinre BCGIK, swiðran D, swiþræn E^2, swiran H
usque		oð ABCFGIJ, oþ DK, oðð H, oþðe E^2
in		on CDE^{2}FJ
finem		ende ABCDE^2*FGHIJK (*L*)

ED: [ ]otas (G)] Notas *Rosier.* uitę (E)] vitae *Harsley.* uite (I)] uitae *Lindelöf.* lętitia (E)] laetitia *Harsley.* letitia (I)] laetitia *Lindelöf.*

OE: þu dydest (I)] *orig.* þu didest: i *altered to* y. of blisse (E^2)] f *on eras.* mid (E^x)] *on eras. by corr. in light brown ink.* andwliten (E^x)] *on eras. by corr. in light brown ink.* þine (E^x) *(1st)*] *on eras. by corr. in light brown ink.* gelustfulnyssa (I)] s. sunt : synt *written in bottom margin below* delec(tationes). gelustfulnesse (E^x)] *on eras. by corr. in light brown ink.* þine (E^2) *(2nd)*] *eras. after word.* ende (E^2)] h *eras. before word.*

LTg: Notas] [ ]otas G: *initial* N *lost.* mihi] michi EJ, C: *orig.* mihi: c *added interl. in light brown ink.* fecisti] fęcisti G. uias] E: a *on eras.* uitae] uitæ BKL; uitę CDEFHJ; uite G, I: *orig.* uitae: a *eras.* adimplebis] E: *small eras. above 1st* i. laetitia] lætitia B; lętitia CDEFGL; letitia HK, I: *orig.* laetitia: *1st* a *eras.* finem] L: n, e, *and left leg of* m *on eras.*

LTu: mihi] michi ιλξςτ*τ, ϱ: c *interl.* uitae] uitę βεζνξοϱυφ; uitæ ϑχ; uite ισςτ*τ. adimplebis] adimpleuis ϑ. me] mę ζ. laetitia] letitia βξσςυ; lętitia εζιλνφ; lætitia ϑ; leticia τ*τ. delectationes] β: *letter eras. after* d, *1st* e *interl.;* dilectatio ϑ: *cf. Weber MSS* α med.

PSALM 16

1

Exaudi		geher *A*I, gehyr *C*DE^{2}F*HJK,* gfher *B,* gehyr ðu *G* (*L*)
domine		drihtyn *C,* drihten E^2, dryht̄ AB,driħt FHJ, driħ G, eala dr̄n I, hlaford K
iustitiam	|	rehtwisnisse A, ryhtwisnesse BD, rihtwisnysse *C*FI, rihtwisnesse G*HJK, mine E^2
meam	|	mine ABCFGIJK, minre H, ryhtwisnesse E^2*
intende		bihald AB, beheald C*G*J, begym DHK, begým F, begem ł beheæld E^2, beseoh ł begem I
deprecationi*	|	boene *AB,* bene *D*FGHJ, bena C, bene ł halsunge I, gebed K, mine E^2 (*L*)
meae*	|	mine *AB*CFGJ, minre *D*H, to mine I, min K, bene *E^2* (*L*)
Auribus		mid earum ACFI, mid earum BDHJ, mid Earum E$^{x/2}$*, mi[ ] earum *G,* earan *K*
percipe		onfoh ABCDE^{2}FGHIJ, opena K
⟨domine⟩		driħ *J*
orationem	|	gebed ABCDFHI, gebeda G, gebedu J, bene K, min E^2
meam	|	min ACFHI, mine BGJ, [ ]nre *K**, gebed E^2*
non		nales AB, nalys C, nalæs GJ, na DE^x*FHIK
in		in AB, on CDE^{2}FGHIJK
labiis		weolerum A, weolorum B, welerum CD*E*^{x}*HJ, welerum FGI, weleran K

dolosis	faecnum A, fæcnum BC, facenfullum DJ, facenfullum HI, facnfullum F, facenfulle E^{x}*G, facnfulle K

ED: eala dn̄n (I)] eala dr*ihten Lindelöf.* meę (E)] meae *Harsley.* [ ]uribus (G)] *Au*ribus *Rosier.* mi[ ] earum (G)] [ ]arum *Rosier.* labíís (E)] labiis *Harsley.*

OE: rihtwisnesse (G)] h *slightly obscured.* ryhtwisnesse (E^{2})] wisnesse *on eras.* mid Earum ($E^{x/2}$)] mid *added outside left grid by corr. in lighter brown ink.* [ ]nre (K)] *letters lost due to excision of initial.* gebed (E^{2})] *eras.* (*16 mm*) *after word.* na (E^{x})] *on eras. in lighter brown ink.* welerum (E^{x})] *on eras. in lighter brown ink.* facenfulle (E^{x})] *on eras. in lighter brown ink.*

LTg: Exaudi] EXaudi A, L: *small eras.* (?) *after* a; EXAudi B; EXAUDI C; [ ]xaudi G: *initial* E *lost,* H: *initial letter lost, traces of blue ink visible;* [ ]Xaudi K: *initial letter excised.* domine] DN̄E C. iustitiam] iusticiam C: *orig.* iustitiam: *2nd* t *deleted by subscript dot,* c *interl. by corr.* intende] inten[ ] G. deprecationi] dep̄cationi D; deprecationem AB, L: *orig.* deprecationi: *final* i *altered to* e, *macron added above: cf. Weber MSS* Mζ moz med, *see GAg.* meae] meę DE; meam AB; meam (?) L: *orig.* meæ: *right side of* æ *partly eras. to form* a, *with remaining letter fragment serving as macron: cf. Weber MSS* ζ moz med, *see GAg.* Auribus] [ ]uribus G: *initial* A *lost;* (A)uribus K: *left leg of* A *excised.* percipe] percipe domine J: domine *crossed through in light ink.* meam (*2nd*)] [ ]m K: *letters lost due to excision of initial.* labiis] labíís E.

LTu: Exaudi] EXAUdi β; EXAUDI λμνξϱς; EXAVDI φ. domine] DN̄E λμνξϱ. iustitiam] IUSTITIAM λξ; IUSTItiam μ; IUStitiam ν; iusticiam τ*τφ; IUSTICIAM ϱ: *orig.* IUSTITIAM: *2nd* T *deleted,* C *interl.* meam (*1st*)] MEAM λξ. deprecationi] depraecationem β: *cf. Weber MSS* Mζ moz med, *see GAu.* meae] meę ν; mee ςτ*; meam β: *cf. Weber MSS* Mζ moz med, *see GAu.* labiis] labis ϑ.

GAg: deprecationi meae] deprecationem meam FGHIJ, ABL: *see LTg;* depræcationem meam K.

GAu: deprecationi meae] depraecationem meam δ, β: *see LTu;* deprecationem meam εζϑιλοπτ; deprȩcationem meam ξ; depracationem meam ψ; dep̄cationem meam μϱσυφχ.

2

De		of *ABCDE*^{x}*FGHIJK (*L*)
uultu		ondwlitan AB, andwlitan CDFH, andwlitum E^{x}*, ánsyne G, ansyne IJK
tuo		ðinum A, þinum BCDE^{x}*FH, þinre GJK, þynre I
iudicium	|	dom ACDFGHIJK, dóm B, minne E^{2} (*L*)
meum	|	minne ABFGJ, min CDHIK, dom E^{2}
prodeat		forðyppeð *A*B, forðyppað C, forðyppe GJ*, yppe DF*H*K, yppæþ E^{2}, forðsteppe I

oculi | egan AHK, eagan BCDFGI, eagon J, mine E^{2}
mei* | min AC, mine BD, ðine F, þine GHIJK, cgæn E^{2}*
uideant gesiað A, geseoð B, gesioþ E^{2}, geseoþ K, geseon *CD*FGHJ, geseon ł bewlatiun I
aequitatem* efennisse *ADH,* efynnysse *C,* efennesse *E*^{2}GJ, efnesse *BK,* efnysse ł rihtwisnesse I, emnyssa F (*L*)

ED: æquitatem (D)] aequitatem *Roeder.* ęquitatem (E)] aequitatem *Harsley.*

OE: of (E^{x})] *on eras. in lighter brown ink.* andwlitum (E^{x})] *on eras. in lighter brown ink.* þinum (E^{x})] *on eras. in lighter brown ink.* forðyppe (J)] r *interl. in lighter ink.* egæn (E^{2})] *on eras.*

LTg: De] de ABCDEL. iudicium] iudiciu L: *macron wanting.* prodeat] A: *orig.* prodiat: i *altered to* e, H: *eras.* (?) *after word, on which punct. is written.* uideant] D: n *interl.* aequitatem] æquitatem BD, K: *letter eras. after* c, *macron added above* e; ęquitatem CEHL.

LTu: De] de βνςτ*. uideant] β: n *interl.* aequitatem] ęquitatem ν; equitatem ςτ.

GAg: mei] tui FGHIJK. aequitatem] aequitates F; ęquitates GJ; equitates I: *letter eras. before 1st* e.

GAu: mei] tui δεζϑιλμξοπϱστυφχψ, ς. aequitatem] aequitates δεμοπϱυ; equitates ζστ, ψ: *scribe first wrote* oequitatis, *altered* o *to* a, *then crossed it out;* æquitates ϑ; ęquitates ιλξφ.

3

Probasti ðu acunnadest A, þu acunnades B, þu acunnudyst C, þu cunnodest GJ, ðu afandudest D, þu afandudest E^{2}**H,* ðu afandodest F, þu afandodest IK
cor | heortan ABCDGHIJK, heorte F, mine E^{2}
meum | mine ABCDFGHIK, minre J, heortæn E^{2}
et ⁊ ABCE^{2}FGH*IJ*K
uisitasti neasades A, neosades B, ðu neosodest DF, þu neosodest GHK, þu neosadest J, þu neosodest me E^{2}*, geneosodyst C, þu geneosadest I
nocte on næht A, on niht BGHJK, on nyht D, on nyhte I, on niehte E^{2}, nihte C, niht F
igne mid fyre ABGIJ, mid fire E^{2}, fyre CDFK, fyrene H
me | me ABCFGJK, ameredest þu E^{2}
examinasti | amearedes A, ðu ameredes B, þu amerydyst C, ðu ameredest D, þu ameredest FGHJ, þu amerodest IK, me ł streddest E^{2}*
et ⁊ ABCDE^{2}FGHIJK

non	|	nis ABF, nys CDI, nan G, na HJK, ne E^{2}
est	|	is E^{2}GHJ*K*
inuenta		gemoeted A*, gemetyd C, gemet BDE^{2}*FGHI, gemett J, funden K
in		in AB, on CDE^{2}FGHIJK
me		me ABCDE^{2}FHIJK, m[ ] G
iniquitas		unrehtwisnis A, unryhtwisnes BD, unrihtwisnys C, unrihtwisnes HK, unrihtwisnysse F, unrihtwisnesse E^{2}*I, unriht GJ

ED: þu acunnades (B)] þu accunnades *Brenner.* on (G) (*2nd*)] [ ] *Rosier.* m[ ] (G)] [ ] *Rosier.*

OE: þu afandudest (E^{2})] afandudest *on eras.* ⁊ (H) (*1st*)] *written below* e *in preceding* mine, *which extends above* et. ⁊ (J)] *written below* n *in* minre *on Lat. line.* þu neosodest me (E^{2})] *1st* e *altered from* i. me ł streddest (E^{2})] t *partly on eras. extending above following* ⁊. gemoeted (A)] *orig.* gemoeteð: *cross-stroke of* ð *eras.* gemet (E^{2})] *eras. after word.* unrihtwisnesse (E^{2})] wis *interl.,* se *added by corr. in brown ink.*

LTg: Probasti] H: *initial letter faint.* est] ést K.

LTu: me (*1st*)] *interl.* ϑ.

4

Ut		ðætte A, þætte *B,* þætte *C,* þæt *DFGH*K, þæt *IJ,* þeð *E*^{2} (*L*)
non		he ne AC, ne BDE^{2}FGHIJ, na K
loquatur		sprece ABCDE^{2}FGHIJ, spece K
os	|	muð *A*B*D*FGHK, mvð C, muþ IJ, min E^{2}
meum	|	min ABCFGHIJK, muþ E^{2}
opera	|	wirc A, werc B, worc C, weorc DFGHJK, weorc ł dæda I*, mænnæ E^{2}* (*L*)
hominum	|	monna ABC, manna DFGHIJK, weorcum E^{2}
propter		fore ABCDHK, for E^{2}*FGIJ
uerba		wordum AC*FI, wordum BDE^{2}H, worde GJ, worda K
labiorum	|	weolura A, welera BDFGHIJK, welyra C, þinræ E^{2}
tuorum	|	ðinra AF, þinra BCDGHIJK, weleræ E^{2}
ego		ic ABCDE^{2}*FGHI*JK
custodiui		heold ABC, geheold DHI, gehyold E^{2}*, gehealde FK, behealde GJ
uias	|	weagas A, wegas BCDFGHIJK, heærde E^{2}
duras	|	ða heardan AB, hierde C, hearde DFGHJK, stiðe ł hearde I, wegas E^{2}

ED: ós (A)] os *Kuhn.* mvð (C)] muð *Wildhagen.*

OE: weorc ł dæda (I)] e *interl.* mænnæ (E2)] *orig. gloss eras.*, mænnæ *written on next line.* for (E2)] *eras. after word.* wordum (C)] u *on eras.* ic (E2)] *eras. before word.* ic (I)] *gloss eras. after word.* gehyold (E2)] yold *on eras.*

LTg: Ut] Vt BCDEFGHIJL. os] ós AD. opera] L: *descenders of* p *and* r *slightly faded.*

LTu: Ut] UT β; Vt ζινξορσςυφχ.

5

Perfice		gefreme AB, gefremy C, gefreme þu G, gefrema þu J, fulfreme DH, Fulfreme E2, fulfrema FIK
gressus	|	gongas *A*BC, stæpas DFG, stepas H, stapas J, stæppas K, stepas ł paþas ł fereldu I*, mine E2
meos	|	mine ABCFGIJK, minum DH, stepæs E2
in		in ABC, on DE2FGHIJK
semitis	|	stigum ACDGHK, stigum BJ, paðum F, siðfætum I, þinum E2
tuis	|	ðinum A, þinum BCDGHJ, þinum FIK, stigum E2
ut		ðæt A, þæt BCI, þæt DFHK, þet E2, þæt þæt G, þæt þe J
non	|	ne ABCDE2*FHI, na K, hi ne G*, hy ne J
moueantur	|	sien onwende AB, syn onwende C, syn onwændende J, s[ ]n onwendende G, syn astyred D, sien astyred E2, syn astyrod F, sin astyred H, syn astyrode ł awende I*, beo astyrud K
uestigia	|	sweðe A, swaþu BK, swaðu DE2, swaðas C, swiðe GJ, fotswaþu F, fotswaþa H, siðstapla ł wegas I (*L*)
mea	|	mine ABCE2FGJK, mina DH, mine ł fots[ ]ðu I*

ED: þæt hi ne (G)] þ[ ] h[ ] *Rosier.* s[ ]n onwendende (G)] s[ ] onwendende *Rosier.* mine ł fots[ ]ðu (I)] mine ł fotswaðu *Lindelöf.*

OE: stepas ł paþas ł fereldu (I)] ł fereldu *written in left margin.* ne (E2)] *eras. before word.* syn astyrode ł awende (I)] *2nd* y *altered from* i (?). mine ł fots[ ]ðu (I)] e *obscured by stain, letters between* s *and* ð *lost due to tight binding.*

LTg: gressus] gressvs A: *orig.* gressos: *deleting dot in center of* o, v *interl. by corr.* uestigia] L: *ascender of* s *slightly faded.*

LTu: gressus] gresus ϑ. tuis] σ: *interl. above eras.* moueantur] δ: n *interl.*

6

Ego		ic ABCFGHIJK, Ic E2
clamaui		cleapede A, cleopode B*D*H, cleopude F, clypode *C*K, clepode I, clipie E2, clypige G, clipige J
quoniam		forðon ABE2, forþon CFJ, forþam G, forðan K, forðan þe I
exaudisti	|	ðu geherdes A, þu geherdes B, þu gehyrdyst C, ðu gehyrdest D, þu gehyrdest FGHIK, þu hididest J, þu me E2

me	|	me ABCFGIJK, gehierdest E^{2}*
deus		god ABCE^{2}FGJK, eala ðu god I
inclina		onhæld A, onheld B, onhyld CDE^{2}*FHI, onhyld þu G, onhild þu J, ahyld K
aurem	|	eare ABCDFHIJ, earan GK, þine E^{2}
tuam	|	ðin AF, þin BC*IJ, þine HK, þin̄ G, eæræn E^{2}
mihi		me A*C*DFGHI*J*K, to me B*E*^{2}
et		⁊ ABCE^{2}FGHIJK (*L*)
exaudi		geher AB, gehyr CFGHIK, gehir J, gehiere E^{2}
uerba	|	word AB*C*FGHIJK, mine E^{2}
mea	|	min ACFGJ, mine BDHIK, word E^{2}

ED: forðon (A)] for ðon *Kuhn*. uerba (C)] uerb[o] *Wildhagen*.

OE: gehierdest (E^{2})] dest *on eras*. onhyld (E^{2})] *orig*. onhild: i *altered to* y, *letter eras. after word*. þin (C)] *eras. after* n.

LTg: clamaui] C: ui *interl*., D: ad te *added interl. after word by glossator and indicated for inclusion*. mihi] michi EJ, C: *orig*. mihi: c *added interl. by corr*. et] L: *scribe began to write* ex, *but only completed top left arm of* x, *which was then altered to* t. uerba] C: a *on eras*.

LTu: inclina] β: l *interl*. mihi] michi ιλςτ*τ, π: c *interl*.

7

Mirifica		gewundra ABCG, gewuldra J, gewundurlęc D, gewundorlæc F, gewundurlæc H*, gewunderlyc E^{2}*, wunderlica K, gemærsa I
misericordias	|	mildheornisse A, mildheornyssa C, mildheortnessa BDH, mildheortnyssa FI, mildheortnesse GJ, mildheortnes K, þine E^{2}*
tuas	|	ðine AF, þine GIJ, þina BCH, ðina D, þin K, mildheortnesse E^{2}
qui	|	se A, ðe D, þe E^{2}*H, þu B, þu þe CGIJ, ðu þe F, þa K
saluos	|	hale ABCDFGHIJK, hæle E^{2}
facis	|	gedoest A*, gedest BCE^{2}*G*J*, dest DFHK, dest ł ðu þe gehælst I
sperantes		ða gehyhtendan A, þa gẹhihtyndan C, gehyhtende B, gehihtende *G*J, hyhtende DE^{2}*H, hihtende IK, ða hopiendan F
in		in AB, on CDE^{2}*FGHIJK
te		ðec A, ðe *B*DE^{2}*F, þe CGHIJK

ED: gehihtende (G)] [ ] *Rosier*.

OE: gewundurlæc (H)] *right leg of* n *obscured.* gewunderlyc (E^{2})] ge *and* erlyc *on eras.* þine (E^{2})] e *on eras.* þe (E^{2})] *on eras.* gedoest (A)] *deleting dot* (?) *below* o. gedest (E^{2})] st *on eras.* (?). hyhtende (E^{2})] *on eras.* on (E^{2})] *on eras.* ðe (E^{2})] *on eras.*

LTg: facis] J: *eras. after* s. sperantes] [ ]perantes G. te] té B.

LTu: misericordias] missericordias ϑ.

8

A		from *AB,* from *C,* fram *DE*^{2}*GJ, fram FHIK (*L*)
resistentibus		ðæm wiðstondendum A, þæm wiðstondendum B, þam wiðstondyndum C, þam wiþstandendum J, þam wiðstandendan G, ꝥa (h)wyderstandendum F*, wiðerstandendum DH*, wiþerstandendum K, wiðerstondende E^{2}, wiðercwiðendum ł agenstandendum I
dexterae	|	ðere swiðra A*, swiðran *BC,* swyþran *F,* swiþran *GIJ,* swyðra *K,* ðinre *D,* þinre H*E*^{2}* (*L*)
tuae	|	ðinre *AF,* þinre *BCGIJK,* swiðran *DH,* swiþren *E*^{2}* (*L*)
Custodi		gehald A, geheald BCD*FGHIJ*K, geheæld E^{2}
me		mec A, me BCE^{2}FGHJK
domine*		dryhten B, drihten E^{2}, dryht̄ A, driħt C, driħ J
ut		swe swe A, swa swa BCG*IJ, swa DFH, swæ E^{2}, þæt swa K
pupillam		sean A, seon BCDFHJ, syon G, þæræ sione E^{2}*, seo IK
oculi		egan AK, eagan BCFI, eagana G, eagena J, eages DE^{2}*H
sub		under ABDE^{2}*FGHIJK,* undyr C
umbra	|	scuan AB, sceade CIK, scade GJ, sceadwe DH, scaduwe F, þinræ E^{2}*
alarum	|	fiðra ABC, fiðera DFHK, fiþræ E^{2}, fyþera J, feðera G, fyðerena I
tuarum	|	ðinra AF, þinra BCDGHIJK, scæde E^{2}
protege		gesild A, gescild BJ, gescyld CD*F*GHIK, gescylde E^{2}
me		me ABCE^{2}FGHIJK

ED: dexterę (E)] dexterae *Harsley.* dextere (I)] dexterae *Lindelöf.* tuę (E)] tuae *Harsley.* tue (I)] tuae *Lindelöf.* swa swa (GIJ)] swaswa *Rosier, Lindelöf, Oess.* protegę (F)] protege *Kimmens.*

OE: fram (E^{2})] *on eras.* ꝥa (h)wyderstandendum (F)] *shoulder of* h *eras.* wiðerstandendum (H)] *cross-stroke of* ð *obscured.* ðere swiðra (A)] *orig.* ðere swiðre: *deleting dots above and below final* e, a *interl.* þinre (E^{2})] *eras. after word.* swiþren (E^{2})] n *in slightly darker ink, possibly added.* swa swa (G)] *1st* w *faded.* þæræ sione (E^{2})] sione *on eras.* eages (E^{2})] *on eras.* þinræ (E^{2})] *orig. gloss eras. above word,* under þinræ *begins above* ala(/rum).

LTg: A] L: *orig.* a: *altered to* A̧ *by corr.;* a ABCDE. dexterae] dextere CDF, I: *letter eras. after* r; dexteræ BKL; dexterȩ EGJ. tuae] tuȩ ACDEFGH; tuæ BKL; tue I: *letter eras. after* u. Custodi] custodi FGHIJK. sub] Sub FGHIJK. protege] protegȩ F: *cauda added in another hand: see LTg note to Ps 15.8* ne (nȩ F).

LTu: A] a βνςτ*; *wanting* τ. dexterae] β: *orig.* dextera: e *added interl.;* dexterȩ ειλνξοπρςφ; dæxtere ζ; dextere στ*τ; dextræ ϑ. tuae] β: *orig.* tua: e *added interl.;* tuȩ ειλξπρςφ; tuæ ϑμ; tue στ*τ. Custodi] custodi δεζϑιλμξοπρστυφχψ. sub] Sub δεζϑιλμξοπρστυφχψ.

GAg: domine] *om.* FGHIK.

GAu: domine] *om.* δειλμξοπρστυφχψ.

9

a — from A, from B, fram FGIK, fram CJ, fræm E^{2}, of DH
facie — onsiene *A*E^{2}, onsine B, ansyne *C*DGHIK, ansine FJ
impiorum — arleasra ABCFHIJK, árleasra G, ærleæsræ E^{2}, arleasa D
qui — ða A, þa BCK, þæ E^{2}*, ða ðe F, þa þe GIJ
me — me ABCE^{2}FGIJK
adflixerunt — swencton AB*CDE*^{2}**FG*K, swæncton *H,* swængton *J,* geswenctun ł wiðsettun *I*

Inimici | fiond A, fiend B, fynd CDFGHIJK, Mine E^{2}
mei | mine ABCDFGHI*JK, fiend E^{2}
animam | sawle ABCDFIJ, saule GHK, mine E^{2}
meam | mine ABCDFGHIJK, sæulæ E^{2}
circumdederunt — ymbsaldun A, ymbsealdon B*C*DF*H,* ymbesealdan K, ymseældon *E*^{2}*,* utan ymbsealdon GJ, ymþrungon ł ymbtrymdon I

ED: fram (G)] fra[ ] *Rosier.* ansyne (G)] [ ]e *Rosier.* çircundederunt (C)] circu[m]dederunt *Wildhagen.* circumdederunt (G)] circumdeder*unt Rosier.*

OE: þæ (E^{2})] *eras. after word.* swencton (E^{2})] *eras. before and after word,* ::::on *visible on next line, with letter before* o *an ascender.* mine (I) (*1st*)] n *malformed.*

LTg: facie] A: *letter eras. after* i; faciae C. adflixerunt] afflixerunt EFGIJ, C: *orig.* adflixerunt: d *deleted by subscript dot,* f *interl. by corr.*, H: *1st* f *interl.* circumdederunt] circundederunt E, C: *eras. to left of 1st* n, H: *orig.* circumdederunt: *right leg of* m *eras. to form* n.

LTu: adflixerunt] afflixerunt εζιλξοπρστ*τυφχ. circumdederunt] circundederunt ειλτ*φ; circūdederunt ϑμρστχ.

10

adipem	smeoru A, smeru *C,* gelynde B, to lynde G, to lynd J, fætnisse ł rysl D, fetnisse ł rysl E²*, fætnysse F*, fætnyssa *I,* fæstnysse H, fætnesse *K*
suum	his AB, hys *C,* heora DFGHIJK, heore E² (*L*)
concluserunt	bilucun A, belucon BJ, belucun C, belúcan *G,* hy belucon H, hi belucan K, hy belucon ł ymbelicton D, hio betiendon ł belucon ł ymbelicton E²*, hi belukon ł hi beclysdon *I,* hi beclýsdon F
os	muð *A*BCDGHI, muþ E²*FJ*K*
eorum	heara A, hira B, heora CDFGHIJK, heore E²*
locutum	spreocende A, sprecende BGJ, sprecynde C, specende K, sprec DE²*, spræc *H*I, hi spræcon F (*L*)
est	wes A, wæs G*J,* is B*K,* ys C
⟨in⟩	in *A,* on *E²** (*D*)
superbia	oferhygde *AB,* ofyrhigde *C,* ofermodnisse *DH,* ofermodignysse *F,* ofermodinesse *K,* ofermodinesse ł on oferhydo *E²**, ofermodines ł oferhygd *G,* on oferhid *J,* ofermetta ł prutscipe ł modignysse I (*L*)

ED: ádipem (I)] adipem *Lindelöf.* ós (A)] os *Kuhn.* ofermodines ł oferhygd (G)] ofermodnes ł oferhygd *Rosier.*

OE: fetnisse ł rysl (E²)] *on eras.* fætnysse (F)] *eras. after* æ, *with remains of descender visible,* t *partly eras.* hio betiendon ł belucon ł ymbelicton (E²)] belucon ł ymbelicton *on eras.* muþ (E²)] *on eras.* heore (E²) (*2nd*)] *on eras.* sprec (E²)] *on eras.* on (E²)] *on eras.*, of *eras. before word.* ofermodinesse ł on oferhydo (E²)] ofermodinesse *on eras.*

LTg: adipem] K: *letter eras. after* d; ádipem CI. suum] C: *orig.* suam: a *deleted by subscript dot,* u *interl. by corr.;* suu L: *macron wanting.* concluserunt] I: *punct. eras. after word;* conc[ ]userunt G. os] ós AK. locutum] loqutum H: *orig.* loculum: c *altered to* q; loculu L: *macron wanting.* est] J: *eras. before* e; ést K. superbia] in superbia A; in superbiam D, E: in *written in diff. hand in darker ink;* superbiam BCFGHJKL: *cf. Weber MSS* MKαη² med.

LTu: adipem] adhipem σ. suum] suam ς. superbia] superbiam δεζιλμνξοπρσςτυφχ; in superbia θ; in superbiam τ*: *cf. Weber MSS* MKαη² med.

11

Proicientes	aweorpende AG, aworpende B, aworpynde C, awerpende I, awurpende J, utawyrpende D, utæwurponde E²*, utawypende F, utaweorpende *H,* utawyrppende K

me — me ABCE^2FGHIJK
nunc — nu ABCD*E*^{2}GHJK, nu ða FI
circumdederunt — ymbsaldun A, ymbsealdun *C,* ymbsealdon DF*H,* ymbseældon E^2*, ymbesealdan K, utan ymbsealdon BGJ, hi ymsettun ł hi ymbðrungon I
me — me *A*BCE^2*FGHJK
oculos | egan AHK, eagan BCDFGI, eagon J, on eorðæn E^2*
suos | heara A, hira B, heora DFGHI*J*K, hys C, hie æsettæn E^2
statuerunt | gesetton ABCGJ, hy asetton D, hi asettun I, hi asetton K, hi setton H, hi [ ](tsto)don F*, hiræ E^2
declinare | onhældan A, onheldan B, onhyldan C, ahyldan DHK, ahyldon F, ⁊ onhyldon G, ⁊ onhildon J, to gehyldanne I, eægæn E^2
in | in A, on BCDFGHIJK, to E^2
terram | eorðan ABCDFHIJ, eorþan K, earðan G, aheldene E^2*

ED: utaweorpende (H)] ut aweorpende *Campbell.* circundederunt (C)] circu[m]dederunt *Wildhagen.* (m)[ ] (A)] me *Kuhn.* hi [ ](tsto)don (F)] hi ætstodon *Kimmens.* eorðan (B)] eordan *Brenner.*

OE: utæwurponde (E^2)] *eras. before word, ascender visible.* ymbseældon (E^2)] ⁊ *eras. before word.* on eorðæn (E^2)] ⁊ *eras. before* on. hi [ ](tsto)don (F)] tsto *and preceding letter obscured by eras.* aheldene (E^2)] *on eras.*

LTg: Proicientes] [ ]roicentes H: *initial* P *lost.* nunc] E: *2 strokes eras. after* nunc, *corresponding to similar strokes in margin, but without marginal note.* circumdederunt] circundederunt C: *eras. after 1st* n, H: *1st* n *interl.* me] (m)[ ] A: *right leg of* m *eras.,* e *eras.* suos] J: *eras. after final* s.

LTu: Proicientes] Proiecientes ϑμ. circumdederunt] circundederunt ιλτ*τφ, ψ: *2nd* de *interl.;* circūdederunt ϑoϱσχ.

12

Susceperunt — onfengun *A,* onfengon BGJ, onfengun C, hy anfengon D, hye onfengon E^2, hi onfengon F, hy afengon H, hi anfengcon *I,* hi afengon K
me — me ABCE^2FGHIJK
sicut — swe swe A, swa swa BCFGHIJ, swa DK, swæ E^2
leo | lea A, leo BGHJK, lyo C, léo F, gære E^2*
paratus | gearu ACK, gearo BDF, geara GJ, geard H, þe is gearuw I, lyo E^2
ad — to ABCDE^2FGHIJK

praedam — herehyðe A*BC*, reaflace *DFGJK*, hreaflace *H*, þere hlowe ł reaflace *E*^{2}*, reaflace ł huðe I (*L*)
et — ⁊ ABCE^{2}FGHIJK
sicut — swe swe A, swa swa BCDGHIJ, swæ swæ E^{2}, swa FK
catulus | hwelp AB*C*DFI, hwælp H, hwelpas GJK, þęre leon E^{2}
leonis | leon AB*C*DH, leona FGJK, þæs leon I, hwelp E^{2}*
habitans — eardiende ABF, eardiynde C, eardgiende DH, eardigende GJ, eardende K, eærdiænde bioð E^{2}*, wuniende I
in — in ABDH, on CE^{2}FGIJK
abditis — degulnissum A, deagolnessum B, digulnyssum C, halum D, halum F, helum H*, healle K, gehildum ł holum E^{2}, behydednessum G, behidednesse J, scræfum ł on dygelnyssum I

ED: Suscéperunt (I)] Susceperunt *Lindelöf.* swa swa (GIJ) (*1st*)] swaswa *Rosier, Lindelöf, Oess.* prędam (G)] predam *Rosier.* p̄dam (K)] prædam *Sisam.* swa swa (BGIJ) (*2nd*)] swaswa *Brenner, Rosier, Lindelöf, Oess.*

OE: gære (E^{2})] e *on eras.,* on *eras. after* e, *eras. before and after word,* þ *visible in initial position.* þere hlowe ł reaflace (E^{2})] ł reaflace *added.* hwelp (E^{2})] *2 letters eras. after word, a lobe and perhaps* s. eærdiænde bioð (E^{2})] *letter eras. after 2nd* æ. helum (H)] e *obscured by crease in leaf.*

LTg: Susceperunt] Suscéperunt I; Susciperunt A. praedam] prædam B; predam DEFHJL; prędam CG; p̄dam K. catulus] cátulus C. leonis] leónis C.

LTu: Susceperunt] Susciperunt ϑ. praedam] prędam ενϱυ; predam ζιλξπϛτ*τ; p̄dam ϑοσφχ.

13

Exsurge — aris *A*B*C*DE^{2}*FH*I*J*K, aris þu G (*L*)
domine — drihten E^{2}FK, dryht̄ A, driħt CH, driħ GJ, eala driht̄ I, domine B
praeueni — forecym A*B**, forecum *CE*^{2}*H,* forecum *D,* forcum *F,* forecum þu *G,* forecum þu *J,* focum *K,* forestæpe ł forhrada *I** (*L*)
eos* — hie ABCE^{2}, hy D, hi FK, hig GJ, hine HI
et — ⁊ ABCDE^{2}FGHIJK
subuerte* — forcer AB, forcyr ðu G, forcir þu J, forceorf C, ferhweorf D, forhwyrf K, forwyrf E^{2}*, awyrtwala F*, underplanta H, understappla ł forscr[ ] I* (*L*)
eos* — hie ABCE^{2}, hy D, hig GJ, hi K, hine FHI (*L*)

Eripe		genere *ABC*, genera *FGJ*, ⁊ genere ł alys *E^2*, alys *DHI*, alys me *K* (*L*)
animam	I	sawle ABCDFIJK, saule G, saul H, mine E^2
meam	I	mine ABCDFGHIJK, sæwle E^2
ab		from A, from B, fram CDFGHJK, fram I, fræm E^2
impio		ðæm arleasan A, þæm eærleæsæ E^2, arleasum BGIJ, arleasum C*D**H, árleasum F, arleasan K
framea*	I	sweorde *A*B, swurde *C*, sword ł meche *E^2**, flane *D*F*H, flana K, þin sweord ł flana I, cocor G, cocorflane J (*L*)
(tuam)*	I	ðine F, þine HIK, þin G, þinre J

ED: aris (E)] Aris *Harsley.* p̄ueni (EK)] preveni *Harsley;* præueni *Sisam.* préueni (H)] preueni *Campbell.* práueni (I)] praeueni *Lindelöf.* understappla ł forscr[ ] (I)] understappla ł forscrænc *Lindelöf.* frámeam (H)] frameam *Campbell.*

OE: forecym (B)] *right leg of* m *faint but visible.* forestæpe ł forhrada (I)] ł forhrada *written above* forestæpe. forwyrf (E^2)] *2nd* r *on eras., letter* (e?) *eras. after word.* awyrtwala (F)] *slightly obscured by eras.* understappla ł forscr[ ] (I)] *letters after final* r *lost to tight binding.* arleasum (D)] *initial* a *on eras. and malformed.* sword ł meche (E^2)] sword *on eras.* flane (F)] *slightly obscured by eras.*

LTg: Exsurge] F: *middle bar and part of bottom of* E *lost;* Exurge ACHJL. praeueni] preueni BDL; preuéni C; p̄ueni EK; préueni FHJ; prȩueni G; práueni I: *letter eras after* á. subuerte] L: supplanta *written above word by corr.: see GAg.* eos (*2nd*)] L: um *written below* os: *see GAg.* Eripe] eripe ABCDEFGHIJL, K: *eras.* (*2 letters*) *after word.* impio] D: *right leg of* m *on eras.* framea] frameam A: *final* m *added by corr.,* E: *letter eras. after* f, L: *final* m *added by corr., with* inimicorum de manu (*v. 14*) *underlined to signal deletion and* m *added to following* tuu, *thus completing* (*without proper agreement*) *v. 13: see GAg;* frámeam C; frameam D: *cf. Weber MSS* Mδη*.

LTu: Exsurge] EXurge β; Exurge δειλνξπρστ*τυφχ. praeueni] prȩueni εζλνρ; p̄ueni θοσφχ; preueni ιξπςτ*τυ. Eripe] eripe βδεθιλμνξοπρσςτ*τυφχψ. framea] frameam τ*.

GAg: eos (*1st*)] eum FGHIJK. subuerte] subplanta FGIK; supplanta HJ, L: *see LTg.* eos (*2nd*)] eum FGHIJK, L: *see LTg.* framea] frameam tuam FGIJK; frámeam tuam H; *for* L *see LTg.*

GAu: eos (*1st*)] eum δεζθιλμξοπρστυφχψ. subuerte] subplanta δεζιμξρστχψ; suplanta θ; supplanta λοπυφ. eos (*2nd*)] eum δεζθιλμξοπρστυφχψ. framea] frameam tuam δεζθιλμξοπρστυφχψ.

14

(ab)*	fram FI, fram K*
inimicorum*	feonda AB*C*DGJ, feondum FIK*, minræ fiondæ E^2 (*L*)

de* of ABCDE^2 (*L*)

manu* | honda AB, handa CDGHIJK, of handa F, þinre E^2 (*L*)

tua* | ðinra A, þinre BCDFI, þinra J, þine GHK, hændæ E^2 (*L*)

Domine Drihten E^2, dryhī AB, drih̄t C*FH*, drih̄ *GJ*, eala drihī I

a from A, from BC, fram DFHK, fræm E^2, fram I

paucis feam AB, feawum CDE^2*J, feawum FGH, fæwum K, weawum I

a* from A, from BC, fram DGHJ, of E^2*FIK (*L*)

terra eorðan ABCD*E*^{2}*GI, eorþan FHJK (*L*)

dispartire* todael A, todæl *C*DFHIK, todiel B, todæl þu GJ, todref *E*^{2}* (*L*)

eos hie ABCE^2*, hi FIK, hig GJ, hy H (*L*)

et* ⁊ ABCE^2* (*L*)

subplanta* gescrenc *ABC*, underplanta D, underga E^2* (*L*)

eos* hie ABC, hy DE^2 (*L*)

in in AB, on CDE^2FGHIJK

uita life ABCDE^2*FGHIJ, wege K*

ipsorum* heara A, hira B, hyra C, heora DFGHIJK, heore E^2* (*L*)

De of ABCD*FHIK*, Of E^2*, fram *GJ*

absconditis | degelnissum A, degelnessum B, digelnyssum C, behyddum D, behyddum FH, bebodenessum G, bebodenessum J, bedigledun ł dygelnyssum I*, hydelse K, þinum E^2

tuis | ðinum A, þinum BCHJ, ðinum D, þinum FGI, þinre K, behyddum E^2*

adimpletus gefylled ABE^2FHI, gefyllyd C, gefylled is D, to gefyllanne G, to gefillenne J, to gefulled K

est is ABDE^2*FGHIJK, ys C

uenter | womb A*B, wamb CDGH*K, wambe IJ, innoð F, hieræ E^2*

eorum | heara A, hira B, hyra C, heora DFGHIJK, wambe E^2*

saturati | gereorde ABC, gefyllede *FI*, gefullede *K*, gefylde *GJ*, hy synd D*H*, hy synt E^2*

sunt | sind A, sint B, synd CFK, syndon I, wæron GJ, gefyllede DH, gefellede E^2*

porcina* ða swinnan A, þa swinnan B, þa swinan C, of fulnisse D, bearn *F*GIJK, of fetnesse ł of swinisse ł fulnisse *E*^{2}*

et ⁊ ABCDE^2*FGIJK

reliquerunt* forleortun A, forleton B, forletan GK, hi forletyn *C*, hi forleton FIJ, hy lyfdon D*E^2* (*L*)

quae* ða A, þa *C*, ðe *D*, þæ *E*^{2}*, þa ðe *B*, lafa F, lafe IK, ⁊ þa lafe G, ⁊ þa lafa J (*L*)

superfuerunt*	to lafe werun A, to lafe wæron B, ofer to lafe wæron C, þærofer wæron D, ðerofer weron E^2, heora FIJK, his G (*L*)
paruulis |	lytlingum AI*, lytlingum BCDK, litlyngum F, litlingum H, litlingas GJ, hire E^2
suis |	heara A, hira B, hyra C, heora DFHIJK, his G, lytlingum ł cyldum E^2*

ED: tue (I)] tuae *Lindelöf.* supplanta (C)] su[b]planta *Wildhagen.* to gefulled (K)] togefulled *Sisam.* quę (E)] quae *Harsley.* superfuerunt (B)] super fuerunt *Brenner.* ðerofer weron (E)] ðer ofer weron *Harsley.*

OE: fram (K) (*1st*)] fre *eras. after word.* feondum (K)] o *altered from* u. feawum (E^2)] *on eras.* of (E^2) (*2nd*)] *on eras.* eorðan (E^2)] *on eras.* todref (E^2)] *on eras.* hie (E^2)] *on eras.* ℸ (E^2) (*1st*)] *on eras.* underga (E^2)] *on eras.* hy (E^2)] *on eras.* life (E^2)] *on eras.* wege (K)] *lemma misread as* uia. heore (E^2)] *on eras.* Of (E^2)] f *on eras.* bedigledun ł dygelnyssum (I)] ł dygelnyssum *written in left margin.* behyddum (E^2)] *on eras.* is (E^2)] *eras. after word.* womb (A)] *orig.* wonb: m *interl., but without deleting dot.* wamb (H)] *eras.* (*of gloss?*) *after word.* hieræ (E^2)] *letter eras. after word.* wambe (E^2)] *on eras.* hy synt (E^2)] *on eras.* gefellede (E^2)] *on eras.* of fetnesse ł of swinisse ł fulnisse (E^2)] *on eras.* ℸ (E^2) (*2nd*)] *on eras.* hy lyfdon (D)] *orig.* hy gelyfdon: ge *eras. but visible.* hy lyfdon (E^2)] *on eras.* þæ (E^2)] *on eras.* lytlingum (I)] y *altered from* i (?). lytlingum ł cyldum (E^2)] ł *interl.*

LTg: inimicorum] C: *small eras.* (?) *after 2nd* i. inimicorum de manu tua] inimicorum de manu tuu L: inimicorum de manu *underlined to signal deletion,* m *added to* tuu (*thus completing [without proper agreement] v. 13*), *and* ab inimicis manus tue *written in right margin: see GAg.* Domine] [ ]omine GH: *initial* D *lost.* a (*2nd*)] L: de *added before word by corr., but without deleting dot below* a: *see GAg.* terra] E: *retraced in darker ink,* L: diuide *written above word by corr.: see GAg note to* dispartire. dispartire] dispartíre C: *small eras. below shoulder of 2nd* r; dispertire EL. dispartire eos et] dispertire eos et L: *underlined to signal deletion: see GAg.* subplanta] L: *underlined to signal deletion: see GAg;* supplanta AB, C: *orig.* subplanta: b *altered to* p. eos (*2nd*)] L: diuide *added* (*2nd time: see note to* terra *above*) *before word.* ipsorum] L: *underlined to signal deletion,* eorum *added by corr. before word: see GAg.* De] de FGHIJK. saturati] Saturati GHIJK; Saturaturati F. porcina] E: por *on eras. by Lat. scribe.* reliquerunt] C: *2nd* e *interl.;* reliquert L: *macron wanting.* quae] quæ B; que CD; quę EL. superfuerunt] superfuert L: *macron wanting.*

Additional Note: *With alterations by corr.,* L (*vv 13–14*) *appears as follows* (*consult notes to individual words above*):

tue
meam ab impio · frameam inimicorum de manu tuu m. ab inimicis man*us*
diuide
D*omi*ne a paucis de a terra dispertire eos · et subplanta
diuide eos in uita eor*um* ipsorum.

LTu: dispartire] dispertire ντ*. subplanta] supplanta ς. De] de δεζϑιλμξοπρστυφχψ. adimpletus] inpletus β; impletum ς. saturati] Saturati δεζϑιλμξοπρστυφχψ. quae] quę ν, que ςτ*.

GAg: inimicorum de manu tua] ab inimicis manus tuę FGK; ab inimicis manus tuae HJ; ab inimicis manus tue I: *final word orig.* tuae: a *eras.*, L: *see LTg.* a (*2nd*)] de FGHIJK, L: *see LTg.* dispartire] diuide FGHIJK, L: *see LTg notes to* terra *and* dispartire. et subplanta] *om.* FGHIJK, L: *see LTg.* eos (*2nd*)] *om.* FGHIJK; *for* L *see LTg and Additional Note.* ipsorum] eorum FGHIJK, L: *see LTg.* porcina] filiis HIJK, F: s *added later on eras.;* filii G. reliquerunt] dimiserunt FGHIJK. quae superfuerunt] reliquias suas FGHIJK.

GAu: inimicorum de manu tua] ab inimicis manus tuae δεζμπρυχψ; ab inimicis manus tuæ ϑ; ab inimicis manus tuę ιλοφ; ab inimicis manus tue ξστ. a (*2nd*)] de δεζϑιλμξοπρστυφχψ. dispartire] diuide δεζϑιλμξοπρστυφχψ. et subplanta] *om.* δεζϑιλμξοπρστυφχψ. eos (*2nd*)] *om.* δζϑιλμξοπρστυφχψ. ipsorum] eorum δεζϑιλμξοπρστυφχψ. porcina] filiis δεζϑιλξοπρστυφχψ; filii μ. reliquerunt] dimiserunt δεζϑιλμξοπρστυφχψ. quae superfuerunt] reliquias suas δεζϑιλμξοπρστυφχψ.

15

Ego		ic ABCDFGHIJK, Ic E^{2}
autem		soðlice ABCFGHI, soþlice DE^{2}J, witodlice K
cum*		mid ABCDE^{2}J, on FGIK
iustitia		rehtwisnisse A, ryhtwisnesse BD, rihtwisnysse CFI, rihtwisnesse GHJ, rihtwisnese K, soþfestnesse E^{2} (*L*)
apparebo		oteawu A, oðiwe DH, oþywe K, ic oðiwe F, æteawe B, ic ætywe *C*, ic ætýwe G, ic ætywde J, ablice ł oðiwe *E^{2}**, beo ætywed ł æteowie I
in*		in AB, on CDE^{2}FGHIJ (*K*)
conspectu*	|	gesihðe AB*G*HIJ, gesihþe C, gesyhðe DF, ansyne *K*, þinre E^{2} (*L*)
tuo	|	ðinre AF, þinre BCDGHIJ, þine K, gesihþe E^{2}
satiabor		ic biom gereorded A, ic beom gereordud C, ic beo gereord B, ic beom gefylled D, ic beo gefylled HIK, ic bio gefylled E^{2}, ic eom gefilled F, ic gefylle G, ic gefille J
dum*		ðonne A, þonne BCDGJ, þonne E^{2}FK, þænne I
manifestabitur*		bið gesweotulad A, bið gesweotolod B, bið gesutulod C, beoð geswutelod G, beoþ geswutulod J, gesweotolod bið D, geswytolod bið K, geswotoloð bið E^{2}*, ætywð F, ætywed bið I (*L*)
gloria	|	wuldur A, wuldor BCDFGHIJ, wvldor K, þin E^{2}
tua	|	ðin *AF*, þin BCDGHIJK, wuldor E^{2}

ED: ic ætýwe (G)] ic ætywe *Rosier.*

OE: ablice ł oðiwe (E2)] *on eras.* geswotoloð bið (E2)] swotoloð *on eras.*, man *eras. after* ge (*note lemma*).

LTg: iustitia] L: *top of ascender of* s *eras., perhaps to make room for Lat. gloss.* apparebo] E: *eras. after word,* C: *orig.* aparebo: *1st* p *interl. by corr.* in] K: *interl. by corr.* conspectu] L: *top of ascender of* s *eras., perhaps to make room for Lat. gloss,* K: *letter eras. after word;* consp̨ectu G. manifestabitur] L: *top of ascender of* b *eras., perhaps to make room for Lat. gloss.* tua] A: *3 lines eras. below, probably orig. title to Ps 17, which is rewritten at top of fol. 21v.*

LTu: iustitia] iusticia τ*τφ. apparebo] π: *1st* p *interl.;* aparebo ϑ. in] χ: *added in left margin.* satiabor] saciabor τ*τ.

GAg: cum] in FGHIJK. in] *orig. om.* K: *see LTg.* dum] cum FGHIJK. manifestabitur] apparuerit HIJK, F: erit *interl. in another hand, eras. after* u; aparuerit G.

GAu: cum] in δεζϑιλμξοπϱστυφχψ. in] *om.* δεζιλμξοπϱστυφψ. conspectu] conspectui ϱ. dum] cum δεζϑιλμξοπϱτυφχψ. manifestabitur] apparuerit δεζιλμξοϱστυφχψ; aparuerit ϑπ.

PSALM 17

2

Diligam		ic lufiu *A*, ic lufie *DE*2, ic lufige *C*F*G*IJ*K*, ic lufuge *H* (*B*)
te		ðe *A*DE2F, þe *C*GHIJK (*B*)
domine		drihtyn *C*, drihten E2, dryhꞇ̄ *A*B, driȟt FH, driȟ GJ (*I*)
uirtus*	|	megen A, mægen BD, mægn C, strengcþ F, strengð ł mægen G, mægn ł strengþ J, strengðe I, strenð K, mine E2 (*L*)
mea	|	min ABCFGHIJK, megne E2

ED: Díligam (H)] DILIGAM *Campbell.* TÉ (B)] Té *Brenner.* uirtus (BE)] virtus *Brenner, Harsley.* strengcþ (F)] strengeþ *Kimmens.*

LTg: Diligam] G: *eras. after word;* DILIGAM BCE, A: *orig.* DILEGAM: *crude* I *written above* E; DIligam K; DILIgam D; Díligam H: *eras. after word.* te] TE AC; TÉ B. domine] I: s. o *interl.;* DN̄E AC. uirtus] L: fortitudo *written below and to right of* uirtus *by corr.: see GAg.*

LTu: Diligam] DILIGAM βιλμϱςφψ. te] TE βλμϱψ. domine] DN̄E λμνϱψ. mea] MEA λ.

GAg: uirtus] fortitudo FGHIJK, L: *see LTg.*

GAu: uirtus] fortitudo δεζϑιμξοπστυφχψ; FORTITUDO λ; FORTITOdo ϱ.

3

Domine*		drihten *E*^{2}FI*, drȳ *A,* dryht̄ *B,* driħt *C*H, driħ GJ (*DL*)
firmamentum	I	trymenis *A*B, trumnys C, trumnes DFH*, trymnesse G, trimnes J, trymnes K, staðolfæstnys ł trumnys I*, þu eært min E^2
meum	I	min ABCDFGH*I*JK, trymnes E^2
et		⁊ ABCE^{2}FGHIJ
refugium	I	geberg A, gebeorg B, gebeorh C, tohyht D, tohiht H, frofor FJ, frofer K, friðstol G, gener ł frofer I, mín E^2
meum	I	min ABCFGHIJK, gescyld ł gehyht E^2
et		⁊ *ABCDE*^{2}FGHIJK (*L*)
liberator	I	gefrigend A, onlesend B, alysynd C, alysend DFHIJK, alýsed G, min E^2
meus	I	min ABCDFGHI*JK, friolsend ł alysend E^2*
Deus	I	god *ABC*F*G*HIJ, min *E*^{2} (*DL*)
meus	I	min ABCFGHIJ, god E^2
adiutor	I	fultum AC, fultum̲ B, fultum ł fylstend I, gefylstend DK, gefylsten H, gefylsta F, gefultumiend GJ, min E^2
meus	I	min AB*C*FGHIJK, gefylstend ł fultumend *E*^{2}* (*DL*)
(et)*		⁊ CE^{2}FGHIJK
sperabo		ic gehyhtu A, ic gehyhte B, ic gehihte CE^2*GI, gehihte J, ic hyhte DH, ic hihte K, ic hopude F
in		in AB, on CDE^{2}FGHIJK
eum		hine ABCDFGHIJ, hin *K,* hiene E^2
Protector	I	gescildend AB, gescyldynd C, gescyldend DF*H*I, gescyld GK, scild J, Min E^2
meus	I	min ABCFGHIJK, scildend E^2*
et		⁊ ABCDE^2*FGHIJK
cornu		horn ABCDE^2*FGHJK, horn ł strengð I
salutis		haelu A, hælo BJ, hæle CDE^2*FGHIK
meae		minre A*CBD*F*GHJIK,* minne *E*^{2}* (*L*)
(et)*		⁊ FGIJK (*L*)
adiutor*		fultum AB, gefylstend D, ⁊ fultumlynd C, gefultumiend J, gefultumig[ ] G, fultumend ł gefelstend E^2*, underfang F, anfengcend ł underfond I*, anfeng K
meus		min ABCE^2*FGI*JK

ED: adiutor (E) (*1st*)] adjutor *Harsley.* hin (K)] *Sisam suggests an* e *eras. after* n. [ ]rotector (H)] Protector *Campbell.* meę (E)] meæ *Harsley.* mee (I)] meae *Lindelöf.* anfengcend ł underfond (I)] andfengcend ł underfond *Lindelöf.*

OE: drihten (I)] s ÷ : is *written before word.* trumnes (H)] *eras. after* m *extending from eras. after* Diligam (*v.* 2) *above.* staðolfæstnys ł trumnys (I)] ł trumnys *written below lemma in bottom margin.* meus (I) (*1st*)] est : is *written in left margin.* friolsend ł alysend (E^2)] *eras. after* friolsend, ł alysend *written above* friolsend. gefylstend ł fultumend (E^2)] gefylstend ł *on eras.* ic gehihte (E^2)] gehihte *on eras.* scildend (E^2)] *eras. after word.* ⁊ (E^2) (*4th*)] *eras. after word.* horn (E^2)] ho *on eras.* hæle (E^2)] *eras. before word.* minne (E^2)] ⁊ *eras. before word.* fultumend ł gefelstend (E^2)] ł gefelstend *written above* fultumend. anfengcend ł underfond (I)] u *closed at top, although not to be taken as* a: *cf. v. 13* gewitun. min (E^2) (*6th*)] *eras. after word.* meus (I) (*5th*)] est : he is *written in left margin.*

LTg: Domine] domine A; dominus BCDL, E: ł e *interl. in lighter brown ink: cf. Weber MSS* V moz med, *see GAg.* firmamentum] A: *final* m *added by corr.* meum (*1st*)] I: *eras. after word.* et (*2nd*)] Et ABCDEL. Deus] deus ABCDEL; [ ]eus G. meus (*3rd*)] meus et CDEL: *cf. Weber MSS* αβ moz med, *see GAg.* eum] K: um *on eras.* Protector] [ ]rotector H. meae] meæ B; meę CDEGJK; męę H; mee I: *letter eras. after 1st* e; meæ et L: et *added interl. by corr.: see GAg.* adiutor (*2nd*)] L: susceptor *added interl. by corr.: see GAg.*

LTu: Domine] dominus βνςτ*: *cf. Weber MSS* V moz med, *see GAu.* et (*2nd*)] Et νςτ*. Deus] deus βνςτ*. meus (*3rd*)] meus et βνςτ*: *cf. Weber MSS* αβ moz med, *see GAu.* eum] eom ο: *orig.* eum: um *deleted,* o *interl.;* eo φ. Protector] [ ]rotector τ*τ: *initial letter wanting.* meae] meę ζινςφ; meæ ϑ; mee στ*τ.

GAg: Domine] dominus FGHIJK, BCDEL: *see LTg.* meus (*3rd*)] meus et FGHIJK, CDEL: *see LTg.* meae] meae et F; meę et GJK; męę et H; mee et I; *for* L *see LTg.* adiutor (*2nd*)] susceptor FGHIJK, L: *see LTg.*

GAu: Domine] dominus δεζϑιλμξοπρστυφχψ, βνςτ*: *see LTu.* meus (*3rd*)] meus et δεζιλμξπρστυφχψ, βνςτ*: *see LTu.* meae] meae et δελμοπρυψ; meę et ζιξφχ; meæ et ϑ; mee et στ. adiutor (*2nd*)] susceptor δεζϑιλμξπρστυφχψ.

4

Laudans		hergende *AB,* hergynde *C,* heregende *D*H, heriende *E^2*FJ, herigende GIK (*L*)
inuocabo		ic gecegu A, ic gecige BCDE^2*GHIJ, ic gecege F, ic clypige K
dominum		drihten E^2IK, dryht̄ AB, driħt CFH, driħ GJ
et		⁊ ABCE^2*FGHIJK
ab		from A, from BC, fram DGHJK, fram FI, fræm E^2*
inimicis	|	feondum ACFGHI, feondum BD, feondon J, feonda K, minum E^2*
meis	|	minum AFGI, minum BCDHJ, mina K, fiondum E^2
saluus	|	hal ABCDGHJK, hal ł gehealden I, ic beo E^2
ero	|	ic biom A, ic beo BCDGHIJK, hæl E^2

OE: ic gecige (E^2)] *on eras.* ⁊ (E^2)] *eras. after word.* fræm (E^2)] *eras.* (*12 mm*) *before word,* ⁊ *eras. before word.* minum (E^2)] *eras. before* u.

LTg: Laudans] laudans ABCDEL.

LTu: Laudans] laudans ςτ*; laudens β; et laudans ν.

5

Circumdederunt | ymbsaldon A, ymbsealdon *CDH,* ymbesealdon K, utan ymbsealdon B*G,* uton ymbsealdon J, ymbtrymdon F, ymbðrungon I, me E^2*
me | me ABCFGHIJK, ymbseældon E^2
gemitus* | geamrunge A, geomrunge C, geomrunga BDJ, geomorunga G, gemerunga K, sár F, sarnyssa I, deæþes E^2*
mortis | deaðes ABGH, deaðys C, deaþes DFIJK, geomrung E^2*
et ⁊ ACE^{2}G*HIJK, et B
torrentes burnan ABCD*F*HJK, burnon G, þæ burnan E^2*, burnan ł flownyssa I
iniquitatis unrehtwisnisse A, unryhtwisnesse BD, unrihtwisnysse *C**F, unrihtwisnesse E^2*H*K,* unrihtwisnyssa I, unrihtes GJ
conturbauerunt | gedroefdon A, gedrefdon BCDFGHJ, gedrefdun I, gedrefdan K, me E^2
me | me ABCFGIJK, gedrefdon E^2

ED: Circundederunt (C)] Circu[m]dederunt *Wildhagen.* [ ]ircundederunt (H)] Circundederunt *Campbell.* geomrunga (B)] geomrunge *Brenner.*

OE: me (E^2) (*1st*)] *eras. before word.* deæþes (E^2)] *on eras.,* ⁊ *eras. before word, over which* d *of gloss is partly written.* geomrung (E^2)] *on eras.* ⁊ (G)] *cropped at top.* þæ burnan (E^2)] burnan *on eras.* unrihtwisnysse (C)] se *written below line, with both letters underdotted.* unrihtwisnesse (E^2)] *on eras., 1st* n *altered from another letter* (*false start of* r?).

LTg: Circumdederunt] [ ]ircumdederunt G: *initial* C *lost;* Circundederunt C: *orig.* Circumdederunt: *left leg of* m *eras. to form* n, *1st* de *interl.;* [ ]ircundederunt H: *orig.* Circumdederunt: *initial* C *lost, 3rd leg of* m *eras.* torrentes] F: *eras. before word.* iniquitatis] C: *orig.* iniquitates: ę *deleted by subscript dot,* i *interl. by corr. in light brown ink,* K: *3rd* i *altered from another letter.*

LTu: Circumdederunt] Circundederunt ελφ; circūndederunt ϱσυτ*; [ ]ircumdederunt τ: *initial letter wanting.*

GAg: gemitus] dolores FGHIJK.

GAu: gemitus] dolores δεζϑιλμξοπϱστυφχψ.

6

Dolores	I	sar ACDGHJK, sár BF, helle E^{2}
inferni	I	helle ABCDGHIK, on helle *F*J, sær E^{2}
circumdederunt	I	ymbsaldon A, ymbsealdon B*CH,* ymbesealdan K, utan ymbsealdon G, uton ymbsealdon J, ymbtrymdon F, ymbtremedun I, hie me E^{2}
me	I	me ABCFGHJK, ymbsealdon E^{2}
praeuenerunt*	I	forecwomon A, forecomon *BCD,* forecoman GJ, forcoman K, forcomon ł abysgodon F, forestopun ł ofðriccetan I, ⁊ me *E*^{2} (*L*)
me	I	me ABCFGIJK, forecomon E^{2}
laquei	I	gerene A, gryne B*, gryn C, grynu DI, grinu FHK, grina J, gegrines G, deæþæs E^{2}
mortis	I	deaðes ABG, deaðys C, deaþes FIJK, deaðe H, gegryno E^{2}

ED: circundederunt (C)] circu[m]dederunt *Wildhagen.* preoccupauerunt (I)] praeoccupauerunt *Lindelöf.*

OE: gryne (B)] y *interl.*

LTg: inferni] F: *2nd* n *interl.* circumdederunt] circundederunt C: *orig.* circumdederunt: *left leg of* m *eras. to form* n; circundederunt H: *1st* n *interl.* praeuenerunt] preuenerunt BDE; prękuenerunt C, L: preoccupauerunt *written interl. by corr.: see GAg.*

LTu: inferni] inferi ζιμπτφψ. circumdederunt] circundederunt ειλτφ; circūndederunt οστ*χ. praeuenerunt] pręuenerunt ν; preuenerunt ςτ*.

GAg: praeuenerunt] preocupauerunt FJ; pręoccupauerunt GH; preoccupauerunt K, L: *see LTg,* I: *orig.* praeoccupauerunt: *1st* a *eras.*

GAu: praeuenerunt] praeoccupauerunt δμυψ; pręoccupauerunt ζλοϱφ, ε: *1st* c *interl.;* preoccupauerunt ϑιπτ, ξ: *1st* c *interl.;* p̄occupauerunt σχ.

7

Et*	⁊ *ABE*^{2}* (*CDL*)
in*	in AB, on CD*E*^{2}*FGHIJK*
tribulatione*	geswencednisse A, geswencednysse *C,* geswince BDGHJK, geswince ł eærfoþnesse *E*^{2}*, gedrefednysse F, gedrefednesse I
mea*	minre A*C*E^{2}*FI, minu̲m̲ BDJ, minum H, minan GK
inuocaui	ic gecede A, ic gecigde BCDH, ic gecigede E^{2}, ic gecige G*J,* ic cege F, ic clepode I, ic clypige K
dominum	dryhten B, drihten E^{2}FK, dryht̄ A, driħt CHJ, driħ G
et	⁊ ABCDE^{2}FGHIJK
ad	to ABCDE^{2}FGHIJK

deum gode ABCDE^{2}FGHIJK
meum minum ABCGI, minum DHJ, mine E^{2}F, minan K
clamaui ic cleopede A, ic cleopode BDE^2*, ic clypode CH, ic clypude F, ic clypige GK, ic clipige J, ic cigde I

Et ⁊ ABCE^{2}F*G*HIJK
exaudiuit he geherde AI, he gehyrde CF*G*K, he gehierde E^2*, he gehirde J, gehyrde DH, he geherge B
de | of ABCDFGHIJK, mine E^2
templo | temple ABCDFGHIJK, stemne E^2
sancto | ðæm halgan A, þæm halgan B, þam halgan CFG, halgan I, haligan K, haligum J, his DH, of his E^2
suo | his ABFIJK, hys C, ðam haligan D, þam haligan H, þæn hælgæn E^2
uocem | stefne ABCDFIK, stæfne HJ, temple E^2
meam | mine ABCDFGHIK, min J
et ⁊ ABCDE^{2}FGHIJK
clamor | cleopung ABD, clypung CFHK, clepung I, clipung J, clypige *G*, mine E^2
meus | min ABCFGHIJK, clipunge E^2
in in AB, on CDE^2*FGHIJK
conspectu | gesihðe ABCG, gesyhðe D, gesihþe FJ, gesyhþe H, ansyne ł on gesihðe I, ansyne K, his E^2
eius | his ABCFGHIJ*K*, gesihþe E^2
introiuit ineode ABDGHIJK, inneode C, ingeode E^2*, infærð F
in in AB, on CDE^{2}FGHJK, to I
aures | earan ABDHJK, earum CF, [ ]ran *G*, his E^{2}I
eius | his ABFGJ*K*, hys C, hine H, eæræn E^2, earum I

ED: mea (C)] méa *Wildhagen*. ic clypige (G)] ic clypig[ ] *Rosier*. ⁊ (G) (*2nd*)] [ ] *Rosier*. clypige (G)] [ ]:pige *Rosier*.

OE: ⁊ (E^2) (*1st*)] *otiose diagonal stroke through top: false start on transposition marks* (*see below*). geswince ł eærfoþnesse minre (E^2)] *written orig. as* geswince minre ł eærfoþnesse: *transposition marks before* minre *and above* eæ. ic cleopode (E^2)] eopode *on eras.* (?). he gehierde (E^2)] d *altered from* e, *final* e *added*. on (E^2) (*2nd*)] *eras. before word*. ingeode (E^2)] ⁊ *eras. before word,* geode *on eras*.

LTg: Et (*1st*)] et ABDL, E: *on eras. in darker ink; om.* C: *see GAg*. in (*1st*)] E: *on eras. in darker ink;* In FGHIJK. tribulatione] C: *small eras.* (?) *after 1st* i, E: tri *on eras. in darker ink*. mea] C: a *malformed at top, surmounted by smudge* (?). inuocaui] J: *orig.* inuacaui: *1st* a *altered to* o. Et (*2nd*)] [ ]t G. exaudiuit] exaudiui[ ] G. clamor] cl(a)mor G: a *split vertically and obscured by paper mount*. eius (*1st*)] eíus K. aures] (a)ures G: a *split vertically and obscured by paper mount.* eius (*2nd*)] eíus K.

LTu: Et (*1st*)] et βτ*; *om.* νς. in (*1st*)] In δεζιλμξοπϱστυφχψ. introiuit] β: *2nd* i *interl.;* introibit δϑ.

GAg: Et (*1st*)] *om.* FGHIJK, C: *see LTg.*

GAu: Et (*1st*)] *om.* δεζιλμξοπϱστυφχψ. Et in tribulatione mea] Cum tribularer ϑ: *cf. Bib. sac. MSS* R*FI.

8

Et* ⁊ ABCD, And E^{2}* (*L*)
commota | onstyred AB, onstyryd C, astyred DE^{2}*H,* astyrod *F,* astyrud *K,* onwended *G,* awænded *J,* wæs *I*
est | wes A, is BE^{2}FGHJ*K,* ys C, astyrod I
et | ⁊ ABFGHIJK, eorþe E^{2}
contremuit | cwęcede A, cwacode B*C,* forhtude DH, forhtode F, forhtodan K, bifode GJ, heo bifode I, ⁊ E^{2}
terra | eorðe ABCDGI, eorþe FJK, eorðan H, forhtæde ł beuede E^{2}* (*L*)
et ⁊ ABDE^{2}*HJ* (*CFGIKL*)
fundamenta | steaðelas A, staðolas BC, staþolas J, ⁊ staðolas *G,* grundweallas D, ⁊ grundweallas *F,* grundwealles H, staþolas ł grundweallas ł grundas I, ⁊ grundweal *K,* grundwealles ł dunæ E^{2}
montium | munta AB*CDFGIJK, mvntas H*, gestæþelungæ *E*^{2}
conturbata | gedroefde A, gedrefde BFI, gedrefede DGHJK, gedrefed C, sindon E^{2}
sunt | sind A, sint B, synd CDFHK, syndon GJ, wæron I*, gedrefede E^{2}
et ⁊ ABCE^{2}FGHJK
commota onstyrede ABE^{2}, onstyryd C, astyrede DH, astyrude F, astyrud K, onwende G, onwænde J (*L*)
sunt sind A, sint B, synd CDFHK, syndon GJ
quoniam forðon ABHJ, forþon C, forþan K, forþon þe E^{2}*, forðon ðe F, forþam G
iratus | eorre A*BDH, yrre CFGK, irre J, god *E*^{2}*
est | is ABFH, ys C, wæs G, he wæs J, him *E*^{2}*
eis | him ABDFGHJ, hi<u>m</u> K, hym C, is *E*^{2}
deus* | god ABC, yrre E^{2}

ED: contremuit (C)] cóntremuit *Wildhagen.* forhtæde ł beuede (E)] forhtæde ł beued*e* *Harsley.* mvntas (H)] muntas *Campbell.* forðon (A)] for ðon *Kuhn.*

OE: And (E^{2})] A *altered from* O. forhtæde ł beuede (E^{2})] d *in* forhtæde *altered from* e, e *added;* beuede *written above following* ⁊, *final* de *in ligature.* munta (B)] u *closed at top.* mvntas (H)] *orig.* montas: v *written above* o, *overlapping letter.* wæron (I)] *remainder of v. 8 (comprising 1st line of fol. 21v) unglossed.* forþon þe god him (E^{2})] *transposition marks written above* for *and after* god; *perhaps intended order is* him forþon þe god (*fol. ends after* quoniam *and* him). eorre] A: *possibly altered from* iorre.

LTg: Et] L: *underlined to signal deletion: see GAg.* commota (*1st*)] Commota FHIJK; [ ]ommota G. est (*1st*)] ést K. contremuit] C: *smudge above* o. terra] L: *eras. after word.* et (*2nd*)] H: *written as* ⁊ (*by glossator?*); *om.* CI; *for* FGKL *see notes to* terra *and* fundamenta, *cf. Weber MSS* med. fundamenta] FGK: *eras.* (*2 letters*) *before word.* montium] montivm E. commota (*2nd*)] comota L. iratus] E: *right leg of* u *retraced in darker ink.* est (*2nd*)] E: *on eras.* eis] E: s *formed from another letter, eras. after word.*

LTu: commota (*1st*)] Commota δεζιλμξοπϱστυφχψ. et (*2nd*)] *om.* βεζινπϱ. montium] monsium β.

GAg: Et] *om.* FGHIJK, L: *see LTg.* deus] *om.* FGHIJK.

GAu: Et] *om.* δεζϑιλμξοπϱστυφχψ. deus] *om.* δεζϑιλμξοπϱστυφχψ.

9

Ascendit		astag AB, astagh D, astagh E^{2}*, astah FHIK, upastah CGJ
fumus		rec AGH, réc D, smec B, smíc F, smic K, smic ł rec C, smic ł réc E^{2}J, smoca I
in		in AB, on CDE^{2}*FGHIJK
ira	I	eorre ADH, irre BJ, yrre CGIK, graman F, his E^{2}
eius	I	his ABFGHIJ*K*, hys C, yrre E^{2}
et		⁊ ABCE^{2}FGHIJK
ignis		fyr ABCDFGHIJK, fir E^{2}*
a	I	from A, from B, fram CGJ, fram FI, of DHK, byrneþ E^{2}
facie	I	onsiene *AB,* ansyne CDF*G*HI*J*K, of E^{2}*
eius		his ABDE^{2}FGHIJ*K,* hys *C*
exardescit*	I	born AB, barn C, abarn GJ, ⁊ abarn I, onbyrnð D, forbærnde F, byrð K, onsiene E^{2}
Carbones	I	colu ABCD*H,* cola *K,* gleda ł cola *F,* gleda *GJ,* gledan *I,* Onheledæ E^{2} (*L*)
succensi	I	onęlde A, onælde BFGI, onælede CDJK, anælede H, sient E^{2}
sunt	I	sind A, synd F, synd CHK, sint B, synt I, wæron GJ, gledæ E^{2}
ab		from ACE^{2}, from B, fram DFGHJK, fram I
eo		him A*DE^{2}F*GH*JK, him BCI

ED: astagh (E)] Astagh *Harsley.* carbónes (H)] carbones *Campbell.* éo (H)] eo *Campbell.* him (I)] him *Lindelöf.*

OE: astagh (E^2)] *on eras.* on (E^2)] *eras. before word.* fir (E^2)] *eras. before word.* of (E^2)] *on eras.* him (A)] i *written below* h.

LTg: eius (*1st*)] eíus K. facie] A: *letter eras. after* i, J: *eras. before word;* facię BG. eius (*2nd*)] C: *eras.* (?) *before word;* eíus K. Carbones] L: *minuscule* c *written in bowl of initial* C; carbones FGIK; carbónes H; carbonos J. eo] éo GH.

LTu: Ascendit] [ ]scendit τ*: *initial letter wanting.* facie] facię ε. exardescit] exardescet ς. Carbones] carbones δεζϑιλμξοπϱστυφχψ. ab eo] habeo ζ.

GAg: exardescit] exarsit FGHIJK.

GAu: exardescit] exarsit δεζϑιλμξοπϱστυφχψ.

10

Et*	⁊ *ABCDE*^{2} (*L*)
inclinauit	he onhaelde A, he onhelde B*I,* he onhylde C, he ahylde D*F*K,* ne ahylde *H,* he onhyldeþ E^2, onhyldeð *G,* ahildaþ *J*
caelos	heofenas A*G,* heofonas *BDFIJ,* heofonæs *E*^{2}*,* heofanas *H,* hefynas *C,* heofenan *K* (*L*)
et	⁊ ABC*E*^{2}FGH*IJK
descendit	ofdune astag *A*B, adune astah CDFH, adun astah E^2*K, ofdune astigeð G, ofdune astigeþ J, niðerastah I
et	⁊ ABCE^2FGHIJK (*D*)
caligo	dimnis A*F,* dimnes BD*G*H, dymnys C, dymnes JK, dimnesse E^2*, is dymnes I
sub	under ABCDE^2*FGHIJK
• pedibus	| fotum ACFGIJ, fotum BDH, fotan K, his E^2*
eius	| his ABDFGHIJ*K,* hys C, fotum E^2

ED: cęlos (E)] caelos *Harsley.* adune astah (C)] aduneastah *Wildhagen.* fotum (D)] fótum *Roeder.*

OE: he ahylde (F)] *eras. after* he. ⁊ (H) (*1st*)] *written below* n *in* heofanas. adun astah (E^2)] *on eras.* dimnesse (E^2)] *by main hand in darker ink.* under (E^2)] *on eras., eras. before word.* his (E^2)] *eras. after word.*

LTg: Et] et ABCDE, L: *underlined to signal deletion: see GAg.* inclinauit] Inclinauit FGHIJK. caelos] cælos BK; cęlos CEFGIJL; celos D, H: *added interl. in smaller hand* (*by glossator?*). et (*1st*)] E: *as* ⁊. descendit] A: *orig.* discendit: *1st* i *altered to* e. et (*2nd*)] *om.* D. caligo] calígo FG. eius] eíus K.

LTu: Et] et βνςτ*. inclinauit] Inclinauit δεζϑιλμξοπϱστυφχψ. caelos] cęlos εζιλξοφ; cælos ϑ; celos σςτ*τ. descendit] discendit βϑ.

GAg: Et] *om.* FGHIJK, L: *see LTg.*

GAu: Et] *om.* δεζϑιλμξοπϱστυφχψ.

11

Et ⁊ ABCE^{2}FGHIJK
ascendit astag AB, he astag D, he æstag E^{2}*, he astah FHK, upastah CGJ, he upastah I
super ofer ABE^{2}FGHI*JK, ofyr C
cherubin cerubim A, cherubin C*F**J, cherubím *G*, cheruphin E^{2} (*I*)
et ⁊ ABCE^{2}FGHIJK
uolauit fleg A, fleag B, fleah J, flieh C, he fleah DE^{2}*FGHI, he fleh K
uolauit fleg A, fleag B, flieh C, fleah FGJ, fleh K, he fleah HI, ⁊ he fleah E^{2}*
super ofer ABCE^{2}FGHIJK
pinnas | fiðru A*B*, fyðru *CI*, fiþera *F*, fiðera *K*, heanessa *DH*, windæ E^{2}, winda *GJ* (*L*)
uentorum | winda ABCDFHIK, feþerum G, fyþerum J, heanesse ł fiþræs E^{2}*

ED: fiðru (B)] fiðra *Brenner.*

OE: he æstag (E^{2})] ag *on eras.* ofer (I) (*1st*)] *otiose mark at shoulder of* r. cherubin (F)] *orig.* cherubim: *right leg of* m *eras.* he fleah (E^{2})] fleah *on eras.* ⁊ he fleah (E^{2})] fleah *on eras.* heanesse ł fiþræs (E^{2})] ł *eras. before* heanesse.

LTg: cherubin] F: *orig.* cherubim: *right leg of* m *eras.;* cherubím G; cherubim I. pinnas] pennas BCDFGHIJKL.

LTu: Et] Aet δ; [ ]t ι*τ: *initial letter wanting.* cherubin] cherubim μ; hiruphin ϑ. pinnas] pennas δεζϑιλμνξοπϱσςτ*τυφχψ.

12

Et ⁊ ABCDE^{2}FGHIJK
posuit sette ABC, he asette DFH, he gesette E^{2}*GIJ, he sette K
tenebras ðeostru A, þeostru B, þystru C*GJ, ðystru FI, ðystro D*, þystro E^{2}H, þystra K
latibulum | heolstur AB, heolstru ł ī C*, digelnysse F, digelnesse G, dygolnessa J, dymhofan ł dymnes ł behydednesse I, his DE^{2}H
suum | his ABFGJ, hys C, [ ]is I*, indiegelnesse DH, digelnesse E^{x}*
in in AB, on CDE^{x}*FGHIJK
circuitu | ymbhwyrfte ABCDE$^{2/x}$*F, ymhwyrfte *H,* ymbehwyrfte K, ymbgange GJ, his I
eius | his ABCDE^{2}*FGHJ*K*, ymbhwyrfte I
tabernaculum geteld ABCGJ, eardungstow DH, eardungstowa ł teld F, eardungstowe E^{2}*I, earddung K
eius his AFGHIJ*K*, hys C

tenebrosa	ðeostre A, þeostre B*, þystre C, þystregu G, þystru J, ðeosterfull DE^{2}*, þeosterfull H, ðeostorfull F, þysterful K, þicce ł ðeostru I
aqua	weter A, wæter BDFHK, weter E^{2}, wætru C, wæteru IJ, wætera G
in	in AB, on CDE^{2}FGHIJK
nubibus	wolcnum AGI, wolcnum BJ, weolcnum C, genipum D, genipum F, genipum HK, genipum ł wolon E^{2}
aeris	lyfte ABCE^{2}H, lyfta K, lyftes FI, lyste D, lyftlicum *G,* liftlicum J

ED: heolstru ł t̄ (C)] heolstru ł (—)tyr *Wildhagen.* [ ]is (I)] his *Lindelöf.* indiegelnesse (H)] in diegelnesse *Campbell.* wolcnum (B)] wolcnum *Brenner.* aeris (D)] aëris *Roeder.*

OE: he gesette (E^{2})] *1st* t *interl., eras. after word.* þystru (C)] *orig.* þustru: *1st* u *altered to* y. ðystro (D)] *written in right margin after* tenebras: þæt is þæt hy hit ne mehton ne hit gemet wæs him eal awreon. heolstru ł t̄ (C)] ł t̄ *written above* tru *in* heolstru. [ ]is (I)] *only ascender visible in initial position.* digelnesse on ymbhwyrfte (E$^{2/x}$)] digelnesse on ymb *added by corr.* (?); *glosses written above* latibulum suum, *while* in circuitu eius *shows eras. extending above words, with* ⁊ *visible above* in, *followed by illegible ascenders.* his (E^{2}) (*2nd*)] ⁊ *eras. before word.* eardungstowe (E^{2})] *on eras.* þeostre (B)] *eras. after word* (*4 letters?*), e *visible in final position, with* r (?) *before.* ðeosterfull (E^{2})] *on eras.*

LTg: circuitu] circumitu H. eius (*1st*)] eíus K. eius (*2nd*)] eíus K. aeris] áeris G.

LTu: posuit] possuit ϑ. aeris] ęris β; æris ϑ.

13

Praefulgore	fore sciman *ABC,* for ligræsce *F,* lygrescas *D,* legrescas *E^{x}**, ligræscas *H,* ligræsca *K,* for leoman *GJ,* toforan ligette ł for lygræscunge I (*L*)
in	in AB, on CDE^{2}*FGHIJK
conspectu |	gesihðe AB*CFG, gesyhðe H, gesihþe J, ansyne IK, his DE^{2}
eius |	his ABFGHIJ*K*, hys C, gesihðe D, gesihþe E^{2}
nubes	wolcen A, wolcnu B, weolcnu C, wolcna GJ, wolcnu ł genipu I, nipu ł wolon E^{2}*, genipu DFH, genipum K
transierunt	leordon *A*BC, ferdon D*G*HJK, færdon E^{2}*, feredon F, gewitun I*
grando	hegel A, hagal B*, hagul F, hagol J, hægl G, hegle ł yft E^{2}, hagol ł hreohnes I, yst DH, micyl C
et	⁊ ABCE^{2}FGHIJK

carbones	I	colu ABCI, gleda DF*H*JK, gledan G, fyres E2*
ignis	I	fyres ABDFGHI*JK, fyrys C, gleden E2*

ED: Pręfulgure (B)] Pręfulgure *Brenner.* Prefulgóre (CH)] Prefulgór[æ?] *Wildhagen;* Prefulgore *Campbell.* Prefulgorę (E)] Pre fulgorae *Harsley.* Prefulgore (F)] Pre fulgore *Kimmens.* carbónes (H)] carbones *Campbell.*

OE: legrescas (Ex)] *on eras. in lighter brown ink.* on (E2)] *eras. before word.* gesihðe (B)] hi *eras. after word.* nipu ł wolon (E2)] *eras. after word, letter traces visible but illegible.* færdon (E2)] don *on eras.* gewitun (I)] u *closed at top, although not to be taken as* a: *cf. v. 3* anfengcend ł underfond. hagal (B)] hagol (?). fyres (E2)] *eras. after word.* ignis (I)] s. sunt : synt *written in left margin.* gleden (E2)] en *on eras.*

LTg: Praefulgore] A: *2nd* u *on eras.;* Pręfulgure B; Prefulgóre H, C: *orig.* Prefulgóra: a *altered to* e *by corr. in light brown ink;* Pręfulgora D; Prefulgorę E: ł u *written in lighter brown ink above* o; Prefulgórę K; Pręfulgore G; Prefulgora J; Prefulgore F, L: *orig.* Prefulguru: *2nd* u *altered to* o, *right stem of 3rd* u *eras., eye added to left stem by corr. to form* e: *cf. Weber MSS* PV2η mozx. eius] eíus K. transierunt] A: *eras. after 1st* n, s *added by corr. before* i *in next line;* transier[ ] G. carbones] carbónes H.

LTu: Praefulgore] Praeuulgore β; Pręfulgore εφ; Pręfulgoriæ ζ; Prefulgoræ ϑ; Prefulgorę ι; Prefulgore λξϱστ*τυ; Pręfulgora ν; Praefulgorę δο; Prefulgora ς. transierunt] transerunt ϑ.

14

Et		⁊ ABCDE2F*G*HIJK
intonuit		hleoðrað AB, hleaðrað C, hleoðrode F, hleoþrode G, hleoþrade J, hlynde DH, hlydde K, swegde I, denede ł þunerode E2*
de		of ABCDE2*FIK, on H, to GJ
caelo		heofene A, heofone *BDH,* heofonæ *E2*,* hefynum *C,* heofonum *F*J, heofenum *G,* heofenum *I,* heofenan *K* (*L*)
dominus		dryhten A, drihten E2*, dryht̄ B, driht́ CF, driht̄ I, drih́ GJ
et		⁊ ABCDE2*FGHIJK
altissimus		se hehsta ABK, se heahsta CD, se heahesta E2*, se hyhsta FG, se heaxta I, se hihsta J, þe hehsta H
dedit		salde A, sealde BCDFGHIJK, gef ł selde E2*
uocem	I	stefne ABCDGHIK, stæfne J, stemne F, his E2
suam	I	his ABFGIJK, hys C, stemne E2 (D*)
(grando)*		hagul F, hagol J, hægl G, storme ł h[ ]gol I*
(et)*		⁊ FGHIJK
(carbones)*		cola F, gledan GK, gleda HJ, gledan ł colu I
(ignis)*		fyres FGH*I*JK

ED: cęlo (E)] caelo *Harsley.* storme ł h[ ]gol (I)] storme ł hagol *Lindelöf.* carbónes (H)] carbones *Campbell.*

OE: denede ł þunerode (E^2)] *on eras.* of (E^2)] o *on eras.* (?). heofonæ (E^2)] *letter eras. after word; Harsley reads* s. drihten (E^2)] *on eras.* ⁊ (E^2) (*2nd*)] *on eras.* se heahesta (E^2)] *on eras.* gef ł selde (E^2)] *eras. after* gef, de *on eras.* suam (D) *gloss eras.* storme ł h[ ]gol (I)] *hole in leaf after* h.

LTg: Et] [ ]t G. caelo] cælo B; cęlo CEFGKL; celo DHI. ignis] I: s. sunt *written in left margin.*

LTu: caelo] cęlo εζιξουφ; cælo ϑχ; celo σςτ*τ.

GAg: suam] suam grando et carbones ignis FGIJKL; suam grando et carbónes ignis H.

GAu: suam] suam grando et carbones ignis δεζϑιλμξοπϱστυφχψ.

15

(Et)*		⁊ FGHIJK
Misit		sende ABC*GK,* sænde *J,* he sende DE^2**H,* he asende *FI*
sagittas		strele A, stræle B, strælas CGJ, flana DFHIK, flane E^2
suas		his ABFGIJK, hys C, his ł strelæ E^2*
et		⁊ ABCE^2FGHIJK
dissipauit	I	tostencte ABCG, tostæncte *J,* he tostencte DFHIK, he hi E^2
eos	I	hie ABCG, hig F*IJ*, hy H, hi *K,* tostencte E^2*
⟨et⟩		⁊ *A*
fulgora		legite *A,* legeto B, lígeta *G**, liggetta J, ⁊ ligettu *C,* legte ł legrescas E^2*, ligettas ł ligrescetunga *I,* legrescas D, legræscas *F,* ligræscas *H,* ⁊ ligræscas *K* (*L*)
multiplicauit		gemonigfaldade A, gemanigfaldode B, gemonigfealdoda C, gemenigfylde DH, gemænifylde F, gemanifealdode G, gemænigfealdode J, he gemonigfældæ E^2*, he gemænifylde I, gemyclude K
et		⁊ ABCDE^2*FGHIJK
conturbauit		gedroefde A, gedrefde BCDFGJ, gedrefede E^2*H, he gedrefde I, drefde K
eos		hie ABCE^2G, hig FJ, hy H, hi IK

ED: fúlgura (H)] fulgura *Campbell.* lígeta (G)] li-geta *Rosier.*

OE: he sende (E^2)] *eras. after gloss.* his ł strelæ (E^2)] *eras. after* ł. tostencte (E^2)] *final* te *on eras.* lígeta (G)] *accent* (?) *malformed.* legte ł legrescas (E^2)] grescas *on eras.* he gemonigfældæ (E^2)] ge *interl., letter eras. after final* æ. ⁊ (E^2) (*2nd*)] *eras.* (*23 mm*) *before word.* gedrefede (E^2)] *2nd* d *on eras.*

LTg: Misit] misit FGHIJK. dissipauit] disipauit J: *orig.* dissipauit: *1st* s *eras.* eos

(*1st*)] KI: *eras. after word* (*original flanking signs* ÷ *and* : *remain in* I); eos et A: et *interl. by corr.: cf. Weber MSS* αγδη moz^{x}. fulgora] G: *descender of* g *lost;* fulgura FIKL, A: *2nd* u *on eras.*, C: *orig*. fulgora: o *deleted by subscript dot,* u *interl. by corr. in light brown ink;* fúlgura H: *accent eras. above 2nd* u: *cf. Weber MSS* γη^{2} moz med.

LTu: Misit] misit δεζϑλιμξοπϱστυφχ. suas] *om*. μ. dissipauit] disipauit ϑ. eos (*1st*)] eos et ϑμ, β: et *added by corr.*, υ: et *eras.*: *cf. Weber MSS* αγδη moz^{x}. fulgora] β: f *added by corr. in ligature with preceding added* et; fulgura ελινξοπϱστ*τφχ. conturbauit] conturbabit β.

GAg: Misit] Et misit FGHIJK.

GAu: Misit] Et misit δεζϑιλμξοπϱστυφχ.

16

Et		⁊ ABCDE^{2}FGHIJK
apparuerunt		oteawdon A, æteawdon B, ætywdon *C*, oðeowdon DH, oðywdon F, ontyndon G, untindon J, ætywdon I, etywdan K, stywdon ł ataudon E^{2}*
fontes	|	waellan A, wællan B, wyllas CDFHK, æsprincg G, æsprinc J, wylsprengas I*, wetræ E^{2}
aquarum	|	wetra A, wætra BD, wætyra C, wætera FGHJK, wætru I, wyllæs *E*$^{2/x}$*
et		⁊ ABC*E*^{x}*FGHIJK
reuelata		onwrigen A, onwrigenc BG, onwrigyne C, awrigene D*E*^{x}*FHK, unwrigene J, unwrogene I
sunt		werun A, wæron BGJ, synd CFI*K, synt *E*^{x}*, sy[ ] *H**
fundamenta		steaðelas A, staðolas BGI, staþolas J, staðylas C, grundweallas DE^{x}FHK
orbis		ymbhwyrftes ABDE^{x}*FI, ymbhwyrftys C, ymbhyrftes H, ymbehwyrftes K, ymbhwyrft GJ
terrae*		eorðan *ABCD*E^{x}*H, eorþan FJK, eorðena G, eorðana I (*L*)
Ab	|	from A, from BC, fram *G*J, fram I, of DF*H*K, Drihten E^{2}
increpatione	|	ðreange A, þreaunga BCFH*K, ðreaunga D, þreaunge I, ceaste GJ, from E^{2}
tua		ðinre ADF, þinre BCGHIJK, þinræ E^{2}
domine	|	drihten G, dryht̄ AB, driħt CFH, driħ J, eala driht̄ I, þrægunge E^{2}
ab		from A, from BC, fram GJ, fram I, of DE^{2}*FHK
inspiratione		onoeðunge A, oneðunge B, oneþgunge D, oneþgunge E^{2}*, onéþunge G, oneðunga H*, ineþunge J, onorþunge I, órðunge F, eðunge C, eþunga K

spiritus	gastes ABDFGIK, gastys C, gæstes E^{2}, gast HJ
irae	earres A, eorres B*DH*, yrrys *C*, yrres *E^{2}*GIK*, irres *J*, graman *F* (*L*)
tuae	ðines A*DE^{2}**, þines B*FG*IJ*K*, þinys *C*, þine H (*L*)

ED: Et (G)] *Et Rosier.* onwrigene (G)] onwrigena *Rosier.* su(n)[ ] (H)] sunt *Campbell.* sy[ ] (H)] sy(nd) *Campbell.* [ ]b (G)] *Ab Rosier.* ceaste (G)] [ ]st: *Rosier.* órðunge (F)] orðunge *Kimmens.* tuę (E)] tuae *Harsley.*

OE: stywdon ł ataudon (E^{2})] ataudon *on eras.* wylsprengas (I)] *orig.* wylspringas: i *altered to* e, y *altered from* i (?). wyllæs (E$^{2/x}$)] læs *on eras. by corr.*, læs (?) *eras. after* wyl-. ⁊ (E^{x}) (*2nd*)] *on eras. by corr.* awrigene (E^{x})] *on eras. by corr.* synd (I)] *orig.* synt: t *altered to* d. synt (E^{x})] *on eras. by corr.* sy[ ] (H)] *final letters lost due to hole in leaf.* grundweallas (E^{x})] *on eras. by corr.* ymbhwyrftes (E^{x})] *on eras. by corr.* eorðan (E^{x})] *on eras. by corr.* þreaunga (H)] *letter* (w?) *eras. after 1st* a. of (E^{2})] *on eras.* oneþgunge (E^{2})] *on eras.* oneðunga (H)] *letter eras. after* ð. yrres (E^{2})] s *on eras., eras. after word.* ðines (E^{2})] nes *on eras.*

LTg: apparuerunt] aparuerunt C. aquarum] E: *retouched due to eras. of orig. gloss.* et] E: *retouched due to eras. of orig. gloss.* reuelata] E: *retouched due to eras. of orig. gloss.* sunt] E: *retouched due to eras. of orig. gloss;* su(n)[ ] H: n *cropped, final letter lost due to hole in leaf.* terrae] terrę A; terre CD; terræ B, L: arum *written interl. by corr.: see GAg.* Ab] [ ]b G, H: *traces of blue ink visible in initial position.* irae] irę CEFGHJK; ire D; iræ L. tuae] tuę CDEFGK; tuæ L.

LTu: apparuerunt] aparuerunt ϑ. fundamenta] ς: ta *interl.* terrae] terrę βν; terre τ*; terrarum ς: *cf. Weber MSS* T*αη. inspiratione] insperatione ϑ. irae] irę εινπϱφ; ire ζξσςτ*τ; iræ ϑ. tuae] tuæ ϑχ; tuę ιξφ; tue σςτ*τ.

GAg: terrae] terrarum FGHIJK, L: *see LTg.*

GAu: terrae] terrarum δεζϑιλμξοπϱστυφχψ, ς: *see LTu.*

17

Misit	sende ABG, he sende CH, he sænde J, he asende DE^{2}*FIK
de	of ABCE^{2}*FGIJK
summo	heanisse A, heanesse B, heanysse CI, heahnesse E^{2}*, ofene D, efene H, yfan K, heofonum F, hean GJ
et	⁊ ABCDE^{2}FGHIJK
accepit	| onfeng AB**G*J, he onfeng C, genam DK, genam H, he genam FI*, me E^{2}
me	| me ABCDFGHIJK, onfeng E^{2}
et	⁊ ABCE^{2}FG*I*J (D**HK*)
adsumpsit	| genom AB, genam *CJ*, to genam *G*, anfeng D*H*, afengc *F*, afenc *K*, upahof *I*, me E^{2}

me	I	me ABCFGHIJK, genæm E[2]
de		of ABCDE[2]*FGIJK
multitudine*	I	menge AB, mænigeo C*, menigo D, manege E[2], wæterum FJ, wætrum I, wætera GK (*L*)
aquarum*	I	wetra A, wætra BC, wætera D, wetere E[2]*, miclum F, menigeo G, manegum IJ

ED: D: *gloss on 2nd* et *eras. and not visible, although Roeder records* ⁊. assumsit (C)] a[d]sumsit *Wildhagen.*

OE: he asende (E[2])] *on eras.* of (E[2]) (*1st*)] *on eras.* heahnesse (E[2])] *on eras.* onfeng (B)] *letter eras. after word.* he geman (I)] *1st* e *interl.* et (*2nd*)] D: *gloss eras.* of (E[2]) (*2nd*)] *eras. after word.* mænigeo (C)] i *interl.* wetere (E[2])] *on eras., eras. before word.*

LTg: accepit] a[ ]cepit G. et (*2nd*)] H: *on eras.*, I: *added interl.* (*by glossator?*), K: *on eras. by corr.* adsumpsit] assumpsit FGIJ; assumsit C: *1st* s *on eras. by corr.*, H: as *on eras.*, K: as *on eras. by corr.* multitudine] L: aquis multis *written interl. by corr.: see GAg.*

LTu: Misit] Missit ϑ. et (*2nd*)] *interl.* σχ; *om.* δμϱυ. adsumpsit] assumpsit δεζιλξο πϱστ*τυφχ; assumsit ϑ. de] ς: a *deleted after word* (*initial letter of following* aquarum *directly below*).

GAg: multitudine aquarum] aquis multis FGHIJK, L: *see LTg.*

GAu: multitudine aquarum] aquis multis δεζϑιλμξοπϱστ*ιυφψ, χ: a *interl.*

18

Eripuit*	generede ABG, he generyde C, he generede E[2]*, he generode FJ, he nerede DHK, he alysde ł he generode I
me	me ABCE[2]FGHJK
de	of ABDE[2]FGHJK, from C, fram I
inimicis	feondum AFGHI*, feondum BCDJK, fyondum E[2]*
meis	minum AFGHI, minum BCDJ, minan K, mine E[2]*
fortissimis	ðæm strongestum A, þæm strongestum B, þam strongystum C, ðam strengestum D, ðam strengestum E[2]*, þam strengestum H, þam strangestum I, þam strengston F, þa strongestan GJ, þam strengustan K
et	⁊ ABCDE[2]*FGHIJK
ab	from A, from BC, fram DE[2]*FGHJK, fram I
his	ðissum A*B*, ðyssum DE[2]*, ðýsum F, ðysum *G,* þisum H, þisum J, þyssu C, þys *K*
qui	ða A, þa BK, þe CD*E*[2]*H, þa ðe F, þa þe GJ, þam þe I
oderunt	fiodon A, feodon B, feodun C, hatedon DE[2]*GH, hatodon J, hatudon F, hatedun I, hatodan K

me		me ABCE^2*FGHIJK
quoniam		forðon ABH, forþon C, forðan ðe F, forþon þe J, forðam þe G, forðan þe I, forþæm þe E^2
confortati*	|	gestrongade AB, gestrongode C, gestrangode F*GJ, hi gestrangode I, hi strængode E^2, he wæron D, hi wæron H
sunt	|	werun A, wæron B, weron E^2, hi wæron C, synd F, synt I, syndon GJ, strangode DH
super		ofer AB*E^{2}FGHIJ, ofyr C
me		me ABCE^{2}FGHIJ

ED: þam strangestum (I)] fram strangestum *Lindelöf.* hís (BG)] his *Brenner, Rosier.* forðon (A)] for ðon *Kuhn.*

OE: he generede (E^2)] he *on eras.* feondum (I)] um *obscured at top.* fyondum (E^2)] *on eras.* mine (E^2)] *on eras.* ðam strengestu͟m (E^2)] *on eras.* ⁊ (E^2)] *on eras.* fra͟m (E^2)] *on eras.* ðyssu͟m (E^2)] *on eras.* þe (E^2)] *on eras.* hatedon (E^2)] *on eras.* me (E^2) (*2nd*)] *on eras.* gestrangode (F)] *final* e *partly effaced.* ofer (B)] *eras.* (?) *after word.*

LTg: his] hís BG; iis K. qui] E: *on eras.*

LTu: Eripuit] ERipuit β. his] iis ιλπτφ. oderunt] hoderunt ς.

GAu: Eripuit] Eripiet μ. confortati] confirmati μ.

19

Praeuenerunt	|	forecomun A, forecomon *BCGJ,* hy forecomon *D,* hi forecomon *FH,* hi forcoman *K,* hi forestopun ł hi forhradodan I, hy Me *E^2* (*L*)
me	|	me ABCFGHJK, forecomon E^2
in		in AB, on CDE^{2}FGHIJK
die		dege A, dæge BCDFGJ*H*I, dæg K, dege E^2
adflictionis	|	geswinces A*BGJ,* geswencys *C,* geswencednisse DH, geswencednysse *F,* geswencednesse *K,* gedrefednysse ł geswencednysse *I**, minre *E^2*
meae	|	mines A*B*GJ, minys *C,* minre *DF*HI*K,* geswincednesse *E^2** (*L*)
et		⁊ ABCE^{2}FGHIJK
factus	|	geworden ABFGHIJ, gewordyn C, gewordon D, gedon K, drihten E^2
est		is ABE^{2}FGHI*K,* ys C, is me J
dominus	|	drihten F, dryht̄ AB, drih́t CG, drih́ HJ, geworden E^2
protector		gescildend AB, gescyldynd C, gescyldend DG*H,* scyldend E^{2}I, scildend J, bewerigend F, frofer K
meus		min ABCDE^2*FGHJK, min ł min beweriend I

ED: on (H)] in *Campbell.* afflictionis (C)] a[d]flictionis *Wildhagen.* meę (E)] meae *Harsley.*

OE: gedrefednysse ł geswencednysse (I)] *top of 2nd* s *faint.* geswincednesse (E^{2})] ed *interl.* min (E^{2})] *on eras.*

LTg: Praeuenerunt] Preuenerunt BCDEFJL, H: *initial* P *faint but visible;* Prępuenerunt G; Præuenerunt K. die] dię H. adflictionis] afflictionis BEFGIJK, C: *1st* f *on eras. by corr.* meae] meæ BK; meę CDEFL. est] ést K. protector] H: tector *on eras.*

LTu: Praeuenerunt] Pręuenerunt ελρυφ; Preuenerunt ζϑιξπσςτ*τ. adflictionis] afflictionis εζιλμξοπρστ*τυφ. meae] meæ ϑ; meę ινφ; mee ξσςτ*τ.

20

Et	⁊ *ABCDE*^{2}*FGHIJK (*L*)
eduxit	utalaedde A, utalædde BC, utgelædde G, he geledde DE^{2}*, he gelædde F*H*IJ, he lædde K
me	me AB*C*E^{2}*FGHIJK
in	in ABJ, on CDE^{2}FGHIK
latitudinem	braedu A, brædu B, bræde C, tobredednesse *D*E^{2}*, tobrædednysse F, tohrædnesse H, tobrædednesse I, bradnesse K, sidhealfe *G*, sydhealfe J (*L*)
saluum	halne ABCDE^{2}*FGHIJ, hal K
me	me ABCFGIK, he me E^{2}*J (*H*)
fecit	doo A, do F, gedo G, gedyde BCJ, dyde E^{2}*K*, he dede ł he gehælde I*
quoniam	forðon ABHJ, forþon C, forðan K, forðæn þe E^{2}, forðon ðe F, forþam þe G, forþan þe I
uoluit	walde *A*, wolde BG, he wolde CDE^{2}*FHIJK
me	me ABCE^{2}FGHIJK

ED: he geledde (E^{2})] he geledd*e Harsley.* forðon (A)] for ðon *Kuhn.*

OE: ⁊ (E^{2})] *on eras.* he geledde (E^{2})] he *on eras.*, de *in ligature and on eras.* me (E^{2}) (*1st*)] *on eras.* tobredednesse (E^{2})] bredednesse *on eras.* halne (E^{2})] *on eras.* he me (E^{2})] *on eras.* he dede ł he gehælde (I)] ł he gehælde *written in right margin.* he wolde (E^{2})] *eras. after* he.

LTg: Et] et ABCDEL. eduxit] ęduxit H. me (*1st*)] C: *eras.* (?) *after word.* latitudinem] G: *orig.* letitudinem: *1st* e *altered to* a; latitudine DL. me (*2nd*)] H: *interl. by glossator and indicated for inclusion in Lat. line.* fecit] K: e *and* t *on eras. by corr., small hole in leaf after* e. uoluit] A: ui *in ligature,* t *and following* me *extend beyond grid.*

LTu: Et] et βνςτ*. me (*1st*)] *interl.* ε. latitudinem] latitudine ζν. fecit] facit ϑ; feciet μ.

GAu: fecit] faciet μ.

21

Et		⁊ ABCE^{2}FGHIJK
retribuit*	I	geedleanade *AB*, geedleanað C, he ageald DFH, he geald K, gesealde GJ, agylt I, me E^2
mihi	I	me AB*C*DFGHI*J*K, geeædleænyde ł ageald *E*^{2}*
dominus		drihten E^{2}K, dryht̄ AB, drih̄t CF, driht̄ I, drih̄ GHJ
secundum		efter AE^2, æfter BDFGHIJK, æftyr C
iustitiam	I	rehtwisnisse A, ryhtwisnesse BD, rihtwisnysse *C*FI, rihtwisnesse GHJK, minre E^2
meam	I	mine AB, minre C*D*FGHIJK, rihtwisnesse E$^{2/x}$*
et		⁊ ABCDE^{2}FGHIJK
secundum		efter AE^2, æfter BDFGIJK, æftyr C, æft<u>er</u> H
innocentiam*		unsceðfulnisse A, unsceðfulnesse B, unsceðfulnysse C, unsceaðfulnesse G, ungescæþfulnesse J, unscyldgunga D, unscyldinesse E^2* clænnysse F, clænsynga K, hluttornysse I (*L*)
manuum	I	honda A, handa BCDFGHIJK, minre E^2
mearum	I	minra ABCDFGHIJK, hændæ E^2
retribuit*	I	geedleanad *A*, geedleanað *B*C, he ageald DFH, forgeald K, he agylt I*, gesette G, gesete J, me E^2
mihi	I	me AB*C*FGHI*J*K, geedleænæde ł ageald *E*^{2}*

ED: mihi (G) (*1st*)] me *Rosier.* iusticiam (C)] iustitiam *Wildhagen.*

OE: geeædleænyde ł ageald (E^2)] ł ageald *added by corr* (?). rihtwisnesse (E$^{2/x}$)] rihtwis *and left leg of* n *on eras. by corr.* unscyldinesse (E^2)] dines *on eras.* he agylt (I)] *orig.* he agilt: i *altered to* y. geedleænæde ł ageald (E^2)] de *on eras.*, ł ageald *added by main hand in slightly darker ink.*

LTg: retribuit (*1st*)] retribuet B, A: *orig.* retribuit : *2nd* i *altered to* e: *cf. Weber MSS* M^{2}T*Q^{2}UXαγδη, *see GAg.* mihi (*1st*)] michi EJ, C: *orig.* mihi: c *interl. by corr.* iustitiam] iusticiam C: *orig.* iustitiam: *2nd* t *altered to* c. meam] D: *eras. after word of mark indicating marginal note.* innocentiam] L: *underlined to signal deletion and* puritatem *added interl. by corr.: see GAg.* retribuit (*2nd*)] retribuet B, A: *orig.* retribuit: *2nd* i *altered to* e: *cf. Weber MSS* M^{2}Q^{2}UXαγδη moz^c, *see GAg.* mihi (*2nd*)] michi EJ, C: *orig.* mihi: c *interl. by corr.*

LTu: mihi (*1st*)] michi ιλϛτ*τ, πϱ: c *interl.* iustitiam] iusticiam τ*τφ, ϱ: *orig.* iustitiam: *2nd* t *deleted,* c *interl.* manuum] manu<u>um</u> ϑ. mihi (*2nd*)] michi ειλϛτ*, πϱ: c *interl.*

GAg: retribuit (*1st*)] retribuet FGHIJK, AB: *see LTg.* innocentiam] puritatem FGHIJK, L: *see LTg.* retribuit (*2nd*)] retribuet FGHIJK, AB: *see LTg.*

GAu: retribuit (*1st*)] retribuet δεζϑιλμξοπϱστυφχψ. innocentiam] puritatem δεζϑιλμξοπϱστυφχψ. retribuit (*2nd*)] retribuet δεζϑιλμξοπϱστυφχψ.

22

Quia — forðon AB, forþon CJ, forðæn E^{2}*, forþam F, forþā *G*K, forðan þe I
custodiui — ic heold ABK, ic geheold CDE^{2}*FHIJ, ic gehcald G
uias — weagas A, wegas BCDE^{2}FGHIJK
domini — dryhtnes B, drihtnys C, drihtnes E^{2}FG, drihtnys I, dryht̄ A, driħt J
nec — ne ABCDE^{2}FGHIJ, na K
impie — arleaslice *A*BCDE^{2}*HK, árleaslice *F*, arlease GJ, unrihtlice ł arlea[ ]lice I*
gessi — ic dyde A*BCDE^{2}*FHK, dyde G, dide J, ne ic dyde I*
a — from A, from BC, fram FI, fram E^{2}*GJK
deo — gode ABCFGIJK, gódvm E^{2}*
meo — minum ACFG, minum BDE^{2}*HIJ, minan K

ED: forðon (A)] for ðon *Kuhn*. forðæn (E)] Forðæn *Harsley*. árleaslice (F)] arleaslicc *Kimmens*. unrihtlice ł arlea[ ]lice (I)] unrihtlice ł arleaslice *Lindelöf*.

OE: forðæn (E^{2})] þe *eras. after word*. ic geheold (E^{2})] heold *on eras*. arleaslice (E^{2})] *on eras*. unrihtlice ł arlea[ ]lice (I)] *letter after 2nd* a *lost to tight binding*. ic dyde (A)] *orig*. ic do: o *altered to form left branch of* y. ic dyde (E^{2})] *on eras*. ne ic dyde (I)] ne *written in left margin,* dyde *orig*. dide: i *altered to* y. fram (E^{2})] *on eras*. gódvm (E^{2})] *on eras*. minum (E^{2})] *on eras*.

LTg: Quia] [ ]uia G: *initial* Q *lost*. impie] A: e *on eras*.; impię F.

LTu: Quia] quia β. nec] nęc ξ. impie] impię ξυ.

23

Quoniam — forðon AB, forþon C, forþæn E^{2}, forðon ðe F, forðan þe I*, forþon þe J, forþā þe G
omnia — alle A, calle BCDFGHIJK, eællæ E^{2}
iudicia — | domas ABCDFGHIJK, his E^{2}
eius — | his ABFGHIJ*K*, hys C, domæs E^{2}
in — in AB, on CDE^{2}FGHIJK
conspectu — | gesihðe ABCDGH, gesyhþe FK, gesihþe J, ansyne ł gesyhðe I, minre E^{2}
meo — | minre ABCDF*GHIJK, gesigþe E^{2}
sunt* — sindun A, syndon C, sint BE^{2}, synd J (*L*)
semper* — aa A, simle B, symle C, æure E^{x}* (*L*)
et — ⁊ ABCE^{2}FGHIJK
iustitias — | rehtwissnisse A, ryhtwisnessa B*D*, rihtwisnyssa *C*FI, rihtwisnesse GJ, rihtwisnessa H, rihtwisnes K, his E^{2}

eius	I	his ABFGHIJ*K*, hys C, rihtwisnesse E^2*
non	I	ic ABC, ic na DIK, ic ne E^{2}FGJ
reppuli	I	on weg ne adraf AB, aweg ne adraf C, adraf *FGJ*, anydde D, anedde E^2*, ic anydde *H*, nydde *K*, awearp ł ⁊ ic ut ne adræfde I
a		from A*E*^{2}, from BC, fram FI, fram GJK
me		me ABCE^{2}FGIJ

ED: forðon (A)] for ðon *Kuhn*. forþæn (E)] Forþæn *Harsley*. forþā þe (G)] forþam þe *Rosier*. iusticias (C)] iustitias *Wildhagen*. répuli (H)] repuli *Campbell*. á (E)] a *Harsley*. awearp ł ⁊ ic ut ne adræfde (I)] *Lindelöf omits* ⁊.

OE: forðan þe (I)] s. sunt : syndon *written in left margin and signaled for inclusion after* þe. minre (F)] *orig.* minne: *2nd* n *altered to* r. æure (E^x)] *added by corr.; initial letter eras.: Harsley suggests* h. rihtwisnesse (E^2)] *on eras.* anedde (E^2)] *on eras.*

LTg: eius (*1st*)] eíus K. iustitias] iusticias C: *orig.* iustitias: *2nd* t *altered to* c; iustitiam D: *cf. Weber MSS* PQ^{2}Uη* med. sunt] L: *underlined to signal deletion: see GAg.* semper] L: *underlined to signal deletion: see GAg.* eius (*2nd*)] eíus K. reppuli] J: *1st* p *interl.*, K: *1st* p *interl. by corr.;* repuli F; répuli H. a] á E.

LTu: Quoniam] [ ]uoniam τ*τ: *initial letter wanting.* iustitias] iusticias τφ, ϱ: *orig.* iustitias: *2nd* t *deleted*, c *interl.;* iusticiam τ*φ. reppuli] εξπχ: *1st* p *interl.*, ζ: *2nd* p *interl.;* repuli ϑ.

GAg: sunt] *om.* FGHIK, L: *see LTg.* semper] *om.* FGHIJK, L: *see LTg.*

GAu: sunt] *om.* δεζιλμξοπϱστυφχψ. semper] *om.* δεζϑιλμξοπϱστυφχψ.

24

Et		⁊ ABCDE^{2}FGHIJK
ero		ic biom A, ic beom C, ic beo BDFGHIJK, Ic bio E^2*
inmaculatus		unwemme AB*CDE*^{2}K, unwæmme *H*, unwæmmed F, unawemmed *I*, unbesmiten GJ
coram*		biom A, beforan BCDGJ, beforæn E^2, mid FIK
eo		him ABE^{2}FGI, hym C, him J, heom K
et		⁊ ABE^{2}FGHIJK, gif *D* (*CL*)
obseruabo	I	ic haldu A, ic healde B*C*K, ic healde ł warnie *D*, ic healde ⁊ warnige H, ic gehealde FI, gehealde GJ, ic me *E*^{2} (*L*)
me	I	me A*B*CFGIJK, geheælde E^2
ab		from AE^2, from BC, fram DFGHJK, fram I
iniquitate	I	unrehtwisnisse A, unryhtwisnesse BD, unrihtwisnysse CFI, unrihtwisnesse GHJK*, minre E^2
mea	I	minre ABDFGHIJK, minr C*, unrihtwisnesse E^2

ED: immaculatus (C)] [in]maculatus *Wildhagen.* minr (C)] minre *Wildhagen: see OE.*

OE: Ic bio (E^{2})] *letter eras. after* o. unrihtwisnesse (K)] *eras. before word,* n *visible in 2nd position; Sisam reads* on?r. minr (C)] *final* e *possibly lost due to trimming of leaf.*

LTg: inmaculatus] immaculatus EI, C: *orig.* inmaculatus: i *connected to* n *to form* m, *additional* i *written in initial position,* H: *orig.* inmaculatus: *middle leg added to* n *to form* m. et] et si L: et *added by corr.;* si CD. obseruabo] L: *orig.* obseruauero: *2nd* u *altered to* b, er *crossed through;* obseruauero CDE. me] B: *orig.* mea: a *eras.*

LTu: inmaculatus] immaculatis εξιλπτ*τυφ, ο: *orig.* inmaculatis: n *deleted,* m *interl.;* īmaculatis σ. coram] ϛ: *orig.* cum: u *altered to* o, or *interl. after* c: *see GAu.* et] si τ*. obseruabo] obseruauero ντ*.

GAg: coram] cum FGHIJK.

GAu: coram] cum δεζϑιλμξοπϱστυφχψ; *for* ϛ *see LTu.*

25

Et		⁊ ABCDE^{2}F*GH*IJK
retribuit*	|	geedleanað *AB*C, he ageald DGHK, he sealde F, geheald J, agelt ł geedleanaþ I, drihten *E*^{2}
mihi		me AB*CDE*^{2}FGHI*J*K
dominus	|	drihtyn C, drihten F, drihtten K, dryht̄ AB, driht H, drih GJ, edleænæþ E^{2}
secundum		efter AE^{2}, æfter BFGHI, æftyr C, æfter JK
iustitiam	|	rehtwisnisse A, ryhtwisnesse BD, rihtwisnysse *C*F, rihtwisnesse GHIJK, minre E^{2}
meam	|	minre ABC*FGHIJK, rihtwisnesse E^{2}*
et		⁊ ABCE^{2}FGHIJK
secundum		efter AE^{2}*, æfter BFGI, æftyr C, æfter HJK
innocentiam*		unsceðfulnisse A, unsceðfulnesse B, unsceðfulnysse C, unsceaðfulnesse G, ungescæþfulnesse J, onscyþenesse ł unscyldgunge E^{2}*, unscyldgunga D, clænnysse F, clænsunga K, hluttornysse ł clænnysse I (*L*)
manuum	|	honda A, handa BCDFGHIJK, minre E^{2}
mearum	|	minra ABCDFGHIJ, minre K, hændæ E^{2}
in		in AB, on CDE^{2}FGHIJK
conspectu	|	gesihðe ABFG, gesyhðe C, gesyhðe D, gesihþe HJ, gesyhðe ł beforan I*, halsunga K*, his E^{2}
oculorum	|	egena A, eagna B, eagyna C, eagena DFG, eagana I, eægnæ E^{2}, eagan H, eagon J, egan K
eius	|	his ABFHIK, hys C, his ł heora G, heora J, gesihþe E^{2}

ED: iusticiam (C)] iustitiam *Wildhagen.*

OE: minre (C)] n *interl.* rihtwisnesse (E^2)] *on eras.* efter (E^2) (*2nd*)] *eras. after word.* onscyþenesse ł unscyldgunge (E^2)] ł unscyldgunge *added by main hand.* gesẏhðe ł beforan (I)] y *altered from another letter* (?). halsunga (K)] *lemma misread as* auspicio.

LTg: Et] H: *initial* E *faint but visible;* [ ]t G: *initial* E *lost.* retribuit] retribuet B, A: *orig.* retribuit: *2nd* i *altered to* e, E: *2nd* i *on eras.: cf. Weber MSS* M^{2}Q^{2}UXαγδη moz^c, *see GAg.* mihi] michi EJ, C: c *added interl. by corr.* iustitiam] iusticiam C: *orig.* iustitiam: *2nd* t *altered to* c. innocentiam] L: *underlined to signal deletion and* puritatem *added interl. by corr.: see GAg.*

LTu: retribuit] retribuet β: *see GAu.* mihi] michi ιλςτ*τ, πϱ: c *interl.* iustitiam] iusticiam τ*τφ, ϱ: *orig.* iustitiam: *2nd* t *deleted,* c *interl.* innocentiam] β: *orig.* innocensiam: s *deleted,* t *interl.* manuum] β: *2nd* u *interl.;* manuum ϑ. eius] est ν.

GAg: retribuit] retribuet FGHIJK, AB: *see LTg.* innocentiam] puritatem FGHIJK, L: *see LTg.*

GAu: retribuit] retribuet δεζϑιλμξοπϱστυφχψ, β: *see LTu.* innocentiam] puritatem δεζϑιλμξοπϱστυφχψ.

26

Cum	mid ABCDFGHIJK, Mid *E*^{2}
sancto	ðone halgan AB, þone halgan C, halgum DHJ, halgum FGI*, hælgum *E*^{2}*,* haligan K
sanctus	halig ABCDFHI, hælig E^2, hali K, ⁊ halige G*J
eris	ðu bis A, ðu bist BDF, þu bist CE^2*GH*J, ðu byst I, ic beo K
et	⁊ ABCE^{2}FGHIJ*K
cum	mid ABCE^{2}FGHIJK
uiro	were ABCDE^2*GHIJ, werum F, weran K
innocente	unscedendum A, unsceððendum B, unsceðþyndum C, unscyldigum D, unscyldigum E^2*F*, unscyldigam H, unscyldugum K, unsceaðfulnesse G, unscæþfulnesse J, unscæððigum I*
innocens	unsceððende AB, unsceðþynde C, unscyldig DE^2*F*HI*K, unscildig J, unsceaðful G
eris	ðu bist ABDF, þu bist C*GH,* þu byst IJK, ðu beost E^2*

ED: Cvm (E)] Cum *Harsley.* ęris (G) (*1st*)] eris *Rosier.* ínnocens (H)] innocens *Campbell.*

OE: halgum (I)] s. homine : menn *written in left margin and signaled for inclusion after* sancto. ⁊ halige (G)] i *interl.* ⁊ (J) (*2nd*)] *written below* bist. were (E^2)] *on eras.* unscyldigum (E^2)] ldigum *on eras.* unscæððigum (I)] *1st* ð *interl.* unscyldig (E^2)] ig *on eras.* ðu beost (E^2)] ðu *on eras.*

LTg: Cum] Cvm E. sancto] E: *gloss eras. above word.* eris (*1st*)] ęris GH. innocente] F: *eras. after 2nd* e. innocens] I: *accent* (?) *above* i; ínnocens H. eris (*2nd*)] G: *eras. before word;* ęris H.

LTu: εζϱφ: *psalm division indicated,* ν: Diuisio psalmi, υ: Gloria patri. Cum] Cvm ιφ.

27

Et	⁊ AB*CE^{2}FGIJK (*DL*)
cum	mid AB*CE^{2}*FGIJK
electo	ðy upahefenan A*, ðy upahæfenan B, þa<u>m</u> upahafynan C, ðam gecorenu<u>m</u> F, gecorenum GI, gecorenu<u>m</u> J, gecorenan K, gecorene E^{2}* (*H*)
electus	upahefen A, upahæfen B, upahafyn C, gecoren DE^{2}*FGHIJK
eris	ðu bist ABD, þu bist CFGJ, þu byst HIK, þu beost E^{2}
et	⁊ ABCE^{2}FGHJK
cum	mid ABCDE^{2}FGHIJK
peruerso	ðy ðweoran A, ðy þweoran B, þon þwuran C, þweorum F, ðrowerum G, þraweru<u>m</u> J, ferhwyrfedu<u>m</u> D*E^{2}, forhwerfedu<u>m</u> H, wyþerwerdum ł mid þweorum I, wiþerwyrdan K
subuerteris*	ðu bist forcerred A, þu bist forcerred B, þu bist forcyrryd C, gecyrred þu bist F, ðu forhwyrfed bist D, þu forhwirfed bist H, þu beost forhwyrwed E^{2}*, forcyrred G, forcirred J, ⁊ þu byst behwyrfed ł miswend I*, wiðerwyrd þu byst K

OE: ⁊ (B) (*1st*)] *on eras. from Lat. line below.* mid (B) (*1st*)] *on eras. from Lat. line below.* mid (E^{2}) (*1st*)] *on eras.* ðy upahefenan (A)] *lemma misread as from* elat- (?); *see also* BC. gecorene (E^{2})] *on eras.* gecoren (E^{2})] ge *on eras.* ferhwyrfedu<u>m</u> (D)] *2nd* e *interl.* þu beost forhwyrwed (E^{2})] beost forhwyrwed *on eras.* ⁊ þu byst behwyrfed ł miswend (I)] s. eris *written in left margin.*

LTg: Et] et ACDEL, B: *on eras.* cum (*1st*)] B: *on eras.*, t *eras. after* ū. electo] E: *eras. after word, most likely from eras. of gloss above;* ęlecto H. electus] ęlectus GH. eris] ęris H. subuerteris] E: *on eras. by corr.;* subuertéris C.

LTu: Et] et βνςτ*. electo] ęlecto ε. electus] ęlectus ε.

GAg: subuerteris] peruerteris FHIJ, G: *orig.* peruersteris: *1st* s *eras.*, K: teris *on eras. by corr.*

GAu: subuerteris] peruerteris δεζιλμξοπϱστυφχψ; peruertes ϑ.

28

Quoniam — forðon ABJ, forþon C, forðan E^{2}*, forþan K, forðon ðe F, forþā þe *G*, forðan þe I

tu — ðu AB, þu CE^{2}*FGIJK

populum — folc ABCDE^{2}*FIK, folcc H, þæt folc GJ

humilem — eaðmod ABH, eaþmod D, eadmod CE^{2}*FGIJK

saluum | hal AB*C*DE^{2}*FHK, þu hal G, þu hale J, gehælst I

facies | gedoest A, gedest BGJ, þu gedest C, dest DE^{2}*HK, ðu dest F

et — ⁊ ABCDE^{2}*FGHJK

oculos — egan AK, eagan BCDE^{2}*FGHI, eagon J

superborum — oferhygdigra AB, oferhydigra G, oferhidigra J, ofyrmodra C, ofermodra DFH, ofermodre E^{2}*, ofermodigra I, ofermodigan K

humiliabis — ðu gehenes A, þu gehenest B, þu gehynyst [ge]eadmodest C/C^{2}*, þu gehynest GJ, þu geniðerast D, þu geniðerast H, þu genyð[ ]rast F*, ⁊ þu geeaðmetst ł þu genyþerast I, geadmodast K, þu geniðarast ł ædmedest E^{2}*

ED: forðon (A)] for ðon *Kuhn*. forðan (E)] Forðan *Harsley*. forþā þe (G)] forþam þe *Rosier*. þu genyð[ ]rast (F)] þu genyðerast *Kimmens*.

OE: forðan (E^{2})] *on eras.* þu (E^{2})] *on eras.* folc (E^{2})] *on eras.* eadmod (E^{2})] *on eras.* hal (E^{2})] *on eras.* dest (E^{2})] *on eras.* ⁊ (E^{2})] *on eras.* eagan (E^{2})] *on eras.* ofermodre (E^{2})] *on eras.* þu gehynyst (C/C^{2})] eadmodest *added interl. in smaller hand in brown ink and signaled for insertion after* ge (= geeadmodest); *by same scribe who wrote* oþþe litlige *at v. 43.* þu genyð[ ]rast (F)] *back of* e (?) *partly visible after* ð. þu geniðarast ł ædmedest (E^{2})] þu geniðarast ł *on eras.*, ædmedest *added.*

LTg: Quoniam] [ ]uoniam G. saluum] C: *eras. after* l.

LTu: facies] facias ς. et] *om.* ϱ.

29

Quoniam — forðon ABF, forþon CE^{2}, forðam G, forðan þe I, forðon þe J (*H*)

tu — ðu ABF, þu CE^{2}GHIJK

inluminas — inlihtes AB, onlihtyst *C*, onlyhtest D*FGK*, onlyhtes *E*^{2}, onlihtest *J*, alyhtest *H*, onlyhst *I**

lucernam | lehtfet A, lehtfæt B, leohtfæt CDFGHJK, leohtfætels ł leohtfæt I, mine E^{2}

meam | min ABCFHIJK, blecernæ ł leohtfet E^{2}

domine | dryht̄ AB, driħt CF, driħ GHJ, hlafor K, min E^{2} (*I*)

deus | god *A*BCFGHJK, eala ðu god I, drihten E^{2}

meus | min ABCFGHIJK, god E^{2}

inlumina — inliht AB, onlyht *CDK,* onlyhte E2, onlihte F, onleoht *H,* onliht *I,* onlyht ðu *G,* onliht þu *J*
tenebras — ðeostru AB, þystru CGI*J, ðystra F, þystra K, ðystro ł swarcunga D, þeostro ł swarcunga H*, swartunge ł þistro E2*
meas — min AG, mine BCE2FIJK

ED: forðon (A)] for ðon *Kuhn.* forþon (E) Forþon *Harsley.* illunas (C)] i[n]lunas *Wildhagen.* illumina (C)] i[n]lumina *Wildhagen.*

OE: onlyhst (I)] *eras. after* h. þystru (I)] *eras. after* r, u *formed from another letter* (?). þeostro ł swarcunga (H)] t *partly obscured by crease in leaf.* swartunge ł þistro (E2)] e *on eras.*

LTg: Quoniam] (Q)uoniam H: *initial* Q *nearly completely lost.* inluminas] illuminas EFIJK, GH: *1st* l *altered from another letter;* illunas C: *orig.* inlunas: *left leg of 1st* n *altered to* l, *right leg eras.* domine] I: *eras. after word,* s. o *written interl.* deus] A: *three letters eras. before word.* inlumina] illumina IK, GH: *1st* l *altered from another letter,* J: *1st* l *on eras., eras. before initial* i, C: *orig.* [ ]nlumina: *initial letter eras., right leg of* n *altered to* l.

LTu: inluminas] illuminas εζϑιλξοπϱστ*τυφχ. inlumina] illumina εζϑιλοπϱστ*τυφχ. tenebras] tenbras υ.

30

Quoniam — forðon ABFJ, forþon C, forðæn E2, forþā *G*K, forðan ðe I
a* — from AG, from B, fram CJ, fræm *E2,* on FIK
te — ðe ABFI, þe *C*E2GJK
eripiar — ic biom genered A, ic beom nered D, ic beo genered BE2GH*, ic beo generyd C, ic beo generod JK, ic gegripen beo F, ic beo alysed I
a — from A, from BC, fram DJK, fram FGHI, fræm *E2**
temptatione — ðe costunge A, costunge BI, costunge D, costnunge CGHJ, costnunga FK, costungum E2
et — ⁊ ABCE2FGHIJ*K*
in — in AB, on CDE2FGHIJK
deo — | gode ABCDFGHIJK, minum E2
meo — | minum AI, minum BCDFGHJ, minan K, gode E2
transgrediar — ic ofergaa A, ic ofergá B, ic ofyrgáá C, ic ofergange DE2*FHK, ic foreleore G, ic foreleose J, ic oforfare ł ofersteppe I*
murum — wall A, weall CDFGHIJ, wællas K, þone weæll E2

ED: forðon (A)] for ðon *Kuhn.* forðæn (E)] Forðæn *Harsley.* á (E) (*1st*)] a *Harsley.* á (E) (*2nd*)] a *Harsley.*

OE: ic beo genered (H)] c *obscured by crease in leaf.* fræm (E^2) (*2nd*)] *eras. after word.* ic ofergange (E^2)] ofergange *on eras.* ic oforfare ł ofersteppe (I)] ł *interl.*

LTg: Quoniam] [ ]uoniam G. a (*1st*)] á E. te] té C. a (*2nd*)] á E. et] K: *written in left margin by main hand.*

GA a (*1st*)] in FGHIJK.

GAu: a (*1st*)] in δεζϑιλμξοπϱστυφχψ.

31

Deus	I	god ABCFG*HIJ*K, Min E^2
meus	I	min ABCFGHIJK, god E^2
inpolluta		unbesmiten A*B*DE*^2**FH, onbesmitende *G*J, onbesmitynnysse *C,* unafilede ł unbesmitene I, vnwemme K (*L*)
uia	I	weg ABCDHK, wegas FGIJ, his E^2
eius	I	his ABFGHIJ*K,* hys C, weg E^2*
eloquia	I	gespreocu A, gesprecu CG, gespreca J, gesprec B, spræca FI, spæca D*H,* spæc K, drihtnes E^2
domini	I	dryhtnes B, drihtnys C, drihtnes F, drihtnys I, drihtenes K, dryht̄ A, driħt H, driħ GJ, gesprecæ E^2
igne		mid fyre ABGI, mid fire J, of fyre DE^2*FH, fyre C, fyr K
examinata		amearad A, amered BE^2*J, ameryd C, amerede DGHK, amerode FI
protector	I	gescildend AB, gescyldynd C, gescyldend D, gescyldend H, gescylden F, he gescylded G, he gescildend J, scyldend I, frofer K, he is E^2
est	I	is ABFGJ*K,* he ys C, he is DHI, scildend E^2
omnium		alra A, ealra BCDFGHIJ, eallan K, eælræ þæræ þe E^2
sperantium	I	gehyhtendra ABG, gehihtendra J, hyhtyndra C, hyhtendra DH, hihtendra I, hihtende K, opiendra F, on E^2
in	I	in AB, on CDFGHIJK, hine E^2
se	I	hine A*B*CDFGHK, him I*, þe J, gehopan E^x*

ED: impolluta (C)] i[n]polluta *Wildhagen.*

OE: unbesmiten (A)] *orig.* unbesmitene: *final* e *eras.* unbesmiten (E^2)] *letter eras. after word.* weg (E^2)] *eras. after word.* of fyre (E^2)] of *interl.* amered (E^2)] *on eras.* him (I)] s. est : is (*with single subscript dot*) *and* s. sunt : synt (*with single subscript dot*) *written in left margin,* s. e : is (*with four subscript dots*) *written in right margin with somewhat large, crudely-formed* ł *or* + *written to right.* gehopan (E^x)] *added by corr.,* ł *eras. after word, continuing into next line* (*18 mm*).

LTg: Deus] [ ]eus H: *traces of blue ink visible in initial position;* Qeus J (Qs̄).

inpolluta] inpulluta DL, E: *eras. after* n; impolluta FG, C: *orig.* inpolluta: *right leg added to* n *to form* m. eius] eíus K. eloquia] ęloquia H. est] ést K. se] sé B.

LTu: inpolluta] β: *orig.* inpuluta: *1st* u *deleted,* o *interl.;* inpulluta ϑν; impolluta ιλξπτ*τφ, ϱ: i *interl.;* ī polluta σ. uia] uie ς. eloquia] ęloquia ς. examinata] exminata ς. se] eum ϑ.

32

<table>
<tr><td>Quoniam</td><td></td><td>forðon AB, forþon CJ, forðæn E^{2}*, forþā G, forþam K, forðon ðe F, forðan þe I</td></tr>
<tr><td>quis</td><td></td><td>hwelc ABH, hwylc CDE^{2}FGK, hwilc IJ</td></tr>
<tr><td>deus</td><td></td><td>god ABCFGHJK, god is E^{2}I</td></tr>
<tr><td>praeter</td><td></td><td>butan ABCDHGI, butæn E^{2}, butan þe K, buton FJ (L)</td></tr>
<tr><td>dominum</td><td></td><td>drihtne CI, dryhtne D, drihten E^{2}K, drihtenes H, dryhī AB, ure drihtne F, úre drihten G, ure driħ J</td></tr>
<tr><td>aut*</td><td></td><td>oððe ABCFGHI, oþðe D, oþþe E^{2}, ⁊ JK</td></tr>
<tr><td>quis</td><td></td><td>hwelc AB, hwylc CDE^{2}FGK, hwilc HIJ</td></tr>
<tr><td>deus</td><td></td><td>god ABCE^{2}FGHJK, god is I</td></tr>
<tr><td>praeter</td><td></td><td>butan ACDHGIK, buton BF, butæn E^{2}, buto J (L)</td></tr>
<tr><td>deum</td><td>|</td><td>gode ABDGHIJ, ure gode F, god C, drihten K, urum E^{2}</td></tr>
<tr><td>nostrum</td><td>|</td><td>urum ACDFGHI, uru<u>m</u> BJ, ure K, gode E^{2}</td></tr>
</table>

ED: forðon (A)] for ðon *Kuhn.* forðæn (E)] Forðæn *Harsley.* urum (A)] uram *Kuhn.*

OE: forðæn (E^{2})] *eras.* (*18 mm*) *before word.*

LTg: Quoniam] I: [ ] e<u>st</u> *written in left margin.* praeter (*1st*)] pręter BGK; preter CDFHIJL. aut] H: *on eras., along with preceding punct. mark,* K: *on eras. by corr.* quis (*2nd*)] K: *on eras. by corr.* deus (*2nd*)] K: *on eras. by corr.* praeter (*2nd*)] præter BK; preter CDFHIJL; pręter G.

LTu: praeter (*1st*)] preter εζϑιοπςτ*τ; pręter λμνξϱφ; p̄ter σχ. praeter (*2nd*)] preter ϑιοςτ*τ; pręter λνπϱφ; p̄ter εζσχ.

GAu: aut] et δεϑμοψ.

33

<table>
<tr><td>Deus</td><td></td><td>god ABCE^{2}FGHI*JK</td></tr>
<tr><td>qui</td><td>|</td><td>se ABCDE^{2}*FHK, se me G, se þe J, þe I</td></tr>
<tr><td>praecinxit</td><td>|</td><td>bigyrde A, begyrde BDFGHJK, begyrede E^{2}*, begerde I, begyrdyð C (L)</td></tr>
<tr><td>me</td><td>|</td><td>me ABCE^{2}FIJK</td></tr>
<tr><td>uirtute</td><td></td><td>mid megne A, mid mægene BI, mid mægyne C, mid mægne GJ, of mægene DH, of megne E^{2}, mægne K, of mihte F</td></tr>
</table>

et ꝛ ABCDE^{2}FGHIJK
posuit sette AK, gesette BCDE^{2}FHI, he gesette GJ
inmaculatam unwemne AB*C*DE^2*K*, unwæmme F*H*, unawemmendne *I*, unbesmitenne GJ
uiam | weg ABCDFGHIJK, minne E^2
meam | minne ABCDFGHIJK, weig E^2

ED: immaculatam (C)] i[n]maculatam *Wildhagen*. unwemne (D)] unwemme *Roeder*.

OE: god (I)] s. e<u>st</u> : he is *written in left margin*. se (E^2)] *on eras*. begyrede (E^2)] y *altered from* i, *eras. after word*.

LTg: Deus] Q<u>eus</u> J (Qs̄). praecinxit] precinxit BCDEK, FH: *letter eras. after* n; prȩcinxit G; precincxit IJL. uirtute] FH: *eras. after* e. inmaculatam] immaculatam IK, C: *orig*. inmaculatam: i *added before* i, *orig*. i *joined with* n *to form* m, H: *orig*. inmaculatam: *middle leg added to* n *to form* m.

LTu: praecinxit] prȩcinxit ελνϱφ; precinxit ζϑξπϛτ*τ; p̄cinxit ισχ. uirtute] uirtutem ς. posuit] possuit ϑ. inmaculatam] immaculatam ειλξπτ*τυφ, o: i *interl., 1st* m *altered from* n, ϱ: i *interl.*

34

Qui se ABCDFHIK, Se E^2*, se þe GJ
perficit* gefremede *AB*GHJ, gefremyde *C*, gefremed *D**, gefremode F, gefremede K, fulfremed *E*^{2}*, gedede ł se ðe fulfremed[ ] I* (*L*)
pedes | foet AB, fet CGHIJ, fét D, fot FK, mine E^2
meos | mine ABCFGIJ, minne K, fet E^2
tamquam swe swe A, swa swa B*C*DF*GH*IJ, swæ swæ *E*^{2}, swa K
cerui* heorutes A, heorotes B, heortys C, heortes DFG, heorta HI, heortas JK, þæs heortes *E*^{2}*
et ꝛ AB*CE^{2}FGHIJK
super ofer ABE^{2}FGHJK, ofyr C, ofor I
excelsa ða hean AB, þa hean C, heanessa DH, heannyssa F, heannessæ G, heannesse J, heahnesse E^2*, heahnesnes K, healice ł heanyssa I*
statuit* gesette AB*C*GJ, he gesette DE^2*FK, gesettende I
me me AB*C*E^{2}FGIJK

ED: gefremed (D)] gefremed<u>e</u> *Roeder*. tanquam (C)] ta[m]quam *Wildhagen*. swa swa (BGIJ)] swaswa *Brenner, Rosier, Lindelöf, Oess*.

OE: Se (E^2)] e *on eras*. gefremed (D)] *letter* (e?) *eras. after* d. fulfremed (E^2)] fr *on* *eras., letter eras. after word.* gedede ł se ðe fulfremed[ ] (I)] se ðe fulfremed[ ] *written in right margin, final word cropped.* þæs heortes (E^2)] heortes *written above eras. of gloss.* ⁊ (B)] *letter* (?) *eras. after word.* heahnesse (E^2)] *on eras.* healice ł heanyssa (I)] heanyssa *written in right margin, although signaled for inclusion before* ofor. he gesette (E^2)] he *on eras.*

LTg: perficit] A: *1st* i *on eras.*, D: *1st* i *on eras.* (*of* e?), E: ic *on eras. by corr.;* perfecit BCL: *cf. Weber MSS* MT*QUδζ, *see GAg.* tamquam] tanquam E, G: n *altered from another letter,* C: *eras. before* n, H: *eras. after* n. cerui] E: i *on eras. by corr.* statuit] státuit C. me] mé C.

LTu: Qui] [ ]ui τ*τ: *initial letter wanting.* tamquam] tanquam εϑιλτ*τφ; tāquam σ.

GAg: perficit] perfecit FGHIJK, BCL: *see LTg.* cerui] ceruorum FGHIJK. statuit] statuens FHIJK; statuens G: *final* s *on eras.*

GAu: perficit] perfecit δεζϑιλμνξοπρστφχψ. cerui] ceruorum δεζιλμξοπρστυφχψ; cerborum ϑ. statuit] statuens δεζϑιλμξοπρστυφχψ.

35

Qui se ABCDH, Se þe E^2, se ðe FI, se þe GJ, þa K
docet* laered *A*, læreð BDGH, læryð C, lereþ E^2, lærde J, læreþ ł tæcð I, tæcð F, doceþ K*
manus | honda A, handa BCDFGHIJK, minæ E^2
meas | mine ABFGIJK, mina C, hændæ E^2
ad to ABCDE^{2}FGHIJK
proelium gefehte AB, gefeohte C*FGHIJ,* gefeohte *D,* gefiohte *E^2,* feohte *K* (*L*)
et ⁊ ACDE^{2}FGHIJLK
posuit* sette AB, he sette K, gesette CJ, he gesette DE^2*F, þu gesettest GHI (*L*)
ut swe swe A, swa swa BDE^2*FGHIJ, swa CK
arcum | bogan ABCDGHIJK, boga F, ercnne ł cyperene E^2*
aereum | ærenne A*B,* ærynne *C,* cyperenne *D,* cypenerre *H,* cyperen *K,* bræsenne I, lyft *F**, lust *GJ,* bogæn *E^2* (*L*)
brachia | earmas *ABC*DGHIJK, earm F, minum E^2
mea | mine A*BCDGHIJ, min F, eærmum E^2

ED: Qui (B)] qui *Brenner.* et (I)] Et *Lindelöf.* swa swa (BGIJ)] swaswa *Brenner, Rosier, Lindelöf, Oess.* ærеum (D)] aereum *Roeder.* ęreum (E)] aereum *Harsley.*

OE: doceþ (K)] *from lemma.* he gesette (E^2)] he *on eras.* swa swa (E^2)] *added,* initial s *on eras.* erenne ł cyperene (E^2)] ł cyperene *added.* lyft (F)] yf *partially obscured by eras.* mine (A) (*2nd*)] m *partly obscured.*

LTg: docet] A: *orig.* docit: i *altered to* e. proelium] prelium DEJL; praelium F; pręlium GHK. posuit] L: *altered by corr. to* posuisti (?—*2nd* s *malformed*): *see GAg.* aereum] æreum BD; ęreum CEFHL, K: *eras. before word;* aérum G; ereum J. brachia] A: *letter* (c?) *eras. after 1st* a, C: *eras. after* i.

LTu: proelium] pręlium εζλνξπφ; prelium ιςτ*τ; p̄lium σχ; praelium υ. aereum] ęreum βζιλξχ; aerium ϑ; ereum σςτ*τ; hęreum φ.

GAg: docet] doces J, G: s *on eras.* posuit] posuisti FGHIJK, L (?): *see LTg.*

GAu: docet] doces ϑ. posuit] posuisti δεζιλμξοπϱστυφχψ; possuisti ϑ.

36

Et		⁊ ABCE^{2}FGHIJK
dedisti		ðu saldes A, ðu sealdes B, þu sealdyst C, ðu sealdest DF, þu seældæs E^2, þu sealdest GHIJK
mihi		me AB*C*D*E*^{2}FGHI*J*K
protectionem		gescildnisse A, gescildnesse BE^2, gescyldnysse CFI, gescyldnesse GH, gescyldnisse D, gescildnessa J, gescyldnes *K*
salutis	|	haelu A, hælo BFJ, hæle CDGIK, þinre E^2
tuae	|	ðinre A*DF*, þinre *BCIJK*, þine *G*, helo *E*^{2} (*HL*)
et		⁊ ABCE^{2}FGHIJK
dextera	|	sie swiðre A, seo swýþre F, seo swiðre GHI, seo swiþre J, seo swiðe D, swiðre BC, swyþre K, þin E^2
tua	|	ðin AFG, þin BCDHIJK, swiþre E^2
suscepit	|	onfeng *A*BCDF, anfeng H, onfenge G, anfengc I, onfengc J, onfenc K, me E^2
me	|	me ABCFGHIJK, onfeng E^2
et		⁊ ABCE^2**FHIJK* (*G*)
disciplina		ðeodscipe AB, þeodscype C, lár D, lar E^2*FGHJK, lar ł steore I
tua		ðin ABF, þin CDE^2*GIJK (*H*)
(correxit)*		ðreade F, þreade J, þu arærdest G, ⁊ gestyrde ł gerihtlæhte I, gerihtllæhte K*
(me)*		me FGJK
(in)*		on FGIJK
(finem)*		ende FGIJK
(et)*		⁊ FHIJK
(disciplina)*		lár F, lar GHJ, seo steor I*, steore K
(tua)*		ðin F, þin GHIJK
ipsa		he ABG, heo CDFHK, hyo E^2*, he silf J, sylfe I (*L*)
me		me ABCE^{2}FGIJK

docuit*		lærde ABDHK, lerde *E*^{2}*, he lærde G, gelærde *C*, gelæreþ J, ⁊ læreð ł tæcð I, tæhte F (*L*)

ED: tuę (EI)] tuae *Harsley, Lindelöf.* seo swýþre (F)] seo swyþre *Kimmens.* Et (G) (*2nd*)] *Et Rosier.* disciplina (G)] *dis*ciplina *Rosier.* ⁊ læreð ł tæcð (I)] *Lindelöf omits* ⁊.

OE: ⁊ (E^2) (*3rd*)] *on eras. of 35 mm.* lar (E^2)] *eras.* (*15 mm*) *after word.* þin (E^2) (*2nd*)] in *on eras.* gerihtllæhte (K)] *as* geriht l læhte. seo steor (I)] seo *written in left margin, but without mark to signal inclusion.* hyo (E^2)] *on eras.* lerde (E^2)] de *on eras.*

LTg: mihi] michi EJ, C: *orig.* mihi: c *interl. by corr.* protectionem] K: *eras.* (*3–4 letters*) *after word.* tuae] tuæ B; tuę CDEFGHIKL. suscepit] suscipit A: *orig.* suscepit: i *written above* e, *but without deleting dot.* et (*2nd*)] Et FGHIJK. tua (*2nd*)] H: *glossed by Lat.* tua. ipsa] L: *underlined to signal deletion and* correxit *added interl. by corr.: see GAg.* docuit] E: *eras. before word;* edócuit C; edocuit L: in finem *added interl. by corr. and* et disciplina tua ipsa me docebit *added after word: cf. Weber MS* M, *see GAg.*

LTu: mihi] michi ιλςτ*τφ, ζπϱ: c *interl.* tuae] tuę ζιξϱφ; tuæ ϑμ; tue σςτ*τ. suscepit] suscoepit β. et (*2nd*)] Et δεζϑιλμξοπϱστυφχψ. docuit] edocuit ς.

GAg: disciplina tua] disciplina tua correxit me in finem et disciplina tua HIJK, F: *2nd* r *in* correxit *interl.;* disciplina tua correxit me in finem [ ] disciplina tua G; *for* L *see LTg note to* docuit. docuit] docebit FGHIJK, L: *see LTg.*

GAu: disciplina tua] disciplina tua correxit me in finem et disciplina tua δεζϑιλμξοπϱστυφχψ. docuit] docebit δεζϑιλμξοπϱστυφχψ.

37

Dilatasti		ðu gebraeddes A, þu gebræddes B, þu gebræddyst C, þu gebreddæst E^2*, þu tobreddest D, ðu tobræddest F, þu tobræddest GHI, ðu tobrædest K, þu abræddest J
gressus	|	gongas ABC, gangas GJ, stæpas DF, stæppas K, stiga ł stæpas ł færel[ ] I*, mine E^2
meos	|	mine ABCDFGHIJK, stepæs E^2
subtus		under ABDE^2*FGHIJK, undyr C
me		me ABCE^{2}FGHIJK
et		⁊ ABCE^{2}FGHIJK
non		ne ABCDE^{2}FGHIJ, na K
sunt		sind A, synd CDFHK, sint B, synt I, synd ł wæron G*, wæron J, sindon E^2
infirmata		geuntrumad AB, geuntrumude CDH, geuntromode E^2, geuntrumode FGJ, geuntrumede I, on seocnesse K
uestigia	|	sweðe A, swaðo B, swaðu CDG, swaþu HJ, swaþa K, uotswaðu F, fotstaplas I, mine E^2
mea	|	mine ABCDFGHIJK, swæþu E^2

ED: Dilatasti (B)] Dilalatasti *Brenner.* stiga ł stæpas ł færel[ ] (I)] stiga ł stæpas ł færeldu *Lindelöf.*

OE: þu gebreddæst (E^{2})] *1st* d *interl. by corr.,* t *added by corr. in darker ink.* stiga ł stæpas ł færel[ ] (I)] ł færel[ ] *written in right margin, final letters lost due to tight binding.* under (E^{2})] *on eras.* synd ł wæron (G)] ł wæron *added in diff.* (?) *hand.*

LTg: gressus] A: u *on eras., letter* (v?) *eras. above* u.

LTu: gressus] gresus ϑ. meos] β: *orig.* meus: o *interl.* uestigia] uistigia ϑ.

38

Persequar		ic oehtu A, ic oehte B, ic iehte C, ic ehte DF*G*HJK, ic ehtige I, ic fylge ł ehte $E^{2/x}$*
inimicos	|	feond *A*FG, fiend B, fynd CDHI*J*, feonda K, minum E^{2}
meos	|	mine *A*BCDFGHIJ, minra K, fiondum E^{2}
⟨animam⟩		sawle *J*
⟨meam⟩		mine *J*
et		⁊ *A*BCE^{2}FGHIJK
conprehendam		gegripo *A,* gegripe B, ic gegripe CDF*GHJ,* ic gegrype *E^{2},* ic gripe *K,* ic gehæftnige ł gelæ[ ] ł gegripe *I**
illos		hie ABE^{2}*, hi CFI, hy DGH, hig J, his K
et		⁊ ABCE^{x}*FGHIJK
non	|	ic ne ABC$E^{2/x}$*, ic na ne I, na DFGHK, ne J
conuertar	|	gecerru A, gecerre B, gecyrre IK, gecirræ E^{2}*, cyrre C, ic gecyrre D*, ic gecyrre FH, beo ic gecyrred G*, beo me gecirred J
donec		ær ðon AB, ær þon C, oðþæt DH, oððæt FG, oþðæt I, oþþæt J, oþþæt K, oðð E^{x}
deficiant		hie aspringað *A*B, hi aspringyn C, hy geteoriað DH, hye geteorieð E^{x}*, hi geteoriað G, hi geteoriaþ FJ, hi ateoriun I

ED: (Perse)quar (G)] Persequar *Rosier.* ic gehæftnige ł gelæ[ ] ł gegripe (I)] ic gehæftnige ł gelæcce ł gegripe *Lindelöf.* ær ðon (B)] ærðon *Brenner.* ær þon (C)] ærþon *Wildhagen.* oðþæt (H)] oð þæt *Campbell.* oþðæt (I)] oþ ðæt *Lindelöf.* oþþæt (J)] oþ þæt J *Oess.* hi geteoriað (G)] [ ] *Rosier.*

OE: ic fylge ł ehte ($E^{2/x}$)] *eras.* (*2 letters*) *before* ic, ł ehte *added by corr. in darker ink.* ic gehæftnige ł gelæ[ ] ł gegripe (I)] *final letters of* gelæ[ ] *lost due to tight binding.* hie (E^{2})] ⁊ *eras. before word.* ⁊ (E^{x}) (*2nd*)] *added by corr. in darker ink.* ic ne ($E^{2/x}$)] ic *added by corr. in darker ink.* conuertar (D)] oþþæt *eras. above word.* gecirræ (E^{2})] *letter eras. before and after word.* beo ic gecyrred (G)] beo *added in diff.* (?) *hand.* hye geteorieð (E^{x})] teorieð *on eras.*

LTg: Persequar] (Perse)quar G: Perse *cropped by tear in leaf.* inimicos] A: o *on* *eras.;* inimicus J. meos] A: o *on eras.;* meos animam meam J. et] A: *eras. after word.* conprehendam] conpraehendam A: *2nd* n *by corr.* (?); comprehendam EIJ, G: *orig.* conprehendam: *right leg added to 1st* n *to form* m, H: *orig.* conprehendam: *middle leg added to 1st* n *to form* m; comprȩhendam K. deficiant] A: ant *by corr.*

LTu: conprehendam] conpraehendam βψ; comp̄hendam εχ; comprehendam ζιλξπτ*; co̲n̲p̄hendam ϑ; conpræhendam μ; cōprehendam ϱτφ, o: *orig.* cōpraehendam: *1st* a *deleted;* cōp̄hendam συ. illos] eos β: *cf. Weber MSS* γδ. donec] donȩc ξ.

39

Adfligam*		ic swencu *A,* ic swence *BDE²/x*,* ic swænce J, ic geswence *C,* ic hy geswence G, ic tobrece F, ic tobryte ł ic tobreke I*, ic tobryte K (*L*)
illos	I	hio A, hie BC, hy DGH, hi FIK, hig J, hye Eˣ*
nec	I	ne ABDEˣ*FGHJ, na K, ne hi ne I, þ̲æ̲t̲ hi ne C
potuerunt*	I	hie magun A, hie magon B, hy magan D, hi magan K, hye ne magen Eˣ*, hi ne magon F, magon *C*HI, magon ł ne mihton G*, mihton J
stare		stondan AB, standan CDFGHIJK, standen Eˣ*
cadent		fallað *A,* feallað *B,* hi feallað *C,* hy feallað *D*H, hi feallaþ FIK, hi feallað G, hie gefeællæþ E², gefeallaþ J (*L*)
subtus		under ABDE²*FGHI*J*K, undyr C
pedes	I	foet AB, fet CFGHJ, fét D, fotum I, fota K, minum E²
meos	I	mine ABCDFGHJ, minum I, minra K, fotum E²

ED: affligam (C)] a[d]fligam *Wildhagen.* Confringam (G)] Confringam *Rosier.* póterunt (G)] porterunt *Rosier.* pót[ ]erunt (H)] poterunt *Campbell.*

OE: ic swence (E²/x)] swence *on eras. by corr.* ic tobryte ł ic tobreke (I)] *initial 4 letters written in left margin before rest of gloss.* hye (Eˣ) (*1st*)] *on eras. by corr.* ne (Eˣ) (*1st*)] *on eras. by corr.* hye ne magen (Eˣ)] *on eras. by corr.* magon ł ne mihton (G)] ł ne mihton *added in diff.* (?) *hand.* standen (Eˣ)] *on eras. by corr.* under (E²)] *on eras.*

LTg: Adfligam] adfligam BDE, A: *eras.* (*ca 4 letters*) *before word,* L: *altered to* co̲n̲fri̲n̲ga̲m̲ *by corr.: see GAg;* affligam C: *1st* f *on eras. by corr.* potuerunt] poterunt C, L: r *altered from* n *by main scribe: cf. Weber MSS* T²PQRUVXδζ, *see GAg.* cadent] Cadent ABCD, L: C *crossed through and minuscule* c *written to right.* subtus] J: b *altered from another letter.*

LTu: Adfligam] adfligam νς; affligam τ*. nec] nȩc ξ. potuerunt] poterunt ν: *cf. Weber MSS* T²PQRUVXδζ, *see GAu.* cadent] Cadent βνςτ*. subtus] suptus ζ.

GAg: Adfligam] Confringam FGHIJK; *for* L *see LTg.* potuerunt] poterunt IJ, CL: *see LTg,* F: *letter eras. after 1st* t; póterunt G; pót[ ]erunt H: *letter eras. after 1st* t.

GAu: Adfligam] Confringam δεζϑιλμξοπϱστυφχψ. potuerunt] poterunt δεζϑιλμξοπϱσυφχ, ν: *see LTu.*

40

Et	⁊ *ABCD*FGHIJK, and *E*^{2}* (*L*)
praecinxisti	ǀ ðu bigyrdes A, þu begyrdes *B,* þu begyrdyst *C,* ðu begyrdest *D,* þu begyrdest *FH,* (þ)u begyrdest *G**, begirdest *J,* þu ymgyrdest *I,* þu gyrdest *K,* megne *E*^{2} (*L*)
me	ǀ me ABCDF*G*HJK, þu me E^{2}
uirtute	ǀ mid megne A, mid mægene B, mid mægne J, mid mihte F, of mægene DGH, mægyne C, mægne K, mid strengþe I, begierdes E^{2}
ad	to ABCDE^{2}*FGHIJK
bellum	gefehte AB, g̲efeohte C, gefeohte DFGHIJ, gefiohte E^{2}, feohte K
⟨et⟩	⁊ *ABFGI* (*KL*)
subplantasti	gescrenctes *A,* þu gescrenctes *B,* þu gescrenctyst *C,* þu forscrængtest *J,* ðu underplantudest *D,* þu underplantodest *F**, þu [ ]nderplantudest *G**, þa underplantudest *H,* þu underplantodes K, ðu beswice ƚ underdulfe ƚ ⁊ ðu forscrænctest I*, þu underwyrtwæledæst *E*^{2} (*L*)
omnes*	alle A, ealle BCD, eælle E^{2} (*L*)
insurgentes	arisende AB, onarisynde C, onarisende DE^{2}*FHI, onrisende K, on[ ]sende G, þa arisendan J
in	in A, on BCDE^{2}*FGHIJK
me	me ABCDE^{2}*FGHIJK
subtus	under AB*E*^{2}*FIJK, undyr C, underneoþan DH, underneoðan G
me	me ABCE^{2}FGIJK

ED: ⁊ (G) (*1st*)] [ ] *Rosier.* p̄cinxisti (E)] precinxisti *Harsley.* (þ)u begyrdest (G)] þu begyrdest *Rosier.* Supplantasti (C)] Su[b]plantasti *Wildhagen.* þu [ ]nderplantudest (G)] þu underplantudest *Rosier.* þa underplantudest (H)] þa underplantu dest *Campbell.*

OE: and (E^{2})] *orig.* ond: o *altered to* a. (þ)u begyrdest (G)] *ascender of* þ *lost.* to (E^{2})] *eras. after word.* þu underplantodest (F)] *partly obscured by eras.* þu [ ]nderplantudest (G)] *letter fragments visible before* n. ðu beswice ƚ underdulfe ƚ ⁊ ðu forscrænctest (I)] ⁊ ðu forscrænctest *written in left margin, 2nd* ƚ *written above* et (*1st word in Lat. line*), *possibly when marginal gloss was added* (*MS:* ƚ ⁊ ðu beswice ƚ underdulfe + ⁊ ðu forscrænctest; *it may be read either as* ⁊ ðu forscrænctest ƚ ⁊ ðu beswice ƚ underdulfe *or in order recorded above*). onarisende (E^{2})] *on eras.* on (E^{2})] *on eras.* me (E^{2}) (*2nd*)] *on eras.* under (E^{2})] *on eras.*

LTg: Et] L: *orig.* et, *altered by corr. to* Et; et ABCE, D: *lemma written at bottom of fol. 24r, gloss at top of fol. 24v.* praecinxisti] præcincxisti B; pręcincxisti C; precincxisti DJ; precinxisti GK, FH: *letter eras. after* n; praecincxisti I; p̄cinxisti EL. me (*1st*)] *lost* G. bellum] F: *orig.* bellum et: et *eras.;* bellum Et AB; bellum et GIK, L: et *added by corr. to right of* S *in* Subplantasti *in next line: cf. Weber MS* ζ*. subplantasti] L: *orig.* Subplantasti: *initial* S *crossed through and minuscule* s *added to right;* Subplantasti DE; Supplantasti C: *orig.* Subplantasti: b *altered to* p; supplantasti ABGH, F: *eras. before word* (*see note to* bellum *above*), J: *eras. before word* (*see* bellum), *with 1st* p *altered from* b. omnes] L: *underlined to signal deletion: see GAg.* subtus] E: bt *retraced in darker ink.*

LTu: Et] et βνςτ*. praecinxisti] pręcinxisti ελνϱ; precinxisti ζϑιξοπσςτ; p̄cinxisti τ*υφχ. bellum] bellum Et β; bellum et ιλξοπϱστφ, εζ: et *interl.: cf. Weber MS* ζ*. subplantasti] Subplantasti νςτ*; supplantasti εζϑιλπτυφχ. subtus] suptus ψ.

GAg: omnes] *om.* FGHIJK, L: *see LTg.*

GAu: omnes] *om.* δεζϑιλμξοπϱστυφχψ.

41

Et		⁊ *ABCE*^{2}*FGIJK (*DL*)
inimicorum*	ǀ	feonda ABCD, fynd FIK, [ ]ynd G, find J, minum E^{2} (*L*)
meorum*	ǀ	minra ABCD, mine FGIJK, fyondum E^{2} (*L*)
dedisti	ǀ	ðu saldes A, þu sealdes B, þu sealdyst C, ðu sealdest D, þu sealdest FGHIJK, þu me E^{2}
mihi	ǀ	me ABCDFGHIJK, seældest E$^{2/x}$*
dorsum		bec A, bæc BCGJ, bæcc DE^{2}HK, on bæcc ł hrícc F, hrygc I
et		⁊ ABCDE^{2}FGHJK
odientes		ða figendan A, þa feogyndan C, feogende B, fænde ł hatigende D*H, hatiende E^{2}*, hatigende F*K*, hatigende ł feogende G, hatigende ł ł ⁊ feogende *J**, ða hatiendan I*
me		me ABCE^{2}*FGHIJK (D*)
disperdidisti		ðu tostenctes A, þu tostenctes B, ðu tostenctyst C, þu tostænctest J, þu forspildest D*E^{2}*H, ðu forspildest F, þu forspildes *K*, þu forspildest ł þu tostenctest G*, ⁊ þu todræfdest ł toscænctest I

ED: hatigende ł ł ⁊ feogende (J)] hatigende ł ⁊ feogende *Oess.* disperdidisti (H)] disperdisti *Campbell.*

OE: ⁊ (E^{2}) (*1st*)] *eras. after word.* odientes me disperdidisti (D)] *glossed in left margin by* Eos qui permanserunt. in obstinatione id est id est on wiþeringe. seældest (E$^{2/x}$)] t *added by corr., eras.* (*18 mm*) *after word.* hatiende (E^{2})] *on eras.* hatigende ł ł ⁊ feogende (J)] *1st* e *in* feogende *altered from* o; *line ends after 1st* ł, *with 2nd* ł *added in* *smaller hand before* ⁊ *in next line.* ða hatiendan (I)] *3rd* a *formed from another letter* (?). me (E^{2}) (*2nd*)] *on eras.* þu forspildest (E^{2})] *eras. after* þu, t *possibly added by corr.* þu forspildest ł þu tostenctest (G)] ł þu tostenctest *added in diff.* (?) *hand.*

LTg: Et] et ABCDEL. inimicorum] L: *altered to* inimicos *by corr.: see GAg.* meorum] L: *altered to* meos *by corr.: see GAg.* mihi] michi J, C: *orig.* mihi: c *interl. by corr.* odientes] K: o *altered from* d; odigentes J. disperdidisti] dispersisti K: sisti *on eras. by corr.*

LTu: Et] et βνςτ*. mihi] michi ιλσςτ*φ, πϱ: c *interl.* odientes] hodientes ς. disperdidisti] disperdedista β; disperdedisti ϑ.

GAg: inimicorum meorum] inimicos meos FGHIJK, L: *see LTg.*

GAu: inimicorum meorum] inimicos meos δεζϑιλμξοπϱστυφχψ.

42

Clamauerunt		cleopedun A, cleopodon B, clypudun C, clypodon J, clypedon K, hy clypodon D*H*, hy clypudon F, hy clypedon G, hi clepodon I, hie clypodon ł cigden $E^{2/x}$*
nec	|	ne ABCFGIJ, na K, næs DH, nes E^{x}
erat	|	wes A, wæs BCGJK, næs FI
qui		se ABE^{x}*, se ðe CFG, se þa J, þa K, þe hi I
saluos		hale ABDFGHIK, hæle E^{2}, halnė J, hine healde C
faceret		dyde ABDH*K, gedyde CE^{2}FG, gedide J, gedyde ł se ðe gehælde I*
ad		to ABCE^{x}*FGI*J*K
dominum		dryhtne B, driħny C, drihtne E^{2}FGI, drihtene K, dryht̄ A, driħ J
nec	|	ne ABCE^{2}FGIJ, na K, he ne DH
exaudiuit	|	he geherde A, he gehierde B, he gehyrde CK, gehyrde DH, he ne gehyrde FGIJ, he hie ne E^{2}
eos	|	hie ABCDH, hig FJ, hy G, hi IK, geherde $E^{2/x}$*

ED: [ ]lamauerunt (H)] Clamauerunt *Campbell.*

OE: hie clypodon ł cigden ($E^{2/x}$)] clypodon *in slightly darker ink,* ł cigden *added by corr.,* don *on eras.,* ⁊ *eras. after word.* se (E^{x})] *eras. after word.* dyde (H)] y *partly obscured by crease in leaf.* gedyde ł se ðe gehælde (I)] s. eos : hi *written in right margin.* to (E^{x})] *eras.* (*30 mm*) *before word.* geherde ($E^{2/x}$)] de *on eras. by corr.*

LTg: Clamauerunt] [ ]lamauerunt H: *only faint traces of initial letter visible.* ad] J: *eras. before word.*

LTu: nec (*both*)] nęc ξ.

43

Et		⁊ ABCE^{2}FGHIJK
comminuam	I	ic gebreocu A, ic gebrece B, ic gebrece oþþe litlige C/C^{2}*, ic forgnide DH, forgride K, ic gewanie ł forcníde F, ic forgnide ł gewanige G*, gewanige ic J, ic gelytlige ł ic tobryte I*, ic hie E^{2}
illos	I	hie ABC, hy D*G*H*, hig *FIJ,* hi *K,* gewænige E^{2}*
ut		swe swe A, swa swa BCDFGHIJ, swæ E^{2}*, swa K
puluerem		dust ABCDFHIK, dust ł myll G*, dust ł mill J, þet dust E^{2}
ante		biforan A, beforan BCDGHIJK, ætforan F, from E^{2}
faciem		onsiene AB, onsine E^{2}, ansyne CDFGHIJK
uenti		windes ABDFGHIK, windys C, wyndes J, þes windes E^{2}
ut		swe swe A, swa swa BCDFGHI, swa JK, ⁊ swæ E^{2}
lutum		lam ABCJ, fen DHK, fenn F, fænn I, fen ł lam G*, þæt fen ł lím E^{2}
platearum		worðigna AC, worðiga B, stræta DFHK, strætena I, þæræ stræte E^{2}*, stræta ł lanena G*, lamena J
delebo	I	ic adilgiu A, ic adilgige BI, ic gedylgie C, ic gedilegige J, ic dilge D, ic dilgie F, ic dilige GK, ic diligie H, ic hie E^{2}
eos	I	hie ABC, hy D*G*H, hig FJ, hi IK, adylge E^{2}

ED: ic gewanie ł forcníde (F)] ic gewanie ł forcnide *Kimmens.* swa swa (BGIJ) (*1st*)] swaswa *Brenner, Rosier, Lindelöf, Oess.* swa swa (GI) (*2nd*)] swaswa *Rosier, Lindelöf.* lutum (F)] lutem *Kimmens.*

OE: ic gebrece oþþe litlige (C/C^{2})] oþþe litlige *added in brown ink by same scribe who added* [ge]eadmodest *at v. 28.* ic forgnide ł gewanige (G)] ł gewanige *added in diff.* (?) *hand.* ic gelytlige ł ic tobryte (I)] y *in* gelytlige *altered from another letter.* hy (G)] *added in diff.* (?) *hand.* gewænige (E^{2})] *2nd* g *altered from* e. swæ (E^{2}) (*1st*)] *eras.* (*of* ⁊?) *before word: cf.* ⁊ swæ *later in verse.* dust ł myll (G)] ł myll *added in diff.* (?) *hand.* fen ł lam (G)] ł lam *added in diff.* (?) *hand.* þæræ stræte (E^{2})] stræte *on eras.* stræta ł lanena (G)] ł lanena *added in diff.* (?) *hand.*

LTg: illos] eos FGHIJK: *cf. Weber MSS* β med, *see also Hebr. Ps 18.43:* delebo eos ut puluerem, *etc.* eos] G: o *altered from another letter.*

LTu: illos] eos δεζλιμξϱσυφχ: *cf. Weber MSS* β med, *see also Hebr. Ps 18.43:* delebo eos ut puluerem, *etc.*

44

Eripies		ðu genes A, þu generes B, þu generyst C*, genera F, þu generast I, þu generedest J, þu Generest ł alysest E^{2}*, ðu alysest D*, þu alysest *G*H, þu alyst K

me — me ABCE^{2}*FGHJK
de — of ABCDE^{2}*FHIJK, ofer G
contradictionibus | wiðcwedenisse A, wiðcwedynnysse C, wiðcwedenessum B, þam wiþcwedennessum J, wiðersacum D, wiðersacum F, wiþersacum H, wiþersacan K, wiðersacan ł of ðam wiðcwedennessum G, wiðercwidelnyssum I, folcæ E^{2}
populi | folces ABDFHI*K, folcys C, folca G, folce J, wiþercwedolnesse ł wiðersacum E^{2}*
constitues — ðu gesetes A, þu gesetes B, þu gesettyst C, ðu gesetst D, þu gesetst E$^{2/x}$*HI, þu gesettest FGJ, þu gesets K
me — me ABCE^{2}FGHIJK
in — in AB, on CDE^{2}FGHIJK
caput | heafud AC, heafod B*D*FG*HJ*, hæfod K, heafod ł on forewearde I, þiode E^{2}
gentium | ðieda A, ðeoda BD, þeoda CFGHIJK, heæfod E^{2}

ED: Eripies (B)] Eripis *Brenner.*

OE: þu generyst (C)] t *interl.* þu Generest ł alysest (E^{2})] þu *added in left margin by main hand; gloss written as* þu Generest me of ł alysest: *transposition marks written after* Generest *and above* alysest *to indicate correct order,* ł alysest *seems added by main hand.* ðu alysest (D)] *letter eras. after 1st* s. me (E^{2}) (*1st*)] *see note to* þu Generest ł alysest. of (E^{2})] *see note to* þu Generest ł alysest. folces (I)] e *on eras.* wiþercwedolnesse ł wiðersacum (E^{2})] ł wiðersacum *added by corr.* (?). þu gesetst (E$^{2/x}$)] st *added on eras. by corr.*

LTg: Eripies] [ ]ripies G. caput] DH: orum *written after gloss, letter eras. before* o *in* H.

LTu: Eripies] ERipies β; [ ]ripies τ: *initial letter wanting.* me (*1st*)] π: *interl.* caput] capud ξς.

45

Populus — folc *A*BCDFGHIK, þæt folc J, þet folc E^{2}
quem — ðæt A, þæt BCFGHK, þæt DJ, þæt þe I, þe E^{2}
non | ic ne ABCE$^{2/x}$*FIJ, na DGHK
cognoui | oncnew A, oncneow BCE^{2}FI, ic gecneow D, ic gecneow GHK, gecneow J
seruiuit | ðeawde A, þeowode BD*FGH, ðeowude C, ðeowde I, þeawode J, þeowwode K, me E^{2}
mihi | me AB*C*FGI*J*K, þeowæde *E^{2}**
(in)* — on FGIK, fram J*
obauditu* | from gehernisse A, from gehernesse B, from gehyrnysse *C,*

		of hlyste *D*, hlyste FHK, hlyste ł fra̲m̲ gehyrnessa G*, gehyrnesse J, gehyrnysse [ ]n heorcnunge I*, from eæræнæ E^2 (*L*)
auris	l	earan ABFK, earen I, earum C, earana G, earena J, earis D, eares H, gehlyste ł hiernesse E^2*
obaudiuit	l	hersumade A, hersumode B, hyrsumude *C*, hyrsumade *G*, hyrsumode *J*, hit gehyrsumode *I*, gehlyste *DF**, gehlystan *K*, me E^2 (*HL*)
mihi	l	me AB*C*FGI*J*K, gehlyste E^2*

ED: obauditu (B)] ob auditu *Brenner.* gehyrnysse [ ]n heorcnunge (I)] gehyrnysse ł on heorcnunge *Lindelöf.*

OE: ic ne ($E^{2/x}$)] ic *by corr., followed by eras.* þeowode (D)] *2nd* o *interl.* þeowæde (E^2)] de *on eras.* fra̲m̲ (J)] *eras. after* a. hlyste ł fra̲m̲ gehyrnessa (G)] ł fra̲m̲ gehyrnessa *added in diff.* (?) *hand,* hyrnessa *in* gehyrnessa *interl. above* earana. gehyrnysse [ ]n heorcnunge (I)] [ ]n heorcnunge *written in left margin, initial letter* (*including* ł?) *lost due to tight binding.* gehlyste ł hiernesse (E^2)] gehlyste ł *added by main hand.* gehlyste (F)] *partly obscured* (*by eras.?*). gehlyste (E^2) (*2nd*)] *on eras. by corr.; eras. extends to end of line, illegible ascenders visible.*

LTg: Populus] A: *orig.* Populum: *deleting dot between 1st two legs of* m, s *interl. by glossator.* mihi (*1st*)] michi EJ, C: *orig.* mihi: c *interl. by corr.* obauditu] L: ob *crossed through by corr., in added interl.: see GAg;* abauditu CDE. obaudiuit] D: *orig.* obediuit: au *interl. by glossator,* e *deleted by subscript dot,* E: a *altered from another letter, 1st* u *written in right margin;* obęditiuit FG, C: *cauda malformed;* obediuit HJK; oboediuit IL. mihi (*2nd*)] michi EJ, C: *orig.* mihi: c *interl. by corr.*

LTu: mihi (*1st*)] michi ιλς, πϱ: c *interl.* obauditu] abauditu ςτ*. auris] aures β. obaudiuit] oboediuit βελμοπϱυφχψ; obediuit δζισςτ; abaudiuit ϑ; obędiuit νξ. mihi (*2nd*)] michi ειλξσςφ, πϱ: c *interl.*

GAg: obauditu] in auditu FGHIJK, L: *see LTg.*

GAu: obauditu] in auditu δεζϑιλμξοπϱστυφχψ.

46

Filii	l	bearn ABCDFGHIJ*K*, fremdæn *E^2*
alieni	l	fremðe A, fremde BCG**K*, fremedu DH, ælfremde F, ælfremede J*, ælfremede ł ælðeodisce I, beærn E^2
mentiti	l	ligende A, leogende BFJ*, leogynde C, lugun DH, lugon K, lugun ł leogende G, alugon I, me E^2
sunt		werun A, wæron BCGJ, synd F, syndon E^2
mihi	l	me AB*C*DFGHI*J*K, liogende *E^2*

filii | bearn ABCFGIJ*K*, fremdæn *E*^{2}*
alieni | fremðe A, fremde BCG*, ælfremde F, ælfremede J*, elelendisce I, beærn E^2
inueterauerunt* | aldadon *A*, ealdedon BGJ, ealdodon D*, ealdodum C, ealdude K, forealdodon I, gehealdene F*, synt E^2
(sunt)* | synd FGK, wæron J, eældigende E^2*
et ⁊ ABCE^{2}FGHIJK
claudicauerunt haltadon A, healtodon BCK, healtedon J*, hy haltodon E^2, hy héaltedon F, hy healtoton H, hy healtodon ł huncetton D, hi healtodon ł hlyncoton G*, ahealtedon ⁊ luncodon I
a from AE^2, from BC, fram DFHJK, fram GI
semitis | stigum ABJ, stigum CI, siðfatum D, siðfatum H, siðfatum ł sti[ ] G, siðfate K, stæpum F, hieræ E^2
suis | heara *A*, hira B, heora CDF*H*, his K, synum ł fram heora paðum I, þinum G, þinum *J*, siðfatum E$^{2/x}$* (*L*)

ED: Filíí (EK)] Filii *Harsley, Sisam.* filii (B)] Filii *Brenner.* filíí (EK)] filii *Harsley, Sisam.* siðfatum ł sti[ ] (G)] siðfatum ł st[ ] *Rosier.*

OE: fremde (G) (*1st*)] *eras.* (?) *after* m. ælfremede (J) (*1st*)] *otiose mark after 1st* e: *cf. Pss 19.7 and 20.8 for similar marks.* leogende (J)] o *interl.* fremdæn (E^2) (*2nd*)] *eras. before word.* fremde (G) (*2nd*)] *eras.* (?) *after* m. ælfremede (J) (*2nd*)] *insertion mark* (?) *after 1st* e, *but no letter visible.* ealdodon (D)] *orig.* ealdedon: *1st* o *interl., but without subscript deleting dot.* gehealdene (F)] *partly obscured by eras.* eældigende (E^2)] g *altered from* e. healtedon (J)] t *on eras.* hi healtodon ł hlyncoton (G)] hi *obscured by small blot.* siðfatum (E$^{2/x}$)] tum *on eras. by corr.*

LTg: Filii] Filíí EK. alieni (*1st*)] aliȩni K. mihi] michi EJ, C: *orig.* mihi: c *interl. by corr.* filii] filíí EK. inueterauerunt] A: *ink begins to lighten after* inu; inueterati sunt E: *see GAg.* suis] A: *written above* tis *in* semitis *by main scribe in smaller hand due to lack of space at end of line,* H: *1st* s *altered from another letter,* J: *1st* s *altered from* t, L: *1st* s *formed from another letter on eras.*

LTu: mihi] michi ιλςτ, πϱ: c *interl.* alieni (*2nd*)] *interl.* ε. inueterauerunt] inueterati sunt τ*: *see GAu.* suis] ς: iuit o *written in next line as false start of v. 47;* tuis ϑ.

GAg: inueterauerunt] inueterati sunt FGHIJK, E: *see LTg.*

GAu: inueterauerunt] inueterati sunt δεζϑιλμξοπϱστυφχψ, τ*: *see LTu.*

47
Uiuit | leafað *A*, leofað *BDFGH*, leofaþ *I**JK, lyfað *C*, Dryhten *E*^{2} (*L*)
dominus | drihtyn C, drihten FGIK, dryht̄ AB, drih̄ J, liofæþ E^2

et ⁊ ABCE^{2}FGHIJK
benedictus | gebledsad A, gebletsod BDFG, se gebletsuda C*, sy gebletsod I, gebletsiaþ J, bletsud H, bletsod K, min E^2
deus god ABCFGIJK, god E^2
meus | min ABCFGIJK, is gebletsot E^2
et ⁊ ABCE^{2}FGHIJK
exaltetur sie uppahefen A, sie upahæfen B, sy upahafyn C, sy upahafen DH, sy upæhafen E$^{2/x}$*, sy upahafon I, si he upahafen G*J, si ahafen K, bið upahafen F
deus god ABCE^{2}FGIJK
salutis hęlu A, hælo BDH, helo E^2, hæle CFGIJ, hæl K
meae minre A*B*C*D*F*GH*I, me *J*, min *E^2*K* (*L*)

ED: [ ]iuit (G)] Uiuit *Rosier.* leofað (B)] leofad *Brenner.* leofaþ (I)] leofað *Lindelöf.* meę (E)] meae *Harsley.*

OE: leofaþ (I)] et e͟s͟t : ⁊ is *written in left margin.* se gebletsuda (C)] *1st* e *interl., eras. after initial* s. sy upæhafen (E$^{2/x}$)] a *altered from* e *by corr.,* n *on eras. by corr.* si he upahafen (G)] he *added in diff.* (?) *hand above* si up-. min (E^2) (*2nd*)] *letter eras. after word.*

LTg: Uiuit] Viuit ABEFHIL; [ ]iuit G: *initial* V *lost, outline visible;* Viuet C, D: *orig.* Viuit: *2nd* i *altered to* e. meae] meæ BK; meę DEGHJL.

LTu: Uiuit] ς: *see LTu note to v. 46* suis; Viuit εζινξοσυφ. meae] meæ ϑ; mee ιστ*τ; meę ξφ.

48
Deus god ABCE^{2}FGJK, þu god I*
qui ðu A, þu BCG, þu ðe DE^2*F, þu þe HIJ, þe K
das | seles A*B*, sylyst C, selst DH, sylst FI, sylest ł sealdest G*, sealdest J, gifst K, me E^2
uindictam* | wrece A, wræce BGJK, wrace CDF, wræca I, selest E^2 (*L*)
mihi | me AB*C*DFG*HI*J*K, wrece *E^2*
et ⁊ ABCDE^{2}FGIJK
subdidisti underðeodes A, underðeoddes B, underðeodest E^2*, þu undyrþeoddyst C, ðu underðeoddest D*F,* þu underþeoddest *J,* ðu onðerþeodyst *I,* þu underþyddest *G,* þu underðydest *K* (*HL*)
populos folc ABCDE^2*F*GH*JK, folctruman I
sub under ABDE^{2}FGIJK, vndyr C
me me ABCDE^2*FGIJK

Liberator	I	gefrigend A, gefreogynd C, aliesend B, alysend DGHI*JK, alýsend *F*, Drihten is E^2 (*L*)
meus		min ABCDE^{2}FGHIJK
dominus*	I	dryht̄ AB, friolsend ł alysend *E*^{2}* (*CL*)
de		of ABCDE^2*FGHIJ, fram K
gentibus*		ðeodum A, ðeodum BD, þeodum C, ðeodum E^2*, feondum *F*GHI, feondum J, freondum K (*L*)
(meis)*		minum FH, minum I, minu[ ] G, minan K, me *J* (*L*)
iracundis		eorsendum A, eorsiendum B, yrsiendum CE^2*, yrsegendum D, yrsigendum F, yrsgendum H, yrsiendum I, yrsigende K, yrsigendum ł fram unrihtwisum G*, fram unrihtwisum J*

ED: uindictam (BE)] vindictam *Brenner, Harsley.* underðeodes (A)] underðeoðes *Kuhn.* popul[ ] (G)] popu*los Rosier.* inim[ ]cis (F)] inimicis *Kimmens.*

OE: þu god (I)] s. o *written before gloss.* þu ðe (E^2)] ðe *interl.* sylest ł sealdest (G)] ł sealdest *added in diff.* (?) *hand.* underðeodest (E^2)] derðeodest *on eras.* folc (E^2)] *eras. before and after word.* me (E^2) (*2nd*)] *on eras.* alysend (I)] tu es : þu eart *written in left margin.* friolsend ł alysend (E^2)] ł alysend *on eras.* of (E^2)] *on eras.* ðeodum (E^2)] *on eras.* yrsiendum (E^2)] *on eras.* yrsigendum ł fram unrihtwisum (G)] ł fram unrihtwisum *added in diff.* (?) *hand.* fram unrihtwisum (J)] *source-text misread, perhaps reading gloss to* iniquo *in v. 49; see also* G.

LTg: das] dás B. uindictam] L: m *crossed through by corr., with 1st leg used to form stem of long* s: *see GAg.* mihi] michi EHJ, C: *orig.* mihi: c *interl. by corr.* subdidisti] L: disti *crossed through by corr. and final* s *added interl.;* subdis FGHIJK. populos] H: *2nd* o *altered from another letter;* popul[ ] G. Liberator] L: *initial* L *crossed through and minuscule* l *written to right;* liberator FGHIJK. dominus] E: *written in left margin,* C: *om.: cf. Weber MSS* αβδη moz^c, L: *underlined to signal deletion: see GAg.* gentibus] L: *underlined to signal deletion, with* inimicis meis *added interl. by corr.: see GAg;* gentibus me J.

LTu: qui] *interl.* o. mihi] michi ιλς, πρ: c *interl.* subdidisti] subdis δεζιλμξοπρστυφχ; subdes ψ; subdidit ϑ. Liberator] liberator δεζιλμξοπρστυφχ. de] di ϑ. iracundis] iracondis ϑ.

GAg: uindictam] uindictas FGHIJK, L: *see LTg.* dominus] *om.* FGHIJK, CL: *see LTg.* gentibus] inimicis meis GHIK, L: *see LTg;* inim[ ]cis meis F: *letter lost after 1st* m, c *cropped due to hole in leaf.* J *reflects neither Ro. nor Ga. tradition: see LTg.*

GAu: uindictam] uindictas δεζϑιλμξοπρστυφχψ. dominus] *om.* δεζϑιλμξοπρστυφχψ. gentibus] inimicis meis δεζϑιλμξοπρστυφχψ.

49

Et	⁊ *ABCE²*FGHJK (*IDL*)
ab	from A, from BC, fram DE²FHJK, fram G*I*
insurgentibus	ðæm arisendum A, þæm arisendum B, þam arisyndum C, þam arisendum G*, þam arisendum J, arisendum H, onarisendum D, onarisendum E²*F, onarisendum ł onræsendum I, onri[ ] *K**
in	in A, on BCDE²*FGHIJ (*K*)
me	me ABCDE²*FGHIJ (*K*)
exaltabis	ðu upahefes A, þu upahefes B, þu upahefyst C, ðu upahefst D, þu úpahefst F, þu upahefst E²*GHI*, upahefest J (*K*)
me	me ABCE²*FGIJK
a	from A, from BC, fram FGJK, fram I, ⁊ fram E²*
uiro	were ABCDE²*GHIJ, werum F, weran K
iniquo	ðæm unrehtwisan A, þan unrihtwisan C, unryhtwisum BD, unrihtwisum FHJ, unrihtwisum E²*GI (*K*)
eripies	generes A, þu generes B, þu generest CE²**G*H, ðu generest D, ðu generast F, þu generast I, þu generedest (*K*)
me	me ABCDE²*FGHIJ (*K*)

ED: ęripies (G)] eripies *Rosier.*

OE: þam arisendum (G)] þam *added in diff* (?) *hand.* onarisendum (E²)] *on eras.* onri[ ] (K)] *partly lost due to section of leaf torn away; glosses to* in me exaltabis *also lost.* on (E²)] *on eras.* me (E²) (*1st*)] *on eras.* þu upahefst (E²)] *on eras.* þu upahefst (I)] up *interl.* me (E²) (*2nd*)] *on eras.* ⁊ fram (E²)] *on eras.* were (E²)] *on eras.* unrihtwisum (E²)] *on eras.*, t *interl.* þu generest (E²)] *on eras.* me (E²) (*3rd*)] *eras. before word.*

LTg: Et] et ABCDEL; *om.* I. ab] Ab I: *eras. between* A *and* b, A *crudely formed.* insurgentibus] ins[ ] K: *partly lost due to section of leaf torn away.* in] K: *lost due to section of leaf torn away.* me (*1st*)] K: *lost due to section of leaf torn away.* exaltabis] K: *lost due to section of leaf torn away.* iniquo] ini[ ] K: *partly lost due to section of leaf torn away.* eripies] K: *lost due to section of leaf torn away.* me (*3rd*)] K: *lost due to section of leaf torn away.* eripies] ęripies G.

LTu: Et] et βθνςτ*λμ; *om.* μυ: *cf. Weber MSS* SKαβγδη moz^c med. ab] Ab μυ. eripies] eripias β.

50

Propterea	foreðon AB, forþon CE²G, forðon DFH, forðan I, forþan JK
confitebor	❘ ic ondetto A, ic ondette B, ic andette CDFGHIJK, on E²*

tibi	I	ðe ABF, þe CDGHIJ, folce E^2 (*K*)
in	I	in AB, on CDF*G*IJ, drihten *E*^{2} (*K*)
populis*	I	folcum AB*GJ, folcum D, folce C, cynrenon F, ðeodum I, ic þe *E*^{2}
domine	I	dryht̄ AB, driħt CF, driħ GJ, eala þu drihten I*, ondette E^2
et		⁊ *A*BCDE^{2}FGHIJK
⟨in⟩		on *D*
nomini	I	noman ABD, naman CFGHIK, on naman J, on þinum E^2
tuo	I	ðinum A, þinum BCDJ, þinum GHI, ðinne F, þinne K, nomæn E^2
psalmum	I	salm A, sealm DE^2*GHJ*K*, sielm C, sealmsong B, sealmlof I, ic sýnge F
dicam	I	ic cweoðu A, ic cweðe BCK, cweðe F, ⁊ ic cweðe I, ic cweþe J, ic secge DGH, ic þe singe E^2

ED: Propterea (E)] Propter ea *Harsley*. foreðon (A)] fore ðon *Kuhn*. forþon (EG)] Forþon *Harsley;* forðon *Rosier*. ⁊ (D)] *no gloss Roeder*. ⁊ ic cweðe (I)] ic cweðe *Lindelöf*.

OE: on (E^2)] *eras. after word*. folcum (B)] *on eras*. eala þu drihten (I)] þu *interl*. sealm (E^2)] *on eras., eras. extends 18 mm after word*.

LTg: tibi] K: *top of* ti, *ascender and top of bowl of* b *lost due to section of leaf torn away*. in] E: *on eras*., G: n *malformed*, K: *lost due to section of leaf torn away*. populis] E: pop *on eras*. et] A: *eras. after word;* et in D: in *added interl. by glossator* (*along with gloss*): *cf. Weber MS* η^2. psalmum] salmum K.

LTu: Propterea] PROPterea β. et] et in β. nomini] in nomini ς; nomine β. psalmum] σ: p *interl.;* salmum β.

GAg: populis] nationibus FGHIJK.

GAu: populis] nationibus δεζϑιλμξοπϱστυφχψ.

51

Magnificans		gemicliende AB, gemicliynde C, gemicelgende D, Gemycligende E^2*, gemiciligende *G*, gemycelgende K, miccligende J, gemicel H, sý gemiclod F, gemicligende ł mærsiende I*
salutare*		haelu A, hælo BDFGI*J*, hæle CK, helo E^2 (*L*)
regis	I	cyninges ABDH, cyningys C, cininges K, kyninges GJ, kyningces I, ðæs cyninges F, his E^2
ipsius*	I	his ABDFGHIJK, hys *C*, kyninges E^2
et		⁊ ACDE^{2}FGHIJK

faciens		donde ABCDGHIJK, doende E^2, wyrcende F
misericordiam	I	mildheortnisse AD, mildheortnesse BGJK, mildheortnysse CI, mildheortnyssa F, mildheornesse H, his E^2
christo	I	criste ABCJ, cristes F, crist̄ G*, cyning D*, cyningc H, cininge K, gecorenu<u>m</u> ł gesmiredu<u>m</u> I, xpistes E^2 (*L*)
suo	I	his AB*CD**FGHIJK, mildhertnesse E^2
dauid		dauide CDE^2*HG, dauides F, dauiðe I, þa<u>m</u> gehalgedon dauide J, n K*
et		⁊ ABCDE^{2}FHIJ*K
semini	I	sede A, sæde BCDE^2*GHK, sæd J, ofspringc ł sæd F, his I
eius	I	his ADE^2*FGHJ*K*, hys C, sæde ł ofsprynge I (*B*)
usque		oð *A*BCFHJK, oþ DI, oððe E^2*, oðþæt G
in		in AB, on CDE^{2}FGJ
saeculum		weoruld A, weorold *B**, worulde *CDGH,* weorulde *F,* worlde *J,* worolde *E^{2}K,* worlde ende I (*L*)

ED: (M)agnificans (G)] *M*agnificans *Rosier.* christo (K)] Christo *Sisam.* dauid (K)] Dauid *Sisam.* dauide (G)] dauid *Rosier.* sęculum (E)] saeculum *Harsley.* scłm (K)] sæculum *Sisam.*

OE: Gemycligende (E^2)] i *altered from* e. gemicligende ł mærsiende (I)] s. e<u>st</u> : he is *written in left margin.* crist̄ (G)] *so MS.* christo suo (D)] *glossed in left margin by* wæs mid iudeu<u>m</u> on geardagu<u>m</u> calra cyninga g<u>e</u>hwelc cristus nemned. om<u>n</u>is rex in antiq<u>ui</u>s dieb<u>us</u> aput iudeos nominabit<u>ur</u> chr<u>istu</u>s. dauide (E^2)] *on eras.; ink somewhat darker, but likely by main hand.* n (K)] *for* nomen. ⁊ (J) (*2nd*)] *written below* n *in* gehalgedon. sæde (E^2)] *on eras.* his (E^2) (*3rd*)] *on eras.* oððe (E^2)] *on eras.* weorold (B)] *orig.* weorolde: *final* e *eras.*

LTg: Magnificans] (M)agnificans G: *initial* M *partly lost.* salutare] L: ar *underlined to signal deletion,* s *added by corr.: see GAg;* salutem J: *cf. Weber MSS* αδη moz. ipsius] C: *1st* s *interl.* (*by corr.?*), *eras. above* u. christo] cristo L. suo] C: *eras. after word.* eius] eíus K; *om.* B. usque] A: ue *added by corr.* saeculum] sæculum B; seculum CGHL; sęculum EF; scłm DJK.

LTu: faciens] ϑ: n *interl.* misericordiam] missericordiam ϑ. dauid] dauit β. semini] semeni ϑ. saeculum] sęculum ειvο; seculum ζςτ; sæculum ϑ; scłm λμξπστ*υφχ.

GAg: salutare] salutes FGHIK, L: *see LTg.* ipsius] eius FGHIJ; eíus K.

GAu: salutare] salutes δεζϑιλμξοπϱστυφχψ. ipsius] eius δεζϑιλμξοπϱστυφχψ.

PSALM 18

2

Caeli		heofenas A*GK*, heofynas *C*, heofonas *DFJ*, heafanas H*, heofones *E*^{2}, heofonas oððe apostoli I (*BL*)
enarrant		asecgað AB*C*, seægæþ ł bodieð E^2*, secgaþ ł reccaþ J, bodiaþ K, bodiað ł cyþað D, bodiaþ ł cyþaþ F, bodiað ł cy(ð)að G*, bodiað ł cyðað H, gecyðaþ I
gloriam	|	wuldur ACD, wuldor BF*G*HIJK, godes E^2
dei	|	godes ABDFGHIJK, godys C, wuldor E^2
et		⁊ ABCDE^{2}FHIJK (*G*)
opera		werc AI*, weorc BCDE^{2}FHJK (*G*)
manuum	|	honda *A*, handa BCDFGHIJK, his E^2
eius	|	his ABDFGHIJ*K*, hys C, hændæ E^2
adnuntiant*		segeð *A*, sægð *BC*, bodiaþ *D*K, bodiað GH, bodaþ J, bodað ł cýþ F, bodað ł cyð I, cyþæþ ł bodiað E^2*
firmamentum		trymenis A, trymenesse B, trumnysse C, trymnesse K, staðol ł trumnisse D, trumnysse ł staðol F, trvmnesse ł staðel ł fesnesse E$^{2/x}$*, staðol ł tru(m)nesse ł rador G*, staþolnesse H, staðolfæstnysse ł roder I, rodor J

ED: CÆLI (C)] CAELI *Wildhagen.* (C)æli (G)] Caeli *Rosier.* heofonas oððe apostoli (I)] heofonas *Lindelöf.* et (G)] *Rosier records* ⁊ *as gloss, but only letter fragments are visible: see LTg note to* et opera. werc (I)] weorc *Lindelöf.* annuntiant (C)] a[d]nuntiant *Wildhagen.* staðol ł tru(m)nesse ł rador (G)] staðol ł trumne ł rador *Rosier; Berghaus* (*p. 15*) *takes* ł rador *as added in contemporary hand.*

OE: heafanas (H)] *eras.* (?) *after 1st* a. seægæþ ł bodieð (E^2)] ł bodieð *added by corr.* (?). bodiað ł cy(ð)að (G)] *cross-stroke of 2nd* ð *not visible.* werc (I)] *orig.* worc: o *altered to* e. cyþæþ ł bodiað (E^2)] *eras.* (*20 mm*) *before* cyþæþ, ł bodiað *added by corr.* (?), ð *on eras.* trvmnesse ł staðel ł fesnesse (E$^{2/x}$)] v *altered from* y, ł staðel *added by corr.* (?), ł fesnesse *on eras. by corr.* staðol ł tru(m)nesse ł rador (G)] *only 1st 2 legs of* m *visible.*

LTg: Caeli] CÆLI BC; CELI DE; Cęli FL; (C)æli G: *initial* C *only partly visible;* Cæli K; Celi J. enarrant] ENARRANT C. gloriam] glori[ ] G. et opera] G: *letter fragments of gloss visible above both words.* manuum] manvum A: v *interl. by corr.* eius] eíus K. adnuntiant] annuntiant C: *1st* n *on eras. by corr.;* annuntiat A: *orig.* annuntiant: *deleting dots above and below 4th* n; adnuntiat BD: *cf. Weber MSS* α moz med, *see GAg.*

LTu: Caeli] CAEli β; Cæli ϑ; CELI ιλςτ*τ; CAELI μνϱ; CAeli ο; Celi σ; CĘLI φ. enarrant] χ: na *interl.;* ENARRANT λμνϱ; ENArrant ς; ęnarrant ε. gloriam] GLORIAM λϱ. dei] DEI λϱ. manuum] χ: *2nd* u *interl.;* manu<u>um</u> ϑ. adnuntiant] adnuntiat ς; annuntiat τ*: *cf. Weber MSS* α moz med, *see GAu.*

GAg: adnuntiant] adnuntiat J, BD: *see LTg;* annuntiat FGI, H: *1st* n *on eras.*, K: *1st* n *on eras. by corr.*, A: *see LTg.*

GAu: adnuntiant] adnuntiat δϑμ, ς: *see LTu;* annuntiat εζιλξπστυχ, ο: *orig.* adnuntiat: d *deleted,* n *interl.*, τ*: *see LTu;* annunciat φ, ϱ: *orig.* annuntiat: *1st* t *deleted,* c *interl.;* adnunciat ψ.

3

Dies	deg A, dæg BCDFGHI, dæges JK, Se deig *E^x**
diei	dege A, dæge BCDH, dæg K, ðam dæge F, þa<u>m</u> dæge GJ, dæges I*, of þem dege E^2
eructuat	roccetteð *A*B, roccytyð *C,* forðroccette *G,* forþracette *J,* belcet DK, belceð E^x*, bealceþ *F*I, elcet *H*
uerbum	word ABCDE^2FGHJK, wurd I
et	⁊ ABC*E^x**FGHIJK
nox	neht A, niht BCFGHIJ, nyht D, nihta K, seo nieht *E^x**
nocti	nehte A, nihte BCF*H*IJ, nyhte D, nihtes G, niht K, þere nieht E^x*
indicat	getacnað AB, geeacnað C, bycneþ D, býcneþ F, bicneð *H,* bycneþ K, bicnað ł gesæde G, gescade J, gecyþeð ł bycneþ *E^x**, gecyð ł gebeacnaþ I*
scientiam	wisdom ABCJ, ingehygd DH, ingehyd K, ingehýd ł gesæd wisdom F, ingehyd ł wisdom G*, wisdom ł ingehyd I, ingehygð ł wit ł wisdom E^x*

ED: forðroccette (G)] *Berghaus (p. 15) takes* roccette *as added in contemporary hand.* uerbum (B)] verbum *Brenner.* índicat (H)] indicat *Campbell.* bicnað ł gesæde (G)] *Berghaus (p. 15) takes* ł gesæde *as added in contemporary hand.*

OE: Se deig (E^x)] *on eras. by corr.* dæges (I)] *eras. after word.* belceð (E^x)] lc *on eras.* ⁊ (E^x)] *on eras. by corr.* seo nieht (E^x)] *on eras. by corr.* þere nieht (E^x)] *on eras. by corr.* gecyþeð ł bycneþ (E^x)] *on eras. by corr.* gecyð ł gebeacnaþ (I)] *eras. before* gecyð. ingehyd ł wisdom (G)] ł wisdom *added in diff (?) hand.* ingehygð ł wit ł wisdom (E^x)] *on eras. by corr.,* ingehygð ł wit *written above* ł wisdom.

LTg: Dies] E: *retraced in darker ink.* eructuat] eructat FGHJ, A: *orig.* eructuat: *deleting dots above and below 2nd* u, C: at *on eras.* (*by main hand?*): *cf. Weber MSS* med. et] E: *retraced in darker ink.* nox] E: *retraced in darker ink.* nocti] H: i *altered from another letter.* indicat] E: *retraced in darker ink;* índicat H.

LTu: eructuat] eructat δζϑιμξοπϱστυφ: *cf. Weber MSS* med.

4

Non	ne ABCDFGHJ, Ne E^2, na K, na gyta I*
sunt	sind A, synd CDFGHK, sint B, sindon E^2, wæron J, nærun I
loquellae	gespreocu A*, gesprecu *G,* gespreca *E^2*,* gesprecene *J,* spræca *BCDFH,* swæca *K,* wordlacu *I** (*L*)
neque	ne *A*BCDE^2*FGHI*, ⁊ na JK
sermones	word ABCDE^2GHJK, wórd ł sprǽca F, spræcu I*
quorum	ðeara A, þara BDGHJK, ðara F, þæræ E^2*, þara þe CI
non	ne ABCDE^2FGHIJ, na K
audientur*	bioð geherde A, beoð gehierde B, beoð gehyrede C, beoþ gehyrede J, bioþ gehired E^2*, synd gehyrede ł ne beoð G*, syn gehyred DH, synd gehyred F, wæron geherde I, synd K
uoces	| stefne AK, stefna BDGI, stæfna CFH, stæfne J, hieræ E^2
eorum	| heara A, hira B, heora CDFGHIJK, stemnæ E^2

ED: ne (G) (*1st*)] [ ] *Rosier.* gesprecu (G)] *Berghaus* (*p. 15*) *takes* ge *as added in contemporary hand.* word (G)] *Berghaus* (*p. 15*) *takes this as added in contemporary hand.* uoces (BE)] voces *Brenner, Harsley.*

OE: na gyta (I)] *orig.* na gita: i *altered to* y. gespreocu (A)] *orig.* gespreoca: a *altered to* u. gespreca (E^2)] a *altered from another letter.* wordlacu (I)] *orig.* wurdlacu: *1st* u *altered to* o. ne (E^2) (*2nd*)] *eras.* (*2 letters*) *after word, ascender visible.* ne (I) (*2nd*)] *eras. after word.* spræcu (I)] cu *on eras.* þæræ (E^2)] *eras. before word.* bioþ gehired (E^2)] *letter eras. after* d. synd gehyrede ł ne beoð (G)] ł ne beoð *added in diff.* (?) *hand.*

LTg: loquellae] loquellæ B; loquelę CDFGH; loquelae I; loquele EJKL. neque] A: *eras.* (?) *above word.* audientur] audiantur L: *see GAg.*

LTu: loquellae] loquelę δελμνοϱφχ; loquele ζιοςτ*τυψ; loquelæ ϑ; loquęle ξ; loquęlę π. audientur] audiantur ν: *cf. Weber MSS* ST²PQUVXαβγδη moz med, *see GAu.*

GAg: audientur] audiantur FGHIJ, L: *see LTg,* K: *2nd* a *on eras. by corr.*

GAu: audientur] audiantur δεϑιλμξοπϱστυφχ, ν: *see LTu;* au audiantur ξ.

5

In	in A, on BCDFGHIJK, On E^2
omnem	alle A, ealle BCDH, eælræ E^2, ealre FIJ, eallre G*, ealra K
terram	eorðan ABCDGHI, eorðæn E^2, eorþan FJK
exiuit	uteode AB*C*DGHJK utgeode E^2*, utfor F, asprang ł ferde I
sonus	swoeg AB, sweg CE^2FIJ, son ł hlisa DH, son ł hlisa ł sweg G*, hlisa K
eorum	heara A, hira B, hyra C, heora DFGHIJK, heore E^2*

et		⁊ ABCDE^{2}*FGHIJK
in		in A, on BCDE^{2}*FGHIJK
fines		endas ABCDH, endes E^{2}*, ende FG*JK, endum ł gemærum I
orbis		ymbhwyrftes ABC*DHI, ymbwyrftes E^{2}*, ymbhyftes F, ymbhwyrfte J, embhwerfte G, embehwyrfte K
terrae		eorðan A*BCDE^{2}*GH*I, eorþan *FJK* (*L*)
uerba		word A*B*CDE^{2}*FGHJK, wurd I
eorum		heara A, hira B, hyra C, heora DE^{2}*FGHIJK

ED: eallre (G)] eall(r)a *Rosier.* uteode (H)] ut eode *Campbell.* in (G) (*OE, 2nd*)] on *Rosier.* terrę (E)] terrae *Harsley.* eorum (A) (*2nd*)] eurum *Kuhn.*

OE: eallre (G)] r *added in diff.* (?) *hand.* utgeode (E^{2})] *on eras.* son ł hlisa ł sweg (G)] ł sweg *added in diff.* (?) *hand.* heore (E^{2})] *on eras.* ⁊ (E^{2})] *on eras.* on (E^{2}) (*2nd*)] *on eras.* endes (E^{2})] *on eras.* ende (G)] *small eras. after word.* ymbhwyrftes (C)] es *interl.* ymbwyrftes (E^{2})] *on eras.* eorðan (E^{2})] *on eras.* word (E^{2})] *on eras.* heora (E^{2})] *on eras.*

LTg: exiuit] C: *eras. after* x. terrae] terræ BK; terrę CEFGHL; terre DJ.

LTu: exiuit] exibit β. terrae] terrę βεινξφ; terre ζστ*τ; terræ ϑ. uerba] β: r *added interl.* eorum] illorum ϑ: *cf. Weber MSS* moz[x].

6

In		in A, on BCDFGHIJK, On E^{2}
sole		sunnan ABCDFGHIJ, sunnæn E^{2}, sunna K
posuit		he sette ABCK, he gesette DE^{2}*FGH, he asette I, gesette J
tabernaculum	ǀ	geteld ABCJ, getelda F, eardunge ł geteld G*, ł eardunge D, eardunge H, eardunga K, eardungstowe I, his E^{2}
suum	ǀ	his ABCDFGHIJK, geteldunge ł ærdunge E^{2}*
et		⁊ ABCE^{2}FGHIJK
ipse		he ABCDE^{2}FHK, he s(y)l(f) *G**, he silf J, he is I*
tamquam		swe swe A, swa swa B*C*DF*GH*IJ, swæ E^{2}, ealswa K
sponsus		brydguma ABCDFGHIK, blidguma J, se brydgumæ E^{2}
procedens		forðgande A, forðgongende B, forþgangynde C*, forþgongende E^{2}, forþgangende J, forðgewitende D*, forþgewitende F, forðgewitende H, forðgewitende ł forðgangeð *G**, forðstæppende I, forðsteppende K
de		of ABCDE^{2}FGHIJK
thalamo	ǀ	brydbure AB*C*FI, brydbrvre K, gyftbure D, giftbure H, giftbure ł brydbure G*, his E^{2}J
suo	ǀ	his ABDFGHIK, hys C, brydhuse J, brydbure ł gyftbure E^{2}*

Exultauit		gefaeh A, gefeh B, gefeoh C, he blissode D*F**K*, he blyssade H, he geblissode I, he winsumæde ł blitsode E^{2}*, he blissade ł wynsumiað *G**, winsumiaþ J
ut		swe swe A, swa swa BCDFGHIJ, swæ swæ E^{2}, swa K
gigans		gigent A, gigant B*CDGH,* etenæs E^{2}, ént *FJ,* se mæsta ł swa swa ent *I**, n *K** (*L*)
ad	|	to AB*C*DFHIJK, to g G*, weg E^{2}*
currendam	|	earnenne A, irnanne B, yrnanne C, yrnenne DGH, ýrnenne F, geyrnenne J, geyrnanne I, yrnnende K, to E^{2}
uiam*	|	on weg ABC, weg DFGIJK, weg his *H*, iernenne E^{2}

ED: tanquam (C)] ta[m]quam *Wildhagen.* swa swa (BGIJ) (*1st*)] swaswa *Brenner, Rosier, Lindelöf, Oess.* he winsumæde ł blitsode (E^{2})] he winsumæd*e* ł blitsode *Harsley.* swa swa (GIJ) (*2nd*)] swaswa *Rosier, Lindelöf, Oess.* to g (G)] to *Rosier.*

OE: he gesette (E^{2})] gesette *on eras.* eardunge ł geteld (G)] ł geteld *added in diff.* (?) *hand.* geteldunge ł ærdunge (E^{2})] teldunge *on eras.*, ł ærdunge *added.* he s(y)l(f) (G)] *descenders of* y *and* f *lost.* he is (I)] s. est *written in left margin.* forþgangynde (C)] *1st* n *interl.* forðgewitende (D)] d *interl.* forðgewitende ł forðgangeð (G)] ł forðgangeð *added in diff.* (?) *hand.* giftbure ł brydbure (G)] ł brydbure *added in diff.* (?) *hand.* brydbure ł gyftbure (E^{2})] *in darker ink.* he winsumæde ł blitsode (E^{2})] *1st* de *in ligature on eras.*, ł blitsode *written above* he winsumæde. he blissade ł wynsumiað (G)] ł wynsumiað *added in diff.* (?) *hand above* blissade. se mæsta ł swa swa ent (I)] ł swa swa ent *written in right margin.* n (K)] *for* nomen. to g (G)] g (*false start?*) *slightly larger than immediate other letters.* weg (E^{2})] *eras. before* (*15 mm*) *and after* (*5 mm*) *word.*

LTg: ipse] ip[ ] G. tamquam] tanquam C: *eras. before* n, G: *orig.* tamquam: *right leg of 1st* m *eras. to form* n, H: n *altered from another letter.* procedens] G: *orig.* procȩdens: *cauda eras.* thalamo] C: *orig.* thalomo: *1st* o *altered to* a. Exultauit] G: *2nd* u *altered from another letter,* K: *2nd* u *on eras. by corr.* gigans] gigas CIJKL, F: *eras.* (?) *after word,* GH: s *altered from another letter, eras. after word.* ad] C: d *interl.* uiam] H: *eras. after word.*

LTu: posuit] possuit ϑ. tabernaculum] β: r *added interl.* tamquam] tāquam συτ; tanquam εϑιλτ*φ. procedens] procens ϑ. thalamo] talamo ψ. Exultauit] Exsultauit ϑ; Exultabit μψ. gigans] gigas δεζϑιλνξοπϱστυφχ.

GAu: uiam] uiam suam ϑμ.

7

a		from A*E*^{2}, from C, fram BDFK, fram HI, fram ł of G*, of J
summo	|	ðæm hean AB, þam hean CG*, hean DF, heon H, þam hean J, heannysse fram þære healican I*, heahnesse K, heofones E^{2}

caelo	I	heofene A, heofone *BDFH,* hefune *C,* heofeñ *G**, heofonum J, heofonan I, heofenes *K,* hihþo *E^2* (*L*)
egressio		utgong AC, utgang BDE^2*FGHJ, utgan K, forðgang ł utfær I*
eius		his ABDE^2*FGHI*J*K*, hys C
et		⁊ ABCDE^2**FGHJK,* ⁊ is *I*
occursus		eftyrn A, eftryne B, æfterryne C, edryne *K,* edryne ł gencyris D, edryne ł gencyr E^2*, edryne l gecnirr H*, geancyr F, his ongengang ł edryne ł gecnyr G*, genryne I, ongængan J (*L*)
eius		his ABCE^{2}FGHIJ*K*
usque		oð ABCFGI, oþ DJK, oððe E^2*H
ad	I	to DE^{2}FGHK, hire I*
summum		hehnisse A, hiehnysse C, heahnesse DE^2*FHK, heanesse BG, heannesse J, heannysse ł I
eius	I	his ABE^2*FGHJ*K,* hys C
nec	I	ne ABCFIJ, n(e) G*, na K, nis DE^2*H
est	I	is ABFGJ*K,* ys C, nis I
qui		se ðe ABCE^2*G, se þe DFHIJ, þa þe K
se		hine A*B*CDE^2*FGHIJ
abscondat		ahyde ABC, behyde DE^2*G*HIJ, behydde *F,* behyt K
a		from A, from BC, fram DFHJ, fram E^2*GI, fra K
calore		haeto A, hæto BC, hætan DGHK, hetan E^2*, hæton F, hæten I, hetum J
eius		his AB*D**E^2*FGHIJK, hys C

ED: á (E)] a *Harsley.* heannysse fram þære healican (I)] heannysse ł fram þære healican *Lindelöf.* cęlo (E)] caelo *Harsley.* edryne l gecnirr (H)] edryne *uel* gecnirr *Campbell.* eus (D)] eius *Roeder.* eius (K) (*3rd*)] eíus *Sisam.*

OE: fram ł of (G)] ł of *added in diff.* (?) *hand above* fram. þam hean (G)] þam *added in diff.* (?) *hand above preceding* fram. heannysse fram þære healican (I)] fram þære healican *written in left margin; Lindelöf records* ł *before* fram, *but none is visible* (*although possibly lost due to tight binding*). heofeñ (G)] *so MS, see v. 9* drihtñ. utgang (E^2)] *on eras.* forðgang ł utfær (I)] ł utfær *written in right margin.* his (E^2) (*1st*)] *written in right margin.* his (I) (*1st*)] s. est : is *written in right margin, with single subscript* (*syntactical*) *dot below* est. ⁊ (E^2)] *on eras.* edryne ł gencyr (E^2)] *on eras.* edryne l gecnirr (H)] *cross-stroke of* ł *wanting.* his ongengang ł edryne ł gecnyr (G)] his ongengang ł *added in diff.* (?) *hand above* edryne ł. oððe (E^2)] *on eras.* hire (I)] *stands above* usque, *followed by* heannysse *and, in next line,* ł *above* eius, *but without gloss.* heahnesse (E^2)] *on eras.* his (E^2) (*3rd*)] *on eras.* n(e) (G)] *eye of* e *lost.* nis (E^2)] *on eras.* se ðe (E^2)] *on eras.* hine (E^2)] *on eras.* behyde (E^2)] *on eras.* behyde (G)] *letter eras. after* y. fram (E^2)] *on eras.* hetan (E^2)] *on* *eras.* eus (D)] ac allum bodað se gast *written after word and extending into right margin.* his (E^2) (*4th*)] *on eras.*

LTg: a (*1st*)] á E. caelo] cælo BK; celo D; cęlo CEFHL, G: *orig.* cęli: i *altered to* o. egressio] ęgressio G. eius (*1st*)] eíus K. et] Et FGHJK, I: s. est *written in left margin.* occursus] K: ursus *on eras.*, L: *letter eras. after* r. eius (*2nd*)] eíus K. est] ést K. se] sé B. abscondat] F: *orig.* abscondit: i *altered to* a. eius (*4th*)] eus D.

LTu: caelo] cęlo ζιξοςφ; cælo ϑ; celo στ*τ. egressio] egresio ϑ. aegressio π. et] Et δεζϑιλμξοπϱστυφχψ. a (*2nd*)] A β, *but not signaling verse division.*

8

Lex	| ęew A, ęe D, æ B*G*I*J, ǽ CF, æe H, Drihtnes E^2* (*K*)
domini	| dryhtnes BD, drihtnys C, drihtnes FHI*, dryht̄ A, driht̄ *G,* driȟ *J,* ę́e E^2 (*K*)
inreprehensibilis*	untelwyrðe *A**, untælwyrðe B*C,* untallic D, antalic F, ungripendlic is *E^2**, unforgripendlicu G, unawemmed I, ungewæmmedlicu J (*L*)
conuertens	gecerrende AB, gecyrrende CGHI, gecyrrende D, gecyrende F, gecirrende J, to gecierrenne *E^2* (*K*)
animas	sawle AFJ, sawla BCHI*, saula DH, saule E^2*, sauwlæ G (*K*)
testimonium	cyðnis A, cyðnes BH, cyþnes D, cyðnysse C, cyþnesse J, gecyþnys F, gecyðnesse G, gecyðnysse I, cyþnes ł witnesse E^2* (*K*)
domini	dryhtnes B, drihtnys CI, drihtnes E^2*, dryht̄ A, driȟt F, godes *GJ* (*K*)
fidele	getreowu *A*B, getreow H, getrywe C, getrywe *I*, getriwe J, getreowful D, getrewful E^2*, getréowfull F, getreowfull G, getrywful K
sapientiam	snyttro BC, wisdom DE^2*H, wisdo(m) K*, wisdom ł snytro F*G**, snitro ł wisdon J, snoternysse ł wisdom I, [ ]ro *A**
praestans	gearwiende A*FGH,* gearwende *B,* gearwiynde *C,* gearuwigende *D,* geærwiende *E^2**, gearwigende *J,* lænende ł tyðiende I*, [ ]gende *K** (*L*)
paruulis	cilde AC, lytlingum BD, lytlingum FH, litlingum ł childvm *E^2**, lytlingum ł eadmodum I, þam litlingum G*, lytlingas K, þam litlan J

ED: [ ]ex (G)] Lex *Rosier.* irreprehensibilis (C)] i[n]reprehensibilis *Wildhagen.* wisdo(m) (K)] wisdom *Sisam.*

OE: æ (I)] s. ÷ : is *written in left margin.* Drihtnes (E^2)] *letter eras. after* t. drihtnes (I)] e *on eras.* untelwyrðe] A: *scribe began to write* untelwr-, *but altered* r *to* y.

ungripendlic (E^{2})] lic *on eras.* sawla (I)] s. est : is *written in left margin, with single (syntactical) subscript dot below* est. saule (E^{2})] *on eras.* cyþnes ł witnesse (E^{2})] *on eras.* drihtnes (E^{2})] *on eras.* getrewful (E^{2})] *on eras.* wisdom (E^{2})] *on eras.*, his *eras. before word.* wisdo(m) (K)] *final letter fragmentary.* wisdom ł snytro (G)] ł snytro *added in diff.* (?) *hand above* wisdom. [ ]ro (A)] *added in left margin, initial letters cropped.* geærwiende (E^{2})] de *on eras.* lænende ł tyðiende (I)] *orig.* lænende ł tiðiende: *1st* i *altered to* y. [ ]gende (K)] *minim visible before* g, *on loss see notes to K at Ps 17.49.* litlingum ł childvm (E^{2})] *on eras.* þam litlingum (G)] þam *added in diff.* (?) *hand.*

LTg: Lex] [ ]ex G: *initial* L *lost;* L[ ] K: *lower portion of* L *visible only: see notes to Ps 17.49.* domini (*1st*)] *on eras.* G; *lost* K: *see notes to Ps 17.49;* dei J: *eras. after word: cf. Weber MSS* γδ moz. inreprehensibilis] E: ilis *on eras. by corr. in dark ink,* L: inmaculata *written above word by corr.: see GAg;* inrepraehensibilis A; irreprehensibilis C: *eras. below shoulder of 1st* r. conuertens] E: con *written by corr. in right margin;* [ ]rtens K: *see notes to Ps 17.49.* animas] an[ ] K: *see notes to Ps 17.49.* testimonium] *lost* K: *see notes to Ps 17.49.* domini (*2nd*)] K: *ascender of* d *lost.* fidele] A: *eras.* (*ca 8 letters*) *after word,* I: *eras. after word* (*of punct.?*). sapientiam] [ ]ientiam A: *added by corr. in left margin of fol. 24v, initial letters cropped: cf.* fidele *above for eras. of last word on fol. 24r;* sapienti[ ] G. praestans] prestans BCDEFGHJKL. paruulis] parvvlis E.

LTu: inreprehensibilis] inrepraehensibilis β; inreprẹhensibilis ν; irreprehensibilis τ*. domini (*2nd*)] *om.* σ. praestans] prẹstans ελνξφ; prestans ζιςτ*τ; p̄stans ϑσχ; præstans μ.

GAg: inreprehensibilis] inmaculata FJ, L: *see LTg;* immaculata GI, H: *orig.* inmaculata: *middle leg added to* n *to form* m; *lost* K: *see notes to Ps 17.49.*

GAu: inreprehensibilis] inmaculata δζϑμχψ; immaculata ειλξπυφ, οϱ: i *interl.;* īmaculata στ.

9

Iustitiae	I	rehtwisnisse A, ryhtwisnessa *BD*, rihtwisnysse *C*, rihtwisnyssa *FI*, rihtwisnessa *H*, rihtwisnesse *J*, (r)iht(w)i(s)ne(ss)e *G**, rihwisnẹs *K*, Drihtnes *E^{2}* (*L*)
domini	I	dryhtnes B̄D, drihtnys C, drihtnes FI*, drihtenes K, drihtñ G*, dryht̄ *A*, driħ J, ryhtwisnesse E^{2}*
rectae		rehtlice *A*, ryhtlice *B*, rihtlice *C*, ryhta *DE^{2}**, rihta *HJ*, rihte *FGIK* (*L*)
laetificantes		blissiende A*BK*, blissiynde *C*, blissigende *J*, gẹblisgende *D*, geblissigende *G*, geblissigendra *F*, geblissiende *E^{2}*HI* (*L*)
corda		heortan ABCDFGHJK, heortæn E^{2}, heortan is *I*

praeceptum — bibod A, bebod BCDE^2*FGHIJK (*L*)
domini — dryhtnes B, drihtnys C, drihtnes E^2*F, dryht̄ A, driħ GJ
lucidum — leht AB, leoht CJ, beorht DFH, beorct K, beorht ł leoht G*, beorht ł scinendlic ł leoht I, bryht E^2*
inluminans — inlihtende A, onlihtende BF*IJ*, onlihtynde *C*, onlyhtende D*E*^{2}**GK*, lyhtende *H*
oculos — egan A*K, eagan BCDFGHI, eægæn E^2, eagon J

ED: Iustitiæ (CE)] Iustitiae *Wildhagen, Harsley.* [ ]ustitię (G)] *Iusti*tię *Rosier.* domini rectæ lætificantes corda præceptum : dryhtnes ryhtlice blissiende heortan bebod (B)] *om. Brenner.* lętificantes (E)] laetificantes *Harsley.* heortan (G)] heorta[ ] *Rosier.* illuminans (C)] i[n]luminans *Wildhagen.* beorht ł leoht (G)] beorht ł leohton *Rosier.* onlyhtende (G)] lyhtende *Rosier.*

OE: (r)iht(w)i(s)ne(ss)e (G)] r *fragmentary, descenders of* w *and 1st* s *lost, descenders of* ss *partly lost.* drihtnes (I)] e *on eras.*, sunt : synt *written in left margin.* drihtñ (G)] *so MS: see v. 7* heofeñ. ryhtwisnesse (E^2)] *on eras.* ryhta (E^2)] *on eras.;* to *incompletely eras. after word: see note to* geblissiende. geblissiende (E^2)] de *on eras.*, ryht[ ]a *eras. after word.* bebod (E^2)] *on eras.* drihtnes (E^2)] *eras. after word extending to end of line.* beorht ł leoht (G)] ł leoht *added in diff.* (?) *hand.* bryht (E^2)] *on eras.* onlyhtende (E^2)] *on eras.* egan (A)] *orig.* egun: u *altered to* a.

LTg: Iustitiae] Iustitiæ BCE; Iustitie JK; Iustitię DFHL; [ ]ustitię G: *initial* I *lost.* domini (*1st*)] A: i *on eras.* rectae] rectæ B; recte DEFGJ; rectę CHKL, A: *cauda added by corr.* laetificantes] lætificantes B; letificantes CDHJKL; lętificantes EFG. corda (I)] s. e<u>st</u> *written in left margin, with single (syntactical) subscript dot below* e<u>st</u>. praeceptum] præceptum B; pręceptum CGK; preceptum DEFHJL. inluminans] E: *eras. above* (inlumi/)nans; illuminans I, C: *eras. before 1st* i, *1st* l *altered from another letter*, G: *1st* l *altered from another letter,* H: *1st* l *on eras.*, J: *orig.* illuminas: s *altered to form left leg of 2nd* n, *right leg of* n *and final* s *added in light brown ink,* K: *orig.* inluminans: *right leg of 1st* n *eras., left leg altered to* l *by corr.*

LTu: Iustitiae] Iustitię εζινξς; Iustitiæ ϑμ; Iusticię φ, ϱ: *orig.* Iustitię: *2nd* t *deleted,* c *interl.;* Iustitie συ; Iusticie τ*τ. rectae] rectę δεμνξϱφ; rectæ ϑχ; recte ζιλοπσςτ*τυ. laetificantes] lętificantes ειλφ; lætificantes ϑ; letificantes νξσςτ*τυ. praeceptum] pręceptum βλνξφ; p̄ceptum εϱσχ; preceptum ζϑιπςτ*τ. inluminans] illuminans εζϑιλξοπϱστ*τυφχ.

10

Timor | ege ABCDFGHIJK, Drihtnes E^2*
domini | dryhtnes B, drihtnes F, drihtnys CI*, drihtenes K*, dryht̄ A, driħt J, driħ GH, hælgæ E^2

sanctus	ǀ	halig A*BCDFGHIJ, hali K, ęge E^{2}
permanet*		ðorhwunað A, ðurhwunað B*D, þurhwunað CF, þurhwunæþ E^{2}, þurhwunaþ J*, þuhwvnaþ K, þurhwuniende GHI
in		in A, on BCFGHIJK
saeculum		weoruld A, weorold *B,* woruld *C,* worulda *FG,* worulde *H,* worlda *I**, worolda *K,* world *J,* aworuld *D,* æworoldæ *E^{2}* (*L*)
saeculi		weorulde A, weorolde *B,* worulde *CF,* worł *E^{2},* woruld *GH,* world *IJ,* worold *K* (*DL*)
iudicia	ǀ	domas ABCDGHIJK, dom F, godes E^{2}
dei*	ǀ	godes AB, godys C, drihtnes FI*J, driħ G, domas *E^{2}*
uera		soðe ABCDGI, soþe E^{2}*FJK, foðe H
iustificata		gerehtwisade A*, geryhtwisode B, gerihtwisude CH*, geryhtwisude D, gerihtwisede *E^{2}**, gerihtwísode F, gerihtwisode I, gerihtwisud K, gerihtwisnesse J, [ ]erih[ ] G
in		in A, on BCDE^{2}FGHIJK
semetipsa		him seolfum A, him selfum B, him sylfum G*, him sylfum J, hyre sylfre CI, hy selfe D, hy sylfe *E^{2}**, hý sylfe F, hy selue H, hi sylfe K

ED: drıħt (J)] drih*tnes Oess.* scłm (EIJK)] seculum *Oess, Harsley;* saeculum *Lindelöf;* sæculum *Sisam.* scłi (FIJK)] seculi *Kimmens, Oess;* saeculi *Lindelöf;* sæculi *Sisam.* worł (E)] worl*de Harsley.* [ ]erih[ ] (G)] [ ]ih[ ] *Rosier.* semetipsa (B)] semet ipsa *Brenner.*

OE: Drihtnes (E^{2})] *eras. after word.* drihtnys (I)] ÷ : is *written in left margin.* drihtenes (K)] *1st* e *malformed,* n *shows stroke ascending from left leg.* halig] A: h *formed from* s (?). ðurhwunað (B)] *initial* ð *obscured by stain.* þurhwunaþ (J)] *2nd* u *altered from* a. worlda (I)] *orig.* worlde: e *altered to* a. drihtnes (I)] s. sunt : synt *written in left margin.* soþe (E^{2})] *eras. before word.* gerehtwisade (A)] *scribe began to write* gerehtwa-, *but altered* a *to* i. gerihtwisude (H)] *2nd* i *malformed.* gerihtwisede (E^{2})] riht *on eras.* him sylfum (G)] u *altered from another letter.* hy sylfę (E^{2})] ę *on eras., eras. after word.*

LTg: saeculum] sæculum B; seculum CGHL; sęculum F; scłm DEIJK. saeculi] sæculi B; seculi CDEGHL; scłi FIJK. dei] domini E: ł dei *written in right margin by corr.: see GAg.* iustificata] E: *eras. above* (iustifi/)cata. semet ipsa] E: *top of* a *retouched due to small eras. above.*

LTu: Timor] [ ]imor τ*: *initial letter wanting.* permanet] βϱ: *orig.* permanens: ns *deleted,* t *added interl.: cf. Weber MSS* MSKT*αβγδζη mozᶜ; permanei ς: *traces of* *eras. letters visible after* i (*minim is perhaps residue of* n *partially eras.*). saeculum] sęculum ιος; seculum πτ; sclm εζθλμξϱστ*υφχ. saeculi] sęculi ινος; seculi πτ*τ; scłi εζθλμξϱσυφχ. dei] domini τ*: ł dei *added interl.: see GAu.* in (*2nd*)] *interl.* π.

GAg: permanet] permanens FHIJ, G: *small eras. after 2nd* n, K: *eras. after word, macron above 2nd* e *and* s *added by corr.* dei] domini FGHIJK, E: *see LTg.*

GAu: permanet] permanens δθμοπϱυχψ. dei] domini δεζιλξοπϱστυφχ, τ*: *see LTu.*

11

<table>
<tr><td>Desiderabilia</td><td></td><td>wilsum ABC, þa wilsuman J, þa winsuman F*, gegyrnendlicȩ D, Gegyrnendlice̲ E^2*, gegyrnendlice H, gegyrendlic K, gegyrnendlice ł þa wilsuman *G**, gewilniendlice I* (*L*)</td></tr>
<tr><td>super</td><td></td><td>ofer ABE^{2}FGHJK, ofyr C, ofor I</td></tr>
<tr><td>aurum</td><td></td><td>gold ABCDE^{2}FGHIJK</td></tr>
<tr><td>et</td><td></td><td>⁊ ABCE^{2}FGHIJK</td></tr>
<tr><td>lapidem</td><td>|</td><td>stan ABCDGHJ, stán F, stane I, stanas K, swiðe E^2*</td></tr>
<tr><td>pretiosum</td><td></td><td>deorwyrðne *A*BDH, diorwiorðne E^2*, deorwurþne FJ, deorwyrðe C, dyrwyrþe *K,* deorwurðum G, deorwyrðum *I*</td></tr>
<tr><td>multum</td><td>|</td><td>swiðe ABCD, swyðe G, swyþe HK, swíþe J, swyþne F, þearle ł swiðlicor I, stæn E^2*</td></tr>
<tr><td>et</td><td></td><td>⁊ ABCDE^{2}FGHIJK</td></tr>
<tr><td>dulciora</td><td></td><td>swoetran A, swetran BDGJ, swetræn E^2, swettran FH, swetra C*K,* swetra ł weorodran I</td></tr>
<tr><td>super</td><td></td><td>ofer ABDE^{2}FGHIJK, ofyr C</td></tr>
<tr><td>mel</td><td></td><td>hunig ABCDE^2*HIJ, húnig F, hyni K, hu[ ]ig G*</td></tr>
<tr><td>et</td><td></td><td>⁊ ABCDE^{2}FHIJK</td></tr>
<tr><td>fauum</td><td></td><td>biobread A, beobread BCDHJ, beobreade I, beobred K, béonbreade F, biebreæd ł hunicamb E$^{2/x}$*, [ ]ead G*</td></tr>
</table>

ED: gegyrnendlice ł þa wilsuman (G)] *Berghaus takes* ł þa wilsuman *as added in contemporary hand.* hu[ ]ig (G)] hunig *Rosier.* biebreæd ł hunicamb (E)] biebreæd ł hvnicamb *Harsley.* [ ]ead (G)] ⁊ beobread *Rosier.*

OE: þa winsuman (F)] winsuman *partly obscured by eras.* Gegyrnendlice̲ (E^2)] gyrnendlic̄ *on eras.* gegyrnendlice ł þa wilsuman (G)] ł þa wilsuman *written above* gegyrnendlice. gewilniendlice (I)] sunt : hi synt *written in left margin, with single (syntactical) subscript dot below* sunt. swiðe (E^2)] *on eras.,* ⁊ *eras. after word (next line).* diorwiorðne (E^2)] ne *on eras.* stæn (E^2)] *eras. after word (1 or 2 letters), followed by eras. to end of line.* hunig (E^2)] *2 letters* (es?) *eras. after word.* hu[ ]ig (G)] *letter after* u *not visible,* ig *obscured by stain.* [ ]ead (G)] *Rosier records* ⁊

beobread *as gloss on* et fauum: *MS is stained here, and gloss as Rosier records it is not visible;* ead *is questionable.* biebreæd ł hunicamb (E$^{2/x}$)] ł hunicamb *on eras. by corr.,* e *eras. after word.*

LTg: Desiderabilia] L: *all except* D *traced over in darker ink, rest of verse (extending beyond writing grid) in same dark ink by main hand;* [ ]esiderabilia G. pretiosum] praetiosum AI; prætiosum K. dulciora] dultiora K.

LTu: pretiosum] prętiosum βεμνϱυ; praetiosum δο; preciosum ιτ*τφψ.

12

Nam*	weotudlice A, witodlice B*D*E^{x}*, witvdlice C, ㇠ witodlice K, witendlice F, ㇠ soðlice I, ㇠ soþlice J (*L*)
et*	㇠ ABCDE^{x}*
seruus	ðeow A*D*E^{x}*F, þeow BCH, þeowa GJK, ðeowa I
tuus	ðin ABDE^{x}*F, þin CGHIJK
custodiet*	haldeð A, healdeð B, healdyð *C,* gehealdeþ J, gehylt *D*E^{x}*FH, gehyld G, gehealt I, hælt K
ea	ða AB, þa CIK, þe J, þ[ ] G, hy *D*E^{x}*H, híg F
in	in A, on BCDE^{x}*FGHIK, mid J
custodiendo*	gehælde AB, gehylde C, gehealdene J, gehealdnysse FI, geheordnisse DH, geheordnesse ł to bewitena E^{2}, heordnesse K, ge(h)[ ] G* (*L*)
illa*	dere A, þære BC, þara I, ða DE^{2}F, þa J, þa ł hy G*, hi<u>m</u> K* (*L*)
retributio	edlean ABCDHJK, edleæn E^{2}*, edléan F, eadlean G, edleanunga I
multa	micel ABDE^{2}HI*, micyl C, mycel K, micclan GJ, manige F

ED: [ ](m) (G)] *Etenim Rosier.* witvdlice (C)] witudlice *Wildhagen.* ge(h)[ ] (G)] geh[ ] *Rosier.*

OE: witodlice (E^{x})] *on eras. by corr.* ㇠ (E^{x})] *on eras. by corr.* ðeow (E^{x})] *on eras. by corr.* ðin (E^{x})] *on eras. by corr.* gehylt (E^{x})] *on eras. by corr.* hy (E^{x})] *on eras. by corr.* on (E^{x})] *on eras. by corr.* ge(h)[ ] (G)] *ascender of* h *lost.* þa ł hy (G)] *Berghaus (p. 16) takes* þa ł *as added in contemporary hand.* edleæn (E^{2})] *eras. after word.* micel (I)] s. e<u>st</u> : is *written in left margin, with single (syntactical) subscript dot below* e<u>st</u>.

LTg: Nam] E: a *retraced in darker ink,* L: *crossed through and* Etenim *written above by corr.: see GAg;* Nám D. seruus] E: us *retraced in darker ink.* tuus] E: tu *retraced in darker ink,* us *on eras. by corr.* custodiet] E: *retraced in darker ink;* custodit C: *cf. Weber MSS* γδη moz^{x} med, *see GAg.* ea] E: *on eras. by corr.* custodiendo] L: *final* o *crossed through,* is *written above by corr.: see GAg.* illa] L: a *crossed through,* is *written above by corr.: see GAg.*

LTu: custodiet] β: e *added interl.;* custodit ν: *see Weber MSS* KTPQUVXγδη moz^{x} med. custodiendo] custo ς.

GAg: Nam et] Etenim FHIJK, L: *see LTg;* [ ](m) G: *2 legs of* m *visible.* custodiet] custodit FGHIJK, C: *see LTg.* custodiendo illo] custodiendis illis FGHIJK, L: *see LTg.*

GAu: Nam et] Etenim δεζϑιλμξοπϱστυφχψ. custodiet] custodit δεζϑιλμξοπϱστφχψ, ν: *see LTu.* custodiendo illa] custodiendis illis δεζϑιλμοπϱστυφχψ; cvstodiendis illis ξ.

13

Delicta	I	scylde A, scylda B, scilda J, scyld C, scyldas DGHK, gyltas F, gyltas ł synna I, hwylc E^{2}
quis	I	hwelc ABH, hwylc CDF, hwilc GJ, la hwylc I, hwa K, ongitt E^{2}*
intellegit	I	ongeteð A, ongiteð B, ongytyð C, ongyteð F*G*, ongiteþ J, ongytt *D*, ongyt *HI**, ynder *K*, gyltes ł scyldes *E^{2}**
ab		from ACE^{2}, from B, fram DFHJK, fram GI
occultis	I	degelnissum A, deagolnessem B, digolnyssum *I*, digolnessum J, digylnisse C, deglum D, diglum FGH, drihlum K, minum E^{2}
meis	I	minum AFGK, minum BDHIJ, minre C, dieglum E^{2}
munda		geclasna A, geclænsa BCJ, geclensæ E^{2}, geclensa I, (ge)clænsa G*, clensa D, clænsa FHK
me		me ABCE^{2}FGHIJK
domine*		dryhten BE^{2}, dryht̄ A, driħt C, driħ *HJ* (*FKL*)

ED: ocultis (I)] occultis *Lindelöf.*

OE: ongitt (E^{2})] *1st* t *on eras., eras. after word.* ongyt (I)] *orig.* ongit: i *altered to* y. gyltes ł scyldes (E^{2})] te *on eras.,* ł scyldes *added by main hand.* (ge)clænsa (G)] ge *not clearly visible.*

LTg: intellegit] intelligit DEGK, H: *2nd* i *on eras.* occultis] ocultis I. domine] FK: *added interl. by corr. in light brown ink,* H: *added by corr.,* L: *underlined to signal deletion: see GAg.*

LTu: intellegit] intelligit εζλξιπτ*τφχ, ο: *orig.* intellegit: *2nd* i *written over 2nd* e, ϱσ: *orig.* intellegit: *2nd* e *deleted,* i *interl.* occultis] ο: *1st* c *interl.;* ocultis ϑνσ.

GAg: domine] *om.* GI, L: *see LTg.*

GAu: domine] *om.* δεζϑλμξοπϱστυφψ, ι: *crossed through.*

14

et ⁊ ABCE^{2}*FGHIJK
ab from AE^{2}*, from BC, fram DHJK, fram FGI
alienis ðæm fremðum A, þam fremdum C, fremdum BDE^{2}*, fremdum G, fremdum HK, fremdum J, ælfremdum F, ælðeodigum I
parce spreara A, spara BCG, spara þu J, ara DHK, ára E^{2}F, ara ł gemildsa I
seruo | ðiowe A, þeowe BCDHJ, ðeowe G, þeowum F, þeowen I, þeowan K, þinum E^{2}*
tuo | ðinum AF, þinum BGH, þinum CIJ, ðinum D, þinne K, þeowe E^{2}

Si gif ABDGHIJK, Gif E^{2}, gef C, gyf F
mei min ADE^{2}*FGHJK, minc BCI
non | ne ABCIJ, na K, hy ne DE^{2}, hi ne FGH
fuerint | bioð A, beoð BDGHI, beoþ *C*FJK, bioþ E^{2}
dominati waldende AB, wealdynde C, wyldende I*, wyldde DF, wylde H, gewylde K, weældænd E^{2}, onwaldende *G**J
tunc ðonne A, þonne BGH, þonne CDE^{2}J, ðonne F, þænne IK
inmaculatus | unwemme AB*C*, ungewemmed DK, ungewæmmed F, on [ ]gewemmed *H**, on ungewemmc ł unbesmiten G*, unbesmiten J, unawemmed I, ic bio E^{2}
ero | ic biom A, ic beom DH, ic beo BCFGIJK, ungewemmed E^{2}
et ⁊ ABCDE^{2}*FGHIJK
emundabor ic biom geclasnad A, ic beo geclæsnod B, ic beo geclænsod C*G*JK, ic beom clænsod DH, ic beo geclænsod ł afeormod I, ic eom geclænsod F, ic beo clensod E^{2}*
a from AE^{2}, from BC, fram DIK, fram FGHJ
delicto scylde A*BCDFGHK, scildum J, scylde ł gyltum E^{2}*, gylte I*
maximo ðere mæstan A, þære mæstan BC, ðam mæstan D, ðam mestan E^{2}*, þam mæstan FG, þam mæstan HJ, þam mæstan ł miclan I, myclum K

ED: spara (G)] swaswa *Rosier.* min (H)] mine *Campbell.* immaculatus (C)] i[n]maculatus *Wildhagen.* i[ ]aculatus (H)] i(mm)aculatus *Campbell.* on [ ]gewemmed (H)] ongewemmed *Campbell.*

OE: ⁊ (E^{2}) (*1st*)] *on eras.* from (E^{2}) (*1st*)] *eras. after word,* þ *visible.* fremdum (E^{2})] em *on eras.* þinum (E^{2})] *eras. after word.* min (E^{2})] *orig.* mine: e *eras.* wyldende (I)] *eras.* (*of gloss*) *follows;* si non dominari fuerint mei : gyf hi ne gewyldaþ min *written in bottom margin.* onwaldende (G)] ł ta *added in later hand after gloss: see LTg note to* dominati. on [ ]gewemmed (H)] *2 letters lost after* n *due to hole in leaf, 2nd letter possibly* n. on ungewemme ł unbesmiten (G)] ł unbesmiten *added in diff.* (?) *hand above* ungewemme. ⁊ (E^2) (*2nd*)] *on eras.* ic beo clensod (E^2)] ic beo *on eras.* scylde (A)] s *written over* h. scylde ł gyltum (E^2)] scylde *on eras.* gylte (I)] y *altered from* i (?). ðam mestan (E^2)] *on eras., macron remains above 2nd* a (mestān).

LTg: fuerint] fuérint C. dominati] G: ł ta *added interl. after gloss in later hand* (= dominata). inmaculatus] immaculatus C: *orig.* inmaculatus: i *linked with* n *to form* m, i *added before orig.* i *by corr.;* i[ ]aculatus H: *letters lost due to hole in leaf, although fragments are visible.* emundabor] ęmundabor G.

LTu: fuerint] fuerit ϑ. dominati] ε: a *interl.* above *2nd* i, τ: ł ta *added interl.* inmaculatus] immaculatus ελξoπτ*υφ, ϱ: i *interl.;* īmaculatus ϑσ.

15

Et		⁊ ABCDE^{2}FGHIJK
erunt		bioð A, beoð BCDFGHI, beoþ JK, bioþ E^2
ut		ðæt A, þæt BGJ, þæt CK, þætte DH, þætte FI, þette E^2
conplaceant		hie gelicien A, hie gelicigen B, hi gelicigyn *C,* gelician *I*,* geliciað D*H,* gelíciaþ F, geliciaþ *K,* gelicieð *E^2*,* ægeliciað ł efnlicien *G*,* hig efenliciant *J*
eloquia		gespreocu A, gespræcu C, gesprecu *G*J, gespreco B, spreca D, sprecæ E^2*, spræca F*H*I, spæce K
oris	|	mudes A, muðes BFGHIJ, muðys C, muþes DK, mines E^2
mei	|	mines ABDFGHIJK, minys C, muþes E^2
et		⁊ ABCE^{2}FGHIJK
meditatio		smeang A, smeaung BCI, smægung K, smeagunge J, gemynd DH, gemínd F, smeæwung ł gemind E^2, gemynd ł smeaung G*
cordis	|	heortan ABCDFGHIJK, minre E^2
mei	|	minre ABCDFG*HIJK, heortæn E^2
in		in A, on BCDE^{2}FGHIJK
conspectu	|	gesihðe ABCH, gesyhðe DG, gesyhþe FK, gesihþe J, gesihðe ł beforan I, þinre E^2
tuo	|	ðinre A, þinre BCDFGHIJK, gesihþe E^2*
semper		aa *A,* simle B, symle CDIJ, simle E^2, sýmle F, symble H, symble ł æfre G, æfre K
Domine		dryhten B, Drihten E^2, dryht̄ A, driht̃ CF, driht̄ I, drih̃ GJ, hlafurd K
adiutor		fultum ABCI, gefylstend D*, gefelstend E^2*, gefultuma F,

	gefylstent H, gefylstent ł gefultumigend G*, gefultumiend J, fylst K
meus	min ABCDE^{2}FGHI*JK
et	| ⁊ ABCE^{2}FGHJK
redemptor	| alesend AB, alysynd C, alysend DE^{2}GHIJ, alýsend F, alynsend *K*
meus	| min ABCDE^{2}FGHJ, ⁊ min I (*K*)

ED: complaceant (C)] co[n]placeant *Wildhagen.*

OE: gelician (I)] *orig.* gelicien: *2nd* e *altered to* a. gelicieð (E^2)] *eras. before word,* ð *on eras.* ægeliciað ł efnlicien (G)] ł efnlicien *added in diff.* (?) *hand.* sprecæ (E^2)] *orig.* gesprecæ: ge *eras.* gemynd ł smeaung (G)] ł smeaung *added in diff.* (?) *hand.* minre (G)] r *interl.* gesihþe (E^2)] *small eras. after word.* gefylstend (D)] s *interl.* gefelstend (E^2)] *eras. after 1st* e. gefylstent ł gefultumigend (G)] ł gefultumigend *added in diff.* (?) *hand above* gefylstent. min (I) (*1st*)] ÷ : is *written in left margin.*

LTg: conplaceant] complaceant EIK, CG: *orig.* conplaceant: *right leg added to 1st* n *to form* m, H: *orig.* conplaceant: *middle leg added to 1st* n *to form* m, J: orig. conplaceant: *right leg added to 1st* n *to form* m, *with macron above* o (= commplaceant). eloquia] ęloquia GH. semper] A: mper *written by corr.,* m *on eras.* redemptor] redempto[ ] K: *letter lost due to excision of initial on fol. 26v.* meus] K: *lost due to excision of initial on fol. 26v.*

LTu: erunt] erant βζ. conplaceant] complaceant εζιξπϱτ*τ; cōplaceant λοσυφχψ. eloquia] ęloquia ε. redemptor] redemtor ψ.

PSALM 19

2

Exaudiat	gehere A*I, gehiere *B,* gehyre *CDFK,* Gehére *E*^{2}*,* gehir J, gehyrde H, gehyrde ł gehyre *G** (*L*)
te	ðe AB*F*GI, þe *C*E^{2}JK
dominus	dryhten B, drihten E^{2}G, dryht̄ A, driȟt *C*F, driht̄ I, driȟ J
in	in A, on BCDE^{2}FGHIJK
die	dego AE^2, dæge BCDFGHIJ, dæg K
tribulationis	geswinces ABGHJ*K,* geswinces D, þinre geswencnesse E^2, geswencednysse I, gedrefednysse CF
protegat	gescilde ABC*, gescylde DE^{2}FHIK, gescylde ł forþecce G*, forþecce J
te	ðe AB, þe CE^{2}FGHIJK
nomen	noma ABD, nama CI, naman FGHJ, nomæ E^2*, nam[ ] *K**

dei | godes ABDFGHIJ, godys C, iæcobes E^{2} (*K*)
iacob | iacefes A, iacobes BDFGHIJ, iacobys C, godes E^{2} (*K*)

ED: t(r)[ ]lationis (K)] tr[ibu]lationis *Sisam.*

OE: gehere (A)] *written in left margin to left of decorated initial.* gehyrde ł gehyre (G)] ł gehyre *added in diff.* (?) *hand.* gescilde (C)] i *interl.* gescylde ł forþecce (G)] ł forþecce *added in diff.* (?) *hand.* nomæ (E^{2})] o *on eras.* nam[ ] (K)] *partly lost due to excision of initial on fol. 26v.*

LTg: Exaudiat] F: t *on eras.;* EXaudiat BDKL; EXAUDIAT CE; [ ]xaudiat G: *initial* E *lost.* te (*1st*)] F: t *on eras.;* TE C. dominus] DN̄S C. tribulationis] t(r)[ ]lationis K: *partly lost due to excision of initial on fol. 26v.* nomen] no[ ] K: *partly lost due to excision of initial on fol. 26v.* dei] K: *lost due to excision of initial on fol. 26v.* iacob] K: *lost due to excision of initial on fol. 26v.*

LTu: Exaudiat] EXAudiat β; EXAUDIAT ιλμνϱτ*τφψ; EXAVdiat ς. te (*1st*)] TE λμνϱψ. dominus] DN̄S λμνϱψ. in] IN λϱ. die] DIE λϱ. tribulationis] TRIBUlationis λ; TRIbulationis ϱ.

3

Mittat sende AC, sænde J, onsende B, he asende DFGH, he ASende E^{2}*, asende he I, he sende K
tibi ðe ABF, þe CE^{2}GIJK
auxilium fultum ABCE^{2}*GHIJ, fultum DF*K*
de of ABCDE^{2}*FGHIJ (*K*)
sancto halgum ABFG, halgum DHJ, hælgum E^{2}*, halgum ł of halignesse I*, halgan C
et ⁊ ABCE^{2}FGHIJK
de of ABCDE^{2}FGHIJK
sion sion AJ, sione B, syon C, syon ł heahnesse E^{2}*, heahnesse D, heahnese K, heahnysse F, heanesse H, heanysse I, heannessum ł seon *G**
tueatur gescilde *A*BJ, gescylde *C*, he gescylde FI*, he behealde *D*E^{2}*HK, he behealde ł gescylde G*
te ðe *A*BF, þe *C*E^{2}GHIJ (*K*)

ED: sion (K)] Sion *Sisam.* þe (G) (*2nd*)] *Berghaus takes this as added in contemporary hand.*

OE: he ASende (E^{2})] he *added in left margin,* AS *larger than surrounding letters.* fultum (E^{2})] *eras. after word.* of (E^{2}) (*1st*)] *eras. before word.* hælgum (E^{2})] um *on eras.* halgum ł of halignesse (I)] ł of halignesse *written in right margin.* syon ł heahnesse (E^{2})] *on eras.*, ł heah *written above* nesse. heannessum ł seon (G)] ł seon *added in diff.* (?) *hand.* he gescylde (I)] y *altered from* i (?). he behealde (E^{2})] *on eras.* he behealde ł gescylde (G)] ł gescylde *added in diff.* (?) *hand.*

LTg: auxilium] auxiliu[ ] K: *partly lost due to excision of initial on fol. 26v.* de] K: *lost due to excision of initial on fol. 26v.* sion] syon G: *orig.* sion: y *written over* i. tueatur] A: ea *extends beyond grid,* tur *added by corr., eras. above word;* tueátur C; tuęatur D. te] A: *added by corr. above* eat *in preceding* tueatur, *eras. above word;* té C; *lost* K: *due to excision of initial on fol. 26v.*

LTu: Mittat] Mitat ϑ. sion] syon ειξτ*τυφ.

4

Memor	|	gemyndig ABCI, he gemyndig DGH, he Gemyndig E^{2}*, he gemindig F, he gemyndi K, sy J
sit	|	sie ABDE^{2}*, sy C*G, sý F, sy he I, sige H, beo K, gemindig J
dominus*		dryhten B, drihtyn C, dryhƮ A (*DEL*)
omnis		alre A, ealre BDGI, eælre E^{2}, eallre *F,* ealra HJ, ealle C, eallan K
sacrificii	|	onsegednisse A, onsægdnesse B, onsægydnysse C, onsægdnysse I, offrunga ł onsægednesse *G**, ofrunga D*K,* ofrunge F, offrunga H, þinre *E*^{2}, þinra J*
tui	|	ðinre ADF, þinre BGHI, þine C, þi(n)[ ] *K**, onseigdnesse E^{2}, onsægednessa J
et		⁊ ABCE^{2}FGHIJ (*K*)
holocaustum	|	onsegdnisse A, onsægdnesse BK, onsægdnysse C, onsægednyssa F, ofrung ł onsægdnis D, offrung ł ⁊ lác G*, offrung *H,* offrunga I, lac *J,* þin E^{2}
tuum	|	ðine A, þine BCIJ, þin DGHK, ðin F, offrung ł onseigdnesse E^{2}*
pingue		gefaettie A, gefættige BC, gefætige G, fætt DF, fett E^{2}, fet H, fæt JK, fæt ł onfengce I
fiat		sie DE^{2}GH*K,* sy IJ, sý ł geweorðe F, gewyrðe C

ED: sacrificíí (EK)] sacrificii *Harsley, Sisam.* þi(n)[ ] (K)] þin[ ] *Sisam.* pingue fiat (ACE)] pinguefiat *Kuhn, Wildhagen, Harsley.* gefætige (G)] *Berghaus takes initial and final* ge *as added in contemporary hand.*

OE: he Gemyndig (E^{2})] he *added in left margin.* sie (E^{2}) (*1st*)] *eras.* (*12 mm*) *after word.* sy (C)] *'squeezed in' between* gemyndig *and* drihtyn. offrunga ł onsægednesse (G)] ł onsægednesse *added in diff.* (?) *hand above* offrunga. þinra (J)] n *interl.*

þi(n)[ ] (K)] *right leg of* n *lost, final letters lost due to excision of initial on fol. 26v.* offrung ł ⁊ lác (G)] ł ⁊ lác *added in diff.* (?) *hand above* offrung. offrung ł onseigdnesse (E2)] g *altered from* d, d *altered from another letter* (*incomplete* n?), *eras. after* d.

LTg: dominus] L: *underlined to signal deletion; om.* DE: *cf. Weber MSS* αβγδη* moz med, *see GAg.* omnis] F: *orig.* omnes: e *eras.*, i *added on eras.*, *with smaller* i *written above.* sacrificii] G: *3rd* i *interl.*; sacrificíí EK. tui] t(u)[ ] K: *partly lost due to excision of initial on fol. 26v, minim visible after* t. et] K: *lost due to excision of initial on fol. 26v.* holocaustum] H: *orig.* olocaustum: h *interl. in hand of Lat. text;* holochaustum J: *2nd* h *interl.* (*by glossator?*). fiat] fiad K.

LTu: dominus] *om.* τ*: *cf. Weber MSS* αβγδη* moz med, *see GAu.* omnis] ξ: i *interl.* holocaustum] holochustim ϑ.

GAg: dominus] *om.* FGHIJK, DEL: *see LTg.*

GAu: dominus] *om.* δεζϑιλμξοπϱστυφχψ, τ*: *see LTu.*

5

Tribuat		selle ABDFH, Selle E2*, sylle CGK*, sy ealle *J,* agylde he I*
tibi		ðe ABF, þe CDE2*GHIJK
dominus*		dryhten B, drihtyn C, drihten E2, dryht̄ A
secundum		efter AE2, æfter BFGIJK, æftyr C, æft<u>er</u> DH
cor	I	heortan ABCDFGHIJK, þinre E2
tuum	I	ðinre ABF, þinre CDGHIJK, heortæn E2
et		⁊ ABCE2FGHIJK
omne		all *A,* eall BCGHI, eal D, eæl E2*, ealle F*J*K
consilium	I	gedaeh A, geðeaht B, geþieht C, geþeaht DFGHIJK, þin E2*
tuum	I	ðin AF, þin BCDGHIJ, þine K, geþeæht E2*
confirmet		getrymme AB, he getrymme DE2*HK, getrymme he I, he getrymð F, he getrymme ł getrymeð G*, getrimed J, gestrongie C

ED: geþeaht (H)] geþeat *Campbell.*

OE: Selle (E2)] *on eras.* sylle (K)] *otiose stroke* (*false start?*) *before word.* agylde he (I)] y *altered from* i (?). þe (E2)] *on eras.* eæl (E2)] le *eras. after word.* þin (E2)] e *eras. after word.* geþeæht (E2)] *eras.* (*8 mm*) *after word.* he getrymme (E2)] me *on eras.* he getrymme ł getrymeð (G)] ł getrymeð *added in diff.* (?) *hand.*

LTg: Tribuat] J: *orig.* Tribuit: *2nd* i *altered to* a; [ ]ribuat G. omne] A: *eras. after word,* J: *small eras. before* n.

LTu: Tribuat] TRibuat β.

GAg: dominus] *om.* FGHIJK.

GAu: dominus] *om.* δεζιλμξοπϱστυφχψ.

6

Laetabimur		we bioð geblissade A, we beoð blissiende *B,* we blissiað *DGH,* we blissiaþ *FJ,* We blissiæþ *E*^{2}, we blissian I*, we geblissiað *K,* we beoð *C* (*L*)
in		in A, on BCDE^{2}FGHIJK
salutari	ǀ	haelu A, hælo BDFHIJ, hæle CGK, þinre E^2
tuo	ǀ	ðinre AB, þinre CDFGHJK, þinre ł on þinum halwen[ ] I*, helo E^2
et		⁊ ABCE^{2}FGHIJK
in		in A, on BCDE^{2}FHIJK
nomine	ǀ	noman AB, naman CDFGHIJ*K, drihtnes E^2
domini*	ǀ	dryhtnes B, drihtnys C, dryht̄ A, namæn E^2* (*L*)
dei	ǀ	godes ABF*G*HIJK, godys C, ures E^2*
nostri	ǀ	ures ABDFGIJ, urys C, ure HK, godes E^2
magnificabimur		we bioð gemiclade A, we beoð gemiclode BE^2*H, we beoð gemiclude C, we beoð gemiclode D, we beoþ gemiclode F, we beoð gemicclode ł we gemiccliað G*, we beoð gemiclade ł gemærsode I, we gemiccliaþ J, we gemycliaþ K

ED: Lȩtabimur (E)] Laetabimur *Harsley.* þinre ł on þinum halwen[ ] (I)] þinre *Lindelöf, but in corrigenda (p. 323)* þinre on þinum halwend.... ures (G)] *Berghaus takes* s *as added in contemporary hand.*

OE: we blissian (I)] a *altered from another letter.* þinre ł on þinum halwen[ ] (I)] ł on þinum halwen[ ] *written in right margin, final word cropped.* naman (J)] *scribe first wrote initial* m, *then used right leg to form* a. namæn (E^2)] a *on eras.* ures (E^2)] *top of* r *by corr. followed by eras.* we beoð gemiclode (E^2)] we beoð gemic *on eras.* we beoð gemicclode ł we gemiccliað (G)] ł we gemiccliað *added in diff.* (?) *hand.*

LTg: Laetabimur] Lætabimur B; Letabimur CDFHL; Lȩtabimur EGJ; Lætabimur K. domini] L: *underlined to signal deletion: see GAg.* dei] de[ ] G: *hole in leaf after* e.

LTu: Laetabimur] Lȩtabimur ειλφ; Lætabimur ϑ; Letabimur ξσςτ*τυ.

GAg: domini] *om.* FGHIJK, L: *see LTg.*

GAu: domini] *om.* δεζιλξοπϱστυφχψ.

7

Impleat	ǀ	gefylleð A, gefillaþ J, gefylle BCDFIK, gefyll H, gefylle ł gefyllað G*, drihten E^2*
dominus	ǀ	dryhten BD, drihten K, dryht̄ A, driht̄ CFH, driht̄ I, drih̄ GJ, gefylle E^2*
omnes		alle A, ealle BCFGHIJK, eællæ E^2

petitiones	|	boene A, boena B, bena *CI*, bene J, gyrnenga D, girninge K, bena ł gýrnynga F, wyrninga G*, wyrnynga H, þinæ E^{2}
tuas	|	ðine AF, þine CIJK, ðina B, þina D, þinre H, þinre ł þine bene G*, benæ ł gyrnenga E^{2}*
nunc		nu ABCDE^{2}GHJK, nu þa FI
cognoui		ic oncneow AB**C*E^{2}*FGIJ, ic ancneow DH, ic geccneow K
quoniam		ðætte A, þætte B, forþon C, forðon D*H,* forþæn E^{2}*, forðan I, forþon J, forþon ðe F, forþam G, forðam K
saluum		halne ABCDFGHI, halue E^{2}*, hale J, hal K
faciet*		doeð AB, gedeþ CDE^{2}FJ, dó ł gedeð G*, dyde K, dyde ł þæt gehælde I* (*L*)
dominus		drihten E^{2}*K, ðryht̄ A, dryht̄ B, drih́t CH, drih́ GJ, drih́t cyníng F
christum	|	crist ABFK, xp̄st C, cyning DH, kyning ł criest *E^{2},* cyning ł crist G*, þone gehalgodon J, his I
suum	|	his ABDE^{2}*FGHJK, hys C, gecorenan ł crist ł kyningc I*
et*		⁊ ABC (*L*)
exaudiet		gehereð A, gehereþ E^{2}*, gehirð B, gehyrð D*H,* gehyreð *G,* gehyrþ *K,* he gehyrð *F,* gehireþ *J,* gehyre C, gehere *I* (*L*)
illum		hine ABCDE^{2}*FGHIJK
de		of ABC*DE^{2}FGHIJK
caelo	|	heofene A*G,* heofone *BDH,* hefone *C,* heofonum *F,* heofonum I, heofenan *K,* his *E^{2}J* (*L*)
sancto	|	ðæm halgan AB, þam halgan G, þæne halgan *C,* þa halgan H, þam halgan J, ðam halgum D, halgum F, hælegæ E^{2}*, halgan I
suo	|	his ABCDFGHIK, heofone E^{2}J*
in		in A, on BCDE^{2}*FGHIJK
potentatibus		maehtum A, mehtum B, mihtum CJ, his miehte ł anweldum E^{2}*, anwealdum D, andwealdum F, andwealdum H, anwealde K, anwealdum ł on mihtum G*, anwealdnyssum ł on mihtigum I*
salus		haelu A, hælo BDGI*J, helo E^{2}, hæle H, hæl CK, hæl[ ] *F**
dexterae	|	swiðran A*BC*I, swyþre *K,* þære swiþran *D*H,* ðære swyþran *F,* þære swyðran *G,* þa swiðran *J,* his *E^{2}* (*L*)
eius	|	his ABCDFGHIJK, swyþre E^{2}

ED: halue (E)] halne *Harsley.* dó ł gedeð (G)] do ł gedeð *Rosier.* christum (K)] Christum *Sisam.* xp̄st (C)] christ *Wildhagen.* anwealdum (G)] *Berghaus takes* m *as added in contemporary hand.* sal[ ] (F)] salu[ ] *Kimmens.* swiðran (B)] swidran *Brenner.*

OE: gefylle ł gefyllað (G)] ł gefyllað *added in diff.* (?) *hand.* drihten (E^{2}) (*1st*)] *on* *eras.* gefylle (E^2)] þ *eras. after word.* wyrninga þinre ł þine bene (G)] ł þine bene *added in diff.* (?) *hand above* wyrninga. benæ ł gyrnenga (E^2)] ł gyrnenga *added,* ł *in right margin,* gyrnenga *on next line above* nu ic on. ic oncneow (B)] *otiose marks before* ic. ic oncneow (E^2)] *2nd* o *altered from* a, *letter eras. after* w. forþæn (E^2)] *eras.* (*15 mm*) *after word.* halue (E^2)] u *on eras.,* a *altered from another letter* (æ?). dó ł gedeð (G)] ł gedeð *added in diff.* (?) *hand.* dyde ł þæt gehælde (I)] y *altered from* i (?). drihten (E^2) (*2nd*)] *on eras.* cyning ł crist (G)] ł crist *added in diff.* (?) *hand.* his (E^2) (*1st*)] ⁊ *eras. before word,* s *on eras.,* ic (?) *eras. after word.* gecorenan ł crist ł kyningc (I)] an *written below* gecoren *in left margin.* gehereþ (E^2)] *letter eras. after* h. hine (E^2)] *on eras.* of (C)] *poorly written outside left grid.* hælegæ (E^2)] *eras. after word.* heofone (J)] *otiose mark after word: cf. Pss 17.46 and 20.8 for similar marks.* on (E^2)] *eras. after word* (⁊?). his miehte ł anweldum (E^2)] ł anweldum *added in right margin and signaled for inclusion.* anwealdum ł on mihtum (G)] ł on mihtum *added in diff.* (?) *hand.* anwealdnyssum ł on mihtigum (I)] ł on mihtigum *written in left margin.* hælo (I)] s. est : is *written in right margin, with single* (*syntactical*) *dot below* est. hæl[ ] (F)] *hole in leaf after* l. þære swiþran (D)] *see Sisam §109.*

LTg: petitiones] C: *scribe orig. began* petitit-, *then altered 3rd* t *to* o. quoniam] H: *eras. after word.* cognoui] congnoui C. faciet] feciet L: *orig.* faciet: a *altered to* e. christum] E: *otiose dot below* t. et] L: *underlined to signal deletion.* exaudiet] Exaudiet FHIK, L: *orig.* exaudiet: *initial* e *altered to* E; Exaudiat J; [ ]xaudiat G: *orig.* [ ]xaudiet: e *altered to* a, *initial* E *lost.* caelo] cælo BKL; celo CDEH; cęlo GJ. sancto] C: *scribe orig. began* sant-, *then altered* t *to* c. salus] sal[ ] F: *hole in leaf after* l. dexterae] dexteræ BL; dexterę CFGH; dextere JK; dextera DE.

LTu: quoniam] *interl.* ε. faciet] faciat ς. exaudiet] Exaudiet δεζιλμξοπρσυχψ; Exaudiat ϑτφ. caelo] cęlo εζιουφ; cælo ϑμ; celo ξσςτ*τ. dexterae] dexterę εζινξοπφ; dexteræ ϑ; dextere σςτ; dextera τ*.

GAg: faciet] fecit FGHIJK. et] *om.* FGHIJK, L: *see LTg.*

GAu: faciet] fecit δεζϑιλμξοπρστυφχψ. et] *om.* δεζϑιλμξοπρστυφχψ.

8

Hii	ðas AB*, þas *CIJ,* ða ł hy *D,* þa ł hy E^2**H,* ða hi *F,* þa *K* (*G*)
in	in AJ, on BCDE^2*FHIK
curribus	creatum A, cratum B, cræteum CGI*, cræteum J, cretum K, wænum ł on cræteum D, wænum ł cræteum F, wægnum ł cræteum H, wenum ł rynum E^2*
et	⁊ ABCDE^2*FGHIJK
hii	ðas AB, þas *CGIJ,* þa *K,* hy *D*E^2*,* hi *FH*
in	in A, on BCDE^2*FGIK
equis	horsum ABE^2*F*GH*I, horsum *C*DJ, horssum *K* (*L*)
nos	we ABCDE^2FGHIJK

autem		soðlice ABCI, soþlice E2FJ, þonne̲ soð[ ] G, witodlice K
in		in A, on BCDE2FHIJK (*G*)
nomine	I	noman AB, naman CDFGHIJ*K, drihtnes E2
domini	I	dryhtnes BD, drihtnys C, drihtnes FI, drihtenes K, dryht̄ A, driħ GJ, nomæn E2*
dei	I	godes ABFGIJ, godys C, ures E2
nostri	I	ures ABDFGHIJK, urys C, godes E2
magnificabimur*		we bioð gemiclade A, we beoð gemiclode B, we beoð gemiclod C, beoð g̲emiclode D, beoð gemiclyde E2*, we gecegað ł cleopiaþ F, we gemiccliað G, we gemiccliaþ J, we clypiað K, geciað I (*L*)

ED: Híí (H)] Hii *Campbell.* crætum (G)] [ ]rætum *Rosier.* autem (G)] aute*m Rosier.* þonne̲ soð[ ] (G)] þonn soð[ ] *Rosier, Berghaus.*

OE: ðas (B) (*1st*)] *otiose marks above* s. þa ł hy (E2)] *eras. after* a (*orig.* þæ?). on (E2) (*1st*)] *on eras.* crætum (I)] s. sunt : synt *written in left margin.* wenum ł rynum (E2)] *on eras.* ꝛ (E2)] *on eras.* hy (E2)] *on eras.* on (E2) (*2nd*)] *on eras.* horsum (E2)] *on eras.* naman (J)] *scribe first began to write initial* m, *but stopped after completing second shoulder and wrote* a, *now in ligature.* nomæn (E2)] o *altered from another letter* (a?). beoð gemiclyde (E2)] e *in* beoð *interl.*, de *on eras.*

LTg: Hii] Híí H; Hi CDEFGIJK. hii] H: *interl.: scribe used stem of preceding tironian* et *as upper part of ascender of* h; hi CDEFIJK, G: *mark* (*long* s?) *inserted after* i. equis] H: *eras. before* s, E: *top of* s *retouched in darker ink due to eras. in line above;* ęquis CL, G: *cauda added later* (*by glossator?*); æquis K. in (*3rd*)] *lost* G. magnificabimur] L: *underlined to signal deletion,* inuocabimus *written above by corr.: see GAg.*

LTu: Hii] Hi δεζιλμνξοπϱτ*τυφχψ. hii] hi δεζιλμνξοπϱτ*τυφχψ; íí σ. equis] æquis ϑ; ęquis νξϱ. domini] *interl.* χ.

GAg: magnificabimur] inuocabimus FHIJK, L: *see LTg;* inuocabimu[ ] G.

GAu: magnificabimur] inuocabimus δεζιλμξοπϱστυφχψ.

9

Ipsi		hie AB, hi CE2HI, hy DGK, hig FJ
obligati	I	gebundne AB, gebundynne C, g̲ewriðene D, gewriðene HK*, gewriðene ł ofergytende G*, ofergýtende F, ofergiton J, geþylmede ł gewriþene I, synt E2
sunt	I	sindun A, sindon B, syndun C, synd DHK, synt I, synt ł wæron G*, wæron FJ, gewriðene E2*
et		ꝛ ABCE2*FGHIJK
ceciderunt		gefeollun A, gefeollon BCJ, gefeollen E2*, hi gefeollon G*,

		hy feollon DH, hi feollon F, hi hruron ł hi feollon *I,* feollan *K*
nos		we ABCDE^{2}FHIJ, we ł us G*
uero		soðlice ABC*HI,* soþlice DE^{2}*FJ,* soð[ ] *G**, witodlice *K*
resurreximus*		aresun A, arisan B, aryson C, we arison DGH, we arisan K, arison FJ, uparyson I, ærysæþ E^{2}
et	|	⁊ ABCE^{2}FGHJK
erecti	|	uparehte AB*C,* arehte DFGH, arærede ⁊ I, arisene K, ryhte E^{2}, þe sind *J*
sumus	|	sindun A, we sint B, we synt D, we synd FGH, we syndon I, we syndo[ ] C*, beoþ K, bioþ gewordene E^{2}, gerehte J

ED: cęciderunt (I)] ceciderunt *Lindelöf.* soðlice (H)] soþlice *Campbell.* soð[ ] (G)] soðlice *Rosier.* we syndo[ ] (C)] we syndon *Wildhagen.*

OE: gewriðene (K)] *eras.* (*1–2 letters*) *after 1st* e. gewriðene ł ofergytende (G)] ł ofergytende *added interl. in diff.* (?) *hand above* gewriðene. synt ł wæron (G)] ł wæron *added in diff.* (?) *hand.* gewriðene (E^{2})] wriðene *on eras.* gefeollen (E^{2})] feollen *on eras.,* o *altered from another letter.* hi gefeollon (G)] ge *added later by glossator* (?). we ł us (G)] ł us *added in diff.* (?) *hand.* soð[ ] (G)] *only letter fragments visible after* ð. we syndo[ ] (C)] o *slightly cropped on right, final letter likely lost due to trimming of leaf.*

LTg: ceciderunt] cęciderunt IK. uero] autem FGHIJK: *cf. Bib. sac. MSS* Ω^{M2}, *Hebr.* erecti] CJ: *initial* e *interl.*

LTu: obligati] χ: b *interl.* uero] autem δζμοπϱστυφχψ: *cf. Bib. sac. MSS* Ω^{M2}, *Hebr.*

GAg: resurreximus] surreximus FGHIJK.

GAu: resurreximus] surreximus δεζιλμξοπϱστυφχψ.

10

Domine		dryhten B, drihten E^{2}, dryhт̄ A, driћ GHJ, s. o eala driћt C*, eala ðu driћt F, o. eala driht̄ I (*K*)
saluum	|	halne ABCDGHIJ, gehalne F, hal *K,* gedo E^{2}
fac	|	do AFHK, dóó C, dó D, gedó B, þu do GJ, do ł gehæl I*, þone E^{2}
regem	|	cyning ABCDGH, cyningc F, kyninc J, cining K, kyningc usserne I, kyning hælne E^{2}
et		⁊ ABCE^{2}FGHIJK
exaudi		geher A, gehier B, gehyr CDIK, gehiere E^{2}, gehýr þu F, gehyr þu GH, gehir þu J
nos		us ABCE^{2}FGHIJ (*K*)
in		in A, on BCDE^{2}FGHIJ (*K*)
die		dege A, dæge BCDFGHIJ, degge E^{2}*, dæg K

in*	in A, on DE^2 (*BCK*)
qua	ðæm A, on ðæm B, þam þe CG, ðam þe DE^2*, þam þe HJ, on þam þe FI, þa K
inuocauerimus	we gecegað A, we gecegeað B, we gecigað C, we geciaþ I, we gecigen DG, we gecegan F, we gecygen H, we gecigan J, we ciað K, we gecygen ł clipien E^2*
te	ðec A, ðe *B*F, þe CDE^2*GHIJK

ED: [ ](a)luum (K)] [s]aluum *Sisam.* þu do...gehyr þu G: *Berghaus takes* þu (*both*) *as added in contemporary hand.* dæge (G)] *Berghaus takes* e *as added in contemporary hand.* ðæm (B)] dæm *Brenner.*

OE: s. o eala driħt (C)] s. o *written outside left grid.* do ł gehæl (I)] ł gehæl *written in left margin.* degge (E^2)] deg *on eras.* ðam þe (E^2)] *on eras.* we gecygen ł clipien (E^2)] *on eras.* þe (E^2)] *on eras.*

LTg: Domine] K: *lost due to excision of initial to Ps 20.* saluum] [ ](a)luum K: *partly lost due to excision of initial to Ps 20, back of* a *visible.* nos] K: *lost due to excision of initial to Ps 20.* in (*1st*)] [ ]n K: *partly lost due to excision of initial to Ps 20.* in (*2nd*)] *om.* BC: *cf. Weber MSS* δ* moz^c, *see GAg.* te] té B.

LTu: die] dię ν. in (*2nd*)] *om.* νς: *cf. Weber MS* δ*, *see GAu.*

GAg: in (*2nd*)] *om.* FGHIJK, BC: *see LTg.*

GAu: in (*2nd*)] *om.* δεζϑιλμξοπϱστυφχψ, νς: *see LTu.*

PSALM 20

2

Domine	eala ðu driħt F*, eala drihten I*, s. o eala driħt *C,* Drihten *E^2,* dryht̄ *A,* driħt H, driħ GJ (*BDKL*)
in	in A, on B*C*DE^{2}FGHIJK (*L*)
uirtute	| megne A, mægene BDGH, mægyne *C,* mægne IJ, mæine K, mihte F, þinum E^2 (*L*)
tua	| ðinum AG, þinum BCDJ, þinum HI, ðin F, þinan K, megne E^2 (*L*)
laetabitur	| bið geblissad A, biþ geblissod *C,* blissað *BDGK,* blyssað *H,* blissaþ *I,* blissiað *F,* blissiaþ *J,* se kyning *E^2* (*L*)
rex	| cyning ABCG, cyningc F, kyningc I, kyninc J, cining K, blissæþ E^2
et	⁊ ABCDE^{2}FGHIJK
super	ofer ABDE^{2}FGHIJK, ofyr C
salutare	haelu A, hælo BD*FGH*IJ, hæle CE^2*K

tuum	ðine AB*F*, þine CDE^{2}*K, þinre *GH*J, þinre þinum halwendan I*
exultabit	gefihð *A***B*, gefihþ C, he blissade *D*F, he blyssode H, [ ]e blissode K*, wynsumæde ł blissade E^{2}*, he blissode ł wynsumiað G*, winsumiaþ J, he blissað ł gefægnaþ I
uehementer	swiðlice ABC, swiþlice J, swyþe K, swiþe ł ðearle E$^{2/x}$*, ðearle DF, þealre H, þearle ł swiðlice G*I

ED: lętabitur (E)] laetabitur *Harsley*. þinre þinum halwendan (I)] þinre ł þinum halwendan *Lindelöf*. [ ]e blissode (K)] [h]e blissode *Sisam*. wynsumæde ł blissade (E^{2})] wynsumæd*e* ł blissade *Harsley*.

OE: F: *small* o *written in bowl of* D *in* Dñe *by glossator.* eala drihten] I: s. o *written before* eala. hæle (E^{2})] *on eras*. þine (E^{2})] *on eras*. þinre þinum halwendan (I)] þinum halwendan *written in left margin*. gefihð (A)] *orig*. gefiht: t *altered to* ð. [ ]e blissode (K)] *initial letter lost due to excision of psalm initial*. wynsumæde ł blissade (E^{2})] *1st* de *on eras. in ligature,* ł blissade *added, with* ł bliss *on eras*. he blissode ł wynsumiað (G)] ł wynsumiað *added in diff.* (?) *hand*. swiþe ł ðearle (E$^{2/x}$)] swiþe ł *added by corr*. þearle ł swiðlice (G)] ł swiðlice *added in diff.* (?) *hand*.

LTg: Domine] DÑe A; DÑE BCDEL; [ ]ÑE K: *initial letter excised*. in] IN CL. uirtute] UIRTVTE C; VIRTVTE L: TE *in ligature*. tua] TVA L. laetabitur] lætabitur B; lętabitur CEIK; letabitur DFGHJL. salutare] FGH: *orig*. salutari: i *altered to* e. tuum] G: *final* ũ *altered from another letter,* F: *orig*. tuo: o *deleted by subscript dot,* ũ *interl. by hand that added* dñe *at Ps 18.13,* H: ũ *on eras*. exultabit] A: b *on eras.;* exultauit BD.

LTu: Domine] DÑE βλμνϱτ*φψ; DOMINE ιτ; DOMINe ς. in] IN λμνϱφψ. uirtute] VIRTUTE λ; UIRTUTE μψ; UIRTUte ν; UIRTVTE ϱ; VIRTVTE φ; virtvte φ. tua] TUA λϱψ. laetabitur] lętabitur εζϑινφ; LETABITUR λ; letabitur ξσςτ*τυ; LAEtabitur ϱ. salutare tuum] salutari tuo ψ. exultabit] exultauit βς. uehementer] uehimenter β; uechimenter ϑ.

3

Desiderium		lust AB, lvst C, gyrninge DFH, gyrnuunge *K**, gyrninge ł willan G*, willan J, gewilnunga I, gewilnunge ł gyrninge E^{2}
animae	|	sawle A*BC*, saule *D*, heortan *FGHIJK*, his *E*^{2} (*I*)
eius	|	his ABDFGHIJ*K*, hys C, sæwle E^{2}
tribuisti	|	ðu saldes A, ðu sealdest BF, þu sealdyst C, þu sealdest DGHIJK*, þu him E^{2}
ei	|	him ACFGHI, him *D*J, his B, seældest E^{2}
et		⁊ ABCDE^{2}FGHJK
uoluntate		willan ABC*J*K, from willan D, fram wyllæn E^{2}*, fram willan *FG*H, fram willan ł gewilnyssa *I*

labiorum	ǀ	weolera A, welera BFGHIJK, welyra C, wellera D, his E^{2}
eius	ǀ	his ABDFGHIJ*K*, hys C, welere ł lippe E^{2}*
non	ǀ	ðu ne AD, þu ne BCFGHJ, þu na I, na K, þu E^{2}
fraudasti	ǀ	bisceredes A*, besceredes B, bescyredyst C, bescyredest DF, becyredest H, bescyrodest K, bescyredest ł þone for(h)te G*, bescyredyst ⁊ ðu ne bepæhtest I*, þrute J, hine ne E^{2}
eum	ǀ	hine ABCDFHIJK, becyredest ł bepehtes E$^{2/x}$*

ED: [ ]esiderium (K)] [d]esiderium *Sisam*. lvst (C)] lust *Wildhagen*. gewilnunge ł gyrninge (E)] Gewilnunga ł gyrninge *Harsley*. labiorum (G)] laborium *Rosier*. bescyredest ł þone for(h)te (G)] bescyredest ł þone :::te *Sisam*^{2}.

OE: gyrnuunge (K)] *1st* u *obscured by stain*. gyrninge ł willan (G)] ł willan *added in diff.* (?) *hand*. þu sealdest (K)] *top of 1st* s *lost due to excision of psalm initial*. fram wyllæn (E^{2})] ⁊ *eras. after* fram. welere ł lippe (E^{2})] pe *on eras., eras. marks below* re. bisceredes (A)] bi *interl.* bescyredest ł þone for(h)te (G)] ł þone for(h)te *added in diff.* (?) *hand,* h *split and fragmentary*. bescyredyst ⁊ ðu ne bepæhtest (I)] ⁊ ðu ne bepæhtest *written in left margin*. becyredest ł bepehtes (E$^{2/x}$)] ł bepehtes *added by corr.*

LTg: Desiderium] [ ]esiderium K: *initial letter lost due to excision of psalm initial.* animae] animæ B; animę CDL; anime E; cordis FGHIJK: *cf. Weber MSS* $\alpha^2\gamma\eta^2$ med *and Bib. sac.* RFIL*, *cf. Hebr. and LXX.* eius (*1st*)] eíus K. ei] ęi D. uoluntate] FI: *eras. after word,* GI: *orig.* uoluntatem: m *eras.;* uoluntatem J. eius (*2nd*)] eíus K.

LTu: animae] animæ ϑ; animę ν; anime ςτ*; cordis δεζιλμξοπϱστυφχψ: *cf. Weber MSS* $\alpha^2\gamma\eta^2$ med *and Hebr.* uoluntate] uoluntatem βζυ. eum] β: u *interl.*

4

Quoniam		forðon ABDFHJ, forþon C, forðæn E^{2}, forþan I, forðam G
praeuenisti		ðu forecwome A, þu forecome *BCE*^{2}**FG,* ðu forecome *D,* þu forcome *K,* þu fore *H,* þu forestope I, þu foredome *J* (*L*)
eum		hine ABCDE^{2}*FGHIJK
in		in A, on BCDE^{2}FGHIJK
benedictione*		bledsunge A, bletsunge BCFGHJK, bletsvnge D*, þinre bletsunge E^{2}*, blætsungum I
dulcedinis		swoetnisse *A**, swetnisse BDH, swetnysse CI, swétnysse F, swetnesse E^{2}GK, swetnessa J
posuisti		ðu settes A, þu settest BE^{2}G, ðu settest D, þu setest K, þu gesettyst C, ðu gesettest F, þu gesettest HJ, þu gesettyst I
in		on BCDE^{2}FGHIJK
capite	ǀ	heafde ABDFGI, heafude C, heafode H, heafod *K,* eafde J, his E^{2}
eius	ǀ	his ABDFGHIJ*K,* hys C, heæfode E^{2}

coronam		beg A, beag B, beah CGJ, hroðgirelan D, hroðgyrelan H, gewuldorbeagod F, wuldorbeag I, cynehelm K, helm ł coruna E$^{2/x}$*
de		of ABCDE^{2}FGHIJK
lapide	I	stane ABCDFGHIJ, stanan K, þæm diorweorþestæn E^2
pretioso	I	deorwyrðum _A_*_B_CH, deorwyrðum D, deorwurþum _G_, deorwyrþum I, deorwurþum J, deor[ ]ðum _F_*, dyrwyrþra K, stænum E^2

ED: forðon (A)] for ðon _Kuhn_. forðæn (E) Forðæn _Harsley_. preuenisti (B)] prevenis _Brenner_. bletsvnge (D)] bletsunge _Roeder_. deor[ ]ðum (F)] deorw--ðum _Kimmens_.

OE: þu forecome (E^2)] come _on eras_. hine (E^2)] _on eras_. bletsvnge (D)] _orig_. bletsonge: o _deleted by subscript dot_, v _interl_. þinre bletsunge (E^2)] þinre _underlined_. swoetnisse (A)] o _interl_. helm ł coruna (E$^{2/x}$)] helm ł _added by corr._, un _on eras_. deorwyrðum (A)] _orig_. deorwyrðem: u _written below 2nd_ e, _but without deleting dot_. deor[ ]ðum (F)] _letters lost due to hole in leaf_.

LTg: praeuenisti] preuenisti BCDEFGHJL; pręuenisti K. dulcedinis] dulcidinis A. capite] K: ite _on eras_. eius] eíus K. pretioso] praetioso A: so _added by corr._; p̄tioso B; prętioso G; pr&[ ]oso F: _hole in leaf after_ &, & _cropped_.

LTu: praeuenisti] preuenisti ζιξσςτ*τ; p̄uenisti ϑο; pręuenisti λνπϱφ. dulcedinis] β: _orig_. dulcidinis: _1st_ i _deleted_, e _interl._; dulcidinis ϑ. posuisti] possuisti βϑ. pretioso] praetioso βου; prętioso ε; p̄tioso ζμξ; p̄ctiosso ϑ: _1st_ s _interl._; precioso ιφ, ϱ: _orig_. pretioso: t _deleted_, c _interl._; p̄cioso τ*τ.

GAg: benedictione] benedictionibus FHIJK; benedictionib[ ] G.

GAu: benedictione] benedictionibus δεζϑιλμξοπϱστυφχψ.

5

Uitam	lif _ABCDFGHIJK_, lyf E^2
petiit	bed _A_, bæd B, he bæd CDFGHIJK, he bed _E_^{2}
(a)*	fram _D_FHJ, fram _E_^{2}*G, from _C_, æt IK (_L_)
(te)*	þe _CDE_^{2}*GHIJ_K_*, ðe F (_L_)
et	⁊ ABCE^2*FGHI_J_ (_K_)
tribuisti	ðu saldes A, ðu sealdes B, þu sealdyst C, ðu sealdest DF*, þu seældest E^2*, þu sealdest GIJK, þu sealdast H
ei	him ABCE^2*FGH, him IJK
longitudinem	lengu A, lengo B, léngo J, lenge C, langnisse DE^2*, langnissa H, langnesse K, langsumnysse F, langsumnyssa I*, langsumnessa ł lengo G*
dierum	dęga _A_, daga BCDFGHJ, dage E^2, dagena I, dagan _K_
in	in A, on BCE^{2}FGHIJ

(saeculum)*	weorulde F, worulde G, woruld H, worlde I, world J
(et)*	⁊ FGHIJ
(in)*	on FGHIJ
saeculum	weoruld A, weorold *B,* woruld *C,* worold *E^2*, weorulda *F,* worulda *GH,* worlda *I**J,* aworuld *D* (*KL*)
saeculi	weorulde A, weorolde *B,* worulde *C,* woruld *FGHJ,* world *IJ,* aworł *E^2* (*DKL*)

ED: lyf (E)] Lyf *Harsley.* petíít a te (E)] petiit a te *Harsley.* té (G)] te *Rosier.* sęculum (G) (*1st*)] seculum *Rosier.* sclm (K) (*1st*)] sæculum *Sisam.* sęculum (E)] saeculum *Harsley.* sclm (K) (*2nd*)] sæculum *Sisam.* sęculi (E)] saeculi *Harsley.* scli (DK)] saeculi *Roeder;* sæculi *Sisam.* aworł (E)] aworl*de Harsley.*

OE: fram (E^2)] *on eras.* þe (E^2)] *on eras.* þe (K)] ⁊ *eras. after word: see LTg note to* et. ⁊ (E^2)] *on eras.* ðu sealdest (F)] t *slightly cropped at top.* þu seældest (E^2)] þu *on eras.* him (E^2)] *on eras.* langnisse (E^2)] *on eras.* langsumnyssa (I)] sum *interl.* langsumnessa ł lengo (G)] ł lengo *added in diff.* (?) *hand above* langsumnessa. worlda (I)] *orig.* worlde: e *altered to* a.

LTg: Uitam] Vitam ABDFGHIK. petiit] petit A; petiit a te CDL; petíít a te E: *cf. Weber MS* β, *see GAg.* et] *interl.* J; *eras.* K. dierum] A: m *added by corr.*, K: *letter eras. after* ū. saeculum] sæculum B; seculum CDH; sęculum EFG; sclm IJKL. saeculi] sæculi B; seculi CH; sęculi EFG; scli DIJK, L: *underlined to signal deletion and* ⁊ in sclm scli *written after word by corr.: see GAg.*

LTu: Uitam] Vitam νξϱσςτ*τυφ. petiit] petiit a te νςτ*: *cf. Weber MS* β, *see GAu.* et] *interl.* ε; *om.* σ. saeculum] sęculum εζινοϱυφ; seculum ςτ; sclm ϑλμξπστ*υχ. saeculi] sęculi ειvϱυφ; seculi οςτ*τ; scli ζϑλμξπσυχ.

GAg: petiit] petiit a te FHIJ, CDL: *see LTg;* petiit a té G; petiit á te K; *for* E *see LTg.* in] in sęculum et in FG; in seculum et in H; in sclm et in IJK; *for* L *see LTg note to* saeculi.

GAu: petiit] petiit a te δεζϑιλμξοπϱστυφχψ, νςτ*: *see LTu.* in] in saeculum et in δψ; in sęculum et in εζιλοφ; in seculum et in μτ; in sclm et in ϑξπϱσυ; in sæculum et in χ.

6

Magna		micel ABDFHI*, Micel E^2, micyl C, mycel K, micel is GJ
est*		is ABE^2, ys C (*L*)
gloria	|	wuldur ADH, wuldor BCFGIJK, his E^2
eius	|	his ABCFGIJ*K,* wuldor E^2*
in		in A, on BCDE^{2}FGHIJK
salutari	|	haelu A, hælo B*DFGHJ, hæle CIK, þinre E^2
tuo	|	ðinre AF, þinre BCDGHJK, þinre ł on ðinum halwendan I, helo E^2

gloriam	wuldur ACDH, wuldor BE^2*FIJK, wuld[ ] *G*
et	⁊ ABCE^{2}FGHIJK
magnum	micelne *A*BDE^{2}GHIJ, micylne C, mycelne F, mycel K
decorem	wlite ABC*D*E^{2}FGHIJK
inpones	ðu onsctes *A,* þu onasetst *I**, ðu asetst DE^2*F, þu asetst H, þu asets K, þu asettesð *G,* þu asettest J, þu setst *B,* onasette *C* (*L*)
super	ofer ABDE^{2}FGHJK, ofyr C, ofor I
eum	hine ABDFGHIJK, hyne C, him E^2

ED: gloriam (G)] glori*am Rosier.* inpones (B)] impones *Brenner.* impones (C)] i[n]pones *Wildhagen.*

OE: micel (I)] *eras. after word,* s. e̲s̲t̲ : is *written in left margin.* wuldor (E^2) (*1st*)] *eras. after word.* hælo (B)] *eras.* (*2 letters?*) *after word.* wuldor (E^2) (*2nd*)] *eras. after word.* þu onasetst (I)] a *interl.* ðu asetst (E^2)] asetst *on eras.*

LTg: est] L: *underlined to signal deletion: see GAg.* eius] eíus K. gloriam] gloria[ ] G. magnum] A: u *on eras. by corr.* decorem] decôrem D. inpones] A: e *on eras. by corr.;* impones GIL, C: *orig.* inpones: i *linked to* n *to form* m, i *added before orig.* i.

LTu: est] *interl.* σ (÷). gloria] ς: *remainder of psalm wanting.* magnum] magnam β. inpones] impones ειξοσφ; ῑpones ϑ.

GAg: est] *om.* FGHIJK, L: *see LTg.*

GAu: est] *om.* δεζϑιλμξοπρτυφχψ.

7

Quoniam	forðon ABHJ, Forðon E^2, forþon CF, forþā G, forðan þe I
dabis	❘ ðu selest AB, þu sylyst C, þu selst DFH, þu sylst GIK, þu sillst J, þu hine E^2
eum	hine ABCDFGHIJ*K,* selest E^2
in	in A, on BCDE^{2}FGHIJK
benedictionem	bledsunge A, bletsunge B*CDE*^{2}FGK, gebletsunge H, bletsungum I, blesunge J (*L*)
in	in AF, on BCE^{2}GHIJK
saeculum	weoruld A, woruld *CH,* world *E*^{2}, weorolde *B,* weorulde *F,* woroldda *K,* worulde ł a *G**, worlde *I,* worlda *J* (*DL*)
saeculi	weorulde A, weorolde *B,* worulde *C,* woruld *GH,* world *IJ,* worul *F,* aworł *E*^{2} (*DKL*)
laetificabis	❘ ðu geblissas A, þu geblissast *BCG**I, ðu geblissast *DF,* ðu geblissas *K,* þu blisast *H,* þu blissast *J,* þu hine *E*^{2} (*L*)
eum	❘ hine ABCFGHIJK, geblissæst E^2
in	in A, on BCDE^{2}FGHIJK

gaudio		gefian A*, gefean BCDFHJ, gefeæn E^2, gefean ł blisse G*, blisse IK
cum		mid ABCDFGHIJ, myd E^2
uultu	ǀ	ondwleotan A, andwlitan BCDH, ándwlitan F, andwlitum ł ansyne G*, ansyne J, þinre E^2, þinum I
tuo	ǀ	ðinum A, þinum BCDFH, þinum ł þinre G*, þinre J, onsine ł andwlitan E^2, andwlytan I

ED: forðon (A)] for ðon *Kuhn.* forþā (G)] forþam *Rosier.* sęculum (G)] seculum *Rosier.* sclm (K)] sæculum *Sisam.* sęculi (E)] saeculi *Harsley.* scli (DK)] saeculi *Roeder,* sæculi *Sisam.* aworł (E)] awor*lde Harsley.* lętificabis (E)] laetificabis *Harsley.*

OE: worulde ł a (G)] ł a *added in diff.* (?) *hand.* þu geblissast (G)] ge *added in diff.* (?) *hand.* gefian] A: g *altered from* i. gefean ł blisse (G)] ł blisse *added in diff.* (?) *hand.* andwlitum ł ansyne (G)] ł ansyne *added in diff.* (?) *hand above* andwlitum. þinum ł þinre (G)] ł þinre *added in diff.* (?) *hand.*

LTg: eum (*1st*)] K: *eras.* (*60 mm*) *after word.* benedictionem] benedictione CDEL: *cf. Weber MSS* KTQ^2VXε moz^x. saeculum] sæculum B; seculum CDEHL; sęculum G; sclm FIJK. saeculi] sæculi B; seculi CHL; sęculi EG; scli DFIJK. laetificabis] lætificabis B; letificabis CDL; lętificabis EFGHJK.

LTu: Quoniam] [ ]oniam τ*: *initial letter wanting.* benedictionem] benedictione ψ: *cf. Weber MSS* KTQ^2VXε moz^x. saeculum] sęculum ιν; seculum πτ*τ; sclm δεζϑλμξϱσυφχ. saeculi] sęculi ινο; seculi πτ*τ; scli δεζϑλμξϱσυφχ. laetificabis] lętificabis ειλνοϱφ; lætificabis ϑ; letificabis ξστ*τυ.

8

Quoniam		forðon ABFJ, forþon C, forþæn þe E^2, forþā þe G, forðan þe I*
rex		cyning ABC, cyningc F, kyningc I, cininc K, se kyning E^2, se cyning G*, se cync J
sperauit*		gehyhteð *A*, gehihtyð C, gehihteð G*, gehihteð hopað I*, gehyhte BD, gehihte H, hihteþ J, geweneþ ł hyhteð *E^2**, hopað F, hopaþ K (*L*)
in		in A, on BCDE^2FGIJ
domino		dryhtne ABD, drihtne FI, drihtny C, drihten E^2, driħt G, driħ J
et		⁊ ABCE^2FGHI*J*K
in		in A, on BCDE^2FG*H*IK (*J*)
misericordia	ǀ	mildheortnisse A, mildheortnesse BDH, mildheortnysse CFI, mildheortness[ ] *G*, milheortnesse K, on mildheortnesse J*, þes hihstæn E^2

altissimi | ðes hestan A, ðæs hehstan BD, þæs hehstan F, þæs hiehstan C, ðæs hyhstan H, þæs heaxstan I, þæs hihstan J*, þæs hyhstan GK, mildheortnesse E^2

non | ne ABCJ, na K, he ne DE^{2}GH, na he ne F, nc byð he na I

commouebitur | bið onstyrcd AB, bið onstyryd C, bið astyred D, byð astyred H, bið astyrod F, bið onstired J, beo astyrud K, bið astyred ł ne b[ ]ð onstyred G*, biþ onwended ł astyred E^2*, astyrod ł ⁊ he ne bið awend I

ED: forðon (A)] for ðon *Kuhn*. forþæn þe (E)] Forþæn þe *Harsley*. forþā þe (G)] forþam þe *Rosier*. gehihteð hopað (I)] gehihteð ł hopað *Lindelöf*. mildheortness[ ] (G)] mildheortne[ ] *Rosier*. commouebitur (G)] commoueb*itur* *Rosier*. bið astyred ł ne b[ ]ð onstyred (G)] bið astyred ł ne bið onstyred *Rosier*.

OE: forðan þe (I)] þe *written in left margin and signaled for inclusion after* forðan. se cyning (G)] se *interl*. gehihteð (G)] ð *added in diff*. (?) *hand*. gehihteð hopað (I)] hopað *written in left margin*. geweneþ ł hyhteð (E^2)] teð *on eras*. on mildheortnesse (J)] *otiose mark* (,) *after* mildheortnesse: *cf. Pss 17.46 and 19.7 for similar marks*. þæs hihstan (J)] *otiose mark* (,) *after* hihstan: *cf. Pss 17.46 and 19.7*. bið astyred ł ne b[ ]ð onstyred (G)] *letter after 2nd* b *obscured by modern repairs;* ł ne b[ ]ð onstyred *added in diff*. (?) *hand*. biþ onwended ł astyred (E^2)] *eras. after* biþ.

LTg: sperauit] L: ui *underlined to signal deletion: see GAg;* sperabit A: b *on eras. by corr.*, E: *orig*. sperauit: u *altered to* b. et] *interl*. J. in (*2nd*)] *interl*. H; *om*. J. misericordia] misericordi[ ] G. altissimi] C: a *altered from another letter*.

LTu: sperauit] sperabit τ*. misericordia] missericordia ϑ.

GAg: sperauit] sperat FGHIJ, K: a *on eras*., L: *see LTg*.

GAu: sperauit] sperat δεζϑιλμξοπϱστυφχ.

9

Inueniatur | sie bið gemoeted A, bið gemeted B, bið gemetyd C, sie gemet D, sý gemet F, si gemet HK, sy gemet I, si gemeted GJ, bio gemet E^2*

manus | hond A, hand BCDFIJK, handa GH, þin E^2*

tua | ðin AF, þin BCDIJK, þinum G, þinum H, hand E^2*

omnibus | allum A, eallum BDHIJ, eallum CFG, eællum E^2, eallan K

inimicis | feondum ACFGHI, feondum BDJ, feondan K, þinum E^2

tuis | ðinum AF, ðinum B, þinum CGI, þinum J, þinan K, þin H, fyondum E^2

dextera | sie swiðre A, seo swiðre C, seo swyðre G, seo swiþre J, seo swiðran H, þeo swiþre D, ðeo swýþre F, swiðra I, swyþre K, hand B, þin E^2

tua | ðin AB, þin CDGHIJK, ðín F, swiþræ E^2
inueniat gemoeteð *A*, gemetað C, gemet *BJ*, gemett F, gemete DI, geméte E^2, gemette K, geme[ ]ð G*
omnes alle A, ealle BCDFGIJK, eælle E^2
qui ða ðe AB, þa þe I, þa CE^2*JK, þe DG, ðe FH
te ðe A*B*DHI, þe CE^2FGJK
oderunt figað A, feodon B, hatedon DGH, hatudon *CF*, hatedun I, hatodon K, fiogæþ ł hatedon E^2, hatodon ł feodon J*
⟨oderunt⟩ [ ]atedon ł feodan *G**

ED: Inueniatur (G)] *I*nueniatur *Rosier.* hand (E)] hànd *Harsley.* eallum (G)] [ ]llum *Rosier.* dextera] de*x*tera *Rosier.* inueniat (G)] inuen*i*at *Rosier.* té (B)] te *Brenner.*

OE: bio gemet (E^2)] *letter eras. after* bio, *eras. (1–2 letters) after* gemet. þin (E^2)] *letter eras. after word.* hand (E^2)] *small eras. after* a, *possibly altered from* æ. geme[ ]ð (G)] *two obscured letters after 2nd* e: *leaf split.* þa (E^2)] *small eras. after* a, *possibly altered from* æ. hatodon ł feodon (J)] ł feodon *written above* hatodon. [ ]atedon ł feodan (G)] ł feodan *added in diff.* (?) *hand.*

LTg: inueniat] A: *letter eras. after* a; inueniet B. te] té B. oderunt] C: *scribe began with* d- *but altered* d *to* o; oderuit F. oderunt ⟨oderunt⟩] G'*s last line on fol. 30v ends* omnes qui te, *with* oderunt *added in blank space following end of v. 8, 4 lines above; oversight led scribe to begin fol. 31r with 2nd* oderunt.

10

Pones | ðu setes A, ðu setst BD, þu setyst C, þu setst FK, þu asetst I, þu gesitest *G*, þu gesettest J, þu hie E^2
eos | hie AB, hi CIK, hy DG, hig FJ, gesetst E^2*
ut swe swe A, swa swa BCDGIJ, swæ swa E^2*, swá swá F, swa K
clibanum ofen AFGIJ, ofn B, ofyn C, fyrðolle DE^2*, cliwen K
ignis fyres ADE^2*GIK, fyrys C, fýres F, fires J, ofn B
in in A, on BCDE^2*FGIJK
tempore tid A, tide BCDFIJK, tyde E^2
uultus | ondwliotan A, andwlitan BCDFI, ansyne GK, ansine J, þinre E^2
tui | ðines *A*B, þines DI, þinys C, ðin F, þinre GK, þine J, onsine ł andwlite E^2
dominus dryhten BE^2*, drihtyn C, drihten F, dryht̄ *A*, drih̄t H, driht̄ I, drih̄ GJ
in in A, on BCDE^2FGHIJK
ira | eorre ABDH, yrre CGJK, yrre ł graman I*, graman F, his E^2

sua	ǀ his ABDFGHIJK, hys C, yrre E^{2}
conturbabit	gedroefeð *A*, gedrefð *B*I, gedrefþ E^{2}, he gedrefð DFG*H*, gedrefyd C, gedrefed J, he drefde *K*
eos	hie ABE^{2}, hy DGH, hi CIK, híg F, hig J
et	⁊ ABCE^{2}*FGHIJK
deuorabit	ǀ forswilgeð *A*, forswilgð B, forswyhð C, forswylhð D, forswilhþ *H*, forspylð F, forswylgeð G, forswelgeþ J, forswylgð *K*, forswelgð ł fornimð I*, fyr E^{2}
eos	hie ABE^{2}, hi CK, hig FIJ, hy GH
ignis	ǀ fyr ABCDGHIK, fýr F, fir J, forswylgþ E^{2}

ED: swa swa (GIJ)] swaswa *Rosier, Lindelöf, Oess.* swá swá (F)] swa swá *Kimmens.* hie (A) (*2nd*)] his *Kuhn.* fyr (G)] fyr[ ] *Rosier.*

OE: gesetst (E^{2})] st *on eras.* swæ swa (E^{2})] swa *on eras.* fyrðolle (E^{2})] ðolle *on eras.* fyres (E^{2})] fyr *on eras.* on (E^{2}) (*1st*)] *on eras.* dryhten (E^{2})] ry *on eras.* (?). yrre ł graman (I)] ł graman *written in right margin.* ⁊ (E^{2})] *eras. after word.* forswelgð ł fornimð (I)] ł fornimð *written in right margin.*

LTg: Pones] [ ]ones G: *initial* P *lost.* tui] A: *added by corr. at end of line.* dominus] A: tui *eras. at beginning of line before word.* conturbabit] AK: *2nd* b *on eras. by corr.*, H: *orig.* conturbauit: *2nd* u *altered to* b; conturbauit B. deuorabit] AK: b *on eras. by corr.*, H: *orig.* deuorauit: *2nd* u *altered to* b.

LTu: clibanum] cliuanum ϑ; clybanum ξ. conturbabit] conturbauit ϑ, β: *orig.* conturbabit: u *interl. above 2nd* b. deuorabit] deuorauit ϑ, β: *orig.* deuorabit: u *interl. above* b.

11

Fructum	ǀ westem A, wæstm BCDFGHIK*, wæstmas J, hieræ E^{2}
eorum	ǀ heara A, hira B, hyra CG, heora DFHIJK, westm E^{2}
de	of ABCDE^{2}*FGHIJK
terra	eorðan ABCDFGHI, eorþan JK, eorþæn E^{2}
perdes	ðu forspildes *A*, þu forspiltst B, þu forspilst CHIK, ðu forspilst F, þu forspildest E^{2}G*J, ðu forswiltst D
et	⁊ ABCE^{2}FGHIJ*K
semen	ǀ sed A, sæd BCDFGHIJK, hieræ E^{2}
eorum	ǀ heara A, hira B, hyra C, heora DFGHIJK, sed E^{2}
a	from A*E*^{2}, fro<u>m</u> BC, fra<u>m</u> DFGHJK, fram I
filiis	ǀ bearnum AGH, bearnu<u>m</u> CDFI, biernu<u>m</u> J, bearn BK, mannæ *E*^{2}*
hominum	ǀ monna AB, manna CDFGHIJK, beærnum E^{2}

ED: þu forspiltst (B)] ðu forspiltst *Brenner.* á (E)] a *Harsley.* filíís (E)] filiis *Harsley.*

OE: wæstm (K)] wæsm *eras. before word.* of (E^2)] *on eras.* þu forspildest (G)] de *added interl. in diff.* (?) *hand.* ⁊ (J)] *written below* forspildest. mannæ (E^2)] a *altered from another letter.*

LTg: perdes] A: *2nd* e *on eras. by corr.* a] á E. filiis] filíís E.

LTu: filiis] filis ϑ.

12

Quoniam	forðon ABJ, forþon CG, Forðæn E^2, forþon ðe F, forðan þe I
declinauerunt	hie onhaeldon A, hi onhyldon C, hy ahyldon DFH, hie ahyldon E^2*, hi ahyldon GK, hi ahyldun I, onheldon B, onhildon J
in	in A, on BCDE^2*FGHIJK
te	ðe ABDFGI, þe CE^2HJK
mala	yfel ABGJK, yfyl C, yfelu DFH, yflu I, yfela E^2
cogitauerunt	ðohtun A, ðohton B, þohton J, hi þohton CG, hy ðohton D, hy þohton E^2*H, hi ðohton F, hi geþohtun I, hi þohtan K
consilium*	geðaeht A, geðeht B, geþeaht CDFGH, geþæht K, geþeahta I, geþeah J, geþeæhtunge ł gerun E^2 (*L*)
quod*	ðæt A, þæt BGH, þæt CDFJ, þeð E^2, þa þe I, þa K
non	hie ne AB, hi ne CFIJ, na DE^2*GHK
potuerunt	maehtun A, mehton B, meahton C, mihton FIJK, hy meahton D, hy mihton GH, hy ne miehton E^2
stabilire	gesteaðulfestian A, gestaðulfæstan C, gestaþolfæston F, gestaþelfæstan J, gestaþolfæstnian ł gestaðelian I, gestalian ł gestaðolfæstan G*, gestaðolian BD, gestathelien E^2, gestaþolian K, gestalian H

ED: forðon (A)] for ðon *Kuhn.*

OE: hie ahyldon (E^2)] *eras. before* hie, a *on eras.* on (E^2)] *eras. before word.* hy þohton (E^2)] *eras.* (*17 mm*) *after gloss.* na (E^2)] *orig.* ne: e *altered to* a. gestalian ł gestaðolfæstan (G)] ł gestaðolfæstan *added in diff.* (?) *hand.*

LTg: consilium] L: u *altered to* a *by corr.,* m *underlined to signal deletion: see GAg.*

GAg: consilium] consilia FGHJK, I: *eras.* (?) *after word,* L: *see LTg.* quod] quę FGHJ; quae I; que K.

GAu: consilium] consilia δεζϑιλμξοπϱστυφχψ. quod] quae δμοπυχψ; quę εζιξϱφ; q̄ ϑ; que λστ.

13

Quoniam	forðon ABFJ, forþon CG, Forðæn E^2, forðan þe I

pones | ðu setes A, ðu setst DF, þu setst H, þu settest G*JK, þu gesetst I, gesetst C, þu s B*, þu hie E^2

eos | hie AB, hi CIK, hy DGH, hig FJ, asetst E^2*

deorsum* bec *A*, bæc C, on bæc BK, on bǽc F, adune DH, niþer ł adune E^2, adune ł ofdune G*, ofdune J, on hricge *I* (*L*)

in in A, on BCDE^2*GHIJK, an F

reliquiis lafum ABCE^2*FI, lafum DH, leafum G, leafum J, lafe *K*

tuis ðinum AF, ðinum B, þinum CDHIJ, þinum E^2*G, þinan K

praeparabis ðu gearwas A, þu gearwast *BHK*, ðu gearwast *D*, ðu gærwest *E^2**, þu gegearwast *CG*J*, þu géarcost *F**, þu gegearkast I (*L*)

uultum ondwleotan A, ondwlitan B, andwlitan CDF, andwliten E^2*, andwlitan ł ansyne G*, andwlita H, anwlitan I*J*K

illorum* heara A, hira B, hyra C, heora DFGHIJK, heore E^2*

ED: forðon (A)] for ðon *Kuhn*. reliquíís (K)] reliquiis *Sisam*. on (I) (*2nd*)] *no gloss Lindelöf*. p̄parabis (E)] preparabis *Harsley*.

OE: þu settest (G)] te *added interl. in diff.* (?) *hand*. þu s (B)] *rest of gloss after* s *not written*. asetst (E^2)] st *on eras.* adune ł ofdune (G)] ł ofdune *added in diff.* (?) *hand above* adune. on (E^2)] *on eras.* lafum (E^2)] *on eras.* þinum (E^2)] *on eras.* ðu gærwest (E^2)] *on eras.* þu gegearwast (G)] *1st* ge *added interl. in diff.* (?) *hand*. þu géarcost (F)] *back of* a *on eras.* andwliten (E^2)] *on eras.* andwlitan ł ansyne (G)] ł ansyne *added interl. in diff.* (?) *hand above* andwlitan. heore (E^2)] *on eras.*

LTg: Quoniam] [ ]oniam G: *initial* Q *lost*. deorsum] A: e *and left side of* o *on eras.*, L: e *obscured by blot: see GAg*. reliquiis] reliquíís K. praeparabis] preparabis BCDFGHJ; præparabis K; p̄parabis EL. uultum] J: *2nd* u *on eras. of* l.

LTu: reliquiis] β: *2nd* i *interl.;* riliquis ϑ. praeparabis] pręparabis βελμνξϱ; preparabis ζϑιπσ; p̄parabis οτ*τφχ.

GAg: deorsum] dorsum FGHIJK, L: *see LTg*. illorum] eorum FGHIJK.

GAu: deorsum] dorsum δεζϑιλμξοπϱστυφχψ. illorum] eorum δεζϑιλμξοπϱστυφψ.

14

Exaltare hefe up A, uphefe B, upphefe C, upahefe DE^2*FH, upahefe þu GJ, si þu upahafen I, afehe K

domine dryhten B, drihten E^2*F, dryht̄ A, driht *C*H, drih̄ GJ (I*)

in in A, on BCDE^2*FGHIJK

uirtute megne AE^2*, mægene BDGHI, mægyne C, mægne JK, mihte F

tua ðinum AF, ðinum B, þinum CDIJ, þinum GH, þine E^2*

cantabimus — we singað ABCDFGH, we singaþ IJK, we singeð E^{2}*
et — ⁊ ABCDE^{2}*FGHIJK
psallemus — singað *AB*C, we singað J, drymað D*G*H, dremað E^{2}*FK, we freadremaþ I
uirtutes | megen A, mægyn C, mægeno B, mægenu DH, mægnu F, mægene G, mægne J, mægna K, strengða I, þine E^{2}*
tuas | ðin A, þin C, ðine BF, þine DHIK, þinum G, þinum J, megne E^{2}

OE: upahefe (E^{2})] *on eras.* domine] I: s. o đ (= drihten *or variant form*) *written in left margin; a single subscript dot links abbreviation with* domine, *which also carries a single subscript dot.* drihten (E^{2})] *on eras.* on (E^{2})] *on eras.* megne (E^{2}) (*1st*)] *on eras.* þine (E^{2}) (*1st*)] *on eras.* we singeð (E^{2})] *on eras.* ⁊ (E^{2})] *on eras.* dremað (E^{2})] *on eras.* þine (E^{2}) (*2nd*)] e *on eras.*

LTg: domine] C: *interl. by main scribe.* psallemus] G: *orig.* sallemus: p *added, with bowl extended above initial long* s; psallimus AB.

LTu: psallemus] psallimus βμ.

PSALM 21

2

Deus — god *AF*GJ, god E^{2}, eala god C*, eala þu god I (*BDK*)
deus — god AB*C*E^{2}FGIJK (*D*)
meus — min AB*C*E^{x}*FGIJK (*D*)
respice — geloca ACJ, loca B, loce E^{2}, beseoh DFHI, beseoh ł beheald ł geloca G*, besceawa K
in* — in A, on BCDE^{2}G*J (*HK*)
me — me ABCDE^{2}FGJK, on me I
quare — forhon A, forhwon BCJ, forwæn E^{2}, hwy D, hwi GHK, forhwý F, forhwi I
me | me ABCFGI, forlete þu E^{2}J, þu me K
dereliquisti | forleorte ðu A, forlete þu CI, þu forlete BGH, ðu forlete DF, forlete K, me E^{2}J
longe — feor ABDFGHIJK, feorr C, fyor E^{x}*
a — from A, from BC, fram DGHJK, fram E^{x}*FI
salute — haelu A, hælo BDFHJ, hæle CGIK, hele E^{x}*
mea — minre ABCDFGHIJK, minra E^{2}
uerba — word *ABCD*FGHI*JK, Word *E^{2}* (*L*)
delictorum | scylda ABCDGHK, scilda J, gylta FI*, minræ E^{2}*
meorum | minra ABCDFGHI*JK, ægyltæ E^{2}*

ED: god (E) (*1st*)] God *Harsley*. á (E)] a *Harsley*. forhon (A)] for hon *Kuhn*.

OE: eala god (C)] s. o *written before* eala, eala *obscured by show-through from fol. 33r but visible*. min (E^{x})] *on eras*. beseoh ł beheald ł geloca (G)] ł geloca *added above* beheald *in diff.* (?) *hand*. on (G)] *added below 1st OE* me *in diff.* (?) *hand*. fyor (E^{x})] *on eras*. fram (E^{x})] *on eras*. hele (E^{x})] *on eras*. word (I)] *orig*. wurd: u *altered to* o. gylta (I)] *orig*. gilta: i *altered to* y. minræ (E^{2})] *eras. after word*. minra (I)] s. synt *written in left margin*. ægyltæ (E^{2})] *possible accent above initial* æ (ǽgyltæ?).

LTg: Deus] DS̄ ABDFK; DEVS C. deus] DEUS C; DS̄ D. meus] MS̄ CD. in] G: i *on eras*. (ī), H: *on eras*., K: *added later by main hand: see GAg*. a] á E. uerba] L: *orig*. Verba: V *crossed through and* u *written after* V *by Lat. glossator;* Verba ABDE; Uerba C.

LTu: Deus] DEVS ιτ; DEUS πς; DS̄ βλμνξϱστ*φ. deus] DEUS π; DS̄ βλμνξϱσφ. meus] MEUS νπ; MS̄ λμξϱσφ. respice] RESPICE λξπϱ; RESPIce μ. me] ME λξπϱ. quare] QVARE ξ; QUAre ϱ. longe] longue ϑ. uerba] Uerba β; Verba νςτ*. delictorum] dilictorum ϑ.

GAg: in] *om*. FI; *for* K *see LTg*.

GAu: in] *om*. δειλοπτψ.

3

Deus	I	god *ABC*F*G*I*JK, min E^{2} (*DL*)
meus	I	min ABCFGIJK, god E^{2}
clamabo		ic cleopiu A, ic clipige BJ, ic clypige C*DFGH, ic clepige I, ic clypie K, ic cige E^{2}
per		ðorh A, þurh BCE^{2}FGHJK, ðurh D, iand I
diem		deg AE^{2}*, dæg BCDFG*H*IJK
(et)*		⁊ FGHIJK
nec*	I	ne ABDE^{2}J, na GHK, ne þu ne C, þu ne I*, ðu ne F
exaudies	I	ðu geheres A, ðu gehierest B, þu gehierest E^{2}*, ðu gehyrest D, þu gehyrest GH, g̲ehyrst C, gehyrest FK, geherst I, gehires J
et		⁊ ABCDE^{2}FGHIJK
nocte		on naeht A, on niht BDG*H*K, on nihte I, on nyht E^{x}*, nihte C, niht FJ
et		⁊ ABCE^{x}*FG*H**IJK
non		nales AB, nalæs FJ, nalys C, na DE^{x}*GHIK
ad		to ABCDE^{x}*FGHIK, on J
insipientiam		unwisdome ABDFHK, unwisdome ł ⁊ nalæs on unwisum G, þan unwisdome C, unwisum̲ J, nanre unsnotornysse I, unsnyternesse ł unwisdóme E^{2}
mihi		me AB*C*FGI*J*K, minre *E^{2}*

ED: díem (H)] diem *Campbell.*

OE: god (I)] þu min *written in left margin.* ic clypige (C)] l *interl.* deg (E^{2})] *eras. after word.* þu ne (I)] e *blotted.* þu gehierest (E^{2})] *eras. before word.* on nyht (E^{x})] *on eras.* ⁊ (*3rd*) (E^{2}H)] *on eras.* na (E^{x})] *on eras.* to (E^{x})] *on eras.*

LTg: Deus] deus ABCDEL; [ ]eus G. diem] díem H; diem ⁊ L: ⁊ *added interl. by Lat. glossator: see GAg.* nocte] H: *followed by eras.* et (*2nd*)] H: *on eras.* mihi] michi EJ, C: *orig.* mihi: c *interl. by corr.*

LTu: Deus] deus βνςτ*. mihi] michi ιξσςτ*τφ, ζπϱ: *orig.* mihi: c *interl. by corr.*

GAg: diem] diem et FGIJK, L: *see LTg;* díem et H. nec] non FGHIJK.

GAu: diem] diem et δεζϑιλμξοπϱστυφχψ. nec] non δεζϑιλμξοπϱστυφχψ.

4

Tu	ðu ABF, þu CE^{2}GIJK
autem	soðlice ABCGI, soþlice E^{2}FJ, witodlice K
in	in A, on BCDE^{2}*FGHIJK
sancto	halgum AFGI, halgu<u>m</u> BHJ, halygu<u>m</u> C, halgan D, hælgæn E^{2}, halinese K
habitas	eardas A, eardast BCDHK, eardest E^{2}, þu eardast G**J*, geeardast I, wunast F
laus	lof ABCDE^{2}FGHIJK
israhel	israhela B, israhel C, israhele F, israela *J,* isra(h)[ ] G*, israele ł haligen *E^{x}**, israelitica bearna *I,* ðæs haligan folces *D**, þæs haligan folces H (*K*)

ED: isrł (DJIK)] israhel *Roeder, Oess;* israel *Lindelöf;* Israhel *Sisam.*

OE: on (E^{2})] *eras. after word.* þu eardast (G)] þu *added in diff.* (?) *hand.* isra(h)[ ] (G)] *ascender of* h *lost.* israele ł haligen (E^{x})] *on eras.* ðæs haligan folces (D)] folces *written below* an *in* haligan, *extending into right margin.*

LTg: habitas] habitans J: see *Weber MSS* moz^{c}. israhel] israel E: *eras. after word;* isrł DIJK.

LTu: israhel] israel ινςτ*; isrł εξοπϱσυ, β: s *interl.*

5

In	in *A*, on *BCE^{x}*FGHIJK* (*DL*)
te	ðe A*B*FH, þe CE^{x}*GIJK
sperauerunt	gehyhtan A, gehyhton B, gehihton *C,* ic gehihte G*J, hyhton D, hihtan K, hyhte H, hyhton ł hopedon E^{x}*, gehihton ł hopedon I, ic hopude F
patres	fedras A, fædras B, fæderas C*DFGHIJK, ure E^{2}

nostri | ure ABCDFGHIJK, federæs E^{2}
sperauerunt gehyhton AB, gehihton *CJ*, hy gehyhton D, hi gehihtun I, hy hyhton GH, hihtan K, hig hopudon F, on þe hy gehopeden $E^{2/x}$*
et ⁊ ABCDE^{2}FGHIJK
liberasti | ðu gefreodes A, ðu alesdes B, ðu alysdest D, þu alysdest FGH, þu alesdest I, þu alisdest J, þu lysdest K, þu gefreodyst C, þu hie E^{2}
eos | hie AB, hy DGH, hig FJ, hi IK, his C, alysdest E^{x}*

OE: on (E^{x})] *on eras.* þe (E^{x})] *on eras.* ic gehihte (G)] ic ge *added in diff.* (?) *hand.* hyhton ł hopedon (E^{x})] *on eras.* fæderas (C)] e *interl.* on þe hy gehopeden ($E^{2/x}$)] hy gehopeden *on eras. by corr.* alysdest (E^{x})] *on eras.*

LTg: In] G: *orig.* in: i *eras., initial* I *written in left margin;* in ABCDEFJKL, H: i *on eras.* te] té B. sperauerunt (*1st*)] C: *1st* e *on eras. by corr.* sperauerunt (*2nd*)] C: *eras.* (*ca 4 letters*) *after 2nd* e.

LTu: In] *as* In *in* εζ, *but not indicating verse division;* in βδϑνξϱσςτ*υχψ. et liberasti eos] *om.* φ.

6
Ad to ABCFGHIJK, To E^{2}
te ðe ABFGHI, þe CE^{2}JK
clamauerunt cleopedon A, clipodon B, clypodun C, clipedon J, clypodon K, hy cleopodon D, hie clipoden $E^{2/x}$*, hy clypedon G, hy clepodon I, ic clypude F, ic clypedon H
et ⁊ ABCDE^{2}FGHIJK
salui hale ABCDE^{2}*FGHIK
facti gewordne AB, gewordyne C, gewordene IJ, hy gewordene D, hy gewordene H, hy gewordene $E^{2/x}$*, hi gewordene FG, gedone K
sunt sind A, sint B, synd CFGK, synt E^{2}, sindon D, syndon HJ, synt ⁊ hi synt gehælde I*
in in A, on BCE^{2}FGHIJK
te ðe ABFH, þe CE^{2}GIJK
sperauerunt gehyhton AB, gehihtun C, hy gehyhton D, hy gehyhton H, hy gehihton G, hi gehihton FI, hie hopodon ł gehihton $E^{2/x}$*, hihton J, hihtan *K*
et ⁊ ABCE^{2}FGHIJK
non | ne ACE^{2}FJ, na DH*K*, na ne G, hi ne I, hie B
sunt | werun A, wæron J, synt CI, synd DFGHK, syndon E^{2}, næron B
confusi gescende ABE^{2}, gescynde CDFGH*I*, gescinde J, gescynd K

ED: consusi (I)] confusi *Lindelöf.*

OE: hie clipoden (E$^{2/x}$)] clipoden *on eras. by corr.* hale (E^{2})] a *altered from* æ. hy gewordene (E$^{2/x}$)] hy *on eras. by corr.* synt ⁊ hi synt gehælde (I)] ⁊ hi synt gehælde *written in right margin.* hie hopodon ł gehihton (E$^{2/x}$)] hopodon ł *on eras. by corr.*

LTg: sperauerunt] K: aue *altered from* unt. non] K: *final* n *added interl. by corr.* confusi] consusi I.

LTu: confusi] confussi ϑ.

7

Ego	ic ABCDF*GH*IJK, Ic E^{2}
autem	soðlice ABCFGHI, soþlice D*J, Soþlice E^{2}*, witodlice K
sum	eam A, eom BCE^{2}GIJK, ic eom DF
uermis	wyrm ABCDE^{2}*FGHIJK
et	⁊ ABCE^{2}FGHIJK
non	nales AB, nalys C, nalæs G*J, na DE^{2}*FHIK (*L*)
homo	mon AB, man FGHJK, mann CDE^{2}*I
obprobrium	edwit *AC,* edwet B, hosp DG_H_*JK, hósp F, ædwít ł hosp E$^{2/x}$*, bysmerung ł hosp *I*
hominum	monna AB, manna CDFGHIJ, manne E^{x}*, mannan K
et	⁊ ABCDE^{x}*FGHIJK
abiectio	aworpnes A, aweorpnes B, aworpnys C, aworpenis D, aworpennys F, aworpennis H, aworpennes K, aworpednysse E^{x}*, aworpenis ł onweg awearp G, onweg awearp J, forwyrpnes ł aworpennys I*
plebis	folces ABDE^{x}*FHI, folcys C, folc GJ

ED: [ ]go (H)] Ego *Campbell.* opprobrium (C)] o[b]probrium *Wildhagen.* abiectio (E)] abjectio *Harsley.*

OE: soþlice (D)] *on eras.* Soþlice (E^{2})] *eras.* (ic?) *after word.* wyrm (E^{2})] *eras. after word.* nalæs (G)] læs *added in diff.* (?) *hand.* na (E^{2})] *eras. after word.* mann (E^{2})] a *altered from* æ. hosp (H)] h *partly effaced.* ædwít ł hosp (E$^{2/x}$)] ædwít ł *on eras., eras. after* hosp. manne (E^{x})] *on eras.* ⁊ (E^{x})] *on eras.* aworpednysse (E^{x})] *on eras.* forwyrpnes ł aworpennys (I)] ł aworpennys *written in right margin.* folces (E^{x})] *on eras.*

LTg: Ego] [ ]go G, H: *initial* E *lost, outline visible only.* non] *om.* L, *but* n[on] *added interl. by Lat. glossator.* obprobrium] opprobrium AHI, C: *orig.* obprobrium: *1st* b *altered to* p.

LTu: obprobrium] opprobrium λοπ, β: *orig.* obprobrium: p *interl. by corr. after* b, *but without deleting mark;* oppbrium εφ.

8

Omnes		alle A, ealle BCDFG*H*IJK, Eælle E^{2}
qui*		ða A, þe C*D, ða ðe B, þa þe E$^{2/x}$* (*L*)
uidebant*	|	gesegun A, gesawon BCD, geseonde IK, geseonde ł þa ðe gesawon G, ða þe gesawon F, þa þe gesawon J, me E^{2} (*L*)
me	|	me ABCGIJK, gesægen E^{2}
aspernabantur*		herwdun A, hèrwdon B, hyrwdon C, hy anscunedan D, tǽldon ł býsmrodon F, forhogodon G, forhogedon J, hyrpæden ł anscunedon E$^{2/x}$*, hlehtredon ł tældun ł hlogon on bysmor I (*L*)
me		me ABCDE^{x}*FGIJ
locuti		spreocende A, sprecende BJ, sprecynde C, specende K, hy spræcon D*H*, hy sprecen E^{2}, hig spræcon F, hy spræco[ ] G*, hi spræcon ł sprecende I*
sunt		werun A, wæron CIJ, hie wæron B, synd K (*G*)
labiis		mid weolerum A, mid welerum C, mid welerum FI, mid welrum B, on welerum J, welleron D, welerum GH, weleras K, mid welleron ł lippen *E^{x}**
et		⁊ ABCE^{x}*FGHIJK
mouerunt		hrisedon AB, hrysydon C, hrysedon DFGH, hrysodon K, weagedon ł rysedon E^{2}*, onwændon J, hi cwehtun I*
caput		heafud AC, heafod B*DH,* heofod E^{x}*, hæfod K, heora heafod FIJ

ED: hy spræco[ ] (G)] *see OE.* s[ ]t (G)] *sunt Rosier.* labíís (E)] labiis *Harsley.*

OE: þe (C)] e *interl.* þa þe (E$^{2/x}$)] a *and 2nd* þ *on eras. by corr.* hyrpæden ł anscunedon (E$^{2/x}$)] den ł anscunedon *on eras. by corr.* me (E^{x}) (*2nd*)] *on eras.* hy spræco[ ] (G)] *perhaps another gloss written above:* spre(?) *followed by tear in leaf and then* [ ]on; *not noted by Rosier.* hi spræcon ł sprecende (I)] hi spræcon *written in left margin.* mid welleron ł lippen (E^{x})] *on eras.* ⁊ (E^{x})] *on eras.* weagedon ł rysedon (E^{2})] *on eras.* hi cwehtun (I)] hi *interl.* heofod (E^{x})] *on eras.*

LTg: Omnes] H: O *nearly completely lost, with faint traces of blue ink visible.* qui] L: *underlined to signal deletion. see GAg.* uidebant] L: bant *underlined to signal deletion,* ntes *interl. by Lat. glossator: see GAg.* aspernabantur] L: *underlined to signal deletion,* deriserunt *interl. by Lat. glossator: see GAg.* locuti] loquti H: *orig.* locuti: c *altered to* q. sunt] s[ ]t G. labiiis] labíís E. caput] H: t *altered from another letter;* capud D.

LTu: me (*1st*)] mę ζ. labiis] labis ϑ. caput] capud ξ.

GAg: qui] *om.* FGHIJK, L: *see LTg.* uidebant] uidentes FGHIJK, L: *see LTg.* aspernabantur] deriserunt FGIK, H: *orig.* diriserunt: *1st* i *altered to* e, J: riser *on eras.,* L: *see LTg.*

GAu: qui] *om.* δεζϑιλμξοπϱστυφχψ. uidebant] uidentes δεζϑιλμξοπϱστυφχψ. aspernabantur] deriserunt δεζϑιλμξοπϱστυφχψ.

9

Sperauit	gehyhteð AB, gehihte C, he gehyhte DH, he gehyhte ł hopade E^{x}*, he gehihte GI, gehihton J, he hihte K, hig hopudon F
in	in A, on BCDE^{2}FGHIJK
domino	dryhtne BD, drihtne CFI, drihten E^{2}G*K, dryht̄ A, driħt H, driħ J
eripiat	| generеð AB, generyð *C*, he generað F, generede J, he alyseþ *D*, he aleseð H, he alysde K, he alyseð ł generede G*, he genereð he generie I*, he hine *E*^{2} (*L*)
eum	| hine ABDFGHIJK, hyne C, generæþ ł alyseþ E$^{2/x}$*
saluum	halne ABCDE^{2}FG*HJ*, hal K, [ ]e gehæle I*
faciat	doe A, dóó *C*, deð *B*, deþ K, he gedeþ DE^{x}*FH, he gedeð ł gedyde G*, gedide J (*L*)
eum	hine ABCE^{x}*FHIJK, hi[ ] G*
quoniam	forðon ABFH, forþon *C*, forðan K, fordan E^{x}*, forþon þe GJ, forðan þe I
uult	he wile ABDE$^{2/x}$*FHI, he wyle C, wyle K, he wile ł wolde G*, he wolde J
eum	hine ABE^{2}FGIJK, hyne C

ED: Sperauit (B)] speravit *Brenner*. on (G)] [ ]n *Rosier*. domino (G)] dom*ino* *Rosier*. drihten (G)] drihtn *Rosier*. he genereð he generie (I)] he genereð ł he generie *Lindelöf*. saluum (BE)] salvum *Brenner, Harsley*. [ ]e gehæle (I)] he gehæle *Lindelöf*. forðon (A)] for ðon *Kuhn*.

OE: he gehyhte ł hopade (E^{x})] he gehyhte *on eras., 1st corr. wrote* ł hopað, *2nd corr. altered* ð *to* d *and added* e. drihten (G)] e *interl.* he alyseð ł generede (G)] ł generede *added above* he alyseð *in diff.* (?) *hand.* he genereð he generie (I)] he generie *written in right margin.* generæþ ł alyseþ (E$^{2/x}$)] ł alyseþ *on eras.* [ ]e gehæle (I)] *written in left margin, initial letter lost due to tight binding* (?); *orig. glosses above* saluum faciat *eras.* he gedeþ (E^{x})] *on eras.* he gedeð ł gedyde (G)] ł gedyde *added above* he gedeð *in diff.* (?) *hand.* hine (E^{x}) (*2nd*)] *on eras.* hi[ ] (G)] *2 minims visible after* i. fordan (E^{x})] *on eras.* he wile (E$^{2/x}$)] he *on eras. by corr.* he wile ł wolde (G)] ł wolde *added above* he wile *in diff.* (?) *hand.*

LTg: eripiat] eripiet CL, D: *orig.* eripiat: a *deleted by subscript dot,* e *interl.*, E: *2nd* e *on eras.* saluum] H: *eras. before word.* faciat] faciet BCL. quoniam] C: m *altered from another letter, with 3rd leg by corr.*

LTu: eripiat] eripiet τ*. faciat] σ: *orig.* faciet: et *deleted,* at *interl.;* faciet τ*.

10

Quoniam	forðon ABF, forþon CGJ, Forðæn E^{2}*, f̄ þe I
tu	ðu AB, þu CDE^{2}FGHIJK
es	earð A, eart BCDFGHIJK*, eært E^{2}
qui	ðu A, þu B, þu þe J, ðu þe I, þe CDE$^{2/x}$*FGH, þa K
abstraxisti*	| atuge ABCK, framatuge DH, framatuge F, framatuge ł [ ] ðe oftuge G*, oftuge J, utatuge ł genyddyst I, me E^{2} (*L*)
me	| me ABCFGIJK, framátuge E^{x}*
de	of ABCDE^{x}*FGHIJK
uentre	wombe AB, wambe C, innoðe DE^{x}*H, innoþe FK, innoþe ł wambehrife G*, wambe ł innoþe ł life J*, rife ł of innoðe I*
spes	hyht AB*D*H, hiht CFIK, hihtes GJ, hope ł hyht E^{x}*
mea	min *A*BCDE^{x}*FGHI*K, mines J
ab	from A, from BC, fram I, fram DE^{x}*FGHJ*K
uberibus	breostum AC, breostum BJ, breosta K, breostwelmum D, breostwylmum FG, breostwylmum H , breostwelmum ł tyten E^{x}*, breostcofan I
matris	modur AC, modor BDFHIJ, moder E^{x}*K, meder G*
meae	minre *ABCDE^{x}*FGH*IJ*K* (*L*)

ED: forðon (A)] for ðon *Kuhn*. f̄ þe (I)] forþan þe *Lindelöf*. framatuge (H)] fram atuge *Campbell*. framatuge ł [ ] ðe oftuge (G)] f[ ]am atuge ł þc oftuge *Rosier*. framátugc (E^{x})] fram átuge *Harsley*. meę (E)] meæ *Harsley*.

OE: Forðæn (E^{2})] forðæn (?): *minuscule and majuscule forms often distinguished only by size*. eart (K)] e *malformed*. þe (E$^{2/x}$)] e *on eras. by corr.* framatuge ł [ ] ðe oftuge (G)] *ascender visible after* ł, *followed by tear in leaf, left side of bowl of* ð *lost;* ł [ ] ðe oftuge *written above* framatuge, *in diff.* (?) *hand*. framátuge (E^{x})] *on eras.* of (E^{x})] *on eras.* innoðe (E^{x})] *on eras.* innoþe ł wambehrife (G)] ł wambehrife *added above* innoþe *in diff.* (?) *hand*. wambe ł innoþe ł life (J)] ł life *written above* wambe. rife ł of innoðe (I)] *1st* i *on eras.* hope ł hyht (E^{x})] *on eras.* min (E^{x})] *on eras.* min (I)] s. es : þu eart *written in left margin*. fram (E^{x})] *on eras.* fram (J)] *written below preceding* mines. breostwelmum ł tyten (E^{x})] *on eras.* moder (E^{x})] *on eras.* meder (G)] *orig.* modor: o *altered to* e *both times, possibly by diff. hand*. minre (E^{x})] *on eras.*

LTg: abstraxisti] L: ab *crossed through,* ex *added interl.: see GAg*. spes] spés D. mea] A: *eras. after word*. meae] meæ BKL; meę CDEG; męę H.

LTu: qui] qvi τ*. meae] meę ειμνξφ; meæ ϑ; mee σςτ*τ.

GAg: abstraxisti] extraxisti FGHIJK, L: *see LTg*.

GAu: abstraxisti] extraxisti δεζϑιλμξοπϱστυφχψ.

11

in		in A, on BCDE^{x}*FGHIJK
te		ðe ABDE^{x}*HI, þe CFGJK
iactatus*	I	aworpen ABE^{x}*FGI, aworpyn C, aswenged D, ic wæs J
sum	I	ic eam A, ic eom BCDE^{x}*FGHI, geworpen J
ex		of ABCDE^{x}*GHIK, on J
utero		innoðe ABC, innoþe IJK, hrife DH, hryfe F, hrife ł of innoðe G*, ingerife E^{x}*
de		of ABCDE^{x}**FGHIK,* ⁊ of *J*
uentre		wombe AB, wambe CK, innoðe DE^{x}*FH, innoðe ł hrife G*, hryfe I, hyre J
matris		modur AC, modor BDFH, moder E^{x}*IK, meder GJ
meae		minre A*BCDE^{2}FGHIJK* (*L*)
deus		god ABCE^{2}*FGIJK
meus		min ABCE^{2}FGIJK
es	I	eart CDE^{2}FGH*JK, ðu AB, þu I
tu	I	ðu CF, þu DE^{2}G*H*JK, earð A, eart BI

ED: in (E)] In *Harsley*. meę (E)] meae *Harsley*.

OE: on (E^{x})] *on eras.* ðe (E^{x})] *on eras.* aworpen (E^{x})] *on eras.* ic eom (E^{x})] *on eras.* of (E^{x}) (*1st*)] *on eras.* hrife ł of innoðe (G)] ł of innoðe *added in diff.* (?) *hand.* ingerife (E^{x})] *on eras.* of (E^{x}) (*2nd*)] *on eras.* innoðe (E^{x})] *on eras.* innoðe ł hrife (G)] ł hrife *added above* innoðe *in diff.* (?) *hand.* moder (E^{x})] *on eras.* god (E^{2})] *small eras. after* d. eart (H)] *eras. before* r, *mostly likely due to eras. of ligature of* st *in* es tu.

LTg: de] De FGHIJK. meae] meæ BKL; meę CDFG, E: *eras. after word;* męę H; mee J. tu] H: *eras. above* t, *most likely of ligature of* st *in* es tu.

LTu: de] De δεζϑιλμξοπϱστυφχ. uentre] uentrę ν. matris] ψ: *interl.* meae] meę ειμνξςφχ; meæ ϑ; mee στ*τ.

GAg: iactatus] proiectus FGHIJK.

GAu: iactatus] proiectus δεζϑιλμξοπϱστυφχψ.

12

Ne	ne ABCD*FGHIJK,* Ne E^{2} (*L*)
discesseris	gewit ðu ADFGI, gewit þu BCE^{x}*JK, gewit *H**
a	from A*E*^{2}, from̲ C, fram̲ BJ, fram FGI, fra K
me	me ABCE^{2}FGIJK
quoniam	forðon AB, forþon CE^{2}, forðon ðe *F,* forþon þe *G,* forðon þe *J,* forþan þe *I* (*HK*)

tribulatio geswinc ABCDGHJK, geswinc ł eærfoþu E2/x*, gedrefednysse F, unrotnysse I
proxima on neoweste A, on neawoste B, on neawyste C, gehende DH, gehende ł neæh E2/x*, gehende ł neah G*, neahlice is ł gehende I, neah J, nihsta F, nyxt K
est is ABEx*FGIJ*K*, ys C
et* ⁊ ABCDE2*J, forðon ðe F, forðan þe I, forþam þe G, forðam K
non | nis ADEx*FHI, nys C, ne B, nan G, na JK
est | is BGJ*K*
qui se ðe ABCG*, se þe FIJ, se E2*, þe DH, þa K
adiuuet gefultume *A,* gefultumige B, gefultumie *C,* fultumge D, fultomie E2/x*, fultmige H, gefultumað F, gefultumigeð G, gefultumiaþ J, gefultumige ł gehelpe I, fylsteþ *K*

ED: á (E)] a *Harsley.* forðon (A)] for ðon *Kuhn.*

OE: gewit þu (Ex)] *on eras.* gewit (H)] *eras. after* t: u *visible beneath* sse *added interl. to lemma below* (*see LTg note to* discesseris). geswinc ł eærfoþu (E2/x)] swinc *on eras. by corr.* gehende ł neæh (E2/x)] gehende *on eras. by corr.* gehende ł neah (G)] ł neah *added above* gehende *in diff.* (?) *hand.* is (Ex)] *on eras.* ⁊ (E2)] *eras. before word.* nis (Ex)] *on eras.* se ðe (G)] *added in diff.* (?) *hand.* se (E2)] *eras. before word.* ſultomie (E2/x)] ie *on eras. by corr., eras. before word.*

LTg: Ne] ne FGHIJK, L: *orig.* Ne: N *crossed through and* n *written after by Lat. glossator.* discesseris] H: sse *interl. on eras. and signaled for inclusion by a stroke: see OE note to* gewit. a] á E. quoniam] Quoniam FGHIJK. est (*1st*)] ést K. est (*2nd*)] ést K. adiuuet] A: *2nd* u *on eras.,* C: iu *on eras.;* adiuuæt K.

LTu: Ne] ne δεζϑιλμξοπϱστυφχ. discesseris] ε: sse *interl.;* disceseris ν. quoniam] Quoniam δεζιλμοπϱστυφχψ. et] quoniam ς: *cf. Weber MSS* αβδεη med, *see GAu.* adiuuet] adiubet β; adiuuat ϑ.

GAg: et] quoniam FGHIK.

GAu: et] quoniam δεζϑιλμξοπϱστυφχψ, ς: *see LTu.*

13

Circumdederunt ymbsaldon AB, ymbsealdon *CDH,* Ymbseældon *E*2, ymbesældan K, utan ymbsealdon *G**, uton ymbsealdon J, hy ymbtrymdon F, ymhwurfon ł ymbsetton ł ymbtrymdon I*
me me ABCE2F*G*IJK (*L*)
uituli | calfur A, cealfru *B*DHJ, calfru F, cealfra G, cealfas CI, cealfa K, monegu E2

multi	I monig A, monige B, mænige CG, menige DH, manige F, mænega I, manega J, maniga K, ceælfæs E²*
tauri	fearras ABCDFGHIJ, feærræs E², færras K
pingues	faette A, fætte BCDE²FGHIJK
obsederunt	I oferseton *A*, ofyrsæton C, ofsæton B, ofsetton J, ofsettun ł ymbsæton I, forsætnodon D, forsætnodon ł ofsæton G*, forsetnodon H, forsetnodan K, forsæton F, me E²
me	I me ABCFGIJK, forsetnoden E²*

ED: Circundederunt (C)] Circu[m]dederunt *Wildhagen.*

OE: utan ymbsealdon (G)] n *in* utan *interl.* ymhwurfon ł ymbsetton ł ymbtrymdon (I)] ł ymbtrymdon *written in bottom margin below lemma.* ceælfæs (E²)] *eras. (20 mm) after word.* forsætnodon ł ofsæton (G)] ł ofsæton *added in diff.* (?) *hand,* ton *written above following OE* me. forsetnoden (E²)] r *on eras. and 'squeezed in,'* no *on eras.*

LTg: Circumdederunt] G: -run *added in black ink on eras. before* t, t *slightly raised above line* (*cf. Ps 21.18* dinumerauerunt); Circundederunt E, C: *orig.* Circumdederunt: *left leg of* m *eras. to form* n, H: *orig.* Circumdederunt: *right leg of* m *eras. to form* n. me (*1st*)] G: *written in same dark ink as* run *in* Circumdederunt; *om.* L. uituli] B: *on eras.* multi] B: *on eras.* obsederunt] A: *orig.* obsiderunt: i *altered to* e.

LTu: Circumdederunt] Circundederunt λφ, ϱ: *orig.* Circumdederunt: *deleting dot below right leg of* m.

14

Aperuerunt	ontyndon ABC*G**J, hy atyndon *D*H, hi atyndon *K,* hy atýwdon F, hi untyndun I, hy atyndon ł upenedon *E²/x**
in*	in A, on BCDE², ofer FGI*JK (*L*)
me	me ABCDE²FGIJK
os	I muð *A*BCFGHI, muþ JK, hioræ E²
suum	I his A, hys C, hira B, heora DFHIJK, muþ E²
sicut	swe swe A, swa swa B*C*DE²/x*FGHIJ, swa K
leo	leo ABFGIJK, lyo C, lye E²
rapiens	reafiende ABDH, reafigynde C, rafigende G, reafigende JK, gripende E²*, grimetende F, hreafiende ł gripende ł gyrretynde I*
et	⁊ ABCDE²FGHIJK
rugiens	grymetiende A, grymetende BI*, grymytiende C, grymetgende DE²*H, grymettigende *G,* grimitigende *J,* gremetgende K, reafigende F

ED: ós (A)] os *Kuhn.* swa swa (GIJ)] swaswa *Rosier, Lindelöf, Oess.*

OE: ontyndon (G)] *in lighter ink.* hy atyndon ł upenedon (E$^{2/x}$)] ł upenedon *on eras. by corr.* ofer (I)] *orig.* ofor: *small cross-stroke added in bowl of 2nd* o *in light brown ink.* swa swa (E$^{2/x}$)] *1st* a *altered from another letter* (æ?), *2nd* swa *on eras. by corr.* gripende (E^{2})] *eras. after word.* hreafiende ł gripende ł gyrretynde (I)] *1st* y *altered from* i (?). grymetende (I)] *orig.* grimetende: i *altered to* y. grymetgende (E^{2})] *eras. after* t.

LTg: Aperuerunt] E: *right leg of 1st* u *and* ert *on eras. by corr.,* K: *shoulder of* r *and* t *on eras.;* Apperuerunt D; Operuerunt G. in] L: *underlined to signal deletion,* super *added interl. by Lat. glossator: see GAg.* os] ós A. sicut] sic C. rugiens] G: *orig.* ruiens: iens *crossed through, with deleting dots above and below,* giens *added to right in same later hand that wrote* deus *at Pss 21.21 and 25.9 and added* r (*interl.*) *at Ps 24.3* irrideant; rugens J.

LTu: Aperuerunt] Apperuerunt β. in] β: n *interl.*

GAg: in] super FGHIJK, L: *see LTg.*

GAu: in] super δεζϑιλμξοπϱστυφχψ.

15

Sicut		swe swe *A*, swa swa *BCD*FGHIJ, swæ swæ *E*^{2}, swa K (*L*)
aqua		weter A, wæter BCDFGHIJK, wætær E^{2}
effusa*		agotene ABDE$^{2/x}$*K, agotyne C, agoten I, utagoten FGJ (*L*)
sunt*		sind A, sint B, synd CDK, siondon E^{2}, ic eom FI, wæron ł ic eom G*, wæron J (*L*)
et		⁊ ABCDE^{2}FG*HIJK
dispersa		tostrogden A, tostrogdne B, tostregde C, tostencede DE$^{2/x}$*K, tostæncede H, tostrede F, tostredde G*, tostridde J, todræfde ł tostænct[ ] ł toworpene I*
sunt		sind A, sint B, synd CDIK, sýnd F, sind H, wæron ł synd G*, wæron J, beoð E^{2}
omnia*		all *A*, ealle BCDFGHIJK, eælle *E*^{x}*
ossa	|	ban ABCFGHIJK, bán D, míne E^{2}
mea	|	min AK, mine BCFGIJ, mina DH, ban E^{2}*
Et*		⁊ CE^{2} (*ABL*)
factum	|	geworden *ABDFGH*, gewordyn C, gewordon *I**, ⁊ geworden *J*, gedo *K**, min E^{2}
est	|	wes A, wæs C, is BFGHIJ*K*, heorte E^{2}
cor	|	heorte ABCDFGHIJK, his E^{2}
meum	|	min ABCFGIJK, geworden E^{2} (*D*)
tamquam		swe swe A, swa swa B*C*DFG*H*IJ, swæ swæ *E*^{2}, swa K

cera | wæx A, weax B*F*GJ, wiex C, wehs DH, wex IK, meltende *E*^{2}
liquifiens* | gemaeltende *A*, gemeltende B, myltynde *C*, meltende *D*H, miltende F, myltende IK, mylted G*, gemilted J, wex *E*^{2} (*L*)
in | in A, on BCDE^{2}FGHIJK
medio | midle ABC, midle ł on middeweardan I*, middele DFGHJ, middum E^{2}, middan K
uentris | wǫmbe ABC, innoðes DFGI, innoþes HJ, innoþe K, mines E$^{2/x}$*
mei | minre ABC*, mines DFGHIJ, min K, innoþes E^{2}

ED: swa swa (GIJ) (*1st*)] swaswa *Rosier, Lindelöf, Oess.* utagoten (J)] utagotene *Oess.* todræfde ł tostænct[ ] ł toworpene (I)] todræfde ł tostæncte ł toworpene *Lindelöf.* Factum (B)] factum *Brenner.* ⁊ geworden (J)] geworden *Oess.* swa swa (GIJ) (*2nd*)] swaswa *Rosier, Lindelöf, Oess.* mylted (G)] [ ]ted *Rosier.*

OE: agotene (E$^{2/x}$)] a *on eras. by corr., eras. after word.* wæron ł ic eom (G)] *written in lighter ink,* ł ic eom *added above* wæron. ⁊ (G)] *written in lighter ink.* tostencede (E$^{2/x}$)] to *on eras. by corr.* tostredde (G)] *written in lighter ink.* todræfde ł tostænct[ ] ł toworpene (I)] *final letter of* tostænct[ ] *lost due to tight binding: only fragment visible.* wæron ł synd (G)] *written in lighter ink,* ł synd *added above* wæron. eælle (E^{x})] *on eras.* ban (E^{2})] *orig.* bæn: æ *altered to* a. gewordon (I)] *orig.* gewurdon: u *altered to* o. gedo (K)] ne *eras. after word.* mylted (G)] m *and* l *cropped at top.* midle ł on middeweardan (I)] ł on middeweardan *written in left margin.* mines (E$^{2/x}$)] es *on eras. by corr.* minre (C)] r *on eras.*

LTg: Sicut] sicut ABCDE; Ssicut L: *orig.* sicut: *initial* S *added by Lat. glossator, following* s *not crossed through.* aqua] C: *scribe began* au-, *then altered* u *to* q. effusa] effusus L: *2nd* u *altered from another letter,* s *added: see GAg.* sunt (*1st*)] sum L: *orig.* sunt: nt *altered to* m: see *GAg.* omnia] E: *small tick after word, with eras. in right margin,* ł uniuersa *interl. on eras.; for* A *see GAg.* Et] et L: *orig.* Et: E *crossed through and* e *written after by Lat. glossator,* t *also (mistakenly) crossed through; om.* AB: *cf. Weber MSS* Σαβγδεζη moz med, *see GAg.* factum] Factum ABFHIJK; [ ]actum G. est] ést K. meum] D: mea *added interl. above* meum *by glossator.* tamquam] tanquam E, C: *orig.* tamquam: *left leg of 1st* m *eras. to form* n, H: *orig.* tamquam: *right leg of 1st* m *eras. to form* n. cera] cęra F. liquifiens] liquefiens A: lique *added by corr. in left margin;* liquescens CDEL: *cf. Weber MSS* βγ med, *see GAg.*

LTu: Sicut] sicut βνςτ*. factum] Factum δεζθιλμξοπϱστυφχψ. tamquam] tanquam ιλτφ, ϱ: *orig.* tamquam: *deleting dot below right leg of 1st* m; tanqvam τ*. cera] cęra εμφ; cæra ϑ; caera νψ. liquifiens] liquescens νςτ*: *cf. Weber MSS* βγ med, *see GAu.*

GAg: effusa] effusus FGHIJK, L: *see LTg.* sunt] sum FGHIJK, L: *see LTg.* omnia] uniuersa A, E: *see LTg.* Et] *om.* FGHIJK, AB: *see LTg.* liquifiens] liquescens FGHIJK, CDEL: *see LTg.*

GAu: effusa] effusus δεζϑιλμξοπϱστυφχψ. sunt] sum δεζϑιλμξοπϱστυφχψ. omnia] uniuersa ϑ, β: *interl. by corr. above* omnia. Et] *om.* δεζϑιλμξοπϱστυφχψ. liquifiens] liquescens δεζιλμξοπϱστυφχψ, νςτ*: *see LTu;* licquescens ϑ.

16

Exaruit*		adrugade A, adrugode B, adrugude C, astiðude DH, Astiðude E^{x}*, astiþude F, astiþude ł heardode G*, aheardode J, adruwode ł forsearode I* (*L*)
uelut*		swe swe A, swa swa *BCD*FGHIJ, swæ swæ *E$^{2/x}$**, swa K (*L*)
testa		tigule A, tigele B, tigle CDE^{x}*FHK, tigle ł lamsceal G*, lamsceal J, blywnys ł crocsceard I
uirtus		megen AE^{x}*, mægen BDGHIJ, mægyn C, mægn K, miht F
mea		min ABCDE^{x}*FGHIJK
et		⁊ AB*CDE*^{2}FGHIJK
lingua	|	tunge ABCDGHIJK, tunga F, mine E^{2}
mea	|	min ABCFGHIJK, tungæ E^{2}
adhesit		ætfalh A, ætfelh B, ætfealh C, ætfylgþ ł togecleouode E$^{2/x}$*, togecleofode DF, togeclefode K, togecleofode ł ætfealh G*, togecleowode H, tocleofode I, toclyfode J
faucibus	|	gomum ACI, gomum B, gomum ł ceacan J, welerum DFHK, welerum ł gomum *G**, minum E^{2}
meis	|	minum AF, minum BCD*G*HIJ, minra K, gómum E^{2}
et		⁊ ABCDE^{2}FGHIJK
in		in A, on BCDE^{2}FGHIJK
puluerem	|	dust *A*BCDH, duste FIK, duste ł on myll G*, dust ł myl J, deæþes *E*^{2}
mortis	|	deaðes ABFGH, deaðys C, deaþes DIJK*, duste *E*^{2}
deduxerunt*		gelaeddon *A*, gelæddon BCGJ, he geleddon D, he geledden *E^{x}**, hí gelæddon F, þu gelæddest I, he lædde K (*L*)
me		me ABC*E^{x}**FGIJK

ED: swa swa (GIJ)] swaswa *Rosier, Lindelöf, Oess.* togecleowode (H)] togecleofode *Campbell* (*but correct in note*).

OE: Astiðude (E^{x})] *on eras. by corr.* astiþude ł heardode (G)] ł heardode *added above* astiþude *in diff.* (?) *hand.* adruwode ł forsearode (I)] ł forsearode *written in left margin.* swæ swæ (E$^{2/x}$)] *final* wæ *on eras. by corr.* tigle (E^{x})] *on eras.* tigle ł lamsceal (G)] ł lamsceal *added above* tigle *in diff.* (?) *hand.* megen (E^{x})] *on eras.* min (E^{x})] *on eras.* ætfylgþ ł togecleouode (E$^{2/x}$)] ł togecleouode *added by corr.,* de *on eras.* togecleofode ł ætfealh (G)] ł ætfealh *added above* togecleofode *in diff.* (?) *hand.* welerum ł gomum (G)] ł gomum *added above* welerum *in diff.* (?) *hand.* duste ł on myll (G)] ł on myll *added in diff.* (?) *hand.* deaþes (K)] *letter* (m?) *eras. before word.* he geledden (E^{x})] *on eras.* me (E^{x})] *on eras.*

LTg: Exaruit] L: Ex *crossed through,* a *altered to* A *by corr.: see GAg.* uelut] D: *orig. om.*: *added interl. by glossator*, E: *added by corr. of Ps 18.10* ł dei, L: tamquam *written interl. by corr.: see GAg;* uelud B. et (*1st*)] CE: *on eras.* faucibus] G: bus *written in lighter ink slightly above line.* meis] G: *written in lighter ink slightly above line.* pulurem] A: m *added by corr.* mortis] E: *on eras. by corr.* deduxerunt] E: *on eras. by corr.*, L: erunt *underlined to signal deletion,* isti *written interl. by corr.: see GAg.* me] E: *on eras. by corr.*

LTu: adhesit] σ: h *interl.;* adhęsit επφ; adhaesit ψ. faucibus] β: u *interl.;* fucibus ϑ. puluerum] limum ϑ: *cf. Weber MS* η.

GAg: Exaruit] Aruit FGHIJK, L: *see LTg.* uelut] tamquam FGIJK, L: *see LTg;* tanquam H: *orig.* tamquam: *right leg of 1st* m *eras. to form* n. deduxerunt] deduxisti FGHIJK, L: *see LTg.*

GAu: Exaruit] Aruit δεζϑιλμξοπϱστυφχψ. uelut] tamquam δεζμξοπσυχψ; tanquam ϑιλτφ, ϱ: *orig.* tamquam: *deleting dot below right leg of 1st* m. deduxerunt] deduxisti δεζϑιλμξοπϱστυφχψ.

17

Quoniam	forðon ABDFH, forþon C, forþon þe J, forþan þe I, Forþæn E^{2}*, forþam G
circumdederunt	ymbsaldon A, ymbsealdon B*CD*F*H*, ymbseældon *E^{2}*, ymbesealdan K, [ ]an ymbsealdon G*, hihton ymbsealdon J, ymbeþrungon I
me	me ABCE^{2}FGIJK
canes |	hundas ABCDFGIJK, hundes H, monigæ E^{2}
multi |	monge A, monige BC, manige DFGH, manege I, mine J, feala K, hundæs E^{2}*
concilium	geðaeht A, geðeaht B, geþeaht CDFHIK, geþeaht ł réd E^{x}*, geþeaht ł gemot G*J
malignantium	awergedra A, awergdra B, awyrgydra C, awyrgedra DGHK, awýrgedra F, awirgedra J, awargedre E^{2}*, yfelcundra ł awirgendra I
obsedit	oset A, ofsæt BJ, asæt C, forsæt ł ofsæt *G**, ofsæt ł y(m)[ ]s[ ] *I**, ofsæton F, forsetnode DH, ofsetnode E^{2}*, forsetton K
me	mec A, me BCE^{2}FGJK
Foderunt	dulfun A, dulfon B, hy dulfon DH, hi dulfon F, hie dulfun E^{2}, hi dulfan K, adulfon C, hy adulfon *G**, adulfon J, hig ðurhðygdon ł hi dulfon ł nægledun I* (*L*)

manus	I	honda A, handa BCDFGHIJK, mine E^{2}
meas	I	mine ABCDFGIJK, mina H, hænde E^{2}
et		⁊ ABCE^{2}FGHIJK
pedes	I	foet A, fet BCDFHIJK, f(e)t G*, mine E^{2}
meos	I	minc ABCFGIJK, fet E^{2}

ED: Quoniam (G)] *Q*uoniam *Rosier*. forðon (A)] for ðon *Kuhn*. circundederunt (C)] circu[m]dederunt *Wildhagen*. obsédit (I)] obsedit *Lindelöf*. forsæt ł ofsæt (G)] forsæ[ ] ł ofsæt *Rosier*. ofsæt ł y(m)[ ]s[ ] (I)] ofsæt ł ymbsæt *Lindelöf*. hie dulfun (E)] Hie dulfun *Harsley*. mine (G) (*1st*)] mi[ ] *Rosier*. ⁊ (G)] [ ] *Rosier*. f(e)t (G)] [ ] *Rosier*.

OE: Forþæn (E^{2})] *eras.* (*12 mm*) *after word*. [ ]an ymbsealdon (G)] he g (?) *visible before* an. hundæs (E^{2})] *eras.* (*22 mm*) *after word*. geþeaht ł réd (E^{x})] *on eras.* geþeaht ł gemot (G)] ł gemot *added in diff.* (?) *hand*. awargedre (E^{2})] *eras. after word*. forsæt ł ofsæt (G)] ł ofsæt *added in diff.* (?) *hand*. ofsæt ł y(m)[ ]s[ ] (I)] *1st 2 legs of* m *visible; word partly lost due to tight binding*. ofsetnode (E^{2})] *eras. after word*. hy adulfon (G)] a *interl*. hig ðurhðygdon ł hi dulfon ł nægledun (I)] hig ðurhðygdon ł *written in left margin*. f(e)t (G)] *eye of* e *not visible*.

LTg: circumdederunt] circundederunt E, C: *orig.* circumdederunt: *left leg of* m *eras. to form* n, H: *orig.* circumdederunt: *right leg of* m *eras. to form* n. obsedit] obsédit I; obse[ ] G. Foderunt] [ ]oderunt G.

LTu: circumdederunt] circundederunt εϑιλφ, ϱ: *orig.* circumdederunt: *deleting dot below right leg of* m. me (*2nd*)] mę ζ.

18

dinumerauerunt		arimdon ABC, arymdon J, hy getealdon D, hi getealdon F, hy getealdan H, hi getealdan K, hy getealdon ł arimdon *G**, ⁊ ærimeden ł tealdon E$^{2/x}$*, hi gerimdon ł getealdon I
omnia		all A, ealle BCDFGHIJK, eælle E^{2}
ossa	I	ban ABCDGHIJK, bán F, mine E^{2}
mea	I	min A, mine BCDFGHIJK, bæn E^{2}

Ipsi	hie AB, hy DHK, hi CE^{2}FJ, hig I* (*G*)
uero	soðlice ABCGHI, soþlice DE^{2}FJK
considerauerunt	sceawedun A, sceawodon B, sceawydon C, besceawodon DFG*HJ, bescæwodon E^{2}, besceawedon I, bescæwodan K
et	⁊ ABCDE^{2}FGI*JK
conspexerunt*	gelocadon A, gelocodon B*C*, beheoldon DI*J, behyoldon E^{x}*, beheoldan K, on beheoldon F, todældon G
me	me *A*BCE^{2}*FGIJK

OE: hy getealdon ł arimdon (G)] ł arimdon *added in diff.* (?) *hand.* ⁊ ærimeden ł tealdon ($E^{2/x}$)] ⁊ *and* ł tealdon *on eras. by corr.* hig (I)] *eras. before word.* besceawodon (G)] w *split and partly obscured.* ⁊ (I)] *slightly obscured by stain.* beheoldon (I)] be *slightly obscured by stain.* behyoldon (E^{x})] *on eras.* me (E^{2})] *eras.* (*13 mm*) *before word.*

LTg: dinumerauerunt] G: t *slightly raised, possibly added later* (*cf. Ps 21.13* Circumdederunt). Ipsi] [ ]psi G. conspexerunt] C: x *on eras.* me] A: *added by corr.*

LTu: dinumerauerunt] σ: nu *interl.*, υ: me *interl.;* denumerauerunt ϑ.

GAg: conspexerunt] inspexerunt FGHIJK.

GAu: conspexerunt] inspexerunt δεζϑιλμξοπϱστυφχψ.

19

diuiserunt	todaeldun *A*, todældon BC, todældan K, hy todeldon E^{2}*, hi todældon I, hi todældon ł sændon J, hy dældan D, hi dældon F, hy dældon G, hy dǽldon H
sibi	him ABCE^{x}*F, him DHJ, hym G, him ł betweox heom I*, heom K
uestimenta	hregl A, hrægl BCG, rægl J, hræglu DH, hregle E^{2}, hrægl ł scrud I, scryd K, réaf F
mea	min ABCGIJK, mín F, mina D, mine E^{x}*H
et	⁊ ABCDE^{2}FGHIJK
super	ofer ABDE^{2}FGHJK, ofyr C, ofor I
uestem	hregl A*, hrægl BC, hrægel K, rægl J, wæd DH, wæda F, wæd ł hrægl G*, reaf I, min E^{2}
meam	min ABCGIJK, mine DFH, hregl ł wed E^{2}
miserunt	sendon ABC, hy sendon DH, hie sendon E^{2}, hi sendon FGK, hi sændon J, ⁊ hig asendon ł hi setton I*
sortem	hlet A, hlét B, hlyt CDFHJ, hlyht E^{2}, hlyt ł hlot I, hlot GK

ED: hy dǽldon (H)] hy dældon *Campbell.* ⁊ hig asendon ł hi setton (I)] *Lindelöf omits* ⁊.

OE: hy todeldon (E^{2})] *2nd* o *on eras.* him (E^{x})] *on eras.* him ł betweox heom (I)] ł betweox heom *written in bottom margin below* sibi. mine (E^{x})] *on eras.* hregl (A) (*2nd*)] *scribe mistakenly added ascender after* h, *over which* r *was written.* wæd ł hrægl (G)] ł hrægl *added in diff.* (?) *hand.* ⁊ hig asendon ł hi setton (I)] ⁊ hig asendon *written above* ł hi setton.

LTg: diuiserunt] A: *eras.* (*2–3 letters*) *before word.*

20

Tu	ðu AF, þu BCE²GHIJK
autem	soðlice ABCGHI, soþlice DE²FJ, witodlice K*
domine	dryhten B, dryhten E², dryhť A, driħt CF, driħ GJ
ne	nales A*B, nalys C, na DK, ne E²FGIJ
longe*	feor ABD, feorr C, feorsa ðu F, do þu feor GJ, afyr þu ł ne afyrsa I*, feor do K, dó E²
facias*	do ðu AB, þu dó D, gedo þu C, þinne E²
auxilium	fultum ABCE²FI**J*K, fultum DH, fu(l)[ ] G*
tuum	ðinne AF, þinne CDGHIJ*K*, fior E²
a*	from A, fram CD, fram GI, fræm *E²* (*FK*)
me*	me ACDE²GI (*FK*)
ad	to ABCDE²FGHIJK
defensionem	gescildnisse A, gescildnesse BJ, gescyldnysse CFI, gescyldnesse DHK, minre gescyldnesse G*, minum E²
meam	minre ABCDFGHIJK, gescyldnesse E²/x*
aspice*	geloca ABC, geloca þu GJ, beseoh DFK, beseoh ł locæ *E²*, beseoh ł bewlata I

ED: fu(l)[ ] (G)] ful[ ] *Rosier.* á (E)] a *Harsley.*

OE: witodlice (K)] d *altered from* t. nales (A)] *small smudge above* e. afyr þu ł ne afyrsa (I)] *eras. after* fyrsa. fultum (I)] *followed by eras. gloss in right margin.* fu(l)[ ] (G)] *top of* l *visible.* minre gescyldnesse (G)] e *of* minre *interl., word added in diff.* (?) *hand.* gescyldnesse (E²/x)] nesse *on eras. by corr.*

LTg: auxilium] ausilium J. tuum] K: *on eras. by corr.* a] F: *on eras. by later hand,* K: *on eras. by corr.: see GAg;* á E. me] F: *on eras. by later hand,* K: *on eras. by corr.: see GAg.* aspice] E: as *on eras. by corr.*

LTu: ne] λ: e *interl.* auxilium] axilium β. defensionem] defentionem ϑ.

GAg: longe facias] elongaueris FHIJK; ęlongaueris G. a me] *om.* J: *for* FK *see LTg.* aspice] conspice FGHIJK.

GAu: longe facias] elongaueris δεϑιλμξοπϱστυφχψ, ζ: *orig.* longaueris: *initial* e *added interl.* a me] *om.* δϑσψ. aspice] conspice δεζϑιλμξοπϱστυφχψ.

21

Erue	genere AB, genere C, genere E², genera FJ, genera ł ales I*, aliða D*H,* aliða ł aliða G*, aliþa K
a	from A, fram BCDHJK, fram *E*ˣ*FGI
framea	sweorde AB, swurde C*I,* sworde Eˣ*, flane D*H*K, flane ł cócere *G**, cocore F, cocore minre J* (*L*)

⟨deus⟩ god *CDJ* (*GL*)
animam | sawle ABC*F*IJK*, saule D, sauwle G, saul H, mine E^2
meam | mine ABCDFGHIK, min J, sæwlæ E^2
et ⁊ ABCDE^2FGHIJK
de | of ABCDFGHIJK, mine E^2
manu | honda AB, handa CDFGHJK, anwealde ł handa I, annesse E^2
canis | hundes ABDGHI*, hundys C, hunda FK, hundas J, of E^2
unicam | ða angan A, þa angan BC, þa ánlican DG, þa anlican H, ða ænlican F, anlican K, ankennan I, sawle þa J*, þes hundes E^2
meam | mine ABCDFJK, miñ G*, mine ł mine anlican I, hændæ E^2

ED: Erue (B)] Eripe *Brenner*. [ ]rue (H)] Erue *Campbell*. genere (E)] Genere *Harsley*. á (E)] a *Harsley*. frámea (I)] framea *Lindelöf*. þa ánlican (G)] þa anlican *Rosier*.

OE: genera ł ales (I)] genera *written in left margin*, e *in* ales *on eras*. aliða ł aliða (G)] ł aliða *added in diff.* (?) *hand, with 2nd* aliða *above following* fram. fram (E^x)] *on eras*. sworde (E^x)] *on eras*. flane ł cócere (G)] ł cócere *added above* flane *in diff.* (?) *hand*. cocore minre (J)] minre *written below* cocore. sawle (K)] s *and descender eras. before word; Sisam reads* sw. hundes (I)] *eras. after word*. sawle þa (J)] *lemma misread as* animam. miñ (G)] *so MS: cf. Ps 18.7* heofeñ, *18.9* drihteñ.

LTg: Erue] [ ]rue H: *traces of blue ink visible in initial position*. a] á E. framea] frámea I, H: *eras. after word;* framea deus CJ, D: deus *interl.;* fframea deus G: deus *added interl.: see LTg note to v. 14* rugiens; framea ds L: *macron not visible*. animam] F: i *interl*.

LTu: Erue] Eruę π. framea] framea deus ιν, σ: *added interl.*, τ: deus *crossed through*.

22
Libera* gefrea A, gefreo *C*, alies B, lys D, alys ðu G, gefriolsæ E^2, gehæl FI, hæs ł alys þu J, hæl K
me me ABCDE^2F*G**IJK
de* of ABCDE^2FG*HIJK
ore | muðe ABCDFG*H, muþe IJK, þes leon E^2
leonis | leon ABC, leonis D*H, leona FJK, lyona G*, þære leon I*, muþe E^2
et ⁊ ABCDE^x*FGHI*J*K
a from A, from B, fram CH*J*K, fram DFGI, from *E*^{2}
cornibus hornum ADFGI, hornum BCH, horne E^2 (*J*)
unicornuorum* anhyrnera AB*C*, anhyrnan K, anhyrnendra DFI, anhyrnedra H, þes anhornede E^x*, anhyrnedra deor[ ] G, anhyrne deora J (*L*)

humilitatem	I	eaðmodnisse AD, eaðmodnesse BH, eaðmodnysse I, eadmodnysse CF, eadmodnesse GJK, minre E^{x}*
meam	I	mine ABCDFGHIJK, eæþmodnesse E^{x}*

ED: gefriolsæ (E)] Gefriolsæ *Harsley*. á (E)] a *Harsley*.

OE: me (G)] *interl.* of (G)] *in lighter ink* (?). muðe (G)] *in lighter ink* (?). leonis (D)] *glossator perhaps copied lemma into gloss.* lyona (G)] y *malformed.* þære leon (I)] *eras. before word,* [ ]e *written in left margin but initial letter lost due to tight binding; O'Neill (p. 88) reads* he *and suggests it indicates alternative masc. gender of* leo. ⁊ (E^{x})] *on eras.* þes anhornede (E^{x})] *on eras.* minre (E^{x})] *on eras.* eæþmodnesse (E^{x})] *on eras.*

LTg: C: *verse initially omitted: added by main hand in blank space after v. 21* meam. me] *interl.* G. et] *on eras.* (?) J. a] *on eras.* (?) J; á E. cornibus] *on eras.* (?) J. unicornuorum] C: *right side of 2nd* u *and* orum *on eras. by corr.;* unicorniorum L: *orig.* unicornuorum: *right side of 2nd* u *eras.*

GAg: Libera] Salua FGHIJK. de] ex FGHIJK. unicornuorum] unicornium FGHIJ, K: ium *on eras. by corr.*

GAu: Libera] Salua δεζθιλμξοπρστυφχψ. de] ex δεζθιλμξοπρστυφχψ. unicornuorum] unicornium δεζιμξορσυχψ; unicornuum λπτφ.

23

Narrabo		ic secgu A, ic secgo B, ic secge C, ic cyþe DK, Ic cyþe $E^{2/x}$*, ic cyðe FI, ic cuþe H, ic cyðe ł ic secge G*, ic secge ł ic recce ł ic cyþe J*
nomen	I	noman ABD, naman CF*GHIJK, þinum E^{2}
tuum	I	ðinne ABF, þinne DGHIJK, þin *C*, nomon E^{2}
fratribus	I	broðrum ACGH, broðrum BD, broþrum J, gebroðrum I, broðra F, broþra K, minum E^{2}*
meis	I	minum ABFGHI, minum CD, minnum J, minan K, broþrum E^{2}
in		in A, on BCDE^{2}FGHIJK
medio		midle ABC, middele DFHJ, midre E^{2}, middere G*, middan IK
ecclesiae		cirican A*J*, circan *B*, cyricean *CG*, circeæn *E^{2}*, getreowfulre gesomnunge *D*, getreoffulre gesomnunge *H*, somnunga *K*, gelaðlunge ł circean *F**, þære gelaðunge *I* (*L*)
laudabo	I	ic hergo A, ic herge BK, ic herige CFGHIJ, ic herige D, ic þe E^{2}
te	I	ðe A*B*, þe *CFGI*JK, herige E^{2}

ED: ęcclesię (E)] aecclesiae *Harsley*. té (GI)] te *Rosier, Lindelöf*.

OE: Ic cyþe ($E^{2/x}$)] cyþe *on eras. by corr.* ic cyðe ł ic secge (G)] ł ic secge *added in diff.* (?) *hand.* ic secge ł ic recce ł ic cyþe (J)] ł ic cyþe *written above* ic secge. naman (F)] *otiose mark before initial* n. minum (E^2)] *eras. before word.* middere (G)] r *malformed.* gelaðlunge ł circean (F)] ł *interl. and signaled for inclusion by stroke between words.*

LTg: tuum] C: m *altered from another letter, perhaps false start of* u. ecclesiae] æcclæsiæ B; æcclesiæ L; ecclesię C; eclesie D; ęcclesię EFGH; aecclesiae I; ecclesie J; ecclesiæ K. te] té BCGI.

LTu: ecclesiae] ecclessię βμ; ecclesie σςτ*τ; ęcclesię ειξφχ; æclesia ϑ; aecclesiae λπϱυ; ęcclesiae ν; ecclesię ο.

24

Qui — ða ðe A, þa þe BC, ge ða D, ge þe E^x*GHIJ, ge ðe F, ge K
timetis — ondreðað A, ondrædað BCI, ondredæþ E^2, ondrædaþ G*J, andræden DH, ondrædan F*, þandrædað K
dominum — dryhten D, drihten E^2IK, dryht̄ AB, driħt CFH, driħ GJ
laudate — hergað AB, hergeað C, herigað D*, heriæþ E^2, heriað FGHI, heriaþ K
eum — hine ABCDE^2F*G**HIJK
uniuersum — all AD, eall BCGHIJ, eæll E^2*, eal K, eall F*
semen | sed A, sæd BCDHK, cyn sæd F*, sæd ł cynn G*, ofspryng ł sæd ł cyn I, cynred J, iæcobes E^2
iacob | iacobes ABIJ, iacobys C, getreowfulra DFH, getreowfulra ł iacobes G*, n K*, sed E^2
magnificate* — micliað ABC, gemicliað D, gemycliæþ E^2, gemicliað F, gewuldriað G, wuldriað I, wuldriaþ JK (*L*)
eum — hine ABCDE^2FHIJK, ge hine *G*

ED: ondrædaþ (G)] ondrædan *Rosier*. iacob (K)] Iacob *Sisam*.

OE: ge þe (E^x)] *on eras., with eras. extending entire line.* ondrædaþ (G)] *orig.* ondrædan: *left leg of 2nd* n *extended above and below line to form stem of crude* þ. ondrædan (F)] a *altered from* u (?). herigað (D)] g *interl.* hine (G)] *gloss and lemma repeated at end of line above.* eæll (E^2)] *small eras. after word.* eall cyn sæd (F)] eall cyn *written above* uniuersum, sæd *written above* semen *in line below.* sæd ł cynn (G)] ł cynn *added in diff.* (?) *hand.* getreowfulra ł iacobes (G)] ł iacobes *added above* getreowfulra *in diff.* (?) *hand.* n (K)] *for* nomen.

LTg: eum (*1st*)] G: *lemma and gloss repeated at end of line above.* magnificate] L: *underlined to signal deletion,* glorificate *written to left by Lat. glossator: see GAg.* eum (*2nd*)] G: *in slightly darker ink.*

GAg: magnificate] glorificate FHIJK, G: *in slightly darker ink,* L: *see LTg.*

GAu: magnificate] glorificate δεζιλμξοπρστυφχψ.

25

Timeat | ondrede A, ondræde BCFIK, andræde DH, ondrædað G*, ondrædaþ J, hine E^{2}

eum | hine ABCDFGHIJK, ondredæ E^{2}*

omne — all A, eall BCF*HI*, eal D, eæl E^{2}, ealle *GJ*K

semen | sed A, sæd BCDFHIK, sæd ł cýnn G*, cynn J, isræhelæ E^{2}*

israhel | israela A*J,* israhela BG, israhelys C, israheles *I**, ealre getreowfulnisse D, ealre getreow H, sed *E²* (*FK*)

quoniam — forðon AB, forþon C, forþæn *E²*, forðan þe I, forðon ðe F, forðon þe J, forþā þe G

non | ne ABI, na FK, he ne C*E*$^{2/x}$*G, he na J (*H*)

spreuit | forhogde AB, forhogode C, forhygede DE^{x}*H, forhígede F, forhigde K, ahyrweð ł forhogede G, ahyrweþ J, [ ]wearp I*

neque — ne ABJ, ⁊ ne DE^{x}*FGH, ⁊ na K, ne ne C

despexit* — forsaeh *A,* forseh *B,* forseah C*D*E^{x}*F*H*K, forsyð he G*, he forsihþ J, for forseah I*

precem* — boene A, bene BDE^{x}*FGJ, bena *C,* halsunge ł gecleopunga ł bene I* (*L*)

pauperum* — ðearfena A*F, þearfena BJ, þearfyna C, þearfæna G*, ðearfna DE^{x}*, þearfan I (*L*)

neque* | ne A*BFGIJ, na K, ⁊ ne D, ne ne C, ⁊ he ne $E^{2/x}$* (*L*)

auertit | forcerreð A, forcirreð B, forcyrryð C, he acyrde D, acyrde E^{x}*, cyrde K, he awende F, he onweg acyrreð G, he aweg cirreð J, he framawende acyrde I*

faciem — onsiene A, onsine B, onsyne DE^{x}*H, ansyne CFGIJK

suam — his ABCDE^{x}*FGIK, hyne H, þyne *J*

a — from AE^{2}, from B, fram CDFGHJK, fram I

me — me ABCDE^{2}FGHIJK

et — ⁊ ABCE^{2}FGHIJK

dum* — mid ðy AB, mid þy þe C, þonne D, þonne E^{x}*H, mid þonne F, þonne (þ)e G*, þone K, þa þa I, þa þe J

clamarem — ic cleapade A, ic clipode B, ic clypode CGHI, ic cleopode DE^{x}*F, ic clipide J, ic clypude K

ad — to ABCDE^{2}FGHIJK

eum — him ABCDE^{2}GHIJK, hím F

exaudiuit | geherde A, he gehirde B, he gehyrde CDGHIJK, he gehýrde F, he me E^{2}

me | me ABCFGIJK, gehirde $E^{2/x}$*

ED: sæd ł cýnn (G)] sæd ł cynn *Rosier*. isrł (EI)] israel *Lindelöf, Harsley*. isrł (K)] Israhel *Sisam*. forðon (A)] for ðon *Kuhn*. forþā þe (G)] forþam þe *Rosier*. [ ]wearp (I)] awearp *Lindelöf*. he framawende acyrde (I)] he framawende ł acyrde *Lindelöf*. þonne (þ)e (G)] þonne þe *Rosier*. þa þa (I)] þaþa *Lindelöf*.

OE: ondrædað (G)] *orig.* ondræde: e *altered to* a, ð *added, in lighter ink of added glosses*. ondredæ (E2)] *orig.* ondredæþ: þ *eras*. sæd ł cýnn (G)] ł cýnn *added in diff.* (?) *hand*. isræhelæ (E2)] s *altered from another letter*. israheles (I)] *orig.* israhelis: *2nd* i *altered to* e. he ne (E2/x)] he *on eras. by corr.* forhygede (Ex)] *on eras.* [ ]wearp (I)] *orig. gloss to* spreuit *eras. and* [ ]wearp *written in left margin, partly lost due to tight binding*. ⁊ ne (Ex)] *on eras.* forseah (Ex)] *on eras.* forsyð he (G)] he *added in diff.* (?) *hand*. for forseah (I)] *gloss eras. after* for, forseah *written in left margin*. bene (Ex)] *on eras.* halsunge ł gecleopunga ł bene (I)] *crude cross* (?) *added in another hand after* bene. ðearfena (A)] *orig.* ðearfene: *final* e *deleted by subscript dot,* a *interl.* þearfæna (G)] *orig.* þearfan: a *altered to* æ, *final* a *added in lighter ink of added glosses*. ðearfna (Ex)] *on eras.* ne (A) (*3rd*)] *gloss eras. before word, descender visible in initial position,* o *perhaps in 2nd position,* r *clearly visible in final position: cf. following* forcerreð. ⁊ he ne (E2/x)] ne *on eras. by corr.* acyrde (Ex)] *on eras.* he framawende acyrde (I)] acyrde *written in left margin*. onsyne (Ex)] *on eras.* his (Ex)] *on eras.* þonne (Ex)] *on eras.* þonne (þ)e (G)] *bottom of bowl and descender of 2nd* þ *lost*. ic cleopode (Ex)] *on eras.* gehirde (E2/x)] de *on eras. by corr.*

LTg: omne] G: *eras. after word,* H: e *altered from* s; omnis J. israhel] isrł EFIJK. quoniam] E: ā *retraced in darker ink*. non] H: *interl.*, E: n̄ *retraced in darker ink*. despexit] DH: *orig.* dispexit: *1st* i *altered to* e; dispexit AB: *cf. Weber MSS* MSKV*γδζ. precem] preces C, L: deprecationem *written below lemma by Lat. glossator: cf. Weber MSS* β moz, *see GAg*. pauperum] pauperis L: *orig.* pauperum: m *crossed through, right minim of 2nd* u *forms stem of* s: *see GAg*. neque] Nec L: *orig.* neque: N *written above* n, c *written above* q, ue *crossed through by Lat. glossator: see GAg*. suam] tuam J.

LTu: Timeat] TImeat β. israhel] israel ιϛ; isrł βεμξοπϱστ*τυχφ. spreuit] spręuit ε. despexit] dispexit β: *cf. Weber MSS* MSKV*γδζ, *see GAu*. precem] pręcem β. suam] tuam π.

GAg: precem] deprecationem FGHIJK, L: *see LTg*. pauperum] pauperis FGHIJK, L: *see LTg*. neque (*2nd*)] Nec FGHIJK, L: *see LTg*. dum] cum FGHIJK.

GAu: despexit] dispexit δεϑοψ, β: *see LTu*. precem] deprecationem δεζϑιλμξοπϱστυφχ; depraecationem ψ. pauperum] pauperis δεζϑιλμξοπϱστυφχψ. neque (*2nd*)] Nec δεζϑιλμξοπϱστυφχψ. dum] cum δεζϑιλμξοπϱστυφχψ.

26

Apud	mid *ABCDFGH*IJK, Myd E2
te	ðe ABF, þe CDE2GHIJK

laus	I lof ABCDFGHIJK, min E2
mihi*	I me AB*CD*, min FGI*JK, lof *E2* (*L*)
in	in A, on BCDE2FGHIJK
ecclesia	I cirican AJ, ciercan *B*, cyrcean C, cercean F, geso*m*nunga *D*, gesomnunga *H*, somnunge *K*, gesamnunge ł cyrican *G**, gelaþunge I, þere miclæn E2 (*L*)
magna	I micelre ABDFGIJ, micylre C, mycelre HK, ciercæn E2
uota	I gehat ABCGHJ, gehát D, behat FI, behæs K, dryhten E2
mea	min ABCFGIK, mine DE2HJ
domino*	I dryhtne B, drihtny C, dryht̄ A, gehát E2*
reddam	ic ageofu A, ic agyfe C, ic agilde BJK*, ic agylde DGH, ic ægilde E2, ic ágylde F, ic agelde I*
(in)*	on FGK, beforan I, ætforan J
coram*	biforan A, beforan BCD, beforæn E2, gesihðe FG, gesihþe J, ansyne K (*L*)
timentibus*	ondredendum A, ondrædendu*m* B, ondrædyndu*m* C, ðam ondredendu*m* D, ðam ondredendum E2, þa ondrædendan G, þa ondrædendra J, ondræddendra F, ondrædendra I, adredende K (*L*)
eum	hine ABCDE2FGI*J*K, hyne H

ED: ondrædendu*m* (B)] ondrædendum *Brenner*.

OE: min (I) (*1st*)] s. e*st* : is *written in bottom margin*. gesamnunge ł cyrican (G)] ł cyrican *added in diff.* (?) *hand above* gesamnunge. gehát (E2)] á *altered from another letter* (æ?). ic agilde (K)] c *malformed*. ic agelde (I)] *orig.* ic agilde: i *altered to* e.

LTg: Apud] A: d *on eras.;* [ ]pud GH; Aput D. mihi] michi C: *orig.* mihi: *small* c *interl. by corr.*, E: *as* m[1], *eras.* (*1–2 letters*) *after word;* mea L: *orig.* mihi: ihi *crossed through,* ea *interl. by Lat. glossator: see GAg.* ecclesia] æcclæsia B; ęcclesia GHL; eclesia DK. coram] L: in conspectu *written interl. by Lat. glossator: see GAg.* timentibus] timentiu*m* L: *orig.* timentibus: b *and* s *crossed through, macron added above* u: *see GAg.* eum] meum J.

LTu: Apud] Aput ϑ. ecclesia] ęcclesia ειοφχ; æclesia ϑ; aecclesia νϱςυ; ecclesia τ*τ.

GAg: mihi] mea FGHIJK, L: *see LTg.* domino] *om.* FGHIJK. coram] in conspectu FGHIJK, L: *see LTg.* timentibus] timentium FGHIJK, L: *see GAg.*

GAu: mihi] mea δεζιλμξοπϱστυφχψ. domino] *om.* δεζϑλμξοπϱτυφψ. coram] in conspectu δεζϑιλμξοπϱστυφχψ. timentibus] timentium δεζϑιλμοπϱστυφχ; timentiim (?) ξ: *left leg of orig.* u *eras.*

27

Edent	I	eatað A, etað BCDGH, étað *F,* etaþ IJ, ætan K, þeærfæn E^{2}
pauperes	I	ðearfan AB, þearfan CDGHIJ, þerfan K, ðearfena F, etæþ E^{2}
et		⁊ ABCDE^{2}FGHIJK
saturabuntur		bið gefylled A, beoð gefyllyde C, beoð g̲efyllede D, bioþ gefillede E^{2}, beoð gefyllede F, beoð gefylled H, beoþ gefylled K, beoð gefylde B, beoþ gefilde J, beoð gefyllede ł gefylde G*, hi beoð gefylde I
et		⁊ ABCE^{2}FGHIJK
laudabunt		hergað ABC, herigað D*E^{x}*, heriað FHJK, heria[ ] G, hi heriaþ ł wurþiað I
dominum		dryhten D, drihten E^{x}*FK, dryht̄ AB, driħt CH, driht̄ I, driħ GJ
qui		ða A, þa ðe BDE^{x}*, þa þe CGHJK, ða ðe F, ða þe I
requirunt		soecað A, secað CDE^{x}*G*H*I, sécað F, secaþ J*K**, sohton B
eum		hine ABCDE^{x}*F*G*HIJK
uiuet*	I	leofað *ABD,* leofaþ J, lyfað *C,* libbað F, libbaþ I, lybbaþ K, hi libbað ł leofað G*, hioræ *E*^{2} (*L*)
cor*		heorte ABCDGHJK, heortan FI, heortæ E^{2} (*L*)
eorum	I	heara A, hira B, hyra C, heora DFGHIJK, lifæþ E^{2}
in		in A, on BCDE^{2}FGHIJ, a K
saeculum		weoruld A, weorold *B,* woruld *C,* world *E*^{2}, worulde̲ *D**, weorulde *F,* worulde *H,* worulda *GJ,* worlda *I,* worolda *K* (*L*)
saeculi		weorulde A*F,* weorolde *B,* worulde *C,* worvlde̲ *D**, woruld *GH,* world *IJ,* worold *K,* æworł *E*^{2} (*L*)

ED: secað (C)] secad *Wildhagen.* hine (G)] *no gloss Rosier.* sclm (EIJ)] saeculum *Lindelöf;* seculum *Oess, Harsley.* worvlde̲ (D)] worulde̲ *Roeder.* scłi (EIJK)] saeculi *Lindelöf;* seculi *Oess, Harsley;* sæculi *Sisam.* æworł (E^{2})] æworl*de Harsley.*

OE: beoð gefyllede ł gefylde (G)] ł gefylde *added above* gefyllede *in diff.* (?) *hand.* herigað (D)] g *interl.* herigað (E^{x})] *on eras.* drihten (E^{x})] *on eras.* þa ðe (E^{x})] *on eras.* secað (E^{x})] *on eras.* secaþ (K)] *eras. after word.* hine (E^{x})] *on eras.* hi libbað ł leofað (G)] ł leofað *added in diff.* (?) *hand,* að *written above* leof. worulde̲ (D)] e *indicated by bar extending from bowl of* d. worvlde̲ (D)] *orig.* worolde̲: v *written above 2nd* o *but without subscript deleting dot,* e *indicated by bar extending from bowl of* d.

LTg: Edent] Aedent F. requirunt] K: unt *on eras. by corr.;* requirent H: *2nd* e *formed from another letter and partly on eras.* eum] eu[ ] G. uiuet] Uiuet D; Viuet BC, A: e *on eras.,* E: e *on eras. in darker ink,* iu *and* t *retraced in darker ink;* Viuent L: *orig.* Viuet: n *added interl. above* t *by Lat. glossator: see GAg.* cor] corda L: *orig.* cor: da *added interl. by Lat. glossator: see GAg.* saeculum] sæculum B; seculum CDGHKL; sęculum F; scłm EIJ. saeculi] sæculi B; seculi CDHL; sęculi FG; scłi EIJK.

LTu: uiuet] Viuet ντ*; uiuit βς. saeculum] sęculum εο; seculum ζς; scłm βϑιλμνξπστ*τυφχ. saeculi] sęculi ενο; seculi ζςτ*τ; scłi βϑιλμξπϱσυφχ.

GAg: uiuet] uiuent FGHIJK, L: *see LTg.* cor] corda FGHIJK, L: *see LTg.*

GAu: uiuet cor] uiuent corda δεζϑιλμξοπϱστυφχψ.

28

Reminiscentur		gemynen *AB,* gemunyn *C,* hy g̲emunað *D,* hy gemunað H, hi gemunað F, hi gemvnað K, hie gemuneð *E$^{2/x}$*,* hi gemunað ł beoð gemyndige G*, beoþ gemindige J, hi beoð gemyndige *I* (*L*)
et		ꝛ ABCDE^{x}*FGHIJK
conuertentur		sien gecered A*, sien gecirde B, syn gecyrryd C, beoð g̲ecyrrede D, beoð gecyrrede E^{x}*FGI, beoð gecyrredde H, beoþ gecirrede J, beoþ gecyrrede K
ad		to ABCDE^{x}*FG*HIJK
dominum		dryhtne BD, drihtny C, drihtne *E^{x}**FHI, drihtene G, drihten K, dryhꞇ̄ A, driħ J
uniuersi		alle A, ealle BCDFGHI*J*K, eællæ E^{2}*
fines	|	gemæru AI, gemcaru F, gemæro B, endas CDHJK, ende ł endas G*, eorþæn E^{2}*
terrae	|	eorðan *ABCDFGHI,* eorþan *JK,* endes *E^{2}* (*L*)
et		ꝛ *ABCDE^{2}FGHIJK* (*L*)
adorabunt		gebiddað ABCDFH, gebiddæþ E^{2}*, gebiddaþ I*K, gebiddað ł weorðiað G*, wurðiaþ ł we gebiddaþ *J*
in		in A, on BCDE^{x}*FGHIJK
conspectu		gesihðe ABCFGIJ, gesyhðe DE^{x}*H, ansyne K
eius		his ABCDE^{x}*FGHIJ*K*
omnes*		alle A, ealle BCDE^{x}*FGIJK (*L*)
patriae*		oeðlas A*B,* eðles C, eþelas *D*K, eþeles *E^{x}*,* hiredas F, onwealdeð G, onwaldaþ J*, hywrædena ł hiwscipas I (*L*)
gentium		ðeoda AFG, þeoda BCDE^{x}*HIJK

ED: uniuer[ ] (G)] uniu*erse Rosier.* terrę (E)] terrae *Harsley.* conspectu (G)] con*s*pectu *Rosier.* gesihðe (G)] gesih[ ]e *Rosier.* ealle (G) (*2nd*)] ea[ ] *Rosier.* oeðlas (B)] œðlas *Brenner.*

OE: hie gemuneð (E$^{2/x}$)] neð *on eras. by corr.* hi gemunað ł beoð gemyndige (G)] ł beoð gemyndige *added in diff.* (?) *hand,* i *interl.* ꝛ (E^{x})] *on eras.* sien gecered (A)] *eras. before word* (*Kuhn sees* h *eras. and* ge *on eras.*). beoð gecyrrede (E^{x})] *on eras.*

to (E^{x})] *on eras.* to (G)] t *slightly obscured by hole in leaf.* drihtne (E^{x})] *on eras.* eællæ (E^{2})] *eras. after word.* ende ł endas (G)] ende ł *added in diff.* (?) *hand.* eorþæn (E^{2})] þ *eras. before word.* gebiddæþ (E^{2})] *eras. before word.* gebiddaþ (I)] *eras.* (?) *before word.* gebiddað ł weorðiað (G)] ł weorðiað *added in diff.* (?) *hand.* on (E^{x})] *on eras.* gesyhðe (E^{x})] *on eras.* his (E^{x})] *on eras.* ealle (E^{x})] *on eras.* eþeles (E^{x})] *on eras.* onwaldaþ (J)] *source-text misread, perhaps reading gloss to* dominabitur *in v. 29; note* G onwealdeð. þeoda (E^{x})] *on eras.*

LTg: Reminiscentur] I: *crude cross* (?) *in left margin,* L: *orig.* reminiscentur: *1st* r *altered to* R; reminiscentur BCD, A: *2nd* n *added by corr.*, E: *1st* r *on eras. in left margin,* remi *retraced in darker ink.* dominum] E: *ascender of* d *on eras. in darker ink.* uniuersi] J: *orig.* uniuersae: i *interl. above* ae, *but without deleting mark.* terrae] I: *crude* ł (?) *written in another hand in left margin;* terrę ACEFGHK; terræ BL; terre DJ. et (*2nd*)] Et ABCDEFGHIJKL. adorabunt] adhorabunt J. eius] eíus K. omnes] L: *underlined to signal deletion,* uniuerse *added interl. by Lat. glossator: see GAg.* patriae] patriæ B, L: *underlined to signal deletion,* familie *added interl. by Lat. glossator: see GAg;* patrię DE.

LTu: Reminiscentur] reminiscentur βν. uniuersi] uniuerse ς. terrae] terrę εζιλνξφ; terræ ϑ; terre σςτ*. et (*2nd*)] Et βδεζιλνξοϱσςτ*τυφχψ. patriae] patrie ςτ*τ.

GAg: omnes] uniuerse F, L: *see LTg;* uniuersę HK; uniuersae IJ; uniuer[ ] G. patriae] familię FGHK; familiae I; familie J, L: *see LTg.*

GAu: omnes] uniuerse δζξστ; uniuersę ειλπϱυφ; uniuersæ ϑχ; uniuersae μοψ. patriae] familiae δζμπυχψ; familię ειλξοϱφ; familiæ ϑ; familie στ.

29

Quoniam		forðon *AB*FJ, forþan *C,* forðan K, forðam G, forðan þe *E*$^{2/x}$*, forðan þe I (*DL*)
domini		dryhtnes B, drihtnys C, drihtnes E^{2}I, dryht̄ A, driħt F, driħ GJ
est		is ABDE^{2}FGHIJ*K*, ys C
regnum		rice ABCDFGHIK, riche *E*^{x}*, ric J
et		⁊ ABCE^{x}*FGHIJK
ipse	ǀ	he ABCDE^{x}*FGHK, he sylf I, he silf J
dominabitur	ǀ	waldeð AB, wealdyð C, wyldeþ D, wyldeð H, waldeþ E^{x}*, wealdeð F, wealdeþ J, wældeð K, gewylt I, [ ]ldeð sylf G*
gentium		ðeada A, ðeoda BFGIK, þeoda CDHJ, ðeode E^{2}

ED: forðon (A)] for ðon *Kuhn.* regnvm (E)] regnum *Harsley.* [ ]ldeð sylf (G)] [ ]yldeð sylf *Rosier.*

OE: forðan þe (E$^{2/x}$)] forðan *on eras.* riche (E^{x})] *on eras.* ⁊ (E^{x})] *on eras.* he (E^{x})] *on eras.* waldeþ (E^{x})] *on eras.* [ ]ldeð sylf (G)] *letter fragment visible before* l, sylf *added in diff.* (?) *hand.*

LTg: Quoniam] L: *orig.* quoniam: q *altered to* Q *by Lat. glossator;* quoniam ABCD, E: q *on eras. in darker ink and retraced.* est] ést K. regnum] regnvm E.

LTu: Quoniam] quoniam βνςτ*.

30

Manducauerunt	eton A, æton BCIJ, hy æton D*H*, hie eton E^{2}*, hi æton FG, hi ætan K
et	⁊ ABCDE^{x}*FGHIJK
adorauerunt	weorðadon A*, weorðodon B, wurþodon J, wurðiað C, gebædon DE^{x}*H, hi gebædon F, gebædan K, togebædon ł weorðedon G*, hi geeaðmededon ł hi gebædon I*
omnes	alle A, ealle BCDFGHIJK, éalle E^{x}*
diuites*	weolie A, welige B, welige CDGJ, welie E^{x}*, fætte F, þa fætten I, ealdras K* (*L*)
terrae	eorðan A*BCDFGH*I, eorþan *JK*, eorðen *E^{x}** (*L*)
in	in A, on BCDE^{x}*FGIJK
conspectu	gesihðe ABCFGI, gesihþe J, gesyhðe D, gesyhðe E^{x}*, ansyne K
eius	his ABCE^{x}*FGIJ*K*, hys H
procident*	forðgað *AB*C, falleð *D*E^{x}**, feallað F, feallaþ HJK, feallað ł foregande G*, gehreosað ł feallað I* (*L*)
uniuersi*	alle A, ealle BCDFGHIJK, eælle E^{2} (*L*)
qui	ða A, þa K, þe DE^{2}, þa ðe BJ, þa þe CI, ða þe F, þa þe ł þær G*, þe þær H
descendunt	astigað *A*BH, advneastigað C, astigað ł ofduneastigað G*, niðerastigað D, niðæræstigæþ E^{2}, nyðerastygað F, niðerastigað I*, nyþerstigaþ K, ofdune stigaþ J
in	in A, on BCDE^{2}FGHJK, to I
terram	eorðan ABCDFGHIJ, eorþàn K, eorðæn E^{2}

ED: terrę (E)] terrae *Harsley*. astigað ł ofduneastigað (G)] astigað ł ofdune astigað *Rosier*. niðerastigað (D)] niðer astigað *Roeder*.

OE: hie eton (E^{2})] *eras.* (*20 mm*) *after* eton. ⁊ (E^{x})] *on eras.* weorðadon (A)] *small eras. above* d, *possibly of cross-stroke.* gebædon (E^{x})] *on eras.* togebædon ł weorðedon (G)] ł weorðedon *added in diff.* (?) *hand.* hi geeaðmededon ł hi gebædon (I)] *orig.* hi geeadmededon ł hi gebædon: *1st* d *altered to* ð. éalle (E^{x})] *on eras.* welie (E^{x})] *on eras.* ealdras (K)] *lemma misread as* principes. eorðen (E^{x})] *on eras.* on (E^{x})] *on eras.* gesyhðe (E^{x})] *on eras.* his (E^{x})] *on eras.* falleð (D)] *2nd* l *interl., gloss added in a 12th-c. hand; for other examples of this hand in* D *see OE note to Ps 2.8* anwaldnesse. falleð (E^{x})] *on eras.* feallað ł foregande (G)] ł foregande *added in diff.* (?) *hand.* gehreosað ł feallað (I)] ł feallað *written in left margin.* þa þe ł þær

(G)] þa *and* ł *added in diff.* (?) *hand.* astigað ł ofduneastigað (G)] ł ofduneastigað *added in right margin in diff.* (?) *hand, 2nd* a *in* astigað *obscured.* niðerastigað (I)] *1st* i *on eras.*

LTg: Manducauerunt] [ ]anducauerunt H: *initial* M *lost.* diuites] L: pinques *added below word by Lat. glossator: see GAg.* terrae] terræ BL; terrę CEFGHJK; terre D. eius] eíus K. procident] D: i *and* e *on eras.*, E: i *and* e *on eras.*, p, d, nt *in darker ink, eras. after word,* L: pro *underlined to signal deletion,* i *deleted by subscript dot,* a *written above* (= cadent): *see GAg;* procedunt B, A: *orig.* procidunt: i *altered to* e: *cf. Weber MSS* εη* moz. uniuersi] L: omnes *added interl. by Lat. glossator: see GAg.* descendunt] A: *orig.* discendunt: i *altered to* e.

LTu: terrae] terrę ειμξοφ; terræ ϑ; terre σςτ*τ. procident] procedent β; procedunt ς: *cf. Weber MSS* εη* moz. descendunt] discendunt ϑ, μ: *orig.* descendunt: i *interl. above 1st* e. terram] terra σ: *macron not written.*

GAg: diuites] pingues FGHIJK, L: *see LTg.* procident] cadent FGHIJK, L: *see LTg.* uniuersi] omnes FGHIJK, L: *see LTg.*

GAu: diuites] pinques δεζϑιλμξοπϱστυφξψ. procident] cadent δεζϑιλμξοπϱστυφξψ. uniuersi] omnes δεζιλμξοπϱστυφξψ, ϑ: *interl.*

31

<table>
<tr><td>Et</td><td></td><td>⁊ ABCFGIJK, Ond E^{2}</td></tr>
<tr><td>anima</td><td>|</td><td>sawul A, sawl BG*, saul DH, sawle CFIJ, sawel K, min E^{2}</td></tr>
<tr><td>mea</td><td>|</td><td>min ABCDFGHIJK, sæwl E^{2}</td></tr>
<tr><td>ipsi*</td><td></td><td>him ABDFI, him HK, hym E^{x}*, heo G*J, sylf C</td></tr>
<tr><td>uiuet</td><td></td><td>leofað ABFG, leofaþ K, lefað C, leofaþ J, liofaþ I, lybbe D, libbe E^{2}H</td></tr>
<tr><td>et</td><td></td><td>⁊ ABCE^{2}FGHIJK</td></tr>
<tr><td>semen</td><td>|</td><td>sed A, sæd BCDGHJK, sæd ł cyn I, ofspringc ł sæd F, min E^{2}</td></tr>
<tr><td>meum</td><td>|</td><td>min BCDFGHIJK, sed E^{2}</td></tr>
<tr><td>seruiet</td><td>|</td><td>ðiowað A, þeowað BDHI, ðeowað F, þeowaþ K, þeowiað G*, þeowiaþ J, þeowie C, him E^{2}</td></tr>
<tr><td>illi*</td><td>|</td><td>him ACDFGHI, him BJK, þewæþ E^{2}</td></tr>
</table>

ED: Et (B)] et *Brenner.*

OE: sawl (G)] *bowl of* w *and* l *by corr.* (?). hym (E^{x}) *on eras.* heo (G)] *orig.* hi: i *altered to* e, o *added by corrector.* þeowiað (G)] i *interl.*

LTg: uiuet] A: e *on eras.* (?).

GAg: ipsi] illi FHIJK, G: *eras. after 2nd* i. illi] ipsi FGHIJK.

GAu: ipsi] illi δεζϑιλμξοπϱστυφχψ. illi] ipsi δεζϑιλμξοπϱστυφχψ.

32

Adnuntiabitur segeð A, sægð B, bið sæd *C,* bið bodad D*H,* bið gebodad *G,* biþ gebodod J, bið gebodad ł cýdd F, bodiaþ *K,* bið gecyd *I,* Bið Cyþæd ł bodad E^{2}*

domino drylitne B, drihtny C, drihtne E^{2}FI*, dryht̄ A, driħ GJ

generatio | cneoris ABDGHJ, cneoriss C, cneornes K, cneorisse ł mægð I, mægðe ł cynrine F, þæ towerdæ E^{2}*

uentura | toword A, toweard BCFIJ, towearde G, toweardu DH, towyrda K, cneowrisse E^{2}

et ⁊ ABCE^{2}FGIJK

adnuntiabunt | secgað *ABC,* bodiað DG, bodiaþ J*K,* to bodiað F, gecyþað *I,* heofonæs E^{2} (*H*)

caeli heofenes A, hefenes *B,* hefynas *C,* heofonas *DFH*I*J,* heofenas *G,* heofenan *K,* cyþæþ ł bodiað *E$^{2/x}$** (*L*)

iustitiam rehtwisnisse A*, ryhtwisnesse BD, rihtwisnysse *C,* rihtwisnysse *F*I, rihtwisnesse E^{x}*GHJ, rihtwisnes K

eius his ABCDE^{x}*FGHIJK

populo folce ABCDFGHIJK, folcæ E^{2}, folc K

qui | ðæt A, þæt B, þæt C, þæt ðe I, þe DGH, þæ E^{2}*, ðe F, þa K, se biþ J

nascetur | bið acenned *A*B, bið acennyd C, byð acenned I*, acenned bið DFGK, acenne bið H, acænned J, geboren bið E$^{2/x}$*

quem ðæt A, þæt BGHI, þæt DK, þet E^{2}, þone C, ðone F, þone þe J

fecit dyde ABDH, dyde de K, he dyde ł þone þe geworhte G*, geworhte CE^{2}*FI*J

dominus drihtyn C, drihten DE^{x}*FG, dryht̄ AB, driħt H, driht̄ I, driħ J

ED: Annuntiabitur (C)] A[d]nuntiabitur *Wildhagen.* Bið Cyþæd ł bodad (E)] Bið cyþæd ł bodad *Harsley.* annuntiabunt (C)] a[d]nuntiabunt *Wildhagen.* cęli (E)] caeli *Harsley.* iusticiam (C)] iusti[t]iam *Wildhagen.*

OE: Bið Cyþæd ł bodad (E^{2})] *1st* d *on eras.* drihtne (I)] *partly eras.* þæ towerdæ (E^{2})] *letter eras. after 2nd* æ. cyþæþ ł bodiað (E$^{2/x}$)] ł bodiað *on eras. by corr.* rehtwisnisse (A)] *orig.* rehtwissnisse: *deleting dot above 2nd* s. rihtwisnesse (E^{x})] *on eras.* his (E^{x})] *on eras.* þæ (E^{2})] *eras. after word.* byð acenned (I)] d *malformed and in darker ink.* geboren bið (E$^{2/x}$)] n *and* bið *on eras., 2nd* e *retraced in darker ink.* he dyde ł þone þe geworhte (G)] ł þone þe geworhte *added above* he dyde *in diff.* (?) *hand.* geworhte drihten (E$^{2/x}$)] drihten *on eras. by corr.,* hte *retraced in darker ink; orig.* drihten geworhte, *with transposition marks* (//). geworhte (I)] ge *interl. in darker ink.*

LTg: Adnuntiabitur] Annuntiabitur I, CK: *1st* n *on eras. by corr.,* H, *1st* n *on eras. in lighter ink,* G: *orig.* Adnuntiabitur: d *crossed through,* n *written above and to left by corr.* et] J: *eras. after word.* adnuntiabunt] annuntiabunt AI, CK: *1st* n *on eras. by*

corr., 2nd t *interl.*, H: *1st* n *on eras. in lighter ink.* caeli] cæli BK; cęli CEFGHL; celi DJ. iustitiam] F: *2nd* ti *interl.;* iusticiam C: *orig.* iustitiam: *2nd* t *altered to* c. nascetur] A: *orig.* nascitur: i *altered to* e.

LTu: Adnuntiabitur] Annuntiabitur εζιλνπϱστ*υχ, ο: *orig.* Adnuntiabitur: d *deleted,* n *interl.;* Annunciabitur τφ; Adnunciabitur ψ. adnuntiabunt] annuntiabunt εζιλξπϱστ*υχ, ο: *orig.* adnuntiabunt: d *deleted*, n *interl.;* annunciabunt τφ; adnunciabunt ψ. caeli] ψ: *interl.;* cęli ειξςυφχ; celi στ*τ, ζ: *orig. om., added interl. by corr.;* cæli ϑ; *om.* δμο: *cf. Weber MSS* αβγεη moz^{c}. iustitiam] iusticiam τ*τφ. nascetur] nascitur β.

PSALM 22

1

<table>
<tr><td>Dominus</td><td></td><td>drihten E^{2}G, driħt CF, dryh̄ A, driħ J (BDK)</td></tr>
<tr><td>regit</td><td>|</td><td>receð AB, recyð C, gerecht D, gereht H, gerehte F, gerecht ł gereceð G*, gereceþ J, gerecþ K, gewissaþ I, me E^{2}</td></tr>
<tr><td>me</td><td>|</td><td>me ABCFG*IJK, gerecht E^{2}*</td></tr>
<tr><td>et</td><td></td><td>⁊ ABCE^{2}FGIJK</td></tr>
<tr><td>nihil</td><td></td><td>nowiht AC, nawuht E^{2}*, nawiht J, naht BDFHIK, naht ł nawiht G*</td></tr>
<tr><td>mihi</td><td></td><td>me ABCE^{2}FGIJK</td></tr>
<tr><td>deerit</td><td></td><td>wonu bið A, wona bið B, wana bið DFGHK, wana biþ J, wane bið E^{x}*, bið wona C, ne byþ wana I*</td></tr>
</table>

ED: déerit (H)] deerit *Campbell.*

OE: gerecht ł gereceð (G)] ł gereceð *added in later* (?) *hand.* me (G) (*1st*)] *added in later* (?) *hand.* gerecht (E^{2})] t *interl.*, ht *on eras. by corr.* nawuht (E^{2})] *small eras. after* a (*orig.* æ?). naht ł nawiht (G)] ł nawiht *added in later* (?) *hand.* wane bið (E^{x})] *on eras.* ne byþ wana (I)] et non deerit ihi (> mihi?) : ⁊ wana ne bið *written in right margin.*

LTg: Dominus] G: D *partly lost;* DN̄S ABCDEK. regit] REGIT C. me] ME C. nihil] nichil EGHJK. mihi] michi EG. deerit] deęrit G; déerit H.

LTu: Dominus] DOMINVS ιπτ; DOMInus ς; DN̄S βλμνξοϱστ*φχ. regit] REGIT νξπϱ; REGET βλμ; reget ζϑ. me] ME λμνξπϱ. et] ET λμξπϱ. nihil] NIHIL λ; nichil ισςτ*τφ; NICHIL ξπ, ϱ: c *added interl.* mihi] michi ις; MICHI λξ, πϱ: c *added interl.* deerit] DEERIT ξ.

2

<table>
<tr><td>in</td><td>in A, on BCDE^{2}FGHIJK</td></tr>
<tr><td>loco</td><td>stowe ABCDFGHIJK, þæræ stowe E^{2}</td></tr>
<tr><td>pascuae</td><td>leswe A, læswe BCFJ, læswen I, fostornoðes DH,</td></tr>
</table>

	fosternoðes *E^{x}**, fosternoþes *K*, fostosnoðes ł læswe he *G* (*L*)
ibi	| ðer A, ðær BFI, þær CDGH, ðer E^{2}, ðar K, þar he J
me	| mec A, me BDFGIJK, he me CE^{2}
collocauit	| gesteaðelade *A*, gestaðolode B, gestaðulode C, gestæþelede E^{2}*, gestaþelodc J, hc gcstaþelode D, he gestaðelode FG*, he gestaþolode H, he gestaþolaþ K, he gelogade I
Super	ofer ABDFGHIJK, Ofer E^{2}, ofyr C
aquam	weter A, wæter BGHIJK, wæt<u>er</u> D, wætyr C, weteræs E^{2}, wæteru F
refectionis	gereodnisse A, gereordnesse BJ, gereordnisse C, gereordnysse I, g<u>e</u>reordunge D, gereordunge $E^{2/x}$*HK, gereordunga F, gereordunge ł gereordnesse G*
educauit	aledde *A**, alædde B, gelædde C, he fedde DF**H*K, he gefedde E^{x}*, he fedde ł he lærde *G**, gelærde J, he geedwistode I
me	mec A, me BCE^{x}*FG*IJK

ED: pascue (I)] pascuae *Lindelöf.*

OE: fosternoðes (E^{x})] *on eras.* gestæþelede (E^{2})] ede *on eras.*, þ *altered from* e *by corr.* he gestaðelode (G)] *orig.* he gestaðelede: *3rd* e *in* gestaðelede *altered to* o *by glossator.* gereordunge ($E^{2/x}$)] ordunge *on eras. by corr.* gereordunge ł gereordnesse (G)] ł gereordnesse *added in diff.* (?) *hand above* gereordunge. aledde (A)] *lemma misread as from* educere (?); *see also* BCGJ. he fedde (F)] f *partly obscured.* he gefedde (E^{x})] *on eras.* he fedde ł he lærde (G)] ł he lærde *added in diff.* (?) *above* he fedde. me (E^{x})] *on eras.* me (G) (*2nd*)] *in slightly lighter ink.*

LTg: pascuae] pascue BDEGIJL; pascuę CFHK. collocauit] conlocauit A. educauit] A: *1st* u *on eras.;* ęducauit GH.

LTu: in] In βν. pascuae] pascuę διλμξφ; pascue ζπϱσϛτ*τυψ; paschuę ν. ibi] ibe β. collocauit] conlocauit βμ; collocabit ψ.

3

animam	sawle *A*BCFGIJK, saule DH, sæwle E^{2}
meam	mine $ABCDE^{x}$*FGHIJK
conuertit	gecerde A, gecerde B, gecyrde CK*, gecirred J, he gecyrde DE^{x}*FGHI
Deduxit	gelaedde A*, gelædde BC, he gelædde FI, he lædde DHK, he ledde E^{x}*, he lædde ł gelædon G*, gelæddon *J*
me	me $ABCE^{x}$*FIJK

super ofer ABE^{2}FGHJK, ofyr C, ofor I
semitam* stige ABCJ, siþfæt ł stige D, siþfæt ł stige H, siðfet ł stige $E^{2/x}$*, siðfæt ł stige G*, paðas FI, wegas K (*L*)
iustitiae rehtwisnisse A, ryhtwisnesse *BD*, rihtwisnysse *CF*I, rihtwisnesse *E^{x}*GHJ*K* (*L*)
propter fore ABDH, for CE^{2}F*G*IJK
nomen | noman ABC, naman DFHIK, nomen G, nama J, his E^{2}
suum | his ABDFGHIJK, hys *C*, nomæn E^{2}*

ED: saule (H)] saul *Campbell.* mine (H)] min *Campbell.* he ledde (E)] He ledde *Harsley.* iusticię (C)] iusti[t]ię *Wildhagen.* iusititię (E)] iustitiae *Harsley.*

OE: mine (E^{x})] *on eras.* gecyrde (K)] g *eras. before word.* he gecyrde (E^{x})] *on eras.* gelaedde (A)] *2nd* d *interl.* he ledde (E^{x})] *on eras.* he lædde ł gelædon (G)] ł gelædon *added in diff.* (?) *hand.* me (E^{x})] *on eras.* siðfet ł stige ($E^{2/x}$)] fet ł stige *on eras. by corr.* siðfæt ł stige (G)] ł stige *added in diff.* (?) *hand.* rihtwisnesse (E^{x})] *on eras.*, ÷ *written after* rihtwis *and before* nesse *in next line.* rihtwisnesse (J)] h *altered from* r. nomæn (E^{2})] o *altered from another letter.*

LTg: animam] A: *2nd* m *added by corr.* Deduxit] duxit J. semitam] semitas L: *final* s *added by corr.: see GAg.* iustitiae] iustitiæ BL; iusititię DEFGHK; iustitie J; iusticię C: *orig.* iustitię: *2nd* t *altered to* c. propter] propte[ ] G. suum] C: *2nd* u *on eras.*

LTu: iustitiae] iusititię ειν$\xi\chi$; iustitiæ μ; iusticiae ϱ: *orig.* iustitiae: *2nd* t *deleted,* c *interl.;* iustitie σ, ς: u *interl.;* iusticie τ*τ; iusticię φ. suum] tuum ς.

GAg: semitam] semitas FGHIJK, L: *see LTg.*

GAu: semitam] semitas δεζϑιλμξοπϱστυφχψ.

4
Nam weotudlice A, weotodlice D, witodlice BHIK, witudlice C, Witotlice E^{x}*, witodlice ł soðlice *G**, soðlice J, soðes F
et ⁊ ABCDE^{x}*FGHIJ
si ðæh ðe A, þeh þe B, þeah þe CJ, ðeh þe I*, gif DHK*, gef E^{x}*, gyf F, gif þeah G*
ambulem* ic gonge AB, ic gange CE^{x}*FJK, ic gange ł fare DG*, ic gange fare H, ic gange oððe fare I
in in A, on BCDE^{2}FGHIJK
medio midle ABCIJ, middele DGH, myddæn E^{2}, middan K, midlunge F
umbrae | scuan A*B*, sceade *C*, scæde *K*, sceaduwe *DFH*, sceadue *I*, sceadu *G*, scadu *J*, deæþes *E^{2}* (*L*)
mortis | deaðes ABF^{2}*GH, deaþes DIJK, deaðys C, sceaduwe E^{x}*
non | ne ABE^{x}*J, na DGHK, ic ne CI (F*)

timebo | ondredu ic A, ondræde ic BE^{x}*J, ic ondræde DGH, ondræde CI, dræde K, [ ]r[ ] F^{2}
mala yfel ABK, yfyl C, yfelu DGHJ, yfæle E^{2}*, yfele F^{2}, yflu I
quoniam forðon ABDF^{2}GJ, forþon CH, forþæn E^{2}, forðan K, forþan þe I
tu ðu AF^{2}, þu BCE^{2}GIJK
mecum mid me ABCDF^{2}GHIK, myd me E^{2}, me mid J
es erð A, eart BF^{2}G*I*JK*, þu eart *C*, bist ł ært E^{2} (*DH*)

Uirga | gerd *AI*, gird *BF*^{2}*J*, gyrd CD*H*K, þin *E*^{2} (*G*)
tua | ðin ABF^{2}, þin CDHIJK, [ ]in G, gierd E^{2}
et | ⁊ ABCDE^{2}F^{2}GHJK, stæf I
baculus | cryc AB, crice C, stæf DGHJK, stef E^{2}F^{2}, ⁊ I
tuus ðin AF^{2}, þin BCDE^{x}*GHIJK
ipsa hie AB, hi CK, hy DE^{x}*H, he F^{2}, þonne hy G*, þonne J, sylfe I*
me me ABCDE^{x}*F^{2}GHIK, æfre J
consolata froefrende A, frefriynde C, afrefrende B, frefredon DE^{x}*F^{2}H, frefrodan K, gefrefrode G, gefrefredun I, frēde J
sunt werun A, wæron J, sint B, synt C, synd ł wæron G*

ED: et si (CDEFGIJK)] etsi *Wildhagen, Roeder, Harsley, Kimmens, Lindelöf, Rosier, Oess, Sisam.* þch þc (B)] þchþe *Brenner.* þeah þe (C)] þeahþe *Wildhagen.* gif þeah (G)] gif ł þeah *Rosier.* umbrę (I)] umbrae *Lindelöf.* forðon (A)] for ðon *Kuhn.* és (H)] es *Campbell.* [ ]in (G)] [ ] *Rosier.*

OE: Witotlice (E^{x})] *on eras.* witodlice ł soðlice (G)] ł soðlice *added in diff.* (?) *hand above* witodlice. ⁊ (E^{x})] *on eras.* ðeh þe (I)] þe *interl.* gif (K)] g (?) *eras. before word.* gef (E^{x})] *on eras.* gif þeah (G) þeah *written in diff.* (?) *hand above* gif. ic gange (E^{x})] *on eras.* ic gange ł fare (G)] gange ł *added in diff.* (?) *hand.* deaðes (F^{2})] *all glosses from* deaðes *until end of psalm* (*i.e., fol. 22v*) *written in 16th-c. hand on eras., with exception of gloss to* in longitudine (*v. 6*). sceaduwe (E^{x})] *on eras.* ne (E^{x})] *on eras.* non (F)] *gloss eras.* ondræde ic (E^{x})] *on eras.* yfæle (E^{2})] e *added by corr.* (?). eart (G)] a *interl. by glossator.* þin (E^{x})] *on eras.* hy (E^{x})] *on eras.* þonne hy (G)] *added in diff.* (?) *hand.* sylfe (I)] þin sylfe gerd *written in right margin.* me (E^{x})] *on eras.* frefredon (E^{x})] *on eras.* synd ł wæron (G)] ł wæron *added in diff.* (?) *hand.*

LTg: Nam] [ ]am G. umbrae] umbræ BL; umbrę CHIK; umbre DEFGJ. es] C: *eras. after word;* és DHK, J: s *altered from another letter and followed by eras.* Uirga] Virga ABEFHIJ, G: V *partly lost.*

LTu: umbrae] umbrę δεζνξϱφ; umbræ ϑ; umbre ιϛστ*τυ. Uirga] Virga ζινξοστ*τυφ.

GAg: ambulem] ambulauero FGHIJK.

GAu: ambulem] ambulauero δεζϑιλμξοπϱστυφχψ.

5

Parasti | ðu gearwades A, þu gearwades B, ðu gearwodest D, þu gearwodest HK, þu gearewodest *G*, þu gegearwudost C, þu giredost F^{2}, þu earwodest J, þu geærwodest beod E^{2}*, þu gearcodest I
in — in A, on BCDE^{2}F^{2}GHJK, beforan I
conspectu | gesihðe ABCF^{2}GH, gesihðe D, gesihþe J, gesyhþe K, minre E^{2}I
meo | minre ABCDF^{2}GHJK, gesihþe E^{2}, gesihðe I
mensam — biod A, beod BCDHK, mýse ł beod F^{2}, beod ł mysan G*, beoþ ł misan J, beod ł beodwyste ł mysan I
aduersus — wið AJ, ongen BC, ongean DE^{x}*HK, ongean ł *G**, ongeanes F^{2}, agen hi ł agenes I
eos — him A, hig F^{2}IJ, hy G, ða BD, þa CE^{x}*HK
qui — ða A, þa K, þe CE^{x}*DH, þa ðe BIJ, ða þe F^{2}, þa þe G
tribulant — swencað AB, swenceað C, swencton DH, swæncton J, geswencton G*, drefað ł swencton F^{2}, geswencaþ ł ða þe gedrefaþ I, drefað K, eærfoþigæþ ł swencton E$^{2/x}$*
me — mec A, me BCE^{x}*F^{2}GIJK

Inpinguasti — ðu faettades A, þu fættodes B, þu gefættudyst *C,* þu afættodost J, þu mæstest D*K,* þu mæsthest H, þu onbryddæs ł mestest E$^{2/x}$*, ðu smiriast F^{2}, þu amæstest ł þu gefætnodest I, [ ]estest [ ]tadest *G**
in | in A, on BCDF^{2}GHIJK, min E^{2}
oleo | ele ABCDF^{2}GHIJK, heæfod E^{2}
caput | heafud AC, heafod *B*D*F*^{2}G*H*IJ, hæfod *K,* on E^{2}
meum | min ABCDF^{2}GHIJK, ele E^{2}
et — ⁊ ABCE^{2}F^{2}GHJK
poculum* | drync AB, drenc CG, drincefæt D, drencfæt K, drencfæc ł calic I, calic F^{2}, þin E^{2}*, þinne J (*L*)
tuum* | ðinne A, þinne B, þin CD, min I, dryncefæt E^{x}*, drinc J (*L*)
inebrians — indrencende A, ondrencende B, druncengende DH, drungniende E^{2}, druncnend F^{2}*, drunccende K, druncigende ł ondrengte G*, drincende ł on druncninge I*, ondrængte J, druncenlæwe C (*L*)
quam — swide A, swiðe BC*, hu DE^{2}F^{2}H, eala hu GJ, ⁊ la hu I
praeclarum* — freaberht A, fræbeorht *BC,* beorht ł mære *D*GH, bryht ł mere *E*^{2}, bearht F^{2}, beoht J, scinende ł hu beorht I (*L*)
est — is ABE^{x}F^{2}GHIJ, ys C

ED: mýse ł beod (F)] myse ł beod *Kimmens*. aduers[ ] (G)] adu*ersus* *Rosier.* Impinguasti (C)] I[n]pinguasti *Wildhagen.* [ ]estest [ ]tadest (G)] [ ]estest ł [ ]tadest *Rosier.* drencfæc ł calic (I)] drencfæt ł calic *Lindelöf.* p̄clarus (K)] præclarus *Sisam.*

OE: þu geærwodest beod (E^{2})] t *possibly added by corr.* beod ł mysan (G)] ł mysan *added in diff.* (?) *hand.* ongean (E^{x})] *on eras.* ongean ł (G)] ł *added in diff.* (?) *hand.* þa (E^{x})] *on eras.* þe (E^{x})] *on eras.* geswencton (G)] ge *added in diff.* (?) *hand.* eærfoþigæþ ł swencton ($E^{2/x}$)] ł swencton *added by corr.,* me (E^{x})] *added by corr.* þu onbryddæs ł mestest ($E^{2/x}$)] ł mestest *added by corr.* [ ]estest [ ]tadest (G)] [ ]tadest *added in diff.* (?) *hand.* þin (E^{2})] *eras. after word.* dryncefæt (E^{x})] *on eras. by corr.* druncnend (F^{2})] *gloss eras. above preceding* meus. druncigende ł ondrengte (G)] ł ondrengte *added in diff.* (?) *hand above* druncigende. drincende ł on druncninge (I)] ł on druncninge *written in left margin.* swiðe (C)] ð *malformed.*

LTg: Parasti] [ ]arasti G. aduersus] aduers[ ] G. Inpinguasti] Impinguasti CK: *orig.* Inpinguasti: *left leg added to 1st* n *by corr. to form* m; [ ]guasti G. caput] F: *orig.* capud: d *deleted by subscript dot,* t *interl.,* H: t *altered from another letter;* capud B, K: *orig.* caput: t *altered to* d. poculum] L: *underlined to signal deletion,* calix *written interl. by corr.: see GAg.* tuum] L: *underlined to signal deletion,* tuus *written interl. by corr.: see GAg.* inebrians] inębrians L. praeclarum] preclarum BCDEL.

LTu: Inpinguasti] [ ]npinguasti ς: *initial wanting;* Impinguasti πτ*τφχ. caput] capud νξυ. praeclarum] pręclarum ν; preclarum ςτ*.

GAg: poculum] calix FGHIJK, L: *see LTg.* tuum] meus FGHIJK. praeclarum] preclarus FHJ; pręclarus G; praeclarus I; p̄clarus K.

GAu: poculum tuum] calix meus δεζϑιλμξοπϱστυφχψ. praeclarum] pręclarus δελϱφ; preclarus ζιπστ; p̄clarus ϑξου; praeclarus μχψ.

6

Et		⁊ ABC$E^{2}F^{2}$HIJK
misericordia	I	milheortniss A, mildheortnis D, mildheortnes BHJ, mildheortnesse F^{2}GK, mildheortnys I, mildheort C, þin E^{2}
tua	I	ðin AF^{2}, þin BCGIJK, þine H, mildheortnesse E^{2}
subsequitur	I	efterfylgeð *A,* æfterfylgeð B*G,* æft<u>er</u>filgeþ *J,* æfterfylgð *F^{2},* æfterfylge *I**,* ofyrfylgð *C,* fylgeð *DHK,* me E^{2} (*L*)
me	I	mec A, me BCF^{2}GHIJK, efterfylgend E^{2}*
omnibus		allum A, eallum BCF^{2}, eallu<u>m</u> DHJ, eællum E^{2}, on eallum GI, eallan K
diebus		degum A, dagu<u>m</u> BDJ, dagum CHI, dægum $E^{2}F^{2}$, dagan G, diebus K
uitae	I	lifes A*BDF²GIJK**,* lifys *C,* liues H, mines *E^{2}* (*L*)
meae	I	mines A*BDGHIJ,* minys *C,* minres F^{2}, minre *K,* lifes *E^{2}* (*L*)

(Et)*	⁊ F^{2}GHIJK
Ut	ðæt *A,* þæt *BGH,* þæt *CDF^{2}IJK,* þet *E^2* (*L*)
inhabitem	ic ineardie A, ic ineardige BC, ic oneardige GJ, ic eardige DF^{2}HK, ic eærdige E^2*, ic wunige I
in	in A, on BCE^{2}F^{2}GIJK
domo	| huse ABCIJK, husu F^{2}G, drihtnes E^2
domini	| dryhtnes B, drihtnys C, drihtnes F^{2}G, drihtnys I, dryht̄ A, driħ J, huse E^2
in	in A, on BCDE^{2}FGHIJK
longitudinem	lengu A, lengo *B,* lenge *CJ,* langan *K,* langnisse *DH,* langnesse *E^x*,* langnesse ł on lenge G*, langsumnysse I, la[ ]sse *F**
dierum	dę(g)a A*, daga BCDF^{2}HI, dagana G, dagena J, dagan K, minræ dægæ E^2

ED: Et (B)] et *Brenner.* uitę (E)] vitae *Harsley.* meę (E)] meae *Harsley.* on (F) (*2nd*)] [ ] *Kimmens.* la[ ]sse (F)] [ ] *Kimmens.* dę(g)a (A)] dęga *Kuhn.*

OE: æfterfylge (I)] y *altered from* i (?). efterfylgend (E^2)] e *eras. after* d, ł e *written below* nd *by main hand.* lifes (K)] *scribe originally began* u-, *then eras. left leg and altered right leg to* l. ic eærdige (E^2)] *eras. after* ic. langnesse (E^x)] *on eras.* langnesse ł on lenge (G)] ł on lenge *added in diff.* (?) *hand.* la[ ]sse (F)] n (?) *visible after* a. dę(g)a (A)] *top of* g *lost.*

LTg: subsequitur] A: *small eras. after* i (*altered from* e?); subsequętur G; subsequetur FHIJK, D: *orig.* subsequitur: i *altered to* e; subsequatur CL: *cf. Weber MSS* PQUVXβγη. uitae] uitæ B; uitę CEFGL; uite DJK, I: *letter eras. after* t. meae] meæ BC; meę DEGJKL; mee I: *orig.* meae: a *eras.* Ut] L: E *added by corr. within lobe of* U: *see GAg;* Vt ABCDE; ut FGHIJK. longitudinem] longitudinem C: *eras. after* ē, H: m *on eras. in lighter ink,* K: *macron* (-nem) *added later;* longitudine BDEFJ: *cf Weber MSS* MS^{2}PXαβγ moz.

LTu: misericordia] missericordia ϑ. subsequitur] subsequetur ϑιπϱστφψ, χ: ue *interl.;* subsequatur νς; subsequętur υ. uitae] uitę βεζινξοφ; uitæ ϑ; uite σςτ*τ. meae] meę εινξφχ; meæ ϑ; mee σςτ*τ. Ut] Vt ν; ut δεζϑιμξοπστυφψ. inhabitem] σ: h *interl.* longitudinem] longitudine βζϑϱτ*υψ: *cf Weber MSS* MS^{2}PXαβγ moz.

GAg: Ut] Et ut FHIJK, I: *eras. after word* (*probably flanking sign* ÷); [ ]t ut G: *initial* E *lost; for* L *see LTg.*

GAu: Ut] Et ut δεζϑιλμξοπϱστυφχψ.

PSALM 23

1

Domini	drihtnys *C*, drihtnes *DF*/F^{2}*III, Drihtnes *E*^{2}, dryht̄ *A*, driħ GJ (*BK*)
est	is ABDE^{2}F^{2}GHIJ*K*, ys *C*
terra	earðe A, eorðe B*C*DF^{2}HI, eorþe JK, sio eorþe E^{2}, teorðan G
et	⁊ ABCDE^{2}F^{2}GHIJK
plenitudo	ſylnis A, fylnes BJ, gefyllydnys C, gefyllednis DH, gefelledness E^{x}*, gefyllednes K, gefyllednisse F^{2}, gefyllednes ł fylnes G*, fulnysse ł gefyllednes I
eius	his ABCJK, hire DE^{2}F^{2}H, hyre GI
orbis	ymbhwyrft ABCDF^{2}G*HI, ymbwyrft E^{2}, ymbehwyrft K, ymbhwyrftes J
terrarum	eorðena ABCE^{x}*F^{2}, eorþena GJ, eorðana DHI, eorþan K
et	⁊ ABCDE^{x}*F^{2}GHIJK
uniuersi	alle A, ealle B*C*DF^{2}GHIJ, ælle E^{x}*, eale K
qui	ða A, þa K, þa ðe BDE^{x}*, þa þe CGHIJ, ða ðe F^{2}
habitant	eardiað ABCDF^{2}GK, eærdiæþ E^{2}*, eardiaþ J, eardigað H, wuniað I
in	in A, on BCDE^{2}F^{2}GHIJK
ea*	hire AH, hyre DI*K, hieræ E^{2}, hyre ł on hine G*, hyne F^{2}, hine J, him B, him C

OE: drihtnes (F/F^{2})] nes *written in 16th-c. hand on eras., as are remainder of glosses to v. 1.* gefelledness (E^{x})] *on eras.* gefyllednes ł fylnes (G)] nes ł fylnes *added in diff.* (?) *hand, with* fylnes *divided after* y *by following* hyre. ymbhwyrft (G)] *otiose superscript stroke after* t. eorðena (E^{x})] *on eras.* ⁊ (E^{x})] *on eras.* ælle (E^{x})] *on eras.* þa ðe (E^{x})] *on eras.* eærdiæþ (E^{2})] i *interl.* hyre (I)] [ ]f him *written in left margin, cropped.* hyre ł on hine (G)] ł on hine *written in diff.* (?) *hand.*

LTg: Domini] DN̄i A; DN̄I CBDEK. est] EST C; ést K. terra] TERRA C. uniuersi] C: *eras. before word.*

LTu: Domini] DOMINI ιτ; DOMIni ϛ; DN̄I βλμνξπρστ*φχ. est] EST λμνξπρ. terra] TERRA λμνξπρ. et (*1st*)] ET λμξπρ. plenitudo] PLENITUDO λξπ; PLENItudo ρ. eius] EIUS ξπ. orbis] ORBIS ξ. terrarum] TERrarum ξ.

GAg: ea] eo FGHIJK.

GAu: ea] eo δεζϑιλξορστυφχψ.

2

(Quia)* forþon J, forðā F, forþan K, forðan þe I, þa þa G
Ipse he ABCDE^{2}**FGHK,* he sylf *I,* he silf *J*
super ofer ABDE^{2}FGHIJK, ofyr Ç
maria sęas *A*B, seas H, sæs DIJ, ses E^{2}, sǽs F, sæ CK, sǽ *G*
fundauit | gesteaðelade A, gestaðolode BI, gestaðolude C, gestaðelode J, gegrundweallude DH, gegrundweallode F^{2}*, gegrundwallede hye ł gestæþolædæ E$^{2/x}$*, gegrundweallude ł gestáðolode G*, grundweallode K
eam* | hie AB, hi C, hine F^{2}*HIJ, hine ł hig G* (*K*)
et ⁊ ABCDE^{2}FGHIJK
super ofer ABDE^{2}FGHJK, ofyr C, ofor I
flumina flodas ABCDGHIJ, flod FK, streæmæs E^{2}
praeparauit gearwað A, gegearwode *BCJ,* he gegearwode *D**FH,* he geærwode *E*^{2}, he gegearowode *G,* gearwode *K,* he gegearkode *I* (*L*)
illam* ða A, þa BC, hy D, hi K, hie E^{2}*, hine FHIJ, hine ł hig G*

ED: sǽ (G)] sæ *Rosier.* mária (G)] maria G. gestaðolode (B)] he gestaðolode *Brenner.* gegrundwallede hye ł gestæþolædæ (E$^{2/x}$)] gegrundwalled*e* hye ł gestæþolædæ *Harsley.* praepauit (I)] praeparauit *Lindelöf.* p̄parauit (K)] præparauit *Sisam.*

OE: he (E^{2})] *eras.* (:s?) *after word.* gegrundweallode (F^{2})] *written in 16th-c. hand on eras.* gegrundwallede hye ł gestæþolædæ (E$^{2/x}$)] gegrundwallede hye ł *on eras. by corr.,* ł *interl.* gegrundweallude ł gestáðolode (G)] ł gestáðolode *added in diff.* (?) *hand above* gegrundweallude. hine (F^{2}) (*1st*)] *written in 16th-c. hand on eras.* hine ł hig (G) (*1st*)] ł hig *added in diff.* (?) *hand.* he gegearwode (D)] d *on eras.* hie (E^{2})] e *on eras.* hine ł hig (G) (*2nd*)] ł hig *added in diff.* (?) *hand.*

LTg: Ipse] ipse FGHIJK. maria] A: *letter eras. after word;* mária G. praeparauit] preparauit BCDEFGHJL; praepauit I; p̄parauit K.

LTu: Ipse] ipse δεζιϑλμξοπϱςτυφχψ. praeparauit] pręparauit βζλνπϱ; preparabit ϑ; preparauit ιξςτ*; p̄parauit οστφ. illam] illum ϑ.

GAg: Ipse] Quia ipse FGHIJK. eam] eum FGHJ, K: u *on eras.;* e[ ] I: *eras. after* e. illam] eum FGHIJ, K: u *on eras.*

GAu: Ipse] Quia ipse δεζιλμξοπϱστυφχψ; quia ipse ϑ. eam] eum δεζϑιλξοπστυφχψ. illam] eum δεζιλοπϱστυφχψ; eam μξ.

3

Quis hwelc ABD, hwylc CE^{2}F*HK,* (h)wilc *G**, hwilc J, la hwilc I
ascendit astigeð A, astigð *B,* astigþ D*, æstigæþ E^{2}, astihð *CFIK,* astah *J**, astah ł astihð *GH*

in		in A, on BCDE^{2}FGHIJK
montem	I	munt ABCDGHJ, munte FI, muntas K, drihtnes E^{2}
domini	I	dryhtnes B, drihtnys C, drihtnes F, dryht̄ A, driħt G, driħ J, dune E^{2} (*K*)
aut		oððe ABCFGH, oþðe DK, oþðæ E^{2}, oþþe I, oþþ J
quis		hwelc AB, hwylc *C*DFHK, hwilc GIJ, wylc E^{2}
stabit		stondeð AB, stondyð C, standeþ DF, standeð H, stænt ł standeð G*, gestandeþ J, stent E^{2}I, stynt K
in		in AB, on CDE^{2}FGHIJ*K
loco	I	stowe ABCDFGHIJK, his E^{2}
sancto		ðere halgan A, þære halgan BCDGH, þere hælgæn E^{2}, halgan F, haligum J, haligre ł halgan I*, halian K
eius	I	his ABCDFGHIJ*K*, stowe E^{2}

ED: [ ]uís (G)] *Q*uis *Rosier.* (h)wilc (G)] hwilc *Rosier.* þere hælgæn (E)] þere ælgæn *Harsley.*

OE: (h)wilc (G)] *ascender of* h *lost.* astigþ (D)] *orig.* astagþ (*or* astag, *with* þ *added?*): i *interl., 2nd* a *deleted by subscript dot.* astah (J)] h *altered from another letter* (*traces of descender visible*). stænt ł standeð (G)] ł standeð *added in diff.* (?) *hand above following* on. on (J) (*2nd*)] *written below* gestandeþ. haligre ł halgan (I)] ł halgan *written in right margin.*

LTg: Quis] K: s *interl.* (*by corr.?*); [ ]uís G; [ ]uis H: *initial* Q *lost.* ascendit] ascendet BCFGHIJK: *cf. Weber MSS* M^{2}PQUVXα med. domini] K: *eras.* (*30 mm*) *after word.* quis] C: *orig.* qui: s *added interl. by corr.* eius] eíus K.

LTu: ascendit] ascendet ζϑιξοπϱσυφχψ, λ: *2nd* e *altered from orig.* i. sancto] *interl.* ϱ.

4

Innocens		unsceððende AB, unsceðþyndc *C,* underigende DFH, þæ underiende E$^{2/x}$*, on underigende ł unsceaðful G*, unscæþful J, unscyldig ł se unscæððiga I*, unscyldige K
manibus		on hondum A, on hondum B, on handum G*I*, on handum J, handum D, handum FH, hand C, hændæ E^{2}, handa K
et		⁊ ABCE^{2}FGHIJK
mundo	I	clænre AB*C*DFH, clænre ł clæne G*, þæ clenæ E^{2}*, clæne J, clænan K, se clænheorta I*
corde	I	heortan ABCDFGHK, heortæn E^{2}, heorte J
qui		se ABC, se þe DE^{2}HIJ, se ðe FG, þa K
non		ne ABCI, na DE^{2}*FHJK, na ne G*
accepit		onfeng *ABC*DE^{2}FH, onfeng ł onfehð G*, afeng K, onfehþ J, nam ł anfengc I

in	in ADF, on BCE²GHIJK
uano	idelnisse *A*, idelnesse B, idylnysse C, ydelnesse E², idel DH*J*K, ydel FI, idel ł idlum G*
animam	I sawle ABCFGHIJK, saule D, his E²
suam	I his ABCDFGHIJ*K, sæwlæ E²
nec	I ne A, na K, ne ne DE²FHI*, ne he ne BCG*J
iurauit	I he swor A, swor BCDE²*HIK, swór F, swor ł swereð G*, sweraþ J
in	in A, on BCDE²*FGH*IJK
dolo	facne ABCDE²*FGHIJ, facn K
proximo	I ðæm nestan A, þæm nihstan BI, þam neahstan C, ðam nextan F, þam nyhstan G, þam nihstan J, nyhtan K, his DE²**H*
suo	I his ABCFGIJK, nehstan D, niehxtæn E², nixstan H

ED: Innocens (B)] innocens *Brenner.* ne ne (D)] nene *Roeder.*

OE: þæ underiende (E^2/x)] deriende *on eras. by corr.* on underigende ł unsceaðful (G)] ł unsceaðful *added in diff.* (?) *hand above* on underigende. unscyldig ł se unscæððiga (I)] se unscæððiga *written in left margin.* on handum (G)] on *added interl. in diff.* (?) *hand.* on handum (I)] *on eras., gloss eras. before* on. clænre ł clæne (G)] ł clæne *added in diff.* (?) *hand.* þæ clenæ (E²)] *2nd* æ *altered from* a *by corr.* se clænheorta (I)] *eras.* (?) *after* clæn. na (E²)] *orig.* ne: a *altered to* e. na ne (G)] ne *added in diff.* (?) *hand.* onfeng ł onfehð (G) ł onfehð *added in diff.* (?) *hand.* idel ł idlum (G)] ł idlum *added in diff.* (?) *hand.* his (J) (*1st*)] hi *on eras.* ne ne (I)] *eras. after 1st* ne. ne he ne (G)] *2nd* ne *added in diff.* (?) *hand.* swor (E²)] *on eras.* (*by corr.?*). swor ł swereð (G)] ł swereð *added interl. in diff.* (?) *hand.* on (E²) (*2nd*)] *on eras.* (*by corr.?*). on (H) (*2nd*)] *otiose horizontal stroke after* n. facne (E²)] *on eras.* (*by corr.?*). his (E²) (*2nd*)] *eras. after word.*

LTg: Innocens] C: *eras. after* I. mundo] C: o *on eras.* accepit] accipit AB; acepit C. uano] A: *orig.* uanu: o *written above final* u, J: o *altered from another letter.* proximo] H: *2nd* o *on eras.*

LTu: Innocens] INnocens β. accepit] accipit βϑ. animam suam] anim suam ψ.

5

Hic	ðes ABD, þes CE²GHIJ*K*, ðæs F
accipiet	onfoeð A, onfehð BDGHI, onfehþ CE²FJ, afehþ K
benedictionem	bledsunge A, bletsunge BCE²IJ, bletsunga DFGHK
a	from A*E²*, from BC, fram F, fram GJ, æt I, of K
domino	dryhtne B, drihtny C, drihtne E²FI, drihtene K, dryht̄ A, drih̕t G, drih̕ J

et	⁊ ABCE²FGHIJK
misericordiam	mildheortnisse AD, mildheortnysse CFHI, mildheortnesse BE²GJK
a	from A, from BC, fram *E*ˣ*I*, fram FGJK
deo	gode ABCEˣ*FGJ*K*, his I
salutari	ðæm halwendan A, þæm halwendan B, þam halwendan C, halwendan *I*, hælo DFGH, hæle Eˣ*JK
suo	his ABDEˣ*FGHJK, hys C, gode I

ED: Hic (G)] *Hic Rosier.* á (E) (*1st*)] a *Harsley.* á (E) (*2nd*)] a *Harsley.*

OE: fram (Eˣ)] *on eras.* fram (I)] *eras. after word.* gode (Eˣ)] *on eras.* hæle (Eˣ)] *on eras.* his (Eˣ)] *on eras.*

LTg: Hic] Híc K. a (*1st*)] á E. a (*2nd*)] á E. deo] K: ō *on eras.* (dō), *word possibly altered from* dño. salutari] I: *eras. above word.*

LTu: misericordiam] missericordiam ϑ: *1st* s *interl.*

6

Haec	ðis AF, þis *BCDGHJK,* þios *E²,* þeos I (*L*)
est	is ABDE²FGHIJ*K*, ys C
generatio	cneoris ABJ, cneoriss C, cneores D, cnyowris E²*, cneowres H, cneornes K, cneoris ł cýnren G*, cneoris ł mægþ I, cynrin F
quaerentium	soecendra A, secendra *BDFGHJ,* secyndra *C,* secændra *E²/ˣ*,* secende I**K* (*L*)
dominum*	dryhten B, drihtyn C, drihten DE², dryhī A, hine FIJK
requirentium*	socendra A, soecendra B, secyndra C, secendra DFGHIJ, secændre E²/ˣ*, secende K
faciem	onsiene AE², onsien B, ansyne CIJK, onsyne D, ansinc F, onsiene H, on ansyne G*
dei	godes ABFGIJK, godys C, iæcobes E²
iacob	iacobes ABFIJ, iacobys C, getreowfulra DH, getreowfulra ł iacobes G, n K*, godes E²

ED: Hęc (E)] Haec *Harsley.* cneoris ł cýnren (G)] cneoris ł cynren *Rosier.* secende (I)] secendra [*or* secendre] *Lindelöf.* e[ ] (G)] eum *Rosier, who records the gloss* h[ ], *although no* h *is visible.* iacob (K)] Iacob *Sisam.*

OE: cnyowris (E²)] *letter eras. after word.* cneoris ł cýnren (G)] cneoris ł *added in diff.* (?) *hand.* secændra (E²/ˣ)] dra *on eras. by corr.* secende (I)] *orig.* secendra: *deleting dots above and below* r, a *altered to* e. secændre (E²/ˣ)] d *blotted,* re *on eras. by corr.* on ansyne (G)] on *added in diff.* (?) *hand.* n (K)] *for* nomen.

LTg: Haec] Hæc BCKL; Hec D; Hęc EHJ; [ ]aec G. est] ést K. quaerentium] quærentium B; querentium CDEGHJKL; quęrentium F.

LTu: Haec] Hęc ειφ; Hæc ϑμχ; Hec ξσςτ; [ ]ec τ*: _initial wanting_. quaerentium] quęrentium δελορφ; querentium ζϑιμξστ*τυ.

GAg: dominum] eum FHIJK; e[ ] G. requirentium] quęrentium F; querentium GHJK; quaerentium I.

GAu: dominum] eum δεζϑιλμξπρστυφχψ. requirentium] querentium δϑιξστ; quęrentium εζλνοπρφ; quærentium μχ; quaerentium υψ.

7

Tollite*		onhebbað ABC, [ ]hebbað ł tohlynnað I*, adoþ D, tadoð H, adoð ł nimað ge G*, nimaþ J, geopeniæþ E^{2}, undo F, undoþ K (_L_)
portas		geatu ABG*, gatu CDFHIJK, gæto E^{2}
principes	|	aldres A, ealdras BFK, aldrys C, aldormen D*, ealdormen GHJ, eala ge ealdras I*, eowre E^{2}*
uestri*	|	eowres _A_, eowre B_D_FGHIJ, eowrys _C_, eoure K, eældormonne _E^{2}*_ (_L_)
et		ꝛ ABCDE^{2}FGHIJK
eleuamini		bioð upahefene A, beoð upahæfene B, beoð upahafyne C, beoð upahafene ł ꝛ uparærað I, upahebbað DFG, upæhebbæþ E^{2}, upahebbaþ H, upahebbaþ ge J, ahebbað K (_L_)
portae	|	geatu A_BG*_, gatu _CDFHIJ_, gata _K_, þæ ecelecæn _E^{2}_ (_L_)
aeternales	|	ecelice A_BCHK_, ecelece _D_, eccelice F, ecelice ł ecnesse _G*_, ecnesse _J_, gæto _E^{2}_ (_IL_)
et		ꝛ ABCE^{2}FGHIJK
introibit		ingaeð A, ingæð BC, ingeþ E^{2}, ingæþ K, ingangeþ DJ, ingangeð F_G_H, infærð ł ꝛ ingangeð I
rex	|	cyning ABCDGH, cyningc F, kyningc I, kyninc J, cining K, se wuldorfestæ E^{2}
gloriae	|	wuldres A_BDFG_HI_JK_, wuldrys C, kyning _E^{2}_ (_L_)

ED: [ ]hebbað ł tohlynnað (I)] ahebbað ł tohlynnað _Lindelöf._ geopeniæþ (E)] Geopeniæþ _Harsley._ beoð upahafene ł ꝛ uparærað (I)] beoð upahafene ł ꝛ up arærað _Lindelöf._ æternales (D)] aeternales _Roeder._ ęternales (E)] aeternales _Harsley._ glorię (E)] gloriae _Harsley._

OE: [ ]hebbað ł tohlynnað (I)] [ ]hebbað _written in left margin, initial letter lost to tight binding._ adoð ł nimað ge (G)] ł nimað ge _added in diff._ (?) _hand above_ adoð. geatu (G) (_1st_)] e _added interl. in diff._ (?) _hand._ aldormen (D)] _eras. after word._ eala ge ealdras (I)] s. o _written below_ eala, ge _interl._ eowre (E^{2})] _eras. after word._

eældormonne (E²)] s *eras. after 2nd* e. geatu (G) (*2nd*)] e *added interl. in diff.* (?) *hand.* ecelice ł ecnesse (G)] ł ecnesse *added in diff.* (?) *hand.*

LTg: Tollite] L: attollite *written between* To *by corr.: see GAg.* uestri] uestras CDEL, A: *orig.* uestri: i *altered to* a, s *added: cf. Weber MSS* η moz, *see GAg.* eleuamini] L: u *on eras.* (?). portae] portæ B; porte CDEGJK; portę FHL. aeternales] I: *gloss above word eras.;* æternales BCDKL; ęternales EGH; eternales J. introibit] introtroibit G: intro *written at end of line,* troibit *at beginning of next line.* gloriae] gloriæ B; glorię DEFGKL; glorie J.

LTu: uestri] uestras νςτ*: *cf. Weber MSS* η moz, *see GAu.* portae] β: r *interl. by corr.;* porte δειπσςτ*τυ; portæ ϑ; portę λνορφ. aeternales] ęternales ειξφ; æternales ϑχ; eternales σςτ*τ. introibit] introiuit β. gloriae] glorię δζξπρφ; gloriæ ϑ; glorie ισςτ*τυ.

GAg: Tollite] Attollite FGHIK, L: *see LTg;* Adtollite J. uestri] uestras FGHIJK, ACDEL: *see LTg.*

GAu: Tollite] Attollite δεζιλμξοπρστυφχψ; Adtollite ϑ. uestri] uestras δεζϑιλμξοπρστυφχψ, νςτ*: *see LTu.*

8

Quis		hwelc AB, hwylc CDF*H**, hwilc E²G, hwil J, la hwilc I, hwæt K
est		is ABDE²FGHIJ, ys C, ic *K*
iste		ðes AF, þes BCDE²HIJK, þæs G
rex	|	cyning ABCDH, cyningc FI, cyninc J, cining K, cyninges G, wuldorfestæ E²
gloriae	|	wuldres A*BCDFHIJK*, wuldor *G*, kyning *E²* (*L*)
dominus		dryhten B, drihten E²F, dryht̄ A, drih̄t G, driht̄ I*, drih̄ J, drih̄t ys C
fortis	|	strong AB, strang CDFGHJK, se stranga I, his mihtig E²
et		⁊ ABCDE²FGHIJK
potens	|	maehtig A, mehtig B, mihtig CFJ, mihti K, se mihtiga I, rice DH, rice ł mihtig G*, stræng E²
dominus		dryhten B, drihten FGI, drihtæn E², dryht̄ A, drih̄t C, drih̄ J
potens		maehtig A, mehtig B, mihtig CFIJ, mihti K, rice DGH, is stræng E²
in		in A, on BCDE²FGHIJK
proelio		gefehte A, gefeohte B*FGH*I*JK*, gefeohte *D*, gefiohte *E²*, gefeoht *C* (*L*)

ED: hwylc (H)] hwyl(c) *Campbell.* glorię (E)] gloriae *Harsley.* glorie (I)] gloriae *Lindelöf.* fortis (G)] for*tis* *Rosier.*

OE: hwylc̨ (H)] c *obscured but visible.* driht̄ (I)] s. est *written before word above line, with* he is *written above.* rice ł mihtig (G)] ł mihtig *added in diff.* (?) *hand.*

LTg: Quis] [ ]uis H: *initial* Q *lost.* est] ést K. gloriae] gloriæ B; glorię CDEFHJKL; glorie G, I: *orig.* gloriae: a *eras.* proelio] C: *1st* o *interl.;* pręlio DF; pręlio EGHJK; plio L.

LTu: est] *interl.* ς. gloriae] glorię εζπφ; gloriæ ϑ; glorie ιξσςτ*τ. proelio] ο: *orig.* praelio: a *deleted, 1st* o *interl.;* prelio ζισςτ*τ; pręlio λνξφ; praelio υ.

9

Tollite*		onhebbað ABC, undo F, undoþ K, Geopeniæþ E^2, openiað G, tadoð H, nimaþ J, ahlinnað ł ahebbað I (*L*)
portas		geatu AB, gatu CFGHIJ, gæto E^2, gata K
principes	|	aldermen A, ealdormen J, aldras BCD, ealdras FGK, ealdres H, eala ge ealdras I*, eowres E^2*
uestri*	|	eowres *A*, eowre B*C*FGIJK, eældormonnes *E*^{2}* (*DL*)
et		⁊ ABCFGIJK, ond E^2
eleuamini		bioð upahefene A, beoð upahæfene B, beoð uppahafyne C, upæhebbæþ E^2, upahebbað F, uppahebbað *G**, upahebbaþ ge J, upahræræð I
portae	|	geatu A, geato *B*, gatu *CDFH*I**J*, geata *G**, ðæ ecelecæn *E*^{2} (*KL*)
aeternales	|	ecelice A*BCF*, ecelice ł ecnesse *G**, ecnesse *J*, ecelican I, ecu *DH*, gæto *E*^{2} (*KL*)
et		⁊ ABCE^{2}FGIJ
introibit		ingaeð A, ingæð BC, ingeþ E^2, ingangeð F, ingangeþ J, insteppeð I, in[ ] *G*
rex	|	cyning ABDG, cyningc FI, cyninc J, cyng C, se wuldorfestæ E^2
gloriae		wuldres A*BFGIJ*, wuldorys C, kyning *E*^{2} (*DHKL*)

ED: [ ]ttolite (G)] Attolite *Rosier.* ęleuamini (G)] eleuamini *Rosier.* ecelice ł ecnesse (G)] ecelice ł [ ]cnesse *Rosier.* aeternales (A)] æternales *Kuhn.* æternales (D)] aeternales *Roeder.* ęternales (E)] aeternales *Harsley.* in[ ] (G)] [ ] *Rosier.* glorię (E)] gloriae *Harsley.*

OE: uppahebbað (G)] up *added above* upp (= upahebbað). geata (G)] e *added interl. in diff.* (?) *hand.* eala ge ealdras (I)] *written in right margin: orig. gloss eras. and* s. o *added on eras. in darker ink.* eowres (E^2)] s *on eras. by corr.* eældormonnes (E^2)] es *on eras. by corr.* gatu (I)] ge *written in right margin; O'Neill (p. 88) suggests it indicates OE is vocative.* ecelice ł ecnesse (G)] ł ecnesse *added in diff.* (?) *hand above* ecelice.

LTg: Tollite] L: Atto *written between* To *by corr.: see GAg.* uestri] uestras CDEL, A: *orig.* uestri: i *deleted by subscript dot,* as *interl.: cf. Weber MSS* moz, *see GAg.* eleuamini] ęleuamini G. portae] portæ B; porte CDEGJK; portę FHL. aeternales] æternales BDKL; eternales CHJ; ęternales EFG. introibit] i[ ] G. gloriae] gloriæ BKL; glorię DEFGH; glorie J.

LTu: principes] principis β: *orig.* principes: i *interl. above* e *by corr.* uestri] uestras νςτ*: *cf. Weber MSS* moz, *see GAu.* portae] β: r *interl. by corr.;* porte δοσςτ*τυ; portę εζλμνξϱφ; portæ ϑι. aeternales] ęternales ειvξφ; æternales ϑ; eternales σςτ*τ. gloriae] glorię βιμξπχ; gloriæ ϑ; glorie σςτ*.

GAg: Tollite] Attollite FIK, L: *see LTg,* H: *1st* t *on eras.;* [ ]ttolite G: *initial* A *lost;* Adtollite J. uestri] uestras FGHIJK, ACDEL: *see LTg.*

GAu: Tollite] Attollite δεζιλμξοπϱστυφχψ. uestri] uestras δεζϑιλμξοπϱστυφχψ, νςτ*: *see LTu.*

10

Quis		hwet A, hwelc B, hwylc CFK, hwilc E^{2}GJ, la hwilc I
est		is ABE^{2}FGIJ*K,* ys C
iste		ðes AF, þes BCE^{2}GIJK
rex	|	cyning ABGH, cyningc FI, cyninc J, cyng C, cinig K, wuldorfestæ E^2
gloriae	|	wuldres A**BFGIJK,* wuldrys *C,* kyning *E^2* (*DHL*)
dominus		dryhten B, drihten E^{2}GI, dryht̄ A, drih̄t CF, drih̄ J
uirtutum		megna *A,* mægna BC, megene D, mægene H, mægen GJ, mægnes K, of meigne E^2*, mægena ł mihta I, mihtig F
ipse		he ABCDE^2*FHIK, he silf J, [ ]lf G
est		is ABDE^{2}FGHIJ*K,* ys C
rex		cyning ACDGHI, kyning E^2, cyningc F, kyninc J, cining K, cyng B
gloriae		wuldres A*BFGHIJK,* wuldrys C, on wuldre *E^2* (*DL*)

ED: Quis (G)] *Quis Rosier.* ipse (G)] *ipse Rosier.* [ ]lf (G)] [ ] *Rosier.* is (G)] [ ] *Rosier.* glorię (E) (*2nd*)] gloriae *Harsley.*

OE: wuldres (A) (*1st*)] r *interl.* meigne (E^2)] *final* e *in darker ink.* he (E^2)] *on eras.*

LTg: est (*1st*)] ést K. gloriae (*1st*)] gloriæ BKL; glorię CDGH; glorie EFJ. uirtutum] A: *in darker ink by main hand.* est (*2nd*)] ést K. gloriac (*2nd*)] gloriæ BKL; glorię DEFGH; glorie J.

LTu: gloriae (*1st*)] glorię βεζιξοπφ; gloriæ ϑμ; glorie σςτ*τ. gloriae (*2nd*)] glorię βεζιξφχ; gloriæ ϑ; glorie σςτ*τ.

PSALM 24

1

Ad		to A*BCD*FGHIJ*K*, To *E*^{2}
te		ðe ABDFGHI, þe *C*E^{2}JK
domine		drihten E^{2}FGI*, dryht̄ AB, drih̄t *C*, drih̄ J
leuaui		ic upahof AE$^{2/x}$*, ic uphof B, ic ahof DFHI, ic ahof ł upahebbe G*, ic uppahebbe *C*, ic upahebbe J, ic ahebbe K
animam	|	sawle ABC*F*GIJ, saule DHK, mine E^{2}
meam	|	mine ABCD*F*GHIJK, sæwle E^{2}

ED: leuaui (G)] lauaui *Rosier.*

OE: drihten (I)] s. o *written in left margin.* ic upahof (E$^{2/x}$)] ahof *on eras. by corr.* ic ahof ł upahebbe (G)] ł upahebbe *added in diff.* (?) *hand partly above* ic ahof.

LTg: Ad] AD BCDEK. te] TE C. domine] DN̄E C. leuaui] LEVAUI C. animam] F: *final* m *partly retraced in diff. hand.* meam] F: *initial* m *retraced in diff. hand.*

LTu: Ad] AD βιλμνξπρςτ*τφ. te] TE λμνξπρςφ. domine] DOMINE π; DN̄E λμνξρφ. leuaui] LEUAUI λμνξπρ. animam] ANIMAM λξπρ. meam] MEAM ξπ.

2

deus	|	god ABCFGIJK, min E^{2} (DL)
meus	|	min ABCFGJK, eala þu min I*, god E^{2}
in		in A, on BCE^{x}*FGIJK
te		ðe ABFG, þe CE^{x}*IJK
confido		ic getreowu A, ic getreowo B, ic getreowe DE^{x}*F, ic getreow H, ic getrywe C, ic truwige ł trywe G*, ic getriwe J, ic gelyfe ł ic truwie I*, ic hihte K (*L*)
non	|	ne AB, na FK, ic na DH, ic ne E^{2}I, þæt ic ne CGJ
erubescam	|	scomiu ic A, scomige ic B, scamie DF, sceamige CH, scæmige E^{2}, sceamige ł ne bysmriað G*, gescamige J*, sy aswæmed ł þæt me ne sceamige I, beo ic K

ED: deus (I)] Deus *Lindelöf.* þæt ic ne (G)] þæt ic *Rosier.*

OE: eala þu min (I)] s. o *written in left margin before* eala. on (E^{x}*)] *on eras.* þe (E^{x}*)] *on eras.* ic getreowe (E^{x}*)] *on eras.* ic truwige ł trywe (G)] ł trywe *added in diff.* (?) *hand above* truwige. ic gelyfe ł ic truwie (I)] ł ic truwie *written in bottom margin below lemma.* sceamige ł ne bysmriað (G)] ł ne bysmriað *added in diff.* (?) *hand.* gescamige (J)] i *and top of 2nd* g *partly obscured.*

LTg: confido] L: *right side of 1st* o *partly lost due to hole.*

LTu: deus] DS̄ ξ. meus] MS̄ ξ. in] IN ξ.

3

Neque	ne ABCJ, ⁊ na DE^{x}**G*HK, ne ne FI
inrideant	bismeriað A, bismriað B, bysmriaþ *J*, bysmrien D*E*^{2}, bysmrian *F*, bysmrigen *H*, bysmren *K*, onbysmrien *G*, tælun ł hlakerian ł gebysmerian *I**, gebysmriyn *C*
me	mec A, me BCE^{2}FGJK
inimici	ǀ feond A, fiend B, fynd CDFGHIJ, fund K, mine E^{2}I
mei	ǀ mine ABCFGJK, fiend E^{2}, fynd I
etenim	⁊ soðlice AB*C*GH, ⁊ soþlice E^{2}J, soþlice D, soðlice I, ⁊ witendlice F, ⁊ witodlice K
uniuersi	alle A, ealle BCDE^{x}*FGHI*JK
qui	ða ðe ABF, þa ðe CDE^{x}*I, þa þe GJ, þa þa K
(sustinent)*	geðyldigað F, onbidað G, onbidaþ J, ðoliað ł anbidiaþ I, uphealdað K
te	ðe BF, þe *G*I*JK, þin C (*H*)
expectant*	bidað AB, gebidað C, geanbidigað *D*, anbidigeð *E*$^{2/x}$* (*L*)
domine*	drihtne E^{x}*, dryhт̄ A, driħt C (*BL*)
non	ǀ ne ABCIJ, na DE^{x}*FHK, næ G
confundentur	ǀ sien gescende *A*B, syn gescynde C, hy beoð g̲escende D*, hy beoð gescynde E^{x}*H, hi ne beoð gescende F, hi ne beoð gescynde G, beoþ gescynde J, beon gescynde I, beon gescynd K

ED: etenim (BH)] et enim *Brenner, Campbell.* té (G)] te *Rosier.*

OE: ⁊ na (E^{x})] *on eras.* tælun ł hlakerian ł gebysmerian (I)] *stray* on *written in top margin well above* h. ealle (E^{x})] *on eras.* ealle (I)] *eras. after word.* þa ðe (E^{x})] *on eras.* þe (I)] *eras. after word.* anbidigeð (E$^{2/x}$)] a *altered from* o *by corr.*, igeð *on eras. by corr.* drihtne (E^{x})] *on eras.* na (E^{x})] *on eras.* hy beoð gescende (D)] g̲escende *orig.* g̲escynde: e *written above* y, *but without subscript deleting dot.* hy beoð gescynde (E^{x})] *on eras.*

LTg: Neque] Nequę G. inrideant] irrideant CEIJK, FH: *1st* r *on eras.*, G: *1st* r *altered from another letter* (n?), *extra* r *added interl.* (= irrrideant) *by another hand: see LTg note on Ps 21.14* rugiens. etenim] étenim C. te] H: t *interl. in lighter ink;* té G. expectant] L: ant *underlined to signal deletion* (*but to apply to entire word*), *and* sustinent te *written by corr. below: see GAg;* exspectant DE. domine] L: *underlined to signal deletion: see GAg; om.* B: *cf. Weber MSS* T^{2}Q^{2}UVXαβγδεη moz med. confundentur] A: entur *added by corr.*

LTu: inrideant] irrideant δειλνξπϱστ*τυφχ. qui] β: i *interl.* expectant] exspectant β.

GAg: qui] qui sustinent FGIJK, H: *2nd* t *interl. in lighter ink,* L: *see LTg note to* expectant. expectant] *om.* FGHIJK, L: *see LTg.* domine] *om.* FGHIJK, BL: *see LTg.*

GAu: qui] qui sustinent δεζϑιλμξοπρστυφχψ. expectant] *om.* δεζϑιλμξοπρστυφχψ. domine] *om.* δεζϑιλμξοπρστυφχψ.

4

Confundantur		sien gescende AB, Sien gescynde E^{2}*, syn gescende F, syn gescynde CI, syn gescinde J, syn gescende ł forscamode̲ D*, syn gescynde ł forscamod G, sin ge̲scynde ł forscamod H, forsceanode K
(omnes)*		ealle FGIJK
iniqui*		ða unrehtwisan A, ða unryhtwisan BD, þa unrihtwisan E$^{2/x}$*GH, þa unrihtwise C, unrihtlice *F*, þa unriht J*, unrihtwisen K, unrihte ðing I (*L*)
facientes*		donde ADGHK, doende BE^{x}*, doynde C, wyrcende ł donde I, fram̲ ðeode F*, fram̲ þeodum̲ *J** (*L*)
uana*		ða idlan AB, þa idlan C, idelu DE^{x}*, ofer ydelnysse F, ofer idel ł æmptig G, ofer idele K, ofer H, ofer do þu J, ofor æmtignysse ł on idel I* (*L*)
uias	|	wegas ABCD*FGHIJK*, þine *E*^{2}
tuas	|	ðine *A*BF, þine CGHIJK, wegæs E^{2}
domine		dryhten B, drihten E^{2}FG, dryht̄ A, driħt C, driħ J (*I*)
notas*	|	cuðe ABC, cuþe D, cuðe gedó ðu G, cuþe gedon J, ætyw K, ðu ætý[ ]e(s)t F*, geswutela I, gedo E^{2} (*L*)
fac*	|	doo A, do B, gedó C, me E^{2} (*L*)
mihi	|	me AB*C*FGI*J*K, cuþe *E*^{2} (*H*)
et		⁊ ABCE^{2}FGHJK
semitas	|	stige A*C*, stiga BJ, siþfatu DK, siðfatu F, siðfatu ł ⁊ stige G*, siþ H, paðas I, þine E^{2}
tuas	|	ðine ABF, þine CDGHIJK, stygæ ł siþfatu E^{2}*
edoce*		lær AB*HJK*, lære D, gelær C*G*, gelere E^{2}, lær ⁊ tæc I*, tǽc *F*
me		me ABCE^{2}FGHIJK

ED: ðu ætý[ ]e(s)t (F)] ðu ætýwdest *Kimmens.* siðfatu ł ⁊ stige (G)] siðfatu ł stige *Rosier.* edocę (F)] edoce *Kimmens.* lær ⁊ tæc (I)] lær ł tæc *Lindelöf.*

OE: Sien gescynde (E^{2})] *eras.* (*12 mm*) *after word.* syn gescende ł forscamode̲ (D)] *orig.* syn gescynde ł forscamode̲: *2nd* y *deleted by subscript dot,* e *written above, final* e *indicated by bar extending from bowl of* d. þa unrihtwisan (E$^{2/x}$)] *eras. after 1st* a, *perhaps altered from* æ, wisan *on eras. by corr.* þa unriht (J)] *dot* (*deleting?*) *above* u *and* n. doende (E^{x})] *on eras.* fram̲ ðeode (F)] *obscured by eras.,* eod *more so.* fram̲ þeodum̲ (J)] *underlined and* doende *written in right margin in later hand.* idelu (E^{x})] *on eras.* ofor æmtignysse ł on idel (I)] ł on idel *written in left margin.* ðu ætý[ ]e(s)t

(F)] *on eras., letters lost after* ý, s *fragmentary.* siðfatu ł ⁊ stige (G)] ł ⁊ stige *added in diff.* (?) *hand.* stygæ ł siþfatu (E2)] ł siþfatu *added* (*by corr.?*). lær ⁊ tæc (I)] *small eras. after* lær.

LTg: iniqui] inique F: *cf. Weber MS* α. iniqui facientes uana] L: *underlined to signal deletion,* omnes iniqua agentes superuacue *added interl. by corr.: see GAg.* uias] A: *added by corr. in left margin,* E: u *on eras. by corr. in left margin;* Vias FGHIJK. tuas (*1st*)] A: *added by corr. in left margin.* domine] I: o *written above word.* notas fac] L: *underlined to signal deletion,* demonstra *added above by corr.: see GAg.* mihi] michi EHJ, C: *orig.* mihi: *small* c *added interl. by corr.* semitas] C: *middle leg of* m *malformed.* edoce] GK: *orig.* doce: *initial* e *added by corr.,* H: *initial* e *added interl. by corr.;* edocę F: *initial* e *and subscript cauda* (?) *of 2nd* e *added in another hand: see LTg note to Ps 15.8* nę.

LTu: iniqui] inique ς. uias] Uias δεζμοπϱφ; Vias ιλξστυχ. mihi] michi ιξπς, ϱ: c *added interl.*

GAg: Confundantur] Confundantur omnes FGHIJK, L: *see LTg note to* iniqui facientes uana. iniqui] iniqua GHIJK, L: *see LTg note to* iniqui facientes uana. facientes] agentes FGIK, H: a *interl.,* J: *underlined* (*cf. OE note to* fram þeodum), L: *see LTg note to* iniqui facientes uana. uana] superuacue FHIJK; superuacuę G, L: *see LTg note to* iniqui facientes uana. notas fac] demonstra FGHIJK, L: *see LTg.* edoce] doce IJ.

GAu: Confundantur] Confundantur omnes δεζθιλμξοπϱστυφχψ. iniqui] iniqua δεζθιλμξοπστυφχψ, ϱ: *orig.* inique: e *deleted,* a *interl.* facientes] agentes δεζθιλμξοπϱστυφχψ. uana] superuacue διλμξοπϱστυφχ, θ: *end of word obscured;* superuacuę ε; superuacuae ζψ. notas fac] demonstra δεζθιλμξοπϱστυφχψ. edoce] doce δεθοπϱυψ.

5

Dirige — gerece ABCDFHK, Gerece E2, gerece þu GJ, gewissa ł gerece ł gelæd I*
me — me ABCE2FGHIJK
in — in A, on BDE2FGHIJK
ueritate | soðfestnisse A, soðfæstnysse CI, soþfæstnisse D, soþfæstnysse F, soðfæstnesse BGH, soþfæstnesse JK, þine E2
tua | ðinre AB, þinre CDG*IJK, ðine F, þine H, soþfestnesse E2
et — ⁊ ABCE2FGIJK (*H*)
doce — lær ABCDHJK, lere E2, lær ðu G*, tǽc *F*, tæc ł lær I*
me — me ABCE2FGHJK
quia — forðon ABDE2, forþon *C*GHJ, forþan F, forðā K, forþan þe I
tu — ðu AB, þu CDE2*FGHIJK
es — earð A, eart BCDFGHIJ, eært E2, ert K

deus		god ABCE^{2}*FGIJK
salutaris*	|	haelend *A*, hælend *B*FIJ, hælynd C, hælend ł scyppend G, hælen K, hælo D, mín E^{2}
meus	|	min ABCDFGHIJK, hælend E^{2}
et		⁊ ABCDE^{x}*FG*H*JK
te		ðe ABDE^{x}*F, þe CHI*JK, to ðe G*
sustinui		ic arefnde AJ, ic aræfnde *B*, ic arefynde C, ic ærefne ł þyldgode E^{2}, ic geþyldgode DFH, ic geþylgode K, ic geþingode G, ⁊ ic forðyldegode ł ic geþolade I*
tota		alne A, ealne BCFJ, æle E^{x}*, ælce DH, ælcne G*, eallan I, ælle K
die		deg AE^{x}*, dæg BCFGJ, dæge DH, dæ K, dæge ł ealne dæg I

ED: et (H) (*1st*)] *Campbell records gloss* ⁊ *where none is visible.* docę (F)] doce *Kimmens.* forðon (A)] for ðon *Kuhn.* ic aræfnde (B)] ic arefnde *Brenner.*

OE: gewissa ł gerece ł gelæd (I)] gewissa *written in left margin.* þinre (G)] r *added interl. in diff.* (?) *hand.* lær ðu (G)] *orig.* lære: e *altered to* ð, u *added in diff.* (?) *hand.* tæc ł lær (I)] *eras. before* tæc *and* lær. þu (E^{2})] u *on eras. by corr.* god (E^{2})] *eras. after word.* ⁊ (E^{x}) (*2nd*)] *on eras.* ðe (E^{x})] *on eras.* þe (I)] *eras. before word.* to ðe (G)] *orig.* te: t *altered to* ð *and* to *added in diff.* (?) *hand.* ⁊ ic forðyldegode ł ic geþolade (I)] ⁊ ic forðyldegode *written in left margin.* æle (E^{x})] *on eras.* ælcne (G)] n *added interl. in diff.* (?) *hand.* deg (E^{x})] *on eras.*

LTg: et (*1st*)] H: *added by glossator.* doce] docę F: *subscript cauda* (?) *added in another hand: see LTg note to Ps 15.8* nę. quia] C: i *interl.* salutaris] saluator AB: *cf. Weber MS* α, *see GAg.* et (*2nd*)] H: *on eras.* sustinui] sustenui B.

LTu: Dirige] Direge β. salutaris] β: t *interl. by corr.*

GAg: salutaris] saluator FGHIJK, AB: *see LTg.*

GAu: salutaris] saluator δεζϑιλμξοπϱστυφχψ.

6

Reminiscere		gemyne ABCDH, gemune E^{x}*F, gemun I*, gemyne þu G*, gemine þu me J, gemildsunga K
miserationum		mildsa A, miltsa B, myldsa C, miltsunga ł ofearmunga D, miltsunga E^{x}*F, mildsunga H, gemiltsungæ G*, gemildsunga I, mildsunga K, on soþfæstnesse J
tuarum		ðinra ABF, þinra CDGHIK, þinre E^{x}*J
domine		dryhten B, drihten E^{2}I*, dryht̄ A, driħt CF, driħ GJ
et		⁊ ABCE^{2}FGHIJK
misericordiae*	|	mildheortnis *A*, mildheortnes *B*, mildheortnysse *C*,

	mildheortnyssa FI, mildheortnesse *D*GJK, gemildheortnesse H, þinre *E*[2] (*L*)
tuae*	ðin *AB*, þine *C*, þinre *D*GHK, ðinra F, þinra I, þynre J, mildheortnesse *E*[2] (*L*)
quae*	ða A*B*, þa *CK*, þe *DE*[x]**FHIJ* (*GL*)
a	from A, from BC, fram I, fram J, of DE[x]*FH, on K (G*)
saeculo	werulde A, weorolde *B*, worulde *CDFGH*, worlde *E*[2]*IJ*, worolde *K* (*L*)
sunt	sind A, sint B, synd CFHK, synd ł wæron G*, wæron J, sindon E[2], syndun I

ED: misericordię (E)] misericordiae *Harley*. tuę (E)] tuae *Harley*. quę (E)] quae *Harley*. que (G)] *que Rosier*. á (E)] a *Harley*. a (G)] *a Rosier*. sęculo (E)] saeculo *Harley*. scło (DFHJ)] saeculo *Roeder;* seculo *Kimmens, Campbell, Oess.*

OE: gemune (E[x])] *on eras.* gemun (I)] *eras. after word.* gemyne þu (G)] þu *added in diff.* (?) *hand.* miltsunga (E[x])] *on eras.* gemiltsungæ (G)] ge *added in diff.* (?) *hand; contrary to Rosier,* æ *is not an addition altered from* a. þinre (E[x])] *on eras.* drihten (I)] o *written before word.* þe (E[x])] *on eras.* of (E[x])] *on eras.* a (G)] *letter fragment of gloss visible, perhaps upper portion of* r *followed by* a. synd ł wæron (G)] ł wæron *added in diff.* (?) *hand.*

LTg: misericordiae] misericordię CE; misericordie D, L: arum *added above* ie *by corr.: see GAg;* misericordia AB. tuae] tuę CE; tue D; tuæ L: arum *written above* æ: *see GAg;* tua AB. quae] quæ B; quę CDEFHK; que GJL. a] á E. saeculo] sæculo B; sęculo EG; seculo CIKL; scło DFHJ.

LTu: miserationum] misserationum ϑ. misericordiae] misericordie ςτ*. tuae] tue ςτ*. quae] quę βεζιvξφ; que σςτ*τ. saeculo] sęculo ειλvξο; seculo πςτ*τ; sçlo δσ; scło ζϑμϱυφχ.

GAg: misericordiae] misericordiarum FGHIJK, L: *see LTg*. tuae] tuarum FGHIJK, L: *see LTg*.

GAu: misericordiae] misericordiarum δεζιλμξοπϱστυφχψ; missericordiarum ϑ. tuae] tuarum δεζϑιλμξοπϱστυφχψ. quae] quia μ.

7

Delicta	scyld ABC, scilde J, scyldas DH, scyldas ł e G*, scylda K, Ægyltæs E[2], gylta F, giltas I
iuuentutis	guiuðu A, geogoðe B, iuguðe *C*, iuguþe K, iuguðhades *DE*[x]*FGH, geoguþhades J, giugoðhades ł iugoðe I (*L*)
(meae)*	minre *CE*[x]*FGI*K, mines J (*DL*)
et	⁊ ABCDE[x]*FGHJK

ignorantiae*		unondcyðignisse A, unondcyðignesse *B*, nytyndnysse *C*, nytennisse *D*, nitenesse *E*^{x}*, nytennyssa FG, nytennissa H, nytenyste K, gymelæsta ł nytennyssa I (*L*)
meae*		minre A*BCDE*^{x}*, minre FGK, ⁊ minre I (*L*)
ne		ne ACDE^{x}**F*GHIJ, no B, na K
memineris		ðu gemynes A, þu gemyne B, gemun þu CK, gemun ðu DFGHI, gemune ðu E^{x}*, gemine J
⟨domine⟩		drihten *E*^{x}*, drih̄t *C* (*DL*)
secundum		efter AE^{x}*, æfter B*FGHI*, æftyr C, æft<u>er</u> *J*, neh *K* (*L*)
magnam*		miclan ABC, micelre D, micle E^{x}*
misericordiam	|	mildheortnisse A*H, mildheortnysse CI, mildheortnyssa F, mildheortnesse BE^{2}GJ, mildheortnessę D, þinre K
tuam	|	ðinre A, þinre BCDE^{2}GHIJ, ðine F, mildheortnesse K*
memor*		gemyndig AB*C*DE^{x}*, gemun ðu F, gemun þu I, gemun G, gemyn K, beo þu gemindig J (*L*)
esto*		bio ðu A, beo ðu B*C**D, byo ðu E^{x}* (*L*)
mei		min ABDE^{x}*FGHIJK
deus*		god ABCE^{2}, ðu F, þu JK (*L*)
Propter		fore ABD, for CE^{2}**FGHIJK* (*L*)
bonitatem	|	godnisse ADH, godnysse CFI, godnesse BGJK*, þinre *E*^{2}
tuam	|	ðine A, þine BF, þinre *C*DGHJK, ðinre I, godnesse E^{2}
domine		dryhten B, drihten E^{x}*FI, dryhꞇ̄ A, drih̄t CG, drih̄ J

ED: meę (E) (*1st*)] meae *Harley*. mee (I)] meae *Lindelöf*. ignorantiæ (D)] ignorantiae *Roeder*. ignorantiæ (E)] ignorantiae *Harley*. ignorantias (G)] ignorantia*s* *Rosier*. meę (E) (*2nd*)] meae *Harley*. nę (F)] ne *Kimmens*. memento (G)] mem*ento* *Rosier*. for (G)] : : : *Rosier*. domine (G)] domin*e* *Rosier*. drih̄t (G)] [ ] *Rosier*.

OE: scyldas ł e (G)] ł e *added in diff.* (?) *hand above* scyldas. iuguðhades (E^{x})] *on eras*. minre (E^{x}) (*1st*)] *on eras*. minre (I)] e *slightly obscured*. ⁊ (E^{x})] *on eras*. nitenesse (E^{x})] *on eras*. minre (E^{x}) (*2nd*)] *on eras*. ne (E^{x})] *on eras*. gemune ðu (E^{x})] *on eras*. drihten (E^{x}) (*1st*)] *on eras*. efter (E^{x})] *on eras*. micle (E^{x})] *on eras*. mildheortnisse (A)] t *interl*. mildheortnesse (K)] *letter* (a?) *eras. after* t. gemyndig (E^{x})] *on eras*., b *eras. after 2nd* g. beo ðu (C)] *written in darker red ink on eras*. byo ðu (E^{x})] *on eras*. min (E^{x})] *added by corr*. for (E^{2})] *on eras*. godnesse (K)] g *eras. before word*. drihten (E^{x}) (*2nd*)] *on eras*.

LTg: iuuentutis] iuuentutis meę CDE; iuuentutis meæ L: *cf. Weber MSS* T*γδη* med, *see GAg*. ignorantiae] ignorantiæ B, D: *orig. final letter eras. after 2nd* a *and eye of* e *added to back of* a *to form* æ, E: *right side of* æ *in darker ink;* ignorantias CL: *cf. Weber MSS* ε med, *see GAg*. meae] meæ B, D: *orig. final letter eras. after* a *and eye of* e *added to back of* a *to form* æ; meę (*2nd*) E; meas CL: *cf. Weber MSS* ε med, *see GAg*. ne] nę

F: *subscript cauda added in another hand: see LTg note to Ps 15.8* nę. memineris] memineris domine CDE, L: domine *underlined to signal deletion.* secundum] L: s *underlined to signal deletion,* S *written above* s *by corr.;* Secundum FGHIJK. memor] C: r *written by corr.,* L: memento *added interl. by corr.: see GAg.* esto] C: *eras. before word,* L: *see note to* memor *above.* deus] L: *underlined to signal deletion,* tu *added interl. by corr.: see GAg.* Propter] L: *initial* P *crossed through,* p *added to right by corr.;* propter FGHIJK. bonitatem] E: *eras. above* boni. tuam] tuan C.

LTu: Delicta] Dilicta ϑ. iuuentutis] iuuentutis meę ν; iuuentutis mee ςτ*: *cf. Weber MSS* T*γδη* med, *see GAu.* ignorantiae] β: e *interl.;* ignorantie ςτ*; ignorantias ν: *cf. Weber MSS* ε med, *see GAu.* meae] meę β; mee ςτ*; meas ν: *cf. Weber MSS* ε med, *see GAu.* memineris] memeneris ϑ; memineris domine ντ*. secundum] Secundum δεζϑιλμξοπρστυφχψ. misericordiam] missericordiam ϑ. Propter] PROPTER β; propter δζιλμξπρστυφχψ; probter ϑ.

GAg: iuuentutis] iuuentutis meę FGJ, CDE: *see LTg;* iuuentutis męę H; iuuentutis mee I: *letter eras. after 2nd* e; iuuentutis meæ K, L: *see LTg.* ignorantiae] ignorantias FGHIJK, CL: *see LTg.* meae] meas FGHIJK, CL: *see LTg.* magnam] *om.* FGHIJK. memor esto] memento FGHIJK, L: *see LTg.* deus] tu FGHIJK, L: *see LTg.*

GAu: iuuentutis] iuuentutis meae δζλμοπρυψ; iuuentutis mee στ, ςτ*: *see LTu;* iuuentutis meę εϑιξφ, ν: *see LTu;* iuuentutis meæ χ. ignorantiae] ignorantias δεζϑιλμξοπρστυφχψ, ν: *see LTu.* meae] meas δεζϑιλμξοπρστυφχψ, ν: *see LTu.* magnam] *om.* δεζϑλμξοπρσυφχψ. memor esto] memento δεζϑιλμξοπρστυφχψ. deus] tu δεζϑιλμξοπρστυφχψ.

8

Dulcis	swoete *A*, swete *BCDE*^{x}*FGHJK, swete ł werod I (*L*)
et	⁊ ABCE^{2}FGHIJK
rectus	reht AB, riht CI*, ryhtwis D, rihtwis E^{2}*FGHJK
dominus	dryhten B, drihtyn C, drihtæn E^{x}, drihten F, driht̄ I, drih̄ GJ, dryt̄ A
propter	fore *ABE*^{2}*D*H, for *C*FGJ, forþan K, forþan ł forðy I (*L*)
hoc	ðissum A, ðissum B, þissum CE^{2}*, þisum J, þam DFGH
legem	aee A, æe H, æ BE^{x}*IJK, ǽ CDF, æ æ G
statuit*	gesette ABJ, gesette ł sealde G, he gesette C*, he sette DE$^{2/x}$*, sylð F*, he sylð I, gef K (*L*)
delinquentibus	gyltendum AC, agyltendum B, ðam agyltendum D, ðam agiltendum E^{x}*, ðam agiltendum F, þam agyltendum GH, þam agiltendum J, þam angyltendum K, agylttendum I
in	in A, on BCDE^{x}*FGHIJK
uia	wege ABCD*E*^{x}*FGHIJK

OE: swete (E^{x})] *on eras.*, ⁊ *visible before word, followed by illegible letter traces.* riht (I)] s. est : is *written in left margin.* rihtwis (E^{2})] sum *eras. after word.* þissum (E^{2})] *1st* s *interl. by corr., eras. after word.* æ (E^{x})] *on eras.* he gesette (C)] *otiose stroke below* e *in* he. he sette ($E^{2/x}$)] *orig.* he gesettes: ge *and final* s *eras.* sylð (F)] *gloss eras. after word.* ðam agiltendum (E^{x})] *on eras.* on (E^{x})] *on eras.* wege (E^{x})] *on eras.*

LTg: Dulcis] dulcis ABCDE, L: D *added above* d *by corr.* propter] Propter ABCDE, L: *initial* P *crossed through,* p *added to right by corr.* statuit] L: dabit *added interl. by corr.: see GAg.* uia] E: *orig.* Quia: Q *eras.*

LTu: Dulcis] dulcis βνςτ*. propter] PROPTER β; Propter νςτ*. in uia] β: *written in left margin by corr.*

GAg: statuit] dabit GHIJK, F: *eras. (ca 7 letters) after word,* L: *see LTg.*

GAu: statuit] dabit δεζθιλμξοπρστυφχψ.

9

Diriget — gereceð *AB*, gereceþ J, he gerecyð *C*, he gerecþ *D*, he gerecþ *E^{x}**, he gerecð FGK, he gerehð H, he gewissað ł he gerehð I* (*L*)

mites* — ða mildan AB, þa mildan C, biliwite D, bilewitte K, bilewite ł eæþmoden *$E^{2/x}$**, manþwære FG, modþwære ł þa manðwæran I* (*L*)

in — in A, on BCDE^{2}FGHIJK

iudicio — dome ABCDFGHIJK, his dome E^{2}

docebit — lereð A, læreð B, he læryð C, he lærð DGH, he lereþ E^{2}*, he læreð K, he lærð ł he tæcð I, lær þu J, he tæcð F

mansuetos* — ða monðwęran A, þa monþwæran B, þa manþwæran C, ða manswæsan D, þam softon E^{x}*, þa bylehwítan F, þa mildan G, þam mildan J, þam liþum I, geðwære K (*L*)

uias | wegas ABCDFGHIJK, his E^{2}

suas | heara A, heora C, his DFGHIJK, ðine *B*, wegæs E^{2}

ED: mansuętos (G)] mansuętos *Rosier.* mítes (H)] mites *Campbell.*

OE: he gerecþ (E^{x})] *on eras.* he gewissað ł he gerehð (I)] he gewissað *written in left margin.* bilewite ł eæþmoden ($E^{2/x}$)] bilewite *on eras. by corr.* modþwære ł þa manðwæran (I)] þa manðwæran *written in right margin.* he lereþ (E^{2})] ⁊ *eras. before* he. þam softon (E^{x})] *on eras.*

LTg: Diriget] diriget CD, E: et *on eras. by corr.,* g *retraced in darker ink;* dirigit AB; Dirigit L: *orig.* dirigit: d *altered to* D: *cf. Weber MSS* βγδη. mites] E: m *retraced in darker ink,* L: mansuetos *added interl. by corr.: see GAg.* mansuetos] L: mites *added interl. by corr.: see GAg.* suas] tuas B.

LTu: Diriget] direget βνς.

GAg: mites] mansuetos FHIJK, L: *see LTg;* mansuętos G. mansuetos] mites FGIJK, L: *see LTg;* mítes H.

GAu: mites] mansuetos δεζϑιλμξοπρστυφχψ. mansuetos] mites δεζϑιλμξοπρστυφχψ.

10

Uniuersae		alle *A*, ealle *BCDFGHI*J*, Eælle *E^2**, ungerim *K* (*L*)
uiae	|	wegas A*BCDFGHIJ*, wega *K*, drihtnes *E^2* (*L*)
domini	|	dryhtnes B, drihtnys CI, drihtnes F, drihtenes G,dryhī A, drih̄ J, wegæs E^2
misericordia		mildheortnis ADH, mildheortnes B, mildheortnys C, myldheortnesse E^2, mildheortnyssa F, mildheortnys I, mildheortnes J, mildheortnesse K, mildheortnes[ ] G
et		⁊ ABCDE^{2}FGHIJK
ueritas		soðfestnis A, soðfæstnys C*FI, soþfæstnis D, soðfæstnis H, soðfæstnes BJ, soþfestnesse E^2*, soþfæstnesse K, soðfæst[ ] *G*
requirentibus		soecendum A, soecendum B, secyndum C, secendum I, ðam secendum D, ðam secendum E^x*, þam secendum FG, þam secendum HJ, þam secendan K
testamentum		cyðnisse A, cyðnesse BGH, cyðnysse C, cyþnisse D, cyþnesse K, cyþnessa J, gecyþnesse E^2, gecyðnysse F, swutulunga ł gecyðnyssa I
eius		his A*B*CDE^{2}FGHIJ*K*
et		⁊ ABCDE^{2}FGHIJK
testimonia		cyðnisse A, cyðnysse C, cyðnessa B, cyþnissa D, cyðnissa H, cyþnes K, gewitnesse E^2, gewitnyssa FI, gewitnesse GJ (*L*)
eius		his ABCDE^{2}FGHIJ*K*

ED: Vniuerse (E)] Universe *Harley*. [ ]niuerse (G)] Vniuerse *Rosier*. Uniuerse (I)] Uniuersae *Lindelöf*. uie (EI)] uiae *Harley, Lindelöf*.

OE: ealle (I)] s. sunt *written in bowl of* U *in* Uniuerse, *with* synt *interl. after initial letter*. Eælle (E^2)] *letter* (s?) *eras. after word*. soðfæstnys (C)] t *interl*. soþfestnesse (E^2)] his (?) *eras. after word*. ðam secendum (E^x)] *on eras*.

LTg: Uniuersae] Vniuersae A; Vniuersi B; Vniuersę CDH; Vniuerse EFL; Uniuerse J, I: *orig*. Universae: a *eras.;* Uniuersę K; [ ]niuerse G: *intitial* V *lost*. uiae] uiæ BL; uię CGHK; uie DEJ, I: *orig*. uiae: a *eras*., F: ui *retraced by same hand responsible for retraced letters of Ps 24.1* animam meam. ueritas] uerita[ ] G. eius (*1st*)] B: *interl. abbreviation;* eíus K. testimonia] L: *1st* i *on eras*. eius (*2nd*)] eíus K.

LTu. Uniuersae] Uniuersę εζλπρυ; Uniuersæ ϑ; Vniuerse ιξς; Vniuersę νσφ;

Vniuersae o; Uniuerse τ*τ. uiae] uię εζνξφ; uiæ ϑμ; uie ισςτ*τ. misericordia] missericordia ϑ. eius (*2nd*)] ipsius ϑ: *cf. Weber MSS* mox[x].

11

Propter		fore AB, for CFGIJK, For E[2]
nomen	I	noman AB, naman CDFGIJK, nama H, þinun E[2]
tuum	I	ðinum AFI, ðinum B, þinum CGH, þinum DJ, þinan K, nomæn E[2]
domine		dryhten BE[2], dryht̄ A, driħt CFG, driħ J (*I*)
propitiaberis		ðu gemildsas A, þu gemiltsast *C*F, ðu gemildsast D, þu gemildsast E[x]*H, ðu gemildsast I, þe gemiltsast ł beo þu arfu[ ] *G**, þu gemidsast K, þu miltsast B, beo þu arful J
peccato	I	synne ABCDH, synnum F, synnum J, synne ł num G*, minre synne ł gylte I*, syna K, minum E[2]
meo	I	minre ABCDH, minu F, minum I, minum J, mine ł num G*, minan K, synnum E[2]
copiosum*	I	genyhtsum AB, genihtsum C, mænigfeald D, mycel FK, micel GIJ, soþlice *E*[2] (*L*)
est		is ABFGJK, ys C, hiræ is *E*[2], heo is I
enim	I	soðlice ABCFGI, soþlice J, witodlice K, manigfeald *E*[2]

ED: nama (H)] nama*n Campbell.* propitiaber[ ] (G)] propitiab*eris Rosier.* þe gemiltsast ł beo þu arfu[ ] (G)] þe gemiltsas ł beo þu arf[ ] *Rosier.*

OE: þu gemildsast (E[x])] *on eras.* þe gemiltsast ł beo þu arfu[ ] (G)] ł beo þu arfu[ ] *added in diff.* (?) *hand.* synne ł num (G)] ł num *added in diff.* (?) *hand above* synne. minre synne ł gylte (I)] minre *written in left margin,* gylte *orig.* gilte: i *altered to* y. mine ł num (G)] ł num *added in diff.* (?) *hand above* mine.

LTg: domine] I: o *written above word.* propitiaberis] propitiaber[ ] G; propitiare C. copiosum] E: *on eras. by corr.,* L: multum est *added interl. by corr.: see GAg.* est] E: *on eras. by corr.* enim] E: *on eras. by corr.*

LTu: Propter] PROPTER β. propitiaberis] propitiaueris β; propiciaberis φψ, ϱ: *orig.* propitiaberis: t *deleted,* c *interl.*

GAg: copiosum] multum FGHIJK, L: *see LTg.*

GAu: copiosum] multum δεζϑιλμξοπϱστυφχψ.

12

Quis	hwelc ABD, hwylc CE[2]F, hwilc G*H*J, la hwilc I, hwæt K
est	is ABDE[2]FGHIJ*K*, ys C
homo	mon AB, man DFHJK, mann CG, se mæn E[2], se man I
qui	se ðe ABCF, se þe GJ, þe DH, ðe I, þa K, se him E[2]

timeat*	I	ondrede A, ondræde BC, andræde DH, ondrædeþ FJ, ondræt GI, drædæð K, drihten E^{2}
dominum	I	dryhten B, drihten FK, dryht̄ A, drih̄t CG, driht̄ I, drih̄ J, ondrede E^{2}
legem		ęe A, æe D, ǽ BCF, æ æ G, æ HIJK, æ ł ewe E$^{2/x}$*
statuit	I	sette AB, he sette K, he gesette CFGI, he gesętt D, he geset H, gesete J, he him E^{2}
ei	I	him AFGHIJ, him BCDK, gesette E^{2}*
in		in A, on B*C*DE^{x}*FGHIJK
uia		wege ABCDE^{2}FGHIJK
quam		ðone A, þone B, þone þe CI, þene K, þam *D*E^{x}*, þam G, ðam ðe F, þam þe J
elegit		geceas AB, he geceas CI*J*, he ceas K, he gecyst DE$^{2/x}$**H*, he gecýst F, he gecyst ł þone þe gecéas *G**

ED: ondrede (E)] ondred*e Harley.* ǽ (B)] æ *Brenner.* he gesętt (D) he gesett *Roeder.* quam (D)] qua *Rosier.* he gecýst (F)] he gecyst *Kimmens.* he gecyst ł þone þe gecéas (G)] he gecyst ł ðone þe gecéas *Rosier.*

OE: æ ł ewe (E$^{2/x}$)] æ ł *on eras. by corr.* gesette (E^{2})] te *on eras.* on (E^{x})] *on eras.* þam (E^{x})] *on eras.* he gecyst (E$^{2/x}$)] he *on eras. by corr.* he gecyst ł þone þe gecéas (G)] ł þone þe gecéas *added in diff.* (?) *hand.*

LTg: Quis] H: s *on eras.* est] ést K. in] C: *orig.* m: *shoulder between 1st and 2nd minim eras.* quam] D: *orig.* qua: *macron added above* a *in slightly diff.* (*russet*) *ink: cf. Weber MSS* T^{2} moz. elegit] ęlegit GH; elegi J: *cf. Weber MS* α.

LTu: Quis] [ ]uis τ*: *initial wanting.*

GAg: timeat] timet FGHIJK.

GAu: timeat] timet δεζϑιλμξοπϱστυφχψ.

13

Anima	I	sawul A, sawl BC*G*, saul DH, sawle FIJ, sawel K, his E^{2}
eius	I	his ABCDFGHIJK, sæwle E^{2}
in		in A, on BCDE^{2}FGHIJK
bonis		godum ABFGHI, godum CJK, gódum D, gode E^{2}
demorabitur		wunað ABCFGH, wunaþ J, wunast D, wvnast K, biþ wunigende E^{2}, þurhwunað I
et		⁊ ABCDE^{2}FGHIJK
semen	I	sed A, sæd B*C*DFGHK, sæþ J, sæd ł cynren I, his E^{2}
eius	I	his ABCDFGHIJ*K*, sed E^{2}
hereditatem*		erfeweardnisse *A*, erfweardnesse B, yrfeweardnysse *C*, yrfeweærdnesse *E^{2}*, erfeweardaþ *D*, erfeweardað H,

erfweardað K, yrfweardnysse F, yrfeweardnesse GJ, geyrfeweardað I (*L*)
possidebit* gesiteð *A*B, gesiteð ł wealdyð C, ǽgende E^{2} (*L*)
terram eorðan ABCDFGHJ, eorðæn E^{2}*, eorþan K, land ł eorðan I

ED: [ ]nima (G)] Anima *Rosier.* hęreditate (E)] haereditate *Harley.*

OE: eorðæn (E^{2})] *eras. before and after word.*

LTg: Anima] [ ]nima G: *initial* A *lost.* semen] C: *1st* e *malformed.* eius (*2nd*)] eíus K. hereditatem] hereditate A, D: *orig.* hereditatem: m *eras.*, L: te *underlined to signal deletion,* tabit *added to left in margin by corr.* (*word division after* a *of lemma,* te *on next line*): *see GAg;* hereditatę C; hęreditate E: *cf. Weber MSS* T^{2}PQ^{2}UVXαγ moz. possidebit] A: *2nd* i *on eras., eras. after* b *and 2nd* i, L: *underlined to signal deletion: see GAg.*

LTu: eius] β: i *interl.* hereditatem] hereditate νςτ*: *cf. Weber MSS* T^{2}PQ^{2}UVXαγ moz. possidebit] posidebit β.

GAg: hereditatem] hereditabit FGHIJK, L: *see LTg.* possidebit] *om.* FGHIJK, L: *see LTg.*

GAu: hereditatem] hereditabit δεζθλξοπστυχψ; hęreditabit ιμϱφ. possidebit] *om.* δεζθιλμξοπϱστυφχψ.

14

Firmamentum trymenis A, trymnes B*GJ, trymynys C, trumnys F, trymnesse E^{2}, truma DK, truma ł strengo H, staðolfæstnys ł trumnys I
est is ABE^{2}FGIJ*K*, ys C
dominus dryhten BE^{2}, drihtyn C, dryht̄ A, driħt FG, driht̄ I, driħ J
timentibus ondredendum A, ondrædendum B, ondrædendum FI, ondrædyndum C, ðam ondrædendum D, ðam ondredendum E^{x}*, þam ondrædendum G, þam ondrædendum HJ, drædendum K
eum hine ABDE^{x}*FGHIJK, hyne C
et ⁊ ABCDFGHI*JK
testamentum cyðnes A*K, cyðnyss C, cyþnis D, cyðnys F, cyðnis H, cyðnesse BG, cyþnesse E^{2}, cyþnessa J, gewitnysse ł gecyðnysse I
ipsius his ABCDE^{2}*GHIJK, hes F
ut ðæt AB, þæt D*E*^{2}FGHJK, þætte C, þætte I
manifestetur sie gesweocelad A, sie gesweotolad B, sy geswutulud C, heo sie geswutelad D*, heo sy geswutelod G, heo sie geswutelad

		E$^{2/x}$*, heo sý geswutelod F, heo sie geswutelod H*, he si geswytelod K, þu si geswutelod J, sy geswutulad ł þæt he beo ge[ ] I*
illis		him ABCGHJ, him DIK, heom E^{2}*F*

OE: trymnes (B)] *faint but visible.* ðam ondredendum (E^{x})] *on eras.* hine (E^{x})] *on eras.* ⁊ (I)] est : is *written in left margin.* cyðnes (A)] *orig.* cyðnis: i *altered to* e. his (E^{2})] *eras. before word,* þ *visible.* heo sie geswutelad (D)] o *interl.* heo sie geswutelad (E$^{2/x}$)] geswutelad *on eras. by corr., eras. (20 mm) after word,* ł *visible after word.* heo sie geswutelod (H)] *eras. after 2nd* o. sy geswutulad ł þæt he beo ge[ ] (I)] ł þæt he beo ge[ ] *written in right margin and cropped.*

LTg: est] ést K. ut] vt E. illis] illi[ ] F: *final letter lost due to burning through of coloured initial on fol. 24v.*

15

Oculi	I	egan AK, eagan BCDFGHI*, eagon J, Min E^{2}
mei	I	mine ABCDFGHIJK, eægæn E^{2}
semper		aa A, simle BF, symle CE^{2}IJ, æfre ł simle G*, æfre K
ad		to ABCE^{2}FGIJK*
dominum		dryhtne B, drihtny C, drihtne E^{2}FGI, drihtene K, dryht̄ A, driħt J
quoniam		forðon ABD, forþon *C*J, forþan K, forþæn þe E^{2}, forðan ðe F, forþan þe I, forþam þe G (*L*)
ipse		he ABCDE^{2}FGHJK, he sylf I
euellet		aluceð *A*B, alucyð C, utaluceð DFG, utaluceþ HJ, utalucð *K*, oferswyþeþ ł utaluceð E^{2}, awyrtwalað ł alysð ł anereð I
de		of ABCDE^{2}FGHIJK
laqueo		girene A, girne B, gryne CFI, grine DGHJK, gegrynum E^{2}
pedes	I	foet AB, fet CDGHIJK, fot F, mine E^{2}
meos	I	mine ABCDGHIJK, minne F, fet E^{2}

ED: forðon (A)] for ðon *Kuhn.* euellet (BE)] evellet *Brenner, Harley.*

OE: eagan (I)] s. sunt : synt *written in left margin.* æfre ł simle (G)] ł simle *added in diff.* (?) *hand above* æfre. to (K)] *false start of* d *after* o.

LTg: quoniam] C: *scribe began to write* quonim, *completing only 1st 2 legs of* m, *which were then altered to* a *and the word completed.* quia L: *cf. Weber MSS* ε moz^{x}. euellet] A: *orig.* euellit: i *altered to* e; ęuellet K.

LTu: laqueo] ς: *orig.*, o *inserted on line, then deleted and* o *added interl.*

16

Respice		geloca ABC, geloca þu J, locæ ł syoh E$^{2/x}$*, beseoh DIK, beseah H, beseoh ł beheald G, beheald F
in		in A, on BCDE^{2}FGHIJK
me		mec A, me BCDE^{2}FGHIJK
et		⁊ ABCE^{x}*FGHIJK
miserere		mildsa *A*JK, miltsa B, myltsæ E^{2}, gemiltsa CDG, gemildsa FI, mildheortnessa H
mei		min ABCDFGHI*, me E^{2}JK
quoniam*		forðon AB, forþon CJ, forþæn E^{2}, forðam F, forþam K, forþā G, forðan þe I
unicus	|	anga AB, se anga J, angan C, anlic DE^{x}*, ænlic F, anglic H, anlic ł se ánga G*, ic eom anlic I, anlipi K
et		⁊ ABCE^{2}FGHIJK
pauper		ðearfa AFGI, þearfa BDHJK, þeærfe E^{2}*, þearfan C
sum	|	eom BCGJK, ic AE^{2}F (*I*)
ego	|	ic BCGJK, eam A, eom F, heom E^{2} (*I*)

ED: locæ ł syoh (E)] Locæ ł syoh *Harley*. forðon (A)] for ðon *Kuhn*. forþā (G)] forþam *Rosier*.

OE: locæ ł syoh (E$^{2/x}$)] ł syoh *added by corr.* ⁊ (E^{x}) (*1st*)] *on eras.* min (I)] *on eras.* anlic (E^{x})] *on eras.* anlic ł se ánga (G)] ł se ánga *added in diff.* (?) *hand above* anlic. þeærfe (E^{2})] *letter eras. after word.*

LTg: miserere] A: *orig.* miserire: *2nd* i *altered to* e. sum ego] I: *eras. above word* (*of gloss?*): *see gloss to* unicus *above.*

LTu: miserere] misserere ϑ.

GAg: quoniam] quia FGHIJK.

GAu: quoniam] quia δεζϑιλμξοπϱστυφχψ.

17

Tribulationes		geswencednisse A, geswencydnysse C, geswinc B, geswinc ł gedeorfu D, gedrefednysse F, gedrefednes K, geswinces GJ, geswincnyssa ł gedrefednyssa I, Eærfoþnesse E^{2} (*H*)
cordis	|	heortan ABCDFGHIJK, minre E^{2}
mei	|	minre ABC*DIJK, mine FGH, heortæn E^{2}
dilatatae*		gebrędde A, gebrædde *BC*, tobrædde *D*, tobredde *E^{2}**, gemænigfylde FIJ, gemænigfealdode G, mænifylde K (*L*)
sunt		sind A, synd CFHK, sint B, synt D, siendon E^{2}*, syndon IJ, sy[ ] *G*

de	of *A*BCDE^{2}*FGHIJK
necessitatibus	nedðearfnissum A, nedðearfnessum B, nydþearfnyssum *C*, niedþeærfum E^{2}*, neadðearfnyssum I, neadþearfum G, nydþearfum J, neadum D, neadum FH, neode K
meis	minum AFG, minum BCDHIJ, mine E^{2}, minre K
eripe*	genere ABCE^{2}, genera F, genere þu G, genera þu J, nere D, nera K, ales ł genera I (*L*)
me	me ABCE^{2}FGJK

ED: dilatatę (E)] dilitatae *Harley*. sun[ ] (G)] su*nt Rosier*.

OE: minre (C)] re *interl*. tobredde (E^{2})] *on eras. from Lat. line below, line reruled.* siendon (E^{2})] *on eras. from Lat. line below, line reruled.* of (E^{2})] *on eras. from Lat. line above, line reruled.* niedþeærfum (E^{2})] *letter eras. after* d.

LTg: Tribulationes] H: *initial* T *partly lost.* dilatatae] dilatatæ B; dilatatę C, E: *written in brown ink by hand appearing on fol. 33r,* l *by main hand,* di *retraced;* dilatate DL. sunt] sun[ ] G. de] A: *eras. (2 letters) before word.* necessitatibus] necesitatibus C. eripe] L: erue *added interl. by corr.: see GAg.*

LTu: Tribulationes] TRibulationes β; [ ]ribulationes ς: *initial wanting*. dilatatae] dilatatę ν; dilatate ς; dilatat β.

GAg: dilatatae] multiplicatę FH; multiplicate GJK; multiplicatae I. eripe] erue GHIJ, L: *see LTg;* ęrue K; eruę F: *subscript cauda added in another hand: see LTg note to Ps 15.8* nç.

GAu: dilatatae] multiplicate δζιξστυ; multiplicatę ελορφ; multiplicatæ ϑ; multiplicatae μπψ, χ: *back of 1st* a *and 2nd* t *faint.* eripe] erue δεζϑιλμξοπρστυφχψ.

18

Uide	geseh A, geseoh *BCFGHIJK*, geseoh *D*, Gesioh *E*$^{?}$* (*L*)
humilitatem |	eaðmodnisse AD, eaðmodnysse I, eaðmodnesse B, eadmodnysse C, eadmodnyssa F, eadmodnesse GJK, eadmodnisse H, mine E^{2}
meam |	mine ABCFGIJK, minre D, min H, eæþmodnesse E^{2}
et	⁊ AB*C*DE^{x}*FGHIJK
laborem	gewin AB, gewinn J, geswinc CDK, geswyngc F, geswing H, gewin ł swinc E^{x}*, geswinc ł gewínn G*, geswinc ł gedeorf I
meum	min ABCD*E*^{x}*FGHIJK
et	⁊ ABCDE^{2}FGHIJK
dimitte	forlet *A*E^{x}*, forlæt *B*DFHJK, forlæt þu G, forlæt ł forgif I, forgyf C

omnia* alle A, ealle BCDE^{x}*FGHIJ, ungerim K (*L*)
peccata* synne AE^{x}*, synna BCDGJ, gyltas FI*, scylda K
mea mine ACE^{x}*FGIJ, mina BDH, minra K

ED: geseoh (F)] geseah *Kimmens.* meum (B)] meam *Brenner.*

OE: Gesioh (E^{2})] G *altered from another letter, lower portion of* h *on eras.* ⁊ (E^{x})] *on eras., line reruled.* gewin ł swinc (E^{x})] *on eras., line reruled.* geswinc ł gewínn (G)] ł gewínn *added in diff.* (?) *hand above* geswinc. min (E^{x})] *on eras., line reruled.* forlet (E^{x})] *on eras., line reruled.* ealle (E^{x})] *on eras., line reruled.* synne (E^{x})] *on eras., line reruled.* gyltas (I)] *orig.* giltas: i *altered to* y. mine (E^{x})] *on eras., line reruled.*

LTg: Uide] L: *eye of* e *lost due to hole;* Vide BDEFGHIJK. et (*1st*)] C: *outline of eras.* U *appears to left of word, probably beginning of repetition of* Uide *above.* meum] E: *small eras. between arms of* u. dimitte] demitte AB: *cf. Weber MSS* MS^{2}Kδη. omnia] L: uniuersa *added interl. by corr.* peccata] L: delicta *added interl. by corr.: see GAg.*

LTu: Uide] Vide ινξστ*τ. dimitte] dimittae ψ; demitte βϑμ.

GAg: omnia] uniuersa FGHIJK, L: *see LTg.* peccata] delicta FGHIJK, L: *see LTg.*

GAu: omnia] uniuersa δεζϑιλμξοπϱστυφχψ. peccata] delicta δεζιλμξοπϱστυφχψ, dilicta ϑ.

19

Respice geloca ABC, geloca þu J, locæ ł beseoh E^{x}*, beseoh D*H*K, beseoh ł beheald *G,* besih ł beheald I, beheald F
inimicos | feond AF, fiend B, fynd CDGHI*K, on fynd J, on mine E^{x}*
meos | mine ABCDGHIJK, minne F, fiend E^{2}*
quoniam forðon ABJ, forþon CG, forðæn E^{2}, forðam F, forðan þe I
multiplicati gemonigfaldade A*, gemonigfealdode B, gemonigfealdude C, gemænifealdode G*, gemænigfyld D, gemænigfyld H, gemænigfylde FJ, hy gemonifeældode E^{2}, hi gemænigfylde I*, mænifealde K
sunt sind *A,* sint B, synt F, synd CGK, hy synt D, he synd H, syndon E^{2}IJ
et ⁊ ABCE^{2}FGHIJK
odio laeððu A, læðþe C, fe(o)unge B*, fioung ł hatunge $E^{2/x}$*, hatunge D, hatunge GHK, hatung *F,* on ł mid hatunge I*
iniquo unrehtwisre A, unryhtwisre B, unrihtwisre C, mid unrihtwisnesse J, unryhtre D, unrihtre FGHI, unryhtæ $E^{2/x}$*, unriht K
oderunt fiedon A, feodon B, feodun C, hy hatedon DE^{x}*H, hi

hatudon F, hi hatodun I, hig hatodon J, hi hatedon ł feodon G*, hatodon K

me mec A, me BCE^{x}*FGHIJK (*L*)

ED: besih ł beheald (I)] besih ł heheald *Lindelöf.* forðon (A)] for ðon *Kuhn.*

OE: locæ ł beseoh (E^{x})] *on eras., line reruled.* fynd (I)] *eras. before word.* on mine (E^{x})] *on eras., line reruled.* fiend (E^{2})] e *eras. after word.* gemonigfaldade (A)] *orig.* gemonigfadade: l *added on ligature of* ad *by glossator.* gemænifealdode (G)] do *interl.* hi gemænigfylde (I)] hi *interl.* fe(o)unge (B)] *right side of* o *wanting.* fioung ł hatunge (E$^{2/x}$)] ł hatunge *on eras. by corr.* on ł mid hatunge (I)] ł mid *written in left margin; insertion mark, however, is placed before* unrihtre. unryhtæ (E$^{2/x}$)] un *on eras. by corr.* hy hatedon (E^{x})] *all but* h *in* hy *on eras. by corr.* hi hatedon ł feodon (G)] ł feodon *interl. above following* me. me (E^{x})] *on eras.*

LTg: Respice] [ ]espice GH. sunt] A: *eras. above* nt, t *added by corr.* odio] F: *letter eras. before word.* me] L: *added by corr.*

LTu: odio] hodio ς. oderunt] hoderunt ς; odierunt ϑ.

20

Custodi hald A, heald B, geheald CDFHIK, Geheæld E$^{2/x}$*, geheald þu GJ

animam sawle ABCFGIJ, saule DE^{x}*HK

meam mine ABCDE^{x}*FGH*I*JK

et ⁊ ABCDE^{x}*FGIJK

eripe* genere ABCE^{x}*, genere DG, genera FIJ, nera K (*L*)

me mec A, me B*CE^{x}**FGIJK (*DL*)

⟨domine⟩ drihtyn *C*, drihten *E^{x}** (*DL*)

non ne ABCGJ, na E^{x}*K, þæt ne F, þæt me ne I*

confundar* biom ic gescended A, beo ic gescended B, beo ic gescynded G, beo ic gescyndeþ J, beo ic gescynd C, ic beo gescynd K, ic beon scynd DE^{x}*, scamige F, scamie ł ic ne aswæme ł na ic beo gescend I* (*L*)

quoniam forðon AB, forþon CGJ, forðan E^{x}*, forðam F, forðon þe I

inuocaui* ic gecede A, ic gecegde B, ic gecigde C, ic gecigde D, ic hopude F, ic gehihte GI, ic hihte JK, ic gecleopode E^{x}* (*L*)

(in)* on FGIJK

te ðe A*B*FI, þe CDE^{x}*GJK

ED: ic beon scynd (E)] ic be onscynd *Harley.* forðon (A)] for ðon *Kuhn.*

OE: Geheæld (E$^{2/x}$)] heæld *on eras. by corr.* saule (E^{x})] *on eras.* mine (E^{x})] *on* *eras.* ⁊ (E^{x})] *on eras.* genere (E^{x})] *on eras.* me (E^{x})] *on eras.* drihten (E^{x})] *on eras.* na (E^{x})] *on eras.* þæt me ne (I)] *written in left margin along with following* scamie. ic beon scynd (E^{x})] *on eras.* scamie ł ic ne aswæme ł na ic beo gescend (I)] scamie *written in left margin after* þæt me ne (*above*), ł ic ne aswæme ł na ic beo gescend *on eras.* forðan (E^{x})] *on eras.* ic gecleopode (E^{x})] *on eras.* þe (E^{x})] *on eras.*

LTg: meam] I: *flanking sign* ÷ *eras. before word.* eripe] L: ue *added below word by corr.: see GAg.* me] me domine CDE, L: domine *underlined to signal deletion: cf. Weber MSS* T^{2}PQUVX moz^{x}. confundar] L: erubescam *added below word by corr.: see GAg.* inuocaui] L: speraui *added interl. by corr.: see GAg.* te] té B.

LTu: me] me domine ντ*: *cf. Weber MSS* T^{2}PQUVX moz^{x}.

GAg: eripe] erue GHIJK, L: *see LTg;* eruę F: *subscript cauda added in another hand: see LTg note to Ps 15.8* nę. confundar] erubescam FGHIJ, K: *3rd leg of* m *by corr.* (*on eras.?*), L: *see LTg.* inuocaui] speraui in FGHIJK; *for* L *see LTg.*

GAu: eripe] erue δεζϑιλμξοπϱστυφχψ. confundar] erubescam δεζϑιλμξοπϱστυφχψ. inuocaui] speraui in δεζϑιλμξοπϱστυφχψ.

21

Innocentes — unsceððende AB, unsceðþynde C, unscyldige DH, unscildige F, unscyldige K, unscyldig ł unsceaðful G*, unscæþfulle J, þæ unscyldie E$^{2/x}$*, þa unscæðþigan I*

et — ⁊ ABCDE^{x}*FG*HI*JK

recti — rehtwise AB, rihtwise CFGJK, ryhtwise D, riht H, þæ rihtwise E^{x}*, ða rihtan I*

adheserunt | ætfelun A, ætfeollon J, ætfulgon B*C**, togeþeoddon DH, togeðeoddon F, togeþeoddan *GK*, geðeodlæhtun ł tocleofedon ł geþeoddon *I**, me E^{2}

mihi | me AB*C*FGI**J*K, etfyolæþ ł togeþeoddon *E*$^{2/x}$*

quoniam* — forðon AB, forþon C, forþæn E^{2}*, forðam F, forþā K, forþā þe G, forðan þe I, forþon þe J

sustinui — ic arefnde *AC*, ic aræfnde *B*, ic aræfnode J, ic forbær E^{x}*, ic forbær ł geþyldgode ł geanbidude D, ic forbær ł geðilgode ł geanbidude H, ic forbær ł geanbidude ł geþyldigode ł ic arǽfnde G, ic forbær ðe ł forðylgode F, ic forbær K, ic geanbidode I*

te — ðe ABF, þe CE^{2}*I*JK

domine* — dryhten B, drihten E^{2}, dryht̄ A, driht́ C (*L*)

ED: forðon (A)] for ðon *Kuhn.* forþā þe (G)] forþam þe *Rosier.* té (I)] te *Lindelöf.*

OE: unscyldig ł unsceaðful (G)] ł unsceaðful *added in diff.* (?) *hand.* þæ unscyldie

(E$^{2/x}$)] die *on eras. by corr.* þa unscæðþigan (I)] *on eras.* ⁊ (E^{x})] *written by corr.* (?). ⁊ (G)] *2nd* ⁊ *written above* r *of following* rihtwise, *apparently because* ð *in added* unsceaðful *obscures original* ⁊. ⁊ (I)] *on eras.* þæ rihtwise (E^{x})] *written by corr.* (?), *eras. after* riht. ða rihtan (I)] *on eras.* ætfulgon (C)] u *on eras.* geðeodlæhtun ł tocleofedon ł geþeoddon (I)] to *in* tocleofedon *written in right margin and signaled for inclusion, 2nd* o *in same word interl.* me (I)] *written in right margin after* mihi. etfyolæþ ł togeþeoddon (E$^{2/x}$)] etfy *on eras. by corr.,* ł togeþeoddon *added by corr.* forþæn (E^{2})] *on eras.* ic forbær (E^{x})] *on eras.* ic geanbidode (I)] g *on eras.* (?).

LTg: adheserunt] K: adh *on eras. by corr.;* adhęserunt CGI. mihi] michi EJ, C: *orig.* mihi: c *interl. by corr.* sustinui] A: *1st* i *on eras.;* sustenui B. te] té I. domine] L: *underlined to signal deletion: see GAg.*

LTu: adheserunt] adhęserunt εμϱφ; adhaeserunt ψ. mihi] michi ιλςτ, πϱ: c *added interl.* sustinui] sustenui ϑ.

GAg: quoniam] quia FGHIJ, K: a *formed from another letter, with eras. before and after.* domine] *om.* FGHIJK, L: *see LTg.*

GAu: quoniam] quia δεζϑιλμξοπϱστυφχψ. domine] *om.* δεζϑιλμξοπϱσυφχψ.

22

Redime*		ales A, alies B, alys CIK, alýs F, alis J, ælys E^{2}*, alyse D, [ ]ys þu *G* (*L*)
me*		me ABCDE^{2} (*L*)
deus	|	god ABCFJI*K, ysræhelæ E^{2} (*G*)
israhel	|	israhela BC, israhela folc F, þeoda israhel G, israhela bearn *I,* israela *J,* geleaful *K,* god *E*^{2} (*H*)
ex		of ABCDE^{2}FGHIJK
omnibus		allum A, eallum BCFGI, eallum DJ, eællum E^{2}, ealle H, eallan K
angustiis*	|	nearenissum A, nearonessum B, nearunyssum C, nearownissum D, næro(ness)[ ] K*, gedrefednyssa F, gescwincum geswinc[ ] ł nearonessum G*, geswincum H, geswincum J, minum *E*^{2}*,* heora I* (*L*)
meis*	|	minum AC, minum BD, heora FJ, his ł heora G, his HK, angsumnesse E^{2}*, gedrefednyssum ł geswincnyssum I* (*L*)

ED: [ ]bera (G)] Libera *Rosier.* ælys (E^{2})] Ælys *Harley.* [ ]ys þu (G)] [ ] *Rosier.* isrł (EHIJK)] israhel *Campbell, Oess;* israel *Harley, Lindelöf;* Israhel *Sisam.* angustíís (E)] angustiis *Harley.* tribulationibus (G)] tribul*a*tionibus *Rosier.* gescwincum geswinc[ ] ł nearonessum (G)] gescwinc[ ] ł nearonessum *Rosier.*

OE: ælys (E^{2})] *on eras., retraced in darker ink.* god (I)] o *written before word.*

næro(ness)[ ] (K)] *lower portions of* ness *lost due to excision of initial on fol. 31r, final letters not visible.* gescwincum geswinc[ ] ł nearonessum (G)] gescwincum *written to right of line,* geswinc[ ] *written to left in line below, hence repetition.* angsumnesse (E[2])] *eras. before word.* heora gedrefednyssum ł geswincnyssum (I)] *orig.* geswinc-nyssum heora, *with* heora *on line above:* ł *added before* geswincnyssum *and* gedrefed-nyssum *added after* heora, *hence order of gloss as recorded above.*

LTg: Redime] L: Libera *added interl. by corr.: see GAg.* me] L: *underlined to signal deletion: see GAg.* deus] d[ ]us G. israhel] isrł ẸHIJK. angustiis] L: tribulationibus *added interl. by corr.: see GAg;* angustíís E. meis] L: suis *added interl. by corr.: see GAg.*

LTu: israhel] israel ιvςτ; isrł δμξοπϱστ*υφχ.

GAg: Redime] Libera FIJK, L: *see LTg,* H: *initial* L *partly retraced in diff. ink;* [ ]bera G. me] *om.* FGHIJK, L: *see LTg.* angustiis] tribulationibus FHIJ, G: a *cropped,* L: *see LTg;* tribu[ ]onibus K: *letters lost due to excision of initial on fol. 31r.* meis] suis FGHIJK, L: *see LTg.*

GAu: Redime] Libera δεζϑιλμξοπϱστυφχψ. me] *om.* δεζϑιλμξοπϱστυφχψ. angustiis meis] tribulationibus suis δεζϑιλμξοπϱστυφχψ.

PSALM 25

1

Iudica — doem *AB*, dem *CD*E[2]*FH*I, dem *K*, dem þu *G*J
me — mec A, me B*C*E[2]FGHIK
domine — dryhten B, drihtyn *C,* drihten E[2]FGK, dryht̄ A, driht̄ I*, driħ J
quoniam — forðon ABDGHJ, forþon C, forþan K, forþan þe E[2], forðan þe I, forþam ðe F
ego — ic ABCE[2]FGHIJK
in — in A, on BCDE[2]FG*H*IK (*J*)
innocentia | unsceðfulnisse *A,* unsceðfulnesse B, unsceðfulnysse C, unscyldignisse DH, unscyldignyssa F, ynscyldinese K, unscyldig[ ]fulnesse G*, unscildig *J,* mynre E[2], minre I
mea | minre *A*BCDFGHK, min *J,* unscyldignesse E[2/x]*, unscæððinysse I
ingressus | ingongende AB, ingongynde C, ingangende J, ic ingange D, ic ingange E[x]*FH, ic inga K, on ingange G, infærde I
sum | ic eam A, ic eom BCGJ
et — ⁊ ABCE[2]FGIJK
in — in A, on BCE[2]FGIJK
domino — dryhtne B, drihtne CFI, drihten E[2]K, dryht̄ A, driħt G, driħ J

sperans	gehyhtende AB, gehihtynde C, gehihtende G*, hyhtende DH, hihtiende I, hihtende K, ic hihte J, hopiende E^{x}*F
non	| ic ne AC, ⁊ ic ne I, ne BJ, na DE^{x}*FGHK
infirmabor	| biom geuntrumad A, beo geuntrumud C, beo geuntrumad I, beo ic geuntrumad B*, beo ic geuntrumod J, ic untrumige ł ne beo ic geuntrumod G*, ic untrumig*e* D, ic untrumie E^{x}*, ic untrumige H, ic untrumge F, ic untrymige K

ED: IVDICA (C)] JVDICA *Wildhagen*. dem (E)] Dem *Harsley*. forðon (A)] for ðon *Kuhn*.

OE: driht̄ (I)] o *written before word*. unscyldig[ ]fulnesse (G)] *cf. Rosier: 'because the MS is badly damaged here, it is uncertain whether the glossator wrote* unscyldigfulnesse *or* unscyldig ł [ ]fulnesse.' unscyldignesse (E$^{2/x}$)] ldignesse *on eras. by corr.* ic ingange (E^{x})] *on eras.* gehihtende (G)] ge *added in diff.* (?) *hand.* hopiende (E^{x})] *on eras.* na (E^{x})] *on eras.* beo ic geuntrumad (B)] t *faint but visible.* ic untrumige ł ne beo ic geuntrumod (G)] ł ne beo ic geuntrumod *added in diff.* (?) *hand.* ic untrumie (E^{x})] *on eras.*

LTg: Iudica] IVdica AD; IUdica B; IVDICA C; Ivdica H; (I)udica F: *initial letter nearly completely lost due to burning from ink;* [ ]udica G; [ ]Vdica K: *initial letter excised.* me] ME C. domine] DN̄E C. in (*1st*)] H: *added interl.*, J: *inserted.* innocentia] A: *eras. after* a; innocentiam J: *cf. Weber MSS* Sαγεη moz. mea] A: *eras. after* a; meam J: *cf. Weber MSS* Sαγεη moz.

LTu: Iudica] IUdica β; IUDICA λμνξπϱς; IUDica σ; IVDICA φ. me] ME λμνξπϱς. domine] DN̄E λμνξπϱ. quoniam] QUONIAM π; QM̄ λμνξϱ. ego] EGO λξπϱ. in (*1st*)] IN λξπϱ. innocentia] INNOCENTIA λξπ; INNOcentia ϱ. mea] MEA ξ. domino] ϰ *begins.* infirmabor] infirmabo ς: *cf. Weber MSS* ζ moz^{c}.

2

Proba	acunna AC, acunne B, gecunna J, [ ]cunna ł fanda *G*, fanda K, afanda D, afa(n)da F*, gefanda I, ofhanda H, Gecosta ł afanda E$^{2/x}$*
me	me ABCE^{2}FGIJK
domine	dr(y)hten B*, drihten E^{2}F, dryht̄ A, drih̄t CG, drih̄ J, hlaford K (*I*)
et	⁊ ABCE^{2}FGHIJK
tempta	costa ABCDE^{x}*HK, costa þu GJ, costna F, gecostna I
me	me ABCE^{x}*FGIJK
ure	bern AE^{x}*, bærn BCDK, bæ(r)n G*, bǽrn F, bearn HJ, onæl ł forswa[ ] ł swæl ł bærn I*

renes		eðre A, ædran BCHK, edran D, edren E^{2}, æddran F, æddran lendenu *G**, lęndenu ł ædran I, lændenu J
meos		mine ABCDE^{2}FGHIJK
et		⁊ ABCDE^{2}FGHIJK
cor		heortan ABDE^{2}GHIJK, heorte CF
meum		mine ABDE^{2}FGHIJK, min C

ED: afa(n)da (F)] afanda *Kimmens*. ofhanda (H)] of handa *Campbell*. bea(r)n (G)] bearn *Rosier*. onæl ł forswa[ ] ł swæl ł bærn (I)] *for* forswa[ ] *Lindelöf gives* forswa---, *but in corrigenda* (*p. 323*) *perhaps* forswæ.... (r)enes (G)] renes *Rosier*. æddran lendenu (G)] æddran ł lendenu *Rosier*. lęndenu ł ædran (I)] lendenu ł ædran *Lindelöf*.

OE: afa(n)da (F)] n *obscured by stain*. Gecosta ł afanda (E$^{2/x}$)] ł afanda *added by corr*. dr(y)hten (B)] *left arm of* y *not visible*. costa (E^{x})] *on eras*. me (E^{x})] *on eras*. bern (E^{x})] *on eras*. bæ(r)n (G)] *descender of* r *lost*. onæl ł forswa[ ] ł swæl ł bærn (I)] ł forswa[ ] *written in right margin and cropped, 2nd* ł *interl*. æddran lendenu (G)] lendenu *written in diff*. (?) *hand above* æddran.

LTg: Proba] [ ]roba G. domine] I: o *written above word*. renes] G: r *cropped*.

LTu: tempta] temta v.

3

Quoniam		forðon AB, forþon CJ, forþā K, forðæn þæ E^{2}, forðam ðe F, forþon þe I, [ ]orþon þe G
misericordia	I	mildheortnis ADH, mildheortnes B*J, mildheortnys C, mildheortnyssa F, mildheortnesse GI, mildheornesse K, þin E^{2}
tua	I	ðin ABDF, þin CGHIJK, myldheortnesse E^{2}
ante	I	biforan A, beforan BCDGHJK, ætforan F, toforan I, is E^{2}
oculos	I	egum A, eagum BC*, eagan ł um G*, eagan DFI, egan HK, eagon J, beforæn E^{2}
meos		minum AE^{2}, minum BCJ, mine DFI, mine ł num G*, minan K (*H*)
est	I	is ABFGIJ*K*, ys C, eægæn E^{2} (*H*)
et		⁊ ABCDE^{x}*FGHIJK
conplacui		ic gelicade A, ic gelicode BE^{x}*F*I*K, ic gelicode D, gelicode *H*, ic gelocade *C**, ic gelicode ⁊ ic efenlicige G*, ic geefenlicige *J*
in		in A, on BCDE^{2}FGHIJK
ueritate	I	soðfestnisse A, soðfæstnysse CFH, soþfæstnisse D, soðfæstnesse BG, soþfæstnesse J, soþfæstnese K, þinre E^{2}I
tua	I	ðinre AD, þinre BCGHJK, ðine F, soþfestnesse E^{2}, soðfæstnesse I

ED: forðon (A)] for ðon *Kuhn*. forðæn þæ (E)] Forðæn þæ *Harsley*. complacui (C)] co[n]placui *Wildhagen*. ic gelicode (E^x)] ic gelicod*e* *Harsley*.

OE: mildheortnes (B)] e *partly faded*. eagum (C)] u *on eras*. eagan ł um (G)] ł um *written above* eagan. mine ł num (G)] ł num *written above* mine. ⁊ (E^x)] *on eras*. ic gelicode (E^x)] *on eras*., de *in ligature*. ic gelocade (C)] *eras. before* l (ge *written on fol. 40r*, locode *on fol. 40v*). ic gelicode ⁊ ic efenlicige (G)] ⁊ ic efenlicige *added in diff.* (?) *hand*, lici *interl.*, ge *below and written after* on *glossing following Lat.* in.

LTg: meos] H: *on eras. in lighter ink*. est] H: *on eras. in lighter ink;* ést K. conplacui] complacui IJ, C: *orig*. conplacui: *right leg added to* n *by corr. to form* m, H: *orig*. conplacui (?), *word followed by eras*.

LTu: misericordia] missericordia ϑ. conplacui] complacui δεπτ*; cōplacui οτχ.

4

Non	|	ic ne ABCDFGHI, Ic ne E^2*, ic na K, ne J
sedi	|	set A, sæt BCDE^x*FGHIK, sæt ic J
in*		in A, on BCDE^{2}J, mid FGHIK
concilio	|	geðaehte A, geðeahte B, geþeahte CFHI, geþeahte D, geþæhte K, geþeahtes ł on gemote G*, gemote J, ydelnesse E^2
uanitatis	|	idelnisse AD, idelnesse BGK, idylnysse C, ydelnyssa F, ydelnisse H, ydelnysse I, ydelnesse J, gemotstowe E^2
et		⁊ ABCDE^{2}FGHIJK
cum		mid ABCDFGHIJK, myd E^2
iniqua		ða unrehtan A, þam unrihtum G, þan unriht C, þæm unrihtberendum E^2, þam unrihte J, unryht B, unryhte D unrihte FHK, unrihte þingc I
gerentibus		ðondum A, dondum BDJ, dondum FGH, doendum C, donde K, ł dondum E^2*, wyrcendum I
non	|	ic in ne AE^2, ic inn ne C, ic ne I, ic no B, na DFGHK, na ic J
introibo	|	ga AC, ingonge B, gængæ E^2, ic gange J, ic ineode DH, ic incode ł ic ne ingange G*, ic fare ł inga F, ic inga K, instæppe ł inga ł ⁊ ic ne fara I

OE: Ic ne (E^2)] *eras.* (*8 mm*) *after* ne. sæt (E^x)] *on eras*. geþeahtes ł on gemote (G)] ł on gemote *added in diff.* (?) *hand above* mid geþeahtes. ł dondum (E^2)] *written above preceding* -berendum. ic ineode ł ic ne ingange (G)] ł ic ne ingange *added in diff.* (?) *hand*.

LTu: in] cum ς: *cf. Weber MSS* δ moz^c, *see GAu*. concilio] consilio ϰ. non] iñ ς.

GAg: in] cum FGHIJ, K: *on eras*.

GAu: in] cum εζϑιϰμξοπϱσυφχψ, ς: *see LTu*.

5

Odiui		ic fiode A, ic feode BC, Ic fiode ł hatude E$^{2/x}$*, ic hatude DFH, ic hatode IJK, ic hatude ł ic feode G*
congregationem*		gesomnunge ABCG, gesomninga D, gesomninge E^{x}*, gesamnunge I, on gesomnunge J, somnunge K, cyrcean F
malignorum*		awergedra A, awirgdra B, awyrgydra C, awyrgedra DE^{2}FG, awirgedra J, awyriede K, yfelcundra ł awyrgendra I
et		⁊ ABCE^{2}FGHIJK
cum		mid ABCDFGHIJK, myd E^{2}
impiis		arleasum ACFGH, arleasum BD, þæm ærleæsum *E^{2}*, þam arleasum I, þam arleasum J, arlæsan K
non	|	ic ne ACE^{2}FIJ, ic no B, na DFGHJK
sedebo	|	sitto A, sitte BE^{2}FI, sette C*, ic gesitte D, ic sitte H, ic sitte ł ne sæt G*, sæt JK

ED: ęcclesiam (G)] ecclesiam *Rosier*. impíís (E)] impiis *Harsley*.

OE: Ic fiode ł hatude (E$^{2/x}$)] c *on eras.*, ł hatude *added by corr. in right margin*. ic hatude ł ic feode (G)] ł ic feode *added in diff.* (?) *hand above* ic hatude. gesomninge (E^{x})] *on eras*. sette (C)] *eras. before 1st* e, *possibly orig.* æ. ic sitte ł ne sæt (G)] ł ne sæt *added in diff.* (?) *hand*.

LTg: impiis] impíís E.

GAg: congregationem] ęcclesiam FGHI; ecclesiam JK. malignorum] malignantium FGHIJK.

GAu: congregationem] ecclesiam δζκμπστψ; ęcclesiam ειλξοφχ; æclesiam ϑ; aecclesiam ϱυ. malignorum] malignantium δεζϑκιλμξοπϱστυφχψ.

6

Lauabo		ic ðwea ABDFI, ic þwea CGJ, Ic ðwea E^{x}*, ic þwæ K, ic swea H
inter	|	betwih AC, betwuh B, betweox DG, betweohx H, betwúx F, betwux I, betweoh J, betwyx K, mine E^{2}
innocentes	|	alle unsceðende A, ealle unsceðþynde C, þa unsceððendan B, unscyldige DF, unscyldig H, þa unscyldige ł unsceðþendan G*, unscyldigum K, unscyldigum I, þam unscildigum J, hænde E^{2}*
manus	|	honda A, handa BCDFGHIJK, betwyoh E^{2}
meas	|	mine ACFGIJK, mina BDH, ðæm unscyldige E$^{2/x}$*
et		⁊ ABCDFGIJK
circuibo*		ic ymbgaa A, ic ymbgá B, ic ymbgáá C, ic ymbgange D, ic ymbgange G, ic ymbgonge E^{2}, ic ymbsylle FJ,

ic ymbehwyrfe ł ⁊ ic ymbtrymme I*, ymbesylle K (*L*)
altare — wibed *A*B, wigbed J, weofud C, weofod FGI, weofed K, wifod E^{x}*, altre DH
tuum — ðin AB, þin CE^{x}*GIJK, þinre D, ðinre F, þine H
domine — dryhten B, drihtyn C, drihten E^{2}F, dryht̄ A, drih̄t G, drih̄ J, eala þu *I**

ED: circúndabo (H)] circundabo *Campbell.*

OE: Ic ðwea (E^{x})] *on eras.* þa unscyldige ł unsceðþendan (G)] ł unsceðþendan *added in diff.* (?) *hand at end of Lat. line above and extending above following* handa. hænde (E^{2})] h *on eras.* ðæm unscyldige ($E^{2/x}$)] unscyldige *on eras. by corr.* ic ymbehwyrfe ł ⁊ ic ymbtrymme (I)] ⁊ ic ymbtrymme *written in right margin.* wifod (E^{x})] *on eras.* þin (E^{x})] *on eras.* eala þu (I)] *written in right margin, any following words presumably lost due to trimming of leaf.*

LTg: circuibo] L: ibo *underlined to signal deletion, macron added above* u, dabo *added interl.: see GAg.* altare] A: *eras. after word.* domine] I: o *written above word.*

LTu: δ: *vv 6–end wanting.* manus] man[ ] ϰ.

GAg: circuibo] circumdabo FGIJK, L: *see LTg;* circúndabo H: *orig.* circúmdabo: *right leg of* m *eras. to form* n.

GAu: δ: *vv 6–end wanting.* circuibo] circumdabo εζϰλμξπϱστυχψ; circūdabo ο; circundabo ιφ.

7

Ut — ðæt *A*, þæt *B*, þæt *CDFGHI*JK, þet E^{2} (*L*)
audiam — ic geheru A, ic gehiere BE^{2}, ic gehyre CFGHK, ic gehyre D, ic gehere I, ic gehire J
uocem — stefne ABDFGIK, stæfne CHJ, stemne E^{2}
laudis | lofes ABDFGHJK, lofys C, lofes ðines I, þines *E^{2}*
tuae* | ðines A, þines *BDJ*, þinys *C*, lofes *E^{2}* (*L*)
et — ⁊ AB*C*FGHIJK, þæt *D*, ⁊ þet *E^{2}*, ⁊ þæt G
enarrem — ic asecgu A, ic asecge BC, ic cyþe D, ic cyðe FHI*, ic cyðe ł þæt ic asecge G, ic gecyþe ł asecge J, ic secge ł cyþe $E^{2/x}$*, bodige K
uniuersa — all A, ealle BCDFGHIJ, eælle E^{2}
mirabilia | wvndur A*, wundru BCDHI, wundra FJ, wuldra G, þine E^{2}
tua | ðin A, ðine BF, þine CGIJ, wundoru E^{2}*

ED: [ ]t (G)] Vt *Rosier.* tuę (E)] tuae *Harsley.*

OE: ic cyðe (I)] *eras. after* ic. ic cyðe ł þæt ic asecge (G)] ł þæt ic asecge *added in diff.* (?) *hand.* ic secge ł cyþe ($E^{2/x}$)] ł cyþe *added by corr.* wvndur (A)] *orig.*

wondur: v *written above* o, *but without deleting dot.* wundoru (E^2)] *final* u *added by corr.*

LTg: Ut] Vt ABCDEFHIL; [ ]t G: *initial* V *lost.* laudis] lavdis E: av *written in right margin.* tuae] tuæ BL; tuę CEJ, tue D. et] ut CDE: *cf. Weber MSS* T* med.

LTu: δ: *verse wanting.* Ut] Vt ινξυφ. tuae] tuę β, υ: *added by corr.;* tuæ ϑ; tue κςτ*. et] ut κτ*: *cf. Weber MSS* med.

GAg: tuae] *om.* FGHIK.

GAu: δ: *verse wanting.* tuae] *om.* εζιλμξοπρστφχψ.

8

Domine — dryhten B, drihtyn C, drihten E^{2}F, dryht̄ A, drih́t *G*, drih́ J, hlaford K (*I*)
dilexi — ic lufade AH, ic lufode BCFIJ, ic lufude DE$^{2/x}$*G, ic lufede K
decorem — wlite ABC*D*E^{2}FGHJK, wurðunge ł wlite I
domus | huses ABDFGHIJK, husys C, þines E^2
tuae | ðines A*BF*I, þines *DGHJK,* þinys C, huses *E^2* (*L*)
et — ⁊ ABCDE^{2}FGIJK
locum — stowe ABCDE^{2}FGHIJK
tabernaculi* — getedes *A,* geteldes *B,* geeardunge *C,* eærdungæ *E^2*, eardunge FGHJK, eardunge ł wununge I (*DL*)
gloriae | wuldres A*BFGH*I*K,* wuldrys C, wulderes *D,* wundres *J,* þines *E^2* (*L*)
tuae | ðines A*BF*I, þinys *C,* þines *DGHK,* þine J, wuldres *E^2* (*L*)

ED: drih́t (G)] dri[ ] *Rosier.* tuę (E) (*1st*)] tuae *Harsley.* glorię (E)] gloriae *Harsley.* tuę (E) (*2nd*)] tuae *Harsley.*

OE: ic lufude (E$^{2/x}$)] ude *on eras. by corr.*

LTg: Domine] G: *ascender of* D *lost,* I: o *written above word.* decorem] decôrem D. tuae (*1st*)] tuæ BL; tuę DEFGHJK. tabernaculi] tabernaculis AB; habitationis CDEL: *cf. Weber MSS* αγεη* moz med, *see GAg.* gloriae] gloriæ B; glorię DEFGHJL; glorie K. tuae (*2nd*)] tuæ BL; tuę CDEFGHK.

LTu: δ: *verse wanting.* Domine] DN̄i β. tuae (*1st*)] tuę εζιξοφ; tuæ ϑ; tue κοςτ*τ. tabernaculi] tabernaculis ς: *cf. Weber MSS* Q*U; habitationis ντ*: *cf. Weber MSS* αγεη* moz med, *see GAg.* gloriae] glorię ειξφ; gloriæ ϑ; glorie κοςτ*τ. tuae (*2nd*)] tuę ειξρφ; tuæ ϑ; tu[ ] κ; tue σςτ*τ.

GAg: tabernaculi] habitationis FGHIK, CDEL: *see LTg;* abitationis J: *3rd* i *altered from another letter.*

GAu: δ: *verse wanting.* tabernaculi] habitationis εζϑικλμξοπρτυφχψ, ντ*: *see LTu.*

9

Ne		ne ABCDFGHIJ, Ne E^{2}, na K
perdas		forspild ðu AB, forspill þu C, forspil ðu DFJ, forspil þu $E^{2/x}$*GH, amyr þu I, forleos K
cum		mid ABCDGHIJK, myd E^{2}
impiis		ðæm arleasum A, þæm ærleæsum *E^{2},* þam arleasum *G,* þam arleasum *J,* þam arleasum I, ðone arleasan F, arleasan *K,* arleasum B*CDH* (*L*)
⟨deus⟩		god *CJ* (*GHL*)
animam	|	sawle ABCFGHIJK, saule D, mine E^{2}
meam	|	mine ABCFGHIJK, sæwle E^{2}
et		⁊ ABCE^{2}FGK
cum		mid ABCFGIJK, myd E^{2}*
uiris		weorum A, werum BD, werum FGHI, wera C, weræ E^{2}, weres J, weran K
sanguinum		bloda ABDF*H,* blode GJK, blodum *C*E^{2}, blodigum I (*L*)
uitam	|	lif ABCDFGHJK, lif ⁊ I, min E^{2}
meam	|	min ABCFGHIJK, lyf E^{2}

ED: impíís (E)] impiis *Harsley.*

OE: forspil þu ($E^{2/x}$)] þu *on eras. by corr.* myd (E^{2}) (*2nd*)] *eras. after word.*

LTg: impiis] K: *1st* i *added later by main hand;* impíís E; impiis deus CJL, G: deus *added interl. in another hand: see LTg note to Ps 21.14* rugiens, H: deus *added interl. in smaller hand.* sanguinum] C: *scribe orig. began* sangun- *but eras. right leg of* n *to form* i, H: *2nd* u *on eras. and altered from* e, L: a *altered from* u *by main hand.*

LTu: δ: *verse wanting.* impiis] impiis deus ν, σ: deus *added interl. by later hand.*

10

In		in *A,* on *BCDE*^{2}FGHIJK (*L*)
quorum		ðeara A, ðara BDFG, þara CHIJ, þæræ E^{2}, þæra K
manibus		hondum A, handum BD, handum CFGHI, hondum E^{2}, handa þe J, handa K
iniquitates	|	unrehtwisnisse A, unrihtwisnysse C, unryhtwisnessa BD, unrihtwisnyssa F, unrihtwisnessa G*, unrihtwisnessæ I, unrihtwisnessc K, unrihtwise J, unriht H, siendon E^{2}
sunt	|	sindun A, syndon I*, synd CFGHJK, sint B, synt D, unryhtnesse E^{2}
dextera	|	seo swiðre *AC,* seo swiþre J, þeo swiþre *D*H, ðeo swýþre F, þeo swiðre G, swiðre *B,* swiðra I, swyðra K, hioræ *E*^{2}* (*L*)

eorum	I heara A, hira B, hyra C, heora DFG*H**IJK, swyþræ E[2]
repleta	gefylled AE[2]FGHIK, gefyllyd C, gefylled D, gefilled J, gefyldu B
est	is ABE[2]FGIJK, ys C
muneribus	geofum AB, gyfum C, of medsceattum D, of medsceattum F, of metsceattum H, of metsceattum ł mid g[ ] G*, mid gifum J, mid lacum I, lacca K, læcum ł medsceattum E[2]

ED: quorum (B)] quoru*m* *Brenner*. eoru[ ] (H)] eor(um) *Campbell*. heora (H)] heo(rum) *Campbell*.

OE: unrihtwisnessa (G)] *letter* (æ?) *written above* a. syndon (I)] d *altered from* t. hioræ (E[2])] *eras. after word.* heora (H)] a *obscured by hole in leaf.* of metsceattum ł mid g[ ] (G)] ł mid g[ ] *added in diff.* (?) *hand.*

LTg: In] in ABCDEL. dextera] Dextera ABCDEL. eorum] eoru[ ] H.

LTu: δ: *verse wanting.* In] in βνςτ*. dextera] Dextera βντ*, ς: *wanting v. 10* Dextera–*end.*

11

Ego	ic *ABCDE*[2]FGHIJK (*L*)
autem	soðlice ABCFGI, soþlice E[2]*J, witodlice K
in	in A, on BCDE[2]*FG*H*I (*J*)
innocentia	I unsceðfulnisse *A*, unsceðfulnesse B, unsceðfulnysse C, unscæþðignes J, unscyldignisse D, unscyldignyssa *F*, unscyldignesse H, unscyldignysse I, unscyldinesse K, unscyldignesse [ ]nsceaðfulnes G*, mynre E[2]
mea	I minre *A*BCDFHIK, min GJ, unscyldinesse E[x]*
ingressus	I ingongende AB, ingongynde C, ic ingangende J, ic ineode DFH, ic ingeode E[x]*, ic ineode ł ingande G*, ineode *K*, instæppende I
sum	I ic eam A, ic eom BG, ic eom C, eom J, ic eom ł ic on ferde I*
redime	ales A, alies B, alys CDFHIK, æles E[2]*, alys þu G*, alis þu J
me	me ABCE[2]FGIJK (*H*)
⟨domine⟩	(*D*)
et	⁊ ABCDE[2]FGHIJK
miserere	mildsa *A*, miltsa B, myltsa C, myltsæ E[2], milsa *K*, gemiltsa D, gemiltsa FH, gemiltsa þu G, gemildsa IJ
mei	min ABCDFGHI*J*, me E[2] (*K*)

ED: ic (E)] Ic *Harsley*. unscyldignesse [ ]nsceaðfulnes (G)] unscyldignesse ł [ ]n-sceaðfulnes *Rosier*. i(n)[ ]sus (K)] in[gre]sus *Sisam*. ic ineode ł ingande (G)] ic ineode ł ingand[ ] *Rosier*. redime domine (D)] redime *Roeder*.

OE: ic (E$^{?}$)] Ic (?). soþlice (E^{2})] ⁊ *eras. after word*. on (E^{2})] *on eras*. unscyldignesse [ ]nsceaðfulnes (G)] *right leg of 1st* n *used to form ascender of* s, *but left uneras. and following* s *written* (*thus* unsscy-), [ ]nsceaðfulnes *added in diff.* (?) *hand*. unscyldinesse (E^{x})] *on eras*. ic ingeode (E^{x})] *on eras*. ic ineode ł ingande (G)] ł ingande *added in diff.* (?) *hand*. ic eom ł ic on ferde (I)] ł ic on ferde *written in left margin*. æles (E^{2})] s *on eras. by corr.*, e *malformed* (*eye of* e *likely retraced after eras., or* e *altered from* i). alys þu (G)] *letter eras.* (?) *before* alys.

LTg: Ego] ego ABCDEL. in] H: *added interl. in main hand*, J: *added in main hand*. innocentia] A: *eras. after word*, F: *2nd* n *interl*. mea] A: *eras. after word*. ingressus] i(n)[ ]sus K: *letters lost due to excision of initial on fol. 31r, right leg of* n *lost*. me] H: *followed by eras.*, D: domine *added interl. in main hand: cf. Weber MS* α^{2}. miserere] A: *orig.* miserire: *2nd* i *altered to* e; miser[ ] K: *letters lost due to excision of initial on fol. 31r*. mei] J: *followed by eras.* (?), K: *lost due to excision of initial on fol. 31r*.

LTu: δς: *verse wanting*. Ego] ego βντ*. autem] λ: *interl*. redime] redeme μ. me] meę ε. miserere] misserere ϑ.

12

Pes	fot ABDE^{x}*_G_*HIJK, fet C, eart _F_
enim*	soðlice ABC, soþlice E^{x}*
meus	min ABCDE^{x}*FGHIJK
stetit	stod ABCDE^{x}*FGHIK, soþlice stod J
in	in A, on BCDE^{2}FGIJK*
uia*	wege ABCD, rihtum E^{2}
recta*	ðæm rehtan A, þan rihtan C, rihtan D, ryhtum B, rihte F, þam rihtan wege G, þam rihtan wege J, rihtum wege ł on rihttinge I*, wege rihtan K, wege _E^{2}_
in	in A, on BCDE^{2}GHIJ, o FK
ecclesiis	cirecum A, circeum _B_, ciricean _C_, cyrceæn _E^{2}_, halgum _D_, halgum ł on ges[ ] _G_*, halgum gesomnungum H, hallian so[ ] _K_*, gesomnunge J, gesamningum ł on gelaþungum _I_*, gelaðungum F
benedicam	ic bledsiu A, ic bletsige BCDHIJ, ic bletsie E^{2}*F, bletsige K, [ ]letsige G
(te)*	ðe FI, þe GJK
dominum*	dryhten B, drihtyn C, drihten E^{2}FG, dryht̄ A, drih̄ J, þv drihten I*

ED: o (F)] on *Kimmens*. ęcclesiis (E)] aecclesiis *Harsley*. [ ]letsige (G)] [ ]ledsige *Rosier*.

OE: fot (E^x)] *on eras.* fot (G)] *eras. after word, letter fragments visible.* min (E^x)] *on eras.* stod (E^x)] *on eras.* on (K)] *otiose mark (false start?) before word.* rihtum wege ł soþlice (E^x)] *on eras.* on rihttinge (I)] ł on rihttinge *written in left margin.* halgum ł on ges[ ] (G)] ł on ges[ ] *added in diff.* (?) *hand.* hallian so[ ] (K)] *letters lost due to excision of initial on fol. 31r.* gesamningum ł on gelaþungum (I)] ł on gelaþungum *written in right margin.* ic bletsie (E^2)] ⁊ *eras. after* ic. þv drihten (I)] o *written before* þv.

LTg: Pes] G: *eras. after word,* F: *initial* P *added later, eras. after word.* recta] E: *eras. after* c, ct *orig. in ligature.* ecclesiis] æcclæsiis B; ęcclesiis CEGI; eclesiis D; eccle[ ] K: *letters lost due to excision of initial on fol. 31r.*

LTu: δς: *verse wanting.* meus] β: *added in right margin by corr.* ecclesiis] ęcclesiis εινξφ, π: *1st* c *interl.;* ęclesiis ζχ; æclesis ϑ; aecclesiis λϱυ.

GAg: enim] *om.* HIJK, FG: *see LTg note to* Pes. uia] *om.* FGHIJK. recta] directo FGHIJK. benedicam] benedicam te FGHIJK. dominum] domine FGHIJK.

GAu: δ: *verse wanting.* enim] *om.* εζϑικλμξοπϱστυφχψ. uia] *om.* εζϑικλξοϱστυφχψ. recta] directo εζϑικλξοπϱστυφχψ. benedicam dominum] benedicam te domine εζϑικλμξοπϱστυφχψ.

PSALM 26

1

Dominus		Drithen *E^x*, drihten HI*, dryhꞇ̄ *A*, driħt *C*F, driħ GJ (*BDKL*)
inluminatio	ǀ	inlihtnis *A*, onlihtnes B, onlihtnys *C*, onlyhtnis D*H*, onlyhtnes *FK*, onlyhtnes ł onlyhtend *G**, onlihtnes ł onlihtingc *I*, onlihtend J, is min *E^3* (*L*)
mea	ǀ	mine *A*, min BCDFGHIJK, onlihtnesse E^3
et		⁊ ABCE^3FGHIJK
salus	ǀ	haelu A, hælo BCDFGHIJ, hæl K, mine E^3 (*L*)
mea	ǀ	min *A*BCDFGHIJK, helæ E^3
quem		ðone AE^3, þone BCDHJK, þonne F, þonne G, hwane I (*L*)
timebo		ic ondredo A, ic ondræde BCFGHJ, ic andræde D, ic me ondrede E^3, ondræde ic I, ic dræde K
Dominus		dryhten *B*, drihten E^3, dryhꞇ̄ A, driħt CF*G*, driħ J
defensor*		gescildend A, gescyldynd C, gescyldend DFI*, is gescyldend G, is gescildend J, is scyldon E^3, sceldend B, gescyld K (*L*)
uitae	ǀ	lifes A*BDFG*HIJ*K*, lifys *C*, mines *E^3* (*L*)

meae	mines A*BDFG*HIJ, minys *C*, lifes E^3 (*KL*)
a	from A, from BC, fram DJK, fram FGHI, for E^3
quo	dæm A, ðæm B, þam CGJ, ðæn E^3, hwam DK, hwam FHI
trepidabo	ic forhtiu A, ic forhtige BCDFGHJK, ic fortie E^3, forhtige ic I

ED: DN̄S (B) (*1st*)] Dn̄a *Brenner*. [ ]ominus (G) (*2nd*)] Dominus *Rosier*. drihten (E^3)] Drihten *Harsley*. uitę (E)] uitae *Harsley*. ðæm (B)] dæm *Brenner*.

OE: drihten (I)] ÷ : is *written in bowl of* D *in* (*1st*) Dominus. onlyhtnes ł onlyhtend (G)] ł onlyhtend *added in diff.* (?) *hand*. gescyldend] I: y *altered from* i (?).

LTg: Dominus (*1st*)] DN̄S ACDEKL, B: D *circled in drypoint, perhaps in preparation for excision*. inluminatio] K: l *eras. after 1st* n, *deleting dots above and below 1st* n, *but not eras.;* INLVMINATIO AL; IILVMINATio C: *orig*. INLVMINAtio: *1st* N *deleted by subscript dot*, l *interl. by corr.;* illuminatio EFI, G: *orig*. inluminatio: *1st* n *altered, then crossed through by 12th-c.* (?) *corr., who then wrote* l *to right of* n, H: *1st* l *on eras*. salus] salvs L. mea] MEA A. quem] qvem L. Dominus (*2nd*)] dominus B; [ ]ominus G. defensor] L: protector *added interl. by Lat. glossator: see GAg*. uitae] uitæ B; uitę CDEL; uite FGK. meae] meæ BCKL; mee DE; meę FG.

LTu: δ: *wanting vv 1–2* mei. Dominus (*1st*)] DN̄S βειλμνξπϱστ*τφχ; DOMINUS ο; DOMInus ς. inluminatio] INluminatio β: o *interl.;* INLUMINATIo μ; INLUMInatio ν; INLVMINATIO ξ; ILLVMINATIO ελ; ILLUMINATIO οπϱ; illuminatio ϑικστ*τυφχ. mea] MEA ελξπϱ. et] ET π. quem] Quem ϱ: *not marking verse division*. defensor] deuensor β. uitae] uitę ειvξυφ; uitæ ϑ; uite κποστ*τ. meae] meę ειvξφ; męę ς; meæ ϑ; mee κστ*τ.

GAg: defensor] protector FGHIJK, L: *see LTg*.

GAu: δ: *wanting vv 1–2* mei. defensor] protector εζϑικλμξοπϱστυφχψ.

2

Dum	ðonne A, þonne BCDJ, ðonne F, þonne G, þonne H, þone K, þænne I, Midþy E^3
adpropiant	toneolicað *A*, genealecað B*I*, genealæcað DE^{x}*FG*H*, genealæcaþ *J*, hi genealæcað *C*, neahlæcaþ *K*
super	ofer $ABDE^3FGHJK$, ofyr C, ofor I
me	me $ABCDE^3FGHIJK$
nocentes	sceððende AB, sceðþynde C, sceþðende DE^{x}*, scæðþende H, scæðende F, scæððiende G, scæþþende J, ða deriendan I, derigende K
ut	ðæt A, þæt BG, þæt CDFHIJK, þet E^3
edant	hie eten *AB*, hi etyn C, hei eten D, hie eton E^3, hie etan *H*, hig etan F, hi etan G, hi etun I, hi eton J, etaþ K

carnes	flæsc ABCDFGHJK, flesc E^{3}, flæscas I
meas	min ACFGJ, mine BDE^{3}HK, mine ł min flæsc I
qui	ða ðe AB, þa þe C*GHI,* þa ðe DE^{3}**FJ,* þa *K* (*L*)
tribulant	swencton B, swæncton J, swenceað C, swencað DHK, swencat E^{x}, swencað ł swencto G*, geswencað I*, drefaþ F
me	me ABCDE^{x}*FGHIJK
inimici	fiond A, fiend B, fynd CDE^{x}*FGHIJK
mei	mine ABCE^{x}FGIJK
ipsi	hie AB, hi C, hy DGHK, hig FJ, ⁊ hi sylfe I
infirmati	| geuntrumede *A,* geuntrumode BFJ, geuntrumude CG, geuntrumede I, geuntrumod K, untrymede D, untrumude H, sint E^{3}
sunt	| sind A, synd CFGHJK, sint B, synt D, syndon I, geuntromode E^{3}
et	⁊ ABCDE^{3}FGHJK
ceciderunt	gefeollun *A,* gefeollon BCJ, hy feollon DH, hig feollon F, hi feollon ł ge G*, hruron ł feollon I, feollan K, gefeælleð E^{3}

ED: appropiant (C)] a[d]propiant *Wildhagen.*

OE: genealæcað (E^{x})] *on eras.* sceþðende (E^{x})] *on eras.* þa ðe (E^{3})] *retraced by corr.* swencað ł swencto (G)] ł swencto *added in diff.* (?) *hand, and extending above following* me. geswencað (I)] ge *interl.* me (E^{x})] (*2nd*)] *on eras.* fynd (E^{x})] *on eras.* hi feollon ł ge (G)] ł ge *added in diff.* (?) *hand above* hi fe-.

LTg: adpropiant] A: *eras. after* i; appropiant IK, C: *1st* p *on eras.,* nqu *written in right margin in same hand (Parkerian) that numbered psalm verses and that can been seen in contents list at front of volume, indicated for insertion after 3rd* p *though it should be for after* i (= appropinquant, *a Roman variant*), H: *1st* p *on eras.;* appropriant J. me (*1st*)] J: *interl. and signaled for inclusion.* edant] ædant B; aedant H. qui] Qui FGHIJK, L: *orig.* qui: q *crossed through and* Q *written above by Lat. glossator.* infirmati] A: *small eras. between crossbars of* f, *with descender formed of 2 strokes as though altered from another letter.* ceciderunt] A: *eras. after 1st* c.

LTu: δ: *wanting vv 1–2* mei. adpropiant] adpropriant β; appropiant εικλξοπϱστ*τυφχ; adpropinquant ϑ: *cf. Weber MSS* βγε mox^{x}. nocentes] innocentes ς. edant] ędant ε. carnes] β: r *interl. by corr.* qui] Qui εζϑικλμξοπϱστυφχψ.

3

Si	gif ABCDGHJK, Gif E^{3}*, gyf F, þeah ðe I
consistant	gestondað ABC, standað DFH, stondæþ E^{3}, standaþ K, standað ł gif geondoð G*, samod standan I, ge undoþ J

aduersum	wið ABC, wiþ J, ongean DE^{x}*H, ongean ł wið G*, togeanes F, togenes K, agen ł togeanes I
me	me ABCE^{3}FGHIJK
castra	ferdwic A, fierdwic B, fyrdwic C, weredu DE^{x}FH, wereda ł fẏrdwic G*, fyrdunga ł fyrdwicu I, feondlic J, werod K
non	ne ABCGIJ, na DE^{x}*FHK
timebit	ondredeð AE^{x}*, ondrædeð BH, ondrædeþ DF, ondrædyþ C, ondrædað G, ondrædaþ J, ondræt I, adræt K
cor	heorte ABCDE^{3}FGHIJK
meum	min ABCDE^{x}*FHIJK, mine G
si	gif ABCDE^{3}**GJK*, gyf *FH*, þeah ðe *I*
exsurgat	ariseð *A*BG*, arisyð *C*, ærisæþ E^{3}, arise *DH*I, aryse F, gearisaþ J, arist K (*L*)
in*	in A, on BCDE^{3}, ongean FJ, ongean ł wið G*, tog togeanes I, togenes K
me	me ABCDE^{3}FGIJK
proelium	gefeht A, gefeoht BC*FGH*IJK, gefeoht *D*, gefioht *E^{3}* (*L*)
in	in A, on BCDE^{3}FGHIJK
hoc	ðis AB, þis CJ, þisum $E^{3/x}$*, ðysum F, þæt DH, þæt I, þæt ł þ[ ]s G*, þam K
ego	ic ABCDE^{3}FGH*IJK
sperabo	gehyhtu AB, gehihte CGIJ, gehyhte ł gewene $E^{3/x}$*, hyhte DH*, hihte K, hopige F

ED: þæt ł þ[ ]s (G)] þæt ł þis *Rosier*.

OE: Gif (E^{3})] hie *eras. after word.* standað ł gif geondoð (G)] ł gif geondoð *added in diff.* (?) *hand above* standað. ongean (E^{x})] *eras. before* gean *in next line* (on/gean). ongean ł wið (G) (*1st*)] ł wið *added in diff.* (?) *hand.* wereda ł fẏrdwic (G)] ł fẏrdwic *added in diff.* (?) *hand above* wereda. na (E^{x})] *on eras.* ondredeð (E^{x})] *on eras.* min (E^{x})] *on eras.* gif (E^{3})] *eras. before word.* ariseð (G)] *according to Rosier,* ð *added in diff. hand.* ongean ł wið (G) (*2nd*)] ł wið *added in diff.* (?) *hand.* þisum ($E^{3/x}$)] þi *on eras. by corr.* þæt ł þ[ ]s (G)] ł þ[ ]s *added in diff.* (?) *hand, with* s *above following* ic: s *written sideways above* i; *scribe possibly took* i *with dual purpose, as serving for* þis *and* ic. gehyhte ł gewene ($E^{3/x}$)] gehyhte ł *added by corr.* ic hyhte (H)] *written above* hoc *on fol. 48v, although* ego sperabo *is on fol. 49r.*

LTg: si] Si FGHIJK. exsurgat] exurgat DL, C: *eras. after* x, a *altered from another letter,* H: *eras. after* x; insurgat A: *cf. Weber MSS* ε moz^{x} med. proelium] prelium DJ, E: *eras. after word, perhaps from OE line above;* prȩlium FGHL.

LTu: Si] SI β. si] Si δεζθικλμξπρσυφχψ; [ ]ι τ: *initial wanting.* exsurgat] β: in *interl. above* ex; exurgat δειλξοστ*τχ, ϱ: *orig*. exsurgat: s *deleted*. proelium] prę̨lium δζλξ; prehelium ϰ; prelium ιστ*τ; praelium υ.

GAg: in] aduersum FGHIJK.

GAu: in] aduersum δεζϑικλμξοπϱστυφχψ.

4

Unam		an A*BCDGHJK*, án *F*, Anes *E*^{3}, an ðing *I*
petii		ic bed A, ic bæd BCD*E*$^{3/x}$*GHIJ*K*, ic beo F
a		from A, from BC, fram *E*^{3}*FG, fram JK, æt I
domino		dryhtne AB, drihtny C, drihtne E^{3}*FI, driħt G, driħ J
hanc		ðas A, þas BCJ, þæs E^{3}, þæt DF*H*K, þæt ł þas G*, þæt an I
requiram		ic soecu A, ic soece B, ic sece CIJ, ic sece ł gegyrnde E$^{3/x}$*, ic gegyrnde D*FH, ic gyrnde ł ic sece G*, ic gyrde K
ut		ðæt A, þæt BG, þæt C*DFHIJK, þet E^{3}
inhabitem	I	ic ineardie A, ic ineardige C, ic oneardige D, ic oneardige GH, ic eardige BJK, ic geeardige ł þæt ic onwunie I*, ic onwunige F, ic on E^{3}
in	I	in A, on BCDFGHI*JK, dryhtnes E^{3}
domo		huse ABCDFGHIJK
domini	I	dryhtnes BD, drihtnys C, drihtnes F, drihtnys I, drihten K, dryhƗ A, driħt GH, driħ J, eærdie E^{3}
omnibus*		allum A, eallum BDFJ, eallum CGI, eælle E^{3}, ealle HK
diebus*		dægum A, dagum BCDJ, dagum FGHI, dægæs E^{3}, dagas K
uitae	I	lifes A*BDFGHIJK,* lifys *C,* mines *E*^{3} (*L*)
meae	I	mines A*BDFGHIJK,* minys C, lifes *E*^{3}* (*L*)
Ut		ðæt A, þæt *BGI,* þæt *CDFH*JK, þet *E*^{3} (*L*)
uideam		ic gese A, ic geseo BCFGHIJK, ic geseo D, ic gesio E^{3}
uoluntatem	I	willan AB*C*DFGHIJK, mines drihtnes E^{3} (*L*)
domini	I	dryhtnes B, drihtnys C, drihtnes FI, drihtenes K, dryhƗ A, driħt G, driħ J, willæn E^{3}
et		⁊ ABCDE^{3}FGIJ
protegar*		ic siem gescilded A, ic sie gescilded B, ic sy gescyldyd C, ic sie gescylded E^{3}, ic sy gescyld D, ic geneosige FIJ, geneosige G
a*		from A*E*^{3}, from BC, fram D
templo*	I	tempe A, temple BC, temple DJ, templ G, tempel I*K, his E^{3} (*L*)
sancto*		ðæm halg(a) A*, þam halgan B, ðam haligan D, þan halgan C, halgæn E^{3}* (*L*)
eius	I	his BCDGIJ*K,* temple E^{3}

ED: petíí (EK)] petii *Harsley, Sisam*. á (E) (*1st*)] a *Harsley*. hánc (H)] hanc *Campbell*. uitę (E)] vitae *Harsley*. meę (E)] meae *Harsley*. á (E) (*2nd*)] a *Harsley*.

OE: ic bæd (E$^{3/x}$)] æd *on eras. by corr.* fram (E^{3})] *retraced by corr.* drihtne (E^{3})] tne *retraced by corr., eras. after word.* þæt ł þas (G)] ł þas *added in diff.* (?) *hand above following* ic. ic sece ł gegyrnde (E$^{3/x}$)] ł gegyrnde *added by corr.* ic gegyrnde (D)] ge *interl.* ic gyrnde ł ic sece (G)] ł ic sece *added in diff.* (?) *hand.* þæt (C) (*1st*)] *eras. before word.* ic geeardige ł þæt ic onwunie (I)] *1st* ge *and* o *on eras.* on (I)] *on eras.* (?). lifes (E^{3})] *top of* f *retouched in darker ink.* tempel (I)] *2nd* e *on eras.* ðæm halg(a) (A)] *2nd* a *partly faded, with back lost* (*Kuhn notes 'Rest cut off; prob.* halgan.'). halgæn (E^{3})] þe (?) *eras. before word.*

LTg: Unam] Vnam BCEFGHIJK. petii] petíí EK. a (*1st*)] á E. hanc] hánc H. uitae] uitæ B; uitę CEFHL; uite DGJK. meae] meæ BL; mee DJ; meę EFK; męę H. Ut] Vt BDEFHIL; [ ]t G. uoluntatem] C: *1st* u *on eras.*; uoluntem L. a (*2nd*)] á E. templo] L: um *added above* o *by Lat. corr.: see GAg.* sancto] L: um *added above* o *by Lat. corr.: cf. Weber MSS* γδ, *but more likely corr. overlooked Gallican omission and sought grammatical agreement independently.* eius] eíus K.

LTu: Unam] Vnam εικνρσ. petii] peti β; petiui ϑ. uitae] uitę εζινξοπφ; uitæ ϑ; uite κσςτ*τ. meae] meæ ϑχ; meę ινξφ; mee σςτ*τ, κ: *fragment ends.* Ut] ς: Ut...eius *wanting.* Ut] Vt ινξυφ. uideam] uidiam ϑ.

GAg: protegar] uisitem FGHIJK. a (*2nd*)] *om.* FGHIJK. templo] templum FGHIJK, L: *see LTg.* sancto] *om.* FGHIJK.

GAu: omnibus diebus] omnes dies ϑμ. protegar] uisitem δεζϑιλμξοπρστυφχψ. a (*2nd*)] *om.* δεζϑιλμξοπρστυφχψ. templo] templum δεζϑιλμξοπρστυφχψ. sancto] *om.* δεζϑιλμξοπρστυφχψ.

5

Quoniam		forðon ABJ, forþon C, forþan K, forðæn þe E^{3}, forðam ðe F, forþam þe G, forðan þe I
abscondit	|	ahydeð AB, ahydyð C, ahydeþ J, he behydde DI, behydde FHK, he behydde ł forðon he ahýdeð G*, me E^{3}
me	|	me ABCFGIJK, gehidde E^{3}
in		in A, on BCDE^{3}FGHIJK
tabernaculo	|	getelde ABCFJ, eardunge ł getelde DH, ear[ ]unge ł geteldes G*, eardungstowe K, his E^{3}I
suo*	|	his ABCDFGHJK, geteldunge E^{3}, bure ł on his eardungstowe ł on his getelde *I*
in		in A, on BCDE^{3}FGHIJK
die		dege AE^{3}, dæge BCDFGHIJ, dæ K
malorum		ðæra yfla A*, þara yfylra C, þæræ yflæ E^{3}, yfla B, yfelra DFGH*IK, yfela J

protexit		gescilde ABE3, gescylde *C*, gescild J, he scylde DFHK*, he gescylde GI
me		me ABCE3FGJK
in		in A, on BCDE3FGHIJK
abscondito		degulnisse A, deagelnesse B, diegulnysse C, dygelnisse D, digelnysse FI, digelnesse G, digelnisse H, digolnesse JK, gedygelnesse E3/x*
tabernaculi	|	geteldes ABFJ, geteældunge E3, in getelde C, eardunge D, eardunge H, earddunga K, ear[ ]unge ł geteldes G*, his I
sui	|	his ABCDE3FGHJK, eardungstowe ł his geteldes I

ED: forðon (A)] for ðon *Kuhn*. in (G) (*1st Lat.*)] on *Rosier*. ear[ ]unge ł geteldes (G)] eardunga ł geteldes *Rosier*.

OE: he behydde ł forðon he ahýdeð (G)] ł forðon he ahýdeð *added in diff.* (?) *hand in blank space at end of line above.* ear[ ]unge ł geteldes (G) (*1st*)] *letter after* r *lost due to hole in leaf,* ł geteldes *added in diff.* (?) *hand.* ðæra yfla (A)] *orig.* ðæm yfla: m *altered to* ra. yfelra (H)] *eras. after* l. he scylde (K)] *orig.* he scyldest: st *eras.* gedygelnesse (E3/x)] dygel *on eras. by corr.* ear[ ]unge ł geteldes (G) (*2nd*)] *letter after* r *lost due to hole,* ł geteldes *added in diff.* (?) *hand, with* ldes *written interl. after following* his.

LTg: suo] I: *eras.* (?) *after word.* protexit] C: *eras. after* p (pro-).

LTu: suo] *om.* ϑ: *cf. Weber MSS* γη*, *see GAu.*

GAu: suo] *om.* ϑ: *cf. Bib. sac. MSS* F2L2.

6

In		in *A*, on *BCDE3*FGHIJK (*L*)
petra		stane ABCDFGHIJK, þæn stænæ E3
exaltauit		upahof ABCJK, he upahof DFHI, he upæhof E3, he upahóf G
me		mec A, me BCE3FGHIJK
(et)*		⁊ FGIJK (*L*)
nunc		nu *ABCD*GHJK, nu þa F, nu ða I, Nu ðonne *E3* (*L*)
autem*		soðlice ABCE3 (*L*)
exaltauit		upahof ABJ, uppahof C, upǽhefþ E3, he upahof I, he upahefð DH, he upahefþ F, he upahefð ł ahóf G, ahof K
caput	|	heafud AC*, heafod B*DFGH*IJ, hæfod K, mín E3
meum	|	min ABCDFGHIJK, hæfod *E3*
super		ofer ABDE3*FGHJK, ofyr C, ofor I
inimicos		fiond A, fiend BE3, fynd CDFGHIJK
meos		mine ABCDE3*FGHIJK

Circuibo*		ic ymbgaa *A*, ic ymbgá *B*, ic ymbgáá *C*, ic ymbga *D*FGHJ, ic ymbgonge *E^3*, ic embega K, ic ymbeode I (*L*)
et		⁊ ABCDE^x*FGHIJK
immolabo*		ageldu ł offrige A/A^2*, agelde B, agylde C, ic ofrige D, ic ofrige HJK, ic offrige E^x*FG, ic offrode I
in		in A*, on BCDE^{3}FGHIJK
tabernaculo	|	getelde ł on eardungstowe A/A^2*, eardungstowe ł getelde G*, eardungstowe ł on his getelde I, getelde *B*CFJ, eardungstowe DH, earddunga K, his E^3
eius	|	his ABCDFGHIJ*K*, geteældunge E^3
hostiam		onsegdnisse A, onsægdnysse C, onsægdnisse DH, onsægednyssa F, onsægdnesse BE^x*I, onsægednesse GJ, lac K
iubilationis*		wynsumnisse ł lofes A/A^2*, wynsumnesse B, wynsumnysse C, lofes D, lofes ł dremes E^x*, mid cleopunge F, mid clypunge H, mid clipunge J, hreamas G, ł hreames ł stefnelofes I*, stefne K
cantabo		ic singu A, ic singe BCE^x*FGIJK, ic synge D, ic syngige H
et		⁊ ABCE^{3}FGHIJK
psalmum		salm AD, sealm BCFGHJ, seælm E^3*, sealmas K, lofsang I
dicam		ic cweoð *A*, ic cweðe BCHI, ic cwiðe E^3, ic cweþe JK, cweðe F, ic cweðe ł ic secge G, ic secge D
domino		dryhtne BD, drihtne CE^{3}FI, drihtene K, driht́ GH*, drih́ J

ED: he upahóf (G)] he upahof *Rosier*. upǽhefþ (E)] upæhefþ *Harsley*. psalmum (G)] psalmu*m* *Rosier*.

OE: heafud (C)] e *interl.* ofer (E^3)] *letter eras. after word.* mine (E^3)] e *added by corr.* ⁊ (E^x)] *on eras.* ageldu ł offrige (A/A^2)] ł offrige *added in 11th-c. hand.* ic offrige (E^x)] *on eras.* in (A) (*2nd*)] i *faint.* getelde ł on eardungstowe (A/A^2)] ł on eardungstowe *added in 11th-c. hand.* eardungstowe ł getelde (G)] ł getelde *added in diff.* (?) *hand.* onsægdnesse (E^x)] *on eras.* wynsumnisse ł lofes (A/A^2)] ł lofes *added in 11th-c. hand.* lofes ł dremes (E^x)] *on eras.* ł hreames ł stefnelofes (I)] *gloss eras. before 1st* ł. ic singe (E^x)] *on eras.* seælm (E^3)] *letter eras. after word.* driht́ (H)] *otiose stroke above* t.

LTg: In] in ABCDEL. me] me et L: et *added interl. by Lat. glossator: see GAg.* nunc] Nunc ABCDE, L: n *written after* N *by Lat. glossator.* autem] L: *underlined to signal deletion: see GAg.* caput] F: *orig.* capud: d *deleted by subscript dot,* t *interl.*, H: t *altered from another letter;* capud DG. meum] mevm E: v̄ *written in right margin by main hand.* Circuibo] circuibo ABCDEL. tabernaculo] B: o *on eras. followed by eras.* eius] eíus K. dicam] A: m *added by corr.* (?).

LTu: In] in βνςτ*; Im δ. nunc] Nunc βνςτ*. caput] capud ξςυ. Circuibo] circuibo βνςτ*. cantabo] Cantabo λ: *but not marking verse division.*

GAg: me] me et FGHIJK, L: *see LTg*. autem] *om*. FGHIJK, L: *see LTg*. Circuibo] Circuiui FIJK; [ ]ircuiui G; Circumiui H. immolabo] immolaui FGHIJK. iubilationis] uociferationis FGHIJK.

GAu: me] me et δεζϑιλμξοπϱστυφχψ. autem] *om*. δεζϑιλμξοπϱστυφχψ. Circuibo] Circuiui δεζϑιλμξοπϱστυφψ; Circumiui χ. immolabo] immolaui δεζϑιλμξοπϱστυφχψ. iubilationis] uociferationis δεζϑιλμξοπϱστυφχψ.

7

Exaudi		geher A, gehier B, gehyr CDF*G*HIK, Gehier E^3*, gehir J
domine		drihten E^3*F, dryht̄ AB, drih̄t CGH, drih̄ J, hlaford K (*I*)
uocem	|	stefne ABCDFGIK, stæfne HJ, mine E^3
meam	|	mine ABFGHIJK, min C, stemne E^3
qua		mid ðere A, mid ðære B, mid þære CI, mid þare HJ, on ðæt ł mid þæ G, on þære D, on ðære F, þæ E^3, þa K
clamaui		ic cleopede A, ic cleopode BD, ic clypode CH, ic clipode IJ, ic clýpude F, ic clypige K, ic clyp[ ] *G*, ic chige ł clypie E$^{3/x}$*
ad*		to ABCE^3*G*J (*FIK*)
te*		de A, ðe *B*, þe CE^{3}J, (ð)[ ] *G** (*FIK*)
miserere		mildsa *A*J, milsa K, mildsæ E^3, miltsa þu *G*, gemiltsa BCDF, gemildsa H, gemiltsa I
mei		min ABCDFHIJ, me E^{3}GK
et		⁊ ABCDE^{3}FGHIJK
exaudi		geher A, gehier B, gehyr CDFGHIK, gehir J, ongehiere E^3
me		mec A, me BCE^{3}FGHIJK

ED: a[ ] (G)] ad *Rosier*. (ð)[ ] (G)] ð[ ] *Rosier*.

OE: Gehier (E^3)] *letter eras. after word.* drihten (E^3)] en *on eras. by corr.* ic chige ł clypie (E$^{3/x}$)] ł clypie *added by corr.* (ð)[ ] (G)] *only stem and cross-stroke of* ð *visible.*

LTg: Exaudi] [ ]audi G. domine] I: o *written above word.* clamaui] clamau[ ] G. ad] F: *added later by corr.*, I: *added by corr. in right margin,* K: *added by corr. in left margin;* a[ ] G: *letter fragments visible after* a. te] B: *on eras.*, F: *added later by corr.*, I: *added by corr. in right margin,* K: *added by corr. in left margin,* G: *lost due to MS damage.* miserere] A: *orig.* miserire: *2nd* i *altered to* e; [ ]iserere G: *minim visible in initial position.*

LTu: Exaudi] EXaudi β. ad te] ϱ: *added by corr.*, χ: *interl.* miserere] misserere ϑ.

GAg: ad te] *orig. om.* FIK: *see LTg.*

GAu: ad te] *om.* δμοψ.

8

Tibi		to ðe AB, to þe HJ, þe CDE^{x}**K, ðe FI (*G*)
dixit		cweð A, cwæð *H*, cwæþ J, ic cwæð *B*, sæde CFK, sægde DE^{x}*, sæde ł cwæð I
cor	|	heorte ABCDFGHIJK, min E^{3}
meum	|	min ABCDFGHIJK, heorte E^{3}
quaesiui*		ic sohte *ABCDE^{x}**FGHJK, sohte I (*L*)
(te)*		ðe F, þe GHI*JK (*L*)
uultum*	|	ondwleotan A, ondwlitan B, andwlitan CD, ansyn FK, ansyne HIJ, ans[ ] G, ðine E^{3} (*L*)
tuum*	|	ðinne A*B, þinne CD, min FIK, mine J, andwlitan E^{x}* (*L*)
uultum*		ondwlitan B, andwlitan C, [ ]ndwleotan A*, ł onsine E^{x}*, ansyne FGI, ansine J, ansyn K (*L*)
tuum*		þinne BC, [ ]nne A, ðine E^{x}*, þine HIJ, ðin F, þin GK (*L*)
domine		dryhten E^{3}*, (dr)yht̄ A*, dryht̄ B, driħt CFGH, driħ J, eala þu dr̄ I*
requiram		i(c s)oecu A*, ic soece B, ic sece CDE^{3}*GIK, ic séce F, ic sete H, ic sohte ł ic sece J

ED: þe (E)] Þe *Harsley*. dixit (G)] dixit *Rosier*. ansyne (H)] *no gloss Campbell*. faciem (H) *no gloss*] ansyne *Campbell*. [ ]ndwleotan (A)] ondwleotan *Kuhn*. [ ]nne (A)] ðinne *Kuhn, noting in apparatus 'From* ðine; *2nd* n *above.'* (dr)yht̄ (A)] dryht̄ *Kuhn*. i(c s)oecu (A)] ic soecu *Kuhn*. ic sete (H)] ic sece *Campbell*.

OE: þe (E^{x})] *on eras.* sægde (E^{x})] *on eras.* ic sohte (E^{x})] *on eras.* þe (I)] *written in left margin along with another* te: *see GAg.* ðinne (A)] *2nd* n *interl.* andwlitan (E^{x})] *on eras.* [ ]ndwleotan (A)] *initial letter obscured.* ł onsine (E^{x})] *on eras.* ðine (E^{x}) (*2nd*)] *on eras.* dryhten (E^{3})] *retraced by corr.* (dr)yht̄ (A)] dr *obscured,* d *visible but not stem of* r. eala þu dr̄ (I)] o *written before* eala. i(c s)oecu (A)] c *and* s *obscured but visible.* ic sece (E^{3})] *eras. after 2nd* e.

LTg: Tibi] [ ]ibi G. dixit] H: t *added in lighter ink;* dixi B: *cf. Weber MS* P. quaesiui] quęsiui C; quesiui ABDE; exquisiuit te L: *orig.* quesiui: ex *added interl. before* q *and signaled for inclusion,* e *deleted by subscript dot,* i *and final* t *added interl.,* te *added interl. by Lat. glossator: see GAg.* uultum tuum uultum tuum] L: facies mea faciem tuam *added interl. by Lat. glossator: see GAg.*

LTu: Tibi] TIbi β. dixit] dixi β: *cf. Weber MS* P. quaesiui] quęsiui βν; quesiui ςτ*.

GAg: quaesiui] exquisiuit te FGH, K: te *interl.,* L: *see LTg;* exquisiuit té I: té *interl. and signaled for inclusion;* exquisiui te J. uultum (*1st*)] facies FGHIJK, L: *see LTg.* tuum (*1st*)] mea FHIJK, L: *see LTg,* G: *lost due to MS damage.* uultum tuum (*2nd*)] faciem tuam FGHIJK, L: *see LTg.*

GAu: quaesiui] exquisiuit δϑοψ; exquisiuit te εμλξστφ, ζπϱυ: te *added interl.;* exquisiui te ι; exquesiuit te χ. uultum tuum (*1st*)] facies mea δεζϑιλμξοπϱστυφχψ. uultum tuum (*2nd*)] faciem tuam δεζϑιλμξοπρστυφχψ.

9

Ne ne A*BCDFGHIJ, Ne E^{3}, na K
auertas acer ðu A, acir ðu B, acyrr þu C, acyrre ðu DE^{x}*, acyr þu H, acyr ðu I, acir þu J, acyrr[ ] (ð)u G*, acyr K, awend ðu F
faciem | onsiene A*B, ansyne CDGHIK, ansine FJ, þine E^{3}
tuam | ðine A, þine BCDGHIJK, ðin F, onsiene E^{3}
a from AE^{3}, from BC, fram FI, fram GHJK
me me *A**BCE^{3}FGHIJK
et* ⁊ ABCE^{3}
ne ne BCDE^{3}FHIJ, na K, [ ]e A*
declines ahaeld ðu A, aheld ðu B, ahyld þu CI, ahyld ðu F, ahyld ðú G, ahild þu J, ahyld K, hyld þu D, ahird þu H, hyld ł becyrre ðu E$^{3/x}$*
in in A, on BCDE^{3}FGHIJK
ira eorre ABDE^{x}*, yrre CGIK, irre HJ, graman F
a from A, from B, fram CDFJK, fram GI (*EH*)
seruo ðiowe A, þeowe BCDE^{x}*FJ, ðeowe G, ðeowum I, ðeowan K, fram þeowe *H*
tuo ðinum AF, ðinum B, þinum CDIJ, þinum G, þine E^{x}H, þinan K

Adiutor fultum ABCJ, fultum H*, gefultuma F, gefylstend D, Gefylstend E^{x}*, gefylstend ł fultum G*, fultum ł gefilsta I, fylstend K
meus min ABCDE^{x}*FGHIJK
esto ðu earð *A,* þu eart *B*H, eart þu J, beo þu *CGK,* beo ðu *D*F, þu beo E^{3}, sy ðu ł beo þu *I** (*L*)
⟨deus⟩ god *B*
⟨domine⟩ drihten *K,* drih́t *C* (*IL*)
ne ne BCDE^{3}FGHIJ, na K
derelinquas forlet ðu A, forlæt ðu BF, forlæt þu CGHIJ, forlæte þu D, forlet þu E^{3}*, forlæt K
me me ABCE^{3}FHIJ, minan K
neque ne ABE$^{3/x}$*GHIJ, ⁊ ne D, ⁊ na K, ny ne C, ne ne F
despicias forseh AK, forseoh DF*H,* forseoh ðu B, forseoh þu CGJ, forSioh þu E$^{3/x}$*, forseoh ðu na ł ne ðu ne forseoh I*
me me ABCDE^{3}FGHIJK

deus — god ABCE^{3}FGHIJK
salutaris* | se halwynde A, se halwenda C, hælend BG*J, hælo DFHK, mine E^{3}, eala þu I
meus | min ABCDFGHJK, hęlo E^{3}, min halwenda god I

ED: acyrr[ ] (ð)u (G)] acyrr[ ] [ ]u *Rosier*. [ ]e (A)] ne *Kuhn*. ahyld ðú (G)] ahyld ðu *Rosier*. á (E) (*2nd*)] a *Harsley*. fultu͟m (H)] fult*um* *Campbell*.

OE: ne (A) (*1st*)] *left leg of* n *obscured by bleed-through from display line of fol. 31r.* acyrre ðu (E^{x})] *on eras.* acyrr[ ] (ð)u (G)] *eye of* e (?) *visible after 2nd* r, *bowl of* ð *visible.* onsiene (A)] o *obscured by bleed-through from display line of fol. 31r.* me (A) (*1st*)] m *obscured by bleed-through from display line of fol. 31r.* [ ]e (A)] *initial letter obscured by bleed-through from display line of fol. 31r.* hyld ł becyrre ðu (E$^{3/x}$)] hyld ł *added by corr.* eorre (E^{x})] *on eras.* þeowe (E^{x})] *on eras.* fultu͟m (H)] *scribe orig. began* fulu- *but altered left leg of 2nd* u *to* t, *added minim at end to complete* u, *and added macron.* Gefylstend (E^{x})] *on eras.* gefylstend ł fultum (G)] ł fultum *added above* gefylstend *in diff.* (?) *hand.* min (E^{x})] *on eras.* sy ðu ł beo þu (I)] ł beo þu *written in left margin.* forlet þu (E^{3})] *eras. after* forlet, þu *in darker ink.* ne (E$^{3/x}$) (*3rd*)] n *retraced in darker ink,* e *on eras. and altered from another letter.* forSioh þu (E$^{3/x}$)] for *on eras. by corr.* forseoh ðu na ł ne ðu ne forseoh (I)] ne ðu ne forseoh *written in left margin.* hælend (G)] n *interl. in diff.* (?) *hand.*

LTg: me (*1st*)] A: e *obscured by bleed-through from display line of fol. 31r.* a (*2nd*)] á E; *om.* H. esto] A: o *on eras.*, D: *orig.* es tu: u *altered to* o; es tu deus B; es tu domine CL; esto domine I: o *written above* domine, K: domine *underlined in brown ink: cf. Weber MSS* η^{2} moz^{x}. despicias] H: *orig.* dispicias: *1st* i *altered to* e.

LTu: ne (*1st*)] nec ϑ. esto] estu νς; esto domine ζϱυ, σ: domine *added interl. in later hand.* despicias] dispicias ψ, β: e *added interl. above 1st* i *by corr.*

GAg: et] *om.* FGHIJK.

GAu: et] *om.* δεζϑιλμξοπϱστυφχψ. salutaris] saluator ϑ: *2nd* a *interl.*

10

Quoniam — forðon ABJ, forþon C, forðæn E^{3}, forþam *G,* forþā K, forðam ðe F, forðon þe I
pater — feder AE^{3}, fæder BDFGIJK, fædyr C, fador H
meus — min ABCDFGHIJK, mín E^{3}
et — ⁊ ABCDE^{3}FGHJK (*I*)
mater — modur AC, modor BDFGHJ, moder E^{3}I*K
mea — min ACDE^{3}FGHJK, ⁊ min I, mea B
dereliquerunt — forleorton A, forleton BC, forletun I, forleton J, hy forleton DE$^{3/x}$*, hý forleton F, hi forleton GH

me	mec A, me BCDE^{3}FGHIJ
dominus	dryhten B, drihten E^{3}F, dryht̄ A, drih́t CG, drih́ J
autem	soðlice ABCE^{3}FGH, soþlice DJ, sodlice I
adsumpsit	genom A, genam *C*, onfeng BF*GH*, anfeng D*E^x**, onfengc *J*, onfeng ł upahof *I* (*K*)
me	mec A, me BCE^{3}FGJ

ED: (Q)uoniam (G)] Quoniam *Rosier*. forðon (A)] for ðon *Kuhn*. forðæn (E)] Forðæn *Harsley*. sodlice (I)] soðlice *Lindelöf*. assumpsit (C)] a[d]sumpsit *Wildhagen*.

OE: moder (I)] ⁊ *eras. before word.* hy forleton (E$^{3/x}$)] hy *added by corr., eras.* (*2 letters?*) *before* forleton, f *retraced in darker ink.* anfeng (E^x)] *on eras.*

LTg: Quoniam] (Q)uoniam G: *bowl of* Q *lost, outline visible.* et] I: *eras.* (⁊?) *above word.* adsumpsit] assumpsit EGIJK, C: *1st* s *on eras. by corr.*, H: *1st* s *on eras.*

LTu: derelinquerunt] derelinquęrunt υ. adsumpsit] assumpsit εζϑιοπϱστ*τυφχ.

11

Legem	aee AH, ęe D, æ BIJK, ǽ CF, Ǽwe E^3, æ æ G
(pone)*	geséte F, gesete HJ, gesette G, asete I, sete K
mihi	me AB*CE^3*FGIJK (*L*)
constitue*	gesete ABCD, gesette E^3* (*L*)
domine	dryhten D, drihten E^{3}F, dryht̄ AB, drih́t CG, driht̄ H, drih́ J, halford K (*I*)
in	in A, on BCDE^{3}FGHIJ, o K
uia	wege ABCDE^{3}FGHIJK
tua	ðinum AE^{3}FI, ðinum B, þinum CDHJ, þinan ł um G*, þinan K
et	⁊ ABCDE^{3}FGHIJK
dirige	gerece AB*CDE^{3}FGHJ, gerece ł gewissa I, rece K
me	mec A, me BCE^3*F*GJK
in	in A, on BCDE^3*FGHIJK
semita	stige ABCJ, siþfæte DH, siðfæte F, siþfæt K, siðfæte ł on stige G*, stigæ ł on siðfæte E$^{3/x}$*, siðfæte ł on pæðe I
recta	ða rehtan A, þa rihtan C, ryhtum D, rihtum F, rihtum HK, rihtum ł rihtre G*, rihtæ E^3, rihtan I, rihte J, ryhtre B
propter	fore ABDGH, for CE^3*FIJK
inimicos	fiendum A, feondum BDHK, feondum CFGIJ, fiondum E^3
meos	minum ACE^{3}GH, minum BDFIJK

ED: Legem (B)] legem *Brenner*. driht̄ (H)] drih́t *Campbell*.

OE: gesette (E^3)] s *and cross-stroke of* tt *retraced in darker ink.* þinan ł um (G)] ł um *added in diff.* (?) *hand above* þinan. gerece (B)] erec *blotted* (*by water stain?*) *but visible.* on (E^3) (*2nd*)] *eras. after word.* siðfæte ł on stige (G)] ł on stige *added in diff.* (?) *hand above* fæte. stigœ ł on siðfœte ($E^{3/x}$)] ł on siðfœte *added by corr.* rihtum ł rihtre (G)] ł rihtre *added in diff.* (?) *hand above* rihtum. for (E^3)] *orig.* fore: e *eras.*

LTg: mihi] L: *underlined to signal deletion,* pone mihi *written by Lat. glossator in left margin: see GAg;* michi E, C: *orig.* mihi C: c *interl. by corr.* constitute] L: *underlined to signal deletion: see GAg.* domine] I: o *written above word.* me] F: *eras. after word.*

LTu: mihi] β: hi *interl. by corr.;* michi ιλξςτ, πϱ: c *added interl.* constitue] constituae ν. semita recta] semitam rectam ν: *cf. Weber MSS* TPQUVX.

GAg: Legem] Legem pone FGHIJK, L: *see LTg note to* mihi. constitue] *om.* FGHIJK, L: *see LTg.*

GAu: Legem] Legem pone δεζθιλμξοπρστυφχψ. constitue] *om.* δεζθιμξοπστυφχψ.

12

Ne	ne ABCDFGHIJ, Ne E^3, na K
tradideris	sele ðu ABD, sele þu E^3H, syle ðu F, syle þu G, sile þu J, gesyle þu C, betæc ðu ł ne sele þu I, sylle K
me	mec A, me BCE^3FGIJK
in	in A, on BCDE^3FGIJK
animas	sawle ACFJ, saule DK, sawla *B*GH, Sæwlæ E^3, sawlum ł on anwealde I
persequentium*	oehtendra A, ehtendra BDG*JK, oiehtyndra C, ehtendræ E^3, gedrefedra F, geswencendra I
me	mec A, me BCE^3FGIJK
quoniam	forðon ABJ, forþon CG, forðæn E^3, forþan K, forðam ðe F, forþon þe I
insurrexerunt	areosun A, onarison BDFGI*J, onaryson C, onarisen H, onrison E^x*, onrisendan K
in	in A, on BCDE^3FGHIJK
me	mec A, me BCDE^3*FGHIJK
testes	geweotan A, gewitan BCI*, gewiton J, cyþras D, cyðras H, cyðeras F, cyþeras K, cyþras ł gewiten $E^{3/x}$*, cyðeras ł gewiton G*
iniqui	unrehte A, unrihte I*, unryhtwise BD, unrihtwise C$E^{3/x}$*FGJ, unrihtwis[ ] H*, unrihtwisnes K
et	⁊ ABCDE^3FGHIJK
mentita	legende A, leogendu B, leogynde C, leogende J, leasfyrhte DE^x*F, lesfyrhte H, leasefyrhte K, leasfeorhte ł leogende G*, alogen ⁊ aleah unrihtwisnys hire *I**

est — wes A, wæs BC*, is E^{x}*FGIJ*K*
iniquitas — unrehtwisnis A, unryhtwisnes BDE^{x}*, unrihtwisnys FI, unrihtwiɛnoɛ GH, unrihtwiɛnoɛɛo J, unrihtwiɛnoɛɛo K, ɛoo unrihtwisnys C
sibi — him ABCE^{x}*HJ, him DFK, h[ ] *G*, heom I*

ED: forðon (A)] for ðon *Kuhn.* unrihtwis[ ] (H)] unrihtwise *Campbell.* alogen ⁊ aleah unrihtwisnys hire (I)] *Lindelöf places added glosses after* heom, *adding* ł *after* alogen.

OE: ehtendra (G)] *in slightly lighter ink.* onarison (I)] on *in slightly darker ink,* on (*separate from gloss*) *with single subscript dot written in left margin corresponding to* in *in* insurrexerunt, *which also shows single subscript dot; additional gloss* (?) *eras. before* onarison. onrison (E^{x})] *on eras.* me (E^{3}) (*3rd*)] *eras. after word.* gewitan (I)] *word eras. after gloss.* cyþras ł gewiten (E$^{3/x}$)] cyþras ł ge *added by corr.* cyðeras ł gewiton (G)] ł gewiton *added in diff.* (?) *hand above* cyðeras. unrihte (I)] e *on eras., eras. after word.* unrihtwise (E$^{3/x}$)] *eras. before word,* wise *on eras. by corr.* unrihtwis[ ] (H)] *base of final letter fragment visible.* leasfyrhte (E^{x})] *on eras.* leasfeorhte ł leogende (G)] ł leogende *added in diff.* (?) *hand above* leasfeorhte. alogen ⁊ aleah unrihtwisnys hire (I)] ⁊ aleah unrihtwisnys hire *written in left margin: inclusion of gloss here seems to be indicated by a stroke, much like an accent, after* alogen *and above* i *in* mentita: *see ED.* wæs (C)] æ *on eras.* is (E^{x})] *on eras.* unryhtwisnes (E^{x})] *on eras.* him (E^{x})] *on eras.* heom (I)] *see ED.*

LTg: animas] B: *2nd* a *blotted* (*by water stain?*) *but visible.* mentita] mentíta I. est] ést K. sibi] si[ ] G.

GAg: persequentium] tribulantium FGHIJK.

GAu: persequentium] tribulantium δεζϑιλμξοπϱστυφχψ.

13

Credo — ic gelefu A, ic geliefe B, ic gelyfe CDFGHIK, Ic geliefe E^{3}*, ic gelife J
uidere — | gesian A, geseon BCDFGHIJK, drihtnes E^{3}
bona — god ABCDE^{3}HK, gód J, godu FGI
domini — | dryhtnes B, drihtnes C*FI, dryht̄ A, driħt G, driħ J, to gesionne E^{3}
in — in A, on BCDE^{3}FGHIJK
terra — | earðan A, eorðan BCDFHJ, eorþan GK, eorðan ł on land I*, liuiendræ E^{3}
uiuentium — | lifgendra AB, lifigendra JK, lifigendum D, lifigendum H, lifgendum ł lyfigendra G*, lybbyndra C, libendra F, libbendra I, eorðæn E^{3}

ED: drihtnes (C)] driht[nys] *Wildhagen*. eorðan ł on land (I)] eorðan *Lindelöf:* on lande *recorded in corrigenda* (*p. 323*); *final* e *perhaps lost due to tight binding.*

OE: Ic geliefe (E^3)] Ic *retraced in darker ink.* drihtnes (C)] *orig.* driħt: *cross-stroke through ascender of* h *eras.*, nes *added.* eorðan ł on land (I)] ł on land *written in right margin: see ED.* lifgendum ł lyfigendra (G)] ł lyfigendra *added in diff.* (?) *hand.*

LTu: Credo uidere] ς: *orig.* Credere: o uid *added interl.*

14

expecta	abid *AB*, geanbida *DFHIJK*, ł abid geanbida C*, ic anbida ł abid *G**, ic onbide E^3 (*L*)
dominum	dryhten B, drihten FI, drihtnes E^3, drihtenes GK, dryht̄ A, driħt C, driht̄ H, driħ J
et*	⁊ CE^3 (*AB*)
uiriliter	werlice ABCDFI, wærlice GHK, werirlice J, ic werlice E^3
age	doo *A*, dóó C, dó BD, do E^3GHIJK, do ðu F
et	⁊ ABCDE^3FGHIJK
confortetur	sie gestrongad A, sie gestrongod B, sy gestrongod C, sy g̲estrangod D, si gestrængod E^3, sy gestrangod FIJ, sie gestrangod H, si gestrangod K*, si gestr[ ]god G*
cor	| heorte ABCDFGHIJK, þin E^3
tuum	| ðin AF, ðín B, þin CGIJK, þinum H, heorte E^3
et	⁊ ABCDE^xFGHIJK
sustine	abid *ABCG**J, geanbida DE^xFHK, geðola ł forðyldiga I
dominum	dryhten B, drihtyn C, drihten *E^x*FHI, drihtenes GK, dryht̄ A, driħ J

ED: exspecta (B)] expecta *Brenner.* ic anbida ł abid (G)] anbida ł abid *Rosier.* driht̄ (H)] driħt *Campbell.* ðín (B)] ðin *Brenner.* geanbida (H)] geanbid *Campbell.*

OE: ł abid geanbida (C)] ł *misplaced.* ic anbida ł abid (G)] ł abid *added in diff.* (?) *hand.* si gestrangod (K)] *orig.* si gestrangode: *2nd* e *eras.* si gestr[ ]god (G)] god *written at beginning of next line, letters after* r *lost to MS damage.* abid (G)] *in lighter ink.*

LTg: expecta] Expecta IJ, H: *eras. after* x, L: *orig.* expecta: *1st* e *altered to* E *by corr.;* exspecta ABDE; Exspecta K; [ ]xpecta F: *initial letter not written;* [ ]xspecta G: *initial letter lost.* et (*1st*)] *om.* AB: *cf. Weber MSS* MQ^2Uαγδεη moz med, *see GAg.* age] Λ: *eras. after word.* sustine] A: i *on eras.;* sustinę G. dominum (*2nd*)] dominvm E.

LTu: expecta] exspecta βμ; Expecta δεζϑιλξοπϱστυφχψ. sustine] exspecta ϑ: *cf. Weber MSS* βγδε$η^2$ moz^c med. dominum] dominvm τ*.

GAg: et (*1st*)] *om.* FGHIJK, AB: *see LTg.*

GAu: et (*1st*)] *om.* δεζϑιλμξοπϱστυφχψ.

PSALM 27

1

Ad	to A*BC*FGIJ*K*, To *E^3** (*D*)
te	ðe ABFG, þe *CE^3*IJK (*D*)
domine	drihten E^3F, dryht̄ AB, drih̄t *C*G, drih̄ J (*I*)
clamaui*	ic cleopiu *A,* ic clipige BJ, ic clypige FHK, ic clypode *C,* ic cleopode D, ic clipode *E^3*,* ic clypode ł ic clypige G*, ic cleopige I (*L*)
deus	| god ABCFGHJK, godd D, min E^3I
meus	| min ABCDFGHJK, god E^3I
ne	ne ABCE^xFGIJ, na DHK
sileas	swiga ðu ABD, swiga þu CE^xHIJK, swýga ðu F, swige ł a þu G*
a	from A*E^3,* from *B,* fram CFGJ, fram K, æt I
me	me ABCE^3FGIJK (*L*)
(nequando)*	þelæs F, þilæs J, hwænne ne G, ahwanne ne I
(taceas)*	ðu suwige F, þu suwige J, suwa þu G, suga þu I
(a)*	fram FGJ, fram I
(me)*	me FGIJ
et	⁊ ABCDE^3FGIJ
ero*	ic biom A, ic beom C, ic beo BD, ic bío E^3 (*L*)
similis*	gelic A*BCDE^3, ic beo gelice FJ, ic beo geanlicod G, ic beo geanlicod I* (*L*)
descendentibus	astigendum *A,* astigendum BJ, þam astigendum G*, þam stigendum D, ðam stigendum F, þam stigendum H, niðyrastigyndum C, niðerstigendum I, þæm niþerstigendum *E^3*,* astigende K
in	in A, on BCDE^3FGHIJK
lacum	seað ABCDFGH, seaþ JK, seþe E^x*, seaðe I

ED: ne (G) (*1st*)] [ ] *Rosier.* á (E)] a *Harsley.* nequando (FJK)] ne quando *Kimmens, Oess, Sisam.*

OE: To (E^3)] *in darker ink, possibly by corr.* ic clipode (E^3)] ode *by corr., possibly on eras.* ic clypode ł ic clypige (G)] ł ic clypige *added in diff.* (?) *hand above* ic clypode. swige ł a þu (G)] ł a *added in diff.* (?) *hand above* swige. gelic (A)] *letter eras. after* e. ic beo geanlicod (I)] an *interl. in lighter brown ink.* þam astigendum (G)] *2nd* a *added interl. in diff.* (?) *hand between* m *and* s. þæm niþerstigendum (E^3)] *ink blotted between* st, gendum *retraced* (?) *by corr.* seþe (E^x)] *on eras.*

LTg: Ad] AD BCDEK. te] TE CDE. domine] I: o *written above word;* DN̄E C. clamaui] L: ui *underlined to signal deletion,* bo *interl.;* CLAMAVI C; clamavi E;

clamabo A: *orig.* clamaui: bo *added interl. by corr.: cf. Weber MSS* MT^{2}εζ med, *see GAg.* a] B: *on eras.;* á E. me] B: m *partly on eras.,* L: ne quando taceas a me *written in right margin by corr., right leg of 1st* n, *1st* e, *and* q *on eras.: see GAg.* ero similis] L: *underlined to signal deletion,* assimilabor *added interl. by corr.: see GAg.* descendentibus] A: *orig.* discendentibus: *1st* i *altered to* e; descendentibvs E.

LTu: Ad] AD βιλμνξπϱσςτ*τφχ. te] TE λμνξπϱςφχ; Te σ. domine] DN̄E λμνξπϱφχ. clamaui] CLAmaui ν; clamabo ς: *cf. Weber MSS* MT^{2}εζ med, *see GAu.* deus] DEUS π; DS̄ λξϱ. meus] MEUS λξπ; MS̄ ϱ. ne] NE ξπ. sileas] SILEAS ξ; silias ϑ. a] A ξ. me] ME ξ. descendentibus] discendentibus β. lacum] lacvm τ*.

GAg: clamaui] clamabo FGHIJK, AL: *see LTg.* me] me nequando taceas a me FGHIJK, L: *see LTg.* ero] *om.* FGHIJK. similis] adsimilabor F; assimilabor GIJK, H: *1st* s *interl. in lighter ink,* L: *see LTg.*

GAu: clamaui] clamabo δεζϑιοστυφψ, ς: *see LTu;* CLAMABO λμξπϱχ. me] me nequando taceas a me δεζϑιλμοπϱστυφχψ. ero] *om.* δεζϑιλμοστυφχψ. similis] adsimilabor δϑμοψ; assimilabor εζιλπϱστυφχ.

2

Exaudi		geher A, gehier B, gehyr *CFIK,* Gehire E^3, gehir *J,* [ ]ehy(r) *G** (*H*)
⟨domine⟩		drihten *F,* driħt *G,* driħ *J* (*HIKL*)
uocem		stefne ABCFGIK, stæfne J, stemne E^3
deprecationis	|	boene AB, bene CDFGHJK, halsunge ł bene I, mines E^3
meae	|	minre *ABCDHIJK,* mine *FG,* gebedes *E^3* (*L*)
dum		ðonne A, þonne BCDFHJK, þonne G, þænne I, midþie E^3
oro	|	ic gebiddu A, ic gebidde BFGHIJ, ic gebidde D, ic me gebidde *C,* ic bidde K, ic to E^3
ad	|	to ABCDFGHIJK, gebidde E^3
te		ðe ABDFG, þe CHIJK
et*		⁊ ABCDE^x* (*L*)
dum		ðonne AE^x*F, þonne BCDHJK, þonne G, þænne I
extollo		ic uphebbu A, ic uphebbe BDE^x*GH, ic upahebbe *C*FI*J, ic hebbe K
manus	|	honda AB, handa CDGHIJ, hand F, m handa K, mine E^3
meas	|	mine ABCFHIJK, mina D, m[ ] *G,* hænde E^3
ad		to ABCDE^{3}FGHIJK
templum	|	temple ABCDFGIJ, temple HK, þinum E^3*
sanctum		halgum AF, halgum J, halygum C, haligum DH, ðæm halgan B, þ[ ]m haligum ł an G*, hælgæn E^3, halgan I, halian K
tuum	|	ðinum AF, ðinum B, þinum CH, þinum DI, [ ]inum G*, þinan K, temple E^3

ED: [ ]ehy(r) (G)] [ ] *Rosier.* meę (E)] meae *Harsley.* mine (G)] min *Rosier.* ic to gebidde (E)] ic togebidde *Harsley.* templum (G)] templ*um Rosier.* þ[ ]m haligum ł an(G)] þam haligum ł an *Rosier.* [ ]inum (G)] ðinum *Rosier.*

OE: [ ]ehy(r) (G)] *descender of* r *not visible, letter fragment visible in initial position.* ⁊ (E^{x})] *on eras.* ðonne (E^{x})] *on eras.* ic uphebbe (E^{x})] *on eras.* ic upahebbe (I)] a *interl.* þinum (E^{3})] *eras. after word, stem of* þ *visible in initial position.* þ[ ]m haligum ł an (G)] ł an *added in diff.* (?) *hand above* um. [ ]inum (G)] *initial letter lost due to hole in leaf.*

LTg: Exaudi] Exaudi domine FGHJK, I: o *written above* domine, L: domine *added interl. by corr.;* [ ]xaudi domine G: *cf. Weber MSS* SKT*X*α^{2}ε med. meae] meę ADEFJK; meæ BCL; męę H; me[ ] G. oro] ora C. et] L: *underlined to signal deletion: see GAg.* extollo] C: *1st* l *on eras.* meas] G: *lost due to MS damage, minim visible.*

LTu: Exaudi] EXaudi β; Exaudi domine δεζιλμξοπρστυφχψ: *cf. Weber MSS* SKT*X*α^{2}ε med. deprecationis] depc̄ationis ϑλοϱστφχ; depraecationis υ. meae] meę ειvϱφ; meæ ϑ; mee ξστ*; męę ς. et] *interl.* v; *om.* τ*: *cf. Weber MSS* αβγδεη moz med, *see GAu.*

GAg: et] *om.* FGHIJK, L: *see LTg.*

GAu: et] *om.* δεζϑιλμξοπρστυφχψ, τ*: *see LTu.*

3

Ne | ne AFIJ, no B, na CDHK, Na E^{x}*
simul — somud A, somod BDE^{x}*, samod CFGHIK, samad J
tradas | sele A, þu selle DE^{x}*H, ðu sylle F, þu syle K, þu sylle ł þu syle G*, sele ðu B, sele þu ł betæc þu I*, ne sile þu J, gesyle þu C
me — mec A, me BCE^{3}*FGIJK
cum — mid ABCDE^{3}*FGHIJK
peccatoribus — ðæm synfullum A, ðæm synfullum B, þæm synfullum C, þam synfullum J, þam sinfullu[ ] G, synfullum D, synfullum E$^{3/x}$*FHI, synfullan K
et — ⁊ ABCDE^{3}FGHIJK
cum — mid ABCDE^{3}FGHIJK
operantibus — wircendum A, wyrcendum BDK, wyrcyndum C, wyrcendum FHI, wircendum J, weorcendum G, þæm wircendum E^{3}
iniquitatem — unrehtwisnisse A, unryhtwisnesse BD, unrihtwisnysse CF, unrihtwisnesse GJK, unrihtwysnysse I, unrihtnesse E^{3}, unriht H
ne — ne ABCDE^{3}FGHIJ, na K
perdas* — forspild ðu AB, forspill þu C, forspil ðu DFGI, forspil ðú E^{3}*, forspil þu HJK
me — me ABCDE^{3}FGIJK

Cum*		mid ABCD, Mid E^{3} (*L*)
his*		ðissum A, þissum B, þissum *C,* þysum E^{3}, þam D (*L*)
qui		ða ðe A*I,* þa ðe B, ða þe *F,* þa þe C*G*J,* þe D*H,* þa *K,* þe her E^{3} (*L*)
loquuntur		spreocað A, sprecað B*C*DFGH*I,* sprecæð E^{3}, sprecaþ *J,* specaþ K
pacem		sibbe ABDE^{3}GHIJK, sybbe CF
cum		mid ABCDE^{3}FGHIJK
proximo	I	ðone nestan A, ðone nihstan B, þam nehstan C, þam neahstan G, þam nixtan I, þam nihstan *J,* nehstan DF, neahstan H, nyxstan K, hirum E^{3}
suo	I	his ABCFGJK, heora DHI, nixtum E^{3}
mala	I	yfel ABJK, yfyl C, yfelu DFH*, yflu I, yfelu ł yfel G*, soðlice E^{3}
autem	I	soðlice ABCFGHI, soþlice DJK, yfel E^{3}
sunt		sind A, sint BE^{3}, synd C (*FGHIJKL*)
in		in A, on BCDE^{3}FGHIJK
cordibus	I	hortum A, heortum BD, heortum CFGH, heortan IJK, hiroæ E^{3}
eorum	I	heara A, hira B, hyra C, heora DFGHI*JK, heortæn E^{3}

ED: forspil ðú (E)] forspil ðu *Harsley.* iís (C)] hís *Wildhagen.*

OE: Na (E^{x})] *on eras.* somod (E^{x})] *on eras.* þu selle (E^{x})] *on eras.* þu sylle ł þu syle (G)] ł þu syle *added in diff.* (?) *hand above* þy sylle. sele þu ł betæc þu (I)] sele *orig.* sile: i *altered to* e. me (E^{3}) (*1st*)] *eras.* (*7 mm*) *after word.* mid (E^{3})] *eras. after word.* synfullum (E$^{3/x}$)] syn *on eras. by corr.,* f *retraced in darker ink.* forspil ðú (E^{3})] ú *on eras. by corr., accent by main hand.* þa þe (G)] þa *written outside left grid.* yfelu (H)] *orig.* yfela: u *written above* a, *but without deleting mark.* yfelu ł yfel (G)] ł yfel *added in diff.* (?) *hand.* heora (I)] s. sun[ ] : sy *written in right margin and cropped.*

LTg: Cum his] L: *underlined by corr. to signal deletion: see GAg.* his] iís C: *orig.* hís: *ascender of* h *eras. to form* i. qui] L: q *altered to* Q *by corr.;* Qui FGHIJK. loquuntur] locuntur CIJ. proximo] J: *orig.* proximi: *final* i *altered to* o. sunt] L: *underlined to signal deletion; om.* FGHJK, I: *see OE note to* heora: *cf. Weber MSS* α med.

LTu: me (*2nd*)] eum τ*. Cum] cum ϑ. qui] Qui δεζϑιλξοπϱστυφψ. loquuntur] locuntur δζϑιμνοςτ*τχ. sunt] *om.* τ*φχ: *cf. Weber MSS* α med.

GAg: Cum his] *om.* FGHIJK, L: *see LTg.*

GAu: perdas] perdideris ϑ. Cum his] *om.* δειλμξοπϱστυφχψ.

4

Da	sele ABDH, Sele E^{3}, syle CF*G*IJK
illis	him ABGH, him CDJK, heom FI, hem E^{3}*

secundum		efter AE³, æfter BFGI, æft<u>er</u> J, æftyr C
opera	I	wercum A, weorcum I, weorce BJ, worc C, weorcu DFH, weorcæ G, weorc K, hioræ E³
eorum*	I	heara A, hira B, hyra C, heora DFG*I*J, arleasa *K**, weorce E³ (*H*)
et		⁊ ABCDE³FGHIJ
secundum		efter AE³, æfter BFGI, æft<u>er</u> DHJ, æftyr C
nequitiam		niðum *AB,* niðas C, niþe J, nearoðancu<u>m</u> *D**, nearoþancu<u>m</u> H, nearuþancum F, nearaþancu<u>m</u> K, nearaþancum ł niðe G*, nearoðancnysse ł mane I, hiore niþhete E³
studiorum*	I	teolunge A, tilunga B, tylvnge C, gecneorþnissa D, wiðmetednyssa F, wiþmetendra J, afundennesse G, gegaderungum ł gemetednessa ł heora afundennysse I*, hioræ E³ (*L*)
ipsorum	I	heara A, hira B, hyra C, heora DFGHJ, gecneorþnisse ł tilengæ E³/x* (*L*)
(Secundum)*		æfter FGK, æft<u>er</u> HJ
(opera)*		weorcæ G*, weorc H, weorcum I, weorce J, weorca K
(manuum)*		handa FGHIJK
(eorum)*		heora FGHIJK
retribue*		geedleana ABC, geedleænæ E³, agyld DH, agild F, agyld ł forgyf I*, gild K, syle GJ (*L*)
illis		him ABCGHJ, hi<u>m</u> D, hem E³, heom FIK
Redde		agef A, agif B, agyf C, agyld D*FH,* Agield E³, agyld ł agyf *G**, ageld *I,* agild *J* (*K*)
retributionem	I	edlean AB*C*DFHJ*K,* eadlean G, edleanunga I, hioræ E³
eorum	I	heara A, hira B, hyra C, heora DFGHIJK, edleænængæ E³
ipsis		him ABCDFGH, hi<u>m</u> K, hem E³*, heom I, hym J

ED: weorcæ (G) (*1st*)] weorca *Rosier.*

OE: hem (E³) (*1st*)] *orig.* him: i *altered to* e. arleasa (K)] *possibly glossing orig.* ipsorum (*see LTg and GAg*), *misread as* impiorum. nearoðancu<u>m</u> (D)] *orig.* nearoðoncu<u>m</u>: *2nd* o *deleted by subscript dot;* a *interl.* nearaþancum ł niðe (G)] ł niðe *added in diff.* (?) *hand above* neara. gegaderungum ł gemetednessa ł heora afundennysse (I)] etednessa *on eras.* gecneorþnisse ł tilengæ (E³/x)] gecneorþnisse ł *added by corr.* weorcæ (G) (*2nd*)] æ *added in diff.* (?) *hand; Rosier suggests* æ *altered from* a. agyld ł forgyf (I)] *orig.* agylt ł forgyf: t *altered to* d. agyld ł agyf (G)] ł agyf *added in diff.* (?) *hand.* hem (E³) (*3rd*)] *orig.* him: i *altered to* e.

LTg: Da] [ ]a G. eorum] K: *on eras. by corr.*, H: e *on eras.*, I: *scribe orig. wrote* & s, *then erased & and altered* s *to* e: *see GAg.* nequitiam] nequitias B, D: *orig.* nequitiam: s *interl. by corr. above* m, *but without deleting mark,* A: *orig.* nequitia: s *added interl. by corr.: cf. Weber MSS* MS *and* PRX. studiorum ipsorum] L: *underlined to signal deletion,* Secundum opera *written in left margin,* manuum eorum *added interl. by corr.: see GAg.* retribue] L: re *underlined to signal deletion: see GAg.* Redde] redde FGHIJK. retributionem] C: *eras. after 1st* i, K: *2nd* e *altered by corr. from* u.

LTu: nequitiam] nequitia ς: *cf. Weber MSS* MS *and* PRX. Redde] redde δεζϑιλμξοπρστφχψ.

GAg: eorum] ipsorum GJ, F: eorum *added interl. in later hand; for* HIK *see LTg.* studiorum] adinuentionum FGHIJK. ipsorum] ipsorum Secundum opera manuum eorum GHIJK, F: opera *added interl. in later hand; for* L *see LTg note to* studiorum ipsorum. retribue] tribue FGHIJK, L: *see LTg.*

GAu: eorum] ipsorum δϑμορυψ. studiorum] adinuentionum δεζϑιλμξοπρστυφχψ. ipsorum] ipsorum Secundum opera manuum eorum δεζϑιλμξοπρστυφχψ. retribue] tribue δεζιλμπρστυφχψ; tibuę ϑ.

5

quoniam		forðon AB, forþon C, forðam *F,* forðon þe E^3, forþam þe *G,* forðan þe *I,* forþon J (*HKL*)
non	|	ne C, na DFHK, hie ne ABE^3, hi ne GIJ
intellexerunt	|	ongetun AC, ongeton B, ongeæton E^3, ongeaton GJ, hy angeaton DH, hí ongeaton F, hi ongeatan K, ageatun I
in*		in A, on BD
opera	|	werc A, weorc BCDFGHJK, worc I, drihtnes E^3
domini	|	dryhtnes B, drihtnys C, drihtnes FI, drihttenes K, dryht̄ A, driħt G, driħ J, weorc E^3
et		⁊ ABCE^3FGIJK
in		in A, on BCE^3FGIJK
opera		werc A, weorc BC, weorcum F, worcum I, weorcæ G*, weorce J, weorca K, his worce E^3
manuum	|	honda AB, handa *C*DFGHIJK, his E^3
eius	|	his ABDFGHIJ*K,* hys C, honde E^3*
non*		ne ABC, na D, hie ne E^3 (*L*)
considerauerunt*		sceawiað *ABC**, hy besceawodon *D**, sceæwodon *E^3** (*L*)
Destrue*		toweorp AB, towurp C*J,* tobrec DHK, Tobrec E^3, tobræc F, toweorp ł tobrec G*, ðu tostencst I (*L*)
illos		hie ABCE^3, hy DGH, hí F, hi IK, hig J
(et)*		⁊ FGHIJK

nec*		ne ABCDE^{3}J, na GHK, ðu na I (*L*)
aedificabis	I	ðu timbres A, ðu timbrest *B,* þu getimbrast F, þu getimbrost *G,* þu ne getimbryst *C,* timbrast *J,* ðu getimbre *D,* þu getimbre *H,* getimbra *K,* gestaðolast I, þu hie ne E^{3} (*L*)
eos	I	hie AB, hy DGH, hí F, hi IK, hig J, him C, getimbre E^{3}

ED: forðon (A)] for ðon *Kuhn*. honde (E)] hond*e* *Harsley*. ędificabis (E)] aedificabis *Harsley*. hie (A) (*3rd*)] his *Kuhn*.

OE: weorcæ (G)] æ *possibly altered from* a. honde (E^{3})] de *in ligature*. sceawiað (C)] i *interl*. hy besceawodon (D)] *translating* considerauerunt, *not* considerant. sceæwodon (E^{3})] *eras. after word, perhaps from marginal gloss below*. toweorp ł tobrec (G)] toweorp ł *added in diff.* (?) *hand*.

LTg: quoniam] L: Q *added interl. above* q *by corr.;* Quoniam FGHIJK. manuum] manuvm C: v *interl*. eius] eíus K. non (*2nd*)] L: *underlined to signal deletion: see GAg*. considerauerunt] L: *underlined to signal deletion: see GAg;* considerant ABCDE: *cf. Weber MSS* MS βελ. Destrue] destrue J; Destrues L: *orig*. Destrue: s *added by corr.: see GAg*. nec] L: *underlined to signal deletion,* et non *added interl. by corr.: see GAg*. aedificabis] ædificabis B; ędificabis CDEH, K: *cauda added by corr.;* edificabis GJL.

LTu: quoniam] Quoniam δεζϑιλξοπϱτ*χψ. in (*2nd*)] β: *added in left margin; om*. ϑ. considerauerunt] considerant βςτ*: *cf. Weber MSS* MS βελ. Destrue] destrue δ; distrue ϑ. aedificabis] ędificabis δειξυφ; ædificabis ϑ; edificabis λνςτ*τ.

GAg: in (*1st*)] *om*. FGHIJK. non considerauerunt] *om*. FGHIJK, L: *see LTg*. Destrue] destrues FI, H: *final* s *added by corr.,* K: *final* s *added later by main hand;* dęstrues G; *for* L *see LTg*. illos] illos et FGHIJK, L: *see LTg note to* nec. nec] non FGHIJK, L: *see LTg*.

GAu: in (*1st*)] *om*. δεζϑιλμξοπϱστυφχψ. non considerauerunt] *om*. δεζϑιλμξοϱστυφχψ. Destrue] destrues ειλξοπϱστυφχψ, ζ: *2nd* s *added interl.;* distrues μ. illos] illos et δεζιλμξοπϱστυφχψ. nec] non δεζϑιλμξοπϱστυφχψ.

6

benedictus	gebledsad A, gebletsod BCD*GHK*, gebletsæd E^{3}, gebletsod is *F*, sy gebletsod *I**, gebletsod sy þu *J*
dominus	dryhten BD, drihtyn C, drihten E^{3}F, dryht̄ A, driħt G, driħ HJ, god K
quoniam	forðon AB, forþon CGJ, forþam K, forðon þe $E^{3/x}$*, forðam ðe F, forðan þe I
exaudiuit	geherde A, gehirde B, gehyrde F, he gehyrde CDGHIK, he gehierde E^{x}*, þu gehirdest J
uocem	stefne ABCDFGIK, stæfne HJ, stemne E^{3}

deprecationis	I	boene AB, bene CDFGHJK, halsunge ł mines gebedes ł minre bene I*, mines E^{3}
meae	I	minre *ACD*H, mine *BFGJ*, mire *K*, gebedes *E^{3}* (*L*)

ED: forðon (A)] for ðon *Kuhn*.

OE: sy gebletsod (I)] s. sit *written before* sy. forðon þe (E$^{3/x}$)] þe *added by corr.* he gehierde (E^{x})] *on eras. by corr.*, ge *eras. before* gehierde. halsunge ł mines gebedes ł minre bene (I)] *otiose mark above* mines.

LTg: benedictus] Benedictus FJK, I: *1st* e *malformed;* [ ]enedictus G, H: *initial* B *lost.* meae] meæ BCKL; meȩ ADFG; mee EJ.

LTu: benedictus] Benedictus δεζϑιλμξοπϱστυφχψ. deprecationis] depc̄ationis ϑμξϱστ*φχ; deprȩcationis β; deprecationis ο: *orig.* depraecationis: *1st* a *deleted;* depraecationis υψ. meae] meȩ ειvξϱφ; meæ ϑ; mee σςτ*τ.

7

Dominus		drihten K, dryht̄ AB*, drih́t CFG, drih́ J, drihten is E^{3}, is I*
adiutor	I	fultum ABCJ, gefylsta DFHI, gefylstend ł fultum G*, fylst K, min E^{3}
meus	I	min AB*CFGIJK, fultum E^{3}*
et		⁊ ABCE^{3}FGIJK
protector	I	gescildend A, gescyldynd C, gescyldend DFGHI*, scildend BJ, frofer K, min E^{3}
meus	I	min ABCF*G*JK, ⁊ min I, scyldend E^{3}
et		⁊ ABCE^{3}HIJ (*FGK*)
in		in A, on BCDE^{3}FGHIJK
ipso		hine ABCE^{3}GI*J, him DFH, him K
sperauit		gehyhteð AB, gehihteð G, gehihteþ J, gehihte CI, gehyhte DH, gehyhte ł geweneþ E$^{3/x}$*, ic hopude F*, hiht K
cor	I	heorte ABCFGIJK, min E^{3}
meum	I	min ABCFGIJK, heorte E^{3}
et		⁊ ABCE^{3}*FGHIJK
adiutus		gefultumad AI, gefultumod BE$^{3/x}$*FGHJK, gefultumod D, gefultumud C
sum		ic eam A, ic eom BDE^{x}*FIJK, ic eom C
Et		⁊ A*B*CE^{3}FGHIJK
refloruit		bleow ABCDGHIJK, bleów F, blostmæt ł bleow E$^{3/x}$*
caro	I	flęsc A, flæsc BCDFGHIJ, flæcs K, min E^{3}
mea	I	min ABDFGHIJK, minum C, flesc E^{3}

et		⁊ ABCDE^{3}FGHIJK
ex		of ABCDE^{3}FGHIJK
uoluntate	I	willan ABCDFGHIJK, minum E^3
mea	I	minum AFHI, minum D, minum ł min G*, min BCJ, minan K, willum E^3
confitebor		ic ondetto A, ic ondette BE^3, ic andytte C, ic andette DFGHIJK
illi*		him ABCE^{3}FGIJ, him DK

ED: drihten is (E)] Drihten is *Harsley.* gescyldend (I)] gescildend *Lindelöf.* meus et (I) (*2nd*)] meus *Lindelöf.* meum (G)] meam *Rosier.*

OE: dryht̄ (B)] *water stain at bottom of* h. is (I)] ÷ (= est) *written in bowl of* D *in* Dominus. gefylstend ł fultum (G)] ł fultum *added in diff.* (?) *hand, with* tum *written above following* min. min (B)] *left leg of* m *obscured by water stain.* fultum (E^3)] *eras. after word.* gescyldend (I)] *orig.* gescildend: i *altered to* y. hine (I)] *orig.* him: *right leg of* m *used to form back of* e, *added in light brown ink.* gehyhte ł geweneþ (E$^{3/x}$)] gehyhte ł *added by corr.* ic hopude (F)] ic *faint but visible.* ⁊ gefultumod (E$^{3/x}$)] *top stroke of* ⁊ *retraced in darker ink,* gefultu *retraced in darker ink,* mod *added by corr., eras. between* ⁊ *and* ge. ic com (E^x)] *on eras.* blostmæt ł bleow (E$^{3/x}$)] blostmæt *partly retraced in darker ink,* ł bleow *added by corr.* minum ł min (G)] ł min *written in diff.* (?) *hand above* minum.

LTg: meus (*2nd*)] meu[ ] G. et (*2nd*)] FG: *added in later hand in left margin,* K: *added in left margin by corr.* Et] et B.

LTu: protector] protecttor ς (protect-/-tor): *orig.* protector: *2nd* t *added in left margin.* et (*2nd*)] ζ: *added interl.* Et] et ς.

GAg: illi] ei FGHIJK.

GAu: illi] ei δεζϑιλμξοπϱστυφχψ.

8

Dominus		drihten F, dryht̄ AB, driħt C, driħ *G*J, drihtnes E^3
fortitudo		strengo ABCDH, stranga K, strengðe F, strengðo E^{3}G, strengð I, getranga J (*L*)
plebis	I	folces ABDFGHK, folcys CI, folc J, his E^3*
suae	I	his A*BCDFGH*I*JK,* folce *E^3* (*L*)
et		⁊ ABCE^{3}FGHIJK
protector		gescildend A, gescyldynd C, gescyldend D, gescyldend GHI*, gescyld E^3, scildend BJ, bewerigend F, frofer K
salutarium*	I	ðeara halwendra A, þara halwendra B*C,* halwendra G, halwændra J, haligra DF, alesednessa ł hælu I, crist E^3 (*L*)

christi | cristes ABI, cristys C, cristenan J, cyninges DG, cyningces F, cyninge H, hiora E^{3}

sui | his ABCDFHIJ, he is ł cristenan his G, helo E^{3}

est is ABCE^{3}FGIJ, he is DH (*K*)

ED: drihtnes (E)] Drihtnes *Harsley.* suę (E)] suae *Harsley.* christi (K)] Christi *Sisam.*

OE: his (E^{3})] hi *blotted at base.* gescyldend (I)] *orig.* gescildend: i *altered to* y.

LTg: Dominus] [ ]ominus G. fortitudo] L: *2nd* o *malformed.* suae] suę BCDEFH; sue GJK; suæ L. salutarium] C: ta *interl.*, L: ationum *added interl. by corr. above* tarium: *see GAg.* est] ést K.

LTu: fortitudo] ϑ: ti *interl.* suae] suę εζιξφ; suæ ϑ; sue σςτ*τ.

GAg: salutarium] saluationum FGHIJ, K: *2nd* u *on eras. by corr.*, L: *see LTg.*

GAu: salutarium] saluationum δεζϑιλμξοπϱστυφχψ.

9

Saluum | hal ABCDGHK, gehæl F, gehæl ł I*, hal þu J, Gedo E^{3}

fac | doo A, dóó C, dó B, do DGHJK, hæl E^{3}

populum* | folc ABCDFGHIJK, þin E^{3}

tuum* | ðin AFI, þin BCDGHJK, folc E^{3}

domine* drihtyn C, drihten E^{3}F, dryht̄ AB, driht́ G, drih́ J (*IK*)

et ⁊ ABCE^{3}FGHIJK

benedic bledsa AC, bletsa BDFGHJK, gebletsæ E^{3}, gebletsa I

hereditatem* | erfweardnisse *A*B, yrfeweardnysse *C,* yrfeweardnisse *D,* yrfweardnyssa F, yrfeweardnesse GJ, yrfeweardnysse I, erfwerdnes K*, þine *E^{3}* (*L*)

tuam* | ðine *A**BI, þine CFGJ, þin K, hyrfeweærdnesse *E^{3}* (*DL*)

et ⁊ ABCDE^{3}FGHIJK

rege rece ABC, rice J, gerece hy ł rice G, gerece DE^{3}HK, gerece þu F, gerece G, gerece ł gewissa I

eos hie ABE^{3}, hi CK, hy DGH, hig F, his J

et ⁊ ABCDE^{3}FGHIJK

extolle uphefe ABJ, upahefe G*I, uppahefe C, ahefe ⁊ ahefe D*, ahefe FHK, genim ł ahefe E$^{3/x}$*

illos hic ABE^{3}, hi CF*K*, hy DG, hig IJ

usque oð *B*CFGHI, oþ DJK, oþþe E^{3}

in on DBCE^{3}FGHJK

saeculum* weorolde *B,* worulde *C,* world ł on ecnisse *E$^{3/x}$**, ecnisse *D,* ecnysse FI, ecnesse HJK, ecnesse ł on worulde G

ED: populum (B)] plebem *Brenner.* hęreditati (E)] haereditati *Harsley.* tuę (E)] tuae *Harsley.* erfweardnisse (B)] erfweardnesse *Brenner.* [ ](sq)ue (B)] usque *Brenner.* œternum (D)] aeternum *Roeder.* ęternvm (E)] aeternum *Harsley.*

OE: gehæl ł (I)] *eras.* (?) *after* ł. erfwerdnes (K)] *orig.* erfwerdnesne: *final* ne *eras.* ðine (A)] i *written below line.* upahefe (G)] upahéfe (?). ahefe ⁊ ahefe (D)] *1st* ahefe *appears on fol. 35r,* ⁊ ahefe *on fol. 35v;* ex *in* extolle *appears on fol. 35r,* tolle *on fol. 35v.* genim ł ahefe ($E^{3/x}$)] ł ahefe *added by corr.* world ł on ecnisse ($E^{3/x}$)] ł on ecnisse *added by corr.*

LTg: domine] K: *added interl. by main hand,* I: o *written above word.* hereditatem] hereditati CDL, A: *orig.* hereditatem: i *interl. above final* e *in later insular hand;* hęreditati E: *cf. Weber MSS* Xε mozx, *see GAg.* tuam] tuę CE; tue D; tuae L, A: *orig.* tuam: e *interl. in later insular hand: cf. Weber MSS* Xε mozx, *see GAg.* illos] K: ill *written by corr. on eras.* usque] [ ](sq)ue B: *initial letter lost* (*fragments visible*), *descenders of* s *and* q *lost due to excision of initial from Ps 28.* saeculum] sæculum B; seculum C: ł in eternum *added in main hand, underlined* (*except* ł) *by another hand in brown ink;* æternum D; ęternvm E: *cf. Weber MSS* med, *see GAg.*

LTu: domine] ζ: *added interl.: see GAu.* hereditatem] hereditati νςτ*: *cf. Weber MSS* Xε mozx, *see GAu.* tuam] tuę ν; tue ςτ*: *cf. Weber MSS* Xε mozx, *see GAu.* et (*2nd*)] Et ϑ. saeculum] sæclm ϑ; seculum ς; ęternum ν; eternum τ*: *cf. Weber MSS* med, *see GAu.*

GAg: hereditatem] hereditati FGHIJK, ADL; *for* E *see LTg.* tuam] tuę FGH, E: *see LTg;* tue K, D: *see LTg;* tuae IJ, AL: *see LTg.* saeculum] ęternum FGH, L; eternum J; aeternum I; æternum K, D: *see LTg; for* E *see LTg.*

GAu: populum tuum] plebem tuam ϑ. domine] *om.* δοψ; *for* ζ *see LTu.* hereditatem] hereditati δζϑλμξοπστυχψ, νςτ*: *see LTu;* hęreditati ειϱφ. tuam] tuae δλμοπϱχψ; tuę εζιξσυφ, ν: *see LTu;* tuæ ϑ; tue τ, ςτ*: *see LTu.* saeculum] ęternum δεζιξφ, ν: *see LTu;* aeternum λμοπϱυχψ; eternum στ, τ*: *see LTu.*

PSALM 28

1

Adferte		tobringað *A,* tobringaþ *J,* bringað *CDGHI,* bryngað *F,* bringaþ *K,* gebringað *Ex,* [ ]ngað *B** (*L*)
domino		to dryhtne A, to drihtny *C,* to drihtne G, dryhtne BD, drihtne E3FHI, drihtene K, driħ J
filii	|	bearn AB*C*DFGHJ, bearn ł eala ge suna I*, sunu K, godes *E3*
dei	|	godes ABFGIJK, godys C, beærn E3
adferte		tobringað *A*B, tobringaþ *J,* bringað *CGK,* bryngað *F,* gebrengæð *E3** (*DHIL*)
domino		to drihtne C, to dryhŧ A, tó dri[ ] G, dryhtne B, drihtne E3F, driħ J

filios | bearn ABCDHJK, bearn ł suna I, sunu F, weþræs ł romma $E^{3/x}$*
arietum | romma AB, ramma *CDFHIJK*, [ ]a G, beærn E^{3}

ED: filíí (E)] filii *Harsley*. tó dri[ ] (G)] to dri[ ] *Rosier*. filios arietum (G)] *filios arie*tum *Rosier*. aríętum (H)] ariętum *Campbell*.

OE: [ ]ngað (B)] *letters lost due to excision of decorated initial from Lat. line*. bearn ł eala ge suna (I)] o *written before* bearn, ł eala ge suna *written in left margin*. gebrengæð (E^{3})] *lower portions of* ge *retraced in darker ink*. weþræs ł romma ($E^{3/x}$)] s ł romma *written by corr., eras. before* r, a *partly on eras.* (*altered from another letter?*).

LTg: Adferte] Afferte AFIJKL, H: *1st* f *on eras. by corr.*, D: *orig.* Adferte: f *written above* d *by 12th-c. hand: for other examples of same hand see OE note to Ps 2.8* anwaldnesse; AFFERTE CE; [ ]fferte G; [ ]te B: *letters lost due to excision of decorated initial*. domino (*1st*)] DN̄O C. filii] FILII C; filíí E. adferte] afferte ACEFGIJKL, H: *1st* f *on eras. by corr.*, D: *orig.* adferte: d *deleted by subscript dot*, f *interl. by 12th-c. hand: see OE note to Ps 2.8* anwaldnesse. arietum] aríetum C; aríętum H.

LTu: Adferte] ADferte β; ADFERTE μ; ADFERte ς; Afferte εζουχ; AFFERTE ιλνξπρστ*τφ. domino (*1st*)] DN̄O λμνξπρ. filii] FILII λμνξπρ. dei] DEI λμξπρ. adferte] afferte ειvορστ*τυφχ; AFFERTE λξπ. domino (*2nd*)] DOMINO π; DN̄O λξ. filios] ζ: s *interl.*; FILIOS ξ. arietum] ARIETUM ξ.

2

Adferte — tobringað *A*, tobringaþ *J*, [ ]bringað *B**, bringað *CG*, bryngað *F*, bringaþ *K*, Gebrengæð E^{3}* (*DHIL*)
domino — to drihtne C, to dryht̄ A, to driħt G, dryhtne B, drihtne E^{3}F, driħ J
gloriam — wuldur ACDH, wuldor BE^{3}FGIJK
et — ⁊ ABCE^{x}*FGH*I*JK
honorem — are AB, are oððe wurðmynt C, weorðmynt F, wyrðmynt IK, arwyrðunge D*, arwurðunge E^{x}*, arw[ ]rðú[ ] *H**, árwurðe ł áre G*
adferte — tobringað *A*, tobringaþ *J*, bringað *CG*, bryngað *F*, bringaþ *K*, gebrengæð E^{3} (*BDHIL*)
domino — to drihtny C, to dryht̄ A, to driħt G, drihten E^{3}, drihtne FI, drihtene K, driħ J (*B*)
gloriam — wuldur A, wuldor BCFGIJK, wundor E^{3}
nomini | noman AB, naman CDFGHIJK, his E^{3}
eius | his ABDFGHIJ*K*, hys C, næmon E^{3}
adorate — wearðiað *A*, wurðiað *C*, wurþiaþ *J*, gebiddaþ *DIK*, Gebiddæþ E^{3}, gebiddað F*H*, togebiddað ł weorðiað G* (*BL*)

dominum		drihtyn C, drihten E^3, drihtne F, dryht̄ A, driħt G, driħ J, to drihtne I, [ ]ten B*
in		in A, on BCDE^{3}FGIJK
aula*	I	halle A, healle BCDGJK, cafertune FI, his E^3 (_L_)
sancta*		ðere halgan A, ðære halgan B*, þære halgan C, haligre D, hæligre E^x*, halgum FG, halgum̲ J, halgan I, halire K (_L_)
eius	I	his ABCFGIJ_K_, hælla E$^{3/x}$*

ED: honore[ ] (H)] honorem _Campbell._ arw[ ]rðú[ ] (H)] arwurðun(ge) _Campbell._ ador[ ]te (H)] adorate _Campbell._

OE: [ ]bringað (B)] _letters lost due to excision of decorated initial from Lat. line of v. 1._ Gebrengæð (E^3)] Ge _and ascender of_ b _retraced in darker ink._ ⁊ (E^x)] _on eras._ arwyrðunge (D)] n _interl._ arwurðunge (E^x)] _on eras._ arw[ ]rðú[ ] (H)] _letter after_ w _lost due to hole in leaf, minim visible after_ ú. árwurðe ł áre (G)] ł áre _interl. above_ árwurðe. togebiddað ł weorðiað (G)] ł weorðiað _added in diff._ (?) _hand._ [ ]ten (B)] _letters lost due to excision of decorated initial from Lat. line of v. 1, cross-stroke of_ t _not visible._ ðære halgan (B)] _1st_ a _written below line._ hæligre (E^x)] hæli _on eras._ hælla (E$^{3/x}$)] lla _on eras. by corr._

LTg: Adferte] Afferte ACEFGIJKL, H: _1st_ f _on eras. by corr.,_ D: _orig._ Adferte: d _deleted by subscript dot,_ f _interl. by 12th-c. hand: see OE note to Ps 2.8_ anwaldnesse; [ ]ferte B: _letters lost due to excision of decorated initial from v. 1, letter fragment visible before_ f. et] I: _eras. above word._ honorem] honore[ ] H: _final letter lost due to hole in leaf._ adferte] B: _word and gloss lost due to excision of decorated initial at beginning of v. 1;_ afferte ACEFGIJKL, H: _1st_ f _on eras. by corr.,_ D: _orig._ adferte: d _deleted by subscript dot,_ f _interl. by 12th-c. hand: see OE note to Ps 2.8_ anwaldnesse. domino (_2nd_)] B: _word and gloss lost due to excision of decorated initial at beginning of v. 1, letter fragment visible._ eius (_1st_)] eíus K. adorate] B: _word and gloss lost due to excision of decorated initial at beginning of v. 1,_ K: _1st_ a _altered from_ o, L: _orig._ Adorate: A _crossed through and_ a _written to right;_ ador[ ]te H: _letter lost due to hole in leaf;_ Adorate ACDE; adhorate J. aula] L: atrio _written interl. by corr.: see GAg._ sancta] L: o _written interl. by corr.: see GAg._ eius (_2nd_)] eíus K.

LTu: Adferte] Afferte εζιλνξοπϱστ*τυφχ. honorem] horem ψ. adferte] afferte εζιλνξοπϱστ*τυφχ. adorate] Adorate βνςτ*.

GAg: aula] atrio FGHIJK, L: _see LTg._ sancta] sancto FGHIJK, L: _see LTg._

GAu: aula sancta] atrio sancto δεζθιλμξοπϱστυφχψ.

3

Uox	I	stefn _AB*CDFGHI,_ stæfn J, stefne K, drihtnes _E^3_
domini	I	dryhtnes B*, drihtnys C, drihtnes _F_G, drihtnys I, dryht̄ A, driħ J, stem E^3

super ofer ABDE^{3}FGHIJK, ofyr C
aquas weter *A*, wæter GJ, wætyru C*, wæteru DFH, weteru E^3*, wætru I*, wætera K (*B*)
deus god *A*BCFGJK, ⁊ godes E^3
maiestatis megendrymmes *A*, mægenðrymmes B, mægynþry<u>m</u>nys C, mægenþry<u>m</u>mes D, mægnþrymmes F, mægenþrymmes GH, mægðrymnysse I, mægenþrymme J, mæþrymmes K, megenþrym E^3
intonuit hleoðrað AB, hleoþriaþ J, hleoðrode C, swegde DF*H*K, onswegde ł hleoðraþ G*, onaswegde I*, ontyneþ ł onswegde E$^{3/x}$* (*L*)
dominus drihtyn C, drihten E^{3}GK, dreyht̄ A, dryh̓(t) B*, drih̓t *F*, drih̓ *J*
super ofer *A*BDFGHIJK, ofyr C, ofor E^3
aquas | weter A, wæter BGJ, wæteru DFH, wætrv C, wætru I, wæteras K, monigo E^3
multas | micel A, micle BC, miccle J, manegu D, manegum H, manega FI, managa K, manega ł micle G*, weteru E^3*

ED: uox (BE)] Vox *Brenner;* vox *Harsley.* domini (F)] domini est *Kimmens: see LTg.* mægenþrymme (J)] mægenþrimme *Oess.* dominus (F)] dominus est *Kimmens: see LTg.*

OE: stefn (B)] t *and* f *obscured,* n *faint but visible.* dryhtnes (B)] tn *nearly lost, right leg of* h *faint but visible.* wætyru (C)] u *added later in red ink.* weteru (E^3) (*1st*)] u *added by corr.* wætru (I)] est : is *written in left margin.* onswegde ł hleoðraþ (G)] ł hleoðraþ *added in diff.* (?) *hand.* onaswegde (I)] s. intonuit : swegde *written in right margin.* ontyneþ ł onswegde (E$^{3/x}$)] ł onswegde *added by corr. below* ontyneþ. dryh̓(t) (B)] *cross-stroke of* t *not visible.* manega ł micle (G)] ł micle *added in diff.* (?) *hand.* weteru (E^3) (*2nd*)] u *added by corr.*

LTg: Uox] uox ABCD, E: *eras. above word;* Vox FGHI. domini] domini est F: est *interl., possibly by hand that added late glosses to v. 5.* aquas (*1st*)] A: *added by corr., s cropped on right;* [ ]quas B: *initial letter and gloss lost due to excision of decorated initial at beginning of v. 1, tail of initial letter visible.* deus] A: *eras. before word (4–5 letters).* maiestatis] A: *eras. after word (2–3 letters).* intonuit] L: *orig.* et intonuit: et *crossed through;* intonu[ ] H: *final letters lost due to hole in leaf.* dominus] J: n *altered from another letter and on eras.;* dominus est F: est *interl., possibly by hand that added late glosses to v. 5.* super (*2nd*)] A: *orig.* sup<u>er</u>: er *added interl. by corr.*

LTu: Uox] Vox ιλξοϱσ; uox βνςτ*. dominus] σ: *interl.*

4
Uox | stefn A*B*CD*FGH*, stæfn J, stefne *K*, stemn *I*, drihtnes *E*^{3}
domini | dryhtnes B, drihtnys C, drihtnes *F*, dryht̄ A, drih̓t G, drih̓ J, stem E^3

in		in A, on BCDE^{3}FGHIJK
uirtute		megne A, mægne J, mægene BDGHI*, mægyne C, megene E^3, milite F, strenþe K
uox	I	stefn ABCFG, stæfn J, is stemn I*, drihtnes E^3
domini	I	dryhtnes B, drihtnys C, drihtnes *F,* dryhτ̄ A, driħ GJ, stem E^3
in		in A, on B*CDE^{3}FGHIJK
magnificentia		micelnisse *A,* micelnesse B*, mycelnysse *C,* micelnessæ E^3, micelnesse J, g̲e̲miclunga D, gemiclunga H, gemyclunga K, mærsungum F, gemicclunge ł on miceln[ ] G*, micelnysse ł on gemiclunga ł on mærsunge I

ED: drihtnes (E) (*1st*)] Drihtnes *Harsley.* stemn (I)] *no gloss Lindelöf.* domini (F) (*both*)] domini est *Kimmens: see LTg.*

OE: mægene (I)] e̲s̲t̲ : is *written in left margin.* is stemn (I)] s. e̲s̲t̲ *written before* is. on (B) (*2nd*)] o *fragmentary.* micelnesse (B)] *right leg of* m *faint.* gemicclunge ł on miceln[ ] (G)] ł on miceln[ ] *added in diff.* (?) *hand.*

LTg: Uox] Vox BEFGHIK. domini (*both*)] domini est F: est *interl. possibly by hand that added late glosses to v. 5.* magnificentia] A: *orig.* magnificentiam: *final* m *eras.;* magnificæntia C.

LTu: Uox] Vox ειν ξςτ*υφ. magnificentia] magnificentiam β: *final* m *added by corr.*

5

Uox	I	stefn *ABCFGH,* stæfn *J,* drihtnes *E^3* (*DIL*)
domini	I	dryhtnes B*, drihtnys C, drihtnes F, dryhτ̄ A, driħt G, driħ J, stem E^3
confringentis		gebreocendes A, gebrecendes *B,* gebrecyndys C, gebrecende E^3, forbrecendis DH, forbrecendes F, forbrocen is G, forbrecende *K,* tobrysiende ł tobrytendes I*, gebringende J
cedros		cederbeamas AB, cederbeamys C, ceodorbeamas I*, ceadarbeamas J, cederbeam F*, þone cedorbeæm E^3, lang̲e̲ stefnas D, lange stefnas *H,* lange stefnas ł cederbeamas *G*,* cedertreow K
et		⁊ ABCDE^{3}FGHIJK
confringet	I	gebriceð *A,* gebricð B, tobrycð C, tobrecð ł tobryt I, forbrihð D, forbryhð H, forbricð F, forbrit K, forbrynð ł gebrycð G*, gebringaþ J, drihten E^3
dominus	I	drihtyn C, drihten IK, dryhτ̄ A, driħt FG, driħ J, dryht[ ] B*, gebriceð E^3

cedros	cederbeamas AC*G*J, cederbeam F*I, cederas DE^{x}, cedras *H* (*L*)
libani	| ðes muntes A, ðæs muntes BC, þæs muntes IIJ, þæs muntas G, ðæs holtes F, þæs holtes I, of libani E^{x}

ED: drihtnes (E)] Drihtnes *Harsley*. confringentes (B)] confringentis *Brenner.* lange stefnas (H)] langestefnas *Campbell.* dryht[ ] (B)] dryhten *Brenner.* libani (K)] Libani *Sisam.*

OE: dryhtnes (B)] tn *malformed.* tobrysiende ł tobrytendes (I)] *eras. after* i. ceodorbeamas (I)] e<u>st</u> : is *written in left margin.* cederbeam (F) (*1st*)] *below gloss is written* cedirtriu *in later cursive hand, possibly same that added* est *interl. in vv 3–4.* lange stefnas ł cederbeamas (G)] ł cederbeamas *added in diff.* (?) *hand.* forbrynð ł gebrycð (G)] ł gebrycð *added in diff.* (?) *hand.* dryht[ ] (B)] *with exception of* h *letters faint.* cederbeam (F) (*2nd*)] *below gloss is written* cedirtreu *in later cursive hand, possibly same that added* est *interl. in vv 3–4.*

LTg: Uox] Vox ABCDEFGHIJL. confringentis] K: *orig.* confringentes: *2nd* e *altered to* i; confringentes B. cedros (*1st*)] cędros GH. confringet] A: *orig.* confringit: *2nd* i *altered to* e. cedros (*2nd*)] cędros GHL.

LTu: Uox] Vox εζινξοϱστ*τφ. cedros (*1st*)] cędros εν; caedros ζμ; cædros χ. confringet] confringit β. cedros (*2nd*)] cędros ενχ; caedros ζμ. libani] lybani ε.

6

Et	⁊ *ABCE*^{x}*FGHIJK (*DL*)
comminuet	gescæneð AB, gescænyð C, gescæneð gewanað H, scæneþ ł gewanaþ J, forgnideþ *D*, forgnideð E^{x}*, forgnidæt *K*, forcnýdeþ F, forgnidet ł gewánað G*, he tocwiesð ł gelytlað I*
eas	hie *A*BE^{3}*, hi *CFK*, hy *DG*, hyg *H*, hig *IJ* (*L*)
tamquam	swe swe A, swa swa B*C*DFG*H*IJ, swæ swæ *E*^{3}*, swa K
uitulum	caelf A, cealf BC*DGHIJK, cealfas F, þet sceælf E^{3}
libani	þæs muntys C, þæs muntes HJ, ðæs holtes F, þæs holtes GI, on libani E^{x}*
et	⁊ ABCDE^{3}**F*GHJK, ⁊ is I*
dilectus	se leofa *AB*C*H, leofne *D*E^{x}*K, leof G, gecorena F, se leofesta ł se gelufoda I, seo leofa ł gecorena J* (*L*)
sicut*	swe swe A, swa swa BCI, swæ swæ *E*^{3}*, on ðam gemete F, on þa<u>m</u> gemete J, ealswa K
filius	sunu *A*BDGHI*J*K, bearn *C*F, beærn *E*^{3}* (*L*)
unicornuorum*	anhyrnra ABH, anhyrneráá C, anhyrna J, anhyrne K, anhyrnedra DI*, anhyrnendra F, anhyrnede ł anhyrna G*, ænhyrnedes diores E^{3}*

ED: tanquam (C)] ta[m]quam *Wildhagen*. swa swa (GIJ) (*1st*)] swaswa *Rosier, Lindelöf, Oess*. libani (K)] Libani *Sisam*. swa swa (I) (*2nd*)] swaswa *Lindelöf*. dilectus (D)] dilectu(m) *Roeder*.

OE: ꝧ (E^{x}) (*1st*)] *on eras*. forgnideð (E^{x})] *eras. after word*. forgnidet ł gewánað (G)] ł gewánað *added in diff*. (?) *hand*. he tocwiesð ł gelytlað (I)] gelytlað *orig*. gelitlað: i *altered to* y. hie (E^{3})] *eras. after word*. swæ swæ (E^{3}) (*1st*)] *1st* sw *retraced in darker ink*. cealf (C)] a *interl*. on libani (E^{x})] *on eras*. ꝧ (E^{3}) (*2nd*)] *eras. after word*. ꝧ is (I)] s. est *written after* is. leofne (E^{x})] *on eras., with eras. extending beyond word*. seo leofa ł gecorena (J)] *otiose mark after* gecorena. anhyrnedra (I)] *eras. after* e. swæ swæ (E^{3}) (*2nd*)] *2nd* s *retraced in darker ink*. beærn (E^{3})] *eras. above* rn *and continuing beyond word*. anhyrnede ł anhyrna (G)] ł anhyrna *added in diff*. (?) *hand*. ænhyrnedes diores (E^{3})] *eras. before* ænhyrnedes, es (*both*) *on eras. by corr.*

LTg: Et] et ABCDEL. comminuet] D: *orig*. comminuit: *2nd* i *altered to* e *by corr.: see OE note to Ps 2.8* anwaldnesse; comminuæt K. eas] AG: a *on eras*., K: a *on eras. by corr.*, HL: *orig*. eos: o *altered to* a, I: *eras. at shoulder and bottom back of* a (*attempt to alter to* eos?); eos CE, D: *orig*. eas: a *altered to* o *by corr.: see OE note to Ps 2.8* anwaldnesse. tamquam] tanquam C: *orig*. tamquam: *left leg of 1st* m *eras. to form* n, H: *small eras. after* n. et] F: *illegible word written interl. by same hand that added late glosses to v. 5*. dilectus] A: u *on eras*., D: *orig*. dilectu: s *added by corr.: see OE note to Ps 2.8* anwaldnesse, L: *orig*. dilectum: m *crossed through*, s *interl. by corr.;* dilectum C. sicut] E: *on eras*. filius] A: u *on eras*., L: *orig*. filios: o *deleted by subscript dot*, u *interl. by corr.;* filios CEJ: *cf. Weber MS* P.

LTu: Ėt] et βνςτ*. comminuet] comminuit β. eas] eos βζ; dominus ς. tamquam] tanquam ϑιλτ*τφ. libani] lybani ε. dilectus] delectus β: *orig*. dilectus: i *altered to* e. filius] filias ς.

GAg: sicut] quemadmodum FGHJK; quemammodum I. unicornuorum] unicornium FGHIJK.

GAu: sicut] quemadmodum δεζϑιλμξοπϱστυφχψ. unicornuorum] unicornium δεζϑλμξοϱσυχψ; unicornvum ιπ: *orig*. unicornium: *2nd* i *deleted*, v *interl.;* unicornuum τφ.

7

Uox	ǀ	stefn AC*F*G, stæfn *HJ*, [ ]t[ ] *B**, drihten *E^{3}* (*IK*)
domini	ǀ	dryhtnes B*, drihtnys C, drihtnes F, dryhꝉ A, driħt G, drihꝉ H, driħ J, stem E^{3}
intercidentis		betwihgongendes A**B**, betwihgongyndys *C*, tosceadendis *DF*, tosceaddendis E^{x}*, toscædende is *K*, tosceaden is ł betweohceorfendes *G**, ł forceorfendes I*, betweohceorfendes *HJ*

flammam | legfyr AB, lægfyr H, leg CDE^{x}*K, lég F, lyg G, lig I, ligræsc J
ignis | fyrys C, fýres *F,* fyrcs DGIK, fircs J, þæm fire E^{3}

ED: [ ]t[ ] (B)] stefn *Brenner.* drihten (E)] Drihten *Harsley.* intercidentis (C)] intercedentis *Wildhagen.* intercidentis (D)] interc[e]dentis *Roeder.* betweohceorfendes (HJ)] betweoh ceorfendes *Campbell, Oess.* flammam (G)] flamman *Rosier.* legfyr (B)] leg fyr *Brenner.* lægfyr (H)] læg fyr *Campbell.* ignis est (F)] ignis *Kimmens.*

OE: [ ]t[ ] (B)] *only* t *and letter fragments visible.* dryhtnes (B)] *faint but visible.* betwihgongendes (AB)] *lemma misread as* intercedentis (?): *see also* C. tosceaddendis (E^{x})] *on eras.* tosceaden is ł betweohceorfendes (G)] ł betweohceorfendes *added in diff.* (?) *hand.* ł forceorfendes (I)] *word eras. before* ł. leg (E^{x})] *on eras.*

LTg: Uox] Vox BEFHIJK. intercidentis] C: *orig.* intercedentes: *2nd* e *altered to* i, G: *eras. after 2nd* i, H: *2nd* i *altered from another letter,* D: *orig.* intercedentis: *2nd* e *altered to* i *by main hand,* F: *orig.* intercidentes: *3rd* e *deleted by subscript dot,* i *interl.,* K: *2nd* i *on eras. by corr.;* intercedentis BJ. ignis] ignis est F: est *interl., possibly by hand that added late glosses to v. 5.*

LTu: Uox] Vox ιvξσςτ*τ. intercidentis] intercedentis ϑ.

8

uox stefn A*C*FG, stæfn HJ, stęfn E^{x}*, ste(f)[ ] B*, is stemn I*
domini drihtnys C, drihtnes E^{3}FH, d[ ]yht[ ]es B*, dryhт̄ A, drih̄ GJ
concutientis tosaecendes A, toscæcyndys C, tosceacyndes *I,* tosceacende F, tos[ ]end[ ] B*, toscecendes astah H, tosettendes astah *J,* hrysiendis DE^{x}*, hrysigendis G, hrysigende *K*
solitudinem* bihygdignisse A, bihygdignesse B, behydignys C, westen DGHIJK, wésten F, on westen E$^{3/x}$*
et ך ABCE^{3}*FG*H*IJK
commouebit onstyreð A, onstyryð C, astyreð DG, onstyrede B, onstired *H,* astyred E^{x}*, astired J, astyrod bið F, astyrað ł towent I, astyraþ K
dominus drihtyn C, drihten E^{3}*K, dryhт̄ AB, drih̄t FG, drih̄ *HJ*
desertum | woesten A, westen BDG*I*IK, westyn C, on westen F, of westen J, onwendeþ westen E^{3}
cades feallað F, fealleð J, þæs landes G, feldes ł ðæs landes I, gefeællende E^{3} (*HK*)

ED: ste(f)[ ] (B)] stefn *Brenner.* d[ ]yht[ ]es (B)] dryhtnes *Brenner.* tos[ ]end[ ] (B)] tos..cend.. *Brenner.* drih̄ (H)] drih̄t *Campbell.* desertum (G)] desert*um Rosier.* cadés (K)] Cades *Sisam.*

OE: stęfn (E^x)] *on eras., e eras. after word, tongue of which intersects following* d. ste(f)[ ] (B)] *top of* f *visible, final letter lost.* is stemn (I)] e<u>st</u> *interl. before* is. d[ ]yht[ ]es (B)] d *faint, following letter lost,* e *faint.* tos[ ]end[ ] (B)] *letter fragments visible after* s. hrysiendis (E^x)] *on eras.* on westen ($E^{3/x}$)] westen *on eras.* ⁊ (E^3)] *eras. after word.* astyred (E^x)] *on eras.* drihten (E^3)] ⁊ *eras. before word.*

LTg: uox] C: x *on eras.* concutientis] I: *eras. above word,* K: *2nd* c *altered from another letter by main hand;* concutientes J. et commouebit dominus desertum cades] H: *added by corr.* cades] cadés K.

GAg: solitudinem] desertum FGHIJK.

GAu: solitudinem] desertum δεϑιλμξοπϱστυφχψ; dertum ζ.

9

Uox | stefn A*B*CF*G*, stæfn J, drihtnes *E*^{3} (*DHIL*)
domini | dryhtnes B, drihtnys C, drihtnes F, dryht̄ A, drih̄t G, drih̄ J, stem E^3
praeparantis gearwiendes A, gearwiyndys *C,* gearwigendes *DJ,* gearwiendes *F,* gegearwigendes *B,* gegearwigendis *G**, geærwiende *E*^{3}, gearwigende *K,* wearwigendes *H,* gearciendes *I* (*L*)
ceruos heoretas A, heortas BCDGHI*K, heorttas F, heortes J, þæ heortes E^3
et ⁊ ABCDE^3FGHI*JK
reuelabit biwrah *A*B,* bewrieh *C,* awriht *D,* awrihð FH*K,* onwreah G, unwreah J, he unwrihð I, to ónwreonne E^3*
condensa ða ðiccan A*, þa ðiccan B, þa þiccan CGJ, þyccettu D, þiccettu F, þyctectu H, þiccettu ł hioræ den $E^{3/x}$*, þiccetu ł ðicnyssa I
et ⁊ ABCE^3FGHIJK
in in A, on BCDE^3FGHIJK
templo | temple ABCFGHIJK, te<u>m</u>ple D, his E^3
eius | his ABCFGHIJ*K,* temple E^3 (*D*)
omnes* alle A, ealle BCDFG*HJK,* eælle E^3, ælc *I**
dicent* cweoðað AB, cweðað CFG, cweþæþ E^3, cwedaþ J, cweð D*HI,* cweþað *K*
gloriam wuldur ACDH, wuldor BE^3FGI*JK

ED: drihtnes (E)] Drihtnes *Harsley.* gegearwigendis (G)] gegearwigend is *Rosier.* heorttas (F)] heorttan *Kimmens.* templo eius (D)] templo *Roeder.*

OE: gegearwigendis (G)] *initial* ge *added in diff.* (?) *hand.* heortas (I)] est : is *written in left margin.* ⁊ (I) (*1st*)] *written to right of eras.* biwrah (A)] *otiose mark after* h. to ónwreonne (E^3)] ó *altered from* n. ða ðiccan (A)] *eras. after* i. þiccettu ł hioræ den (E$^{3/X}$)] þiccettu ł *added by corr.* ælc (I)] *small eras. above* c. wuldor (I)] *written in bottom margin:* ⁊ sæcgað ealle wuldor on his temple.

LTg: Uox] Vox BDEGHIL. praeparantis] preparantis BCDEFHIJL, K: ntis *on eras. by corr.;* pręparantis G. reuelabit] A: b *on eras.*, D: *orig.* reuelauit: *2nd* u *altered to* b, K: *orig.* reuelauit: *2nd* u *altered to* b *by corr.;* reuelauit BC. eius] D: *interl. by same* (?) *corr. as seen earlier in psalm* (*e.g. v. 6*). eius] eíus K. omnes] H: s *formed from another letter, eras. after word,* I: *orig.* omnis: i *altered to* e, K: *orig.* omnis: i *altered to* e *by corr.* dicent] H: nt *on eras. in lighter ink,* K: nt *on eras. by corr.,* I: *orig.* dicet: *crude* n *interl. and signaled for inclusion.*

LTu: Uox] Vox ειν ξϱϱυφ. praeparantis] preparantis δζθιξς; pręparantis λνοπϱσ; p̄parantis τ*τυφχ. reuelabit] reuelauit βς: *cf. Weber MSS* MKT^{2}Qαγε med. templo] μ: l *interl.* omnes] ϱ: *orig.* omnis: i *deleted,* e *interl.* dicent] ζξϱ: *orig.* dicet: n *added interl.* gloriam] gloria β.

GAu: omnes] omnis δψ. dicent] dicet δμψ.

10

Dominus	driħtnes F, drihtæn E^3, dryht̄ AB, driħt C, driħ J (*G*)
diluuium	cwildeflod AB*C, cwyldeflod J, [ ]wildeflod G, flod DE^{3}HIK, flód F
inhabitat*	ineardað A, oneardað *B*CFH, oneardaþ DK, oneærdæþ E^3*, oneardað ł oneardian G*, oneardian I, onheardian J
(facit)*	deþ FJK, deð I, he deð G
et	⁊ ABCDE^{3}FGHIJK
sedebit	siteð AB, sityð C, sit DFHK, sitt I, sit ł siteð G*, sitteþ J, onsitt E^3*
dominus	dryhten B, drihten E^{3}FK, dryht̄ A, driħt CG, driħ J
rex	cyning ABCG, kining E^3, cyningc F, kyningc I, cyninc J, cining K
in	in A, on BCDE^{3}FGHIJK
aeternum	ecnisse *AD*, ecnysse *CF*I, ecnesse *BGHJK*, eccnesse *E^3* (*L*)

ED: drihtæn (E)] Drihtæn *Harsley.* æternum (D)] aeternum *Roeder.* ęternum (E)] aeternum *Harsley.*

OE: cwildeflod (B)] il *faint but visible.* oneærdæþ (E^3)] *eras.* (*15 mm*) *before word.* oneardað ł oneardian (G)] ł oneardian *added in diff.* (?) *hand.* sit ł siteð (G)] ł siteð *added in diff.* (?) *hand.* onsitt (E^3)] *orig.* ondsitt: d *eras.*

LTg: Dominus] [ ]ominus G. inhabitat] inhabitet B. aeternum] ęternum ACEFGHL; æternum BDK; eternum J.

LTu: inhabitat] inhabitet ς. aeternum] β: r *interl. by corr.;* ęternum ειλνξφ; æternum ϑ; eternum σςτ*τ.

GAg: inhabitat] inhabitare facit FGHIK; inhabitare fecit J: *cf. Weber MS* ε^2.

GAu: inhabitat] inhabitare facit δεζϑιλμξοπϱστυφχψ.

11

Dominus		dryhten B, drihten FK, drihtnes E^3, dryht̄ A, drih̄t CG, drih̄ J
uirtutem		megen AE^3, mægen BDGH*JK,* mægn C, mægen ł strencðe I, mihtig F
populo	I	folce ABCDFGHI, folc JK, his E^3
suo	I	his ABCDFGHIJK, folce E^3
dabit		seleð A, sylyð C, seleoð E^3, sýlð F, selð I, syleþ J, sylþ K, s[ ]ð B*, he syleð G
et*		⁊ ABCDE^3, drih̄t FG, drih̄ J (*L*)
benedicet		bledsað *A,* bletsað BCDF, bletsaþ H, bletsast K, he bletsað G, gebletsæð E^3, gebletsað I, bletsunge J
populum*		folc ABCDE^3*FGK, folce IJ (*L*)
suum*		his ABCFGIJK, hys E^x (*L*)
in		in A, on BCDE^{3}FGHIJK
pace		sibbe A*B*E^{3}FGHIJK, sybbe CD

ED: drihtnes (E)] Drihtnes *Harsley.* mægen (H)] *Campbell prints gloss above* Dominus.

OE: s[ ]ð (B)] *medial letters obscured by stain.* folc (E^3)] þine (?) *eras. before word.*

LTg: uirtutem] K: *orig.* uirtutum: um *altered to* em *by main hand;* uirtutum J. et] L: *crossed through: see GAg.* benedicet] A: *orig.* benedicit: *2nd* i *altered to* e. populum] populo L: *orig.* populum: m *underlined to signal deletion,* o *interl. above 2nd* u: *see GAg.* suum] suo L: *orig.* suum: m *underlined to signal deletion,* o *interl. above 2nd* u: *see GAg.* pace] p[ ] B: *letters lost due to excision of decorated initial from fol. 31r.*

GAg: et] dominus FGHIJK, L: *see LTg.* populum] populo FGHIJK, L: *see LTg.* suo] FGHIJK, L: *see LTg.*

GAu: et] dominus δεζϑιλμξοπϱστυφχψ. populum suum] populo suo δεζϑιλμξοπϱστυφχψ.

PSALM 29

2

Exaltabo ic uphebbu *A,* ic uphebbe *B*GJ, ic upphebbe *C,* ic upahebbe I, ic ahebbe *D*FH, Ic ahebbe *E^x*, ic ahæbbe *K* (*L*)
te ðec A, ðe BFI, þe *C*E^{x}GI
domine drihten E^{3}FK, dryht̄ AB, driħt *C*G, driħ J (*I*)
quoniam forðon ABJ, forþon CG, forðæn E^3, forðam F, forþan K*, forðan þe I*
suscepisti | ðu onfengc A*B,* þu onfenge C*G*J, þu afenge DFHK, ðu anfenge I, þu me E^3
me | me ACFGIJK, onfenge E^3 (*B*)
nec d ne A, ne BCDE^{x}FGHIJ, na K
delectasti ðu gelustfullades *A,* ðu gelustfullodes B, þu gelustfulludyst C, ðu na tobreddest *D,* þu na tobreddest H, þu na tobręddest E$^{3/x}$*, ðu na tobræddest F, þu na tobræddest K, þu na tobred ł tobrædd[ ] *G**, þu ne gelustfulladest tobræddest I*, þu tobræddest *J*
inimicos | feond A, fiend B, fynd CDFGHIJK, mine E^3
meos | mine ABCFGIJK, fiend E^3
super ofer AD*E^3*F*G*HIJK, ofyr C, of[ ] *B**
me mec A, me CDE^{3}FHJK (*B*)

ED: quonim (G)] quoniam *Rosier.* forðon (A)] for ðon *Kuhn.* þu na tobred ł tobrædd[ ] (G)] þu na tobred ł tobræ[ ] *Rosier.* þu ne gelustfulladest tobræddest (I)] þu ne gelustfulladest ł tobræddest *Lindelöf.* super (G)] super *Rosier.*

OE: forþan (K)] f *altered from* þ. forðan þe (I)] þe *interl.* þu na tobręddest (E$^{3/x}$)] þu na to *and final* t *by corr.,* na to *on eras.* þu na tobred ł tobrædd[ ] (G)] *2nd* d *in* tobrædd[ ] *written above 1st* d; ł tobrædd[ ] *written above* bred *in* tobred. þu ne gelustfulladest tobræddest (I)] tobræddest *written in left margin, 1st* t *partly cropped.* of[ ] (B)] *final letters lost due to excision of decorated initial on fol. 31r.*

LTg: Exaltabo] EXaltabo ABDKL; EXALTABO CE. te] TE C. domine] I: o *written above word;* DN̄E C. quoniam] quonim G. suscepisti] suscepis[ ] B: *final letters lost due to excision of initial on fol. 31r;* suscepist[ ] G. me (*1st*)] B: *lost due to excision of initial on fol. 31r.* delectasti] A: *orig.* dilectasti: *1st* i *altered to* e, D: *orig.* dilatasti: *1st* i *altered to* e, *1st* a *deleted, and* ec *interl. by corr.: see OE note to Ps 2.8* anwaldnesse; delectast[ ] G; dilatasti J. super] svper E; super G; su[ ] B: *final letters lost due to excision of initial on fol. 31r.* me (*2nd*)] B: *lost due to excision of initial on fol. 31r.*

LTu: Exaltabo] EXaltabo β; EXALTABO ιλμνξπρτφχ; EXALtabo ς. te] TE λμνξπρχ. domine] DN̄E λμνξπρ. quoniam] QUONIam ρ. suscepisti] SUSCEPISTI λξπ;

suscipisti ϑ. me (*1st*)] ME ξπ. nec] NEC ξ. delectasti] β: *orig.* dilectasti: *1st* i *altered to* e, o: *orig.* dilatasti: delectasti *added interl. by corr.*; dilectasti ϑ.

3

Domine | dryht̄ AB, driħt CFG, driħ J, hlaford K, Min E^3 (*I*)
deus | god ABCFGIJK, drihten E^3
meus | min ABCFGIJK, god E^3
clamaui | ic cleopade A, ic cleopode BD, ic clypude C, ic clýpode F, ic clypode HK, ic cleopede I, ic clypode ł ic clypig[ ] G*, ic clipige J, to E^3
ad | to ABCFIJK, þe E^3
te | ðe ABFG, þe CIJK, ic chige ł cleopode E$^{3/x}$*
et ⁊ ABCDE^{3}FGHIJ*K*
sanasti | ðu gehaeldes A, ðu gehældes B, þu gehældyst C, ðu g̲e̲hældest F, ðu gehældest I, þu gehældest J*, ðu hældest D, þu hældest GHK, þu me E^3
me | mec *A*, me BCFGHIJK, gehęldest E^3*

ED: ⁊ (H)] *no gloss Campbell.* me (H)] *no gloss Campbell.*

OE: ic clypode ł ic clypig[ ] (G)] ł ic clypig[ ] *added in diff.* (?) *hand.* ic chige ł cleopode (E$^{3/x}$)] ł cleopode *added by corr.* þu gehældest (J)] h *closed at bottom.* gehęldest (E^3)] d *interl.*

LTg: Domine] I: o *written above word.* et] æt K: *letter eras. before word* (*Sisam reads* S). me] A: *eras. after word.*

4

Domine drihten *E^3*, dryht̄ *AB,* driħt *C*F, driħ GJ (*DHIL*)
abstraxisti* ðu atuge A, þu atuge BCDF, þu agute J, þu widtihx E^3*, þu utgelæddest GI*, þu alæddest K (*L*)
ab from AE^3, fro̲m̲ B, fra̲m̲ CDFGJK, fram I
inferis* helwearum A, helwarum FG, helwaru̲m̲ *B*DE^x*, hellwaru̲m̲ C, helle IJK
animam | sawle ABCDFGHIJ, saule K, mine E^3
meam | mine ABCDFGHIJK, sæwle E^3
saluasti | ðu gehaeldes A, þu gehældes B, þu gehældyst C, þu gehældest IJ, ðu hældest D, þu hældest GH*K,* gehæl F, ⁊ þu me E^3
me | mec A, me BCFGJK, geheldest E^3*
a from A, fro̲m̲ BC*E^3*, fra̲m̲ DFGHJK, fram I
descendentibus dunestigendum *A*C, ofdune astigendu̲m̲ B, ofdune astigende J, stigendu̲m̲ DH, stigendum ł fra̲m̲ dune ofastigendu̲m̲ G,

	astigendum F, þæm niþerstigendum E^3, niðerastigendum I*, nyþerstigendum K
in	in A, on BCDE^{3}FHIJK, [ ]n G
lacum	seað ABCDGH, seaþ JK, seaðe FI, þone Seæþ E^3

OE: þu widtihx (E^3)] *letter eras. before* þu. þu utgelæddest (I)] *1st* t *altered from* g, *1st and 2nd* u, *and 1st* e *on eras.*, ut ge *written again in left margin.* helwarum (E^x)] *eras. after word.* geheldest (E^3)] d *interl.* niðerastigendum (I)] a *interl.*

LTg: Domine] I: o *written above word;* domine BCDE, A: *written in left margin outside of grid by corr.*, L: *orig.* domine: d *crossed through and* D *written by corr. to left;* [ ]omine H: *initial* D *lost.* abstraxisti] L: *underlined to signal deletion*, eduxisti *written in right margin: see GAg.* inferis] infęris B. saluasti] K: *letter eras. before word.* a] á E. descendentibus] A: *orig.* discendentibus: *1st* i *altered to* e.

LTu: Domine] domine βνςτ*. me] β: e *interl. by corr.* descendentibus] ϑ, β: discendentibus: *1st* i *altered to* e.

GAg: abstraxisti] eduxisti FIJK, L: *see LTg;* ęduxisti GH. inferis] inferno FGHIJK.

GAu: abstraxisti] eduxisti δεζϑιλμξοπϱστυφχψ. inferis] inferno δεζϑιλμξοπϱστυφχψ.

5

Psallite		singað ABCGH, syngað DF, Singæð E^3, singaþ IJK
domino		dryhtne B, drihtny C, drihtne E^{3}FI, drihtene K, dryht̄ A, driħ GJ
sancti	|	halge A, halige B, halige DFH, halgan CI, halignesse GJ, his E^3*
eius	|	his ABCFGIJ, is *K,* hælgum E^3
et		⁊ ABCDE^{3}FGHIJK
confitemini		ondettað AB, ondettæþ E^3, andyttað C, andettaþ IJ, andetaþ K, geandettað DGH, ic andette F
memoriae		gemydde A, gemynde *BCIJ,* gemynd *FK,* ðam gemynde *D,* þam gemynde *GH,* mid geminde *E^3* (*L*)
sanctitatis	|	halignisse AD, halignysse CFI, halignesse BHJ, halinesse GK, his E^3
eius	|	his ABCDFGHIJ*K,* hælignisse E^3*

ED: memorię (E)] memoriae *Harsley.* memorie (I)] memoriae *Lindelöf.*

OE: his (E^3) (*1st*)] *eras. before word.* hælignisse (E^3)] *retraced in darker ink by corr.*

LTg: eius (*1st*)] eíus K. memoriae] memoriæ B; memorie JK, I: *orig.* memoriae: a *incompletely eras.;* memorię DEFGHL, C: ię *on eras.* eius (*2nd*)] eíus K.

LTu: memoriae] β: *final* e *interl. by corr.;* memorię εζιμξοπσυφχ; memoriæ ϑ; memorie ςτ*τ.

6

Quoniam		forðon ABJ, forþon C, Forðæn E^3, forþam F, forþā K, forþam þe *G,* forðan þe I
ira		eorre ABDH, yrre CGI, irra J, eorre biþ E^3*, graman F
in		in A, on BCDE^3*FGHIJK*
indignatione	I	ebylgðu A, æbylgðe B, æbylhðe C, æbylgnisse D, ebylgnesse E^3, æbylignysse F, æbilignesse J, æbygilgnesse H, æbylinesse K, æbilinesse ł on æfðuncan G*, his I
eius	I	his ABCDE^{3}FGHJ*K,* æbylgnysse I*
et		⁊ ABCDE^{3}FGHIJK
uita		lif ABCDFGHIJK, lyf E^3
in		in A, on BCDE^{3}FGHIJK
uoluntate	I	willan ABCDFGHIJK, his E^3
eius	I	his ABCDFGHIJ*K,* willæn E^3
Ad		æt ABGJ, oð C, on DF*H*K, On E^3, to I
uesperum		efenne A, æfenne BGI, æfynne C, æfen DFHJK, ðon ęfen E^3
demorabitur		wunað ABCDGH, wunaþ FJK, bið wuniende E^3, ðurhwunað I*
fletus		wop ABCDFGIJ*K,* wóóp E^3
et		⁊ ABCDE^{3}FGHIJK
ad		to ABCE^{3}J, on DFGHIK
matutinum		margentide A, morgentide B, morgyntide C, morgen K, degred D, dægred FHI, dægred ł on mergen G*, to mergen ł on dægred J, þæm uhtlicum ł dægred $E^{3/x}$*
laetitia		blis A*BDE^{3}FJK,* bliss *CG,* blisse I (*HL*)

ED: [ ]uoniam (G)] Quoniam *Rosier.* forðon (A)] for ðon *Kuhn.* on (G) (*2nd*)] [ ]n *Rosier.* willan (G)] [ ]llan *Rosier.* ælf̄ (I)] *O'Neill* (*p. 92*) *suggests* ælf[remed].

OE: eorre biþ (E^3)] o *perhaps altered from another letter by main hand.* æbilinesse ł on æfðuncan (G)] *2nd* i *interl.,* ł on æfðuncan *added in diff.* (?) *hand.* æbylgnysse (I)] e̲s̲t̲ : is *written in left margin.* ðurhwunað (I)] *below* demorabitur, *in bottom margin, is written* ælf̄, *and above that* elcaþ, *with* e *lining up above* f̄: *see ED.* dægred ł on mergen (G)] ł on mergen *added in diff.* (?) *hand.* þæm uhtlicum ł dægred ($E^{3/x}$)] ł dægred *added by corr.*

LTg: Quoniam] [ ]uoniam G: *initial* Q *lost, outline visible.* in (*1st*)] F: *on eras. by corr.,* G: *added by corr.,* H: *added interl. by glossator,* K: *added interl. by corr.* eius (*1st*)] eíus K. eius (*2nd*)] eíus K. Ad] [ ]d H: *initial* A *lost.* fletus] K: s *partly cropped on right due to excision of initial on fol. 34v.* laetitia] lætitia B; lętitia CFGHJL; letitia DEK.

LTu: in (*1st*)] *interl.* ϱ; *om.* ς (in/dignatione *for* in indignatione). indignatione] β: g *interl. by corr.* Ad] τ*τ: *initial wanting.* matutinum] matudinum ϑ. laetitia] lętitia ειλμ; lætitiæ ϑ; letitia ξσϛυ; laeticia ϱ: *orig.* laetitia: *2nd* t *deleted and* c *interl.;* leticia τ*τ; lęticia φ.

7

Ego		ic ABCFGIJK, Ic E³*
autem		soðlice AB*C*E³FG, soþlice J, witolice K
dixi		ic ceð A, cwæð BC, cwęð E³, cwæþ J, cweþe K, sæde F, sæde ł cwæð G*I
in		in A, on BCDE³FGHIJK
mea*	}l	minre AB*CD*E³FGHIJ, minr[ ] K* (*L*)
abundantia*	}l	genyhtsumnisse A, genyhtsumnesse *B,* genihtsumnysse C, genihsumnisse *D,* genihtsumnisse *E³,* genihtsumnysse FI, genihtsumnesse GK, genihtsumnesse HJ (*L*)
non		ne ABCJ, na DFGHK, ic ne I, þet ic me ne E³
mouebor		biom onstyred A, beom ic onstyred B, beom ic onstyryd C, beo ic astyrud K, ic beom astyred D, ic beon astyrod F, beo astyrod I*, ic beo gestyred GH, beo ic astired J, onwende ł astyred E³/x*
in		in A, on BCDE³FGHIJK
aeternum		ecnisse *AD,* ecnesse *BE³GHJK,* ecnysse *CF*I* (*L*)

ED: æternum (D)] aeternum *Roeder.* ęternum (E)] aeternum *Harsley.*

OE: Ic (E³)] *orig.* ic: i *altered to* I *by main hand.* sæde ł cwæð (G)] ł cwæð *added in diff.* (?) *hand.* minr[ ] (K)] *final letter lost due to excision of initial on fol. 34v.* beo astyrod] *orig.* astirod: i *altered to* y. onwende ł astyred (E³/x)] ł astyred *added by corr.* ecnysse (I)] *eras.* (?) *after* c.

LTg: autem] C: *abbreviation used by orig. scribe; corr. added* autem *interl.* mea] C: a *malformed and followed by eras.* b, L: *underlined to signal deletion, with* mea *added interl. by Lat. glossator above* tia *in following* habundantia: *see GAg.* abundantia] habundantia BDEL. aeternum] ęternum AEFGH; æternum BDKL; eternum C.

LTu: abundantia] habundantia βντ*. aeternum] ęternum βειμξφ; æternum ϑ; eternum σϛτ*τ.

GAg: mea abundantia] abundantia mea HI; habundantia mea FGJ, L: *see LTg note to* mea; habundantia me[ ] K: *final letter lost due to excision of initial on fol. 34v.*

GAu: mea abundantia] abundantia mea ειμοπϱφψ; habundantia mea δζϑλξστυχ.

8

Domine		drihten E³F, dryhť AB, driħt C*FG, driħ J (*HI*)
in		in A, on BCDE³FGHIJK
bona*	l	godum A, godum BCD, þinum E³ (*L*)

uoluntate	I	willan ABCDFGHIJK, goðæn E^3
tua	I	ðinum AFI, ðinum B, þinum DJ, þinum H, þin C, þinre G, þinan K, willæn E^3
praestitisti		ðu gearwades A, ðu gearwodes *B,* ðu gearwodest *D,* þu geærwedest *E*^{3}*, þu gearwodest *FJK,* þu gegearwodyst *C,* þu gegearwodest *GH,* ðu lændest ł ðu getyþodest I (*L*)
decori	I	wlite ABCDFGHIJ, of wlite K, minum E^3
meo	I	minum ACFG, minum BDIJ, minu[ ] H*, minre K, wlite E^3
uirtutem		megen A, mægen BDGHIJ, mægyn C, mǽgn F, strenðe K, þin męgen E^3
auertisti		ðu forcerdes A, þu forcerdes B, þu forcyrdyst C, þu forcirdest *J,* ðu acyrdest D, þu acyrdest *GHK,* þu ǽwirfdes E^3, þu awændest *F,* ðu awendest *I* (*L*)
faciem	I	onsiene AB, ansyne CFGIJK, onsyne D, onsine H, þine E^3
tuam	I	ðine ABF, þine CIJK, þinre GH, onsine E^3
a		from A, from BC, fram *E*^{3}I, fram FGHJK
me		me ABCE^{3}FGHIJK
et		⁊ ABCE^{3}FGHIJK
factus		geworden ABDFHI*J, gewordyn C, gewordene G, ic geworden E^3, gedon K
sum		ic eam A, ic eom BCFIJ, eom E^3*K, synd ł ic eom G*
conturbatus		gedroefed A, gedrefed BE^{3}FGHJK, gedrefyd C, gedrefed D, gedrefod I

ED: minu[ ] (H)] minum *Campbell.* þin męgen (E)] þin megen *Harsley.* þu ǽwirfdes (E)] þu æwirfdes *Harsley.* á (E)] a *Harsley.* synd ł ic eom (G)] syn[ ] ł ic eom *Rosier.*

OE: drih̄t (C)] s. o *written before word.* þu geærwedest (E^3)] t *interl. by corr.* minu[ ] (H)] *hole in leaf after* u, *letter fragments visible* (*2 minims*). geworden (I)] *orig.* gewurden: u *altered to* o. eom (E^3)] *on eras.* synd ł ic eom (G)] ł ic eom *added in diff.* (?) *hand.*

LTg: Domine] H: *eras. after word,* I: o *written above word.* bona] L: *underlined to signal deletion: see GAg.* praestitisti] prestitisti BCDEFHJKL; pręstitisti G. auertisti] Auertisti FGHIJK, L: *orig.* auertisti: a *altered to* A *by Lat. glossator.* a] á E.

LTu: praestitisti] prestitisti δζϑιπςτ*τ; pręstitisti ελμνξϱσφ; p̄stitisti χ. auertisti] Auertisti δεζϑιλμξοπϱσυφχψ; [ ]uertisti τ*: *initial letter wanting.*

GAg: bona] *om.* FGHIJK, L: *see LTg.*

GAu: bona] *om.* δεζϑιλμξοπϱστυφχψ.

9

Ad	|	to ABCFGIJK, drihten E^3
te	|	ðe ABFG, þe CIJK, to E^3
domine	|	dryht̄ AB, driħt CFG, driħ J, hlaford K, þe E^3 *(I)*
clamabo		ic cleopiu A, ic clipige BJ, ic clypige CDH, ic cliepie E^3, ic clepige I, ic clypode F, ic clypode ł ic clypige G*, i clypige K
et		⁊ ABCDE^{3}FGHIJK
ad		to ABCDE^{3}FGIJK
deum	|	gode ABCDFGHIJ, drihtene K, minum E^3
meum	|	minum ACFGI, minum BDHJ, minan K, godum E^3
deprecabor		ic biddu A, ic biddo B, ic bidde CDFGHJ, ic gebidde IK, ⁊ ic bio biddende E^3

OE: ic clypode ł ic clypige (G)] ł ic clypige *added in diff.* (?) *hand.*

LTg: domine] I: o *written above word.*

LTu: deprecabor] depraecabor β; dep̄cabor ϑμξοστχ.

10

Quae		hwelc *AB*, hwylc *CDE^3*FHK*, hwilc *G*, la hwilc I, hilc *J* *(L)*
utilitas		nyttnis A, nyttnys C, nytnis DGH, nytnys F, nytnes K, netnesse E^3*, nytto B, neteo J, nytwyrðnes I*
in		in A, on BCDE^{3}FGHIJK
sanguine	|	blode A*B*CDFGHJK, minum E^{3}I
meo	|	mine A, minum CFGH, minum BDJ, minan K, blode E^{3}I
dum		ðonne AF, þonne BE^x*, þonne CDHJ, þonne G, þænne IK
descendo		ic astigo A, ic astige *BJ*, ic nyðyrastige *C*, ic niðærstige E^3*, ic stige niðer *D*, ic stige nyðer F, ic stige niþer H, nyðer G, ic gewende ł þonne ic niþerastige I, ic nyþerstige K
in		in A, on BCDE^{3}FGHIJK
corruptionem		gebrosnunge ABC, brosnunga DFH, brosnungæ G, brosnunge I, brotsnunge K, geblosnunge J, gegripnesse ł on brosnunga E$^{3/x}$*
Numquid		ah AB, hune ł cwyst ðu *C*, cwyst ðu D, cwyst þu *HK*, cwyst þu la F, cweþst þu la I, cwyst þu ł ac G*, ac cwistu la J, Is þes wén þet *E^3*
confitebitur	|	ondetteð AB, andyttyþ C, andettað D, andetteþ H, ic andette F, ic andette ł andettað G*, geandetteð I*, andetta J, andetaþ K, ic þe E^3
tibi	|	ðe ABF, þe DGHIJK, þe þe C, ondette þe E$^{3/x}$*

puluis — dust ABDE^{x}*FGHIK, dvst *C*, dust ł mil J
aut — oððe ABCFGHIJ, oþðe DE^{x}*K
adnuntiabit — seged *A*, sægð *BC*, bodaþ *DE^{x}*K*, bodað *H*, bodað ł cyð *F*, he bodað ł segð G*, bodaþ ł cyþeþ ł segþ J, gecyþ hit *I*
ueritatem — soðfestnisse A, soðfæstnisse H, soðfæstnysse CI, soþfæstnisse DE^{x}, soþfæstnysse F, soðfæstnesse BG, soþfæstnesse J, soþfæstnese K
tuam — ðine AB, þine CDE^{x}FGHIK, þinre J

ED: quæ (D)] quae *Roeder.* quę (E)] quae *Harsley.* descendo (C)] d[i]scendo *Wildhagen.* gegripnesse ł on brosnunga (E)] gegripnesse ł onbrosnunga *Harsley.* Nunquid (C)] Nu[m]quid *Wildhagen.* hune ł cwyst ðu (C)] hune ł cwystðu *Wildhagen.* cwyst ðu (D)] cwystðu *Roeder.* cwyst þu (H)] cwyst *Campbell.* andetteþ (H)] þu andetteþ *Campbell.* dvst (C)] dust *Wildhagen.* annuntiabit (C)] a[d]nuntiabit *Wildhagen.* þine (G)] *no gloss Rosier.*

OE: hwylc (E^{3})] *on eras., possibly by corr.* netnesse (E^{3})] *2 letters eras. before word, 2nd of which is* t. nytwyrðnes (I)] e͟s͟t͟ : is *written in left margin.* þonne (E^{x})] *on eras.* ic niðærstige (E^{3})] nið *retraced in darker ink,* ær *in darker ink, eras. before* stige *in next line.* gegripnesse ł on brosnunga (E$^{3/x}$)] ł on brosnunga *added by corr.* cwyst þu ł ac (G)] ł ac *added in diff.* (?) *hand.* ic andette ł andettað (G)] ł andettað *added in diff.* (?) *hand.* geandetteð (I)] *1st* t *interl.* ondette þe (E$^{3/x}$)] þe *written by corr.* dust (E^{x})] *eras. before word.* oþðe (E^{x})] *on eras.* bodaþ (E^{x})] *on eras.* he bodað ł segð (G)] ł segð *added in diff.* (?) *hand.*

LTg: Quae] Quę FH, J: *cauda added by glossator;* Que K; [ ]uae G; quae A; quæ BD; quę CE; Quæ L: *orig.* quæ: Q *interl. by corr.* sanguine] sangui B. descendo] C: *orig.* discendo: i *altered to* e *by corr.;* discendo BD. Numquid] Nunquid E, H: *small eras. after* n, C: *orig.* Numquid: *left leg of* m *eras. to form* n, K: *orig.* Numquid: *right leg of* m *eras. to form* n. puluis] C: *eras. after* p. adnuntiabit] annuntiabit BDFI, A: b *on eras.,* H: *1st* n *on eras.,* CEK: *1st* n *on eras. by corr.*

LTu: Quae] Quę εζϑιμξφ; Que στ; quę βνς; que τ*. sanguine] β: i *interl. by corr.* descendo] discendo βϑ. Numquid] Nunquid εζιφ. puluis] pulues ϑ. adnuntiabit] adnuntiauit β; annuntiabit εζιλξπστ*τυχ, ο: *orig.* adnuntiabit: d *deleted,* n *interl.;* annunciabit φ, ϱ: *orig.* annuntiabit: *1st* t *deleted,* c *interl.;* adnunciabit ψ. ueritatem] ueritate μ.

11

Audiuit | geherde AB, gehyrde CDFGHIK, gehirde J, drihten E^{3}
dominus | drihtyn C, drihten FIK, dryht̄ AB, driħt G, driħ HJ, gehierde E^{3}*

et	⁊ ABCE^{3}FGHIJK
misertus	I mildsiendie A, mildsiend K, mildsigende *J*, miltsiende B, miltsiynd C, gemiltsode DG, gemildsod F, he gemildsode I, mildsode H, is E^3
est	I is AFJ*K*, ys C, is ł miltigende wæs G*, wæs B, miltsigende E^3
mihi*	me AB*CDE^3*JK, min FGI
dominus	drihtyn C, drihten E^{3}F, dryhт̄ AB, drih̃t G, drih̃ J
factus	I geworden ABDFGHIJ, gewordyn C, gedon K, is E^3
est	I is ABFGIJ*K*, ys C, geworden E^3
adiutor	I fultum ACJ, fultu<u>m</u> B, to fultume F*, gefylstend DH, gefylstend ł fultum *G**, fultumiend ł fultum I*, fylstend K, ge min E$^{3/x}$*
meus	I min ABCGHIJK, minum F, fultumend ł gefylstend E$^{3/x}$*

ED: drihten (E) (*1st*)] Ɖrihten *Harsley*. adiutor] audiutor *Rosier*.

OE: gehierde (E^3)] de *on eras. by corr.* is ł miltigende wæs (G)] ł miltigende wæs *added in diff.* (?) *hand.* to fultume (F)] *eras. between* lt. gefylstend ł fultum (G)] ł fultum *added in diff.* (?) *hand.* fultumiend ł fultum (I)] fultumiend *written in right margin.* ge min (E$^{3/x}$)] ge *added by corr.* fultumend ł gefylstend (E$^{3/x}$)] ł gefylstend *added by corr. above* fultumend.

LTg: misertus] J: *1st* s *interl. by glossator.* est (*1st*)] ést K. mihi] michi E, C: c *interl. by corr.* est (*2nd*)] ést K.

LTu: misertus] missertus ϑ. mihi] michi ςτ*. adiutor] adiutorr ς (adiuto‹/r).

GAg: mihi] mei FGHIJK.

GAu: mihi] mei δεζιλμξοπϱστυφχψ.

12

Conuertisti	ðu gecerdes AB, þu gecyrdyst CH, ðu gecyrdest D, ðu gecirdest E^3, þu gecyrdest *FG*K, þu gecirdest J, þu gecerdest ł þu ahwyrfdest ł þu awendest I*
planctum	I wop ABCIJ, heof DFH, heof ł wop G*, geomerunga K, minne E^3
meum	I minne ABDFGJ, mine K, min C, minne ł mine heofunge I*, heof E^3*
in	in A, on BCDE^{3}FGJK, to I
gaudium	gefean A*B*CFJ, g<u>e</u>fean D, gefeæn E^3*, blisse ł on gefean *G**I*, blisse K
mihi	mc AB*CE^3**FHI*J*K
conscidisti	ðu toslite *A*, þu toslite BC*GHI, þu tosclite J, ðu slite D, þu slite FK, þu tostlite ł curfe E$^{3/x}$*

saccum | sec A, sæc BIJ, sæcc *C,* heran D, hæran FHK, hæran ł sæc G*, mine *E*^{3}
meum | minne ABCIJ, mine DFG*HK, sęc ł hæran E$^{3/x}$*
et ⁊ ABCDE^{3}FGIJK
praecinxisti* | bigyrdes A, begyrdyst *C,* ðu bigyrdes *B,* þu begyrdest *D*K, þu ymbsealdest F, þu ymbsealdest ł ymbsettest I, þu ymbtrym[ ] G, ymbsillende J, me *E*^{3} (*L*)
me | me ABCFGIJK, begierdest me E$^{3/x}$*
laetitia mid blisse A*BC*I, of blisse *D,* on blisse *E*^{x}, blisse *FGHJK* (*L*)

ED: m^{1} (E)] michi *Harsley.* me[ ]m (G)] m*eam Rosier.* mine (G)] mi[ ]ne *Rosier.* þu ymbtrym[ ] (G)] þu ymbtr:[ ] *Rosier.* lętitia (E)] laetitia *Harsley.*

OE: þu gecerdest ł þu ahwyrfdest ł þu awendest (I)] þu gecerdest ł *and* ł þu awendest *written in left margin.* heof ł wop (G)] ł wop *added in diff.* (?) *hand.* minne ł mine heofunge (I)] ł mine heofunge *written in right margin.* heof (E^{3})] o *retraced in darker ink and partly on eras., cross-stroke of* f *in darker ink.* gefeæn (E^{3})] eæn *retraced in darker ink.* blisse ł on gefean (G)] ł on gefean *added in diff.* (?) *hand.* blisse ł on gefean (I)] ł on gefean *written in right margin.* me (E^{3})] *in darker ink.* þu toslite (C)] *eras. after 2nd* t. þu tostlite ł curfe (E$^{3/x}$)] stlite ł *added by corr.* (*read as* þu tostlite ł curfe > þu tostlite ł tocurfe). hæran ł sæc (G)] ł sæc *added in diff.* (?) *hand.* mine (G)] *hole after* i. sęc ł hæran (E$^{3/x}$)] ł hæran *added by corr.* begierdest me (E$^{3/x}$)] me *added by corr.*

LTg: Conuertisti] F: tis *added on eras. by corr.;* [ ]nuertisti G. gaudium] B: a *on eras.* (*before gloss was entered*); gaud[ ] G. mihi] michi J, C: c *interl. by corr.;* m^{1} E. conscidisti] A: *eras.* (*2 letters?*) *before word.* saccum] C: *orig.* saccam: *2nd* a *altered to* u; saccvm E. meum] me[ ]m G. praecinxisti] precincxisti BC; precinxisti EL; pręcinxisti D. laetitia] lætitia B; lętitia CEFGL; letitia DHJK.

LTu: mihi] michi λξς, πϱ: c *added interl.* praecinxisti] pręcinxisti ν; precinxisti ςτ*. laetitia] lętitia βειλν; lætitia ϑ; letitia μξσς; lęticia ϱ: *orig.* lętitia: *2nd* t *deleted and* c *interl.;* leticia τ*τ; lęticia φ.

GAg: praecinxisti] circumdedisti FGIJK; circundedisti H: *small eras. after* n.

GAu: praecinxisti] circumdedisti δεζϑιλμξοπϱστυχψ; circundedisti φ.

13
Ut ðæt *A,* þæt *B,* þæt *CDE*^{x}*F*G*H*I*K,* ⁊ *J* (*L*)
cantem* singe *AB*CI, ic synge D, ic singe *E*^{x}*F*GHK, singaþ J
tibi ðe ABF, þe CDE^{3}GHIJK
gloria wuldur ABDH, wuldor CE^{3}FGIJK
mea min ABCDE^{x}FGHIJK

et ⁊ *A*BE^{x}FGHIJK, þæt C
non | ic ne *A*BCE$^{3/x}$*IJ, na DFGHK
conpungar | biom inbryrd A/A^{3}*, beo onbryrded BJ, beom geinbryrdyd *C*, ic beom abryrd D, ic ne beo abrýrd F, ic beo abryrd *H*, ic beo abryrded G, beo abryd *K**, síe ł ne beo onbryrd E$^{3/x}$*, beo gewitnod *I** (*L*)

domine | drihtyn *C*, drihten F, dryht̄ *AB*, driht́ GH, drih́ J, eala þu dr̄ I*, Min *E*^{3} (*D*)
deus | god ABCFGHIJ, drihten E^{3}
meus | min ABCFGHIJ, god E^{3}
in in A, on BCDE^{3}FGHIJK
aeternum ecnisse A*D*, encynsse *C*I, écnysse *F*, ecnesse *BE*^{3}**GHJK* (*L*)
confitebor ic ondettu A, ic ondette BE^{3}, ic andytte C, ic andette D*F*GHIJK
tibi ðe ABFI, þe CDE^{3}GHJK

ED: þæt (G)] ðæt *Rosier.* compungar (C)] co[n]pungar *Wildhagen.* biom inbryrd (A)] biom inbr *Kuhn: see OE.* æternum (D)] aeternum *Roeder.* ęternum (E)] aeternum *Harsley.*

OE: ic ne (E$^{3/x}$)] ic *written by corr.* biom inbryrd (A/A^{3})] *leaf cropped; a late hand added* yrd *in pencil on next line to complete gloss.* beo abryd (K)] *2 letters* (br?) *eras. before* beo. síe ł ne beo onbryrd (E$^{3/x}$)] ł ne beo *added by corr.* beo gewitnod (I)] *with additional Lat. gloss* ł plangat. eala þu dr̄ (I)] o *written before* eala. ecnesse (E^{3})] *left leg of* n *malformed.*

LTg: Ut] Vt FI; ut ABCDE, L: *orig.* ut: V *interl. by corr.*; [ ]t G; Et J. cantem] A: *orig.* cantet: *final* t *on eras., crossed through in pencil and* m *interl. by corr.*; cantet B: *cf. Weber MSS* QRXαγλ moz, *see GAg.* et] A: e *on eras.* non] A: *eras. after initial* n. conpungar] L: *eras. before word;* compungar IK, C: *orig.* conpungar: *right leg added to 1st* n *by corr. to form* m, H: *orig.* conpungar: *middle leg added to 1st* n *to form* m. domine] Domine ABCDE. aeternum] æternum BDKL; ęternum CEFGH; eternum J. confitebor] F: or *on eras. by corr.*

LTu: Ut] Vt ιξϱστ; ut βνςτ*φ. conpungar] compungar ειλπ, οϱ: *orig.* conpungar: *1st* n *deleted, macron added above* o; cōpungar χ. domine] DNe βτ*; Domine νς. aeternum] ęternum ειvξσφ; æternum ϑ; eternum ςτ*τ.

GAg: cantem] cantet FGHIJK, B: *see LTg.*

GAu: cantem] cantet δεζϑιλμξοπϱτυφχψ.

PSALM 30

2

In		in *A,* on *BCD*FGHIJ*K,* On *E^{3}*
te		ðe ABDF, þe *CE^{3}*GHIJK
domine		dryhten A, drihten E^{3}, dryht̄ B, driħt *C*FG, driħ HJ (*I*)
speraui		ic gehyhte AB, ic gehihte *C*G*I, ic hyhte DH, ic hihte JK, ic hopude F, ic gewene ł hyhte $E^{3/x}$*
non	|	ne ABC, na DFGHJK*, na ne I, þet ic ne E^{3}
confundar	|	biom ic gescended A, beom ic gescyndyd C, beo ic gescended B, ic g̲e̲scend beo D, ic gescynd beo HK, ic gescynded beo G, ic ne beo gescend F, beo ic gescynded ł þ̲æ̲t̲ ic ne beo gescænd I, sie gescynd E^{3}*, ic beo gescynd J
in		in A, on BCDE^{3}FGHIJK
aeternum		ecnisse A*D,* ecnysse *C,* écnysse *F,* ecnesse *BE^{3}GH*I*JK* (*L*)
in		in A, on BCDE^{3}FGHIJK
tua*	}	ðire A, þinre BCE^{3}GHIJK, ðinre D, ðine F (*L*)
iustitia*	}	rehtwisnisse A, rihtwisnysse CFI, ryhtwisnesse BD, rihtwisnesse GJ*K, unrihtwisnesse H, soþfestnesse E^{3}
libera		gefrea A, gefreo C, gefriolsæ ł alys $E^{3/x}$*, alies B, alys DFGHIK, alis J
me		me ABCDE^{x}*FGHJK
et*		⁊ ABCE^{x}* (*L*)
eripe*		genere AB, genery C, nere DE^{x}* (*L*)
me*		me ABCE^{x}* (*L*)

ED: æternum (D)] aeternum *Roeder.* ęternum (E)] aeternum *Harsley.*

OE: ic gehihte (G)] ge *added interl. in diff.* (?) *hand.* gewene ł hyhte ($E^{3/x}$)] ł hyhte *added by corr.* na (K)] *otiose mark* (*false start?*) *before word.* sie gescynd (E^{3})] *orig.* sie gescynde: *final* e *eras.* rihtwisnesse (J)] n *altered from* r. gefriolsæ ł alys ($E^{3/x}$)] ł alys *on eras. by corr.* me (E^{x}) (*1st*)] *on eras.* ⁊ (E^{x})] *on eras.* nere (E^{x})] *on eras.* me (E^{x}) (*2nd*)] *on eras.*

LTg: In] IN ABCDE; [ ]N K: *initial letter excised.* te] TE CE. domine] I: o *written above word;* DN̄E C. speraui] SPERAVI C. aeternum] æternum BDKL; ęternum CEFGH; eternum J. tua] L: *underlined to signal deletion,* tua *written written above* iustitia *and signaled to come after word: see GAg.* et eripe me] L: *underlined to signal deletion: see GAg.*

LTu: In] IN βϑιλμνξπϱςτ*τφχ. te] TE βλμνξπϱςφ. domine] DN̄e β; DOmine ς; DN̄E λμνξπϱ. speraui] SPERAUI λμνξπϱ. non] NON λξπϱ. confundar] CONFUNDAR λξπ; CONFVNdar ϱ. in] IN ξ. aeternum] ęternum ειvφ; æternum ϑ; ETERNUM ξ; eternum σςτ*τ. iustitia] iusticia τ*τ.

GAg: tua iustitia] iustitia tua FGHIJK, L: *see LTg*. et eripe me] *om*. FGHIJK, L: *see LTg*.

GAu: tua iustitia] iustitia tua δεζιλμξοπσυχψ; iusticia tua τφ, ϱ: *orig*. iustitia tua: *2nd* t *deleted*, c *interl*. et eripe me] *om*. δεζιλμξοπϱστυφχψ.

3

Inclina		onhaeld A, onheld B, onhyld CIJ, Onhyld E^{3}*, ahyld DF*GHK*
ad	I	to ABCDFGHIJK, þin E^{3}
me	I	me ABCDFGHIJK, eæræ E^{3}
aurem	I	eare ABCDFHIJ, earan GK, to E^{3}
tuam	I	ðin AF, þin BCHIJ, þine GK, me E^{3}
adcelera		hreaða *AC,* hrada *B,* efst *DH,* efest *K,* efst ł nealæce *F,* efst ł raðe *G**,* geefst ł hrada *I,* raþe *J,* ⁊ þu hredlice ł efest *E*$^{3/x}$* (*L*)
ut		ðæt A, þæt CDFHIJ, þæt GK, þætte B
eripias*	I	ðu generge A, þu generige BFJ, ðu generige C, ðu nere D*, þu nera K, þu nerige GH*, nere E^{x}*, ðu alyse I (*L*)
me		mec *A,* me CDE^{x}*FGHJK
Esto		bia ðu A, beo ðu BD, beo þu CFGHJ, béo þu E^{x}*, beo K, sy þu I
mihi		me AB*CE*^{x}*FGI*J*K
in		in A, on BCE^{x}*FGIJ
deum		god ABCGJ, gode E^{x}*FI
protectorem		gescildend ABJ, gescyldynd C, gescyldend D, gescyldend E^{3}*F*G*H, gescyld K, scyldendum ł on beweriendum I
et		⁊ ABCE^{3}FGHIJK
in		in A, on BCDE^{3}FGHIJK
locum*		stowe ABCDE^{3}, huse FGHIJK (*L*)
refugii		geberges A, gebeorges BJ, gebeorhnysse C, gebeorges ł rotnesse ł generes G*, rotnisse D*E*^{x}*H, rotnysse F, rotnesse *K,* generes I
ut		ðæt A, þæt CFGJK, þæt I, þætte B, oþþet E^{3}*
saluum	I	halne ABCDGH, þu halne F, þu gehæle I*, þu me E^{3}, þu me halne J, hal K
me	I	mec A, me BCFGIJK, hæle E^{3}
facias	I	ðu gedoe A, þu gedo B, gedo þu C, gedó E^{3}, gedo J, þu dó D, þu do GH, do FK

ED: béo þu (E)] Béo þu *Harsley*. refugií (E)] refugii *Harsley*. refugíí (K)] refugii *Sisam*. gebeorhnysse (C)] gebeorhnysse *Wildhagen*.

OE: Onhyld (E^{3})] *orig*. Onhylde: e *eras*. efst ł raðe (G)] ł raðe *added in diff*. (?) *hand*. ⁊ þu hredlice ł efest (E$^{3/x}$)] ł efest *added by corr*. ðu nere (D)] g *eras*. *after* ðu.

þu nerige (H)] *orig.* þu generige: ge *eras. but visible.* nere (E^{x})] *on eras.* me (E^{x}) (*2nd*)] *on eras.* béo þu (E^{x})] *on eras., accent may be trace of eras. letter.* me (E^{x}) (*3rd*)] *on eras.* on (E^{x})] *on eras.* gode (E^{x})] *on eras.* gescyldend (E^{3})] ge *added by corr.* gebeorges ł rotnesse ł generes (G)] gebeorges ł *and* ł generes *added in diff.* (?) *hand.* rotnisse (E^{x})] *on eras.* oþþet (E^{3})] *eras. before word.* þu gehæle (I)] hæl *on eras.* (?).

LTg: Inclina] [ ]nclina G, K: *initial letter lost due to excision of initial in v. 2* (*fol. 34v*). adcelera] acelera A: *orig.* adcelera: d *eras.;* accelera BCEFGHIJKL, D: *orig.* adcelera: d *altered to* c. eripias] L: ipi *underlined to signal deletion,* u *added interl. by Lat. glossator: see GAg.* me (*2nd*)] A: *added by corr.* mihi] michi EJ, C: *orig.* mihi: c *interl. by corr.* protectorem] G: *otiose descending stroke after 1st* o. locum] L: *underlined to signal deletion,* domum *added interl. by corr.: see GAg.* refugii] refugií E: *accent above 1st* i *lost due to eras. above;* refugíí K.

LTu: Inclina] INclina β; inclina ϑ. adcelera] accelera δεζιλμνξοπϱσςτ*τυφχψ; et celera β. Esto] esto ϑι. mihi] michi ιλςτ*τ, πϱ: c *added interl.*

GAg: eripias] eruas FGHIJK, L: *see LTg.* locum] domum FGHIJK, L: *see LTg.*

GAu: eripias] eruas δεζϑιλμξοπϱστυφχψ. locum] domum δεζϑιλμξπϱστυφχψ.

4

Quoniam		forðon ABJ, forþon C, Forðæn E^{3}, forþā G, forðam ðe F, forðan þe I
firmamentum*	|	trymenis A, trymnes B, trumnys C, tru<u>m</u>nis D, strengð FI, strengþ K, strenþ J, strengð ł miht G*, mine E^{3} (*L*)
meum*	|	min ABCDFGHIJK, trimnesse E^{3}
et		⁊ ABCE^{3}FGHIJK
refugium	|	geberg A, gebeorg B, gebeorh CJ, frofr DH, frofor F, frofer K, frofer ł gebeorh G*, gener ł frofre I, min *E^{3}*
meum	|	min ABCDFGHIJK, gescyld E^{3}
es	|	eart CFJK, west *E^{3},* beo G, ðu AB, þu *I*
tu	|	þu CE^{3}J*K,* ðu F, þu ł þu eart G*, earð A, eart BI
et		⁊ ABCE^{3}FGJK (*I*)
propter		fore ABDH, for CE^{3}FGIJK
nomen	|	noman AB, naman CDFGHIJK, þinum E^{3}
tuum	|	ðinum AF, þinu<u>m</u> BCDH*J,* þinum GI, þinan K, nomæn E^{3}
⟨domine⟩		driħ *J*
dux*	|	ladtow A*, latteow B, latþeow CD, þu lætst F, þu læddest G, þu lædest H, ⁊ þu gelædst I, gelændest J, lædest K, mín E^{3} (*L*)
mihi*	|	me AB*C*FGIJK, lættþeow *E^{3}** (*L*)
eris*		ðu bist A, þu bist BE^{3}, þu byst C
et		⁊ ABCE^{3}FGHIJK

enutries	I foedes A, foedest B, fedyst C, feddest J, þu fedest DH, ðu fedest F*, þu feddest *GK*, þu gefedst I, þu me E³
me	I me ABCFGHIJK, afeddest E³

ED: forðon (A)] for ðon *Kuhn*. refugivm (E)] refugium *Harsley*. és (E)] es *Harsley*. m¹ (E)] michi *Harsley*. ęnutries (G)] enutries *Rosier*.

OE: strengð ł miht (G)] ł miht *added in diff.* (?) *hand*. frofer ł gebeorh (G)] ł gebeorh *added in diff.* (?) *hand*. þu ł þu eart (G)] ł þu eart *added in diff.* (?) *hand*. ladtow (A)] *orig.* ladtod: *final* d *deleted by subscript dot,* w *interl. by glossator*. lættþeow (E³)] ttþ *in darker ink*. ðu fedest (F)] d *altered from another letter*.

LTg: firmamentum] L: *underlined to signal deletion,* fortitudo *added interl. by corr.: see GAg*. refugium] refugivm E. es] I: es *written again in left margin;* és E. tu] K: u *obscured by stain*. et (*2nd*)] I: *eras. above word: see gloss to* dux. tuum] tuum domine J. dux] L: *underlined to signal deletion,* deduces *added interl. by corr.: see GAg*. mihi] L: *underlined to signal deletion,* me *added interl. by corr.: see GAg;* michi C: *orig.* mihi: c *interl. by corr.;* m¹ E. enutries] K: *2nd* e *on eras.;* ęnutries G.

LTu: Quoniam] QM̄ β. mihi] michi ς.

GAg: firmamentum meam] fortitudo mea FGHIJK; fortitudo meam L: *see LTg*. dux mihi eris] deduces me FGHIJK, L: *see LTg*.

GAu: firmamentum meam] fortitudo mea δεζϑιλμξοπϱστυφχψ. dux mihi eris] deduces me δεζϑιλμξοπϱστυφχψ.

5

Et*	⁊ ABCD
educes	utalędes *A*, utalædest *B*, utalædyst C, ðu lædest D*F*, þu læddest *GK*, þu lædest *H*, þu gelædst *I*, þu gelæddest *J*, læddest þu E³*
me	mec A, me CE³FGHIJK
de	of ABCDEˣ*FGHIJK
laqueo	gerene A, gryne CDEˣ*, grine FGIJK, gyrne B
isto*	ðisse A, ðissu<u>m</u> B, þissum CEˣ*, þysu<u>m</u> DGH, þysum I*, þisu<u>m</u> J, ðam F
quem	ða A, þa CE³K, þy D, ðe F, þæt BJ, þ<u>æt</u> G, þ<u>æt</u> ðe I*
occultauerunt*	I gedegladon A, gedeglydon C, bedegledon B, bedægledon G, bedigledon J*, hy dygledon D*, hi digelodan K, hi behyddon FI, me E³ (*L*)
mihi	I mec A, me B*C*DFG*HIJ*K, gedieledon *E³**
quoniam	forðon ABE³, forþon CJ, forþā G, forðam K, forðam ðe F, forðan þe I*
tu	ðu ABF, þu CDEˣG*H*IJK

es	earð A, eart BCFG*H*IJK, art *E*^{x}
protector	gescildend A, gescyldynd C, gescyldend DE^{x}GHI, scildend BJ, scyld K, bewerigend F
meus	min ABCDE^{x}*FGHIJK
domine*	drihten E^{3}, dryhт̄ AB, driħt C

ED: tú (H)] tu *Campbell.* forðon (A)] for ðon *Kuhn.* és (E)] es *Harsley.*

OE: læddest þu (E^{3})] *in darker ink, possibly orig. gloss 'freshened up.'* of (E^{x})] *on eras.* gryne (E^{x})] *on eras.* þissum (E^{x})] *eras. after 2nd* s. þysum (I)] *eras. after* y. þ<u>æt</u> ðe (I)] ðe *on eras.* bedigledon (J)] l *altered from another letter.* hy dygledon (D)] *orig.* hy dyglodon: *1st* o *deleted by subscript dot,* e *interl.* gedieledon (E^{3})] *letter eras. after 2nd* e. forðan þe (I)] þe *interl.* min (E^{x})] *on eras.*

LTg: educes] Aeduces F; Educes GHIJK; educis AB. occultauerunt] L: absconderunt *added interl. by corr.: see GAg.* mihi] michi EHJ, C: *orig.* mihi: c *interl. by corr.* tu] tú H. es] és EH.

LTu: educes] Educes δεζϑιλμξοπϱστυφχψ. mihi] michi ιλςχ, ϱ: c *added interl.* quoniam] Quoniam ϱ: *not indicating verse division.* domine] *om.* ς: *cf. Weber MSS* Κα*γ moz^{c}, *see GAu.*

GAg: Et] *om.* FGHIJK. isto] hoc GIJ; hóc K: *crossed through,* FH: *lemma eras.: cf. Weber MSS* γλ moz^{x}. occultauerunt] absconderunt FGHIJK, L: *see LTg.* domine] *om.* FGHIJK.

GAu: Et] *om.* δεζϑιλμξοπϱστυφχψ. isto] hoc δεζϑιλμξοπϱστυφψ; *om.* χ: *eras. after* laqueo. occultauerunt] absconderunt δεζϑιλμξοπστυφχψ. domine] *om.* δεζϑιλμξοπϱστυφχψ, ς: *see LTu.*

6

In		in *A,* on *BCDE^{3}*FGHI*JK
manus	|	honda AB, handa CDFGHK, handum I, hand<u>um</u> J, þine E^{3}
tuas	|	ðine AF, þine C, þina B, þinre G*, þinra K, þinum I, þin<u>um</u> *J*, hænde E^{3} (*H*)
⟨domine⟩		driħ *J*
commendo*		ic bibiodu A, ic bebeode BCDFGH, ic beode J, ic etfeste ł ic bebeode þe E$^{3/x}$*, ic befæste ł betæce [ ]c bebeode I*, ic betæce *K*
spiritum	|	gast AB*C*DFGHIJK, mine E^{3}
meum	|	minne ABCDFGIJK, mine H, gæst E^{3}
redemisti	|	ðu alesdes *A,* þu aliesdes *B,* þu alysdyst *C,* þu alysdest *DG*HIK*, ðu alysdest F, þu alisdest J, þu me *E^{3}* (*L*)
me	|	mec A, me BCFGIJK, alisdest E^{3}*
domine		drihtyn C, drihten E^{3}F, dryhт̄ AB, driħ GJ (*I*)

deus	god ABCE^{3}FGIJK
ueritatis	soðfestnisse A, soðfæstnysse CI, soþfæstnisse DH, soþfæstnys F, soðfæstnesse BG, soþfæstnese K, on soðfestnesse E^{3}, soþfæst J

ED: ic befæste ł betæce [ ]c bebeode (I)] ic befæste ł betæce ł bebeode *Lindelöf.*

OE: on (I)] *faint but visible.* þinre (G)] r *added interl. in diff.* (?) *hand.* ic etfeste ł ic bebeode þe ($E^{3/x}$)] *3rd* e *added in darker ink,* þe *added by corr.* ic befæste ł betæce [ ]c bebeode (I)] bebeode *written in left margin, back of 3rd* c *cropped.* þu alysdest (K)] *eras.* (?) *after 1st* s. alisdest (E^{3})] t *added by corr.*

LTg: In] in ABCDE. tuas] H: *eras.* (*3 letters?*) *after word.* commendo] K: *orig.* commendabo: ab *eras.*, F: *see GAg.* tuas] tuas domine J: *cf. Weber MS* γ: in manibus tuis commendo domine. spiritum] C: *1st* i *formed from another letter: eras. of descender visible.* redemisti] G: redemisti me domine deus ueritatis *in darker ink,* L: R *crossed through,* r *written to right by corr.;* Redemisti ABCDE. domine] I: o *written above word.*

LTu: In] in βν. tuas] tuas domine ϑς: *cf. Weber MS* γ: in manibus tuis commendo domine. redemisti] Redemisti βνςτ*; redimisti ϑ. me] *interl.* ϱ.

GAg: commendo] commendabo F: *orig.* commendo: *2nd* o *deleted by subscript dot,* dabo *interl. by corr.*

GAu: commendo] commendabo δζοψ.

7

Odisti	ðu fiodes *A*, þu feodes *B*, þu feodyst *C*, þu feodest J, þu fiodes ł hatudest *$E^{3/x}$**, ðu hatudest *D*, þu hatudest FGH, ðu hatodest I, þu hatoddest K (*L*)
obseruantes	haldende A, healdende BJK, healdynde C, beweardgende DFH, beweardigende G, þæ beweardgende $E^{3/x}$*, þa begymendan I
uanitatem*	idelnisse A, idylnysse C, ydelnysse F, idelnesse BDE^{3}JK, idelnessa GHI, idelnesse J (*L*)
superuacue	idellice *A*B, ofyr idyllice C, ofer idellice J, ofer unnytlice DGH, ofer unnyt FK, ofer þæ emettgæn ł unnytlice $E^{3/x}$*, on idel ł unnytlicu *I*

Ego	ic ABCDF*G*HIJK, Ic E^{3}
autem	soðlice ACE^{3}*FG, soþlice DHJ, soð B, witolite K
in	in A, on BCE^{3}FGIJK
domino	dryhtne B, drihtne CFI, drihten E^{3}K, dryht̄ A, drih̄t G, drih̄ I
sperabo*	ic gehyhtu A, ic gehyhte B, ic gehihte CG*, gehihte IJ, ic hihte F, hyhte DE^{x}*H, hihte K (*L*)

ED: ofyr idyllice (C)] ofyridyllice *Wildhagen.*

OE: þu fiodes ł hatudest (E$^{3/x}$)] ł hatudest *added by corr.* þæ beweardgende (E$^{3/x}$)] beweardgende *by corr.* ofer þæ emettgæn ł unnytlice (E$^{3/x}$)] ł unnytlice *added by corr.* soðlice (E^{3})] *eras. (22 mm) after word.* ic gehihte (G)] ic ge *added in diff.* (?) *hand.* hyhte (E^{x})] *on eras.*

LTg: Odisti] odisti ABDE, C: *eras. after* d, L: O *written above* o *by corr.* uanitatem] L: m *crossed through and* s *added to right by corr.: see GAg.* superuacue] A: *letter eras. after 2nd* u; superuacuae I. ego] [ ]go G. sperabo] L: bo *crossed through and* ui *written interl. by corr.: see GAg.*

LTu: Odisti] odisti βνςτ*. superuacue] superuacuae βδ; superuacuę ζλξ; superuacuæ ϑ.

GAg: uanitatem] uanitates FGIJK, H: *orig.* uanitatis: *2nd* i *altered to* e, L: *see LTg.* sperabo] speraui FGHIJK, L: *see LTg.*

GAu: uanitatem] uanitates δεζϑιλμξοπϱστυφχψ. sperabo] speraui δεζϑιλμξοπϱστυφχψ.

8

Exultabo	ic gefie A, ic gefeo BCJ, ic fægnie D, ic fægnige FHK, ic fægni[ ] *G,* ic winsumie ł fægnie *E$^{3/x}$*,* ic blissige I
et	⁊ ABCDE^{3}FGHIJK
laetabor	blisie A, blissie *C*,* blissige *BDGJ,* blissiæ *E^{3},* ic blissige *FK,* bliðgge *H,* ic gladige I (*L*)
in	in A, on BCDE^{3}FGHIJK
tua* }	ðinre AB, þinre CDGHIK, ðine F, þin J, þire E^{3}*
misericordia* }	mildheortnisse AD, mildheortnysse CI, mildheortnessæ E^{3}, mildheortnyssa F, mildheortnesse BGHJK
quia*	forðon *ABD*H, forþon *C*GJ, Forðæn *E^{3},* forðam F, forþan K, forþan þe I* (*L*)
respexisti	gelocades A, þu gelocades B, þu gelocodyst C, þu gelocodest J, þu gesawe DGH, þu gesege K, þu beheolde F, þu gelocedes ł sawe E$^{3/x}$*, þu beheolde ł þu besawe I*
humilitatem	eaðmodnisse AD, eaðmodnesse B, eæþmodnesse E^{3}, eaðmodnysse I, eadmodnysse C, eadmodnyssa F, eadmodnesse GHJK
meam	mine ABCDE^{x}*FGHIJK
saluam*	hale ABCD, hæle J, ⁊ hele E^{3}, gehæle F, þu hældest G, þu gehældest I*, hældest K (*L*)
fecisti*	ðu dydes A, þu dydes B, þu dydyst C, ðu dydest D, me gedydest E^{3} (*L*)
de	of ABCDE^{3}FGHIJK
necessitatibus	nedðearfnissum A, nydþearfnyssum C*, neadðearfnyssum I,

		nedðearfnessum B, nydþearfnessum J, minum niedþeærfnessvm ł nedum E$^{3/x}$*, nedum D, nedum FH, nede K, neadum ł neadnessum G
animam		sawle ABCFGIJ, saule DHK, sæwle E^{3}
meam		mine ABCE^{3}FGHIJ, minre K

ED: ic winsumie ł fægnie (E)] ic winsumie ł fægcnie *Harsley*. lętabor (E)] laetabor *Harsley*. þire (E)] þine *Harsley*. forðon (A)] for ðon *Kuhn*.

OE: ic winsumie ł fægnie (E$^{3/x}$)] ł fægnie *added by corr.* blissie (C)] *2nd* i *interl. in red in main hand.* þire (E^{3})] orig. þine: *left leg of* n *extended to form* r. forþan þe (I)] *written in left margin.* þu gelocedes ł sawe (E$^{3/x}$)] ł sawe *on eras. by corr., eras. (5–6 letters) after word.* þu beheolde ł þu besawe (I)] *stem of 1st* þ *formed from another letter, bowl of 2nd* þ *and* u *on eras.*, heolde *written in left margin.* mine (E^{x})] *on eras.* þu gehældest (I)] *2nd* e *on eras.*, st *added later by glossator.* nydþearfnyssum (C)] u *altered from another letter.* minum niedþeærfnessvm ł nedum (E$^{3/x}$)] v *altered from* e, ł nedum *added by corr.*

LTg: Exultabo] exultab[ ] G; exultabor E: *cf. Weber MSS* αγ. laetabor] lætabor BK; lętabor CEFG; letabor DHJL. quia] Quia ABCDL; Qvia E. saluam] L: m *underlined to signal deletion, but with expected Gallican variant not provided: see GAg.* fecisti] L: *underlined to signal deletion: see GAg.*

LTu: laetabor] lętabor εϑιλνφ; letabor ξσςτ*τυχ. quia] Quia βνς; Qvia τ*.

GAg: tua misericordia] misericordia tua FGHIJK. quia] Quoniam FGHIJK. saluam fecisti] saluasti FGHIJK; for L *see LTg*.

GAu: tua misericordia] misericordia tua δεζιλμξοπϱστυφχψ; missericordia tua ϑ. quia] Quoniam δεζϑιλμξοπϱστυφχψ. saluam fecisti] saluasti δεζϑιλμξοπϱστυφχψ.

9

Nec		ne *ABCDE*^{x}FG*H*IJ, na K (*L*)
conclusisti		biluce A, beluce ðu B, beluce þu C, beluc þu J, ðu na beluce DE^{x}, þu na beluce GH*K*, þu na beclysdest F, þu ne beclysdest I
me		me ABCDE^{x}FGHIJ
in		in A, on BCDE^{x}FGIJK (*H*)
manus*	I	honda AB, handa CD*K*, handum *F*G, handum J, handum ł on anwealde I, fiondæs E^{3} (*HL*)
inimici	I	feondes ABDFGHI, feondys C, feondum J, feonda K, hændum E^{3}
statuisti		ðu gesettes *A*, þu gesettes *B*, þu gesettyst *C*I, ðu gesettest *D*, ðu gesettest F, þu gesettest *E*^{3}GHJK (*L*)
in	I	in A, on BCDFGHIJK, mine E^{3}

loco	I	stowe ABCDFGHJK, felde ł on stowe I, fęt E^3
spatioso	I	rumre ABCHJK, rumre ł widgilre D, rumre ł widgylre G, wídgylre F, bradum ł on bradre sto[ ] I*, on E^3
pedes	I	foet AB, fet CFGHIJK, fét D, stowe E^3
meos	I	mine ABCFGHIJK, rumre ł widgilre E^x*

OE: bradum ł on bradre sto[ ] (I)] ł on bradre sto[ ] *written in right margin, last word cropped.* rumre ł widgilre (E^x)] rumre ł wid *on eras.*

LTg: Nec] Nęc H; nec ABCDE, L: N *written above* n *by corr.* conclusisti] K: n *interl. by corr.* in (*1st*)] H: *eras. after word.* manus] H: *eras.* (*2 letters*) *after* n, F: *orig.* manibus: ibus *crossed through and abbreviation for* us *added by corr.*, K: *orig.* manibus: ibus *deleted by subscript dots, abbreviation for* us *added interl.*, L: ibus *written above* us *by corr.: see GAg.* statuisti] Statuisti ABCDEL.

LTu: Nec] οσυ: c *interl.;* nec βνςτ*. me] *om.* ς. statuisti] Statuisti βνςτ*. spatioso] spacioso τ*τφψ.

GAg: manus] manibus GIJ, L: *see LTg; for* FHK *see LTg.*

GAu: manus] manibus δεζιλμξοπϱτυψ.

10

Miserere		mildsa *AHJK*, miltsa *G*, miltsæ *E^3**, gemiltsa *B*F, gemyltsa *C*, gemildsa I (*DL*)
mihi*		me AB*CE^3*GHK, min FIJ
domine		dryhten B, drihten E^3, dryht̄ A, driht C, drih̄t F, drih̄ GHJ, hlaford K (*I*)
quoniam		forðon ABJ, forþon CE^3, forðā F, forþā K, forþā þe G, forðan þe I*
tribulor		ic biom geswenced A, ic beom geswencyd C, ic geswenced b[ ] *G*, ic swenced beo H, ic eom geswenced B, swencende K, ic senged beom D, ic gedrefed beo F, ic iem geeærfoþod E^3, ic eom gedrefod I, ic eom gespræneced J
conturbatus		gedroefed *A*, gedrefed *BD*GHJ, gedrefyd *C*, Gedrefed *E^3*, gedreued K, geswenced F, astyrod I* (*L*)
est		is ABDE^{3}FGHIJ*K*, ys C
in	I	in A*, on BCDFGHIJK, min E^3*
ira	I	eorre ABDH, yrre CGIJK, graman F, egæ E^3*
oculus	I	ege A, eage BCIJ, eage D, eagan FGH, egan K, for E^3
meus	I	min ABCFIJ, mine GH, minan K, irre E^3
anima		sawul A, sawl BCGHI, saul D, sæul E^3*, sawle FJ, sawel K
mea		min ABCDFGHIJK, mín E^3

et	ᴛ ABCE^{x}FGHIJK
uenter	womb AB, wamb CK*, wambe J, innoð DE^{3}FGHI
meus	min ABCE^{x}*FGHIJK

ED: m[1] (E)] michi *Harsley*. dryhten (B)] dryht*en* *Brenner*. forðon (A)] for ðon *Kuhn*. forþā þe (G)] forþam þe *Rosier*. ic geswenced b[ ] (G)] ic geswenc:þ *Rosier*.

OE: miltsæ (E^{3})] m *eras. after word.* forðan þe (I)] e *interl.* astyrod (I)] *orig.* astirod: i *altered to* y. in (A)] *small eras. before* i. min (E^{3}) (*1st*)] e *eras. after word.* egæ (E^{3})] *letter* (n?) *eras. after word.* sæul (E^{3})] *eras. after word.* wamb (K)] *eras. (10 mm) before word,* w *visible in initial position.* min (E^{x})] (*2nd*)] *eras. before word.*

LTg: Miserere] miserere BCDE, L: M *written above* m *by corr.*, A: *orig.* miserire: *2nd* i *altered to* e; [ ]serere G; Misere K. mihi] m[1] E: *letter eras. after word;* michi C: *orig.* mihi: c *interl. by corr.* domine] I: o *written above word.* tribulor] tribul[ ] G. conturbatus] Conturbatus ABCDEL. est] ést K.

LTu: Miserere] miserere βνςτ*; Misserere ϑ. mihi] michi ς. conturbatus] Conturbatus βνςτ.

GAg: mihi] mei FGHIJK.

GAu: mihi] mei δεζϑιλμξοπϱστυφχψ.

11

Quoniam	forðon ABJ, forþon C, forþam K, forðæn þe E^{3}, forðam ðe F, forþam þe G, forðan þe I
defecit	asprong ABC, teorode DE^{x}*, ateorode FIK, geteorode GHJ
in	I in A, on BCDFGIJK, min E^{3}
dolore	I sare ABCDFGIJK, lyf E^{3}
uita	I lif ABCDFGHIJK, on E^{3}
mea	I min ABCDFGHIJK, særæ E^{3}
et	ᴛ ABCDE^{3}FGHIJK
anni	I ger AC, gear BDFGHJK, gearas I, mine E^{3}
mei	I min AFK, mine BCDGHIJ, geær E^{3}
in	on BCDE^{3}FGHIJ
gemitibus	geamringum *A*, geomrungum B*H*, geomrungum D, giomrungum E^{3}, geomrungum F, geomorungum G, geomrunge CJ, geomerunga K, geomrungum ł on siccetum I
Infirmata	geuntrumad A, geuntrumod BDFGHIJ, geuntrumud C, Geuntrumed E^{3}, geuntrumed K
est	is ABDE^{3}FGHIJ*K*, ys C
in	in A, on BCDE^{3}FGHIJ, o K

paupertate	ðearfednisse A, ðearfednesse B, þearfydnysse C, þearfednesse J, ðearflicnisse D, þeærflicnisse E3/x*, þearflicnysse F, þearflicnesse GH, þearflicnesnes K, yrmðe I
uirtus	megen A, mægen BDExHJ, mægyn C, mægn K, mægen ł miht GI, miht F
mea	min ABCDE3*FGHIJK
et	⁊ ABCDE3FGHIJK
ossa	ban ABCGHIJK, bán DF, bæn E3
mea	min AK, mine BCDEx*FGHIJ
conturbata	gedroefed A, gedrefed DH, gedrefde BF, gedrefyde C, gedrefede E3GJK, gedrefode I
sunt	sind A, synd CGHK, sýnd F, sint B, synt DExI, syndon J

ED: forðon (A)] for ðon *Kuhn*. Infirmata (B)] infirmata *Brenner*. ðearfednesse (B)] ðearfnesse *Brenner*.

OE: teorode (Ex)] *on eras*. þeærflicnisse (E3/x)] licnisse *on eras. by corr., with eras. extending into next line* (*10 mm*). min (E3) (*2nd*)] ⁊ *eras. before word,* e *eras. after word.* mine (Ex) (*2nd*)] *on eras.*

LTg: gemitibus] A: us *added by corr.*, H: *eras. after 1st* i. est] ést K.

LTu: uita] uitæ ϑ. mea] meæ ϑ. Infirmata] INfirmata β.

12

Super	ofer ABDFGHJK, ofyr C, Ofer E3, ofor I
omnes	alle A, ealle BC*D*FGHIJK, eællæ E3
inimicos	ǀ fiond A, fiend B, fynd CDFGIJK, feond H, mine E3
meos	ǀ mine ABCDFGHIJK, fiend E3
factus	geworden ABEx*FGHIJ, gewordyn C, geworden D, gedon K
sum	ic eam A, ic eom BCDEx*FGHIJK
obprobrium	edwit *A*B**C*, hosp DEx*FG*HIJK*
(et)*	⁊ FGHI
uicinis	nehgehusum A, nehgeburum B, nehgeburum C, neahgeburum D, neahgeburum Ex*FI, neacheburum G, neacheburum H, neahheburum J, ⁊ nehgeburan *K*
meis	minum AEx, minum BCDGHIJ, minan K
nimium*	swiðe ABG, swyðe K, swiðust C, swið D, to swiðe Ex, ðearle F, þearle IJ (*L*)
et	⁊ ABCDExFGHIJK
timor	ege ABCDExFGHIJK
notis	cuðum ABCGH, cuþum D, cuþum E3I, cuðe F, cuþe J, cuþan K
meis	minum AEx*FGH, minum BCDI*J, minan K

Qui		ða AB, þa CJK, þa ðe DFH, ða þe E[3]*, þa þe GI
uidebant	I	gesegun A, gesegan K, gesawon BCDFGHJ, gesawun I, me E[3]
me	I	mec A, me BCDFGHIJK, gesiowon E[x]*
foris*		ute ABCD*E[3]*FGHK, ut IJ
fugiebant*		flugun A, flugon B*C*HI, flegan J, hie flugon D*E[3/x]**, hi flugon FG, hi flugan K (*L*)
a		from A*E[3]*, fro<u>m</u> BC, fra<u>m</u> DHJ, fram FGI, fra K
me		me ABCDE[3]FGHIJK

ED: meos (C)] *emos Wildhagen.* opprobrium (C)] o[b]probrium *Wildhagen.* cuðum (B)] cuðu<u>m</u> *Brenner.* Qui (B)] qui *Brenner.* mec (A)] me *Kuhn.* á (E)] a *Harsley.*

OE: geworden (E[x])] *on eras.* ic eom (E[x])] *on eras.* edwit (B)] t *blotted.* hosp (E[x])] *on eras.* neahgeburum (E[x])] h *altered from another letter.* minum (E[x]) (*2nd*)] *on eras.* minu<u>m</u> (I) (*2nd*)] *written in right margin and cropped:* ic eom geworde[ ] hosp ofer eal[ ] mine fynd ⁊ [ ] minum nea(h)[ ]burum þearl[ ] minum cuþ[ ]: *letter fragment* (o *or* e?) *visible after* ⁊, *ascender of* h *visible.* ða þe (E[3])] a *altered from another letter.* gesiowon (E[x])] iow *on eras.* hie flugon (E[3/x])] ugon *on eras. by corr.*

LTg: Super] [ ]uper G: *initial* S *lost, outline visible.* omnes] oms D: *no macron visible.* obprobrium] opprobrium AHI, C: *orig.* obprobrium: b *altered to* p *by corr.,* K: *orig.* obprobrium et: et *eras.* uincis] K: et *eras. before word.* nimium] L: *underlined to signal deletion and* ualde *written above by corr.: see GAg.* foris] foras E: *cf. Weber MSS* α med, *see GAg.* fugiebant] C: i *interl.,* E: ba *altered from other letters;* fugebant L: bant *underlined to signal deletion and* runt *written interl. by corr.: see GAg.* a] á E.

LTu: Super] SUper β. obprobrium] opprobrium λφ; opproprium ε, β: *orig.* obproprium: *1st* p *interl. above* b. uidebant] uiderunt ϑ: *cf. Weber MS* γ.

GAg: obprobrium] obprobrium et FG; opprobrium et II: et *added by glossator,* I: et *interl.* nimium] ualde FGHIJK, L: *see LTg.* foris] foras FGHIJK, E: *see LTg.* fugiebant] fugerunt FHIJ, K: *letter eras. after* g, L: *see LTg;* fugierunt G: *cf. Weber MS* δ, *Bib. sac. MSS* RQΦ[RGV]G*, *etc.*

GAu: obprobrium] obprobrium et δζϑιλμξϱτχψ, o: *1st* b *altered from* p; opprobrium et φ, π: *1st* p *altered from* b, et *interl.* nimium] ualde δεζϑιλμξοπϱστυφχψ. foris] foras δεζιλμξοπϱστυφχψ. fugiebant] fugerunt δεζϑιλξοπϱστυφχψ; fugierunt μ: *cf. Weber MS* δ, *Bib. sac. MSS* RQΦ[RGV]G*, *etc.*

13

Excidi*	ic gesnerc *A,* ic geswearc *B,* ic forcearf *C,* ic g<u>e</u>feol *D,* ic gef(eo)l F*, ic gefeoll J, ⁊ ic gefeol *E[3/x]**, forgytelnesse GI (*L*)
(datus)*	geseald FIJ, forgifen ł geseald G, gifen K (*L*)
(sum)*	ic eom FGIJ (*L*)

tamquam		swe swe A, swa swa B*C*DFG*H*IJ, swæ swæ *$E^{3/x}$**, swa K
mortuus		dead ABDE^{x}*GH, deað CF, deaþ J, se deada I (*L*)
a		from A, from BC, fram DFHJ, fram *E^{x}**GI
corde		heortan ABCDFGHIJ, heortæn E^{3}
et*		⁊ ABCDE^{3} (*L*)
factus	|	geworden AB*FIJ,* gewordyn C, worden D*GH,* don *K,* ic eom E^{3} (*L*)
sum	|	ic eam A, ic eom BDFGHIJK, ic eom C, geworden E^{3}
sicut*		swe swe A, swa swa BCFGHIJ, swæ swæ E^{3}, swa K
uas	|	fet A, fæt BCDFGHIJK, þet forlore $E^{3/x}$*
perditum	|	forloren A*BDFGHJK, forloryn *C,* forspilled ł forloren I*, fęt E^{3}

ED: éxcidi (C)] excidi *Wildhagen.* ic gef(eo)l (F)] ic gefeol *Kimmens.* tanquam (C)] ta[m]quam *Wildhagen.* forgifen ł geseald (G)] forgifen ł forseald *Rosier.* swa swa (GIJ) (*both*)] swaswa *Rosier, Lindelöf, Oess.* á (E)] a *Harsley.*

OE: ic gef(eo)l (F)] *gloss partly eras., lower portions of* eo *visible.* ⁊ ic gefeol ($E^{3/x}$)] gefeol *on eras. by corr.* swæ swæ ($E^{3/x}$)] *2nd* swæ *added by corr.* dead (E^{x})] *on eras., eras. after word.* fram (E^{x})] *on eras.* þet forlore ($E^{3/x}$)] forlore *on eras. by corr.* forloren (A)] *2nd* o *altered from another letter.* forspilled ł forloren (I)] ł forloren *written in left margin.*

LTg: Excidi] éxcidi C; excidi ABDE, L: *underlined to indicate deletion,* obliuioni datus sum *written in right margin by corr.: see GAg.* tamquam] tanquam E, C: *orig.* tamquam: *left leg of 1st* m *eras. to form* n, H: *eras. after* n. mortuus] L: *orig.* mortuos: *2nd* o *altered to* u. a] á E. et] L: *crossed through: see GAg.* factus] L: f *altered to* F *by corr.;* Factus FGIJK, H: *initial* F *nearly completely lost.* perditum] pérditum C.

LTu: Excidi] excidi νςτ*; excide β. tamquam] tanquam ϑιλστ*τφ. mortuus] mortuos β; mortus ϑ. et] β: *interl. by corr.* factus] Factus δεζϑιλμξπστυφχψ.

GAg: Excidi] obliuioni datus sum FGHIJK, L: *see LTg.* et] *om.* FGHIJK, L: *see LTg.* sicut] tamquam FGIJK; tanquam H: *eras. after* n.

GAu: Excidi] obliuioni datus sum δεζϑιλμξοπϱστυφχψ. et] *om.* δεζϑιμξοπϱσυφχψ. sicut] tamquam δεζμξοπϱυχψ; tanquam ϑιλστφ.

14

Quoniam	forðon ABD*HJ,* forþon C*G,* Forðæn E^{3}, forþā *K,* forðam ðe *F,* forðan þe *I* (*L*)
audiui	ic geherde AI, ic gehierde B, ic gehyrde CFHK, ic gehyrde D, ic gehierda E^{3}*, ic gehirde J, gehyrde G
uituperationem	telnisse A, tælnesse B, tælnysse C, tælnessa J, tale DE^{3}*K,

	tále ł tælnyssa F, tælnesse ł tale G, hosp ł tælnessa ł tale I
multorum	monigra AB, mænigra C, manigra DE^3*FHJ, manegra GIK
(commorantium)*	wundriendra ł standendra F, wunigendra ł standendra J, wunigendra G, wuniendra I
(in)*	on FGJ, abutan ł on I
circumhabitantium*	ymbeardiendra AB, ymbeardgendra D, ymbeærdiendra E^3*, ymbeardungra *C*, ymbhwýrfte F, ymbhwyrftc GJ, ymbhwyrte I* (*L*)
In	in A, on BCDF*G*HIJK, On E^3
eo	ðon AB, þone C, ðam D, ðam F*G*, þam H, þæm I, þam JK, him E^3
dum	ðonne A, þonne BI*, þonne C, ðonne F, þa DHJK, ða E^x*, þam *G*
congregarentur*	bioð gesomnade A, beoð gesomnode B, beoð gesomnude C, hy gesomnodon E$^{3/x}$*, hy gæderedon ł somnodon D, hi gederedon ł somnodon F, hi gegaderodon G, hy gæde redon H, hi gæderodan K, hig samod comon ł ł þonne hi gesamnodon I*, hig comon ł somnodon J (*L*)
omnes*	alle A, ealle BCD, eælle E^3 (*L*)
simul	somud A, somod B, samod ĊFI, somed E^3, ætsomne D, ætsomne GHJK
aduersum*	wið ABC, ongean D*E^x**GHJ, agen I, togeanes FK
me	me ABCE^{3}FGHIJK, mec D
ut*	ðæt A, þæt BC, þæt D, þet E^3 (*L*)
acciperent*	hie onfoen A, hie onfon B, hi onfon C, onfoh J, hy anfengen D, hie onfeangen E$^{3/}$*, onfengon G, anfengan K, underfoh F, geniman I (*L*)
animam |	sawle ABCFGHIJK, saule D, mine E^3
meam |	mine ABCDFGHIJK, sæwle E^3
consiliati	geðaehtende A, geðehtende B, geþiehtigynde C, hy geþeahtedon DGH, hy geþeahtiende E^3*, hi geþeahtudon F, hi geþeahtodon I, hi geþehtodon K, geþeahtende ł rædende J*
sunt	werun A, hi wæron C, sint B, synd FGJ, sindon E^3

ED: forðon (A)] for ðon *Kuhn*. éo (G)] eo *Rosier*. hig samod comon ł ł þonne hi gesamnodon (I)] hig samod comon ł þonne hi gesamnodon *Lindelöf*. somed (E)] Somed *Harsley*.

OE: ic gehierda (E^{3})] da *on eras. by corr.* tale (E^{3})] *eras. below gloss extending rest of line.* manigra (E^{3})] *on eras., eras. (21 mm) after word.* ymbeærdiendra (E^{3})] e *eras. after* b, *eras. before* e *in next line* (ymb/eærdiendra), ra *on eras. by corr.* ymbhwyrte (I)] e *malformed.* þonne (I)] *on eras.* ða (E^{x})] *on eras.* hy gesomnodon (E$^{3/x}$)] hy *on eras. by corr., 2nd* o *on eras. of* e, on *on eras. by corr.* hig samod comon ł ł þonne hi gesamnodon (I)] ł þonne hi gesamnodon *written in left margin,* hig samod com *on eras.* ongean (E^{x})] onge *on eras.* hie onfeangen (E$^{3/x}$)] onfeangen *by corr.*, gen *on eras.* hy geþeahtiende (E^{3})] hy *written in left margin by main hand.* geþeahtende ł rædende (J)] ł rædende *written above* geþeahtende.

LTg: Quoniam] L: Q *crossed through and* q *written to right by corr.;* quoniam FGHIJK. circumhabitantium] C: h *interl. by corr.,* L: *underlined to signal deletion and* commorantium in circuitu *written in right margin: see GAg.* In] [ ] G. eo] éo G. dum] G: u *altered from another letter.* congregarentur] L: *underlined to signal deletion and* couenirent *interl. by corr.: see GAg.* omnes] L: *underlined to signal deletion: see GAg.* aduersum] adversum E. ut] L: *underlined to signal deletion: see GAg.* acciperent] L: nt *underlined to signal deletion: see GAg.*

LTu: Quoniam] QM̄ β; quoniam δεζϑιλμξοπϱστυφχψ. In] IN β.

GAg: multorum] multorum commorantium FGHIJK, L: *see LTg note to* circumhabitantium. circumhabitantium] in circuitu FGJK, I: *eras. after* circuitu, L: *see LTg;* in circumitu H. congregarentur] conuenirent FGHIJK, L: *see LTg.* omnes] *om.* FGHIJK, L: *see LTg.* ut] *om.* FGHIJK. acciperent] accipere FGHIJK, L: *see LTg.*

GAu: multorum] multorum commorantium δεζϑιλμξοπϱστυφχ; multorum comorantium ψ. circumhabitantium] in circuitu δεζϑιλμξοπϱστυφχψ. congregarentur] conuenirent δεζϑιλμξοπϱστφχψ. omnes] *om.* δεζϑιλμξοπϱστυφχψ. aduersum] aduersus ϑμ. ut] *om.* δεζϑιλμξοϱστυφχψ. acciperent] accipere δεζϑιλμξοπϱστυφχψ.

15

Ego	ic ABCDFGHIJK, Ic E^{3}
uero*	soðlice ABCE^{3}FGI, soþlice DHJ, witodlice K (*L*)
in	in A, on BCE^{3}FGIJK
te	ðe ABFI, þe CE^{3}GJK
speraui	gehyhte A, ic gehyhte B, ic gehihte CJ, ic hyhte DH, ic hihte FG, hihte K, gewene ł hyhte E$^{3/x}$*, hopode I
domine	dryhten A, drihten E^{3}F, drihtene H, dryht̄ B, drih́t CG, drih́ J (*I*)
dixi	ic cweð AE^{3}*, ic cwæð BCDGH, ic cweþe J, ic cwæþ K, ic cwæð ł ic sæde I, sæde F
tu*	}ǀ ðu ABF, þu C*E^{3}*GIK (*L*)
es*	}ǀ earð A, eart BCIK, eært *E^{3},* earþu J, beo F, be G (*L*)
deus*	}ǀ god ABCFGIJK, min E^{3} (*L*)
meus*	}ǀ min ABCFGIJK, god E^{3} (*L*)

ED: tú (E)] tu *Harsley*. és (E)] es *Harsley*.

OE: gewene ł hyhte (E$^{3/x}$)] ł hyhte *added by corr.* ic cweð (E^{3})] *orig.* ic cweðe: *final* e *eras.*

LTg: uero] L: *underlined to signal deletion,* autem *interl. by corr.* domine] I: o *written above word.* tu] tú E. es] és E. tu es] L: *underlined to signal deletion,* es tu *written interl. after* meus *by corr.: see GAg.*

LTu: speraui] β: *orig.* sperabo: o *crossed through,* ui *interl. by corr.*

GAg: uero] autem FGHIJK, L: *see LTg.* tu es deus meus] deus meus es tu FGHJK, I: *with gloss in order:* min god þu eart, L: *see LTg.*

GAu: uero] autem δϑιλξοπρσυφχψ. tu es deus meus] deus meus es tu δεζϑιλμξοπρσυφχψ.

16

in		in A, on BCDE^{3}FGHIJK
manibus	|	hondum A, hondum B, handum CDGHJ, handum FI, handen K, þinum E^{3}
tuis	|	ðinum AF*, þinum CGI, þinum BDHJ, þinan K, hændum E^{3}
tempora*	|	tide AC, tida BD, hlýt F, hlot GJ*, hlyta I, sint mine E^{3} (*L*)
mea*	|	mine ACI*, mina BD, min FG, minre J, tidæ E^{3} (*L*)
Libera*		gefrea A, gefreo C, alies B, alyse D, Gefriolsæ ł alyse E^{3} (*L*)
me*		me ABCE^{3} (*L*)
et*		⁊ ABCE^{3} (*L*)
eripe		genere ABCE^{3}, genera *FJ,* nere D*GH,* alys ł genera *I,* alys *K* (*L*)
me		me ABCE^{3}FGHJK
de		of ABCDE^{3}FGHIJK
manibus*	|	hondum A, handum CD, handum GH, handa FJK, anwealde ł of hande I, manu *B,* minræ E^{3} (*L*)
inimicorum		feonda ABCDFGHIJK, fiondæ E^{3}
meorum	|	minra A*BCDFGHIJK, hændum *E^{3}*
et		⁊ ABCDE^{3}FGHIJK
a		from AC*E^{3},* from B, fram DGHJK, fram FI
persequentibus	|	oehtendum A, ehtendum BDK, ehtendum FGJH, iehtyndum C, ehtiendum I, me E^{3}
me	|	me ABCDFGHIJK, ehtendum E^{3}

ED: á (E)] a *Harsley.*

OE: ðinum (F)] ð *altered from* t. hlot (J)] *added in later hand.* mine (I)] s. sunt : synt *written in right margin.* minra (A)] *orig.* menra: i *interl., but without deleting dot below* e.

LTg: tempora] L: *underlined to signal deletion,* sortes *interl. by corr.: see GAg.* mea] L: *underlined to signal deletion,* mee *interl. by corr.: see GAg.* Libera me et] L: *underlined to signal deletion,* Eripe me *interl. by corr.: see GAg.* eripe] Eripe FGHIJK. manibus (*2nd*)] L: ibus *underlined to signal deletion,* u *interl. by corr.;* manu B: see *GAg.* meorum] E: eorum *on eras.* a] á E.

LTu: eripe] Eripe δεζϑιλμξοϱστυφ.

GAg: tempora] sortes FGHIJK, L: *see LTg.* mea] meę FG, J: *cauda added by glossator;* męę H; meae I; meæ K; *for* L *see LTg.* Libera me et] *om.* FGHIJK, L: *see LTg.* manibus] manu FGHIJK, BL: *see LTg.*

GAg: tempora] sortes δεζϑιλμξοπϱστυφχψ. mea] meae δζλμοπϱυχψ; meę ειξφ; meæ ϑ; mee στ. Libera me et] *om.* δεζϑιλμξοπϱστφχψ. manibus] manu δεζϑιλμξοϱστχψ.

17

Inlumina*		inliht A, onleht B, onlyht *C*DFK, Onlihtæ E^3, onleoht I*, onliht J, onlustra G*H* (*L*)
faciem	I	onsiene AB, ansyne CGK, onsyne DH, ansine FIJ, þine E^3
tuam	I	ðine A, þine BCGHIJK, þin F, onsiene E^3
super		ofer ABE^{3}FGI*JK, ofyr C
seruum	I	(ði)ow A*, ðeow BCF, þeow DHJ, þeowan G, ðeowan I, þewan K, þinne E^3
tuum	I	ðinne AF, þinne BCDGJK, þine H, þinum I, þiow E^3
et*		⁊ ABCE^3
saluum	I	halne ABDGHJK, haline C, ⁊ halne F, gehæl I, gedo E^3
me		mec A, me BCE^{3}FGIJK
fac	I	doa A, do BFGJK, gedo C, hælne E^3
in		on BCDE^{3}FGHIJK
tua*	}	ðinre AFI, þinre BCDE^{3}GHJ, þ K*
misericordia*	}	mildheortnisse ADI, mildheortnysse C, mildheortnyssa F, mildheortnesse BE^{3}GHJK

ED: Illumina (C)] I[n]lumina *Wildhagen.* ofer (I)] ofor *Lindelöf.* (ði)ow (A)] ðiow *Kuhn.* haline (C)] halme *Wildhagen.* in (A) (*Lat.*) *no gloss*] in : in *Kuhn.*

OE: onleoht (I)] *2nd* o *interl.* ofer (I)] *orig.* ofor: *fine cross-stroke in lighter brown ink in lobe of 2nd* o. (ði)ow (A)] *small eras. results in loss of most of bowl of* ð *and lower half of* i. þ (K)] *eras. after letter.*

LTg: Inlumina] L: mina *underlined to signal deletion,* stra *written interl. by corr.: see GAg;* Illumina C: *eras. before and after* ll.

LTu: Inlumina] INlumina β; Illumina τ*.

GAg: Inlumina] Inlustra F, L: *see LTg;* [ ]nlustra G: *initial* I *lost, outline visible;*

Illustra IJK, H: *eras. after* I, *1st* l *formed from leg of another letter.* et] *om.* GHIJK, F: *eras.* (?). tua misericordia] misericordia tua FGHIJK.

GAu: Inlumina] Inlustra δζμψ; Illustra εϑιλξοπϱστυφχ. et] *om.* δεζϑιλμξοπϱσυφχψ. tua misericordia] misericordia tua δεζιλμξοπϱστυφχψ; missericordia tua ϑ.

18

domine		dryhten B, drihten E^3, dryht̄ A, driħt CG, driħ J, eala ðu driħt F (*I*)
non*	|	ne ABC*F*, na D*GHJK*, þæ̲t̲ *I*, þet ic ne E^3
confundar	|	biom ic gescended A, beom ic gescyndyd C, beo ic gescended B, ic beo gescind J, ic ne beo gescynd I, sie gescynd E^3, ic gescamige DK, ic gesceamige GH, ic ne scamige F
quoniam		forðon ABDE^{3}HJ, forþon CG, forðan K, forðam ðe F, forðan þe I
inuocaui	|	ic gecede A, ic gecigde BDGI, ic gecige CJ, ic gecege F, ic gecigde þe H, ic clypude K, ic þe E^3
te	|	ðec A, ðe BFG, þe CDHIJK, chide E^3*
Erubescant		scomien A, scomigen B, scamigyn C, scamigen D, Sceæmigen *E*^{3}*, sceamian F, sceamigen GHK, scamige J, sceamian ł syn gescend I*
impii		arlease ABCDGH, ðam̲ árleasan F, ða arleasan I, arleasan JK, ærleæsum *E*^{3}
et		⁊ ABCDE^{3}FGHIJK
deducantur		sien gelędde A, sien gelædde B, syn gelædde CJ, Sien geledde E^3, beon ge̲leded D, beon gelæded G*H, beon gelæd F, beon gelæde K, beon hi gelædde I
in		in A, on BCDE^{3}FHK, o[ ] *G*, in on J, to I
infernum		helle ABCDE^{3}F*G*HIJK

ED: forðon (A)] for ðon *Kuhn.* ic gecigde þe (H)] ic gecigdeþe *Campbell.* impíí (E)] impii *Harsley.* deducantur (B)] deducentur *Brenner.*

OE: chide (E^3)] d *altered from another letter by corr.* Sceæmigen (E^3)] þe *or* þæ *eras. after word.* sceamian ł syn gescende (I)] sceamian *written in left margin.* beon gelæded (G)] *top of ascender of* d *lost both times due to tear in leaf.*

LTg: domine] I: o *written above word.* non] F: *orig.* nec: ec *deleted by subscript dot, macron added above* n, o *written in left margin;* n̄ GK: *letter eras. after* n, H: *eras. after word,* I: e *eras. after* n̄, *deleting dot below eras., macron added.* Erubescant] Ervbescant E. impii] impíí E. in] i[ ] G: *minim visible after* i. infernum] [ ]fernum G.

LTu: non] nec δξ: *orig.* ne: c *added interl.: see GAu.* Erubescant] ERubescant β.
GAu: non] ne πρυ.

19

muta	dumbe A*B*CDE^{3}FHIJK, dumba G
efficiantur*	sien gefremed A, sien gefremede B, syn gefremyde *C*, gewerþen D, geweorðe F, geweorþe J, gewurðun I, gewyrþan K, Sien geworðen E^{3}*, synd ł gewurðe G, syn H
labia	weolere A, weleras BDE^{x}*GHIJK, welyras C, welerum F
dolosa	faecne A, fæcne BC, facenfulle DE^{x}*HIJ, facnfulle FK, facen[ ] G
quae	ða A*B*, þa *CK*, þe *DE^{x}*H*, ða ðe *F*, þa þe *GIJ* (*L*)
loquuntur	spreocað A, sprecað BCDE^{3}*FGHI, sprecaþ *J*, spcað *K* (*L*)
aduersus	wið ABC, ongean DGHJ, ongen E^{x}*, togeanes F, togenes I*K*
iustum	ðæm rehtwisan A, þam rihtwisan C, þone ryhtwisan B, ryhtwisne D*E^{x}*, rihtwisne FH, rihtwise GK, rihtwisum I, riht J
iniquitatem	unrehtwisan A, unryhtwisnesse BD, unrihtwisnesse E$^{3/x}$*HJ, unrihtwisnysse CFI, unrihtwisnes K* (*G*)
in	in A, on BCDE^{x}FGHIJK
superbia	oferhygde AB, ofyrhigde *C*, ofermodnisse DE^{x}*, ofermodnesse GH, ofermodignysse F, ofermodinesse K, modignisse I, oferhidig J
et	⁊ ABCDE^{3}FGHI*JK
(in)*	on FGHJ, an on I*
contemptu*	forhogadnisse *A*, forhogodnysse C, forhogunge B, forsewennisse DE^{x}*, forsawennesse I*, unðeawum F, unþeawum J, unþeawe GH (*L*)

ED: quæ (D)] quae *Roeder.* quę (E)] quae *Harsley.* [ ]niquitat[ ]m (G)] iniquitatem *Rosier.*

OE: Sien geworðen (E^{3})] n *in* geworðen *added by corr., letter eras. after word.* weleras (E^{x})] *on eras.* facenfulle (E^{x})] *on eras.* þe (E^{x})] *on eras.* sprecað (E^{3})] að *on eras. by corr.* ongen (E^{x})] *on eras.* ryhtwisne (D)] n *interl.* ryhtwisne (E^{x})] *on eras.* unrihtwisnesse (E$^{3/x}$)] *1st* s *interl.*, wi *and* nesse *on eras. by corr.* unrihtwisnes (K)] un *eras. before word* (*i.e.*, un *written at end of line above, then eras. and word begun again on next line*). ofermodnisse (E^{x})] *partly on eras.* (ofermod?). ⁊ an on forsawennesse (I)] *written above* ne *in* abusione *and extending into right margin; orig. gloss above* abusione *eras.* forsewennisse (E^{x})] *on eras.*

LTg: muta] B: *eras. after* u. efficiantur] C: ci *interl.* quae] quæ BD; que C; quę E; Quę FGH, L: *orig.* quę: Q *interl. by corr.;* Quae I; Que JK. loquuntur] locuntur JKL.

aduersus] áduersus K. iniquitatem] [ ]niquitat[ ]m G. superbia] C: *ascender eras. above* p. contemptu] A: emptu *written by corr.,* L: in abusione *added interl. by corr.: see GAg.*

LTu: quae] quę βν; que τ*; Quae δοπϱυψ; Quę εζϑιλξφχ; Quæ μ; Que στ. loquuntur] locuntur δϑμνοπσυψ; loquntur ς.

GAg: efficiantur] fiant FGHIJK. contemptu] in abusione FGHI, L: *see LTg,* J: *orig.* in abussione: *1st* s *eras.;* in habusione K: *letter eras. after* u.

GAu: efficiantur] fiant δεζϑιλμξοπϱτυφχψ. contemptu] in abusione δεζιλμξοπϱστυφχψ; in abussione ϑ.

20

Quam		swiðe ABC, swiþe J, hu DE^{3}GHK, la hu FI
magna		micel ABDE^{3}*G*I*J, micyl C, mycel FK, micell H
multitudo		mengu A, mengeo B, mænigeo CF, mænigo J, menego DH, manega G, manigo K, monigfealdnes ł mycelnes I*, is þin menigo E^{3}
dulcedinis*	|	swoetnisse *A,* swetnysse CF, swetnisse *D,* swetnesse BGHJ, swetnes K, swetnesse ł werodnes I, þinre E^{3}
tuae	|	ðinre A*F,* þinre *BCDGH*I*J,* þin *K,* swetnesse *E^{3}* (*L*)
domine		drihten E^{3}GJ, dryht̄ AB, drih́t CF (*I*)
quam		ða A, þa BCD*F*GHIJK, þe E^{3}
abscondisti	|	ðu ahydes A, þu ahyddyst C, ahyddes B, þu behyddest DGHI*J, ðu behyddest F, behyddest K, ondredendum E^{3}
timentibus	|	ondredendum A, ondrædendum̲ B, ondrædendum FI, ondrædyndum̲ C, þa ondrædendum̲ G, ðam̲ ondrædendum̲ D, þam̲ ondrædendum H, ondrædende JK, þæ E^{3}
te	|	ðe A, þe BCDFGHIJ*K,* þu behiddest E^{3}
et*		⁊ ABCDE^{3} (*L*)
perfecisti	|	ðu gefremedes A, þu gefremedes B, þu gefremydyst C, ðu fulfremedest D, þu fulfremadest *F,* þu fulfremedest *GH,* þu fulfremodest *I,* þu fremedest *J,* þu fremodest *K,* þu hie E^{3}
eam*	|	ða A, þa B, þe C, hy D, hig I, hi K, him̲ FJ, him G, fulfremedest E^{3}* (*L*)
(qui)*		þa þe FI, þe GHJ, þa K
sperantibus*	|	gehyhtendum A, gehyhtendum̲ B, gehihtendum C, þam̲ hyhtendum̲ D, hopiað F, hihtað GIK, hyhtað H, hihtaþ J, on E^{3} (*L*)
in	|	in A, on BCFGIJK, þe E^{3} (D*)
te	|	ðec A, ðe BFG, þe CIJK, gewenende ł hyhte E$^{3/x}$*
in		in A, on BCDE^{3}FGHJK, beforan ł on I

conspectu		gesihðe ABCFGHIJ, gesyhðe D, gesihþe E^{3}, ansyne K
filiorum	I	bearn ACJ, bearna BDFGHIK, mænnæ E^{3}
hominum	I	monna AB, manna CDFGHIJK, beærnæ *E^{3}*

ED: tuę (E)] tuae *Harsley.*

OE: micel (I)] est : is *written in left margin.* monigfealdnes ł mycelnes (I)] nes *in* mycelnes *written below* el. þu behyddest (I)] *orig.* þu behiddest: i *altered to* y. fulfremedest (E^{3})] t *interl.* (*by corr.?*). in (*1st Lat.*)] D: *gloss eras.*: on (?) *plus a 3rd letter.* gewenende ł hyhte ($E^{3/x}$)] ł hyhte *on eras. by corr.*

LTg: magna] G: na *partly obscured.* dulcedinis] dulcidinis AD: *cf. Weber MSS* δλ, *see GAu.* tuae] tuæ BL; tuę CDEFGHJK. domine] I: o *written above word.* quam] F: m *partly obscured by stain.* te] té K. et] L: *underlined by corr. to signal deletion: see GAg.* perfecisti] Perfecisti FHIJK; [ ]erfecisiti G: *initial* P *lost, outline visible.* eam] L: is qui *interl. by corr.*: *see GAg.* sperantibus] L: tibus *underlined to signal deletion,* t *added by corr. after* n (*line division after* sperant): *see GAg.* hominum] hominvm E.

LTu: tuae] tuę εινξϱςφ; tuæ ϑμ; tue στ*τυ. quam] Quam ϱ: *not indicating verse division.* perfecisti] Perfecisti δεζϑιλμξοπϱστυφχψ. eam] ea β.

GAg: et] *om.* FGHIJK, L: *see LTg.* eam] eis qui FGHIJK, L: *see LTg.* sperantibus] sperant FGHIJK, L: *see LTg.*

GAu: dulcedinis] dulcidinis ϑ. et] *om.* δεζϑιλμξοπϱστυφχψ. eam] eis qui δεζϑιλμξοπϱστυφχψ. sperantibus] sperant δεζϑιλμξοπϱστυφχψ.

21

Abscondes		ðu ahydes A, þu ahydest B, ðu ahydyst C, þu behydest D, ðu behydst F, þu behyddest GK, þu behydst HI, þu behiddest J, ðu gehyddest E^{3}*
eos		hie ABE^{3}, hi CK, hy DGH, hig FIJ
in		in AD, on BCE^{3}FGIJK
abditu		degulnisse *A,* deagolnesse B, digylnysse C, dygelnisse *D,* dygelnesse *$E^{3/x}$**, digelnysse *F,* digelnesse *G,* dygolnyssa *I**, digolnesse *JK* (*L*)
uultus*	I	ondwleotan A, ⁊wlitan B, andwlitan CD, anwlitan K, ansyne FGIJ, þinre E^{3} (*L*)
tui*	I	ðines AB, þinys C, þines D, ðinre F, þinre GIJK, onsiene E^{3} (*L*)
a		from A*E^{3},* from B, fram CDFHJ, fram GIK
conturbatione		gedroefednisse A, gedrefydnysse C, gedrefednisse D, gedrefednysse FI, gedrefednesse BGH, gedrefnesse E^{3}, drefednesse K, wiþersæce J*
hominum		monna AB, manna CDFGHIJK, mænnæ E^{3}

Proteges	ǀ	gescildes A, ðu gescildes B, þu gescyldyst C, þu gescildest FJ, þu scyldst DH, þu scyldes G, þu scyldest *K,* þu gescylst I, ðu hie E³
eos	ǀ	hie AB, hi CK, hy DGH, hig FIJ, gecildest E³
in		in A, on BCDE³FGHIJK
tabernaculo	ǀ	getelde AB*C*F, getelde ł on eardungstowe J*, eardungstowe DGH, eardunga K, þinre E³, þinum I
tuo	ǀ	ðinum A, þinum B, þinum C, þinre DGJ, eærdungstowe E³/ˣ*, bure *I* (*FHK*)
a		from A, from B, fram CDGHJ*K,* fram FI, fron *E³*
contradictione		wiðcwedenisse A, wiþcwidenesse B, wiðcwedennysse C, wiðersæce D, wiðersace FG, wiþersæce HJK, awergednysse ł wiðercwydelnesse I, þæm wiðercweðelum E³
linguarum		geðieda A, geðeoda B, tungyna *C,* tungana DFI*, tungena GJ, tunga H, tungan K, tungum E³

ED: á (E) (*1st*)] a *Harsley.* gecildest (E)] ge[s]cildest *Harsley.* á (E) (*2nd*)] a *Harsley.* fron (E)] from *Harsley.* wiþcwidenesse (B)] wiðcwidnesse *Brenner.*

OE: ðu gehyddest (E³)] t *added by corr.* dygelnesse (E³/ˣ)] dygel *on eras. by corr.* dygolnyssa (I)] *orig.* digolnyssa: i *altered to* y. wiþersæce (J) (*1st*)] *source-text misread, perhaps reading gloss to* contradictione *below.* getelde ł on eardungstowe (J)] on eardungstowe *written above* getelde ł. eærdungstowe (E³/ˣ)] stowe *on eras. by corr.* tungana (I)] *eras. before word.*

LTg: abditu] A: u *on eras.,* L: ditu *underlined to signal deletion,* scondito *added interl. by corr.* (= abscondito); ábditu D; abditv E; abscondito FGIJK: *cf. Weber MSS* αβγ, *Bib. sac. MSS* MQ²W, *etc.* uultus] L: *underlined to signal deletion,* faciei *added interl. by corr.: see GAg.* tui] L: *underlined to signal deletion,* tue *added interl. by corr.* a (*1st*)] á E. Proteges] K: s *interl. by corr.* tabernaculo] C: ta *interl.* tuo] F: *added interl. by corr.,* H: *on eras. by corr.,* I: *written in right margin and signaled for inclusion,* K: *interl.* (*by main hand?*). a (*2nd*)] á EK. linguarum] C: a *interl.*

LTu: Abscondes] [ ]bscondes σ: *initial wanting.* abditu] abditv τ*; abdito ζψ; abscondito δειλμξοπϱστυφ, χ: *orig.* abdito: scon *interl.: cf. Weber MSS* αβγ. tabernaculo] βϑ: r *interl. by corr.* tuo] *om.* ελ, ι: *deleted by 4 subscript dots.*

GAg: uultus] faciei FHIJK, L: *see LTg;* facięi G. tui] tuę FGHK; tuae IJ; *for* L *see LTg.*

GAu: uultus] faciei δεζϑιλμξοπϱστυφχψ. tui] tuae δεζμπϱχψ; tuæ ϑ; tuę ιλξοφ; tue στ.

22

Benedictus	gebledsad A, gebletsod BCFGJK, gebletsod D, Gebletsod E³*, gebletsad H, sy gebletsod I*
dominus	drihten E³FK, dryhτ̄ AB, driħt CG, driħ J

quoniam		forðon ABDHJ, forþon C, forðæn E^{3}, forþam G, forþam ðe F, forðan þe I
mirificauit		gemiclade A, gemiclode B, he gemiclode C, gemicclode J, wuldrude D, wuldrede $E^{3/x}$*, wuldrode F, wuldrade G, wuldrada H, he gemærsode I, wyldre K
misericordiam	|	mildheortnisse A, mildheortnysse CF, mildheortnesse BDGHJK, his E^{3}I
suam	|	his ABDFGHJK, hys C, mildheortnysse I, his mildheortnesse E^{3}
(mihi)*		me FGIJK (*L*)
in		in A, on BCDE^{3}FGHIJK
ciuitate	|	cestre AC, ceastre BDFGHJK, birig ł on ceastre ł on *I*, ymbstandendræ E^{3}*
circumstantiae*	|	ymbstondnisse A, ymbstondnesse *B*, ymbstandnesse *D*, ymbstandynnysse *C*, gewealledre F*, ymbtrymed[ ] G, ymbtrym(e)dre ceastre I*, gewealledre J, þære ceæstre *E^{3}* (*L*)

ED: forðon (A)] for ðon *Kuhn*. birig ł on ceastre ł on ymbtrym(e)dre ceastre (I) birig ł on ceastre trumre ł on ymbtrymedre ceastre *Lindelöf*. circunstantię (C)] circu[m]stantię *Wildhagen*. circumstantiæ (D)] circumstantiae *Roeder*. circumstantię (E)] circumstantiae *Harsley*.

OE: Gebletsod (E^{3})] *blot after* s. sy gebletsod (I)] s. sit *written in left margin*. wuldrede ($E^{3/x}$)] drede *on eras. by corr.*, l *altered from another letter by corr.* ymbstandendræ (E^{3})] a *malformed, perhaps false start of* æ. gewealledre (F)] *obscured by eras., upper portion of* a *lost*. ymbtrym(e)dre ceastre (I)] *1st* e (?) *cropped, back visible.*

LTg: suam] L: mihi *added after word by corr.: see GAg*. ciuitate] I: u *on eras.* circumstantiae] circumstantiæ BD; circunstantię C: *orig.* circumstantię: *left leg of* m *eras. to form* n; circumstantię EL.

LTu: misericordiam] missericordiam ϑ. circumstantiae] circumstantię ν; circumstantie ςτ*.

GAg: suam] suam mihi FGHK, I: *eras. after* mihi, L: *see LTg;* suam michi J. circumstantiae] munita FGHIJK.

GAu: suam] suam mihi δεζθμοπσυψ; suam michi ιλξτφ, ϱχ: c *added interl.* circumstantiae] munita δεζθιλμοϱστυφχψ.

23

Ego	ic ABCDFGHIJK, Ic E^{3}
autem	soðlice ABCE^{3}FGHI, soþlice J, witodlice K
dixi	ic cweð A, cwæð BCHIK, cweð D, cwęð E^{3}, cweðe J, cwæð ł sæde G, sæde F

in		in A, on BC*DE^{x}*FGHI
pauore*		fyrhtu A, fyrhto BCD, forhtunge I*, utgange GH (F**L*)
(mentis)*	I	modes FGK, minre E^{3}*, mines I (*L*)
meo*	I	minre ABCHDJ, mines FGK, firhte E^{3}, modes I (*L*)
proiectus	I	aworpen ABDFGHIK, aworpyn C, orwene J, ic eom E^{3}
sum	I	ic eam A, ic eom BCDFGHIJK, aworpen E^{3}
a		from A*E^{3}, from B, fram CDFJK, fram GI
uultu*		ondwleotan A, ondwlitan B, andwlitan CD, onsine E^{3}*, ansyne FGIK, ansine J (*L*)
oculorum	I	egena A, eagna B, eagena DFGJ, eagyna C, eagana HI, egan *K*, þinræ E^{3}
tuorum	I	ðinra AF, þinra BDHIJK, þinre C*G*, eægænæ E^{3}
Ideo		forðon ABDHJ, forþon CE^{3}FG, forðan I, forðam K
exaudisti		ðu geherdes A, ðu gehirdes B, þu gehierdes E^{3}, þu gehyrdyst C, þu gehyrdest DFGHK, þu geherdest I, þu gehirdest J
uocem		stefne ABCDFGIK, stæfne HJ, stemne E^{3}
deprecationis*	I	boene *A*B, bene CK, halsunga DH, halsunga ł gebeda G, gebedes FIJ, minre E^{3}
meae	I	minre *ABCD*K, minra *GH*, mines *F*IJ, bene *E^{3}* (*L*)
dum		mið ðy A, mid ðy B, þonne CDHJ, ðonne F, þonne E^{x}*G, þane K, þa þa I
clameram		ic cleopiu A, ic clipigo B, ic clypige CK, ic clepedo E^{3}*, ic clipige J, ic clypode DGH, ic clypude F, ic clepode I
ad		to ABCDE^{3}FGHIJ*K*
te		ðe ABCDFI, þe E^{3}GHJK

ED: on ofe(r)stigenysse (I)] on oferstigenysse *recorded by Lindelöf in corrigenda* (*p. 323*). eagana (H)] eagena *Campbell.* tuoru[ ] (G)] tuor*um Rosier.* þinre (G)] þinr[ ] *Rosier.* forðon (A)] for ðon *Kuhn.* forþon (E)] Forþon *Harsley.* mea (A)] meae *Kuhn.* þa þa (I)] þaþa *Lindelöf.*

OE: on (C)] n *interl.* on (E^{x})] *on eras.* forhtunge (I)] on ofe(r)stigenysse *written in bottom margin below* eius quoniam (*last word on fol. 38r*), *but without indication of lemma* (*see* excessu *in GAg notes to* pauore meo), *descender of* r *lost.* excessu (F)]: *gloss eras., letter fragments visible.* minre (E^{3})] *left leg of* m *on eras. by corr.* from (A)] ro *altered from other letters.* onsine (E^{3})] *eras. before word, perhaps long* s. þonne (E^{x})] *on eras.* ic clepedo (E^{3})] *eras. before* ic, *2nd* e *altered from* i, do *on eras. by corr.*

LTg: pauore meo] L: *underlined to signal deletion,* excessu mentis mee *added interl. by corr.: see GAg.* uultu] L: *underlined to signal deletion,* facie *added interl. by corr.* oculorum] óculorum K. tuorum] tuoru[ ] G. deprecationis] deprębcationis A. meae] mea A: *orig.* meae: *final* e *deleted by subscript dot;* meæ BCL; meę DEFG; męę H. ad] ád K.

LTu: tuorum] meorum τ. Ideo] τ*τ: *initial wanting*. exaudisti] χ: ti *interl.* deprecationis] depręcationis β. meae] meę βεινξςφ; meæ ϑ; mee στ*τ.

GAg: pauore meo] excessu mentis meę FG; excessu mentis męę H; excessu mentis meae IJ; excessu mentis meæ K; *for* L *see LTg*. uultu] facie FHIJK, L: *see LTg;* facię G. deprecationis] orationis FGHIJ; órationis K.

GAu: pauore meo] excessu mentis meae δζμοπϱυχψ; excessu mentis meę ειλξφ; excessu mentis meæ ϑ; excessu mentis mee στ. uultu] facie δεϑιλμξοπϱστυφχψ; facię ζ. deprecationis] orationis δεζϑιλμξοπϱστυφχψ.

24

Diligite	I	lufiað ABCDFGHI, lufiaþ JK, drihtæn E^{3}
dominum	I	drihten DHK, dryht̄ AB, driħt CFG, driht̄ I, driħ J, lufiæþ E^{3}
omnes		alle A, ealle BCDFGHIJK, eælle E^{3}
sancti	I	halge A, halige BD, halige FGHJK, haligan C, halgan I, his E^{3}
eius	I	his ABCDFGHIJ*K*, hælge E^{3}
quoniam		forðon ABE^{3}FJ, forþon C, forþam G, foðam K*, forðan þe I
ueritatem*	I	soðfestnisse A, soðfæstnysse CI, soþfæstnisse D, soþfæstnysse F, soðfæstnesse BG, soþfæstnesse *H*JK, hi secæð E^{3}
requiret	I	soeceð *A*, soecð B, secyð C, seceþ J, secð DGI, sécþ F, secþ H, soðfestnesse E^{3}, soþfæstnesse K
dominus	I	dryhten A, dryht̄ B, driħt CF, driħ GJ, ⁊ E^{3}
et	I	⁊ ABCFGHIJK, drihten E^{3}
retribuet		geedleanað *A*BC, geedleanaþ J, edlenæð E^{3}*, he agylt DFGH, he agelt I*, forgylt ⁊ K
his*		ðeossu A, ðissum B, þam *C*D$E^{3/x}$* (*L*)
qui*		þa A*, ða B, þam C, þe DE^{3} (*L*)
abundanter		genyhtsumlice A*B*, genihtsumlice *CDFJ*, genihtsumlice *G*H*K*, geinehtsumnesse *E*^{3}, genihtsumlice ł hetollice I (*L*)
faciunt*		dooð A, doð BC, doþ DE^{3}, þam wyrcendum F, wercendum I*, dondum GH, þam dondum J, donde K (*L*)
superbiam		oferhygd AB, ofyrhigd C, ofermodnisse D, ofermodinesse $E^{3/x}$*, ofermodnesse GH, ofermodignysse F, ofermodinese K, ofermodigan J, modignysse I

ED: forðon (A)] for ðon *Kuhn*. íís (C)] his *Wildhagen*. ofermodnesse (G)] [ ]modnesse *Rosier.*

OE: foðam (K)] *letter* (n?) *eras. after word*. edlenæð (E^{3})] ⁊ *eras. before word*. he agelt (I)] *2nd* e *altered* (?) *from* i. þam ($E^{3/x}$)] am *on eras. by corr.* þa (A)] þ *on* *eras., possibly altered from another letter.* wercendum (I)] *orig.* wircendum: i *altered to* e. ofermodinesse ($E^{3/x}$)] modinesse *on eras. by corr.*

LTg: eius] eíus K. ueritatem] H: *eras. after word.* requiret] A: *orig.* requirit: *2nd* i *altered to* e. retribuet] A: *orig.* retribuit: *2nd* i *altered to* e. his] L: *underlined to signal deletion: see GAg;* íís C: *eras. before word, vestiges of ascender* (?) *visible* (*altered by corr.?*). qui] L: *underlined to signal deletion: see GAg.* abundanter] habundanter BDEGJKL. faciunt] L: entibus *added interl. by corr.: see GAg.*

LTu: Diligite] χ: t *altered from* l, e *interl.* requiret] requirit βϑ. abundantur] habundantur βδϑνξσςτ*τυ.

GAg: his qui] *om.* FGHIJK, L: *see LTg.* faciunt] facientibus FHIJK, L: *see LTg;* facientibu[ ] G.

GAu: ueritatem] ueritates ϑμψ. his qui] *om.* δεζϑιμλξοπϱστυφχψ. faciunt] facientibus δεζϑιλμξοπϱστυφχψ.

25

Uiriliter	|	werlice *ABDFI,* wærlice *CGHK,* ærlice J, doþ E^3 (*L*)
agite	|	doð ACGHI, doþ'DK, dóþ F, doð ge B, doþ ge J, werlice E^3
et		⁊ ABCE^3*FGHIJK
confortetur		sie gestrongad A, sy gestrongud C, sie gestrangod DH, sie gestronged E^3*, sy gestrangod FI, bið gestrongod B, biþ gestrangod J, beo gestrangod K, si gestyrod G
cor	|	heorte ABCDFGHIJK, eowre E^3
uestrum	|	eower ABDFGHJ, eowyr C, eowor I, heortæn E^3
omnes		alle A, ealle BCDFGHIJK, eælle E^3
qui		ða ðe AB, þa þe C, ða þe F, þa ðe J, þe DGH, þæ E^3, þa K, ge þe I*
speratis		gehyhtað AB, gehihtað C, gehihtaþ J, hihtaþ F, hihtað IK, hyhten DH, hihten G, geweneþ hyhten $E^{3/x}$*
in		in A, on BCDE^x*FGHIJK
domino		dryhtne ABD, drihtny C, drihtne FI, drihtene H, drihten E^3K, drih́t G, drih́ J

ED: doð ge (B)] ðod ge *Brenner.*

OE: ⁊ (E^3)] *in darker ink.* sie gestronged (E^3)] ie *on eras., 1st* g *retraced in darker ink.* ge þe (I)] *eras. after final* e. geweneþ hyhten ($E^{3/x}$)] hyhten *on eras. by corr.* on (E^x)] *on eras.*

LTg: Uiriliter] Viriliter ABCEFGIKL.

LTu: Uiriliter] Viriliter ινξσςυ.

PSALM 31

1

Beati eadge *A*B, eadige *CD*F*G*HI*J, ædige *E^{x}*, eadi *K*
quorum ðeara A, þara B*C*, ðæra I, þæra K, þara þe DE^{x}*HJ, ðara þe F, þara ðe G
remissae forletne A, forlætne *B*, forlætene I*J*, forgyfyne *C*, forgifene *DH*, forgyfene *F*, forgefene *E$^{3/x}$*, forgifennesse *G*, þa forgifene *K* (*L*)
sunt sind AH, synd FGJK, sint BE^{3}, synt CD, þe synt I
iniquitates unrehtwisnisse A, unryhtwisnessa BD, unrihtwisnysse F, unrihtwisnessa GH, unrihtwisnyssa I, unrihtwisnesse J, unrihtwinesa K, unrihtwisnys C, hioræ unrihtwisnesse E$^{3/x}$*
et ⁊ ABCDE^{3}FGHIJK
quorum ðeara A, þara BJ, þæra K, þara þe CFGH, ðara þe DE^{x}*, ðæra þe I
tecta | biwrigen A, bewrigene BDE^{x}*FGHJ, bewrigyne C, bewrogene K, synt I
sunt | sind AH, synd FJ, sint B, synt CDE^{x}*, syn[ ] G, bewregone ł oferwrigene I
peccata synne A, synna BCDE^{x}*GIJK, synd F, na H

ED: ædige (E)] Ædige *Harsley*. þara ðe (G)] þara þe *Rosier*. unrihtwisnessa (G)] [ ]rihtwisnessa *Rosier*. sunt (G) (*2nd*)] sun*t* *Rosier*. syn[ ] (G)] sy *Rosier*. peccata (G)] *peccata* *Rosier*.

OE: eadige (I)] s. s<u>unt</u> : synt *written in upper lobe of* B *in* Beati. þara þe (E^{x})] *on eras.* forgefene (E$^{3/x}$)] gefene *on eras. by corr.* hioræ unrihtwisnesse (E$^{3/x}$)] twisnesse *by corr.* ðara þe (E^{x})] *on eras.* bewrigene (E^{x})] *on eras.* synt (E^{x})] *on eras.* synna (E^{x})] *on eras.*

LTg: Beati] BEati ADK; BEATI CE; [ ]eati G. quorum (*1st*)] QVORUM C. remissae] remissę BDFH; remisse CEGJKL.

LTu: Beati] BEATI ιλμνϱςτ*τχψ. quorum (*1st*)] QUORUM λμνϱψ; QUORVM χ. remissae] remissę δενοφ; REMISSĘ λϱ; remisæ ϑ; remisse ιξπσςτ*τυψ; REmissæ μ; REmissae χ. sunt] SUNT λϱ.

2

Beatus eadig A*B*CDF*G*HI*J, Eadig E^{3}, eadi K
uir wer ABCDE^{3}FGHJK, se wer I
cui ðæm A, þæm B, þam C, þa<u>m</u> HJ, þa<u>m</u> ðe D, þa<u>m</u> þe F, þam þe GI, þæm þe E^{3}, þa K
non ne ABCGI*J, na FK, na ne DE^{x}*H

inputauit		geteleð *A*B, getelyð *C*, getealde J, tealde ł þe ne talode *I*, ætwiteþ *DF*, ætwiteð E^{x}*, ætwíteð G, atwiteþ *H*, ætwit *K* (*L*)
dominus		drihtyn C, dryhten E^{x}*, drihten FI, dryht̄ AB, drih́t G, drih́ J
peccatum		synne *A*BCD*G*HIJ, synna FK, his synnæ E^{3}
nec	|	ne ABCIJ, na K, ⁊ nis D*H*, ⁊ nys F, ⁊ ne E^{x}*, nan G
est	|	is ABGJ*K*, ys C, nis E^{x}*I
in		in A, on BCDE^{x}*FGIJK
ore*		muðe ABCDE^{x}*, gaste FGIJK (*L*)
eius		his ABCDE^{3}*FHIJK (*G*)
dolus		facen ABF, facyn C, facn DE^{x}*HJ, faken I, fac K, fa[ ] G

ED: na ne (D)] nane *Roeder.* atwiteþ (H)] ætwiteþ *Campbell.* spiritu (G)] spiratu *Rosier.* fa[ ] (G)] *no gloss Rosier.*

OE: eadig (I)] s. e<u>st</u> : is *written in left margin.* ne (I) (*1st*)] e *on eras.* na ne (E^{x})] *on eras.* ætwiteð (E^{x})] *on eras.* dryhten (E^{x})] *on eras.* ⁊ ne (E^{x})] *on eras.* nis (E^{x})] *on eras.* on (E^{x})] *on eras.* muðe (E^{x})] *on eras.* his (E^{3})] *touched up in darker ink by corr.* facn (E^{x})] *on eras.*

LTg: Beatus] [ ]eatus B: *initial letter not written in MS,* G: *initial letter lost.* inputauit] inputabit CFL, H: b *on eras.;* imputauit DEI; imputabit A: b *on eras.,* K: im *interl. by corr.,* b *altered from* u. peccatum] A: m *added by corr.;* pecc(a)[ ]m G: *bowl of* a *visible.* nec] nęc H. est] ést K. ore] L: spiritu *interl. by corr. after* eius: *see GAg.* eius] G: *letter fragments of gloss visible.*

LTu: Beatus] beatus ϑ. inputauit] inputabit ψ; īputabit ϑ; imputauit ιλπϱστ*τυφ, ε: *orig.* inputabit: n *altered to* m, b *altered to* u (*malformed*), οχ: *1st* i *interl.;* imputabit μ. nec] nęc ξ.

GAg: ore] spiritu FGHIJK, L: *see LTg.*

GAu: ore] spiritu δεζϑιλμξοπϱστυφχψ.

3

Quoniam		forðon *A*BJ, forþon C, Forþæn E^{3}, forþam G, forþā K, forðam ðe F, forðan þe I*
tacui		ic swigade A, ic swigode BDGHIK, ic swýgode F, ic swigude C, ic swigie E^{3}*, ic singode J
inueterauerunt	|	aldadon A, ealdodon BCDJ, ealdedon H, on ealdodon F, on ealdedon G, on ealdinge K, forealdodon I, ⁊ eælle E^{3}
omnia*	|	all A, ealle BCD*I*, mine E^{3}
ossa		ban ABCDFGHIJK, bæn E^{3}
mea	|	min AG, mine BCDFHIJK, eældiæþ E^{3}
dum		mid ðy A, mid þy þe C, þon<u>ne</u> BDHJ, ðonne F, þonne

		GK*, mid þy þonne E$^{3/x}$*, þa þa I (*M*)
clamarem		ic cleapade A, ic clipode BJ, ic clypode CDFGHI*, ic clypude K, ic clipie to ðe E^{x}*
tota		alne A, ealne BCFJ, ealle K, ælce DGH, ælce ł allan E^{x}*, singallice ł ealne I*
die		deg A, dæg BCFJK, dæge DGH, deige E$^{3/x}$*, d[ ] I*

ED: forðon (A)] for ðon *Kuhn.* on ealdedon (G)] onealdedon *Rosier.* mid þy þonne (E)] midþy þonne *Harsley.* þa þa (I)] þaþa *Lindelöf.* d[ ] (I)] dæg *Lindelöf.*

OE: forðan þe (I)] e *interl.* ic swigie (E^{3})] swigie *touched up in darker ink by corr.* þonne (K)] þæ *eras. before word.* mid þy þonne (E$^{3/x}$)] þonne *added by corr.* ic clypode (I)] *orig.* ic clipode: *2nd* i *altered to* y. ic clipie to ðe (E^{x})] *on eras.* ælce ł allan (E^{x})] *on eras.* singallice ł ealne (I)] ealne *written in right margin.* deige (E$^{3/x}$)] ige *on eras. by corr.* d[ ] (I)] *written in right margin, partly lost due to tight binding.*

LTg: Quoniam] A: *macron added by glossator* (Qūm). omnia] I: *written in left margin: see GAg.* dum] M *begins mid-verse.*

LTu: Quoniam] quoniam ϑ.

GAg: omnia] *om.* FGHJK; *for* I *see LTg.*

GAu: omnia] *om.* δεζϑιλμξοπϱστυφχψ.

4

Quoniam		forðon ABDJ, forþon C*G*, Forðæn E^{3}, forþā K, forðam ðe F, forþan þe I
die		deges A, dæges BDFGHIJ, dægys C, deges E^{3}, dæg K
ac		⁊ ABCDE^{3}FGHIJ*K*
nocte		naehtes A, nihtes BFGIJ, nihtys C, nyhtes D, niehtes E^{3}, nihte K, rihtes H
grauata		gehefegad A, gehefygod C, gehefgod B, gehefegod DFGHIJK, gehefogod E^{3} (*M*)
est		is ABDE^{3}FGHIJ*K*, ys C
super		ofer ABDE^{3}FGHJK, ofyr C, ofor I
me		me ABCE^{3}FGIJK
manus	|	hond A, hand BCDFHI, handa GJ, han K, þin E^{3}* (*M*)
tua	|	ðin ABF, þin CDIK, þine GHJ, hænd E^{3}*
conuersus	|	gecerred AB, gecyrryd C, gecyrred F, gecirred J, gecerrod ł gewend I, gehwyrfed DGH, gehwyfed K, ⁊ ic eom E^{3}
sum	|	ic eam A, ic eom BDFGHIJK, ic eom C, gewyrfed E^{3}
in		in A, on BCDE^{3}FGHIJKM^{2}*
aerumna		ermðu *AB,* yrmðe *C,* yrmþum *J,* angnisse *D,* agnysse *F,* angnesse *HK,* angnisse *M*^{2}*, ahnesse *G,* geriwo ł on

angnisse *$E^{3/x}$**, gehrorenesse ł yrmðum *I* (*L*)
(mea)* minre CJK, min F, mine GE^{x}*, minum I
dum ðonne AF, þon<u>ne</u> BCDHJ, þonne E^{x}*K, þanne I (*M*)
confringitur* bið gebrocen AB, bið gebrocyn *C*, bið tobrocen *D**E^{x}*FGH, biþ tobrocen JK, tobrocen bið I
spina ðorn A*, þorn C, hrycg BDFG, hryrcg H, hricg M^{2}, ricg J, hrig K, hrygcban E^{x}*I

ED: forðon (A)] for ðon *Kuhn.*

OE: þin (E^{3})] *orig.* þine: e *eras.* hænd (E^{3})] *orig.* hændæ: *final* æ *eras.* on angnisse (M^{2})] *written in right margin, 2nd* n *interl.* geriwo ł on angnisse ($E^{3/x}$)] ł on angnisse *added by corr.* mine (E^{x})] *on eras.* þonne (E^{x})] *on eras.* bið tobrocen (D)] *gloss eras. after* tobrocen. bið tobrocen (E^{x})] *on eras.* ðorn (A)] *understanding* spina *as* 'thorn' *vs* 'spine, backbone'; *see also* C. hrygcban (E^{x})] *on eras.*, c *interl.*

LTg: Quoniam] A: *macron added by glossator* (Qūm); [ ]uoniam G. ac] ác K. grauata] grauâta M. est] ést K. manus] M: u *blotted.* aerumna] erumna ABDFGHL; erumpna IJK; erumna mea CDL, M: mea *added by corr.;* erumpna mea E: *cf. Weber MS* ε^{2}, *see GAg.* dum] M: m *blotted.* confringitur] C: *2nd* n *interl.*, D: *eras.* (*4 letters*) *after word.*

LTu: conuersus] Conuersus λ, *but not signaling verse division.* aerumna] erumna βελμνσφχ; herumna δ; erumpna mea ϑιξτυ, ο: p *interl.;* erumna mea ς; erumpna mea τ*: *cf. Weber MS* ε^{2}, *see GAu.*

GAg: aerumna] erumna mea FGH, CDL: *see LTg;* erumpna mea IJK, E: *see LTg.* confringitur] configitur FGHIJK.

GAu: aerumna] herumna mea δ; erumna mea ελμπσφχ, ς: *see LTu;* aerumna mea ζψ; erumpna mea ϑιξοϱτυ, τ*: *see LTu.* confringitur] configitur δεζιλμξοπϱστυφχψ; confringitur mihi ϑ (*variant*).

5
Delictum | scyld ACDFG*H*, scild J, scylde BK, gylt I*, Mine E^{3}
meum | min AC, mine BK, minne DFGHIJ, egyltæs E^{3}
cognitum | cuðe ABCG, cuþe J, cuþne DK, cuðne FHI, ic dide E^{3}
tibi ðe ABF, þe CE^{3}GIJK
ſeci | ic dyde ABCDFGHI*, ic dide J, dyde K, oncnæwe E^{3}*
et ⁊ $ABCDE^{3}$FGHIJK
iniustitias* | unrehtwisnisse A, unrihtwisnysse *C*I, unryhtwisnessa BD, unrihtwisnesse J, on unrihtwisnesse G*, unri(h)[ ](ss)e H*, rihtwisnyssc F, rihtwisncs K, mine E^{3} (*L*)
meas* | mine ABCDFGHIJ, min K, unsoðfestnesse E^{3} (*L*)
non | ic ne $ABCE^{3}$I, na DFGHJK

operui*	I	oferwrah AB, oferwreah CDE^{3}*, ic oferwreah J, bewreah K, ic ne behydde F, ic behydde G, behydde I, ic ne hydde H (*L*)
Dixi		ic cweð A, ic cwæð BC*DGH, Ic cweð E^{3}*, ic cwęð I, ic cwæþ K, ic sæde F, he cw̄ J
pronuntiabo*		ic forðsegcgo A, ic forðsecgo B, ic forðsecge *C*, ic bodige D, ic andette FGIJK, þet ic sege ł bodige $E^{3/x}$*
aduersum		wið ABC, ongean DFGH, ongean ł wiþ $E^{3/x}$*, agen I, togeanes J, togenes *K*
me		me ABE^{3}FGHIJK, me me C (*L*)
iniustitias*	I	unrehtwisnisse A, unrihtwisnysse *C*I, unryhtwisnissa D, unryhtwisnessa B, on unrihtwisnessa GH, on unrihtwisnesse JK, rihtwisnysse F, ⁊ mine E^{3} (*L*)
meas*	I	mine ABCFI, minre DJK, minra G, mina H, unsoþfestnesse E^{3} (*L*)
domino		dryhtne B, drihtne FI, drihten E^{3}H, driħt CG, driħ J, from dryht̄ A
et		⁊ ABCDE^{3}FGHIJK
tu		ðu ADF, þu BCE^{3}GHIJK
remisisti		geedleanedes A, geedleanudyst C, forlete BE^{3}J, forgefe D, forgeafe FGIK, fo[ ]eafe *H**
impietatem		arleasnisse A, arleasnysse *C*FI, arleasnesse BDE^{3}*GHJ, arlæsnesse K
cordis*	I	heortan ABCD, synne FGHI, synna J, minre E^{3} (*L*)
mei	I	minre ABCDFHJ, mine GI, heortæn E^{3} (*L*)

ED: [ ]elictum (H)] Delictum *Campbell.* iniusticias (C) (*1st*)] iniusti[t]ias *Wildhagen.* unri(h)[ ](ss)e (H)] unrih(twisne)sse *Campbell.* he cw̄ (J)] he cw*æþ Oess.* iniusticias (C) (*2nd*)] iniusti[t]ias *Wildhagen.* tú (E)] tu *Harsley.* remisisti (H)] r(e)misisti *Campbell.* fo[ ]eafe (H)] forgeafe *Campbell.*

OE: gylt (I)] y *altered from* i (?). ic dyde (I)] *orig.* ic dide: *2nd* i *altered to* y. oncnæwe (E^{3})] *eras. (2 letters) before word.* on unrihtwisnesse (G)] w *altered from* r. unri(h)[ ](ss)e (H)] *right leg of* h *lost and ascenders of* ss *lost due to hole in leaf.* oferwreah (E^{3})] *on eras., perhaps by main hand.* ic cwæð (C)] æ *malformed.* Ic cweð (E^{3})] *orig.* Ic cweðe: *final* e *eras.* þet ic sege ł bodige ($E^{3/x}$)] ł bodige *by corr.*, g *in* sege *altered from* e. ongean ł wiþ ($E^{3/x}$)] ongean ł *by corr.* fo[ ]eafe (H)] *descender visible after* o. arleasnesse (E^{3})] *on eras. by main hand, initial* a *altered from* æ (?).

LTg: Delictum] [ ]elictum H. iniustitias (*1st*)] iniusticias C: *orig.* iniustitias: *2nd* t *altered to* c *by corr.;* iustitiam L: *orig.* iustitias: s *underlined by corr. to signal deletion, macron added above* a: *see GAg.* meas (*1st*)] meā L: *orig.* meam: *final* m *underlined by corr. to signal deletion, macron added above* a: *see GAg.* operui] L: *underlined by* *corr. to signal deletion,* abscondi *added interl.: see GAg.* pronuntiabo] pronuntiábo C. aduersum] áduersum K. me] L: *added interl. by corr.* iniustitias (*2nd*)] iniusticias C: *orig.* iniustitias: *2nd* t *altered to* c *by corr.,* E: *letter eras. after* n; iniustitiam L: *orig.* iniustitias: s *underlined by corr. to signal deletion, macron added above* a: *see GAg.* meas (*2nd*)] meā L: *orig.* meam: *final* m *underlined by corr. to signal deletion, macron added above* a: *see GAg.* tu] tú E. remisisti] H: *split in leaf, but letters visible.* impietatem] impiętatem C. cordis mei] L: *underlined by corr. to signal deletion,* peccati mei *written to right by corr.: see GAg.*

LTu: Delictum] Dilictum ϑ. iniustitias (*1st*)] iniusticiam τ*φ. aduersum] aduersus μ. pronuntiabo] pronunciabo τ*. iniustitias (*2nd*)] iniustias β; iniusticias τ*. domino] β: *orig.* domine: o *interl. above* e *by corr.*

GAg: iniustitias meas (*1st*)] iniustitiam meam FGIJK, L: *see LTg;* iniu[ ] meam H: *hole in leaf due to burn-through from fol. 53v.* operui] abscondi FGHIJK, L: *see LTg.* pronuntiabo] confitebor FGHIJK. iniustitias meas (*2nd*)] iniustitiam meam GHIJK, F: *orig.* iustitiam meam: in *added interl. by corr.,* L: *see LTg.* cordis] peccati FGHIJK, L: *see LTg.*

GAu: iniustitias meas (*1st*)] iniustitiam meam δεζϑιμξoπυψ; iniusticiam meam τφ, ϱ: *orig.* iniustitiam meam; iustiam meam χ. operui] abscondi δεζϑιλμξoπϱστυφχψ. pronuntiabo] confitebor δεζϑιλμξoπϱστυφχψ. iniustitias meas (*2nd*)] iniustitiam meam δεϑιμξoσυφχψ, ζ: in *interl.;* iniusticiam meam τφ, ϱ: *orig.* iniustitiam meam. cordis] peccati δεζϑιλμξoπϱστυφχψ.

6

Pro		fore ABC, for DF*GH*IJKM^2, For E^3
hac		ðissum A, þissum BC, þisum E^3, þisum J, ðysse DG, þysse *M*^{2}, ðyssere F, dysse *H**, þisre I*, þys K
orabit		gebideð A*B*, gebidyð C, gebiddaþ J, gebiddæþ E^3, gebed *D*, gebæd FK, gebied H, ġebit GI (*M*)
ad	I	to ABCFGIJ*K*, eælle E^3
te	I	ðe ABF, þe CGIJK, hælige E^3
omnis	I	all A, ealle CFGJK, ælc DHI, æghwylc B, to E^3
sanctus	I	halig ABDFGH, halige *C*J, halga I*, þe E^3
in		in A, on BCDE^x*FGHIJK
tempore	I	tid A, tide BCDE^x*FGHJ*K*, timan I
oportuno	I	geliplice *A,* gelimplice C, gelimplicre B, gelimplicre ł gehiþlicre J*, gehyþelicre DE^x*F, gehyðelicre *H,* gehyþelicre M^2, gehyþelicre ł ondafenlicre G, geþyllicre K*, geþæslicum ł on gedafenlicre tide I
uerumtamen		þeahhweðre soðlice *A/A*^{2}*, ðeahhweþre Soðlice þonne E$^{3/x}$*, hwæðre soðlice B, hwæðere soðlice *C,* hwæþere soþlice *J,*

	þeahhwæðre *I*, ðeahhweþre *D*, ðeahhwæþere *F*, þeahhwæðere *G*, þeahhwæþere *H*, þehhwæðere *K* (*LM*)
in	in A, on BCDE^{x}*FGHIJKM^{2}
diluuio	cwildeflode AC, cwildflode B, flode D*E*^{x}*FGHIKM^{2}, cealdum flote J
aquarum	wetra A, wætra BCDHI, wętra E^{3}*, wætera FGJK
multarum	micelra A, micylra C, monigra B, manigra DFHJK, manegra GI, monigræ E^{3}
ad	to A*B*CDE^{3}FGHIJK
eum	him A*B*CE^{3}FGHI, him DJK
non	ǀ to ne ABC, na DE^{3}FGHJK, hi ne I
adproximabunt	ǀ geneolaecað A, genealæcað *CI*, togenealæcað D, togeneælecæþ E^{3}*, togenealæcað *FH*, togenealæceð G, genealæhton B, togenealæhton J, nealæcaþ *K*

ED: [ ]ro (H)] Pro *Campbell.* dysse (H)] ðysse *Campbell.* hác (H)] hac *Campbell.* orabit (D)] ora[u]it *Roeder.* uerumtamen (BE)] verum tamen *Brenner, Harsley.* þeahhweðre soðlice (A)] þeah hweðre soðlice *Kuhn.* ðeahhweþre (D)] ðeah hweþre *Roeder.* þeahhwæðere (G)] þeah hwæðere *Rosier.* þeahhwæþere (H)] þeah hwæþere *Campbell.* þeahhwæðre (I)] þeah hwæðre *Lindelöf.* approximabunt (C)] a[d]proximabunt *Wildhagen.*

OE: dysse (H)] *cross-stroke of* ð *not visible.* þisre (I)] s. impietatem : arleasnesse *written in left margin.* halga (I)] *orig.* haliga: i *deleted by subscript dot and eras.* on (E^{x}) (*1st*)] *on eras.* tide (E^{x})] *on eras.* gelimplicre ł gehiþlicre (J)] *3rd* i *interl.* gehyþelicre (E^{x})] *on eras.* geþyllicre (K)] *orig.* geþyldlicre: *deleting dot below and left of* d. þeahhweðre soðlice (A/A^{2})] þeah *added in 11th-c. hand.* ðeahhweþre Soðlice þonne (E$^{3/x}$)] ðeahhweþre *and* ne *on eras. by corr.* on (E^{x}) (*2nd*)] *on eras.* flode (E^{x})] *on eras.* wętra (E^{3})] *eras.* (*30 mm*) *after word.* togeneælecæþ (E^{3})] *letter eras before* g.

LTg: Pro] [ ]ro GH. hac] M: *orig.* hoc: o *altered to* a *by corr.;* hác H. orabit] D: *orig.* orauit: u *altered to* b; orauit BM. ad] ád K. sanctus] C: c *interl.* tempore] temporæ K. oportuno] A: no *added by corr.;* opportuno H: *orig.* oportuno: *1st* p *added interl. by glossator.* uerumtamen] A: *eras.* (*2 letters?*) *before word;* uerúmtamen C; uerŭmtamen M; Verumtamen I, F: *letter eras.* (p?) *after 1st* m, L: *orig.* uerumtamen: V *added interl. by corr. above initial* u; uerumptamen D; Verumptamen G; Uerumptamen J, K: *orig.* Uerumptamem: *final* m *altered to* n; Veruntamen H: *eras. after 1st* n. diluuio] E: *eras. after 1st* u. ad] B: *on eras.* eum] B: *on eras.* adproximabunt] approximabunt IK, C: *1st* p *on eras. by corr.*, H: *1st* p *on eras.*, F: *orig.* adproximabunt: d *altered to* p.

LTu: orabit] orauit βςψ. oportuno] opportuno λπ, ξ: *2nd* p *interl.*, ϱ: *1st* p *interl.* uerumtamen] Uerumtamen δζϑμπτχψ; Veruntamen ειλφ; Uerumptamen ξϱ;

Verumtamen ο; Ueruntamen σ; Verumptamen υ. diluuio] diluvio χ. adproximabunt] approximabunt ειλξορστ*τυφχ.

7

Tu	ðu AF, þu BC*E*^{3}GIJK
es	earð *A**, eart BCFGIJK, eært *E*^{3}
mihi*	me *ABC*, min *E*^{3} (*L*)
refugium	geberg A, gebeorg B, gebeorh C, frofor ł gebeorh J, frofr D*E*^{x}*HM^{2}, frofer GK, gener FI (*L*)
(meum)*	min FGIJK
a	from A, fro<u>m</u> B, fra<u>m</u> CDE^{x}*FGJM^{2}, fram I, a K
pressura*	ferðrycednisse A*, oferðryccednesse B, ofyrþriccydnysse *C*, ofðriccednysse D, ofþriccednysse *M*^{2}, ofðriccednisse E^{x}*, gedrefednysse F*I, gedrefednesse K, oferfrecednessum G, geswince J (*L*)
quae	sie A, se *C*, se ðe F, se þe *J*, seo *B*, seo þe I, þa þe *G*, þa *HK*, þe *E*^{x}* (*DL*)
circumdedit	ymbseled salde A, ymbsylyð *C*, ymbsalde B, ymbsealde DE^{x}**H*J, ymbsealdan G, ymbtrymdon ł sealdon F, ymsette ł ymbsealde I, ymbesealde K
me	me ABCDE^{x}*FGHIJK
exultatio	wynsumnis AC, wynsumnes B, winsu<u>m</u>nes J, blis DE^{x}*FHK, blis ł wynsumnes G*, upahæfdnes I*
mea	min ABCDE^{x}*FGHI*JK
redime*	ales A, alies B, alys CIK, alis J, alyse DE^{x}*, lys G, genera F (*L*)
me	mec A, me BCE^{x}*FGIJK
a	from A, fro<u>m</u> BC, fra<u>m</u> DHJK, fram *E*^{x}*FGI (*M*)
circumdantibus	ymbsellendum A*E*^{3}*, ymbsellendu<u>m</u> BD*H*, ymbsyllyndu<u>m</u> *C*, ymbsyllendum F, ymbsyllendu<u>m</u> J, ymbesyllendu<u>m</u> K, ymbsealdendu<u>m</u> ł ymbsyllendum G*, ymsittendum ł ymbsellendu<u>m</u> I
me	me ABCFGHIJK

ED: Tú (E)] Tu *Harsley*. Tu (G)] *Tu Rosier*. és (E)] es *Harsley*. m^{1} (E)] michi *Harsley*. gedrefednysse (F)] gederefednysse *Kimmens*. quę (E)] quae *Harsley*. circundedit (C)] circu[m]dedit *Wildhagen*. á (E)] a *Harsley*. circundantibus (C)] circu[m]dantibus *Wildhagen*.

OE: earð (A)] *order of text and gloss is* mihi es: me earð: *see LTg*. frofr (E^{x})] *on eras*. fra<u>m</u> (E^{x})] *on eras*. ferðrycednisse (A)] *letter eras. after* y. ofðriccednisse

(E^x)] *on eras.* gedrefednysse (F)] *orig.* gederefednysse: *2nd* e *eras.* þe (E^x)] *on eras.* ymbsealde (E^x)] *on eras.* me (E^x) (*1st*)] *on eras.* blis (E^x)] *on eras.* blis ł wynsumnes (G)] ł wynsumnes *added in diff.* (?) *hand, with* nes *after following* min. upahæfdnes (I)] *lemma misread as* exaltatio. min (E^x)] *on eras.* min (I) (*2nd*)] s. es : þu eart *written in left margin.* alyse (E^x)] *on eras.* me (E^x) (*2nd*)] *on eras.* fram (E^x)] *on eras.* ymbsellendum (E^3)] y *retouched in darker ink, eras. before word.* ymbsealdendum ł ymbsyllendum (G)] ł ymbsyllendum *added in diff.* (?) *hand.*

LTg: Tu] Tú E. es mihi] mihi es A: *cf. Weber MSS* Σαγδε moz. es] és E. mihi] L: *underlined by corr. to signal deletion: see GAg;* michi C: c *interl. by corr.;* m^1 E. refugium] L: meum *added interl. by corr.: see GAg;* refugivm E. pressura] C: *2nd* s *interl., eras. below* e (*perhaps of cauda*), L: *underlined by corr. to signal deletion,* tribulatione *added interl.: see GAg;* praessura M: *orig.* praesura: *2nd* s *interl. by corr.* quae] quæ B; quę CEG; que DHJKL. circumdedit] circundedit H, C: *orig.* circumdedit: *left leg of* m *eras. to form* n. redime] L: *underlined by corr. to signal deletion,* erue *added interl.: see GAg.* a] á EM. circumdantibus] circundantibus E, C: *orig.* circumdantibus: *left leg of* m *eras. to form* n, H: *eras. after 1st* n.

LTu: Tu] TU β. mihi] michi ς; m^1 τ*. pressura] pręssura ν; presura ς. quae] quę βεζινξϱφ; que σςτ*τ; q̄ ϑ. circumdedit] circundedit λ; circ̄dedit ϑ. exultatio] exaltatio βϑ. mea] *interl.* σ. circumdantibus] circundantibus ϑιλφ.

GAg: mihi] *om.* FGHIJK, L: *see LTg.* refugium] refugium meum FGHIJK, L: *see LTg.* pressura] tribulatione FGHIJK, L: *see LTg.* redime] erue FHIJK, L: *see LTg;* erueę G.

GAu: mihi] *om.* δεζϑιλμξοπϱστυφχψ. refugium] refugium meum δεζϑιλμξοπϱστυφχψ. pressura] tribulatione δεζϑιλμξοπϱστυφχψ. redime] erue δεζϑιλμξοπϱστυφχψ.

8

Intellectum		ondget A, ondgit B, ondgyt C, Ondgiet E^3*, andgyt DIK, ongyt F, andgit HJ, on andgyte *G*
dabo*	}	ic sellu A, ic selle BDHI*, ic sylle CG, ic sille J, syle F, do K, ic þe E^3
tibi*	}	ðe ABF, þe CGHIJK, selle E^3
et		⁊ ABCDE^3FGHIJK
instruam	|	getimbru ł lære A/A^2*, getimbrige C, ic getimbre B, ic getimbrige J, ic lære DFG*H*IK, ic þe E^3
te	|	ðe ABF, þe CDG*H*IJK, lære E^x*
in		in A, on BCDFGHIJKE^3
uia	|	wege ABCDFGHIJK, þisum E^3
hac	|	ðissum A, ðissum B, þissum C, þisum J, þy D, þys GH, ðæm I, þam K, wege E^3* (*F*)

qua	ðæm A, þam C, on ðæm B, on þam J, þe DE^{3}*GHI, þa K, his F
ingredieris*	ðu ingæst ABK, þu ingæst *C*, þu gegæst J, þu gæst I, ðu in ongangest D, þu in ongangest E^{3}*, ðu onstæpst F, þu stepst G, þu stæpst H (*L*)
firmabo	ic getrymmu *A*, ic getrymme B, ic getrymme CE^{3}FGIK, ic getrymme D, ic getrimme HJ
super	ofer ABDE^{3}FGHIJK, ofyr C
te	ðe A*BF, þe CDE^{3}GHIJK
oculos	egan A*K, eagan BCDE^{x}*FGHI, eagon J
meos	min A, mine BCDE^{x}*FGHIJK

ED: gradiéris (FGH)] gradieris *Kimmens, Rosier, Campbell.* þu stæpst (H)] þu stepst *Campbell.*

OE: Ondgiet (E^{3})] O *written by corr.* ic selle (I)] *orig.* ic sille: *2nd* i *altered to* e. getimbru ł lære (A/A^{2})] ł lære *added in 11th-c. hand.* lære (E^{x})] *on eras.* wege (E^{3})] *eras. after word.* þe (E^{3})] *written above eras.* þu in ongangest (E^{3})] *written above eras.* ðe (A) (*3rd*)] a *or false start after word.* egan (A)] *orig.* egen: a *interl. above 2nd* e, *but without deleting mark.* eagan (E^{x})] *on eras.* mine (E^{x})] *on eras.*

LTg: Intellectum] [ ]ntellectum G. instruam] H: *eras. after* m. te] H: *eras. after* e. hac] F: *on eras. by corr.* ingredieris] ingredíeris C; gradieris L: *orig.* ingredieris: in *underlined by corr. to signal deletion,* a *added interl. above 1st* e: *see GAg.* firmabo] A: *added interl., possibly by corr.*

GAg: dabo tibi] tibi dabo FGHIJK. ingredieris] gradiéris FGH; gradieris IJ, K: a *on eras. by corr.,* L: *see LTg.*

GAu: dabo tibi] tibi dabo δεζϑιλμξοπρστυφχψ. ingredieris] gradieris δεζϑιλμξοπρστυφψ, χ: *orig.* gredieris: *1st* e *deleted.,* a *interl.*

9

Nolite	nyllað A, nyllað ge B, nellað ge C, nellaþ ge J, nellen ge D, nellen ge HE^{x}*, nylle ge F, nelle ge *G*I, nelle þu K
fieri	bion A, beon BCDE^{x}*FGHIJ, gewyrþan K
sicut	swe swe A, swa swa BCFIJ, swa DE^{x}*GHK
equus	hors AB*C*DE^{3}*FG*HIJK
et	⁊ ABCDFGHIJK (*E*)
mulus	mul A*BCDFGHI, mulas JK, ⁊ mul E^{3}
in*	in A, on BCDE^{3} (*L*)
quibus	dæm A, ðæm B, þæm E^{3}, þam CG, ðam DF, þam HK, on þam J, þam þe I

non	ǀ nis *ADFI*, nys C, nes H, ne BJ, nan G, na K, nis nenig E^{3}
est	ǀ is BGJ*K*
intellectus	ondget A, ondgit B, andgyt CDFI*K, andgit HJ, ontgiet E^{3}, on andgyte G
In	in A, on BCDF*G*HIJKM^{2}, On E^{3}*
freno*	bridelse ABJ, bridylse C, þæm bridle E^{3}, bitole D, bytole M^{2}, gewealde F, walde H, walde ł on bridelse G*, hælftre ł on wealdleðre I*, geahle K (*L*)
et	⁊ ABCDE^{3}FGHIJK
camo*	haelftreo A, hælftre B*C*, walde D, on þęre walde *$E^{3/x}$**, bitole FH, bitole ł midle G*, bridle K*, bridle ł ⁊ midle I*, midle J, ⁊walde M^{2} (*L*)
maxillas	cecan A, ceacan BCFGIJK, ceocan DE^{x}*HM^{2}
eorum	heara A, hira B, hyra C, heora DFGHIJK, heoræ E^{3}
constringe	geteh ł gewriþ A/A^{2}*, geteoh B*C*J, gewrið I, gewrið ł gebind DF, gewryð ł gebind $E^{3/x}$*, gewirð ł gebind H, gewrið ł gebind ł geteoh G*, gebint K
qui	ða AB*, þa CDE^{x}*GHJK, ða þe F, þa þe I
non	to ne ABCJ, na DE^{x}*FGHK, ne I
adproximant	genehlaecað A, genealæc[ ]ð B*, genealæcað *C*, genealæcaþ *I*, togenealecað DE^{x}*, togenealæcað *F*G, togenealæcaþ *HK*, genealæhton *J* (*M*)
ad	to ABCDE^{3}FGHIJ
te	ðe ABCD, þe E^{3}FGHIJK

ED: swa swa (IJ)] swaswa *Lindelöf, Oess.* In (B) (*Lat.*)] in *Brenner.* ęquus (G)] equus *Rosier.* approximant (C)] a[d]proximant *Wildhagen.* genealæc[ ]ð (B)] genealæcað *Brenner.* togenealæcaþ (K)] to genealæcaþ *Sisam.*

OE: nellen ge (E^{x})] *on eras.* beon (E^{x})] *on eras.* swa (E^{x})] *on eras.* mul (A)] ul *on eras. in 11th-c. hand.* andgyt (I)] *orig.* andgit: i *altered to* y. On (E^{3})] *lower part of* O *retouched by corr.* walde ł on bridelse (G)] ł on bridelse *added in diff.* (?) *hand.* hælftre ł on wealdleðre (I)] ł on wealdleðre *written in bottom margin below* chamo. on þęre walde ($E^{3/x}$)] walde *added by corr.* bitole ł midle (G)] ł midle *added in diff.* (?) *hand.* bridle (K)] r *altered from* b. bridle ł ⁊ midle (I)] ł ⁊ midle *written in bottom margin below* freno. ceocan (E^{x})] *on eras.* geteh ł gewriþ (A/A^{2})] ł gewriþ *added in 11th-c. hand.* gewryð ł gebind ($E^{3/x}$)] ryð ł gebind *on eras. by corr., eras.* (*11 mm*) *after* gebind. gewrið ł gebind ł geteoh (G)] ł geteoh *added in diff.* (?) *hand.* ða (B)] *on crease: cross-stroke of* ð *not visible, top of* a *not visible.* þa (E^{x})] *on eras.* na (E^{x})] *on eras.* genealæc[ ]ð (B)] *letter after* c *lost, bowl of* ð *obscured by crease.* togenealecað (E^{x})] *on eras.*

LTg: Nolite] G: N *partly lost.* equus] ęquus CG; aequus F. et (*1st*)] *om.* E. in] L: *underlined by corr. to signal deletion: see GAg.* non (*1st*)] A: on *interl. by corr.* est] ėst K. In] [ ]n G. freno] L: chamo *added interl. by corr.: see GAg.* camo] L: freno *added interl. by corr.: see GAg;* chamo E, C: h *interl. by corr.* constringe] C: e *on eras.* (?). adproximant] approximant IK, H: *1st* p *on eras.*, C: *1st* p *on eras. by corr.*, FJ: *orig.* adproximant: d *altered to* p; adproximabunt M: *orig.* adproximant: bu *interl.: cf. Weber MS* χ.

LTu: equus] æquus ν; ęquus ξ; equis ς. In] IN β. camo] chamo τ*. constringe] χ: *2nd* n *interl.;* contringe ϑ. adproximant] approximant εζιλξοπϱτ*τυφχ; adproximabunt ν: *cf. Weber MS* χ.

GAg: in] *om.* FGHIJK, L: *see LTg.* freno] camo GHK, F: *spiritus asper added interl. after* c (cꜸ-amo); chamo IJ, L: *see LTg.* camo] freno FGHIJK, L: *see LTg.*

GAu: in] *om.* δεζϑιλμξοπϱστυφχψ. freno] chamo δεζιλξοπϱστυφχψ; camo ϑμ. camo] freno δεζϑιλμξοπϱστυφχψ.

10

Multa	monge A, monige BC*, manige F, managa I, monig J, Monigo ł fela E^{3}, fela DH, feala K, fela ł monige *G*
flagella	drea A, ðrea B, þreaunga C, þrean J, swingela ł þrean G, swingella DH, swíngla F, swingla I*, swípo ł swingella E^{3}
peccatorum*	synfulra ABCD, synfullra G, synfulles FH, þæs synfullan I*, synfullan J, synfulla K, þæræ firenfulræ ł synfulra E^{3} (*L*)
sperantes*	gehyhtende AB, gehihtynde C, gehihtende GJ, hyhtende DH, hihtende E^{3}K, þane hihtenden I, hopiende F (*L*)
autem	soðlice ABCI, soþlice E^{3}FJ, witodlice K (*G*)
in	in A, on BCDE^{3}FHIJK (*G*)
domino	dryhtne AB, drihtny C, drihtne FI, drihten E$^{3/x}$*K, driħt GH, driħ J
misericordia	mildheortnis ADE$^{3/x}$*, mildheortnes B*H*K, mildheortnysse C, mildheortnyssa F, mildheortnes[ ] G*, mildheortnisse I, mildheortnesse J
circumdabit	ymbseleð AB, ymbsylyð *C*, ymbesylð K, ymbselð utan DE$^{3/x}$*, ymbselþ utan *H*, ymbutan sylþ F, ymbs[ ]lð ł ymbsyleð G*, ymbsyleþ J, ymsitt ł ymbselleð hi utan I

ED: [ ]ulta (G)] Multa *Rosier.* mildheortnes (B)] mildheortnesse *Brenner.* mildheortnes[ ] (G)] mildheortne[ ] *Rosier.* circundabit (C)] circu[m]dabit *Wildhagen.*

OE: monige (C)] *eras. after* i. swingla (I)] *top of* a *partly lost due to hole in leaf* þæs synfullan (I)] *orig.* þæs sinfullan: i *altered to* y, s. sunt : synt *written in left margin.* drihten (E$^{3/x}$)] ten *on eras. by corr.* mildheortnis (E$^{3/x}$)] mildh *on eras. by corr.*

(*perhaps entire word*). mildheortnes[ ] (G)] *not clear whether more letters follow.* ymbselð utan (E$^{3/x}$)] ymbselð *on eras. by corr.* ymbs[ ]lð ł ymbsyleð (G)] *fragment of* e (?) *visible after 1st* s.

LTg: Multa] [ ]ulta G. peccatorum] peccatoris L: *orig.* peccatorum: m *crossed through, right minim of* u *altered to* s *by corr.: see GAg.* sperantes] sperantem L: *orig.* sperantes: *final* s *crossed through, macron added above* e *by corr.: see GAg.* autem] G: *letter fragments of gloss visible above word.* in] G: *letter fragments of gloss visible above word.* misericordia] H: *eras. after word.* circumdabit] circundabit C: *orig.* circumdabit: *left leg of* m *eras. to form* n; circúndabit: H: *eras. after* n.

LTu: misericordia] missericordịa ϑ. circumdabit] circundabit ειλφ; circ̄dabit ϑ.

GAg: peccatorum] peccatoris FGHIJK, L: *see LTg.* sperantes] sperantem FGHIJK, L: *see LTg.*

GAu: peccatorum] peccatoris δεζϑιλμξοπϱστυφχψ. sperantes] sperantem δεζϑιλμξϱστυφχψ.

11

Laetamini		blisiað A, blissiað *BCIK,* geblissiað *DF,* geblyssiað *H,* geblissiað ge *G,* we blissiæð *E^3,* blissigende J (*L*)
in		in A, on BCDE^{3}FGHIJK
domino		dryhtne AB, dryhtny C, drihtne DE^{3}FI, drihten K, driħt GH, driħ J
et		⁊ ABCDE^{3}FGHIJK
exultate		gefiað A, gefeoð BC, gefeoge J, fægniað DE^x*FGH, fægniað ge I, fægennian K
iusti		rehtwise A, ryhtwise BD, rihtwise CE^x*FGHJK, rihtwisan I*
et		⁊ ABCE^{3}FGHIJK
gloriamini	I	wuldriað ABCDFGHI, wuldriende J, wuldrian K, eælle E^3
omnes	I	alle A, ealle BCDFGHIJK, wuldriæd E^3
recti	I	rehte AB, rihte I, rihtheorte C, ryhtwise D, rihtwise FGHJK, on rihtre E^3
corde	I	on heortan AB, on heortan ł þa rihtgeþancodan I*, heortan FGHJK, heortæn E^3

ED: Lętamini (E)] Laetamini *Harsley.* Lętamni (G)] Lętamini *Rosier.*

OE: fægniað (E^x)] *on eras.* rihtwise (E^x)] *on eras.* rihtwisan (I)] a *on eras.* on heortan ł þa rihtgeþancodan (I)] *2nd* a *in* rihtgeþancodan *altered from* o.

LTg: Laetamini] Lætamini BK; Lętamini CEF; Letamini DHL; Lętamni G.

LTu: Laetamini] Letamini βϑσςτ*τ; Lętamini ειυφ.

PSALM 32

1

Gaudete*	gefioð *A,* gefeoð *BC,* gefeoþ J, gefeogað *DM*[2], fægniað GH, fægniaþ K, fægniað ge I, gefeinigað *E*ˣ*, blissiað F (*L*)
iusti	rehtwise A, ryhtwise BDEˣ*, rihtwise *C*FGHJK, rihtwisan I* (*L*)
in	in A, on B*C*DEˣ*FGHIJK (*L*)
domino	dryhtne BD, drihtny C, drihtne Eˣ*FHI, drihten K, dryht̄ A, driħt G, driħ J (*L*)
rectos	rehtwise A, ryhtwise BD, rihtwise CFGHM[2], ryhwise Eˣ*, rihtwisan K, rihtwisum ł þam rihtum I, riht J (*L*)
decet	gedeofenað A, gedafenað CG, gedafenaþ J, gedafenað ł gerist I, gerist DEˣ*M[2], geríst F, ger(i)sþ H*, gerisæð K, geda B* (*L*)
conlaudatio*	efenherenis A, efenherenes B, efynherenys *C,* somodhering DEˣ*, samodhering M[2], samodherunga I, herung FK, hering *H,* herung ł herenesse G, hirenes J (*L*)

ED: [ ]xultate (H)] EXULTATE *Campbell.* ryhwise (E)] ryh[t]wise *Harsley.* ger(i)sþ (H)] gerisþ *Campbell.* collaudatio (C)] co[n?]laudatio *Wildhagen.*

OE: gefeinigað (Eˣ)] *on eras.* ryhtwise (Eˣ)] *on eras.* rihtwisan (I)] an *on eras.* (?). on (Eˣ)] *on eras.* drihtne (Eˣ)] *on eras.* ryhwise (Eˣ)] *on eras.* gerist (Eˣ)] *on eras.* ger(i)sþ (H)] i *fragmentary.* geda (B)] *rest of gloss not written.* somodhering (Eˣ)] *on eras.*

LTg: Gaudete] GAudete A; GAudête M; GAVdete BD; GAUDETE CE; GAVDETE L: Exultate *added interl. by corr.: see GAg.* iusti] IUSTI C; IVSTI L. in] IN CL. domino] DÑO L. rectos] RECTOS L. decet] DECET L. conlaudatio] CONLAVDATIO L; collaudatio C: *eras. after 1st* o, *1st* l *formed from another letter,* H: col *on eras.*

LTu: Gaudete] GAUDETE βν; GAUdete ςτ*. iusti] IVSTI λ; IUSTI μνϱψ. in] IN λ. domino] DOMINO ϱ; DÑO λ. conlaudatio] collaudatio ϑλστ*χ.

GAg: Gaudete] Exultate FGIJ, L: *see LTg;* EXultate K; [ ]xultate H: *initial* E *lost.* conlaudatio] laudatio FGIJK.

GAu: Gaudete] Exultate δεζξοπσυχ; EXultate ϑ; EXULTATE ιλμϱτ; EXVLTATE φ; EXSULTATE ψ. conlaudatio] laudatio δεζμξοπϱτυφψ, ι: *orig.* collaudatio: col *deleted by subscript dots.*

2

Confitemini	ondettað AB, Ondettæþ E[3]*, andyttað C, andettað DFG, andettaþ *H*IJ, andetaþ K

domino	dryhtne B, drịhtny C, drihtne E^{3}FI, drihtene K, dryht̄ A, driħt G, driħ J
in	in A, on BCDE^{3}FGHIJK
cithara	citra *A*, cytran *B*, hearpan *CD*FGIJ*K*, heapan *H*, eærpungum *E^{3}* (*LM*)
in	in A, on BCDFGIJK, ⁊ on E^{3}
psalterio	hearpan ABD, sealmsange C, saltere FIJK, psalterum E^{3}, salte[ ] G*
decem	ten A, tien B, tyn C*D*FGHIJ*K*M^{2}, tyen E^{x}*
cordarum	strenga *ABC*DE^{x}**FGHM^{2}*, strengum I, strengan *K*, strengodan *J*
psallite	singað ABCDGHIK, singæþ E^{3}*, syngað F, singaþ J
ei*	him ABCDE^{3}FGIJ, him K

ED: salte[ ] (G)] salte *Rosier.* cordarum (CI)] c[h]ordarum *Wildhagen;* chordarum *Lindelöf.* tyn strenga (F)] tynstrenga *Kimmens.* tyn strengum (I)] tynstrengum *Lindelöf.* tyn strengan (K)] tynstrengan *Sisam.*

OE: Ondettæþ (E^{3})] *retraced in darker ink.* salte[ ] (G)] *descender* (*of* r?) *visible after* e. tyen (E^{x})] *on eras.* strenga (E^{x})] *on eras.* singæþ (E^{3})] *eras. before word.*

LTg: Confitemini] [ ]onfitemini H: *initial* C *lost.* cithara] M: *orig.* cythara: y *deleted by subscript dot,* i *interl.;* cythara ABCDEHKL. decem] K: *eras. after 2nd* e, *macron added by corr.;* decim D. cordarum] C: *orig.* chordarum: h *eras.,* F: *spiritus asper* ($^{\text{l-}}$) *added interl. after* c, H: *letter eras. after* c; chordarum BGJKLM, A: *caroline* h *interl.*

LTu: cithara] cythara δεζιλοπϱσυφχψ. cordarum] chordarum β; c$^{\text{l-}}$odarum εο: *spiritus asper interl.*

GAg: ei] illi FGHIJK.

GAu: ei] illi δεζϑιλμξοπϱστυφχψ.

3

Cantate		singað ABCDGHI, Singæþ E^{3}, syngað F, singaþ JK (*M*)
ei		him ACDE^{3}FGHIK, him BJ
canticum	|	song AB, sang *C*JK, cantic DGH, cantícc F, lofsang I, niewne E^{3}
nouum	|	neowne AB, niwne CDGHIJK, níwne F, song E^{3}
bene		wel ABCDGHJK, well FI, and wel E^{3}*
psallite		singað ABCDGHIJK, singæþ E^{3}, syngað F
ei		him CDE^{3}FGHI, him BJK (*A*)
in		in A, on BCDE^{x}*FGJK, mid I
iubilatione*		wynsumnisse A, wynsumnesse B, wynsumnysse *C*, wyndreame ł on lofe DE^{x}*, stemne hludre F, hludre stefne ł

on gehreord gleawnesse ł on hreame I*, hreame G, stæfne J, stefne wyndreama K (*LM*)

OE: and wel (E^{3})] *orig.* ond wel: o *altered to* a. on (E^{x})] *on eras.* wyndreame ł on lofe (E^{x})] *on eras.*, l *eras. before 1st* o. hludre stefne ł on gehreord gleawnesse ł on hreame (I)] ł on hreame *written in left margin.*

LTg: Cantate] Cantâte M. canticum] C: *initial* c *on eras.* ei (*2nd*)] *om.* A: *cf. Weber MSS* γη. iubilatione] C: *2nd* i *interl.*, L: uociferatione *added by corr. in right margin: see GAg;* iubilatiône M.

LTu: Cantate ei] Cantatei δ.

GAg: iubilatione] uociferatione FGHIJK, L: *see LTg.*

GAu: iubilatione] uociferatione δεζθιλμξοπϱστυφχψ.

4

Quoniam* forðon ABD, forþon CJ, forþā K, Forðæn þe E^{3}, forðā þe F, forþam þe G, forðan þe I
rectus* reht A, ryht B, riht CE^{3}FGHIJK, ryhtwis D (*L*)
est is ABDE^{3}FGH*I**JK, ys C
sermo* | word ABCFGHIJ, sprec ł word D, wor K, drihtnes E^{3} (*L*)
domini | dryhtnes B, drihtnys C, drihtnes FI, dryht̄ A, driħt GH, driħ J, gode K, word E^{3}
et ⁊ ABCDFGHI*JK, and E^{3}*
omnia all A, ealle BCDF*G*HIJK, eælla E^{3}* (*M*)
opera | werc A, weorc B*C*DFGHJK, worc I, his E^{3}
eius | his ABCDFGHIJ*K*, weorc E^{3}
in in A, on BCDE^{x}*FGHIJK
fide geleafan ABCDFGHIJK, lofe E^{x}*

ED: forðon (A)] for ðon *Kuhn.*

OE: is (I)] *on eras.* ⁊ (I)] s. sunt : synt *written in right margin.* and (E^{3})] *orig.* ond: o *altered to* a. eælla (E^{3})] a *in darker ink.* on (E^{x})] *on eras.* lofe (E^{x})] *on eras.*

LTg: rectus] L: s *crossed through, macron added above* u: *see GAg.* est] I: *on eras.;* ést K. sermo] L: *underlined to signal deletion,* uerbum *added interl. by corr.* omnia] M: *2 letters eras. after* i, *2nd of which is* a; om[ ] G. opera] C: o *on eras.* eius] eíus K.

LTu: rectus] rectum ς: *see GAu.*

GAg: Quoniam] Quia FGIJK, H: *initial letter faint but visible.* rectus] rectum FGHIJK, L: *see LTg.* sermo] uerbum FGHIJK, L: *see LTg.*

GAu: Quoniam] Quia δεζθιλμξοπϱστυφχψ. rectus] rectum δεζθιλμξοπϱστυφχψ, ς: *see LTu.* sermo] uerbum δεζθιλμξοπϱστυφχψ.

5

Diligit — lufað ABFJ, he lufude C, he lufað DGHI, he lufæþ E^{3}, he lufaþ K (*M*)

misericordiam — mildheortnisse AD, mildheortnesse BGHIJK, milheortnysse C, miltheortnesse E^{3}, mildheortnysse F

et — ⁊ ABCE^{3}FGIJK

iudicium — dom ABCDFGHIJK, drihtnes dóm E^{3}

misericordia — mildheortnisse A, mildheortnysse CF, mildheortnesse BGJ, of mildheortnisse D, of mildheortnessae H, mid mildheortnesse I, mildheortnes K, his mildheortnesse E^{3}

domini — dryhtnes B, drihtnys C, drihtnes FI, drihtenes K, dryht̄ A, drih̄t G, drih̄ J, drihtnes E^{3}

plena — ful ABE^{3}JK, full CDFGI

est — is ABDE^{3}FGIJ*K*, ys C

terra — eorðe ABCDFGIJ, eorþe E^{3}K

LTg: Diligit] Díligit M. est] ést K.

LTu: Diligit] β: *orig.* Dilegit: i *interl. above* e *by corr.* misericordiam] missericordiam ϑ. misericordia] missericordia ϑ.

6

Uerbo — | worde A*BC*, word *FJK,* of worde *DGH,* mid worde *I,* drihtenes *E*^{3} (*LM*)

domini — | dryhtnes B, drihtnys C, drihtnes F, dryht̄ A, drih̄t G, drih̄ J, godes K, wordes E^{3}

caeli — heofenas A, heofonas *BIJ,* hefynys *C,* heofenes *DG,* heofones F*H,* heofenenes *K,* ⁊ heofonæs *E*^{3} (*L*)

firmati — | getrymede ABDGHIKM^{2}, getrymyde C, getrýmde F, getrimede J, Sient E^{3}

sunt — | sind AJ, synd CDFGHK, sint B, syndon I*, getrimede E^{3}

et — ⁊ ABCE^{3}FGHI*JK

spiritu — gaste ABC, gast DFGHJK, mid gaste I*, on gaste E^{3}

oris — | muðes ABDFGI, muðys C, muþes HJ, muþe K, his E^{3}

eius — | his ABCDFGHIJ*K*, muðes E^{3}

omnis — all A, eall B*C*DGI*, eæll E^{3}, ealle FHJK

uirtus — | megen A, mægen BDHJ, mægyn C, mæg K, mægen ł miht GI, mihta F, hioræ E^{3} (*M*)

eorum — | heara *A,* hira B, heora CDFGHIJK, megen E^{3}

ED: cęli (E)] caeli *Harsley.* spiritu (G)] spi*ritu Rosier.*

OE: worde (A)] d *altered from* ð *by eras. of cross-stroke.* worde (C)] *eras. after* e.

syndon (I)] d *altered from* t. ⁊ (I)] *eras. after word.* mid gaste (I)] *written in right margin.* eall (I)] *on eras.*

LTg: Uerbo] uerbo ABCDELM; Verbo FGHIJK. caeli] cæli BK; cęli CEGHL; celi DJ. eius] eíus K. omnis] C: i *on eras.* uirtus] M: *letter* (e?) *eras. after word.* eorum] A: e *on eras.*

LTu: Uerbo] Verbo ειλξσφ; uerbo βνςτ*. caeli] cęli ειλξορςφ; cæli ϑμ; celi στ*τ.

7

Congregans	gesomnende A, gesomniende B, Gesomniende E[3], gesomniynde C, gesomnigende DF*HJ*, gesamnigende *G,* gesamniende I*, gesomnigen K
sicut	swe swe A, swa swa BCDGHIJ, swæ swæ E[3/x]*, swá swá F, swa K
in	in AJ, on BCDE[x]*FGHIK
utrem*	cylle AB, cylle ł bytte C, bytt DE[x]*, bytte *F*GHI*K,* on cille J
aquas	weter A, wæter BJ, wætyr C, wæteru DFH, wætere E[x]*, wætru I, wætera GK
maris	sæs ABDE[x]*HJ, sæys C, sæ GIK, sǽs F
ponens	settende ABDFGH*JKM*[2], settynde C, gesettende E[3]I
in	in A, on BCDE[3]*FGHIJK
thesauris	goldhordum ABFI, goldhordu̲m̲ CDE[3]**H**, goldhord J, golhord K, hordum gold G
abyssos	neolnisse A, neolnyssa B, nywulnysse C, néowelnýsse F, neolnysse *J,* on niwolnesse ł grundas E[3/x]*, grundas *DG*HK*M*[2], diopnyssa ł nywelnyssa I* (*L*)

ED: swa swa (GIJ)] swaswa *Rosier, Lindelöf, Oess.*

OE: gesamniende (I)] s. e̲s̲t̲ : he is *written in left margin.* swæ swæ (E[3/x])] *2nd* swæ *on eras. by corr.* on (E[x]) (*1st*)] *on eras.* bytt (E[x])] *on eras.* wætere (E[x])] *on eras.* sæs (E[x])] *on eras.* on (E[3]) (*2nd*)] *orig.* þone: þ *and* e *eras.* goldhordu̲m̲ (E[3])] ū *by corr.* goldhordu̲m̲ (H)] *gloss eras. after word.* on niwolnesse ł grundas (E[3/x])] ł grundas *added by corr.* diopnyssa ł nywelnyssa (I)] ł nywelnyssa *written in right margin.*

LTg: Congregans] H: *initial letter faint but visible;* [ ]ongregans G. utrem] F: *orig.* utre: *macron added above* e *by corr.,* K: *eras. after* e, *macron added by corr.: see GAg.* ponens] pones J. thesauris] H: i *on eras.* abyssos] D: *small eras. above* y; abissos GJ; abysos LM.

LTu: thesauris] thesauros ς; thesuris ϑ. abyssos] β: *orig.* abissos: y *interl. above* i *by corr.,* χ: *1st* s *interl.;* abisos ϑ; abissos ξτ*τ; abyssus σ.

GAg: utrem] utre GIJ, H: *eras. after* e; *for* FK *see LTg.*

GAu: utrem] utre δειλμξοπρστυφχψ, ζ: m *eras.*

8

Timeat	| ondrede A, ondræde BCDF*G*HK, ondræda I, ondrædende J, drihten E^3
dominum	| dryhten B, drihten I, dryht̄ A, dryħt C, driħt FG, driħ J, him ondrędæþ *E^3*
omnis	all A, eall BCDFGI, eælle E^3, ealle HJ, eal K
terra	eorðe ABCFGI, eorþe E^{3}HK, eorþan J
ab	from AE^3, from C, fram DFGHJK, fram I, fr[ ]m B*
ipso*	him ACE^{3}FGHI, him *D*JK (B*)
autem	soðlice ABCE^{3}F, [ ](o)ðlice G*, soþlice J, witodlice IK
commoueantur	bioð onstyred A, beoð onstyrede B, beoð onstyryde C, beoð astyrode I*, beoþ onstirede J, beon astyrede DH, beon astyrode FG, beon astyrude K, bid onwended E^3
uniuersi*	alle A, ealle BCD
et*	⁊ ACD, ond E^3 (*B*)
omnes	alle A, ealle CDFGHIJK, eælle E^3 (*B*)
qui*	ða A, þe D, ða ðe B, þa þe C, þæ þe E^3
habitant*	eardiað ABC, geondeardiaþ D, oneardiaþ J, oneardigende FGH*, oneardende K, eærdigæþ on E^3*, onwuniende I
orbem	ymbhwyrst A, ymbhwyrft BCFGHIJ, ymbhwyrt D, ymbhwirfte E^3, ymbehwyftes K

ED: fr[ ]m (B)] from *Brenner.* ipso (B) *no gloss visible*] him *Brenner.* [ ](o)ðlice (G)] [ ]ðlice *Rosier.*

OE: fr[ ]m (B)] *letter after* r *lost (fading?).* ipso (B)] *fragment of gloss ascender visible, specks of ink visible after ascender.* [ ](o)ðlice (G)] o *partly lost.* beoð astyrode (I)] *orig.* beoð astirode: i *altered to* y. oneardigende (H)] *bowl of 1st* d *partly lost due to hole in leaf.* eærdigæþ on (E^3)] *eras. after* on.

LTg: Timeat] [ ]imeat G. dominum] dominvm E. ipso] D: *orig.* ipsa: a *deleted by subscript dot,* o *interl.* et] *om.* B. omnes] *om.* B.

GAg: ipso] eo FGHJK; éo I. uniuersi et] *om.* FGHIJK. qui] *om.* FGHIJK. habitant] inhabitantes FGHIJK.

GAu: ipso] eo δεζϑιλμξοπρστυφχψ. uniuersi et] *om.* δεζϑιλμξοπρστυφχψ. qui] *om.* δεζϑιλμξοπρστυφχψ. habitant] inhabitantes δεζϑιλμξοπρστυφχψ.

9

Quoniam	forðon AB, forþon C, Forþæn E^3*, fordon þe F, forþam þe G, forðan þe I, forþon þe J
ipse	he ABCDE^{3}FGHK, he sylf I
dixit	cweð AE^3, cwæð BCDGHIK, cweþ J, sæde F

et	⁊ ABCDE^{3}FGHIJK
facta	| werun A, wæron C, gewordene BDE^{x}*FGHJ, geworhta ł gewurdone I*, gedone K
sunt	| geworden A*, gewordyne C, wæran B, synd DFGJK, sind E^{3}H, synt I
ipse	hie A, he BCE^{x}*FGHIJK
mandauit	et A, bebead BCDE^{x}*FGHIJK (*M*)
et	⁊ ABCDFGHIJK, and E^{3}*
creata	gecwicad A, gecwicade B, gecwicode C, gescapen D, gesceapene GIK, gesceæpene E^{3}, gesceapen H, gescapene J, sceapene F
sunt	werun A, wæron B, synd CFK, hy synt D, hy synd E^{x}*GH, hig synt I*, syndon J

ED: forðon (A)] for ðon *Kuhn*. fordon þe (F)] forðon þe *Kimmens*. forþam þe (G)] forþam *Rosier*.

OE: Forþæn (E^{3})] *eras. after word.* gewordene (E^{x})] *on eras.* geworhta ł gewurdone (I)] geworhta *written in left margin,* u *closed at top, but not altered from* o. geworden (A)] o *altered from another letter.* he (E^{x}) (*2nd*)] *on eras.* bebead (E^{x})] *on eras.* and (E^{3})] a *altered from another letter* (?). hy synd (E^{x})] *added by corr.* hig synt (I)] hig *written above* synt.

LTg: mandauit] mandâuit M.

LTu: Quoniam] Quia ψ.

10

Dominus	drihten E^{3}I, drhiten K, dryht̄ AB, driħt CF, driħ J (*GH*)
dissipat	tostenceð AB, tostencyð C, tostencþ D, tostencð FHI*K*, to[ ]cað G*, tostencte E^{3}, tostænced J
consilia	geðæht A, geðeaht B, geþeaht CDE^{x}*FGHJ, geþæht K, geþeahtas I
gentium	ðieda A, þeoda BCDGHJK, ðeoda FI, þiodæ E^{3}
reprobat	wiðceoseð AB, wiðcyosyð C, he wiðcyst DG*H,* he wyðcyst E^{x}*, he wið-cist M^{2}, he wiðcwyð F, he asceonaþ ł he awyrpð I, wiþsaceð J
autem	soðlice ABCE^{x}*FGI, soþlice J, witodlice K
cogitationes	geðohtas ABF, geþohtas CDE^{x}*GHK, geþoht J, smeaunga ł geþohta I
populorum	folca ABCDF*G*HIJK, þæræ þiodæ ł folca E$^{3/x}$*
et	⁊ ABCE^{3}FGHIJ
reprobat	wiðceoseð AB, wiðceosyð *C,* he wiðceoseð DH, he

		wiðceoseþ K, h[ ] wið-ceoseð M^2*, h[ ] [ ]ðceoseð *G*, wiðceoþað J, wiðcostode E^3, he wiðcẃyþ F, he hiscð ł ⁊ he onscunað I*
consilia		geðaeht A, geðeht B, geþeaht CDFGHJK, geþeahtas I, þære geþoht $E^{3/x}$*
principum		aldermonna A, ealdormonna B, ealdormanna CJ, aldra DE^x*, ealdra *G*HI, eldra K, ealdrum F

ED: [ ]ominus (G)] *Dominus Rosier.* drihten (E)] Drihten *Harsley.* réprobat (H)] reprobat *Campbell.* autem (B)] *om. Brenner.* soðlice (B)] *om. Brenner.* re[ ]robat (G)] reprobat *Rosier.* h[ ] wið-ceoseð (M)] h[e] wið-ceoseð *Brock.* geþeaht (H) (*2nd*)] geþeat *Campbell.*

OE: to[ ]cað (G)] to *questionable, bowl of* ð *partly cropped by tear in leaf.* geþeaht (E^x)] *on eras.* he wyðcyst (E^x)] *on eras.* soðlice (E^x)] *on eras.* geþohtas (E^x)] *on eras.* þæræ þiodæ ł folca ($E^{3/x}$)] þiodæ *retraced in darker ink,* ł folca *on eras. by corr.* h[ ] wið-ceoseð (M^2)] *letter after* h *lost due to crease in leaf.* he hiscð ł ⁊ he onscunað (I)] ⁊ he onscunað *written in left margin.* þære geþoht ($E^{3/x}$)] geþoht *on eras. by corr.* aldra (E^x)] *on eras.*

LTg: Dominus] H: D *faint but visible;* [ ]ominus G. dissipat] disipat K. reprobat (*1st*)] réprobat H. populorum] popul[ ] G. reprobat (*2nd*)] réprobat C; re[ ]robat G: *descender visible after* e. principum] princip[ ] G.

11

Consilium		geðaeht A, geðeaht B, geþeht C, geþeaht DFHIJK, geþeæht E^3*, geþeah[ ] *G*
uero*		soðlice BCFGI, soþlice DE^x*HJ, soðl[ ] A*, witodlice K
domini		dryhtnes B, drihtnes C*E^x*F, drihtenes K, dryht̄ A, drih̉ GJ
manet*	}	wunað ABCDFG*I,* wunaþ HJ, wunæþ E^3*, wynað K
in*	}	in A, on $BCDE^3$FGHIJK
aeternum*	}	ecnisse AD, ecnesse *BE^3G*HJK, ecnysse *C*FI (*L*)
cogitationes	|	geðohtas ABI*, geþohtas CDFGHJK, his E^3
cordis		heortan ABCDFGHIJ, heortæn E^3, heortas K
eius	|	his ABCDFHIJ*K,* geþoht E^3*
in		in A, on BCE^x*FIJK, [ ]n *G*
saeculum*		weoruld A, weorold *B,* woruld *C,* aworuld *D,* alra world *$E^{3/x}$*,* mægþe F, cynrenne G, cynrene K, cynren J, cnosle ł on cynne I (*LM*)
(et*)		⁊ FGIJ
saeculi*		weorulde A, weorolde *B,* worulde *C,* æworold *E^3,* cynryne F, cynren GJ, cnosle ł ⁊ cynne ł on mægþe I (*DML*)

ED: geþeaht (H)] geþeat *Campbell.* uero (BE)] vero *Brenner, Harsley.* soðl[ ] (A)] soðli *Kuhn.* drihtnes (C)] driht*nys Wildhagen* (drihty[nys] *with* nes *interl. above* nys *in corrigenda, p. xxii*). ęternum (E)] aeternum *Harsley.* sęculum (E)] saeculum *Harsley.* alra world (E)] alraworld *Harsley.* sęculi (E)] saeculi *Harsley.*

OE: geþeæht (E^{3})] t *retraced in darker ink.* soþlice (E^{x})] *on eras.* soðl[ ] (A)] *final letters obscured by ink stain.* drihtnes (C)] nes *added in red by corr., small eras. to right of ascender of* h. drihtnes (E^{x})] *on eras., eras.* (*18 mm*) *after word.* wunæþ (E^{3})] wu *retraced in darker ink.* geðohtas (I)] o *on eras.* geþoht (E^{3})] *gloss eras. after word* (*21 mm*). on (E^{x}) (*2nd*)] *on eras.* alra world (E$^{3/x}$)] alra *by corr.,* l *in* world *retouched in darker ink.*

LTg: Consilium] [ ]onsilium G. manet] I: manent *written in left margin by glossator and underdotted by single dot, perhaps to replace* (?) manet *in text.* aeternum] æternum B; ęternum CEL, G: *cauda questionable.* eius] eíus K. in (*2nd*)] *lost* G. saeculum saeculi] sæculum sæculi B; seculum seculi CD, L: generatione et generatione *added interl. by corr.: see GAg;* sęculum sęculi E; sclm scli M.

LTu: aeternum] æternum ϑ; eternum ξ; ęternum ς; eternvm τ*. saeculum saeculi] sęculum saeculi β; sęculum scli ν; seculum seculi ςτ*.

GAg: uero] autem FGHIJK. manet in aeternum] in ęternum manet FH, J: *cauda added by glossator,* G: *cauda questionable;* in aeternum manet I; in æternum manet K. saeculum saeculi] generatione et generationem GI; generatione et generatione JK, H: *eras. after final* e, F: *orig.* generatione et generationem: m *deleted by 3 subscript dots,* L: *see LTg.*

GAu: uero] autem δεζϑιλμξοπϱστυφχψ. manet in aeternum] in aeternum manet δζοπϱυχψ; in ęternum manet ειλμφ; in eternum manet ξστ. saeculum saeculi] generatione et generationem δεζιλμξοπϱυφψ; generatione et generatione ϑστχ.

12

Beata — eadigu A, eadegu B, eadige CJ, eadig DFGHI*, Eædig E^{3}, eadi K
gens — ðiod A, þeod BCFGH, ðeod D, þiod E^{3}*, seo þeod I, þeoda JK
cuius — ðere A, þære BC, þæs ðe DF, ðæs þe G, þæs þe HI, þes ðę E^{3}, þæs JK
est — is ABDE^{3}FGHIJ*K*, ys C
dominus | drihten FIK, dryht̄ AB, driħt C, driħ GJ, hioræ E^{3}
deus | god ABCFGIJK, drihten E^{3}
eorum* | heara A, hira B, hyra C, heora D, his FGIJ, is K, god E^{3} (*L*)
populus — folc *AB*CDE^{3}FGHI*K, folce J
quem — ðæt AB, þæt C, þe DFHI, þæt þe G, þœt þc I, þa K, þem E^{3}*
elegit | geceas ABFG*H*, gecies C, geces D, he geceas IJK, drihten *E^{x}**
dominus* | dryht̄ AB, driħt C, gesceæs *E^{3}*

in — in A, on BCDE^{x}*FGHIJK
hereditatem — erfeweardnisse A, erfweardnesse B, yrfeweardnysse *C*I, yrfeweardnis DE^{x}*, yrfwyrdnysse F, yrfeweardnesse GHJ, yrfwyrdnesse K
sibi — him ABCE^{x}*FGHJ, him DK, him sylfum I

OE: eadig (I)] est : is *written in left margin.* þiod (E^{3})] *orig.* þioð: *cross-stroke of* ð *eras.* folc (I)] s. est beatus : is eadig *written in left margin.* þem (E^{3})] *gloss eras. before word.* drihten (E^{x})] *on eras.* on (E^{x})] *on eras.* yrfeweardnis (E^{x})] *on eras.* him (E^{x})] *on eras.*

LTg: est] ést K. eorum] L: eius *added interl. by corr.: see GAg.* populus] populum AB: *cf. Weber MSS* SKγδεζηλ. elegit] E: t *retraced in darker ink;* ęlegit H. dominus (*2nd*)] E: *on eras. by corr.* in] E: *on eras. by corr.* hereditatem] E: *on eras. by corr.;* hęreditatem C. sibi] E: s *retraced in darker ink.*

LTu: populus] populum β. quem] *interl.* ϑ. hereditatem] hęreditatem ειϱφ.

GAg: eorum] eius FGHIJ, L: *see LTg;* eíus K. dominus (*2nd*)] *om.* FGHIJK.

GAu: eorum] eius δεζϑιλξοπϱστυφχψ. dominus (*2nd*)] *om.* δεζϑιξπϱστυφχψ.

13

De | of ABCDF*G*H*IJK, drihten E^{3}
caelo | hiefene A, hefnum *C,* heofone *BDFH,* heofenan *GK,* heofonum *I,* eofonum *J,* of E^{3} (*L*)
prospexit* | gelocade A, gelocode BCDGHJ, gelocað K, beheold F, beseah I, hefonum E^{3}
dominus | drihten IK, dryht̄ AB, driħt CF, driħ GJ, gelocode $E^{3/x}$*
et* — ⁊ ABCDE^{3}
uidit — gesaeh A, geseah BD$E^{3/x}$*FGHJK, he geseah CI
omnes — alle A, ealle BCDFGHIJK, eællæ E^{3}
filios | bearn ABCFIJK, suna DG, sunu H, monnæ E^{3}
hominum | monna AB, manna CDFGHIJK, beærn E^{3}

ED: drihten (E)] Drihten *Harsley.* celo (I)] caelo *Lindelöf.*

OE: of (F)] *written in left margin.* gelocode ($E^{3/x}$)] *eras. before word,* ge *and* ode *on eras. by corr.* geseah ($E^{3/x}$)] *back of* a *retraced,* h *on eras. by corr., eras. after word.*

LTg: De] H: D *faint but visible.* caelo] cælo B; celo CHJK, I: *orig.* caelo: a *eras.;* cęlo DEFGL.

LTu: caelo] cęlo βεϑιμξουφ; celo σςτ*τ.

GAg: prospexit] respexit FGHIJK. et] *om.* FGHIJK.

GAu: prospexit] respexit δεζϑιλμξοπϱστυφχψ. et] *om.* δεζϑιλμοπϱστυφχψ.

14

De		of *ABCD*FGHI, on J, be *E^3* (*M*)
praeparato		ðæm gegearwedan A, þæm gegearwodan *B*, þan gegearwudan *C*, þam gegearwedon *J*, gearwudre *DH*, gegærwod *K*, þere gearwunge *E^3*, gearcunge *F*, gegearcodre *I*, arwurdre *G* (*L*)
habitaculo	|	eardunghuse ABCJ, eardunge DFGH, earddunge K, wununge ł eardungstowe I, his E^3 (*M*)
suo	|	his ACDFGHIJK, eardunge E^3
respexit		gelocað AB, gelocaþ J, he gelocode C*DH, beheold F, ⁊ he locode E$^{3/x}$*, he locode G, he beseah ł he bewlatode I, beseah K
super		ofer ABE^{3}FGHJK, ofyr C, ofor I
omnes		alle A, ealle BCDFGHIJK, eælle E^3
qui		ða ðe AB, þa þe CI, þa ðe F, þe DE^{3}GH, þam þe J, þa K
habitant		eardiað ABCDFG, eærdiæþ E^3, eardigað H, eardiaþ J, earddiað K, eardiað ł wuniað I
orbem*		ymbhwyrft ABC, ymbhwyrt D, on ymbhwirft E^3*, eorðan FI, on eorðan G, on eorþan JK (*L*)

ED: p̄parato (E)] preparato *Harsley*. preparato (G)] preparatio *Rosier*. he locode (G)] he locade *Rosier*.

OE: he gelocode (C)] e *in* he *altered from* g. ⁊ he locode (E$^{3/x}$)] ode *on eras. by corr.* on ymbhwirft (E^3)] *orig.* on ymbhwirfte: e *eras.*

LTg: De] [ ]e G; de ABCDEM. praeparato] I: ae *malformed;* preparato BCDFGHJKL; p̄parato E. habitaculo] M: u *malformed.* orbem] L: terram *interl. by corr.: see GAg.*

LTu: De] de βνςτ*. praeparato] preparato ϑπς; p̄parato ιστ*τχ; pręparato λνξϱ.

GAg: orbem] terram FGHIJK, L: *see LTg.*

GAu: orbem] terram δεζϑιλμξοπϱστυφχψ.

15

Qui		se ABCDF*H*K, Se E^3, þe G, se þe I
finxit		gehiewade A*, gehiwode B*J*, gehiwude *C*, gehywode I*, hiwode DE^x*GHK, hywode F (*L*)
singillatim		wrixendlice AB, wrixiyndlice C, wrixendlice J, todæledlice D*FHK*, todælendlice *G*, Sienderlice E^3*, synderlice I*
corda	|	heortan ABDFGHI, heorte CJK, hioræ E^3*
eorum	|	heara A, hira B, hyra C, heora DFGHIJK, heortæn E^3
qui		se ABCDFG*HK*, se þe IJ, þæ E^3
intellegit		ongiteð AB, ongytyð C, ongiteþ J, angetæþ *E^3**, angyt D*H**K*, ongyt *FG*, ongytt *I**

in*		in A, on BCDE^x* (*L*)
omnia		all A, eall B, ealle CDE^xFGHIJK
opera	I	werc A, weorc BCDFGHJK, worc I, hioræ E^3
eorum	I	hiera A, hira B, heora CDFGHIJ, hera K, weorc E^3

ED: singillatim (H)] singilatim *Campbell.*

OE: gehiewade (A)] w *altered from another letter* (?). gehywode (I)] y *altered from* i (?). hiwode (E^x)] *on eras., otiose stroke after* e. Sienderlice (E^3)] *eras. before word* (*ca 4 letters*) *and eras. after word* (*ca 6 letters*). synderlice (I)] y *altered from* i (?). hioræ (E^3) (*1st*)] *gloss eras before word* (*ca 7 letters*), *of which final letter is* e, h *retouched in darker ink.* angetæþ (E^3)] *orig.* ongetæþ: o *altered to* a *by corr.* angyt (H)] *possibly* andgyt, *although letter* (?) *obscured by wear and modern repairs.* ongytt (I)] y *altered from* i (?).

LTg: Qui] H: *initial letter faint but visible.* finxit] C: x *on eras.;* fincxit JL. singillatim] F: n *interl. by corr.,* H: *orig.* singilatim: *1st* l *interl.;* singilatim K; singulatim G. qui] qu[ ] H: *final letter lost due to hole in leaf.* intellegit] F: *orig.* intelleget: *deleting mark below 3rd* e, i *interl. by corr.;* intelligit IK, G: *2nd* i *altered from another letter,* E: *2nd* i *on eras.,* H: *2nd* i *on eras.* (?). in] L: *crossed through by corr.: see GAg.*

LTu: singillatim] β: *orig.* singulatim: il *interl. above* u *by corr.*, ε: *2nd* l *interl.;* singulatim ϑ: *cf. Weber MS* η. intellegit] intelligit εϱστ*τφχ.

GAg: in] *om.* FGHIJK, L: *see LTg.*

GAu: in] *om.* δεζϑιλμξοπϱστυφχψ.

16

Non	I	ne ABCF, Ne E^3, na DGHK, nis na I
saluabitur*	I	bi gehęled A, bið gehæled BDFGHK, byð gehæled C, gehæld I, gehiwode J*, biþ se kining *E^3* (*L*)
rex	I	cyning ABCG, cyningc F, cyninc J, cining K, se kyningc I, geheled E^3*
per		ðorh A, þurh BCDE^3FGHIJK
multam	I	micel ABDGHJ, mycyl C, mycel F, micele I, mycle K, his E^3
uirtutem	I	megen A, mægen BDF*HJ*, mægyn C, mægen ł miht G, mægen ł mihte I, strengðe K, micle E^3* (*M*)
suam*	I	his ABCD, megen E^3 (*L*)
nec*		ne ACDE^3, nec B (*L*)
(et)*		⁊ FGHJ
gigans		gigent A, gigant B*C*D**GH*, ent *F*, ént *J*, se ormæta *I*, entas *K*, se eten *E^3* (*LM*)
(non)*		ne EFJ, na GHK, ⁊ ne I
saluus*	I	hal ABCD, biþ hal J, bið gehæled FG, byð gehæled H, beoþ

		gehæled K, bið na geholpen I, bið E³
erit*	I	bið ABCD, geheled E³
in		in A, on BCDE³FGHIJK
multitudine		mengu A, mengeo B, mænigeo CG, menigo D, mængo H, mænigo J, micelnysse F, mycelnesse ł menigo E³/X*, mænigfealdnysse ł micelnysse I, mycle K
fortitudinis*	I	streng A, strengo B, strenge C, strangnisse D, mægnes F, mægenes G, mægennes I, mægne JK, his E³ (*L*)
suae	I	his *ABDFGIJK,* hys *C,* streingþo *E³* (*HL*)

ED: mænigfealdnysse ł micelnysse (I)] mænigfealdnysse ł micelnysse *Lindelöf.* suę (E)] suae *Harsley.*

OE: gehiwode (J)] *source-text misread, perhaps reading gloss to* fincxit *in v. 15.* geheled (E³)] *ascender of* h *retouched in darker ink.* micle (E³)] *top of* l *retouched in darker ink.* gigant (D)] n *interl.* mycelnesse ł menigo (E³/X)] ł menigo *added by corr.*

LTg: saluabitur] E: bitur *on eras. by corr.,* L: bi *crossed through by corr.: see GAg.* uirtutem] H: *left leg of* m *partly obscured by hole in leaf;* uirtûtem M. suam] L: *crossed through by corr.: see GAg.* nec] L: *crossed through by corr.,* et *added interl.: see GAg.* gigans] gigas CEFGIJL, H: *letter eras. after* a, K: n *orig. added interl. after* a, *then eras.,* M: *orig.* gigans: n *deleted by super- and subscript dots: cf. Weber MS* ε, *Bib. sac. MSS* F²IQ²Φ^PG²Ψ^B2, *etc.* saluus erit] L: non saluabitur *added interl. by corr.: see GAg.* fortitudinis] L: uirtutis *added interl. by corr.: see GAg.* suae] suę ABEFH, I: *cauda partly obscured by stain;* sue CDJK; suæ L; tsuę G.

LTu: multam] β: *orig.* multum: a *interl. above 2nd* u *by corr.* gigans] gigas δεϑιλνξοπϱστ*τυχ; gygas φ. multitudine] χ: ti *interl.* suae] suæ ϑ; suę ινξφχ; sue ςτ*τ.

GAg: saluabitur] saluatur FHI, K: *orig.* saluator: or *eras.,* ur *abbreviation added by corr.,* L: *see LTg;* saluator G: *orig.* saluatur: *2nd* u *altered to* o. uirtutem suam nec] uirtutem et FGHIJK, L: *see LTg.* saluus erit] non saluabitur FGHIJK, L: *see LTg.* fortitudinis] uirtutis FGHIJK, L: *see LTg.*

GAu: saluabitur] saluatur δεζιλμξοπϱστυφχψ. uirtutem suam nec] uirtutem et δεζϑιλμξοπϱστυφχψ. saluus erit] non saluabitur δεζϑιλμξοπϱστυφχψ. fortitudinis] uirtutis δεζιλμξοπϱστυφχψ.

17

Falsus*	leas ABDFGIJ, leæs E³*, leas ł untemed C*, styppede K* (*L*)
equus	hors ABCDE³FGHIJK (*L*)
ad	to ABCDE³FGHI*JK
salutem	haelu A, hæle CIK, hælo BDFGHJ, hęlo E³
in	in A, on BCDE^X*FGIJK
abundantia	genyhtsumnisse A, genyhtsumnesse *B,* genihtsumnysse *C,*

	genyhtsumnisse *D,* geniehtsumnesse E^{3}, genihtsumnyssa F, genihtsumnesse *GK,* genihtsumnysse I, genihtsumnesse *J,* ungenihtsumnisse H (*LM*)
autem	soðlice ABCE^{3}G, soþlice FJ, witodlice K
uirtutis	megnes A, mægenes BHI, mægynys C, mægenis D, megenes E^{3}*, mægnes J, mæones K, mihta F, mihte G
suae	his *ABDE$^{3/x}$*FGHIJK,* hys *C* (*L*)
non	ne ABCE^{3}GIJ, na DFK
erit*	bið ABC, bioþ E^{3}, hit bið D (*L*)
saluus*	halu A, hal BCDE$^{3/x}$*, hælo F, bið gehæled GK, biþ gehæled J, byð gesund ł ne bið he na geholpen I (*L*)

ED: abundantia (C)] [h]abundantia *Wildhagen.* suæ (D)] suae *Roeder.* suę (E)] suae *Harsley.*

OE: leæs (E^{3})] *eras. before word,* æn (?) *eras. after word.* leas ł untemed (C)] ł untemed *written above* leas. styppede (K)] *see Sisam §80.vi.* to (I)] *partly obscured by stain.* on (E^{x})] *gloss eras. before word.* megenes (E^{3})] *gloss eras. before word.* his (E$^{3/x}$)] s *on eras. by corr.* hal (E$^{3/x}$)] *eras. after* a, l *on eras. by corr., followed by eras.*

LTg: Falsus] L: sus *crossed through,* lax *added interl. by corr.: see GAg.* equus] J: *eras. after 1st* u; aequus G; æquus L. abundantia] C: *orig.* habundantia: h *eras.;* habundantia BDFGJKLM. suae] suæ BDL; suę CEFGH, J: *cauda added by glossator;* sue K. erit saluus] L: non saluabitur *added interl. by corr.: see GAg.*

LTu: equus] aequus ν; ęquus ξ. abundantia] habundantia βζϑνξσςυχ. suae] suę βειvξυφ; suæ ϑ; sue σςτ*τ.

GAg: Falsus] Fallax FHIJK, L: *see LTg;* [ ]allax G. erit saluus] saluabitur FGHIJK, L: *see LTg.*

GAu: Falsus] Fallax δεζϑιλμξοπϱστυφχψ. erit saluus] non saluabitur δεζϑιλμξοπϱστυφχψ.

18

Ecce	sehðe AB, efnenu C, efne FIK, in gesyhþe DE^{x}*, in gesihðe H, on gesihðe G, gesihþe J
oculi	egan A, eagan BC*DE^{x}*FGHI, eagon J, egan K
domini	dryhtnes B, drihtnes E^{x}*FI, drihtenes K, drihten C*, dryht̄ A, driȟt G, driȟ J
super	ofer ABE^{x}*FGI*JK, ofyr C
timentes*	ða ondredendan A, þa ondrædyndan C, þa ondrædendan I, ondrædende BH, andredende DE^{x}*, ondrædendum F, me ondrædende GJ, drædende K
eum	hine ABCDE^{x}*FHI*JK, hi[ ] G (*L*)

(et)* ⁊ FGIJK
(in)* on FGIJ
(eis)* him FGJ, ðæm I, heom K
(qui)* se ðe F, þa þe G, þe IJ, þa K
sperantes* gehyhtende AB, gehihtynde C, hyhtende DE^{x}*, hihtað GK, hihtaþ J, gehihtiaþ I*, hopað F (*L*)
autem* soðlice ABC, soþlice E^{x}* (*LM*)
in* in A, on BCDE^{x}*I, ofer FGHJK (*L*)
misericordia | mildheortnisse ADE^{x}*, mildheortnysse C, mildheortnyssa F, mildheortnesse BGJK, his I
eius | his ABCDE^{x}*FGJK, mildheortnysse I

ED: in gesihðe (H)] ingesihðe *Campbell.*

OE: in gesyhþe (E^{x})] *on eras.* eagan (C)] *1st* a *interl.* eagan (E^{x})] *on eras.* drihtnes (E^{x})] *on eras.* drihten (C)] en *added in red by corr.* ofer (E^{x})] *on eras.* ofer (I)] *orig.* ofor: *2nd* o *altered to* e. andredende (E^{x})] *on eras.* hine (E^{x})] *on eras.* hine (I)] s<u>unt</u> : synt *written in left margin.* hyhtende (E^{x})] *on eras.* gehihtiaþ (I)] *eras. after 2nd* h. soþlice (E^{x})] *on eras.* on (E^{x})] *on eras.* mildheortnisse (E^{x})] *on eras.* his (E^{x})] *on eras.*

LTg: eum] L: et in eis qui *added interl. by corr.: see GAg.* sperantes] L: es *underlined to signal deletion: see GAg.* autem] L: super *added interl. after word by corr.: see GAg,* M: *eras. (5 letters?) after word.* in] L: *underlined to signal deletion: see GAg.*

LTu: autem] β: *orig.* autem in domino et: domine et *crossed through.* misericordia] missericordia ϑ. eius] β: i *interl.*

GAg: timentes] metuentes GHIJK, F: *on eras. by corr.* eum] eum et in eis qui FGHIJK, L: *see LTg: cf. Bib. sac. MSS* F^{2}Q^{2}G*, *Weber MSS* moz. sperantes] sperant FGHIJK, L: *see LTg.* autem] *om.* FGHIJK, L: *see LTg.* in] super FGHIJK, L: *see LTg.*

GAu: timentes] metuentes δεζιλμξοπρστυφχψ. eum] et in eis qui δεζϑιλξοπρστυφχψ: *cf. Bib. sac. MSS* F^{2}Q^{2}G*, *Weber MSS* moz; eum qui μ. sperantes] sperant δεζϑιλμξοπρστυφχψ. autem] *om.* δεζϑιλμξοπρστυφχψ. in] super δεζϑιλμξοπρστυφχψ.

19
Ut ðet *A,* þæt *BC,* þ<u>æt</u> *DE^{x}*FG*IJK (*HLM*)
eripiat* he generge *C,* he generige BGJ*, he ge[ ] A*, generige F, he nerige DE^{x}*K, he generige ł alyse I (*L*)
a from A, fra<u>m</u> BDE^{x}*FGHJK, fram I, of C
morte deaðe ABCE^{x}*FGHI, deaþe DJK
animas sawle AFJK, sawla BCI, saula D, saule E^{x}*, sawla ł e G*, sawlas H

eorum heara A, hira B, heora CDFGHIJK, hioræ E^{3}
et ⁊ ABCDE^{x}*FGHIJK
alat foedeð AB, fedyð C, fedeþ J, fede D*E^{x}*FGH, fedde K, he afet I
eos hie AB, hi CK, hy DE^{x}*GH, hig FIJ
in in A, on BCDE^{x}*FGHIJ, of K
fame hungre ABCDE^{3}*GHIJK, ungre F

ED: hie (A)] his *Kuhn.*

OE: þæt (E^{x})] *on eras.* he generige (J)] *2nd* g *altered from* r, *shoulder of which forms back of following* e. he ge[ ] (A)] *eras. (2–3 letters) after 2nd* e. he nerige (E^{x})] *on eras.* fram (E^{x})] *on eras.* deaðe (E^{x})] *on eras.* saule (E^{x})] *on eras.* sawla ł e (G)] ł e *added in diff. (?) hand.* ⁊ (E^{x})] *on eras.* fede (D)] fet *written in left margin in 11th-c. hand as gloss on* alat *in marginal commentary.* fede (E^{x})] *on eras.* hy (E^{x})] *on eras.* on (E^{x})] *on eras.* hungre (E^{3})] *retraced in darker ink.*

LTg: Ut] Vt FGH, L: *orig.* ut: V *added interl. by corr.;* ut ABCDEM. eripiat] C: *orig.* ęripiat: *cauda eras.*, L: eruat *added interl. by corr.: see GAg.*

LTu: Ut] Vt ιξσυφ; ut βνςτ*.

GAg: eripiat] eruat FGHIJ, K: e *by corr.*, L: *see LTg.*

GAu: eripiat] eruat δεζϑιλμξοπϱτυφχψ.

20

Anima | sawul A, sawl BCD*G*I, sawla F, saul H, sawle JK, soþlice E^{3}
autem* | soðlice ABC, ure E^{3}
nostra | ur A, ure BCDFGHIJK, sæule E^{3}
sustinet abideð ABG, abidyð C, abydeþ J, anbidaþ I, forbyrdigað DF*H*, forbyrdigað ł geðolað E^{x}*, bewarað K (*M*)
dominum dryhten D, drihten E^{x}*HK, dryht̄ AB, driħt CFG, driħ J
quoniam forðon ABE^{x}*J, forþon C, forðan K, forðam ðe F, forþam þe *G*, forþi þe I
adiutor fultum ABC, fultum JK, he fultumiend I, gefylsta DE^{x}*FGH
et ⁊ ABCDE^{x}*FGHIJK
protector gescildend ABE$^{3/x}$*J, gescyldynd C, gescyldend D, gescyldend FGHI*, frofer K
noster ur A, ure BCDE^{x}*FGHIJK
est is ABFIJ*K*, ys C, he is DE^{x}*GH

ED: soþlice (E)] Soþlice *Harsley.* forðon (A)] for ðon *Kuhn.*

OE: forbyrdigað ł geðolað (E^{x})] *on eras.* drihten (E^{x})] *on eras.* forðon (E^{x})] *on* *eras.* gefylsta (E^x)] *on eras.* ⁊ (E^x)] *on eras.* gescildend (E^{3/x})] ge *on eras. by corr.,* cildend *retraced in darker ink.* gescyldend (I)] y *altered from* i (?). ure (E^x) (*2nd*)] *on eras.* he is (E^x)] *on eras.*

LTg: Anima] [ ]nima G. sustinet] H: *final* t *on eras.;* sústinet M: et *on eras.* quoniam] quia G. est] ést K.

LTu: sustinet] σ: *final* t *interl.*

GAg: autem] *om.* FGHIJK.

GAu: autem] *om.* δεζϑιλμξοπϱστυφχψ.

21

Et*	⁊ A*BCDE^x**, forðon F, forþon J, forþā K, forþā þe G, forðan þe I (*LM*)
in	in A, on BCDE^x*FGIJK
ipso*	him ABCDE^x*FG, hi<u>m</u> IJK (*L*)
laetabitur	bið geblissad A, bið geblissud *C,* blissað *BGHIK,* blissiað *DF,* blissiaþ *J,* blissiad *E^x** (*L*)
cor	heorte ABCDE^x*FGHIJK (*M*)
nostrum	ur *A,* ure BCDE^x*FGHIJ
et	⁊ ABCE^x*FGHIJK
in	in A, on BCDE^x*FGHIJK
nomine	noman ABE^x*, naman CDF*GHIJK
sancto	ðæm halgan A, ða<u>m</u> halgan B, halgan CI*, haligu<u>m</u> D, halgu<u>m</u> E^x*, halgum FGH, halgu J, halian K
eius	his ABCDE^x*FGHIJ*K*
sperauimus	we gehyhtað *A*B, we gehihtað *CI,* we gehihtaþ *J,* we hyhtað *DE^x*F,* we hihtað GK, we hyhtaþ *H* (*M*)

ED: forþā þe (G)] forþam þe *Rosier.* lętabitur (E)] laetabitur *Harsley.*

OE: ⁊ (E^x) (*1st*)] *on eras.* on (E^x) (*1st*)] *on eras.* him (E^x)] *on eras.* blissiad (E^x)] *on eras.* heorte (E^x)] *on eras.* ure (E^x)] *on eras.* ⁊ (E^x) (*2nd*)] *on eras.* on (E^x) (*2nd*)] *on eras.* noman (E^x)] *on eras.* naman (F)] *orig.* namam: *right leg of final* m *eras. to form* n. halgan (I)] an *on eras., 2nd* a *obscured.* halgu<u>m</u> (E^x)] *on eras.* his (E^x)] *on eras.* we hyhtað (E^x)] *on eras.*

LTg: Et] L: *underlined to signal deletion,* Quia *added interl. by corr.: see GAg;* et BCDEM. ipso] L: eo *added interl. by corr.: see GAg.* laetabitur] lætabitur B; lętabitur CEFG; letabitur DHJKL. cor] cór M. nostrum] A: ostrum *added by corr.,* trum *interl.* eius] eíus K. sperauimus] sperabimus EFIJ, ADM: b *on eras.,* CH: *orig.* sperauimus: *1st* u *altered to* b.

LTu: Et] et βνςτ*. laetabitur] lętabitur βειλμσφ; letabitur δξςτ*τυ; lætabitur ϑ.

nomine] inomine ϑ. sancto] ς: c *interl.* sperauimus] ε: *orig.* sperabimus: b *altered to* u; sperabimus λξστ*.

GAg: Et] Quia FHIJK, L: *see LTg;* [ ]uia G: *initial* Q *lost.* ipso] eo FGHIJK, L: *see LTg.*

GAu: Et] Quia δεζϑιλμξοπρστυφχψ. ipso] eo δεζϑιλμξοπρστφχψ.

22

Fiat	I	sie AB, sy CD*G*HJ, si K, geweorðe F, gewurðe I, drihtæn E^{3}
domine*	}I	dryhten A, drihten F, dryht̄ B, driħt C, driħ GJ, Sie E^{3} (*IL*)
misericordia*	}I	mildheortnis ADH, mildheortnes BK, mildheortnys CI, mildheortnyssa F, mildheortnesse GJ, þin E^{3}
tua*	}I	ðin AB, þin CDFGHIJK, mildheortnes E^{3} (*L*)
super		ofer ABDE^{3}FGHIJK, ofyr C
nos		us ABCD*E^{3}*FHIJK (*G*)
sicut*		swe swe A, swa swa B*C*DI, swæ swæ *E$^{3/x}$**, ealswa K, on ðam gemetum F, on þa<u>m</u> gemete J (*L*)
sperauimus		we gehyhtað *A*B, we gehihtað C*, we gehihtaþ J*, we hyhton D*E^{x}*, we hihton G, we hihtað K, gehyhton H, we gehihtaþ ł we hopiaþ I, þe we hopudon F (*M*)
in		in *A*, on BCDE^{x}FGH*I*JK
te		ðe *A*BDF, þe CE^{3}**G*HIJK (*M*)

ED: drihtæn (E)] Drihtæn *Harsley.* nos (G) *lost*] n*os Rosier.* swa swa (I)] swaswa *Lindelöf.* quemadmodum (I)] quemammodum *Lindelöf.* t[ ] (G)] te *Rosier.*

OE: swæ swæ (E$^{3/x}$)] *gloss eras. after 1st* swæ, *with* e *visible in final position, 2nd* swæ *by corr.* we gehihtað (C)] we ge *added in red by corr.* we gehihtaþ (J)] i *altered from* l. þe (E^{3})] þ *retouched in darker ink.*

LTg: Fiat] [ ]iat G. domine] I: o *written above word,* L: *underlined to signal deletion: see GAg.* tua] L: domine *added interl. by corr. after word: see GAg.* nos] E: s *on eras. by corr.,* G: *only initial minim visible.* sicut] E: *on eras. by corr.;* quemadmodum CL: *cf. Weber MS* η, *see GAg.* sperauimus] E: *initial* s *retraced in darker ink;* sperabimus AM: b *on eras.* in] A: *written by corr.,* I: n *on eras.* te] A: *written by corr.;* tê M; t[ ] G: *letter fragment visible after* t.

LTu: misericordia] missericordia ϑ. sperauimus] sperabimus ϱ.

GAg: domine misericordia tua] misericordia tua domine FGHIJK, L: *see LTg.* sicut] quemadmodum FHJK, CL: *see LTg,* I: *orig.* quemammodum: *2nd* m *deleted by 3 subscript dots, crude* d *written interl.;* [ ]modum G.

GAu: domine misericordia tua] misericordia tua domine δεζιλμξοπρστυφχψ. sicut] quemadmodum δεζϑιλμοπρστυφχψ.

PSALM 33

2

Benedicam		ic bledsiu *A,* ic bletsige *BCDHIJK,* Ic bletsige *E^x,* ic bletsie F, b[ ] *G* (*M*)
dominum		drihten E^3HK, dryht̄ AB, driħt *C*FG, driħ J
in		in A, on BCDE^3FGHIJK
omni		alle A, ealle BCJ, eallre F, ælcre DHI, ælcere G, eallan K, egwilc E^3
tempore		tid AB*C*E^3, tide DFGHIJ, tidan K
semper		aa *A,* simle BE^3, symle CDHIJ, symble F, æfre GK
laus	|	lof ABCDFGHIJK, his E^3*
eius	|	his ABCDFGHIJ*K,* lof E^3*
in		in A, on BCDE^3FGHIJK
ore	|	muðe *A*BCDFGHI, muþe JK, minum E^3
meo	|	minum ACFGI*, minum BDHJ, minan K, muðie E^3

ED: B[ ]edicam (G)] Benedicam *Rosier.* [ ]enedicam (H)] BENEDICAM *Campbell.*

OE: his (E^3)] s *retraced in darker ink.* lof (E^3)] *retraced in darker ink.* minum (I)] s. sit : syn *written in left margin.*

LTg: Benedicam] BEnedicam ABK; BENEDICAM CE; BENedîcam M; B[ ]edicam G; [ ]enedicam H: *initial* B *lost: outline visible.* dominum] DN̄M C. tempore] teporė C. semper] A: *orig.* semper: er *added by corr.* eius] eíus K. ore] A: e *by corr.* (*on eras.?*).

LTu: Benedicam] BENedicam β; BENEDICAM ιλμνϱτφχ; BENEdicam ς. dominum] DN̄M λμϱχ. in] IN λϱ. omni] OMNI λϱ. tempore] TEMpore λϱ.

3

In		in A, on B*C*DFGHIJK, On E^3
domino		dryhtne ABD, drihtny C, drihtne E^3FHI, drihten K, driħ GJ
laudabitur		bið hered ABD, bið heryd C, biþ hered E^3*, byð hered H, bið herod K, bið gcherod F, bið gehered G, ł bið gehered I*, biþ gehered J
anima	|	sawul A, sawl BCDI, sawla F, sawle GJ, saul H, sawel K, min E^3
mea	|	min ABCDFHIJK, mine G, sawle E^3
audiant		geheren A, gehieren B, gehyryn C, gehyren DH, gehyran FK, geheran I, gehiran J, gehyrað G, hie geheren $E^{3/x}$* (*L*)
mansucti		ða monðueran A, ða monþwæran B, þa manþwæran CJ, þa manðwæran I, þa geþwæran K, þæ geþwernesse ł bilewitan

	$E^{3/x}$*, þa bilewitan D, þa bilewittan M^2, ða bylewitan F*, þa bilwitan *G*, þa bylwitan H
et	⁊ ABCDE^{x}*FGHIJK
laetentur	blissien A*DH*, blissigen *B*, blissiyn *C*, blissiæn *$E^{3/x}$**, blissian *FJK*, blissien *G*, fægniun ł ⁊ blissian hig I (*L*)

ED: mine (G)] *no gloss Rosier.* ða bylewitan (F)] ða bylehwitan *Kimmens.* lętentur (E)] laetentur *Harsley.*

OE: biþ hered (E^3)] *letter eras. after* h, *eras. after word with traces of* e *in final position.* ł bið gehered (I)] *word eras. before* ł. hie geheren ($E^{3/x}$)] *letter eras. after 2nd* h, eren *on eras., final letter orig.* þ. þæ geþwernesse ł bilewitan ($E^{3/x}$)] ł bilewitan *on eras. by corr.* ða bylewitan (F)] *orig.* ða bylehwitan: h *eras.* ⁊ (E^x)] *added in left margin.* blissiæn ($E^{3/x}$)] n *on eras. by corr.*

LTg: In] C: *eras. after* I. audiant] L: *orig.* audiunt: *2nd* u *altered to* a. mansueti] mansuęti G. laetentur] lætentur B; lętentur CEFGH; letentur DJKL.

LTu: In] IN χ. laetentur] lętentur βειvσφ; lætentur ϑ; letentur λξςτ*τυ.

4

Magnificate	micliað ABC, gemicliað DH, geMicliæþ $E^{3/x}$*, gemicliað M^2, gemiccliað G, gemiccliaþ J, gemycliað K, gemicliað ł mærsiaþ I*, mærsiað F
dominum	dryhten A, drihtæn E^3, drihtne F, drihten K, dryht̄ B, driht́ C, drih́ GJ
mecum	mid me ABCDE^{3}FGHIJK
et	⁊ ABCDE^{3}FGHIJK
exaltemus	uphebbað we AB, uppahebbyn we *C*, upahebban we *J*, we upahebben D*H*, we upæhebbæn E^3, upahebbað F*K*, upahebban G, uton ahebban I (*M*)
nomen	| noman AB, naman CDFGHIJ*K*, his E^3
eius	| his ABCDFGHIJ*K*, nomæn E^3
in	on IK
inuicem*	betwinum A, betweonum B, betweonum GJ, us betweonan C*, us betwéonan F, eow betweonan D, eow betwionum $E^{3/x}$*, þæt sylfe IK

ED: ⁊ (G)] *no gloss Rosier.* upahebban (G)] *no gloss Rosier.* betweonum (B)] betweonum *Brenner.*

OE: geMicliæþ ($E^{3/x}$)] ge *added by corr.,* M *retouched on left.* gemicliað ł mærsiaþ (I)] l *obscured by stain.* us betweonan (C)] o *interl.* eow betwionum ($E^{3/x}$)] *gloss eras. before* eow, *initial* e *perhaps by main hand,* be *by corr.,* t *altered from* o *by main hand.*

LTg: exaltemus] CJ: *orig.* exultemus: *1st* u *altered to* a, H: *orig.* exeltemus: *2nd* e *altered to* a, K: *orig.* exultemus: u *deleted by subscript dot,* a *interl. by main hand;* exaltêmus M. eius] eíus K.

LTu: inuicem] inficem β.

GAg: inuicem] idipsum FGHIJK.

GAu: inuicem] idipsum δεζϑιλμξοπϱτυφχψ, σ: id *interl.*

5

Inquisiui*		ic sohte ABCDF*GHIK, Ic sohte $E^{3/x}$*, ic sohte ł rece J (*L*)
dominum		drihten E^{3}K, dryht̄ AB, driħt CFG, driħ J
et		⁊ ABCE^{3}FGHIJK
exaudiuit	I	he geherde A, he gehirde BJ, he gehyrde CDFGHIK, he me E^{3} (*M*)
me	I	me ABCFGHJK, gehirde E^{3}
et		⁊ ABCDE^{3}FGHIJK
ex		of ABCDE^{3}FGHIJK
omnibus		allum A, eallum BCGHIJ, eallum D, eællum E^{3}, ealre F, eallan K
tribulationibus	I	geswencednissum A, geswencednessum B, geswencydnyssum C, geswæncednessum J, geswincum D, geswincum H, geswincum ł gedrefednessum G, gedrefednyssum FI, geswican K, minum E^{3}
meis	I	minum AGI, minum BCDHJK, minun F, eærfoþnessum E^{3}
eripuit	I	generede A, he generede BJ, he generyde C, he nerede DGHK, he nerode F, he alysde I, he me E^{3}
me	I	me ABCFGIJK, generede $E^{3/x}$*

OE: ic sohte (F)] hte *on eras., eras.* e *visible after* e. Ic sohte ($E^{3/x}$)] *MS* In/quisiui : Ic/sohte: Ic *eras. before* sohte (*on same line*), *2nd* Ic *added in line above by corr.* generede ($E^{3/x}$)] *orig.* genereð: ð *altered to* d, *final* e *added by corr.*

LTg: Inquisiui] L: Ex *written by corr. after* I: *see GAg.* exaudiuit] exaudîuit M.

LTu: Inquisiui] INquisiui β.

GAg: Inquisiui] Exquisiui FGHIK, J: *orig.* Exquisiuit: t *eras.*, L: *see LTg.*

GAu: Inquisiui] Exquisiui δεζιλμξοπϱστυφχψ; Exquessiui ϑ.

6

Accedite	togenehlaecað A, genealæceað B, genealæcað CF*G*H, genealæcað D, genealæcaþ I, genealæceþ J, Genealæcet E^{x}*, neahlæcað K
ad	to ABCDE^{x}*FGHIJK

eum — him ABCE^{x}*FGHIK, him DJ
et — ⁊ ABCDE^{3}FGGIJK
inluminamini — bioð inlihte A, beoð onlihte B, beoþ onlihte *J,* beoð onlyhtyde *C,* hie bioþ onlihte E^{3}, ge beoð alyhte *D,* ge beoð onlihte F*I,* ge beoð onlyhte *H,* ge beoð alyhte K, onlyhte ge beoð G
et — ⁊ ABCDE^{3}FGJK
uultus* — ondwleotan A, ondwlitan B, andwlitan CDE^{x}*J, ansyne FK, ansena I, doð G (*L*)
uestri* — eowre ACDE^{x}*FGHJK, eowere I (*L*)
non — ne *A*BCDE^{x}*FGHJ, ⁊ ne I, na K
erubescent* — scomien A, scomigen B, gesceamiyn C, asceamiað D, onsceæmiæþ E^{3}, beoð gescende FGH, beoð gescænde I, beoþ gescynde J*, forwyrð K (*L*)

ED: him (J)] him *Oess.* illuminamini (C)] i[n]luminamini *Wildhagen.* onlyhte ge beoð (G)] onlyhte gebeoð *Rosier.* facies (G)] facie*s Rosier.*

OE: Genealæcet (E^{x})] *on eras.* to (E^{x})] *on eras.* him (E^{x})] *on eras.* andwlitan (E^{x})] *on eras.* eowre (E^{x})] *on eras.* ne (E^{x})] *on eras.* beoþ gescynde (J)] o *altered from* ð *or* d.

LTg: Accedite] G: *initial* A *partly lost.* inluminamini] illuminamini DIJ, CH: *orig.* inluminamini: *initial* i *eras., shoulder of 1st* n *eras. and right leg used to form 1st* l. uultus] L: facies *added above by corr.: see GAg.* uestri] uestre L: *orig.* uestri: i *altered to* e *by corr.* non] A: on *interl. by corr.* erubescent] L: *underlined to signal deletion,* confundentur *written to right by corr.: see GAg.*

LTu: Accedite] Aaccedite μ. inluminamini] illuminamini εζιλξοπρστ*τυφχ.

GAg: uultus] facies FGHIJK, L: *see LTg.* uestri] uestrę FH; uestrae IJ; uestre GK, L: *see LTg.* erubescent] confundentur FGHIJK, L: *see LTg.*

GAg: uultus] facies δεζϑιλμξοπρστυφχψ. uestri] uestrae δμοπρυχ; uestrę εζιλξφψ; uestræ ϑ; uestre στ. erubescent] confundentur δεζϑιλμξοπρστυφχψ.

7
Iste — ðes AE^{3}FI, þes BCDGHJK
pauper — ðearfa AB, þearfa CDFGHIJ, þeærfæ E^{3}, þærfa K (*M*)
clamauit — cleopede A, cleopode BDGH, clypode CFJ, clipæde E$^{3/x}$*, clepode I, clypede K
et — ⁊ ABCE^{3}FGIJK
dominus — dryhten B, drihten E^{3}, dryht̄ A, driħt CFGI, driħ J (*H*)
exaudiuit | geherde A, gehirde BJ, gehyrde CDFGHIK, hiene E^{3} (*M*)
eum | hine ABCDFGHJK, gehyrde E$^{3/x}$*
et — ⁊ ABCE^{3}FGHIJK

ex* of ABCDE^{3}*FGI*JK, iof H*
omnibus allum A, eallum BCFGHI, eallum DJ, eællum E^{3}, eallan K
tribulationibus | geswencednissum A, geswencednessum B, geswencednyssum C, geswæncednessum J, geswincum DH, geswincan K, geswincum ł gedr[ ]nessum G, gedrefednyssum F, geswincfulnyssum I, his E^{3}
eius | his ABCDFGHIJK, eærfoþnessum ł geswincum E$^{3/x}$*
liberauit* gefriode A, he gefreode C, aliesde B, alysde E^{x}K, he alysde D, he gehæleþ F, hælde G, he gehælde IJ
eum hine ABCFGHIJ, hiene he alysde ł gefriolsæþ E$^{3/x}$*

ED: iof (H)] lof *Campbell.*

OE: clipæde (E$^{3/x}$)] *orig.* clipæð: ð *altered to* d, e *added by corr.* gehyrde (E$^{3/x}$)] *orig.* gehireþ: i *altered to* y *by corr.,* d *written over orig.* r *and* r *added in line above,* þ *eras.* iof (H)] *serif of initial letter not a common feature of this scribe; letter rises slightly above line of* of *but is certainly not* l. eærfoþnessum ł geswincum (E$^{3/x}$)] ł geswincum *added by corr.,* ge *on eras.* hiene he alysde ł gefriolsæþ (E$^{3/x}$)] he alysde ł *added by corr.*

LTg: pauper] pâuper M. dominus] H: *eras. after word.* exaudiuit] exaudîuit M. ex] F: *orig.* de: d *deleted by subscript dot,* x *interl. in light brown ink,* I: *eras. before* e, x *interl.: see GAg.*

GAg: ex] de GJ; *for* FI *see LTg.* liberauit] saluauit FGHIJ, K: ui *on eras. by corr.,*

GAu: ex] σ: *orig.* de; de δεζϑιμορυφψ, χ: *by corr.* liberauit] saluauit δζιλμξοπρστυφχψ; saluabit εϑ.

8

Inmittet | insende A, onsende B*C,* onsænde *J,* asende *DK,* asend F, onasendeð G, asendeð *M*^{2}, asendep *H**, gesent *I**, drihten *E*^{3}
angelum* | engel ABDGHI*J*K, engyl C, ængel F, onsendeð *E*^{3}
dominus* drihtyn C, drihtnes FGI, drihtenes K, dryht̄ AB, drih̄ J, his englon *E*^{3}
in in A, on BCDFGHIJK
circuitu ymbhwyrfte ABCDFGIJ, ymbhwyrftte *H,* embehwyrfte K*, ymbhwyrfte ł gænge E$^{3/x}$*
timentium | ondredendra A, ondrædendra BDGHI, ondrædyndra C, ondrædendum F, ondrædende J, adrædendra K, hine E^{3}
eum | hine ABCFGHIJK, ondredende E^{3}
et ⁊ ACDE^{3}FGHIJK
eripiet | genereð A, he genereð CD, he genereþ H, he generaþ FJ, he generað I, generigeð G, he alyseþ K, he hie E^{3}
eos | hie A, hi CK, hig FIJ, hy GH, genereþ E^{3}

ED: Immittet (C)] I[n]mitted *Wildhagen*. asendep (H)] asendeþ *Campbell*.

OE: asendep (H)] *no ascender visible to form* þ. gesent (I)] *eras.* (?) *before word.* embehwyrfte (K)] *letter eras. after* f (*Sisam records* 'e *with* t *above eras.*'). ymbhwyrfte ł gænge ($E^{3/x}$)] ymbhwyrfte ł *added by corr.*, n *retouched in darker ink.*

LTg: Inmittet] D: ł i *interl.* (= Inmittit): *see v. 15 below for similar instance: cf. Weber MSS* KT* moz, HKM: *orig.* Inmittit: *last* i *altered to* e; Inmittit J, E: *orig.* Inmittet: i *interl. above* e *by corr.*; Immittet C: *orig.* Inmittet: *minim added by corr. to left of* n *to form* m; Immittit I; Inmittit J. angelum] E: m *on eras. by corr.*, J: *eras. after* ū (*of* s?): *see GAg*. dominus] E: *minim eras. after* n (dominus): *see GAg*. circuitu] circumitu H.

LTu: Inmittet] INmittit β; Inmittir ς; Inmittit φχ. circuitu] circumitu ε.

GAg: angelum] angelus FGHIK; *for* J *see LTg*. dominus] domini FGHIK; *for* E *see LTg*.

GAu: angelum] angelus δεζθιλξοπρστυφχψ. dominus] domini δεζθιλξοπρστυφχψ.

9

Gustate		bergað A, birgeað B, birgaþ J, byrgað ł etað C, onbyrgað DFH*M*[2], Onbirgæþ $E^{3/x}$*, onbyriaþ I*, abyriaþ K, ongebyrigeað *G*
et		⁊ ABCE^{3}FGHIJK
uidete		gesiað A, geseoð BCDFGHIK, gesioþ E^{3}, geseoþ J
quoniam		ðætte A, þætte B, þæt I, forþon C, forðon J, forðam ðe F, forþon þe G, hu E^{3}
suauis		wynsum ABCDGHIK, winsum E^{3}F, winsum J
est	ǀ	is ABFGIJ*K*, ys C, drihten E^{3}
dominus	ǀ	dryhten B, drihten GIK, dryht̄ A, driht̄ C, driȟt F, driȟ J, is E^{3}
beatus		eadig ABCDFGHI*J, eadi K, eædig biþ E^{3}
uir		wer ABCDFGHIJ*K, Se wer E^{3}
qui		se A, se ðe BFI, se þe CJ, þe DE^{3}H, þa þe G, þa K
sperat		gehyhteð AB, gehihtað G, gehihtaþ J, hihtaþ I, hihtæþ K, gehiht C, gehyht DE^{x}*H, hopað F
in		in A, on BCDE^{x}*FGIJK
eum*		hine ABCD*E*^{x}*F, him GI, him JK (*M*)

OE: Onbirgæþ (E)] On *added by corr.* onbyriaþ (I)] y *altered from* i (?). eadig (I)] s. est : is *written in left margin.* wer (J)] *orig.* wegr: g *eras.* gehyht (E)] *on eras.* on (E)] *on eras.* hine (E)] *on eras.*

LTg: Gustate] Gustâte M; [ ]ustate G. est] ést K. eum] E: ū *on eras.*, M: um *blotted.*

GAg: eum] eo FGHIJK.

GAu: eum] eo δεζθιλμοπρστυφχψ.

10

Timete	ondredað A, ondrædað CF*G*H, ondrædaþ DIJK, Ondredæþ E[3], ondrædað ge B (*M*)
dominum	drihten E[3]FGK, dryht̄ AB, driħt C, driħ J
omnes	alle A, ealle BCDFGIJ, eælle E[3], eale K
sancti	ǀ halge A, halige BCDGHJ, hali K, halgan FI, his E[3]
eius	ǀ his ABCFGHIJ*K*, hælige E[3]
quoniam	forðon ABDJ, forþon *C*, forðæn E[3], forðam ðe F, forþam þe G, forðan þe I
nihil*	nowhit AC, naht B, næniguht D, nenigwyht *E[x]**, nis FI, nan is G, ne is J, na is K (*L*)
deest*	wonu A, wona BC, wana DE[x]*, wanhafnes F, wanhafolnes I, wanbæfennes J, onhæfenlyste G, on wædla K* (*L*)
timentibus	bið ðæm ondredendum A, bið ondrædendum B, bið ondrædyndun C, is ðam ondrædendum̲ D, is ðam ondredendum E[x]*, þam̲ andrædendum G*, þam̲ adrædendum̲ H, ondrædendum FI, ondrædendum̲ J, adrædenden K
eum	hine ABCDE[x]*FGIJK

ED: forðon (A)] for ðon *Kuhn*. eum (G)] eu*m Rosier.*

OE: nenigwyht (E[x])] *by corr., with* wyht *on eras.* wana (E[x])] *on eras.* on wædla (K)] d *altered from* l (?). is ðam ondredendum (E[x])] *on eras.* þam̲ andrædendum (G)] *1st* n *interl.* hine (E[x])] *on eras.*

LTg: Timete] G: *initial letter faded and vellum partly translucent;* Timête M. eius] eíus K. quoniam] C: o *malformed.* nihil] L: ihil *underlined to signal deletion, macron added above* n: *see GAg;* nichil E. deest] L: de (*but not* e̲s̲t̲) *underlined to signal deletion,* inopia *written above following* timentibus: *see GAg.*

LTu: Timete] TImete β. eius] β: i *interl.* nihil] nichil ςτ*. timentibus] ς: *2nd* i *interl.*

GAg: nihil] non est FGHIJ, L: *see LTg;* non ést K. deest] inopia FGHIJK, L: *see LTg.*

GAu: nihil] non est δεζϑιλμξοπϱστυφχψ. deest] inopia δεζϑιλμξοπϱστυχψ.

11

Diuites	weolie A, welige BCDFGJ, wælige E[3/x]*, þa weligan I, welegan K (*M*)
eguerunt	weðladon A, wædlodon BCI, wædledon J, beþorfton DE[x]*F*H*K, beþorfton ł wædlodon *G**
et	⁊ ABCDE[3]FGHIJK
esurierunt	hyngradun A*, hingrydon C, hyngredon BD, hingredon J, hingrodan K, hy hyngredon *E[x]**, híg hyngredon F, hy hingredon G*H*, him hingrode I* (*M*)

inquirentes | socende A, soecende B, secynde C, secende J, ða secendan D, þa secendan FI, þa secenda GH, þa secende K, þa Soþlice $E^{3/x}$*
autem | soðlice ABCFG, soþlice HJ, witodlice K, secende E^3
dominum dryhten D, drihten E^3*FIK, dryht̄ AB, driht̄ C, drih̄t GH, drih̄ J
non ne ABCDE^3*FGIJ, na K
deficient* aspringað ABC, geteoriað DE^x*, atteoriað F, beoð gewanede G, beoð gelytlode ł gewanode I*, onteoriaþ J, lytliað K (*LM*)
omni ængum ABC, eallu̳m̳ DH, eællum $E^{3/x}$*, eallum FG, ælcum I, ænigu̳m̳ ł eallu̳m̳ J, ealle K
bono gode ABCFGH, góde DJ, gode ł nanes godes I*, god K, godum $E^{3/x}$*

ED: híg hyngredon (F)] hig hyngredon *Kimmens.* þa secenda (G)] þa secend[ ] *Rosier.* minuen[ ] (G)] minue*ntur Rosier.*

OE: wælige ($E^{3/x}$) wæ *by main hand,* lige *on next line on eras. by corr.* beþorfton (E^x)] *on eras.* beþorfton ł wædlodon (G)] ł wædlodon *added in diff.* (?) *hand.* hyngradun (A)] g *interl.* hy hyngredon (E^x)] *on eras.* him hingrode (I)] e *altered from* a, *eras.* (*of* n?) *after* e. þa Soþlice ($E^{3/x}$)] þa *added by corr.* drihten (E^3)] *eras. after word.* ne (E^3)] *eras. before word.* geteoriað (E^x)] *on eras.* beoð gelytlode ł gewanode (I)] y *altered from* i (?). eællum ($E^{3/x}$)] um *added by corr.* gode ł nanes godes (I)] ł nanes godes *written in right margin.* godum ($E^{3/x}$)] um *added by corr.*

LTg: Diuites] Dîuites M. eguerunt] G: g *altered from* u; ęguerunt H. esurierunt] E: *tops of* sur *retouched in darker ink due to eras. of orig. gloss;* ęsurierunt H; esurierunt M: *orig.* aesurierunt: a *deleted by dots above and below letter.* deficient] L: minuentur *added interl. by corr.: see GAg;* deficiet M: *orig.* deficient: n *deleted by dots above and below letter.*

LTu: eguerunt] eugerunt ξ. esurierunt] essurierunt ϑ.

GAg: deficient] minuentur FHIJK, L: *see LTg;* minuen[ ] G.

GAu: deficient] minuentur δεζϑιλμξοπϱστυφχψ.

12
Uenite cumað *ABC*DF*GHI,* Cumæþ *E³,* cumaþ *J*K (*LM*)
filii bearn ABCDFHJK, beærn *E³,* bea(r)n G*, ge bearn I*
audite geherað AI, gehirað B, g̲ehyrað C, gehyrað DFGHK, gehieræþ E^3, gehiraþ J (*M*)
me me ABCE^3FGHIJK
timorem | ege ABCDFGHIJK, drihtnes E^3 (*M*)
domini | dryhtnes BD, drihtnys CI, drihtnes F, drihtenes H*K,* dryht̄ A, drih̄ GJ, ege E^3

docebo	I	ic læru AC, ic lære BDFGHIJK, ic eow E^3 (*M*)
uos	I	eow ABCDFGHIJK, lęre E^3

ED: [ ]enite (G)] *Venite Rosier.* cumað (G)] *no gloss Rosier.* filíí (E)] filii *Harsley.* bea(r)n (G)] [ ]earn *Rosier.*

OE: bea(r)n (G)] *shoulder and right side of* r *lost.* ge bearn (I)] o *written before* ge.

LTg: Uenite] Uenîte M; Venite ABEHIJL; [ ]enite G. filii] filíí E. audite] audîte M. timorem] timôrem M. domini] d[ ] K: *letters lost due to excision of initial on fol. 38v, macron visible.* docebo] docêbo M.

LTu: Uenite] Venite ιvξοϱσςτ*τυφ.

13

Quis		hwelc AB, hwylc CF, hwilc E^3*GHJ*, la hwilc I, hwæt DK
est		is ABDE^{3}FGHIJ*K*, ys C
homo		mon AB, man FJK, mann GH, se man C*I, se mon E^3
qui		se ABJ, se ðe CF, se þe E^{3}I, þe DGH, þa K
uult		wile ABCDE^{3}FGHIJ, wyle K
uitam		lif ABCDE^{3}FGHI*JK
et*		⁊ ABCD*K*, ond E^3
cupit*		willað A, wilnað BD, willnað C, wilnæþ E^3, lufað F, lufaþ J, þe lufað I, adylgode G, l[ ] *K** (*L*)
uidere*	}I	gesian A, geseon BCDFGHIJK, gode E^3
dies*	}	dægas A, dagas BCDGHIJK, dægæs E^3, dæges F
bonos	I	gode ABCDFGHIK, gód J, tó gesionne E^3

OE: se man (C)] se *interl. in red by corr.* lif (I)] s. qui : se *written in left margin.* l[ ] K: *letters lost due to excision of initial on fol. 38v, minim visible after* l.

LTg: Quis] H: *eras. after* s; [ ]uis G. est] ést K. cupit] L: *underlined to signal deletion,* Et qui diligit *added interl. by corr.: see GAg.* et] *eras.* K: *see GAg.* uidere dies] L: *underlined to signal deletion,* dies uidere *added interl. by corr.: see GAg.*

GAg: ct] *om.* FGHIJ; *for* K *see LTg.* cupit] diligit FGHIJ, L: *see LTg;* d[ ]git K: *letters lost due to excision of initial on fol. 38v.* uidere dies] dies uidere FGHIJK, L: *see LTg.*

GAu: et] *om.* δεζϑιλμξπϱστυφχψ. cupit] diligit δεζιλμξοπϱστυφχψ. uidere dies] dies uidere δεζιλμξοπϱστυφχψ.

14

Cohibe*		bewere AB*CDE*^{3}F, bewera K, geheald ł [ ]we G, geheald J, forbeod ł forhafa ł bewere I* (*LM*)
linguam	I	tungan ABCDFGHJK, tun(g)an *I**, þine E^3

tuam	I	ðine AF, þine BCDGHIJK, tungæn E^3
a		from A**E*^{3}*, from B, fram CDFHJK, fram GI (*M*)
malo		yfle ABE^{3}I, yfyle C, yfele DFGJK, yuele H
et		⁊ ABCDE^{3}FHJK (*G*)
labia	I	weolure A, weleras BDHI*JK*, welyras C, welerum F, þine E^3 (*G*)
tua	I	þine BCGHIJK, ðinum F, weleræs E^3
ne	I	ðy læs AB, þe læs C, þilæs þe J, ne DH, þæt ne F, þet hie ne E^3, þæt hig ne I*, na K (*G*)
loquantur	I	sprecen AD*E*^{3}, sprecon FI, sprecan G, specan HK, hie sprecen B, hy sprecyn C, hi sprecan J
dolum		facen ADE^x*FGH, facn BK, facyn C, faken I, yfel ł facn J

ED: tun(g)an (I)] tungan *Lindelöf.* á (E)] a *Harsley.* a (G)] *a Rosier.* malo (G)] *malo Rosier.* þe læs (C)] þelæs *Wildhagen.*

OE: forbeod ł forhafa ł bewere (I)] ł bewere *written in bottom margin below lemma.* tun(g)an (I)] *bottom of* g *lost due to eras. between lemma and gloss.* from (A)] r *altered from* o. weleras (I)] s. prohibe : forbeod *written in left margin.* weleras (K)] *eye of 1st* e *lost due to excision of initial on fol. 38v.* þæt hig ne (I)] hig *written above* þæt, *otiose mark after* n. facen (E^x)] *on eras.*

LTg: Cohibe] L: Pr *added after* C: *see GAg,* E: *majuscule* P *followed by 2 letters eras. before* C, M: *orig.* Coibe: h *interl.;* Cóibe C. linguam] I: *eras. between lemma and gloss.* a] á EM. et] *lost* G. labia] *lost* G. ne] G: *letter* (a?) *visible as part of gloss.* loquantur] E: *eras. after* tur, *orig. macron visible.*

LTu: Cohibe] Chohibe β.

GAg: Cohibe] Proibe FK; Prohibe HIJ, L: *see LTg;* Prohib[ ] G.

GAu: Cohibe] Prohibe δεζϑιλμξοπϱστυφχψ.

15

Deuerte	acer *A*, acir B, acyrr CG, acyr ł gewít *D,* acer ł gewit E^x*, gecyr *F,* gecir J, awend ł gecyr *I*, gewit *K* (*H*)
a	from A*E*^{3}*, from B, fram CDFGHJK, fram I (*M*)
malo	yfle ABDE^{3}I, yfele CGHJK, yfelu F
et	⁊ ABCDE^{3}FGHIJK
fac	doa A, dó BD, do CE^{3}FGHIJK
bonum	god ABCDE^3*FGHIK, gód J
inquire	soec AB, sec CE^3*HIK, séc D, sece J, sec ðu F, andsec G (*M*)
pacem	sibbe ABFGHIJK, sybbe CD
et	⁊ ABCDFGHIJK, and E^3*

sequere*	fylg A*BDH, fylge *C*I*, fyli K, fyle ðu F, filige ł fili G, filige J, folgæ E^3 (*LM*)
eam	ða AB, þa DHI, þære C, þare J, ðam F, hy G, hiere E^3, hyre K

ED: acer ł gewit (E)] Acer ł gewit *Harsley.* á (E)] a *Harsley.*

OE: acer ł gewit (E^x)] *on eras.* from (E^3)] f *retouched in darker ink.* god (E^3)] *eras.* (*14 mm*) *after word.* sec (E^3)] *orig.* sece: *final* e *eras.* and (E^3)] *orig.* ond: o *altered to* a *by main hand.* fylg (A)] g *interl.* fylge (I)] y *altered from* i (?).

LTg: Deuerte] D: ł i *written interl. before gloss* (= Diuerte): *see v. 8 above for similar instance;* Diuerte AH: i *on eras.*, F: *orig.* Deuerte: *1st* e *deleted by subscript dot,* i *interl. in light brown ink,* I: *orig.* Deuerte: *1st* e *altered to* i, K: *eras. after* i, *perhaps altered from another letter.* a] á EM. inquire] inquîre M. sequere] C: *eras. before 2nd* e, L: se *on eras. and underlined to signal deletion,* perse *added after* se: *see GAg,* M: *orig.* sequire: i *altered to* e.

LTu: Deuerte] Diuerte ζιπστχ.

GAg: sequere] persequere FGHIJK, L: *see LTg.*

GAu: sequere] persequere δεζιλμξοπρστυφχψ.

16

Oculi	ǀ	egan AK, eagan BCDF*G*HI, eagon J, drihtnes E^3
domini	ǀ	dryhtnes B, drihtnys CI*, drihtnes F, drihtenes K, dryht̄ A, drih̄t G, drih̄ J, eægæn E^3
super		ofer ABDE^3FGHIJK, ofyr C
iustos		rehtwise A, ryhtwise BD, rihtwise CFGHK, rihtwisnesse J, þa rihtwisan I, þæ Soþfestæn E^3
et		⁊ ABCDE^3FGHIJK
aures	ǀ	earan ABCDFGHIJK, his *E^3*
eius	ǀ	his ABCDFGHIJ*K*, eæræn E^3
ad*		to ABDE^3, on *C*F*G*H*I*J*K*
preces	ǀ	boene AB, bene FJ, benum C*G*HI, benum D, gebedan K, hioræ E^3 (*M*)
eorum	ǀ	heara A, hira B, hyra C, heora DFGHIJ, heoran K, bene E^3

ED: drihtnes (E)] Drihtnes *Harsley.*

OE: drihtnys (I)] s. sunt : synt *written in left margin.*

LTg: Oculi] [ ]culi G. aures] avres E. eius] eíus K. ad] F: *orig.* in: *deleted by subscript dots,* ad *interl. in light brown ink,* H: *altered from another word* (in?), K: *on eras. by corr.,* ł in *written in left margin.* preces] M: *eras. after* r; pręces G.

LTu: preces] praeces βυ; præces μ; p̄ces χ.

GAg. ad] in GIJ; *for* FHK *see LTg*

GAu: ad] in δϑιμορυψ.

17

Uultus* | ondwleotan *A*, andwlitan *FJ*, ondwlita *B*, andwlita *CDGI**, andwilita *H*, ansyne *K*, Soðlice *E^{3}* (*L*)
autem* | soðlice ABCFGI, soþlice J, witodlice K, andwlita E^{x}*
domini dryhtnes B, drihtnes E^{x}*FI*, drihtenes K, dryht̄ A, driħt C, driħ GJ
super ofer ABFGJK*, ofyr C, ofor E^{x}*I
facientes ða dondan A, þa dondan BJ, þa doyndan C, donde DE^{x}*GHK, þa wyrcende F, ða wyrcendan I*
mala yfel ABGJK, yfyl C, yfelu DE^{x}*F, yuelu H, yflu I
ut ðet A, þæt BI, þæt CDFGHJK, þet E^{3}
perdat he forspilde ABCE^{3}, he forspille DFGHJ, he fordo ł forspille I, forspille K
de of ABCDFGHIJK, on E^{3}
terra eorðan ABCDFGHJ, eorðæn E^{3}, eorþan K, lande I
memoriam gemynd ABCDFHI*K*, gemind E^{3}*J, gemyndyg G
eorum heara A, hire B, hyra C, hire E^{x}*, heora DFGHIJK

OE: andwlita (I)] d *interl.* andwlita (E^{x})] *on eras.* drihtnes (E^{x})] *on eras.* drihtnes (I)] s. est : is *written in left margin.* ofer (K)] ansyne *eras. after word.* ofor (E^{x})] *on eras.* donde (E^{x})] *on eras.* ða wyrcendan (I)] an *on eras.* (?). yfelu (E^{x})] *on eras.* gemind (E^{x3})] *gloss eras. before word.* hire (E^{x})] *on eras.*

LTg: Uultus] Vultus ABCDEFGIJKL; [ ]ultus H: *initial* V *lost: outline visible.* memoriam] K: ri *altered from another letter* (m?), *macron added by corr.*

LTu: Uultus] Vultus ζινσς.

GAu: Uultus] Facies ϑ. autem] *om.* ϑ.

18

Clamauerunt | cleopedon A, clipodon B, clypodon CDJK, clypedon GH, clepodon I, hi clypudon F, ðæ soðfestæn E^{3}*
iusti | rehtwise A, ryhtwise B, rihtwise CDFGHJK, þa rihtwisan I, clipiæþ E^{3}
et ⁊ ABCE^{3}FGIJK
dominus drihten E^{3}IK, dryht̄ AB, driht̄ C, driħt F, driħ GJ
exaudiuit | geherde A, gehierde B, gehyrde CDFGHIK, gehirde J, hi E^{3} (*M*)

eos	hie A*B, hi CK, hy DGH, híg F, hig IJ, gehireþ E^{3}*
et	⁊ ABCE^{3}FGHJK
ex	of ABCDE^{3}*FGHIJK
omnibus	allum A, eallum BDHJ, eallum CFGI, eællum E^{3}, eallan K
tribulationibus	geswencednissum A, geswencednessum B, gescwencednyssum C, geswæncednessum J, geswincum DH, geswincum G, geswince K, gedrefednyssum FI, eærfoþnessum ł geswincum $E^{3/x}$*
eorum	heara A, hira B, hyra C, heora DE^{x}FGHIJK
liberauit	gefrede A, gefreode C, aliesde B, he alysde DFGHJ, he aliesde $E^{3/x}$*, ⁊ he alesde I, alysde K (*M*)
eos	hie AB, hi CK, hy DE^{x}*GH, hig FIJ

OE: ðæ soðfestæn (E^{3})] *letter eras. after* n. hie (A)] i *written below line.* gehireþ (E^{3})] *eras. above gloss, perhaps of underdotting of lemma above* (iusti): *cf. parallel Hebr. text, which retains underdotting.* of (E^{3})] f *in darker ink of corr.* eærfoþnessum ł geswincum ($E^{3/x}$)] *gloss eras. before* eærfoþnessum, ł *added by corr.,* geswincum *added by diff. corr., with* cum *on eras.* he aliesde ($E^{3/x}$)] a *by corr.,* lies *by main hand,* d *altered from* t, e *added (retraced?), eras. after word.* hy (E^{x})] *on eras.*

LTg: exaudiuit] exaudîuit M. liberauit] liberâuit M.

19

Iuxta	neh AB, nieh C, neah DF*G*HJK, Neæh E^{3}, gehende I
est	is ABE^{3}FGIJ*K*, ys C
dominus	drihtyn C, drihten E^{3}F, dryht̄ AB, driħt G, driħ J
his	ðissum A, þysum B, þisum J, þam *C*G, ðam F, þæm *D*I, þæm H, þam K, þem E^{x}* (*M*)
qui	ða A, þe *C*DE^{x}*GHIK, ðe F, ða ðe B, þa þe J
tribulato	geswencedre ABDE^{x}*, geswencyde C, geswéncede F, geswencede G, geswencendne H, geswæncede J, geswente K, gedrefede I
sunt	sind A, synd CFGHJK, sint B, synt E^{x}*I
corde	on heortan ACI, heortan BDE^{x}*FGHJK
et	⁊ ABCE^{x}*FGHJK (*I*)
humiles	eaðmode ABCDE^{x}*H, eadmodan F, eadmode GJK, þa eaðmodan I
spiritu	on gaste ABD*E^{x}**I, of gaste C, gaste FHK, gast G, gastas J
saluabit	gehaeleð A, gehælð B, he gehælð C, he gehæleð D*F*H*, he gehelþ E^{3}*, hi gehæleð G, he gehælð K, ⁊ he gehælð I, beoð gehæled J (*M*)

ED: [ ]uxta (G)] Iuxta *Rosier.* iís (C)] [h]ís *Wildhagen.*

OE: þem (E^{x})] *on eras.* þe (E^{x})] *on eras.* geswencedrc (E^{x})] *on eras.* synt (E^{x})] *on eras.* heortan (E^{x})] *on eras.* ⁊ (E^{x})] *on eras.* eaðmode (E^{x})] *on eras.* on gaste (E^{x})] *on eras.* he gehæleð (H)] *eras. before initial* h. he gehelþ (E^{3})] *initial* h *retouched by corr.*

LTg: Iuxta] [ ]uxta G. est] ést K. his] hís M; hiis D; iís C: *orig.* hís: *ascender of* h *eras. to form* i: *cf. Weber MSS* SK² med. qui] C: i *interl.* et] I: *gloss* (⁊?) *eras. above word.* spiritu] spiritv E. saluabit] saluâbit M; saluauit F.

LTu: his] iis επ.

20

Multae	mong A, monige *B*J,* Monigæ E^{3}, mænige *CDGH,* manige *FK,* fela *I* (*L*)
tribulationes	geswenced A, geswencydnys C, geswencednessa B, geswæncednessa J, geswinc DGH, swinc K, gedrefednysse F, gedrefednessa I, eærfoðnesse E^{3}
iustorum	rehtwisra A, ryhtwisra BD, rihtwisra CFGIJK, rihtwis H, þæræ soðfestræ E^{3} (*M*)
et	⁊ ABCE^{3}FGHIJK
de	of ABCDFGHIJK, be E^{3}
his* }	ðissum A, ðyssum B, þissum *C,* þysum I, þisum E^{3}, þisum J, þys *K,* ðam *D,* ðam F, þam GH (*M*)
omnibus* }	allum A, eallum BCFGI, eallum DHJ, eællum E^{3}*, eallan K
liberauit	gefreað *A,* gefreoð *C,* aliesde B, alysde *JK,* alyseþ *DE^{x}*,* alyseð *GH,* he aliseð *F,* ⁊ alesð *I* (*LM*)
eos	hie AB, hi CK, hig FIJ, hy G, hem E^{x}*
dominus	drihtyn C, drihten E^{x}*F, dryht̄ AB, driħt G, driħ J (*K*)

ED: monige (B)] menige 'oder monige?' *Lindelöf*². iís (C)] [h]ís *Wildhagen.* liberauit (F)] liberabit *Kimmens.*

OE: monige (B)] *right side of* o *incomplete, but enough of a stroke is made to indicate* o *and not* e (*see ED*). eællum (E^{3})] *gloss eras. after word.* alyseþ (E^{x})] *on eras.* hem (E^{x})] *on eras.* drihten (E^{x})] *on eras.*

LTg: Multae] I: s. sunt *written in left margin;* Multæ B; Multę CDFGH; Multe EJKL. iustorum] iustôrum M. his] hís KM; hiis D; iís C: *orig.* hís: *ascender of* h *eras. to form* i: *cf. Weber MSS* S med. liberauit] F: *orig.* liberabit: *2nd* b *eras.,* u *on eras.;* liberâbit M: *orig.* liberâuit: u *on eras., then deleted and 2nd* b *interl.;* liberabit CDEGHIJL, A: *2nd* b *on eras.,* K: *orig.* liberauit: u *altered to* b *by corr.* dominus] K: *gloss eras.*

LTu: Multae] Multe διξπσςτ*τ; Multę ελνρυφψω; Multæ ϑ. liberauit] liberabit ϑινξοστ*τχψω, ε: *2nd* b *altered from* u.

GAg: his omnibus] omnibus his FGHIJ; omnibus hís K.

GAu: his omnibus] omnibus his δεζϑιλμξοπρστυφχψω. dominus] *om.* ϑ.

21

Dominus* } dryhten B, drihtyn C, drihten FK, dryht̄ A, drih̄t G, drih̄ J, ðrihten E^{3}* (*M*)
custodit* } haldeð A, healdeð B, healdyð *C,* healdað J, gehealdeþ DE^{x}*, gehealdeð GH, geheald F, gehealt I, gehealdæt K (*M*)
omnia all A, ealle BCDE^{x}*FGHIJK
ossa ban ABCDFGHIJK, bæn E^{3}*
eorum heara A, hira B, hyra C, heora DE^{x}*FGHIJK
unum an ABCDE^{x}*GHIJK, án F(*M*)
ex of ABCDE^{x}*FGHIJK
eis* ðæm A, þæm B, þam *C*G, ðam̲ *D,* ðam *E^{x}*F, þam̲ HJK, ðisum I*
non ne *A*BCDE^{x}FGHIJ, na K
conteretur bið fordręsted A, bið forþræstyd C*, bið forðræstet B, bið tobrocen DE$^{3/x}$*F*G*H, biþ tobrocen J, bið tobryt ł ne bið na tobrocen I, tobryrð K (*M*)

ED: custodit (C)] castodit *Wildhagen.*

OE: ðrihten (E^{3})] ð *retraced in darker ink by corr.* gehealdeþ (E^{x})] *on eras.* ealle (E^{x})] *on eras.* bæn (E^{3})] *ascender of* b *retouched in darker ink.* heora (E^{x})] *on eras.* an (E^{x})] *on eras.* of (E^{x})] *on eras.* ðisum (I)] *letter eras. after* s. bið forþræstyd (C)] *1st* r *interl.* bið tobrocen (E$^{3/x}$)] bið to *by corr.*

LTg: custodit] C: u *malformed; custôdit* M. unum] ûnum M. eis] iis C: *2nd* i *interl.;* hiis D; his EL: *cf. Weber MSS* SK^{2} *and* moz^{c}, *see GAg.* non] A: on *interl. by corr.* conteretur] M: *orig.* conterîtur: i *altered to* e; conterętur G.

LTu: Dominus] [ ]ominus τ*. eis] his νςτ*: *cf. Weber MSS* SK^{2} *and* moz^{c}, *see GAu.*

GAg: Dominus custodit] Custodit dominus FGHIJK. eis] his FGHIJ, EL: *see LTg;* hís K; *for* CD *see LTg.*

GAu: Dominus custodit] Custodit dominus δεζιλμξοπρστυφχψω. eis] his δζϑιλμξοπρστυφχψω, νςτ*: *see LTu;* iis ε.

22

Mors deað ABCF*G*HIK, deaþ DE^{x}*J
peccatorum synfulra ACDE^{x}*FGHIJ, synfylra B, synfulla K (*M*)
pessima se wyrresta AB, se wyrrysta *C,* se wyrsta I*, se wirresta J, wyrst D*E^{x}**FGHK, sæmust ł wyrst M^{2}* (*L*)
⟨est⟩ ys *C,* is *E^{x}** (*L*)

et ⁊ ABCE^{x}*FGHIJK
qui ða ða A, þa ðe BDE^{x}*J, þa þe CGHI, ða ðe F, þa K
oderunt figað A, feogeað BC, hatedon DE^{x}*GH, hatudon F, hatodun I, hatodon JK (*M*)
iustum ðone rehtwisan A, þone ryhtwisan B, þone rihtwisan C, þane rihtwisan I, rihtwissan K, þone rihtwisum J, ryhtwise DE^{x}*, rihtwisne FH, rihtwisre G
delinquent agyltað ABC, ⁊ agyltað I*, he agyltað D, hy agyltað G, hí agyldeþ F, he agyteð H, agitaþ J, hi agylt K, he forlet E^{3}*

OE: deaþ (E^{x})] *on eras.* synfulra (E^{x})] *on eras.* se wyrsta (I)] s. est : is *written in left margin.* wyrst (E^{x})] *on eras.* sæmust ł wyrst (M^{2})] id est *precedes gloss.* is (E^{x})] *on eras.* ⁊ (E^{x})] *on eras.* þa ðe (E^{x})] *on eras.* hatedon (E^{x})] *on eras.* ryhtwise (E^{x})] *on eras.* ⁊ agyltað (I)] *orig.* ⁊ agiltað: i *altered to* y. he forlet (E^{3})] *gloss eras. before word.*

LTg: Mors] [ ]ors G. peccatorum] peccatôrum M. pessima] pessima est CEL: *see Weber MSS* T^{2}PQ*RVXλ *and OE note to* se wyrsta (I). oderunt] odérunt M.

LTu: pessima] pessima est νςτ*: *see Weber MSS* T^{2}PQ*RVXλ. oderunt] hoderunt ς. delinquent] ϑ: *2nd* n *interl.*

23
Redimet | aleseð *A*B, alysyð C, alesð I, aliseþ J, alyseð K, alyseð ⁊ F, alyseð ł nereð DG, alyseþ ł nereð H, ðrihten E^{3}
dominus | drihten K, dryht̄ AB, driħt CFGH, driħ J, ælised E^{3}
animas sawle ACK, sæwle E^{3}*, sawla BDFGIJ, saula H (*L*)
seruorum ðiowa A, þeowa C, ðeowa B, þeowra DGHJ, þiowræ E^{3}*, ðeowena F, ðeowana I, þeowan K (*M*)
suorum his ABCDE^{x}*IJ, hys H, heora FGK
et ⁊ ABCE^{x}*FGHIJ*K*
non | ne ABC, na DE^{x}*GHJK, hi na F, he na ne I (*M*)
derelinquet* | forleteð *A,* forlæteð B, forlætað CI, forlæteþ F, forlætæð K, forlæteþ he D, forleateþ he *E^{x}*,* forlætað he G, forlæteð he H, forlæten J (*LM*)
omnes alle A, ealle BCDE^{x}*FGHIJK (*M*)
qui ða ðe AB, þa þe CGHIJ, þa ðe D, ða þe F, þæ þe E^{x}*, þa K
sperant gehyhtað AB, gehihtað *C,* gehihtaþ J, hyhtað DH, hihtað GK, hyhtat E^{x}*, hihtiaþ ł hopiaþ *I*,* hopiað F
in in AF, on BCDE^{x}*GHIJ (*K*)
eum* hine ABDE^{x}*F, hyne C, þe H, him GI, him J

ED: hihtiaþ ł hopiaþ (I)] hihtaþ ł hopiaþ *Lindelöf, but see p. 52, n. 8.*

OE: sæwle (E^{3})] *eras.* (?) *after word.* þiowræ (E^{3})] r *interl.* his (E^{x})] *on eras.* ⁊ (E^{x})]

on eras. na (E^{x})] *on eras.* forleateþ he (E^{x})] *on eras.* ealle (E^{x})] *on eras.* þæ þe (E^{x})] *on eras.* hyhtat (E^{x})] *on eras.* hihtiaþ ł hopiaþ (I)] *2nd* i *interl.* on (E^{x})] *on eras.* hine (E^{x})] *on eras.*

LTg: Redimet] A: *orig.* Redimit: *2nd* i *altered to* e. animas] *om.* L, *added interl. by corr.* seruorum] seruôrum M. et] [ ]t K: e *lost due to excision of initial to Ps 34 below* (*fol. 38v*). non] nôn M. derelinquet] A: *3rd* e *on eras.*, M: et *blotted,* E: *orig.* derelinquent: *2nd* n *eras.*, L: re *underlined to signal deletion,* n *added interl. above* t: *see GAg.* omnes] M: nes *on eras.* sperant] C: n *interl.*, I: p *on eras.* in] K: i *and left leg of* n *lost due to excision of initial to Ps 34 below* (*fol. 38v*).

LTu: Redimet] β: *orig.* Redemet: i *interl. above 2nd* e.

GAg: derelinquet] delinquent FGHIJK, L: *see LTg.* eum] eo FGHIJK.

GAu: derelinquet] delinquent δεζιλμξοπρστυφχψω; dilinquet ϑ. eum] eo εζϑιλξοπρστυφχω.

PSALM 34

1

Iudica	doem *AB*, dem *CDE^{x}*FGHIJ*K* (*M*)
domine	drihten E^{3}*I*, dryht̄ AB, driħt *C*F, driħ FGJ
nocentes	ðа sceððendan A, þa sceððendan B, þa sceðþyndan C, þa unscæþþigan J, deriende DE^{x}*H, derigende FGK, þa deriendan I
me	me ABCE^{x}*FGHIJK
expugna	oferfeht AB, oferfeoht J, ofyrfeoht *C,* oferwin DE^{x}*F*G*K, ofer-win M^{2}, oferwin ł H, gewin ł oferwin I
inpugnantes*	ðа onfehtendan A, þa onfehtendan B, þa onfeohtyndan C, onwinnende DFG*H*KM^{2}, onwinnendes E^{x}*, þa onawinnendan ł onwinnende *I,* oferfeohtendan J
me	mec A, me BCE^{x}*FGHIJK

ED: IVDICA (C)] JVDICA *Wildhagen.* Iudica (G)] *I*udica *Rosier.* oferwin ł (H)] oferwin *Campbell.*

OE: drihten (E^{3})] *gloss eras. after word, letter traces visible.* drihten (I)] o *written before word.* deriende (E^{x})] *on eras.* me (E^{x}) (*1st*)] *on eras.*, s:yþ *eras. before word: see gloss to* nocentes. oferwin (E^{x})] *on eras.* onwinnendes (E^{x})] *on eras.* me (E^{x}) (*2nd*)] *on eras.*

LTg: Iudica] IVdica ABD; IVDICA CE; Ivdica J; IUdica M; [ ]Vdica K: *initial letter excised.* domine] DNE C. expugna] C: g *altered from another letter* (n?); expugn[ ] G. inpugnantes] impugnantes I, H: m *on eras.*

LTu: Iudica] IUDica β; IUdica ϑ; IVDICA ιςτ*τφ; IUDICA λμνρχψ. domine] DÑE λμνϱχψ. nocentes] NOCENTES λνϱχ; NOCENtes μψ. me (*1st*)] ME λϱχ. expugna] EXPUGNA λ. inpugnantes] impugnantes ιλτ*τυφω, ξ: m *interl.*, ο: i *interl.*

GAu: inpugnantes] expugnantes δμχψ.

2

Adprehende		gegrip *A**B*CDE*^{3}F*H**JKM*^{2}, gegrip ł gelæc *I* (*G*)
arma		wepen A, wæpn BCDGHJK, wepn E^{3}*, wǽpn F, wæpna I
et		⁊ ABCDE^{3}FGHIJK
scutum		sceld AB, scyld CDFGHIK, Scild E^{3}*, scild J
et		⁊ ABCDE^{3}FGHIJK
exsurge		aris *A*B*CDFH*IJ, aras K, Æris *E*^{3} (*GLM*)
in	I	in A, on BCDHIJK, to F, me E^{3}
adiutorium	I	fultum A*C*DJ, fultum BK, fultume FI, ful[ ]um H*, on E^{3} (*G*)
mihi	I	me AB*C*DFGHI*JK*, fultum *E*^{3} (*M*)

ED: Apprehende (C)] A[d]prehende *Wildhagen.* gegrip (E)] Gegrip *Harsley.* wæpn (G)] *no gloss Rosier.* Æris (E)] æris *Harsley.* exurge (F)] exsurge *Kimmens.* ex[ ]urge (G)] e*x*surge *Rosier.* [ ]torium (G)] *adiu*torium *Rosier.* ful[ ]um (H)] fultum *Campbell.*

OE: gegrip (A)] *letter eras. after* e (*perhaps* y *or* w?). gegrip (H)] *eras. after* e, *perhaps from Lat. line below.* wepn (E^{3})] *eras. before word.* Scild (E^{3})] *eras. before word.* ful[ ]um (H)] *letter after* l *lost due to hole in leaf.*

LTg: Adprehende] Adpraehende AM; Apprehende DIJ, C: *1st* p *on eras. by corr.*, H: *1st* p *on eras.*, K: *1st* p *altered from another letter;* Ap̄hendite E; [ ]de G. exsurge] M: s *on eras.;* exurge ACEL, F: *orig.* exsurge: s *deleted by subscript dot,* H: *eras. after* x; ex[ ]urge G: *letter fragments of gloss visible above word.* adiutorium] C: *2nd* i *interl.;* [ ]torium G. mihi] M: *eras. after 1st* i; michi EJK, C: *orig.* mihi: c *interl. by corr.*

LTu: Adprehende] Adpręhende βν; Apprehende εζιλξϱστ*τ, ο: *orig.* Adpraehende; Adpraehende μψ; Appręhende υ; Ap̄hende φχω. exsurge] exurge δειλξπτ*τυφχ, ϱ: *orig.* exsurge. mihi] michi ισςτ*τ, χ: c *interl.;* m[1] φ.

3

Effunde	ageot ABCF*G*K, ageot ut DHM^{2}, Ægiot ut E$^{3/x}$*, tobræd I*, asænd J
frameam	sweord AB, swurd C, sword E^{x}*, swurd ł wrace *I*, sweord ł mece *J*, flane DHM^{2}, flana K, flane mine G, cocor minne F*
et	⁊ ABCE^{3}*FGHIJK
conclude	biluc A, beluc BCDFHJKM^{2}, belucc G, beluc ł betiene E$^{3/x}$*, beluc ł beclys I
aduersus	wið ABC, wiþ J, ongean DE^{x}*H, on[ ]an G, togeanes FK,

	agen ł togeanes I
eos	him A, hic B, hi CK, hy DE^{x}*GH, híg F, hig IJ
qui	ða ðe A, þa ðe BJ, þa þe CFI, þe DE^{3}G, þa K, þe me H
me* }	me ABDE^{3}*GHIJK, min CF (*L*)
persequuntur* }	oehtað AB, iehtað C, ehtað *DF***K**, ehtaþ HJ, eahtað E^{x}*, l ehtað G*, ehtiað I (*LM*)
dic	cweð ABC, cweþ JK, cweðe F, sege DE^{x}*GHIM^{2}
animae	to sawle A*BJ*, sawle *CDFGH*, sæwle *E*^{3}, sawel *K*, to sawle I (*L*)
meae	minre A*BCDE*^{x}*IJ*K*, min *F*, mine *G* (*HL*)
salus	hælu A, hælo BDFGHIJM^{2}, helo E^{3}, hæl C, hæle K
tua	ðin ABF, þin CDE^{x}*GHIJK*
ego	ic ABCDE^{x}*FGHIJK
sum	eam A, eom BCDE^{x}*FGHIJK

ED: [ ]ffunde (G)] *Effunde Rosier.* ageot (G)] *no gloss Rosier.* angetoh (I) (*see* tobræd *in OE*)] *not noted by Lindelöf.* frámeam (I)] frameam *Lindelöf.* flane mine (G)] flane *Rosier.* aduersus (G)] a*du*ersus *Rosier.* on[ ]an (G)] [ ]an *Rosier.* l ehtað (G)] ehtað *Rosier.* sawle (G)] *no gloss Rosier.* meæ (D)] meae *Roeder.* meę (E)] meae *Harsley.* mine (G)] *no gloss Rosier.*

OE: Ægiot ut (E$^{3/x}$)] ut *on eras. by corr., followed by eras. of gloss.* tobræd (I)] angetoh *written in left margin.* sword (E^{x})] *on eras.* cocor minne (F)] *eras. but visible.* ⁊ (E^{3})] *eras. before word.* beluc ł betiene (E$^{3/x}$)] luc ł be *by corr.* ongean (E^{x})] *on eras.* hy (E^{x})] *on eras.* me (E^{3})] *gloss eras. after word.* ehtað (F)] *eras. before word.* ehtað (K)] *letter eras. after word.* eahtað (E^{x})] *on eras.* l ehtað (G)] l = ł *without cross-stroke?* sege (E^{x})] *on eras.* minre (E^{x})] *on eras.* þin (E^{x})] *on eras.* þin (K)] *orig.* þinre: re *eras.* ic (E^{x})] *on eras.* eom (E^{x})] *on eras.*

LTg: Effunde] [ ]ffunde G. frameam] J: r *interl. by glossator;* frámeam I. me] L: *underlined to signal deletion: see GAg.* persequuntur] L: me *added interl. above* ur *by corr.: see GAg;* persecuntur DKM. animae] animæ B; anime CDEFJK; animę GHL. meae] meæ BDKL; meę CEFG; męę H.

LTu: persequuntur] persecuntur δμνοςχω; persequntur ϑ. animae] animę βδεϑμνοπχψω; anime ιξσςτ*τ. meae] meę εϑινξπςφω; mee στ*τ; meæ χ.

GAg: me persequuntur] persequuntur me FGHI, L: *see LTg;* persecuntur me JK.

GAu: me persequuntur] persecuntur me δμοσχω; persequuntur me εζιλξπρυψ; persequntur me ϑ.

4

Confundantur	sien gescilde A*, sien gescende B, syn gescynde C, syn gescænde J, gescamigen DE^{x}*, gesceamigan G,

		gesceamien *H,* gescæmigen K, gescamien M^{2}, gesceamian ł gescende F, beon gescynde ł [ ]camigan hi I*
et		⁊ ABCDE^{3}FGHIJKM^{2}
reuereantur		onscunien *A,* onscunigen B, onscamiyn C, onscuman ł ondrædan J, wandien D*HKM^{2}, wandian G, cirrede ł wandien E$^{3/x}$*, aðracian ł ⁊ sýn geunarode F, anðracian I
inimici*	|	feond A, fiend B, fynd CD, mine E^{3} (*L*)
mei*	|	mine ABCD, fiend E^{3} (*L*)
qui*		ða A, þa ðe BD, þa þe C, þæ þe E^{3}
quaerunt*		soecað *A,* seceað *C,* secað *D,* secæþ *E^{3},* sohton *B,* secende GJ, ða secendan F, þa secendan I, þa secað K (*LM*)
animam	|	sawle ABCDFGHJK, sawle ł licaman I, mine E^{3}
meam	|	mine ABCFGHIJK, sæwle E^{3}
Auertantur		sien forcerred A, syn forcyrryd C, sien forcirde B, sin gecyrrede D, syn gecyrrede FGM^{2}, sýn gecyrrede H, sy gecirred J*, sin gecyrred K, Sien gewirfede ł sin gecyrrede E$^{3/x}$*, syn gehwyrfed ł gecyrran I
retrorsum		on bec A, on bæc BCK, on bæcc J, underbecling D, underbæclincg G, underbæcling H*, underbæclinc M^{2}, underbæcc F, underbæc I, on bęcling E^{3}
et		⁊ ABCDFGHIJKM^{2}, ond E^{3}
erubescant*		scomien A, scomigen B, scamiyn C, scæmige E^{3}, gesceamian FG, gesceamien H, beon gescynde I, syn gescænde J, hy ablysygen D, ablysien M^{2}, forwyrðan K (*L*)
qui*		ða A, ða ðe B, þa þe C, þa ðe D, þæ þe E^{3} (*L*)
cogitant*	|	ðencað A, þencað BD, þenceað C, þam þéncendan F, þa þencendan I, þencende JK, sprecende G, me E^{3} (*L*)
mihi	|	me AB*C*FGI*J*K, þencæþ *E^{3}*
mala		yfel ABJK, yfyl C, yfelu DFG, yuelu H, yflu I, yfeles E^{3}

ED: [ ]onfundantur (H)] Confundantur *Campbell.* gescamigen (E)] Gescamigen *Harsley.* beon gescynde ł [ ]camigan hi (I)] beon gescynde ł scamigan hi *Lindelöf.* qūrunt (E)] querunt *Harsley.* sýn gecyrrede (H)] syn gecyrrede *Campbell.* underbæcc (F)] under bæcc *Kimmens.* underbæc (I)] under bæc *Lindelöf.* m^{1} (E)] michi *Harsley.*

OE: sien gescilde (A)] *lemma misread as* defendere. gescamigen (E^{x})] *on eras.* beon gescynde ł [ ]camigan hi (I)] [ ]camigan hi *written in left margin, letter fragment visible in initial position.* wandien (D)] *orig.* wandian: *2nd* a *deleted by subscript dot,* e *interl.* cirrede ł wandien (E$^{3/x}$)] ł wandien *added by corr.* sy gecirred (J)] *descender of* y *malformed.* Sien gewirfede ł sin gecyrrede (E$^{3/x}$)] ł sin gecyrrede *added by corr. above* Sien gewirfede. underbæcling (H)] *small eras. after* g.

LTg: Confundantur] [ ]onfundantur H: *initial* C *lost*. reuereantur] A: *3rd* e *on eras. by corr.* inimici] L: *underlined to signal deletion: see GAg*. mei] L: *underlined to signal deletion: see GAg*. quaerunt] quęrunt A; querunt BCDM; qūrunt E; querentes L: *orig*. querunt: e *added above 2nd* u *by corr. and* es *added to end of word: see GAg*. erubescant] L: *underlined to signal deletion,* confundantur *added interl. by corr.: see GAg*. qui] L: *underlined to signal deletion: see GAg*. cogitant] L: es *added at end of word by corr.: see GAg*. mihi] michi J, C: *orig*. mihi: c *interl. by corr.;* m^1 E.

LTu: quaerunt] querunt βςτ*; quęrunt ν. mihi] michi ιλξσςφ, πϱ: c *interl.;* m^1 τ*τ.

GAg: inimici mei] *om*. FGHIJK, L: *see LTg*. qui (*1st*)] *om*. FGHIJK. quaerunt] quęrentes F; querentes HJK, L: *see LTg;* quaerentes I; queren[ ] G. erubescant] confundantur FGHIJK, L: *see LTg*. qui (*2nd*)] *om*. FGHIJK, L: *see LTg*. cogitant] cogitantes FGHIJK, L: *see LTg*.

GAu: inimici mei] *om*. δεζϑιλμξοπϱστυφχψω. qui (*1st*)] *om*. δεζϑιλμξοπϱστυφχψω. quaerunt] querentes δϑιξστ; quęrentes εζλμπϱφω; quaerentes ουχψ. erubescant] confundantur δεζϑιλμξοπϱστυφχψω. qui (*2nd*)] *om*. δεζϑιλξοπϱστυφχψω. cogitant] cogitantes δεζϑιλμξοπϱστυφχψω.

5

<table>
<tr><td>Fiant</td><td></td><td>sien AB, syn C, hy syn DH, Sin hic E^3*, hy synd G, synd J, g̲e̲weorðe F, gewyrðan K, beon hig ł gewurðun hig I*</td></tr>
<tr><td>tamquam</td><td></td><td>swe swe A, swa swa BCDFGHIJ, swæ E^3, swa K</td></tr>
<tr><td>puluis</td><td></td><td>dus A, dust BCDFGHIK, dust ł myll J, þęt dust E^3</td></tr>
<tr><td>ante</td><td></td><td>biforan AB, beforan CDGHIJK, beforæn E^3, ætforan F</td></tr>
<tr><td>faciem</td><td></td><td>onsiene AB, onsíne E^3, ansyne CDFGJK, ansiene H, ansene I</td></tr>
<tr><td>uenti</td><td></td><td>windes ABDFGHIJK, windys C, þes windes E^3</td></tr>
<tr><td>et</td><td></td><td>⁊ ABCE^3FGHJK (I*)</td></tr>
<tr><td>angelus</td><td>|</td><td>engel ABDGHIJK, engyl C, englas F, drihtnes E^3</td></tr>
<tr><td>domini</td><td>|</td><td>dryhtnes B, drihtnys C, drihtnes F, dryht̄ A, drih́t G, drih́ J, engel E^3</td></tr>
<tr><td>adfligens*</td><td>|</td><td>swencende ABDG, swencynde C, swæncende J, gewriðende ł geswencendæ ł genyrwiende I*, hie E^3 (L)</td></tr>
<tr><td>eos</td><td>|</td><td>hie AB, hi C, hy DGH, hig FIJ, swencende E^x*</td></tr>
</table>

ED: tanquam (C)] ta[m]quam *Wildhagen*. swa swa (GIJ)] swaswa *Rosier, Lindelöf, Oess*. affligens (C)] a[d]fligens *Wildhagen*.

OE: Sin hie (E^3)] *orig*. Sien hie: *1st* e *eras*. beon hig ł gewurðun hig (I)] beon hig ł *written in left margin*. et (I)] s. et sit : ⁊ sy *written in top margin*. gewriðende ł geswencendæ ł genyrwiende (I)] ł genyrwiende *written in right margin*. swencende (E^x)] *on eras*.

LTg: tamquam] tanquam E, C: *orig*. tamquam: *left leg of 1st* m *eras. to form* n, H:

eras. after n. puluis] H: *added above line by glossator.* adfligens] L: *underlined to signal deletion,* coartans *added by corr. in blank space after* eos: *see GAg.* affligens D, C: *1st* f *on eras. by corr.*

LTu: tamquam] tanquam εθιστ*τφ. angelus] β: *orig.* angelos: o *deleted,* u *interl.* adfligens] affligens τ*.

GAg: adfligens] coartans FGHIK, J: *eras. after* o, L: *see LTg.*

GAu: adfligens] coartans δεζθιλμξοπρστυφχψω.

6

Fiant*	sien AB, syn CDF, Sin E^{x}*, sig G, sie H, synd J, gewurðe I, gewyrðe K* (*L*)
uiae*	wegas A*BCDE^{x}**FJ, weg GHIK (*L*)
eorum*	heara A, hira B, hyra C, heora DE^{x}*FGIJK*
tenebrae	ðeostre A*B,* þystre *CK*,* þystro *DE^{x}*GH,* ðystra *F,* þystru I, þeostru *J** (*LM*)
et	⁊ ABCE^{x}*FGHIJK
lubricum	glidd AB, glid C, glidd ł sclidd J*, slidornis DHM^{2}, slidornes G, slidernes K, stlidornis E^{x}*, slipore F, slipor ł asceonigendlic I
et	⁊ ABCE^{x}*FGHJK
angelus	ængel A*, engel BDGHIJK, engyl C, angel E^{x}*, ænglas F
domini	dryhtnes B, drihtnys C, drihtnes E^{x}*FI, drihtenes K, dryht̄ A, driħ GJ
persequens	oehtende AB, iehtynde C, ehtende DE^{x}*FGHJK, ehtiende I (*M*)
eos	hie ABE^{x}*, hi C, hig FIJ, hy GH, heora K

ED: uiæ (D)] uiae *Roeder.* weg (G)] wæg *Rosier.* tenebræ (D)] tenebrae *Roeder.* slidornes (G)] slipornes *Rosier.* hie (A)] his *Kuhn.*

OE: Sin (E^{x})] *on eras.,* h *visible after word.* gewyrðe (K)] *eras. after word.* wegas (E^{x})] *on eras.* heora (E^{x})] *on eras.* heora (K)] *orig.* heoran: n *eras.* þystre (K)] þe *eras. before word.* þystro (E^{x})] *on eras.* þeostru (J)] s *altered from* r. ⁊ (E^{x}) (*1st*)] *on eras.* glidd ł sclidd (J)] *2nd* i *altered from* l. stlidornis (E^{x})] *on eras.* ⁊ (E^{x}) (*2nd*)] *on eras.* ængel (A)] æ *malformed.* angel (E^{x})] *on eras.* drihtnes (E^{x})] *on eras.* ehtende (E^{x})] *on eras.* hie (E^{x})] *on eras.*

LTg: Fiant] L: n *underlined to signal deletion: see GAg.* uiae] uiæ BD; uię CL; uie E. tenebrae] tenebræ BD; tenebrę CFHL; tenebre EGJK; ténebrae M. persequens] pérsequens M.

LTu: Fiant] υ: n *interl.* uiae] uie ςτ*; uiæ υ. tenebrae] tenebrę βενπφω; tenebre διξσςτ*υ; tenebræ θ.

GAg: Fiant] Fiat FGIJ, K: *orig*. Fiant: n *eras.*, L: *see LTg;* (F)iat H: F *partly lost*. uiae] uia FGHIJK. eorum] illorum FGHIJK.

GAu: Fiant] Fiat δεζθξχψ. uiae] uia δεζθιλμξοπρστφχψω. eorum] illorum δεζθιλμξοπρστφχψω.

7

Quoniam		forðon AB, forþon CJ, Forðæn E^3, forðā þe F, forþā G, forþy þe I
gratis		bi ungewyrhtum AB, bc ungewyrhtum C, by ungewirhtum J, gifum D, gifum E^x*GH, gife K, buton F, hi buton gewyrhtum ł butan geearnung[ ] I*
absconderunt		ahyddon AB, ahyddun C, ahiddon J, hy hyddon DE^x*, hyddon K, hi behyddon F, hy behyddon GH, behyddon I
mihi		me AB*CE^x**FGIJ*K*
⟨in⟩		on *CJ*
interitum		forwyrd AB*C*DI*J*, forwirð E^3*, on forwýrde F, on forwyrd *H*K, on foreweardum G (*M*)
laquei	|	girene A, girne B, grynys C, grines DE^x*FGHK, grina J, heora I
sui	|	heara A, hira B, heora DE^x*JK, his CFGH, grines I (*M*)
uane*		idellice *A*B, idyllice C, on idel DE^x*I, ofer ydel F, ofer idel G, ofer on idel J, ofer idelnes K (*L*)
exprobrauerunt		edwittun A, edwitan BG, oðwiton C, edwit J, hy hyspton DE^x*FH, hi hyspton K, hi asceonodon ł hi hyspton I
animam	|	sawle ABDFGHIJ, saule K, sawl C, mine E^3
meam	|	mine ABCFGHIK, minre J, sawle E^3

ED: forðon (A)] for ðon *Kuhn*. on foreweardum (G)] onforeweardum *Rosier*.

OE: gifum (E^x)] *on eras.* hi buton gewyrhtum ł butan geearnung[ ] (I)] ł butan geearnung[ ] *written in right margin and cropped.* hy hyddon (E^x)] *on eras., traces of 3 letters* (we:?, *last of which is descender*) *visible before word.* me (E^x)] *on eras.* forwirð (E^3)] *retraced in darker ink.* grines (E^x)] *on eras.* heora (E^x)] *on eras.* on idel (E^x)] *on eras.* hy hyspton (E^x)] *on eras.*

LTg: mihi] K: *final* i *on eras. and followed by eras.;* michi E, C: *orig.* mihi: c *added interl. by corr.* interitum] H: *eras. before word,* M: *eras.* (*2 letters?*) *after* n, C: *orig.* in interitum: in *deleted by 2 subscript dots;* in interitu J. sui] M: *eras. after word.* uane] A: *letter eras. after* n, L: *underlined to signal deletion and* superuacue *added interl. by corr.; see GAg.*

LTu: mihi] michi ιλςτ*τ, πρ: c *interl.;* m¹ φ. interitum] in interitum βθς, υ: in *interl.* uane] uanę β; *om.* ς.

GAg: uane] superuacue FHIJK, L: *see LTg;* superuacuę G.

GAu: uane] supcruacue δεζιλμξϱστυφχψω, o: *orig.* superuacuae; superuacuæ ϑ; superuacuę π.

8

Ueniat	cyme A*BC,* cume *DFHJK,* Cumo *E*^{3}***, cumað *G,* becume *I* (*L*)
illis*	him ACFG, him BDHJK, hem E^{3}*, heom I (*L*)
laqueus	giren A, gryn BCDI, grin E^{3}*FGHJK
quem	ða AB, þa J, þe CI, þæt DFHK, þæt G, þet E$^{3/x}$*
ignorant*	hie neoton A, hie nyton B, hi nyton *C*I, hy ne gecnawað D, hi ne gecnawaþ E^{x}*, hy ne gecnæwað GH, hi ne gecnawon F, hi na gecnawan K, hig ne gecnawaþ J (*LM*)
et	⁊ ABCE^{x}*FGHIJK
captio	geheftednis A, gehæftednes B, gehæftydnys C, gehæftedne J, hæftnunga F, gegripennis DE^{x}*HM^{2}, gegripen G*, gegrip K, feng ł deað I
quam	ða *A*B, þa *C,* þe I, þane D*K,* þare þæ E$^{3/x}$*, þone þe F, þone þa J, þa þæ G (*M*)
occultauerunt*	gedegladon A, gedeglodon B, gediglodon C, hie gedigledon E^{3}, hy dygledon D, he behydde FG, hi behyddun I, he behidde J, hi hydan K (*L*)
adprehendat*	gegripeð *A*B, gegripyð *C,* gegripeð G, gegripaþ *J,* gegripe *DH*K,* gegripæ *E*^{3}**,* to gegripe *F,* ⁊ gegripe *I* (*M*)
eos*	hie AB, hi CK, hy DE^{x}, hine FGJ, hyne H
et	⁊ FGHIJK (*ABCDEM*)
in	in A, on BCDE^{3}FGHIJK
laqueum*	girene *AB*, gryne *CD*, grine FGHIJ, grin *K**, grino E^{3}* (*M*)
incidant*	ingefallen hie A, ingefallen B, ongefeallyn *C**, hy ongehreosen D, hi hreosun I, feallan F, feallað G, fealleþ J, fealle H, fælle K, hie gefeælled E^{3} (*LM*)
in	in A, on BCDE^{3}FGHIJ
idipsum*	ðæt ilce *AB,* þæt ylce C, þæt selfe D, þæt sylfe F*I,* þæt selue *H,* þet selfe E^{3}, þæt sylfe ł on þæt ilce *J,* hi sylfe ł on þæt ylce G* (*KM*)

ED: captio (G)] capt*io Rosier.* gegripen (G)] gegr[ ] G. adp̄hendat (E)] adprehendat *Harsley.* laqueum (D)] laque[o] *Roeder.* íncidant (C)] incidant *Wildhagen.* idipso (A)] id ipso *Kuhn.* idipsum (E)] id ipsum *Harsley.*

OE: Cumo (E^{3})] *orig.* Cumon: n *eras.* hem (E^{3})] *orig.* him: i *altered to* e. grin (E^{3})]

orig. gegrino: ge *and* o *eras.: see* grino *below.* þet ($E^{3/x}$)] et *by corr., eras.* e *visible 1–2 letter spaces after word.* hi ne gecnawaþ (E^{x})] *on eras.* ⁊ (E^{x})] *on eras.* gegripennis (E^{x})] *on eras.* gegripen (G)] gegrípen[ ] (?). þare þæ ($E^{3/x}$)] þare *added by corr. in left margin.* gegripe (H)] *eras. after final* e, *perhaps from Lat. line below.* gegripæ (E^{3})] hie ge *eras. before word,* geg *in darker ink,* :n *eras. after word.* grin (K)] *letter* (ł?) *eras. after word* (*note lemma*). grino (E^{3})] *eras.* (*2 letters*) *before word* (g *or* ge?), g *retraced in darker ink.* ongefeallyn (C)] *2nd* e *interl. in red* (*by corr.?*). hi sylfe ł on þæt ylce (G)] ł on þæt ylce *added in diff.* (?) *hand.*

LTg: Ueniat] Veniat BCDEGHIJL, K: a *on eras. by corr.* illis] L: s *crossed through by corr.: see GAg.* ignorant] L: *2nd* n *underlined by corr. to signal deletion: see GAg;* ignórant CM. quam] AK: a *on eras. by corr.,* M: a *on eras.;* quem C. occultauerunt] L: *underlined to signal deletion,* abscondit *added interl. by corr.: see GAg.* adprehendat] adpraehendat AM; apprehendat DIJ, H: *1st* p *on eras.,* C: *orig.* adprehendat: d *deleted by subscript dot and* p *added interl.;* adp̄hendat EF; aprehendat K. et (*2nd*)] M: *orig. om., added by corr.; eras.* E; *om.* ABCD: *cf. Weber MSS* MS. laqueum] D: *orig.* laqueo: o *altered to* u *with macron added above,* K: ū *on eras. by corr.;* laquevm M: *orig.* laqueo: v̄ *interl.;* laqueo ABC: *cf. Weber MSS* βε moz, *see GAg.* incidant] M: *orig.* incedant: e *crossed through and* i *added interl.,* L: cadat *added interl. by corr.: see GAg;* íncidant C. idipsum] M: ū *followed by eras.;* idipso AB: *cf. Weber MS* δ; ipsum IJ, HK: ū *on eras.: cf. Weber MSS* γεζη med.

LTu: Ueniat] Veniat ζινξ. laqueus] β: *orig.* laqueos: u *added interl. above* o *by corr.* quam] quem β. adprehendat] apprehendat εζιλπρτ*τφ; adprę̨hendat ν; appraehendat ου; appræhendat χ; adpraehendat ψ. et (*2nd*)] *om.* β. laqueum] laqueo βς: *cf. Weber MSS* βε moz. incidant] β: *orig.* incedant: i *added interl. above* e *by corr.* idipsum] ipsum ζλξοπρτυφχψ, σ: ū *interl.*

GAg: illis] illi FGHIJK, L: *see LTg.* ignorant] ignorat FGHIJK, L: *see LTg.* occultauerunt] abscondit FGHIJK, L: *see LTg.* eos] eum FGHIJK. laqueum] laqueo G, ABC: *see LTg; for* DKM *see LTg.* incidant] cadat FGIJK, H: *orig.* cadet: e *altered to* a, L: *see LTg.* idipsum] ipso FG.

GAu: illis] illi δεζθιλμξοπρστυφχψ. ignorant] ignorat δεζθιρσ. occultauerunt] abscondit δεθιλμξοπρστυφχψ. adprehendat] conp̄hendat θ. eos] eum δεζθιλμξοπρστυφχψ. laqueum] laqueo θ. incidant] cadat δεζθιλμξοπρστυφψ. idipsum] ipso δεθιμ.

9

Anima	I sawul A, sawl BCD*G***H*I, sawla F, sawle J, sawel K, Soðlice E^{3}
autem	I soðlice ABCFG, soþlice J, min E^{3}
mea	I min ABDFGHIJK, mine C, sæwle E^{3}*

exultabit gefið *A,* gefihð *B,* gefeoð C, blissode *D*E^{x}*FG*H*K, geblissað I, upahefþ J (*M*)
in in A, on BCDE^{x}*FGHIJ
domino dryhtne AB, drihtne CDE^{x}*FI, drihtene H, drih̄t G, drih̄ J
et* ⁊ ABCDHIJK
delectabitur bið gelustfullað A, bið gelustfullad B, bið gelustfullud C, bið gelustfullod DGHJ, bið gelusfullod F*, heo gelustfullað I, lustfulleð E$^{3/x}$*, lustfullude K
super ofer ABDE^{3}FGHI*JK, ofyr C
salutare* | haelu A, hæle CK, hælo BDFGHJ, halwendan I, his E^{3} (*M*)
eius* | his ABDFGHJK, hys C, hire I, helo E^{3} (*M*)

ED: [ ]nima (GH)] Anima *Rosier, Campbell.* exultauit (B)] exultabit *Brenner.* exultabit (D)] exulta[u]it *Roeder.* domino (G)] domino *et Rosier.* bið gelusfullod (F)] bið gelusfufullod *Kimmens.* ofer (I)] ofor *Lindelöf.*

OE: sawl (G)] *top of* s *slightly cropped.* sæwle (E^{3})] *gloss eras. after word.* blissode (E^{x})] *on eras.,* þy *eras. before word.* on (E^{x})] *on eras.* drihtne (E^{x})] *on eras.* bið gelusfullod (F)] *orig.* bið gelusfufullod (?): f *and left leg of* u (?) *eras. after* s. lustfulleð (E$^{3/x}$)] full *retraced in darker ink,* eð *on eras. by corr.* ofer (I)] *orig.* ofor: *cross-stroke added by corr. through 2nd* o *to form* e.

LTg: Anima] [ ]nima G, H: *fragment of initial* A *visible.* exultabit] AD: b *on eras.,* H: b *altered from another letter,* M: *orig.* exultâuit: *2nd* u *deleted,* b *interl.;* exultauit B. salutare] M: *eras. above* e *over which is written light* 'x' *in brown ink.* eius] M: *orig.* eus: i *interl. by main hand followed by light* 'x' *in red ink* (*to mark error?*).

LTu: exultabit] exultauit βς. et] *interl.* βζσχ. delectabitur] dilectabitur ϑ.

GAg: et] *om.* FG. salutare] salutari FGHIJK. eius] suo FGHIJ; súo K.

GAu: et] *om.* δμοπρψ. salutare] salutari δεζϑι. eius] suo δεζϑιλμξοπρστυφχψ.

10
Omnia all A, ealle BCDFGHIJK, Eælle E^{3}
ossa | ban ABCDFGHIJK, mine E^{3}
mea | min A, mine BCFGIJK, bǽn E^{3}
dicent cweodað A, cweoðað B, cweðað CFH, cweþað DK, cweþæð E^{3}, cweðaþ G*IJ
domine drihten E^{3}FI*, dryht̄ AB, drih̄t CG, drih̄ J
quis hwelc ABD, hwilc E^{3}GHJ, hwylc K, hwylc is *C*F, hwilc is I*
similis | gelic ABCDE^{3}*FGHJK, þin I
tibi* | ðe ABF, þe CDE^{3}JK, þin G, gelica I
eripiens genergende A, g̲e̲nergynde C, generigende B*FJ,* neriende D*H,* nerigende *G*E^{3}*, nerigend *K,* alesende *I* (*L*)

inopem	weðlan A, wædlan BJK, on wædlon C*, þane wædlan I*, unspedigne DE[x]*FG*H*M[2]
de	of ABCDE[3]FGHIJK
manu	honda AB, handa CDFGHJK, hænde E[3], anwealde I
fortioris*	strongran A*BC, strengran DE[3/x]*FGHJ, strengra I, strangra K (*LM*)
eius	his AB*C*DE[x]*FHIJ*K*, h[ ] G
egenum	weðlan A, wædlan BCJ, wedlæn ł elþeodigne E[3/x]*, elþeodigne D, ælðeodigne F*G*, ælþeodigne H, þane wreccan I (*M*)
et	⁊ ABCE[3]*FGHIJ
pauperem	ðearfan *A*F, þearfan BCDGJ, þeærfæn E[3], þearfan ł H, þone ðearfan I* (*K*)
a	from A*E[3]*, from B, fram CDFHJ, fram GI
rapientibus*	❘ ðæm reafiendum A, ðæm reafiendum B, þam reafgyndan C, þam reafigendum J, reafiendum D, reafigendum FGH, him E[3], rypendum ł bereafiendum I*
eum	❘ hine ADFGHIJ, him BC, reafiendum E[x]*

ED: ínopem (H)] inopem *Campbell.* eius (G)] ei*us Rosier.* h[ ] (G)] *no gloss Rosier.* þearfan (C)] pearfan *Wildhagen.* á (E)] a *Harsley.*

OE: cweðaþ (G)] *orig.* cweðan: n *altered to* þ. drihten (I)] o *written before word.* hwilc is (I)] s. est *written in right margin.* gelic (E[3])] *eras. before and after word.* nerigende (E[3])] d *on eras. by main hand.* on wædlon (C)] on *eras. but visible.* þane wædlan (I)] w *on eras.* (?). unspedigne (E[x])] *on eras.* strongran (A)] *orig.* stronges: *deleting dot below* e *and to right of* s, ran *interl. by glossator.* strengran (E[3/x])] *eras. before word,* ran *on eras. by corr.* his (E[x])] *eras. after word.* wedlæn ł elþeodigne (E[3/x])] ł elþeodigne *added by corr.* ⁊ (E[3])] *eras. after word: 1st letter is* þ. þone ðearfan (I)] ne *interl.* rypendum ł bereafiendum (I)] ł be *on eras.* (?). reafiendum (E[x])] *on eras.*

LTg: quis] C: *orig.* qui: s *added by corr.* eripiens] L: E *addd above initial* e *by corr.;* Eripiens FGHIJK. inopem] ínopem H. fortioris] L: is *crossed through by corr.,* um *added interl.: see GAg;* fortiôris M. eius] C: *eras. before word;* eíus K. egenum] egênum M; aegenum G. pauperem] A: *otiose dot between 2nd and 3rd leg of* m, K: ē *on eras. by main hand.* a] á E.

LTu: tibi] β: *final* i *interl.* eripiens] Eripiens δεζϑιμξοπρστυφχψ. inopem] inopum ς. pauperem] β: *orig.* pauperum: *2nd* u *deleted,* e *interl. by corr.*

GAg: tibi] tui FGHIK. fortioris] fortiorum FGHIJK, L: *see LTg.* rapientibus] diripientibus FGHIJK.

GAu: tibi] tui δεζιλμξπρστυφχψ. fortioris] fortiorum δεζιλμξοπρστυφχψ. rapientibus] diripientibus δεζιλμξοπρστυφχψ; deripientibus ϑ: *1st* e *interl.*

11

Exsurgentes* arisende *A*BDFGHIJ, arisynde *C*, Ærisende E^{3}* (*LM*)
testes cyðeras ABG, cyðyras C, cyþeras J, cyþras DE^{x}*, cyðras FH, gewitan ł cyþeras I*
iniqui unrehte A, unryhte B, unrihte CIJ, unryhtwise DE^{x}*, unrihtwise F*G*H
quae ða A*B*, þe *C*, þa *D*E^{x}**GH*, ða *F*, þa þing þe I* (*JKL*)
ignorabam ic nysse AB, ic nyste CDE^{x}*FGHI, ic nesse J (*K*)
interrogabant frugnon AB, frunon C, on frinon J, hy ahsodon D, hy acsodon E^{x}, hi ahsodon F, hi ahsedon H, hi axsodan K, axodon I, [ ]odon G*
me mec A, me BCE^{x}*FGHJK

ED: Exurgentes (A)] Exsurgentes *Kuhn*. Exurgentes (C)] Ex[s]urgentes *Wildhagen*. [ ]rgentes (G)] *Sur*gentes *Rosier*. ini[ ]ui (G)] ini*qu*i *Rosier*. quæ (D)] quae *Roeder*. quę (E)] quae *Harsley*. [ ]odon (G)] *no gloss Rosier*.

OE: Ærisende (E^{3})] *eras. (20 mm) after word.* cyþras (E^{x})] *on eras.* gewitan ł cyþeras (I)] ł cyþeras *written in right margin.* unryhtwise (E^{x})] *on eras.* þa (E^{x})] *on eras.* þa þing þe (I)] *orig.* þa þinc þe: c *altered to* g. ic nyste (E^{x})] *on eras.* hy acsodon (E^{x})] *on eras.* [ ]odon (G)] *descender visible before 1st* o. me (E^{x})] *on eras.*

LTg: Exsurgentes] M: *1st* s *on eras.;* Exurgentes A: *orig.* Exsurgentes: *deleting dot above 1st* s, C: s *eras. after* x; Surgentes L: *orig.* Exurgentes: Ex *underlined to signal deletion,* S *added interl. by corr.: see GAg.* iniqui] ini[ ]ui G. quae] quæ BD; quę CEFGHL; que JK. ignorabam] K: *right leg of* m *on eras., followed by eras.*

LTu: Exsurgentes] EXsurgentes β; Exurgentes τ*τ. quae] quę βεινξϱςφ; que στ; q̄ ϑτ*; quæ χ. ignorabam] ignorabant β: *2nd* a *altered from another letter,* nt *interl. by corr.*

GAg: Exsurgentes] Surgentes FIJK, L: *see LTg;* [ ]rgentes G; [ ]urgentes H: S *lost.*

GAu: Exsurgentes] Surgentes δεζϑιλμξοπϱσυχψ.

12

Et* ⁊ *ABC*E^{x}* (*DLM*)
retribuebant geedleanedun A, geedleanodon B*J*, geedleanydon C, aguldon DE^{3}*FGH*, hi aguldon *I*, hi aguldan *K* (*L*)
mihi me AB*C*DE^{x}*FGHIJ*K*
mala yfel ABIJK, yfyl C, yfelu DE^{x}*FG, yuelu H
pro fore ABDH, for CE^{x}*FGIJK
bonis godum ABFI, godu<u>m</u> J, gode CE^{x}*H, god K, go[ ] G
et* ⁊ $ABCE^{x}$* (*LM*)
sterilitatem unbeorednisse *A*, unberendnysse C, unwæstmbærnesse *B*J, wæstmbærnysse I*, stedignisse DE^{x}*, stedignysse F,

	stedignesse G*H*, stedinese K
animae	sawle A*BCDE*^{x}**FGHIJK* (*LM*)
meae	minre A*BCDE*^{x}*F*H*IK, mine *GJ* (*L*)

ED: Retribuębant (G)] Retribuebant *Rosier.* go[ ] (G)] *no gloss Rosier.* wæstmbærnysse (I)] wæstbærnysse *Lindelöf* (*but correct in appendix, p. 323*). meæ (D)] meae *Roeder.* meę (E)] meae *Harsley.*

OE: ⁊ (E^{x})] *on eras.* me (E^{x})] *on eras.* yfelu (E^{x})] *on eras.* for (E^{x})] *on eras.* gode (E^{x})] *on eras.* ⁊ (E^{x})] *on eras.* wæstmbærnysse (I)] *translating* insterilitatem. stedignisse (E^{x})] *on eras.* sawle (E^{x})] *on eras.* minre (E^{x})] *on eras.*

LTg: Et] et ABCDEM, L: *underlined by corr. to signal deletion: see GAg.* retribuebant] retribvebant E; Retribuebant FHIJK, L: R *added interl. by corr. above* r; Retribuębant G. mihi] michi EK, C: *orig.* mihi: c *added interl. by corr.* et] M: *added interl. by corr.,* L: *underlined by corr. to signal deletion: see GAg.* sterilitatem] H: *orig.* sterelitatem: *2nd* e *altered to* i; sterelitatem AB: *cf. Weber MSS* KRQ^{2} ε moz^{x}. animae] animæ BL; animę CDFGHM; anime EJK. meae] meæ BDL; meę EGH.

LTu: Et] *om.* β; et νςτ*. retribuebant] Retribuebant δεζϑλξοπστυφχψ. mihi] michi ιςτ*φ, πϱχ: c *interl.;* m^{1} λστ. sterilitatem] sterelitatem βε. animae] anime δζπσςτ*τ; animę ειλνξφ; animæ ϑ. meae] meę ειλνξςφ; meæ ϑχ; mee στ*τ.

GAg: Et] *om.* FGHIJK, L: *see LTg.* et] *om.* FGHIJK, L: *see LTg.*

GAu: Et] *om.* δεζϑιλμξοπϱστυφχψ. et] *om.* δεζϑιλμξοϱστυχψ.

13

Ego	ic ABCFGIJK, Ic E^{3}
autem	soðlice ABC*E*^{3}FGI, soþlice J, witodlice K
dum*	ðonne A, þonne BF, þonne CDE^{3}*HJK, þonne G, ða þa I
mihi	me AB*CE*^{3}FGIJK
molesti	hefic AC, hefige BFGHJKM^{2}, hefige D, wiðertyme ł hefigtyme I*, unyþgiende E^{3}
essent	werun A, wæren BD, wæron CFJ, weron E^{3}, wæran HK, wæ[ ]n *G**, hi wærun I
induebam*	ic gegerede AB, ic gegyryde C, gegirede J, ic scrydde DE$^{3/x}$*FGK, ic scridde H, wæs ymbscryd I* (*L*)
me*	mec A, me BCE^{x}
cilicium*	mid heran *A,* mid hæran *B*CFI*, of hæran *D*G, of hæron H, of heron *E*^{3}, hæran JK (*LM*)
et*	⁊ ABCDE^{3} (*L*)
humiliabam	ic geeaðmodade A, ic geeaðmodode B, geeadmodude C, ic geadmodode *J,* ic eaðmedde D*GH,* ic geeaðmette *FI,* ic ædmedde *K,* ic eæðmodde E^{3}*

in		in A, on BDE^{3}FGHIJK, o C
ieiunio		festenne A, fæstenne BH, fæstynne C, fæstene DFGI*K*, festenum E^{3}, westene J
animam	I	sawle ABCDFGHIJ, sauwle K, mine E^{3}
meam	I	mine ABCDFGHIJK, sæwle E^{3}
et		⁊ ABCE^{3}FGHIJK
oratio	I	gebed ABCDFGHK, gebeda J, min E^{3}I
mea	I	min ABCFGHK, mine J, gebed E^{3}I
in		in A, on BCDE^{3}FGHIJK
sinu*		seate A, sceate B, bearme *C**J, bearm DH, bearn G, bosm E^{x}*, bosme FIK (*LM*)
meo*		minum AB*C*G, minum *D*E^{x}*FH*I*J, minan K (*LM*)
conuertebatur*		sie forcerred *A*, sie forcirred *B*, se forcyrryd *C*, sy gecyrred *D*FGH, si gecirred E$^{3/x}$*, ⁊ byð gecyrred ł gecyrre I*, sy gecirred ł gehwirfed J, gecyrraþ K (*LM*)

ED: dum (D)] cum *Roeder.* þonne (G)] þonne *Rosier.* ða þa (I)] ðaþa *Lindelöf.* esse[ ]t (G)] essent *Rosier.* wæ[ ]n (G)] wær[ ]n *Rosier.* ic scrydde (G)] ic scyrdde *Rosier.* (H)umiliabam (G)] Humiliabam *Rosier.* [ ]umiliabam (H)] Humiliabam *Campbell.*

OE: þonne (E^{3})] *eras. before word.* wiðertyme ł hefigtyme (I)] ł hefigtyme *written above* wiðertyme. wæ[ ]n (G)] *descender visible after* æ. ic scrydde (E$^{3/x}$)] scrydde *on eras. by corr., letter* (y?) *eras. after* c. wæs ymbscryd (I)] *eras.* (on?) *before* wæs. mid hæran (I)] an *on eras.* ic eæðmodde (E^{3})] *eras.* (*1–2 letters*) *after* ic, o *altered by corr. from another letter, 2nd* d *altered from* e, *final* e *added.* bearme (C)] *some red ink after final* e, *probably otiose.* bosm (E^{x})] *on eras.* minum (E^{x})] *on eras.* si gecirred (E$^{3/x}$)] si *on eras. by corr.* ⁊ byð gecyrred ł gecyrre (I)] ł gecyrre *written in right margin, with* y *altered from* i (?).

LTg: autem] avtem E. mihi] michi E, C: *orig.* mihi: c *interl. by corr.* essent] esse[ ]t G. induebam] L: m *underlined to signal deletion,* r *added interl. by corr.: see GAg.* cilicium] cilicio ABCDELM: *cf. Weber MSS* Q^{2}U^{2}Xε moz, *see GAg.* et (*1st*)] L: *underlined to signal deletion: see GAg.* humiliabam] Humiliabam FIJK; (H)umiliabam G: *ascender of* H *lost;* [ ]umiliabam H: *initial* H *lost.* ieiunio] K: ie *interl. by main hand in darker ink.* sinu] sinum CL; sinum M: *macron added by corr.* (?): *cf. Weber MSS* MTα med: *see GAg.* meo] I: o *partly on eras., altered from* u; meum CL; mevm D: *orig.* meo: o *deleted by subscript dot and* v̄ *added interl.,* M: *orig.* meo: v̄ *interl.: cf. Weber MSS* MTα med, *see GAg.* conuertebatur] conuertetur BCDL, A: *orig.* conuertitur: i *altered to* e; conuertêtur M: *cf. Weber MSS* ST^{2}*γδζη* med, *see GAg.*

LTu: Ego] EGo β. mihi] michi ιλςτ*τφ, χ: c *interl.;* m^{1} σ. cilicium] cilicio βνς: *cf. Weber MSS* Q^{2}U^{2}Xε moz, *see GAu.* et (*1st*)] Et ϑ. humiliabam] Humiliabam δεζιλμξοπρστυφχψ. sinu] sinum ν: *cf. Weber MSS* MTα med, *see GAu.* meo] meum ν: *cf. Weber MSS* MTα med, *see GAu.* conuertebatur] confertetur β; conuertetur νςτ*: *cf. Weber MSS* ST^{2}*γδζη* med, *see GAu.*

GAg: dum] cum FGHIJK. induebam] induebar FGHIJK, L: *see LTg.* me] *om.* FGHIJK. cilicium] cilicio FGHIJK, ABCDELM: *see LTg.* et (*1st*)] *om.* FGHIJK, L: *see LTg.* sinu] sinum FG, H: m *on eras.*, K: *macron above* u *by corr.*, CLM: *see LTg.* meo] meum FGL, H: um *on eras.*, K: ū *by corr.*, CL: *see LTg; for* DM *see LTg.* conuertebatur] conuertetur FGHIJK, ABCDL: *see LTg; for* M *see LTg.*

GAu: dum] cum δεζϑιλμξυπρστυφχψ. induebam] induebar δεζϑιλμξοπρστυχψ. me] *om.* δεζϑλμξορστυχψ. cilicium] cilicio δεζϑιλμξορστυφχψ, βνς: *see LTu.* et (*1st*)] *om.* δεζιλξρστυχψ. sinu] τ: ł nū *interl.;* sinum εϑιξοχ, ν: *see LTu.* meo] τ: ł ū *interl.;* meum εϑιξ, ν: *see LTu;* mevm ο. conuertebatur] conuertetur δεζϑιλμξοπρστυφχψ, νςτ*: *see LTu.*

14

Sicut* — swe A, swa BCJ, swa swa DFGHI, Swæ suæ $E^{3/x}$*, ealswa K (*L*)

proximum — ðone nestan A, þone nihstan B, þone nehstan *C,* þæm neaxtan I, þone nihtan J, niextæn E^{3}*, nehstan F, gesybne *D,* gesibbe GH, gesibne K (*LM*)

⟨et⟩ — ⁊ *CE³* (*DLM*)

sicut* — swe A, swa BCJ, swæ E^{3}, swa swa DFG, ⁊ swa swa I, ⁊ swa K (*L*)

fratrem | broður A, broðor BCD*F*G, broþor H, broðra J, broðer K, urne E^{3}, urum I

nostrum | urne ABDK, ure CFGHJ, broþur E^{3}, breþer I

ita* — swe A, swa BCDGHIJK, swá F, swæ E^{3}

conplacebam — ic gelicie A, ic gelicige CG, gelicige B*J,* ic gelicode D, ic gelicode F*HK,* ic licode $E^{3/x}$*, ic blissode ł ic gelicode *I,* quemde M*

tamquam* — swe swe A, swa swa B*CDE*ˣFGHIJK (*L*)

lugens — hiofende A, heofende BDH*JK,* heofiynde C, heofendæ E^{3}*, heofigende FG, heofiende ł wepende I

et — ⁊ ABCFGHIJK

contristatus — geunrotsad A, geunrotsod BD*E³**FHJK, geunrotsvde C, ungerotsod G, ungerotsod ł gedrefed I

ita* — swe A, swa BCDFGHIJK, swæ E^{3} (*L*)

humiliabar — ic wes geeaðmodad A, ic wæs geeaðmodod *B,* ic wæs geeaðmodvd C, ic wæs geeadmeded J, ic geeaðmedde DFH, ic geeæðmedde $E^{3/x}$*, eadmette G, ic me geeadmette ł ic wæs geeadmet I*, ic geædmede K (*M*)

ED: tanquam (C)] ta[m]quam *Wildhagen.* swa swa (GI) (*1st*)] swaswa *Rosier, Lindelöf.* swa swa (G) (*2nd*)] swaswa *Rosier.* ⁊ swa swa (I)] ⁊ swaswa *Lindelöf.* swa swa (GI) (*3rd*)] swaswa *Rosier, Lindelöf.* swa swa (J)] swaswa *Oess.*

OE: Swæ suæ (E$^{3/x}$)] suæ *on eras. by corr.* niextæn (E^{3})] i *in darker ink.* ic licode (E$^{3/x}$)] ode *on eras. by corr.* quemde (M)] *written in red in right margin.* heofendæ (E^{3})] ⁊ *eras. after word.* geunrotsod (E^{3})] *letter* (⁊?) *eras. before word* (*eras.* ⁊ *after* heofendæ *is on line above*), g *retouched in darker ink.* ic geeæðmedde (E$^{3/x}$)] *eras. after* ic, ð *altered from another letter by main hand, 1st* d *on eras.*, de *added on eras. by corr.* ic me geeadmette ł ic wæs geeadmet (I)] ł ic wæs geeadmet *written in left margin.*

LTg: Sicut] L: Quasi *added by corr. below word: see GAg.* proximum] proximum et CDE, M: et *interl. by corr.*, L: et *underlined by corr. to signal deletion: cf. Weber MSS* εζη^{2} moz^{x}. sicut] L: quasi *added by corr. below word: see GAg.* fratrem] F: e *on eras.* conplacebam] complacebam HI; complacebam J: *orig.* conplacebam: n *eras.*, K: *letter eras. after* ā, *macron added by corr.* tamquam] L: *underlined to signal deletion,* quasi *added interl. by corr.: see GAg;* tanquam E, C: *orig.* tamquam: *left leg of 1st* m *eras. to form* n. lugens] K: *letter eras. after* g; lugiens J. contristatus] E: tus *on eras.* ita (*2nd*)] L: sic *added interl. by corr.: see GAg.* humiliabar] humiliabor BM.

LTu: proximum] proximum et ςτ*: *cf. Weber MSS* εζη^{2} moz^{x}. conplacebam] β: *orig.* conplaceuam: b *interl. above* u *by corr.;* complacebam ι; cōplacebam φ. tamquam] tanquam τ*.

GAg: Sicut] Quasi FGHIJK, L: *see LTg.* sicut] quasi FGHIJK, L: *see LTg.* ita (*1st*)] sic FGHIJK. tamquam] quasi FGHIJK, L: *see LTg.* ita (*2nd*)] sic FGHIJ, L: *see LTg;* síc K.

GAu: Sicut] Quasi δεζϑιλμξοπρστυφχψ. sicut] quasi δεζϑιλμξοπρστυφχψ. ita (*1st*)] sic δεζϑιλμξοπρστυφχψ. tamquam] quasi δεζϑιλμξοπρστυφχψ. ita (*2nd*)] sic δεζϑιλμξοπρστυφχψ.

15

(Et)*	⁊ FGIJK
Aduersum	wið AB, wiþ ł ongean *J,* ongen C, ongean DE^{x}**GH,* ongen *K,* agen *I,* togeanes *F* (*L*)
me	me ABCDE^{3}FGHIJK
laetati	geblissade A, geblissode *BJ,* geblissude *C,* geblissodan *K,* hy blissodon *DE$^{3/x}$*GH,* híg blissodon *F,* ⁊ hig blissodon *I** (*L*)
sunt	werun A, wæron BJ, synd GK
et	⁊ AB*E*^{3}FGHIJK (*CL*)
conuenerunt	tosomne bicwomun A, tosomne becomon B*C*FG, tosomne becomon *D,* tosomne becomen *E^{x}*,* tosomne becoman HK, tosomne comon J, gesamnodon hi ł ⁊ hi samod comon I (*L*)

⟨et⟩	⁊ *CE^{3}* (*DL*)
congregauerunt*	gesomnadon A, gesomnodon BC, gesomnode J, hy gegæderedon DE^{x}*, gegaderode FG, gegadorede I, gegæderede K (*L*)
(sunt)*	synd FGJK, synt I
in*	in A, on BCDE^{3}, ofer FGJK, ofor I (*L*)
me	mec A, me BCDE^{3}FGJK
flagella	ðrea AB, þreat J, swingylla C, swingella DH, swyngla F, swingela GK, swingla I, swipæn ł swyngla E$^{3/x}$*
et	⁊ ABCE^{x}*FGIJK
ignorauerunt*	hie hit nyston AB, hi hyt nyston C, ic hit niste J, hy nyston DE^{x}*, hi nyston K, ic nyste FI, ic nyste ł ic ne gecneow G (*L*)

ED: ongean (E)] Ongean *Harsley.* lętati (EI)] laetati *Harsley, Lindelöf.*

OE: ongean (E^{x})] *on eras.* hy blissodon (E$^{3/x}$)] hy *added by corr. in left margin,* odon *on eras. by corr.* ⁊ hig blissodon (I)] blissodon *on eras.* tosomne becomen (E^{x})] *on eras.* hy gegæderedon (E^{x})] *on eras.* swipæn ł swyngla (E$^{3/x}$)] *eras. before* swipæn, ngla *on eras. by corr.* ⁊ (E^{x}) (*3rd*)] *on eras.* hy nyston (E^{x})] *on eras.*

LTg: Aduersum] aduersum FGHIJK, L: *eras. after word.* laetati] lætati BK; lętati CDEFGIL; letati HJ. et (*1st*)] E: *added by corr.; om.* CL. conuenerunt] conuenerunt et CDEL. congregauerunt] L: ue *underlined to signal deletion,* ta *added interl. after* a *by corr.,* s *added interl. above 2nd* r: *see GAg.* in] L: super *added interl. by corr.: see GAg.* ignorauerunt] L: erunt *underlined to signal deletion,* i *added interl. above* u *by corr.: see GAg.*

LTu: Aduersum] aduersum δεζϑιλμξοπστυφχψ. me] mę π. laetati] lętati ειφ; lætati ϑ; letati ξοςτ*τυ. et (*1st*)] *interl.* ε. conuenerunt] conuenerunt et νςτ*.

GAg: Aduersum] Et aduersum FGHIJK. congregauerunt] congregati sunt G, F: *orig.* congregata sunt: *final* a *deleted by subscript dot,* i *interl. by corr.;* congregata sunt IJK, H: *orig.* congregati sunt: i *deleted by subscript dot and* a *added interl.,* L: *see LTg.* in] super FGHIJK, L: *see LTg.* ignorauerunt] ignoraui FGHIJK, L: *see LTg.*

GAu: Aduersum] Et aduersum δεζϑιλμξοπϱστυφχψ. congregauerunt] congregati sunt επψ; congregata sunt δζϑιλμξστυφχ, οϱ̣: *orig.* congregati sunt. in] super δεζϑιλμξπϱστυφχψ. ignorauerunt] ignoraui δεζϑιλμξοπϱστυφχψ.

16

Dissoluti*	tolesde A, toliesde B, tolisede J, tolysyde C, tolysede DK, Tolysede E^{3}, tostencte FGI*, tostencede H (*L*)
sunt	sind AE^{3}*, synd CGHJK, sint B, synt F, hy synd D, hig synt I

nec	ne ABCDE^{x}*F*G*HI*JK
conpuncti	geinbryrde AB*C*, geinbride J, he abryrde DG*H*, hy abryrde *E^{x}**, hi abrydde *K*, hi onbryrde *F*, onbryrde M^{2}, hi ne synt abryrde *I*
sunt*	sind AE^{x}*, synd C, sint B, synt D
temptauerunt	costadon A, costodon B*C*J, hi costodon ł costnodo[ ] I*, hy fandedon DE^{x}*GHM^{2}, hi fandedon F, hi fandodan K
me	mec A, me BCFGIJK
et*	⁊ ABC (*EL*)
deriserunt*	bismeradon A, bismrodon B, bysmrydon C, bysmredon DM^{2}, bismeredon hie E$^{3/x}$*, ⁊ bysmrodon F, hy hypston G, hi tældon ł onscægdon ł hig hyspton I, hig fandodon J (*L*)
(me)*	me FGI
derisu*	mid bismerunge A, mid bismrunge B, of bysmrunge *C*, of hleahtre DE^{x}*, mid hleahtre F, mid leahtre J, mid hospe G, mid bismero ł mid hospe I (*L*)
striderunt*	grymetadon A, grymetodon B, grymytydon ł gurunn C*, hi grymetedon G, hi grimetodon I, hig grennodon J, hy gristbitoton D, hi gristbitoton M^{2}, hy gristbitedon E^{x}*, hi grundon F (*L*)
in*	in A, on BCDE^{x}*, ofer FGJK, ofor ł agen I (*L*)
me	mec A, me BCDE^{x}*FGIJK
dentibus	mid toðum ACFI, mid toðum B, toþum DHJ, toþum E^{3}, toðum G, toþan K
suis	heara A, hira B, heora CDE^{x}FGHIJK

ED: nęc (G)] nec *Rosier.* compuncti (C)] co[m]puncti *Wildhagen.* hi costodon ł costnodo[ ] (I)] hi costodon ł costnodon *Lindelöf.* derisu (C)] d[i]risu *Wildhagen.*

OE: tostencte (I)] *gloss* (?) *eras. before word extending into left margin.* sind (E^{3}) (*1st*)] *eras. after word.* ne (E^{x})] *on eras.* ne (I) (*1st*)] e *on eras.* hy abryrde (E^{x})] *on eras.* sind (E^{x}) (*2nd*)] *on eras.* hi costodon ł costnodo[ ] (I)] *final letter lost due to tight binding.* hy fandedon (E^{x})] *on eras.* bismeredon hie (E$^{3/x}$)] eredon *on eras. by corr.* of hleahtre (E^{x})] *on eras.* grymytydon ł gurunn (C)] ł gurunn *interl. above* tydon *in* grymytydon. hy gristbitedon (E^{x})] *on eras.* on (E^{x})] *on eras.* me (E^{x})] *on eras.*

LTg: Dissoluti] L: ipati *added interl. by corr.: see GAg.* nec] nęc G. conpuncti] compuncti C: *orig.* conpuncti: *1st* n *eras., macron added above* o; compuncti EI, F: *orig.* conpuncti: *1st* n *deleted by subscript dot, macron added above* o, H: *orig.* conpuncti: *middle leg added to 1st* n *to form* m, *eras. after* i, *otiose stroke above* i, K: *letter eras. after* ō, *macron added by corr.* temptauerunt] temtauerunt C: *letter eras. after* a. et] E: *written by corr.* (?). et deriserunt] L: *underlined to signal deletion,* subsunnauerunt me *added interl. by corr.: see GAg.* derisu] C: *orig.* dirisu: *1st* i *altered to* e, L: *underlined to signal deletion,* subsannatione *added interl. by corr.: see GAg.* striderunt] L: frenduerunt *added interl. by corr.: see GAg.* in] L: *underlined to signal deletion,* super *added interl. by corr.: see GAg.*

LTu: conpuncti] compuncti ιτ*τ, ξ: om *interl.;* cōpuncti λφ.

GAg: Dissoluti] Dissipati FGHIJK, L: *see LTg.* sunt (*2nd*)] *om.* FGHIJK. et] *om.* FGHIJK. deriserunt] subsannauerunt me FGHJK, I: e *in* me *on eras.*, L: *see LTg.* derisu] subsannatione FHI, K: *orig.* subsanatione: *macron added above 1st* a *by corr.*, L: *see LTg;* subsanatione GJ. striderunt] frenduerunt FGHI, K: *1st* n (*malformed*) *by corr.*, L: *see LTg;* freduerunt J. in] super FGHIJK, L: *see LTg.*

GAu: Dissoluti] Dissipati δεζθιλμξοπρστυφχψ. sunt (*2nd*)] *om.* δεζθιλμξοπρστυφχψ. et] *om.* δεζιλμξοπρστυφχψ. deriserunt] subsannauerunt me δεζθιλμξοπρστυφψ; sussanauerunt me χ. derisu] subsannatione δεζθιλμξοπρστυφψ; succanatione χ. striderunt] frenduerunt δεζθιλμξοπρστυφχψ. in] super δεζθιλμξοπρστυφχψ.

17

Domine		drihten E^{3}F, dryht̄ AB, driht́ C, driȟ GJ (*I*)
quando		hwonne ABE^{3}, hwanne C, hwænne J, ahwænne F, þonne D, þonne GHIK
respicies		gelocas ðu AB, gelocast þu C, þu gelocast D, þu gelocast HK, þu locast G, locast þu J, forelocæst þu E^{3}, behealts ðu F, þu beseohst I (*M*)
restitue		gesete AB, gesete CFI*K, gesette J, eft gesete DH, eft gesette *G*, þet þu gesette E^{3} (*M*)
animam	|	sawle ABCDFGHIJK, mine E^{3}
meam	|	mine ABCFGHIJK, sæwle E^{3}
a		from A*E*^{3}, from B, fram CDHJ*K*, fram FGI (*M*)
malefactis*	|	yfeldedum A, yfeldædum BD, yfeldædum FG, yfyldædum C, yueldædum H, yfeldæda JK, awyrgednysse I, hioræ E^{3} (*LM*)
eorum	|	heara A, hira B, hyra C, heora DFGHI*JK, yflum dęđum E^{3}
et*		⁊ CE^{3} (*ABLM*)
a		from A, from B*E*^{3}, fram CDHJK, fram FGI (*M*)
leonibus	|	leom AB, leonum CFGH, leonum DJ, leon K, deoflum ł fram leonum I, ænnesse E^{3} (*M*)
unicam		ða angan AB, þa angan CJ, anlican DGHK, ænlican F, anlican ł annysse I*, þæræ leonæ E^{3}
meam		mine ABCDFGHIJK

ED: drihten (E)] Drihten *Harsley.* á (E) (*both*)] a *Harsley.* yueldædum (H)] yuel dædum *Campbell.*

OE: gesete (I)] *eras. before word: scribe possibly began gloss* (*writing* ges), *noted intrusion of* st *ligature from below, then eras. and began again to avoid ligature.* heora (I)] *eras. before word.* anlican ł annysse (I)] anlican *extends into left margin.*

LTg: Domine] I: o *written above word.* respicies] respícies M. restitue] restituę G; restititue M. a (*1st*)] K: *on eras.;* á EM. malefactis] M: *orig.* malifactis: *1st* i *altered to* e, L: i *added interl. above* e *by corr.,* f *altered to* g, nitate *added interl.: see GAg.* et] M: *added by main scribe in smaller hand,* L: *underlined by corr. to signal deletion; om.* AB: *cf. Weber MSS* SKαβγδζη, *see GAg.* a (*2nd*)] á EM. leonibus] M: *orig.* lionibus: *1st* i *altered to* e.

LTu: restitue] restituae ψ; restitues βϑ: *cf. Weber MSS* ε moz^{x}.

GAg: malefactis] malignitate FGHIJK, L: *see LTg.* et] *om.* FGHIJK, AB: *see LTg; for* LM *see LTg.*

GAu: malefactis] malignitate δεζϑιλμξοπϱστυφχψ. et] *om.* δεζϑιλμξοπϱσυφχψ.

18

Confitebor	I	ic ondetto AB, ic andytte C, ic andette DFGHIJK, Ic þe E^{3}
tibi	I	ðe ABF, þe CGJK, andette E^{3}
domine*		drihten E^{3}, dryht̄ AB, driħt C (*L*)
in		in A, on BCDE^{3}FGHIJK
ecclesia		cirican AJ, circan *B,* cyrycean C, haligre gesomninga D, haligre gesomnunga *H,* haligre gesamnunge *G,* halgre somninga *E^{x}*,* gesomnunga K, gelaðunge *FI* (*L*)
magna		micelre ABDE^{x}*GHJ, micylre C, mycelre FK, myclre I*
in		in A, on BCDE^{x}*FGHIJK
populo	I	folce ABCDE^{x}*FGHJK, hrorenum folke ł on swarum folce I*
graui	I	hefigum AE^{x}*FGH, hefigum BDJK, hefygum C
laudabo	I	ic hergu A, ic herge BC, ic herige D, ic herige FGHIJK, ic þe E^{3}
te	I	ðe A*BF*, þe CGHIJK, herige E^{3}

ED: ęcclesia (E)] aecclesia *Harsley.* halgre somninga (E)] halgresomninga *Harsley.*

OE: halgre somninga (E^{x})] *on eras.* micelre (E^{x})] *on eras.* myclre (I)] *orig.* miclre: i *altered to* y. on (E^{x}) (*2nd*)] *on eras.* folce (E^{x})] *on eras.* hrorenum folke ł on swarum folce (I)] ł on swarum folce *written in right margin.* hefigum (E^{x})] *on eras.*

LTg: domine] L: *underlined to signal deletion: see GAg.* ecclesia] æcclæsia B; ęcclesia EFHIL; ęcclesia G: *cross-stroke through* l *wanting.* te] té B.

LTu: ecclesia] ęcclesia ειvφχ; æclesia λ, ϑ: i *interl.;* aeclessia πϱυ. laudabo] β: *orig.* ladabo: u *interl. by corr.*

GAg: domine] *om.* FGHIJK, L: *see LTg.*

GAu: domine] *om.* δεζλμξϱυτχψ.

19

Ut*	ðæt *AB*, þæt *CD*, þet $E^{3/x}$* (*L*)
non	ne *A*BC*G*, na D$E^{3/x}$**FJK*, þæt *I* (*H*)
insultent*	bismcrien A, bismrien B, bysmriyn C, bysmrigen D, bysmerigen E^{x}*, oferbismrigan F, oferblissiað G, oferblissian K, ofer ne blissiun I, ofergefean J (*LM*)
in*	in A, on BCDE^{3} (*L*)
me*	mec A, me B*CDE*^{3}FGIJK (*L*)
⟨inimici⟩	fynd *C* (*LM*)
⟨mei⟩	mine *C* (*LM*)
qui	ða ðe AB, þa þe CE^{x}*FGHIJ, þa ðe DK
aduersantur	wiðerbrociað AB, wiðerbrociað C, wiðerbrecaþ J, wiþerweardiað DE^{x}*F, wiðerwerdiað H, wiðerweardi[ ]ð *G**, wiðewyrddiað K, wiðriað I
mihi	me AB*CDE*^{x}*F*GH*IJ*K*
inique	unrehtlice A, unryhtlice BD, unrihtlice C*E*^{x}**G*HIJ, on unriht F, unrihtte K
qui	ða ðe ABI, þa þe CG, þa ðe FJ, þa DE^{x}*HK
oderunt	fiað A, feoð C, feogað B, hatedon DE^{x}*GH, hatudon F, hatodun I, hatodon JK
me	me ABCE^{x}*FGHIJK
gratis	bi ungewyrhtum A, be ungewyrhtum C, butan gewyrhtum B, buton gewyrhtum G, buton gewirhtum J, buton geearnungum F, butan geearnungum I, orceapungum DH, orceawunga K*
et	⁊ ABCE^{x}*FGH*I*JK
annuebant*	becnadon A, beacnodon B, bycnodon C, bycnedon DE^{x}*, becnodon F, bicnedon GH, bicnodon J, hig beacniað I, bycnunga K (*L*)
oculis	mid egum AE^{x}*, mid eagum BCDH, mid eagum I, mid eagon J, eagan F, eagon G, egan K

ED: oferbismrigan (F)] ofer bismrigan *Kimmens.* wiðerweardi[ ]ð (G)] wiðerweardiað *Rosier.* iniquę (E)] iniquae *Harsley.* be ungewyrhtum (C)] be ungewyrhtu*m Wildhagen.*

OE: þet ($E^{3/x}$)] þ *on eras. by corr.* na ($E^{3/x}$)] *orig.* ne: e *altered to* a *by corr.* bysmerigen (E^{x})] *on eras.* þa þe (E^{x})] *on eras., eras. (32 mm) before gloss.* wiþerweardiað (E^{x})] *on eras.* wiðerweardi[ ]ð (G)] *letter after 2nd* i *lost due to hole.* me (E^{x}) (*2nd*)] *on eras.* unrihtlice (E^{x})] *on eras.* þa (E^{x})] *on eras.* hatedon (E^{x})] *on eras.* me (E^{x}) (*3rd*)] *on eras.* orceawunga (K)] s *eras. before word.* ⁊ (E^{x})] *on eras.* bycnedon (E^{x})] *on eras.* mid egum (E^{x})] *on eras.*

LTg: Ut] Vt ABCDE, L: *underlined by corr. to signal deletion: see GAg.* non] A: on *interl. by corr.,* L: *initial* n *altered to* N *by corr.;* Non FGHIJK. insultent] M: ns *on eras.,* L: *underlined by corr. to signal deletion,* supergaudeant *added interl. by corr.: see GAg.* in] L: *underlined by corr. to signal deletion: see GAg.* me (*1st*)] E: *orig.* me inimici mei: inimici mei *deleted by underdotting;* me inimici mei C, M: inimici mei *added by corr. in right margin,* L: me *underlined to signal deletion,* michi *added interl. by corr.,* inimici mei *crossed through* (*see Hebr. Ps 35.19*): *see GAg.* aduersantur mihi] G: *written 3 lines above and signaled for inclusion by* ħ. mihi] michi EHK, C: *orig.* mihi: c *added interl. by corr.* inique] iniquę EG. et] I: *crude* ł *or cross written in left margin.* annuebant] L: eb *underlined to signal deletion,* u *added above 2nd* a *by corr.: see GAg.*

LTu: Ut] Vt ν. non] Non δεζϑιλμξοπϱστυφψ. me] ν: *orig.* me inimici mei: inimici mei *crossed through;* me inimici mei β. mihi] michi ιλϛτ*τ, ϱχ: c *interl.;* m^{1} σφ. inique] iniquę ιξ; iniqui ϑ. oderunt] hoderunt ς. annuebant] annueuant β: *orig.* annuebant: b *crossed through,* u *interl. by corr.*

GAg: Ut] *om.* FGHIJK, L: *see LTg.* insultent] supergaudeant FGHIJK, L: *see LTg.* in] *om.* FGHIJK, L: *see LTg.* me (*1st*)] mihi FGHIJK; *for* L *see LTg.* annuebant] annuunt FGHIJK, L: *see LTg.*

GAu: Ut] *om.* δεζϑιλμξοπϱστυφχψ. insultent] supergaudeant δεζιλμξοπϱστυφχψ; supergaudiant ϑ. in] *om.* δεζϑιλοπϱσυχψ. me (*1st*)] mihi δεζϑουψ; michi ιτ, πϱχ: c *interl.;* m^{1} λξσφ. annuebant] annuunt δεζιλμξοπϱστυφχψ; annunt ϑ.

20

Quoniam	forðon ABJ, forþon C, Forðæn þe E^{3}, forðam ðe F, forþan þe I, forþam G
mihi	me AB*C*D*E*^{3}FGH*J*K
quidem	efne ABCJ, witodlice DE^{3}GHK, witedlice F, soðlice I
pacifice	sibsumlice ABK, sibsumlice J, sybsumlice C, gesybsumlice D, gesybsumlice F, gesibsumlice E^{3}GI, gesibsumlice H (*M*)
loquebantur	spreocað A, sprecað B, hi sprecaþ J, spræcon C, hy spræcon DG, he spręcon E^{3}*, hi spræcon FHI, spæcan K
et	⁊ ABCDE^{3}FGIJK
super*	ofer ABDE^{3}*, ofyr C, on FGIJK (*L*)
iram*	eorre ABD, yrre CE^{3}, irre J, graman F, yrsunge G, hatheortnysse I, hatheotnesse K (*L*)

(terrae)*	eorðan FG, eorþan JK, þære eorðan I
(loquentes)*	sprecende FIJ, specende K
dolose*	faecenlice A, facenlice B, facynlice C, facenfullicȩ D, facenfullice E^{x}*, facen F, faken I, facn JK (*L*)
cogitabant	ðohtun A, ðohton B, þohton *C,* hy þohton DG, hi þohton FJK, hy þohtan H, hy þohten E$^{3/x}$*, hi þohton ł smeadun I

ED: forðon (A)] for ðon *Kuhn*. loquebantur (G)] loqu*e*bantur *Rosier.* loque[ ]tes (G)] *l*oque*n*tes *Rosier.*

OE: he sprȩcon (E^{3})] he *written by corr.* (?). ofer (E^{3})] *gloss eras. after word.* facenfullice (E^{x})] *on eras.* hy þohten (E$^{3/x}$)] hy *on eras. by corr.*

LTg: mihi] michi EJ, C: *orig.* mihi: c *added interl. by corr.* pacifice] pacífice M. super] L: *underlined to signal deletion,* in *added by corr. after word: see GAg.* iram] L: *underlined to signal deletion,* iracunda terre *added interl. by corr.: see GAg.* dolose] L: *underlined to signal deletion,* dolos *added interl. by corr.: see GAg.* cogitabant] C: co *interl.*

LTu: mihi] michi ιλξςτ*τ, πχ: c *interl.;* m^{1} φ.

GAg: super] in FGHIJK, L: *see LTg.* iram] iracundia terrȩ loquentes FH; iracundia terrȩ loque[ ]tes G; iracundia terrae loquentes I: *eras. after* terrae, *possibly of* : (*note* ì *before word*); iracundia terre loquentes JK, L: *see LTg.* dolose] dolos FGHIJ, K: *2nd* o *on eras.*, L: *see LTg.*

GAu: super] in δεζιλμξοπϱσυφχ, ψ: *interl.* iram] iracundia terrae loquentes δζμυχψ; iracundia terrȩ loquentes ειλξοπϱφ; irac<u>on</u>dia terræ loquentes ϑ; iracundia terre loquentes στ. dolose] dolos δεζϑιμοπϱστυφχψ.

21

(Et)*	⁊ FGHIJK
Dilatauerunt	gebrȩddon A, gebræddon BC, hie gebreddon E^{3}, geblæddon *J,* hy tobreddon D, hi tobræddon *F,* hy tobrædden *G,* hy tobræddon *H,* hig tobræddun *I,* hi tobræddan *K,* hi tobræddon M^{2} (*L*)
in*	in A, on BCE^{3}, ofer FGIJK (*L*)
me	me ABCE^{3}FGJK
os	muð *A*BCDFG*H*I, muþ J*K,* heoræ E^{3}* (*M*)
suum	his A, hira B, hyra C, heora DFGHIJK, muð E^{3}
dixerunt	cwedon A, cwædon BJ, hi cwædon CF, hy cwædon D*G*H, hie cwedon E^{3}, hi cwædun I, hi cwædan K
euge	wel ðe A, wel þe ł gefeh C, eala DFI, egele *K,* ealá gefeoh J*, gefeoh BH, gefea ł eala ł wellawel G, eulæ E^{3}

euge — wel ðe A, wel þe C, eala FI, ealá gefeoh J*, gefeoh B, eule E^{3} (*K*)

uiderunt — gesegan AK, gesegon B, geseagon J, gesawon CDFGHI, hie gesæwæn E^{3}

oculi — | egan AK, eagan BCDF*G*HI, eagon J, uræ E^{3}

nostri — | ur A, ure BCDFGHIJK, eægæn E^{3}

ED: ós (AH)] os *Kuhn, Campbell.* dixeru[ ]t (G)] dixer*unt Rosier.* gefea ł eala ł wellawel (G)] gefea ł eala ł wellawe *Rosier.*

OE: heoræ (E^{3})] *orig.* hiræ: o *interl.,* i *altered to* e. ealá gefeoh (J) (*both*)] gefeoh *written above* eala.

LTg: Dilatauerunt] L: Et *added. by corr. before word: see GAg;* dilatauerunt FGHIJK. in] L: *underlined to signal deletion,* super *added interl. by corr.: see GAg.* os] ós AHKM. dixerunt] dixeru[ ]t G: *minim visible after* u. euge (*both*)] eúge K. oculi] ocu[ ] G: *letter fragment visible after* u.

LTu: Dilatauerunt] dilatauerunt δεζϑιλμξοπϱστυφχ.

GAg: Dilatauerunt] Et dilatauerunt FGHIJK, L: *see LTg.* in] super FGHIJK, L: *see LTg.*

GAu: Dilatauerunt] Et dilatauerunt δεζϑιλμξοπϱστυφχψ. in] super δεζϑιλμπϱστυχψ.

22

Uidisti — ðu gesege *A,* ðu gesawe *BF**, þu gesege K, þu gesawe *DHIJ,* þu geseæwe *E^{3},* þu gesawe *G,* ge þu gesawe *C* (*LM*)

domine — drihten $E^{3/x}$*, dryht̄ AB, driħt CFG, driħ J (*I*)

ne — ne ABCDE^{x}*FGHIJM^{2}, na K

sileas — swiga ðu *A*B, swiga þu CE^{x}*HJKM^{2}, swiga ðu DG*, swigo þu J, swuga þu F, suwa þu I

domine — drihten E^{3}, dryhṫ *A**, dryht̄ B, dryħt C, driħt F, driħ GJ (*I*)

ne — ne ABCDE^{3}FGHIJM^{2}, na K

discedas — gewit ð A, gewit ðu BCD, gewit þu $E^{3/x}$*FGHIJK, gewit þu M^{2}

a — from A, from B, fram CD*E^{x}*FHJ, fram GIK (*M*)

me — me ABCDE^{3}FGHIJK

ED: á (E)] a *Harsley.*

OE: ðu gesawe (F)] ðu *written in left margin.* drihten ($E^{3/x}$) (*1st*)] en *added by corr., cross-stroke of* t *retraced.* ne (E^{x})] *on eras.* swiga þu (E^{x})] *on eras.* swiga ðu (G)] g *altered from* ð. dryhṫ (A)] *abbreviation indicated by dot above* t, *likely the start of a macron.* gewit þu ($E^{3/x}$)] wit *by corr.*

LTg: Uidisti] Vidisti FHIJ, L: *orig.* uidisti: u *altered to* V *by corr.;* uidisti ABCDEM; [ ]idisti G. domine (*1st*)] I: o *written above word.* sileas] A: *eras.* (*2 or 3 letters*) *after word, with* d *visible as 1st letter.* domine (*2nd*)] A: *added by corr. in left margin at beginning of new line,* I: o *written above word, eras. after word, possibly of* : (*note* ÷ *before word*). a] á EM.

LTu: Uidisti] Vidisti ζιλσ; uidisti βνςτ*. domine (*2nd*)] *interl.* ε.

23

Exsurge		aris A*B*C*DFG*H*JK, Aris *E^3**, uparis I (*LM*)
domine*		drihten E^3, dryht̄ AB, driħt C
et		⁊ ABCE^3FGHIJK (*M*)
intende		bihald A, behald B, beheald CDGHJM^2, beheæld E^3, begim F, begem I, ongyt K
iudicium*	I	dom ACDFGHJK, dóm B, dome I, minne E^3 (*L*)
meum*	I	minne ACDFGHJK, minum BI, dóm E^3 (*L*)
deus	I	god ABCDFGHIJK*, min E^3
meus	I	min ABCDFGHJK, eala þu min I*, drihten E^3
et		⁊ ABCFGHIJK
dominus	I	dryhten D, drihten FHK, dryht̄ AB, driħt CG, driħ J, god E^3
meus		min ABCE^3*FGHIJK
in		in A, on BCDGHJK, to I
causam	I	intingan ABCFGJK, intingæn E^3, ðing ł intingan D, þyng ł on intingan H, minum I
meam	I	minne ABG*H, mine CF, minum̲ J, minan K, min E^3, intingan I

OE: aris (A)] *otiose stroke below* i. Aris (E^3)] *orig.* Arise: e *eras.* god (K)] o *malformed.* eala þu min (I)] o *written before* eala. min (E^3) (*2nd*)] ⁊ *eras. before word, eras. after word.* minne (G)] *fragment of gloss written in right margin,* t *visible.*

LTg: Exsurge] Exurge CEL, H: *eras. after* x, M: *hole in leaf after* x *due to eras.* et (*1st*)] M: *inserted by corr.* iudicium] L: um *underlined to signal deletion,* o *added interl. by corr.: see GAg.* meum] L: um *underlined to signal deletion,* o *added interl. by corr.: see GAg.*

LTu: Exsurge] EXsurge β; Exurge δειλξπρτ*τυφχ. iudicium] β: *orig.* iudecium: e *crossed through,* i *interl. by corr.* meum] mmeum β.

GAg: domine] *om.* FGHIJK. iudicium] iudicio FGI, H: o *altered from another letter, eras. after* o, K: *1st* o *interl., then eras. and written on eras. by corr.,* L: *see LTg.* meum] meo FGI, H: o *altered from another letter, eras. after* o, K: *1st* o *interl., then eras. and written on eras. by corr.,* L: *see LTg.*

GAu: domine] *om.* δεζθιλμξοπρστυφχψ. iudicium meum] iudicio meo δεζθιλμξοπρστυφχψ.

24

Iudica		docm AB, dem CDE^{3}FGHIJK
me		me ACE^{3}FGHIJK
domine*		drihten E^{3}, dryht̄ AB, driħt C (*L*)
secundum		efter AE^{3}, æfter BJ, æfter DFGHIK, æftyr C
misericordiam*	I	mildheortnisse A, mildheortnysse C, mildheortnesse BD, rihtwisnysse FI, rihtwisnesse GJ, rihtwisnes K, þinre E^{3} (*L*)
tuam*	I	ðinre ABF, þinre CDGHIK, minre *J*, mildheortnesse E^{3}
domine	I	dryhten D, dryht̄ AB, driħt CGH, driħ J, eala ðu driħt F, hlaford K, min E^{3} (*I*)
deus	I	god ABCFGHJK, drihten E^{3}, min I
meus	I	min ABCDFGJK, mi(n) *H**, god E^{3}I
ut*		þæt A, þæt CDM^{2}, þet E^{3}, ðætte B, ⁊ FGIJK (*L*)
non	I	ne ABC, na DE^{x}*FGJKM^{2}, hi ne I
insultent*	I	bismerien AE^{x}*, bismrigen B, bysmriyn C, bysmrien ł hyspen D, hyspen *M^{2}*, oferfægnian F, ofergefean J, oferblissigend G, oferblissian K, geblission I (*L*)
in*		in A, on BCDE^{3} (*L*)
me*		mec A, me BCDE^{3}FGHJK, ofor me I (*L*)
inimici*	I	feond A, fiend B, fynd CD, mine E^{3} (*L*)
mei*	I	mine ABC, fiend E^{3} (*L*)

ED: Iudica (C)] Judica *Wildhagen.* dem (E)] Dem *Harsley.* mi(n) (H)] min *Campbell.* oferfægnian (F)] ofer fægnian *Kimmens.*

OE: mi(n) (H)] *right leg of* n *lost due to hole in leaf.* na (E^{x})] *on eras.* bismerien (E^{x})] *on eras.*

LTg: domine (*1st*)] L: *underlined to signal deletion: see GAg.* misericordiam] L: *underlined to signal deletion,* iusticiam *added interl. by corr.: see GAg.* domine (*2nd*)] I: o *written above word.* meus] H: s *partly lost due to hole in leaf.* ut] L: *underlined to signal deletion,* et *added interl. by corr.: see GAg.* insultent] M: ns *on eras.,* L: *underlined to signal deletion,* supergaudeant *added interl. by corr.: see GAg.* in] L: *underlined to signal deletion: see GAg.* me (*2nd*)] L: *underlined to signal deletion,* michi *added interl by corr.: see GAg.* inimici mei] L: *underlined to signal deletion: see GAg.*

GAg: domine (*1st*)] *om.* FGHIJK, L: *see LTg.* misericordiam] iustitiam FGHIJK, L: *see LTg.* tuam] meam J. ut] et FGHIJK, L: *see LTg.* insultent] supergaudeant FGHIJ, L: *see LTg.* in] *om.* FGHIJK, L: *see LTg.* me (*2nd*)] mihi FGIJK; michi H, L: *see LTg.* inimici mei] *om.* FGHIJK, L: *see LTg.*

GAu: domine (*1st*)] *om.* δεζθιλμξοπϱστυφχψ. misericordiam] iustitiam δεζθιλμξοπσυχψ; iusticiam τφ, ϱ: *orig.* iustitiam. tuam] meam ϑ. ut] et δεζϑιλνξοπϱστυφχψ. insultent] supergaudeant δεζιλμξοπϱστυφψ; supergaudiant ϑ. in] *om.* δεζϑιλμξοπϱστυφψ. me (*2nd*)] mihi δεζϑμουψ; michi ιλ, πϱ: c *interl.;* m[1] ξστφχ. inimici mei] *om.* δεζϑιλμξοπϱστυφχψ.

25

Nec* — ne *ABC*FI*J, na GHK, ne ne *DE*^{x}* (*LM*)
dicant — cweðen ABH, cweðyn C, cweþen DK, cweðan F, cwedæn E^{3}*, cweðat J, cweðun hig I, ic cweðe G
in — in A, on BCDE^{3}FGHIJK
cordibus | heortum ACFI, heortum BDJ, heortan GHK, hioræ E^{3}
suis | heara A, hira B, hyra C, heora DFHIJ, his GK, heortæn E^{3}
euge — wel ðe AB, wel þe C, eala ł wellawel DE^{x}*H, ealla ł wellawel G, eala F, ealá J, egel K, wel wel ł eala eala I*
euge — wel ðe AB, wel þe C, eala F, ealá J
animae | sawle A*BCDFGJK,* sawla *I,* saul *H,* ure *E*^{3} (*L*)
nostrae | ure *ABCFGHIJK,* urre *D,* sæwle *E*^{3} (*L*)
nec — ne A*B*E^{3}FIJ, na K, ne ne CDG, nen H
dicant — cweðen AB, cweðyn C, cweþen DHK, cweðan F, cwedæn E^{3}*, cwædan G, hi ne cweþan I, cweþaþ J
obsorbuimus* — we forswelgað *AB,* we forswulgun C, we forswulgon F*, we forswulgun I, we fofswelgað G, forswelgaþ J, we besencton DE$^{3/x}$*M^{2}, forniman K (*L*)
eum — hine ABDFGHIJ, hyne CE^{x}*

ED: ne ne (D) (*both*)] nene *Roeder.* animę (E)] animae *Harsley.* anime (I)] animae *Lindelöf.* nostrę (EI)] nostrae *Lindelöf, Harsley.* absorbuimus (B)] absorbimus *Brenner.*

OE: ne (I)] n *altered from another letter.* ne ne (E^{x})] *on eras., eras. before word.* cwedæn (E^{3}) (*1st*)] n *on eras. by corr.* eala ł wellawel (E^{x})] *on eras.,* l *eras. after* l *in* eala. wel wel ł eala eala (I)] id est bene bene *written before gloss.* cwedæn (E^{3}) (*2nd*)] n *on eras. by corr.* we forswulgon (F)] *descender of* w *lost due to eras. in Lat. line below.* we besencton (E$^{3/x}$)] w *altered from* þ *by corr.,* e *retouched,* besencton *on eras. by corr.* hyne (E^{x})] *on eras.*

LTg: Nec] L: *orig.* nec: n *altered to* N *by corr.,* ec *underlined to signal deletion,* on *added interl. by corr.: see GAg;* nec ABCDEM. animae] animæ BL; animę CDEH; anime FGIJK. nostrae] A: ostrae *added by corr.;* nostræ BL; nostre CGJ; nostrę DEFHIK. nec] ne B. obsorbuimus] L: *underlined to signal deletion,* deuorauimus *added interl. by corr.: see GAg;* absorbuimus AB: *cf. Weber MSS* SRαβδη med.

LTu: Nec] nec βνςτ*. animae] anime δξσςτ*τ; animę εζιλμνπϱυφχ; anima ϑ. nostrae] nostrę δειλνξϱυφ; nostre σςτ*τ; nostræ χ; nostra ϑ.

GAg: Nec] Non FGHIJK, L: *see LTg*. obsorbuimus] deuorauimus GHIJ, F: *orig.* deborauimus: b *altered to* u, L: *see LTg;* deuorabimus K.

GAu: Nec] Non δεζϑιλμξοπϱστυφψ. obsorbuimus] deuorabimus δεζιλοπϱστ; deuorauimus ϑμξυφχψ.

26

Erubescant — scomien A, scamigen B, scamiyn C, Scæmien E^{3}, sceamian F, scamian J, ablysigen DK, ablissigen G, ablysien H, syn gescynde ł ablysian ł scamian I

et — ⁊ ABCE^{3}FGHIJK

reuereantur — onscunien *A,* onscunigen B, onscuniyn C, onscunian J, arweorðien DG, arweorþien E^{x}*H, arwyrþian K, aðracian F, anðracian I*

simul — somud A, somod B, samod CFIJK, ætgædere DGH, ætgedere *E^{x}**

qui — ða A, ða ðe B, þa þe CGHIK, þa ðe DE^{x}*J, þam ðe F

gratulantur — blissiað A*BCI, blissiaþ J, þanciað DE^{x}*FGH, ðanciað K

malis | yflum AB, yfelum DE^{x}*J, yfelum G, yfyla C, yfelu F, yuelum H, yfeles K, for minum I

meis | minum ABFGH, minum DE^{x}*J, minra C, mines K, yflum I

induantur — sien gerede A, sien gegerede B, syn gegyryde C, syn gegirede *J,* syn gescrydde D*FGHI,* Sin gescrydde E$^{3/x}$*, sin gescrydde *K* (*L*)

pudore* — scome A, scame B, sceame C, mid sceame ł mid gescændnysse I, forwandunge DE^{x}*, mid gescendnysse F, mid gescændnesse G, mid gescildnesse J (*LM*)

et — ⁊ ABCE^{x}*FGHIJK

reuerentia — awescnisse *A,* æwiscnesse B, æwiscnysse C, arweorþunge DE^{x}*, arweorþunga H, arwurðunga G, arwyrþðunga K, arwurþnesse J, unwurþunge F, anðracunge I

qui — ða ðe A, þa þe CIJK, ða ða B, þa þæ G, þe DE^{x}*FH

magna* — miclan AB, micyl *C,* mætu *DE^{x}**H, yfel FJ, yfelwillendnessa G, yfelcunda I (*LM*)

loquuntur — spreocað A, sprecað BCFG, sprecaþ I*J,* specaþ E^{x}*, specað HK (*LM*)

aduersum* — wið AB, ongen C, ongean DE^{x}*, ofer FGIJ, ofen K (*L*)

me — me ABCDE^{x}*FGIJK

ED: somod (B)] somoð *Brenner.*

OE: arweorþien (E^{x})] *on eras.* anðracian (I)] *eras. after 1st* n. ætgedere (E^{x})] *on eras.* þa ðe (E^{x})] *on eras.* blissiað (A)] *orig. gloss to* gratulantur *eras.,* blissiað *written to right.* þanciað (E^{x})] *on eras.* yfelum (E^{x})] *on eras.* minum (E^{x})] *on eras.* Sin gescrydde (E$^{3/x}$)] *letter eras. after* i, gescrydde *on eras. by corr.* forwandunge (E^{x})] *on eras.* ⁊ (E^{x}) *(2nd)*] *on eras.* arweorþunge (E^{x})] *on eras.* þe (E^{x})] *on eras.* mætu (E^{x})] *on eras.* specaþ (E^{x})] *on eras.* ongean (E^{x})] *on eras.* me (E^{x})] *on eras.*

LTg: reuereantur] A: *3rd* e *on eras.* simul] E: *eras. after word.* induantur] Induantur FGHIJK, L: *orig.* induantur: i *altered to* I *by corr.* pudore] L: *underlined to signal deletion,* confusione *added by corr. in right margin: see GAg;* pudôre M. reuerentia] A: n *on eras. by corr.* magna] maligna CDEL, M: *orig.* magna: li *added interl.: cf. Weber MSS* T*Q^{2}R^{2}δε, *see GAg.* loquuntur] locuntur JLM. aduersum] L: *underlined to signal deletion,* super *added interl. by corr.: see GAg.*

LTu: reuereantur] β: *3rd* e *interl.* induantur] Induantur δεζθιλμξπρστυφχψ. magna] maligna ςτ*: *cf. Weber MSS* T*Q^{2}R^{2}δε, *see GAu.* loquuntur] locuntur δθμντ*χ; loquntur ς. aduersum] aduersus θ.

GAg: pudore] confusione FGHIJK, L: *see LTg.* magna] maligna FHIJK, CDELM: *see LTg;* malingna G. aduersum] super FGHIJK, L: *see LTg.*

GAu: pudore] confusione δεζιλμξοπρστυφχψ; confussione θ. magna] maligna δεζθιλμξοπρστυφχψ, ςτ*: *see LTg.* aduersum] super δεζιλμξοπρστυφχψ.

27

Exultent	gefiað A, gefeoð BCJ, fægnien DE^{x}*H, fæignien *G,* fægnian K, blissian F, blissiun I
et	⁊ ABCDE^{3}FGHIJK
laetentur	blissiað A*BC,* blissiæþ *E^{3},* geblissien *D,* blissigen *G,* blissien *H,* blissian *K,* fægnian *F,* fægniun I, gehihtaþ *J* (*L*)
qui	ða AB, þa þe CGHI, þa ðe DFJK, þa þe þæ þe E$^{3/x}$*
uolunt	willað ABCDGHIJ, wyllað FK, willæþ E^{3}
iustitiam	rehtwinisse A, ryhtwisnesse BD, rihtwisnysse *C*FI, ryhtwisnisse E^{x}*, rihtwisnesse GHJK
meam	mine ABCFGHIJK, min DE^{x}*
et	⁊ ABCE^{x}*FGHIJK
dicant	cweoðað A, cweðað BCG, cweþað J, cweðaþ K, cweðaþ hig I, cweþen DE^{x}*H, cweðan F
semper	aa A, áa B, symle CDE^{x}*IJ, symble FH, symble ł æfre G, æfre K
magnificetur	sie miclad A, sie gemiclod BDH, Síe gemiclod E^{3}*, sy gemiclud C, si gemicclod G, sy gemicclod J, si gemyclod K, sy gemiclud ł si gemærsod I, sy gemærsod F (*M*)
dominus	drihten DE^{3}FK, dryht̄ AB, driħt CH, driħ GJ
qui	ða A*, þa B, þa þe CGHI, þa ðe DE^{x}*FJK
uolunt	willað ABDE^{x}*GI, willaþ J, willad C, wyllað FK, wylloð H

pacem sibb A, sibbe BFGHIJK, sybbe CDE^{x}* (*M*)
serui ðeowes AB, þeowys C, þeowes DE^{x}*GHJ, ðeowan FI, þeowan K
eius his ABDE^{x}*FGHIJK, hys C

ED: fægnien (E)] Fægnien *Harsley.* lętentur (E)] laetentur *Harsley.* willað (H)] wyllað *Campbell.* iusticiam (C)] iusti[t]iam *Wildhagen.* si gemicclod (G)] sy gemicclod *Rosier.* drih̄ (G)] *no gloss Rosier.* willad (C)] willað *Wildhagen.*

OE: fægnien (E^{x})] *on eras.* þa þe þæ þe (E$^{3/x}$)] þa þe *on eras. by corr.,* þæ þe *in line below by main hand.* ryhtwisnisse (E^{x})] *on eras.* min (E^{x})] *on eras.* ⁊ (E^{x}) (*2nd*)] *on eras.* cweþen (E^{x})] *on eras.* symle (E^{x})] *on eras.* Síe gemiclod (E^{3})] *gloss eras. before* Síe. ða (A) (*2nd*)] *eras.* (?) *before word.* þa ðe (E^{x})] *on eras.* willað (E^{x})] *on eras.* sybbe (E^{x})] *on eras.* þeowes (E^{x})] *on eras.* his (E^{x})] *on eras.*

LTg: Exultent] [ ]xultent G: *initial* E *lost.* laetentur] lætentur BL; lętentur CEFG; letentur DHJK. iustitiam] iusticiam C: *orig.* iustitiam: *2nd* t *altered to* c. magnificetur] magnificêtur M. pacem] pâcem M.

LTu: Exultent] Exsultent ϑψ. laetentur] lętentur ειλνφ; letentur ϑξσςτ*τυ. iustitiam] iusticiam τφ.

28
Sed* | ah AB, ac *C*, ⁊ eac DE^{x}* (*L*)
et | ⁊ ABC*FGIJK* (*H*)
lingua mid tungan A, tungan F, tunge B*C*DE^{x}*GHIJK
mea min A*BCDE^{x}*GHIJK, mine F
meditabitur bið smegende A, bið smeagende B, bið smeagynde C, biþ smeagende J, smeægendæ E^{3}, smeað DFGH, smæð K, smeage I
iustitiam | rehtwisnisse A, ryhtwisnesse B, rihtwisnysse *C*FI, ryhtwisnisse D, rihtwisnesse HJ, rihtwisnes K, rihtwise G*, þine E^{x}*
tuam | ðine AB, þine CDFGHIJK, ryhtwisnesse E^{x}*
tota alne A, ealne BCFIJ, ælce DGH, ælle K, ęlce E^{3}*
die deg A, dæg BCFIJK, dei E^{x}*, dæge DGH
laudem | lof ABCDFGHIJK, þin E^{x}
tuam | ðin ABF, þin CDGHIJK, lof E^{x}

ED: iusticiam (C)] iusti[t]iam *Wildhagen.*

OE: ⁊ eac (E^{x})] *on eras.* tunge (E^{x})] *on eras.* min (A)] *letter eras. after* n. min (E^{x})] *on eras.* rihtwise (G)] *letter eras. after* s, *descender visible.* þine (E^{x})] *on eras.* ryhtwisnesse (E^{x})] *on eras.* ęlce (E^{3})] *eras. before word, initial* e *but not cauda retouched in darker ink.* dei (E^{x})] i *has form of* j.

LTg: Sed] C: *orig.* Set: t *altered to* d, L: *underlined to signal deletion: see GAg.* et] Et FGHIJK. lingua] C: *eras. after* g. iustitiam] iusticiam C: *orig.* iustitiam: *2nd* t *altered to* c.

LTu: et] Et δεζϑιλμξοπϱστυφχψ. iustitiam] iusticiam τ*τφ. laudem] lavdem ι.

GAg: Sed] *om.* FGHIJK, L: *see LTg.*

GAu: Sed] *om.* δεζϑιλμξοπϱστυφχψ.

PSALM 35

2

Dixit	cweð *A*, cwæð B*CD*H, Cwæð *E*x*, cwæþ J*, cw̄ F, cwæ K, sæde ł cwæð GI*
iniustus	se unrehtwisa A, se unryhtwisa B, se unrihtwisa *C*DFGHIJ, se unrihtwise *E*x*, þe unrihtwisa K
ut	ðætte A, þætte B, þætte C, þæt DI, þæt FG*J*K, þet E3 (*H*)
delinquat	he forlæte C, he forlet ł agylte E3/x*, agylte B, he agylte D, he agylte FGHI, he agulde K, þe agilde J
in	in A, on BCDE3FGHIJK
semetipso	him seolfum A*, him selfum B, hym sylfum C, him Selfum E3, him sylfum FI, him sylfum J, selfum him D, selfum him H, sylfum him *G,* sylfum him K
non	ǀ nis ABDFHI, nys C, nan G, ne *E3*J, na K
est	ǀ is *E3**GJ*K*
timor	ege ABCDFGHIJK, ęge *E3*
dei	godes ABFGIJK, godys C (*E*)
ante	biforan A, beforan BCDGHIJK, beforæn E3/x*, ætforan F
oculos	ǀ egum A, eagum BC, eagan DFGHI, eagon J, egan K, his E3
eius	ǀ his ABDFHIJ*K*, hys C, [ ]is G*, eægum E3

ED: cw̄ (F)] cwæþ *Kimmens.* semetipso (B)] semet ipso *Brenner.* se(me)[ ]i(p)so (G)] semetipso *Rosier.* [ ]is (G)] *no gloss Rosier.*

OE: Cwæð se unrihtwise (Ex)] Cwæð se un *by one corr.,* rihtwise *by another on eras.* cwæþ (J)] *blue ink of* D *in* Dixit *over* cw *in* cwæþ. sæde ł cwæð (I)] sæde *written in bowl of* D *in* Dixit. he forlet ł agylte (E3/x)] forl *retraced in darker ink,* ł agylte *added by corr.* him seolfum (A)] *scribe orig. began* him seof- *but corrected* f *to* l. is (E3)] *eras. after word (16 mm).* beforæn (E3/x)] be *added by corr.* [ ]is (G)] *minim visible before* i, *stroke (otiose?) visible after* s.

LTg: Dixit] DIxit A; DIXIT CDE. iniustus] E: us *abbreviation partly eras. from eras. above and rewritten by corr.;* INIVSTUS C. ut] H: *eras. after word,* J: non *eras. after word.* semetipso] se(me)[ ]i(p)so G: me *partly lost due to hole in leaf, letter lost after*

2nd e, *descender of* p *lost.* non] *on eras.* E. est] *on eras.* E; ést K. timor] *on eras.* E. dei] *on eras.* E. eius] eíus K.

LTu: Dixit] DIXIT βιλμνϱςτ*τφχ. iniustus] INIUSTUS λμνϱχ. ut] UT λϱ; ut non υ: non *interl.* delinquat] DELINQUAT λϱ.

3

Quoniam		forðon ABDJ, forþon C*G*, forðæn E^{3}*, forþam ðe F, forþan ðe I
dolose		faccenlice A, facenlice BJ, facynlice C, facenfullice D, facenfullice FHI, facenfullic E^{x}*, facenfulle G
egit		dyde ABK, he dyde CDFG*H*I, he dide E^{x}*J
in		in A, on BCDE^{x}*FGHIJK
conspectu	|	gesihðe ABCFG, gesyhþe D, gesiehðe E^{3}, gesihð H, gesihþe J, gesyhðe K, his I
eius	|	his ABCDE^{x}FGHJ*K*, gesyh[ ] I*
ut		ðæt AB, þæt CHI, þæt FK, þætte D, þette E^{x}* (*G*)
inueniret*		gemoette A, he gemette B*C*E^{x}*FK, he gemette D, gemet G, he gemette ł þæt si gemet I (*LM*)
iniquitatem*		unrehtwisnisse A, unrehtwisnesse B, unrihtwisnysse *C*FI, unryhtwisnesse D, unrihtwisnesse E^{x}*J, unrihtwisnesse K, unrihtwisne H, unrihtwis G* (*L*)
suam*		his ABE^{x}*FGHIJK, hys C (*L*)
et*		⁊ ABCE^{x}*K, to FIJ (*L*)
odium		laeðu A, læððe B, læþþe J, læðþa C, hatunge DE^{x}*FH, hatunga IK (*G*)

ED: forðon (A)] for ðon *Kuhn.* forðæn (E)] Forðæn *Harsley.* gesyh[ ] (I)] gesyhþe *Lindelöf.* inueniret (BE)] inveniret *Brenner, Harsley.*

OE: forðæn (E^{3})] *eras. after word.* facenfullic (E^{x})] *on eras.* he dide (E^{x})] *on eras.* on (E^{x})] *on eras.* gesyh[ ] (I)] *letters lost due to tight binding.* þette (E^{x})] *on eras.* he gemette (E^{x})] *on eras.* unrihtwisnesse (E^{x})] *on eras.* unrihtwis (G)] *top of* s *cropped.* his (E^{x}) (*2nd*)] *on eras.* ⁊ (E^{x})] *on eras.* hatunge (E^{x})] *on eras.*

LTg: Quoniam] [ ]uoniam G. egit] ęgit H. eius] eíus K. ut] *lost* G. inueniret] C: in *interl.*, L: ret *crossed through by corr.*, atur *written below: see GAg;* inuenîret M. iniquitatem] L: *1st* t *and* tem *underlined for deletion,* s *added interl. after* a *by corr.: see GAg;* iniqutatem C. suam] L: *underlined for deletion,* eius *added interl. by corr.: see GAg.* et] L: *underlined for deletion,* ad *added interl. by corr.: see GAg.* odium] *lost* G.

GAg: inueniret] inueniatur FHIJK, L: *see LTg;* [ ]nueniatur G. iniquitatem] iniquitas FGHIJK; *for* L *see LTg.* suam] eius FGHIJ, L: *see LTg;* eíus K. et] *lost* G; ad FHIJ, K: *on eras. by corr.,* L: *see LTg.*

GAu: inueniret] inueniatur δεζιλμξοπϱστυφχψ, ϑ: *2nd* n *interl.* iniquitatem suam] iniquitas eius δεζϑιλμξοπϱστυφχψ. et] ad δεζιλμξοπϱστυφχψ.

4

Uerba		word A*BCDFH*JK, Word *E*^{3}, wurd *I*, wo[ ]d *G* (*L*)
oris	|	muðes ABFHI, muþes DGJK, mine C, his E^{3} (*M*)
eius	|	his ABCDFGHIJ*K*, muðes E^{3}
iniquitas		urrehtwisse A, unryhtwisnes BD, unrihtwisnyss C, unrihtwisnys FI, unrihtwisnes GHJK, unrihtwisnesse E$^{3/x}$*
et		⁊ ABCDE^{x}*FGHIJK
dolus		facen ABFI*, facn CDE^{x}**G*H*JK
noluit		nalde A, nolde BCJK, he nolde DE^{x}*F*HI (*G*)
intellegere		ongeotan A, ongitan B**CDFHI*J, ongetan *E^{x}**, ongytan G, understandan *K*
ut		ðæt AB, þæt CDE^{x}*HIJ, þæt FGK
bene	|	wel A*, well I, he wel BCDFGHJK, he węl E^{x}*
ageret	|	dyde ABCDGHK, dide FJ, dede E^{x}*, he dede I (*M*)

ED: Verba (G)] Verba *Rosier.* [ ]erba (H)] Verba *Campbell.* urrehtwisse (A)] unrehtwisse *Kuhn, who notes that the* n *may be an* r.

OE: unrihtwisnesse (E$^{3/x}$)] wisnesse *on eras. by corr.* ⁊ (E^{x})] *on eras.* facen (I)] s. sunt : synt *written in left margin.* facn (E^{x})] *on eras.* facn (H)] a *orig. obscured by ascender of* d *of lemma, scribe then added 2nd* a *above 1st.* he nolde (E^{x})] *on eras.* he nolde (F)] *letter* (l?) *eras. after 1st* e. ongitan (B)] t *blotted* (*by water stain?*). ongetan (E^{x})] *on eras.* þæt (E^{x})] *on eras.* wel (A)] *eras. before word.* he węl (E^{x})] *on eras.* dede (E^{x})] *on eras.*

LTg: Uerba] Verba BDEFGIL; [ ]erba H: *initial* V *lost.* oris] ôris M. eius] eíus K. dolus] dolu[ ] G. noluit] *lost* G. intellegere] intelligere CEI, F: *orig.* intellegere: *2nd* e *deleted by subscript dot,* i *interl. by corr.,* HK: *orig.* intellegere: *2nd* e *altered to* i. ageret] ágeret M.

LTu: Uerba] Verba ιvξοϱσ. dolus] μ: *remainder of psalm wanting.* intellegere] intelligere εζιλοπϱσυχ.

5

Iniquitatem	unrehtwisnisse *A*, unryhtwisnesse *BD*, unrihtwisnysse *C*FI, unrihtwysnisse *E^{x}**, unrihtwisnesse GHJK (*LM*)
meditatus	smegende A, smeagende BJ, smeagynde C, smægendę K, he smeade DE$^{3/x}$*FGH, he smeadde I
est	is ABJ*K*, he wæs C (*H*)
in	in A, on BCDE^{3}FGHIJK

cubili	|	bedcleofan AB, bedclyfan *J,* inclyfan C, incleofe D*H,* incleofum F, incleofan *K,* incleo[ ] *G,* his E^{3}I (*M*)
suo	|	his ABCDF*HJK, bedcliofum E^{3}*, incofan ł on his c[ ]fan I* (*G*)
adstetit		ætstod *ABCJK,* he ætstod *DFGHI,* he Etstod *E*^{x}* (*LM*)
omni		allum A, eallum BK, eallum *C,* ælcum D, ælcum *F*GHI, on eallum J, eælle E^{3}
uiae		wege A*BCDFG*HI*K,* wegæs *E*^{3}*,* wegum *J* (*L*)
non		noht *A*BC, na DFGHIK, ne E^{3}*, naht J
bonae		gode A*BC,* godé *J,* godum *D,* godum *FGHK,* god *E*^{3}*,* godum ł ælcum yfelum wege *I** (*L*)
malitiam		hete AB*C*J, hetenið ł yfelnisse E$^{3/x}$*, yfelnisse D, yfelnysse *F,* yfelnesse GHIK
autem		soðlice *A*BCE^{3}FG, soþlice J, witodlice IK
non	|	ne *A*BJ, na DE^{x}*FGHK, he ne CI
odiuit	|	fiede A, feode BCJ, he hatode DE$^{3/x}$*H, he hatude F, he hatede G, hatode IK

ED: ést (H)] est *Campbell.* cubíli (HK)] cubili *Campbell, Sisam.* cubi[ ] (G)] cub*ili Rosier.* incofan ł on his c[ ]fan (I)] incofan ł on his clyfan *Lindelöf.* Astitit (C)] A[d]stitit *Wildhagen.* godé (J)] gode *Oess.* maliciam (C)] mali[t]iam *Wildhagen.*

OE: unrihtwysnisse (E^{x})] *on eras.* he smeade (E$^{3/x}$)] he *and* de *by corr., 2nd* e *altered from* i. his (F)] i *altered from* s. bedcliofum (E^{3})] f *on eras. by corr.* incofan ł on his c[ ]fan (I)] *letters after 2nd* c *lost due to tight binding.* he Etstod (E^{x})] he *added by one corr.,* od *added by other corr. on eras.* ne (E^{3})] *eras. after word.* godum ł ælcum yfelum wege (I)] ł ælcum yfelum wege *written in left margin.* hetenið ł yfelnisse (E$^{3/x}$)] ł yfelnisse *added by corr.* na (E^{x})] *on eras.* he hatode (E$^{3/x}$)] hatode *on eras. by corr.*

LTg: Iniquitatem] L: *orig.* iniquitatem: *initial* i *altered to* I *by corr.;* iniquitatem ABCDEM. est] ést HK. cubili] J: *letter eras. after final* i; cubíli HK; cubîli M; cubi[ ] G. suo] *lost* G. adstetit] Adstitit ABL; Ádstitit M: *1st* i *on eras.;* Astitit E, C: *letter eras. after* A; Asstitit D: *orig.* Adstitit: d *altered to* s; astitit F, H: *letter eras. after* s; adstitit GJ; asstitit I; ádstitit K. omni] C: i *on eras.,* F: *orig.* omno: *deleting dot below final* o, *then* o *eras.,* i *interl. by corr.* uiae] uiæ B; uię CDFGL; uie EJK. non (*1st*)] A: on *interl. by corr.* bonae] bonæ BL; bonę CDFGHI; bone EJK. malitiam] F: *2nd* a *on eras., final* m *added by corr.;* maliciam C: *orig.* malitiam: t *altered to* c. autem] A: *orig. macron above* e *eras.,* m *added by corr.* non (*2nd*)] A: *interl. by corr.*

LTu: Iniquitatem] iniquitatem βνςτ*. adstetit] Adstitit νς, β: *orig.* Adstetit: i *interl. above* e; Astitit τ*φ; astitit ειλοπστυχ, ζ: *wanting from* omni *to end of psalm;* asstitit ϱ; adsti[ ]it δ: *letter eras.;* astetit ψ; a[ ] ξ. uiae] uię ενξϱσςυφ; uiæ ϑ; uie ιτ*τ. bonae] bonę βενπϱσφ; bonæ ϑ; bone ιξτ*τ. malitiam] maliciam φ. odiuit] hodiuit ς.

6

Domine		drihten E^{3}, dryht̄ AB, driħt CF, driħ *G*J, hlaford K (*I*)
in		in A, on BCDE^{3}FGHIJK
caelo		heofene A, heofone *B,* hefone *C,* heofone *DH,* hefonum *E^{3},* heofonum *FI,* heofonum̲ *J,* heofenan *G,* heofenen *K* (*L*)
misericordia	|	mildheortnis A, mildheortnes BHK, mildheortnyss C, mildheortnis D, mildheortnyssa F, mildheortnesse GJ, mildheortnys I, þin E^{3}
tua	|	ðin AB, þin CDFGH*IJK, mildheortnes E^{3}*
et		⁊ ABCDE^{3}FGHIJK
ueritas	|	soðfestnis A, soðfæstnyss C, soþfæstnis D, soðfæstnys F, soðfæstnes BHI, soþfæstnes K, soðfæstnesse G, soþfæstnesse *J,* þin E^{3}
tua	|	ðin ABFI, þin CGHJK, soðfestnes E^{3}
usque		oð ABCFGHJ, oþ DIK, oþþet E^{3}
ad		to DE^{x}FGHJK
nubes		wolcen A, wolcn B, wolcne J, þam wolcne C, wolcn ł genipum̲ $E^{3/x}$*, wolcnum ł oð þa genipu I, g̲enipum̲ D, genipum FGH, genippan K

ED: drihten (E)] Drihten *Harsley.* cælo (D)] caelo *Roeder.* cęlo (E)] caelo *Harsley.* þin (H) (*1st*)] *no gloss Campbell.*

OE: þin (H) (*1st*)] *written below preceding gloss.* mildheortnes (E^{3})] l *on eras.* wolcn ł genipum̲ ($E^{3/x}$)] ł genipum̲ *added by corr.*

LTg: Domine] I: o *written above word;* [ ]omine G. caelo] cælo BDKL; cęlo CEFGHIJ. ueritas] ueritate J.

LTu: caelo] cęlo δεινξοφ; cælo ϑ; celo σςτ*τ. misericordia] missericordia ϑ. nubes] nu[ ] ξ.

7

Iustitia	|	rehtwisnis A, rihtwisnys *C*F, ryhtwisnes BD, rihtwisnes *H*IK, rihtwisnesse GJ, þin E^{3}
tua	|	ðin AF, þin BCDGHIJK, soþfestnes E^{3}
sicut		swe swe A, swa swa BCDGHIJ, swæ swæ $E^{3/x}$*, swa FK
montes	|	muntas ABCDGH, muntes I, munt JK, duna F, godes E^{3}
dei	|	godes ABFGI*JK, godys C, dún ł muntas $E^{3/x}$*
et*		⁊ CE^{3} (*ABM*)
iudicia	|	domas ABCDFGHIJ, dom K, þine E^{3}
tua	|	ðine ABF, þine CDIJ, þin GHK, domæs E^{3}*
abyssus		niolnis *A,* neolnes B, nywyllnysse C, neowelnys F,

	neowelnes J, deopnis ł niowelnesse E$^{3/x}$*, deopnis D, deopnys G, deopnes H, deopnessa I, deop *K* (*LM*)
multa	micelu AB, micclu J, micyle C, micel I, micellu ł felafeald F, felafeald DGH, felafæald E^{x}, swyþe K
Homines	men ABHJK, Men E^{3}, menn CDGI, mann F
et	⁊ ABCDE^{3}FGHIJK
iumenta	neat ABC, nytenu DGHI, niteno E^{3}, nitenu F, nytena JK
saluos*	hale ABCD, þu hæle E^{3}, ðu gehælst F, þu gehælst G*I, þu gehældest J, þu hælest K
facies*	ðu does A, þu dest BCD, gedest E^{3}
domine	drihten E^{3}F, dryht̄ AB, driħt C, driħ GJ, hlaford K (*IM*)

ED: Iusticia (C)] Iusti[t]ia *Wildhagen.* [ ]ustitia (H)] Iustitia *Campbell.* swa swa (GIJ)] swaswa *Rosier, Lindelöf, Oess.* micellu ł felafeald (F)] micellu ł fela feald *Kimmens.*

OE: swæ swæ (E$^{3/x}$)] *1st* swæ *added by corr.* godes (I)] e̲s̲t̲ : is *written in left margin.* dún ł muntas (E$^{3/x}$)] ł muntas *added by corr.* domæs (E^{3})] *eras. after word.* deopnis ł niowelnesse (E$^{3/x}$)] deopnis ł *added by corr.,* niow *retraced in darker ink.* þu gehælst (G)] *in lighter ink, added in diff.* (?) *hand.*

LTg: Iustitia] Iusticia C: *orig.* Iustitia: *2nd* t *altered to* c; [ ]ustitia H. et (*1st*)] *on eras.* M; *om.* AB: *cf. Weber MSS* Sαβγδεη moz med, *see GAg.* abyssus] A: u *on eras.,* K: *orig.* abyssos: o *altered to* u *by main hand;* abysus LM. Homines] omines J: *initial letter wanting.* domine] I: o *written above word,* M: *orig.* domini: *final* i *altered to* e.

LTu: Iustitia] Iusticia τ*τφ. abyssus] abissus ϑξτ*τ; abyssos β; abysus ν. multa] *lost* ξ. Homines] [ ]omines τ*τ: *initial wanting.*

GAg: et (*1st*)] *om.* FGHIJK, AB: *see LTg.* saluos facies] saluabis FGHIJK.

GAu: et (*1st*)] *om.* δεϑιλξοπϱστυφχψ. saluos facies] saluabis δεϑιλξοπϱστυφχψ.

8

quemadmodum	to ðæm gemete AB, to þæm gemete C, on þa̲m̲ gemete J, on þam gemetum F, swa swa DE^{x}*HK, swa swa to þæm gemete G*, la hu swiðe *I*
multiplicasti	gemonigfaldade A, ðu gemonigfaldodes B, þu gemonigfealdodyst C, þu gemenigfyldest D, þu gemonigfeældeæst E^{x}*, ðu gemænigfyldest F, þu gemænigfyldest H, þu gemonigfyldest J, þu gemænigfyldest ł mænigfealdast G*, ðu mænifyldst K, þu gemiclodest I

misericordias*	I	mildheortnisse A, mildheortnyssa C, mildheortnissa D, mildhcortnysse F, mildheortnessa B, mildheortnesse GIJK, þine E^{3} (*L*)
tuas*	I	ðine AFI, þine CJK, ðina B, þina *D,* þinre G, mildheortnesse E^{3}
deus		god ABCDE^{3}FGJK (*I*)
Filii	I	bearn ABCD*G*HIJ, sunu FK, Mænnæ *E*^{3}
autem	I	soðlice ABCFG, soðlice I, soþlice J, witodlice K, beærn E^{3}
hominum	I	monna AB, manna CDFGHIJK, soðlice E^{x}
in		in A, on BCDE^{3}FG*JK, under I
protectione*		gescildnisse AE^{3}*, gescyldnysse C, gescyldnisse D, gescildnesse BJ, gescyldnesse G*, wæfelse F, wæfelse ł on gescyldnesse I, helunge K (*LM*)
alarum	I	fiðra ABC, fiþera D, fyðera FGH, fyþera J, fiðera K, þinræ E^{3}, þinra I
tuarum	I	ðinra ABF, þinra CDGHJK, fiþræ E^{3}, fiþera I
sperabunt		gehyhtað AB, gehihtað C, gehihtaþ J, hyhtað DH, hihtað FGK, hyhtat ł gewenæþ E$^{3/x}$, hopiaþ I

ED: quemadmodum (I)] quemammodum *Lindelöf.* swa swa to þæm gemete (G)] swaswa to þæm gemete *Rosier.* Filíí (E)] Filii *Harsley.* [ ]ilii (G)] Filii *Rosier.* tegmine (I)] tegmien *Lindelöf.* gescildnisse (E)] geScildnisse *Harsley.*

OE: swa swa (E^{x})] *on eras.* swa swa to þæm gemete (G)] to þæm gemete *added in diff.* (?) *hand.* þu gemonigfeældeæst (E^{x})] *eras.* (*18 mm*) *before* þu. þu gemænigfyldest ł mænigfealdast (G)] ł mænigfealdast *added in diff.* (?) *hand.* on (G)] *in lighter ink, added in diff.* (?) *hand.* gescildnisse (E^{3})] *1st* s *slightly larger than normal.* gescyldnesse (G)] *in lighter ink, added in diff.* (?) *hand.* hyhtat ł gewenæþ (E$^{3/x}$)] hyhtat ł *added by corr., with eras.* (*14 mm*) *before word.*

LTg: quemadmodum] I: *orig.* quemammodum: *1st* d *interl. above 2nd* m. tuas] tua D. deus] I: o *written above word.* Filii] Filíí E; [ ]ilii G: *initial* F *lost.* protectione] L: tegmine *added interl. by corr.: see GAg;* protectiône M.

LTu: quemadmodum] quemadmodu[ ] ξ; quemammodum υ, o: *orig.* quemadmodum.

GAg: misericordias] misericordiam FGHIJK. tuas] tuam FGHIJK. protectione] tegmine FGIJK, H: *small eras. after final* e, L: *see LTg.*

GAu: misericordias] misericordiam δειλξοπϱστυφχψ; missericordiam ϑ. tuas] tuam δεϑιλξοπϱστυφχψ. protectione] tegmine δεϑιλξοπϱστυφχψ.

9

Inebriabuntur		bioð geindrencte *A*, beoð geindrencte *C*, beoð ondrencte *B*, beoð ondrængte J, beoð druncnude *D*, beoð druncnode *G*, beoð druncnude H, beoð druncene F, beoð druncnigende K, ondruncniende *E*[3], hig beoð gefyllede ł hig beoþ gedrencte I (*LM*)
ab		from A, from B, fram C, fram J, of DFGHK, ⁊ of E[3/x]*, for I
ubertate		breostum A*C, genyhtsumnesse B, genihtsumnisse D*, genihtsumnisse H, genihtsumnisse I, genyhtsumnisse E[x]*, genihtsumnysse F, genihtsumnesse GK, nihtsumnesse J
domus	I	huses ABDFGHIJK, husys C, þines E[3]
tuae	I	ðines A*BF*, þinys C, þines *DGIJK*, þine *H*, huses *E*[3] (*L*)
et		⁊ ABCDE[3]FGHIJK
torrente		burnan AB, of burnan CDE[x]*FGHIJ, of burnnan K
uoluntatis	I	willan AB*CDFGHJK*, þines E[3], þinre *I*
tuae	I	ðines A*BF*, þinys *C*, þines *DGH*J, þinre *K*, willæn E[3], wynsumnysse *I* (*L*)
potabis		drences A, þu drencst BDGH, þu drenctyst C, þu drencæst E[3/x]*, þu drenctest F, þu dreccest J, þu dreintes K, ⁊ þu scæncst I (*M*)
eos		hie AB, hi CK, hí F, hy DE[x]GH, hig I, his J

ED: tuæ (D) (*1st*)] tuae *Roeder*. tuę (E)] tuae *Harsley*. tuæ (D) (*2nd*)] tuae *Roeder*.

OE: ⁊ of (E[3/x]) of *on eras. by corr.* breostum (A)] *understanding* uber *as* 'breast' *vs* 'abundance'; *see also* C. genihtsumnisse (D)] geniht *on eras.* genyhtsumnisse (E[x])] *on eras. by corr.* of burnan (E[x])] *on eras.* þu drencæst (E[3/x])] *orig.* hi drincæs: hi *altered to* þu *by corr.*, i *in* drincæs *altered to* e *and* t *added.*

LTg: Inebriabuntur] L: *orig.* inebriabuntur: *initial* i *altered to* I *by corr.;* Inębriabuntur G; inebriabuntur ABCDEM. tuae (*1st*)] tuæ BDL; tuę EFGHJ; tue K. uoluntatis] uolutatis C; uoluptatis GHI, K: *orig.* uoluntatis: n *altered to* p *by corr.* tuae (*2nd*)] tuæ BD; tuę CGHIL, F: t *on eras.;* tue K. potabis] potàbis M.

LTu: Inebriabuntur] inebriabuntur βςτ*. tuae (*1st*)] tuæ ϑ; tuę ιvξουφ; tue σςτ*τ. uoluntatis] uoluptatis ξο. tuae (*2nd*)] tuæ ϑ; tuę ιλvξυφχ; tue στ*τ.

10

Quoniam	forðon AB*J, forþon C, Forþæn E[3], forþam G, forðam ðe F, forðan þe I
apud	mid *A*BCDFGHIJ*K*, mit E[3]
te	ðe ABF, þe CE[3]GIJK

<table>
<tr><td>est</td><td></td><td>is ABE^{3}FGIJK, ys C</td></tr>
<tr><td>fons</td><td>|</td><td>waelle A, welle BI, wylle CDF, wille H, wyl K, lifes E^3</td></tr>
<tr><td>uitae</td><td>|</td><td>lifes ABDFGHIK, lifys C, lif J, wielle E^3 (L)</td></tr>
<tr><td>et</td><td></td><td>⁊ ABCFGIJ, ond E^3 (K)</td></tr>
<tr><td>in</td><td></td><td>in A, on BCDE^{3}FGHIJK</td></tr>
<tr><td>lumine</td><td>|</td><td>lehte A, leohte BCDFGH, liohte I, lyhte J, leoht K, þinum E^3</td></tr>
<tr><td>tuo</td><td>|</td><td>ðinum AF, ðinum B, þinum CJ, þinum GI, þinan K, liohte E^3</td></tr>
<tr><td>uidebimus</td><td></td><td>we gesiað A, we geseoð BCDHIK, we geseoþ J, we gesioþ E^3, þe geseoð G, we gesawon F</td></tr>
<tr><td>lumen</td><td></td><td>leht A, leoht BCDFGHJK, lioht E^{3}I</td></tr>
</table>

ED: forðon (A)] for ðon *Kuhn*. uitę (E)] vitae *Harsley*.

OE: forðon (B)] *1st* o *faint but visible*.

LTg: apud] A: d *on eras. by corr.*; aput K. est] ést K. uitae] uitæ B; uitę CDEFGHKL; uite J. et] K: *on eras. by corr.* lumine] A: e *on eras.*

LTu: apud] aput υ. uitae] uitę βειvοπσφ; uitæ ϑ; uite ξςτ*τυ. et] *om.* δ. in lumine] illumine ϑ, ε: il *by corr.*

11

<table>
<tr><td>Praetende</td><td></td><td>ðene AB, aðene CF, aþena J, astrece ł þene DG, astrece ł þe H, astrece K, aspread ł þene E^x*, aræc ł sele ł tobræd I (L)</td></tr>
<tr><td>misericordiam</td><td>|</td><td>mildheortnisse A, mildheortnysse CF, mildheortnesse BDGHIJK, þine E^3</td></tr>
<tr><td>tuam</td><td>|</td><td>ðine ABF, þine CGHIJ, þinre K, mildheortnesse E^3</td></tr>
<tr><td>scientibus</td><td>|</td><td>weotendum A, witendum BDH, wityndum C, witendum F*GJ, witende K, ongitendum ł witendum I, þe E^3</td></tr>
<tr><td>te</td><td>|</td><td>ðec A, ðe BF, þe CDGHIJK, witendum E^3*</td></tr>
<tr><td>et</td><td></td><td>⁊ ABCFGHIJK</td></tr>
<tr><td>iustitiam</td><td>|</td><td>rehwisnisse A, rihtwisnysse CF, ryhtwisnesse BD, rihtwisnesse GHIJ, rihtwisnes K, þine E^3</td></tr>
<tr><td>tuam</td><td>|</td><td>ðine ABF, þine CIJ, þinre G, þin K, soðfestnesse E^3</td></tr>
<tr><td>his</td><td></td><td>ðissum A, þissum C, ðysum B, þisum J, þam DGH, þam E^3, ðam F, þæm I, ðan K (M)</td></tr>
<tr><td>qui</td><td></td><td>ða AB, þa þe CI, þe DE^{3}GHJK, ðe F</td></tr>
<tr><td>recto</td><td></td><td>rehte AB, rihte CE^{3}FIJ, ryhtwisere D, rihtwise G, rihtwisse HK</td></tr>
<tr><td>sunt</td><td>|</td><td>sind A, synd CFGJK, sint B, synt I, heortæn E^3</td></tr>
<tr><td>corde</td><td>|</td><td>on heortan AB, on hyra heortan C, heortan DFGH*JK, heortan ł ða rihtgeþancodan I*, sindon E^3</td></tr>
</table>

ED: aspread ł þene (E)] Aspread ł þene *Harsley*. iusticiam (C)] iusti[t]iam *Wildhagen*. iiś (C)] [h]ſs *Wildhagen*.

OE: aspread ł þene (E^{x})] aspread *on eras*. witendum (F)] e *altered from* t. witendum (E^{3})] *letter eras. after* n. heortan (H)] *bottom of left leg of* n *lost due to hole*. heortan ł ða rihtgeþancodan (I)] ł ða rihtgeþancodan *written in right margin*.

LTg: Praetende] Prætende B; Pretende CDEFGHIJKL. te] té B. iustitiam] iusticiam C: *orig*. iustitiam: *2nd* t *altered to* c. his] hís M; iiś C: *orig*. hís: *ascender of* h *eras. to form* i; hiís K: *1st* i *interl. by main hand*.

LTu: Praetende] υ: nde *interl.;* Pretende βδϑιοσςτ; Prętende ελνϱφ; [ ]retende τ*: *initial wanting*. misericordiam] missericordiam ϑ. iustitiam] iusticiam τ*τφ. his] iis ελπφχ.

12

Non	ne ABCDFGHIJ, Ne *E^{3}*, na K
ueniat	cyme ABC, cume DE^{3}FGHJK, becume I
mihi	me AB*CDE^{3}*FGHI*K*, to me J
pes	fot ABC*D*E^{3}*FGHJK, fot ł angin I*
superbiae	oferhygde A*B*, ofyrhigde *C*, oferhidig *J*, ofermodnisse *DH*, ofermodinesse *E^{x}**, ofermodignysse *FI*, ofermodignesse *G*, oferermodines *K* (*L*)
et	⁊ ABCE^{x}*FGHIJK
manus	hond A, hand BCDE^{x}*HK, handa FGJ, hand ł anweald I
peccatorum*	synfulra ABDE^{x}*FGK, synfullys C, synfulles J, þæs synfullan I* (*M*)
non	ne ABCDE^{x}*FGHJ, na K, ⁊ ne I
moueat	onwendeð AB, onwendyð *C*, onwændaþ J, styrige DE^{x}*F, astyrige GI*K, astirige H
me	mec AD, me BCE^{x}*FGHJK

OE: fot (E^{3})] ot *retouched in darker ink*. fot ł angin (I)] ł angin *written in right margin*. ofermodinesse (E^{x})] *on eras*. ⁊ (E^{x})] *on eras*. hand (E^{x})] *on eras*. synfulra (E^{x})] *on eras*. þæs synfullan (I)] þæs *written in bottom margin below* peccatoris. ne (E^{x})] *on eras*. styrige (E^{x})] *on eras*. astyrige (I)] *orig*. stirige: a *interl., 1st* i *altered to* y. me (E^{x})] *on eras*.

LTg: Non] E: on *on eras*. mihi] michi EK, C: *orig*. mihi: c *interl. by corr*. pes] pés D. superbiae] superbiæ B; superbię CDFGHIKL; superbie EJ. peccatorum] peccatôrum M. moueat] moueant C: n *interl*.

LTu: mihi] michi ιξςτ*τ, ϱ: c *interl.;* m^{1} φ. superbiae] superbię ειντξυφ; superbiæ ϑ; superbie σςτ*τ.

GAg: peccatorum] peccatoris FGHIK, J: i *altered from* e, *eras. after* i.

GAu: peccatorum] peccatoris δεϑιλοπϱτυφχψ; peccatori[ ] ξ.

13

Ibi		ðer AE^{3}, ðær BCF, þær DGHI, þar JK
ceciderunt		gefeollun A, gefeollon BJ, hie gefiollon E^{3}, feollon CF, feollan K, hrurun ł feollon D, hruron ł feollon G*H*, feollun gehruron I*
omnes*		alle A, ealle BCD, eælle E^{3}
qui		ða ðe AB, þa þe CGI, þa ðe JK, þæ þe E^{3}, þe DH, þa F
operantur		wircað A*J*, wyrceað BCI, wyrcað DGH, wircæþ E^{3}, wyrcendan F, worhtton K
iniquitatem		unrehwisnisse A, unrihtwisnysse CFI, unryhtwisnesse D, unrihtwisnesse $E^{3/x}$**G*HJK, unryhtwisnes B
expulsi	|	on weg adrifene A, aweg adrifene B, aweg adrifyne C, aweg ł utadrifene J, utacnyssed DH, utacnýsed F, utascofene I, utanydde K, hi sint E^{3} (*G*)
sunt	|	sind A, synd CJK, sint B, synt I, hy synd D, hi synd F, hy sind H, [ ]nd G, utacnyssed $E^{3/x}$*
nec	|	ne ABD*H*I, na K, hi ne C, hy ne G, ne hi ne FIJ, þæt hie ne E^{3}
potuerunt	|	hie maegon A, hie magon B, magon J, mihton CFG, mihtun I, mihtan K, mæhton $E^{3/x}$*, hy meahton D, hi mihton H
stare		stondan *A*DK, stondon E^{3}, standan BCFHI, standa[ ] *G**, standon J

ED: feollun gehruron (I)] feollun ł gehruron *Lindelöf.* [ ]i (G)] *expulsi Rosier.* utacnyssed (H)] ut acnyssed *Campbell.* [ ]nd (G)] *no gloss Rosier.* standa[ ] (G)] stan[ ] *Rosier.*

OE: feollun gehruron (I)] gehruron *written above* feollun. unrihtwisnesse ($E^{3/x}$)] wisnesse *added by corr.* utacnyssed ($E^{3/x}$)] uta *interl. by corr.,* ssed *added.* mæhton ($E^{3/x}$)] hton *on eras. by corr.* standa[ ] (G)] *letter fragment (bowl?) visible after 2nd* a.

LTg: ceciderunt] cęciderunt H. operantur] J: n *interl. by glossator.* iniquitatem] iniquitate[ ] G. expulsi] [ ]i G. nec] nęc H. stare] A: *title for Ps 36 eras. and written on fol. 39r;* star[ ] G.

LTu: omnes] *om.* ς: *see GAu.* nec] nęc ξ.

GAg: omnes] *om.* FGHIJK.

GAu: omnes] *om.* δεϑιλξοπϱσυφχ, ς: *see LTu.*

PSALM 36

1

Noli	nyl ðu AB, nelle þu *CJ*, nelle ðu *D*, nelu *K*, nylle þu FHI, Nelle þu þe *$E^{3/x}$**, [ ]u *G* (*M*)
aemulari	elnian *AB*, elnian ł ellenwondian *C**, onhyrigan *D*, onhyrian *GHK*, onscuniæn *E^{3}*, onbyrgan *F**, geeuenlæcan *I*, efnian *J* (*L*)
inter*	betwih AB, betwioh E^{3}, betwux C, betweox DH, betweax G, on FK, mid I, ⁊ J (*L*)
malignantes*	awergde AB, awyrgyde C, þa awyrgendan DH, þæm awyrgendan $E^{3/x}$*, þam awyrgedan G, þam awyrgendum I, ða awyrigede K, yfelwyllendum F, yfelsacigan J (*L*)
neque	ne ABCDE^{x}*GHI, ne ne F, ⁊ na J
aemulatus*	elnende A*B*, elniynde *C*, onhyred *DE^{x}**, ándian F, þu ne anda GH, geeuenlæc I (*L*)
fueris*	ðu sie AB, þu sy C, þu beo DE^{x}*
facientes	donde ABJK, doynde C, ða dondan DE^{x}*, þa dondan H, þam dondum F, þa<u>m</u> dondan G, þu wyrcende I
iniquitatem	unrehtwisnisse A, unryhtwisnesse B, unrihtwisnysse CF, unrihtwisnesse DGHIJ, unrihtwisnes K*, unrihtnesse E^{3}

OE: Nelle þu þe ($E^{3/x}$)] Nelle þu *by corr.* elnian ł ellenwondian (C)] on *interl.* onbyrgan (F)] *orig.* onhyrgan: h *altered to* b. þæm awyrgendan ($E^{3/x}$)] awyrgendan *by corr.* ne (E^{x})] *on eras.* onhyred (E^{x})] *on eras.* þu beo (E^{x})] *on eras.* ða dondan (E^{x})] *on eras.* unrihtwisnes (K)] ne *eras. after word.*

LTg: Noli] NOLI CE; NOli DKM; [ ]oli G. aemulari] A: i *on eras. by corr.;* EMVLARI C; emulari BDEFGHIJK; æmulari L. inter] L: ter *underlined to signal deletion: see GAg.* malignantes] L: tes *underlined to signal deletion,* ibus *written below: see GAg.* aemulatus] emulatus BCDE, L: zelaueris *added interl. by corr.: see GAg.*

LTu: ζ: *wanting vv 1–14* trucident, μ: *wanting vv 1–9.* Noli] NOLi βς; NOLI ιλνϱτ*τχψ. aemulari] emulari βδϑιξπστ*τυφ; EMULARI λϱχ; ęmulari ε; Æmulari ν; EMulari ς; AEMULARI ψ. aemulatus] emulatus βςτ*; ęmulatus ν.

GAg: inter] in FGHIJĶ, L: *see LTg.* malignantes] malignantibus FHIJK, G: *lower loop of* g *wanting*, L: *see LTg.* aemulatus] zelaueris FGHIJK, L: *see LTg.* fueris] *om.* FGHIJK.

GAu: inter] in δεϑιξοπσυφχψ; IN λϱ. malignantes] malignantibus δεϑιξοπστυφχψ; MALIGNANtibus λϱ. aemulatus] zelaueris δεϑιλξοπϱστυφχψ. fueris] *om.* δεϑιλξοπϱστυφχψ.

2

Quoniam	forðon A*B*J, forþon C, Forðæn E^{3}, forðan K, forðon þe I, forðam ðe F, forþam G
tamquam	swe swe A, swa swa B*C*DG*H*IJ, swá swá F, swæ swæ *E^{3}**, swa K
faenum	heg A*BCDE^{x}*FH,* hyg *G,* hig *IK,* híg *J* (*L*)
uelociter	hreðlice A, hrædlice BCDFGHI, hreadlice E^{x}*, rædlice J, snellice K
arescent	adrugiað AB, adrugað F*K,* adrugiað G, adruwiað C, adruwaþ J, hy adrugiað D, hi adrugiað H, hy adrigiað E^{x}*, hi adruwiað ł forseariaþ I (*M*)
et	⁊ ABCE^{x}*FGJK
sicut*	swe swe A, swa swa BCD*E^{x}**I, on ðam gemete F, on þam gemete J, to þam gemetes G, ealswa K (*L*)
holera	| leaf AB*C,* blæda ł leæf *E^{x}*,* bleda D*FH,* blæda *K,* blæda ł wy[ ] *G,* wyrta *IJ* (*M*)
herbarum	| wyrta ABCD*E^{x}**H, wýrta F, wyrtta K, weorta ł gærs G*, felda ł blæda wyrtena I*, gærswyrta J
cito	hreðe AB, hraðe C, raðe D*E^{x}**GH, raþa J, hrædlice F, hwætlice I, sona K
cadent*	fallað AB, feallyð C, feallað FK, feallaþ J, hreosað ł fеælleþ *E^{x}*,* hi feallaþ ł hreosað I, hreosað DGH

ED: forðon (A)] for ðon *Kuhn.* tanquam (C)] ta[m]quam *Wildhagen.* swa swa (GIJ)] swaswa *Rosier, Lindelöf, Oess.* swa swa (I) (*2nd*)] swaswa *Lindelöf.* décident (H)] decident *Campbell.*

OE: swæ swæ (E^{3})] *eras. before and after gloss.* heg (E^{x})] *on eras.* hreadlice (E^{x})] *on eras.* hy adrigiað (E^{x})] *on eras.* ⁊ (E^{x})] *on eras.* swa swa (E^{x})] *on eras.* blæda ł leæf (E^{x})] *on eras.* wyrta (E^{x})] *on eras.* weorta ł gærs (G)] ł gærs *added in diff.* (?) *hand.* wyrta felda ł blæda wyrtena (I)] ł blæda wyrtena *written in right margin.* raðe (E^{x})] *on eras.* hreosað ł feælleþ (E^{x})] *on eras.*

LTg: Quoniam] [ ]m̄ B: *initial letter not written.* tamquam] tanquam E, C: *orig.* tamquam: *left leg of 1st* m *eras. to form* n, H: *orig.* tamquam: *right leg of 1st* m *eras. to form* n. faenum] foenum BDEIL; fęnum CFG; fenum HJK. arescent] M: *orig.* arescint: i *altered to* e; árescent K. sicut] E: *retraced in darker ink,* L: quemadmodum *added interl. by corr.: see GAg.* holera] E: *retraced in darker ink;* olera CFGHIJK, M: *orig.* holera: h *deleted by subscript dot.* herbarum] E: herba *retraced in darker ink.* cito] E: it *retouched in darker ink.* cadent] E: *ascender of* d *retouched in darker ink.*

LTu: tamquam] tanquam εϑιλτ*τ. faenum] foenum δεϑλνοπϱφχ; fęnum ιξσυ;

fenum ςτ*τψ. uelociter] β: *orig.* felociter: u *written above* f *by corr.* holera] ϑυ: *spiritus asper* (ꟷ) *interl.;* olera ιπϱστ*φ. cito] cyto ξ. cadent] decident τ*: *see GAu.*

GAg: sicut] quemadmodum GHIJK, F: *eras. after word,* L: *see LTg.* cadent] decident FGI; décident H: *orig.* décidant: a *altered to* e, *although now taking on appearance of* æ, K: *orig.* decidant: a *altered to* e *by main hand;* decidant J.

GAu: sicut] quemadmodum δεϑιλξπϱστυφχψ; quemammodum o: *orig.* quemadmodum. cadent] decident δεϑιξοπϱστυφχψ, τ*: *see LTu.*

3

Spera	gehyht ABCD*H*, gehiht GIJ, hiht K, Gewene ł hyht $E^{3/x}$*, hopa F
in	in A, on BCE^{3}FGIJK
domino	dryhtne B, drihtne CFGI, drihten E^{3}K, dryht̄ A, drih́ J
et	⁊ ABCE^{3}FGHIJK
fac	doa A, doá C, dó BF, do DE^{x}GHIJK
bonitatem	godnisse ADH, godnesse BE^{3}JK, godnysse CI, gódnysse F, godnessæ G
et	⁊ ABCE^{3}JK (*FGHI*)
inhabita	inearda AB, onearda CF, onearde G, earda DH, earda on K, þu eærdest E^{3}, onwuna I
terram	eorðan ABCDFGH, eorþan JK, on eorðæn E^{3}, on gelaðunge I
et	⁊ ABCE^{3}FGHIJK
pasceris	ðu bist foeded AB, þu byst fedyd *C*, þu bist feded *F*, þu bist fed DE^{3}**H*, þu bist fett G, ðu bist gefed *I*, þu gefed byst K, þu bist J (*M*)
in	in A, on BCDE^{3}FGHIK
diuitiis	| weolum A, welum BCFGH, welum D, his *E*^{3}I, estan K* (*M*)
eius	| hire ADH, his BCFG*K*, welum E^{3}, welum þæt is on godes rice I

ED: [ ]p[ ]ra (H)] Spera *Campbell.* dó (B)] do *Brenner.* pascéris (HI)] pasceris *Campbell, Lindelöf.* diuitíís (E)] divitiis *Harsley.* eius (G)] ei*us Rosier.*

OE: Gewene ł hyht ($E^{3/x}$)] ł hyht *added by corr. above* Gewene. þu bist fed (E^{3})] *eras. after word (7 mm), tongue of* e *visible in final position.* estan (K)] *lemma misread as* deliciis (?).

LTg: Spera] [ ]p[ ]ra H: *initial* S *lost, letter fragments visible after* p. fac] E: *on eras.* et (*2nd*)] F: *added by corr.,* HI: *interl.; om.* G. pasceris] pascéris CFHI; pascêris M. diuitiis] M: s *altered from another letter;* diuitíís E. eius] eíus K.

LTu: et (*1st*)] β: *crossed through; om.* ι. inhabita] inabita λ. diuitiis] β: *orig.* diuitis: *4th* i *added interl. by corr.*

4

Delectare		gelustfulla ABCDF*G*HIJK, Gelustfullæ E^{3}*
in		in A, on BCDE^{3}FGHIJK
domino		dryhtne B, drihtny C, drihtne DFI, drihtæn E^{3}, drihten K, dryht̄ A, drih̄t GH, drih̄ J
et		⁊ ABCE^{3}FGHIJK
dabit	|	seleð A, sylyð C, he seleð B, he selð D, he sylþ FH, he sylð GI, he silleþ J, he gifð K, he þe E^{3}
tibi	|	ðe ABFI, þe CGHJK, seleþ E^{3}
petitionem*		boene AB, bena C, bene E^{3}J, gyrninge DG, gyrningce F, girninge H, gewilnunga ł gyrningce ł bena I*, wilnunga K (*M*)
cordis	|	heortan ABCDFGHIJK, þinre E^{3}
tui	|	ðinre A, þinre BCGIJK, þines D, ðines F, þin[ ] H*, heortæn E^{3}

ED: þin[ ] (H)] þin(es) *Campbell.*

OE: Gelustfullæ (E^{3})] þ *eras. after word.* gewilnunga ł gyrningce ł bena (I)] ł bena *written above* gyrningce. þin[ ] (H)] *letter fragment visible after* n, *letters lost due to hole in leaf.*

LTg: Delectare] [ ]electare G: *initial* D *lost.* petitionem] petitiônem M.

LTu: Delectare] Dilectare βϑ. dabit] dauit ϑ.

GAg: petitionem] petitiones FHIJK; pętitiones G.

GAu: petitionem] petitiones δεϑιλξοπϱστυφχψ.

5

Reuela		onwrih A, onwreoh BC, awreoh DGHIK, Awrioh $E^{3/x}$*, unwreoh FJ (*M*)
ad*		(*ABCDELM*)
dominum*		dryhtne *AB,* drihtne *DFE*^{3}*I, drihtene K, drih̄t *C*GH, drih̄ J (*LM*)
uiam	|	wig A, weg BCDFGHIJK, þinne E^{3}
tuam	|	ðinne ABF, þinne CDGH*IJK, weg E^{x}
et		⁊ ABCE^{3}FGHIJK
spera		gehyht AB, gehiht CI, gehihte J, hyht DH, hiht GK, hopa F, gewene ł hyht $E^{3/x}$*
in		in A, on BCDE^{3}FGHIJK
eum*		hine ABDE^{3}FGJ*K,* hyne CH, him I
et		⁊ ABCDFGHIJK, ond E^{3}
ipse		he ABCDE^{3}*FGHJK, he sylf I
faciet		doeð AB, deð CE^{3}FGK, deþ DHJ, deð þæt her æfter is gesett I

OE: Awrioh ($E^{3/x}$)] *orig.* Onwrioh: O *altered to* A, n *eras.* drihtne (E^{3})] *eras. before word.* þinne (H)] *1st* n *altered from* r. gewene ł hyht ($E^{3/x}$)] *added by corr.* he (E^{3})] *eras. after word.*

LTg: Reuela] Reuêla M. ad] *om.* ABCDEL; *eras.* M: *cf. Weber MSS* T^2 med, *see GAg.* dominum] domino ABCDELM: *cf. Weber MSS* T^2 med, *see GAg.* eum] K: um *on eras.*

LTu: ad] *om.* ντ*: *cf. Weber MSS* T^2 med, *see GAu.* dominum] domino ντ*: *cf. Weber MSS* T^2 med, *see GAu.*

GAg: ad] *om.* FGHIJK, ABCDEL: *see LTg.* dominum] domino FGHIJK, ABCDELM: *see LTg.* eum] eo FGIJ, H: *small eras. after* o.

GAu: ad] *om.* δεϑιλξοπϱστυφχψ, ντ*: *see LTu.* dominum] domino δεϑιλξοπϱστυφχψ, ντ*: *see LTu.* eum] eo εϑιλξπϱστυφχ, ο: *orig.* eum.

6

Et — ⁊ ABCE^{3}FGHIJK
educet — utalędeð A, utalædeð B, utalædyð C, utalædeþ J, he gelædeþ DF, he gelædeð GH, he gelæt I, he lædet K, he ðe ledeþ E^{3} (*M*)
tamquam* — swe swe A, swa swa B*C*DFJ, swæ swæ E^{3}, hwilc G, swilce I, ealswa K
lumen — leht A, leoht BCDFGHIJK, þet lioht E^{3} (*M*)
iustitiam | rehtwisnisse A, ryhtwisnesse BD, rihtwisnysse *C*FI, rihtwisnesse GHJK, þinre E^{3}
tuam | ðine ABF, þine CHIJK, þinre G, soðfestenesse E^{3}
et — ⁊ ABCE^{3}FGHIJK
iudicium | dom ACDFGHIJK, dóm B*, ðinne E^{3}
tuum | ðinne ABF, þinne CDGHIJK, dom E^{3}
sicut* — swe A, swa BK, swa swa CDFGIJ, swæ swæ E^{3}* (*L*)
meridiem — on midne deg *A*, on midne dæg *B*C, midne dæg J, middæg DFGHIK, middeig E^{3}* (*M*)

ED: tanquam (C)] ta[m]quam *Wildhagen.* swa swa (J) (*1st*)] swaswa *Oess.* iusticiam (C)] iusti[t]iam *Wildhagen.* swa swa (GIJ) (*2nd*)] swaswa *Rosier, Lindelöf, Oess.*

OE: dóm (B)] *accent faint but visible.* swæ swæ (E^{3})] *2nd* swæ *by corr.* (?). middeig (E^{3})] æn *eras. before word* (*Harsley reads* on), *2–3 letters eras. after* d.

LTg: educet] edûcet M. tamquam] tanquam C: *orig.* tamquam: *left leg of 1st* m *eras. to form* n. lumen] lûmen M. iustitiam] iusticiam C: *orig.* iustitiam: *2nd* t *altered to* c. sicut] L: tamquam *added interl. by corr.: see GAg.* meridiem] merídie<u>m</u> M: *orig.* merídie: *macron added, eras.* (?) *after 2nd* e; meridie AB: *cf. Weber MSS* SKαβ moz^x.

LTu: Et] *lost* ξ. educet] [ ]ducet ξ. tamquam] tanquam τ*. lumen] β: *added in right margin by corr.* iustitiam] iusticiam τ*τφ. meridiem] meridie β.

GAg: tamquam] quasi FGHIJK. sicut] tamquam FGIJK, L: *see LTg;* tanquam H: n *altered from another letter.*

GAu: tamquam] quasi δεϑιλξοπϱστυφχψ. sicut] tamquam δξοπϱυχψ; tanquam ϑιλστφ, ε: n *interl.*

7

Subditus	ǀ	underðioded A, underðeoded B, underþeodyð C, underþeod D*GHK,* underðeod *FI,* underþeodeþ *J,* Beo ðu $E^{3/x}$* (*L*)
esto	ǀ	bio ðu A, beo ðu BDI, beo þu CF*GHK, bo du J, drihtne E^{3}
domino	ǀ	dryhtne B, drihtne DFHI, drihtene K, dryhī A, driħt *C*G, driħ J, underþied E^{3}
et		⁊ ACE³FGIJK (*H*)
obsecra*		halsa ABCDE^{x}**K, bide FG, gebide I, gebide þe J (*LM*)
eum		hine ABCDE^{x}**FGIK, to him J
ne*	ǀ	ne AC, na DE^{x}**, nylle ðu F, nelle ðu G, nelle þu IJK (*L*)
aemulatus*	ǀ	elnende A, elniynde *C,* onhyre ðu *DE^{x}***, onhyrian G, hyrian K, byrgan F, geeuenlæcan I, efnian J (*BL*)
fueris*	ǀ	ðu sie AB, þu sy C (*L*)
(in)*		on FGIJK
eum*		hine ABCDE^{x}**F, him G, hi<u>m</u> JK, þæm I (*L*)
qui		se ABCJ, þe D*E^{x}**I, ðe F, þa þe G, þa K
prosperatur		bið gesundfullad AB, bið gesundfullud C, bið gesundfullod DF, byð gesundfullod I, biþ gesundfullod J, bið gesunfullod *E^{x}***, he bið gesundfullod H, beoð gesundfullod G, beoð gesundfullud K
in		in A, on BCD*E^{x}***FGHIJK
uia		wege ABCDFG*H*IJK, wæge *E^{x}**
sua		his ABCDE^{x}**FG*H*IJK
in		in A, on BCDE^{x}**FGHIJK
homine		men ABE^{x}**HIJK, menn CDFG
faciente		dondum ABF, doyndum C, dondu<u>m</u> DE^{x}**H, donde GJK, wyrcende I
iniquitatem*		unrehtwisnisse A, unryhtwisnesse BD, unrihtwisnysse CF, unrihtwisnesse E^{3}*HJK, unrihtwisnes G, unrihtwisnyssa I (*L*)

ED: subditus (I)] Subditus *Lindelöf.* bo du (J)] bodu *Oess.*

OE: Beo ðu ($E^{3/x}$)] Beo *by corr.,* ðu *retraced by corr.* beo þu (F)] *eras. before* beo. halsa (E^{x})] *on eras., letter eras. after* l. hine (E^{x}) (*1st*)] *on eras.* na (E^{x})] *on eras.* onhyre ðu (E^{x})] *on eras.* hine (E^{x}) (*2nd*)] *on eras.* þe (E^{x})] *on eras.* bið gesunfullod (E^{x})] *on eras.* on (E^{x}) (*1st*)] *on eras.* wæge (E^{x})] *on eras.* his (E^{x})] *on eras.* on

(E^{x}) (*2nd*)] *on eras.* men (E^{x})] *on eras.* dondum (E^{x})] *on eras.* unrihtwisnesse (E^{3})] *1st* s *interl.*

LTg: Subditus] L: *initial* S *crossed through by corr. and minuscule* s *added between* Su; subditus FGHIJK. domino] C: *final* o *on eras.* (?). et] H: *on eras.* obsecra] L: ora *added interl. by corr.: see GAg;* óbsecra M. ne] L: Noli *added interl. by corr.: see GAg.* aemulatus] æmulatus B; emulatus CDE, L: tus *underlined to signal deletion,* ri *added interl. by corr.: see GAg.* fueris] L: *underlined to signal deletion: see GAg.* eum] L: in eo *added interl. by corr.: see GAg.* qui] E: i *retraced in darker ink.* prosperatur] E: *retraced in darker ink.* in] E: *retraced in darker ink.* uia] E: *retraced in darker ink,* H: *eras. after* a. sua] H: *eras. after* a. iniquitatem] L: iniusticias *added interl. by corr.: see GAg.*

LTu: Subditus] subditus δεϑιλξοπϱστυφψ. aemulatus] ęmulatus ν; emulatus ςτ*.

GAg: obsecra] ora FGHIJK, L: *see LTg.* ne] Noli FHIJK, L: *see LTg;* [ ]oli G: *initial* N *lost.* aemulatus fueris eum] emulari in eo FHJK, L: *see LTg;* ęmulari in eo G; aemulari in eo I. iniquitatem] iniustitias FGHIJK; *for* L *see LTg.*

GAu: obsecra] ora δεϑιλξοπϱστυφχψ. ne] Noli δεϑιλοπϱστυφχψ; [ ]oli ξ. aemulatus fueris eum] emulari in eo δϑιλξπϱστυφχ; ęmulari in eo ε; aemulari in eo οψ. iniquitatem] iniustitias δεϑιλξοπϱσυχψ; iniusticias τφ.

8

Desine — blin A*B, forlæt ł blin *C**, ablin *DGHI*JK, Ablin E^{3}, ablin ðu F (*M*)
ab — from AE^{3}, from BC, fram DFHJK, fram GI
ira — eorre AB, yrre *C*DFGHIK, irre J, yrræ E^{3}
et — ⁊ ABCE^{3}FGHIJK
derelinque — forlet *A*E^{3}, forlæt BCD*F*GHIJK
furorem — hatheortnisse AD, hatheortnesse BGHJ, hatheortnysse CFI, hatheortnes K, hatheornesse *E^{x}** (*M*)
ne* — I ne ABCD, na E^{x}*, nylle þu F, nelle þu IJK (*L*)
aemuleris* — I elna ðu A*B,* elna þu *C,* elnian J, anhyre ðu *DE^{x}*,* anhyrigan K, [ ]h(y)rian G*, onbyrgan F, geeuenlæcan I (*LM*)
ut — þætte A, ðætte B, þætte C, þæt DE^{x}*FGIJK (*H*)
nequiter* — nohtlice AB*C,* nearolice DE^{x}* (*L*)
facias* — ðu doe A, ðu dó B, þu do CE^{x}*, þu dó D, þu wyrge F, þu wirige J, þu beo yfelwillende G, þu beo awerged s. mid deofle I, ðu beo acursod K

ED: Désine (HI)] Desine *Campbell, Lindelöf.* hatheornesse (E^{x})] hatheor[t]nesse *Harsley.* æmuleris (D)] aemuleris *Roeder.* [ ]h(y)rian (G)] [ ]rian *Rosier.* malignéris (I)] maligneris *Lindelöf.*

OE: blin (A)] *eras. after* l. forlæt ł blin (C)] ł blin *written in left margin.* hatheornesse (E^x)] *on eras.* na (E^x)] *on eras.* anhyre ðu (E^x)] *on eras.* [ ]h(y)rian (G)] *top of* y *visible.* þæt (E^x)] *on eras.* nearolice (E^x)] *on eras.* þu do (E^x)] *on eras.*

LTg: Desine] C: *eras.* (a?) *before final* e, D: *final* e *on eras.;* Désine HIM. ira] C: *orig.* iret: et *altered to* a. derelinque] A: n *interl. by corr., final* e *on eras.,* F: re *interl. by corr.* furorem] E: fu *retraced in darker ink;* furôrem M. ne] L: *underlined to signal deletion,* noli *added interl. by corr.: see GAg.* aemuleris] æmuleris BCD; aemulêris M; emuleris E, L: eris *underlined to signal deletion,* ari *added interl. by corr.: see GAg.* ut] H: *on eras.* nequiter] L: maligneris *added interl. by corr.: see GAg;* nęquiter C: *cauda unclear.*

LTu: Desine] [ ]ne ξ. aemuleris] ęmularis ν; emuleris ςτ*.

GAg: ne] noli FGHIJK, L: *see LTg.* aemuleris] emulari FHJK, L: *see LTg;* ęmulari G; aemulari I. nequiter facias] maligneris FGHJK, L: *see LTg;* malignéris I.

GAu: ne] noli δεϑιλξοπϱστυφχψ. aemuleris] emulari ϑιλξπϱστυφχ; ęmulari ε; aemulari δοψ. nequiter facias] maligneris δεϑιλξοπϱστυφχψ.

9

Quoniam	forðon ABJ, forþon C, Forðæn *E^3**, forðam F, forðan I, forþan K, for G
qui	ða AB, þa C, þe D, þa ðe FJK, þa þe GI, þæ þe *E^3*
nequiter*	nohtlice AB*C,* nearolicȩ D, heteniþ *E^3* (*LM*)
agunt*	doð ABC, doþ D*E^x**, wyrgað F, wyrgeað K, wiriaþ J, beoð awerged I, beoð yfelwillende G
exterminabuntur	biað abreotte A, beoð abreotte B, beoð abrytte C, beoþ abrytte J, beoð geteorode D*E^x**GH, beoþ geteorode F, beoð geterode K, hi beoð ut asceofan I (*M*)
qui*	ða AB, þa C, þa ðe DE^x*
(sustinentes)*	þa geþyldigan F, þa geþildigan J, forþyldigendan G, anbidiende ł þoliende I, uphealden K
uero*	soðlice ABCFG, soþlice DE^x*J, witodlice K*
expectant*	abidað ABC, geanbidiað D*E^x** (*LM*)
dominum	drihten E^x*FK, dryht̄ AB, driћt CG, driћ J
ipsi	he A, hie BE^3, hi *C*FK, hy DGH, hig J, þa I
hereditate*	erfewordnisse A, yrfeweardnysse *C,* yrfeweardnisse *D,* yrfeweardnesse J, yrfeweærdnesse E^3, yrfweardnesse B, yrfweardnysse F, [ ]rfeweardnesse G, geyrfweardiaþ ł geahniąð I, eorfwerddiaþ K (*LM*)
possidebunt*	gesittað AB, wealdað C, agun D, agon E^3*
terram	eorðan ABCFGHJ, eorðæn E^3, eorþan K, land ł ece lif I*

ED: forðon (A)] for ðon *Kuhn*. þa geþildigan (J)] þa ge þildigan *Oess*. hereditate (D)] hereditatem *Roeder*. hereditabunt (G)] *here*ditabunt G. [ ]rfeweardnesse (G)] yrfeweardnesse *Rosier*.

OE: Forðæn (E^{3})] F *and* r *retraced by corr*. doþ (E^{x})] *on eras*. beoð geteorode (E^{x})] *on eras*. þa ðe (E^{x})] *on eras*. soþlice (E^{x})] *on eras*. witodlice (K)] d *altered from* t. geanbidiað (E^{x})] *on eras*. drihten (E^{x})] *on eras*. agon (E^{3})] *orig*. ægon: æ *altered to* a, *eras. after word*. land ł ece lif (I)] ł ece lif *extends into right margin*.

LTg: Quoniam] E: m *retouched in darker ink*. qui (*1st*)] E: *retouched in darker ink*. nequiter] E: equiter *retouched in darker ink*, L: malignantur *added interl. by corr.* (agunt *remains undeleted*): *see GAg;* nęquiter C; néquiter M. agunt] E: *retouched in darker ink*. exterminabuntur] E: exter *retouched in darker ink;* exterminabúntur M. ipsi] C: *final* i *on eras*. expectant] E: ectant *retouched in darker ink*, L: sustinetes autem *added interl. by corr.* (qui uero *remains undeleted although implied by addition of* autem): *see GAg*, M: *orig*. exspectant: s *eras*. hereditate] D: *orig*. hereditatem: *macron above final* e *eras*., L: possidebunt *added interl. by corr.*: *see GAg;* hęreditate C; heredităte M: *eras. after final* e.

LTu: Quoniam] [ ]m̄ ξ. expectant] exspectant β. dominum] *interl*. σ. hereditate] hereditatem βς.

GAg: nequiter agunt] malignantur FGHIJK; *for* L *see LTg note to* nequiter. qui uero expectant] sustinentes autem FGHIJK; *for* L *see LTg note to* expectant. hereditate] hereditabunt FGHIJK. possidebunt] *om*. FGHIJK.

GAu: nequiter agunt] malignantur δεϑιλξοπϱστυφχψ. qui uero expectant] sustinentes autem δεϑιλξοπϱστυφχψ. hereditate] hereditabunt δϑλξοπστυχψ; hęreditabunt ειϱφ. possidebunt] *om*. δεϑλξπϱτσυφχψ.

10

(Et)*	⁊ FGHIJK
Pusillum	} lytel *A*B, lytyl C, lytelfæc *D*E^{x}*FGH, lytelfec K, ł scortlice ł lytelfæc I, litel lyht hwon J (*LM*)
adhuc	} nu get A*B, nu gyt CDE^{x}*GH, nu gýt F, is nu gyt I, nu git J, gyt K
et	⁊ ABCE^{3}*FGIJK
non	ne ABCE^{3}*GIJ, na FK
erit	bið ABCDE^{3}**F*GHK, byð I, biþ J
peccator	se synfulla ABIJ, synfull CDFG, synful E^{x}*HK
et	⁊ ABCE^{3}FGHIJK
quaeres	soeces *A*, secyst *C*, secest *DE^{3}K*, secst *GH*, ðu soecest *B*, ðu sécst *F*, þu secst I, þu secest *J* (*LM*)
locum	| stowe ABCDFGHIJK, his E^{3}
eius	| his ABCDFGHIJ*K*, Stowe E^{3}*

(et)*	⁊ FHIJK
nec*	ǀ ne ABCJ, na DE³*FHK, ⁊ ne G, ðu ne I
inucnies	ǀ ðu gemotes A, ðu gemetest B, þu gemetest E³/ˣ*F, þu gemetyst C, ðu gemetst D, þu gemetst H*, bið gemet G, biþ gemeted J, gemetst I, findest K

ED: ⁊ (G) (*1st*)] *no gloss Rosier.* lytelfæc (E)] lytel fæc *Harsley.* ł scortlice ł lytelfæc (I)] ł scortlice ł lytel fæc *Lindelöf.* nu gyt (CEG)] nygyt *Wildhagen, Harsley, Rosier.* nu git (J)] nugit *Oess.* eius (G)] eius et *Rosier.*

OE: lytelfæc (Eˣ)] *on eras.* nu get (A)] t (*malformed*) *added by corr., possibly over another letter.* nu gyt (Eˣ)] *on eras.* ⁊ (E³) (*1st*)] *gloss eras. before word.* bið (E³)] sy (?) *eras. before word.* synful (Eˣ)] *on eras.* Stowe (E³)] *gloss eras. after word.* na (E³)] *orig.* ne: e *altered to* a *by corr.* þu gemetest (E³/ˣ)] þu ge *by corr.,* s *on eras.* þu gemetst (H)] *orig.* þu gemestst: *1st* s *eras.*

LTg: Pusillum] A: *eras. after 1st* u, D: *orig.* Pussillum: *1st* s *eras.,* L: Et adhuc pusillum *added interl. by corr. above* Pusillum: *see GAg;* Pusíllum M: *orig.* Pussíllum: *1st* s *eras.* et (*1st*)] E: *retouched in darker ink.* non] E: *retouched in darker ink.* erit] F: i *on eras.* quaeres] quęres BFG, A: *orig.* quęris: i *altered to* e, H: s *altered from another letter and followed by eras.;* quæris C; quæres L: *orig.* quæris: i *altered to* e *by corr.;* queris DE; queres JK; quaeris M. eius] eíus K.

LTu: quaeres] queris βςτ*; queres δϑιξστυ; quęres ελοπϱφψ; quæres μ; quęris ν. eius] β: i *interl.*

GAg: Pusillum adhuc et] Et adhuc pusillum et FHIJK, L: *see LTg note to* Pusillum *above;* [ ]t adhuc pusillum et G. eius] eius et FGHIJ; eíus et K. nec] non FGHIJK.

GAu: Pusillum adhuc et] et adhuc pusillum et δ; Et adhuc pusillum et εϑιλμξοπϱστυφχψ. eius] eius et δεϑιλμξοπστυφχψ. nec] non δεϑιλμξοπϱστυφχψ.

11

Mansueti	ða monðuaeran A, ða monðwæran B, þa manþwæran C, þa manðwæren I, þa manþwæron J, þa geþwæran DEˣ*H, ða geþwæran F, geþwæran K, [ ]ran *G**
autem	soðlice ABCFG, soþlice Eˣ*J, witodlice K
possidebunt*	gesittað ABC, agun DEˣ*, hí yrfweardiað F, yrfcweardnesse GJ*, geyrfweardiað I, erfwerdiað K (*L*)
terram	eorðan ABCDEˣ*FJ, eorþan HK, e[ ] G*, heofonrice I
et	⁊ ABCDE³*FGHIJK
delectabuntur	bioð gelustfullade A, beoð gelustfullode B, beoð gelustfullude C, gelustfullode beoþ J, gelustfulliað DE³/ˣ*FGHK*, hig gelustfulliað I* (*M*)
in	in AF, on BCDE³*GHIJK

multitudine		menge A, mengo B, mænigeo C, mænigfealdnisse DH, manigfealdnisse E^{x}*, mænigfealdnesse G, mænigfealdre J, mycelnysse FI, mycelnesse K
pacis		sibbe ABE^{3}*GHIJK, sybbe CDF

ED: yrfeweardnesse (G)] yrfeweardnes[ ] *Rosier.* e[ ] (G)] eorða[ ] *Rosier.* gelustfulliað (G)] lustfulliað *Rosier.*

OE: þa geþwæran (E^{x})] *on eras.* [ ]ran (G)] r *questionable.* soþlice (E^{x})] *on eras.* agun (E^{x})] *on eras.* yrfeweardnesse (J)] *otiose mark above* y. eorðan (E^{x})] *on eras.* e[ ] (G)] *letter fragments visible after* e. ⁊ (E^{3})] *eras. (15 mm) after word.* gelustfulliað (E$^{3/x}$)] g *and 1st* l *retouched in darker ink,* iað *on eras. by corr.* gelustfulliað (K)] *left leg of 2nd* u *obscured by stain.* hig gelustfulliað (I)] *1st* g *on eras.* on (E^{3})] *eras. before word.* manigfealdnisse (E^{x})] *on eras.* sibbe (E^{3})] *possibly by corr.*

LTg: Mansueti] G: *left leg of* M *lost.* possidebunt] L: hereditabunt *added interl. by corr.: see GAg.* delectabuntur] M: *orig.* dilectabuntur: i *altered to* e.

LTu: delectabuntur] dilectabuntur ϑ.

GAg: possidebunt] hereditabunt FGHIJK, L: *see LTg.*

GAu: possidebunt] hereditabunt δϑλμξοπστυχψ; hȩreditabunt ειϱφ.

12

Obseruabit		haldeð *A*B, healdyð C, healdeþ J, begimð D*H,* begymð FG, begimþ E^{x}*K, begymeþ ł besihð I (*M*)
peccator		se synfulla ABCFGHIJ, þe synfulla DE^{x}*, þe synfula K
iustum		ðone rehtwisan A, ðone ryhtwisan B, þone rihtwisan C, þæne rihtwisan I, þone rihtwisan J, ryht D, riht E^{x}*GHK, rihtwisne *F*
et		⁊ ABCE^{x}*FGIJK
fremet*		grymetad *A*, grymetað BD, grimetað E^{x}*, grymmyttað C, gremettiaþ K, he grýstbitað F, gristbitað G*, gristbidaþ J, ⁊ he gristbitaþ I (*LM*)
super		ofer ABDE^{x}*FGHJK, ofer I, ofyr C
eum		hine ABCDE^{x}*FGHIJK
dentibus	ǀ	mid toðum ABC, [ ]id toðum F*, toþum DE^{x}*HJK, toðum G, mid his I
suis	ǀ	his ABCDE^{x}GHK, heora FJ, toðum I

ED: [ ]bseruabit (H)] Obseruabit *Campbell.* [ ]stum (F)] iustum *Kimmens.*

OE: begimþ (E^{x})] *on eras., descender visible beneath* b, ð *beneath* e. þe synfulla (E^{x})] for *followed by* s *or* þ *visible beneath* e, f *beneath* f. riht (E^{x})] *on eras.* ⁊ (E^{x})] þ *or* r *visible beneath gloss.* grimetað (E^{x})] *on eras.* gristbitað (G)] að *obscured by* *modern repairs.* ofer (E^x)] *on eras.* hine (E^x)] *on eras.* [ ]id toðum (F)] *initial letter lost due to hole in leaf.* toþum (E^x)] *on eras.*

LTg: Obseruabit] AM: *2nd* b *on eras.;* [ ]bseruabit H: *initial* O *lost.* iustum] [ ]stum F: *letters lost due to hole in leaf, fragments of initial 2 letters visible.* fremet] L: stridebit *added interl. by corr.: see GAg;* fremebit A: *2nd* e *on eras.,* bit *interl. by corr.,* M: b *on eras.,* it *added by corr.: cf. Weber MS* γ.

LTu: fremet] fremit β.

GAg: fremet] stridebit FGHIJK, L: *see LTg.*

GAu: fremet] stridebit δεϑιλμξοπϱστυφχψ.

13

Dominus	drihtyn *C,* drihten *E^x*I,* dryht̄ *AB,* drih̄t F*G,* drih̄ J (*DLM*)
autem	soðlice ABCG, soþlice E^x*FJ, soðlice I, witodlice K
inridebit	bismerað A, bismrað B, bysmryð *C,* bysmraþ *J,* onhyscþ *D,* onhyscð *E^x*H,* onhysc *G,* onhnyscþ *F,* gehyscð ł tælþ *I,* ahyscð *K* (*L*)
eum	hine ABCFGIJ, him E^x*
quoniam	forðon ABJ, forþon C, forðan K, forðam ðe F, forðan þe E^x*I*, forðam G
prospicit	gelocað ABC, gelocaþ J, he foresceawað DGH, he forsceawað E^x*, he forscæwaþ K, beforan sceawað F, he gesihð I (*M*)
quod	ðæt AB, þæt CDE^{3}HK, þæt FGI, þæt þe J
ueniet	cymeð AB, cymyð C, cumeð DE^x*G*H,* cymeþ FJ, cymð *IK*
dies	deg A, dagas CK, dæg BDFG*HIJ, dęg E^x*
eius	his ABDE^x*FGHI*J*K,* hys C

ED: [ ]ominus (G)] Dominus *Rosier.* irridebit (C)] i[n]ridebit *Wildhagen.* forðon (A)] for ðon *Kuhn.* ueniat (I)] ueniet *Lindelöf.*

OE: drihten (E^x)] *on eras.* soþlice (E^x)] *on eras.* onhyscð (E^x)] *on eras.* him (E^x)] *on eras.* forðan þe (E^x)] *on eras.* forðan þe (I)] þe *interl.* he forsceawað (E^x)] *on eras.* cumeð (E^x)] *on eras.* dæg (G)] *otiose stroke above* d. dęg (E^x)] *on eras.* his (E^x)] *on eras.* his (I)] s. ut punietur : þæt he byð gecwylmed *written in right margin, followed by* Dies iudicii ł dies ire; y *in* gecwylmed *altered from* i.

LTg: Dominus] L: *orig.* dominus: D *added interl. by corr.;* [ ]ominus G; dominus ABCDEM. inridebit] irridebit DEFGIJKL, C: *1st* r *altered from another letter,* H: *small eras. after 1st* r, *perhaps altered from* n. prospicit] M: *1st* i *on eras.* ueniet] H: *2nd* e *on eras.;* ueniat I: *orig.* ueniet: et (&) *deleted by subscript dot,* a *interl.;* ueniæt K: æ *on eras.* eius] eíus K.

LTu: Dominus] dominus βνςτ*; [ ]n̄s ξ. inridebit] irridebit ειλνξοπρστ*τυφχ, β: *orig.* inridebit: *1st* r *written above* n *by corr.* quoniam] quia ϑ. prospicit] prospicet ϑ. quod] quoniam ϑ. ueniet] ueniat τφ.

14

Gladium — sweord ABDE^{x}*FGHJ, swyrd C, swurd K, swurd ł facen I

euaginauerunt — gebrugdun A, gebrudon BC, gebrudon ł getugon J, of sceaðe atugon DE$^{3/x}$*FH, of sceðe atugon *G,* of sceaþe tugan K, utatugon I

peccatores — ða synfullan AB, þa synfullan DFGIJ, þæ synfullan E^{x}*, þa synfullum H, synfulle CK

tetenderunt* — ðenedon *A*B, aþenydon C, æþenedon E^{3}, aþenedon J, hy aþenedon DH, hi aðenedon F, hi aþenedon GK, hig aðenodun I, tinde M* (*L*)

arcum | bogan ABCDFGHIJKM*, hioræ E^{3}

suum | his AF, hira B, hyra C, heora DGHIJK, bogæn E^{3}

ut — ðæt A, þæt B, þæt C*DFGHIJK,* þet E^{3} (*L*)

deiciant* — hie awurpen AB, hi awurpon C, hy awyrpen D, hi æwiorpen E^{3}*, hig awurpon J, hi awurpon ut G, hy awyrpen ut H, hi utaweorpan F, hi awyppen K, hi bepæcan I (*L*)

inopem* } weðlan A, wædlan BJK, wædla C, wædlan ł ⁊ þone hafenleasan I*, unmagan DE^{x}*H, unmagon F, hu magon G (*LM*)

et — ⁊ ABCDE^{x}*FGHIJK

pauperem* } ðearfan AF, þearfan BCDGHK, þearfon J, þone þearfan I, wedlen ł þearfan E$^{3/x}$* (*L*)

ut — ðæt A, þæt CDE^{x}*FI*K, þæt GH, þætte B, þæt þe J

trucident — hie cwaelmen A, hie cwelmen B, hy cwelmen E^{x}*, hi gecwylmyn C, hy cwylmen *D*,* hi cwylmen F, hy cwylmen *H,* hi cwylmian J, hi cwelmman *K,* hy wylmen G, hi gecwylmian ł þæt hi ofbeatun I* (*M*)

rectos | ða rehtheortan A, ða ryhtheortan B, þa rihtheortan C, ryhtwise DE^{x}*, rihtwise HJ, rihtwisse K, rihtwisre G, rihte FI

corde | on heorte DH, on hiortæn E$^{3/x}$*, heortan F*G*JK, on heortan ł ða rihtgeþancodan I (*M*)

ED: sweord (E)] Sweord *Harsley.* intenderunt (A)] tenderunt *Kuhn.* tinde bogan (M)] tinde *Ber.* Vt (IJ)] ut *Lindelöf;* Ut *Oess.*

OE: sweord (E^{x})] *on eras.* of sceaðe atugon (E$^{3/x}$)] of sceaðe *on eras. by corr.* þæ synfullan (E^{x})] *on eras., eras.* (*18 mm*) *before* þæ. tinde bogan (M)] *gloss and lemma* (tetendit . tinde bogan) *written in right margin in red ink.* hi æwiorpen (E^{3})] *eras. after* hi. wædlan ł ⁊ þone hafenleasan (I)] ł ⁊ þone hafenleasan *written above* wædlan. unmagan (E^{x})] *on eras.* ⁊ (E^{x})] *on eras.* wedlen ł þearfan ($E^{3/x}$)] ł þearfan *added by corr.* þæt (E^{x})] *on eras.* hy cwclmcn (E^{x})] *on cras.* hy cwylmen (D)] *2nd* y *interl.* þæt hi gecwylmian ł þæt hi ofbeatun (I)] þæt hi gecwylmian *written at end of line above.* ryhtwise (E^{x})] *on eras.* on hiortæn ($E^{3/x}$)] on *on eras.*

LTg: euaginauerunt] ęuaginauerunt G. tetenderunt] intenderunt A: *orig.* tetender(unt): u *on eras.*, nt *added by corr.*, in *added interl. above 1st* t, L: in *added interl. by corr.: see GAg.* ut (*1st*)] Vt FGIJK, H: *initial letter nearly completely lost,* L: *orig.* ut: u *altered to* V *by corr.* deiciant] L: ici *underlined to signal deletion,* cipi *added interl. by corr.: see GAg.* inopem] L: *underlined to signal deletion,* paupere (*without macron*) *added interl. by corr.: see GAg;* ínopem M. pauperem] L: *underlined to signal deletion,* inopem *added interl. by corr.: see GAg.* trucident] H: *orig.* trucidant: a *altered to* e, *although taking on appearance of* æ; trucîdent M: *orig.* trucîdant: a *altered to* e; trucidænt K; trucidant D: *cf. Weber MSS* MKTRUX. corde] G: d *altered from* o, M: *1 leaf wanting* (*containing vv 15–38*).

LTu: Gladium] [ ]ladium ξ. ut (*1st*)] Ut δεθμξοπτυψ; Vt ιλρσφχ. deiciant] β: *orig.* deciant: *1st* i *added interl. by corr.* trucident] βρ: *orig.* trucidant: e *written above* a *by corr.;* trucidant ς.

GAg: tetenderunt] intenderunt FGHIJK, AL: *see LTg.* deiciant] decipiant FGHIJK, L: *see LTg.* inopem et pauperem] pauperem et inopem FGHIK; pauperem et in inopem J: ī *interl. by corr. after* in *in* inopem; *for* L *see LTg.*

GAu: tetenderunt] intenderunt δεθιλμξοπρστυφχψ. deiciant] decipiant δεθιλμξοπρστυφχψ. inopem et pauperem] pauperem et inopem δεθιλμξοπρστυφχψ.

15

Gladius	I	sweord ABDFGHJ, swyrd CK, swurd I, hioræ E^{3}
eorum	I	heara A, hira B, hyra C, heora DFGHIJK, sweord E^{3}
intret		ingaeð A, ingæð BCK, ingæþ J, inga DFGHI, ongeþ E^{3}
in		in A, on BCDE^{3}FGHIJK
cor*	I	heortan ABCDFGHIJK, heoræ *$E^{3/x}$** (*L*)
ipsorum	I	heara A, hira B, hyra C, heora DFGHIJK^{2}, heortæn E^{3}
et		⁊ ABCFGHIJK^{2}, ond E^{3}
arcus	I	boga ABCDGHIK^{2}, bogan F*J,* hioræ E^{3}
eorum	I	heara A, hira B, hyra C, heora DFGHIJK^{2}, bogæ E^{3}
conteratur*		bið forðrested A, bið forðræsted B, beoð forþræstyde C, bið tobryt *D*F, biþ tobrit J, si tobryt G, sy tobrocen ł beo tobryt I, tobrecha K^{2}, bið gebrocen *E^{3}* (*L*)

ED. cór (E)] cor *Harsley*.

OE: heoræ ($E^{3/x}$)] he *on eras. by corr.*

LTg: Gladius] [ ]ladius G. intret] C: *small eras. after* i. cor] L: da *added interl. by* *corr.: see GAg;* cór E. arcus] J: r *formed from another letter* (c?). conteratur] L: fringatur *added interl. by corr. above* teratur: *see GAg;* conteretur D, E: ał conteretur *written in left margin by corr.*

LTu: conteratur] conteretur ς.

GAg: cor] corda FGHIJK, L: *see LTg.* conteratur] confringatur FGHIJK, L: *see LTg.*

GAu: cor] corda δεζϑιλμξοπϱστυφχψ. conteratur] confringatur δεζϑιλμξοπστυφχψ.

16

Melius   bettre A, betre B, betyre C, betere DFGHJK^{2}, betre I, Selre ł betere E$^{3/x}$*
est   is ABDE^{3}FGHIJ*K*^{2}, ys C
modicum   lytel ABK^{2}, lytyl C, litel J, medmicel DE^{3}GHI, gehwæde F
iusto   ðæm rehtwisan A, ðæm ryhtwisan B, þan rihtwisan C, þam ryhtwisan D, þam rihtwisan E^{x}*I, þam rihtwisan FGJ, þam rihtwisan H, þam rihtwise K^{2}
super   ofer ABDE^{x}*FGHI, ofyr C, ofar K^{2}, þan ofer J
diuitias   weolan AB, welan CDE^{x}*HIJ, weligum F, wædlan G, welas K^{2}
peccatorum   synfulra ABCI*K^{2}, synna DE^{x}*FGH, þam sinfullan J*
multas   monge A, monige BJ, mænige CGH, mænige D, manige E^{x}*, manegum F, fela ł manega I, feola K^{2}

OE: Selre ł betere (E$^{3/x}$)] ł betere *added above* Selre *by corr.* þam rihtwisan (E^{x})] *on eras.* ofer (E^{x})] *on eras.* welan (E^{x})] *on eras., orig.* of *eras. before word,* l *visible beneath* a. synfulra (I)] *orig.* synfulran: *final* n *eras.* synna (E^{x})] *on eras.* þam sinfullan (J)] *2nd* l *written over partially completed letter* (a?). manige (E^{x})] *on eras.*

LTg: est] ést K.

LTu: iusto] iustum β.

17

Quoniam   forðon ABJK^{2}, forþon C, Forðæn E^{3}, forðam ðe F, forþam þe G, forþan þe I (*H*)
brachia   earm *A*BFJ, earmas CDE^{x}*GHK^{2}, earmas ł modignys I
peccatorum   synfulra ABCDE^{x}*FGHIJK^{2}
conterentur   sien forðręsteð A, syn forþræstyd C, sien forðræste B, beoð tobrocene DE^{x}*GH, beoþ tobrocene F, beoþ tobrytte ł beoð tobrocene I*, biþ forþræst ł tobrocen J, tobrecað K^{2}
confirmat   getrymeð ABD, getrimeð E^{x}*, getrymmeþ F, getrymð I*, getrimeþ J, a getrymmeð G, a getrymeþ H, getrymyd C, trymað *K*^{2}
autem   soðlice ABCFGIK^{2}, soþlice E^{x}*J

iustos	ða rehtwisan A, ða ryhtwisan B, þa rihtwisan I, rihtwisan J, rihtwis C, ryhtwise D, rihtwise Ex*FG*H*, rihtwisa K2
dominus	drihten Ex*FHK2, dryht̄ AB, driht̄ C, drih̄ J, d[ ]h̄ G

ED: [ ]uoniam (H)] Quoniam *Campbell.* forðon (A)] for ðon *Kuhn.* d[ ]h̄ (G)] drih̄ *Rosier.*

OE: earmas (Ex)] *on eras.* synfulra (Ex)] *on eras.* beoð tobrocene (Ex)] *on eras.* beoþ tobrytte ł beoð tobrocene (I)] *gloss eras. before* ł beoð, beoþ tobrytte *written in right margin below* ł beoð tobrocene. getrimeð (Ex)] *on eras.* getrymð (I)] y *altered from* i (?). soþlice (Ex)] *on eras.* rihtwise (Ex)] *on eras.* drihten (Ex)] *on eras.*

LTg: Quoniam] H: [ ]uoniam H: *initial* Q *lost but for fragments.* brachia] A: *eras. after 1st* a. confirmat] K: a *interl. above eras.* iustos] H: *orig.* iustus: *2nd* u *altered to* o.

LTu: peccatorum] pecatorum ϑ. confirmat] confirmet ϑ.

18

Nouit	wat AB*J*, gecnæwð C, gecneow K2, can DEx*F*G*H, can ł wat I
dominus	drihten Ex*FHIK2, dryht̄ AB, driht̄t CG, drih̄ J
uias*	weagas A, wegas BC*D*Ex*, dæges F, dæg G, dagas IJ, dages K2 (*L*)
inmaculatorum	unwemra ABC, unwæmme J, onwemmendra D*E*x*, onwæmmedra F, onweämendra *H,* unwemmendra G, unwæmmæddre *K*2, ungewæmmedre *I**
et	⁊ ABCE3FGHIJK2
hereditas	| erfewordnis A, yrfweardnes B, yrfeweardnys *C,* yrfeweardnis DH, yrfweardnys FI, yrfeweardnes J, hyrfeweardnesse G, yrfa K2, hiræ *E*3
eorum	| heara A, hira B, hyra C, heora DFGHIJK2, yrfæweærdnis E3/x*
in	in A, on BCDE3FGHIJK2
aeternum	ecnisse A*D,* ecnysse *CF*I*K*2, ecnesse *B*E3*GHJ* (*L*)
erit	bið ABCDFGH, biþ J, he byð I, weorð K2, ƀid E3*

ED: can (E)] Can *Harsley.* hęreditas (E)] haereditas *Harsley.* æternum (D)] aeternum *Roeder.* ƀid (E)] bið *Harsley.*

OE: can (Ex)] *on eras.* drihten (Ex)] *on eras.* wegas (Ex)] *on eras.* onwemmendra (Ex)] *on eras.* ungewæmmedre (I)] *gloss eras. before word.* yrfæweærdnis (E3/x)] nis *on eras. by corr.* ƀid (E3)] *cross-stroke through* b.

LTg: Nouit] J: *eras. after* o; [ ]ouit G. uias] D: u *on eras.* (?); dies L: d *altered from* u, e *altered from another letter: see GAg.* inmaculatorum] immaculatorum EIK, H:

middle leg added to n *to form* m. hereditas] hęreditas CE. aeternum] æternum BDKL; ęternum CFGH; eternum EJ.

LTu: inmaculatorum] immaculatorum ειλπσφ. hereditas] hęreditas ειϱφ. aeternum] ęternum βειvφ; æternum ϑ; eternum ξσςτ*τ.

GAg: uias] dies FGHIJK, L: *see LTg*.

GAu: uias] dies δεζϑιλμξοϱστυφχψ.

19

Non	I	ne ABC*G*J, Ne E^{3}, na DFHK, hi ne I
confundentur	I	bioð gescende *A*, bioþ gescende E^{3}, beoð gescende B, beoð gescynde CI, beoð gescænde J, hy beoð gescynde DH, beoþ hi gescende F, hy ne beoð gescynde G, hi beoþ gescynd K
in		in A, on BCDE^{3}FGHIJK
tempore	I	tid AB, tide CDFGHJ, tida K, timan I, þere yflen E^{3}
malo	I	yfle AB, yfylre C, yfelre DHG, yfelra J, yfelu F, yflum I, yuela K, tyde E^{3}
et		⁊ ABCE^{3}FGHJK
in		in A, on BCDE^{3}FGHIJK
diebus	I	dægum A, dagum BDJ, dagum CFGHI, dagan K, þæm hingriendum E^{3}
famis	I	hungres AB, hungrys C, hungres DFGHIJK, dægum E^{3}
saturabuntur		bioð gefylde A, beoð gefylde B, beoþ gefilde J, beoð gefyllyde C, bioð gefillede E^{3}*, beoþ gefyllede K, hi beoð gefyllede F, hy beoð gefyllede G, hi beoþ gefyllede *I**, hy beoð fyllede DH

ED: diebus (E)] diebis *Harsley.*

OE: bioð gefillede (E^{3})] *eras. before word.* hi beoþ gefyllede (I)] *orig.* hi beoþ gefillede: *2nd* i *altered to* y.

LTg: Non] G: *left leg of* N *partly lost.* confundentur] A: e *on eras.* saturabuntur] I: *eras. before word.*

20

quoniam*	forðon ABJ, forþon *C,* forðæn E^{3}, forþan K, forðam þe F, forþam þe G, forþan þe I (*L*)
peccatores	synfulle ABCDFGHK, synfullæn $E^{3/x}$*, þa synfullan IJ
peribunt	forweorðað ABG, forwurðað C, forweorþað D, forwiorþæþ E^{3}, forwyrþað H, forwurþeð J, forwyrðað K, forweorðaþ ł losiað I, losiað F*

Inimici	feond A, fiend B, fynd CDE^{x}*FGHIJK (L)
autem*	soðlice ABGI, soþlice CE^{x}*FJ, witodlice K (*L*)
domini	dryhtnes B, driħtnys C, drihtnes E^{x}*F, dryht̄ A, driħt G, driħ J
mox	sona ABDE^{x}*FGHJK, sona ł þærrihte I, raðe C
⟨ut⟩	(*FJL*)
honorati*	gearade AB, gearode C, gearweorþode DE^{x}*, geárwurðode F, gearwvrþode H, gearwurþode IJ, gegeárwurðode G, gearwyrðude K (*L*)
(fuerint)*	beoð FGHJK, þonne hi beoð I* (*L*)
et	⁊ ABCE^{x}*FGHIJK
exaltati	upahefene A, upahæfene B, uppahafyne C, upahafene D*E^{x}*FGH*J, upahafone I, anhauene K
fuerint*	biað A, beoð BCDE^{x}* (*L*)
deficientes	aspringende ABJ, aspringynde C, geteoriende D, geteoriend E^{x}*, geteriende H, geteorigende *F*, geteorigende ł aspringende G, ateoriende I, geteorian K
ut*	swe swe A, swa swa BCDE^{x}*GI, swa K, swa swa ł sona ł on þam gemete J, on ðam gemete F
fumus	rec A, smec BI, smic CDE^{3}*GHJK, smíc F
deficient	hie aspringað AB, hi aspringað C*, he geteorað DE^{x}*, hy geteoriað H, hig geteoriað J, hy geteoriað ł hi aspringað G, ateorað F, ateoriað I, aterat K*

ED: forðon (A)] for ðon *Kuhn.* forþam þe (G)] forþam *Rosier.* fynd (E)] Fynd *Harsley.* driħtnys (C)] drihtnys *Wildhagen (but correct in corrigenda, p. xxii).* gearwvrþode (H)] gearwurþode *Campbell.* defici[ ]tes (F)] deficientes *Kimmens.* swa swa (GI)] swaswa *Rosier, Lindelöf.* swa swa ł sona ł on þam gemete (J)] swaswa ł sona ł on þam gemete *Oess.*

OE: synfullæn ($E^{3/x}$)] syn *on eras. by corr.*, f *retouched,* þ: *and* s: *or* f: *visible before word.* losiað (F)] *stray* ð *following word.* fynd (E^{x})] *on eras.* soþlice (E^{x})] *on eras.* drihtnes (E^{x})] *on eras.* sona (E^{x})] *on eras.* gearweorþode (E^{x})] *on eras.* þonne hi beoð (I)] s. cum *written in left margin.* ⁊ (E^{x})] *on eras.* upahafene (D)] *small eras. after* p. upahafene (E^{x})] *on eras.* upahafene (H)] *orig.* upahefene: *1st* e *deleted by subscript dot,* a *interl.* beoð (E^{x})] *on eras.* geteoriend (E^{x})] *on eras.* swa swa (E^{x})] *on eras.* smic (E^{3})] *eras. before word.* hi aspringað (C)] r *interl.* he geteorað (E^{x})] *on eras.* aterat (K)] *letter eras. before word.*

LTg: quoniam] L: quia *added interl. by corr.: see GAg.* autem] L: uero *added interl. by corr.: see GAg.* mox] mox ut J, F: ut *interl. by corr.,* L: vt *interl. by corr.: cf. Bib. sac. MSS* I?M*W^{c}, *etc.* honorati] L: ific *added interl. by corr. after* r, fuerint *added interl. by corr. after word: see GAg.* fuerint] L: *underlined to signal deletion: see GAg.* deficientes] defici[ ]tes F: *letters lost due to hole, fragments visible, including eye of* e.

LTu: Inimici] INimici β. honorati] honorati fuerint β: *cf. Weber MSS* βζ. fuerint] *om.* β: *cf. Weber MSS* βζ.

GAg: quoniam] quia FGHIJK, L: *see LTg.* autem] uero FGHIJ, L: *see LTg.* honorati] honorificati fuerint FGIJK, H: *eras. after* fuerint, L: *see LTg.* fuerint] *om.* FGHIJK, L: *see LTg.* ut] quemadmodum FGHJK; quemammodum I.

GAu: quoniam] quia δεζϑιλμξοπϱστυφχψ. autem] uero δεζϑιλμξοπϱστυφχψ. honorati] honorificati fuerint δεζϑιλμξοπϱστυφχψ. fuerint] *om.* δεζϑιλμξοπϱστυφχψ. ut] quemadmodum δεζϑιλμξπϱστφχψ; quemammodum υ, ο: *orig.* quemadmodum.

21

Mutuatur* bið onwende A*, bið onwendende *B,* byð C, borgað DE^{x}*GH, borgaþ IJK, adumbað F* (*L*)

peccator se synfulla ABDE^{x}*GIJ, se synfvlla C, se syn[ ]a F*, synfulla H, þe synfulla K

et ⁊ ABCE^{3}FGIJK

non ne ABCE^{3}GJ, na FIK

soluit* onleseð *AB,* onsælyð *C,* agylt *D*F, gylt K, alyseð ł ne gyldeð G, gefyllð ł he ne agylt I*, gildeþ ł ne sileþ J, ł agylt bið ælised $E^{3/x}$* (*L*)

iustus se rehtwisa A, se ryhtwisa BD, se rihtwisa HIJ, se rihtwise E^{x}*, se riht[ ] G*, rihtwis CK, rihtwisa F

autem soðlice ABCFG, soþlice E^{x}*J, witodlice K

miseretur mildsað A, mildsaþ JK, miltsað BG, gemildsað I, bið gemildsod C, ofearmað DE^{x}*F

et ⁊ ABCDE^{x}*FGIJK (*H*)

commodat* geðwaerað A, geþwaerað B, geþwærað C, alenð DE^{x}*, geleanað F, læneþ J, agylt GH, agilt K, tiþað I

ED: se syn[ ]a (F)] se synfulla *Kimmens.* soluet (BE)] solvet *Brenner, Harsley.*

OE: bið onwende (A)] *lemma misread as* Mutatur; *see also* B. borgað (E^{x})] *on eras.* adumbað (F)] *eras. but visible, otiose stroke after* a. se synfulla (E^{x})] *on eras.* se syn[ ]a (F)] *letters lost due to hole in leaf, fragments of 2 letters visible before* a *and fragment of descender visible after* n. gefyllð ł he ne agylt (I)] ł he ne agylt *written above* na gefyllð, *1st* y *altered from* i (?). ł agylt bið ælised ($E^{3/x}$)] ł agylt *added by corr.* (*orig.* ne / bið ælised > ne ł agylt / bið ælised). se rihtwise (E^{x})] *on eras.* se riht[ ] (G)] *fragments of 3 letters visible after* t. soþlice (E^{x})] *on eras.* ofearmað (E^{x})] *on eras.* ⁊ (E^{x}) (*2nd*)] *on eras.* alenð (E^{x})] *on eras.*

LTg: Mutuatur] E: *letter* (m?) *eras. after* a, L: bi *added by corr. below* at: *see GAg;* Muatur B. soluit] L: soluet *added above following* autem, *apparently due to lack of*

space above soluit *for alteration;* soluet BCDE, A: e *on eras.: cf. Weber MSS* S*Καβγδ moz^{x}, *see GAg.* et (*2nd*)] H: *eras. after word.*

LTu: Mutuantur] Motabitur ϑ. peccator] pecator ϑ. soluit] soluet νςτ*: *cf. Weber MSS* S*Καβγδ moz^{x}, *see GAu.*

GAg: Mutuatur] Mutuabitur FHIJK, L: *see LTg;* [ ]utuabitur G. soluit] soluet FGHIJK, ABCDEL: *see LTg.* commodat] tribuet FHIK; tribuit G; retribuet J: *cf. Weber MSS med.*

GAu: Mutuantur] Mutuabitur δεζιλμξοπρστυφχψ. soluit] soluet δεζϑιλμξοπρστυφχψ, νςτ*: *see LTu.* commodat] tribuet δεζϑιλμξοπρστυφχψ.

22

Quoniam*		forðon ABC, forþon J, Forðæn E^{3}, forþā K, forþā þe F, forþan þe I (*L*)
benedicentes	|	bledsiende A, bletsiende BFH, bletsiynde C, bletsigende D, bletsigende K, þa bletsiendan I, bletsigende beoþ J, hine *E^{3}*
eum*	|	hine ABCDK, him FGI, him J, bletsiende E^{3} (*L*)
possidebunt*		gesittað AB, wealdað C, agun DE^{x}*, yrfweardiað F, yrfeweardnesse GJ, geahniað ł yrfweardiaþ I* (*L*)
terram		eorðan $ABCE^{x}$*FH, eorþan J, land I (*G*)
maledicentes		wercweoðende A, wergende B, cursiynde C, yfelcwedelginde DH, yfelcweþelginde E^{x}*, yfelcweþende F, yfelcwedende G, yfelcweðende J, yfelcweþendan K, þa wyrgendan I*
autem		soðlice ABCFG, soþlice E^{x}*HJ, witodlice *K**
illum*		hine $ABCE^{x}$*F, him GIK, him J
disperient*		forweorðað AB, forwurðað C, forweorðaþ DF, forworðaþ E^{x}*, forwurðaþ I, forweorðað ł tostencte beoð G, forwurðaþ ł tostænce beoþ J, forwyrþan K (*L*)

ED: Quia (G)] *Q*uia *Rosier.* forðon (A)] for ðon *Kuhn.* maledicentes (C)] malędicentes *Wildhagen.* forweorðað ł tostencte beoð (G)] forweordað ł tostencte beoð *Rosier.*

OE: agun (E^{x})] *on eras.* geahniað ł yrfweardiaþ (I)] weardiaþ *written in right margin and signaled to come after* yrf. eorðan (E^{x})] *on eras.* yfelcweþelginde (E^{x})] *on eras.* þa wyrgendan (I)] y *altered from* i (?). soþlice (E^{x})] *on eras.* witodlice (K)] od *nearly completely lost, cross-stroke of* t *lost due to stain.* hine (E^{x}) (*2nd*)] *on eras.* forworðaþ (E^{x})] *on eras.*

LTg: Quoniam] L: uia *added interl. by corr. after* Q: *see GAg.* benedicentes] E: *small eras. after* i. eum] L: um *underlined to signal deletion, anticipated* i *not added: see GAg.* possidebunt] L; posside *underlined to signal deletion,* heredita *added interl. by corr.: see GAg.* terram] terra[ ] G: *letter fragments* (rð?) *of gloss visible.* autem] K:

aut *retraced in darker ink over stain.* disperient] L: bunt *added interl. by corr. above* ent: *see GAg.*

LTu: maledicentes] malædicentes ϑ.

GAg: Quoniam] Quia FGHIJK, L: *see LTg.* eum] ei FGHIJK; *for* L *see LTg.* possidebunt] hereditabunt FGHIJK, L: *see LTg.* illum] ei FGHIJK. disperient] disperibunt FGHIJK, L: *see LTg.*

GAu: Quoniam] Quia δεζϑιλμξοπϱστυφχψ. eum] ei δεζϑλμξοπϱστυφχψ. possidebunt] hereditabunt δζϑλμξοπστυχψ; hęreditabunt ειϱφ. illum] ei δεζϑιλμξοπϱστυφχψ. disperient] disperibunt δεζϑιλμξοπϱστυφχψ.

23

A*	from A, from B, From E^{3}, fram CD, fram F, beforan K, [ ]foran G, beforan ł mid I, mid J (*L*)
domino*	dryhtne B, drihtne CDE^{3}I*, drihtene K, dryht̄ A, drih́t G, drih́ J (*L*)
gressus	gong A, stapas B, stæpas CE^{x}FGHJK, stepas D, stæpas ł færeldu I*
hominis	monnes AB, mannys C, mannes DGHIK, monnæs E$^{3/x}$*, manna FJ
dirigentur	bioð gereht *A,* beoð gerehte BC, beoð gerihte DG*H,* beoþ gerihte E^{x}*, beoþ gerehte FJ, beoð gereht *K,* beoð gerihtlæhte I
et	⁊ ABCE^{x}*FGHIJK
uiam	weg ABCDFGHIJ, wæg E^{x}*, wegas K
eius	his ABCDFGHIJ*K*
cupiet*	gewillað *A,* gewilnað B*C,* he gewilnað ⁊ he wile I*, he wilnað DK, he wilnæþ E$^{3/x}$*, wilnað G, wilnaþ J, he wyle F (*L*)
nimis*	swiðe ABC, swiþe DE^{3} (*L*)

ED: he gewilnað ⁊ he wile (I)] he gewilnað ł ⁊ he wile *Lindelöf.*

OE: drihtne (I)] ne *interl.* stæpas ł færeldu (I)] ł færeldu *written in right margin.* monnæs (E$^{3/x}$)] s *added by corr.* beoþ gerihte (E^{x})] *on eras.* ⁊ (E^{x})] *on eras.* wæg (E^{x})] *on eras.* he gewilnað ⁊ he wile (I)] ⁊ he wile *written in left margin.* he wilnæþ (E$^{3/x}$)] he *on eras. by corr.*

LTg: A] L: pud *added interl. by corr. after* A: *see GAg.* domino] L: o *underlined to signal deletion,* m *added interl. by corr.: see GAg.* dirigentur] A: e *on eras.,* n *interl. by corr.,* H: n *interl.,* K: n *on eras.* eius] eíus K. cupiet] A: *orig.* cpiet: u *squeezed in, partly covering* c; cupit C, L: *underlined to signal deletion,* uolet *added interl. by corr.: see GAg.* nimis] L: *underlined to signal deletion: see GAg.*

LTu: gressus] gresus ϑ. dirigentur] dirigintur β: *orig.* dirigentur: i *written above* e *by corr.;* dirigctur δ.

GAg: A] Apud HIJK, L: *see LTg,* F: *orig.* Aput: t *altered to* d; [ ]pud G. domino] dominum FGHIJK, L: *see LTg.* cupiet] uolet FGHIJ, L: *see LTg.* nimis] *om.* FGHIJK, L: *see LTg.*

GAu: A] Apud δεζϑιμξοπρστυφχψ; Apđ λ. domino] dominum δεζϑιλμξοπρστυφχψ. cupiet] uolet δεζϑιλμξοπρστυφχψ. nimis] *om.* δεζϑιλμξοπρστυφχψ.

24

Cum	ðonne A, þonne BE^{x}**G*HI, þonne CDJ, ðonne F, þon K*
ceciderit	gefalleð AB, gefeallyð C, gefealleþ J, hreoseþ DE^{x}*, hreosað K, reoseð *F,* ahreoseð G, ahreoseþ H, he fylð [ ] riht[ ]sa I*
iustus*	se rehtwisa A, se ryhtwisa B, se rihtwisa C*E^{x}*FG, rihtwis J (*HK*)
non	ne ABCFGIJ, na DE^{x}*K
conturbabitur*	bið gedroefede A, beoð gedrefyde C, bið gedrefed B, hy bið gedrefed D, hi bið gedrefed E^{x}*, sy he gedrefed FJ, bið totwysed G, bið tocwysed I, beoð gæderod K* (*L*)
quia	forðon ABDE^{x}*, forþon CJ, forðan FK, forþan H, forðam G, forþan þe I
dominus	dryhten E^{x}*, drihten K, dryht̄ AB, driħt CG, drħt F, driħ J
firmat*	trymeð ABDE^{x}*, trymmað C, getrimeþ J, set F, underleigð G, underwriðaþ ł set I, underset K (*L*)
manum	hond A, hand BCDE^{x}*F, handa GHIJK (*L*)
eius*	his ABDE^{x}*FGIJK, hys C, heora H (*L*)

ED: þon (K)] þonne *Sisam.* [ ] riht[ ]sa (I)] se rihtwisa *Lindelöf* (*n. 1*). bið totwysed (G)] bið tocwysed *Rosier.* forðon (A)] for ðon *Kuhn.*

OE: þonne (E^{x})] *on eras.* þon (K)] *eras. above* n, *perhaps of macron.* hreoseþ (E^{x})] *on eras.* he fylð [ ] riht[ ]sa (I)] [ ] riht[ ]sa *written in left margin, letters lost due to tight binding.* se rihtwisa (C)] se *added in red by corr.* se rihtwisa (E^{x})] *on eras.* na (E^{x})] *on eras.* hi bið gedrefed (E^{x})] *on eras.* beoð gæderod (K)] *lemma misread as* colligetur. forðon (E^{x})] *on eras.* dryhten (E^{x})] *on eras.* trymeð (E^{x})] *on eras.* hand (E^{x})] *on eras.* his (E^{x})] *on eras.*

LTg: Cum] (C)um G: C *mostly lost.* ceciderit] F: *initial* c *added* (?) *by main scribe in smaller hand.* iustus] H: *interl. in later hand,* K: *interl. in main hand.* conturbabitur] L: turbabitur *underlined to signal deletion,* lidetur *added interl. by corr.: see GAg.* firmat] L: *underlined to signal deletion,* supponit *added interl by corr.: see GAg.* manum] L: *eras. after* n. eius] L: *underlined for deletion,* suam *added interl. by corr.: see GAg.*

LTu: ceciderit] cecidirit ϑ.

GAg: iustus] *om.* I: *see OE gloss to* ceciderit. conturbabitur] collidetur FGHJK; *for* L *see LTg.* firmat] supponet F: ł nit *added interl. by corr.;* subponet G; supponit HIK, L: *see LTg;* subponit J. eius] suam FGHIJK, L: *see LTg.*

GAu: iustus] *om.* δεζιλμξοπϱστυφψ. conturbabitur] collidetur εζιλξοπϱστυφχ; conlidetur δϑμψ. firmat] supponit διλϱτυφχψ, o: *orig.* subponit; subponit εμξπσ; subponet ζ; suponit ϑ. eius] suam δεζϑιλμξοπϱστυφχψ.

25

Iuuenior*	I	gungra A, geongra B, ieongra *C*, gyngra *D*F, gingra K, iung GJ, iungling I, Ic wes *E*^{3} (*L*)
fui	I	ic wes A, ic wæs BCDFGHIJK, giongre E$^{3/x}$*
et*		⁊ ABCE^{x}K, ⁊ soðlice GHJ, witendlice F, witodlice I
senui		ic aldade A, ic ealdode BCDFIJK, ic eældode E^{3}, ealdode G, ealdod *H*
et		⁊ ABCE^{3}FGHIJK
non	I	ic ne ABCE^{3}IJ, na DFGHK
uidi	I	gesaeh A, geseh B, geseah CFIJK, ic geseah G, ic seah DH, seæh E^{3}
iustum		ðone rehtwisan A, þone ryhtwisan B, þone rihtwisan I, þonę rihtwisan J, rihtwisne CFGH, ryhtwisne DE^{x}*, rihtwise K
derelictum		forletenne A, forlætenne BDIJ, forlætynne C, forlætene FGHK, forlætęnne E^{x}*
nec		ne ABCFGIJ, na E^{x}*, nan K
semen		sed A, sæd BCDE^{x}*FGHIJK
eius		his ABDE^{3}FGHIJ*K*, hys C
egens*		weðliende A, wædliende B, wædliynde C, þearfende D, þarfende E^{3}*, secende FGIJK (*L*)
pane*		hlaf *AB*CFGHIJK, hlafe D, hlæfe E^{3} (*L*)

OE: giongre (E$^{3/x}$)] re *on eras. by corr.* ryhtwisne (E^{x})] *on eras.* forlætęnne (E^{x})] *on eras.* na (E^{x})] *on eras.* sæd (E^{x})] *on eras.* þarfende (E^{3})] *possibly added by corr.*

LTg: Iuuenior] Iunior CDEL: *cf. Weber MSS* T^{2}QRδχλ moz med, *see GAg.* senui] H: *eras. after word, perhaps of punct.* eius] eíus K. egens] L: querens *added below word by corr.: see GAg.* pane] panem AB, L: m *added after* e *by corr.: cf. Weber MSS* SKαβδζλ moz med, *see GAg.*

LTu: derelictum] derilictum ϑ.

GAg: Iuuenior] Iunior GHIJK, F: *stray* l *written before word by glossator,* CDEL: *see LTg.* et (*1st*)] etenim FGHIJK. egens] quęrens F; querens GHJK, L: *see LTg;* quaerens I. pane] panem FGHIJK, ABL: *see LTg.*

GAu: Iuuenior] Iunior δεζϑιλμνξοπϱστυφχψ. et (*1st*)] etenim δεζιλμξοπϱστυφχψ. egens] quęrens δελοϱφ; quċrens ζϑιξστχ; quaerens μπυψ. pane] panem δεζϑιλμξοπϱστυφχψ.

26

Tota — alne A, ealne BCFJ, ælce DGH, Elce E^{3}, eale I*K
die — deg A, dæg BCFJK, dæge DG*H, deie E^{3}, dæg ł symle I
miseretur — mildsað AC, miltsað B, he mildsað K, he miltsað F, milsaþ J, he miltseoþ $E^{3/x}$*, he gemildsað I*, heo feormað D, hi ofearmað GH
et — ⁊ ABCE^{3}*FGHIJK
commodat — geþwærað AC, geðwærað B, lænð DF*G*H, lænþ E^{x}*, læneð K, he lænð I, gegearwaþ J
et — ⁊ ABCDE^{3}FGHIJK
semen | sed A, sæd BCDFGHJK, cyn I, his E^{3}
eius* | his ABDFIJK, hys C, hiora G, sed E^{3}
in — in A, on BCDE^{3}FGHIJK
benedictione — bledsunge A, bletsunge BCDE^{3}FGHIJK
erit — bið ABCDF*GH*K, byð I, biþ E^{3}J

OE: eale (I)] *written in left margin.* dæge (G)] d *altered from* t. he miltseoþ ($E^{3/x}$)] he *and* oþ *added by corr., 2nd* e *on eras.* he gemildsað (I)] *2nd* e *interl.* ⁊ (E^{3}) (*1st*)] *top stroke retraced in darker ink.* lænþ (E^{x})] *on eras.,* g: *eras. before word.*

LTg: commodat] comodat G. erit] ęrit GH.

LTu: miseretur] misseretur ϑ.

GAg: eius] illius FGHIJK.

GAu: eius] illius δεζϑλμξοπϱσυφχψ.

27

Declina — onhaeld A, onheld B, Onheld E^{3}*, ahyld CDFGH, ahyld ł gecyr I, ahild ł abuh ł gecir J, abuh K (*L*)
a — from AE^{3}, from B, fram DFHJK, fram GI, of C
malo — yfle A*BCE^{3}I, yfele DFGJ, yuele HK
et — ⁊ ABCE^{3}FGHIJK
fac — doo A, do BC*D*E^{3}FGHIJ, don K
bonum — god ABCDE^{3}FGHIK, gód J
et — ⁊ ABCE^{3}FGHIJK
inhabita — inearda AB, onearda CFJK, onwuna D*G*HI, onwune ł eærdæ $E^{3/x}$*
in — in A, on BCE^{3}FGIJK

saeculum — weoruld A, weorold *B*, woruld *C*, world *E*^{3}, aworuld *DH*, worulde *F*, worulda *G*, worlda I*J*, worolde *K* (*L*)
saeculi — weorulde A, weorolde *B*, worulde *C*, woruld *FG*, world *IJ*, æworld *E*^{3} (*DHKL*)

ED: scłm (EFJ)] seculum *Harsley, Kimmens, Oess.* scłi (EJ)] seculi *Harsley, Oess.*

OE: Onheld (E^{3})] *orig.* Onhilde ge: i *altered to* e *by corr., final* e *in* Onhilde *eras.*, ge *eras.* yfle (A)] l *formed from another letter.* onwune ł eærdæ (E$^{3/x}$)] *orig.* ond(?) eærdæ: *letter* (d?) *eras. after* n, wune ł *added by corr.*

LTg: Declina] L: *divisio psalmi*: diuisio sancti benedicti abbatis. fac] fác D. inhabita] inhabi[ ] G. saeculum] sæculum BKL; seculum CDGH; scłm EFJL. saeculi] sæculi B; seculi CDFGHK; sęculi I; scłi EJL.

LTu: Declina] εφ: *divisio psalmi.* saeculum] sęculum βλνοπ; sæculum ϑ; seculum ς; scłm ειμξστ*τυφχ. saeculi] sęculi ζλνοπ; sæculi ϑ; seculi ς; scłi δειμξστ*τυφχ.

28

Quoniam* — forðon ABJ, forþon C, forðan E$^{3/x}$*, forðā F, forþan K, forþā þe G, forðan þe I (*L*)
dominus — drihten E^{3}K, dryhт̄ AB, driћt CFG, driћ J
amat — lufað ABCDFGHIK, lufaþ J, lufæþ E^{3}
iudicium — dom ABCDFGHIJK, dóm E^{3}
et — ⁊ ABCE^{3}FGHIJK
non | ne ABC, na DE^{x}*FGHJK, he ne I
derelinquet | forleteð *A*, forlæteð BG, forlætyð C, forlæteþ DFJK, forlætæþ E^{x}*, forlætet H, forlæt I
sanctos | halge AB, halige CDGHJK, halgan FI, his E^{3}*
suos | his ABCFIJK, hys G, hælgæn E^{3}
in — in A, on BCE^{3}FGIJK
aeternum — ecnisse A, ecnesse *BE*^{3}*GJK*, ecnysse *C*I, écnysse *F*, æfre *DH* (*L*)
conseruabuntur — bioð gehaldne A, beoð gehaldne B, beoð gehealdynne *C*, hy beoð gehealdene D, hi beoð gehealdene FI, hi beoþ gehealdene K, hy bioþ gehældene E^{3}, hy beoð gehealdene GH, beoð geealdene J

Iniusti — ða unrehtwisan A, þa unryhtwisan B, þa unrihtwisan CIJ, unrihtwisan K, unryhtwise DE^{x}*, unrihtwise F*G*, unriht H
autem* — soðlice ABC, soþlice E^{x}*
punientur — bioð wicnade A, beoð witnode B, beoð cnysyde C, beoð witnode DFH, beoþ witnode K, beoð gewitnode E^{x}*GI, beoþ gewitnode J

et	⁊ ABCE^{x}*FGHIJK
semen	scd A, sæd BCDE^{x}*FGHJK, sæd ł cyn I
impiorum	arleasra ACDGHIJ, árleasra F, arleasa B, arlæsra K, ærleæsræ E^{3}*
peribit	forweorðeð A, forwyrðyð C, forweorþeð D*H*J, forweorþeþ E^{3}, forwyrðaþ K, forweorð G, forwyrð BI, losað F

ED: [ ]uia (H)] Quia *Campbell.* forðon (A)] for ðon *Kuhn.* forðan (E)] Forðæn *Harsley.* forþā þe (G)] forþam þe *Rosier.* æternum (D)] aeternum *Roeder.* ęternum (E)] aeternum *Harsley.* beoð gehaldne (B)] beoð gehaldene *Brenner.* peribi[ ] (H)] peribit *Campbell.*

OE: forðan ($E^{3/x}$)] an *by corr., with* a *written over another letter.* na (E^{x})] *on eras.* forlætæþ (E^{x})] *on eras.* his (E^{3})] *eras. after word.* unryhtwise (E^{x})] *on eras.* soþlice (E^{x})] *on eras.* beoð gewitnode (E^{x})] *on eras.* ⁊ (E^{x}) (*2nd*)] *on eras.* sæd (E^{x})] *on eras.* ærleæsræ (E^{3})] *ca 7 letters eras. before word,* ræ *visible in final position.*

LTg: Quoniam] L: uia *added interl. after* Q *by corr.: see GAg.* derelinquet] derelinquit A. aeternum] æternum BDKL; ęternum CEFGH; eternum J. conseruabuntur] C: a *interl.* Iniusti] G: I *partly lost.* peribit] peribi[ ] H: *final letter lost due to hole in leaf.*

LTu: derelinquet] χ: re *interl.;* derilinq̄t ϑ. aeternum] ernum β; ęternum ειvξφ; æternum ϑ; eternum στ*τ. Iniusti] INiusti β.

GAg: Quoniam] Quia FGIJK, L: *see LTg;* [ ]uia H: *initial* Q *lost, letter fragments visible.* autem] *om.* FGHIJK.

GAu: Quoniam] Quia δεζϑιλμξοπϱστυφχψ. autem] *om.* δεζϑιλμξοπϱστφχψ.

29

Iusti	ða rehtwisan A, þa rihtwisan CIJ, rihtwisan K, ryhtwise DE^{x}*, rihtwise FGH, ða unryhtwisan B
uero*	soðlice ABC, soþlice E^{x}*FHJK (*L*)
hereditate*	erfewordnisse A, erfweardnesse *B,* yrfeweardnysse *C,* yrfeweardnisse *D,* yrfeweardnesse GJ, yrfeweærdeiesse *E^{3}*,* yrfweardiað F, erfwerdiað K, geahniaþ ł yrfweardiaþ I* (*L*)
possidebunt*	gesittað ABC, agan D, ægon E^{3} (*L*)
terram	eorðan ABCDFGHJ, eorðæn E^{3}*, on eorða K, land I
et	⁊ ABCE^{3}FGHIJK
inhabitabunt	ineardiað AB, oneardiað CDGH, oneærdæþ E^{3}, oneardiaþ JK, oneardað F, hig onwuniaþ I
in	in A, on BCE^{3}FGHIJK
saeculum	weoruld A, weorold *B,* woruld *CH,* world *E^{3},* weorulde *F,* aworuld *D,* worlde *I,* worlda *GJ,* worolde *K* (*L*)

saeculi   weorulde A, weorolde *B,* worulde *CF,* world *IJ,* aworlde *E^{3},* woruld *G* (*DHKL*)
super   ofer ABDE^{3}FGHIJK, ofyr C
eam   hie A, hiea B, hine *CF,* hy DE$^{3/x}$**H,* hig J, hi[ ] G, hi *K,* þæt land I

ED: hęreditate (E)] haereditate *Harsley.* sclm (EIJK)] saeculum *Lindelöf;* seculum *Harsley, Oess;* sæculum *Sisam.* scli (EFIJK)] seculi *Harsley, Kimmens, Oess;* saeculi *Lindelöf;* sæculi *Sisam.* eam (C)] e[u]m *Wildhagen.* hi[ ] (G)] *no gloss Rosier.*

OE: ryhtwise (E^{x})] *on eras.* soþlice (E^{x})] *on eras.* yrfeweærdeiesse (E^{3})] *eras.* (*ca 28 mm*) *before word,* fe *visible in final position.* geahniaþ ł yrfweardiaþ (I)] diaþ *interl.* eorðæn (E^{3})] on *eras. before word.* hy (E$^{3/x}$)] y *altered from another letter by corr., followed by added punctus and letter eras. after word.*

LTg: uero] L: autem *added interl. by corr.: see GAg.* hereditate] L: te *underlined to signal deletion,* bunt *added interl. by corr.: see GAg;* hęreditate CE; hereditatem BD: *cf. Weber MSS* MSKX. possidebunt] L: *underlined to signal deletion.* saeculum] seculum CGHL; sęculum F; sclm BDEIJK. saeculi] seculi CDGHL; scli BEFIJK. eam] CHK: *orig.* eum: u *altered to* a, F: *orig.* eum: u *deleted by subscript dot,* a *interl.*

LTu: hereditate] hereditatem β. saeculum] sæculum ϑ; sęculum νς; sclm βδειλμξοπστ*τυφχ. saeculi] sęculi ζνο; seculi ς; scli δεϑιλξπστ*τυφχ.

GAg: uero] autem FGHIJK, L: *see LTg.* hereditate possidebunt] hereditabunt FGHIK, J: *eras. after word,* L: *see LTg.*

GAu: uero] autem δεζϑιλμξοπρστυφχψ. hereditate possidebunt] hereditabunt δζϑιλμξοστυχψ; hęreditabunt ερφ; haereditabunt π.

30

Os   muð *ABCD*FG, Muð *E^{3},* muþ HIJ*K*
iusti   ðes rehtwisan A, ðæs ryhtwisan B, þæs rihtwisan CJ, ryhtwises DE^{x}*, rihtwises FGH, rihtwises ł þæs rihtwisan I*, rihtwis K
meditabitur   bið smead A, smeað CFI, smeaþ J, smæþ K, bið smeagende B, smeað ł gemyneð DGH, smeað ł gemyneþ E^{x}*
sapientiam   snyttru A, snyttro BC, wisdom DE^{x}*FGHIJK
et   ⁊ ABCE^{3}FGHIJK
lingua   I tunge ABCD*G*HIJK, tunga F, his E$^{3/x}$*
eius   I his ABDFHIJ*K,* hys C, tunge E^{3}
loquetur   spriced *A,* spriceð B, sprycð C, spricþ E^{3}*, sprecð D*G*H, sprecþ FI, spreceþ J, spycð K
iudicium   dom ACDFGIJK, dóm BE^{3}H

ED: Ós (AE)] Os *Kuhn, Harsley.* tunge (G)] tung[ ] *Rosier.* eius (G)] *eius Rosier.*

dóm (H)] dom *Campbell.*

OE: ryhtwiscs (E^{x})] *on eras.* rihtwises ł þæs rihtwisan (I)] ł þæs rihtwisan *written in left margin.* smeað ł gemyneþ (E^{x})] *on eras.* wisdom (E^{x})] *on eras.* his ($E^{3/x}$)] s *by corr., eras. before and after word.* spricþ (E^{3})] *gloss eras. after word, stem visible in initial position, followed by 2 letters and* e.

LTg: Os] Ós ADEK. lingua] ling[ ] G. eius] eíus K. loquetur] A: *orig.* loquitur: i *altered to* e; loquȩtur G.

LTu: loquetur] loquitur β.

31

Lex	I	ae ACIJK, ǽ BDF, æ æ *G*, æe H, Godes E^{3}*
dei	I	godes ABDFGHIJK, godys C, ǽ E^{x}
eius		his ABC$E^{3/x}$*FGHIJ*K*
in		in A, on BCDE^{3}FGHIJK
corde	I	heortan ABCDFG*IJK, heorte H, his E^{3}*
ipsius	I	his ABCDI*JK, he F, him GH, heortæn E^{3}
et		⁊ ABCFGHIJK, ond E^{3}
non		ne ABCE^{3}I*J, na FGHK
subplantabuntur		bioð gescrenote *A,* beoð gescrencte *BC,* beoð gestrængte _J*,_ underplantade ł ⁊ ne beoð gescrencte G*, beoð underdolfene ł ⁊ ne beoð forscrǽncte _I*,_ underplantade beoð D, underplantude beoð *FH,* underplantode *K,* bioþ underwirtwælede ł plantade _$E^{3/x}$*_
gressus	I	gongas ABC, stæpas DGI, stepas H, stapas J, stæppas K, færelda F, his E^{3}
eius	I	his ABFGHIJ*K,* hys C, stepæs E^{3}

ED: supplantabuntur (C)] sub[b]plantabuntur *Wildhagen.* underplantade ł ⁊ ne beoð gescrencte (G)] underplantade ł ne beoð gestrencte *Rosier.*

OE: Godes (E^{3})] s *retouched in darker ink.* his ($E^{3/x}$) (*1st*)] hi *by corr., possibly retracing orig.* hi. heortan (G)] *orig.* heorten: *2nd* e *altered to* a. his (E^{3}) (*2nd*)] s *by corr., eras. after word* (ræ?; *orig.* hiræ?). his (I) (*2nd*)] s. e͟s͟t : is *written in left margin.* ne (I) (*1st*)] e *on eras.* beoð gestrængte (J)] b *altered from* n. underplantade ł ⁊ ne beoð gescrencte (G)] ł ⁊ ne beoð gescrencte *added in diff.* (?) *hand.* beoð underdolfene ł ⁊ ne beoð forscrǽncte (I)] ł ⁊ ne beoð forscrǽncte *written in left margin.* bioþ underwirtwælede ł plantade ($E^{3/x}$)] ł plantade *added by corr.* (= underplantade).

LTg: Lex] [ ]ex G. eius (*1st*)] eíus K. subplantabuntur] supplantabuntur ABEHIJK, CF: *orig.* subplantabuntur: *1st* b *altered to* p. eius (*2nd*)] eíus K.

LTu: subplantabuntur] β: *orig.* supplantabitur: un *written above* i *by corr.;* supplantabuntur δεϑιλξπϱσςτ*τυφψ, o: *orig.* subplantabuntur. gressus] gresus ϑ.

32

Considerat		sceawað ABC, besceawað DFGH, besceawaþ J, bescewaþ K, beosceawaþ E^{x}*, besceawaþ ł bewlataþ I
peccator		se synfulla ABCFIK, se sinfulla J, þe synfulla DE^{x}*, synfulla H, synfullan G
iustum		ðone rehtwisan A, ðone ryhtwisan B, þone rihtwisan C, þonne rihtwisan F, þone rihtwisan J, þone rihtwisne I, ryhtwisne DE^{x}*, rihtwisne GH, rihtwise K
et		⁊ ABCE^{3}FGHIJ
quaerit		soeceð *AB,* secyð *C,* seceþ *J,* secð *DGH,* secþ *E^{3},* sécð *F,* sehð *K,* he secð *I** (*L*)
perdere*	|	forspildan AB, forspillan CD, adydan G, dydan K, cwýlmian F, tocwylmianne I*, to forspillanne J*, hine E^{3} (*L*)
eum	|	hine ABCDFG*H*IJK, tóforspillan E$^{3/x}$*

ED: Considerat (G)] Considerat *Rosier.* besceawað (G)] [ ]wað *Rosier.* tocwylmianne (I)] to cwylmianne *Lindelöf.*

OE: beosceawaþ (E^{x})] *on eras.* þe synfulla (E^{x})] *on eras.* ryhtwisne (E^{x})] *on eras.* he secð (I)] he *interl.* tocwylmianne (I)] *orig.* tocwilmianne: *1st* i *altered to* y. to forspillanne (J)] r *altered from* f. tóforspillan (E$^{3/x}$)] lan *on eras. by corr.,* e *eras. after word.*

LTg: quaerit] queret B, A: *orig.* querit: i *altered to* e; querit CDEGHJKL; quęrit F; quærit I. perdere] L: mortificare *added interl. by corr.: see GAg.* eum] H: u *altered from another letter.*

LTu: peccator] pecator ϑ. quaerit] queret ιμ; quęrit δενϱυφ; querit ϑξσςτ*τ, β: *orig.* queret: i *written above 2nd* e *by corr.*

GAg: perdere] mortificare FHIJK, G: e *obscured,* L: *see LTg.*

GAu: perdere] mortificare δεζϑιλμξοπϱστυφχψ.

33

Dominus	|	drihtyn *C,* dryht̄ *AB,* (d)riħt *G*,* driħ J, soþlice *E^{3}** (*DL*)
autem	|	soðlice ABCFGH, soþlice JK, drihten E^{3}
non		ne ABCE^{3}GIJ, na DFHK
derelinquet		forleteð *A,* forlæteð BDG, forlæteþ FHJ, forlætyð C, forlet E^{3}, forlæt IK
eum		hine ABFGHIJK, hyne C, hiene E^{3}
in		in A, on BCDE^{3}FGHIJK
manibus*	|	hondum A, hondum B, handum CFGH, handum DJ, handan *K,* hande ł anwealde I, his E^{3}
eius	|	his ABCFG*H*IJ*K,* hondum E^{3}
nec		ne ABE^{3}GIJ, ne ne CF, na ne DK, na H

damnabit	I	geniderað A, geniðerað *B,* genyðrað C, genyþrað *DF,* genyðreð *H,* genyðereð *G,* genyþerað J, he genyðrað ł ne he ne fordemþ *I**, hynð *K,* hine ne E^{3}
eum	I	hine ABDFGHIJK, hyne C, geniðræþ E^{3}
cum		ðonne A, þonne BCDJK, þonne FH, þænne I, mid þy E^{3}
iudicabitur	I	bið omed A, bið doemed B, byð demyd C, bið gedemed J, bið gedemd I, demed bið DFK, demed byð H, [ ]med b[ ]ð G, him E^{3}
illi	I	him ABCFGHIJ, him DK, bið demend E^{3}*

ED: (d)riħt (G)] *no gloss Rosier.* soþlice (E)] Soþlice *Harsley.* na ne (D)] nane *Roeder.* [ ]ampnabit (G)] *dampnabit Rosier.* cum (B)] cum *Brenner.* mid þy (E)] midþy *Harsley.* [ ]med b[ ]ð (G)] [ ]med bið *Rosier.*

OE: (d)riħt (G)] *ascender of* d *lost.* soþlice (E^{3})] þ *retouched by corr.* he genyðrað ł ne he ne fordemþ (I)] he genyðrað ł *on eras.* (?), fordemþ *written in left margin.* bið demend (E^{3})] *orig.* bið demende: *final* e *eras.*

LTg: Dominus] E: *eras. after* D; [ ]ominus G; dominus ABCDL. derelinquet] A: *3rd* e *on eras. by corr.* manibus] K: ibus *on eras. by corr.* eius] H: *small eras. after* i; eíus K. damnabit] dampnabit BDFHIK; [ ]ampnabit G: *letter fragment visible in initial position.*

LTu: Dominus] dominus βνς. derelinquet] derelinquit β: *orig.* derelinquet: i *written above 3rd* e *by corr.* nec] nęc ξ. damnabit] damnauit β; dannabit ε; dampnauit ι; dampnabit ξρσςτ*τυ.

GAu: manibus] manus δλμψ.

34

Expecta		abid *AB,* gebid C, abid ł geanbida J, geanbida *DFGHIK,* GeOnbide E$^{3/x}$*
dominum		drihtyn C, dryhten D, drihten E$^{3/x}$*K, dryht̄ AB, driħt FGH, driħ J
et		⁊ ABCE^{3}FGHIJK
custodi		gehald A, geheald BDFGHIJK, geheæld E^{3}, heald C
uias*	I	wegas ABCD, weg FGHIJK, his *E^{3}* (*L*)
eius	I	his ABDF*G*HIJ*K,* hys C, wegæs E^{3}
et		⁊ ACDE^{3}FGHIJK (*B*)
exaltabit		hefeð up A, he upahefð CDFGHI, he upahefeð E$^{3/x}$*, he upahefaþ J, he uphef K, ⁊ uphefeð B
te		ðe *AB,* þe CDE^{3}*FGHIJK
ut		þæt ABK, þæt CDE^{3}*F, þæt þe J, swa swa I
inhabites*		ðu ineardie A, ðu ineardige B, þu inneardige C, ðu oneardige

	D, þu oneærdige $E^{3/x}$*, earddige K, þu yrfweardige F, mid yrfwerdnesse G, mid yrfweardnysse I, yrfeweardnesse J (*L*)
(capias)*	onfo FJ, þu underfehst I*, (þ)u underfeh[ ] G*
terram	eorðan ABCD*F*J, eorðæn E^{3}, eorþan K, eorðe GH, land I
cum	ðonne A, ðonne B, þonne CDF, þonne E^{x}*GHK, þænne I, forðon J
pereunt*	forweorðað *AB*FH, forwurðaþ C, forweorþað DE^{x}*J, furwurðað G, forwyrðaþ I, forwyrðað K (*L*)
peccatores	ða synfullan AB, þa synfullan I, þa sinfullan J, synfullan K, synfulle CDE^{x}*GH, se synfulla F
uidebis	ðu gesist A, þu gesihst BFIJ, þu gesihst CDE^{x}*, gesyhst K, þu ge H, þu ge[ ] *G*

ED: Exspecta (B)] Expecta *Brenner.* u[ ]am (G)] uiam *Rosier.* ei[ ] (G)] eius *Rosier.* his (G)] *no gloss Rosier.* swa swa (I)] swaswa *Lindelöf.* hereditate (F)] hereditatem *Kimmens.* (þ)u underfeh[ ] (G)] þu underfeh[ ] *Rosier.*

OE: GeOnbide ($E^{3/x}$)] Ge *added by corr., final* e *on eras.* drihten ($E^{3/x}$)] en *on eras. by corr.,* s *eras. after word.* he upahefeð ($E^{3/x}$)] *eras. (2 letters?) after* he, a *interl. by corr.,* ð *added.* þe (E^{3})] *letter eras. after word.* þæt (E^{3})] *retraced by corr.* (?) *with cross-stroke added; eras. before word, with* þ *visible; eras. after word.* þu oneærdige ($E^{3/x}$)] þu on *added by corr.,* ige *by another corr. on eras.* þu underfehst (I)] þu underfe *on eras.* (þ)u underfeh[ ] (G)] *bowl of* þ *not visible.* þonne (E^{x})] *on eras.* forweorþað (E^{x})] *on eras.* synfulle (E^{x})] *on eras.* þu gesihst (E^{x})] *on eras.*

LTg: Expecta] A: *orig.* Exspecta: s *deleted by superscript dot;* [ ]xpecta G; Exspecta BDK. uias] uiam L: *letter eras. after* a, *macron added above* a *by corr.: see GAg.* eius] eíus K; ei[ ] G. et (*2nd*)] *om.* B. te] A: *eras. but visible;* té B. inhabites] L: in *and* bites *underlined to signal deletion,* a *altered to* er, editate capias *added by corr. after* r: *see GAg.* terram] F: *orig.* terre: re *underlined to signal deletion,* ram *interl. by corr.* pereunt] L: eunt *underlined to signal deletion,* ierint *added interl. by corr.: see GAg;* pereant B, A: *orig.* periant: i *altered to* e. uidebis] uidebi[ ] G.

LTu: Expecta] Exspecta βϑμ. exaltabit] exaltauit β. pereunt] pereant ς, β: *orig.* pereunt: u *crossed through by corr.,* a *interl.*

GAg: uias] uiam FHIJK, L: *see LTg;* u[ ]am G. inhabites] hereditate capias GIK, L: *see LTg,* F: *orig.* hereditatem capias: m *crossed through and deleted by subscript dot,* H: *orig.* hereditate capies: *4th* e *altered to* a; hereditatem capias J. pereunt] perierint FGHIJK, L: *see LTg.*

GAu: uias] uiam δεζϑιλμξοπρστυφχψ. inhabites] hereditate capias δζϑλμξοπστυχψ; hęreditate capias ειρφ. pereunt] perierint δεζϑιλμξοπρστυφχψ.

35

Uidi — ic gesch *B*K, ic geseah *CFHIJ*, ic geseah *D*, Ic geseæh *E*^{3}, ic geseo *G* (*AL*)

impium — asan *A*, ðone arleasan B, þone arleasan CJ, arleasne DE^{x}*FGHK, arleasne ł þone arleasan I*

superexaltatum — upahefenne A, upahæfenne B*, upahafenne I*, ofyrahafynne C, geuferudne D, ofer geuferudne E^{x}*, ofer geúforudne F, ofer upahafenne GJ, ofer ahafene *K*, ofer H

et — ⁊ ABCDE^{x}*FGHIJK

eleuatum — upahefenne A, upahæfenne B, uppahafenne C, upahafenne DE^{x}**G*H, úpahafene F, upahafenne J, upahafen K, tobædne ł geuferodne I

super* — ofer ABDE^{x}*, ofyr C, swa swa FGIJ, swa K

cedros — cederbeamas ABJ, cederbeam F, beamas C, cedertreow D, cedartreow *G*H, cedertryw I, cedertrowes E^{x}*, n K*

libani — þæs holtes F, ðæs wuda ł cederbeamas þæs holtes I, n K*

ED: U[ ] (A)] Uidi *Kuhn*. [ ]mpium (A)] impium *Kuhn*. ofer geuferudne (E)] ofergeuferudne *Harsley*. swa swa (GIJ)] swaswa *Rosier, Lindelöf, Oess.* cedartreow (GH)] cedar treow *Rosier, Campbell*. libani (K)] Libani *Sisam*.

OE: arleasne (E^{x})] *on eras.* arleasne ł þone arleasan (I)] ł þone arleasan *written in left margin.* upahæfenne (B)] æ *blotted.* upahafenne (I)] up *on eras.* ofer geuferudne (E^{x})] *on eras.* ⁊ (E^{x})] *on eras.* upahafenne (E^{x})] *on eras.* ofer (E^{x})] *on eras.* cedertrowes (E^{x})] *on eras.* n (K) (*both*)] *for* nomen.

LTg: Uidi] U[ ] A: *letters lost due to stain;* Vidi BCDEFGHIL. impium] [ ]mpium A: *initial letter lost due to stain.* superexaltatum] K: *eras. after word.* eleuatum] ęleuatu[ ] G. cedros] cędros G.

LTu: Uidi] Vidi ιvoϱσυφ. cedros] caedros ζ; cędros v. libani] liuani ϑ.

GAg: super] sicut FGHIJK.

GAu: super] sicut δεζϑιλμξοπϱστυφχψ.

36

(Et)* — ⁊ *AB*FGHIJK

Transiui — ic leorde *AB*, ic geleorde C, ic ofereode D*GHK*, ic oferfor *F*, ic for *J*, ic geode *I*, Ic ferde ł ofereode *E*^{3}

et — ⁊ ABCDE^{x}*FGIJK

ecce — sohðe AB, sihðe CG, on gesihðe D, on gesyhðe E^{x}*, on gihðe H, efne FIJK

non — ne ABCJ, na K, he næs I*, he næs ł na DE^{x}*, he næs ⁊ F, he næs ł ne G, he nes ł na H

erat | wes *AE*^{x}*, wæs B*CDGHJK* (*I*)
(et)* ⁊ *AB*G
quaesiui ic sohte *ABCDE*^{x}**FG*I**J*, ⁊ ic sohte *HK* (*L*)
eum hine ABCDE^{x}*FGHIJK
et ⁊ ABCE^{3}FGIJK
non | ne ABE^{3}, ne ny C, na DGHJK, nis FI*
est | wes A, wæs BC, is ł nis DH, is E^{3}GJ*K*
inuentus gemoted A, gemoeted B, gemeted J, gentus C, gemet DE$^{3/x}$*HI, ongemet F, ongemett G, funden K
locus | stow ABCDFGHJ, stowe I, stede K, his E^{3}
eius | his ABDFGHIJK, hys C, stow E^{3}

ED: on gihðe (H)] ongihðe *Campbell.*

OE: ⁊ (E^{x}) (*1st*)] *on eras.* on gesyhðe (E^{x})] *on eras.* he næs (I)] *eras. after* he *and* næs; *see also LTg note to* erat. he næs ł na (E^{x})] *on eras.* wes (E^{x})] *on eras.* ic sohte (E^{x})] *on eras.* ic sohte (I)] ⁊ *eras. before gloss.* hine (E^{x})] *on eras.* nis (I)] *another* nis *written in bottom margin below* non est. gemet (E$^{3/x}$)] ge *added by corr., eras.* (*2 letters*) *after word.*

LTg: Transiui] transiui EFGHIJK; Et transiui AB: *cf. Weber MSS* Mαβγδ, *see GAg.* erat] H: *eras. after word,* I: & : ⁊ *eras. after word,* K: et *eras. after word;* erat et AB: *cf. Weber MSS* SKαβγδ moz^{c}. quaesiui] quęsiui G, A: ę *on eras. by corr.,* F: *eras. before word;* quesiui BCDEHJL, K: *eras.* (*2 letters*) *before word.* est] ést K.

LTu: Transiui] TRansiui β; transiui δεζθιλμξοπϱστυφχ. quaesiui] quęsiui βενοϱφ; quesiui δθιξσςτ*τ. erat] erat et β: *cf. Weber MSS* SKαβγδ moz^{c}, *see GAu.*

GAg: Transiui] Et transiui FGHIJK, AB: *see LTg.* erat] erat et G, AB: *see LTg; for* IK *see LTg.*

GAu: Transiui] Et transiui δεζθιλμξοπϱσσυφχψ; [ ]t transiui τ: *initial wanting.* erat] erat et μοπϱσχψ, β: *see LTu.*

37

Custodi hald A, heald BCJ, geheald DF*G*HIK, Geheæld E^{3}
ueritatem* soðfestnisse A, soðfæstnysse C, soþfæstnisse D, soðfæstnesse B, soðfestnesse E^{3}, soþfæstnesse J, on soðfæstnesse G, unsceaððignysse F, unscyldignysse I, unscyldige K (*L*)
et ⁊ ABCDE^{3}FGHIJK
uide geseh A, geseoh BCDFGHIJK, gesioh E^{3}
aequitatem efennisse A*DE*^{x}**H*, efynnysse *C*, efennesse *BGJ*, efnesse *K*, emnysse F, rihtwisnysse ł efnesse I* (*L*)
quoniam forðon ABJ, forþon C, forðæn E^{3}, forþan K, forþam þe F, forðam þe G, forðan þe I

sunt	sind A, synd CFGHJK, sint B, synt DI, Sient E^3
reliquiae	lafe A*C*, lafa *BDFGHJK*, þa lafa ł gemynd I, forletnesse ł laue *$E^{3/x}$** (*L*)
homini	menn ACDG*H*, men BIJ, manna F, mon E^3*, ealle *K**
pacifico	ðæm sibsuman AB, þam sybsuman C, þam sibsuman J, gesybsumum D, geSibsumum $E^{3/x}$*, gesibsumum FGI, gesibsumum H, gesibsume K

ED: ęquitatem (E)] aequitatem *Harsley*. æquitatem (D)] aequitatem *Roeder*. forðon (A)] for ðon *Kuhn*. reliquiæ (D)] reliquiae *Roeder*. reliquię (E)] reliquiae *Harsley*.

OE: efennisse (E^x)] *on eras.* rihtwisnysse ł efnesse (I)] m *written above* f *but without deletion mark* (= emnesse). forletnesse ł laue ($E^{3/x}$)] ł laue *added by corr.* mon (E^3)] *eras. after word.* ealle (K)] *lemma misread as* omni. geSibsumum ($E^{3/x}$)] ge *and* mum *added by corr.*, mum *on eras.*

LTg: Custodi] [ ]ustodi G. ueritatem] L: innocentiam *added interl. by corr.: see GAg.* aequitatem] æquitatem BDL; equitatem CJK; ęquitatem EGH. reliquiae] reliquiæ BD; reliquię CEFGHL; reliquie JK. homini] H: *final* i *altered from another letter,* K: h *interl. by corr.*

LTu: aequitatem] ęquitatem βεινξφ; æquitatem ϑ; equitatem σςτ*τυ. reliquiae] reliquię βειμνξορυφ; reliquiæ ϑ; reliquie σςτ*τ.

GAg: ueritatem] innocentiam FGHIJK, L: *see LTg.*

GAu: ueritatem] innocentiam δεζϑιμξοπρσυφχψ.

38

Iniusti	| ða unrehtan A, ða unryhtan B, þa unrihtan J, þa unrihtwisan CFGHI, þa unryhtwisan D, unrihtwisan K, þa unrihtsan C, Soðlice E^3
autem	| soðlice ABCG, soþlice FJ, þæ unryhtwise E^3
disperient*	forweorðað ABFGH, forwurðað C, forweorðaþ DJ, forwiorþeþ E^3, forwyrðað K, losiað ł forwurðaþ I
simul	somud A, somod BDE^3H, samod CFIJ, samod ætgædere G*, ætsomne K
reliquiae	lafe A*C*, lafa *BDE^3FGHJK*, gemynd ł þa lafa I* (*L*)
impiorum	arleasra ABCDFGHIK, ærleæsræ E^3, arlearra J
peribunt*	forweorðað AB, forwurðað CF, forweorþað D, forweorðaþ J, forwiorþeþ E^3, forwyrþað K*, forwurðaþ ł forðfaraþ I, forðfarað G

ED: Iniusti (B)] iniusti *Brenner.* samod ætgædere (G)] samod ł ætgædere *Rosier.* reliquię (E)] reliquiae *Harsley.*

OE: samod ætgædere (G)] *2nd* d *formed from another letter.* gemynd ł þa lafa (I)] þa *interl.* forwyrþað (K)] *2nd* r *interl.*

LTg: reliquiae] reliquiæ B; reliquię CDEFGHKL; reliquie J: li *interl. in light brown ink of gloss.*

LTu: Iniusti] INiusti β. reliquiae] reliquiæ ϑ; reliquię ινξορυφ; reliquie πσςτ*τ. impiorum] o: *initial* i *interl.*

GAg: disperient] disperibunt FGIJK, H: *small eras. after word.* peribunt] interibunt FGHK, I: in *on eras.*

GAu: disperient] disperibunt δεζϑιλμξοπρστυφχψ. peribunt] interibunt δεζιλμξοπρστυφχψ.

39

Salus	I	haelu A, hæl CI, hælo BDFG*H*JK, Soðlice E^3 (*M*)
autem	I	soðlice ABCG, soþlice FJ, soþis DH, witodlice K, helo E^3
iustorum		rehtwisra A, ryhtwisra B, rihtwisra *C*FGHIJ, ryhtwisra D, rihtwisan K, þæræ soþfestræ E^3
a		from A, from B, fram CFGJ, æt I, to *E^3** (*KM*)
domino		dryhtne B, drihtne E^{3}FGI, drihten K, dryht̄ A, drih́t C, drih́ J
est*		ịs ABDE^3*I**, ys C (*L*)
et		⁊ ABCE^{3}GI*JK
protector	I	gescildend ABJ, gescyldynd C, gescyldend F*H, gescyld DGK, gescyldnes ł beweriend I, hioræ E^3
eorum	I	heara A, hira B, hyra C, heora DGHIJK, heora is *F,* gescild E$^{3/x}$*
est*		is ABE^{3}G, ys C, he is D (*L*)
in		on ABCDE^{3}FGIJK
tempore		tid AB, tide CDE^{3}FGHJK, timan ł on tide I
tribulationis		geswinces ABDGHJ, geswincys C, gedrefednysse FI, gedrefednesse K, eærfoðnesse E^3 (*M*)

ED: [ ]alus (H)] Salus *Campbell.* á (E)] a *Harsley.*

OE: to (E^3)] *on eras.* is (I)] *gloss and lemma written in left margin.* ⁊ (I)] est : ⁊ he is *written in right margin.* gescyldend (F)] *ascender of 1st* d *obscured by stain.* gescild (E$^{3/x}$)] ge *added by corr.*

LTg: Salus] M: *1 leaf wanting containing vv 15–38*; [ ]alus H. iustorum] C: *interl., with gloss above.* a] á EKM. est (*1st*)] I: *lemma and gloss written in left margin,* L: *crossed through by corr.: see GAg.* eorum] F: *eras. after word.* est (*2nd*)] L: *crossed through by corr.: see GAg.* tribulationis] tribulatiônis M.

LTu: est (*1st*)] β: *interl. by corr.* tempore] temporę ξ.

GAg: est (_1st_)] I: _orig. om.: see OE and LTg; om._ FGHJK, L: _see LTg._ est (_2nd_)] _om._ HIJK, F: _see LTg note to_ eorum, L: _see LTg._

GAu: est (_1st_)] _om._ δεζϑιλμξοπϱστυφχψ. est (_2nd_)] _om._ δέζιλμοπϱστυφχψ.

40

Et	⁊ _A_BCE^{x}*F_G_IJK
adiuuabit	gefultumeð A, gefultumað BC, gefultumaþ J, geful[ ]umaþ ł gehelpeð I*, gefylsteð DG, gefylsteþ E^{x}*FHK
eos	hie AB, hi C, hy DE^{x}*H, hig IJ, híg F, him G, his K*
dominus	drihtyn C, drihten E^{x}*K, dryht̄ AB, drih̄t F, drih̄ GJ
et	⁊ ABCE^{x}*FGIJK
liberabit	gefreoð _AB_C, alyseþ DFH, alyseð E^{x}*G, aliseþ _J_, he alysð I, alys K (_M_)
eos	hie AB, hi CE^{3}*K, hy DGH, híg F, hig IJ*
et	⁊ ABCE^{3}*FGJK
eripiet*	genereð ABCE^{3}GH, genereþ D, generað FI, generaþ J, nera K (_L_)
eos	hie AB, hi C_K_, hy DE^{x}GH, híg F, hig J
a	from AE^{3}, from B, fram CDFH_J_K, fram GI (_M_)
peccatoribus	synfullum _A_CE$^{3/x}$*FG_HI_, synfullum BDJ, synfullan K
et	⁊ _A_BCE^{3}FGIJK
saluos*	hale ABCDE^{x}*K, he gehæleð FJ, gehælð G, he gehælð I (_L_)
faciet*	gedoeð AB, he gedeð C, gedeþ DE^{x}* (_L_)
eos	hie AB, hi CK, hy DE^{x}*GH, híg F, hig IJ
quoniam*	forðon ABDHJ, forþon CG, forþæn E^{3}, forþā K, forðam ðe F, forðan þe I
sperauerunt	gehyhton AB, hi gehihtun C, hi gehihta J, hy hyhton DH, hi hihton GK, gewenæþ ł hihton E$^{3/x}$*, hi gehyhtun ł hopodon I, hi hopudon F
in	in A, on BCDE^{3}FGHIJK
eum*	hine ABDE^{3}FHJK, hyne C, him GI (_L_)

ED: geful[ ]umaþ ł gehelpeð (I)] gefultumaþ ł gehelpeð _Lindelöf._ forðon (A)] for ðon _Kuhn._

OE: ⁊ (E^{x}) (_1st_)] _on eras._ geful[ ]umaþ ł gehelpeð (I)] geful[ ]umaþ ł _written in left margin, letter after 1st_ l _lost due to tight binding._ gefylsteþ (E^{x})] _on eras._ hy (E^{x}) (_1st_)] _on eras._ his (K)] _top of_ s _incomplete._ drihten (E^{x})] _on eras._ ⁊ (E^{x}) (_2nd_)] _on eras._ alyseð (E^{x})] _on eras._ hi (E^{3})] _gloss eras. before word._ hig (J)] g _altered from another letter._ ⁊ (E^{3}) (_3rd_)] _by corr.?_ hy (E^{x}) (_3rd_)] _added by corr._ synfullum (E$^{3/x}$)] _eras._ (_10 mm_) _before word,_ syn _on eras. by corr.,_ f _retouched._ hale (E^{x})] _on_ *eras.* gedeþ (E^{x})] *on eras.* hy (E^{x}) (*3rd*)] *on eras.* gewenæþ ł hihton ($E^{3/x}$)] ł hihton *added by corr., eras. after* i, *small eras. before 2nd* h.

LTg: Et] G: E *mostly lost;* et A: *added in left margin by corr.* liberabit] A: *2nd* b *on eras.,* M: *orig.* liberauit: u *deleted,* b *interl.;* liberauit BJ. eripiet] L: ipiet *underlined to signal deletion,* uet *added interl. by corr.* eos (*3rd*)] K: *eras. after word.* a] J: p *eras. after word;* á M. peccatoribus] A: us *added by corr.,* H: *small eras. after word (perhaps of punct.),* I: *eras. after word.* et (*3rd*)] A: *interl. by corr.* saluos] L: os *underlined to signal deletion,* abit *added interl. by corr.: see GAg.* faciet] L: *underlined to signal deletion: see GAg.* eum] L: u *altered to* o *by corr.,* m *underlined to signal deletion: see GAg.*

LTu: Et] [ ]t σ. liberabit] liberauit βτ*τ.

GAg: eripiet] eruet FGHIJK, L: *see LTg.* saluos faciet] saluabit FGHIK, L: *see LTg;* saluauit J. quoniam] quia FGHIJK. eum] eo FGHIJK, L: *see LTg.*

GAu: eripiet] eruet δεζϑιλμξοπρστυφχψ. saluos faciet] saluabit δεζϑιλμξοπρστυφχψ. quoniam] quia εζϑιλμξοπρστυφχψ; qui δ: *letter eras. after* i. eum] eo εζϑιλμξοπρστυφχψ.

PSALM 37

2

Domine	dryhten E^{3}, dryht̄ *AB*, driħt *C*G, driħ *J*, eala ðu driħt F*, eala þu drihten I* (*KM*)
ne	nales AB, nalys *C*, ne DE^{3}FI, na HJK
in	in A, on B*C*DE^{x}*GHIJK
ira*	eorre ABDE^{x}*, yrre *C*K, hatheortnysse F, hatheortnesse GHJ, hatheortnys I
tua*	ðinum A, ðinum B, þinum *C*DE^{x}*, ðín F, þinre GHIJ, þinan K
arguas	ðrea AB, þrea C, þu ðreage D*H*, þu ðreage E^{x}*, þu þreage GJ, ne ðrea ðu F, ðrea þu I, þræa K
me	me ABCE^{x}*FGHIJK
neque	n A, ne BCI, ne ne F, ⁊ na DGHJK, na E^{x}*
in	in A, on BCDE^{x}*FGHIJ
furore*	hatheortnisse A, hatheortnesse BDE^{x}*, yrre CFIK, irre J, yrrum G, yrrum H (*L*)
tuo*	ðinre AB, þinre DE^{x}*, þinum CHJ, þynum F, þinum GI, þinan *K*
corripias	geðrea AB, geþrea C, þu nyrewe DE^{x}*, þu nerige G, þu nerewe H, ne nyrwa ðu F, þu nirewest J, nyrwest me K, styr ðu I
me	mec AB, me CE^{x}*FGHIJK

ED: dryhten (E)] Dryhten *Harsley*. ðín (F)] ðin *Kimmens*.

OE: eala ðu driħt (F)] o *written in bowl of* D *in* Domine. eala þu drihten (I)] þu *interl.* on (E^x) (*1st*)] *on eras.* eorre (E^x)] *on eras.* þinum (E^x)] *on eras.* þu ðreage (E^x)] *on eras.* me (E^x) (*1st*)] *on eras.* na (E^x)] *on eras.* on (E^x) (*2nd*)] *on eras.* hatheortnesse (E^x)] *on eras.* þinre (E^x)] *on eras.* þu nyrewe (E^x)] *on eras.* me (E^x) (*2nd*)] *on eras.*

LTg: Domine] J: *otiose stroke above* n; DN̄E ABCEK; DN̄e M. ne] NE C. in (*1st*)] IN C. ira] IRA C. tua] TVA C. arguas] argvas H. furore] L: ira *added interl. by corr.*: *see GAg*.

LTu: Domine] DN̄E βλμϱτ*ψ; DOMINE ιντ; DOMIne ς. ne] NE ιλμνϱψ. in (*1st*)] IN ιλμνρψ. tua] TUA ν. arguas] argvas ε; ARGUAS λ; ARguas ϱ. me (*1st*)] ME λ.

GAg: ira] furore FGHIJK. tua] tuo FGHIJ, K: u *altered from* a (?). furore] ira FGHIJ, K: a *on stain and retouched,* L: *see LTg*. tuo] tua FGHIJ, K: t *on stain and retouched.*

GAu: ira] furore δεζϑιξοπστυφχ; FVRORE λμϱ; FURORE ψ. tua] tuo δεζϑιμξοπστυφχψ; TVO λϱ. furore] ira δεζϑιλμξοπϱστυφχψ. tuo] tua δεζϑιλμξοπϱστυφχψ.

3

Quoniam		forðon ABJ, forþon C, Forðæn E^3, forþam G, forðam ðe F, forþan þe I
sagittae		strele A, stræla *B*, strælas *CJ*, flana *D*FH*I**K*, flanan *G*, þine E^3 (*L*)
tuae		ðine A*BF*, þine *C*IJ*K*, þina *DH*, þinan *G*, strele ł flane $E^{3/x}$* (*L*)
infixae	|	gefestnade A, gefæstnode *BJK*, onafæstnode *C*I, ongefæstnode *DFGH*, on me E^3 (*L*)
sunt		sind A, synd CDGHJK, sint BE^3, synt FI
mihi	|	me A*B*C*DFGHIJK, gefestnode E^3*
et		ꝧ ABCE^3FGHIJK*
confirmasti		getrymedes A, getrimedest J, ðu getrymedes B, þu getrymydyst C, þu getrymedest D, þu getrimedest E^3*, þu getrymdest F, þu getremedest GH, þu getrymedest I*, þu getrymdest K
super	|	ofer ABDFGHIJK, ofyr C, þin E^3*
me	|	mec A, me BCFGHIJK, hænd E^3*
manum	|	hond A, hand BCDFK, handa GHIJ, ofer E^3
tuam	|	ðine ABFK, þine CGHIJ, me E^3

ED: forðon (A)] for ðon *Kuhn*. sagittę (E)] sagittae *Harsley*. tuę (E)] tuae *Harsley*. m¹ (E)] michi *Harsley*.

OE: flana (D)] *orig.* flane: e *deleted by subscript dot,* a *interl.* flana (I)] fl *on eras.* strele ł flane (E$^{3/x}$)] ł flane *added by corr.* me (A)] *eras. after* m. gefestnode (E^{3})] d *perhaps altered from* ð. ⁊ (K)] þ *followed by 2 illegible letters eras. after word* (*Sisam* '?þug'). þu getrimedest (E^{3})] *final* t *added by corr.* þu getrymedest (I)] y *altered from* i (?). þin (E^{3})] *orig.* þine: e *eras.* hænd (E^{3})] æ (?) *eras. after word.*

LTg: sagittae] sagittæ B; sagittę CDEFHL; sagitte GJ; sagittæ K. tuae] tuæ BL; tuę CDEFGHK. infixae] infixæ B; infixę CFGHKL; infixe DEJ. mihi] m[1] E; michi C: *orig.* mihi: c *interl. by corr.*

LTu: sagittae] sagittę ειλμνοϱφ; sagittæ ϑ; sagitte ξσςτ*τυ. tuae] tuę ειλνςυφ; tuæ ϑ; tue ξστ*τ. infixae] infixę δεινπϱφψ; infixe ζξσςτ*τυ; infixæ ϑ. mihi] michi ιλςτ, ϱ: c *interl.;* m[1] ξπστ*φ.

4

Nec*	|	ne ABCJ, na DGK, Na E$^{3/x}$*, nys F, nis H, nis na I (*L*)
est	|	is ABDE^{x}*GJ*K*, ys C
sanitas		haelu A, hælo BDFGHIJ, hæl CK, hælþe E^{x}*
in		in A, on BCDE^{x}*FGHIJK
carne		flesce A, flæsce BCDE^{x}*FGHIJK
mea		minum *A*GH, minum BCDIJ, mina E^{x}*, mine F, minan *K*
a		fro A, from B, fram CFJ, fram I, of DE^{x}*HK, on G (*M*)
uultu*		ondwleatan A*, andwlitan BDE^{x}*K, ⁊wlitan C, ansyne FGHI, ansine J (*L*)
irae		eorres *ABDE^{x}*H,* yrres *CG*I, irres *J,* yrre *FK* (*LM*)
tuae		ðines A*B,* þinys *C,* þines *DE^{x}*GHI*J, ðine *F,* þinre *K* (*LM*)
et*		⁊ CE^{3} (*AB*)
non	|	nis *A*DH, nys CFI, ne BE^{3}J, na GK
est	|	is BE^{3}GJ*K*
pax		sib ABFJK, sybb CD, sibb GH, syb I, sibbe E^{x}*
ossibus		banum ACFGIJ, banum BDE^{x}*H, bannan K
meis		minum AFGHI, minum BCDE^{x}*J, minan K
a		from A, from B, fram CFJ, fram I, of D*E*^{x}*GHK (*M*)
facie		onsiene A, onsine *B,* ansyne CDFGHIJK, ansine E$^{3/x}$* (*M*)
peccatorum	|	synna ABCDFGHIJK, minræ E^{3}
meorum	|	minra ABCDFGHIJ, minan K, Sinnæ E^{3}

ED: a ffacie (G)] affacie *Rosier.* irę (EG)] irae *Harsley;* ire *Rosier.* tuę (E)] tuae *Harsley.* á (E) (*2nd*)] a *Harsley.*

OE: Na (E$^{3/x}$)] a *on eras. by corr.* is (E^{x}) (*1st*)] *on eras.* hælþe (E^{x})] *on eras.* on (E^{x})] *on eras.* flæsce (E^{x})] *on eras.* mina (E^{x})] *on eras.* of (E^{x}) (*1st*)] *on eras.* ondwleatan (A)] *1st* n *interl.* andwlitan (E^{x})] *on eras.* eorres (E^{x})] *on eras.* þines

(E^{x})] *on eras.* sibbe (E^{x})] *on eras.* banu<u>m</u> (E^{x})] *on eras.* minu<u>m</u> (E^{x})] *on eras.* of (E^{x}) (*2nd*)] *on eras.* ansine ($E^{3/x}$)] an *on eras. by corr.*

LTg: Nec] L: on *added interl. after* N *by corr.: see GAg.* est (*1st*)] ést K. mea] A: a *on eras. by corr.*, K: *eras.* (*25 mm*) *after word.* a (*1st*)] á M. uultu] L: facie *added interl. by corr.: see GAg.* irae] iræ BL; irę CDEFGHM; ire JK. tuae] tuæ BC; tuę DEFGHJKM; tue L. et] *om.* AB: *cf. Weber MSS* αβγδ, *see GAg.* non] A: on *interl. by corr.* est (*2nd*)] ést K. a (*2nd*)] á EM. facie] faciæ B; facię M.

LTu: in] *om* ϑ. carne] carni ϑ. mea] meæ ϑ. irae] ire δσςτ*τι; irę ειvξπφ; iræ ϑ. tuae] tuę εζινξπρυφ; tuæ ϑ; tue σςτ*τ.

GAg: Nec] Non FGHIJK, L: *see LTg.* uultu] facie FIJ, L: *see LTg;* facię HK; ffacie G. et] *om.* FGHIJK, AB: *see LTg.*

GAu: Nec] Non δεζϑιλμξοπρστυφχψ. uultu] facie δεζιλμξορστυφχψ; faciæ ϑ; facię π. et] *om.* δεζϑιλμξοπρστχψ.

5

Quoniam — forðon ABFJ, forþon C, Forþæn E^{3}, forþam G, forþan þe I*
iniquitates | unrehtwisnisse *A*, unrihtwisnysse CF, unryhtwisnessa BD, unrihtwisnessa I, unrihtwisnesse J, unrihwisnesse K, on unrihtwisnesse G, onrihtwisnessa H, minc E^{3}
meae | mine *ACIJK*, mina *BD*, minre *FG*, unrihtnesse E^{3} (*HL*)
superposuerunt* — ofergesetton ABJ, ofyrgesettyn *C*, ofersetton D, oferseton $E^{3/x}$*, ofersett[ ]n G*, ofer stæpas F*, ofer HK, oferferdon I* (*L*)
(sunt)* — synd FG*J
caput | heafud AC, heafod *BDFHIJ*K, [ ]eafod G, min E^{3}
meum | min ABCDF*H*JK, min ł ofer min andgit I, heæfod E^{3} (*G*)
⟨et⟩ — (*H*)
sicut — swe swe A, swa swa BCDE^{x}*GHIJ, swá swá F, swa K
onus — byrðen AB*F*H, byrðyn C, byrþen DIK, b[ ]rðen G*, byrþe E^{x}*, bynden J
graue — hefig *A*BDFHJK, hefige CE^{x}*I, hefig[ ] *G* (*M*)
grauatae — gehefegade A*B*, gehefygode *C*, gehefegode *DFHJK*, gehefogode E^{3}*I* (*GLM*)
sunt — sind A, synd CF*G*HJK, sint B, hy synd D, hi synt I, sindon E^{3}
super — ofer *A*BDE^{3}FGHI*JK, ofyr C
me — mec AD, me BCE^{3}FGHIJK

ED: forðon (A)] for ðon *Kuhn.* meæ (D)] meae *Roeder.* meę (E)] meae *Harsley.* ofergesetton (J)] ofer gesetton *Oess.* synd (G) (*1st*)] *no gloss Rosier.* caput (G)] *caput Rosier.* [ ]eafod (G)] *no gloss Rosier.* meum (G)] meam *Rosier.* meum (I)] meum et *Lindelöf.* swa swa (GIJ)] swaswa *Rosier, Lindelöf, Oess.* grauę (E)] gravae *Harsley.* grauatę (E)] gravatae *Harsley.* g[ ] (G)] *grauate Rosier.* synd (G) (*2nd*)] [ ]nd *Rosier.* ofer (I)] ofor *Lindelöf.*

OE: forþan þe (I)] *eras. after* þe. oferseton ($E^{3/x}$)] seton *on eras. by corr.* ofersett[ ]n (G)] *2 letters follow* n, *2nd of which is* e; *space of ca 11 mm separates* t *and* n, *although there is no damage to leaf.* ofer stæpas (F)] oferstæpas (?). oferferdon (I)] ferdon *on eras.* synd (G) (*1st*)] *top of* s *partly lost.* swa swa (E^{x})] *on eras.* b[ ]rðen (G)] *crease in leaf after* b. byrþe (E^{x})] *on eras.* hefige (E^{x})] *on eras.* ofer (I)] *orig.* ofor: *cross-stroke added to 2nd* o *to form* e.

LTg: iniquitates] A: s *on eras.* meae] A: *final* e *on eras.;* meæ BDL; meę EFGJK, H: ę *interl.* superposuerunt] L: posuer *underlined to signal deletion,* gresse *added interl. by corr.,* s *added interl. before 3rd* u *to form* sunt: *see GAg;* supposuerunt C: *cf. Weber MS* λ. caput] F: t *altered from another letter,* H: *eras. after word;* capt B. meum] G: *tops of* eum *cropped;* meum et H: et *interl.* graue] A: *letter eras. after* u; grauę EG; gráue M. grauatae] grauatæ B; grauatę CEFHIKM; grauate JL, D: e *on eras.;* g[ ] G: *rest of word obscured by paper mounts and by show-through from fol. 45r.* sunt (*2nd*)] [ ]nt G: *minim visible before* n. super] A: *orig.* super: er *interl. by corr.*

LTu: meae] meę βειvξςφ; meæ ϑ; mee στ*τ. meum] meum et υ. onus] honus ς. graue] grauę ιξ. grauatae] grauatę δεζιλνξϱσφ; grauatæ ϑμυχ; grauati β: *orig.* gruati: a *added interl. by corr.;* grauate πςτ*τ.

GAg: superposuerunt] supergressę sunt FHK; supergresse sunt GJ, L: *see LTg;* supergressae sunt I.

GAu: superposuerunt] supergressę sunt δελοπϱσφχψ; supergressae sunt ζμ; supergresæ sunt ϑ; supergresse sunt ιξτυ.

6

Conputruerunt*	fuladun ł rotedan A*, fuladon B, fuludon *C,* afulodon J, rotodon D*E*^{x}*GK, rotudon F, rotode H, forrotodon I (*L*)
et	ᴝ ABCE^{x}*FGHJ
deteriorauerunt*	wyrsadon A, wyrsodon BCDE^{x}*J*K,* gebrosnode F, hy gewemmede G, hi gemmede H, gewemmede I* (*L*)
(sunt)*	synd FGHJ, ᴝ hig synt I
cicatrices	wundsweðe *A,* wundswaðu B*C,* dolhswaðo DFH, dolswaðo E^{x}*, dolhswaþo K, dolhswaða G, dolhswaþa J, dolcswaþu I, dolgsuaþhe *M**
meae	mine *ABCDE*^{x}**FGIJK,* m[ ]ne *H** (*L*)
a	from *A,* from B, fram CFJ*K,* fram I, of DE^{x}*GH (*M*)
facie	onsiene A*B,* ansyne CDE^{x}**FG*K, ansiene H, ansene I, ansyne *J*

insipientiae	unwisdomes A*BDE*^{x}**FGHJ*, unwisdomys *C*, unsnoternesse I, unwisnesse *K* (*L*)
meae	mines A*BDE*^{x}**FGJ*, minys *C*, mire *K*, minre ł mines unwisdomes I* (*HL*)

ED: Computruerunt (C)] Co[n]putruerunt *Wildhagen.* Putruerunt (G)] P*u*truerunt *Rosier.* rotodon (G)] [ ]rotodon *Rosier.* meę (E) (*1st*)] meae *Harsley.* mine (G)] [ ]e *Rosier.* m[ ]ne (H)] mine *Campbell.* á (K)] a *Sisam.* a ffacie (J)] affacie *Oess.* meæ (D)] meae *Roeder.* meę (E) (*2nd*)] meae *Harsley.*

OE: fuladun ł rotedan (A)] ł rotedan *added in 11th-c. hand.* rotodon (E^{x})] *on eras.* ך (E^{x})] *on eras.* wyrsodon (E^{x})] *on eras.* gewemmede (I)] *1st* e *on eras.* dolswaðo (E^{x})] *on eras.* dolgsuaþhe (M)] *written in red in right margin, preceded by* plagę uestigia. mine (E^{x})] *on eras.* m[ ]ne (H)] *letter lost due to hole in leaf.* of (E^{x})] *on eras.* ansyne (E^{x})] *on eras.* unwisdomes (E^{x})] *on eras.* mines (E^{x})] *on eras.* minre ł mines unwisdomes (I)] ł mines unwisdomes *written in left margin.*

LTg: Conputruerunt] L: Con *underlined to signal deletion,* P *added interl. by corr.: see GAg;* Computruerunt C: *orig.* Conputruerunt: *right leg added to 1st* n *to form* m; Conpvtruerunt E. deterioriauerunt] L: corrupte sunt *added interl. by corr.: see GAg.* cicatrices] A: *1st* i *on eras.,* C: *orig.* cycatrices: y *deleted by subscript dot,* i *interl.,* M: *orig.* cycatrices: y *deleted,* i *interl.* meae (*1st*)] A: *added by corr.;* meæ BL; meę DEFGJK, H: *eras. below* e, *perhaps of cauda.* a] A: *eras.* (*3–4 letters*) *before word;* á KM. facie] facię BFG; ffacie J. insipientiae] insipientiæ B; insipientię CDEGHK; insipientie JL. meae (*2nd*)] meæ BCDKL; meę EF, H: *eras. below* e, *perhaps of cauda;* mee GJ.

LTu: cicatrices] cycatrices ξ. meae (*1st*)] meę ζινξπςφ; meæ ϑ; mee στ*τ. facie] faciae βζ. insipientiae] insipientię βεινξοφ; insipientiæ ϑ; insipientie στ*τυ. meae (*2nd*)] meę εινξοςφ; meæ ϑμχ; mee στ*τ.

GAg: Conputruerunt] Putruerunt FGHIJK, L: *see LTg.* deteriorauerunt] corruptę sunt FGHK; corruptae sunt I; corrupte sunt J, L: *see LTg.*

GAu: Conputruerunt] Putruerunt δεζιλμξοπϱστυφχψ; Putrierunt ϑ. deteriorauerunt] corruptę sunt δελϱφ; corruptae sunt ζμοπχψ; corruptæ sunt ϑ; corrupte sunt ιξστυ.

7

Miseriis*	ermðum AB, yrmþu<u>m</u> CGJ, of yrmðu<u>m</u> D, of yrmþum *E*^{3}, of yrmðan K, earm F, wrecca I (*LM*)
(factus)*	geworden FIJ, geswenced G, gedon K
adflictus*	geswenced *ADE*^{x}*, gescenced *B*, geswencyd *C* (*L*)
sum	ic eam AI, ic eom BCDE^{x}*FGJ
et	ך ABCDE^{x}*FGIJK
turbatus*	gedroefed A, gedrefed BDE^{3}*F*GJK, gedrefyd C, gebiged I (*L*)

sum	ic eam A, ic eom BCFIJ, eom GK
usque	oð ABCDF*G*HIJ, oþ E^x*K (*L*)
in	in A*, on BCDE^x*GJ
finem	ende ABCDFGHJK, ęnde E^x*, ænde I
tota	alne A, ealne BCFJ, ælce DGH, eal K, alla E^x*, æfre ł symle I
die	deg A, dæg BCE^x*FJK, dæge DGH
contristatus	geunrotsad A, geunrotsod BDE^x*FGHI*J*, geunrotsud C, unrotsod K
ingrediebar	ic ineode ABCDE^x*F*G*HJK, ic geode ł ic inferde I* (*M*)

ED: Miseríís (E)] Miseriis *Harsley.* [ ]iser (G)] Miser *Rosier.* of yrmþum (E)] Of yrmþum *Harsley.* yrmþu<u>m</u> (C)] yrmþum *Wildhagen.* gedrefed (F)] efed *partly eras.* ic ineode (G)] ic ineod: *Rosier.*

OE: geswenced (E^x)] *on eras.* ic eom (E^x)] *on eras.* ⁊ (E^x)] *on eras.* gedrefed (E^3)] *gloss eras. after word.* gedrefed (F)] efed *partly eras.* oþ (E^x)] *on eras.* in (A)] *faint but visible.* on (E^x)] *on eras.* ęnde (E^x)] *on eras.* alla (E^x)] *on eras.* dæg (E^x)] *on eras.* geunrotsod (E^x)] *on eras.* ic ineode (E^x)] *on eras.* ic geode ł ic inferde (I)] *orig.* ic geode ł ic inferdæ: æ *altered to* e.

LTg: Miseriis] L: iis *underlined to signal deletion: see GAg;* Miseríís E; Misériis M. adflictus] C: *deleting dot below* d (?), *letter* (?) *interl. in brown ink,* L: adfli *underlined to signal deletion,* fa *added interl. by corr.: see GAg;* afflictus ABD; aflictus E. turbatus] L: curuatus *added interl. by corr.: see GAg.* usque] L: q *altered from another letter* (t?); usquę G. contristatus] J: *letter eras. after 2nd* t. ingrediebar] ingrediębar G; ingrêdiebar M.

LTu: adflictus] afflictus τ*.

GAg: Miseriis] Miser factus FGHIJK, L: *see LTg notes to* Miseriis *and* adflictus; [ ]iser factus G. adflictus] *om.* FGHIJK. turbatus] curuatus FGHIJK, L: *see LTg.*

GAu: Miseriis] Miser factus δεζϑιλμξοπϱστυφχψ. adflictus] *om.* δεζϑλμξοπϱστυφχψ. turbatus] curuatus δεζιλμξοπϱστυφχψ; curbatus ϑ.

8

Quoniam	forðon ABJ, forþan CK, forðam F, forþæn þe E^3*, forþam þe G*, forþan þe I
anima*	sawul A, sawl BCDG, sæwl E^3, sawle J, lendenu I, lendena K (*L*)
mea*	min ABCE^x*FGJ, mine IK (*L*)
conpleta*	gefylled ABD*E*^{x}*G, gefyllyd *C,* gefilled J, gefyllede FI*K (*L*)
est*	is ABDE^x*J, ys C, is ł synd G*, synd FK, synt I
inlusionibus	bismernissum A, bismernessu<u>m</u> B, bysmyrnyssy<u>m</u> *C,*

	bysmrungum DE[x]*, bismrungum *H*, besmyrnessum J, on bysmrungum *F*, on bysmrungum G, mid hospe ł bismrungum *I* (*KM*)
et	⁊ ABCE[x]*FGIJK
non	ǀ ne AB, na DE[x]*GHJK, nys CI, nis F
est	ǀ wes A, is BDE[x]*GHJ*K*
sanitas	haelu A, hæl CK, hælo BDFGHIJ, hælþe E[x]*
in	in A, on BCDE[3]FGHIJK
carne	ǀ flaesce A, flæsce BCDFGHIJ, flæce K, minum E[3]
mea	ǀ minum ACGH, minum BDIJ, mine F, mina K, flescum E[3]

ED: forðon (A)] for ðon *Kuhn*. forþæn þe (E)] Forþæn þe *Harsley*. completa (C)] co[n]pleta *Wildhagen*. gefylled (B)] gefyllod *Brenner*. illusionibus (C)] inlusionibus *Wildhagen*.

OE: forþæn þe (E[3])] *eras. after* þe. forþam þe (G)] *descender of* f *obscured*. min (E[x])] *on eras*. gefylled (E[x])] *on eras*. gefyllede (I)] *orig*. gefillede: i *altered to* y. is (E[x]) (*1st*)] *on eras*. is ł synd (G)] ł synd *added in diff*. (?) *hand*. bysmrungum (E[x])] *on eras*. ⁊ (E[x])] *on eras*. na (E[x])] *on eras*. is (E[x]) (*2nd*)] *on eras*. hælþe (E[x])] *on eras*.

LTg: anima] L: *underlined to signal deletion*, lumbi *added interl. by corr.: see GAg*. mea] L: a *deleted by subscript dot*, i *interl. by corr.: see GAg*. conpleta] completa C: *orig*. conpleta: n *eras., macron added above* o *by corr.;* completa E, L: co *underlined to signal deletion*, i *added interl. by corr.,* a *deleted by subscript dot*, i *added interl. by corr.: see GAg*. inlusionibus] F: ł il *interl. above* in *by corr.;* inlusiônibus M; illusionibus I, C: *orig*. inlusionibus: *initial* i *eras., left leg of 1st* n *used to form* i, *right leg of 1st* n *used to form 1st* l, H: *1st* l *altered from another letter, eras. before word*, K: *initial* i *eras., right leg of 1st* n *altered to* l, *left leg of 1st* n *used to form* i. est (*2nd*)] ést K.

LTu: conpleta] completa τ*. inlusionibus] illusionibus εζϑιξοπϱστ*τυφχ.

GAg: anima mea] lumbi mei FGHIJK, L: *see LTg*. conpleta] impleti FHIJ; implęti G; impleti K, L: *see LTg*. est (*1st*)] sunt FGHIJK.

GAu: anima mea] lumbi mei δεζϑιλμξοπϱστυφχψ. conpleta est] impleti sunt δεζιλμξοπϱστυφχψ; inpleti sunt ϑ.

9

Incuruatus*	gebeged *A*B, gebigyd C, gebiged DK, gebyed E[x]*, gebrigged J, gebenged G, gewæht F, geswenced I (*LM*)
sum	ic eam AI, ic eom BCFGJ, ic am E[x]
et	⁊ ABCE[3]FGIJK
humiliatus	gehened ł geeadmet A/A[2]*, gehened B, geaðmed C, geeaðmed DH, geeæðmed E[x]*, geeadmet FG, geeadmed JK, geeaðmeded I

sum	ic eam A, ic eom BCGIJK, ic e[ ]m F*, ic am E^{x}
usquequaque*	hu lenge swiðu ł agehwær A/A^{2}*, a hu lenge swiðor B, a swa leng swa swiðor C*, agehwær D, agehwar E^{x}*, ðearle F, swiðe GIJ, swyþe K (*LM*)
rugiebam	ic grymetede A, ic grymetode B, ic grymytyde *C*, ic grymetede D, ic grymetede E^{x}*, ic grýmetede F, ic grymettede *K*, ic grymet[ ]de H*, grymetede G, ic getrimmeþe J, ic weop ic gyrmde I*, granode ł asten *M**
a	from A, from B, fram FJ, for CI, of DE^{x}*GHK (*M*)
gemitu	gearmrunge A, geomrunge B, geomrunge CHIJ, geomrunga DE^{x}*F, geomorunge G, geomerunge K
cordis	heortan ABCDGHIJK, heortæn E^{3}, heorta[ ] *F**
mei	minre ABDE^{x}*FGIJ*K*, minr[ ] C*, min[ ] H*

ED: ic e[ ]m (F)] ic eom *Kimmens.* usquequaque (B)] usque quaque *Brenner.* ic grymet[ ]de (H)] ic grymetede *Campbell.* ic weop ic gyrmde (I)] ic weop ł ic gyrmde *Lindelöf.* heorta[ ] (F)] heortan *Kimmens.* minr[ ] (C)] minre *Wildhagen.* min[ ] (H)] minre *Campbell.*

OE: gebyed (E^{x})] *on eras., eras. after* y. gehened ł geeadmet (A/A^{2})] ł geeadmet *added in 11th-c. hand.* geeæðmed (E^{x})] *on eras.* ic e[ ]m (F)] *letter after* e *lost due to repairs.* hu lenge swiðu ł agehwær (A/A^{2})] ł agehwær *added in 11th-c. hand.* a swa leng swa swiðor (C)] *initial* a *interl.* agehwar (E^{x})] *on eras.* ic grymetede (E^{x})] *on eras.* ic grymet[ ]de (H)] *letter after* t *obscured by crease in leaf.* ic weop ic gyrmde (I)] ic gyrmde *written in left margin.* granode ł asten (M)] *written in red in left margin.* of (E^{x})] *on eras.* geomrunga (E^{x})] *on eras.* heorta[ ] (F)] *letter after* a *lost due to repairs, minim visible.* minre (E^{x})] *on eras.* minr[ ] (C)] *final letter not visible, perhaps hidden by strip in gutter.* min[ ] (H)] *letter fragment visible after* n.

LTg: Incuruatus] L: *underlined to signal deletion and* Afflictus *added interl. by corr.: see GAg,* M: *2nd* u *malformed;* incurbatus A. usquequaque] L: *underlined to signal deletion and* nimis *added interl. by corr.,* M: nimis *written in red in right margin: see GAg.* rugiebam] C: i *interl.,* K: i *inserted by corr.;* rugiêbam M. a] á M. cordis] F: d *partly obscured by repairs.* mei] K: i *altered from another letter* (?).

LTu: Incuruatus] INcurbatus β. rugiebam] ϑ: i *interl.*

GAg: Incuruatus] Afflictus FGHIJK, L: *see LTg.* usquequaque] nimis FGHIJK, LM: *see LTg.*

GAu: Incuruatus] Afflictus δεζϑιλξοπϱστυχ; Adflictus μφψ. usquequaque] nimis δεζϑιλμξοπϱστυφχψ.

10

Et*	⁊ *ABCE^{x}**, drih̄t G, drih̄ J (*DLM*)

ante   biforan A, beforan BCDE^{x}*GHIJK, ætforan F
te   ðe ABF, þe C**E*^{x}*GIJ (*M*)
est*   is ABE^{x}*, ys C (*L*)
omne   all A, eall BCGHI, eal D, æl E^{x}*, ealle F, is eall J, eallan K
desiderium   lust ł gewilnung A/A^{2}*, lust BC, gewilnung DE^{x}*GHJ, gewilnunga K, gew[ ]lnunga F*, wilnung I
meum   min ABCDE^{3}GHI*J, mine F, minre K
et   ⁊ ABCE^{x}*FGIJK
gemitus   gemrung A, geomrung BDE^{x}*HJ, geonrung C, geomorung G, geomrungum F, wop ł geomrung I, gemerunga K
meus   min ABCDE^{x}*GHIJK, mine F
a   from A, from B, fram CDE^{3}FGHI*J*K* (*M*)
te   ðe ABDFI, þe CE^{3}GHJK
non | nis AHI, nys CF, ne BE^{3}, na GJK
est | is BE^{3}*GJ*K*
absconditus   ahyded AB, ahided J, behyd CF, behydd D*G*HI, behid E^{3}*, behud K (*M*)

ED: desiderium (H)] desideri(u)m *Campbell.* gew[ ]lnunga (F)] gewilnunga *Kimmens.* absconditus (H)] abscon(d)itus *Campbell.* behydd (G)] behy[ ] *Rosier.*

OE: ⁊ (E^{x}) (*1st*)] *on eras.* beforan (E^{x})] *on eras.* þe (C) (*1st*)] *added in red by corr.* þe (E^{x}) (*1st*)] *on eras.* is (E^{x}) (*1st*)] *on eras.* æl (E^{x})] *on eras.* lust ł gewilnung (A/A^{2})] ł gewilnung *added in 11th-c. hand.* gewilnung (E^{x})] *on eras.* gew[ ]lnunga (F)] *letter after* w *lost due to repairs.* min (I) (*1st*)] est : is *written in left margin.* ⁊ (E^{x}) (*2nd*)] *on eras.* geomrung (E^{x})] *on eras.* min (E^{x}) (*2nd*)] *on eras.* fram (I)] *shoulder of* r *and* a *on eras.* is (E^{3}) (*2nd*)] *eras. after word.* behid (E^{3})] *eras. before and after word.*

LTg: Et] et ABCDELM. te (*1st*)] E: *on eras.;* tê M. est (*1st*)] L: *underlined to signal deletion: see GAg.* a] á KM. est] ést K. absconditus] abscónditus M; abscondit[ ] G.

LTu: Et] et βνςτ*. omne] Domine τ*.

GAg: Et] Domine FGHJK, I: o *written above word.* est (*1st*)] *om.* FGHIJK, L: *see LTg.*

GAu: Et] Domine δεζϑιλμξοπϱστυφχψ. est (*1st*)] *om.* δεζϑιλμξοπϱστυφχψ.

11
Cor | heorte ABCFGIJK, Min E^{3}
meum | min ABCDFGHIJK, heortæn E^{x}*
conturbatum   gedroefed A, gedrefed BDE^{3}*F*GHI*J*K, gedrefyd C
est   is ABDE^{x}FGHIJ*K,* ys C
in*   in A, on BCDE^{3} (*L*)

me*		me ABCDE^{3} (*L*)
et*		⁊ ABCE^{3} (*L*)
deseruit*		forleort A, forlet BCDE^{x}*IK, forlæt FGH, ⁊ forlæt J (*L*)
me		mec A, me BCE^{x}*FIJK, m[ ] *G*
fortitudo*		strengu AB, streng C, strengo DE^{3}, miht F, mægen I, mægn K, mægen ł miht G, mægen ł strengð J (*L*)
mea		min ABCDE^{x}FGHIJK
et		⁊ ABCE^{x}*FGIK
lumen		leht A, leoht BCDFGHJK, lioht E^{3}, leoht ł gescead I (*M*)
oculorum	|	egena A, eagyna C, eagana DH, eagena GJ, eagna BI, [ ]agena F*, egan K, minræ E^{3}
meorum	|	minra AB*C*DFHIJ, minr[ ] G, egænæ minre E$^{3/x}$*
(et)*		⁊ FGIJ
(ipsum)*		þæt sylfe F, þæt silfe J, he sylf G, þæt leoht I
non	|	nis ABDHI, nys F, na CGJK, ne E^{3}
est	|	ys C, is E^{3}GJ*K*
mecum		mid me ABCDE^{3}FGHIJK

ED: [ ]agena (F)] eagena *Kimmens.*

OE: heortæn (E^{x})] *on eras.* forlet (E^{x})] *on eras.* me (E^{x})] *on eras.* ⁊ (E^{x}) (*2nd*)] *on eras.* [ ]agena (F)] *initial letter lost due to repairs.* egænæ minre (E$^{3/x}$)] minre *by corr.*

LTg: conturbatum] F: m *obscured by repairs, middle leg of* m *not visible,* J: con *on eras. in lighter brown ink of gloss.* est (*1st*)] ést K. in] L: *underlined to signal deletion: see GAg.* me (*1st*)] L: *underlined to signal deletion: see GAg.* et (*1st*)] L: *underlined to signal deletion: see GAg.* deseruit] L: seruit *underlined to signal deletion,* reliquit *added interl. by corr.: see GAg.* me (*2nd*)] m[ ] G. fortitudo] L: *underlined to signal deletion,* uirtus *added interl. by corr.: see GAg.* lumen] lûmen M. meorum] C: or *interl.* est (*2nd*)] ést K.

LTu: mea] β: *added in right margin by corr.*

GAg: in me et] *om.* FGHIJK, L: *see LTg.* deseruit] dereliquit GHIJ, K: *eras. before word,* L: *see LTg,* F: *orig.* dereliquid: *final* d *deleted by subscript dot,* t *interl.* fortitudo] uirtus FGHIJK, L: *see LTg.* meorum] meorum et ipsum FGHIJ; meorum et ípsum K.

GAu: in me et] *om.* δεζϑιλμξοπϱστυφχψ. deseruit] dereliquit δεζιλμξπϱτφχψ; deriliquit ϑο; dereliquid συ. fortitudo] uirtus δεζϑλμξοπϱστυφχψ. meorum] meorum et ipsum δεζϑιλμξοπϱστυφχψ.

12

Amici	|	freod A, friend B, frynd DFG*H*IK, frind J, fynd C, Mine E^{3}* (*M*)
mei	|	mine ABCDFGHIJK, frend E^{3}*

et ⁊ ABCE^{3}FGHIJK
proximi | ða nestan A, þa nehstan B, þa neahstan C, þa nihstan J, nehstan F, nyxstan K, magas DGH, mine E^{3}I
mei | mine ABCFGJK, nixtan E^{3}, nyhstan I
aduersum wið ABC, ongean DGH, ongen E^{x}*, agen I, togeanes FJ*K* (*M*)
me me ABCE^{3}FGHIJK
adpropiauerunt* tolehlaecað *A*, tonealæhton B, togenealæhton J, genealæhton CFGI, genealehton DH, geneælęcton E^{3}*, neahlætan K (*M*)
et ⁊ ABCE^{3}FGIJK
steterunt stodon ABCDE^{3}*FGHJ, stodan K, hi stodon I (*M*)
et ⁊ ABCE^{3}**FGHIJK* (*L*)
(qui)* þa þe FIJ, þa K
proximi* | ða nestan A, þa nehstan B, þa neahstan C, neahstan D, neah K, wiþ F, wið I, betweox G, sohton J*, mine E^{3} (*L*)
mei* | mine ABC, me FGIJK, þæ niextæn E^{3} (*L*)
(erant)* wæron FJ, wærun I, wæran K, hy wæron G
a* (*ELM*)
longe feor ABDK, feórr F, fer E$^{3/x}$*, feorran CGI, afeorrod J
steterunt stodon ABCDE^{3}IJ, stodan K, hi stodon G, ætstodon F

ED: appropiauerunt (C)] a[d]propiauerunt *Wildhagen.* et proximi mei a longe steterunt (B)] *om. Brenner.* ⁊ þa nehstan mine feor stodon (B)] *om. Brenner.* [ ]t (G)] Et *Rosier.* á (E)] a *Harsley.* steterunt (G)] steterun*t Rosier.*

OE: Mine (E^{3})] e *on eras. by corr., eras. after word.* frend (E^{3})] *in darker ink* (*by corr.?*). ongen (E^{x})] *on eras.* geneælęcton (E^{3})] ge *in darker ink,* ne *retraced in darker ink.* stodon (E^{3})] *eras. after word.* ⁊ (E^{3}) (*3rd*)] *eras. after word.* sohton (J)] *source-text misread, perhaps reading gloss to* querebant *in v. 13.* fer (E$^{3/x}$)] er *on eras. by corr., eras. after word.*

LTg: Amici] H: *orig.* Imici: *green initial* I *altered to* A *in brown ink;* Ámici M. aduersum] M: m *altered from another letter;* áduersum K. adpropiauerunt] A: *eras. after* i, *which may itself have been formed from stem of eras. letter,* M: *orig.* adpropriauerunt: *2nd* r *crossed through by corr.;* appropiauerunt C: *1st* p *altered from another letter: cf. Weber MSS* med. steterunt (*1st*)] stéterunt M. et (*3rd*)] L: *underlined to signal deletion,* Et *added interl. by corr.;* Et FHIJK; [ ]t G: *fragment of initial* E *visible.* proximi] L: *underlined to signal deletion,* qui iuxta *added interl. by corr.: see GAg.* mei] L: *underlined to signal deletion,* me erant *added interl. by corr.: see GAg.* a] L: *underlined to signal deletion,* de *added interl. by corr.: see GAg;* á EM.

LTu: proximi (*1st*)] β: *orig.* proxmi: *1st* i *added interl. by corr.* aduersum me] *interl.* μ. adpropiauerunt] appropriauerunt τ*. et (*3rd*)] Et δεζϑιλμξοπστυχψ.

GAg: adpropiauerunt] adpropinquauerunt FGJ; appropinquauerunt I, H: *1st* p *altered from another letter,* K: *1st* p *altered from* d. proximi mei] qui iuxta me erant FGHIJK, L: *see LTg*. a] de FGHIJK, L: *see LTg*.

GAu: adpropiauerunt] adpropinquauerunt δϑμψ; appropinquauerunt εζιλξπρστυφχ, o: *orig*. adpropinquauerint. proximi mei] qui iuxta me erant δεζϑιλμξοπρστυφχψ. a] de δεζϑιλμξοπρστυφχψ.

13

Et | ⁊ ABCE^{x}**FGHJK,* strengðe *I* (*L*)
uim | ned A, nied B, nyd CDE^{x}*FGH, nyde K, ⁊ I, me J
faciebant dydun A, dydon BCDE^{3}FH, didon J*, dydan K, hy dydon G, worhton I
qui ða A, ða ðe B, þa þe CE^{3}*GHIK, þa ðe DFJ
quaerebant sohton *ABCDE^{3}*FGHIJ,* sohtan *K* (*LM*)
animam | sawle ABCDF*G*H*J*K, mine E^{3}I
meam | mine ABCDFGHJK, sæwle E^{3}, sawle I
et ⁊ ABCE^{3}*FGIJK* (*HL*)
qui ða AF, þa CDHK, þæ E^{3}*, ða ðe B, þa þe G, þa ðe IJ
inquirebant sohton ABCDE^{3}*FGHIJ, sohtan K
mala yfel ABE^{3}JK, yfyl C, yfelu DFGI, yuelu H
mihi me AB*CDE*^{x}*FG*H*IJK
locuti spreocende A, sprecende BJ, sprecynde C, hy spræcon DG, hye sprecen E^{3}*, hi spræcon F*H,* hi spæcan K, spræcon I
sunt werun A, wæron BC, synd J
uanitatem* idelnisse AD, idylnysse C, ýdelnysse F, idelnesse BE^{3}GJK, ydelnesse H, idelnyssa I (*L*)
et ⁊ ABCE^{3}FGJK
dolos facen *A*BF, facyn C, facnu DI, facne E^{x}*, facn GHJK (*M*)
tota alne A, ealne BCFJ, ælce DGH, elce E^{3}, ealla K, symle ł ealne I
die deg A, dæg BCFIJK, dæge DGH, dei E^{3}*
meditabantur werun smegende *A*, wæron smeagende BJ, wæron smegynde C, hy smeadon DGH, hye smeæiden $E^{3/x}$*, hi smeadon F, ⁊ hi smeadun I, smædan K

ED: et (&) (I) (*1st*)] Et *Lindelöf.* anima[ ] (G)] animam *Rosier.* mine (G)] *no gloss Rosier.* Et (F)] et *Kimmens.* ýdelnysse (F)] ydelnysse *Kimmens.*

OE: ⁊ (E^{x}) (*1st*)] *on eras.* nyd (E^{x})] *on eras.* didon (J)] n *malformed: cf. Ps 38.10* minne. þa þe (E^{3})] *on eras. perhaps by corr.,* l *visible beneath* e. sohton (E^{3}) (*1st*)] soh *retraced in darker ink.* þæ (E^{3})] *eras. after word.* sohton (E^{3}) (*2nd*)] soh *retraced in darker ink.* me (E^{x})] *on eras.* hye sprecen (E^{3})] h *altered from another* *letter,* ye *on eras. by corr., eras.* (*15 mm*) *after gloss.* facne (E^{x})] *on eras.* dei (E^{3})] i *given form of* j. hye smeæiden ($E^{3/x}$)] h *altered from another letter,* y *altered from* i, *1st* e *on eras. by corr.,* id *by corr.,* g *eras. after* d, de *eras. after* n (< ?smeægende).

LTg: Et] L: E *underlined and crossed through to signal deletion,* e *written to right;* et FGHIJK. quaerebant] querebant ABCDEGHJLM; quębrebant FIK. animam] G: anima[ ]: *2 minims of final letter visible;* anima J. et (*1st*)] L: Et *added interl. by corr.;* Et FGHIJK. mihi] michi EH, C: *orig.* mihi: c *interl. by corr.* locuti] loquti H: *orig.* locuti: c *altered to* q. uanitatem] L: m *underlined to signal deletion,* s *added interl. by corr.: see GAg.* dolos] A: *2nd* o *on eras.,* M: *2nd* o *altered from another letter.* meditabantur] A: *2nd* a *on eras.*

LTu: Et] et δεζϑιλμξοπϱστυφχψ. quaerebant] quębrebant βελνοϱφψ; querebant διμξπσςτ*τυ; q̄rebant ϑ. et (*1st*)] Et δεζϑιλμξοπϱστυφχ. inquirebant] inq̄rebant ϑ. mihi] michi ιλςτ*τ, ϱ: c *interl.;* m[1] ξσφ. meditabantur] β: *orig.* meditabuntur: *1st* u *crossed through,* a *interl. by corr.*

GAg: uanitatem] uanitates FHIJK, L: *see LTg,* G: *orig.* uenitates: *1st* e *altered to* a.

GAu: uanitatem] uanitates δεζιλμξοπϱστυφχψ.

14

Ego		ic ABCFGIJK, Ic E^{3}
autem		soðlice ABCE^{3}FGH, soþlice DJ, witodlice K
uelut*		swe swe A, swa swa BCDFGHIJ, swæ swæ *$E^{3/x}$**, swa K* (*L*)
surdus		deaf ABCDFGHI, deæf E^{3}, deafe J, deafa K*
non	|	ic ne ABCJ, na DE^{x}*FGHK, ne I
audiebam	|	geherde A*, gehyrde IJK, ic gehyrde DFH, ic geherde $E^{3/x}$*, ic gehyrd[ ] *G,* gehiere B, geþristlæcte C (*M*)
et		⁊ ABCE^{3}FGIJK
sicut		swe swe A, swa swa BCDFGHIJ, swæ swa $E^{3/x}$*, swa K
mutus		dumb ABCDE^{3}FGHJ, se dumba I, dumba K
qui*		se ABCDK, Se E^{3} (*L*)
non		ne ABCE^{3}J, na DFGHIK
aperuit*		ontyneð *A*B, ontynde C, ontinde J, ontyende $E^{3/x}$*, atiende *D,* atynde GH, opniende F, geopnigende I, openedde K (*L*)
os	|	muð *AB*CDFGHK, muþ J, his *E^{3}*I (*M*)
suum	|	his ABCDGHJK, ic eom F, muð E^{3}I

ED. ic (G)] *no gloss Rosier.* uelud (E)] velud *Harsley.* swa swa (GIJ) (*1st*)] swaswa *Rosier, Lindelöf, Oess.* audieba[ ] (G)] audieb*am Rosier.* ic gehyrd[ ] (G)] ic gehy[ ] *Rosier.* swa swa (GIJ) (*2nd*)] swaswa *Rosier, Lindelöf, Oess.* ós (AE)] os *Kuhn, Harsley.*

OE: swæ swæ ($E^{3/x}$)] *2nd* swæ *on eras. by corr.* swa (K) (*1st*)] *otiose stroke* (*false start?*) *before word.* deafa (K)] *orig. gloss eras.* (*18 mm*) *and* deafa *written above eras.* na (E^{x})] *on eras.* geherde (A)] herde *written in 11th-c. hand on eras.* ic geherde ($E^{3/x}$)] ne *eras. after* ic (*cf. A* ic ne), g *in darker ink,* de *on eras. by corr.* swæ swa ($E^{3/x}$)] swa *on eras. by corr.* ontyende ($E^{3/x}$)] ende *on eras. by corr.*

LTg: uelut] uelud E, L: tamquam *added interl. by corr.: see GAg.* audiebam] audiêbam M; audieba[ ] G. qui] L: *underlined to signal deletion: see GAg.* aperuit] D: *orig.* operuit: o *deleted by subscript dot,* a *interl.,* L: uit *underlined to signal deletion,* iens *added interl. by corr.: see GAg;* aperiet A: *cf. Weber MSS* Sβ. os] ós ABEM.

LTu: surdus] sordus ϑ. aperuit] aperuet β: *orig.* aperuit: e *written above* i *by corr.*

GAg: autem] tamquam FGIJK, L: *see LTg;* tanquam H: n *altered from another letter.* qui] *om.* FGHIJK, L: *see LTg.* aperuit] aperiens FGHIJK, L: *see LTg.*

GAu: autem] tamquam δεζμξοπρσυχψ; tanquam ϑιλτφ. qui] *om.* δεζϑιλμξοπστυχψ. aperuit] aperiens δεζϑιλμξοπρστυφχψ.

15

Et		⁊ ABCF*G*HIJ, Ond E^{3}
factus	|	geworden A*BDFGHIJK, gewordyn C, ic eom E^{3}
sum	|	ic eam A, ic eom BCFGHIJ, eom K, geworden E^{3}
ut*		swe swe A, swa swa BDFGHIJ, swæ swæ $E^{3/x}$*, swa CK
homo		mon ABE^{3}*, mann CG, man DFHIJK
non		no AB, ne *C*E^{3}, na DFGHIJK
audiens		geherrende A, gehierende $BE^{3/x}$*, gehyrende CFI, g̲e̲hyrende D, gehirende J, gehyrende K, gehyrde GH
et		⁊ ACE^{3}FGHIJK
non	|	nabbende A, næbbende B, næbbynde *C,* na DFGHIJK, ne E^{3}
habens	|	hæbbende DFGIJ, hębbende E^{x}*, hæbende K, libbende H
in		in A, on $BCDE^{3}$FGHIJK
ore	|	muðe ABCDFGHJ, muþe IK, his $E^{3/x}$*
suo		his ABCDFGHIJK, muðe E^{3}
increpationes*		ðreange *A,* þreaunge *BC,* þreagunge GJ, þreaunga I, streorspreca D, steorspæce K, hleoþrunga F*, on geþræorspreca $E^{3/x}$* (*LM*)

ED: swa swa (GIJ)] swaswa *Rosier, Lindelöf, Oess.* na (I) (*2nd*)] ne *Lindelöf* (*but correct in appendix, p. 323*).

OE: geworden (A)] *orig.* geworðen: *cross-stroke of* ð *eras.* swæ swæ ($E^{3/x}$)] *2nd* swæ *on eras. by corr.* mon (E^{3})] *eras.* (*13 mm*) *after word.* gehierende ($E^{3/x}$)] ende *by corr., partly on eras.* hębbende (E^{x})] bb *on eras.* his ($E^{3/x}$)] is *on eras. by corr.*

hleoþrunga (F)] *obscured by eras. but visible.* on geþræorspreca ($E^{3/x}$)] æ *partly on eras.*, o *on eras.*, *2nd* r *added by corr.*, spreca *by corr.*

LTg: Et] [ ]t G. non (*2nd*)] Non C. increpationes] L: redargutiones *added interl. by corr.: see GAg;* increpatiónes M; increpationem AB: *see Weber MS* β.

LTu: increpationes] increpationem β: *orig.* increpationes: m *written above* s *by corr.*

GAg: ut] sicut FGHIJK. increpationes] redargutiones FGHIJK, L: *see LTg.*

GAu: ut] sicut δεζθιλμξοπρστυφχψ. increpationes] redargutiones δεζθιλμξοπρτυφχψ; reddargutiones σ.

16

Quoniam   forðon ABFJ, forþon C, forðæn E^{3}*, forþam *G*, forðan þe I
in   in A, on BCDE^{3}*F*GHIJK
te   ðe ABDF*GH, þe CE^{3}IK (*M*)
domine   drihten E^{3}*, dryht̄ AB, driħt CFG, driħ J (*I*)
speraui   ic gehyhte AB, ic gehihte CIJ, ic hyhte DE^{x}*H, ic hihte GK, ic hopude F
dixi*   ic cweð AE^{x}*, ic cwæð BCD (*L*)
tu   ðu ABF, þu CDE^{x}*GHIJK (*M*)
exaudies   ð geheres A*, gehieres B, gehyrst CDHJK, geherest I, gehirsþ E^{3}, gehyrdest F, ge(h)yr[ ] *G**
domine   drihten E^{3}, dryht̄ AB, driħt CF, driħ J, eala þu drihten I*, hlaford K, [ ]i[ ] G*
deus | god ABCE^{3}FGJK, min I
meus | min ABC$E^{3/x}$*FGJK, god I (*H*)

ED: forðon (A)] for ðon *Kuhn.* forðæn (E)] Forðæn *Harsley.* tú (E)] tu *Harsley.* ge(h)yr[ ] (G)] gehyr[ ] *Rosier.* [ ]i[ ] (G)] driħt *Rosier.* ms (H)] meus *Campbell.*

OE: forðæn (E^{3})] f *retraced in darker ink.* on (E^{3})] *in darker ink.* on (F)] *written below* forðon. ðe (F)] *written below line of gloss.* drihten (E^{3}) (*1st*)] en *retraced* (?) *in darker ink by corr.* ic hyhte (E^{x})] *on eras.* ic cweð (E^{x})] *on eras.*, e *eras. after word.* þu (E^{x})] *on eras.* ð geheres (A)] *Kuhn takes* ð *as 'Partial repetition of* ðu.' ge(h)yr[ ] (G)] *ascender of* h *not visible.* eala þu drihten (I)] s. o *written before* eala. [ ]i[ ] (G)] *mostly lost due to hole in leaf.* min ($E^{3/x}$)] in *on eras. by corr.*

LTg: Quoniam] G: Q *partly lost.* te] tê M. dixi] L: *underlined to signal deletion: see GAg.* domine] I: s. o *written above word.* tu] tú E; tû M. exaudies] exaudie[ ] G. meus] ms H: *lacks macron.*

GAg: dixi] *om.* FGHIJK, L: *see LTg.*

GAu: dixi] *om.* δεζθιλμξοπρστυφχψ.

17

Quia forðon ABF, forþon CJ, forþā K, forðæn E^{3}, forþā þe *G*, forþan þe I (*H*)
dixi ic cweð A, ic cwæð BCGHK, ic cweþe J, ic sæde FI, sæde ł cwiþe E$^{3/x}$*
ne* ne *A*C, ðylæs B, þylæs DFGH, þyles E^{3}*, þilæs J (*M*)
aliquando* ahwonne *A**D*E*^{x}*, ahwanne I, hwonne B*C*FHJ, hwænne GK (*LM*)
insultent* bismerien A, bismrigen B, bysmriyn C, hyspen DE^{x}*, oferblissian F, oferblissiað GK, þæt ofer ne blissiun I, ofergefean J (*LM*)
in* in A, on BCDE^{3} (*L*)
me* mec A, me BCDE^{3}FGIJK (*L*)
inimici | feond A, fiend B, fynd CDFHIJK, on fynd G, mine E^{3}
mei | mine ABCDFGHIJK, fiend E^{3}
et ⁊ ABCE^{3}*FGJK
dum mid ðy AB, mid þy C, þonne DHJ, ðonne F, þonne E^{x}*GIK
commouerentur* bioð onstyrede A, beoð onstyrede B, beoð onstyryde C, beoð astyrede I, beoþ astirede J, wæron astyrede DH, weron astyrede E^{x}*, wæron astyrode F, wæran astyrud K, wær[ ]n G (*L*)
pedes | foet AB, fet CE^{3}FGHJK, fét D, mine I
mei | min A, mine BCDE^{x}FGHJK, fet I
in* in A, on BCDE^{3}, ofer F*GIJK (*L*)
me me ABCDE^{3}FGIJK
magna ða miclan ł fela A/A^{2}*, ða miclan B, þa miclan C, mycelu F, miclu I, fela DE^{x}*GH, feala K, monige J
locuti spreocende A, sprecende BFJ, sprecynde *C,* hy spræcon D*H**, hy sprecen E$^{3/x}$*, ⁊ hig spræcon *I,* hi spæcan K, hy (s)pr[ ] G*
sunt sind A, synd CJ, sint B, wæron F

ED: Quia (B)] quia *Brenner.* [ ]uia (GH)] Quia *Rosier, Campbell.* forðon (A)] for ðon *Kuhn.* forðæn (E)] Forðæn *Harsley.* nequando (FJ)] ne quando *Kimmens, Oess.* ðylæs (B)] ðy læs *Brenner.* ne ahwonne (A)] *Kuhn notes alternate gloss:* 'a and u also added below line, to read ahuonne'; *Kuhn misreads* ali *as* a *and* u; *added letters pertain not to OE gloss but to lemma, which is altered from* nequando *to* ne aliquando. mid þy (C)] midþy *Wildhagen.* locuti (C)] lo[q]u[u]ti *Wildhagen.* sunt (G)] *sunt Rosier.*

OE: sæde ł cwiþe (E$^{3/x}$)] sæde ł *on eras. by corr.,* cwi *retraced by corr.* þyles (E^{3})] þ *and* les *retraced by corr.* ahwonne (A)] *orig.* honne: a *and* w *interl. by glossator.*

ahwonne (E^{x})] *on eras.* hyspen (E^{x})] *on eras.* ⁊ (E^{3})] *retouched by corr.* þonne (E^{x}) *on eras.* weron astyrede (E^{x})] *on eras.* ofer (F)] e *partly obscured by repairs.* ða miclan ł fela (A/A^{2})] ł fela *added in 11th-c. hand.* fela (E^{x})] *on eras.* hy spræcon (H)] *top of* s *lost due to eras. in Lat. line above.* hy sprecen (E$^{3/x}$)] hy *on eras. by corr.* hy (s)pr[ ] (G)] s *partly lost,* a *or part of* æ *visible after* r.

LTg: Quia] [ ]uia G, H: *outline and fragments of* Q *visible.* ne aliquando] M: ali *on eras. by corr. of Ps 38.8* tamquam nihil, A: *orig.* nequando: ali *added interl. by glossator: see ED, cf. Weber MSS* βδη*, *see GAg,* E: aliqñ *on eras. by OE corr.,* L: ali *underlined to signal deletion: see GAg;* ne alíquando C. insultent] L: supergaudeant *added interl. by corr.: see GAg,* M: ins *on eras.* in me (*1st*)] L: michi *added interl. by corr.: see GAg.* commouerentur] L: re *underlined by corr. to signal deletion: see GAg.* in (*2nd*)] L: *crossed through by corr.,* super *added below line: see GAg.* locuti] C: *orig.* loquuti: q *altered to* c, *2nd* u *eras.;* loquti H: *orig.* locuti: c *altered to* q; loquuti I.

LTu: ne aliquando] nequando β: *orig.* ne aliquando: ali *deleted by corr.: see GAu.* insultent] β: *orig.* inultent: s *added interl. by corr.* commouerentur] commouentur τ*: *see GAu.*

GAg: ne aliquando] nequando FGHIJK, L: *see LTg.* insultent] supergaudeant FHIJK, L: *see LTg;* supergaudea[ ] G. in (*1st*)] *om.* FGHIJK, L: *see LTg note to* in me. me (*1st*)] mihi FGHIJK; michi L: *see LTg note to* in me. commouerentur] commoueantur JK, F: a *on eras. by corr.,* H: a *on eras.;* commouentur I, L: *see LTg;* comm[ ] G. in (*2nd*)] super FGHIJK, L: *see LTg.*

GAu: ne aliquando] nequando δεζϑιλμξοπρστυφχψ, β: *see LTu.* insultent] supergaudeant δεζϑιλμξοπρστυφχψ. in (*1st*)] *om.* δεζϑιλμοπρσφψ. me (*1st*)] mihi δεζϑμουχψ; michi ιξτ, πρ: c *interl.;* m^{1} λσφ. commouerentur] commoueantur ϑρχ, δ: a *interl.;* comouentur ε: *letter space after* c; commouentur ζιλμξοπστυφψ, τ*: *see LTu.* in (*2nd*)] super δεζϑιλμξοπρστυφχψ.

18

Quoniam	forðon ABCJ, forðam FK, fordæn E^{3}, forþam þe G, forþon þe I
ego	ic ABCE^{3}FGIJK
ad*	to ABCD*E*^{3}*, on FGIJK (*L*)
flagella	ðream AB, swingyllan C, swingellu͞m DHK, swingellum GE^{3}*, s(w)inglum F*, swinglum ł to swipum I, þreaswingu͞m J (*M*)
paratus	gearu AC, gearo BDE^{x}FH, geara GJ*, gæra K, gearuw I
sum	ic cam A, ic com CDE^{x}HJ, ic co(m) G*, com BI
et	⁊ ABCE^{3}*FGIJK
dolor	| sar ABCDGHJK, sár F, sær E^{3}, is sar I*

meus		min ABCDE^{x}*FGHIJK
ante*		biforan A, beforan BCI, ongean DE^{x}*, on FGJK (*L*)
(conspectu)*	I	gesyhþe FK, gesihðe GJ, minre I
me*	I	me ABCDE^{3}, minre FGJK, ansyne I (*L*)
est*	I	is ABDE^{3}, ys C (*L*)
semper		aa A, á B*, symle CDHIJ, simle E^{3}, symble F, æfre ł simble G, æfre K

ED: forðon (A)] for ðon *Kuhn.* fordæn (E)] Fordæn *Harsley.* swingellum (H)] swingell*um Campbell.* s(w)inglum (F)] swinglum *Kimmens.* ic eo(m) (G)] ic eom *Rosier.*

OE: to (E^{3})] *eras.* (*12 mm*) *before word, cross-stroke of* t *and* o *retraced, eras.* (*8 mm*) *after word.* swingellum (E^{3})] swi *and left leg of* n *retraced in darker ink, eras. after 1st* l (swingel/lum). s(w)inglum (F)] *descender of* w *not visible due to repairs.* geara (J)] e *altered from* a. ic eo(m) (G)] *2 minims visible after* o. ⁊ (E^{3})] *eras. after word.* is sar (I)] s. est *written before* is. min (E^{x})] *on eras.* ongean (E^{x})] *on eras.* á (B)] *accent faint but visible.*

LTg: ad] E: *retouched in darker ink,* L: *underlined to signal deletion: see GAg.* flagella] flagélla M: *eras. after final* a. ante] L: *underlined to signal deletion,* in conspectu *added interl. by corr.: see GAg.* me] L: *underlined to signal deletion,* meo *added interl. by corr.: see GAg.* est] L: *underlined to signal deletion: see GAg.*

LTu: sum] *om.* υ.

GAg: ad] in FGHIJK, L: *see LTg.* ante] in conspectu GHIJK, F: *1st* c *partly obscured by repairs,* L: *see LTg.* me] meo FGHIJK, L: *see LTg.* est] *om.* FGHIJK, L: *see LTg.*

GAu: ad] in δεζϑιλμξοπϱστυφχψ. ante] in conspectu δεζϑιλμξοπϱστυφχψ. me] meo δεζϑιλμοπϱστυφχψ. est] *om.* δεζϑιλμξοπϱστυφχψ.

19

Quoniam	forðon AB, forþon CJ, forðæn E^{3}, forðon ðe F, forþam K, for þære G
iniquitatem	unrehtwisniss A, unrihtwisnysse C, unryhtwisnesse BD, unrihtwis[ ]ysse F*, unrihtwisnesse E$^{3/x}$*GHJK, unrihtwisnisse I
meam	mine ABCDE^{x}*FGHI, minre JK
ego*	ic ABCDE^{x}* (*L*)
pronuntio*	forðsegcga A, forðsecge B*C*, cyþe DE^{x}*, ic cyðe FG, ic cyþe HIK, to cyþenne J (*L*)
et	⁊ ABCE^{x}*FGIJK
cogitabo	ðenco A, þence B, ic þence CGHIJK, ic ðence F, ic þynce DE^{x}*

pro fore AB, for CDE^{x}*FGHIJK
peccato scylde AB, synne CDGHIK, s(y)nne *F**, sinne E^{3}*, synnum J
meo minre ABCDGHIK, minne E^{x}, minum F, minum J

ED: forðon (A)] for ðon *Kuhn*. forðæn (E)] Forðæn *Harsley*. unrihtwis[ ]ysse (F)] unrihtwisnysse *Kimmens*. pronuncio (C)] pronun[t]io *Wildhagen*. s(y)nne (F)] synne *Kimmens*.

OE: unrihtwis[ ]ysse (F)] *letter after* w *obscured by repairs, minim visible*. unrihtwisnesse ($E^{3/x}$)] wisnesse *on eras. by corr.* mine (E^{x})] *on eras.* ic (E^{x})] *on eras.* cyþe (E^{x})] *on eras.* ⁊ (E^{x})] *on eras.* ic þynce (E^{x})] *on eras.* for (E^{x})] *on eras.* s(y)nne (F)] *right arm of* y *lost due to repairs.* sinne (E^{3})] e *retouched by corr., eras. after word.*

LTg: ego] L: *underlined to signal deletion: see GAg.* pronuntio] L: *underlined to signal deletion,* annuntiabo *added interl. by corr.: see GAg;* pronuncio C: *orig.* pronuntio: t *altered to* c. peccato] F: e *partly obscured by repairs.*

LTu: pronuntiabo] v: bo *interl.*

GAg: ego pronuntio] adnuntiabo FGJ; annuntiabo I, HK: *1st* n *on eras.*, L: *see LTg.*

GAu: ego pronuntio] adnuntiabo δϑμψ; annuntiabo εζιλξπστυφχ, ο: *orig.* adnuntiabo; annunciabo ϱ: *orig.* annuntiabo.

20

Inimici | feond A, fiend B, fynd CDF*G*HIJK, Soþlice E^{3}
autem | soðlice ABCFG, soþlice J, witod K, mine E^{3}
mei | mine ACDGH*I*JK*, m[ ]ne F*, fiend E^{3} (*B*)
uiuent lifgað A, lifgeað B, lifiað D, lyfiað *G,* liuiað H, lybbað C, libbað *FI*, liebbæþ ł lifiað $E^{3/x}$*, lufigende *J* (*K*)
et ⁊ A*BCE^{3}FGIJK
confortati* gestrongade A, gestrongode B, gestrangode CDGJ, gestrængode Ė^{3}, gestrangodde K, geuntrumode F, getrymede ł gestrangede I (*L*)
sunt sind A, synd CDGH*JK, sint B, synt F, Sient E^{3}, hig synt I
super ofer ABDE^{3}FGHJ, ofyr C, ofor I, ofe K
me me ABCDE^{3}FGJK
et ⁊ ABCE^{3}FGHIJK
multiplicati gemonigfaldade A, gemonigfaldode B, gemænigfealdode CJ, gemonigfeældode E^{3}, gemenigfylde DH, ge[ ]ænifylde *F**, gemænigfealde G, gemænigfylde I, gemanifyl *K*
sunt sind A, synd CFGJK, sint B, synt I, sindon E^{3}
qui ða ðe *A*F, þa ðe BD, þa þe CGHIJ, þæ þe E^{3}, þa K
oderunt | fiedon A, feodon BC, hatedon DGH, hatudon F, hatedun I, hatodon J, hatiað K, me E^{3}

me | mec *A*, me BCFGIJK, fiogæþ ł hatedon $E^{3/x*}$
inique unrehtlice A, unryhtlice B, unryhtlice D, unrihtlice CF*G*JK, unrihtlice ł unwislice I, on unriht E^{3}

ED: meí (I)] mei *Lindelöf.* uíuvnt (I)] uiuunt *Lindelöf.* m[ ]ne (F)] mine *Kimmens.* ge[ ]ænifylde (F)] gemænifylde *Kimmens.*

OE: mine (K)] *gloss eras. after word.* m[ ]ne (F)] *letter after* m *lost due to repairs.* liebbæþ ł lifiað ($E^{3/x}$)] ł lifiað *added by corr.* ꝥ (A) (*1st*)] *malformed* (*scribe began to write* g?). synd (H)] *top of* n *partly obscured due to hole in leaf.* ge[ ]ænifylde (F)] *letter lost after 1st* e *due to repairs, letter fragments visible.* fiogæþ ł hatedon ($E^{3/x}$)] ł hatedon *added by corr.*

LTg: Inimici] [ ]nimici G. mei] *om.* B; meí I. uiuent] F: e *altered from another letter,* K: *on eras., with* e *altered from* u; uiuvnt I: *orig.* uiuent: e *eras., with deleting dot below,* v *interl.;* uiuunt GJ: *cf. Weber MSS* γη med. confortati] L: fortati *underlined to signal deletion,* firmati *added interl. by corr.: see GAg.* multiplicati] F: m *obscured by repairs,* K: pli *interl. by corr., perhaps also retraced.* qui] A: *on eras.,* me *eras. after word: cf. Weber MSS* αβγ med. me (*2nd*)] A: *interl. by corr.* inique] iniquę G.

LTu: Inimici] η *begins here.* uiuent] uiuunt πϱφ; uiu[ ]nt λ: *letter eras.* et (*2nd*)] *om.* υ. oderunt me] hoderunt me ς, η: *orig.* me hoderunt: *words transposed;* odierunt me ϑ. inique] iniqui η; iniquę λ.

GAg: confortati] confirmati FGHIJK, L: *see LTg.*

GAu: confortati] confirmati δεζϑιλμξοπϱστυφχψ.

21

Qui ða AB, þa CDFJK, ðæ þe E^{3}, þa þe G, þa ðe I*
retribuebant* | geedleanedon ł aguldon A/A^{2}*, geedleanodon BCGJ, aguldon D, aguldan K, agyldaþ I, forguldon F, me *E^{3}*
mihi* | me AB*C*J, edleæniæþ ł agyldon *$E^{3/x}$**
mala yfel ABJK, yfylu C, yfelu $DE^{3/x}$*FGI, yuelu H
pro fore AB, for CDE^{3}FGHIJK
bonis godum ACFGI, godum BJ, godon DE^{x}, god H, gode K
detrahebant hi teldon A, hy tældon DE^{x}*GH, hi tældon F, hi tældan K, tældon BCJ, tældun I
mihi me $ABCDE^{x}$*FGHIJK
quoniam forðon $ABDE^{x}$*HJ, forþon CG, forþam K, forðam ðe F, forðan þe I
subsecutus* esterfylgende *A**, æfterfylgende B, æftyrfylgynde C, æfterfiligende G, æfterfiligende J, ic fylgde DFI, ic fylide K, fylgende E^{3} (*L*)
sum* ic eam A, ic eom BC (*L*)

iustitiam* rehtwinisse A, rihtwisnysse *C*, ryhtwisnesse BD, godnysse FI, godnesse JK, ic eo[ ] godnesse ł rihtwisnesse G, rithwisnesse sind ł soðfestnesse E$^{3/x}$* (*L*)

ED: mihi (B) (*2nd*)] me *Brenner.* m^{1} (E)] michi *Harsley.* forðon (A)] for ðon *Kuhn.*

OE: þa ðe (I)] ðe *malformed.* geedleanedon ł aguldon (A/A^{2})] ł aguldon *added in 11th-c. hand.* edleæniæþ ł agyldon (E$^{3/x}$)] ł agyldon *added by corr.* yfelu (E$^{3/x}$)] u *added by corr.* hy tældon (E^{x})] *on eras.* me (E^{x}) (*2nd*)] *on eras.* forðon (E^{x})] *on eras.* esterfylgende (A)] *Kuhn notes: 'From* fylgende; ester (*for* efter) *above; ? contemporary.'* rithwisnesse sind ł soðfestnesse (E$^{3/x}$)] rithwisnesse *added by corr.*, ł *added by corr. in left margin* (*gloss to* subsecutus sum iustitiam *orig. read* fylgende sind soðfestnesse).

LTg: retribuebant] E: *2nd* e *on eras.* (?). mihi (*1st*)] michi C: *orig.* mihi: c *interl. by corr.;* m^{1} E. mihi (*2nd*)] michi E. subsecutus] A: sub *interl.*, L: *underlined to signal deletion,* sequebar *added interl. by corr.: see GAg.* sum] L: *underlined to signal deletion: see GAg.* iustitiam] L: *underlined to signal deletion,* bonitatem *added interl. by corr.: see GAg;* iusticiam C: *orig.* iustitiam: *2nd* t *altered to* c.

LTu: mihi (*1st*)] β: *final* i *interl.;* michi ς; m^{1} τ*. detrahebant] η *ends after* detra-. mihi (*2nd*)] michi ιλςτ*τ, ϱ: c *interl.;* m^{1} φ. iustitiam] iusticiam τ*.

GAg: retribuebant] retribuunt FGHIJK. mihi (*1st*)] *om.* FGHIK. subsecutus sum] sequebar FGHIJK, L: *see LTg.* iustitiam] bonitatem FGHIJK, L: *see LTg.*

GAu: retribuebant] retribuebunt λ; retribuunt δεζιμξοπϱστυφχψ; retribunt ϑ. mihi (*1st*)] *om.* δεζϑιλμξοπϱστυφχψ. subsecutus sum] sequebar δεζϑιλμξοπϱστυφχψ. iustitiam] bonitatem δεζϑιλμξοπϱστυφχψ.

22

Ne* ne ACFGHIJ, Ne E^{3}, na *K*, e B
derelinquas forlet ðu A, forlet þu E^{3}, forlæt ðu BI, forlæt þu C*F*GJK, forlæte ðu D, forlæte þu H
me me ABCE^{3}FGIJK
domine drihten E^{3}, dryht̄ AB, driħt CFG, driħ J, eala þu I* (*H*)
deus | god ABCFGJK, min E^{3}I
meus | min ABCFGJK, god E^{3}I
ne ne ABCE^{3}FGHIJ, na K
discesseris gewit ðu ABC, gewit þu FIJ, gewite ðu DE^{x}*, gewite þu G, gewite þe þu H, gewit K (*M*)
a from AE^{3}, from B, fram CHJK, fram FGI (*M*)
me me ABCE^{3}FGHIJK

ED: de(r)[ ]linquas (F)] der-linquas *Kimmens.*

OE: eala þu (I)] s.o s.o *written before* eala *above* domine deus. gewite ðu (E^{x})] *on eras.*

LTg: Ne] K: e *on eras.* derelinquas] de(r)[ ]linquas F: *shoulder of* r *not visible, hole in leaf after* r. domine] H: *small eras. after word.* discesseris] disceseris M. a] á M.

LTu: discesseris] disceseris ν.

GAg: Ne] Non GI.

GAu: Ne] non ιμοφ; Non δεζπτυψ.

23

Intende — bihald *A*, behald *B*, beheald *CDG*HJ, beheæld *E^3*, begym F*, begem *I*, ongyt K (*LM*)
in — in A, on BCDE^xFGHJK, to I
adiutorium | fultum ABCFGHJ, fultu<u>m</u> D, fultume *K*, minne E^3, minum I
meum | minne ABCDFGHJ, minan K, fultum E^3, fultume I
domine — drihten E^3, dryhꝉ̄ AB, driħt *C*FG, driħ J (*I*)
deus* — god ABCE^3FGJK
salutis | halu A, hælo BIJ, hæle CDFGHK, mine E^3
meae | minre A*BCDFH*IJK, mine *G*, helo *E^3* (*L*)

ED: [ ]ntende (I)] Intende *Lindelöf.* meȩ (E)] meae *Harsley.*

OE: begym (F)] *followed by hole in leaf.*

LTg: Intende] intende ABCDEM, L: i *altered to* I *by corr.;* [ ]ntende G, I: *initial letter eras.* adiutorium] ádiutorium K. domine] C: *eras. after* i, I: s. o *written above word.* meae] meæ BCL; meȩ DEFGH.

LTu: Intende] intende βνς. deus] *interl.* δ. meae] meȩ ειξςφ; meæ ϑ; mee στ*τ.

GAg: deus] *om.* I.

GAu: deus] *om.* εζϑμυ.

PSALM 38

2

Dixi — ic cweð *A*, ic cwæð *BCDG*H, Ic cwæð *E^x*, ic cweþe J, ic sæde F*I (*KLM*)
custodiam — ic haldu *A*, ic healde *BCJ*, ic <u>ge</u>healde D, ic gehealde F*G*HIK, ic gehælde E^3 (*LM*)
uias | wegas ABCDF*G*HIJK, minne E^3 (*LM*)
meas | mine BCDFGHIJK, mi[ ] A*, wegæs E^3 (*L*)
ut — ðet A, þæt BG, þ<u>æt</u> CDFHIJK, þet E^3
non | ic ne ABCDE^3FGHIJ, ic na K
delinquam | agylte AB*C*DFGHI, agilte J, gylde K, forlete ł agylte $E^{3/x}$* (*L*)
in — in A, on BCDE^3FGHIJK

lingua	I	tungan ABCDFGIK, tunga HJ, minræ E^{3} (*L*)
mea	I	minre ACDGHIJK, mine BF, tungæ *E^{3}*
Posui		ic sette ABCDFJK, ic asette H, Ic asette $E^{3/x}$*, asette *G,* ic gesette I
ori	I	muðe ABCDFG, muþe IJK, muð H, minum E^{3}
meo	I	minum AFI, minum BCDGHJ, minan K, muþe E^{3}
custodiam		gehaeld A, geheld B, ic gehealde F, gehealdnesse J, geheordunga DE^{3}*GH, geheord K, hyrde C, hyrdnesse I
dum*		ðonne A, þonne BCDHJK, þonne E^{x}*, ðonne F, þonne G, þa þa I
consistit*		gestondeð AB, gestondyð C, gestandeð G, gestandeþ J, standeþ D, standað E^{x}*, standeð F, stande K, samod stod I (*LM*)
peccator		se synfulla $ABCDE^{x}$*FGHIJ
aduersum		wið *A*BC, wiþ ł ongean J, ongean DE^{x}*GH, agen I, togeanes F (*K*)
me		me $ABCE^{3}$FGHIJ

ED: CVSTODIAM (B)] custodiam *Brenner.* mi[ ] (A)] mine *Kuhn.* [ ]osui (G)] Posui *Rosier.*

OE: ic sæde (F)] *written in bowl of* D *in* Dixi. mi[ ] (A)] *eras. from scraping of gold leaf obliterates final letters of gloss.* forlete ł agylte ($E^{3/x}$)] ł agylte *added by corr.* Ic asette ($E^{3/x}$)] asette *by corr.* geheordunga (E^{3})] *eras. before word, gloss perhaps partly on eras., retraced by corr.* þonne (E^{x})] *on eras.* standað (E^{x})] *on eras.* se synfulla (E^{x})] *on eras.,* y *altered from* u (?). ongean (E^{x})] *on eras.*

LTg: Dixi] DIXI ABCEGKLM; DIXi D. custodiam (*1st*)] CVSTODIAM ABCL; cvstodiam J; CUSTODIAM GM. uias] VIAS L; UIAS GM. meas] MEAS L. delinquam] delinqvam L; delinguam C. lingua] lingva L. mea] E: *orig.* meo: o *altered to* a. Posui] [ ]osui G: *fragment of initial* P *visible.* consistit] L: it *underlined to signal deletion,* eret *added interl. by corr.: see GAg;* consistet M: *orig.* consistit: *2nd* i *altered to* e *by corr., otiose mark above* st. aduersum] aduersūs A: *macron above* u: *cf. Weber MSS* αβζηλ; áduersum K.

LTu: δ: *vv 1–10 wanting;* ς: *vv 1–6* uani(tas) *wanting.* Dixi] DIXI βιλμνρτ*τφχψ. custodiam (*1st*)] CUStodiam β; cvstodiam ε; CVSTODIAM λ; CUSTODIam μ; CUSTODIAM νρχψ. uias] VIAS ρ. meas] MEAS ρ. non] β: *added by corr. in left margin.* aduersum] aduersus ϑ: *cf. Weber MSS* αβζηλ.

GAg: dum] cum GHIJK, F: *eras. in bowl of* u. consistit] consisteret FGHIJK, L: *see LTg.*

GAu: dum] cum εζϑιλμξοπρστυφχψ. consistit] consisteret εζϑιλμξοπρστυφχψ.

3

Obmutui		ic adumbade A*C*, ic adumbode B, ic adumbode J, ic adumbude D, Ic ǽdumbede E^{3}, ic adumbede F, ic adumbude *GH*, ic advmbude *K*, ic adumede *I*
et		⁊ ABCE^{3}*FGIJK
humiliatus		geeaðmodad A, geeaðmodod B, geeaðmodud C, geeaðmed D, geædmed E^{3}*, geeæðmet I, eadmedde F, geeadmedde G, geeadmed HK, eadmod J
sum		ic eam A, ic eom BCD$E^{3/x}$*FG*H*IJ
et		⁊ ABCDE^{x}*FGHIJK
silui		ic swigade A, ic swigode BCDFGHIJK, ic swigeode $E^{3/x}$* (*M*)
a		from A, from BC, fram D*E^{x}*FHJ*K*, fram I, fra[ ] G* (*M*)
bonis		godum AE^{x}HIK, godum BCDF, gódu J, god[ ] G*
et		⁊ ABCE^{3}FGIJK
dolor	|	sar ABCDGHIJK, sár F, min E^{3}
meus	|	min ABCDFGHIJK, sær E^{3}
renouatus		geedneowad AB, geedniwud C, geedniwod DE^{x}*FGHIJ, geniwod K
est		is ABFHIJ*K*, ys CE^{x}*

ED: Ommutui (C)] O[b]mutui *Wildhagen.* [ ]bmutui (G)] Obmutui *Rosier.* fra[ ] (G)] fram *Rosier.* á (E)] a *Harsley.* god[ ] (G)] g[ ] *Rosier.* renouatus (BE)] renovatus *Brenner, Harsley.*

OE: ⁊ (E^{3}) (*1st*)] *eras. after word.* geædmed (E^{3})] *orig.* geædmeded: *final* ed *eras.* ic eom ($E^{3/x}$)] eom *on eras. by corr.* ⁊ (E^{x}) (*2nd*)] *on eras.* ic swigeode ($E^{3/x}$)] ic *on eras. by corr.,* g *altered from* c, o *retouched or on eras. by main hand.* fra[ ] (G)] *macron not visible.* god[ ] (G)] *letter fragments visible after* d. geedniwod (E^{x})] *orig.* ge *retouched, rest on eras. by corr.* ys (E^{x})] *on eras.*

LTg: Obmutui] [ ]bmutui G: *initial* O *lost;* Ommutui I, C: *1st* m *on eras. by corr.,* H: *1st* m *on eras.: cf. Weber MS* δ; Ombmutui K: *orig.* Obmutui: *1st* m *inserted by corr. (glossator) but* b *not deleted.* sum] H: *punct. mark eras. after word.* silui] sílui M. a] á EKM. est] ést K.

LTu: δ: *vv 1–10 wanting;* ς: *vv 1–6* uani(tas) *wanting.* Obmutui] Ommutui ειλμπρφχ, ο: *orig.* Obmutui: b *deleted,* m *interl.*

4

Concaluit		hatade AB, hatode CGH, ic hatode K, hatude D, hatud E^{x}*, gehatude F, gehatode J, wearmode ł gehæt wæs ł ahatode I*
cor	|	heorte ABCDFHIJK, heortan G, min E^{3} (*M*)
meum	|	min ABCDFHIJK, mine G, heortæ E^{3}

intra binnan ABC, binnon J, on DE^{3}GHK, on in F, wiðinnan I
me me ABCDE^{3}FGHIJK
et ⁊ ABE^{3}CFIJK (*G*)
in in A, on BCE^{3}FKI (*G*)
meditatione | smeange A, smeaunge BCDHI, smeaungum F, [ ]meaunge *G,* smeagung J, swmegung K, mire E^{3}* (*M*)
mea | minre ABCD*G*H*I*, mine F, min JK, Smeægunge E^{3}
exardescit born A, barn BC, abarn *J,* byrnð *DF*G*HK,* ⁊ abyrnð *I,* bierned *E^{3}*
ignis fyr ABCE^{3}*FGHI, fýr D, swa fyr JK

ED: binnan (C)] binnam *Wildhagen.* et in : [ ] (G)] ⁊ on *Rosier.* [ ]editatione (G)] *me*ditatione *Rosier.* mire (E)] mi[n]re *Harsley.* exardescit (D)] exardesc[e]t *Roeder.*

OE: hatud (E^{x})] *on eras.* wearmode ł gehæt wæs ł ahatode (I)] wearmode *written in left margin.* mire (E^{3})] *letter eras. after* i. fyr (E^{3})] *eras. before word,* f *retraced in darker ink.*

LTg: cor] cór M. et in] G: *glosses lost due to hole in leaf.* meditatione] meditatiône M; [ ]editatione G. mea] H: *small eras. after word.* exardescit] D: i *formed from another letter,* E: i *on eras.;* exardescet FIJ, HK: *orig.* exardescit: i *altered to* e.

LTu: δ: *vv 1–10 wanting;* ς: *vv 1–6* uani(tas) *wanting.* in] μ: *interl.* exardescit] exardescet εζιλξοπρστ*τυφχ.

5
Locutus | spreocende A, sprecende BFJ, sprecynde C, ic sprec D, ic spræc *HI**, ic spæc K, [ ]ræc *G,* Ic eom E^{3}
sum | ic eam A, ic eom BF, ic eom C, ic eon J, sprecende E^{3}
in in A, on BCDE^{3}FGIJK (*M*)
lingua | tungan ABCDFGIJK, tunga H*, minre E^{3} (*M*)
mea | minre ABCDGHIJK, mire F, tungon E^{3} (*M*)
notum | cuð *A*CK, cuðne BFH, cuþne DIJ, cuðe G, gedo E^{3}
mihi* } me AB*CDE^{3}*FGHIJK
fac* }| doa A, dó B, do CDFHIJK, cuþe E^{3}
domine drihten E^{3}F, dryht̄ AB, driht́ CG, drih́ J, hlaford K (*I*)
finem ende ABCDE^{x}FGHIJK
meum minne ABCFGHIJK, minne D, minn E^{x}
et ⁊ ABCE^{x}*FGIJK* (*HL*)
numerum rim AB, gerim K, getæl C, getell I, getæl ł gerim D, getæl ł gerim E^{x}G, getel ł gerim FH, gerim ł getæl J
dierum | dæga A, daga BCDHK, dagena FG, dagana I, dagas J, minræ E^{3}

meorum | minra ABCDFGHIK, heora *J,* daga E^{3}*
quis — hwelc ABDE^{x}*, hwylc *CG,* hwilc *HI*J, la hwy F*, hwa K (*L*)
est — is ABDFGHJ*K,* ys CE^{x}*, hit is I*
ut — ðæt A, þæt BG, þæt CDFHIJK, þet E^{3}*
sciam — ic wite ABCD$E^{3/x}$*FGIJ, ic wi[ ] H*, wite K
quid — hwet AE^{3}, hwæt BCDFGHIJK
desit — wone sie A, wona sie B, wana sy CIJ, wana sie DE^{x}*H, wana sý F, wana si GK (*M*)
mihi — me AB*CDE*^{x}*FGHIJK

ED: [ ]ræc (G)] [ ]æc *Rosier.* tunga (H)] tunga(n) *Campbell.* me (G) (*1st*)] [ ]: *Rosier.* qui (C)] qui[s] *Wildhagen.* hwylc (G)] hwil[ ] *Rosier.* is (G)] [ ]s *Rosier.* ic wi[ ] (H)] ic wite *Campbell.*

OE: ic spræc (I)] [ ]æc *written in left margin, but lost due to tight binding, a gloss following* spræc *eras., letter fragments visible above* sum. tunga (H)] *loop of* g *from* ignis *in line above intersects top of* a *in* tunga, *although no macron seems intended.* daga (E^{3})] *orig.* dagæ: æ *altered to* a. hwelc (E^{x})] *on eras.* la hwy (F)] *hole in leaf after* hwy. ys (E^{x})] *on eras.* hit is (I)] hit *interl.* þet (E^{3})] *eras. before and after word,* t *retouched.* ic wite ($E^{3/x}$)] ic *on eras. by corr.,* wite *retouched.* ic wi[ ] (H)] *final letters obscured by hole in leaf.* wana sie (E^{x})] *on eras.* me (E^{x}) (*2nd*)] *on eras.*

LTg: Locutus] Loqutus H: *orig.* Locutus: c *altered to* q; Loquutus I; [ ]us G. in] M: *on eras.* lingua] M: *on eras.* mea] M: *on eras.* notum] A: u *on eras. by corr.* mihi (*1st*)] michi E, C: *orig.* mihi: c *interl. by corr.* domine] I: o *written above word.* et] L: E *added to left of* e *by corr.;* Et FGHIJK. meorum] eorum J. quis] qui CGHI: *letter eras. after* i, L: *orig.* quis: s *eras.: cf. Weber MSS* αγ. est] ést K. desit] dêsit M. mihi (*2nd*)] michi E, C: *orig.* mihi: c *interl. by corr.*

LTu: δ: *vv 1–10 wanting;* ϛ: *vv 1–6* uani(tas) *wanting.* notum] β: *orig.* notam: a *deleted,* u *interl.;* notam ο. mihi (*1st*)] michi τ*. et] Et εζθιλξοπϱσυφψ. mihi (*2nd*)] michi ιλξστ*τφ, πϱ: c *interl.*

GAg: mihi fac] fac mihi FGIJK; fac michi H.

GAu: mihi fac] fac mihi θζμουχψ; fac michi ιτ, πϱ: *2nd* c *interl.;* fac m^1 ελξσφ.

6
Ecce — sehðe AB, on gesihðe D, On gesihðe E^{x}*, on gesihþe J, efnenu C, efne FIK, efne gesihðe G (*H*)
ueteres* — alde A, ealde BCDE^{x}*, gemetegode FJ, gemetelice ł getælfæste ł ametendlice I*, gemet K (*L*)
posuisti — ðu settes A, þu settes B, þu settest DGJK, ðu settest F, þe settest H, þu gesettyst C, þu gesettest E^{3}, þu asettest I

dies ǀ dęgas A, dagas BCDFGHIJK, minne E^{3}
meos ǀ mine ABCDFGHIJK, dægæs E^{3} (*L*)
et ⁊ ABCE^{3}FGHIJ*K*
substantia ǀ spoede *A*, speda C, spoed B, sped DFGHJ, is sped ł edwist *I*, genihsumnes K, mine E^{3}
mea ǀ mine AC, minne F, min BDGHIJK, spedæ E^{3}
tamquam swe swe A, swa swa B*C*DF*GH*IJ, swæ swæ *E^{3}**, ealswa *K*
nihil* nowiht A*C*, naht BDFJK, næht *E^{3}**, nan þing GI (*L*)
ante biforan A, beforan BCDFGHIJ, beforæn *E^{3}*, bef K*
te ðe ABDF, þe C*E^{3}*GHIJ (*K*)
est* bið AB, ys C, is *E^{3}** (*L*)

Uerumtamen ah hweðre *A*, ah hwæðre *B*, ac þeahhwæðere *C*, þeahhwæþre *DH**, þeahhweþre *E^{x}**, ðeahhwæþere *F*, þeahhwæðere *G*, þeahhwæþere *J*, swa þeah *K* (*IL*)
uniuersa al A, eall BFGHI*J, ealle C, eal D, eæll E^{3}*, ungerim K
uanitas idelnis ADH, idelnes BGK, ydelnys F, idylnyssa C, ydelnessæ E^{3}, idelnesse J, ydelnys ł awendendnys *I**
omnis ylc A, ælc CDF*G*HIJK, eælc E^{3}*, æghwelc B
homo mon AB, mann CDI, man E$^{3/x}$*FGHJK
uiuens lifgende A, lifiende D, liuiend[ ] H*, lifigende FG, libbende BE^{3}IK, lybbynde C, leofað J

ED: [ ]cce (H)] Ecce *Campbell.* tanquam (C)] ta[m]quam *Wildhagen.* tā̄quam (K)] tamquam *Sisam.* swa swa (GIJ)] swaswa *Rosier, Lindelöf, Oess.* té (K)] te *Sisam.* Verumtamen (B)] Verum tamen *Brenner.* Ueruntamen (C)] Ueru[m]tamen *Wildhagen.* Verumtamen (F)] Verumptamen *Kimmens.* þeahhwæþre (DH)] þeah hwæþre *Roeder, Campbell.* þeahhweþre (E)] þeah hweþre *Harsley.* þeahhwæðere (G)] þeah hwæðere *Rosier.* þeahhwæþere (J)] þeah hwæþere *Oess.* liuiend[ ] (H)] liuiend(e) *Campbell.*

OE: On gesihðe (E^{x})] *on eras.* ealde (E^{x})] *on eras.* gemetelice ł getælfæste ł ametendlice (I)] ł ametendlice *written in right margin.* swæ swæ (E^{3})] *2nd* swæ *by corr.* (?). næht (E^{3})] *eras. before word,* n *retouched by corr.* bef (K)] f *separated from* e *by space of 7 mm.* is (E^{3})] *retouched by corr.* þeahhwæþre (H)] *descender of 2nd* þ *lost due to eras. in Lat. line below.* þeahhweþre (E^{x})] *on eras.* eall (I)] *gloss eras. after word.* eæll (E^{3})] *eras. after word.* ydelnys ł awendendnys (I)] s. e<u>st</u> : is *written in right margin.* eælc (E^{3})] c *on eras. by corr., gloss retouched.* man (E$^{3/x}$)] an *on eras. by corr.,* m *retouched.* liuiend[ ] (H)] *hole in leaf after* d, *letter fragments visible.*

LTg: Ecce] [ ]cce H: *fragments and outline of initial* E *visible.* ueteres] L: mensurabiles *added interl. by corr.: see GAg.* et] K: *added in left margin by corr.* substantia] I: s. e<u>st</u> *written in left margin,* A: an *on eras. by corr.* tamquam] tanquam E, C: *orig.* tamquam: *left leg of 1st* m *eras. to form* n, G: *orig.* tamquam: *right leg of*

1st m *eras. to form* n, H: n *formed from another letter;* tāquam K. nihil] L: um *added by corr. after* l: *see GAg;* nichil E, C: *orig.* nihil: c *interl. by corr.* ante] E: *on eras.* te] E: *on eras.;* té K: *accent added later.* est] E: *on eras.*, L: *underlined by corr. to signal deletion: see GAg.* Uerumtamen] Verumtamen ABDIL, F: *letter eras. after 1st* m; Ueruntamen C: *orig.* Uerumtamen: *left leg of 1st* m *eras. to form* n, H: *eras. after 1st* n; Veruntamen E; Verumptamen G, K: *eras. after word, stroke* (*otiose?*) *above 1st* m, en *written by corr., although orig. macron above 2nd* m *by main hand* (*cf. v. 7*); Uerumptamen J. uanitas] I: s. est : is *written in right margin.* omnis] om[ ] G.

LTu: δ: *vv 1–10 wanting;* ς: *vv 1–6* uani(tas) *wanting.* posuisti] possuisti ϑ. tamquam] tanquam εϑιλτ*φ. nihil] nichil τ*. Uerumtamen] Verumtamen ν; Veruntamen ισφ; Ueruntamen λ; Verumptamen ξυ; Uerumptamen τ*τ; Ueruntame ε.

GAg: ueteres] mensurabiles FGHIJK, L: *see LTg.* nihil] nihilum FI, L: *see LTg;* nichilum GHJK. est] *om.* FGHIJK, L: *see LTg.*

GAu: ueteres] mensurabiles εζϑιλμξοπϱστυφχψ. nihil] nihilum εζϑμοπυχψ; nichilum ιλξστφ, ϱ: c *interl.* est] *om.* εζϑιλμξοπϱστυχψ.

7

Quamquam*	ðaeh ðe *A,* þeh ðe *B,* þieh þe *C,* þeah ðe *D,* þeæh þe *E^{3},* þeahhwæþere F, þeahhwæðere G, ł þeahhwæþre I*, soþlice J, swa þeah K (*LM*)
in	in A, on BCDE^{x}*FGHIJ
imagine	| onlicnisse A, onlicnesse B, anlicnysse C*F,* anlicnesse DG*HJK,* hiwe ł on anlicnesse I, godes E^{3}
dei*	| godes AB, godys C, onlicnesse E^{3} (*L*)
ambulet*	gonge A*B,* gange D, gænge E^{3}*, gæð C, þurhfærð FGJ, gindfærð I, forþgæð K (*L*)
homo	mon A, mann CDGI, man FHJK, Se mon E^{3} (*B*)
tamen*	hweðre A, hwæðre B, hwæþre D, hweþre E^{3}, þiehhwæðre C, ac F, ac he is G, ⁊ I, sit K* (*L*)
uane*	idellice AB, idyllice C, on idel DGJ, on ydel E^{3}*FI (*L*)
conturbabitur*	bið gedroefed A, bið gedrefed BFG, bið gedrefyd C, biþ gedrefed J, he bið gedrefed D, he bioþ gedrefed $E^{3/x}$*, ac he is gedrefed I* (*L*)
Thesaurizat	goldhordað A*BC, goldhordaþ J, Goldhordæþ E^{3}*, he goldhordaþ D*H*I, he goldhordað *K,* [ ]es goldhordað F*, þe goldhordað G (*M*)
et	⁊ ABCDE^{3}FGHIJK
ignorat	nat ABCDFGHJ, he nat I, nat he K, he ne wæt E^{3} (*M*)
cui	hwæm ABI, hwam CJK, hwam DE^{x}*FGH

congreget*	gesomnað A*B*, he gesomnað *C*GI, he gesomnaþ *J*, he somnað DH, he somnaþ *E*^{x}*, hit gædcrað ł somnað F, he gæderað K (*LM*)
ea	ða A, þa CDE$^{3/x}$*FG*H*JK, þa þing I (*B*)

ED: quanquam (C)] qua[m]quam *Wildhagen.* þeh ðe (B)] þehðe *Brenner.* þieh þe (C)] þiehþe *Wildhagen.* þeah ðe (D)] þeahðe *Roeder.* þeæh þe (E)] þeæhþe *Harsley.* þeahhwæðere (G)] þeah hwæðere *Rosier.* imagine (F)] imaginem *Kimmens.* [ ]hesaurizat (H)] Thesaurizat *Campbell.* Thesaurízat (K)] Thesaurizat *Sisam.* [ ]es goldhordað (F)] ðes goldhordað *Kimmens.*

OE: ł þeahhwæþre (I)] *written in right margin, orig. gloss eras.* on (E^{x})] *on eras.* gænge (E^{3})] *letter eras. after word.* sit (K)] *lemma misread as* sedet. on ydel (E^{3})] on *in darker ink,* l *retraced in darker ink.* he bioþ gedrefed (E$^{3/x}$)] he *on eras. by corr.,* bioþ *retraced in darker ink.* ac he is gedrefed (I)] *eras. after* is. goldhordað (A)] *orig.* golðhordað: *cross-stroke of 1st* ð *eras.* Goldhordæþ (E^{3})] *eras. before word.* [ ]es goldhordað (F)] *letter fragment visible in initial position,* s *obscured by eras. but visible.* hwam (E^{x})] *on eras.* he somnaþ (E^{x})] *on eras., eras. after* n. þa (E$^{3/x}$)] *orig.* þæ: æ *altered to* a.

LTg: Quamquam] quamquam BD, L: *underlined (fol. 25r) to signal deletion,* Verumtamen *added by corr. in left margin of fol.* 25v: *see GAg;* quanquam E, A: n *on eras. by corr.,* C: *eras. after* n; qvamquam M: *orig.* tamquam: t *altered to* q, v *interl.: cf. Weber MSS* HMKQ*. imagine] HK: *eras. after word,* F: *orig.* imaginem: *final* m *underlined and crossed through: cf. Weber MSS* βγδ moz med. dei] L: *underlined by corr. to signal deletion: see GAg.* ambulet] L: *underlined to signal deletion,* pertransit *added interl. by corr.: see GAg;* ambule[ ] B: *final letter lost due to excision of initial letter from fol. 43r.* homo] B: *lost due to excision of initial letter from fol. 43r.* tamen] L: *underlined to signal deletion,* sed ⁊ *added interl. by corr.: see GAg.* uane] L: *underlined to signal deletion,* frustra *added above by corr.: see GAg.* conturbabitur] L: bi *underlined by corr. to signal deletion: see GAg.* Thesaurizat] M: *eras. after* s; Thesaurízat K: *accent and* t *added by corr.;* [ ]hesaurizat H: *initial* T *lost, outline visible.* ignorat] ignôrat M. congreget] congregat BCELM, J: t *in smaller hand in lighter brown ink, possibly by glossator: cf. Weber MS* η². ea] H: *eras. after word,* B: *lost due to excision of initial letter from fol. 43r.*

LTu: δ: *vv 1–10 wanting.* Quamquam] quamquam νς; quanquam τ*; tamquam β: *cf. Weber MSS* MKQ*. in] *om.* ς. imagine] ymagine ξ; imaginem βς: *cf. Weber MSS* MSKXβγδ moz med. congreget] congregat ϑς: *cf. Weber MS* η².

GAg: Quamquam] Verumtamen FI, L: *see LTg;* Verumptamen G, K: *stroke (otiose?) above 1st* m *(cf. v. 6)*; Veruntamen H: *eras. after 1st* n; Uerumtamen J. dei] *om.* FGHIJK, L: *see LTg.* ambulet] pertransit FGHIJK, L: *see LTg.* tamen] sed et

FGHIK; sed J: *eras.* (?) *after word,* L: *see LTg.* uane] frustra FGHIJK, L: *see LTg.* conturbabitur] conturbatur FGHIJK, L: *see LTg.* congreget] congregabit FGHIJK.

GAu: Quamquam] Ueruntamen εσφ; Uerumtamen ζϑμπϱχψ; Veruntamen ιλ; Verumptamen ξτυ; Verumtamen ο. dei] *om.* εζϑιλμοπϱστυφχψ. ambulet] pertransit εζϑιλμξοπϱστυφχψ. tamen] sed et εζϑιλμξοπϱστυφχψ. uane] frustra εζϑιμξοπϱστυφχψ. conturbabitur] conturbatur εζϑιλμξοϱστυφχψ; conturbatus π. congreget] congregabit εζιλμξοπϱστυφχψ.

8

Et		⁊ *ABCE*^{3}FGHIJ*K* (*DLM*)
nunc		nu ACDE^{3}GHJ, nx B, nu ða *F,* nu þa I, nuc K
quae		hwet A, hwæt *BC,* hwæt ł hwilc I*, hwilc ł hwæt *J,* hwelc *D,* hwylc *FH,* hwilc *E*^{3}*G,* hwa *K* (*L*)
est		is ABE^{3}FGHIJ*K,* ys C
expectatio	|	bad AB, anbid C, andbid K, anbidung *D*F*G*HI, ic abad ł anbidung J, min E^{3}
mea	|	min ABCDFG*H*IJK, anbidung E$^{3/x}$*
nonne		ah ne AB, hu ne C, hu ne nu DE^{x}*HJ, hu nu FK, ac ne G, ne wenstu la I
dominus		drihten E^{x}*I, dryht̄ AB, drih́t CFG, drih́ J
et		⁊ ABCE^{x}*FGIJK
substantia		sie spoed A, spoed B, sped DE^{x}*FGHJK*, speda C, sped ł edwist I
mea		min *A*BDE^{x}*FGHIJK, mine C
tamquam*		swa swa B*C*D, swæ swæ *E*^{3} (*ALM*)
nihil*		noht B, naht D, næht *E*^{3}, nowiht *C* (*ALM*)
ante*		biforan A, beforan BCDIK, beforæn E^{3}, fram F, toforan G, mid J (*L*)
te		ðe ABDF, þe CE^{3}GIJK (*L*)
est		is ABDE^{3}FGHIJK, ys C (*L*)

ED: quę (E)] quae *Harsley.* exspectatio (G)] expectatio *Rosier.* hu ne (C)] hune *Wildhagen.* hu ne nu (DHJ)] hunenu *Roeder, Campbell, Oess.* tanquam (C)] ta[m]quam *Wildhagen.*

OE: hwæt ł hwilc (I)] ł hwilc *written above* hwæt. anbidung (E$^{3/x}$)] a *altered from* o *by corr.,* bidung *on eras. by corr.* hu ne nu (E^{x})] *on eras.* drihten (E^{x})] *on eras.* ⁊ (E^{x}) (*2nd*)] *on eras.* sped (E^{x})] *on eras.* sped (K)] *eras. before word.* min (E^{x})] *on eras.*

LTg: Et] L: *orig.* et: e *altered to* E *by corr.;* et ABCDEKM. nunc] F: c *added above line in smaller hand.* quae] quæ B; quę CDEFHKL; que GJ. est (*1st*)] ést K. expectatio] exspectatio DG. mea (*1st*)] H: *small eras. after word.* mea (*2nd*)] A:

eras. (ca 12 letters) after word. tamquam] L: *underlined by corr. to signal deletion: see GAg;* tanquam E, C: *orig.* tamquam: *left leg of 1st* m *eras. to form* n, M: *on eras. by corr. of Ps 37.17* ali(quando); *om.* A: *cf. Weber MSS* αγδη* moz med, *see GAg.* nihil] L: *underlined by corr. to signal deletion,* M: *on eras. by corr. of Ps 37.17* ali(quando); nichil C: *orig.* nihil: c *interl. by corr.;* nichilum E: *cf. Weber MS* M; *om.* A: *cf. Weber MSS* αγδη* moz med, *see GAg.* ante te est] L: *underlined to signal deletion,* apud te est *added interl. by corr. above preceding* tamquam: *see GAg.*

LTu: δ: *vv 1–10 wanting.* Et] et βνςτ*. quae] que βϑσςτ*; quȩ ειλνξο. expectatio] exspectatio ϑ, β: *orig.* expectatio: s *added interl. by corr.* nonne dominus] non Domine dominus τ*: *initial* D *added mistakenly.* tamquam] tanquam τ*τ. nihil] nichil ς; nichilum τ*.

GAg: tamquam] *om.* FGHIJK, A: *see LTg; for* L *see LTg.* nihil] *om.* FGHIJK, A: *see LTg; for* L *see LTg.* ante] apud FGHIJK, L: *see LTg.*

GAu: tamquam] *om.* εζϑιλμξοπϱστυφχψ. nihil] *om.* εζϑιλμξοπϱστυφχψ. ante] apud εζϑιλμξοπϱστυφχψ.

9

Ab		from AE^3, from B, fram CDHJK, fram FGI
omnibus		allum A, eallum BDHJ, eallum CFGI, eællum E^3, eallan K
iniquitatibus	|	unrehtwisnissum A, unryhtwisnessum BD, unrihtwisnessum G, unrihtwisnyssum CI, unrihtwisnessum HJ, unrihtwisnysse F, unrihtwisnesse K, minum E^3 (*M*)
meis	|	minum AG, minum BCDHIJ, min F, minre K, unrihtwisnesse $E^{3/x}$*
eripe*		genere $ABCE^3I$, genera FJ, nere DH, nera GK (*LM*)
me		mec A, me BCE^3FGHJK
obprobrium		edwit *ABC*, hosp DE^3G*H***I*K, hósp F, hosp ł edwit J
insipienti		ðæm unwisan A, þæm unwisan B, þam unwisum J, þam unrihtwisan C, unwisum DK, unwisum GH, unwinsum F, þam unwitan ł unwisum I, ⁊ unsnytro ł unwisum $E^{3/x}$*
dedisti	|	ðu saldes A*, ðu sealdes B, þu scealdyst C, þu sealdest DGHIJK, ðu sealdest F, þu me $E^{3/x}$*
me	|	mec A, me BCDFGHJK, Seældest E^3

ED: from (E)] From *Harsley.* me (G) (*1st Lat.*)] me *Rosier.* me (G) (*1st OE*)] m[ ] *Rosier.* opprobrium (C)] o[b]probrium *Wildhagen.*

OE: unrihtwisnesse ($E^{3/x}$)] wisnesse *on eras. by corr.* hosp (H)] *descender of* s *eras.* ⁊ unsnytro ł unwisum ($E^{3/x}$)] ł unwisum *on eras. by corr.* ðu saldes (A)] *top of* u *closed.* þu me ($E^{3/x}$)] þu *on eras. by corr.*

LTg: iniquitatibus] M: *orig.* iniquitabus: ti *interl. by corr.* eripe] L: pe *underlined to* *signal deletion,* ue *added interl. by corr.: see GAg;* éripe M. obprobrium] opprobrium AHI, C: *orig.* obprobrium: *1st* b *altered to* p.

LTu: δ: *vv 1–10 wanting.* obprobrium] opprobrium εζλπφ, βο: *orig.* obprobrium: p *written above 1st* b *by corr.*

GAg: eripe] erue FGHIJK, L: *see LTg.*

GAu: eripe] erue εζϑιλμξοπϱστυφχψ.

10

Obmutui — ic adumbade A*C*, ic adumbode B*IJ*, ic adumbude D, Ic ædumbude *E*^{3}, ic adumbude FG*H*, ic swigude K

et — ⁊ ABCDE^{3}FGHIJK

non | ne ABC, na DFGHJK, ic ne E^{3}I

aperui | ontynde ABC, ontinde E^{3}, ic atynde DF*G*H, ic untine J, geopnade I, openode K (*M*)

os | muð *A*BCFGH, muþ *D*IJ*K*, minne *E*^{3} (*M*)

meum | minne ABDFG*H*IJ*K, min C, muð E^{3}

quoniam — forðon ABCJ, forþon *G*, forðæn E^{3}, forðam ðe F, forðan þe I*, forðan K

tu — ðu ABD, þu CE^{3}FGHIJK (*M*)

fecisti — dydest *A*BDE$^{3/x}$*FGHJK, dedyst C, geworhtest ł ðu dydest I*

me* — (*ABCELM*)

ED: Ommutui (C)] O[b]mutui *Wildhagen.* ós (AE)] os *Kuhn, Harsley.* quonia[ ] (G)] quoni*am Rosier.* forðon (A)] for ðon *Kuhn.* forþon (G)] forþo[ ] *Rosier.*

OE: minne (J)] *2nd* n *malformed: cf. Ps 37.13* didon. forðan þe (I)] e *interl.* dydest (E$^{3/x}$)] st *on eras. by corr.* geworhtest ł ðu dydest (I)] ł ðu dydest *written in left margin.*

LTg: Obmutui] Obmvtui E; Ommutui I, C: *1st* m *on eras. by corr.,* H: mm *on eras.: cf. Weber MSS* PQVXγδ. aperui] áperui M; operui G. os] ós ADEKM. meum] H: *eras. after word.* quoniam] quonia[ ] G. tu] tú M. me] *eras.* AM; *om.* BCEL: *cf. Weber MSS* Mα^{2}η* moz^{c} med, *see GAg.*

LTu: δ: *vv 1–10 wanting.* Obmutui] Ommutui ειλπϱχ, ο: *orig.* Onmutui. me] *om.* νςτ*: *cf. Weber MSS* α^{2}η* moz^{c} med, *see GAu.*

GAg: me] *om.* FGHIJK, ABCELM: *see LTg.*

GAu: me] *om.* εζϑιλμξοπϱστυφχψ, νςτ*: *see LTu.*

11

amoue — awend ABC, awænd *J*, astyre DE^{3}F*H*K, astyra G, afyr I (*M*)

a — frome A, from B, fram CD*E*^{3}FHJK, fram GI (*M*)

me	me BCDE^{x}*FGHIJK
plagas	witu ABDFGH, wite CE^{x}*J, wita K, swingla ł witu I*
tuas	ðin A, þin C, ðine BI, þine DE^{x}*FGHJK

ED: ámoue (H)] amoue *Campbell.* á (E)] a *Harsley.*

OE: me (E^{x})] *on eras.* wite (E^{x})] *on eras.* swingla ł witu (I)] ł witu *written in right margin.* þine (E^{x})] *on eras.*

LTg: amoue] ámoue HJM. a] á EM. me] mé J.

12

A	from *A,* fram *BCDE^{3}*HJK, fram F*G*I (*LM*)
fortitudine	strengu A, strenge BC, strengo DE^{x}*H, strengðe FI, strengðo G, strenþe K, strengþe ic awænde J*
enim*	soðlice ABC, soþlice D, soþlice E^{x}* (*L*)
manus	honda AB, handa CFGHIJK, hande DE^{x}*
tuae	ðine A*F,* þine *CGJ,* ðinre *B,* þinre *DE^{x}*H*I*K* (*L*)
ego	ic ABCDE^{x}*FGHIJK
defeci	asprong AB, asprang C, geteorode DE^{x}*, geteorode FG*H,* ateorode IK, geteorige J
in	in A, on BCDE^{x}*FGHIK, innon J
increpationibus	ðreangum A*, þreaungum B, þreaunge CK, ðreaungum I, þreagungum J, þeangum ł steorum D, þeangum ł steorum H, steorum ł on þræwunge $E^{3/x}$*, þeawum ł steorum G, on grapunge ł steorum F*
Propter	fore ABD*H,* for *C*FGIJK,* For E^{3} (*L*)
iniquitatem	unrehtwisnisse A, unryhtwisnesse BD, unrihtwisnysse CFI, unrihtwisnesse E^{x}*GHJK
corripuisti	ðu ðreades AB, þu þreadyst C, þu ðreadest I, þe ðu þreadest J, þu nyrwdest DE^{x}*HK, þu nýrwdest F, þu nyruwdest G
hominem	mon AB, mann CDFGH, mæn E^{3}*, mannan I, mine men *J*
et	⁊ ABCE^{x}**FGIJK* (*H*)
tabescere	aswindan ABC, swindan FJ, swind[ ]n G, weorpian D, aswindan ł weorpian E^{x}*, aswarcan ł acwinan ⁊ aydlian ł aswindan I*, weor K
fecisti	ðu des A, þu dydes B, þu dydyst C, ðu dydest DF, þu dydest GHI*K, þu didest E^{x}*J
sicut	swe A, swa BGIK, swa swa CDFI, swæ swæ $E^{3/x}$*
araneam	gongeweafran *A,* gongewefran *B,* gangewæfre *C*,* gangewefram G, gangenwefram J, rengan ł attorcoppin D*, attercoppan *E^{x}*,* ætterloppan ł ryngan I, ceosol K*

animam sawle ABCDFGHIJ, sæwle E^{x}*, sawel K
eius his ABDE^{x}FGHIJ*K*, hys C

Uerumtamen ah hweðre A, ah hwæðre *B,* ac þeahhwæðere *C,* þeahhwæþre *D,* þeahhwæðre *GH,* þeahhwæþere *J,* þahhwæþre *E^{x}*,* þeahhwæð[ ] *F**, soðlice ł þeahhwæðre *I,* swa þeah *K* (*L*)
uniuersa* all AE^{x}*, eal B, eall CD (*L*)
uanitas* idelnis AD, idelnes B, idylnys C, on ydelnysse F, ydelnessæ E^{3}*, idelnesse J, idel GK, on ydel I (*L*)
(conturbatur)* bið gedrefed F, is gedrefed I, [ ]efed is G, gedrefed K
omnis ylc A, ælc CDE^{3}FGHI, æghwelc B, æghwilc J, ealle K
homo mon ABE^{3}, mann CDFI, man GHJ, men K
uiuens* lifgen A, lifgende D, liuiende E^{3}*, libbende B, lybbynde C (*L*)

ED: á (E)] a *Harsley.* [ ] (G)] A *Rosier.* tuæ (D)] tuae *Roeder.* tuę (E)] tuae *Harsley.* on (G)] *no gloss Rosier.* steorum ł on þræwunge (E)] steorum ł onþræwunge *Harsley.* þeawum ł steorum (G)] weawum ł steorum *Rosier.* ⁊ (G)] *no gloss Rosier.* swind[ ]n (G)] *no gloss Rosier.* swa swa (C)] aw swa *Wildhagen.* swa swa (I)] swaswa *Lindelöf.* rengan ł attorcoppin (D)] rengan *Roeder.* Verumtamen (B)] Verum tamen *Brenner.* Veruntamen (C)] Veru[m]tamen *Wildhagen.* uerum[ ]men (F)] uerum- -amen *Kimmens.* ac þeahhwæðere (C)] ac þeah hwæðere *Wildhagen.* þeahhwæþre (D)] þeah hwæþre *Roeder.* þeahhwæðre (GH)] þeah hwæðre *Rosier, Campbell.* þeahhwæþere (J)] þeah hwæþere *Oess.* þahhwæþre (E)] þah hwæþre *Harsley.* þeahhwæð[ ] (F)] þeahhwæðer– *Kimmens.*

OE: strengo (E^{x})] *on eras.* strengþe ic awænde (J)] ic awænde *perhaps influenced by gloss to* ámoue *in v. 11.* soþlice (E^{x})] *on eras.* hande (E^{x})] *on eras.* þinre (E^{x})] *on eras.* ic (E^{x})] *on eras.* geteorode (E^{x})] *on eras.* on (E^{x})] *on eras.* ðreangum (A)] *orig.* ðreange: u *written above 2nd* e *by glossator,* m *added.* steorum ł on þræwunge ($E^{3/x}$)] steorum ł *on eras. by corr.* on grapunge ł steorum (F)] on grapunge *obscured by eras. but visible.* for (C)] o *interl.* unrihtwisnesse (E^{x})] *on eras.* þu nyrwdest (E^{x})] *on eras.* mæn (E^{3})] *eras. before word.* ⁊ (E^{x})] *on eras.* aswindan ł weorpian (E^{x})] *on eras.* aswarcan ł acwinan ⁊ aydlian ł aswindan (I)] ⁊ aydlian ł aswindan *written in left margin.* þu dydest (I)] y *altered from* i (?). þu didest (E^{x})] *on eras.* swæ swæ ($E^{3/x}$)] *2nd* swæ *on eras. by corr.* gangewæfre (C)] a *interl.* rengan ł attorcoppin (D)] ł attorcoppin *written in left margin in 11th-c. hand,* attorcoppa *also written in right margin as gloss on 1st word of marginal gloss:* Aranea per aera opera sua scrutatur et anima mea per superna etiam precepta. attercoppan (E^{x})] *on eras.* ceosol (K)] *lemma misread for* harenam. sæwle (E^{x})] *on eras.* þahhwæþre (E^{x})] *on eras.* þeahhwæð[ ] (F)] *2 letter fragments visible after* ð, *followed by hole in leaf.* all (E^{x})] *on eras.* ydelnessæ (E^{3})] *eras. before word.* liuiende (E^{3})] *final* e *blotted.*

LTg: A] L: *orig.* a: *altered to* A *by corr.;* a ABCD; á EM; *lost* G. enim] L: *underlined* *by corr. to signal deletion: see GAg.* tuae] tuæ BDL; tuę CEGHJK; tue F. defeci] H: *eras. after word.* Propter] C: p *interl.;* propter GHIJK, L: *orig.* Propter: P *crossed through and* p *added to right.* hominem] hominum J. et] Et GHIJK; E[ ] F: *letter lost due to hole in leaf.* araneam] C: *eras. before word;* aranea A; areanea B: *cf. Weber MSS* SKXβγη moz. eius] eíus K. Uerumtamen] Verumtamen BDL; Veruntamen E, C: *orig.* Verumtamen: *left leg of 1st* m *eras. to form* n; uerumptamen GK; ueruntamen H: *eras. after 1st* n; uerumtamen IJ; uerum[ ]men F: *medial letters lost due to hole in leaf.* uniuersa uanitas] L: *underlined to signal deletion,* uane conturbatur *added interl. by corr.: see GAg.* uiuens] L: *underlined by corr. to signal deletion: see GAg.*

LTu: A] a βνςτ*. fortitudine] fortitudinem β: *orig.* fortitudine: m *added interl. by corr.* tuae] tuę βειλνπφ; tuæ ϑμ; tue ξστ*; tua ς. increpationibus] [ ]repationibus ϑ. Propter] propter δεζϑιλμξοπϱστυφχψ. corripuisti] ϑ: ti *interl.* et] Et δεϑιλμξοπσφχψ. tabescere] β: *orig.* tabescerem: m *crossed through by corr.* fecisti] fęcisti ε. araneam] haraneam ο; haranea β. Uerumtamen] Verumtamen ν; uerumtamen δεζϑμοπϱ; ueruntamen ιλσφ; uerumptamen ξτυ; Uerumptamen ςτ*.

GAg: enim] *om.* FGHIJK, L: *see LTg.* uniuersa] *om.* FGHIJK, L: *see LTg.* uanitas] uane conturbatur FHIJK, L: *see LTg;* uane [ ]turbatur G. uiuens] *om.* FGHIJK, L: *see LTg.*

GAu: enim] *om.* δεζϑλμξοπϱστυχψ. uniuersa] *om.* δεζϑλμξοπϱστυχψ. uanitas] uane conturbatur δεζϑιλμξοπϱστυφχψ. uiuens] *om.* δεζϑιλμξοπϱστυφχψ.

13

Exaudi		geher *A*, gehier *B*, gehyr *CD*F*H*IK, gehir *E*^{3}*J, [ ]r G (*LM*)
deus*		god ACE^3 (*BL*)
orationem	I	gebed ABCDFHIK, gebeda GJ, min E^3* (*M*)
meam	I	min ABCDF*H*IK, mine GJ, bed E^3 (*L*)
(domine)*		driht F, drih GJ, hlaford K
et		⁊ ABCE^{3}FGIJK (*D*)
deprecationem	I	boene AB, bena C, bene FGJ, halsunge ł bene I, gebeda K, mine E^3 (*DM*)
meam	I	mine ABCFGIJK, bene E^3 (*D*)
auribus		mid earum AFGHI, mid earum BDJ, mid eærum E^3, earum C, earan K
percipe		onfoh ABCE^{3}GHJ, anfoh D, onfog I, underfoh F, untyn K (*M*)
lacrimas	I	tearas ABCDFGHIJK, mine E^3*
meas	I	mine ABCDFGHIJK, teæræs E^3
ne		ne ABCDE^3*FGIJ,* na *K* (*HL*)
sileas		swiga ðu ABDF, swiga þu CGJ, swigæ þu E^3, swiga K, suwa þu I

a* from AC*E^3*, from B, fram D (*LM*)
me* me ABCDE^3 (*L*)

Quoniam forðon AB*J*, forþon C*G*, forþæn E^3, forðā *F*, forþi þe *I* (*HK*)
incola* londleod AB, landleod *C*, wræca D, wræcce E^x*, wrecca H, wreocan K, utlende FJ, þearfa ł þearfena G*, elelendisc I
ego ic ABCDE^x*FGHIJK
sum ic eam A, eom BCDE^x*FGHJK, eom I
apud mid *ABC*DE^3FGHIJ, beforan K
te ðe ABF, þe CE^3GHIJ, þan K (*M*)
in* in A, on BCDE^3
terra* eorðan ABCD, eorðæn E^3
et ⁊ ABCDE^3FGHIJK
peregrinus elðeoðig A, elðeodig B, elþeodig CDH, elþidig E^3*, ælðeodig FG, ælþeodig J, ælþeodi K, ælðeodig ł wræcca I (*M*)
sicut swe swe A, swa swa BCDFGHIJ, swæ swæ E^3, swa K
omnes alle A, ealle BCDFGHIJK, eælle E^3
patres | fedras A, fædras BC, fæderas DFGHIJK, mine E^3
mei | mine ACDFGHIJK, ealle B, fedras E^3

ED: et deprecationem meam (D)] *om. Roeder.* á (E)] a *Harsley.* forðon (A)] for ðon *Kuhn.* apud (C)] apu[t] *Wildhagen.* ælðeodig ł wræcca (I)] elðeodig ł wræcca *Lindelöf.* swa swa (GIJ)] swaswa *Rosier, Lindelöf, Oess.*

OE: gehir (E^3)] *orig.* gehire: *final* e *eras.* min (E^3)] *letter eras. after word.* mine (E^3) (*2nd*)] *eras. before word.* wræcce (E^x)] *on eras.* þearfa ł þearfena (G)] ł þearfena *added in diff.* (?) *hand.* ic (E^x)] *on eras.* eom (E^x)] *on eras.* elþidig (E^3)] *2nd* i *actually suspended* i *from lemma.*

LTg: Exaudi] exaudi ABCDEM, L: E *written to left of* e *by corr.;* [ ]xaudi H: *initial* E *lost, outline visible.* deus] L: *underlined by corr. to signal deletion; om.* B: *cf.* *Weber MSS* αβγδ*ηλ moz med, *see GAg.* orationem] oratiônem M. meam (*1st*)] H: *eras. after word,* L: domine *added interl. by corr.: see GAg.* et deprecationem meam] *om.* D, *but added in bottom margin in 12th-c. hand: see note to Ps 2.8* andwaldnesse *for other examples;* et depraecatiônem meam M. percipe] pércipe M. ne] Ne FHIJK, L: *orig.* ne: n *altered to* N *by. corr.;* [ ]e G: *initial* N *lost.* a] L: *underlined by corr. to signal deletion: see GAg;* á EM. me] L: *underlined by corr. to signal deletion: see GAg.* Quoniam] quoniam FGHIJK. incola] íncola C. apud] A: d *on eras.,* C: *orig.* aput: t *altered to* d. te] té M. peregrinus] peregrínus M.

LTu: Exaudi] exaudi βνςτ*. deprecationem] depraecationem βψ; dep̄cationem εθμσυφχ. ne] Ne δεζθιλμξοπρστφχψ. a] β: *added by corr. in left margin.* Quoniam] quoniam δεζθιλμξοπρσφχψ. apud] aput βς.

GAg: deus] *om.* FGHIJK, B: *see LTg; for* L *see LTg.* meam] meam domine FGHJK, I: o *written above* domine, L: *see LTg.* a me] *om.* FGHIJK, L: *see LTg.* incola] aduena FGHIJ, K: *final* a *on eras.* in terra] *om.* FGHIJK.

GAu: deus] *om.* δεζϑιλμξοπϱστυχψ. meam] meam domine δεζϑιλμξοπϱστυφχψ. a me] *om.* δεζϑιμξοπϱστυφχψ. incola] aduena δεζϑιλμξοπϱστυφχψ. in terra] *om.* δεζϑιλμξοπϱστυφχψ.

14

Remitte	forletað *A**, forlæt BDFGHJK, Forlet E³, forlæt ł forgif I, forgyf C
mihi	me ABCD*E*³FGHJK
ut	ðæt A, þæt BF, þæt CDGHIJK, þet E³
refrigerer	ic sie gecoeled A, ic sie gecoled B, ic sy gecelyd C, ic bio æcęled E³, ic si gecylled ł þæt ic si gehyrt G*, ic gecele *D*FK, ic gecelere H, ic gereste ł þæt ic beo aceled I*, ic si gescildig ł ⁊ þæt ic si gehyrt J (*M*)
priusquam	ær ðon AB, ær þon C, ær þam þe DHJ, er þæm þe E³/ˣ*, ær þam þe F*G, ær ðæm þe I, ær þæm K (*M*)
eam*	ic gewite *A*BC, ic gange DEˣ*J, ic ga K, ic habbe G, ic F*, ic gewite ł ær ðan þe ic fare I
et	⁊ ACE³FGHIJK
amplius	męe A, má B, ma CDE³*FGHJKO, siððan I
non	ǀ ic ne ABCDE³FGHIJO, na K
ero	ǀ biom A, beom C, beo BDFGHIJK, bio E³*O

ED: Forlet (E)] forlet *Harsley.* refrigerer (D)] refrigerem *Roeder.* ic gecelere (H)] ic gecele *Campbell.* ær ðon (B)] ærðon *Brenner.* ær þon (C)] ærþon *Wildhagen.* ær þam þe (DHJ)] ærþampe *Roeder;* ærþam þe *Campbell, Oess.* ær þam þe (FG)] ærþam þe *Kimmens, Rosier.* ær þæm (K)] ærþæm *Sisam.* ábeam (I)] abeam *Lindelöf.* non (C)] enon *Wildhagen.*

OE: forletað (A)] *written outside left grid.* ic si gecylled ł þæt ic si gehyrt (G)] ł þæt ic si gehyrt *added in diff. hand.* ic gereste ł þæt ic beo aceled (I)] aceled *interl.* er þæm þe (E³/ˣ)] þe *on eras. by corr.* ær þam þe (F)] *orig.* ær þam þa: *final* a *altered to* e. ic gange (Eˣ)] *on eras.* ic (F)] *see GAg note to* eam. ma (E³)] *orig.* mæ: æ *altered to* a, *eras. before word.* bio (E³)] *eras. after word.*

LTg: Remitte] A: *eras. above word: see OE note to* forletað. mihi] michi E. refrigerer] D *orig.* refrigerem: r *added in 12th-c. hand after* ē (*see note to Ps 2.8* anwaldnesse *for other examples*): *cf. Weber MSS* Sαβγ; refrígêrer M. priusquam] M: *2 letters eras. in right margin and signaled to follow lemma: cf. note to* eam. eam] abeam A: m *added by corr.: cf. Weber MSS* S²γη med, *see GAg.*

LTu: mihi] michi ιλξςτ*τ, πϱ: c *interl.;* m^1 τ*φ. refrigerer] β: *orig.* refrigerem: m *crossed through by corr., final* r *interl.* eam] abeam β: ab *added by corr.: cf. Weber MSS* S^{2}γη med, *see GAu.*

GAg: eam] abeam HJK, A: *see LTg;* ábeam I; abe[ ] F: *hole in leaf after* e; habeam G.

GAu: eam] abeam δεζϑιλοπϱτυφχψ, β: *see LTu;* habeam μξ.

PSALM 39

2

Expectans		bidende *AB,* bidynde *C,* biddende ł geanbidod J, geanbidigende *D*G, Geanbidigende *E*^{3}, geanbidiende *H,* geanbida F, anbidiende I*, anbidigende *K* (*LM*)
expectaui		ic abad ABGJ, ic abád *C,* ic anbad DFHK, ic onbad E^3, ic anbidode I
dominum		dryhten D, drihten FHIK*, drihtnæs E^3, dryhт̄ AB, driħt CG, driħ J
et		⁊ ABCE^3FGIJK
respexit*	ǀ	gelocade A, gelocode BC, he beheold D, beheold K, he begymde FG, he begimde J, he beseh ł he begemde I, me E^3
me*	ǀ	mec A, me BCDFGJK, to me I, forlocede ł he beheold $E^{3/x}$*

ED: EXpectans (A)] EXspectans *Kuhn.* anbidiende (I)] anbidende *Lindelöf.*

OE: anbidiende (I)] *2nd* i *interl.* drihten (K)] n *partly eras.* (?), *possibly ink flaked off.* forlocede ł he beheold ($E^{3/x}$)] ł he beheold *added by corr.*

LTg: Expectans] H: *letter eras. after* x; EXPECTANS E; EXpectans KL, A: *orig.* EXspectans: *faint deleting dot above 1st* s; EXspectans M; [ ]spectans B: *letters lost due to excision of initial from fol. 43v;* EXSPECTANS C; Exspectans D: *1st* s *interl.* expectaui] exspectaui C.

LTu: Expectans] EXPECTANS ιλμνϱτ*τφ, ψ: *orig.* EXSPECTANS; EXPECtans ς; EXpectans χ; EXSPectans β; EXspectans ϑ. expectaui] EXPECTAUI λϱ; EXPECtaui μ; EXpectaui ψ: *orig.* Exspectaui; exspectaui ϑ; EXspectaui ν.

GAg: respexit] intendit FGHIJK. me] mihi FGIJK; michi H.

GAu: respexit] intendit δεζϑιλξοπϱστυφχψ. me] mihi δεζϑοπυχψ; michi ιλσφ, ϱ: c *interl.;* m^1 ξτ.

3

Et	⁊ *ACE*^{3}FGHIJK (*BDLM*)
exaudiuit	geherde A, gehyrde C, gehierde $E^{3/x}$*, he gehyrde DFGHJK, he geherde I, hirde B* (*M*)

deprecationem*	I	boene AB, bene CDFGJK, bena I, mine *E^{3}* (*M*)
meam*	I	minc ABCDFGIJK, bene E^{3}
et		⁊ ACE^{3}FGHIJK (*B*)
eduxit	I	utalaedde A, utalædde J, alædde B*, utgelædde C, he gelædde DFGHI, he lædde K, me E^{3}
me	I	mec A, me BCFGIJK, utgelędde E$^{3/x}$*
de		of ABCDE^{3}FGHIJK
lacu		seaðe ABCDFGHJ, seæþe E^{3}, seaþe I, seþe K
miseriae		ermða A, ermðe *B,* yrmðe *CDFGIK,* yrmþe *HJ,* yrmðæ *E^{3}** (*L*)
et		⁊ ABCE^{x}*FGHIJK
de		of ABCDE^{3}FGHIJK
luto		lame ABCJ, fenne DE^{x}*HIK, fénne F, fænne G
fecis		derstan A, dærstan BC, drosna DE^{x}*HK, drósna F, drosnan I, dide ł geworhte J
Et		⁊ ABCE^{3}FGHIJK (D*)
statuit		sette ABJ, gesette C, he gesette DE$^{3/x}$*FGHI, he sæt K
supra	I	ofer ABD*FGH*I**J*K,* ofyr C, mine E^{3}
petram	I	stan ABCDFGHJK, stane I, fet E^{3}
pedes	I	foet AB, fet CDFGHIJK, ofer E^{3}
meos	I	mine ABCDFGHIJK, stǽn E^{3}
et		⁊ ABCE^{3}FGHIJK
direxit		gerechte A*, gerehte BCE^{3}JK, he gerehte CFGH*, he gerehte ł ⁊ he gerihtlæhte I*
gressus	I	gongas ABC, gangas J, stæpas DFGH, stæppas K, stæpas ł færeldu I*, mine E^{3}
meos		mine *A*BCDFGHIJK, stapæs E^{3}*

ED: dep̄cationem (E)] deprecationem *Harsley.* supra (B)] super *Brenner.* ofer (I)] ofor *Lindelöf.* gerechte (A)] gerec hte *Kuhn.*

OE: gehierde (E$^{3/x}$)] *orig.* gehierð: *cross-stroke of* ð *eras.,* e *added by corr.* hirde (B)] *possibly initial* ge *lost due to excision of initial from fol. 43v.* alædde (B)] *impossible to tell if* ut *preceded word, since hole from excised initial extends to before gloss.* utgelędde (E$^{3/x}$)] de *by corr.* yrmðæ (E^{3})] *eras. before word.* ⁊ (E^{x}) (*3rd*)] *on eras.* fenne (E^{x})] *on eras.* drosna (E^{x})] *on eras.* Et (*2nd*)] D: [ ]gnes / [ ]am (> [an]gnes[s]am?) *written in 11th-c. hand in left margin as gloss on* erumnis *in marginal commentary: cf. Ps 43.19, where* [an]gnessum *glosses* in erumnis *in marginal commentary.* he gesette (E$^{3/x}$)] he *by corr.* ofer (I)] *orig.* ofor: *2nd* o *altered to* e. gerechte (A)] *eras.* (*3 letters?*) *after* c. he gerehte (H)] ge *interl.* he gerehte ł ⁊ he gerihtlæhte (I)] *1st* he *interl.* stæpas ł færeldu (I)] ł færeldu *written in right margin.* stapæs (E^{3})] *orig.* stepæs: e *altered to* a.

LTg: Et (*1st*)] et ACDELM; [ ] B: *lost due to excision of initial from fol. 43v.* exaudiuit] exaudîuit M. deprecationem] depraecatiônem M; dep̄cationem E. et (*1st*)] [ ]t B: e *mostly lost due to excision of initial* (*fol. 43v*). miseriae] miseriæ BL; mis̀erię CDFGHJK; miserie E. supra] F: *orig.* super: ra *added interl. by corr.*, H: *orig.* super: *cross-stroke through descender of* p *eras.*, ra *interl.*, K: *eras. after* p, ra *abbreviation added by corr.* meos (*2nd*)] A: o *on eras.*

LTu: Et (*1st*)] et βϑνςτ*. deprecationem] depręcationem β. miseriae] miserię βενξϱυφ; misseriæ ϑ; miserie ισςτ*τ. fecis] faecis μ. supra] super βχ.

GAg: deprecationem] preces FGHIJK. meam] meas FGHIJK.

GAu: deprecationem] preces δζϑξοπϱστψ; praeces εμ; pręces λ; p̄ces υφχ. meam] meas δεζϑλμξοπϱστυφψ.

4

Et		ㄱ *ABCE^{3}*FGHIJK (*DLM*)
inmisit		insende A, onsende BCK, he onsende DF*H*, he onsænde J, he ondsende E$^{3/x}$*, he onasende I, he onsette G (*M*)
in		in A, on BCDE^{3}FGHIJK
os	|	muð *ABDGJK*, muþ H, muðe *C*I, muþe F, mine *E^{3}* (*M*)
meum	|	minne AB*GHJ, minne D, minum CIK, minum F, múð E^{3}*
canticum	|	song AB, sang CK, sang ł cantic J, cantic DGH, canticc F, lofsang I, niwne E^{3}
nouum	|	niowne A, niwne BCDGHIK, nywne FJ, song E^{3}
hymnum*		ymen ABD, ymynsang *C,* leoð FI, lofsang GK, mid flæsce J, and ymnæd *E^{3}**
deo	|	gode ABCFGHIJK, gode D, urum E^{3}
nostro	|	urum *A*BCDFGI, urum H, ure JK, gode E^{3}
Uidebunt	|	gesioð A, geseoð *BC*GIJ*,* geseoð *D,* geseoþ *H,* we geseoð F, gesegan *K,* Monegæ *E^{3}*
multi	|	monge AB, mænige CG, monige D, monige HJ, manige F, manege I, maniga K, gesioð E^{3}
et		ㄱ ABCE^{3}FGHIJK
timebunt		ondredað A, ondrædað BCDGH, ondrædaþ FJ, ondredæþ E^{3}, hig ondrædaþ I*, ondredan K
et		ㄱ ABCE^{3}FGIJK
sperabunt		gehyhtað ABD, gehihtað CGH, gehihtaþ J, gewenæþ ł gehihtað E$^{3/x}$*, hihtað ł ㄱ hig hopiað I, hihttan K (*F*)
in		in A, on BCE^{x}FGIJK
domino		dryhtne B, drihtne CFI, drihten E^{3}K, dryhт̄ A, driht́ G, drih́ J

ED: [ ]t (G)] Et *Rosier.* ós (AE)] os *Kuhn, Harsley.* spera(b)[ ]t (F)] sperabunt *Kimmens.* drihtne (I)] drihten *Lindelöf* (*but correct in appendix, p. 323*).

OE: he ondsende (E$^{3/x}$)] he *added by corr.,* ⁊ *eras. before* ondsende. minne (B)] *2nd* n *interl.* múð (E^{3})] *accent light.* and ymnæd (E^{3})] *orig.* ond ymnæd: o *altered to* a. geseoð (C)] s *malformed.* geseoð (J)] *eras. after 1st* e. hig ondrædaþ (I)] i *on eras.* gewenæþ ł gehihtað (E$^{3/x}$)] ł gehihtað *added by corr.*

LTg: Et] [ ]t G: *initial* E *lost;* et ABCDELM. inmisit] H: *initial* i *interl.,* M: *otiose mark above* m. os] ós ACDEKM. hymnum] ymnum CE. nostro] A: stro *by corr.* Uidebunt] Videbunt BDEHIJK; [ ]idebunt G: *initial* V *lost.* sperabunt] spera(b)[ ]t F: *letters lost due to hole in leaf: fragments of* b, *minim before* t, *and letter fragment of gloss visible.*

LTu: Et] et βςτ*. inmisit] immisit ειφ, ο: *orig.* inmisit: *initial* i *interl.,* n *altered to* m. hymnum] ymnum βτ*. deo] do ζ: *suspension mark wanting.* Uidebunt] Videbunt ινξοσφ; Videnbunt ε.

GAg: hymnum] carmen FGHIJK.

GAu: hymnum] carmen δεζϑιλμξοπϱστυφχψ.

5

Beatus eadig ABCDFGHI*J, Eædi E^{3}, eadi K (*M*)
uir wer ABC*DE^{3}FGHIJK
cuius ðes A, ðæs B, þæs CJK, þæs ðe D, þæs þe FHI, þes ðe E$^{3/x}$*, þær þe G
est | is ABDFGHIJ*K,* ys C, næma E^{3}
nomen | noma AB, nama CDFGHI, naman JK, is E^{3}
domini drylitnes B, drihtnys C, drihtnes E^{3}FI, drihtenes K, dryht̄ A, driħt G, driħ J
spes | hyht ABDH, hiht CFGIJK, his E^{3}
eius* | his ABCD*F*GHIJ*K,* hiht E^{3}*
et ⁊ ABCDE^{3}FGIJK
non | ne ABCGJ, na DE^{x}*FHK, he ne I
respexit | gelocað ABC, gelocode J, beseah DGHIK, beseah ł locæde E$^{3/x}$*, beheold F
in in A, on BCDE^{3}FGHIJK
uanitatem* idelnisse A, idelnesse *B*GJ, idylnysse *C,* idelnissa *D,* ydelnesse *E^{3},* ydelnysse F, ydelnessa H, idelnese K, idelnyssum I (*LM*)
et ⁊ ABCE^{3}FGIJK
in* in A, on BCE^{3}*J (*D*)
insanias woedenheortnisse A, wedenheortnessa B, wedynheortnysse *C,*

swæceheow DH, on spæceheow F, wedendum E^{3}, on gewitleastum *G*, on wodnessum I, wændan J, on hwispræce K
falsas | lease ABDFGHK, liese C, leæsingum E^{3}, leasum ł gewitlystum̲ I*, þa leasan J

ED: ei(u)s (F)] eius *Kimmens*.

OE: eadig (I)] is *written in left margin*. wer (C)] *descender of* r *written over what appears to be beginning of another letter*. þes ðe (E$^{3/x}$)] ðe *added by corr*. hiht (E^{3})] *in darker ink*, ht *on eras. by corr*. na (E^{x})] *on eras*. beseah ł locæde (E$^{3/x}$)] beseah ł *added by corr*. on (E^{3}) (*2nd*)] *eras. after word*. leasum ł gewitlystum̲ (I)] ł gewitlystum̲ *written above* leasum.

LTg: Beatus] Beâtus M. est] ést K. eius] eíus K; ei(u)s F: *right leg of* u *and top of* s *lost due to hole in leaf*. uanitatem] uanitate B: *cf. Weber MSS* S*X moz^{x}; uanitates CDEL, M: s *added by corr*.: *cf. Weber MSS* αβγδη moz^{c} med, *see GAg*. in (*2nd*)] *om*. D: *cf. Weber MSS* αβδη moz med, *see GAg*. insanias] C: in *on eras*.; i(n)sanias G: *right left of 1st* n *lost*.

LTu: uanitatem] uanitates ντ*, β: *orig*. uanitate: s *added interl. by corr*.: *cf. Weber MSS* αβγδη moz^{c} med, *see GAg*. in (*2nd*)] β: *added interl. by corr*.; *eras*. ν; *om*. ς: *see GAg*.

GAg: uanitatem] uanitates FGHIJK, CDELM: *see LTg*. in (*2nd*)] *om*. FGHIK, D: *see LTg*.

GAu: eius] ipsius ϑ. uanitatem] uanitates δεζϑιλμξοπϱστφψ, χ: te *interl*., βντ*: *see LTg*; uanitate υ. in (*2nd*)] *om*. δεζϑιλμξοπϱστυφχψ, ς: *see LTg*; *for* ν *see LTg*.

6

Multa — feolu A, fela BCDFGHJ, feala I, Monegæ E^{3}, maniga K
fecisti | ðu dydes A, þu dydes B, þu dydest FGH, dydyst C, dydest I*K, didest J, þu DE^{3}
tu | ðu ABF, þu CGHIJK, dydest D*E$^{3/x}$**
domine — drihten E^{3}I*, dryht̄ AB, driħt CFG, driħ J
deus | god ABCFGJK, min E^{3}I
meus | min ABCFGJK, god E^{3}I
mirabilia | wundur ABC, wundor J, wunder K, wundru DH, wundra FI, wuldra G, þinræ E^{3}
tua | ðin A, þin CJK, ðine F, þine G*I*, wundræ E^{3} (*H*)
et — ⁊ ABCE^{3}FGHIJK
cogitationibus | geðohtum AI, geðohtum̲ B, geþohtum CFGHJ, geþohtum̲ D, geþancas K*, þinum E^{3} (*M*)
tuis | ðinum AF, ðinum̲ B, þinum CG, þinum̲ DHJ, on þinum I, þine K, geþohtum E^{3}

non	I	nis AH, nys F, ⁊ nis I, ne BJ, na CDE^{x}*K, nan G
est	I	is BDE^{3}GJ*K*, ys C
quis*		hwelc ABDE^{x}*H, hwylc CFG, hwilc I*J*, hyl K
similis	I	gelic ABDE^{3}GHIJK, ys gelice C, is F
(sit)*	I	gelic F, sy GIJ, si H, bið K
tibi		ðe ABF, þe CDE^{x}GHJK, þe se þe si gelic þe I*
Adnuntiaui		ic segde *AB,* ic sægde *C,* ic sæde J, ic cyþde *DH,* Ic cyþde $E^{3/x}$*, ic cyþe F, ic cydde *G,* ic forekydde *I,* ic bodode K
et		⁊ ABCDE^{3}FGHIJK
locutus	I	spreocende A, sprecende B*I*J, sprecynde C, specende K, ic sprec D, ic spræc FG*H,* ic eom E^{3}
sum	I	ic eam A, ic eom BCJ, ic eom ł ⁊ ic spræc I, eom K, sprecende *E*^{3}
⟨et⟩		⁊ *E*^{3}
multiplicati		gemonigfaldade A, gemonigfaldode B, gemonifældode E^{3}, gemonigfealdode J, gemænigfealdode C*, gemęnigfylde D, gemænigfylde FG*HI, gemænifælde K (*M*)
sunt		sind A, sint B, synd CDFGHJK, hi synt I, sien E^{3}*
super		ofer ABDE^{3}FGHIJK, ofyr C
numerum		rim AB, getel ł gerim C, getæl ł gerim J, getela ł gerím F, gerim DGH, gerim̲ K, gerym E^{3}*, getele I

ED: tú (E)] tu *Harsley.* þe se þe si gelic þe (I)] þe ł se þe si gelic þe *Lindelöf.* Annuntiaui (C)] A[d]nuntiaui *Wildhagen.* ic eom ł ⁊ ic spræc (I)] ic eom ł ic spræc *Lindelöf.*

OE: dydest (I)] y *altered from* i (?). dydest ($E^{3/x}$)] *orig.* dydes: t *added by corr.* drihten (I)] o *written before word.* geþancas (K)] þu *eras. after* ge. na (E^{x})] *on eras.* hwelc (E^{x})] *on eras.* þe se þe si gelic þe (I)] se þe si gelic þe *written in right margin.* Ic cyþde ($E^{3/x}$)] de *on eras. by corr.* gemænigfealdode (C)] o *malformed.* gemænigfylde (G)] *otiose mark after* y. sien (E^{3})] *orig.* sient: t *eras.* gerym (E^{3})] *letter eras. after* e.

LTg: tu] tú E. tua] I: *stray* n *in left margin.* tua] H: *9 small pen-strokes after word.* cogitationibus] cogitatiônibus M. est] ést K. quis] J: s *interl.* Adnuntiaui] [ ]dnuntiaui G: *initial* A *lost;* Annuntiaui ABDI, C: *1st* n *on eras. by corr.,* H: *1st* n *on eras.* locutus] loqutus H: q *possibly altered from* c; loquutus I. sum] sum et E: et (*as* ⁊) *added in left margin: cf. Weber MS* M. multiplicati] M: *eras. before word.*

LTu: Adnuntiaui] Annuntiaui εζλξπϱστ*τυχ, o: *orig.* Adnuntiaui; Annunciaui φ. sum] sum et τ*.

GAg: quis] qui FI, H: *eras. after word.* similis] similis sit FGHIK, J: sit *on eras.*

GAu: quis] qui ειστχ, ψ: *orig.* quis. similis] similis sit δεζϑιλμξοπϱστυφχψ.

7

Sacrificium		onsegdnisse *A,* onsægdnesse *B*GH, onsægdnysse *C,* onsægdnisse *D,* onsegidnisse *$E^{3/x}$*,* onsægednyssa F, onsægednesse JK, ofrunge I (*LM*)
et		⁊ ABCE^{3}FGHIJK
oblationem		onsegdnisse A, onsægdnysse I, ofrunge B, ofrunga FJ, ofrung K, ofrunge ɫ oflętan D, oflætan ɫ offrunga G, oflætan C, ofletan H, tobrengnesse ɫ ofrunge $E^{3/x}$*
noluisti		naldes ðu A, noldyst þu C, þu noldes B, þu noldest D*G*HJK, ðu noldest $E^{3/x}$*, þu noldyst I, þu nol[ ] *F**
corpus*	I	lichoman ABD, lichama C, licaman ɫ earan I*, earan FGJK, soðlice E^{3} (*L*)
autem	I	soðlice ABCGH, soþlice DFJ, witodlice K, lichomon E^{3}*
perfecisti	I	ðu gefremedes *A,* þu gefremedes B, þu gefremydyst C, þu gefremodest J, þu fulfremedest DFGH, þu sealdest ɫ ðu fulfremedest I, fulfremedest K, þu me E^{3}*
mihi	I	me AB*C*DFGHIJK, fulfremedest *$E^{3/x}$**
Holocausta*	I	onsegdnisse A, onsægdnessa B, onsægdnysse C, ansægdnissa D, onsægednyssa F, onsægednesse JK, onsæignesse G, onsægnissa H, ofrunge I, Eæc swilce E^{3} (*L*)
etiam*	I	ec swelce A, eac swelce BD, iec swylce *C,* ⁊ FGJK, ansægidnisse ɫ offrunge $E^{3/x}$* (*L*)
pro		fore ABE^{3}, for CDFGIJK
delicto*		scylde ABC, scyld<u>e</u> D, scyld ɫ gylt E^{x}*, scilde ɫ for sinne J, synne FGI, synnan K (*M*)
non	I	ðu ne A, þu ne BCI, na DE^{x}FGHJK
postulasti	I	bede A, bæde BCIK, þu bæde DGH, þu bede E^{3}, ðu ne bæde F, þu ne bæde J

ED: Sacrificium (G)] *S*acrificium *Rosier.* nolui[ ] (F)] noluis-- *Kimmens.* þu noldest (G)] þu nolde *Rosier.*

OE: onsegidnisse ($E^{3/x}$)] egi *retraced,* dnisse *on eras. by corr.* tobrengnesse ɫ ofrunge ($E^{3/x}$)] ɫ ofrunge *added by corr.* ðu noldest ($E^{3/x}$)] *orig.* ðu noldes: t *added by corr.* þu nol[ ] (F)] *letters lost after* l *due to hole in leaf.* licaman ɫ earan (I)] i<u>d</u> <u>est</u> corpus *written interl. by glossator.* lichomon (E^{3})] *gloss eras. before word.* þu me (E^{3})] *eras. before* þu. fulfremedest ($E^{3/x}$)] *orig.* fulfremedes: t *added by corr.* ansægidnisse ł offrunge (E[3/x])] ansægidnisse ł *added by corr.* scyld ł gylt (E[x])] scyld *added by one corr.*, ł gylt *added by another on eras.*

LTg: Sacrificium] L: *orig.* sacrificium: S *added before* s *by corr.;* sacrificium ABCDEM. noluisti] nolui[ ] F: *letters lost after* i *due to hole in leaf, letter fragment visible after* i; nolu[ ] G. corpus] L: *underlined to signal deletion,* aures *added interl. by corr.: see GAg.* perfecisti] A: er *interl. by corr., although cross-stroke through descender of* p (= per) *not eras.* mihi] michi E, C: *orig.* mihi: c *interl. by corr.* Holocausta] Holocaustum L: *cf. Weber MSS* δ*η, *see GAg.* etiam] C: *eras. after* t, L: iam *underlined to signal deletion: see GAg.* delicto] M: *orig.* dilicto: *1st* i *altered to* e, i *on eras., possibly altered from another letter.*

LTu: Sacrificium] sacrificium βνς. mihi] michi ιλξσςτ*τ, ϱ: c *interl.* Holocausta] [ ]olocausta τ*: *initial wanting.*

GAg: corpus] aures FGHIJK. Holocausta] Holocaustum FHIK, L: *see LTg;* [ ]olocaustum G: *initial* H *lost;* Holochaustum J. etiam] et FGHIJK, L: *see LTg.* delicto] peccato FGHIJK.

GAu: corpus] aures δεζϑιλμξοπϱστυφχψ. Holocausta] Holocaustum δεζιλμξοπϱτυφχψ; Holachaustum ϑ; Olocaustum σ. etiam] et δεζϑιλμξοπϱσφχψ. delicto] peccato δεζϑιλμξοπϱστυφχψ.

8

tunc	ða A, þa BC, þonne DHJ, þonne E[3]FG, ðonne ł þa I, þænne K
dixi	ic cweð A, ic cwæð BC, ic cwæþ IJK, ic sægde D, ic sædge E[x]*, ic sæde FGH
ecce	sehðe AB, efne nu C, efne FGIJK, on gesihðe D, on gesihðe E[x]*, onsæde H
uenio	ic cumu A, ic cume BCDE[3]FGHIJK
In	in A, on BCDF*G*HIJK, On E[3]
capite	heafde ABDFGH, hæfade C*, heæfde E[3], eafde J, heafod K, forewerd I (*M*)
libri	boec AB, boc F, bec C, béc J, boces DGH, bocan K*, þere boces E[3/x]*, þære boc ł on heafde bæc I*
scriptum	awriten ABDE[3]GHIJ, awrityn C, gewriten FK
est	is ABDE[3]FGHIJ*K*, ys C
de	bi AB, be CDE[3]FGHIJ, of K
me	me ABCDE[3]FGHIJK

ED: efne nu (C)] efnenu *Wildhagen.* In (BG)] in *Brenner; In Rosier.* on (G)] *no gloss Rosier.* heafde (G)] *no gloss Rosier.*

OE: ic sædge (E^{x})] *on eras.* on gesihðe (E^{x})] *on eras.* hæfade (C)] a *interl.* bocan (K)] *orig.* bonan: *attempt made to alter letter, but remains malformed.* þere boces (E$^{3/x}$)] *orig.* þere boce: s *added by corr.* þære boc ł on heafde bæc (I)] ł on heafde bæc *written in left margin.*

LTg: In] G: *top of* I *partly lost.* capite] cápite M. est] ést K.

LTu: libri] β: *added by corr. in left margin.*

9

ut		ðæt A, þæt BG, þæt CDFHJK, þet E^{3}
faciam*		ic doe *A*, ic dó BE^{3}, ic doó C, ic do DFGHJ, don K, [ ]c geworhte I*
uoluntatem	|	willan AB*C*DFGHIJK, þinne E^{3}
tuam	|	ðinne A, þinne BCFG*I*JK, þinne D, þinre H, willæn E^{3}
deus	|	god ABCFGHJK, min E^{3}, eala þu min I
meus	|	min ABCGJK, minne F, god E^{3}I (*H*)
uolui		ic walde A, ic wolde BDE$^{3/x}$*FGHIJK, ic wylle C
et		⁊ ABCDE^{3}FGHIJK
legem	|	æ *A*BCIJK, ęe D, ǽ F, ææ G, æe H, þine E^{3}*
tuam	|	ðine ABF, þine DIJK, þin CG, ǽé ł ewe E$^{3/x}$* (*H*)
in		in A, on BCDE^{3}FGHIJK
medio		midle ABCJ, middele DFGH, midre E^{3}, middan IK
cordis	|	heortan ABCDFGHIJ, heorta K, minre E^{3}
mei	|	minre ABDI*JK, mine CFG, (m)ine *H**, heortæn E^{3}

ED: [ ]c geworhte (I)] ic geworhte *Lindelöf.* ææ (G)] æ æ *Rosier.* (m)ei (H)] mei *Campbell.* (m)ine (H)] mine *Campbell.*

OE: [ ]c geworhte (I)] *written in left margin, letter lost in trimming, orig. interl. gloss eras.* ic wolde (E$^{3/x}$)] wolde *on eras. by corr.* þine (E^{3})] ne *retraced in darker ink.* ǽé ł ewe (E$^{3/x}$)] ǽé ł *on eras. by corr.* minre (I)] s. posui : ⁊ ic gesette *written in left margin.* (m)ine (H)] *left leg of* m *lost due to hole in leaf.*

LTg: faciam] A: m *added by corr.* uoluntatem] C: n *on eras.* tuam (*1st*)] I: *eras. after word.* meus] H: *interl. by glossator.* legem] A: m *added by corr.* tuam (*2nd*)] H: *lost due to hole in leaf.* mei] (m)ei H: *left leg of* m *lost due to hole in leaf.*

LTu: meus] *interl.* δ.

GAg: faciam] facerem FGHIJK.

GAu: faciam] facerem δεζθιλμξοπρστυφχψ.

10

Bene*		wel ABCD, Wel E^{3}

nuntiaui*		ic segde A, ic sægde B*C*, ic sæde ł ic bodige J, ic bodude DE$^{3/x}$*FGH, ic bodode IK
iustitiam	|	rehtwisnisse A, ryhtwisnesse BD, rihtwisnysse *C*FI, rihtwisnesse GHJ, rihtwisnes K, þine E^{3}
tuam	|	ðine AB, þine CDFGIJK, þinre H, ryhtwisnesse E^{x}*
in		in A, on BCDE^{3}FGIJK
ecclesia	|	cirican AJ, cyricean C, cercean F, crcan *B,* haligre ge̲som̲nunga D, somnunga K, gelaðunge ł cyrican *G,* gelaðunge I, þere miclæn *E^{3}* (*H*)
magna	|	micelre ABDFGJ, micylre C, myclre I*, mycelre K, cierceæn E^{3}*
ecce		sehðe AB, efne nu C, efne FIJK, on ge̲sihðe̲ D, on gesihðe H, geseoh þe G, eællæ E^{3}
labia	|	weolure A, weleras B*DFGHIJ, welyras C, lippan K, mine E^{3}
mea	|	mine A*BCDGHIJK weleræs E^{3}
non	|	ic ne ABCE^{3}IJ, na DFK, ne G, [ ]a H*
prohibebo	|	biwergu A, biwerge B, bewerige *C,* beweriwe J, bewerie ł forbeode E$^{3/x}$*, ic forbeode D**FGH,* forbeode I, ic forbead K (*M*)
domine		dryhten *A,* drihten *E^{3},* dryht̄ *B,* driħt *C*FG, driħ J, hlaford K (*DILM*)
tu		ðu AB, þu CE^{3}FIJK, þu þe G
cognouisti*		oncneowe AB, oncnewe E^{3}, ancneowe D, gecnewe C, wistest FI, ealle þing wast G, wast JK

ED: nunciaui (C)] nun[t]iaui *Wildhagen.* Wel ic bodude (E)] Welic bodude *Harsley.* iusticiam (C)] iusti[t]iam *Harsley.* ęcclesia (E)] ecclesia *Harsley.* efne nu (C)] efnenu *Wildhagen.* on gesihðe (H)] ongesihðe *Campbell.* weleras (B)] weloras *Brenner.* [ ]a (H)] (n)a *Campbell.*

OE: ic bodude (E$^{3/x}$)] bodude *on eras. by corr.* ryhtwisnesse (E^{x})] *on eras.* myclre (I)] y *altered from* i (?). cierceæn (E^{3})] *2nd* e *blotted.* weleras (B)] *eye of 1st* e *filled in, possibly an* o. mine (A)] *orig.* minne: *deleting dot above 1st* n. [ ]a (H)] *initial letter lost due to hole in leaf.* bewerie ł forbeode (E$^{3/x}$)] ł forbeode *added by corr.* ic forbeode (D)] *eras. after* ic.

LTg: nuntiaui] nunciaui C: *orig.* nuntiaui: t *altered to* c. iustitiam] iusticiam C: *orig.* iustitiam: *2nd* t *altered to* c. ecclesia] æcclæsia B; ęcclesia EGH. prohibebo] F: h *interl.;* proibebo CH; prohibêbo M. domine] I: o *written above word;* Domine ABCDELM

LTu: nuntiaui] nunciaui τ*. iustitiam] iusticiam τ*τφ. ecclesia] ęcclesia εινοπφχψ; æcclesia ϑ; aecclesia λϱςυ. mea] ς: a *interl.* prohibebo] proibebo β: *orig.* preibebo: *1st* e *crossed through,* o *written above by corr.* domine] Domine βνςτ*.

GAg: Bene] *om.* FGHIJK. nuntiaui] Adnuntiaui FGJ; Annuntiaui I, H: *1st* n *on eras.*, K: *orig.* Adnuntiaui: d *deleted by subscript dot,* n *interl.* cognouisti] scisti FGHIJK.

GAu: Bene] *om.* δεζϑιλμξοπϱστυφχψ. nuntiaui] Adnuntiaui δϑμψ; Annuntiaui εζιλξπϱστυχ, ο: *orig.* Adnuntiaui; Annunciaui φ. cognouisti] scisti δεζϑιλμξοπϱστυφχψ.

11

Iustitiam	I	rehtwinisse *A,* rehtwisnesse *B,* rihtwisnysse *C*FI, ryhtwisnesse *D,* rihtwisnesse GHJ, rihtwisnes K, þine *E^{3}* (*LM*)
tuam	I	ðine A, þine BCDFGHIJK, rihtwisnesse E^{x}*
non	I	ic ne ABCI, ic na J, na DE^{x}*FHK, ne G
abscondi	I	ahydde *A*BC, ahide J, ic behydde DFGH, behydde I, ic hydde K, ic gehydde E^{3}*
in		in A, on BCDE^{3}FGHIJ*K*
corde	I	heortan ABCDFGHIJK, minre E^{3}
meo	I	minre ABCDGHIJK, mine F, heortæn E^{3}
ueritatem	I	soðfestnisse A, soðfæstnesse BG, soðfæstnysse CFI, soþfæstnisse D, soðfæstnisse H*, soþfæstnesse J, soþfæstnes K, þine E^{3}
tuam	I	ðine A, þine BCFIJ, þinre G, þinne H*, þin K, soðfestnesse E^{3}
et		⁊ ABCE^{3}FGHIJK
salutare	I	haelu *A,* hælo BDGHI*J, hæle CFK, þine E^{3}
tuum	I	ðine A, þine BCDFJK, þinre GH, þine ł þinne halwend[ ]n I*, helo E^{3}
dixi		ic segde A, ic sægde B, ic sæde CDIJ, ic cwæð DG*H*K, ic cweð E^{3}*
Non	I	ne ABCGJ, na DFHK, Ic ne E^{3}
celaui*	I	hel ic AB, hæl ic *C,* hæl ic ł ic ne dyrnde ic J*, ic hydde DK, ic ne behydde F, ic behydde GH, behydde $E^{3/x}$*
misericordiam	I	mildheortnisse A, mildheortnesse BDGHJK, mildheortnysse CFI, þine E^{3}
tuam	I	ðine ABF, þine CDIJK, þinre GH, mildheortnesse E^{3}
et		⁊ ABCE^{3}FGHJK
ueritatem	I	soðfestnisse *A,* soðfæstnesse BGHK, soðfæstnysse C, soþfæstnisse D, soþfæstnysse F, soþfæstnesse J, þine E^{3}
tuam	I	ðine AF, þine BCDJ, þinre GHK, ⁊ þine I, soþfestnesse E^{3}
a		from AE^{3}, from B, fram CDFHJ, fram GI, fam K (*M*)
synagoga*	I	gesomnunge AB, gesomnunga *D,* gesamnunge C, somnunga K, gesomnunge ł gegaderunge J*, gegaderunge F, geþeahte GI, þeahte H, micelræ E^{3}

multa* | micelre ABDGHJ, micylre C, mycelre FK, miclum I, gemotstowe ł gesom̲nunga E[3/x]*

ED: iusticiam (C)] iusti[t]iam *Wildhagen.* salutare (A)] salutarem *Kuhn.* tuum (G)] tuu*m* *Rosier.* hælo þine ł þinne halwend[ ]n (I)] hælo þine ł þinne halwendan *Lindelöf.*

OE: rihtwisnesse (E[x])] *on eras.* na (E[x])] *on eras.* ic gehydde (E[3])] *eras. after* ic. soðfæstnisse (H)] *small eras. before word.* þinne (H)] *orig.* þinre: r *altered to* n. hælo þine ł þinne halwend[ ]n (I)] *scribe orig. wrote* hælo þinne, *then added* ł *and wrote* halwend[ ]n þine *in right margin, with* þine *in line above; letter after* d *obscured by sewing.* ic cweð (E[3])] e *blotted,* e *eras. after* cweð. hæl ic ł ic ne dyrnde ic (J)] *2nd* n *interl.* behydde (E[3/x])] hydde *on eras. by corr.* g̲e̲som̲nunge ł gegaderunge (J)] gegaderunge *written above* fram̲ g̲e̲som̲nunge ł. gemotstowe ł gesom̲nunga (E[3/x])] stowe *on eras. by corr.,* ł gesom̲nunga *added by corr. on next line.*

LTg: Iustitiam] iustitiam ABDLM, E: *eras. before word;* iusticiam C: *orig.* iustitiam: *2nd* t *altered to* c. abscondi] A: n *by corr.* in] n K. salutare] A: *orig.* salutarem: *fine stroke through* m *by corr.: cf. Weber MSS* βγ. dixi] H: *eras. after word.* celaui] cęlaui C. ueritatem *(2nd)*] A: m *by corr.* a] á M. synagoga] sinagoga D.

LTu: Iustitiam] iustitiam βνς; iusticiam τ*τφ. celaui] cęlaui ς. misericordiam] missericordiam ϑ. synagoga] β: *orig.* sinagoga: i *crossed through by corr.,* y *interl.;* sinagoga τ*.

GAg: celaui] abscondi FGHIJK. synagoga] concilio FGHIJK. multa] multo GHIJK, F: *orig.* multa: a *altered to* o.

GAu: celaui] abscondi δεζϑιλμξοπϱστυφχψ. synagoga multa] concilio multo δεζϑιλμξοπϱστυφχψ.

12

Tu | ðu ABE[3], þu CFGIJK (*D*)
autem | soðlice ABCE[3]G, soþlice FJ, witodlice IK
domine | drihten E[3], dryht̄ AB, driht CFG, drih J (*I*)
ne | nales AB, nalys C, nalæs J, na DFK, ne E[3]GHI
longe | feor ABDGHJK, feorr CF, afyrsa I, do þu *E[3]*
facias | doa ðu A, do þu BJ, þu do DFGH, do K, feorr C, fior E[3]
misericordias* | mildheortnisse A, mildheortnessa B, mildheortnyssa CF, mildheortnesse D, miltsunga G, mildsunga IK, mildsunge J, þine E[3]
tuas | ðine A, þine CGIJK, ðina B, þina D, mildheortnesse E[3]
a | frome *AE[3]*, from̲ B, fram̲ CDFGJ, fram HIK (*M*)
me | me BCDE[3]FGHIJK (*A*)
misericordia | mildheortnis A, mildheortnes BGK, mildheortnys CI, mildheortnis DH, mildheortnyssa F, mildheortnesse J, þine E[3]*

tua	|	ðin AB, þin CDGHIJK, mildheortnesse E^3
et		⁊ ABCE^3FGHIJK
ueritas	|	soðfestnis A, soðfæstnes *B*GI, soðfæstnys C, soþfæstnis D, soþfæstnys F, soþfæstnes K, soðfæst H, soþfæstnesse J, þine E^3
tua	|	ðin AB, þin CDFGHIK, þine J, soðfestnessæ E^3
semper		aa A, simle BE^3, symle CDHJ, symble FGI, æfre K
susceperunt	|	onfengun *A,* onfengon BCI, onfenc J, hy afengon DGH, hi afengon F, anfengan K, hy me $E^{3/x}$* (*M*)
me	|	me ABCDFGHJK, onfengon E^3 (*M*)

ED: miltsunga (G)] miltsunge *Rosier.* á (E)] a *Harsley.*

OE: þine (E^3) (*2nd*)] ⁊ *eras. before word.* hy me ($E^{3/x}$)] hy *added by corr.*

LTg: Tu] D: u *on eras.* domine] I: o *written above word.* longe] E: *eras. before word.* a] á EM. me (*1st*)] A: *2 dots* (:) *to right of* e. susceperunt] M: *small eras. above and below 1st* e; susciperunt A. me (*2nd*)] M: *eras. after word.*

LTu: Tu] TU β. ne longe] ne e longe ϑ: *cf. Weber MSS* ζ med. misericordia] missericordia ϑ. semper] *om.* ς. susceperunt] susciperunt ϑ.

GAg: misericordias] miserationes FGHIJK.

GAu: misericordias] miserationes δεζϑιλμξοπϱστυφχψ.

13

Quoniam		forðon AB, forþon CJ, Forðæn E^3, forðan ðe F, forðan þe I, forþam þe *G*
circumdederunt	|	ymbsaldon A, ymbsealdon B*C*DFG*H*J, ymbesealdon K, ymsettun ł ymbsealdon I, me *E^3*
me	|	me ABCFGHIJK, ymbseældon E^3
mala		yfel ABE^3G, yflu CI, yfelu DFJ, yuelu H, yuela K
quorum		ðeara A, þara BCDGHJ, ðara F, þæræ E^3, þæra I, þeara K
non	|	ne ABE^3J, nys CF, nis DHI, nan G, na K
est	|	wes A, wæs B, is E^3GJ*K*
numerus		rim AB, gerim ł getæl J, getel C, getell I, gerim DE^3GHK, gerym F
conprehenderunt	|	bifengon *A,* befengon B*C,* befengon ł gegripon *J,* hy gegripun D*H,* hi gegripon F, hy gegripon G, hi gegipan K, gegripun ł gehæfton *I*, me *E^3* (*M*)
me	|	me ABCFGHJK, gegrypon E^3*
iniquitates	|	unrehtwisnisse *A*, unryhtwisnessa BD, unrihtwisnysse F, unrihtwisnessa GH, unrihtwisnyssa I, unrihtwisnesse J, on unrihtwisnysse *C**, on unrihtwisnesse K, mine E^3

meae	I	mine ABFGHIJ, minre CK, unrihtnesse *E*^{3} (*DL*)
et		⁊ ABCFGIJK, ond E^{3}
non	I	ic ne ABCIJ, na DE^{x}*FGHK
potui	I	maehte A, mehte B, mihte CIJK, ic mehte D, ic mihte GH, ic ne mihte E$^{3/x}$*, ic ne myhte F
ut		ðæt A, þæt BG, þæt CDFHIJK, þet E^{3}
uiderem		ic gesege A, ic gesawe BCDFGHJK, ic hie gesæwe E^{3}, ic hi gesawe I (*M*)
Multiplicati*		gemonigfaldade A, gemonigfaldode B, gemonigfealdode CJ, hy gemænigfylde D, hy Gemonifældode E^{3}, hy gemænigfylde GH, gemænigfylde FI*, gemanifealde K
sunt		sind A, sint BE^{3}, synd CDFGHJK, hig synt I
super		ofer ABDE^{3}FGHIJK, ofyr C
capillos		loccas ABCDFGHIJK, loccæs E^{3}
capitis	I	heasdes A, heafdes BDFGIJK, heafdys C, hefdes H, mines E^{3}
mei	I	mines ⁊ *A*, mines BDFGHIJK, minys C, heæfdes E^{3}
et		⁊ BCE^{3}FGJK (*A*)
cor	I	heorte ABCDFGHIJ, heort K, min E^{3} (*M*)
meum	I	min ABCDFGHIJK, heorte E^{3}
dereliquit	I	forleort A, forlet BHK, forlæt *C*DFGJ, ⁊ forlet I, me E^{3}
me	I	me ABCFGHJK, forlet E^{3} (*L*)

ED: forðon (A)] for ðon *Kuhn*. circundederunt (C)] circu[m]dederunt *Wildhagen*. comprehenderunt (C)] conprehenderunt *Wildhagen*. cōprehenderunt (E)] comprehenderunt *Harsley*. iniquitates (C)] iniquitat[i]s *Wildhagen*. meæ (D)] meae *Roeder*. meę (E)] meae *Harsley*. uiderem (B)] videam *Brenner*. Multiplicatę (C)] Multiplicat[i] *Wildhagen*.

OE: gegrypon (E^{3})] *right arm of* y *in darker ink* (*altered from* i?). on unrihtwisnysse (C)] un *interl.* na (E^{x})] *on eras.* ic ne mihte (E$^{3/x}$)] ic *on eras. by corr.*, t *retraced, final* e *on eras., eras. after word.* gemænigfylde (I)] *orig.* gemænigfilde: *2nd* i *altered to* y.

LTg: Quoniam] [ ]uoniam G: *initial* Q *lost.* circumdederunt] circundederunt E, C: *orig.* circumdederunt: *left leg of* m *eras. to form* n, H: *eras. after 1st* n. est] ést K. conprehenderunt] conpraehenderunt A; comprehenderunt IJ, C: *orig.* conprehenderunt: *1st* n *deleted by subscript dot, macron added above* o, H: *orig.* conprehenderunt: *middle leg added to 1st* n *to form* m; conpraehenderunt M; cōprehenderunt E. iniquitates] A: ui *on eras.*, C: *orig.* iniquitatis: *4th* i *altered to* e. meae] meæ BD; meę CEFL, H: *eras. below 1st* e. uiderem] uidêrem M. Multiplicati] Multiplicatę C: *orig.* Multiplicati: *final* i *altered to* ę: *cf. Weber MSS* MS^{2}PQ*Rγδλ, *see GAg*. et (*2nd*)] A: *deleted by superscript dots.* cor] cór M. dereliquit] C: *2nd* i *interl.* me (*3rd*)] mé L.

LTu: circumdederunt] circundederunt ελτ*φ. quorum] ψ: u *interl.* conprehenderunt] comp̄henderunt ϑο, ε: m *altered from* n; comprehenderunt ζξπϱτ; cōprehenderunt ιλτ*φχ; conp̄henderunt μ; cōp̄henderunt υ. meae] mee δστ*τ; meę ειvξυ; meæ ϑ. dereliquit] deriliquit ϑ.

GAg: Multiplicati] Multiplicatę FK, C: *see LTg*, H: *orig.* Multiplicati: *final* i *altered to* ę; Multiplicate G; Multiplicatae I.

GAu: Multiplicati] Multiplicatę δειλοϱφχ; Multiplicatæ ϑ; Multiplicate ξστ*υ; Multiplicatae ψ.

14

Conplaceat		gelicað AB, gelicige *CFGIJK*, gelicige D, gelicige $E^{3/x}$*, gelicie *H*
tibi		ðe ABF, þe CE^{3}GHIJK
domine		drihten E^{3}F, dryht̄ AB, driħt CG, driħ J (*I*)
ut		ðæt A, þæt BG, þæt CDFHIJK, þet E^{3}
eripias*	|	ðu generge A, þu generge C, ðu generige B, þu generige J, ðu nerige D, þu nerige FGHK, þu generige ł alyse I, þu me E^{3}
me	|	mec A, me BCFGHIJK, generie $E^{3/x}$*
domine		drihten E^{3}F, dryht̄ AB, driħt CG, driħ J (I)
in*		in A, on $BCDE^{x}$*, ⁊ to F, to GHIJK
auxilium*	|	fultum AC, fultum BD, fylstanne FH, fylstanne ł fultumienne G, gehelpanne ł to fultume I, gefultumigenne J, fultumiendum K, mine E^{x}*
meum*	|	minne ABC, me FGIJK, fultum E^{3}
respice		geloca ABCDGHJ, gelocæ $E^{3/x}$*, beseoh FIK

ED: Complaceat (C)] Co[n]placeat *Wildhagen.* Cōplaceat (E)] Complaceat *Harsley.* domine (H) (*2nd*)] Domine *Campbell.* fylstanne ł fultumienne (G)] fylstanna ł fultumienne *Rosier.*

OE: gelicige ($E^{3/x}$)] ḡ *and* cige *on eras. by corr., 1st* i *retraced.* on (E^{x})] *on eras., eras.* (*22 mm*) *before word.* mine (E^{x})] *on eras.* gelocæ ($E^{3/x}$)] ge *added by corr.*

LTg: Conplaceat] Complaceat IJ, C: *orig.* Conplaceat: *right leg added to* n *to form* m, H: *orig.* Conplaceat: *middle leg added to* n *to form* m, K: *orig.* Conplaceat: *macron added by corr. above* o, *but* n *not deleted;* Cōplaceat E. domine (*both*)] I: o *written above word.*

LTu: Conplaceat] Complaceat ζιξϱστ*υ; Cōplaceat λτ*χ.

GAg: eripias] eruas FGHIJK. in] ad FGHIJ; ád K. auxilium] adiuuandum FGHIJ; ádiuuandum K. meum] me FGHIJK.

GAu: eripias] eruas δεζϑιλμξοπϱστυφχψ. in auxilium meum] ad adiuuandum me δεζϑιλμξοπϱστυχψ.

15

Confundantur sien gescende ABD, Sien gescende $E^{3/x}$*, syn gescynde CIJ, sýn gescende F, sien gescynde H, sin gescend K, gecyrred *G*

et ⁊ ABCDE³*FGHIJK

reuereantur onscunien *A*, onscunigen B, sceamiyn C, scamian J, hy forwandian D, hi forwandian F*, hy forwandien H, forwandud *K*, hy forwand[ ] *G*, gewirfede ł forwandian $E^{3/x}$*, anþracian I

simul somud A, somod BDE³*H, samod CFIJ, [ ]mod ł [ ]tgæ[ ] *G**, ætgædere K

qui ða ðe AB, þa þe CGI, þa ðe FHJ, þe þe D, ðæ þe E³, þa K

quaerunt soecað *AB*, secað *CDFGHIJK*, secæþ *E³* (*L*)

animam | sawle ABCDFGHIJK, mine E³

meam | mine ABCDFHIJK, m[ ] G, sæwle E³

ut ðæt A, þæt BJ, þæt CE³FGHIK (*D*)

auferant hie afirren AB, hi afyrryn C, hi æfyrren E³, hy afyrren H, afyrran J, hi ofbredon F, hy awyrsian G, hig ætbredan ł afyrran I* (*D*)

eam hie ABE^{x}, hi C, híg F, hy GH, hig IJ (*D*)

Auertantur* sien forcerred A, syn forcyrryde C, sien gecirde B, syn gecyrred DFG, Sien gecirrede E³, sin gecyrred HK, syn gecirrede J, gecyrran I

retrorsum on bec A, on bæc BCK, on bæcc J, on bæcling I, underbecling $DE^{3/x}$*, underbæclincg G, underbæcling H, underbæc F

et ⁊ ABCE³FGIJK

erubescant* scomien A*, scamigen B, scamiyn C, scamian J, ablysien ł forscamien D, forscæmien ł ablysien $E^{3/x}$*, ablysigen K, hi forhradian F*, hy forwandian GH, anþracian ł ⁊ ablysian I

qui ða A, þa HK, ða ðe B, þa þe CGI, þa ðe DFJ, þæ þe E³

cogitant* | ðencað AB, þencyn C, þohton D, wyllað FK, wilniað ł willaþ I, willaþ J, willan G, me E³

mihi | me ABCDFGHIJK, þencæþ *E³*

mala yfel ABK*, yfyl C, yfelu DFGIJ, yuelu H, yfeles E³

ED: [ ](m)ul (G)] *s*imul *Rosier.* [ ]mod ł [ ]tgæ[ ] (G)] [ ]mod ł ::g[ ] *Rosier.* þæt (H)] þæt *Campbell.* underbecling ($E^{3/x}$)] under becling *Harsley.* underbæc (F)] under bæc *Kimmens.*

OE: Sien gescende ($E^{3/x}$)] *2nd* e *in* gescende *altered from* i, s *interl. by corr.* ⁊ (E³) (*1st*)] *malformed, another* ⁊ (?) *eras. after gloss.* hi forwandian (F)] *obscured by eras.*

but visible. gewirfede ł forwandian (E$^{3/x}$)] ł forwandian *added by corr.* somod (E^{3})] o *(both) altered from other letters, 2nd perhaps* e. [ ]mod ł [ ]tgæ[ ] (G)] e *(part of* æ?) *visible before* t, *bowl (of* d?) *visible after* æ. hig ætbredan ł afyrran (I)] ł afyrran *written in right margin.* underbecling (E$^{3/x}$)] becling *added by corr.* scomien (A)] *orig.* somien: c *interl. by corr.* forscæmien ł ablysien (E$^{3/x}$)] for *and* n ł ablysien *by corr.* hi forhradian (F)] forhradian *obscured by eras. but visible.* yfel (K)] mala *eras. before word.*

LTg: Confundantur] [ ]onfundantur G: *initial* C *lost.* reuereantur] A: *orig.* reueriantur: i *altered to* e; reueantur K; reuerea[ ] G. simul] [ ](m)ul G: *left leg of* m *not visible.* quaerunt] quęrunt AFIK; querunt BCDEGHJL. ut] D: *added in right margin in later hand on eras.* auferant] D: *added in right margin in later hand.* eam] D: *added in right margin in later hand.* mihi] michi E, C: *orig.* mihi: c *interl. by corr.*

LTu: quaerunt] querunt δϑιξσςτ*τυ; quęrunt εζνπφ; q:runt β. mihi] michi ιλσς, πϱ: c *interl.;* m^{1} τ*τφ.

GAg: Auertantur] Conuertantur FGHIJK. erubescant] reuereantur FHIJK; reue(r)eantur G: *shoulder of 2nd* r *lost.* cogitant] uolunt FGHIJK.

GAu: Auertantur] Conuertantur δεζϑιλμξοπϱστυφχψ. erubescant] reuereantur δεζϑιλμξοπϱστυφχψ. cogitant] uolunt δεζϑιλμξοπϱστυφχψ.

16

Ferant		forðberen AB, forðberyn ł berað C*, forþberan J, hy beren DE^{x}*, hí beran F, hi beren H, hi breran K, hi beran ł feriun I*, hy berað G
confestim		sona A*BC, sona rædlice J*, hrædlice DFGHK, hredlice E^{3}*, hræddlice I
confusionem	|	scome AC, scame B, scamu J, sceame ł gescendnesse I, gescyndnesse DGHK, gescendnysse F, here E^{3}* *(M)*
suam	|	his ACDFGHK, hira B, heora IJ, gesciendnesse E^{3}
qui		ða A, þa BDHK, þa þa C, þæ þe E^{3}, ða ðe F, þa þe GI, þa ðe J
dicunt	|	cweoðað A, cweðað BCG, cweþað DHJK, cweðaþ I, cweðan F, me E^{3}
mihi	|	me A*C*DFG*H*IJK, to me B, cweðæþ *E^{3}*
euge		wel ðe A*B, wel þe CJ, eala DFGH, ealæ E^{3}*, wegla weg ł wala wa ł eala eala I, egele K
euge		wel ðe AB, wel þe CJ, eala DFGH, ealæ E^{3}*

ED: m^{1} (E)] michi *Harsley.*

OE: forðberyn ł berað (C)] ł berað *written in left margin.* hy beren (E^{x})] *on eras.* hi beran ł feriun (I)] ł *interl.* sona (A)] *gloss eras. before word.* sona rædlice (J)] *orig.* fona rædlice: *cross-stroke of* f *eras. to form* s. hredlice (E^{3})] h *altered or retouched by* *corr., eras.* (*10 mm*) *before word.* here (E^3)] *orig.* hire: i *altered to* e. wel ðe (A) (*1st*)] *final* e *malformed, more like* æ. ealæ (E^3) (*both*)] a *on eras. by corr.*

LTg: confusionem] confusiônem M. mihi] michi H, C: *orig.* mihi: c *interl. by corr.*; m^1 E.

LTu: confusionem] confussionem ϑ. mihi] michi λξσςτ, πϱ: c *interl.*; m^1 τ*φ.

17

Exultent — gefen A, gefeon BC, gefeogen DH, gefagen *G*, gefægnian K, fægnian F, Gehihtæþ E^3, geblissiun I, gefeodon J

et — ⁊ ABCDE^{3}FGIJK

laetentur — blissien A*DH*, blissigen *BG*, blissiyn *C*, blissian *FJK*, blissiæþ *E^3*, fægniun I* (*L*)

(super)* — ofer FGIJK

(te)* — þe FGJK, te I

(omnes)* — ealle FGIJK

qui* — ða A, ða ðe B, þa þe *C*, þa ðe D, þæ þe *E^3*

quaerunt* — soecað *AB*, seceað C, secað *D*, secæþ *E^3*, þa secendan FI*, þa secað K, secende GJ (*LM*)

te — ðec A, ðe B, þe CDE^{3}GIJK

domine* — drihten E^3, dryht̄ AB, driħt C

et — ⁊ ABCDE^{3}FGHIJK

dicant — cweoðað A, cweðað BC, cweþað J, cweþaþ K, hy cweþen D, hie cweðæn *E^3**, hy cweðen H, hi cweðan F, hy cwædan G, cweðun hig I

semper — aa A, áa B, symle CDIJ, simle E^3, symble FH, æfre ł symble G, æfre K

magnificetur — sie gemiclad A*, sie gemiclod B, sý gemyclod F, si gemicclod J, gemiclod sie *D*, gemiclæd sie E$^{3/x}$*, gemiclod sy G, gemicelod sie H, gemyclud si K, sy gemærsod CI

dominus — dryhten B, drihten DE^{3}FH, drhten K, dryht̄ A, driħt CG, driħ J

qui — ða AB, þa CJK, þa ðe D, ðæ þe E^3, ða þe F, þa þe GI

diligunt — lufiað ABCDFGHI, lufiæþ E^3, lufiaþ J, luuað K (*M*)

salutare | haelu *A*, hælo BDFGHIJ, hæle CK, þine E^3

tuum | ðine AF, þine BCDGHJK, þine ł þinne halwendan I*, helo E^3

OE: fægniun (I)] i *interl.* þa secendan (I)] *2nd* a *on eras., final* n *in same lighter ink.* hie cweðæn (E^3)] n *on eras. by corr.* sie gemiclad (A)] *1st* e *malformed.* gemiclæd sie (E$^{3/x}$)] d *and* sie *added by corr.* þine ł þinne halwendan (I)] þinne halwendan *written in left margin.*

LTg: Exultent] [ ]xultent G: *initial* E *lost*. laetentur] lætentur B; letentur CDEHJK; lętentur FGL. qui] E: *on eras*. quaerunt] quęrunt AM; querunt BCDEL. dicant] E: *letter eras. after* i (di/cant). magnificetur] D: n *on eras*. diligunt] dîligunt M. salutare] A: *eras.* (*2 letters*) *after word.*

LTu: Exultent] Exsultent ϑψ. laetentur] lętentur εϑν; letentur ςτ*. quaerunt] querunt βςτ*τ.

GAg: laetentur] lętentur super te omnes FG; letentur super te omnes HJK; laetentur super te omnes I. qui (*1st*)] *om*. FGHIJK. quaerunt] quęrentes FGK; querentes HJ; quaerentes I. domine] *om*. FGHIJK.

GAu: laetentur] laetentur super te omnes δζμοχψ; lętentur super te omnes εϑιλπφ; letentur super te omnes ξστυ. qui (*1st*)] *om*. δεζξυφχψ. quaerunt] querentes δειξστ; quęrentes ζλμορφ; q̄rentes ϑ; quaerentes υχψ. domine] *om*. δεζϑιμξοστυφχψ.

18

Ego		ic ABCDFGHIJK, Ic E^{3}
uero*		soðlice ABCE^{3}GI, soþlice DFJ, witodlice K
egenus*		weðla A, wædla BCDFJK, wedlæ E^{3}, wædliga G, wædla ł medgylda I (*M*)
(sum)*		ic eom FGJ, eom HIK
et		⁊ ABCDE^{3}FGHIJK
pauper		ðearfa AF, þearfa BCDGHIJK, ðeærfæ E^{3}
sum*		ic eam A, ic eom C, eom BDE^{3}
dominus		drihten E^{3}F, dryht̄ AB, drih̄t CG, drih̄ J
curam*	|	gemnisse A, gemnesse B, gymnysse C, hoge D, carefull F, carful G, ymbhydig ł carful I*, hævæð E^{3}*
habet*	|	hafað AC, hæfð BD, is FGIJ, hoge ł gemenne E$^{3/x}$*
mei		min ABCE^{3}*F*GJ, mines I (*M*)
Adiutor		fultum AC, fultum̲ BJK, gefultum E^{3}, fultumiend I, gefylsta DFGH
meus		min ABCDE^{x}**F*GHIJK
et		⁊ ABCDE^{x}*FGIJK
liberator*		gefrigend A, aliesend B, alysend DE^{x}*, onlysynd C, gescyldend FG, gescildend J, scyldend I*, frofer K
meus		min ABCDE^{3}*F*GIJK
es*	}|	wes A, beo ðu *B*, beo C, eart FGHIJK, þu DE^{x}*
tu*	}|	ðe A, þu CGHIJK, ðu F, eart DE^{x}* (*B*)
domine*	|	dryhten A, drihten E^{3}, dryht̄ B, drih̄t C, god FGJK, eala þu min I*
(meus)*	|	min FGJK, god I

ne	ne ABCDE^3FGHIJ, na K
tardaueris	leata ðu A, lata ðu B, lata þu CJ, lætæ þu E^3, ylde þu D, yld þu GH, yld ðu ł ne lata ðu þæt F, ylde þu ł ne lata ðu I, yld K

OE: ymbhydig ł carful (I)] *small eras.* (?) *after 2nd* y, ł carful *written in left margin.* hævæð (E^3)] v *altered from another letter, ascender visible.* hoge ł gemenne ($E^{3/x}$)] hoge ł *added by corr.* min (E^x)] *on eras.* ⁊ (E^x) (*2nd*)] *on eras.* alysend (E^x)] *on eras.* scyldend (I)] y *altered from* i (?). þu (E^x)] *on eras.* eart (E^x)] *on eras.* eala þu min (I)] o *written before* eala.

LTg: egenus] egênus M. mei] F: *letter eras. before word,* M: *orig.* me: i *added by corr.* meus] F: *small eras. after word.* es tu] esto B.

LTu: dominus] deus ς: *cf. Weber MSS* $βη^2$. es tu] es ϑ.

GAg: uero] autem FGHIJK. egenus] mendicus sum FGHIJK. sum] *om.* FGHIJK. curam habet] sollicitus est FGHIJ; sollicitus ést K. liberator] protector FGHIJK. es tu] tu es FGHIJK. domine] deus meus FGHIJK.

GAu: uero] autem δεζϑιλμξοπρστυφχψ. egenus] mendicus sum δεζϑιλξοπρστυφχψ, μ: sum *interl.* sum] *om.* δεζϑιλξοπρστυφχψ. curam habet] sollicitus est δεζϑιλμξοπρστυφχψ. liberator] protector δεζϑιλμξοπρστυφχψ. es tu] tu es δεζιλμξοπρστυφχψ; es ϑ. domine] deus meus δεζϑιλμξοπρστυφχψ.

PSALM 40

2

Beatus	eadig *ACDE^x*GHI*J, eadi *K*, eadig bið *B*F (*M*)
qui	se ABC, se ðe BF, se þe DE^3HIJ, þa þe G, þa K
intellegit	ongiteð AB, ongytyð *C*, ongyteð *F*, ongyteþ J, ongytað G, ongeteþ E^3, angyteð D, angyteþ *H*, angytað *K*, undergyt *I** (*M*)
super	ofer ABDE^3FGHIJK, ofyr C
egenum	weðlan A, wædlan BCJ, þæm wædlan *I*, þone wedlæ E^3, elþeodigne DH, ælþeodigum F, eallþeodigne *G*, ælþeodian K (*M*)
et	⁊ ABCDE^3FGHIJK
pauperem	ðearfan ABF, þearfan CDGHIJK, þone þeærfæn E^3
in	in A, on BCDE^3FGHIJK
die	dege A, dæge BCDFGHIJ, dage $E^{3/x}$*, dæg K
mala	yflum AI, yflum B, yfelum *D*, yfelum G, yuelum H, yflun *C*, yfylu F, yfle *E^3**, yfel J, yuela K
liberabit	gefreað *A*, gefreoð *B*C, gefreoþ ł alisseþ J, alyseþ D, alyseð GHK, alysþ *F*, alysð I, drihtæn E^3 (*M*)

eum		hine ABCDFGHJK, hyne I
dominus	|	drihtyn C, drihten HJK, dryht̄ AB, driȟt G, hi gefriolsæð ł alyseð E$^{3/x}$*

ED: [ ]eatus (G)] Beatus *Rosier.* ęgenum (G)] egenum *Rosier.* egénum (I)] egenum *Lindelöf.* yfylu (F)] yfelu *Kimmens.*

OE: eadig (I)] est : is *written in upper lobe of* B *in* Beatus. undergyt (I)] y *altered from* i (?). dage (E$^{3/x}$)] age *by corr.* yfle (E^{3})] hiræ *eras. before word,* le *in darker ink, letter eras. after word.* hi gefriolsæð ł alyseð (E$^{3/x}$)] ł alyseð *added by corr.*

LTg: Beatus] BEAtus A; BEatus BDKM; BEATVS C; BEATUS E; [ ]eatus G. qui] QVI C. intellegit] INTELLEgit C; intéllegit M; intelligit FI, H: *2nd* i *altered from another letter,* K: *orig.* intellegit: e *deleted by subscript dot,* i *interl.* egenum] ęgenum G; egénum I; egênum M. mala] malo CDE: *cf. Weber MSS* K^{2}Q^{2}UVXα. liberabit] A: *2nd* b *on eras. by corr.,* F: *2nd* b *formed from another letter,* M: *2nd* b *on eras.;* liberauit B.

LTu: Beatus] BEAtus β; BEATVS ιϛφ; BEATUS λμνϱτ*τχψ. qui] QUI λμνϱχψ. intellegit] intelligit εζξοστ*τυφχ; INTELLIGIT λ, ϱ: *orig.* INTELLEGIT; INTELlegit μψ; INtellegit ν. super] SUPER λ. egenum] aegenum δ. mala] malo βϛ: *cf. Weber MSS* K^{2}Q^{2}UVX. liberabit] liberauit ϑσϛυ.

3

Dominus		drihten E^{3}, dryht̄ A*B*, driȟt CFG, driȟ J
conseruet		gehaldeð AB, gehealdeð DFGH, geheældeð E^{3}*, gehealde C, gehealt IK, gehæleþ J
eum		hine ABC*D*E^{3}FGHIJK
et		⁊ ABCDE^{3}FGHIJK
uiuificet		gelifesteð A, geliffæstað BDFGH, geliffesteð E^{3}*, geliffæftað C, geliffæstaþ J, he geliffæst I*, liffest K (*M*)
eum		hine ABCDE^{3}FGHIJK
et		⁊ ABCDE^{3}FGIJK
beatum		eadigne ABCDGHI, eædigne E^{3}, eadige J, eadi K, seadigne F (*M*)
faciat		gedoeð *A*B, gedoþ J, gedóþ E^{3}*, gedó *C,* he gedeþ *D*I, he gedeð *H*G, he deþ F, deð K (*LM*)
eum		hine ABCE^{3}FGIJK
et*		⁊ ABCDE^{3}
emundet*		geclasnað A, geclæsnað B, geclænsað C, he aclensað D, he geclensæð E$^{3/x}$*
in		in A, on BCDE^{3}FGHIJK
terra		eorðan ABCDFGHJK, eordæn E^{3}, lande I
animam*	|	sawle ABCD, his E^{3}
eius*	|	his ABCD, sæwle E^{3}

et ⁊ ABCDE^{3}FGHIJK
non | ne ABCJ, na DFGHK, he na I, hine E^3
tradat | seleð AB, silleþ J, gesylle C, he selð D, he seleþ F, he sylð G, he silþ H, sylþ IK, ne E^3
eum | hine ABCDFGHIJK, seleð E^3*
in in A, on BCDE^{3}FGIJK
manus* hond AB, handa CDK, hændæ E^3, sawle FG, sawla J, anwealde I
inimici* | feond A, feondes BD, feonda CFIJ, on feonde G, feoda K, his E^3
eius | his ABCDFGIJ*K*, fiondæs E^3*

ED: [ ]n̄s (B)] dn̄s *Brenner.* geliffæftað (C)] geliffæstað *Wildhagen.* faciat (B)] faci[e]t *Wildhagen.*

OE: geheældeð (E^3)] ð *on eras. by corr.* geliffesteð (E^3)] ð *on eras. by corr., eras. after word, with* e *visible in final position.* he geliffæst (I)] he *interl.* gedóþ (E^3)] þ *added by corr.* he geclensæð (E$^{3/x}$)] he *and* ð *added by corr., eras. after word.* seleð (E^3)] ð *retouched by corr.* fiondæs (E^3)] s *added by corr.*

LTg: Dominus] [ ]n̄s B: *initial* D *not written.* eum (*1st*)] D: *on eras.* (?). uiuificet] uiuíficet M. beatum] beâtum M. faciat] C: *2nd* a *on eras. by corr.,* H: *2nd* a *altered from another letter,* M: *2nd* a *on eras., eras. above letter with fine* x *above;* faciet ADL: *cf. Weber MS* Tmoz^x. eius (*2nd*)] eíus K.

LTu: Dominus] DN̄S β. faciat] faciet βϑςυ: *cf. Weber MSS* Tmoz^x.

GAg: et emundet] *om.* FGHIJK. animam eius] *om.* FGHIJK. manus inimici] animam inimicorum FGHIJK.

GAu: et emundet] *om.* δεζϑιλμξοπϱστυφχψ. animam eius] *om.* δεζϑιλμξοπϱστυφχψ. manus inimici] animam inimicorum δεζϑιλμξοπϱστυφχψ.

4
Dominus drihten E^{3}K, dryht̄ AB, driħt CG*, driħ J
opem weolan A, welan BCJ, spede DFGH, spæde E^3, speda K, fultu<u>m</u> IJ
ferat bireð AB, beryð C, biraþ J, bringeð DE^5*, bryngað F, bringeþ K, bringe GH, bring I
illi him ACE^5*GHI, hi<u>m</u> BDFJK
super ofer ABDE^5*FGIJK, ofyr C
lectum bed ABGHIJK, bedd CDE^5*F
doloris sares ABDE^5*GHJ, sarys C, sar F*, saris ł sarnesse I, sarinesse K
eius his ABCD*E*^{5}*FGHIJ

uniuersum alle A, ealle BCDFGHJK, eall I, ælle E^{5}*

stratum strene A, streone BJ, stræte C, stræle DGH, stræla F*, strele E^{5}*, strælum K, strecednes ł reste I (*M*)

eius his ABCDE^{5}*F*G*HIJ*K*

uersasti ðu gecerdes A, þu gecirdes B, þu gecyrdyst C, gecyrdest K, þu gecirdest ł þu gehwirfdest J, þu acyrdest DE^{5}*GH, ðu acyrdest F, þu awendest I

in in A, on BCDE^{5}*FGHIJK

infirmitate | untrynisse A, untrymnesse B, untrumnysse CF, untrumnesse DE^{5}G, untrumnesse HJ, seohnesse K, his *I*

eius | his ABCDE^{5}FGHJ*K*, untrumnysse I

ED: untrumnysse (I)] untrymnysse *Lindelöf* (*but correct in appendix, p. 323*).

OE: driȟt (G)] *bowl of* d *slightly cropped at bottom due to hole in leaf.* bringeð (E^{5})] *on eras.; Ps 40.4* bringeð–*40.10* ic hyhte (*last verse of fol. 72v and all of fol. 73r*) *written by scribe* E^{5}, *who works as corrector elsewhere.* him (E^{5})] *on eras.* ofer (E^{5})] *on eras.* bedd (E^{5})] *on eras.* sare (E^{5})] *on eras.* sar (F)] es *added in pencil after* r. his (E^{5}) (*1st*)] *on eras.* ælle (E^{5})] *on eras.* stræla (F)] *obscured by eras. but visible.* strele (E^{5})] *on eras.* his (E^{5}) (*2nd*)] *on eras.* þu acyrdest (E^{5})] *on eras.* on (E^{5})] *on eras.*

LTg: eius (*1st*)] E: us *on eras.* stratum] strâtum M. eius (*2nd*)] eíus K; ei[ ] G. infirmitate] I: *2nd* i *on eras., top of 1st* t *lost due to hole.* eius (*3rd*)] eíus K.

LTu: doloris] dolores β. uniuersum] uniuersi ς. stratum] strati ς.

5

Ego ic ABCDE^{5}FGHIJKL

dixi ic cweð A, cweð DE^{5}, cwæð BHIL, cwæþ F, cweþe JK*, sæde C (*G*)

domine dryhten DE^{5}, drihten FKL, dryht̄ *A*B, driȟt C*G*, driȟ HJ (*I*)

miserere mildsa *AC*HJK, miltsa B, gemiltsa DE^{5}FGI, gemildsa L (*M*)

mei min ABCDE^{5}FHIJL, me K, m[ ] G*

sana hael A, hæl DE^{5}HKL, gehæl BCIJ, halo F

animam sawle ABCDE^{5}FGHIJKL

meam mine *A*BCDE^{5}FGIJKL, min H

quia* forðon ABD, forþon J, forþan CL, forðan E^{5}*K*, forþam G, forðā F, forðan þe I

peccaui ic syngade A, ic syngode DE^{5}GKL, ic singode FH, ic gesyngode BC, ic gesingode *J*, ic agylte I*

tibi ðe ABF, þe CDE^{5}GHIJKL

ED: ic (G) (*1st*)] *no gloss Rosier.* driħt (G)] [ ]riħt *Rosier.* sana (G)] *sana Rosier.* meam (G)] *meam Rosier.* mine (G)] [ ]ine *Rosier.* forðon (A)] for ðon *Kuhn.*

OE: cweþe (K)] *1st* e *interl.* m[ ] (G)] *letter fragments visible after* m. ic agylte (I)] y *altered from* i (?).

LTg: dixi] *lost* G. domine] A: *eras.* (*2 letters*) *after word,* I: o *written above word;* [ ]mine G. miserere] A: *orig.* miserire: *2nd* i *altered to* e; miserêre M; mserere C. meam] A: *final* m *added by corr.* quia] K: *on eras. by corr.* peccaui] J: *otiose stroke in lobe of 2nd* c.

LTu: domine] domine et β. miserere] misserere ϑ. sana] υ: na *interl.*

GAg: quia] quoniam GI, F: ł quia *interl. by corr.*

GAu: quia] quoniam δεμξοπϱυψ.

6

Inimici	feond A, fiend B, fynd CDF*G*HIJK, fynd E^{5}
mei	mine ABCDE^{5}GIJK, min FH
dixerunt	cwedon A, cwædon BJ, cwædun I, cwædan K, cwædon ł sægdon D, cwædon ł sædon H, cweðon ł sægdon E^{5}, sædon CF, sædon ł cwædon G
mala	yfel ABGJK, yfyl C, yfelu DFI, yuelu H, yfela E^{5}
mihi	me AB*C*FGIJK, to me *E^{5}*
quando	hwonne ABDE^{5}H, hwænne CFIJ, h[ ]e *G**, þænne K
morietur	swilteð AB, swilteþ J, sweltyð C, swelteð DE^{5}*G*H, sweltaþ F, swelteþ K, swelt he I (*M*)
et	⁊ ABCDE^{5}FGHIJK
periet*	forweorðeð ABH, forweorþeð D, forwurðyþ C, forwerþeð E^{5}, forwyrðeð G, forwirþeð J, forwyrð IK, losað F
nomen	noma ABD, nama CE^{5}FGHIK, naman J (*M*)
eius	his ABDE^{5}FGHIJ*K*, hys C (*M*)

ED: fynd (E)] Fynd *Harsley.* q[ ]ando (G)] quando *Rosier.* moriętur (G)] morietur *Rosier.*

OE: h[ ]e (G)] *part of descender visible after* h.

LTg: Inimici] [ ]nimici G. mihi] michi E, C: *orig.* mihi: c *interl. by corr.* quando] q[ ]ando G. morietur] moriętur G; moriêtur M. nomen] nômen M. eius] eíus K; eîus M.

LTu: Inimici] INimici β. mihi] michi ιλξϛτ*τψ, ιϱ: c *interl.;* m^{1} σ.

GAg: periet] peribit FGHIJK.

GAu: periet] peribit δεζϑιλμξοπϱσυφχψ.

7

Et	⁊ ABDE^{5}FGIJK, ⁊ gif C
(si)*	gyf FI, gif JK
ingrediebantur*	inneodan A, ineodon B, inneodon C, hí inneodon F, hi ineodon G, hy eodon in D, hy geoden in E^{5}, he ineode I, ineode J, hi ingaþ K* (*M*)
ut	ðæt A, þæt B, þæt CDE^{5}FGHIJK
uiderent*	hie gesegen A, hie gesawen B, hi gesawon CF, hy gesawon D, hy gesawan E^{5}, he gesawe GHJ, he geseawe I, hi gesigan K
uana	ða idlan A, þa idlan BCJ, idelu DE^{5}GHK, ydel F, ydelnyssa I (*M*)
locutum*	spreocende A, sprecende B, sprecynde C, gesprec DE^{5}K, gespræc F, hi spraecon G, he spræc I, spræc J
est*	wes A, wæs C
cor	heorte ABCDE^{5}FG*IJK (*M*)
eorum*	heara A, heora DE^{5}, hira B, hyra C, his FGIJK
congregauerunt*	gesomnadon A, gesomnodon B, gesamnedon C, gesamnode I, hy gederedon D, hy gaderedon E^{5}, gegaderode F, he gegaderode G, he gegaderede H, gesomnode ł gegadorodon J*, hi gegæderada K
iniquitatem	unreht A, unryhtwisnesse BDE^{5}, unrihtwisnysse CFI, unrihtwisnesse GHJK
sibi	him ABCE^{5}FGHIJ, him DK
Et*	⁊ ABCDE^{5}
egrediebantur*	uteodon ABC, hy eodon D*GH*, hí eodon *F,* hig eodon *J,* hi eodan K, hy geodon E^{5}, he forðstop ł he ferde *I*
foris*	ut *ABCDE*^{5}FGHIJK (*LM*)
et	⁊ ABCDE^{5}FGIJK
loquebantur*	werun spreocende A, wæron sprecende B, wæron specynde C, hy spræcon DG, hy sprecon E^{5}, spræcon F, spæcan K, he spræc I*, hi spræcon J

ED: loquębatur (G) (*1st*)] loquebatur *Rosier.*

OE: hi ingaþ (K)] *eras. after 1st* i, *orig. macron visible beneath eras.* heorte (G)] *final* e *faint but visible.* gesomnode ł gegadorodon (J)] *1st* do *interl.* he spræc (I) (*2nd*)] e *interl.*

LTg: ingrediebantur] ingrediebántur M. uana] uâna M. cor] cór M. foris] foras BCDEL, M: *fine* x *in red interl. above* a, A: *orig.* foris: i *altered to* a: *cf. Weber MSS* αβγδζη moz^{c} med, *see GAg.*

LTu: foris] foras ςτ*, β: as *by corr.: see GAu.*

GAg: Et (*1st*)] Et si FGHIK. ingrediebantur] ingrediebatur FHIJK; ingrediębatur G. uiderent] uideret FGHIJK. locutum est] loquebatur FIJK, H: ue *on eras.;* loquębatur G. eorum] eius FGHIJ; eíus K: *eras. after word, perhaps of punct.* congregauerunt] congregabit J, F: u *added interl. above* b *with insertion mark at line* (= congregauit); congregauit GHIK. Et (*2nd*)] *om.* FGHIJK. egrediebantur] Egrediebatur FGIJK; (E)grediebatur H: E *partly lost, outline visible.* foris] foras FGHIJK, ABCDELM: *see LTg.* loquebantur] loquebatur FHIJK; loquębatur G.

GAu: Et (*1st*)] Et si δεζϑιλμξοπϱστυφχψ. ingrediebantur] ingrediebatur δεζϑιλμξοπϱστυφχψ. uiderent] uideret δεϑιλ. locutum est] loquebatur δεζϑιλμξοπϱστυφχψ. eorum] eius δεζϑιλμξοπϱστυφχψ. congregauerunt] congregauit δεζϑιοπστφχψ; congregabit λμξϱυ. Et egrediebantur] Egrediebatur δεζϑιλμξοπϱστυφχψ. foris] foras δεζϑιλμξοπϱστυφχψ, βςτ*: *see LTu.* loquebantur] loquebatur δεζϑιλμξοπϱστυφχψ.

8

simul*	somud A, somod BDE^5, samod C
in	in A, on BCDE^{5}F, samod ł on I
unum*	anisse A, annesse B, annysse C, an DE^5, þæt sylfe FI, him betweonan G*, him betweonum J (*M*)
(Aduersum)*	togeanes FK, ongean GH, agen I, wiþ ł ongean J
(me)*	me FGHIJK
susurrabant	hyspton *A*B, hyspton ł runedon *C,* hy bysmredon *D*E^5, bysmrodan K, hy bysmredon ł grimetedon G, hy bysmredon ł grymetodon *H*,* ðohton F*, þohton J, hwastredun ł wiðercwyddedon I*
Omnes	alle A, ealle BCD*FGHIJK,* aelle E^5
inimici	feond A, fiend B, fynd CDE^{5}FGHI*JK
mei	mine ABCDE^{5}FGHIJK
aduersum*	wið AB, ongen C, ongean DE^{5}FG, agen I, wiþ ł ongean J, togeanes K
me	me me A, me BCE^{5}FGIJK
cogitabant	ðohton AB, þohton CDE^5*GHJ, þohtan K, hi ðohton F, hi þohton I
mala	yfel ABGJK, yfylys C, yfelu DE^{5}FI, yuelu H
mihi	me AB*CDE*^{5}FGHIJK

ED: idipsum (I)] id ipsum *Lindelöf.*

OE: him betweonan (G)] *otiose mark above* o. hy bysmredon ł grymetodon (H)] grymetodon *written below following* ealle. ðohton (F)] *obscured by eras. but visible; source-text misread, perhaps reading gloss to* cogitabant *below: see also* J. hwastredun ł wiðercwyddedon (I)] ł wiðercwyddedon *written in right margin.* fynd (I)] d *faint but visible.* þohton (E^5)] h *altered from another letter.* me (K) (*2nd*)] *otiose stroke above* e.

LTg: unum] ûnum M. susurrabant] D: *orig.* susurrabunt: *3rd* u *deleted by subscript dot,* a *interl.*, H: *1st* r *interl.;* sussurrabant C: *2nd* r *interl.;* susurrabunt A: *cf. Weber MS* M. Omnes] omnes FGHIJK. mihi] michi E, C: *orig.* mihi: c *interl. by corr.*

LTu: susurrabant] υ: *1st* r *interl.;* sussurabunt βς. Omnes] omnes δεζϑιλξοπϱυφχ. mihi] michi ιλξςτ*τ, ϱ: c *interl.;* m^1 σφ.

GAg: simul] *om.* FGHIJK. unum] idipsum Aduersum me FGHIJK.

GAu: simul] *om.* δεζϑιλμξοπϱτσυφχψ. unum] idipsum Aduersum me δεζϑιλμξοπϱστυφχψ. aduersum] aduersus ϑμ.

9

uerbum	word ABCDE^5*FGHIJK*
iniquum	unreht A, unryht B, unriht CJ, unryhtwis D, unrihtwís F, unrihtwis E^{5}HI*K*, unrihtwisnes G
mandauerunt*	onbudun ABC, hy bebudon D, hy bebudan E^5, hi gesetton FJ, hi gesetton G, hi gesettan I (*M*)
aduersum	wið AB, ongen CK, ongean DE^{5}GJ, agen ł togeanes I, togeanes F
me	me ABCDE^{5}FGIJK
Numquid	ah AB, cwyðst þu *C,* cwyþst þu la *F,* cwyst þu D*E^{5}K,* cwyst ðu *G,* cwist þu *J,* cwystu *H,* wenst þu la ł cwæþst þu la *I**
qui	se A, se ðe BC, se þe DE^{5}FGHI*J, þe K
dormit	hneapað A, hnappað BC, hnappaþ J, hnæppað F, slæpð DGIK, slapð E^5*, slæfð H
non	to ne AB, to na J, ne CDE^{5}FGHI*, na K
adiciet	geeceð A, geiceð B, geiceþ J, geycyð C, geycþ he na I*, geycþ he ł teohað DE^5, geycþ he ł teohhað G, geycð he ł teohað *H,* teohað K, geteohað he F
ut	þæt ABK, þæt CDE^{5}FGHI*J
resurgat	arise A, he arise BCDE^{5}FGH*J*K, eftarisė I

ED: Numquid (B)] numquid *Brenner.* Nunquid (C)] Nu[m]quid *Wildhagen.* cwyðst þu (C)] cwyðstþu *Wildhagen.* cwyst þu (DE)] cwystþu *Roeder;* Cwystþu *Harsley.* cwyst ðu (G)] cwyst þu *Rosier.*

OE: wenst þu la ł cwæþst þu la (I)] ł cwæþst þu la *written in left margin*. se þe (I)] *eras*. (?) *before* se. slapð (E^{5})] p *on eras*. ne (I)] *on eras*. (?). geycþ he na (I)] geycþ he *on eras*. (?). þæt (I)] *eras*. (?) *before word*.

LTg: uerbum] Uerbum FJK; Verbum GHI. iniquum] K: in *altered from* m *by main hand*. mandauerunt] mandauérunt M. Numquid] Nunquid E, C: *orig*. Numquid: *left leg of* m *eras. to form* n; numquid IJK; nunquid GH: *orig*. numquid: *right leg of* m *eras. to form* n; nũquid F. adiciet] H: *orig*. adiciat: *2nd* a *altered to* e, *but malformed*. resurgat] J: a *altered from another letter*.

LTu: uerbum] Uerbum δεζϑλμπϱτυψ; Verbum ιξοσχ. Numquid] numquid δζμοπσχ; nunquid εϑιτφ; Nunquid τ*; nũquid υ. adiciet] adiciat ϑσ.

GAg: mandauerunt] constituerunt FGHIJK.

GAu: mandauerunt] constituerunt δεζϑιλμξοπϱσυφχψ.

10

<table>
<tr><td>etenim</td><td></td><td>⁊ soðlice ABCG, ⁊ soþlice HJ, soþlice D, soðlice I, soðliche E^{5}, witendlice F, ⁊ witodlice K</td></tr>
<tr><td>homo</td><td></td><td>mon AB, mann CDE^{5}, man FGHIJK</td></tr>
<tr><td>pacis</td><td></td><td>sibbe ABGHJK, sybbe CDE^{5}FI (M)</td></tr>
<tr><td>meae</td><td></td><td>minre ABCDE^{5}FGHIJK (L)</td></tr>
<tr><td>in</td><td></td><td>in A, on BCDE^{5}FGHIJK</td></tr>
<tr><td>quo</td><td></td><td>ðæm AB, þæm I, þam CFGH, þam JK, ðam DE^{5}</td></tr>
<tr><td>sperabam*</td><td></td><td>ic gehyhte AB, ic gehihte J, gehihte C, ic hyhte DE^{5}*H, ic hihte GK, ic gehihte ł on þane þe ic hopode I*, ic hopie F (M)</td></tr>
<tr><td>qui</td><td></td><td>se ðe ABCGI, se þe FHJ, se D, þa K, þæ þe E^{3}</td></tr>
<tr><td>edebat</td><td></td><td>et ACH, æt BDE^{3}FGIJ, eet K (M)</td></tr>
<tr><td>panes</td><td>|</td><td>hlafas ABCDHIJ, hláfas F, hlaf GK, mine E^{3}*</td></tr>
<tr><td>meos</td><td>|</td><td>mine ABCDFHIJ, minne GK, hlǽf E^{3}</td></tr>
<tr><td>ampliauit*</td><td></td><td>gemonigfaldade A, gemonigfaldode B, gemonigfealdode C, he geycte D, he geycte ł monigfeældode E$^{3/x}$*, sý mycelod F, miclode I*, gemicclode J, he gemyclað K, gemærsode G (M)</td></tr>
<tr><td>aduersum*</td><td></td><td>wið ABC, ongean DE^{3}*, ofer FGJK, ofor I</td></tr>
<tr><td>me</td><td></td><td>me ABCDE^{3}FGIJK</td></tr>
<tr><td>subplantationem</td><td></td><td>gescrencednisse A, gescrencednesse BC, gescræncednesse J, bygswæc D, bygswec H, bygspæc F*, bigspæc K, byg[ ] swencednesse G, underþidnesse E^{3}, hleohræscnesse ł forscæncednysse I (M)</td></tr>
</table>

ED: etenim (BE)] et enim *Brenner, Harsley.* mine (E)] minne *Harsley.*

OE: ic hyhte (E^{5})] *hand* E^{3} *recommences after this gloss.* ic gehihte ł on þane þe ic hopode (I)] ł on þane *written in right margin.* mine (E^{3})] *orig.* minne: *1st* n *deleted by subscript dots.* he geycte ł monigfeældode (E$^{3/x}$)] he geycte ł *added by corr.* (E^{5}). miclode (I)] *eras.* (?) *before word.* ongean (E^{3})] *partly on eras.* bygspæc (F)] *partly obscured by eras. but visible.*

LTg: etenim] étenim C; Etenim FGHIJK. pacis] pâcis M. meae] meæ BL; meę CDFG, H: e *altered from* ę; mee E. in quo] iniquo J: *2nd* i *interl.* sperabam] sperâbam M. edebat] edêbat M; ędebat G. ampliauit] amplîauit M. aduersum] A: *eras. above 2nd* u, m *added by corr.* me] A: *added by corr.* (?). subplantationem] supplantationem ABC̣HIJ, D: *1st* p *on eras.*, E: *2nd* p *on eras.;* supplantatiônem M; subpla[ ]onem G.

LTu: etenim] Etenim δεζϑιλμξπϱστυχψ. meae] meę ειvπςφ; meæ ϑ; mee ξστ. edebat] edebant ς. subplantationem] supplantationem εζϑιλνξοϱστ*τυφχψ.

GAg: sperabam] speraui FGHJK, I: *eras. after word.* ampliauit] magnificauit FGHIJK. aduersum] super FGHIJK.

GAu: sperabam] speraui δεζϑιλμξοπϱστυφχψ. ampliauit] magnificauit δεζιλμξοπϱστυφχψ; magnificabit ϑ. aduersum] super δεζϑμξπϱστυφχψ.

11

Tu	ðu ABE^{3}, þu CF*G*IJK
autem	soðlice ABCE^{3}GI, soþlice FJ, witodlice K
domine	drihten E^{3}K, dryht̄ AB, drih̄t CFGJ (*I*)
miserere	mildsa *A*HJK, miltsa BDG, miltsæ E^{3}, gemyltsa C, gemiltsa FI (*M*)
mei	min ABCFI*J, me E^{3}GK
et	⁊ ABCDE^{3}FGHIJK
resuscita	awece ABCDHK, awrece GJ, awrecce me F, arær I, æwece ł arer E$^{3/x}$*
me	me ABCDE^{3}FGHJK
et	⁊ ABCDE^{3}FGHIJK
retribuam	ic geedleaniu A, ic geedleanige C, ic agilde B, ic agylde DE$^{3/x}$*FGH, ic agilde J, agilde K, ic forgelde I
illis*	him ACDFGHJ, him BK, heom I, hem ł geeædleænie E$^{3/x}$*

OE: min (I)] *eras.* (?) *after word.* æwece ł arer (E$^{3/x}$)] ł arer *added by corr.* (E^{5}). ic agylde (E$^{3/x}$)] agylde *added by corr.* (E^{5}). hem ł geeædleænie (E$^{3/x}$)] hem ł *added by corr.* (E^{5}).

LTg: Tu] (T)u G: *crossbar of* T *lost.* domine] I: o *written above word.* miserere] A: *orig.* miserire: *2nd* i *altered to* e; miserêre M.

LTu: miserere] misserere ϑ. resuscita] suscita ς.

GAg: illis] eis FGHIJ; eís K.

GAu: illis] eis δεζιλμξοπϱτυφχψ; eius σ.

12

In	in A, on *B*CDFGHIJK, On *E*[3]
hoc	ðissum A, ðyssum B, þyssum C, þisum J, þam DE[3/x]*FG, þam HK, þæm I
cognoui	ic oncneow A*BCE[3]*FGHIJ, ic ancneow D, ic acneow K
quoniam	ðætte AB, þætte DE[x]*H, þæt GI, þæt K, forþon C, forðon J, forðam ðe F
uoluisti	| ðu waldes A, þu woldes B, þu woldyst C, þu woldest DFGIJK, þu þoldest H, þu me E[3]
me	| mec A, me BCDFGHIJK, woldest E[3]*
quia*	forðon ABDHJ, forþan C, forðæn E[3], forþam G, forðam K, forðan þe I
non	ne ABCGIJ, na DE[x]*FHK
gaudebit	gefið A, gefihð B, gefeoþ J, blissað CDE[x]*GHK, blissaþ I, fægnian F (*M*)
inimicus	se feond A, feond BCDGHK, fiond E[3], fynd FIJ
meus	min ABCDE[x]*FGHIK, mine J
super	ofer ABDE[3]FGHJK, ofyr C, ofor I
me	me ABCE[3]FGHIJK

ED: forðon (A)] for ðon *Kuhn*. meus (G)] meu*s Rosier*.

OE: þam (E[3/x])] am *by corr.* ic oncneow (A)] eo *obscured by stain but visible.* ic oncneow (E[3])] e *altered from* æ, ow *on eras. by corr.* þætte (E[x])] *on eras.* woldest (E[3])] t *added by corr.* na (E[x])] *on eras.* blissað (E[x])] *on eras.* min (E[x])] *on eras.*

LTg: In] in B; IN E. gaudebit] gaudébit M.

LTu: In] IN β.

GAg: quia] quoniam FHIJK; [ ]uoniam G.

GAu: quia] quoniam δεζιμξοπϱστυφχψ.

13

(Me)*	me FGIJK
Propter* }	forðon A, forþon C, forþa K, fore BDE[3]H, for FGIJ (*M*)
innocentiam* }|	unsceðfulnisse A, unsceðfulnesse B, unsceðfulnysse C, unsceaðfulnesse G, unscæððinesse I, unscæþignesse J, unscylde DFH, unscyldygum K, minre E[3]

autem*	}|	soðlice A*BCFGI, soþlice̲ D, soþlice HJ, witodlice K, unscyþenesse E^3
meam*	|	mine A, minre BC*D, sodlice E^3
suscepisti	|	ðu onfenge ABF, þu onfenge CIJ*, þu anfenge DH, þu afenge K, ðu onfen[ ] *G,* þu me E^3 (*M*)
me*	|	mec A, me BCD, onfenge E^3
et		⁊ ABCE^{3}FGHIJK
confirmasti	|	getrymedes AB, getrymdest K, þu getrymydyst *C,* ðu getrymedest D, ðu getrymdest F, getrimedest J, þu getrymedest H, þu getrymodest I, þu getryme G, me E^3
me	|	mec A, me CFGIJK, getrymedest E^3*
in		in A, on BCDE^{3}FGHIJK
conspectu	|	gesihðe ABCDFGI, gesyhðe HK, gesihþe J, þinre *E^3*
tuo	|	ðinre ABF, þinre CDGHIJK, gesihþe E^3
in		in A, on BCDE^{3}FGHJK, a butan I
aeternum		ecnisse *A,* ecnesse *BDE^{3}GJK,* e[ ]nesse *H**, ecnysse *CF,* ende ł on ecnesse I (*L*)

ED: forðon (A)] for ðon *Kuhn.* fore (E)] Fore *Harsley.* æternum (D)] aeternum *Roeder.* ęternum (E)] aeternum *Harsley.* e[ ]nesse (H)] ecnesse *Campbell.*

OE: soðlice (A)] *orig.* soðlece: i *interl. above 1st* e. minre (C)] re *added in red by corr.* þu onfenge (J)] o *malformed.* getrymedest (E^3)] *final* t *added by corr.* (?). e[ ]nesse (H)] *letter after initial* e *obscured by blot.*

LTg: Propter] M: ter *on eras.* suscepisti] M: *orig.* suscipisti: *1st* i *altered to* e; suscepi[ ] G. confirmasti] cofirmasti C. conspectu] conspectv E. aeternum] ęternum ACEFH; æternum BDKL; eternum GJ.

LTu: suscepisti] suscipisti ϑ. aeternum] ęternum βειvφ; æternum ϑ; eternum ξστ*τ.

GAg: Propter innocentiam autem meam] Me autem propter innocentiam FGIJK, H: *letter eras. after 1st* e. me (*1st*)] *om.* FGHIJK.

GAu: Propter innocentiam autem meam] Me autem propter innocentiam δεζιλμξοπϱστυφχψ; Me autem probter innocentiam ϑ. me (*1st*)] *om.* δεζϑιλμξοπστυχψ.

14

Benedictus	gebledsad A, gebletsad B, Gebletsæd E^3, gebletsod DHIJK, sy gebletsod CF, si gebletsod *G*
dominus	dryhten A, drihten E^{3}FK, dryht̄ B, driħt CG, driħ J
deus	god ABCE^{3}FGJK
israhel	israhela B*D*F*G*H, israela J, israhele *E^3,* israelys C, geleaffulra K

a	from A, from BC, fram DFHJK, fram GI (*EM*)
saeculo	weorulde A, weorolde *B*, worulde *CDFH*, worlde *IJ*, worolde *K*, woru[ ] *G*, æworld *E*^{3} (*L*)
et	ℸ ABCDE^{3}FGHIJK
usque*	oð AB*C*D, oþ J, oþþe E^{3}
in	in A, on BDE^{3}FGHIJK
saeculum	weoruld A, weorolde *B*, worulde *CDFGH*, worlde *E*^{3}*IJ*, worolde *K* (*L*)
fiat	sie ABDH, sy CG*J*, þæt si K, beo hit F, gewurðe I, si swæ E^{3}
fiat	sie ABH, sy CG, sý hit swa F, gewurðe ł sy þæt I, swa *J*, si swæ E^{3}

ED: isrł (DE)] israhel *Roeder;* israel *Harsley.* israhel (K)] Israhel *Si.* á (E)] a *Harsley.* sæculo (D)] saeculo *Roeder.* scło (EIJ)] saeculo *Lindelöf;* seculo *Harsley, Oess.* scłm (EHIJ)] seculum *Harsley, Campbell, Oess;* saeculum *Lindelöf.*

LTg: Benedictus] [ ]enedictus G. israhel] isrł DEG. a] á EM. saeculo] sæculo BD; seculo CGHK; sęculo FL; scło EIJ. usque] usquę C. saeculum] sæculum B; seculum CDGK; sęculum FL; scłm EHIJ. fiat fiat] fiad fiad J.

LTu: israhel] israel ς; isrł βδειμνξοπστ*τυφχ. saeculo] sęculo βινο; sæculo ϑ; seculo λπς; scło δεμξστ*τυφχ. saeculum] sęculum βνοφ; sæculum ϑ; seculum λπς; scłm δεζιμξστ*τυχ.

GAg: usque] *om.* FGHIK.

GAu: usque] *om.* δεζϑιλξπϱστφχψ.

PSALM 41

2

Sicut*	swe swe *A*, swa swa *BC*DI, Swæ E^{3}, ealswa K, on þam gemete F, on ðam gemete G, on þam gemete J, on þa gemete H (*M*)
ceruus*	} heorut A, heorot B, heort *C*DFHIJK, heortan G, Se heort E^{3}
desiderat*	} gewillað A, gewilnað *BC*, gewilnaþ I, wilnað DFG, wylnæþ E^{3}*, wilnaþ HK, wilniaþ J
ad	to ABCDE^{3}FG*HIJ*K*
fontes	| waellum A, wiellum B, wyllun C, wyllum D, wyllum G, willum H, wyllan F, willan J, wylle K, wyllsprengum I, þes weteres E^{3}
aquarum	| wetra A, wætra BCDI, wætera FGHJK, willæn E^{3} (*M*)
ita	swę A, swa BDFGHIJK, swæ E^{3}, swa swa C
desiderat	gewillað A, gewilnað B*C*IJ, wilnað DFGHK, wilnæþ E^{3}

anima	ǀ	sawul A, sawl BCDGI, sawle FJ, saul H, sawel K, min E^3
mea	ǀ	min ABCDFGHIJK, sæwl E^3
ad		to ABCE^{3}FGHIJK
te		ðe ABF*H,* þe CE^{3}GIJK
deus		god ABCFGHJK, eala þu god I*, drihten E^3

ED: swa swa (I)] swaswa *Lindelöf.* heortan (G)] heort *Rosier.* aquarum (G)] aquar*um* *Rosier.* min (D)] mín *Roeder.* té (H)] te *Campbell.* deus (G)] de*us* *Rosier.*

OE: wylnæþ (E^3)] yl *on eras. by corr.,* l *retraced.* to (G)] *hole in bowl of* o. eala þu god (I)] o *written before* eala.

LTg: Sicut] SIcut AB; SICVT C; Sícut M. ceruus] CERVVS C. ad (*1st*)] ád K. aquarum] aquârum M. desiderat] DESIDErat C. te] té H.

LTu: Sicut] SICUT βν; SICVT ς. ceruus] Ceruus β; CERUUS ν. desiderat] DEsiderat ν.

GAg: Sicut] Quemadmodum FGHJ; Quemammodum I; QUemádmodum K. ceruus desiderat] desiderat ceruus FGHIJK.

GAu: Sicut] Quemadmodum δεζθπστυ; QVEMadmodum ι; QVEMADMODVM λφ; QUEMADMODUM μϱψ; QUEMADMOdum χ; Quemammodum ο: *orig.* Quemadmodum: *1st* d *deleted, 2nd* m *interl.* ceruus desiderat] desiderat ceruus δεζθιμξοπστυφχψ; DESIDERAT CERVVVS λ; DESIDErat ceruus ϱ.

3

Sitiuit	ǀ	ðyrsteð A*B,* þyrst C, ðyrste DF, þyrste GI*, þyrsthe *H,* þirteþ J, þyrststeð K, Min E^3
anima		sawul A, sawl BDG, sawle CFIJK, sæwle E^3, saul H
mea	ǀ	min ABDGHI, mine C, minre FJK, þirsteþ E^3
ad		to ABCDE^{3}FGHIJK
deum	ǀ	gode A*BCDFGHIJ, drihten K, þæm lifiendæn E^3
(fortem)*		wyll F*, wylle I, wyl K, swiðe G
uiuum	ǀ	ðæm lifgendan AB, þam lyfgyndan *C,* þam lifigendum J, lifgende D, lifigende FK, lyuiende G*, lifiendum H, libbendum I, gode *E^3* (*M*)
quando		hwonne ABDH, hwænne C*E^3*FGIJK
ueniam		ic cyme A, ic cume BCDE^{3}FGHJK, cume ic I
et		⁊ ABCDE^{3}FGHIJ (*K**)
parebo*		oteawe A, æteawe B, ætywe *C,* etiewe *E^3,* ætýwe G, ætiwe J, ic æteowie I, oþeowe *D,* oðywe *F,* þeowe *H* (*LM*)
ante		biforan A, beforan BCGHIJK, beforæn E^3, befon D, ætforan F
faciem	ǀ	onsien A, onsiene B, ansyne CDFIJK, ansiene H, ansyn[ ] G, godes E^3
dei	ǀ	godes ABGHIJK, godys C, onsiene E^3

ED: [ ]itiuit (B)] Sitivit *Brenner.* lyuiende (G)] lyuien[ ] *Rosier.* uiuum (G)] uiuu*m Rosier.* faciem (G)] facie*m Rosier.*

OE: þyrste (I)] y *altered from* i (?). gode (A)] *otiose stroke above* g (*altered from another letter?*), *a cross-stroke through ascender of* d *eras.* (?). wyll (F)] *added by corr. on eras.* lyuiende (G)] *final* e *written below* d. et (K)] ⁊ *eras. above word.*

LTg: Sitiuit] H: ti *interl.* (*by glossator?*); [ ]itiuit B: *initial letter om., although* S *in* SIcut *extends to beginning of this verse and may have been intended to serve as initial* S *in* [S]itiuit *as well.* uiuum] C: *eras. after 3rd* u, E: *on eras. by corr.;* uîuum M. quando] E: qua *retouched by corr.* et] K: *gloss eras.: see OE and GAg note to* parebo. parebo] parêbo M; apparebo CDEL: *cf. Weber MSS* αβλ moz.

LTu: et] *om.* ϑ. parebo] apparebo νςτ*, υ: *orig.* parebo: ap *interl.: cf. Weber MSS* αβλ moz, *see GAu.*

GAg: deum] deum fontem GHIJK, F: fontem *retraced by corr.: cf. Bib. sac. MSS* I^{2}M^{2}Q^{2}DΩ, *etc.* parebo] apparebo GHIJ, F: *1st* p *interl. by corr.,* H: ap *interl.* (*by glossator?*), K: *on eras. by corr., gloss eras.,* CDEL: *see LTg.*

GAu: deum] deum fortem δϑμψ, ο: ƚ n (> fontem) *interl.;* deum fontem εζλπϱστυφχ, ι: vel fortem *interl.,* ξ: *eras. after* o, n *interl.* parebo] apparebo ειλξπστχ, νςτ*: *see LTu;* aparebo ϑ; *for* υ *see LTu.*

4

Fuerunt	I	werun A, wæron BCDFGIJ, weron H, wæran K, Me E^{3}
mihi	I	me AB*C*DFGHIJK, weron *E^{3}*
lacrimae	I	tearas A*BCDFGHIJK,* mine *E^{3}* (*L*)
meae	I	mine A*BCDFGH*IJ*K,* teæræs *E^{3}* (*L*)
panes		hlafas ABCDFG*H*IJK, hlæfæs E^{3} (*M*)
die		deges A, dæges BFIJK, dægys C, on dæg DGH, on dege *E^{3}**
ac		⁊ ABCD*E^{3}*FHIJK, and G
nocte		naehtes A, nihtes BFIJK, nyhtys C, on niht DGH, on niehte E^{3}*
dum		ðonne AF, þonne BG, þonne CDE^{x}*HJ, þænne I, þon K
dicitur		bið cweden ABDFGK, byð cweden H, biþ cweden J, bið gecwedyn C, bið cweðend E^{3}, is gesæd I
mihi		to me AB, me *CDE^{x}**FGHIJK
cotidie		deghwæmlice A, dæghwæmlice C, dæghwamlice DFHK, dæghwamlice GI, dægwamlice J, dæghwæm B, ęlce deg E^{3}*
ubi		hwer AE^{3}, hwær BCDFI, hwar GHJK (*I*)
est		is ABDE^{3}FGHIJK, ys C
deus	I	god ABCFGHIJK, godd D, þin E^{3}
tuus	I	ðin AF, þin BCDGHIJK, god E^{3}

ED: lacrimæ (D)] lacrimae *Roeder.* lacrimę (E)] lacrimae *Harsley.* meæ (D)] meae *Roeder.* meę (E)] meae *Harsley.*

OE: on dege (E^{3})] *letter eras. after gloss.* on niehte (E^{3})] *letter eras. after gloss.* þonne (E^{x})] *eras. after word.* me (E^{x})] *on eras.* ęlce deg (E^{3})] *letter eras. after gloss.*

LTg: mihi (*1st*)] michi E, C: *orig.* mihi: c *interl. by corr.* lacrimae] lacrimę BCEFHKL; lacrimæ D; lacrime GIJ. meae] meæ BDL; meę CEFGK, H: ę *interl.* panes] H: a *altered from* e, M: *orig.* panis: i *altered to* e *by corr.* die] E: *on eras. by corr.* ac] ác E: *on eras. by corr.* mihi (*2nd*)] michi E, C: *orig.* mihi: c *interl. by corr.* ubi] úbi L.

LTu: mihi (*1st*)] michi ζιλξςτφ, πϱ: c *interl.;* m^{1} στ*. lacrimae] lacrimę ειμνξπϱσφ; lacrimæ ϑχ; lacrime ςτ*τυ. meae] meę εινξσςφχ; meæ ϑ; mee τ*. panes] ο: *orig.* panis: i *deleted*, e *interl.;* panis β: *cf. Weber MSS* αδε^{2}ηλ moz^{c}, *see GAu.* mihi (*2nd*)] michi ιλξςφ, ϱ: c *interl.;* m^{1} πστ*τ. cotidie] cotidię ξ.

GAu: panes] panis β: *see LTu.*

5

Haec ðas A, þas *BDE^{x}*GHJK,* þysys *C,* þyssa F, þas þing I (*L*)
recordatus gemyndig ABCF, ic gemunde DE$^{3/x}$*GHIK, gemunnende J
sum ic eam A, ic eom BCFGJ
et ⁊ ABCDE^{x}FGHIJK
effudi ageat AB*C*, ægeæt E^{3}, oneat J, ic ageat DFHIK, ic ongeat G
in in A, on BCDE^{3}FHIJK
me me ABCDE^{3}FGHIJK
animam | sawle ABCDFGIJK, saule H, mine E^{3}
meam | mine ABCDFG*H*IK, min J, sæwle E^{3}
quoniam forðon ABDH, forþon CJ, forðæn E^{3}, forðan ðe F, forþan þe I, forþam G, forðam K
ingrediar* ic inga A, ic ingá B, ic innga C, ic ingange D, ic ingænge E^{3}, ic ga K, ic fare FGJ, ic gewite I
in in A, on BCDE^{3}FGHIJK
locum stowe ABCE^{3}FGHIJK, stow D
tabernaculi geteldes ABDGHJK, geteldys C, getelda F, eærdunge ł geteldes E$^{3/x}$*, bures ł eardungstowes ł geteldes I
admirabilis wundurlic *AB,* wundorlic CJ, wundurlices D, to wunderlices F, wundorlices E^{3}*I,* wundyrlices K, wuldorlices G, wulderli[ ]es H* (*M*)
usque oð AB*C*FGHIJK, oþ DE^{3}
ad on DFGHJ, to IK
domum | godes hus A, hus BDFGHJ, hvs C, huse I, huses K, godes E^{3}
dei | godes ABDFGHIJK, godys C, hus E^{3}
in in A, on BCDE^{3}*FGHIJK*

uoce		stefne ABCDGHIK, stæfne J, stemne E^{3}F
exultationis		wynsumnisse A, wynsumnesse B, wynsumnysse *C*, winsumnesse J, blisse ł winsumnesse $E^{3/x}$*, blisse DF*GH*I, blise K (*M*)
et		⁊ ABCDE^{3}FGHIJK
confessionis	I	ondetnisse A, ondetnesse B, andytnysse C, andetnisse DH, ánddetnysse F, anddetnesse G, andetnysse I, andetnesse JK, swegie E^{3} (*M*)
sonus	I	swoeg AB, sweg CDFGHIJK, onddetnesse E^{3} (*M*)
epulantis		symbliendes *AB*, symbliyndys C, symbligendis J, wistfulgend ł simliende $E^{3/x}$*, gewistfulgend D*H*, gewistfulligend *G**, wistfulgend F, mærsiendes ł ł wistfulliendes I*, wistfullend *K* (*LM*)

ED: Hæc (D)] Haec *Roeder.* Haec (G)] *Haec Rosier.* Hęc (E)] Haec *Harsley.* [ ]ec (H)] Hec *Campbell.* forðon (A)] for ðon *Kuhn.* wulderli[ ]es (H)] wulderli(c)es *Campbell.* ęxultationis (G)] exultationis *Rosier.* mærsiendes ł ł wistfulliendes (I)] mærsiendes ł wistfulliendes *Lindelöf.*

OE: þas (E^{x})] *on eras.* ic gemunde ($E^{3/x}$)] ic *and* unde *on eras. by corr.*, m *retraced.* eærdunge ł geteldes ($E^{3/x}$)] ł geteldes *added by corr.* wulderli[ ]es (H)] *letter fragment visible after* i. blisse ł winsumnesse ($E^{3/x}$)] blisse ł *added by corr.* wistfulgend ł simliende ($E^{3/x}$)] wistfulgend ł *added by corr.* gewistfulligend (G)] *1st* l *interl.* mærsiendes ł ł wistfulliendes (I)] ł wistfulliendes *written in right margin,* s. est : is *written in left margin.*

LTg: Haec] Hęc CEJ; Hæc BDKL; [ ]ec H: *outline of initial* H *visible.* effudi] effúdi C. meam] me[ ] H: *hole in leaf after* e. admirabilis] admirábilis M; ammirabilis ABI. usque] C: *orig.* usquę: *cauda eras.* in (*3rd*)] In FGHIJK. exultationis] C: a *malformed* (*false start of* i?), H: *2nd* i *formed from another letter;* ęxultationis G; exultatiônis M. confessionis] confessiônis M. sonus] sónus M. epulantis] ępulantis AGH; æpulantis BL; aepulantis KM.

LTu: Haec] Hęc ειξσφ; Hec τ*; Hæc χ. tabernaculi] tabenaculi χ. admirabilis] ammirabilis ιϱυ, β: *orig.* admirabile: d *and* e *deleted,* m *and* is *interl.*, o: *orig.* admirabilis: d *deleted,* m *interl.* in (*3rd*)] In δεζϑιλμξοπϱστυφχψ. exultationis] exsultationis ψ. epulantis] aepulantis βυχ.

GAg: ingrediar] transibo FGHIJK.

GAu: ingrediar] transibo δεζϑιλμξοπϱστυφχψ.

6

Quare	forhwon ABCJ, forhwy D$E^{3/x}$*, forhwý F*, forwhi GHIK (*L*)
tristis	unrot ABCDFGHIJK, sari ł unrot $E^{3/x}$*

es	earðu A, eart ðu B, eart þu CE[x]I*JK*, eart DF*GH* (*M*)
anima	sawul A, sawl BCDG, sawle FJ, saul H, sawel K, min E[3], eala þu min *I*
mea	min ABCDFG*H*JK, Sæwl E[3], sawl *I*
et	⁊ ABCDE[3]FGHIJ (K*)
quare	forhon A, forhwon BCFJ, forwæn E[3], forhwy DH, forhwi GK, hwi I
conturbas	gedroefdes ðu A, gedroefes ðu B, gedrefdyst þu C*, gedrefest þu E[3]IJ, drefst DFGH, drefst þu K
me	me ABCDE[3]FGHIJK
Spera	gehyht *AB*, gehiht *C*, ic gehihte J, hyht *DE*[x]*H, hiht G*K*, hopa F, hopa ł gehyht I* (*LM*)
in	in A, on BCDE[3]FHIJK
deum*	gode AFGHIJ, god BCDE[3]K
quoniam	forðon ABD*FJ*, forþon C, forðæn E[3], forðan *K*, forðan þe *I*, forþam *G*
⟨adhuc⟩	nu gít *F*, nu gyt *I*, nu git *J*, na gyt *G* (*HK*)
confitebor	ic ondetto AB*, ic andette CDGIJK, ic ændette E[3], ic ándete F, ic ande H (*M*)
illi	him ABCE[3]FGHJ, hi<u>m</u> DIK
salutare	haelu A, hælo BDFGHJ, hæle CK, helo E[3], se halwenda I (*M*)
uultus	ondwlitan AB, andwlitan DFGH, anwlitan IK, onwlitan J, onsien ł andwlitan E[3/x]*, hiwys C
mei	minis A, minys C, mines BDE[x]*GHI*J, minne F, mine K

ED: forhwon (A)] for hwon *Kuhn.* forhwy (DE) (*1st*)] for hwy *Roeder;* Forhwy *Harsley.* ęs (G)] es *Rosier.* és (H)] es *Campbell.* forhon (A)] for hon *Kuhn.* forhwy (D) (*2nd*)] for hwy *Roeder.* Spera (FG)] spera *Kimmens;* Spera *Rosier.* forðon (A)] for ðon *Kuhn.* adhúc (H)] adhuc *Campbell.* nu git (J)] nugit *Oess.*

OE: forhwy (E[3/x])] hwy *on eras. by corr.,* r *retraced.* forhwý (F)] f *with ascender above top stroke.* sari ł unrot (E[3/x])] sari ł *on eras. by corr.* et (K)] ⁊ *eras. to make room for later punct.* gedrefdyst þu (C)] þu *added by corr. in red ink.* hyht (E[x])] *on eras.* hopa ł gehyht (I)] y *altered* (?) *from* i. ic ondetto (B)] forð *eras. before* ic; *note preceding* forðon. onsien ł andwlitan (E[3/x])] ł andwlitan *added by corr.* mines (E[x])] ne *on eras.* mines (I)] s. e<u>st</u> : is *written in right margin: as in other psalters* I *joins v. 7* deus meus (*here omitting* et) *to v. 6, and links marginal addition* est (*underdotted once*) *with* deus meus (*underdotted twice*).

LTg: Quare] Quáre L. es] ęs G; és HJKM. mea] H: *punct. after word on eras.,* I: s. o *written before word.* Spera] K: S *on eras. by corr.;* spera ABCDELM. quoniam] quoniam adhuc FGIJK; quoniam adhúc H: *cf. Bib. sac. MS* F^2 *and Hebr.* confitebor] confitêbor M. salutare] salutâre M.

LTu: Spera] spera βτ*. quoniam] quoniam adhuc δεζϑιλμξοπϱσυφχ: *cf. Bib. sac. MS* F^2 *and Hebr.*

GAg: deum] deo FGHIJK.

GAu: deum] deo δεζϑιλξοπϱστυφχψ.

7

et*	⁊ ABCDE^3*FGHJK
deus	god ABCDE^3*FGJK, godes H, min I
meus	min ABCDE^{3}F*G**JK, god I
A*	from AE^3, from C, fram BDF, fram K, to GHIJ
me	me ABCDE^{3}FGHIJK (*M*)
ipso*	seolfum A, selfum B, selfum D, sylfum C, sylfum FGI, syluum H, silfum E^{3}J, sylfan K
anima	sawul A, sawl BCDG, Sæwl E^3, saul FH, sawle IJ, sawel K
mea	min ABCDE^{3}FGHIJK
turbata*	gedroefed A, gedrefedu B, gedrefyd C, gedrefed DE^{3}FGHIJK
est	is ABDE^{3}FGHIJK, ys C
propterea	forðon ABD, forþon CFGHJ, forþan E$^{3/x}$*IK
memor	gemyndig ABCDFGHI, gemindig J, gemindy E^3, gemyndi K
ero	ic biom A, ic beom C, ic beo BDE^{x}FGHIJK
tui	ðin AB, þin CDE^{3}FGHIJK
domine*	ðryhten A, drihten E^x*, dryht̄ B, drih́t C
de	of ABCDE^3*FGHIJK
terra	eorðan ABCDE^3*FGH, eorþan J, eorþan K, lande I
iordanis	iordanys C, iordænis E^3, iordane J, ðære éa F, þære ea GI, n K* (*M*)
et	⁊ ACE^{3}FI
hermonis*	hermonys C, hermonis E^3, ánathema F, n K* (*IM*)
a	from A*E^3*, fram BCDHJK, fram FGI* (*M*)
monte	munte AB*CD**GH, muntte J, monte K*, dune E^{3}FI
modico	ðæm lytlan A*, þæm lytlan B, þæm lytlan C, þam litlan ł medmicclan J, medmiclum DF, medmiclum GH, medmycel K, unmicelre E$^{3/x}$*, gehwædre I

ED: from (E) (*1st*)] From *Harsley.* forðon (A)] for ðon *Kuhn.* me ipsum (K)] meipsum *Sisam.* iordanis (K)] Iordanis *Sisam.* ermoníím (K)] Ermoniim *Sisam.* hermoníím (H)] hermoniim *Campbell.* á (E)] a *Harsley.*

OE: ⁊ (E^{3}) (*1st*)] ond *eras. after word.* god (E^{3})] *retraced* (?). min (G)] u͟m͟ *perhaps visible after* n. forþan ($E^{3/x}$)] *eras. after* for, þ *retraced,* an *on eras. by corr.* drihten (E^{x})] *on eras.* of (E^{3})] *retraced by corr., small eras. after* f. eorðan (E^{3})] eor *retraced by corr.* n (K) (*both*)] *for* nomen. fram (I)] *eras. after word.* munte (D)] te *written above* n *to avoid interference from Lat. marginal gloss.* monte (K)] *letter* (u?) *eras. after* o. ðæm lytlan (A)] an *obscured by stain but visible.* unmicelre ($E^{3/x}$)] un *by corr.,* micelre *retraced.*

LTg: meus] meu[ ] G. me] mé M. iordanis] iordânis M. hermonis] hermônis M: *orig.* ermônis: h *inserted by corr.;* hermoniim I: *gloss eras. above word.* a] á EM. monte] C: te *interl.*

LTu: A] *om.* τ*. propterea] ϑ: ea *interl.* hermonis] ermonis β.

GAg: et (*1st*)] *om.* I: *see OE note to v. 6* mines. A] Ad FHIJK; [ ]d G. ipso] ipsum FGHIJK. turbata] conturbata FGHIJK. domine] *om.* FGHIJK. hermonis] ermoniim F; ermoníím K: ii *altered from* u, *accents added;* hermoniim I, G: *crude extra minim added to* m *in slightly lighter brown ink;* hermoníím H: h *and final* m *interl.;* hermonin J.

GAu: et (*1st*)] *om.* δεζμοπφχψ. A] Ad δεζϑιλμξοπρστυφχψ. ipso] ipsum δεζϑιλμξοπρστυφχψ. turbata] conturbata δεζϑιλμξοπρστυφχψ. domine] *om.* δεζϑιλμξοπρστυφχψ. hermonis] hermonim δ; hermoniim εζιλμξοπρτφχψ, υ: *2nd* i *interl.;* hermonin ϑ; ermonum σ.

8

Abyssus	niolnis A, neolnes B, neolnys C, neolnessa J, [ ]ywelnes ł deopnys I*, deopnes DGK, Dyopnes E^{x}, deopnys F, deopnis H (*LM*)
abyssum	niolnisse A, neolnesse B, neolnysse C, neowelnysse F, neolnys J, deopnesse D, diopnesse E^{x}, deopnysse G, deopnisse H, deopnissa I*, of deopnesse K (*LM*)
inuocat	geceð A, gecegð B, gecigyð *C,* gecigð *I*, gecigeþ J, cigð DG*H,* cég F, oncigaþ K, chieð E^{3}*
in	in AD, on BCE^{3}FGHIJK
uoce	stefne ABCDE^{3}GIK, stæfne HJ, stemne F (*M*)
cataractarum	ðeotena A*, þeotena B, þeotyna C, wæterædrana DH, wæter-ædrana M^{2}*, wæterædrena F, wæteræddrena G, wæterædran K, wæterþeotena IJ, geheftræ rihtræ ł wæterædrana $E^{3/x}$*, forsceta M*

tuarum ðinra AF, þinra BCDGHJK, þinræ E^3*, þinra ł þinra wætcrædrana I*
omnia all A, ealle BC*FGHIJ*K, ealla D, eællæ E^3
excelsa ða hean A, þa hean BC, þa heán J, hea DH, heage K, heannyssa F, heannessa *G,* heanyssa I, hihþo E^3
tua ðin A, þin G, þine BCE^{3}FIJK, þina DH
et ⁊ ABCDE^{3}FGHIJK
fluctus yðe AC, yða BFG, yþa DE^{3}HIJ, flod K
tui ðine AF, þine CDE^{3}GIJ, ðina B, þin HK
super ofer ABDE^{3}FGHIJ, ofyr C, ofor K
me mec A, me BCDE^{3}FGHIJK
transierunt leordun A, leordon B, gewiton C, foron DGH, foron ł ferdon J, ferdon ł gewiton F^3*, gewiton urnun ł ferdon I*, ferdan K, ferdon E^3

ED: [ ]ywelnes ł deopnys (I)] nywelnes ł deopnys *Lindelöf.* ínuocat (HI)] inuocat *Campbell, Lindelöf.* deopnissa (I)] deopnisse *Lindelöf, but see p. 68, n. 3.* þinra ł þinra wæterædrana (I)] þinra ł þinra wæteredrana *Lindelöf, but see p. 69, n. 1.* gewiton urnun ł ferdon (I)] gewiton ł urnun ł ferdon *Lindelöf.*

OE: [ ]ywelnes ł deopnys (I)] *initial letter lost due to tight binding.* deopnissa (I)] *orig.* deopnisse: *final* e *altered to* a. chieð (E^3)] *eras. before word.* ðeotena (A)] *orig.* ðeotene: *final* e *deleted by subscript dot,* a *interl.* wæter-ædrana (M^2)] *orig.* wæter-ædrena: a *interl. above 2nd* e. geheftræ rihtræ ł wæterædrana (E$^{3/x}$)] rihtræ ł wæterædrana *added by corr.* forsceta (M)] cataracte forsceta. catarecte aquam concludunt *written in red ink in right margin in context.* þinræ (E^3)] þinr *retraced* (?). þinra ł þinra wæterædrana (I)] ł þinra wæterædrana *written in right margin,* ana *on eras.* ferdon ł gewiton (F^3)] *added in pencil in OE characters in late hand* (*Spelman?*). gewiton urnun ł ferdon (I)] ł ferdon *written in bottom margin below lemma.*

LTg: Abyssus] Abysus L, M: *additional* s *inserted after* y *by corr., but later eras.* abyssum] abysum L, M: *additional* s *inserted after* y *by corr., but later eras.* inuocat] ínuocat CHI. uoce] uôce M. omnia] Omnia FGHIJ. excelsa] exscelsa G.

LTu: Abyssus] Abisus ϑ; Abysus ν; Abissus ξτ*τ. abyssum] abisum ϑ; abysum ν; abissum ξτ*τ; ad abyssum μ: *cf. Weber MSS* ηλ (*Ga. sub ast.*). omnia] Omnia δεζϑλμξοπϱστυφχψ. transierunt] transerunt ϑ.

9

In in A, on BCDFHIJK, On E^3 (*G*)
die dege AE^3, dæge BCFIJK, dæg DGH
mandauit onbead A, bebead BCDHIJK, he bebead F, bebeæð E^3

dominus		drihten DK, dryhten E^{3}, dryht̄ AB, drih̄t *C*FG, drih̄ HJ
misericordiam	I	mildheortnisse AD, mildheortnesse BE^{3}HJK, mildheortnysse CF, mil[ ] *G*, his I
suam	I	his ABDE^{3}FGHJK, hys C, mildheortnysse *I*
et		⁊ ABCDE^{3}FGHI*J*K
⟨in⟩		on *J*
nocte		on naeht A, on niht BDE$^{3/x}$*H, on nihte I, nihte CF, niht GJK
declarauit*		gebirhte A, gebyrhte B, gefræbeorhtude C, he gesweotolode DE^{x}* (*M*)
(canticum)*		cantic FGH, cantic ł sang J, sang K, lofsang I
(eius)*		his FGHIJK
Apud		mid *A*B*C*DF*G*HIJK, Mid E^{3}
me		mec A, me BCDE^{3}FGHIJK
oratio		gebe A, gebed BDE^{3}FGHIJK, gebede C
deo		gode ABDE^{3}FGHI, godys C, godes J, god K
uitae	I	lifes _BDE$^{3/x}$*GHI_J_K_, lifys *C*, lif *F*, mines A (*L*)
meae	I	mines _BDE$^{3/x}$*FGHI_*J_K_, minys *C*, lifes A (*L*)

ED: die (G)] *d*ie *Rosier.* dæg (G)] *no gloss Rosier.* mandauit (G)] mandaui*t Rosier.* mil[ ] (G) mi[ ] *Rosier.* Apud (C)] Apu[t] *Wildhagen.* uitę (E)] vitae *Harsley.* uite (I)] uitae *Lindelöf.* meæ (D)] meae *Roeder.* meę (E)] meae *Harsley.* mee (I)] meae *Lindelöf.*

OE: on niht (E$^{3/x}$)] on *added by corr.* he gesweotolode (E^{x})] sweotolode *on eras.* lifes (E$^{3/x}$)] es *added by corr.* mines (E$^{3/x}$)] es *added by corr.* mines (I)] s. e̲s̲t̲ : is *written in left margin.*

LTg: In] *lost* G. dominus] C: *eras.* (?) *after* i. misericordiam] miser[ ] G. suam] I: s *on eras.* et] et in J: *cf. Weber MSS* moz^{x}. declarauit] declârauit M. Apud] A: d *on eras. by corr.*, C: *orig.* Aput: t *altered to* d; [ ]pud G. uitae] uitæ BK; uitę CDEGHL; uite F, I: *orig.* uitae: a *eras.* meae] meæ BDL; meę CEFGHK; mee I: *orig.* meae: a *eras.*

LTu: In] IN β. misericordiam] missericordiam ϑ. nocte] in nocte ϑ. oratio] oracio σ. uitae] uitę βινξφ; uite εσςτ*τχ; uitæ ϑ. meae] meę βεινξςφχ; meæ ϑ; mee στ*τ.

GAg: declarauit] *om.* FGHIJK. nocte] nocte canticum eius FGHIJ; nocte canticum eíus K.

GAu: declarauit] *om.* δεζϑιλμξοπρστυφχψ. nocte] nocte canticum eius δεξιλμξοπρστυφχψ; in nocte canticum eius ϑ.

10

dicam	ic cweoðu A, ic cweðe BCIK, cweþe J, ic cwiþe E^{3}, ic secge DFGH (*M*)

deo	gode ABCE^{3}FGH, to gode IJ, god K*
susceptor	ondfenga A, ondfengend B, andfenge CG, andfeng D, onfeng E^{3}, anfeng HIK, andfengc J, underfang F
meus	min ABCDE^{3}FGHIJK
es	ðu earð A, ðu eart B, þu eart CDG*H*I, þu ært E^{x}*, eart FJ, is *K* (*M*)
Quare	forhwon ABJ, forhwan C, forhwy D, forhwý F, forhwi E^{x}*GHI*K (*LM*)
me*	mec A, me BCDE^{x} (*M*)
oblitus	ofergeotul AB, ofyrgyttol C, þu ofergete DE^{x}, þu ofergeate FGH, forgeate þu I*, foreate þu J, forgyten K
es	earð A, ðu eart B, eart þu C, eart *K,* þu H (*JL*)
et*	⁊ ABCDE^{x}, me FJ, min GHIK
⟨et⟩	⁊ *IJ* (*HK*)
quare	forhwon ABJ, forhwan C, forhwý F, forhwi E^{x}GIK (*M*)
me*	mec A, me BCE^{x}
reppulisti*	onweg adrife ðu A, þu aweg adrife *B,* aweg adryfe C, þu utanyddest *D,* þu utawyltest ł anyldest E^{x}*
et*	⁊ ABCE^{x}
quare*	forhwon AB, forhawn C, forhwi E^{x}
tristis*	unrot ABCDK, unrot ł sári E^{x}, ge[ ]rot G*, geunrotsod HI, drefst F*, drefst unrote J
incedo	ic ingaa A, ic ingá B, ic innga C, ic gange DE^{x}*F*G*HK,* ic ingange J, gesteppe ic ł ga ic I (*M*)
dum	ðonne ABFK, þonne CDE^{x}HJ, þonne G, þænne I
adfligit	swenceð *AB,* swencyð *C,* swencð *DE^{x}F,* swingð *G,* swincg *H,* swænceþ *J,* geswencð *I,* swenð *K*
me	mec A, me BCE^{x}FGIJK (*M*)
inimicus	fiond AE^{3}*, feond BCDFGHIK, fynd mine J (*M*)

ED: gode (F)] god *Kimmens.* és (H)] es *Campbell.* forhwon (A) (*all*)] for hwon *Kuhn.* forhwy (D)] for hwy *Roeder.* forhwi (E^{x}) (*1st*)] For hwi *Harsley.* forhwi (G) (*1st*)] forhw[ ] *Rosier.* onweg adrife ðu (A)] on weg adrife ðu *Kuhn.* þu aweg adrife (B)] þu awegadrife *Brenner.* þu utawyltest ł anyldest (E)] þu utawyltest ł anyld*e*st *Harsley.* contristat<u>us</u> (G)] contristat*us Rosier.* ge[ ]rot (G)] *no gloss Rosier.* affligit (C)] a[d]fligit *Wildhagen.*

OE: god (K)] *letter* (e?) *eras. after word.* þu ært (E^{x})] *on eras.* forhwi (E^{x}) (*1st*)] *letter eras. before word.* forhwi (I) (*1st*)] *gloss eras. after word.* forgeate þu (I)] *on eras.* þu utawyltest ł anyldest (E^{x})] de *in ligature.* ge[ ]rot (G)] *bottoms of 4 minims* (un?) *visible after* e (> geunrot?). drefst (F)] *source-text misread, perhaps read gloss to* conturbas *in v. 12; see also* J. fiond (E^{3})] *retraced by corr.*

LTg: dicam] dîcam M. es (*1st*)] és HKM. Quare] Quáre L; Quâre M. me (*1st*)] mé M. es (*2nd*)] és JKL. quare (*1st*)] quâre M. reppulisti] repulisti B; reppullisti D: *2nd* l *interl.* incedo] incędo FH; incædo K; incêdo M. adfligit] affligit ABDEFGHIJK, C: *1st* f *on eras. by corr.* me (*3rd*)] mê M. inimicus] inimîcus M.

LTu: Dicam] dicam βδεζϑιλμνξοπϱσςτ*τυφχ. et (*2nd*)] *interl.* v. adfligit] affligit εζιλξοπϱστ*τυφχ.

GAg: me (*1st*)] *om.* FGHIJK. et (*1st*)] mei FGJ; mei et IJ, H: et *interl.*, K: *added by corr.: cf. Bib. sac. MSS* VDΩ, *etc.* me (*2nd*)] *om.* FGHIJK. reppulisti et quare] *om.* FGHIJK. tristis] contristatus FGHIJK.

GAu: me (*1st*)] *om.* δεζϑιλμξοπϱστυφχψ. et (*1st*)] *om.* ε; mei ϑιμξυχψ; mei et λοϱστφ, δζπ: et *interl.* me (*2nd*)] *om.* δεζϑιλμξοπϱστυφχψ. reppulisti et quare] *om.* δεζϑιλμξοπϱστυφχψ. tristis] contristatus δεζϑιλμξοπϱστυφχψ.

11

<table>
<tr><td>Dum</td><td></td><td>ðonne A, þonne B*E*^{x}*GHK, þon<u>ne</u> CDFJ, þænne I</td></tr>
<tr><td>confringuntur</td><td></td><td>bioð gebrocen A, beoð gebrocene B, beoð gebrocyne *C,* beoð tobrocene DFH, bioð tobrocene E$^{3/x}$*, beoð tobrocenne G, beoþ tobrocenne J, beoð tobrocone I, biþ tobrocen K (*M*)</td></tr>
<tr><td>omnia*</td><td></td><td>all A, ealle BCD, eælle E^{3}</td></tr>
<tr><td>ossa</td><td></td><td>ban ABCDFGHIJK, bǽn E^{3}</td></tr>
<tr><td>mea</td><td></td><td>min ABK, mine CDE^{3}FGHIJ</td></tr>
<tr><td>exprobrauerunt</td><td>|</td><td>edwiton A, oðwiton C, hyspton *B,* hy hypston D, he hypston H, hy hyspton F, hi hyspton G, hi hispton J, hi hospton K, hisctun ł gebysmredon I, me E^{3} (*M*)</td></tr>
<tr><td>me*</td><td>|</td><td>mec A, me BCFGHIJK, edwitodon E^{3} (*M*)</td></tr>
<tr><td>qui</td><td></td><td>ða A, þa CK, þa ðe B, ða þe F, þa þe GIJ, ðe D, þe E^{3}H (*M*)</td></tr>
<tr><td>tribulant</td><td></td><td>swencað ABDFGHK, swenceað C, swæncaþ J, eærfoþodon ł swencað E$^{3/x}$*, gedrefað I</td></tr>
<tr><td>me</td><td></td><td>mec A, me BCDE^{3}FGHJK</td></tr>
<tr><td>(inimici)*</td><td></td><td>fynd FGIJK, feond H</td></tr>
<tr><td>(mei)*</td><td></td><td>mine FGHIJK</td></tr>
<tr><td>dum</td><td></td><td>ðonne AB, þon<u>ne</u> CD*FJ,* þonne *G,* þone *K,* þænne *I,* midþi E^{3} (*H*)</td></tr>
<tr><td>dicitur*</td><td></td><td>bið cweden ABDK, bið cwedyn C, bið cweþende E^{3}, cweþan F, hi cweðaþ I, cweþaþ hig J, hi secgað G</td></tr>
<tr><td>mihi</td><td></td><td>to me AB, me *CDE^{3}F*GHIJK</td></tr>
<tr><td>per</td><td></td><td>ðorh A, þurh BCDE^{3}FGHJ, ðurh K, gind I</td></tr>
</table>

singulos		syndrie A, Syndrie E^{3}, syndrige BCDJK, ænlipige F, seon GH, synderlicum ł ænlipie I
dies		dægas AB, dagas CDFGJK, dæges H, dægæs E^{3}, dæge I
ubi		hwer AE^{3}, hwær BCDFGHI*, hwar JK (*L*)
est		is ABDE^{3}FGHIJ*K*, ys C
deus	|	god ABCDE^{3}FGHJK, þin I
tuus	|	ðin ABF, þin CDE^{3}GHJ, ure K, god I

ED: mi[ ] (G)] michi *Rosier.* dum (E)] um *Harsley.*

OE: þonne (E^{x})] *on eras.* bioð tobrocene (E$^{3/x}$)] to *on eras. by corr., rest retraced in darker ink.* eærfoþodon ł swencað (E$^{3/x}$)] ł swencað *added by corr.* hwær (I)] *eras. before word.*

LTg: Dum] Dvm E. confringuntur] C: frin *on eras.;* confringúntur M. exprobrauerunt] exprobrauérunt M; exprobauerunt B. me (*1st*)] mê M. qui] quî M. dum] Dum FGHIJK. mihi] michi E, C: *orig.* mihi: c *interl. by corr.,* G: *orig.* mihi: c *added by corr in light brown ink.* ubi] úbi L. est] ést K.

LTu: dum] Dum δεζθιλμξοπρστυφχψ. mihi] michi ιξτ, πρ: c *interl.;* m^{1} λτ*φ.

GAg: omnia] *om.* FGHIJK. me (*1st*)] mihi FHIJK; mi[ ] G: *3 letters after* i *cannot be made out distinctly.* me (*2nd*)] me inimici mei FGHIJK. dicitur] dicunt FGHIJK.

GAu: omnia] *om.* δεζθιλμξοπρστυφχψ. me (*1st*)] mihi δεζθμοχψ; michi ς, πρ: c *interl.;* m^{1} ιλνξστυφ. me (*2nd*)] me inimici mei δεζιλμξοπρστυφχψ. dicitur] dicunt δεζθιλμξοπρστυφχψ.

12

Quare		forhwon ABCJ, forhwy D*F*G, forhwi E$^{3/x}$*HI*K* (*M*)
tristis	|	unrot ABCDE^{3}FGHJ*K*, eart þu I
es	|	earðu A, eart ðu B, eart þu C, eart J, is *D*E^{3}FG*H*, unrot I (K**M*)
anima	|	sawul A, sawl BCD, saul F, sæul E^{3}*, sawle GHJ, sawel K, eala þu min I*
mea	|	min BCDE^{3}FK, myn J, mine G*H*, him A, sawl I*
et		⁊ ABCDE^{3}FGHIJ (*K*)
quare		forhwon ABJ*, forhwan C, forwæn E^{3}, forhwy D, forhwý F, forhwi GH, hwi IK (*M*)
conturbas		gedroefes ðu A, gedrefst ðu B, gedrefyst þu C, gedrefest þu I, gedrefst þu J, þu gedrefest E$^{3/x}$*, drefst DFHK*, gedrefst G
me		mec A, me CDE^{3}*FGIJK

Spera gehyht *AB*, gehiht CIJ, hyht *D*E^{x}*, hihte G, hyhte H, hiht K, hopa F (*M*)
in in A, on BCDE^{3}FGHIJK
deum* god ABCDE^{3}K, gode FGHIJ
quoniam forðon ABDHJ, forþon C, forþæn E^{3}*, forðan ðe F, forðan þe I, forðam G
(adhuc)* na gýt F, na gyt G, nu git IJ, gyt K
confitebor ic ondetto A, ic ondette B, ic andytte C, ic andette DGHIJK, ic ændette E^{3}, ic andete F (*M*)
illi him ACE^{3}FGHIJ, him BDK
salutare haelu A, hælo BDFGHJ, hæle CK, helo E^{3}, hælo ł þone halwendan I (*M*)
uultus ondwleotan A, ondwlitan B, andwlitan CDFGHI*J, anwlitan K, ondwlite E^{3}
mei mines ABDE$^{3/x}$*FGHJK, minys C, minre I
et | ⁊ ABCE^{3}FGHJK, god *I*
deus | god ABCE^{3}FGHJK, ⁊ I
meus min ABCDE^{3}FGHIJK

ED: forhwon (A) (*both*)] for hwon *Kuhn.* forhwy (D) (*both*)] for hwy *Roeder.* forhwi (E)] Forhwi *Harsley.* és (H)] es *Campbell.* min (E)] *Harsley notes final letter eras.* forhwon (A) (*both*)] for hwon *Kuhn.* forhwy (D) (*both*)] for hwy *Roeder.* forðon (A)] for ðon *Kuhn.* nu git (J)] nugit *Oess.*

OE: forhwi (E$^{3/x}$)] hwi *on eras. by corr.* es (K)] eart *eras. above word.* sæul (E^{3})] sæu *retraced* (?) *by corr.* eala þu min (I)] s. o *written before* eala, u min *on eras.* sawl (I)] *on eras.* forhwon (J) (*2nd*)] *scribe began* forho- *and corrected 2nd* o *to* w. þu gedrefest (E$^{3/x}$)] st *on eras. by corr.* drefst (K)] *eras. before word, perhaps of* dref *or* drif. me (E^{3})] *retraced by corr.* hyht (E^{x})] *on eras.* forþæn (E^{3})] æn *retraced by corr.* andwlitan (I)] *eras. before word.* mines (E$^{3/x}$)] es *added by corr.*

LTg: Quare] Quâre M; [ ]uare F: *initial letter lost due to damage to bottom left of leaf;* quare K. tristis] K: *final* s *interl.* es] K: *gloss eras.;* és DHM. mea] H: *punct. after word on eras.* et (*1st*)] K: *gloss eras.* quare] quâre M. Spera] spera ABDM. confitebor] confitêbor M. salutare] salutâre M. et (*2nd*)] I: *eras. before and after word* (?).

LTu: Quare] quare δσ. et (*2nd*)] *interl.* ε.

GAg: deum] deo FGHIJ; dō K: *macron by main hand,* o *by corr.* quoniam] quoniam adhuc FGHJ, IK: *eras. after* adhuc, *most likely of flanking sign* (※ *precedes word in both cases*).

GAu: deum] deo δεζθιλξοπϱστυφχψ. quoniam] quoniam adhuc δεζθιλμξοπϱστυφχψ.

PSALM 42

1

Iudica doem *AB*, dem *CD*E^{3}F*GH*I*, dem þu J, [ ]em *K** (*M*)
me mec A, me B*C*E^{3}FGHIJ*K*
deus god AB*C*DE^{3}FGHJK, þu god I*
et ⁊ ABCE^{3}FGHIJK
discerne toscad ABJ, toscead CD*E*^{3}FGH, toscæd K, totwæm ł toscead I
causam intingan ABCDFGHI, íntíngan J, intingæn E^{3}, intinge K
meam minne ABCDE^{3}FGHI, mínne J, mine K
de of ABCDE$^{3/x}$*FGHI*JK
gente | ðeode ABDFGK, þeode CHJ, þiode E^{3}, unhaligre I*
non noht AB, naht CGJ, na K (*I*)
sancta | haligre ABJ, haligra C, halig G, halire K, unhaligre DFH, unhæligre E$^{3/x}$*, þeode I*
ab from A, from B, fram CDHJK, fram FGI, fræm E^{3}
homine men ABDE^{3}*G*HJK, menn CI, mannum F
iniquo unrehtum A, unrihtum C, unryhtwisum B, unryhtwisum D, unrihtwisum FGHI, unrihtwisum E$^{3/x}$*JK
et ⁊ ABCDE^{x}*FGHIJK
doloso facnum A*, facnum C, facenfullum BH, facenfullum DGJ, fakenfullum I, facenfullen E^{x}*, facenfulle F, facfullan K
eripe* genere ABE^{3}, genery C, genera FIJ, nere DGH, nera K*
me me ABCDE^{3}FGHIJK (*M*)

ED: [ ]udica (G)] Iudica *Rosier.* discernę (E)] discerne *Harsley.* íntíngan (J)] intingan *Oess.* mínne (J)] minne *Oess.*

OE: dem (I)] *eras. before word.* [ ]em (K)] *initial letter lost due to excision of initial from fol. 48r.* þu god (I)] o *written before* þu. of (E$^{3/x}$)] f *on eras. by corr.* of (I)] *on eras.* unhaligre (I)] *on eras.* unhæligre (E$^{3/x}$)] un *and* igre *on eras. by corr., eras. (2 letters?) before* h. þeode (I)] *on eras.* unrihtwisum (E$^{3/x}$)] *eras. (2 letters?) before word,* twisū *on eras. by corr.* ⁊ (E^{x}) (*2nd*)] *on eras.* facnum (A)] a *partly obscured by blot of red ink.* facenfullen (E^{x})] *on eras.* nera (K)] r *eras. before word.*

LTg: Iudica] IVdica AB; IVDICA C; Ivdica DH; IUdica M; [ ]udica G: *initial* I *lost;* [ ]Vdica K: *initial letter excised from fol. 48r.* me (*1st*)] K: *on eras. by main hand. 2 minims and* c *visible after word;* ME C. deus] DEVS C. discerne] discernę E. non] NOn I. homine] hom[ ] G. me (*2nd*)] mê M.

LTu: Iudica] IUdica βϑ; IUDICA ιλμνϱτχψ; IVdica ς. me (*1st*)] ME λμνϱςχψ. deus]

DS̄ λμνϱχψ. et (*1st*)] ET λμνϱψ. discerne] DISCERNE λϱ; DISCERne ν. causam] CAUSAM λ. meam] MEAM λ. doloso] ε: so *interl.*

GAg: eripe] erue FHIJK; ęrue G.

GAu: eripe] erue δεζϑιλμξοπϱστυφχψ.

2

Quia	forðon ABDHJ, forþon F, forþan C*K*, forðæn E^{3}*, forþā þe G, forþan þe I*
tu	ðu ABE^{3}, þu CDFGHIJK (*M*)
es	earð A, eart BCFGHIJK, eært E^{3} (*M*)
deus	god ABCDE^{3}FGHJK
meus*	min ABCDE^{3}
et*	⁊ ABCDE^{3}
fortitudo	strengu A, strengo B, streng C, strang F, freamiht DH, freamiht ł strengð G*, strencð I, strengþ J, strenð K, strengþo E^{3} (*M*)
mea	min ABCDE^{3}*FHIJK
quare	| forhwon ABJ, forwæn E^{3}, forhwi CGHK, forhwy D, forhwý F, hwi I
me	| me ABCE^{3}JK, forwurpe þu me I (*G*)
reppulisti	| onweg adrife ðu A, þu aweg adrife *B*, þu aweg drife *J*, aweg adrefe þu *C*, þu anyddest DG*HK*, þu anydest F, ðu ædrife ł ðu aryddest E$^{3/x}$*, ł forhwi utaðygdest þu me I* (*M*)
et	⁊ ABCDE^{3}FGHIK (*J*)
quare	forhwon ABCJ, forwæn E^{3}, forhwy DF, forhwi GK, forhwi I, for H
tristis	unrot ABCDE^{3}FGHIJK
incedo	ic inga A*C*DE^{x}**F**HJ, ic ingá B, ic gange G, ga ic I*, ic ga *K* (*M*)
dum	ðonne AF, þonne BH, þonne CDE^{x}*J, ðonne K, þonn[ ] G*, þænne I
adfligit	swenceð A*B*, swencð *DE^{x}**, swéncð *F*, swencþ *H*, swænceþ *J*, swenð *K*, s[ ]nc(ð) *G**, geswencyð *C*, geswencð *I*
me	mec A, me BCDE^{x}*FGHIJK
inimicus	se feond A, feond BCDFGHK, fiond E^{3}, fynd I, fynd mine J (*M*)

ED: Quia (BG)] quia *Brenner; Quia Rosier.* forðon (A)] for ðon *Kuhn.* forðæn (E)] Forðæn *Harsley.* forþā þe (G)] forþam þe *Rosier.* forhwon (A) (*both*)] for hwon *Kuhn.* forhwy (D) (*both*)] for hwy *Roeder.* me (G) (*1st Lat.*)] m*e Rosier, who also* *records gloss as* m[ ]: *see LTg note to 1st* me. reppulisti (G)] reppulisti *Rosier.* onweg adrife ðu (A)] on weg adrife ðu *Kuhn.* affligit (C)] a[d]fligit *Wildhagen.* afflígit (H)] affligit *Campbell.* s[ ]nc(ð) (G)] sw:ncð *Rosier.*

OE: forðæn (E3)] r *and bottom of* ð *retraced by corr.* forþan þe (I)] þe *written in left margin.* freamiht ł strengð (G)] n *interl.* min (E3)] *orig.* mine: e *eras.* ðu ædrife ł ðu aryddest (E3/x)] ł ðu aryddest *added by corr.* ł forhwi utaðygdest þu me (I)] *written in right margin.* ic inga (Ex)] *on eras.* ic inga (F)] inga *obscured by eras. but visible.* ga ic (I)] *eras. after* ic. þonne (Ex)] *on eras.* þonn[ ] (G)] *hole after 2nd* n, *traces of letter fragments visible.* swencð (Ex)] *on eras.* s[ ]nc(ð) (G)] *descender visible after* s, *cross-stroke of* ð *not visible.* me (Ex) (*2nd*)] *on eras.*

LTg: Quia] K: Q *partly cropped on left.* tu] tú M. es] és M. fortitudo] fortitûdo M. me (*1st*)] G: *letter fragments of gloss visible interl.* reppulisti] reppulísti M; repulisti BCJK, H: *letter eras. after* e. et (*2nd*)] *om.* J. incedo] C: in *on eras.* (?); incêdo M; incędo FK. adfligit] affligit BDEFGIJK, C: *orig.* adfligit: d *eras., 1st* f *by corr.;* afflígit H. inimicus] inimîcus M.

LTu: Quia] Qua ε. reppulisti] χ: *1st* p *interl.;* repulisti ϑ. et (*2nd*)] *om.* μ; *interl.* πχ. incedo] incędo ξ. adfligit] affligit εζιλξπϱστ*τυφχ.

GAg: meus] *om.* FGHIJK. et (*1st*)] *om.* FGHIJK.

GAu: meus] *om.* δεζιλμξοπϱστυφχψ. et (*1st*)] *om.* δεζιλμξοπϱστυφχψ.

3

Emitte	onsend ABC, onsænd J, asend DFG*H*IK, Asend E3/x*
lucem	leht A, leoht BCDFGHIJK, lioht E3 (*M*)
tuam	ðin AE3, þin BCDFGHIJK
et	⁊ ABCDE3FGHIJK
ueritatem	soðfestnisse A, soðfæstnesse BGK, soðfæstnysse CFI, soþfæstnisse D, soðfestnesse E3/x*, soþfæstnesse HJ (*M*)
tuam	ðine AF, þine BCDE3/x*IJK, þin GH
ipsa	hie A, hiie B, hi CK, hy DEx*GH, hig J, hig sylfe I*, þa F
me	mec A, me BCDExFGHIJK
deduxerunt	gelaedon A, gelæddon BCJ, gelæddun I, læddon DFGH, lædon K, leddon Ex*
et	⁊ ABCDE3FGHIJK
adduxerunt	togelaeddon A, togelæddon BCDFGHJ, togelædon K, togeleddon E3/x*, hig gebrohton I*
in	in A, on BCDE3FGHIJK
monte*	munte ABCFGI, munt DHJK, dune E3 (*L*)
sancto*	ðæm halgan A, ðam halgan B, þam halgan *C*, haligne DGHK, halig F*, halgum I, halgum J, hælgæn *E3/x** (*L*)

tuo* ðinum A, ðinum B, þinum *C*FI, þinum J, þinne DGHK, ðine $E^{3/x}$* (*L*)
et ⁊ ABCDE^{3}FGHIJK
in in AI, on BCDE^{3}FGHJK
tabernaculo* | getelde AB*C*FJ, eardunge *D*H, earddunge K, eærdunge E^{3}*, eardunge ł on getelde G, to þinum I (*L*)
tuo* | ðinum AF, ðinum B, þinum *C*, þínum J, þine *D*H, ðine E^{3}*, þinre G*K, bure ł geteldum I (*L*)

ED: [ ]mitte (H)] Emitte *Campbell.* togelæddon (B)] to gelæddon *Brenner.* scm (C)] sanctum *Wildhagen.* þínum (J)] þinum *Oess.*

OE: Asend ($E^{3/x}$) send *on eras. by corr.* soðfestnesse ($E^{3/x}$)] se *added by corr.* þine ($E^{3/x}$)] e *by corr.* hy (E^{x})] *on eras.* hig sylfe (I)] *eras. before* hig. leddon (E^{x})] *on eras.* togeleddon ($E^{3/x}$)] don *on eras. by corr.* hig gebrohton (I)] *eras. before* hig. halig (F)] *eras. after word.* hælgæn ($E^{3/x}$)] *eras.* (*11 mm*) *before word,* hæ *retouched by corr.,* lgæn *by corr.* ðine ($E^{3/x}$) (*1st*)] ð *retouched,* ine *on eras. by corr., letter eras. after* i. eærdunge (E^{3})] dunge *retraced by corr.* ðine (E^{3}) (*2nd*)] *eras. before word, letter eras. after* n. þinre (G)] *descender of* r *lost as result of eras. in Lat. line below.*

LTg: Emitte] [ ]mitte H: *outline and fragments of initial* E *visible.* lucem] lûcem M. ueritatem] ueritâtem M. monte] montem CL: *cf. Weber MSS* MTPQRUVXαγδηλ moz^{c} med, *see GAg.* sancto] E: o *on eras.;* sanctum L; scm C: *macron wanting: cf. Weber MSS* MTPQRUVXαγδηλ moz^{c} med, *see GAg.* tuo (*1st*)] E: *eras. after word;* tuum CL: *cf. Weber MSS* MTPQRUVXαγδηλ moz^{c} med, *see GAg.* tabernaculo] E: o *altered from another letter,* D: o *on eras., eras. after word;* tabernaculum CL: *cf. Weber MSS* MR moz^{c}. tuo (*2nd*)] E: o *altered from another letter,* D: o *on eras., eras. after word;* tuum CL: *cf. Weber MSS* MR moz^{c}.

LTu: monte] montem v: *cf. Weber MSS* MTPQRUVXαγδηλ moz^{c} med, *see GAu.* sancto] sanctum v: *cf. Weber MSS* MTPQRUVXαγδηλ moz^{c} med: *see GAu.* adduxerunt] ϑ: *1st* d *interl.* tabernaculo] tabernaculum v: *cf. Weber MSS* MR moz^{c}. tuo (*2nd*)] tuum v: *cf. Weber MSS* MR moz^{c}.

GAg: monte sancto tuo] montem sanctum tuum FGHIJK, CL: *see LTg.* tabernaculo] tabernacula FGIK, H: *orig.* tabernaculo: o *altered to* a. tuo (*2nd*)] tua FIK, G: a *added later on eras.,* H: *orig.* tuo: o *altered to* a.

GAu: monte sancto] montem sanctum δεζϑιλμξοπϱστυφχψ, v: *see LTu.* tuo (*1st*)] tuum δεζϑιλμξοπϱστυφχψ. tabernaculo tuo] tabernacula tua δεζϑιλμξοπϱστυφχψ.

4

(Et)* ⁊ FGHIJK
Introibo ic ingaa A, ic ingá B, ic inga CD*GHIJK,* Ic ingonge E^{3}*, ic infare *F* (*M*)

ad to ABCDE^{3}FGHIJK

altare wibede *A*B, wigbede C, weobede D, weofode FGIJ, weofede H, weofæde K, wifode E$^{3/x}$* (*M*)

dei godes ABDE^{3}FGHIJK, godys C

ad to ABCDE^{3}FGHIJK

deum gode ABCDE^{3}FGHIJ, drihtene K

qui se ABJ, þe CDE$^{3/x}$*F*G*H, se þe I, þa K

laetificat geblissað *ABCDFGHIK*, geblíssaþ *J*, geblissiæð *E*^{3} (*LM*)

iuuentutem | iuguðe A*C*, iuguþe J, giogoðe BE^{3}*, geogoðe DH, geoguðe G, on iuguðe F, ieogoðe K, mine I (*M*)

meam | mine ABCDE$^{3/x}$*FGHJK, ylde oþþe mine niwnysse ł iuguþe I (*M*)

Confitebor ic ondetto AB, ic andette CDFHIJK, Ic ændette E^{3}, anddette *G* (*M*)

tibi ðe ABE^{3}F, þe CDGHIJK

in in A, on BCDE^{3}FGHI*J*K

cithara citran *AB*, hearpan *CD*F*GHI*J, heærpæn *E*^{3}, hearppan *K* (*LM*)

deus god ABCDE^{3}FGHJK

deus | god ABCD*E^{3}GHJK, min I*

meus | min ABCDE^{3}FGHJK, god I

ED: [ ]ui (G)] qui *Rosier.* lętificat (E)] laetificat *Harsley.* geblissað (G)] blissað *Rosier.* geblíssaþ (J)] geblissaþ *Oess.* geoguðe (G)] geoguð *Rosier.* ín (J)] in *Oess.*

OE: Ic ingonge (E^{3})] ingo *retraced by corr.* wifode (E$^{3/x}$)] f *on eras. by corr.* þe (E$^{3/x}$)] þ *on eras. by corr.* giogoðe (E^{3})] *eras. before word.* mine (E$^{3/x}$)] e *on eras. by corr., eye of* e *visible after word.* god (D) (*2nd*)] o *blotted and another* o *written interl. by glossator.* min (I)] o *written before* min.

LTg: Introibo] Introîbo M; introibo FGHIJK. altare] A: *letter* (m?) *eras. after* e; altâre M. qui] [ ]ui G: *descender of initial letter visible.* laetificat] lætificat B; letificat CHL; lętificat DEFGJK; laetíficat M. iuuentutem] C: *eras. after* i; iuuentûtem M: *orig.* iuuentûte: *macron added: cf. Weber MSS* Xα moz^{x}. meam] M: *orig*, mea: *macron added: cf. Weber MSS* Xα moz^{x}. Confitebor] Confitêbor M; [ ]onfitebor G. in] ín J. cithara] cithára M; cythara ABCDEGHIKL.

LTu: Introibo] INtroibo β; introibo δεζϑιλμξοπϱστυφχψ. laetificat] lętificat ελνπφ; lætificat ϑ; letificat ιξσςτ*τυ. cithara] cythara δεζιλνϱσυχ, ο: *1st* a *interl.*

GAg: Introibo] Et introibo FHIJK; [ ]t introibo G.

GAu: Introibo] Et introibo δεζϑιλμξοπϱστυφχψ.

5

quare		forhwon ABCJ, forwæn E^{3}, forhwy DH, forhwý F, forhwi GI, hwi K (*L*)
tristis		unrot ABCD*FGHIJ, unrosast K, sari E^{x}*
es		earðu A, eart ðu B, eart þu CI, ðu eart D, þu eart G*H*, þu ært E^{x}*, eart J, is F (*KM*)
anima	|	sawul A, sawl BCDGH, Sæwl E$^{3/x}$*, saul F, sawle J, sawel K, þv min I*
mea	|	min ABCDE^{3}FGHJK, sawle I*
et		⁊ ABCDE^{3}FGHIJK
quare		forhwon ABC, forwæn E^{3}, forhwy DFH, forhwi GIJK
conturbas		gedroefes A*, ðu gedrefest B, gedrefyst þu C*, gedrefest þu E$^{3/x}$*, gedrefst þu I*J, þu drefst DGH, drefst FK
me		me ABCDE^{3}FGHIJK
Spera		gehyht AB, gehiht C, hyht D, hiht K, hihte G*H*, ic hihte J, hopa F, hopa ł gehiht I*, Gewene ł hyht E$^{3/x}$*
in		in A, on BCDE^{3}FGHIJK
deum		god ABCDE^{3}*JK*, gode *FGHI*
quoniam		forðon ABDGHJ, forþon C, forðæn E^{3}, forðam K, forðam ðe F, forþan þe I
(adhuc)*		nu gýt F, nu gyt I, nu git J, na gyt G, gyt K
confitebor		ic ondettu A, ic ondetto B, ic andytte C, ic andette DFHIJK, ic ændette E^{3}, ic anddette G
illi		him ACE^{3}FGHI*, him BDJK
salutare		haelu A, hælo BDFGHJ, hæle CK, helo E^{3}, se halwenda I
uultus	|	ondwleotan A, ondwlitan B, ondwlitæn E$^{3/x}$*, andwlitan CDFGHJ, ansyne K, mines I
mei	|	mines ABF, minys C, min DE^{3}GHJ, mine K, andwlitan I
et		⁊ ABCDE^{3}FGHIJK
deus	|	god ABCDE^{3}FGHJK, min I
meus	|	min ABCDE^{3}FG*H*JK, god I

ED: forhwon (A) (*1st*)] for hwon *Kuhn.* forhwy (D) (*1st*)] for hwy *Roeder.* és (H)] es *Campbell.* forhwon (A) (*2nd*)] for hwon *Kuhn.* forhwy (D) (*2nd*)] for hwy *Roeder.* [ ]pera (H)] Spera *Campbell.* forðon (A)] for ðon *Kuhn.* nu git (J)] nugit *Oess.* ms (H)] meus *Campbell.*

OE: unrot (D)] *on eras.* sari (E^{x})] *on eras.* þu ært (E^{x})] *on eras.* Sæwl (E$^{3/x}$)] wl *on eras. by corr.,* Sæ *retraced.* þv min sawle (I)] s. o *written after* sawle. gedroefes (A)] d *on eras.* gedrefyst þu (C)] þu *added by corr.* gedrefest þu (E$^{3/x}$)] s *partly retraced,* t *on eras. by corr.,* þu *added by corr.* gedrefst þu (I)] s *interl.* hopa ł gehiht

(I)] hopa *written in left margin.* Gewene ł hyht (E$^{3/x}$)] G *on eras. by corr.,* ł hyht *added by corr.* him (I)] ÷ (> est) : he is *written in left margin.* ondwlitæn (E$^{3/x}$)] æ *retouched,* n *added by corr.*

LTg: quare (*1st*)] quáre L. es] és HKM. Spera] [ ]pera H: *outline of initial* S *visible.* deum] deo FGHIJK: *cf. Weber MSS* PQRUVγδ^{2}. meus] ms H: *macron wanting.*

LTu: deum] deo λϱτφ: *cf. Weber MSS* PQRUVγδ^{2}. quoniam] quoniam adhuc ς: *see GAu.* et (*2nd*)] *om.* φ.

GAg: quoniam] quoniam adhuc FGHIJ, K: *small eras. after* adhuc, *perhaps of flanking sign* (:); *note* ※ *before word.*

GAu: quoniam] quoniam adhuc δεζϑιλμξοπϱστυφχψ, ς: *see LTu.*

PSALM 43

2

Deus		god *ACE*^{3}**F*GH*I*J (*BDKM*)
auribus		mid earum AB*C*F, mid earum J, earum DGHI, eærum E^{3}*
nostris		urum ACE^{3}FG, urum BDHJ, mid urum I, ure K
audiuimus		we geherdun *A,* we gehirdon BJ, we gehyrdon CDFGHI*, we gehierdon E^{3}, we gehyrddan K
⟨et⟩		⁊ *A*
patres	¦	fedras A, fædras BC, fæderas DFJK, faderes E^{3}*, fæderes GH, ure I
nostri	¦	ure ABCDE^{3}FHJK, ures G, fæderas I
adnuntiauerunt		segdun *A,* sægdon *B,* sægdun *C,* bodedon *DGH,* bobodan *K,* bododon ł sædon J, hý bududon ł cyddon F, cyþdon ł bodedon *E*$^{3/x}$*, gecyddun *I*
nobis		us ABCDE^{3}FGHIJK
Opus		werc A, weorc BDF*G*HIJK, worc C, Weorc E^{3}*
quod		ðæt A, þæt BD, þæt CFGHJ, þæt þe I, þa K, ðet E^{3}
operatus		wircende A, wyrcende BJ, þu wyrcynde C, þu wercende ł weorhtest I*, þu worhtest DE^{x}*FH, ðu worhtest K, þu worhtes G
es		ðu earð A, ðu eart B, þu eart J, eart C, þu bist ⁊ þu eart G, wære I (*HKL*)
in		in A, on BCDE^{3}*FGHIJK
diebus		dægum AF, dagum BDJ, dagum CE^{3}*GHI, dagan K
eorum		heara A, hira B, hyra C, heora DFGHIJK, hieræ E^{3}
et*		⁊ ABCD, ond E^{3} (*IK*)
in		in A, on BCDE^{3}*F*GHIJK

diebus	dægum A, dagum BDHJ, dagum CE[3]*FGI, dagan K
antiquis	ðæm alldum A, þam ealdum C, ealdum BD, ealdum G*H*IJ, eældum E[3/x]*, ealum F*, ealdan K

ED: þu wercende ł weorhtest wære (I)] þu wercende wære ł weorhtest *Lindelöf.* és (H)] es *Campbell.* þu bist ⁊ þu eart (G)] þu bist ł þu eart *Rosier.* antíquis (H)] antiquis *Campbell.* ealum (F)] eallum *Kimmens.*

OE: god (E[3])] *added by corr.* (?). eærum (E[3])] eæ *retouched by corr.* we gehyrdon (I)] *orig.* we gehyrdun: u *altered to* o. faderes (E[3])] *orig.* federes: *1st* e *altered to* a *by corr.* cyþdon ł bodedon (E[3/x])] ł bodedon *added by corr., eras. above 3rd* o. Weorc (E[3])] *orig.* Wiorc: i *altered to* e. þu wercende ł weorhtest (I)] ł weorhtest *written above* wercende. þu worhtest (E[x])] *on eras.* on (E[3]) (*1st*)] *eras. before word.* dagum (E[3]) (*both*)] *orig.* dægum: æ *altered to* a. eældum (E[3/x])] *eras. before word,* um *on eras. by corr.* ealum (F)] *orig.* eallum: *2nd* l *eras.*

LTg: Deus] F: eus *written in bowl of* D, I: s. o *written in bowl of* D; DEVS CE; DS̄ ABDKM. auribus] AURIBVS C. audiuimus] audiuimus et A: *cf. Weber MSS* T[2]PQRUVXη[2] moz. adnuntiauerunt] annuntiauerunt ABEI, C: *orig.* adnuntiauerunt: d *deleted by subscript dot,* n *added interl. by corr.,* DHK: *1st* n *on eras.* Opus] [ ]pus G. es] és HKL. et] I: *added later,* K: *interl. by corr.* in (*2nd*)] F: *eras. before word.* antiquis] antíquis H.

LTu: Deus] DS̄ βλμνϱχψ; DEVS ι; DEUS ςτ*τ. auribus] AURibus β; AURIBUS λμνχψ; AURIBVS ϱ. nostris] NOSTRIS λμνϱ; NOStris ψ. audiuimus] AUDIUIMUS λϱ. patres] PAtres λ. adnuntiauerunt] annuntiauerunt εζιλξπστ*υχ, β: *orig.* adnuntiauerunt: n *interl. above* d, o: *orig.* adnuntiauerunt: d *deleted,* n *interl.;* annunciauerunt τφ, ϱ: *orig.* annuntiauerunt: *1st* t *deleted,* c *interl.* et] *interl.* ζψ.

GAg: et] *om.* GHJ, F: *see LTg note to 2nd* in.

GAu: et] *om.* δεμοπϱυχ.

3

Manus	honda A, handa GH, hond B, hand CDE[3]*FIJK
tua	ðine *A,* ðin BE[3]*, þin CDFHIJK, þinra G
gentes	ðeode A, þeode C, ðeoða B, þeoda DHIJ, ðeoda FGK, ðiodæ E[3]
disperdit	tostenceð *AB,* tostencyð *C,* forspilde *DE[3]K,* forspýlde *F,* forspildet *H**, forspildon *G,* forspilde ł tostæncte *I,* tostænced *J* (*LM*)
et	⁊ ABCDE[x]FGHIJK
plantasti	ðu geplantades A, þu geplantodest I, þu plantodes B, ðu plantodest D, þu plantodest GH, þu plantudost F, ðu plantodost J, þu plantodes *K,* plantodyst C, þu plantodest ł wirtwælædæst E[3/x]*

eos	hie ABE^{3}, hi CK, hy *D*GH, hig FIJ
adflixisti	ðu swentes A, þu swenctyst *C,* þu swenctest D*FGH,* ⁊ þu swenctes B, ⁊ þu swængtest *J,* ðu geswenctest *I,* þu swenctes *K,* ðu gebigdest ł swenctest E$^{3/x}$*
populos	folc ACBCDFGHJK, folctruman I (*E*)
et	⁊ ABCDE^{x}FGHIJK
expulisti	onwcg adrife ABC, weg adrife J, þu utædrife E$^{3/x}$*, ðu utanyddest D, þu utanyddest FGH, þu utaneddest I*, utanyddest *K*
eos	hie ABE^{3}, hi C, hy DGH*, hí F, hig IJ (*K*)

ED: forspýlde (F)] forspylde *Kimmens.* onweg adrife (A)] on weg adrife *Kuhn.* þu utanyddest (H)] þu ut anyddest *Campbell.*

OE: hand (E^{3})] *orig.* hænd: æ *altered to* a *by corr., letter* (e *or* æ?) *eras. after word.* ðin (E^{3})] *letter* (e *or* æ?) *eras. after word.* forspildet (H)] *letter eras. after* l. þu plantodest ł wirtwælædæst (E$^{3/x}$)] þu plantodest ł *added by corr., eras.* ⁊ *visible beneath* ł (*which stands above* & *in MS*), *3rd* t *added by corr.* ðu gebigdest ł swenctest (E$^{3/x}$)] *1st* t *added by corr., 1st* s *retouched,* ł swenctest *added by corr., eras. after* ł. þu utædrife (E$^{3/x}$)] þu ut *by corr., 1st* u *and* ut *on eras.* þu utaneddest (I)] ut *interl.* hy (H)] *written below preceding* utanyddest, *which is written to avoid ascenders in* expulisti.

LTg: tua] A: *letter eras after* a. disperdit] disperdet AB, E: et *on eras.,* M: *orig.* disperdit: *2nd* i *altered to* e; disperdidit CDFGHIJKL: *cf. Weber MSS* αγ moz^{x} med, *cf. Bib. sac. MSS* I^{2}M^{2}ΦUG^{2}K^{2}ΨBVDΩ. plantasti] K: *right leg of* n *lost due to excision of initial from fol. 48r.* eos (*1st*)] eas D: *orig.* eos: a *interl.* adflixisti] afflixisti FGHIJK, C: *orig.* adflixisti: d *deleted by subscript dot,* f *added interl. by corr.* populos] E: *2nd* o *altered from another letter.* expulisti] expulis[ ] K: *letters lost due to excision of initial from fol. 48r.* eos (*2nd*)] K: *lost due to excision of initial from fol. 48r.*

LTu: disperdit] disperdet τ*; disperdidit λμνξπϱσςτυφχ: *cf. Weber MSS* αγ moz^{x} med. adflixisti] afflixisti εζϑιλξοπϱστ*τυφχ.

4

Non*	nales AB, nalys C, nalæs J, na DGHK, Na E^{x}*, ne FI
enim	soðlice ABCE^{x}*FGI, soþlice DHJK
in	in A, on BCDE^{3}*FGHIJK
gladio	sweorde ABDE^{3}*FGHIJK, swurde C
suo	his ABCDE^{3}*FGHJK, heora I
possidebunt*	gesittad A, gesittað B, settan K, wealdað C, hy agon D*E$^{3/x}$**GH, hi agon ł besæton J, hí ahnodun F, hi geanwealdedan I (*LM*)

terram — eorðan ABCDFGHI*K*, eorðæn E^{3}, eorþe J
et — ⁊ ABCDE^{3}FGHIJK
brachium — earm *A*BCDFGHJK, eærm E^{3}, earmas I
eorum — heara A, hira B, hyra C, heora DFGHIJK, hioræ E^{3}
non — ne ABCE^{3}FGIJ, na DHK
saluabit — gehæleð AB, gehæleþ *J,* gehælð C, gehęlð E^{3}, hæleþ D, hæleð G*H,* hælþ F, gehęlde *I,* hælde *K* (*M*)
eos — hie ABE^{3}, hi CK*, hy DGH, híg F, hig IJ

Sed — ah AB, ac CDF*G*HIK*J, Ac E$^{3/x}$*
dextera — sie swiðre A, seo swiðre BI, seo swyþre F, swiðre CE^{3}H, swiþre DJ, sweoðre G, swyðre K
tua — ðin ABDE^{3}F, þin CGHIJK
et — ⁊ ABCDE^{3}FGHIJK
brachium — earm *A*BCDFGHIK, eærm E^{3}, dom J
tuum — ðin ABF, þin CDE^{3}GH*I*JK
et — ⁊ ABCDE^{3}FGHIJK
inluminatio — inlihtnis A, onlihtnes BJ, onlyhtnys *C,* onlyhting D*H,* onliehting E^{3}*, onlyhtinge *F*K, onlytlincg G, onlihtingc ł leohtnes *I*
uultus* — ondwleotan A*, ondwlitan B, andwlitan CDFGIJK, andhwlitan H*, andwlitan ł onsien E$^{3/x}$*
tui* — ðines AB, þinys C, þines DE$^{3/x}$*FIK, þin GHJ
quoniam — forðon ABHJ, forþon C, forðā K, forðæn E^{3}, forþon þe G, forðon þe I
conplacuit* — gelicade A, gelicode B*C*DGJK, gelicæde *E$^{3/x}$*,* þu gelicodest FI, gelicodest H
tibi* — ðe ABE^{3}, þe CD
in — in A, on BCDE^{3}FGHIJK
illis* — him AE^{3}FGHJ, him BD, hym C, heom I, heo[ ] K*

ED: illuminatio (C)] i[n]luminatio *Wildhagen.* forðon (A)] for ðon *Kuhn.* complacuit (C)] conplacuit *Wildhagen.*

OE: Na (E^{x})] *on eras.* soðlice (E^{x})] *on eras.* on (E^{3}) (*1st*)] *eras.* (*16 mm*) *before word.* sweorde (E^{3})] *retouched by corr.* his (E^{3})] is *retouched by corr.* hy agon (E$^{3/x}$)] hy *added by corr.*, a *altered from* æ. hi (K)] *otiose dot after* i. ac (K)] *otiose stroke before word.* Ac (E$^{3/x}$)] A *altered from* Æ, c *on eras. by corr.* onliehting (E^{3})] ing *retouched by corr.* ondwleotan (A)] *1st* n *interl.* andhwlitan (H)] *orig.* andhwiltan: i *altered to* l, l *altered to* i. andwlitan ł onsien (E$^{3/x}$)] andwlitan ł *added by corr.* þines (E$^{3/x}$)] es *added by corr.* gelicæde (E$^{3/x}$)] d *altered from* ð (?), *final* e *added by corr.* heo[ ] (K)] *final letter lost due to excision of initial from fol. 48r.*

LTg: possidebunt] E: b *malformed,* L: u *on eras.;* possidebant M: a *altered from another letter,* i *altered to* e, *then altered to* i *by corr.* terram] terr[ ] K: *letters lost due to excision of initial from fol. 48r.* brachium (*1st*)] A: *letter eras. after* a. saluabit] saluauit IJKM, H: *2nd* u *altered from another letter.* Sed] [ ]ed G. brachium (*2nd*)] A: *letter eras. after* a. tuum] I: *eras. after word.* inluminatio] illuminatio I, CH: *orig.* inluminatio: i *eras., bridge connecting legs of 1st* n *eras., right leg of orig.* n *used to form* l, F: il *on eras.* conplacuit] complacuit E; co<u>m</u>placuit C: *orig.* conplacuit: n *deleted by subscript dot, macron added above* o *by corr.*

LTu: saluabit] saluauit εζϑμπϱχψ. inluminatio] illuminatio εζιλξοπϱστ*τφχ. conplacuit] complacuit ςτ*.

GAg: Non] Nec FGHIJK. possidebunt] possederunt G, FHIK: *orig.* possiderunt: i *altered to* e; possiderunt J. conplacuit] conplacuisti FG, K: n *interl. by corr.;* complacuisti IJ, H: *orig.* conplacuisti: *middle leg added to* n *to form* m. tibi] *om.* FGHIJK. illis] eis FGHIJ; ei[ ] K: *final letter lost due to excision of initial from fol. 48r.*

GAu: Non] Nec δεζιλμοπϱστυφχψ; Nęc ξ. possidebunt] possederunt δεζιλμξοϱστυφχ; possiderunt πψ. uultus tui] faciei tuæ ϑ. conplacuit] conplacuisti δζϑμψ; complacuisti ειξοπϱτχ; cōplacuisti λυφ; placuisti σ. tibi] *om.* δεζϑιμξοπϱστυφχ. illis] eis δεζϑιλμξοπϱστυφχψ.

5

Tu		ðu ABE^{3}*F, þu CDGHIJK (*M*)
es		earð A, eart BCDFGHIJK, eært E^{3} (*M*)
ipse		se ilca A*BCJ, self DE^{x}*H, sylf FGI, þe sylfa K
rex		cyning ABDGHI, cyningc F, cyninc J, cining K, cing C, king E^{3}
meus		min ABCDE^{3}FGHIJK
et		ꝺ ABCE^{3}FGHIJK
deus		god ABCE^{3}FGHIJK
meus		min ABCE^{3}FGHIJK
qui	I	þu ðe DE^{3}*, þu þe GHI, ðu ðe F, þa K
mandas	I	ðu onbude AB, þu onbude J, þu bebydst C, bebeodest DFGHIK, bebíódest E$^{3/x}$*
salutem*		haelu A, hælo BDFGHIJ, hæle CK, hęlo E^{3}
iacob		iacobe CF, iacobes GIJ, israhel ł iæcobe E$^{3/x}$*, n K*

ED: iacob (K) Iacob *Sisam.*

OE: ðu (E^{3})] *retouched by corr.* se ilca (A)] *letter eras. after* e. self (E^{x})] f *on eras.* þu ðe (E^{x})] *eras. after* þu. bebíódest (E$^{3/x}$)] t *added by corr.* israhel ł iæcobe (E$^{3/x}$)] israhel ł *added by corr.* n (K)] *for* nomen.

LTg: Tu] Tú M. es] és M.

LTu: Tu] TU β.

GAg: salutem] salutes FGHIJK.

GAu: salutem] salutes δεζϑιλμξοπϱστυφχψ.

6

In	in A, on BCDFGHIJK, On E^{3}
te	ðe ABDF, þe CE^{3}GHIJK
inimicos	fiond AE^{3}, fiend B, fynd CDFGHJK, feond I
nostros	ure ABCDE^{3}FGHIJK
uentilauimus	we windwiað AB_C*J,_ we windwioð _E$^{3/x}$*,_ we awindfiað _DH,_ we awyndwiað _F,_ we awindwiað _K,_ we windwiað ł we todrifað _G*,_ we onblawaþ ł we windwiaþ _I_ (_LM_)
(cornu)*	hornu F, horn J, mid horne I, heorte G, hor K
et	ˀ ABCE^{3}FGIJK
in	in A, on BCE^{3}FGIJK
nomine	noman _A_B, nomæn E^{3}, naman CFGIJK
tuo	ðinum AF, þinum BJ, þinum CI, þinre G, þinan K, þin E^{3}
spernimus*	we forhycgað _A,_ we forhycgað BC_D_FH, we forhicgað G, we forhicgaþ K, we forhycgað ł we forseoð I*, we forhicgaþ ł we forseoþ J, we forhogyen _E$^{3/x}$*_ (_LM_)
insurgentes	arisende AB, onarisynde C, onarisende DGH, onærisonde E$^{3/x}$*, onrisende K, onarisendum F, þa onarisendan I*, arisende J
in	in A, on BCDE^{3}FGHIJK
nos*	us ABCDE^{3}FGHIJK

OE: we windwiað (C)] _2nd_ i _interl._ we windwioð (E$^{3/x}$)] we _added by corr., eras. (8 mm) after_ d, _3rd_ w _on eras. by corr., 2nd_ i _retraced._ we windwiað ł we todrifað (G)] we windwiað _added in diff._ (?) _hand in blank space above_ uentilabimus; ł we todrifað _written in next line above_ heorte (_glossing_ cornu). we forhycgað ł we forseoð (I)] ł we forseoð _written in left margin._ we forhogyen (E$^{3/x}$)] fo _and_ hogyen _on eras. by corr.,_ r _retraced._ onærisonde (E$^{3/x}$)] _initial_ on _and_ nde _added by corr., 2nd_ n _on eras._ þa onarisendan (I)] _orig._ þa onarisenden: _2nd_ e _altered to_ a.

LTg: uentilauimus] uentilabimus CDEFGHIJKL, M: _orig._ uentilauimus: _2nd_ u _deleted,_ b _interl._ nomine] A: _orig._ nomini: _final_ i _altered to_ e. spernimus] A: _eras._ (_3–4 letters?_) _after word,_ M: _orig._ spernemus: _2nd_ e _altered to_ i; spernemus DEL: _cf. Weber MSS_ αδεηχ med, _see GAg._

LTu: In] IN β. uentilauimus] uentilabimus δεζιμνξοπϱσςτ*τυφχψ. spernimus] spernemus ςτ*: _cf. Weber MSS_ αδεηχ med, _see GAu._ in (_2nd_)] _om._ μ.

GAg: uentilauimus] uentilabimus cornu FGHIJK. spernimus] spernemus FGHIJK, DEL: _see LTg._ nos] nobis FGHIJK.

GAu: uentilauimus] uentilabimus cornu δεζιλξοπϱστυφχψ; uentilauimus cornu ϑ. spernimus] spernemus δεζϑιλνξοπϱστυφχψ, ςτ*: *see LTu.* nos] nobis δεζϑιλμξπϱστυφχψ.

7

Non	nales A*B, nalys C, nalæs J, na F*G*HIK, Ne E^{3}*
enim	soðlice A*BCE^{3}*GHIJ, soþlice F, witodlice K
in	in A, on BCDE^{x}GHIJK, mid F
arcu	bogan AB*C*DE^{x}GHIK, bogum F, bogu<u>m</u> J
meo	minum AFGI, minu<u>m</u> BCDE^{x}HJ, minan K
sperabo	ic gehyhto *A*, ic gehyhte BDH, ic gehihte CG*, ic gehihte ł ic ne hopie I*, ic hihte FJ, hihte *K*, ic gewene E$^{3/x}$*
et	⁊ *A*BCDE^{3}FGHIJK
gladius	sweord ABDE^{3}FGHIJ, swurd C, swyrd K
meus	min ABCDE^{3}FGHIJK
non	ne ABCE^{3}FGJ, na HK, na ne I
saluabit	gehaeleð A, gehæleð B, gehæleþ J, gehælð C, geheleð E^{3}, hælð DFGHK, gehelpeð ł ne gehælð I
me	me ABCE^{3}FGHIJK

OE: nales (A)] l *altered from* s. Ne (E^{3})] N *retouched by corr., eras. after word.* soðlice (A)] *orig.* soðliye: y *deleted by subscript dot,* c *interl.* soðlice (E^{3})] *retouched by corr.* ic gehihte (G)] *base of* t *lost due to hole in leaf.* ic gehihte ł ic ne hopie (I)] ł ic ne hopie *written in left margin.* ic gewene (E$^{3/x}$)] ic *added by corr.*

LTg: Non] [ ]on G. arcu] C: *eras. after word.* sperabo] A: *eras.* (*3 letters? 1st* = c) *after word,* K: *eras. after word, in margin and not immediately following lemma.* et] A: *letter eras. after word.*

8

Liberasti*	ðu gefreades A, ðu gefreodes B, þu gefreodyst C, ðu gefriolsedes E^{3}, þu alysdest D, þu gehældest FGIJ, þu hældest K
enim	soðlice ABCE^{3}GI, soþlice FHJ, witodlice K
nos	usic A, us B*CDE^{3}FGHIJK
ex*	of ABCE^{3}*J, fra<u>m</u> DFI, fram GK
adfligentibus	ðæm swencendum A, þæm swencendu<u>m</u> B, þam swencyndum *C*, ðæm swencendu<u>m</u> *E*^{3}, swencendu<u>m</u> *DH**, swencendum *FG*, swencedu<u>m</u> *K*, geswencendum *I*, þa<u>m</u> unswæncendu<u>m</u> *J*
nos	usic A, us BCE^{3}FGHIJ*K* (*D*)
et	⁊ ABCE^{3}FHIJK

eos*	ða AB, þa CDE^{3}
qui*	ða A, ða ðe B, þa þe C, þe DE^{x}*
nos*	usic A, us BCDE^{3}
oderunt*	fiedon A, feodon B, feodun *C,* feodan D, fiodon E^{3}, hatigende FJK, ha[ ](n)d[ ] G, þa hatigendan I
(nos)*	us FGIJK
confudisti	ðu gesteaðelaðes A*, þu gestaðylodyst C, þu gescendes B, þu gescyndest DGHK, ðu gescyndest E^{3}*, þu gescendest FI, þu gescændest J

ED: ha[ ](n)d[ ] (G)] *no gloss Rosier.* þu gescyndest (G)] þu g[ ]scyndest *Rosier.*

OE: us (B) (*1st*)] *eras. before word.* of (E^{3})] *retouched by corr.* swencendum (H)] *1st* n *interl.* þe (E^{x})] *on eras.* ðu gesteaðelaðes (A)] *lemma misread as* fundasti; *see also* C. ðu gescyndest (E^{3})] t *added by corr.* (?).

LTg: adfligentibus] affligentibus DFGHIJK, C: *orig.* adfligentibus: d *deleted by subscript dot, 1st* f *added interl. by corr.,* E: *1st* f *altered from another letter.* nos (*2nd*)] nós DK. oderunt] odérunt C.

LTu: Liberasti] LIberasti β. adfligentibus] affligentibus εζλξοπρστυφχ. oderunt] hoderunt ς.

GAg: Liberasti] Saluasti FGHIJK. ex] de FGHIJK. eos qui nos] *om.* FGHIJK. oderunt] odientes nos FGHIJK.

GAu: Liberasti] Saluasti δεζθιλμξοπρστυφχψ. ex] de δεζιλμξοπρστυφχψ. eos qui nos] *om.* δεζθιλμξοπρστυφχψ. oderunt] odientes nos δεζθιλμξοπρστυφχψ.

9

In	in A, on BCFGIJK, On E^{3}
deo	gode ABCE^{3}GIJ, god K, dæge F
laudabimur	we bioð here A, we beoð herede B, we beoð heryde C, we beoþ herede DE^{x}*, we beoð herede H, we beoþ herode K, we beoð geherode FI, we beoð geherede J, we heredon G
tota	allne A, alne E$^{3/x}$*, ealne BC, ælcne J, ælce DFGH*, ealle K, æfre ł ealne I
die	deg AE^{3}*, dæg BCGIJK, dæge DFH (*M*)
et	⁊ ABCE^{3}FGIJK
in	in A, on BCE^{3}FGIJK
nomine	noman *A*B, naman CFGIJK, namæn E^{3} (*H*)
tuo	ðinum AF, ðinum B, þinum CE^{3}GI, þinum J, þinan K
confitebimur	we ondettað AB, we andettað CDFGH, we andettaþ IJK, we ændetteþ E$^{3/x}$*

in — in A, on BCDE^{3}FGHJK, a butan I
saecula* — weorulðe A, weorolde *B,* worulde *C*FG, worulda *D*H, worlde J, worolde *E^3*K, ende ł on weorlde I (*L*)

ED: nomin(e) (H)] nomine *Campbell.* scła (E)] secula *Harsley.* scłm (IJ)] saeculum *Lindelöf;* seculum *Oess.*

OE: we beoþ herede (E^x)] *on eras.* alne (E$^{3/x}$)] n *on eras. by corr.* ælce (H)] *small eras. after* e. deg (E^3)] *letter eras. after word.* we ændetteþ (E$^{3/x}$)] we *added by corr., eras. after* we, þ *added by corr.* (?).

LTg: die] M: i *faint.* nomine] A: *orig.* nomini: *final* i *altered to* e; nomin(e) H: *hole in leaf after 2nd* n, *letter fragments visible in final position.* saecula] sæcula B; secula CDL; scła E.

LTu: In] IN β. saecula] secula ς; scła βντ*τ.

GAg: saecula] sęculum FK; seculum GH; scłm IJ.

GAu: saecula] sacculum ζμϱχψ; sęculum λ; scłm δεϑιξοπσυφ.

10
Nunc — nu ABCD*G*HJK, Nu E^3, nu þa FI
autem — soðlice ABCE^{3}FGI, soþlice J, witodlice K
reppulisti — onweg adrife A, þu aweg adrife B, þu onweg adrife *C,* þu aweg drife *J,* ðu anyddest D, ðu aneddest E$^{3/x}$*, þu anyddest G*HK,* ðu andettest F*, þu utawurpe ł aneddest I
et — ⁊ ABCDE^{3}FGHIJK
confudisti — ðu gescendes A*, ðu gescendest F, þu gescyndest I, gescendes B, gescyndyst C, gescændest J, ðu gescindest ł drefdest E$^{3/x}$*, ðu gedrefdest D, þu gedrefdest GH, gedrefdest K
nos — usic A, us BCE^3*FGHIJK, ús D
et — ⁊ ABCDE^{3}FGHIJK
non — | ne ACE^3, na DFGHJK, ðu no B, þu ne I
egredieris — | gæst ABC*I,* þu utgæst DFGH, utgæst K, þu ne gæst J, utgængest E$^{3/x}$* (*M*)
deus — god ABCE^{3}FJ (*GIK*)
in — in A, on BCDE^{3}FGHIJK
uirtutibus — | megnum AE^3, mægnum J, mægnum CF, mægenum BH, mægenum D, mægenum ł mihtum G, urum I, strenðe K
nostris — | urum ACE^{3}FGJ, urum BDH, mihtum I, ure K

ED: onweg adrife (A)] on weg adrife *Kuhn.* egrediéris (I)] egredieris *Lindelöf.*

OE: ðu aneddest ($E^{3/x}$)] aneddest *on eras. by corr.* ðu andettest (F)] andettest *obscured by eras. but visible, eye of 1st* e *lost.* ðu gescendes (A)] *letter eras. before* g. ðu gescindest ł drefdest ($E^{3/x}$)] *1st* st *and* ł drefdest *added by corr.* us (E^{3})] *retraced by corr.* utgængest ($E^{3/x}$)] st *on eras. by corr.*

LTg: Nunc] [ ]unc G. reppulisti] C: *orig.* repulisti: *2nd* p *interl. by corr.;* repulisti J, H: *letter eras. after* e, K: *orig.* reppulisti: *1st* p *eras.* egredieris] egrediéris I; egredîeris M. deus] I: *interl. by glossator,* K: *interl. by corr.; om.* G: x *written in brown ink above line marks omission, fragmentary and perhaps otiose stroke appears in left margin.*

LTu: reppulisti] χ: *1st* p *interl.;* repulisti ϑ. deus] *interl.* ζ; *om.* μ.

11

Auertisti	ðu forcerdes A, þu forcerdes B, þu forcyrdyst C, þu forcirdest J, þu acyrdest DGHI*K, ðu acyrdest $E^{3/x}$*F
nos	usic A, us BCDE^{3}FGHI*J*K
retrorsum	on bec A, on bæc BCK, underbecling D, underbæcling H, underbæclincg G, underbæc FI, underbæcc J, on beclinc E^{3}*
prae*	fore A*BDE³**, for *C,* æfter FGIK, æfter J (*LM*)
inimicis*	fiondum A, feondum BDJ, feondum CFI, fiondum *E³**, feondan K, on fynd G
nostris*	urum AC*E³**FGIJ, urum BD, uran K
et	⁊ ABCDE^{3}FGIJK
eos*	ða AB, þa E^{x}* (*CDL*)
qui	ða A, þa K, ðe D, þæ E^{3}, þa ðe BJ, þa þe CGI, ða ðe F
nos* }	usic A, us BC*E³*FGHIJK
oderunt* }	fiedon A, feodon B, feodun C, hatedon DGHI, hatudon F, hatodon JK, fiodon ł hatedon *E³/x**
diripiebant	gereafadon A, gereafodon B, gereafydon C, hy reafodon DH, hi reafedon F, hy reafedon G, hi reafodon K, hyo reafodon E^{x}*, gegripon ł gelahton I, gedrefodon ł gegripon J
sibi	him ABCE^{3}FHIJ, him DK, hi G

ED: nós (J)] nos *Oess.* underbæc (FI)] under bæc *Kimmens, Lindelöf.* prę (E)] prae *Harsley.* on fynd (G)] *no gloss Rosier.* et eos (D)] et *Rosier.*

OE: þu acyrdest (I)] *orig. gloss to* Auertisti *eras.,* þu acyrdest *written in right margin;* yr *underlined and* wæn *written above* cyrdes, *indicating formation of 2nd gloss:* þu awændest. ðu acyrdest ($E^{3/x}$)] ðu *retraced, eras. after* u, acyr *on eras. by corr.* on beclinc (E^{3})] on bec *retouched.* fore (E^{3})] re *retraced.* fiondum (E^{3})] *retraced.* urum (E^{3})] *retraced.* þa (E^{x})] *on eras.* fiodon ł hatedon ($E^{3/x}$)] ł hatedon *added by corr.* hyo reafodon (E^{x})] *on eras. by corr.*

LTg: nos (*1st*)] nós J. prae] M: e *faint;* prę B, C: *orig.* pre: *cauda added in same red ink as gloss*, E: *on eras.;* pre DL. inimicis] E: is *on eras.* nostris] E: nr̄ *retraced,* is *on eras.* eos] D: *added interl. by corr.; om.* CL: *cf. Weber MSS* TRαβγδεηχ moz med, *see GAg.* nos oderunt] oderunt nos E: *cf. Weber MSS* αβη med, *see GAg.*

LTu: prae] prę βν; pre ςτ*. eos] *om.* ν: *cf. Weber MSS* TRαβγδεηχ moz med, *see GAu.* oderunt] hoderunt ς. diripiebant] diripuebant ς.

GAg: prae] post FGHIJK. inimicis nostris] inimicos nostros FGHIJK. eos] *om.* FGHIJK, CL: *see LTg.* nos oderunt] oderunt nos FGHIJK, E: *see LTg.*

GAu: prae] post δεζϑιλμξοπϱστυφχψ. inimicis nostris] inimicos nostros δεζϑιλμξοπϱστυφχψ. eos] *om.* δεζϑιλμξοπϱστυφχψ, ν: *see LTu.* nos oderunt] oderunt nos δεζϑιλμξοπϱστυφχψ.

12

Dedisti — ðu saldes A, ðu sealdes B, þu sealdest DFG*H*IJK, þu g̲esealdyst C, ðu geseældest E^{3}
nos — usic A, us BCDE^{3}FGHIJK
tamquam — swe swe A, swa swa B*C*DF*GH*IJ, swæ swæ *E*^{3}, swa K
oues — scep ABCI, sceap DFGHJK, Sceæp E^{3}
escarum — metta ABDF*GIJ*, mettæ E^{3}, mettas *C*K
et — ⁊ ABCE^{3}FGIJK
in — in A, on BCDE^{3}FGHIJK
gentibus — ðeodu A, ðeodum BGI, þeodum CF, þeodum̲ DHJ, þeoda K, ðiodum E^{3}
dispersisti | ðu tostrugde A, þu tostrugde B, þu tostregdyst C, þu tostenctest DFHK, þu tostencgtest G, þu tostænctest J, þu gindstræidest ł ⁊ þu tostænctest I, ðu us E^{3}
nos | usic A, us BCFHIJK, u[ ] G*, tostenctest E^{3}

ED: [ ]edisti (H)] Dedisti *Campbell.* þu g̲escealdyst (C)] þu gescealdyst *Wildhagen.* ðu geseældest (E)] þu geseældest *Harsley.* swa swa (GIJ)] swaswa *Rosier, Lindelöf, Oess.* oues (BE)] oves *Brenner, Harsley.* ęscarum (I)] escarum *Lindelöf.* u[ ] (G)] us *Rosier.*

OE: u[ ] (G)] *small hole in leaf after* u, *letter fragment visible.*

LTg: Dedisti] [ ]edisti H: *outline of initial* D *visible.* tamquam] tanquam E, C: *orig.* tamquam: *left leg of 1st* m *eras. to form* n, G: *orig.* tamquam: *right leg of 1st* m *eras. to form* n, H: *eras. after* n. escarum] escárum C; ęscarum GI.

LTu: tamquam] tanquam ϑιϑτ*τφ. escarum] ęscarum νο.

13

Uendidisti — ðu bibohtes *A**, ðu bebohtes *B*, þu bebohtyst *C*, þu bohtest J, þu becyptest *DFGH*, þu beceptest ł þu sealdest *I**, þu sealdest K, ðu sældest ł cyptest *E*$^{3/x}$* (*L*)

populum — folc ABCDE^{3}FGHIJK

tuum — ðin A, þin BCDE^{3}FGHIJK

sine — butan ABCDGIK, buton E^{3}FHJ

pretio — weorðe *ABDFG*, weorþe H, wiorðe *E*^{3}, wurðe CJ, wyrþe *K*, feo ł weorðe I* (*M*)

et — ⁊ ABCE^{3}FGHIJK

non — | ne ABCE^3, na GJK, næs DFI, nas *H**

fuit — | wes AE^3, wæs BCJK, næs G

multitudo — mengo A, mengeo B, mænigeo CFG, menegeo H, menego D, menigo E^3, mænigo J, manigo K, mycelnys ł mæniu I*

in — in AC, on BDE^{3}FGHIJK

commutationibus — onwendednissum A, onwendednessum B, onwendydnysse C*, behwearfum D, behwearfum GH, behærfum K, beþe[ ]rfum *F**, stirengum ł behwearfum E$^{3/x}$*, behwearftum ł on awændednyssum I, gewændednessum J (*M*)

eorum* — heara A, hira B, hyra C, heora DFHIK, hyora G, hioræ E^3, heore *J*

⟨nostris⟩ — hure *J*

ED: þu beceptest ł þu sealdest (I)] þu beceptest ł sealdest *Lindelöf.* beþe[ ]rfum (F)] beþearfum *Kimmens.*

OE: ðu bibohtes (A)] *1st* b *altered from* h (?). þu beceptest ł þu sealdest (I)] þu beceptest *in left margin,* ł *written in same ink as marginal gloss.* ðu sældest ł cyptest (E$^{3/x}$)] sældest *on eras. by main hand,* ł cyptest *added by corr.* feo ł weorðe (I)] ł weorðe *in lighter ink.* nas (H)] *lower part of stem of* s *lost due to hole in leaf.* mycelnys ł mæniu (I)] ł *crudely formed.* onwendydnysse (C)] *eras. after 2nd* n, *traces of red ink visible, 2nd* s *interl.* beþe[ ]rfum (F)] *eras. but visible except for letter after 2nd* e, *of which lower loop is lost.* stirengum ł behwearfum (E$^{3/x}$)] ł behwearfum *added by corr.*

LTg: Uendidisti] A: *2nd* i *on eras. by corr.;* Vendidisti BCDEGHIL. pretio] A: *letter eras. after* r; prętio GK; precio E; praetio M. non] no[ ] H: *final letter lost due to hole in leaf.* commutationibus] M: *1st* u *on eras.;* comutationibus F. eorum] eorum nostris J: nostris *added by glossator: a Gallican variant but without deletion of* eorum.

LTu: Uendidisti] Vendidisti ειυσυχ. pretio] prętio βν; precio ιτ*τφ, ϱ: *orig.* pretio: t *deleted,* c *interl.;* praetio μ. commutationibus] commotationibus β.

GAu: eorum] nostris ϑ.

14

Posuisti	ðu settes AB, þu settest FGJK, þu gesettyst C, ðu gesettest E^{3}*, þu gesettest I*, þu asettest D, þu asette H
nos	usic A, us BCDE^{3}FGIJK
in*	in A, on BCDE^{3}
obprobrium	edwit *AB**C*J, edwite *E^{3}*, hosp DFG, iosp *H*, to hospe *I*, on hosp K
uicinis	nehgehusum AB, niehgeburum C, neahgeburum DH, neæhgeburum E$^{3/x}$*, neahgeburum FG, nehgeburum I, neahheburum J, nehgeburan K
nostris	urum A*C*E^{3}FGI, urum BDHJ, uran K
(subsannationem)*	on forhogunge F, for leahtre G, for leahtrum J, tale ł bysmur ł on hlacerungum I
(et)*	⁊ FGIJ
derisu*	mid bismerunge A, mid bismrunge B, mid bysmrunge C, mid bysrunge G, mid bismrum J, of hlæhtre D, of hleahtre FH, hleahter I, of leahtrum *E$^{3/x}$** (*LM*)
et*	⁊ ABCDE^{3}
contemptu*	forhogadnisse A, forhogunge B*C*D, hyrwnesse ł hogunge *E$^{3/x}$** (*LM*)
his	ðissum A, ðissum *B*, þam CD, ðam E$^{3/x}$*, þam FG, þam H, þæm I, þa J (*KM*)
qui	ða A, ðæ E^{3}, þe CDFGHJ, ða ðe B, þa þe I
(sunt)*	synd FG, synt I
in	in A, on BCDE^{3}FGHJ
circuitu	ymhwyrfte A, ymbhwyrfte BCDFGHJ, ymbegænge E^{3}, onbutan I
nostro	urum AFG, urum BCD*HJ*, ure E^{3}, us ł on urum ymbhwyrfte I*
sunt*	sin[ ] *A**, sint B, synd CJ, sindon E^{3}

ED: þu gesettyst (C)] þu gesettyst *Wildhagen.* opprobrium (C)] o[b]probrium *Wildhagen.* uicinis (G)] uicinus *Rosier.* derísum (H)] derisum *Campbell.* s[ ] (A)] su *Kuhn.* sin[ ] (A)] sin *Kuhn.*

OE: ðu gesettest (E^{3})] *final* t *added by corr.* þu gesettest (I)] ge *interl.* neæhgeburum (E$^{3/x}$)] hgeburum *added by corr.*, h *altered from* n. of leahtrum (E$^{3/x}$)] of *on eras. by corr.* hyrwnesse ł hogunge (E$^{3/x}$)] ł hogunge *added by corr.* ðam (E$^{3/x}$)] am *on eras. by corr.* us ł on urum ymbhwyrfte (I)] *scribe began to write* yb *of* ymbhwyrfte, *but having written only ascender of* b, *used it to form left leg of* m. sin[ ] (A)] s *malformed, end of word lost due to trimming of leaf.*

LTg: obprobrium] opprobrium AEI, CH: *orig.* obprobrium: *1st* b *altered to* p *by corr.* nostris] C: o *malformed.* derisu] derisum ELM: *cf. Weber MSS* TQRUX, *see GAg.* contemptu] contemtu C; contemptum ELM: *cf. Weber MSS* TQRUX. his] hiis K: *orig.* his: *1st* i *interl. by corr.;* hís BM. nostro] H: *eras. after word: cf. GAg.* sunt] s[ ] A: *letter fragment visible after* s, *end of word lost due to trimming of leaf.*

LTu: Posuisti] Possuisti ϑ. obprobrium] opprobrium εϑιλοπτ*τφ. derisu] derisum τ*: *cf. Weber MSS* TQRUXχ, *see GAu.* contemptu] contemptum ντ*: *cf. Weber MSS* TQRUX. his] iis λπφ.

GAg: in (*1st*)] *om.* FGHIJK. nostris] nostris subsannationem et FGHIK; nostris subsanationem et J. derisu] derisum FGIJK, ELM: *see LTg;* derísum H: *orig.* dirísum: *1st* i *altered to* e. et contemptu] *om.* FGHIJK. qui] qui sunt FGIK, H: sunt *interl.* sunt] *om.* FGHIK.

GAu: in (*1st*)] *om.* δεζϑιλμξοπϱστυφχψ. nostris] nostris subsannationem et δεζϑιλμξοπϱστυχψ; nostris sussanationem et φ. derisu] derisum δεζϑιλμξοπϱτυφχψ. et contemptu] *om.* δεζϑιλμξοπϱστυφχψ. qui] qui sunt δεϑοϱσυχψ. sunt] *om.* δεϑπϱτυχψ.

15

Posuisti	ðu settes AB, þu settest FJK, þu asettest G, þu asettes *H,* ðu gesettyst C, ðu gesettest E^{3}*, þu gesettest I
nos	usic A, us BCE^{3}FGHIJK
in	in A, on BCDE^{3}FGHIJK
similitudinem	gelicnisse A, gelicnesse BDE^{3}GHJK, gelicnysse CFI
gentibus	ðiodum A, ðeodum BCF, ðiodum E^{3}, þeodum I, þeodum J, ðeoda G, þeoda K
commotionem	onwendnisse A, onwendnesse B, ondwendnysse *C,* æwendnesse ł styringe *E$^{3/x}$**, styringe *D*HK, styrunga F, styrunge *G,* stirunge *J,* cweccunge I* (*LM*)
capitis	heafdes A*BDFGHIJ, heafudys C, heæfdes E^{3}, heafdest K
in	on *B*DE^{3}FGHIJK (*C*)
plebibus*	we gefyllað A**C**, folcum *B*DHK, folcum FGIJ, ðiodum ł folcum E$^{3/x}$*

ED: [ ]osuisti (H)] Posuisti *Campbell.* ðu gesettyst (C)] ðu gesettyst *Wildhagen.*

OE: ðu gesettest (E^{3})] *final* t *added by corr.* æwendnesse ł styringe (E$^{3/x}$)] ł styringe *added by corr.* cweccunge (I)] *gloss eras. after word.* heafdes (A)] d *interl.* we gefyllað (AC)] *glossator takes lemma as* inplebibus (< impleo). ðiodum ł folcum (E$^{3/x}$)] ł folcum *added by corr.*

LTg: Posuisti] [ ]osuisti H: *outline of initial* P *visible.* commotionem] G: *1st* o *altered* *from* u (?), *followed by eras.* (*2 letters*), L: *2nd* o *altered from* u, *followed by eras.* (*2 letters*): *cf. Weber MSS* MK; commutationem CJM; commotationem D: *orig.* commutationem: u *deleted by subscript dot,* o *interl.,* E: *2nd* o *altered from another letter.* in plebibus] B: *2nd* b *on eras.,* C: *underlined in pencil, with* implebimus *written in margin in late hand: see OE.*

LTu: Posuisti] possuisti ϑ.

GAg: plebibus] populis FGHIJK.

GAu: plebibus] populis δεζϑιλμξοπϱστυφχψ.

16

Tota	alne AE³*, ealne BCIJK, ælce DFH, (æ)lce *G**
die	deg A, dæg BCIJK, dæge DFGH, dei E³*
uerecundia	scomu AB, sceame C, scamu E³G*J, sceamung K, aswarnung D, aswærnung H, aswærnunga F*, min aswarnung ł I*
mea	min ABCDE³FGHJK, min scamu I*
contra	wið AB, wiþ J, ongen C, ongean D*Eˣ*FGHK*, togeanes I
me	me ABCDE³FGHIJK
est	is ABE³F*G*HIJ*K*, ys C
et	⁊ ABCE³FGHIJK
confusio	gedroefednis *A*, gedrefednes B, gedrefydnyss C, gedrefednesse J, gescyndnis DH, gescindnes E³, gescendnys F, gescyndnes GK, hosp ł gescyndnys I*
uultus*	ondwleotan A, ondwlitan B, andwlitan CDH, anwlitan GI*, ansyne FJK, onsien ł andwlitan E³/ˣ*
mei*	mines ABDE³/ˣ*GH, minys C, mine FJ, mines ł minre ansyne I*, minre K
operuit*	oferwrah AB, ofyrwreah C, oferwreah DEˣ*FGJ, ofwreah H, oferwreag I, bewreh K
me	mec A, me BCE³FGHIJK

ED: alne (E)] Alne *Harsley.* ęst (G)] est *Rosier.* gescyndnes (G)] gescyndes *Rosier.*

OE: alne (E³)] *letter eras. before word.* (æ)lce (G)] *left side of* æ (?) *fragmentary and obscured by pigment from coloured initial.* dei (E³)] i *has form of* j. scamu (G)] *perhaps written in diff. ink, of type used for hyphen at v. 15* commo-tionem *and v. 16* uere-cundia. aswærnunga (F)] ærnunga *partly eras. but visible.* min aswarnung ł min scamu (I)] *written in bottom margin below* uerecundia mea. ongean (D)] e *interl.* ongean (Eˣ)] *on eras.* ongean (K)] a *malformed, perhaps false start of* n. hosp ł gescyndnys (I)] ge *interl.* onsien ł andwlitan (E³/ˣ)] ł andwlitan *added by corr.*

anwlitan mines ł minre ansyne (I)] ł minre ansyne *written above* anwlitan mines. mines ($E^{3/x}$)] n *retraced,* es *added by corr.* oferwreah (E^{x})] *on eras.*

LTg: Tota] [ ]ota G. est] ęst G; ést K. confusio] A: n *written by corr.*

LTu: uerecundia] β: *orig.* uerecondia: o *crossed through,* u *interl.;* uerecondia ϑ. confusio] confussio ϑ.

GAg: uultus] faciei FGHIJK. mei] meę FGJ, H: ę *interl. by corr.;* meae IK. operuit] cooperuit FGHIJK.

GAu: uultus] faciei δεζϑιλμξοπϱστυφχψ. mei] meae δζμοπϱυχψ; meę ειλξσφ; mee τ. operuit] cooperuit δεζϑιλμξοπϱστυφχψ.

17

A	from A, from BC, fram E^{x}*FJK, fram I, of DGH (*M*)
uoce	stefne ABCDGHIK, stæfne J, stemne E^{3}F
exprobrantis	eðwetendes A, edwitendes BG, edwityndes *C,* hyspendes DE^{x}*F, hyspendest H, hysspende K, hiscendre ł hyspendes I*, hispendra ł edwites J
et	⁊ ABCE^{3}FGHIJK
obloquentis	wiðspreocen A, wiðsprecendes BJ, wiðsprecyndys C, ongeansprecendes DE^{x}*FGH, ongeanspecende K, besprecendre ł ofersprecendes I
a	from A*E^{3},* fram BCF*J,* fram I, of D*G*H (*M*)
facie	onsiene AB, onsine *E^{3},* ansyne CDF*G*H, ansene I, ansine *J* (*M*)
inimici	feondes ABDFGHIJ, feondys C, fiondæs E^{3}*, feonda K
et	⁊ *A*BCDE^{3}FGHIJK
persequentis	oehtendes A, ehtendes BI*J, iehtyndys C, of ehtendes *D*FGH, from ehtendes E^{3}*, ehtende K

ED: fram (E)] Fram *Harsley.* ongeansprecendes (DG)] ongean sprecendes *Roeder;* ongeansprecen *Rosier.* á (E)] a *Harsley.* of ehtendes (DH)] ofehtendes *Roeder, Campbell.*

OE: fram (E^{x})] *on eras.* hyspendes (E^{x})] *on eras.* hiscendre ł hyspendes (I)] hyspendes *written in left margin.* ongeansprecendes (E^{x})] *on eras.* fiondæs (E^{3})] s *added by corr.* ehtendes (I)] *gloss eras. before word.* from ehtendes (E^{3})] *2nd* e *retouched,* s *added by corr. on eras.*

LTg: A] Á M. exprobrantis] C: *2nd* r *interl.* a facie] á facie E, M: *letter eras. after* e; affacie GJ. et (*2nd*)] A: *eras.* (*1 letter?*) *after word.* persequentis] D: *orig.* a persequentis: a *eras.*

LTu: facie] β: *orig.* uoce: facie *added interl.;* faciae ε.

18

Haec — ðas A*B*, þas CDFG*HJK*, ðæs *E*^{3}, þas þing *I* (*L*)
omnia — all A, ealle BCDFGHIJK, eællæ E^{3}
uenerunt — cwomun A, comon BCE^{3}FHIJ, comun D, coman K, acomon G
super — ofer ABFGHIJK, ofyr C
nos — usic A, us BCE^{3}GHIJK, nos F
et* — ⁊ ABCE^{3}, na FK, ne I
obliti — ofergeotele A, ofergitole BJ, ofyrgytule C, ofergiten DFG, ofergyten H, ofergitende E^{3}, forgytele I*, forgytene K
non* — | we ne ACDE$^{3/x}$*, ne *B*
sumus — | sind A, synd C, sint we B, we synd K, syndon D, sindon E$^{3/x}$, we syndon F, we ne syndon G*, we ne sindon H, we ne synt ł ne we ne forgeaton I*
te — ðec A, ðe *B*E^{3}*, þe CFGIK (*D*)
et — ⁊ ABCE^{3}FGHIJK
inique — unrehtlice A, unryhtlice BD, unrihtlice C*E*$^{3/x}$*GHIJ, on unrihtlice *F*, unriht K
non — | we ne ACDE^{3}FGHI, ne BJ, na K
egimus — | doð A, doð we B, doþ we J, dydon CDFG*H*, deden E$^{3/x}$*, dedun I*, dydan K
in — in A, on CDE^{3}FGHIJK, o[ ] *B**
testamento — cyðnisse A, cyðnysse CF, cyþnisse D, cyðnesse GH, ciþnesse J, cyþnesse E^{3}K, gecyðnysse ł gewitnysse I (*B*)
tuo — ðinre A, þinre BCDGHIJK, ðine E^{3}, þine F

ED: Hæc (D)] Haec *Roeder.* Hęc (E)] Haec *Harsley.* Hec (I)] Haec *Lindelöf.* iniquę (E)] iniquae *Harsley.* inique (F)] iniqus *Kimmens.*

OE: forgytele (I)] y *altered from* i (?). we ne (E$^{3/x}$)] we *added by corr.* we ne syndon (G)] *1st* e *and 1st* n *on crease.* we ne synt ł ne we ne forgeaton (I)] ł ne we ne forgeaton *written in right margin.* ðe (E^{3})] ð *altered from another letter by main hand.* unrihtlice (E$^{3/x}$)] *eras. before word,* tlice *on eras. by corr.* deden (E$^{3/x}$)] *2nd* d *altered from* ð, en *added by corr.* dedun (I)] *orig.* didun: i *altered to* e. o[ ] (B)] *letter fragment visible after* o, *lost due to excision of decorated initial on fol. 48v.*

LTg: Haec] Hæc BDK; Hec I: *orig.* Haec: a *eras.;* Hęc EL; [ ]ęc H: *outline of initial* H *visible.* non (*1st*)] B: o *cropped, 2nd* n *nearly completely lost due to excision of decorated initial on fol. 48v.* te] té BD. inique] F: *orig.* iniqus: que *added interl. by corr.;* iniquę E. egimus] H: ı *on eras.* in] i[ ] B: *letter after* i *lost due to excision of decorated initial on fol. 48v.* testamento] B: *lost due to excision of decorated initial on fol. 48v.*

LTu: Haec] Hęc ινξφ; Hec στ*τ. et (*2nd*)] *interl.* χ. inique] iniquę ιπ. egimus] ęgimus ε.

GAg: et (*1st*)] nec FGIJK; nęc H. non (*1st*)] *om.* FGHIJK.

GAu: et (*1st*)] nec δεζϑιλμξοπϱτυφχψ. non (*1st*)] *om.* δεζϑιλμνοπϱστυφχψ.

19

Et ⁊ *ABCE^{3}*FGHIJK (*DLM*)
non ne ABCE^{3}J, na DFGHIK
recessit gewat ABCDE^{3}FGHIJK
retro on bec ADE^{3}, on bæc BCFGHJ, onder bæc I, bæftan K
cor heorte ABCDE^{3}FGHIJK (*M*)
nostrum ur A, ure CDE^{3}FHIJK, u[ ] *B**, urum G
et ⁊ *ABCE^{3}*FGHIJK (*DLM*)
declinasti ðu onhældes A, ðu onheldes B, þu onhyldyst C, þu ahyldest DG*HK, ðu ahyldest F, ðu aheldest E$^{3/x}$*, þu ahyldest ł þu awendest I, þu onlisdest J
semitas stige AC, stiga BJ, stigæ ł siþfatu E$^{3/x}$*, siþfatu DK, siðfatu H, siðfata G, paðas FI
nostras ure ACDFGHIJK, ura B, uræ E^{3}
a from A*E^{3}*, from B, fram CDFHJK, fram GI
uia | wege ABCDFGHIJK, ðinum E^{3}
tua | ðinum A, ðinum B, þinum CD*HJ, þinum GI, ðynum *F*, þinan K, wege E^{3}

ED: þu ahyldest (G)] þu : hyldest *Rosier.* á (E)] a *Harsley.*

OE: u[ ] (B)] *rest of word lost due to excision of decorated initial on fol. 48v.* þu ahyldest (G)] *top of* a *partly lost.* ðu aheldest (E$^{3/x}$)] aheldest *on eras. by corr.* stigæ ł siþfatu (E$^{3/x}$)] ł siþfatu *added by corr.* þinum (D)] [ ]gnessum (> angnessum, *cropped by trimming) in left margin as gloss in 11th-c. hand on* erumnis *in marginal commentary:* id est a exemplo uię tuę. quia sicut in erumnis fuisti ita ⁊ nos [*etc.*].

LTg: Et] et ABCDELM; [ ]t G. cor] cór M. nostrum] n[ ] B: *lost due to excision of decorated initial on fol. 48v.* et] Et ABCDELM. a] á E. tua] F: *eras. after word.*

LTu: Et] et βνςτ*. et] Et βνςτ*.

20

Quoniam forðon *AB*HJ, forþon *C,* [ ]orðon *G,* forðæn *E^{3},* forþam K, forðan þe I (*DLM*)
humiliasti ðu geeaðmodades A, ðu geeaðmodadyst C, þu geeaðmeddes B, þu geeaðmeddest D, ðu geeæðmeddest E^{3}*, þu geeadmeddest GHJK, ðu geeadmettest F, þu geeaðmettest I*
nos usic A, us BCE^{3}GHIJ*K*
in in A, on BCDE^{3}FGHIJK

loco	stowe ABCDE^{3}FGHIJK
adflictionis	geswinces *ABC**, geswinces ł geswæncednesse *J*, geswencednisse D*H*, geswencednysse *F*, geswencendnysse *I*, geswencednesse *E^{3}*K*, [ ]nesse *G**
et	⁊ ABCDE^{3}FGHIJ*K
operuit*	oferwrah AB, ofyrwreah C, oferwreah DE^{x}*FGHIJ, bewreah K
nos	usic A, us BCDE^{3}FGHJ*K*
umbra	scua A, sceadu BCHIK, scadu DE$^{3/x}$*FGJ
mortis	deaðes ABFHI, deaðys C, deaþes DJK, deæþes E^{3}, dea[ ] *G*

ED: Quoniam (I)] quoniam *Lindelöf.* forðon (A)] for ðon *Kuhn.* mo[ ] (G)] mo*r*tis *Rosier.*

OE: ðu geeæðmeddest (E^{3})] t *added by corr.* þu geeaðmettest (I)] test *on eras.* geswinces (C)] n *interl. in red ink by corr.* geswencednesse (E^{3})] ed *interl. by corr.* [ ]nesse (G)] *letter fragments visible before* n. ⁊ (J)] *below* ne *in preceding* geswæncednesse. oferwreah (E^{x})] *on eras.* scadu (E$^{3/x}$)] cadu *on eras. by corr.*

LTg: Quoniam] quoniam ABCDELM; [ ]uoniam G: *fragment of initial letter visible.* nos (*1st*)] nós K. adflictionis] afflictionis ABEFHIJK, C: *1st* f *interl. by corr.;* [ ]ctionis G. nos (*2nd*)] nós K. mortis] mo[ ] G.

LTu: Quoniam] quoniam βνςτ*. adflictionis] afflictionis δεζιλξοπϱστ*τυφχ.

GAg: operuit] cooperuit FGHIJK.

GAu: operuit] cooperuit δεζϑιλμξοπϱστυφχψ.

21

Si	gif ABCDG*H*I*JK, Gif E^{3}, gyf F
obliti	| ofergeotulæ A*, ofyrgytule C, ofergitole J, ofergitelende B, we ofergeaton DFGH, we ofergeatan K, we forgytaþ I*, we sien E^{3}
sumus	| we sind A, we synd C, we beoð B, we beoþ J, ofergitende E^{3}
nomen	noma A, noman B, naman CDFGHIJK, nomon E^{3}
dei	godes ABE^{3}FGHIJK, godys C
nostri	ures ABE^{3}GHIJ, urys C, ure FK
et	⁊ ABCE^{3}FGHIJK
si	gif ABCDE^{3}GHIJK, gyf F
expandimus	we aðennað AB, we aþeniað CDG*H*JK, we áþenıæð E^{3}*, we aðeniað F, we astreccaþ I
manus	honda A, handa BDFGHI*JK, hænde E^{3}, hand C
nostras	ure ACE^{3}GIJK, ura BDFH
ad	to ABCE^{3}FGIJK

deum gode ABCE^{3}FIJ*, godum K, god[ ] *G*

alienum ðæm fremðan A, ðæm fremdan B, þam fremdan C, fremedum D, fremdum E^{3}**G*, fremdum H, ælfremedum F, ælfremedum IJ (*M*)

ED: expándimus (H)] expandimus *Campbell*.

OE: gif (I)] *stray* ð *written in left margin: cf. v. 22* þas ðing. ofergeotulæ (A)] *orig.* ofergeotulu: *final* u *altered to* æ. we forgytaþ (I)] ytaþ *on eras.* we áþeniæð (E^{3})] þ *on eras. by corr.* handa (I)] *gloss eras. before word* (?), *eras. after final* a. gode (J)] *orig.* godes: s *eras.* fremdum (E^{3})] *eras. before word.*

LTg: Si] [ ]i H: *outline of initial* S *visible.* expandimus] expándimus H. deum] deu[ ] G. alienum] alięnum G; álienum M.

22

Nonne ah ne AB, ac na J, hu ne CG, hwu ne E^{3}*, hu ne nu DH, la hu ne I, hu nu FK (*L*)

deus god ABCE^{3}FGHIJK

requiret soeceð *A*, secyð C, secæþ E^{3}, seceþ J, soecð B, secð DFGHIK (*M*)

ista ðas AB, þas CDG*H*K, ðæs E^{3}, ðes F, þa J, þas ðing I*

ipse he ABCDE^{3}FGHJK, he sylf I*

enim soðlice ABCFGI, soþlice HJ, witolice K, eællengæ E^{3}

nouit wat ABDGHIJ, wát F, oncnew C, cnaweð E^{x}, gecnæwð K

occulta* ða deglan AB, þa diglan C, deglu D, diglæ E^{3}*, díglu F, diglu I, digle J, digelnessa G, gehydde K, ⁊ c H*

cordis heortan A*BCDFGHJK, heortæn E^{3}, þære heortan I

Quoniam forðon AB, forþon CJ, forðæn E^{3}*, forþan þe F, forðan þe I, forþam G, forþā K

propter fore ABD*E^{3}*H, for CFGIJ

te ðe ABE^{3}F, þe CGHIJ

morte* mid deaðe AB, deaðe C, deaþe D, deæde E^{3}*

afficimur* we biað geswencte A, we beoð geswencte B, we beoð geswencte C, we beoð wæcede D, we bioþ gewordene $E^{3/x}$*, deade we beoð F, deade we beoþ J, deaþe we beoþ wæcede K, we synt gecwylmberode I*

tota* alne A, ealne BCIJ, ælce DFGH, elce E^{3}, ælle K

die deg AE^{3}*, dæg BCDIJK, dæge FG*H*

aestimati getalde A, getealde *BCJ*, gewenede *DFGHK*, we synt getealde gewenede *I**, we bioþ *E^{3}* (*L*)

sumus | we sind AJ, we synd CFGH, we sint B, we synt D, we syndon I*, we sund K, gewenende E[3]
ut* swe swe A, swa swa BCFGHI*J*, swa DK, swæ E[3]*
oues scep ABCE[3], sceap DFG*H*IJ*K*
occisionis ofslegenisse A, ofslægenisse B, ofslegennisse DH, ofslegennysse F, ofslegennesse G, ofslcgcnesse K, ofscleacnesse J, ofslegyn C, acweællednesse E[3/x]*, to gesnide ł snides I* (*M*)

ED: hu ne (C)] hune *Wildhagen*. hu ne nu (DH)] hunenu *Roeder, Campbell*. ipse (I)] Ipse *Lindelöf*. forðon (A)] for ðon *Kuhn*. forðæn (E)] Forðæn *Harsley*. propte (E)] propte[r] *Harsley*. we beoð g̲e̲swencte (C)] we beoð geswencte *Wildhagen*. æstimati (D)] aestimati *Roeder*. estimati (F)] aestimati *Kimmens*. we synt getealde gewenede (I)] we synt getealde ł gewenede *Lindelöf*. swa swa (GIJ)] swaswa *Rosier, Lindelöf, Oess*. oues (BE)] oves *Brenner, Harsley*.

OE: hwu ne (E[3])] *on eras*. þas ðing (I)] *stray* ð *written after* ðing: *cf. v. 21* gif. he sylf (I)] f *interl*. diglæ (E[3])] *eras. before and after word*. ⁊ c (H)] *tironian* et *dissimilar to form typically employed: upper stroke terminates in slight downward curve;* c, *written to left of ascender of* b *of lemma, remains unexplained: possibly to be read as otiose stroke plus* ic (?). heortan (A)] *otiose dot below* o. forðæn (E[3])] f *by corr. over another letter*. deæde (E[3])] *orig*. deæðe: ð *altered to* d. we bioþ gewordene (E[3/x])] we *added by corr*. we synt gecwylmberode (I)] mber *on eras*. deg (E[3])] *orig*. dege: *final* e *eras*. we synt getealde gewenede (I)] gewenede *written in bottom margin*. we syndon (I)] *written in bottom margin*. swæ (E[3])] *eras. after word*. acweællednesse (E[3/x])] lednesse *on eras. by corr*. to gesnide ł snides (I)] ł snides *written in bottom margin*.

LTg: Nonne] Nónne L. requiret] AM: *orig*. requirit: *2nd* i *altered to* c. ista] H: *small eras. after word*. propter] propte E. die] H: *eras. after* i, e *formed from another letter*. aestimati] æstimati BDK; ęstimati CGHI; estimati EL, F: *orig*. aestimati: a *deleted by subscript dot*. ut] J: *eras. before word*. oues] H: *orig*. ouis: i *altered to* e; óuis K. occisionis] M: *orig*. occissionis: *1st* s *eras*.

LTu: requiret] requirit β. enim] *interl*. ε. occulta] oculta ν. die] dię ν. aestimati] ęstimati βν; estimati ζϑιξϱσϛ*τφ. occisionis] occissionis ϑ.

GAg: occulta] abscondita FGHIJK. morte afficimur] mortificamur FIK, G: *2 letters eras. after* a, *with dash inserted in their place*, H: ti *interl*.; mortificabimur J. ut] sicut FGHIK.

GAu: occulta] abscondita δεζϑιλλξοπϱστυφχψ. morte afficimur] mortificamur δεζϑιλμξοπϱστυφχψ. tota] omni ϑ. ut] sicut ϑιλμξοπϱστυφχ

23
Exsurge aris *AB*C*D*G*H*J*K*, Aris E[3]*, áris *F*, uparis I (*L*)

quare	forhwon AB, hwænne *C,* forwæn E^{3}, forhwy DH, forhwý F, forhwi GIK, forðon J (*L*)
obdormis	heppas ðu A*, hneppast ðu B, hnappast þu C, hnappas þu ł hwi slæpst þu I, slapest þu DH, slæpst þu FGJ*K,* slepest þu $E^{3/x}$*
domine	dryhten B, drihten E^{3}*K,* dryht̄ A, driħt CFG, driħ J (*HI*)
exsurge	aris *A**B*CD*F*G*H*IJK, Æris *E^{3}* (*L*)
et	⁊ CFGHIJK (*AB*)
ne	ne ABCDE^{3}FGHJ, ut ne I, na K
repellas	forspild ðu AB, forspill þu C, forspil þu J, anyd þu DFGH, anyd þu ł ⁊ ne ædrif þu E^{3}*, adræf þu ł aned þu I*, wer *K**
nos*	usic A, us BCE^{x}* (*M*)
usque*	oð ABC, oþ D, oððe E^{3}
in	on DE^{3}FGHIJK
finem	ende ABCDE^{3}FGHIJK

ED: Exurge (F)] Exsurge *Kimmens.* exurge (F)] exsurge *Kimmens.* forhwon (A)] for hwon *Kuhn.* forhwy (D)] for hwy *Roeder.* dryhten (B)] dryht*en Brenner.* Æris (E)] æris *Harsley.*

OE: Aris (E^{3})] *orig.* Æris: Æ *altered to* A, *retouched by corr.* heppas ðu (A)] h *altered from another letter.* slepest þu ($E^{3/x}$)] est þu *added by corr.* aris (A) (*2nd*)] *small eras. above* i. anyd þu ł ⁊ ne ædrif þu (E^{3})] *2nd* þu *added by corr.* adræf þu ł aned þu (I)] *2nd* a *malformed.* wer (K)] r *altered from* w. us (E^{x})] *eras. before word.*

LTg: Exsurge] Exurge ACL, F: *orig.* Exsurge: s *deleted by subscript dot,* H: *eras. after* x. quare] C: *orig.* quarę: *cauda eras.;* quáre L. obdormis] K: ob *interl. by main hand.* domine] H: *small eras. after word, perhaps of punct.,* I: s. o *written above word,* K: nis *in* occisionis (*v. 22*) *orig. written at line end eras. and added to* occisio- *above by glossator.* exsurge] exurge CEL, A: *eras.* (*1–2 letters*) *after word,* F: *orig.* exsurge: s *deleted by subscript dot,* H: *eras. after* x. et] *om.* B, A: *see note to* exsurge *above.* repellas] reppellas K: *2nd* p *interl. by corr.* nos] M: *interl. by corr.*

LTu: Exsurge] β: ge *interl.;* Exurge δειλξπστ*τυφχψ, ϱ: *orig.* Exsurge: s *deleted.* obdormis] dormis ζϱ. exsurge] exurge δειλπτ*τυφχψ, ϱ: *orig.* exsurge: s *deleted.* nos] *om.* β.

GAg: nos usque] *om.* FGHIJK.

GAu: nos usque] *om.* δεζθιλμξοπϱστυφχψ.

24

Quare	forhwon ABJ, forhwan C, Forwæn E^{3}*, forhwý F, forhwi GHIK
faciem	onsiene AB, onsíéne E^{3}*, onsyne D, ansyne CFGHIJK

tuam — ðine ABD, þine CE^xGHIJK, ðyn F
auertis — ðu forcerrest A, þu forcerrest B, þu forcerryst C*, þu forcirrest J, acyrst ðu D, acyrst þu H, þu acyrst G, acyrst K, awendst þu FI, æhwirfst þu E^{3/x}*
obliuisceris — ðu ofergeotelas A, ðu ofergeotelast B, þu ofyrgytolast C, þu ofergitest J, ofergitest D*H*, ofergitest E^3*, ofergytest F, þu ofergytest G, ⁊ forhwi forgetst þu I, forgytst K (*M*)
inopiam* | wedelnisse *A*, wædelnesse B, wædlan C, on wædlungum J, unspede DGHK, on unspede F, unspede ł wedlæn E^{3/x}*, ure I
nostram* | ure *A*BCDE^3FGHK, urum J, hæfenlyste ł ure wanhæfelnesse I
et — ⁊ ABCDE^3FGHIJK
tribulationem* | geswencednisse *A*, geswencednesse B, geswencydnysse C, geswinc D, geswincg G, geswing H, geswinces K, swinc J, eærfoðnesse ł swinc E^3, gedrefednysse F, ure I
nostram* | ure *A*BCDE^3FGHJK, drefednesse I

ED: forhwon (A)] for hwon *Kuhn.* obliuiscerís (H)] obliuisceris *Campbell.*

OE: Forwæn (E^3)] F *retouched by corr.* onsíéne (E^3)] *final* e *added by corr.* þu forcerryst (C)] cer *interl.* æhwirfst þu (E^{3/x})] t *and* þu *added by corr.* ofergitest (E^3)] s *retouched, final* t *added on eras. by corr.* unspede ł wedlæn (E^{3/x})] unspede ł *added by corr.,* de *and* ł *on eras.*

LTg: obliuisceris] obliuiscerís H; obliuiscéris M. inopiam] A: m *on eras.* nostram (*1st*)] A: m *on eras.* tribulationem] A: m *added by corr.* (?). nostram (*2nd*)] A: *added by corr.* (?).

GAg: inopiam] inopię FGIJK; inopiae H. nostram (*1st*)] nostrę FHIK; nostre GJ. tribulationem] tribulationis FGHIJK. nostram (*2nd*)] nostrę FGHK; nostrae I; nostre J.

GAu: inopiam] inopię δεζιλμξπϱφ; inopiæ ϑ; inopiae οψ; inopie στυχ. nostram (*1st*)] nostrae δζοπϱυχψ; nostrę ειλμξφ; nostræ ϑ; nostre στ. tribulationem] tribulationis δεζϑιλμξοπϱστυφχψ. nostram (*2nd*)] nostrae δεζμοπϱυχψ; nostræ ϑ; nostrę ιλξφ; nostre στ.

25

Quoniam — forðon ABJ, forþon C, forðæn E^3, forðan ðe F, forþam G
humiliata — geeaðmodad A, geeaðmododu B, geeaðmeded I, geeadmed CFG, geadmed K, geeaðmed DH, geeæðmæd *E^3**, geeadmodod J
est — is ABD*E^x*FGHIJ*K*, ys C

in — in A, on BCD*E*^{3}*FGHJK, to I
puluere — dusðe A, duste BCDE^{3}*FGH, dvste K, duste ł to eorðan I*, dust ł on myl J
anima | sawul A, sawl BDG, sawle CJ, sæule E^{3}*, saul FH, sawel K, ure I
nostra | ur A, uru B, ure CDE^{3}FGHJK, sawl I*
adhesit* — ætfalh A, ætfealh BC, etfylhð ł clyuode E$^{3/x}$*, geclyfode D, forswulgon F*, forswolgon J, forswolhgen K, gelimod G, gebiged ł forglendrad ł gelimod I* (*M*)
(est)* — is FGIJK
in — in A, on BCDE^{3}FGJK, to I
terra — eorðan ABCDGI, eorðæn E^{3}, eorþan JK, lande F
uenter — womb AB, wamb C, wambe IJ, wamb ł innoð E$^{3/x}$*, innoð DGK, inoð H, innoðes F
noster — ur A, ure BCDE^{3}GHIJK, ures F

ED: forðon (A)] for ðon *Kuhn.* forðæn (E)] Forðæn *Harsley.*

OE: geeæðmæd (E^{3})] d *on eras.* on (E^{3}) (*1st*)] *retraced by corr.* duste (E^{3})] d *retouched by corr.* duste ł to eorðan (I)] ł corpus licama *written after* eorðan. sæule (E^{3})] l *on eras.* sawl (I)] e<u>st</u> : is *written in left margin.* etfylhð ł clyuode (E$^{3/x}$)] ł clyuode *added by corr.* forswulgon (F)] *eras. but visible.* gebiged ł forglendrad ł gelimod (I)] forglendrad *suggests confusion with* (con)glutitus: *see also* FJK. wamb ł innoð (E$^{3/x}$)] wamb ł *added by corr.*

LTg: humiliata] E: *final* a *retraced.* est] E: *on eras. by corr.* in (*1st*)] E: *on eras. by corr.* adhesit] adhaesit M.

LTu: est] ést K.

GAg: adhesit] conglutinatus est FGHI; conglutínatus est J; conglutinatus ést K.

GAu: adhesit] conglutinatus est δεζϑιλμξοπϱστυφχψ.

26

Exsurge — aris *AB*C*DFGH*JK, Æris E^{3}*, uparis I (*LM*)
domine — drihten E^{3}FK, dryht̄ AB, driħt C, driħ GJ (*I*)
adiuua — gefultume A, gefultuma BCJ, gefultumæ E^{3}*, gefylst D*FG*H*, andfylst K, gehelp I
nos — us ABCDE^{3}FGHIJK
et — ⁊ ABCDE^{3}FGHIJK
libera* — gefrea A, gefreo BC, alys ł friolsæ E$^{3/x}$*, alys DGHK*, alýs F, alis J, alys ł genera I
nos — us ABCE^{3}FGHIJK
propter — fore ABDE^{3}H, for CFGIJK*

nomen	nomen A, noman B, naman CDFGHIJK, nomæn E^{3}
tuum	ðinum ABE^{3}F, þinu<u>m</u> C, þinum IJ, þinan GK, þin H

ED: Exurge (C)] Ex[s]urge *Wildhagen.* Exurge (F)] Exsurge *Kimmens.* ádiuua (H)] adiuua *Campbell.*

OE: Ǣris (E^{3})] Ǣ *retouched.* gefultumæ (E^{3})] f *retouched.* gefylst (D)] s *interl.* alys ł friolsæ (E$^{3/x}$)] alys ł *added on eras. by corr.* alys (K)] me *eras. after word.* for (K)] *eras. after word (7 letters).*

LTg: Exsurge] Exurge AL, C: *orig.* Exsurge: s *eras.*, F: *orig.* Exsurge: s *deleted by subscript dot,* H: *eras. after* x, M: *orig.* Exsurge: s *crossed through.* domine] I: s. o *written above word.* adiuua] ádiuua H.

LTu: Exsurge] EXsurge β; Exurge δειλξπστ*τυφχ, ϱ: *orig.* Exsurge: s *deleted.*

GAg: libera] redime FGHIK.

GAu: libera] redime δεζϑιλξοπϱστυφχψ; redeme μ.

PSALM 44

2

Eructuauit*	roccetteð *AB**, roccyttyð *C,* belcette *DE^{x}*HK, bealcetteð F, bealcatte I, forðlæteð ł utroccetteð G, forlæteþ J (*LM*)
cor	heorte AB*C*DE^{3}*FGHIJK (*M*)
meum	min ABDE^{3}FGHIJK
uerbum	word ABCDE^{3}FGHIJK
bonum	god ACE^{3}FGHIK, gód BDJ
dico	| ic cweoðu A, cweðe F, cweþe J, cwiðe E^{3}, secge CDGH, ic BIK
ego	| ic ACDE^{3}FGHJ, cweðe B, cweþe K, sæcge I
opera	werc AB, weorc CDFGHIJK, wiorc E^{3}
mea	min ABC*F*GHIJ, mine DE^{3}K
regi	cyninge ABCDGHJ, kiningc E^{3}, kyninge I, cininge K, ðæs cyninges F
Lingua	tunge AB*C*DFGHIJK, Tunge E^{3}
mea	min ABCDE^{3}FGHI*JK
calamus	hreod *A*BCI, writingfeþer D, writingfeþere E^{x}*, writingcfyðer F*, writingfeðer G, writeingfeðer *H,* writincfeþer K, reod writefæder J (*M*)
scribae	writ *A*BCGJ,* boceres *D,* boceras *IK,* gewriteres *E$^{3/x}$** (*FHLM*)
uelociter	hreðlice A, hrædlice BCDFGHIK, hredlice E^{3}, rædlice J
scribentis	writendes *A*BDE^{3}HIJ, writyndys C, wrytendes F, writende GK

ED: ERuctuáuit (A)] Eructuauit *Kuhn.* [ ]ructauit (B)] [ ]ructavit *Brenner.* cálamus (H)] calamus *Campbell.* writingcfyðer (F)] writingc fyðer *Kimmens.* reod writefæder (J)] reodwrite fæder *Oess.* scribę (C)] scribe *Wildhagen.*

OE: roccetteð (B)] *letter fragment visible before* r. heorte (E^{3})] *final* e *added by corr.* min (I) (*3rd*)] s. est : is *written in left margin.* writingfeþere (E^{x})] *on eras.* writingcfyðer (F)] *obscured by eras. but visible.* writ (A)] *lemma misread as* scribe; *see also* BCGJ. gewriteres (E$^{3/x}$)] eres *on eras. by corr.*

LTg: Eructuauit] ERuctuáuit A: *2nd* u *on eras. by corr.;* [ ]ructauit B: *decorated initial excised;* ERVCTAUIT C; Eructauit D, L: *letter eras. after 1st* t; ERVCTAVIT E; ERuctuauit M. cor] COR C; cór M. mea (*1st*)] F: a *on eras.* Lingua] Linga C. calamus] A: u *on eras.,* s *interl.;* cálamus H, M: u *altered from another letter,* s *added.* scribae] scribę ABCDFGHLM; scribe EIJK. scribentis] A: *2nd* i *on eras.*

LTu: Eructuauit] ERUCTUauit β; ERVCTAuit ς; ERVCTAVIT τ*. cor] COR λμνϱψ. meum] MEUM λϱ. uerbum] UERBUM λ. scribae] scribe βδζιμπσςτ*τ; scribę ελνξϱυφχψ; scribæ ϑ. scribentis] scribentes β.

GAg: Eructuauit] Eructauit FGHIJ, DL: *see LTg;* ERuctauit K; *for* BCE *see LTg.*

GAu: Eructuauit] Eructauit δεϑξοπσυ; ERVCTAVIT ιτ; ERUCTAUIT λμνϱτφχψ.

3

Speciosus	wlitig ABCDGHJ, Wlitig E$^{3/x}$*, wlytig F, wliti K*, wynsum ł æþele ł ænlic ł wlitig I*
forma	on hiowe A, on hiwe BCIJ, heow DE$^{3/x}$*, heaw G, hyw H, hiw K, heap F*
prae	fore *ABDE^{3}H,* for *CFGJK,* toforan *I* (*L*)
filiis	bearnum AGI, bearnum BCDFHJ, beærnum *E^{3},* bearna K
hominum	mona A*, monna B, manna CDFGHIJK, mænnæ *E^{3}*
diffusa	togoten ABD*G*HJ, togotyn C, togoton K, ægoten E^{3}, agoten F, gindgoten I
est	is ABE^{3}FGHIJ*K,* ys C
gratia	geofu A, gefu B, gyfu CK, gifu DE^{3}GHJ, gyfe F, gife I
in	in A, on BCDE^{3}FGHIJK
labiis	weolerum A, welerum BDHJ, welerum CFGI, welrum *E^{3},* weleran K
tuis	ðinum AB, þinum CFGHI, þinum DE^{3}JK
Propterea	forðon ABD, forþon C*H,* forðæn E^{3}, forðan *I,* forþan *K,* forþam *G,* forþā *J,* forða *F*
benedixit	bledsade A, bletsode BDFHJK, bletsude C, he bletsode G, gebletsode E$^{3/x}$*I
te	ðe AB, þe CDE^{3}FGHIJK

deus	god ABCE^{3}FGHIJK
in	in A, on BCDE^{3}FGHIJK
aeternum	ecnisse A, ecnesse *BDE^{3}GHJK*, ecnysse *CF*I (*L*)

ED: filíís (E)] filiis *Harsley.* labíís (E)] labiis *Harsley.* forðon (A)] for ðon *Kuhn.* forðæn (E)] Forðæn *Harsley.* forþā (J)] forþa*m Oess.* æternum (D)] aeternum *Roeder.* ęternum (EG)] aeternum *Harsley;* eternum *Rosier.*

OE: Wlitig (E$^{3/x}$)] it *retouched,* ig *on eras. by corr.* wliti (K)] *gloss eras. before word.* wynsum ł æþele ł ænlic ł wlitig (I)] es : þu eart *written in left margin.* heow (E$^{3/x}$)] ow *on eras. by corr.* heap (F)] *obscured by eras. but visible.* mona (A)] *scribe began* mom-, *then used right leg of 2nd* m *to form bowl of* a. gebletsode (E$^{3/x}$)] ode *on eras. by corr.*

LTg: prae] præ B; pre CDEGHIJK; prę L. filiis] filíís E. hominum] hominvm E. diffusa] difusa G. est] ést K. labiis] labíís E. Propterea] propterea FGHIJK. aeternum] ęternum CEFGHL; æternum BDK; eternum J.

LTu: prae] pre εζϑσςτ*; prę λνξπϱ; p̄ ιτυφχ. filiis] filis ϑ. diffusa] ν: *1st* f *interl.* labiis] labis ϑ. Propterea] PRQPTERea β; propterea δεζϑιλμξτυφχψ. aeternum] ęternum ειλμνξφ; æternum ϑ; eternum στ*τ.

4

accingere	begyrd ABC, begird *J*, ymbgyrdan D**FH*, ymbegyrdan *K*, sy ðu ymbgyrd *I*, to begirdænne E^3 (*G*)
gladium*	| sweord A*B*J, swvrdc *C*, sweorde *DE^3*FGH, swyrde K, mid þinum I (*LM*)
tuum*	| ðin A*B*, þin J, þinu͟m *CD*H, ðinu͟m *E^3*, þinum G, þinan K, þyðum F, swurde I (*LM*)
circa*	ym A, ymb B*CE^3, ymbe D, ofer FGIJK
femur	lendan A, lendna *B*, lendynu C, lændena J, þæ lendeno E^3, þeoh DG*H*IK, ðeoh F
(tuum)*	ðinum F, þinre H, þin GI, þine J, þinan K
potentissime	ða maehtgestan A, þa mihtgestan B, þa mihtigystan C, mihtiglice F, mihtigliche ł þeoh riclicost E$^{3/x}$*, riclicost DK, riclicost ł fromlicost H, riclice ł stranglice ł riclicost I, ri[ ] ł fremlicost *G*

ED: Ac[ ]e (G)] Accingere *Rosier.* þin (G)] þ[ ] *Rosier.*

OE: ymbgyrdan (D)] *orig.* ymbgyrdon: o *deleted by subscript dot,* a *interl.* ymb (B)] *word eras. after* b. mihtigliche ł þeoh riclicost (E$^{3/x}$)] *eras. before gloss*, ig *retouched* (*on eras.?*), liche ł þeoh *on eras. by corr.*

LTg: accingere] Accingere FHIJK; Ac[ ]e G. gladium] B: um *on eras.;* gladio

CDEL, M: *orig.* gladium: u *altered to* o, m *eras.*: *cf. Weber MSS* ε^{2}η moz^{x}, *see GAg.* tuum] B: t *on eras.;* tuo CDEL, M: *orig.* tuum: *2nd* u *altered to* o, m *eras.*: *cf. Weber MSS* ε^{2}η moz^{x}, *see GAg.* femur] femvr H: *orig.* femor: v *interl.;* femor B. potentissime] [ ]tissime G: *letter fragments visible before* t.

LTu: accingere] Accingere δεζιλμξοπστυφχ; Acingere ϑ. gladium] gladio ντ*: *cf. Weber MSS* ε^{2}η moz^{x}, *see GAu.* tuum] tuo ντ*: *cf. Weber MSS* ε^{2}η moz^{x}, *see GAu.* femur] uemur β.

GAg: gladium] gladio FGHIJK, CDELM: *see LTg.* tuum] tuo FGHIJK, CDELM: *see LTg.* circa] super FGHIJK. femur] femur tuum FIJK; femvr tuum H; femur tuu[ ] G.

GAu: gladium] gladio δεζϑιλμξοπϱστυφχψ, ντ*: *see LTu.* tuum] tuo δεζϑιλμξοπϱστυφχψ, ντ*: *see LTu.* circa] super δεζϑιλμξοπϱστυφχψ. femur] femur tuum δζιλμξοπϱστυφχ; femor tuum ϑ, ε: *orig.* femur tuum: o *interl. above 1st* u; faemur tuum ψ.

5

Speciem*	ǀ heow A, hiw B*C*J, wlite *D*FHK, Wlite *E^{3}**, mid þinum I (*LM*)
tuam*	ǀ ðin AB, þin *C*JK, þinum *D*H, þinum FG, ðinne *E^{3}*, hiwe ł wlite I (*LM*)
et	⁊ ABCDE^{3}FGHIJK
pulchritudinem*	fegernisse A, fegernesse *E^{3}*, fægernesse BGJ, fægernysse *C*F, fægernisse *D*H, fægernysse I, fægernes K (*LM*)
tuam*	ðine A*B*C*, þine GJ, þinre *D*HI, ðin FK, dine *E^{3}* (*LM*)
intende	behald A*B, beheald CJ, beheæld E^{3}, behead *K*, beloca ł beheald D, he loca ł beheald H, [ ]heald ł loca *G*, begym F, begem I
prospere	gesundfullice ABE^{x}*FGHJ, gesyndfullice K, gesvntfullice D*, gesundfullice ł gespediglice I, gelystfullice C
procede	forðgaa A, forðga BC, forþga J, forðgewit DFGK, forðgæwit E$^{3/x}$*, forð H, forðstæpe I
et	⁊ ABCE^{x}*FGHIJK
regna	ricsa ABC, rixsa K, rixa DGHIJ, rixæ E$^{3/x}$*, rice F*
Propter	fore ABCDH, Fore E^{3}, for F*G*IJK
ueritatem	soðfestnisse A, soðfæstnesse BGI, soðfæstnysse C, soþfæstnesse DJ, Soðfestnesse E^{3}*, soþfæstnysse F, soðfæstnisse H, soþfætnesse K*
et	⁊ ABCE^{3}FGIJK
mansuetudinem	monðwernisse A, monðwærnesse B, manþwærnysse C, manþwærnesse IJ, geþwærnisse DH, geþwernesse E^{3}, geþwærnysse F, geþwærnesse K, gehwærnesse *G*

et	⁊ ABCE^{3}FGHIJK
iustitiam	rechtwisnisse A, ryhtwisnesse B, rihtwisnysse *C,* rihtwisnesse E$^{3/x}$*GHIJ, ryhtwisnes D, rihtwisnys F, rihtwisnes K
et	⁊ ABCDE^{3}*FGIJK
deducet	gelaedeð A, gelædeð B*G*H, gelædyð C, gelædeþ DFJK, geledeþ E^{3}, gelæt I
te	ðec A, ðe *BF,* þe CDE^{x}GHIJ*K*
mirabiliter	wundurlice AD, wundorlice BCFGI*J,* wundorliche E$^{3/x}$*, wunderlice K, wundur H
dextera	sie swiðre A, seo swiðre B*D, seo swyðre FG, seo swiþre HJ, swiðre CE^{3}I, swyþre K
tua	ðin ABE^{3}, þin C*DFGHIJK

ED: Specie (G)] Specie *Rosier.* [ ]pecie (H)] Specie *Campbell.* he loca ł beheald (H)] beloca ł beheald *Campbell.* gesvntfullice (D)] gesuntfullice *Roeder.* iusticiam (C)] iusti[t]iam *Wildhagen.*

OE: Wlite (E^{3})] W *retouched, eras. after* W. ðine (A)] ð *altered from* t. behald (A)] l *interl.* gesundfullice (E^{x})] sundfullice *on eras.* gesvntfullice (D)] *orig.* gesintfullice: *1st* i *deleted by subscript dot,* v *interl.* forðgæwit (E$^{3/x}$)] forðgæ *retouched,* wit *on eras. by corr.* ⁊ (E^{x}) (*2nd*)] *on eras.* rixæ (E$^{3/x}$)] x *on eras. by corr.,* æ *altered from* e *by main hand.* rice (F)] *eras. but visible.* Soðfestnesse (E^{3})] f *retouched.* soþfætnesse (K)] *letter eras. before word.* rihtwisnesse (E$^{3/x}$)] rihtwis *on eras. by corr.* ⁊ (E^{3}) (*5th*)] *eras. after word.* wundorliche (E$^{3/x}$)] liche *added by corr.* seo swiðre (B)] eo *obscured by stain but visible.* þin (C) (*2nd*)] *orig.* þine: e *eras.*

LTg: Speciem] Specie CDEL, M: *orig.* speciem: m *eras.: cf. Weber MSS* δεη*λT med, *see GAg.* tuam (*1st*)] tua CDEL, M: *orig.* tuam: m *eras.: cf. Weber MSS* δεη*λT med, *see GAg.* pulchritudinem] pulchritudine CDE, M: *orig.* pulchritudinem: m *eras.;* pulc$^{|-}$ritudine L: *spiritus asper* ($^{|-}$) *interl.: cf. Weber MSS* γδεη*λT moz^{c} med, *see GAg.* tuam (*2nd*)] tua CDEL, M: *orig.* tuam: m *eras.: cf. Weber MSS* γδεη*λT moz^{c} med, *see GAg.* intende] K: in *on eras. by corr., eras. after word;* [ ]tende G. Propter] [ ]ropter G: *outline of initial* P *visible.* manṣuetudinem] mansuętudinem G. iustitiam] iusticiam C: *orig.* iustitiam: *2nd* t *altered to* c. deducet] G: *2nd* d *altered from* n. tc] té BK. mirabiliter] J: *minim* (*false start*) *after* r, *over which* a *is written.*

LTu: Speciem tuam] Specie tua ντ*: *cf. Weber MSS* δεη*λT med, *see GAu.* pulchritudinem tuam] pulchritudine tua ντ*: *cf. Weber MSS* γδεη*λT moz^{c} med, *see GAu.* Propter] P<u>ROPTER</u> β. iustitiam] iusticiam τ*τφ, ϱ: *orig.* iustitiam: *2nd* ṭ *deleted,* c *interl.*

GAg: Speciem] Specie IJK, CDELM: *see LTg,* F: *final* e *on eras.,* G: S *partly cropped;* [ ]pecie H: *outline of initial* S *visible.* tuam (*1st*)] tua GHIJK, CDELM: *see LTg,* F: t *on eras.* pulchritudinem] pulchritudine FGHIJK, CDELM: *see LTg.* tuam (*2nd*)] tua FGIJK, CDELM: *see LTg,* H: *orig.* tue: e *altered to* a.

GAu: Speciem] Speciae δ; Specie εζϑιλμξοπϱστυφχψ, ντ*: *see LTu.* tuam (*1st*)] tua δεζϑιλμξοπϱστυφχψ, ντ*: *see LTu.* pulchritudinem] pulchritudine δεζϑιλμξοπϱστυφχψ, ντ*: *see LTu.* tuam (*2nd*)] tua εζϑιλξοπϱστυφχψ, ντ*: *see LTu;* tua et μ, δ: et *interl.*

6

Sagittae	strele A, stræla *B*, strælas *J*, strelæ ł flane *E*$^{3/x}$*, flana *CDFG**HIK* (*L*)
tuae	ðine A*E*^{3}*F,* ðina *B,* þine *CDGH*IJ*K* (*L*)
acutae	scearpe A*BCDFGH*I***K*, sceærpe *E*^{3}, scearp *J* (*LM*)
potentissime*	ða maehtgestan A, þa mihtgestan B, þa mihtegystan C, ðes mihtigestæn E^{3}*, þa ricustan D
populi	folc ABDE^{3}GHIJK, folcys C, folces F
sub	under ABDE^{x}*FGHIJK, undyr C
te	ðe ABE^{3}*, þe CFIJK
cadent	fallað A, feallað BCDFGH, fealleþ J, fællaþ K, gefealleþ E^{3}*, hreosaþ I (*M*)
in	in *A,* on BCDE^{3}*FGHIJK (*M*)
corda*	heortan *ABCDFGHIJK,* heortæn *E*^{3}* (*LM*)
inimicorum	fionda A, feonda BCDFHIJK, on feonde G, find E^{3}
regis	cyninges ABDGHJ, cyningys C, kyninges I, cininga K, þes kinges E^{3}, ðæs cyningces F

ED: Sagittę (E)] Sagittae *Harsley.* tuæ (D)] tuae *Roeder.* tuę (E)] tuae *Harsley.* cordæ (E)] cordae *Harsley.*

OE: strelæ ł flane (E$^{3/x}$)] ł flane *added by corr.* flana (G)] *1st* a *faint but visible.* scearpe (I)] s. <u>sunt</u> : synt *written in left margin.* ðes mihtigestæn (E^{3})] ð *written in left margin (form of* ð *differs slightly from main hand, but same ink; possibly added later).* under (E^{x})] *on eras.* ðe (E^{3})] *retraced.* gefealleþ (E^{3})] ge *retraced.* on heortæn (E^{3})] *MS* h̋eortæn ő n: *transposition marks indicate revised order.*

LTg: Sagittae] Sagittæ B; Sagittę CDEFGHJKLM. tuae] tuæ BD; tuę CEFGHKL. acutae] acutę CDFGHLM; acute EJ; ácute K. cadent] M: t *on eras.* in] A: *added interl. by corr.,* M: *on eras. by corr.* corda] H: *orig.* corde: e *altered to* a, K: a *on eras. by corr.;* cordæ E; corde BDIL, A: e *on eras. by corr.,* M: c *on eras.: cf. Weber MSS* ST^{2}Q*RVδη moz^{c} med.

LTu: Sagittae] Sagittę ειλμνξϱυφχ; Sagittæ ϑ; Sagitte πσςτ*τ. tuae] tuę βεινξφ; tuæ ϑμ; tue σςτ*τ. acutae] acutę εινξϱφ; acute σςτ*τ. corda] corde τ*: *cf. Weber MSS* ST^{2}Q*RVδη moz^{c} med, *see GAu.*

GAg: potentissime] *om.* FGHIJK.

GAu: potentissime] *om.* δεζϑλμξοπϱτυφχψ. corda] corde ϑλμξοπϱτφψ, τ*: *see LTu.*

7

Sedis	seld A*B, setl *CDGHIJK*, sétl *F*, Setle E$^{3/x}$* (*LM*)
tua	ðin AB, þin CDGHI*JK, þín E^{3}, ðín F
deus	god ABCE^{3}FGJK (*I*)
in	in A, on BCDE^{3}FGHIJK
saeculum	weoruld A, weorold *B*, woruld *CDH*, woroldæ *E^{3}*, worulde *F*, worulda *G*, worlda *IJ*, worolde *K* (*L*)
saeculi	weorulde A, weorolde *B*, worulde *C*, woruld *DFGH*, world *E^{3}IJ* (*KL*)
uirga	gerd A, gird BJ, gyrd CDFGHIK, gierd E^{3}
recta*	reht A, ryht BD, riht CE^{3}K, rihtingce F, rihttinge G, steore ł lare ł rihtinge I*
est*	is ABDE^{3}, ys C
uirga	ger A, gird BE^{3}J, gyrd CDFGK, gyrde I
regni	rices ABDE^{3}FIJK, ricys C, rice GH
tui	ðines ABF, þinys C, þines DE^{3}IJK, þin GH

ED: sclm (EHIJ)] seculum *Campbell, Harsley, Oess;* saeculum *Lindelöf.* scli (DEJK)] saeculi *Roeder;* seculi *Harsley, Oess;* sæculi *Sisam.* gyrd (H)] gyrde *Campbell.*

OE: seld (A)] *orig. gloss eras.*, seld *written to left on eras.* Setle (E$^{3/x}$)] *final* e *added by corr.* þin (I)] s. est : is *written in left margin.* steore ł lare ł rihtinge (I)] s. est : is *written in right margin.*

LTg: Sedis] Sedes BCDEFGHIJKL, A: *orig.* Sedis: i *altered to* e, M: es *on eras.*: *cf. Weber MSS* αζη moz med. deus] I: s. o *written above word.* saeculum] sæculum B; seculum CDG; sęculum FK; sclm EHIJL. saeculi] sæculi B; seculi CGHI; sęculi F; scli DEJKL.

LTu: Sedis] Sedes δεζϑιλμνξοπϱστ*τυφχψ: *cf. Weber MSS* αζη moz med. saeculum] sęculum ενο; seculum ϑπς; sclm βιλμξστ*τφχ; sęlm δ. saeculi] sęculi ενοπ; sæculi ϑ; seculi ς; scli βιμξστ*τυφ; sęli δ.

GAg: recta est] directionis FGHIJK.

GAu: recta est] directionis δεζϑιλμξοπϱστυφχψ.

8

Dilexisti	ðu lufedes A, ðu lufodes B, þu lufudyst C, þu lufudest DH, ðu lufodest E$^{3/x}$*F, þu lufedest GK*, þu lufodest *IJ*
iustitiam	rehtwisnisse A, ryhtwisnesse BD, rihtwisnysse CF, rihtwisnesse E$^{3/x}$*GHIJ, rihtwisnes K
et	˥ ABCDE^{3}FGHIJK
odisti	feodes AB, feodyst C, þu fiodest ł hatudest E$^{3/x}$*, ðu hatudes D, þu hatudest FGH, þu hatodest I, atodest J, hatodest K

iniquitatem	unrehtwisnisse *A*, unryhtwisnesse BD, unrihtwisnysse CF, unrihtwisnesse E$^{3/x}$*GHIJK
propterea	forðon *A*BDF, forþon CG*HJ, forþan IK, foreðæn E^{3}
unxit	smirede ABE^{3}, smyryde C, smyrede DG*H*, smerede F, smyrode I, smyrude K, he smerede *J* (*LM*)
te	ðec A, þe CFGHIJK, ðe E^{3} (*B*)
deus	god ABCE^{3}FGHIJK
deus	god ABCE^{3}GIJ
tuus	ðin ABE^{3}, þin CGHIJK, ðín F
oleo	mid ele ABIJ, mid éle F, ele CK, of ele DE$^{3/x}$*GH (*M*)
laetitiae	blisse A*BCDE^{x}FGH*I*JK* (*L*)
prae	fore A*BE^{x}*, for *CDFGHJK*, toforan *I* (*L*)
consortibus	I gefoerraedennum A, geferrædennum B*, geferrædenum J, geferrædynum C, gehlyttum D, gehlyttum GH, gehlytum F, gehlytan K, efnlinge E^{x}*, þinum I
tuis	I ðinum AF, ðinum B, þinum CG, þinum HJ, þinan K, þine E^{x}, efenhlyttum I

ED: [ ]ilexisti (I)] Dilexisti *Lindelöf.* iustitiam (C)] iusti[t]iam *Wildhagen.* forðon (A)] for ðon *Kuhn.* lęticię (E)] laeticiae *Harsley.* letitię (F)] lętitię *Kimmens.*

OE: ðu lufodest (E$^{3/x}$)] es *retraced,* t *added by corr.* þu lufedest (K)] *letter* (f *or* s) *eras. after 1st* e. rihtwisnesse (E$^{3/x}$)] rihtwis *on eras. by corr.*, nesse *retraced.* þu fiodest ł hatudest (E$^{3/x}$)] *1st* t *added by corr.*, ł hatudest *added by corr.* unrihtwisnesse (E$^{3/x}$)] wisnesse *added by corr.* forþon (G)] *2nd* o *altered from* a, *1st* o *touched up in diff. ink.* of ele (E$^{3/x}$)] of *added by corr.* geferrædennum (B)] ennū *on eras., 2nd* n *possibly altered from* r, u *eras. after* u. efnlinge (E^{x})] *on eras.*

LTg: Dilexisti] [ ]ilexisti I: *letter fragment visible in initial position.* iustitiam] C: *orig.* iusticiam: c *altered to* t *by corr.* iniquitatem] A: prop *eras. after word and added by corr. in next line.* propterea] A: prop *added by corr.: see note to* iniquitatem *above.* unxit] uncxit HJLM. te] té B. oleo] M: *letter* (?) *eras. after final* o. laetitiae] lætitiæ B; lętitię C; laetitię D; lęticię E; letitię FG, H: *eras. after word, traces of red ink visible;* letitie J; letitiæ L; lætitię K. prae] præ B; pre CEFGHIJ; prę DKL.

LTu: iustitiam] iusticiam τ*τφ, ϱ: *orig.* iustitiam: *2nd* t *deleted,* c *interl.* odisti] hodisti ς. propterea] probteria ϑ. oleo] β: e *interl.;* holeo ϑ. laetitiae] lętitię βεν; laetitię ζπχ; lętitiæ ϑ; laetitiæ μ; letitię ξυ; letitie σςτ*; lęticię φ; lætitiae ψ; *om.* τ. prae] prę βνϱφ; pre δζϑλπς; p̄ ιμξστ*τυχ.

9

Murra	myrre *A*B, mirre *C*, Murræ *E^{3}**, myrra *J*, herba *H*, wyrtgemange *I*, n *K** (*DFGLM*)

et	⁊ ABE^{3}*CIJ
gutta	dropa ABCI, swete dropen E^{x}*, n K*
et	⁊ ABCE^{3}*FI
cassia	smiring AB, smyring *C,* swete wirt *E^{x}*,* swéte wyrt F, ðysma *I,* n K* (*GHJ*)
a	from AE^{3}, from B, fram CI, fram J, of DFGHK (*M*)
uestimentis	hreglum A, hræglum BDH, hræglum *C*G, ræglum J, reafum FI, hrægele K, girelæn E^{3}
tuis	ðinum ABF, þinum CDHJ, ðinum E^{3}, þinum GI, þinan K
a	from AB, fram CGJ, fram I, of DE^{x}*K, to F (*M*)
gradibus*	stepum A, stæpum BD, stæpum C, stapum E^{x}*, stæppum K, eallum F, husum GIJ
eburneis	elpanbaennum *A,* elpanbænnum B*, elpenbænenum *G*I, elpenbænenum *H,* ylpanbænynum C, aelpenbænenum D, ælpenbanenum E^{x}*, elpenbanum *F,* elpendbana *K,* yrpenbanum J (*M*)
ex	of ABCDE^{x}*FGHIJK
quibus	ðæm AB, þam CGHI, ðam DE^{x}*F, þam JK
te* }	dec A, ðe BF, þe GHIJ (*CEM*)
delectauerunt* }	gelustfulladun A, gelustfullodon BC*FJ, gelustfulludon DHI, gelustfulladon E^{x}*, gelustfulledon G, gelustfullodan K

ED: (M)yrra (I)] Myrra *Lindelöf.* ðysma (I)] þysma *Lindelöf.* ebúrneis (H)] eburneis *Campbell.*

OE: Murræ (E^{3})] *retraced by corr.* n (K) (*all*)] *for* nomen. ⁊ (E^{3}) (*1st*)] *retraced by corr.* swete dropen (E^{x})] *on eras.* ⁊ (E^{3}) (*2nd*)] *retraced by corr.* swete wirt (E^{x})] *on eras.* of (E^{x}) (*1st*)] *on eras.* stapum (E^{x})] *on eras.* elpanbænnum (B)] *orig.* elbanbænnum: *1st* b *altered to* p. ælpenbanenum (E^{x})] *on eras.* of (E^{x}) (*2nd*)] *on eras.* ðam (E^{x})] *on eras.* gelustfullodon (C)] *eras. between* on, *right side of* o *written in red ink of corr.* gelustfulladon (E^{x})] d *on eras. by corr.,* on *added.*

LTg: Murra] Myrra DFGKLM; (M)yrra I: M *fragmentary;* Mirra CEHJ, A: *eras. after* M (*orig.* Murra?): *cf. Weber MSS* moz. cassia] C: *orig.* casia: *1st* s *interl. by corr.,* E: ia *on eras. by corr.;* casia GIJ, H: *eras. after 1st* a. a (*1st*)] á M. uestimentis] C: *eras. after 1st* i. a (*2nd*)] á M. eburneis] A: *orig.* aeburneis: a *eras.;* aeburneis F; ęburneis G; ebúrneis M, H: *small eras. afer word, possibly of punct.;* æburneis K. te] E: *on eras. by corr.;* té M; *om.* C.

LTu: Murra] Myrra δεζλμορσςυχψ; Mirra ινξπτ*τ. cassia] ν: *1st* s *interl.;* casia ειλξοπρσςτυφχ. a (*1st*)] *interl.* ν. eburneis] ęburneis ν. te delectauerunt] delectauerunt te δ.

GAg: gradibus] domibus FGHIJK. te delectauerunt] delectauerunt te GHIJ, F: *orig.* delictauerunt te: i *altered to* e, K: *small eras. after* te.

GAu: gradibus] domibus δεζϑιλμξοπϱστυφχψ. te delectauerunt] delectauerunt te δεζϑιλμξοπϱστυφχψ.

10

filiae — dohtur A, dohtor *BJ,* dohtra *CDFGHIK,* dohtre E^{x}* (*L*)
regum — cyninga ABCDFGHJ, ciningæ E^{3}, kyninga I, cininga K
in — in A, on BCDE^{x}*FGHIJK
honore — are ABCJ, arweorþnisse D, arwurnisse E^{x}*, wurþnysse F, weorðnesse G, weorðnisse H, wyrðmynte I, wyrðmunt K
tuo — ðinre ABE^{3}F, þinre CDGHJ, þinum I, þinan K

Adstetit — ætstod *ABCDFGHIJK,* Etstod E^{3}* (*LM*)
regina — cwoen A, cwen B*C*DGJK, cwén FH, Sio cwen E^{3}, kquen ł hlæfdige I
a — to AB*C*DFG*JK,* æt I (*M*)
dextris — swiðran ABCIJ, swyðran K, þam swyþran D, ðam swyðran FG, þan swiðran H, ðeræ swiðræn E^{3}
tuis — ðire A, ðinre B, þinre CJ, þinum DGH*I,* ðinum F, þinan K, þines E^{3}
in — in A, on BCDE^{3}FGHIJK
uestitu | gegerelan AB, gegyrylan *C,* gegyrelan DGH, girelæn E^{3}, gegirlan J, gýrlan F, gyrlan K, ofergyldum I*
deaurato | bigyldum A, begyldum B, begyldun C, begildum J, gegyldum D*F*GH, gegyldan K, hrægle I*, of golde E^{3}
circumamicta* — ymbswapen AB, ymbswapyn *C,* ymbgyrd D$E^{3/x}$*, ymbsealde F, em(b)eseald K*, ymbsealdon J, ymbtrymd G, ymb H, ymbsett I (*M*)
uarietate — misenlicnisse A, missenlicnesse B, missynlice C, mislicnisse D$E^{3/x}$*H, mislicnysse F, mislicnesse *G*K, mid fagnesse ł missonlicnysse I, fægernesse ł missenlicnesse J

ED: filiæ (D)] filiae *Roeder.* filię (E)] filiae *Harsley.* arwurnisse (E)] arwur[ð]nisse *Harsley.* Astitit (C)] A[d]stitit *Wildhagen.* ætstod (G)] [ ]stod *Rosier.* cwén (H)] cwen *Campbell.* gegyrelan (G)] gegyrela[ ] *Rosier.* em(b)eseald (K)] embeseald *Sisam.*

OE: dohtre (E^{x})] h *on eras.* on (E^{x}) (*1st*)] *on eras.* arwurnisse (E^{x})] *on eras.* Etstod (E^{3})] od *on eras.* (*by corr.?*). ofergyldum (I)] y *altered from* i (?). hrægle (I)] in de[ ] : on ofer[ ] *written in left margin* (*note* deaurato). ymbgyrd ($E^{3/x}$)] gyrd *on eras. by corr., eras.* (*22 mm*) *after word.* em(b)eseald (K)] *ascender of* b *lost due to eras. in Lat. line above.* mislicnisse ($E^{3/x}$)] ni *on eras. by corr.,* sse *added.*

LTg: filiae] filiæ BDL; filię CGHJK, E: *eras. before word.* Adstetit] Adstitit BDEFJKL, A: *1st* i *written by corr. on eras.;* Ádstitit M; [ ]dstitit G: *cf. Weber MSS* βT moz; Astitit C: *eras.* (d?) *after* A, H: *eras. after* A; Asstitit I. regina] regína C. a] CK: *eras. after word;* á M; ad J. tuis] I: *eras. after word.* uestitu] uestítu C. deaurato] F: *eras. after word.* circumamicta] C: *eras. after* u, *right leg of 1st* m *possibly by corr.;* circumámicta M. uarietate] uariętate G.

LTu: filiae] filiæ ϑ; filię ινξυφ; filie ςτ*τχ. Adstetit] Astitit εζιξπϱστ*τυφχ, ο: *orig.* Asstitit: *1st* s *deleted;* Adstitit λνς; Astetit ψ. deaurato] deaurata ς.

GAg: circumamicta] circumdata FIJK, G: *initial* c *and right leg of* u *on eras., right leg of* m *on eras., all of which touched up in lighter brown ink;* circúndata H: *eras. after* n.

GAu: circumamicta] circumdata δζϑιμξοπϱστυχψ; circundata ελφ.

11

Audi	geher ABI, gehyr CD*G*HK, gehýr F, Gehier E^{3}, gehir J
filia	dohtur A, dohtor BCDE^{x}*GHJ, dohter I*K, dohtra F
et	ᛩ ABCDE^{3}FGHIJK
uide	geseh AB, geseoh CDFGHIJK, gesioh E^{3}
et	ᛩ ABCDE^{3}FGHIJK
inclina	onhaeld A, onhield B, onhyld CFIK, onhild E^{3}J, ahyld DGH
aurem	eare ABCDFGHIJ, eære E^{3}, earan K
tuam	ðin ABF, þin CDE^{3}GHIJ, þine K
et	ᛩ ABCDE^{3}FGHIJK
obliuiscere	forget A, forgit BIJ, forgyt CK, ofergyt DFGH, ofergit E^{3}*
populum	folc ABCDE^{3}FGHIJK
tuum	ðin ABE^{3}F, þin CGHIJK
et	ᛩ ABCE^{3}*FGHIJK
domum	gehusscipe A, hus BCDE^{3}*FGHIJK
patris	feadur A, fæder BIJK, fædrys C, federes E$^{3/x}$*, fæderas F, fæde[ ]es G*
tui	ðines AB, þinys C, þines E^{3}FGI*JK

ED: [ ]udi (G)] Audi *Rosier.* fæde[ ]es (G)] f[ ] *Rosier.* þines (G)] *no gloss Rosier.*

OE: dohtor (E^{x})] *on eras.* dohter (I)] o *written before word.* ofergit (E^{3})] it *on eras.* ᛩ (E^{3}) (*4th*)] *retraced.* hus (E^{3})] *retraced.* federes (E$^{3/x}$)] es *added by corr.* fæde[ ]es (G)] *letter fragment visible after 1st* e. þines (I)] [ ]uis d<u>eu</u>s : [ ]in god *written in left margin.*

LTg: Audi] [ ]udi G: *outline of initial* A *visible.*

LTu: obliuiscere] obliuisceres β. populum] populvm ι.

12

Quoniam*	forðon AB, forþon C, forðæn E3, ⁊ FGIJK
concupiuit*	gewillade A, gewilnode BC, gewilnade D, gewilnæde E3/x*, gewilnað FGK, gewilnaþ IJ
rex	cyning ABCG, cyningc F, kining E3*I, cinning K, se cininc J
speciem*	hiow A, hiw BCDK, wlite ł hiw E3/x*, wlite FGHIJ
tuam*	ðin AB, þin CHK, ðinne E3F, þinne IJ, þinum G*
quia*	forðon AB, forþon CJ, forðæn E3, forþan K, forðon ðe F, forþan þe I, forþo[ ] G
ipse	he ABCDE3FGHJK, se sylfa I
est	is ABE3FGIJK, ys C
dominus	dryhten A, drihten E3, dryht̄ B, driħt CFGI, driħ J, god K
deus	god ABCE3FGJ (*KM*)
tuus	ðin ABE3, þin CFGJK (*IM*)
et	⁊ ABCE3FGHIJK
adorabunt	I weorðiað AB, weorðiaþ J*, wurðiað *C*, gebiddaþ D, gebiddað FGHK, hi gebiddaþ I*, hine E3
eum	I hine ABCDFGIJK, gebiddæþ E3

ED: forðon (A) (*1st*)] for ðon *Kuhn.* forðæn (E)] Forðæn *Harsley.* forðon (A) (*2nd*)] for ðon *Kuhn.* forþo[ ] (G)] for[ ] *Rosier.* tuus] *om. Lindelöf.* adorabunt (G)] adorabun*t Rosier.*

OE: gewilnæde (E3/x)] de *on eras. by corr.* kining (E3)] *eras. before word.* wlite ł hiw (E3/x)] ł hiw *added by corr.* þinum (G)] *bowl and descender of* þ *faint.* weorðiaþ (J)] o *malformed.* hi gebiddaþ (I)] *eras. after word.*

LTg: deus] K: *interl. by main hand,* M: *on eras.* tuus] M: *on eras.*, I: *interl.* adorabunt] C: *eras. after* d.

LTu: Quoniam] QM̄ β. rex speciem] β: *orig.* respiem: x *interl. after 1st* e, ec *interl. after* p. deus] *interl.* δζ. adorabunt] adora ϑ.

GAg: Quoniam] Et FGIJK; [ ]t H: *traces of blue ink visible in initial position.* concupiuit] concupiscet FGHIJK. speciem] decorem FGHIJK. tuam] tuum FGHIJ, K: *eras. after word.* quia] quoniam FGHIJK.

GAu: Quoniam] Et δεζϑιλμξοπϱστυφχψ. concupiuit] concupiscet δεζϑιλμξοπϱστυφχψ. speciem tuam] decorem tuum δεζϑιλμξοπϱστυφχψ. quia] quoniam δεζϑιλμξοπϱστυφχ.

13

(Et)*	⁊ FGIJK

filiae	dohtur A, dohtor *BJ,* dohtra *CFHK,* dohtora *D,* dohtore E^{x}*, dohtru I, bearn ł dohtor *G* (*L*)
tyri	ðes londes A, ðæs londes B, þæs londes *C,* þæs landes G*J,* mægðe F, tiriscan I, tire E^{3}, n K*
in	in A, on $BCDE^{3}FGHIJK$
muneribus	gefum AB, gyfum C, gifum G, gifum J, lacum DFHI, lacum K, læcum E^{3}

Uultum	ondwleotan A, ondwlitan *B,* andwlitan *CDFHJK,* anwlitan *GI,* Onsin ł andwliton $E^{3/x}$*
tuum	ðinne ABF, þinne CGIJ, þine K, ðin E^{3}
deprecabuntur	biddað ABC, biddaþ J, bioð biddende E^{3}, beoð bedene DH, beoþ bedene F*, [ ]eoð gebedene *G,* halsiað ł biddaþ I*, bedene K (*M*)
omnes*	alle A, ealle BCDJ, eællæ E^{3} (*GM*)
diuites	weolie A, welige $BCDE^{3}FGHJK$, þa weligan I
plebis	folces $ABDE^{3}FGHIJ$, folcys C, folcces K

ED: filiæ (D)] filiae *Roeder.* filię (E)] filiae *Harsley.* tyri (K)] Tyri *Sisam.* déprecabuntur (E)] deprecabuntur *Harsley.*

OE: dohtore (E^{x})] *on eras.* n (K)] *for* nomen. Onsin ł andwliton ($E^{3/x}$)] ł andwliton *added by corr.* beoþ bedene (F)] d *obscured but visible.* halsiað ł biddaþ (I)] s. omnes : ealle *written in right margin.*

LTg: filiae] filię CEGHL; filiæ BDK; filie J. tyri] tiri CJ. Uultum] Vultum BCDE; uultum FGHIJK. deprecabuntur] déprecabuntur E; depraecabuntur M; [ ]pręcabuntur G. omnes] G: *added by same later hand that wrote* X *after Ps 43.10* egredieris, M: n *interl.* plebis] pleb[ ] G.

LTu: filiae] filię βεν; filiæ ϑ; filie ςτ*. tyri] tiri ϑ. Uultum] Vultum ς; uultum δεζϑιλμξοπϱστυφχψ. deprecabuntur] depraecabuntur βυ; depc̄abuntur ιμξοσχ. omnes] *interl.* υ; *added* χ. diuites] diuitis β.

GAg: filiae] Et filiae FI; Et filię G; Et filie J; (E)t filię H: E *nearly completely lost, outline visible;* Et filiæ K. omnes] *om.* FK, I: *see OE note to* halsiað ł biddaþ.

GAu: filiae] Et filiae δζμοπϱψ; Et filię ειλξφ; Et filiæ ϑ; Et filie στυχ. omnes] *om.* δεζϑλμξοπϱφψ, ι: *deleted by underdotting.*

14

Omnis	all *A,* eall *B*IJ, eal *D*K, eæl E^{3}*, eally *C,* ealle FH (*GLM*)
gloria	wuldur *A*CDH, wuldor $BE^{3}GIJK$, wuldra F
eius	his $ABCDE^{3}FGHI$*JK

filiae dohtur A, dohtor *BCJ,* dohtora *D*E^{x}*, dohtra F*GHI**K* (*L*)

regum* cyning A, cyninga BCD, ciningæ E^{3}, þæs cyninges F, cyninges GJ, kyninges I, cininges K

ab from AB, from E^{3}*, fram C, fram J, fra[ ] G, þanon DF, þanan H, of K (*I*)

intus innan ABCDFHK, inran J, on innen $E^{3/x}$*, wiðinnan *I* (*G*)

in in *A,* on *BCD*FGHIJK, On E^{3}* (*LM*)

fimbriis feasum A, fæsum BC, fesum *J,* fnædum *DH**, fnædum G, fnedum E^{x}*, fnádum F, fnadum I, fnadan *K* (*M*)

aureis gyldnum A, gyldnum B, gyldynum C, gyldenum DHK, gyldenum E^{3}FGI, gildenum J

ED: filiæ (D)] filiae *Roeder.* filię (E)] filiae *Harsley.* fra[ ] (G)] f[ ] *Rosier.* In (B)] in *Brenner.* on (G)] *no gloss Rosier.* fimbríís (EK)] fimbriis *Harsley, Sisam.*

OE: eæl (E^{3})] *eras. after word.* his (I)] debet : sceal *written in left margin.* dohtora (E^{x})] *on eras.* dohtra (I)] þæs *written in right margin.* from (E^{3})] *retraced by corr.* on innen ($E^{3/x}$)] on *on eras. by corr.*, in *retraced,* nen *on eras. by corr.* On (E^{3})] n *retraced.* fnædum (H)] *orig.* fnædum: *left and middle leg of* m *eras., right leg used as interl.* i *for lemma below, macron then added by corr.* fnedum (E^{x})] f *retraced,* nedum *on eras.*

LTg: Omnis] [ ]mnis G; omnis BCDELM, A: i *on eras. by corr.* gloria] A: *eras. after word.* filiae] filiæ BDK; filie J; filię EGHIL, C: *eras. after 2nd* i. ab] áb I. intus] in[ ] G. in] In ABCDELM. fimbriis] D: *orig.* fembriis: e *eras., 1st* i *on eras.,* M: *2nd* i *on eras.,* H: *orig.* fimbris: *3rd* i *interl.: see OE note to* fnædum; fimbríís EK; fimbreis J.

LTu: Omnis] omnis βνϛτ*. gloria] gloriæ ϑ. filiae] filię εινξυφ; filiæ ϑ; filie ϛτ*τχ. in] In βνϛτ*. fimbriis] fimbreis βμς.

GAg: regum] regis FGHIJK.

GAu: regum] regis δεζϑιλμξοπϱστυφχψ.

15

circumamicta ymbswapen ABGJ, ymbswapyn C, ymbcæfed DH, ymbecæfæd K, ymbhángen F, ymbgyrd ł cæfed $E^{3/x}$*, ymbgyrd ł ymbwæfd I (*M*)

uarietate* misenlicnisse A, missenlicnesse BD, missynlicnysse *C,* missenlihnesse $E^{3/x}$*, mislicnesse K, missenlicnessum G, missenlicnessum H, mid missenlicum ł mid fagnyssum I, mid fægernysse F, mid fægernesse J

Adducentur	sien togelaeded A, sien togelædde B, syn togelædyd C, si togelædde J, beoð gelædde DFG*H*, beoþ gelædde K, To bioð geledde E^3, beoþ gebrohte I
regi	cyninge ABDGH, cininge CK, kininge E^3*, cyningce F, cyninc J
uirgines	fęmnan A, fæmnan CFGH, fæmnan D, fæmnena J, femnæn ł medenan $E^{3/x}$*, mædenu I, mægdena K
postea*	efter ðon A*E^3*, æfter ðon B, æftyr þon C, æfter ðan D, æfter þam F, æfter þam G, æfter þan H, æfter þam J*, æfter ðam K, æfter hyre I (*L*)
proximae	| ða nestan A, þa nihstan *BJ*, þa nehstan *C*, þa nehstan *G*, neahstan *DH*, nyhstan *F*, nixtum *E^3*, nyxstan *K*, hyre *I* (*LM*)
eius	| his ABCDFGHJ*K*, his E^3, nextan I
adferentur	sien tobroht AB, syn tobrohte *CJ*, beoð togelædde *DFH*, beoð gelædde *K*, beoð gedæled *G*, beoþ geferode *I*, to bioð borene *E^3*
tibi	ðe ABE^3F, þe CDGHIJK

ED: postea (A)] post ea *Kuhn*. post eam (H)] posteam *Campbell*. æftyr þon (C)] æftyrþon *Wildhagen*. æfter ðan (D)] æfterðan *Roeder*. proximę (C)] proxime *Wildhagen*.

OE: ymbgyrd ł cæfed ($E^{3/x}$)] gyrd ł cæfed *on eras. by corr.* missenlihnesse ($E^{3/x}$)] miss *retraced*, lih *on eras. by corr.* kininge (E^3)] *letter eras. after word.* femnæn ł medenan ($E^{3/x}$)] ł medenan *added by corr.* æfter þam (J)] æ *malformed, both words on eras. of* þa nihsta[ ]: *see following gloss.*

LTg: circumamicta] circumámicta M. uarietate] C: *scribe began* uarit-, *then altered* t *to* e. Adducentur] H: A *faint but visible*. postea] post eam EL: *cf. Weber MSS* αβλTPQ moz, *see GAg*. proximae] proximæ B; proximę CDFHIKM; proxime EGJL. eius] eíus K. adferentur] afferentur DFGHIK, C: *orig.* adferentur: d *deleted by subscript dot, 1st* f *interl. by corr.*, E: ł of *interl. by corr.* (> offerentur); offerentur J.

LTu: postea] post eam τ*: *cf. Weber MSS* αβλTPQ moz, *see GAu*. proximae] proxime δισςτ*τ; proximę εζνξορυφ; proximæ ϑ. adferentur] afferentur εζϑιλνξπρστυφ, ο: *orig.* adferentur: d *deleted*, f *interl.*; afOferentur τ* (af/Of-): *initial wrongly entered, cf.* τ *v. 16* Offerentur.

GAg: uarietate] uarietatibus FHIJK; uariętatibus G. postea] post eam FGHIK, EL: *see LTg*.

GAu: uarietate] uarietatibus δεϑιλμξοπρστυφχψ. postea] post eam δεζϑιλμξοπρστυφχψ, τ*: *see LTu*.

16

(Adferentur)* beoð togelædde F, beoþ gelædde K, syn togebrohte G, hig beoð gebrohte I*, sin tobrohte J
in in A, on BCDE^{3}FGHIJK
laetitia blisse A*BCDFGHIJK*, blissæ *E^{3}* (*L*)
et ⁊ ABCDE^{3}FGHIJK
exultatione wynsumnisse A, wynsumnesse B, wynsumnysse C, winsumnesse J, on gefægnunge H, on gefægnunge K, gefægnunge DG, gefægnunga F, on hyhte ł gefægnunge $E^{3/x}$*, mid glædnysse ł ⁊ fægnunge I
adducentur sien togelaeded A, sien togelædde B, syn togelædyde C, syn togelædde J, hy beoð gelæd DH, hy bioð geledde $E^{3/x}$*, hi beoð gelædde F, hy beoð gelædde G, hig beoð gebrohte I*, beoð gelæd K
in in A, on BCDE^{3}FGHIJK
templum tempel AC, templ BDGHJ, temple E^{3}FIK (*M*)
regis cyninges ABDGHJ, cyningys C, kininges E^{3}, cininges K, ðæs cyngces F, þæs kyninges I

ED: lęticia (C)] lęti[t]ia *Wildhagen.* lætitia (D)] laetitia *Roeder.* lętitia (E)] laetitia *Harsley.*

OE: on hyhte ł gefægnunge ($E^{3/x}$)] ł gefægnunge *added by corr.* hy bioð geledde ($E^{3/x}$)] hy *on eras. by corr.* hig beoð gebrohte (I)] *orig.* hig beoð brohte: ge *written in left margin.*

LTg: laetitia] lætitia BDK; lęticia C: *orig.* lętitia: *2nd* t *altered to* c; lętitia EFG; letitia HJL. templum] templo M: *cf. Weber MSS* ε moz.

LTu: laetitia] lętitia ειν; lætitia ϑ; letitia λξσςυ; leticia τ*τ; lęticia φ. templum] β: *orig.* templo: um *interl.*

GAg: in (*1st*)] Afferentur in FGIJK; [ ]fferentur in H: *initial* A *lost, outline visible.*

GAu: in (*1st*)] Adferentur in δψ; Afferentur in εζϑιλξπρσυφχ, ο: *orig.* Adferentur in: d *deleted, 1st* f *interl.;* Offerentur in τ, *cf.* τ* *v. 15* AfOferentur.

17

Pro | fore ABDE^{3}H, for CF*G*JK, fæderum I
patribus | feodrum A, fædrum B, fædrun C, fæderum DHJK, fæderum FG, federum E^{3}, for I
tuis ðinum AE^{3}, þinum BCDJ, þinum FGHI, þinan K
nati acende ABDH, acænde J, acennyde C, acænede F, accened G, cynnede E^{3}, geborene IK*

sunt	sind A, sint BE^{3}, synd CFGJ, synt I
tibi	ðe ABE^{3}K, þe CFGHIJ
filii	bearn ABCIJ, beærn *E^{3},* suna DGH, sunu F, synu K
constitues	ðu gesetes A, þu gesetest BE$^{3/x}$*, þu gesettest GHIJ, þu gesettyst C, ðu gesettest K, þu gesetst DF
eos	hie ABE^{3}, hi CK, hy DGH, hig FIJ
principes	aldermen A, aldormen D, ealdormon B, ealdormenn C, eældormen E^{3}, ealdormen FGHJ, ealdermen K, ealdras I
super	ofer ABDE^{3}FGHIJK, ofyr C
omnem	alle A, ealle BCDFGHIJK, eælle E^{3}
terram	eorðan ABCDFGHIJK, eorðæn E^{3}

ED: fore (E)] Fore *Harsley.* filíí (E)] filii *Harsley.*

OE: geborene (K)] *false start of letter before word (ascender).* þu gesetest (E$^{3/x}$)] þu *and* st *added by corr.,* g *retouched.*

LTg: Pro] [ ]ro G. filii] filíí E.

LTu: constitues] ψ: *1st* s *interl.* eos] *interl.* ϱ.

18

Memores*	gemyndge AB, gemyndige CD, Gemindyge E^{3}*, gemyndig FI, gemindig J, gemyndi *K,* si ðu gemyndig *G* (*H*)
erunt*	bioð AE^{3}, beoð BD, hi beoð C, ic beo FI*K,* beo ic J (*GH*)
nominis	noman AB, naman CDFGHIJ*K, næmon E^{3}
tui	ðines A, þines *BD*FG*HIJ*K, þinys *C,* þin *E^{3}* (*L*)
⟨domine⟩	dryhten *B,* drihten *E^{3},* driħt *C,* driħ *J* (*DL*)
in	in A, on BCDE^{3}FGIJK
omni	ylcre A, ælcre BC, ælcere GJ, ælcum I, ealre DF, eallan K, eællum E^{3}, [ ]re H*
generatione	cneorisse ABDE^{x}J, cneorysse C, cneoresse H, cneoresse ł cynre[ ] G*, mægþe F, cnosle ł cynrene I (*L*)
et	⁊ ABCDE^{3}*F*GIJ
progenie*	cynne *AB*CE^{x}*, cynrine F, forecynrene D, cneoresse ł cynrenne G, cnosle ł cneorisse I, cneorisse J (*LM*)
Propterea	forðon ADFH, forþon *C,* foreðæm B, foreðæn E^{3}, forþam G, forðan I, forþā JK
populi	folc ABCDE^{3}FGJK, ⁊ folc H, folctruman I
confitebuntur	ondettað AB, andytað C, andettað DFGH, ondettæþ E^{3}, andettaþ IJ, andetteð K

tibi	ðe ABE^{3}F, þe CDGHIJK
in	in A, on BCDE^{3}FGHIJK
aeternum	ecnisse A*DH,* ecnesse *BE*^{3}**GJK,* ecnysse *CF*I (*L*)
et	⁊ ABCE^{3}FGIJK
in	in A, on BCDE^{3}FGIJK
saeculum	weoruld A, weorold *B,* woruld *C,* aworuld *DH,* worold *E*^{3}*,* worulda *FG,* worlda I*J,* worolde *K* (*L*)
saeculi	weorulde A, weorolde *B,* worulde *C,* aworł *E*^{3}*,* woruld *FG,* world I*J,* worold *K* (*DHL*)

ED: naman (H)] namn *Campbell.* [ ]re (H)] re *Campbell.* forðon (A)] for ðon *Kuhn.* foreðæm (B)] fore ðæm *Brenner.* foreðæn (E)] Foreðæn *Harsley.* forþā (J)] forþa*m* *Oess.* æternum (D)] aeternum *Roeder.* ęternum (E)] aeternum *Harsley.* scłm (CDEJ)] saeculum *Roeder, Wildhagen;* seculum *Harsley, Oess.* scłi (EJ)] seculi *Harsley, Oess.* aworł (E)] aworl*de Harsley.*

OE: Gemindyge (E^3)] ge *in darker ink* (*by corr.?*). naman (J)] *orig.* maman: *right leg of 1st* m *eras. to form* n. [ ]re (H)] *eras. before* r. cneoresse ł cynre[ ] (G)] ł cynre[ ] *added in diff.* (?) *hand.* cynne (E^x)] *on eras.* ecnesse (E^3)] *final* e *on eras.*

LTg: Memores] G: s *altered from another letter and followed by eras.,* H: *orig.* Memor: M *faint but visible,* es *interl.,* K: es *on eras. by corr.: see GAg.* erunt] G: *2 insertion marks by corr. after word,* H: *eras. after* r, unt *added,* K: *on eras. by corr.: see GAg.* tui] H: *following punct. on eras.;* tui domine BCDEJL: *cf. Weber MSS* TQUVX moz^x med. generatione] generationę L. et (*1st*)] F: *on eras.* progenie] A: *eras. after* i, M: *orig.* progeniae: a *deleted by dot within and above bowl;* progenię BL. Propterea] C: *2nd* e *interl.* aeternum] æternum BDKL; ęternum CEFG; eternum H. saeculum] sæculum B; sęculum F; seculum GHKL; scłm CDEJ. saeculi] sæculi B; seculi CDGHKL; sęculi F; scłi EJ.

LTu: Memores] ϱ: es *interl. by corr.: see GAu.* erunt] ϱ: *orig.* ero: o *deleted,* unt *interl. by corr.: see GAu.* tui] tui domine νςτ*: *cf. Weber MSS* TQUVX moz^x med. Propterea] P<u>RO</u>Pterea β. aeternum] eternum βστ*τ; ęternum ειμνξφ; æternum ϑς. in (*3rd*)] *interl.* ς. saeculum] sæculum ϑ; sęculum νο; seculum ς; scłm ειμξπστ*τυφχ. saeculi] sæculi ϑ; sęculi λνο; seculi πς; scłi ειμξστ*τυφχ.

GAg: Memores erunt] Memor ero FIJ; *for* GHK *see LTg.* progenie] generatione FGHJK; generationem I.

GAu: Memores erunt] Memor ero δεϑμξοσυψ; *for* ϱ *see LTu.* progenie] generatione δεζϑιλμξοστχψ; generationem πϱυ.

PSALM 45

2

Deus	god *ABCF*GHI*J, God *E*^{x} (*BKLM*)
noster	ur *A,* ure B*CD*E^{3}FG*HI*J*K* (*L*)
refugium	geberg A, gebeorg B, gebeorh *C,* frofr DH, frofer GK, gener F, gener ł frofre I*, gebeorh ł gener J, gescildent ł frofr E$^{3/x}$*, rotnys M^{2} (*L*)
et	⁊ ABCDE^{3}FGHIJK
uirtus	megen AE^{3}, mægen BDGHJ, mægyn C, mægn K, mægen ł ⁊ miht I*, miht F (*L*)
adiutor	fultum ACI, fultum BJ*K,* fultumend E^{3}*, gefylsta DFG, gefylstað H (*L*)
in	in A, on BCDE^{3}FGHIJKM^{2}
tribulationibus	geswencednissum A*, geswencednessum B, geswencydnysse C, geswincum DGH, geswincum J, gedrefednysse F, drefednesse K, gedrefednyssum M^{2}, gedeorfnyssum ł on gedrefednyssum I, swincum ł eærfoþnessum E$^{3/x}$* (*L*)
quae	ða AB, þa *CDFGHJK,* þæ *E*^{3}*,* þa þa I (*LM*)
inuenerunt	gemoetun *A,* gemetton B*CD*E^{3}*FJ, gemitton G, gemittan H, gemetan K, onbecomon I
nos	usic A, us BCDE^{3}FGHIJK
nimis	swiðe ABCE^{3}GHIJ, swiþe D, swyþe FK (*L*)

ED: D[ ] (B)] Ds *Brenner.* quae (B)] quæ *Brenner.* quę (E)] quae *Harsley.*

OE: god (I)] s. est : is *written in bowl of* D *in* Deus. gener ł frofre (I)] *orig.* gener ł frofere: *3rd* e *eras.* gescildent ł frofr (E$^{3/x}$)] ent ł frofr *added by corr.* mægen ł ⁊ miht (I)] ł *interl.,* est : he is *written in right margin,* h *faint.* fultumend (E^{3})] *eras.* (*1–2 letters*) *before word.* geswencednissum (A)] *orig.* geswencednisse: um *written by glossator above final* e, *subscript deleting stroke* (?) *below.* swincum ł eærfoþnessum (E$^{3/x}$)] swincum ł *added by corr.* gemetton (E^{3})] *eras.* (*1–2 letters*) *before word.*

LTg: Deus] DS̄ ACFKLM; DEUS E; D[ ] B: *neither* s *nor macron visible.* noster] H: r *on eras. by corr.;* Noster A; NOSTER CJL. refugium] REFVgium C; REFVGIVM L. uirtus] virtvs L. adiutor] ádiutor K; adivtor L. tribulationibus] tribvlationibvs L. quae] que CJ; quę DEFGHM; quæ L; quæ̨ K. inuenerunt] A: *eras. after* r, unt *interl. by corr.* C: *small eras. after* i. nimiꞅ] L: *eras. after* ꞅ, ꞅ *perhaps formed from another letter, with another stroke made to extend descender below line.*

LTu: Deus] DEVS ς; DEUS τ*τ; DS̄ βειλμνϱφχψ. noster] Noster β; NR̄ ελ; NOSTER μνϱφψ. refugium] REFVGIUM ε; REFVGIVM λ; REFUgium μψ; REFUGIum ν; REFUGIUM ϱ. et] ET εϱ. uirtus] UIRTVS ε. quae] quę βεινξϱφ; que ϑσςτ*τχ.

3

Propterea		forðon ADFH, forþon G, forðæm B, forþan CK, forðan I, forðæn E^{3}*, forþā J*
non	|	we ne ABCE^{3}J, na DFGHK, we us ne I
timebimus	|	ondredað A*, ondrædað BC, ondredæð E^{3}, ondrædaþ IJ, we ondrædað G, we andrædað H, we adrædaþ D, we adrædað F, ondrædað we K
dum		ðonne AF, þonne BG, þonne CDE^{x}HJ, þænne I, donne K
conturbabitur*		bið gedroed A, bið gedroefed B, bið gedrefyd C, biþ gedrefed F, bið gedrefed G, bið drefed D, beoð gedrefed E$^{3/x}$*, bið dreued K, byð astyrod I, byð H, biþ J
terrae		orðe ABCE^{3}F, eorþe JK, seo eorðe *I,* eorðan G*H*
et		⁊ ABCE^{3}FGHIJK
transferentur		bioð forcerred *A,* beoð forcirrede *B,* beoð forcyrryd C, beoþ forcired ł ⁊ forlorene ł ⁊ forlætene beoþ J*, beoð borene DHK, beoð borne F, beoð geborenne G, bioð oferfarende ł borene E$^{3/x}$*, þonne beoð geferede I (*M*)
montes		muntas ABDFGHJK, mvnntas C, muntes ł duna I*, dunæ E^{3}
in		in A, on BCDE^{3}FGHIJK
cor		heortan ABCDFGHIJ*K,* heortæn E^{3} (*M*)
maris		sæs ABDE^{3}*FHIJK, sæys C, sæ G

ED: forðon (A)] for ðon *Kuhn.* forðæm (B)] for ðæm *Brenner.* forðæn (E)] Forðæn *Harsley.* forþā (J)] forþa*m Oess.*

OE: forðæn (E^{3})] *letter eras. after* r. forþā (J)] þā *eras. between* for *and* þā. ondredað (A)] *small eras. after* r. beoð gedrefed (E$^{3/x}$)] beoð *on eras. by corr.,* gedre *retraced, letter* (e?) *eras. after final* d. beoþ forcired ł ⁊ forlorene ł ⁊ forlætene beoþ (J)] ⁊ forlætene beoþ *written above* forcired ł ⁊ forlorene. bioð oferfarende ł borene (E$^{3/x}$)] ł borene *added by corr.* muntes ł duna (I)] ł duna *written in right margin in lighter ink.* sæs (E^{3})] *initial* s *retouched* (*altered from another letter?*), *letter eras. after word.*

LTg: terra] HI: *eras. after* a. transferentur] A: *2nd* e *altered from another letter,* M: *orig.* transferuntur: *1st* u *on eras., 2nd* e *interl. above 1st* u; transferuntur B. cor] K: *eras. after word;* cór M.

LTu: Propterea] PROPterea β. conturbabitur] conturbabuntur ς. transferentur] transferuntur β: *orig.* transferentur: *2nd* e *deleted by subscript dot,* u *interl.*

GAg: conturbabitur] turbabitur FGHIJK.

GAu: conturbabitur] turbabitur δεζϑιλμξοπστυφχψ.

4

Sonauerunt	hleoðradan A, hleoðrodon *BC*, swegdon D*FGH*I*K*, Swegdon *E^{3}**, swegdon ł hleoþredon *J*
et	⁊ ABCE^{3}FGHIJK
turbatae	gedroefde *A*, gedrefde *B*, gedrefyde *C*, gedrefede *DE^{3}*FGHJK*, gedrefode *I* (*L*)
sunt	werun A, sint B, Sint E^{3}, synd CFGHJK, synt DI, hig synt I
aquae	weter A, wæter *BGHJK*, wætru *CI*, wæteru *D*, wetere *E^{3}**, wætera *F* (*L*)
eius*	his ABCE^{3}, heora FGIJK
conturbati	gedroefde A, gedrefde B, gedrefyde C, gedrefede DE^{3}FGHJK, astyrode I*
sunt	werun A, sint BE^{3}, synd CFGHJK, synt I*
montes	muntas ABCDGHJK, dunæ E^{3}, duna FI*
in	in A, on BCDE^{3}FGHIJK
fortitudine	fyrhtu AC, strengo B, strangnisse DH, Strangnysse E$^{3/x}$*, strangnesse G, strencgþe F, strengðe I, strengþe J, strenðe K
eius	his ABCDE^{3}FGIJK, [ ]s H*

ED: Sonuerunt (F)] Sonauerunt *Kimmens*. turbatæ (D)] turbatae *Roeder.* sunt (J)] suut *Oess.* aquæ (D)] aquae *Roeder.* aquę (E)] aquae *Harsley.* [ ]s (H)] h(i)s *Campbell.*

OE: Swegdon (E^{3})] *retraced by corr.* gedrefede (E^{3})] *final* e *on eras. by corr.* wetere (E^{3})] *final* e *added by corr.* astyrode (I)] y *altered from* i (?). synt (I) (*2nd*)] sy *on eras.* duna (I)] *eras. before word.* Strangnysse (E$^{3/x}$)] rangnysse *on eras. by corr.* [ ]s (H)] *ascender visible in initial position, followed by hole in leaf.*

LTg: Sonauerunt] E: a *on eras., 1st* u *retouched;* Sonuerunt BGHK: *letter eras. after 1st* n, FJ: *orig.* Sonauerunt: a *eras.: cf. Weber MSS* αβ med. turbatae] turbatæ BD; turbatę CFGHIKL, A: ę *written by corr. on eras.;* turbate EJ. aquae] aquæ BDL; aquę CEFGHIK; aque J.

LTu: Sonauerunt] Sonuerunt ϑφ, δεζοχ: *letter eras. after 1st* n. turbatae] turbatę εζνϱφ; turbatæ ϑ; turbate ιξσςτ*τυ. aquae] aque βϑςτ*τ; aquę ειvξοϱφ. fortitudine] π: ti *interl.*

GAg: eius (*1st*)] eorum FGHIJK.

GAu: eius (*1st*)] eorum δεζϑιλμξοπϱστυφχψ.

5

Fluminis	flodes ABDF*G*HIJ, flodys C, flod *K*, Streæmæs ł flodes E$^{3/x}$*
impetus	onraes A, onræs BCDF*G*HJK, onres E^{x}, ryne I
laetificat	geblissað A*BCDFK*, geblissæþ *E^{3}*, geblissaþ *HJ*, a geblissað *G*, gegladaþ *I* (*L*)

ciuitatem	cestre AC, ceastre BFG, ceaster DH*K*, ceæstre E^{3}, ceastra J, burg I
dei	godes ABDE^{3}FIJK, godys C (*G*)
sanctificauit	gehalgað AB, gehalgaþ J, halgað K, gehalgode CI*, he gehælgæde E$^{3/x}$*, he halgude DH, he halgode F, [ ]halgode *G* (*M*)
tabernaculum	geteld ABDFGHJ, getyld C, geteld ł eærdungstowe E$^{3/x}$*, bur ł geteld I, eardunga K
suum	his ABCDE^{x}F*G*HIJK
altissimus	se hesta A, se hehsta B, se hiehsta C, se heahsta I, ðu hehsta D, þu hihsta E^{x}, þe hyhsta H, þu hyhsta K, hehsta *G**, þas hyhstan F, þæs hihstan J

ED: lætificat (D)] laetificat *Roeder.* lętificat (E)] laetificat *Harsley.* [ ]tificauit (G)] *sanct*ificauit *Rosier.* his (G)] hi[ ] *Rosier.* [ ]simus (G)] *altissi*mus *Rosier.* hehsta (G)] [ ]ta *Rosier.*

OE: Streæmæs ł flodes (E$^{3/x}$)] mæs *by corr.*, ł flodes *on eras. by corr.* gehalgode (I)] *eras. before word.* he gehælgæde (E$^{3/x}$)] he *by corr.*, gehælgæde *retraced* (*or all by corr.?*). geteld ł eærdungstowe (E$^{3/x}$)] geteld ł *added by corr.* hehsta (G)] *any preceding letters likely lost due to damage to leaf.*

LTg: Fluminis] K: *small eras. of ligature between* um; [ ]luminis G. impetus] impętus G. laetificat] lætificat BD; letificat CHL; lętificat EFGIJK. ciuitatem] K: *eras.* (*2 letters?*) *after 2nd* i (tatem *on next line*). dei] *lost* G. sanctificauit] M: *orig.* sanctificabit: b *on eras., then* b *deleted by dot in bowl and* u *interl.;* [ ]tificauit G. suum] suu[ ] G. altissimus] [ ]simus G.

LTu: laetificat] lętificat εϑινϱφ; letificat λξσςτ*τυ. sanctificauit] sanctificabit β.

6

Deus	god *ABCE^{3}*FI*JK (*DGLM*)
in	in A, on BCDE^{3}FHIJK, [ ]n *G*
medio	midle ABCE^{3}, middele DFGHJ, middan IK
eius	his ABCFGJ*K*, hire DI, hise E^{3}, hyre H
non |	ne ABCE^{3}FGHJ, na K, heo ne I
commouebitur |	bið onstyred *A*B, bið onstyryd C, bið onstired J, bið astyred DG, byð astyred H, bið astyrod F, bið astyrud K, bið onwenden ł astired E$^{3/x}$*, byð awend ł ne bið heo na astyrod I
adiuuabit	gefultumeð *A*, gefultumað *BCD*FH, gefultumaþ IJ*K*, fu[ ]tumað *G**, gefultumat *E^{3}* (*LM*)
eam	hie ABDE^{3}K, hig FJ, hi G, hy H, hyg I*, þa hi C
deus	god ABCE^{3}FGIJ

uultu*		mid ondwleatan A, mid andwlitan BC, andwlitan D, andwlitan ł onsine $E^{3/x}$*, mergen G, morhgen K, on ærne mergen F, on ærne morgen ł on dægered I, on mergen J
suo*		his ABCDE^{3}, on æfen F*, on ærne G, on æfengloman J, dæired K

ED: [ ]n (G, *Lat.*)] *in Rosier.* ne (H)] *ne Campbell.* Adiuuabit (C)] Adiuuauit *Wildhagen.* fu[ ]tumað (G)] [ ]tumað *Rosier.*

OE: god (I)] s. e<u>st</u> : is *written in left margin.* bið onwenden ł astired ($E^{3/x}$)] ł astired *added by corr.* fu[ ]tumað (G)] *any preceding letters likely lost due to damage to leaf.* hyg (I)] y *altered from* i (?). andwlitan ł onsine ($E^{3/x}$)] andwlitan ł *added by corr.* on æfen (F)] *eras. but visible.*

LTg: Deus] *lost* G; deus ABCDELM. in] [ ]n G. eius] eíus K. commouebitur] Commouebitur A. adiuuabit] ádiuuabit K; [ ]diuuabit G; Adiuuabit BCDELM; Adiuuauit A.

LTu: Deus] deus βνςτ*. adiuuabit] Adiuuabit βνςτ*.

GAg: uultu suo] mane diluculo FGIJK, H: lu *interl.*

GAu: uulto suo] mane diluculo δεζϑιλμξοπϱστυφχψ.

7

Conturbatae		gedroefde *A,* gedrofde *B,* gedrefde *C,* gedrefede *DE^{3}FGHIJK* (*LM*)
sunt		sin A, sint BE^{3}, synd CFGHJK, syndon I
gentes		ðeade A, ðeoda B, þeoda CDFG*HIJK, ðiodæ E^{3}
et	I	⁊ ABCE^{3}FGHJK, ahylde I
inclinata	I	onhaelde A, onhelde B, onhylde CF, onhilde E^{3}, onylde J, ahylde DG*H*K, ⁊ I
sunt		sind A, sint BE^{3}, synd CFGJK, syndon I
regna		rice AE^{3}G, ricu BCDFI, rica K
dedit		salde AB, sealde DFGHJK, Selde $E^{3/x}$*, he sealde CI
uocem		stefne *A*BCDE^{3}*GIK, stæfne HJ, stemne F
suam		his ABCDE^{3}FGHIJK
altissimus*		se hehsta AB, se hiehsta C, se heahsta D, se hihsta $E^{3/x}$*
et*		⁊ ABCE^{x}
mota		onstyred AB, onstyryd C, onstired J, astyred DE^{x}*GH, astyrod FI, astyrud K
est		is AE^{3}FGHIJ*K,* ys C, wæs B
terra		corðe ABCFGIJ, eorþe E^{3}*K*

ED: conturbatæ (B)] conturbata *Brenner.* conturbatę (E)] conturbatae *Harsley.* Conturbatę (G)] Conturbate *Rosier.*

OE: þeoda (G)] *followed by 3 light minims.* Selde ($E^{3/x}$)] de *on eras. by corr.* stefne (E^{3})] *retraced.* se hihsta ($E^{3/x}$)] se *on eras. by corr., eras. after* hihsta. astyred (E^{x})] *on eras.*

LTg: Conturbatae] conturbatę CELM, A: ę *on eras. by corr.;* conturbatæ B; conturbate D; Conturbatę FHK, G: *initial* C *shows as transparent on leaf, but visible;* Conturbate J. inclinata] H: *final* a *on eras.* uocem] A: m *added by corr.* est] ést K. terra] K: *eras. after end punct.*

LTu: Conturbatae] conturbatae β; conturbatę ν; Conturbatę εζιλξοπϱφ; Conturbatæ ϑ; Conturbate στυχ; Conturbata ς; conturbate τ*. et (*1st*)] *om.* μ.

GAg: altissimus et] *om.* FGHIJK.

GAu: altissimus et] *om.* δεζϑιλμξοπϱστυφχψ.

8

Dominus	drihten E^{3}I, dryht̄ AB, driħt CFG, driħ J (*H*)
uirtutum	megna A, mægna BJ, mægena HI*, mægyna C, megena D, megene E^{3}, mægen K, mægena ł miht G, mihtig F
nobiscum	mid us ABCDE^{3}FGHIJK
susceptor	ondfenga AB, andfenga C, andfenge G, andfengc I*, onfeng E^{3}*, andfeng J, anfeng K, anfond D, andfeond H, underfang F
noster	ur *A,* ure BCDE^{3}FGHIJ
deus	god ABCE^{3}FGIJ
iacob	iacobys C, iacobes E^{3}FGIJ, n K*

ED: susceptor (G)] suscept*or Rosier.* iacob (K)] Iacob *Sisam.*

OE: mægena (I)] est : is *written in left margin.* andfengc (I)] is *written in right margin.* onfeng (E^{3})] *eras. before word.* n (K)] *for* nomen.

LTg: Dominus] H: D *nearly completely lost.* noster] A: *eras. after* n, oster *interl. by corr.*

9

Uenite	cumað *ABCDGH,* cumaþ FIJK, Cumæþ *E^{3}*
et	⁊ ABCDE^{3}FGHIJK
uidete	gesiað A, geseoð BCDFGHI, geseoþ JK, gesioð E^{3}
opera	werc AB, worc C, weorc DFGHJK, wiorc E^{3}, dæda ł worc I*
domini	dryhtnes B, drihtnys C, drihtnes E^{3}F, dryht̄ A, driħt G, driħ J
quae	ða *AB,* þa *CDE^{x}*K,* þe *FHJ,* þa þa I* (*GL*)
posuit	sette ABCJ, he sette DFHK, he gesette $E^{3/x}$*GI
prodigia	tacen A, tacyn C, tacnu H, foretacen B, foretacn J, foretacnu DG, foretacne $E^{3/x}$*, foretacna F, foretacna ł beacna I*, þæt foretacn *K* (*M*)

super	ofer ABDE^{3}FGHIJK, ofyr C
terram	earðan A, eorðan BCDE^{3}*FGIJ, eorþan HK

ED: quę (E)] quae *Harsley.* quę : *no gloss* (G)] þe *Rosier.* he gesette (G)] gesette *Rosier.*

OE: dæda ł worc (I)] ł *interl.* þa (E^{x})] *on eras.* þa þa (I)] *orig.* þa þe: e *altered to* a. he gesette ($E^{3/x}$)] he *on eras. by corr.* foretacne ($E^{3/x}$)] tacne *by corr., final* e *on eras.* foretacna ł beacna (I)] ł beacna *written in right margin.* eorðan (E^{3})] *possibly* eorðæn, *with* æ *partly obscured by tail attached to* p *in* prodigia *in line above.*

LTg: Uenite] Venite ABDEGHI. quae] quę CDEFGHKL, A: ę *on eras. by corr.;* quæ B; que J. prodigia] K: ut *eras. before word,* M: *stem of* p *faint.*

LTu: Uenite] Venite ζινξσφ. quae] quę ειμνξϱφχ; quæ ϑ; que σςτ*τ. posuit] possuit ϑ.

10

Auferens	afirrende AB, afyrrynde C, afyrrende D*GH,* Afyrrende E^{3}, affirrende J, afyrsa F, afyrsiende I*, afeorsende K
bella	gefeht AB, gefeoht CFJ, gefioht E^{3}, gefeohtu DGH, gewinn I
usque	oð ABCDGH, oþ JK, oððe F, oðða I, oððet $E^{3/x}$*
ad	oð AF, on D, to E^{3}K
fines*	endas ABCDJ, endes $E^{3/x}$*, ende FGHK, ende ł gemæru I*
terrae	eorðan A*BCDFGH,* eorþan I*JK,* eorðæn *E^{3}* (*L*)
arcum	bogan *A*BCDHIJK, bogæ E^{3}, boga FG
conteret	forþreste A*, forðræsteð B, forþræstyð C, forþræsteþ J, he forbryteð DE^{x}*, he forbryteþ *H,* he forbryteð G, forbrytte K, tobryteð F, he tobryt I
et	⁊ ABCE^{3}FGHIJK
confringet	gebriceð *A*B, gebricð $E^{3/x}$*, gebrecyð C, gebreceþ J, he tobricð DI*, he tobrycð F, tobrycð G, tobricð HK
arma	wepen A, wæpen BD, wæpnu CH, wepnæ E^{3}, wǽpnu F, wæpna GK, wæpn J, gewæpnu I
et	⁊ ABCE^{3}FGHIJK
scuta	sceldas ABI*, scyldas C, scildas J, scyld *D*FGHK, scylde E^{3}*
conburet	forberneð *A,* forbærneð B, forbærnyð *C,* forbærnð *K,* he forbærneð *DFGH,* he forbernþ *E^{3},* forbærned *J,* he forswælð *I*
igni	fyr *A*K, fyre CF, mid fyre BIJ, of fyrę *D,* on fyre $E^{3/x}$*, fyres G

ED: terrę (E)] terrae *Harsley.* eorðæn (E)] eorðan *Harsley.* cónteret (H)] conteret *Campbell.* wǽpnu (F)] wæpnu *Kimmens.* scylde (E)] scyld*e Harsley.* comburet (C)] co[n]buret *Wildhagen.*

OE: afyrsiende (I)] e<u>st</u> : he is *written in left margin*. oððet ($E^{3/x}$)] t *added by corr*. endes ($E^{3/x}$)] s *added by corr*. ende ł gemæru (I)] ł gemæru *written after following* eorþan *but signaled to come after* ende. forþreste (A)] *orig*. forwreste: w *altered to* þ. he forbryteð (E^{x})] forbryteð *on eras*. gebricð ($E^{3/x}$)] c *retouched*, ð *on eras. by corr*. he tobricð (I)] e *interl*. sceldas (I)] e *altered from* i (?). scylde (E^{3})] de *in ligature*. on fyre ($E^{3/x}$)] on *and* e *added by corr*.

LTg: Auferens] (A)uferens G: A *fragmentary*, H: A *nearly completely faded, crossbar lost*. terrae] terræ BL; terrę CDEFGHK; terre J. arcum] A: m *added by corr.* (?). conteret] cónteret H. confringet] A: *orig*. confringit: *2nd* i *altered to* e. scuta] D: *eras. after* t, a *interl. above* t *by corr*. conburet] A: buret *written by corr.*; co<u>m</u>buret C: *letter eras. after* o, *macron added by corr.*; comburet DEFIJ, H: *orig*. conburet: *middle leg added to* n *to form* m; conburret K: *orig*. comburret: *right leg of* m *eras. to form* n. igni] A: ig *written by corr.*, D: *orig*. igne: e *altered to* i.

LTu: Auferens] ς: s *interl*. terrae] terrę ειμνξοφ; terræ ϑ; terre σςτ*τ. conburet] cōburet ελ; comburet ζιϱ.

GAg: fines] finem FGKHIK.

GAu: fines] finem δεζιλμξπϱστυφχψ.

11

<table>
<tr><td>Uacate</td><td></td><td>aemetgiað A, æmetgiað B, æmtigað C, geæmtigað DGH, geemtiæð E³, geæmtiaþ K, geæmtiað eow FI, geæmtigaþ eow J (L)</td></tr>
<tr><td>et</td><td></td><td>⁊ ABCD*E³FGHIJK</td></tr>
<tr><td>uidete</td><td></td><td>gesiað A, geseoð BCDFGHIK, geseoþ J, gesioð E³</td></tr>
<tr><td>quoniam</td><td>|</td><td>forðon AJ, forþon C, forðæn E³, forðan ðe F, forþam G, ðætte B, þ<u>æt</u> DHI</td></tr>
<tr><td>ego</td><td>|</td><td>ic ABCDFGHIJK, þ<u>æt</u> ic E³/ˣ*</td></tr>
<tr><td>sum</td><td></td><td>eam AI, eom BCDE³FGJK, eo<u>m</u> H</td></tr>
<tr><td>deus</td><td></td><td>dryhт̄ AB, god CE³FGIJ</td></tr>
<tr><td>exaltabor</td><td></td><td>ic biom upahefen A, ic beom upahæfen B, ic beo uppahæfyn C, ic bio uphæfen E³/ˣ*, ic beo upahafen FJ, ic beo upahofon I, ic beo<u>m</u> upahefd D, ic beo upahefd GH, ic beo uphefd K</td></tr>
<tr><td>in</td><td></td><td>in A, on BCDE³FGHIJK</td></tr>
<tr><td>gentibus</td><td></td><td>ðiodum AE³, ðeodum B, þeodum CFGHIJ, þeodu<u>m</u> D, þeode K (M)</td></tr>
<tr><td>et</td><td></td><td>⁊ ABCE³FGIJK</td></tr>
<tr><td>exaltabor</td><td></td><td>ic biom upahefen A, ic beo upahæfen B, ic beo uppahafyn C, ic beo upahafen FGJ, ic beo upahofon I, bið uphæfen E³</td></tr>
<tr><td>in</td><td></td><td>in A, on BCDE³FGHIJ</td></tr>
<tr><td>terra</td><td></td><td>eorðan ABDCGI, eorþan HJ, eorðæn E³, lande F</td></tr>
</table>

ED: geemtiæð (E)] gecmtiæþ *Harsley*. forðon (A)] for ðon *Kuhn*. ín (I)] in *Lindelöf*.

OE: ⁊ (D)] *eras. but visible*. þæt ic (E$^{3/x}$)] þæt *added by corr*. ic bio uphæfen (E$^{3/x}$)] ic *on eras. by corr.*, o *altered from another letter* (ð? *ascender eras.*); *cf.* bið uphæfen *below*.

LTg: Uacate] Vacate ABCDEFHIKL, J: *orig*. Uacata: *final* a *altered to* e; (V)acate G: *left arm of* V *lost*. quoniam] C: *small eras. after* n. deus] dominus A. in] ín I. gentibus] D: s *written above line by main hand*, H: *eras. after word*, M: t *faint but visible*. terra] terram G.

LTu: Uacate] Vacate ινϱυφχ.

12

Dominus	drihten E^{3}HI, dryht̄ AB, driht̄ C, driħt F, driħ GJ
uirtutum	megna A, mægna CI, mægena BGH*J, megena D, megen E^{3}, mægen K, mihtig F
nobiscum	mid us ABCD*E*^{3}FGHI*JK
susceptor	ondfenga AB, andfenga C, andfenge G, onfeng E^{3}, anfond DK, anfeond H, anfoend J, underfang F, ⁊ andfangol I
noster	ur *A*, ure BCDE^{3}FGHI*JK
deus	god BCE^{3}FGHIJK
iacob	iacobes BE^{3}FGIJ, iacobys *C*, n K*

ED: uirtutum (BE)] virtutum *Brenner, Harsley*. nobiscvm (E)] nobiscum *Harsley*. iacob (K)] Iacob *Sisam*.

OE: mægena (H)] *orig*. mægenu: a *interl. above* u, *but without subscript deleting dot*. mid us (I)] is *written in left margin*. ure (I)] is *written in right margin*. n (K)] *for* nomen.

LTg: nobiscum] nobiscvm E. noster] A: *eras. after* n, oster *interl. by corr.* iacob] C: a *interl.*

LTu: nobiscum] nobiscvm ι.

PSALM 46

2

Omnes	alle *A*, ealle *BC*DFGHJ*K, ælle *E*^{x}, eala ge ealle I*
gentes	ðiode A, ðeoda BFI, þeoda *C*DGHJK, ðioðæ E^{3}
plaudite	plagiað A, plegað *C*, plegiað ge B, blissiað DFGHM^{2}, blissiaþ *J*K, hafetiað I, heofæð ł blissiad E$^{3/x}$*
manibus	mid hondum A, mid hondum B, mid handum CFI, handum DJ, handum G*HK, hændum E^{3}

iubilate	wynsumiað AC, wynsumiað ge B*, winsumiæþ E^{3}, gefeogiað DM^{2}, gefeogiaþ HJ, drymað FG, dremað K, fægniaþ ł freadremaþ I*
deo	gode ABCDE^{3}FGHIJ, god K
in	in A, on BCDE^{3}FGHIJK
uoce	stefne ABCDE^{3}GIK, stæfne HJ, stemne F
exultationis	wynsumnisse A, wynsumnesse B, wynsumnysse C, wynsumnesse ł blisse I, blisse DGHJKM^{2}, blissiað F, hihte ł blisse E$^{3/x}$*

ED: Ones (B)] Omnes *Brenner.* OM̄S (E)] Omnes *Harsley.*

OE: ealle (J)] *initial* e *and part of* a *beneath rubicated* O. eala ge ealle (I)] s. o *written in bowl of* O *in* Omnis. heofæð ł blissiad (E$^{3/x}$)] ł blissiad *added by corr.* handum (G)] *right leg of* n *faint.* wynsumiað ge (B)] *written as* p.sumiað ge: *see v. 6* wynsumnesse. fægniaþ ł freadremaþ (I)] fægniaþ *written in left margin.* hihte ł blisse (E$^{3/x}$)] ł blisse *added by corr.*

LTg: Omnes] OMnes A; OM̄S CE; Ones B. gentes] GENTES C. plaudite] C: i *on eras.*, J: *eras. before* d.

LTu: Omnes] OMNes β; OMNES λμνϱςτ*τψ; OM̄S ιφχ. gentes] GENTES λμνϱχψ. plaudite] PLAUDITE λϱ. manibus] MANIBUS λ.

3

Quoniam	forðon ABJ, forþon C, forðæn E^{3}, forðam ðe F, forþam *G*, forði þe I (*H*)
deus*	god ABCE^{3}J, drihten IK, drih̄t F*G
summus*	heh A, heah BDE^{x}*, hieh C, se hehsta FI*, hehsta K, se healica G (*M*)
terribilis	egesful AB, egysfull C, egeful I, egeslic E^{3}F, bregendlic DHK, bregenlic J, bregenlic ł egeful G
et*	⁊ BCDE^{3} (*A*)
rex	cyning *A*BDGH, cyng C, cing E^{3}, cyngc F, cyningc I*, kyninc J, cinn K
magnus	micel *A*BDE^{3}GHJ, micyl C, mycel FK, mære I
super	ofer ABDE^{3}FGHIJK, ofyr C
omnes*	alle A, ealle BCDE^{3}GHJK, ealre FI
deos*	godas ABCDE$^{3/x}$*, eorðan FGHIJ, eorþā K

ED: forðon (A)] for ðon *Kuhn.* forðæn (E)] Forðæn *Harsley.* drih̄t (F)] g drih̄t *Kimmens.* rex (G)] *r*ex *Rosier.*

OE: drih̄t (F)] *incompletely formed* g (*comprising body, but lacking headstroke and* *finish on tail) written before* d, *taken here as false start of* god. heah (E^{x})] *on eras.* se hehsta (I)] s. est : is *written in bottom margin.* cyningc (I)] s. est : he is *written in bottom margin.* godas (E$^{3/x}$)] a *altered from another letter,* s *added by corr.*

LTg: Quoniam] [ ]uoniam G, H: *outline of initial* Q *visible.* summus] M: *orig.* sumus: *macron added.* et] *om.* A: *see GAg.* rex] A: *written in left margin by corr.* magnus] A: mag *written in left margin by corr.*

LTu: deus] dominus ς: *cf. Weber MSS* αη med, *see GAu.* summus] sumus β. et] *om.* ς. rex] *om.* ς. magnus] *om.* ς: *see GAu.*

GAg: deus] dominus FGHIK. summus] excelsus FGHIJK. et] *om.* FGHIJK, A: *see LTg.* omnes deos] omnem terram FGHIJK.

GAu: deus] dominus δεζιλμξοπρστυφχψ, ς: *see LTu.* summus] excelsus δεζϑιλμξοπρστυφχψ. et] *om.* δεζϑιλμξοπρστυφχψ, ς: *see LTu.* omnes deos] omnem terram δεζϑιλμξοπρστυφχψ.

4

Subiecit	underðeodde AB, undyrþeodde C, he underþeodde D, he underþeodde FG*HI*J, he underðeodde I, he Underþeod E$^{3/x}$*, underþyd K
populos	folc ABCDE^{3}*F*GHJK, folctruman I
nobis	us ABCDE^{3}FGHIJK
et	⁊ ABCE^{3}FGHIJK
gentes	ðiode A, þeode C, ðeode F, þeoda BDGHIJK, ðiodæ E^{3}
sub	under ABDE^{3}FHIJK, undyr C, un[ ]r G*
pedibus	fotum *A*CFGHI, fotum BDJ, fota K, ſet E^{3}
nostris	urum *A*CFGI, urum BDJ, ure E^{3}HK

ED: un[ ]r (G)] *no gloss Rosier.*

OE: he Underþeod (E$^{3/x}$)] he *added by corr.,* þeod *on eras. by corr.* un[ ]r (G)] *ascender visible after* n.

LTg: Subiecit] H: *initial letter faint but visible.* populos] F: *orig.* populus: *2nd* u *deleted by subscript dot,* o *interl.* pedibus] A: us *written by corr.* nostris] A: ostris *written by corr.*

LTu: populos] ϱ: *orig.* populus: *2nd* u *deleted,* o *interl.*

5

Elegit	geceas *A*K, he geceas CDFGHIJ, he Geceæs E$^{3/x}$* (*B*)
nos*	usic A, us CDE^{3}FGHIJK
in*	in A, on CDE^{3}
hereditatem	erfe A, yrfeweardnysse *C,* yrfeweardnisse D, yrfeweærdnesse

	E^3, yrfweardnysse F, yrfeweardnesse GI*J, erfwerdnesse K, on yrfeweardnisse H
sibi*	him ACE^3, him D, his FGIJK
speciem	hiow A, hiw CE^{3}GJK, heow D, hyw H, hyw ł wlite I, wlite F
iacob	iacobys C, iacobes E^{3}FGIJ, n K*
quam	ðæt *A,* þæt *C,* þe *DG***HJ,* se þe F, þæne þe *I,* þa K, ðone *E^3*
dilexit	he luade A, he lufude CDFH, he lufode E$^{3/x}$*GJ, he lufede IK

ED: hęreditatem (E)] haereditatem *Harsley.* iacob (K)] Iacob *Sisam.* d[ ]lexit (G)] d*il*exit *Rosier.*

OE: he Geceæs (E$^{3/x}$)] he *added by corr., eras. after 1st* e *in* Geceæs. yrfeweardnesse (I)] *eras.* (?) *before word.* n (K)] *for* nomen. þe (G)] *ascender of* þ *faint but visible.* he lufode (E$^{3/x}$)] he *on eras. by corr.*

LTg: B: *v. 5 wanting.* Elegit] elegit A. hereditatem] hęreditatem CE. quam] quem ACDEIJ, H: e *on eras. by corr.* dilexit] d[ ]lexit G.

LTu: in] *om.* ς: *cf. Weber MSS* moz^x med, *see GAu.* hereditatem] hęreditatem ειϱφ. quam] quem ιλ, υ: *orig.* quam: e *written above* a.

GAg: nos] nobis FGHIJK. in] *om.* FGHIJK. sibi] suam FGHIJK.

GAu: nos] nobis δεζϑιλμξοπϱστυφχψ. in] *om.* δεζϑιλμξοπϱστυφχψ, ς: *see LTu.* sibi] suam δεζϑιλμξοπϱστυφχψ.

6

Ascendit	astag AB, astah CDFH*IJK, Æstigæþ E^3, [ ]h *G*
deus	god ABCE^{3}FGIJK
in	in A, on BCDE^{3}FGHIJKM^2
iubilatione*	wynsumnisse A, wynsumnesse B*, wynsumnysse C, winsumnesse ł dræme E$^{3/x}$*, wynndreame D, wyndreame FHJM^2, wyndreama G, wyndream K, swiðlicre blisse ł on fægnunge I*
et*	⁊ ABCE^{3}FGJ
dominus	drihtyn C, drihten E^{3}GHIK, dryht̄ AB, driht́ F, drih́ J
in	in A, on BCDE^{3}FHIJK
uoce	stefne ABCDE^{3}F*G*K, stæfne HJ, gehreorde ł on stefne I
tubae	beman *AB**I, byman *CDFGHK,* bimæn *E^3* (*JL*)

OE: astah (H)] in celos *written after word by glossator.* wynsumnesse (B)] *written as* p.sumnesse: *see v. 2* wynsumiað ge. winsumnesse ł dræme (E$^{3/x}$)] ł dræme *added by corr.* swiðlicre blisse ł on fægnunge (I)] ł on fægnunge *written in left margin.* beman (B)] a *written below line.*

LTg: Ascendit] [ ]dit G. uoce] uocę G. tubae] tubę ACFGH; tubæ BL; tube DEJK.

LTu: iubilatione] ι: ati *by corr.*, onc *interl.* et] *interl.* ξ. uoce] ζ: *orig.* uocae: a *deleted by subscript dot.* tubae] tubę ειvξοπρφ; tubæ ϑ; tube σςτ*τυ.

GAg: iubilatione] iubilo FGI, H: o *partly on eras., eras.* (*5 letters*) *after word,* J: *orig.* iubila: a *altered to* o, *eras.* (*5 letters*) *after word,* K: o *on eras., eras.* (*5 letters*) *after word.* et] *om.* HK.

GAu: iubilatione] iubilo δεζϑιλμξοπρστφχψ. et] *om.* δεζϑιλμοπρστυφχψ.

7

Psallite	singað AC*GIK, Singæð E^{3}, sýngað F, singað ge B, syngan ge D, singan ge HJ
deo	gode ABCE^{3}FGIJK
nostro	urum *A*CFGI, urum *B,* ure E^{3}J, uran K
psallite	singað ABCI, singæþ E^{3}, syngað F, singaþ K, ł singað ge D*, singað ge G, singaþ ge HJ,
psallite	singað ABCDHK, singæþ E^{3}, syngað F, singaþ J, sing[ ] G, dremaþ ł singaþ I
regi	cyninge ABDJ, cininge C, kininge E^{3}, cyningce FI, cyninge G, cininge K, cyning H
nostro	urum *A*BCE^{3}GI, ure J, uran K
psallite	singað ACGIK, singæþ E^{3}, syngað F, singaþ HJ, singað ge B

OE: singað (C) (*1st*)] *eras. after* n. ł singað ge (D)] *as alternate to* syngan ge *above.*

LTg: nostro] A: stro *interl. by corr.,* B: *interl. by glossator.*

LTu: Psallite] sallite τ: *initial letter wanting.*

8

Quoniam	forðon ABJ, forþon CF, forðæn E^{3}, forþam G, forðā K (*I*)
rex	cyning ABDGH*I**, cining C, kining E^{3}, cyningc F, cininc J, cining K
omnis	alre A, ealre BCDHIJK, eallre FG, ælre E^{x}* (*M*)
terrae	eorðan A*BCDFGH,* eorðæn *E*^{3}*,* eorþan I*JK* (*L*)
deus	god ABCFGHIJK, is god $E^{3/x}$*
psallite	singað ACGK, syngað F, singaþ IJ, singæþ E^{3}, singað ge B
sapienter	snotterlice A, snotorlice B, snotyrlice C, snytro ł wisliche $E^{3/x}$*, wislice ł snotorlice I, wislice DGHJ, wyslice F, wærlice K

ED: forðon (A)] for ðon *Kuhn.* forðæn (E)] Forðæn *Harsley.* terrę (E)] terrae *Harsley.* terræ (H)] terre *Campbell.*

OE: cyning (I)] *eras. before word.* ælre (E^{x})] ælr *on eras.* is god (E$^{3/x}$)] is *on eras. by corr.* snytro ł wisliche (E$^{3/x}$)] ł wisliche *added by corr.*

LTg: Quoniam] I: m̅ *on eras.* rex] I: re *on eras.*, e<u>st</u> *written in left margin.* omnis] M: s *added.* terrae] terræ BL, H: *orig.* terra: *eye of* e *added to* a *to form* æ; terre CJ; terrę DEFGK.

LTu: terrae] terrę εινξφ; terræ ϑ; terre σ; terra ς. psallite] psallitę π.

9

Regnauit	ricsað *ABCDGH,* Rixæþ *E^{3},* rixað F*I**, rixsaþ J, rixsað *K* (*LM*)
dominus*	drihtyn *C,* drihtæn *E^{3},* dryħ A, dryhī B, god FGIJK (*LM*)
⟨in⟩	on *C* (*ELM*)
⟨aeternum⟩	ecnyssse *C* (*ELM*)
super	ofer ABFGIJK, ofyr C, on ofer E$^{3/x}$*
omnes*	alle A, ealle BCD, eælle E^{3}
gentes	ðeode A, ðeoda *B*F, þeoda CDGHIJK, þiodæ E^{3}
deus	god ABCE^{3}FGI*J (*M*)
sedet	siteð AB, sityð C, sitt DE^{3}, sítt *F,* sit *G*HIJK
super	ofer ABDE^{3}FGHIJK, ofyr C
sedem	seld AB, setle CDE^{3}FHIJ, setl G, setlt K
sanctam	halig A, hali K, ðæt halge B, halgan CFI, halgā D, hæligā E^{3}*, haligan GHJ
suam	his ABCDE^{3}FGHIJK

ED: halgā (D)] halga*m Roeder.* hæligā (E)] hæliga*m Harsley.*

OE: rixað (I)] a *altered from another letter* (o?). on ofer (E$^{3/x}$)] on *added by corr.* god (I)] *gloss eras. after word.* hæligā (E^{3})] gā *in slightly darker ink.*

LTg: Regnauit] Regnabit CDEIL, AM: b *on eras.*, G: b *altered from another letter*, K: *orig.* Regnauit: u *altered to* b; [ ]egnabit H: b *altered from another letter.* dominus] E: in ęternum *written after, but crossed through and its gloss eras.;* dominus in ęternum C; dominus in æternum L, M: in æternum *added interl.: cf. Weber MS* T^{2}. gentes] B: d<u>eu</u>s *eras. after word* (*following* deus *written on next line*). deus] *added* M. sedet] F: *orig.* sedit: i *deleted by subscript dot,* e *interl., small eras. after* t, G: *orig.* sedit: i *altered to* e.

LTu: Regnauit] Regnabit εϑιλμνξοπϱσςτ*τυφχ. dominus] dominus in ęternum ν: *cf. Weber MS* T^{2}. sedet] sedit ϑ.

GAg: dominus] deus FGHIJK. omnes] *om.* FGHIJK.

GAu: dominus] deus δεζϑιλμξοπϱστυφχψ. omnes] *om.* δεζϑλμξοπϱστυφχψ.

10

Principes	aldermen A, ealdormen BCDF*G*HJ, Eældormen E[3], ealderemen K, ealderas I
populi*	folces ABD*E[3]**GHJK, folcys C, folca FI*
conuenerunt*	gesomnadon A, gesomnodun C, tosomne comon B, tosomne becomon D, tosomne becomen E[x]*, gesamnode ł gegaderode I, gegadorode F, gegaderode G, gegædcrode K
(sunt)*	synd FGK, syndon I
cum	mid A*BCE[3]FGHIJK
deo	gode ABCDE[3]FGHIJK
abraham	abrahames ABGHIJK, abrahamys C, abræhæmes E[3], habrahames D
quoniam	forðon ABJ, forþon C, forðæn E[3], forþā G, forþan þe I
dii	godas ABCD*E[3]*FGIJK
fortes	stronge ABC, strange DFG*HJK, strænge E[3], þa strangan I*
terrae	eordan A, eorðan *BDFGH*I, eorþan *JK,* eorðe *C,* on eorþen *E[3/x]** (*L*)
nimium*	swiðe ABCD, swiþe E[3], swyþe K, swiðlice G*I, þearle F
eleuati	upahefene A, upahæfene B, uppahafyne C, upahafene DF*G*HIJ, upæhæfen E[3], ahauene K
sunt	werun A, wæron B, synd CFHJK, synt D, synd ł wæron G*, sindon E[3], syndon I

ED: forðon (A)] for ðon *Kuhn.* abraham (K)] Abraham *Sisam.* díí (E)] dii *Harsley.* terræ (D)] terrae *Roeder.* terrę (E)] terrae *Harsley.*

OE: folces (E[3])] *eras. before and after word.* folca (I)] *eras. before word.* tosomne becomen (E[x])] *on eras.* mid (A)] *orig.* me: e *altered to* d, i *written below line between* md. strange (G)] n *interl.* þa strangan (I)] *orig.* þa strangen: e *altered to* a. on eorþen (E[3/x]) on *and final* n *added by corr.* swiðlice (G)] *added by diff.* (?) *hand.* synd ł wæron (G)] ł wæron *added by diff.* (?) *hand.*

LTg: Principes] [ ]rincipes G. populi] E: i *on eras.* dii] díí E. terrae] terræ BDKL; terrę CEFGH; terre J. eleuati] ęleuati G.

LTu: populi] populorum ς: *cf. Weber MSS* αβγη* moz[c], *see GAu.* abraham] habraham β. fortes] fortis β. terrae] terrę ειμνξοπφ; terræ ϑ; terre σςτ*τ.

GAg: populi] populorum FGHIJK. conuenerunt] congregati sunt FGHIJK. nimium] uehementer FGHIJK.

GAu: populi] populorum δεζϑιλμξοπρστυφχψ, ς: *see LTu.* conuenerunt] congregati sunt δεζϑιλμξοπρστυφχψ. nimium] uehementer δεζϑιλμξοπρστυφχψ.

PSALM 47

2

Magnus — micel *AB*DGH, micyl *C*, mycel F*K*, micell J, Michel E^x, mære ł micel I*
dominus — drihtyn *C*, drihten E^x*IK, dryht̄ AB, driħt FG, driħ J
et — ⁊ ABCE^3FGHIJK
laudabilis — hergedlic A, hergendlic BE^3, hergyndlic *C*, heriendlic DHJ, herigendlic FGIK
nimis — swiðe ABCDHJ, swyðe FG, swyþe K, swiðlic I, swide E^3
in — in A, on BCDE^3FGHIJK
ciuitate — cestre AC, ceastre BDFGHIJK, ceæstre E^3
dei — godes ABE^3FGI, godys C, gode J
nostri — ures ABFGI, urys C, ure E^3, urum J
in — in A, on BCDE^3FGHIJK
monte — munte ABCDFGHIJK, dunæ E^3
sancto — ðæm hagan A, ðam halgan B, þam halgan C, haligum DHJ, halgum FG, halgan I, hælie E^3
eius — him A, his BCDE^3FGHIJ

ED: eius (B)] suo *Brenner.*

OE: mære ł micel (I)] s. est : is *written in left margin.* drihten (E^x)] *by corr.* (?).

LTg: Magnus] MAGnus AB; MAGNVS C; MAGNUS E; MAgnus K. dominus] DN̄S C. laudabilis] lavdabilis C.

LTu: Magnus] MAGNUS βλμνϱτ*τψ; MAGNVS ιφ; MAGNus ς. dominus] DN̄S λμνϱψ. et] ET λμνϱψ. laudabilis] LAUDABILIS λ; LAUDAVIlis ϱ; LAUdabilis ψ.

3

Dilatans* — gebradende A, gebrædynde C, gebredende E^3*, abrædende B, tobrædende D, timbrigend F, staðeligend G, staðeliend I*
exultationes* — wynsumnisse *A*, wynsumnesse B, wynsumnysse *C*, upahefednissa D, upahafennesse GK, upahefennisse H*J*, upahaf[ ]lyssa F*, blisse I, hyhtes *E^x** (*M*)
uniuersae — alre A, ealre *BCDGH*I*J*, ealra *K*, eælle *E^3*, ealle *F* (*LM*)
terrae — eorðan A*BCFG**H*I*JK*, eorðe *E^3* (*DL*)
mons* — se munt AB, munt CD, muntas F*H*, mu(n)tes *G**, muntes *I*, mutes *K*, munt ł dune $E^{3/x}$*
sion — sion AB*E^3*G, sionys C, siones FI*, n K*
latera — on sidan ABC, sidan G*I*K, siden E^x*, side DF*HJ*

aquilonis	noðdaeles A, norðdæles BDGHI*, norðdælys C, norðdeles E^{x}*, norðdælas F, norþdæles K, norþdæl J
ciuitas	cestre A, ceaster BDFH, ceast̄ I*, cestyr C, ceæster E^{3}, ceastre GJK
regis	cyninges ABD*GH, cyningys C, kininges E^{3}, cyningas F, cyningces I, cininges K*, cininge J
magni	ðes miclan *A,* ðæs miclan B, þæs miclan *C,* þæs miclan F, micles DHJ, miceles E^{3}, mycellæs K, miceles ł þæs micclan G*, micelan ł þæs mæran cyninges I*

ED: exultationes (C)] exultation[i]s *Wildhagen.* exultatione (H)] exaltatione *Campbell.* upahaf[ ]yssa (F)] upahafennyssa *Kimmens.* uniuersæ (D)] uniuersae *Roeder.* uniuersę (E)] universae *Harsley.* terræ (D)] terrae *Roeder.* terrę (E)] terrae *Harsley.* mu(n)tes (G)] muntes *Rosier.* sion (K)] Sion *Sisam.* ceast̄ (I)] ceastre *Lindelöf.*

OE: gebredende (E^{3})] *final* e *added by corr.* staðeliend (I)] s. est : he is *written in left margin.* upahaf[ ]yssa (F)] *eras. but partly visible, 3–4 letters eras. after* f. hyhtes (E^{x})] *on eras.* eorðan (G)] e *altered from* t. mu(n)tes (G)] *right leg of* n *not visible.* munt ł dune (E$^{3/x}$)] munt ł *added by corr.*, dune *on eras. by main hand.* siones (I)] s. sunt : syndon *written in left margin.* n (K)] *for* nomen. sidan (G)] *orig.* side: e *altered to* a, n *added in lighter brown ink.* sidan (I)] *eras. before word.* siden (E^{x})] *on eras.* norðdæles (I)] s. est : is *written after word.* norðdeles (E^{x})] *on eras.* ceaster (I, *as* ceast̄)] *orig.* ceastre: re *deleted by subscript dots, macron added above* t (ceast̄ṛẹ). cyninges (D)] *orig.* cyningas: e *interl. above* a, *but without subscript deleting mark.* cininges (K)] *2nd* i *and* g *partly eras. due to eras. in Lat. line above.* miceles ł þæs micclan (G)] ł þæs micclan *added in diff.* (?) *hand.* micelan ł þæs mæran cyninges (I)] cyninges *written as* cyngs̄.

LTg: exultationes] CM: *orig.* exultationis: *2nd* i *altered to* e, E: s *added by corr.;* exultationis AJ: *see Weber MS* ε, *see GAg.* uniuersae] uniuersæ BD; uniuerse CJ, F: ł *interl. by corr. followed by eras.;* uniuersę GHKLM, E: uni *on eras.* terrae] terræ BDL; terrę CEGHK; terre J, F: ł [ ]a *interl. by corr. and eras.* mons] G: *eras. after* n, H: s *altered from another letter, eras. after word,* I: s *added by glossator, eras. after word,* K: *eras. (2 letters?) after word,* s *on eras.; for* F *see GAg.* sion] syon E. latera] H: *final* a *altered from another letter.* magni] A: agni *written by corr.,* C: a *interl.*

LTu: exultationes] exultationis μς, π: *cf. Weber MS* ε, *see GAu.* uniuersae] uniuersę ειν̄ξϱφ; uniuersæ ϑ; uniuerse σςτ*τυ. terrae] terrę ειν̄ξοϱσφ; terræ ϑ; terre πςτ*τ. mons] ϱ: *orig.* montis: tis *deleted,* s *interl.;* mon δ: *eras. after word,* monte θ. *cf. Weber MS* δ*. sion] syon ειξσςτ*υφ. latera] latere ς.

GAg: Dilatans] Fundatur FHJK; Fundatvr I: *orig.* Fundator: o *deleted by subscript dot,* v *interl.;* [ ]undatur G. exultationes] exultatione FGHIK; *for* AJ *see LTg, see also*

Bib. sac. MSS M*Φ^{vp2}. mons] montis F: ł mons *interl. by corr.; for* GHIK *see LTg, see also Bib. sac. MSS* M*Q*$\Phi^{p2}G^{2}$.

GAu: Dilatans] Fundatur δεζϑιλμξοπρστυφχψ. exultationes] exultatione δεζιλξορστυφχψ; exsultatione ϑ; *for* π *see LTu, see also Bib. sac. MSS* M*Φ^{vp2}. mons] montes μου. mons sion] montesion ψ.

4

Deus	god ABCE^{3}FGIJK
in	in A, on CDE^{3}FGIJK
gradibus*	gradum A, stæpum CF, stæpum D, stepum E^{3}, stæppum K, husum GI, huse J
eius	hire AB, his CDE^{3}FGHIJ*K*
dinoscitur*	bið oncnawen ABI, bið oncnawyn *C*, bið tocnawen DF, bið tocnæwen G, byð tocnewen H, biþ tocnewen J, biþ gecnawen K, bioð gitende ł cnawen *$E^{3/x}$** (*LM*)
dum*	ðonne A, þonne BI, þonne CDE^{x}*HJK, þon[ ] G, mid F
suscipiet	onfoeht A, onfehð CG, he onfehð BI, he anfehð D, he anfehþ HJ, he afehð FK*, he onfoð $E^{3/x}$*
eam	hie ABDE^{x}*, hi C, hí F, hig IK, hine *G*, his J (*H*)

OE: bioð gitende ł cnawen ($E^{3/x}$)] *1st* i *retraced, eras. above* o, ð *added by corr.* (*altered from* bið), *2nd* e *and* ł cnawen *added by corr.* þonne (E^{x})] *on eras.* he afehð (K)] f *altered from* t. he onfoð ($E^{3/x}$)] he *added by corr.* hie (E^{x})] e *on eras.*, hi *retraced* (?).

LTg: eius] eíus K. dinoscitur] E: *2nd* i *on eras.;* dinoscetur CL, M: *orig.* dinoscitur: *2nd* i *altered to* e. eam] H: *orig.* eum: u *altered to* a; *lost* G.

GAg: gradibus] domibus FGHIJK. dinoscitur] cognoscetur FGHIJK. dum] cum FHIJK; cu[ ] G.

GAu: gradibus] domibus δεζϑιλμξοπρστυφχψ. dinoscitur] cognoscetur δεζϑιλμξοπρστυφχψ. dum] cum δεζϑιλμξοπρστυφχψ.

5

Quoniam	forðon ABJ, forþon C, forðæn E^{3}, forðon ðe F, forðon þe I, forþam þe G
ecce	sehðe AB, sihþe J, on gesihðe D, on gesihðe GH, efne CFIK, eællengæ E^{3}
reges	cyningas A*BCDFHI, cyninges G, kininges E^{3}, cininges J, ciningas K
terrae*	eorðan A*BCG*, eorðe *E^{3}* (*DFHKL*)
congregati	gesomnade A, gesomnode BH, gesamnude C, gesomnude D,

	gesomnede E^{3}, gesamnode *G*I, gesomnode J, gegaderode F, gegæderode K
sunt	sind A, sint B, synd CDFHJK, beoð ł sint E$^{3/x}$*, syndon I (*G*)
et*	⁊ ABCE^{3}
conuenerunt	gesomnadun A, tosomne becomon B, tosomne comon J, ⁊ somne coman K, becwomon C, togædere becomun D, togædere becomon GH, togedere comen E^{x}*, hi togædere becomon I, hy comon F
in	in A, on BCDE^{3}FGHIJK
unum	annisse A, annesse BIJ, annysse C, an DGHK, án F, ænum E^{3}

ED: forðon (A)] for ðon *Kuhn*. forðæn (E)] Forðæn *Harsley*. on gesihðe (H)] ongesihðe *Campbell*. terrę (E)] terrae *Harsley*.

OE: cyningas (A)] i *written below line*. beoð ł sint (E$^{3/x}$)] beoð ł *added by corr*. togedere comen (E^{x})] *on eras*.

LTg: terrae] terræ BL; terrę CDEG, F: *added by corr*., H: *on eras. by corr.*, K: *added interl. by corr.: see GAg*. congregati] congrega[ ] G. sunt] *lost* G.

LTu: terrae] terræ ϑ; terrę νχ; terre ςτ*. et] *om*. τ*: *see GAu*. conuenerunt] δ: ne *interl*.

GAg: terrae] *om*. IJ; *for* FHK *see LTg*. et] *om*. FGHIJK.

GAu: terrae] *om*. δεζιλμξπϱστυφψ, ο: *orig*. terrę: *underlined to signal deletion*. et] *om*. δεζιλμξοπστυφχψ, τ*: *see LTu*.

6

Ipsi	hie AB, hi CK, hy DE$^{3/x}$**G*H, hig IJ, he F
uidentes	gesiende AE^{3}, geseonde BCDFGHIJK
tunc*	ða AB, þa DE^{3}*, þonne C, swa FGIJ
admirati	wundriende ABE^{3}J, wundriynde C, wundrigende F, wundrudun D*K*, wundredun H, wundredan *I**, wundrudan *K*, wundrode G
sunt	sindun A, synd CFG, sind J, sint E^{3}, wæron B
conturbati	gedroefde A, gedrefde BDF, gedrefyde C, gedrefede E^{3}GHIJK
sunt	sindun A, hig syndon I, synd CFGK, sint E^{3}, wæron BJ
et*	⁊ ABCE^{3}
commoti	onstyrede *A*B, onstyryde C, astyre D, astyrode FG, astyrede HI, astryrude K, onsti[ ] J*, onfarede ł astyrede E$^{3/x}$*
sunt	sind A, synd CFGK, sint E^{x}*, hig syndon I, wæron BJ

OE: hy ($E^{3/x}$)] *orig.* hi: i *altered to* y *by corr.* þa (E^{3})] *eras. after* a (< þæ?). wundredan (I)] *eras. before word,* a *on eras., gloss* (?) *eras. after word.* onsti[ ] (J)] rde *eras. after* i (> onstirde). onfarede ł astyrede ($E^{3/x}$)] far *retraced,* ł astyrede *added by corr.* sint (E^{x}) (*3rd*)] *on eras.*

LTg: Ipsi] [ ]psi G. admirati] ádmirati K; ammirati I. commoti] A: *otiose dot below 1st* m.

LTu: admirati] χ: d *interl.;* ammirati ερσυ, ο: *orig.* admirati: d *deleted,1st* m *interl.*

GAg: tunc] sic FGHIJ; síc K. et] *om.* FGHIJK.

GAu: tunc] sic δεζθιλμξοπρστυφχψ. et] *om.* δεζιλμξοπρστυφχψ.

7

tremor	cwaecung A, cwacung BC, cwacung ł bifung ł ege J, fyrhto K, fyrhto ł bifong D, firhto ł bifung $E^{3/x}$*, fyrhtu ł bifung G, fyrhto ł bifung H, fy[ ] bifung I*, bifung F, befeng J
adprehendit	bifeng *A*, befeng B*C*J, gegrap DG*H*K, gegráp *F,* begrap *I,* gegripþ E^{3} (*M*)
eos	hie ABE^{3}, hi CK, hy DGH, híg F, hig IJ
Ibi	ðer AE^{3}, ðær BF, þær CDGHI*, þar JK
dolores	sar A*BCGHJK, sár F, Sár E^{3}*, saru D, sarnessa I (*M*)
sicut*	swe A, swa K, swa swa BCDGIJ, swa swæ $E^{3/x}$*
parturientis	cennende ABG, cennynde C, cænnende ł eacnigende *J,* eacniendis DF*, æcniendes E^{x}*, eacniende K, eacnigendes wifes I

ED: apprehendit (C)] a[d]prehendit *Wildhagen.* Sár (E)] Sar *Harsley.* swa swa (GIJ)] swaswa *Rosier, Lindelöf, Oess.* eacniendis (F)] eacniend is *Kimmens, taking* is *as induced by lemma.*

OE: firhto ł bifung ($E^{3/x}$)] ł bifung *added by corr., letter eras. after* g. fy[ ] bifung (I)] *rest of word after* y *eras.* þær (I)] *eras. after word,* s. <u>sunt</u> : synt *written in left margin* (*Lindelöf records* sunt : syndon). sar (A)] *orig.* far: *cross-stroke eras. to form* s. Sár (E^{3})] *orig.* Sǽr: ǽ *altered to* á, *accent faint but visible.* swa swæ ($E^{3/x}$)] swa *added by corr.* eacniendis (F)] is *eras. but visible,* is *separated from* eacniend *by 5 letter spaces.* æcniendes (E^{x})] *on eras.*

LTg: adprehendit] adpręhendit M, A: rę *interl. by corr.;* apprehendit EFI, C: *1st* p *on eras. by corr.,* H: *1st* p *on eras.* dolores] M: *orig.* doloris: i *altered to* e. parturientis] J: *eras.* (?) *after 1st* i.

LTu: tremor] Tremor θ. adprehendit] adpraehendit β; apprehendit ειλπρτ*τυ; apprae-hendit ζ, ο: *orig.* adpraehendit: *1st* d *deleted,* p *interl.;* adpprehendit θ; adp̄hendit μ; appręhendit ξ; ap̄p̄hendit σφχ. parturientis] parturientes β.

GAg: sicut] ut FGHIJK.

GAu: sicut] ut δεζϑιλμξοπϱστυφχψ.

8

in	in A, on BCDE^{3}FGHIJK
spiritu	gaste ABCDFGHIJ, gast K, gastæ E^3
uehementi	strongum AB, strangum CJ, swiþlicu DK, swýþlicu F, swiþlicum H, swiðlicum I, swiðlicum ł strangu<u>m</u> G*, swiþe E^3
conterens*	forðręstende *A*, forðræstende B, forþræstynde *C*, forþræstende *J*, forbrytende DF*GH*, þu forbretest *I*, forbrytte *K*, brecende E^3 (*M*)
naues	sceopu A, scipu BGIJ, scypu CDF, scypa E^x*, scyp K
tharsis	ðes londes A, ðæs londes B, þæs landys C, þæs landes GJ, tharsis E^3, tarso F, on tarsen I, n K*

ED: in (I)] In *Lindelöf.* conteres (C)] contere[n]s *Wildhagen.* tharsis (K)] Tharsis *Sisam.*

OE: swiðlicum ł strangu<u>m</u> (G)] ł strangu<u>m</u> *added in diff.* (?) *hand.* scypa (E^x)] *eras. before word.* n (K)] *for* nomen.

LTg: conterens] A: *orig.* conteres: *2nd* n *interl. by corr.*, M: *orig.* conteris: i *altered to* e, *2nd* n *interl.;* conteres C: *cf. Weber MSS* PQRUγδεη moz^x, *see GAg.*

LTu: uehementi] uechimenti ϑ; uehementis β. conterens] ς: s *interl.;* conteres τ*: *cf. Weber MSS* PQRUγδεη moz^x, *see GAu.* tharsis] tarsis ϑπ.

GAg: conterens] conteres FGHIJK, C: *see LTg.*

GAu: conterens] conteres εϑοπϱτφχψ, τ*: *see LTu.*

9

Sicut	swe A, swa BCJK, swæ E^3, swá swá F, swa swa GI
audiuimus	we geherdun A, we gehirdon BE^{3}J, we gehyrdon CFGH, we gehyrdun D, we geherdon I, we gehyrdan K
ita*	swe A, swa BCDIJK, swæ E^3, swá F, ⁊ swa G
et*	⁊ ABCDE^3
uidimus	gesegun *A,* gesegan *K,* we gesegon B, we gesawon CDFGHIJ, we gesæwon E$^{3/x}$*
in	in A, on BCDE^{3}FGHIJK
ciuitate	cestrę AC, ceastre BDFGHIJK, ceæstre E^3
domini	dryhtnes B, drihtnys C, drihtnes FI, drihtenes K, drihten E^3, dryht̄ A, driħ J, [ ]riħ[ ] *G*
uirtutum	megna A, mægena BDH, mægna CK, megene E^3*, mægen J, mihta *F,* miht ł mægena G, mægna ł mihta I

in	in A, on BCE^{3}FGIJK
ciuitate	cestre AC, ceastre BFGIJ, ceæstre E^{3}, ceastra K
dei	godes ABE^{3}FIJ, godys C, g[ ] G
nostri	ures ABFIJ, urys C, ure DE^{3}H, ur[ ] *G*
deus	god ABCE^{3}FGHIJK
fundauit	gesteaðelade A, gestaðolode B*C*, gestæðolode E$^{3/x}$*, gestaðelode G, gestaþelode H*J, gestaðolede I, gestaþolode K, gestaðale D, gestaðela F
eam	ða *A*, þa C, hie B, hy DE$^{3/x}$*GH, hi FK, hig IJ
in	in A, on BCDE^{3}FGHIJK
aeternum	ecnisse A*D*, ecnesse *BE^{3}GHIJK*, ecnysse *CF* (*L*)

ED: swa swa (GI)] swaswa *Rosier, Lindelöf.* sic (H)] sie *Campbell.* in (G) (*1st*)] *in Rosier.* [ ]omini (G)] *domini Rosier.* [ ]riħ[ ] (G)] *no gloss Rosier.* g[ ] (G)] *no gloss Rosier.* æternum (D)] aeternum *Roeder.* ęternum (E)] aeternum *Harsley.* ęternu[ ] (G)] ętern*um Rosier.* ecnesse (G)] ecnes[ ] *Rosier.*

OE: we gesæwon (E$^{3/x}$)] we *interl. by corr.* megene (E^{3})] *final* e *added by corr.* gestæðolode (E$^{3/x}$)] lode *on eras. by corr.* gestaþelode (H)] *2nd* e *possibly formed from another letter.* hy (E$^{3/x}$)] *orig.* hi: i *altered to* y *by corr., eras.* (*3 letters?*) *after word.*

LTg: uidimus] A: u *on eras. by corr.,* K: *eras.* (*of punct.*) *after word.* ciuitate (*1st*)] ciuita[ ] G. domini] [ ]omini G. uirtutum] F: *small eras. after word.* nostri] n[ ]ri G. fundauit] fundaut C. eam] A: m *interl. by corr.* aeternum] æternum BDKL; ęternum CEFH; ęternu[ ] G; eternum J.

LTu: aeternum] ęternum εινξφ; æternum ϑ; eternum σςτ*τ.

GAg: ita] sic FGHIJK. et] *om.* FGHIJK.

GAu: ita] sic δεζϑιλμξοπϱστυφχψ. et] *om.* δεζϑιλμξοπϱστυφχψ.

10

Suscepimus	we onfengun *A*C, we onfengon BHIJ, We onfengon E^{3}, we anfengon DK, we afengon F, we o[ ]ngon *G* (*M*)
deus	god ABCDE^{3}FGHI*JK
misericordiam	mildheortnisse AD, mildheortnesse BE^{3}GHIJK, mildheortnysse CF
tuam	ðine ABF, þine CE^{3}GIJK
in	in A, on BCDE^{3}FGHIJK
medio	midle ABCFI, middele DHJK, mi[ ]dele G, middæn E^{3}
templi	temples *A*BGI, templys C, templis D, templis H, temple E^{3}FK, temple J
tui	ðines AB, þinys C, þines GI, ðin F, þinum J, þinan K, þin E^{3}

ED: Susc[ ]pimus (G)] Suscepimus *Rosier.* mi[ ]dele (G)] middele *Rosier.* te<u>m</u>plis (H)] templis *Campbell.* þines (G)] *no gloss Rosier.*

OE: god (I)] o *written before word.*

LTg: Suscepimus] M: *orig.* suscipimus: *1st* i *altered to* e; Suscipimus A: *1st* i *on eras. by corr.;* Susc[ ]pimus G. templi] tepli A: *not clear that macron was eras.*

LTu: Suscepimus] Suscipimus βϑ. misericordiam] missericordiam ϑ.

11

Secundum	efter A, æfter BFGHIK, æftyr C, æft<u>er</u> DJ, Efter E³*
nomen	noman AB, naman CDFGHIJK, nomæn E³
tuum	ðinu<u>m</u> AB, þinum CHI, þinu<u>m</u> DGJ, ðinum E³F, þinan K
deus	god ABCDE³FGJ
ita*	swe A, swa BCDFGHIJK, swæ E³
et	⁊ ABCE³FGJK
laus	lof ABCDE³FGHIJK
tua	ðin ABF, þin CDE³GHI*JK
in	in A, on BCDE³FGHJK, eac swilce on I
fines	endas ABDGHJ, endys C, ende E³FK, gemęru<u>m</u> I*
terrae	eorðan *ABCDFGH,* eorþan *JK,* eorðæn *E³,* eorðe I (*L*)
iustitia	rehtwisnisse *A,* ryhtwisnesse *B*D, rihtwisnysse *C*F, rihtwisnesse Eˣ*GH*J*K, mid rihtwisnesse I
plena	ful AJK, full BCDE³FGHI
est	is ABDE³FGHIJ*K,* ys C
dextera	sie swiðre A, seo swiðre D, seo swyþre F, seo swyðre G, sco swiþre H, se swiðre J, swiðre BI, swiðræ E³, swyþre K, swiðran C
tua	ðin ABE³, þin CDFGHIJK

ED: terræ (D)] terrae *Roeder.* terrę (E)] terrae *Harsley.* iusticia (C)] iusti[t]ia *Wildhagen.*

OE: Efter (E³)] E *partly beneath gold of* S(ecundum), *showing gloss entered first.* þin (I)] s. e<u>st</u> : is *written in left margin.* gemęru<u>m</u> (I)] eac swylce – on gemæru<u>m</u> *written in bottom margin below* fines, *with* & *written below* eac. rihtwisnesse (Eˣ)] *on eras.*

LTg: terrae] terræ BD; terrę CEFGHKL; terre J. iustitia] iusticia C: *orig.* iustitia: *2nd* t *altered to* c; iustitiae A; iustitiæ B; iustitea J. est] ést K.

LTu: laus] lus ϑ. terrae] terræ ϑ; terrę ινξϱφ; terre σςτ*τ. iustitia] iusticia τ*τφ, ϱ: *orig.* iustitia: *2nd* t *deleted,* c *interl.*

GAg: ita] sic FGHIJ; síc K.

GAu: ita] sic δεϑιλμξοπϱστυφχψ.

12

Laetetur blissie A*C,* blissige *BIJ,* sy geblissod *DG,* sy blissod *H,* si geblissod *K,* blissiæþ *E*^{3}*,* blissa *F* (*L*)

mons se munt AB*J,* munt CDGHI, mvnt K, munt ł dún E^{3}, dune F

sion sion AG**J,* syon *E*^{3}*,* sionys *C,* siones FI, n K*

et ⁊ ABCDE^{3}FGHIJK

exultent gefen A, gefeon BC, gefon J, gefeogen D, gefeogen H, fægnigan F, fægnian I, hihtæþ ł fæogen E$^{3/x}$*, ymbclyppað G, sin glædod K

filiae dohtur A, dohtor *B,* dohtra *CFGHJK,* dohtora *D,* dohtre *E*^{x}*, dohtru I (*L*)

iudae iudæn *E*^{3}*,* iudiscan I, iude *J,* n *K** (*ABCDFGHL*)

propter fore ABDHJ, for CE^{3}*FGIK

iudicia domas ABIJ, dome CE^{3}, domum DFG, domum H, doma K

tua ðine AB, þine E$^{3/x}$*IJ, þinum CG, þinum DH, ðinum F, þinra K

domine drihtyn C, drihten E^{3}FI*, dryħ A, dryht̄ B, driħt G, driħ J

ED: Lætetur (D)] Laetetur *Roeder.* Lętetur (E)] Laetentur *Harsley.* syon (C)] sion *Wildhagen.* sion (K)] Sion *Sisam.* filiæ (D)] filiae *Roeder.* filię (E)] filiae *Harsley.* iudæ (D)] iudae *Roeder.* iudę (EK)] iudae *Harsley;* Iudę *Sisam.*

OE: sion (G)] *added in diff.* (?) *hand.* n (K) (*both*)] *for* nomen. hihtæþ ł fæogen (E$^{3/x}$)] ł fæogen *added by corr.,* o *on eras.* dohtre (E^{x})] *on eras.* for (E^{3})] *letter* (e?) *eras. after word.* þine (E$^{3/x}$)] e *added by corr.* drihten (I)] o *written before word.*

LTg: Laetetur] Lætetur BDK; Lętetur EFGHL, C: *orig.* Lętętur: *cauda below 2nd* e *eras.;* Letetur J. mons sion] monsion J. sion] syon E, C: *orig.* sion: i *deleted by subscript dot,* y *interl.* filiae] filiæ BD; filię CEFGHKL; filie J. iudae] iudę ACEHKL; iudæ BD; iude FGJ.

LTu: Laetetur] Lætetur βϑ; Lętetur εινφ; Letetur ξσςτ*τυ. sion] syon ειξσςτ*τυφ. exultent] exsultent ϑ. filiae] filię ειν ξπυφ; filiæ ϑ; filie στ*τ. iudae] iudę ενξϱςυφ; iudeę ζ; iudæ ϑ; iude ιστ*τ.

13

Circumdate ymbsellað ABD, ymbsyllað *CH,* Ymbsellæð *E*^{3}*,* ymbsylla(ð) *G*,* ymbsillaþ J, ymbsealdon F, embesyllað K, ymbtrymmaþ I

sion sion *E*^{3}J, n K* (*H*)

et ⁊ ABCE^{3}FGHIJK

complectimini clyppað *ABC,* ymbclyppað *DH,* ymbclyppaþ IJ, ymbcleopton F, ymbeclyppað *K,* hi cleoppað G*, bewindæþ ł ymbclyppað E$^{3/x}$* (*LM*)

eam hie AB, hi CK, hy DE$^{3/x}$*GH, hig FIJ

narrate	secgað ABC, secgæþ ł cyþað $E^{3/x}$*, cyþað DK, cyðað GH, cyðaþ I, cyþaþ J, cyþaþ þe F
in	in A, on BCDE^{x}*FGHIJK
turribus	torrum AC, torrum B, stypelum D, stepelum E^{x}*, stypelum FH, stæpulum G, styplum I, stipelum J, stypelas K
eius	hire ABI, his CDE^{3}FGHJ*K*

ED: Circundate (C)] Circu[m]date *Wildhagen.* Circúndate (H)] Circundate *Campbell.* ymbsylla(ð) (G)] ymbsyllað *Rosier.* sión (H)] sion *Campbell.* sion (K)] Sion *Sisam.* complectimini (C)] co[n]plectimini *Wildhagen.*

OE: ymbsylla(ð) (G)] *cross-stroke of* ð *not visible.* n (K)] *for* nomen. hi cleoppað (G)] *added in diff.* (?) *hand.* bewindæþ ł ymbclyppað ($E^{3/x}$)] ł ymbclyppað *added by corr.* hy ($E^{3/x}$)] *orig.* hi: i *altered to* y *by corr.* secgæþ ł cyþað ($E^{3/x}$)] ł cyþað *added by corr.* on (E^{x})] *on eras.* stepelum (E^{x})] *on eras. by corr.*

LTg: Circumdate] Circundate E, C: *orig.* Circumdate: *left leg of* m *eras. to form* n, G: *orig.* Circumdate: *right leg of* m *eras. to form* n; Circúndate H: *small eras. after* n, *initial* C *barely visible.* sion] sión H; syon E. complectimini] H: *orig.* conplectimini: *middle leg added to 1st* n *to form* m; conplectimini DKL, A: *1st* i *on eras.;* conplectemini M: i *written above 2nd* e, *then crossed through with light* x (> conplectimini); complectimini C: *orig.* conplectimini: n *eras. and macron added above* o. eius] eíus K.

LTu: Circumdate] Circundate ελτφ. sion] syon ειξςτ*τυφ. complectimini] conplectimini βεϑνψ; conplectemini μ; cōplectimini σφ, o: *orig.* cōplectemini: *2nd* e *deleted,* i *interl.*

14

Ponite	settað *ABD*FGH, settaþ *C*JK, settæþ *E^{3}*, asettað I (*LM*)
corda	heortan ABDFGHIJK, heartan C, heortæn E^{3}
uestra	eowre ABCFGHIJK, eowra D, eowræ E^{3}
in	in A, on BCDE^{3}FGHIJ, o K
uirtute	megne A, mægene BGHJ, mægne CF, mægenu *D,* megen E^{3}, strengþe K, hire I
eius	his A*C*DE^{3}FG*H*JK, hire B, mægne ł mihte I
et	⁊ ABCE^{3}FGHIJK
distribuite	todaelað A, todælað BCD*H*K, todælaþ I*J,* todeleð E^{x}*, todælað ðe F, todælað þe G
gradus*	stepas A, stæpas BCD, stepæs E^{3}, hus FGJK, husrædenne I
eius	hire ABI, his CDE^{3}FGHJ*K*
ut	ðæt AB, þæt CFI*K, þætte D, þætte GHJ, ðette E^{3}
enarretis	ge asecgen AB, ge asecgað C, ge segæn ł cyþen $E^{3/x}$*, ge cyþen DHJ, ge cyþan FIK, ge cyðan *G*

in	in A, on BCDE^{3}FGHIJK
progenie	cynne *ABC*, forecynrene D*G*HJ, cynryne F*, cynrene K, cneorisse ł mægðe I, cneowrise ł cynrede E$^{3/x}$*
altera	oðrum *A*DE^{x}*FG, oðrum BC, oþrum H, oþrum J, oðre I*, oþra K

ED: uirtute (D)] uirtute[s] *Roeder.* distribúite (H)] distribuite *Campbell.* domus (I)] domos *Lindelöf.* þætte (G)] þæt *Rosier.* ge segæn ł cyþen (E)] gesegæn ł cyþen *Harsley.* ge cyþen (H)] gecyþen *Campbell.* ge cyþan (F)] gecyþan *Kimmens.* ge cyðan (G)] te gecyðan *Rosier.*

OE: todeleð (E^{x})] *on eras.* þæt (I)] *eras. after word.* ge segæn ł cyþen (E$^{3/x}$)] ł cyþen *added by corr.* cynryne (F)] *1st* y *partly obscured, break in descender.* cneowrise ł cynrede (E$^{3/x}$)] *2nd* e *and* ł cynrede *added by corr.* oðrum (E^{x})] *added by corr.* oðre (I)] e *altered from another letter* (?).

LTg: Ponite] ponite ABCDELM. uirtute] D: *orig.* uirtutes: s *eras.* eius (*1st*)] C: *eras.* (*4 letters?*) *after word,* H: *small eras. after word, perhaps of punct.* distribuite] distribúite H; distribuíte J. eius (*2nd*)] eíus K. enarretis] ęnarretis G. progenie] progeniæ B; progenię G; progeniem A: *letter eras. after* i, *macron by corr.* (?): *cf. Weber MSS* URγδη moz^{c}. altera] alteram A: *macron* (*by corr.?*) *written to right of final* a, *not above it: cf. Weber MSS* URγδη moz^{c}.

LTu: Ponite] ponite βνςτ*. progenie] progenię βξ.

GAg: gradus] domus IJ, F: ł mons *interl. by corr.;* domos G: *orig.* domus: u *altered to* o, H: os *interl.,* K: *2nd* o *on eras. by corr.: cf. Bib. sac. MSS* F^{2}L*M^{2}G^{2}K, *etc.*

GAu: gradus] domus δεζθιλμξοπϱστυφχψ.

15

Quoniam	forðon ABJ, forþon CF, Forðan E^{3}, forþam G, forðon þe I
hic	ðes AB, þes CDE^{3}FGHI*K*, þæs J
est	is ABE^{3}*FGIJK, ys C
deus	god A*B*CE^{3}FGIJK
(deus)*	| god *B*J, ure I
noster	| ur *A*, ure BCE^{3}FGJK, god I
in	in A, on BCDE^{3}FGHIJK
aeternum	ecnisse A*H*, ecnesse *BDE^{3}G*I*JK*, ecnysse *CF* (*L*)
et	⁊ ABCDE^{3}FGIJK
in	on BCDE^{3}FGIJK
saeculum	weorund A, weorold *B*, woruld *C*, worold *E^{3}*, worulde *DFH*, worulda *G*, weorlda *I*, worlda *J* (*KLM*)
saeculi	weorulde A, weorolde *B*, worulde *CH*, worvlde *D**, woroldde *K*, woruld *FG*, world *J*, weorl *I*, aworoł *E^{3}* (*LM*)

et*	⁊ ABCE[3]
ipse	he ABCE[3]FGJK, he sylf I
reget	receð AB, recyð *C,* recþ DF, recð GH, rehtð K, gerecet E[3], gewissað I, seceð J
nos	usic A, us BCDE[3]FGHIJ*K*
in	in A, on BCDE[3]FGHIJK
saecula	weorulde A, weorolde *B,* worulde *CF,* worulda *DH,* woruld *G,* weorlde *I,* worlda *J,* worolde *E[3]K* (*LM*)

ED: forðon (A)] for ðon *Kuhn.* æternum (D)] aeternum *Roeder.* ęternum (E)] aeternum *Harsley.* sęculum (E)] saeculum *Harsley.* sclm (FIJ)] seculum *Kimmens, Oess;* saeculum *Lindelöf.* sęculi (E)] saeculi *Harsley.* scli (FIJ)] seculi *Kimmens, Oess;* saeculi *Lindelöf.* worvlde (D)] worulde *Roeder.* aworoł (E)] aworol*de Harsley.* sæcula (D)] saecula *Roeder.* scła (EIJK)] saecula *Harsley, Lindelöf;* secula *Oess;* sæcula *Sisam.*

OE: is (E[3])] s *retouched by corr.* worvlde (D)] *orig.* worolde: *2nd* o *deleted by subscript dot,* v *interl.*

LTg: hic] híc K. deus] deus deus B: *cf. Weber MSS* τ*η* moz[c], *see GAg.* noster] A: os *on eras. by corr.,* ter *interl. by corr.* aeternum] æternum BDKL; ęternum CEFGHJ. saeculum] sæculum B, K: *only fragment of* s *shows, excised along with initial to psalm below* (*fol. 52r*); seculum CGHL; sęculum DE; sclm FIJM. sæculi] sæculi B; seculi CGHL; sęculi DEK; scli FIJM. reget] regit C. nos] nós K. saecula] sæcula BD; secula CGHL; sęcula F; scła EIJKM.

LTu: aeternum] ęternum βειvξσφ; æternum ϑ; eternum ςτ*τ. saeculum] sęculum vo; seculum ςτ*; sclm βεζιμξπρστυφχ; sæculum ϑ. saeculi] sæculi ϑ; seculi λπςτ*; sęculi o; scli βεζιμvξρστυφχ. saecula] sęcula βειοφ; sæcula ϑ; secula ςτ*τ; scła δλvξπσχ.

GAg: deus] deus deus FHIJK, B: *see LTg.* et (*2nd*)] *om.* FGHIJK.

GAu: deus] deus deus δεζϑιμξπρστυφχψ, λ: *1st* deus *interl.* et (*2nd*)] *om.* δϑλμπρσφχ.

PSALM 48

2

Audite	geherað *A*I, gehirað *B*J, gehyrað *CE[x]FG,* gehyrað *D,* gehyraþ H*K*
haec	ðas A*B,* þas *CDFGHJK,* ðæs *E[3],* þas þingc *I* (*L*)
omnes	alle A, ealle B*C*DFGHJK, eælle E[3], ge ealle I*
gentes	ðeode AB, þeoda CDHIK, ðeoda FG, ðiodæ E[3], þeodum J
auribus	mid earum ACFI, mid earum B, mid eærum E[3/x]*, earum DJ, earum GH, earan K
percipite	onfoð ACDE[3]GHI, onfoþ JK, onfoð ge B, underfoh F
(omnes)*	ealle FGIJK

qui	ða ðe A, þa þe CFG, þæ ðe E$^{3/x}$*, þe DHJ, ge ðe B, ge þe I, þa K
habitatis	eardiað ABCFG, eærdiæþ E^{3}, oneardiað I, bugiað DH, bugiaþ J, bogiaþ K
orbem	ymbhwyrf A, ymbhwyrft BCDGHJ, ymbhwyrfte I, ybhwyrfte F, on ymbwirft E$^{3/x}$*, ymbe K

ED: hæc (D)] haec *Roeder.* hȩc (E)] haec *Harsley.* hec (I)] haec *Lindelöf.*

OE: ge ealle (I)] s. o *written before gloss.* mid eærum (E$^{3/x}$)] mid *added by corr.* þæ ðe (E$^{3/x}$)] ðe *added by corr.* on ymbwirft (E$^{3/x}$)] on *added by corr.*

LTg: Audite] AVdite ABD; AVDITE C; AUDITE E; [ ]udite G; [ ]Udite K: *initial letter excised.* haec] HĘC C; hȩc EHJ; hæc BDKL; hec G, I: *orig.* haec: a *eras.* omnes] OMNES C.

LTu: Audite] AUdite βχ; AVDITE ιςτ*τφ; AUDITE λμνϱψ. haec] HAEC λμνϱψ; hæc ϑ; hȩc ιπςφ; hec σ. omnes] OMNES λνϱ; OMnes μψ. gentes] GENTES λϱ.

GAg: percipite] percipite omnes FGHIJK.

GAu: percipite] percipite omnes δεζϑμξοϱστυφχψ.

3

Quique	gehwelce AB, gehwylce I, gehwilce J, hwylce C, ⁊ gefylce E^{x}*, swa hwilc *G*, ⁊ ge D*H*K, þe ⁊ ge F
terriginae	eorðcende *ABC*, eorþware *DF*, eorðware *HK*, eorðwaru *G*, eorðware ł eordcende *E*^{x}*, eorcinne *J*, eorðbogiendan *I* (*LM*)
et	⁊ ABCE^{3}FGHIJK
filii	bearn ABCDGHIJ, beærn *E*^{3}, sunu FK
hominum	monna AB, manna CDFGHIJK, mænnæ E^{3}
simul*	somud A, somod B, samod CJ, semed E^{3}, ætgædere D (*FHIK*)
in	in A, on BCDE^{3}GHIJK, an F
unum	annesse ABI, annisse J, an CDGHK, æn E^{3}, anum F
diues	weolig A, welig BCDE^{3}GHJ, weli F, se welega I, rice K
et	⁊ ABCDE^{3}FGHIJK
pauper	ðearfa ABF, þearfa CD*G*HJ, þeærfæ E^{3}, se ðearfa I, ðearfan K

ED: [ ]uique (H)] Quique *Campbell.* terrigenȩ (D)] terriginȩ *Roeder.* filíí (E)] filii *Harsley.* paup[ ] (G)] pauper *Rosier.*

OE: ⁊ gefylce (E^{x})] *on eras.* eorðware ł eordcende (E^{x})] *on eras.*

LTg: Quique] Quiquȩ G; [ ]uique H: *outline of initial* Q *visible.* terriginae] A: *eras. above* nae; terrigine B; terigenȩ C; terrigenȩ F; DH: *orig.* terriginȩ: *2nd* i *altered to* e;

terrigene EIL, G: *orig.* terrigine: *2nd* i *altered to* e; terriginę JM; terrigęne K. filii] filíí E. simul] F: *added by corr.*, H: *added interl. by corr.*; símul I: *added by corr. in left margin;* [ ]mul K: *initial letters lost due to excision of initial above.* pauper] paup[ ] G.

LTu: terriginae] terrigine διμςτ*τ, β: *1st* e *interl.*; terriginę εζϱ; terriginæ ϑ; terrigenę λσυφχ; terigenę ν; terrigene ξπ; terrigenae ο. simul] ξχ: *added interl. by corr.*: *see GAu.*

GAg: simul] *orig. om.* FHI: *see LTg.*

GAu: simul] *om.* δεζϑλμοπϱσυφψ, ι: *deleted by underdotting; for* ξχ *see LTu.*

4

Os	muð *A*BCGI, muþ FJ, Muð E^{3} (*DKLM*)
meum	min ABCDE^{3}FGHIJK
loquetur	spriceð *A*B, spricð DH, sprecþ F, sprecð E^{3}*G, spycð K, sprecaþ J, spræc C, bið sprecende ł sprecð I (*M*)
sapientiam	snytru A, snytro B, snytro ł wisdom E$^{3/x}$*, wisdom CDFGHJK, snotornesse ł wisdom I*
et	⁊ ABCE^{3}FGJK
meditatio	smeang A*, smeaung BCI, smeagung J, smægyng K, smeæung ł gemynd E$^{3/x}$*, gemynd DFGH
cordis	heortan ABCDFGHIJK, heorte E^{3}
mei	minre ABDE^{3}FIJK, minys C, mine G
prudentiam	gleawnisse ABDH, gleawnysse CF, gleawnesse I, gleawnisse ł wisdom E$^{3/x}$*, gleawnesse ł snoternes G, geleawnesse J, snoternesse K

ED: Ós (A)] Os *Kuhn.* Ós (B)] os *Brenner.* meditatio (G)] med*i*tatio *Rosier.* gemynd (G)] gemynde *Rosier.*

OE: sprecð (E^{3})] ð *on eras. by corr.* snytro ł wisdom (E$^{3/x}$)] ł wisdom *added by corr.* snotornesse ł wisdom (I)] s. e̲s̲t̲ : is *written after* wisdom. smeang (A)] n *interl.* smeæung ł gemynd (E$^{3/x}$)] ł gemynd *added by corr.* gleawnisse ł wisdom (E$^{3/x}$)] gleawnisse ł *added by corr.*

LTg: Os] Ós ADLM; [ ]s K: *initial letter lost due to excision of initial above, fragment visible as well as accent (extending above* s*), gloss lost.* loquetur] AM: *orig.* loquitur: i *altered to* e.

LTu: loquetur] loquitur β. prudentiam] prudentia ι: *orig.* prudentiam: m *deleted by underdotting.*

5

Inclinabo	ic onhaeldu A, ic onhældo B, Ic Onhilde E$^{3/x}$*, ic ahylde *C*DF*H*IK, on ic ahylde G, ic onhidde J
ad*	to ABCDE^{3}, on FGIJK

similitudinem*	gelicnisse AD, gelicnesse BE^{3}, gelicnysse C, bigspelle F, bispelle GJ, bigspel K, bigspellum I
aurem	eare ABCDFHJ, eære E^{3}, earan GIK
meam	min ABCDE^{3}FHJ, mine GIK
aperiam	ic ontynu A, ic ontyne BCI, ic ontine E^{3}, ic atyne DFGH, ic untine J, ic openige K
in	in A, on BCE^{3}FGIJK
psalterio	hearpan AB, saltyre C, saltere DFGHJK, spaltere E^{3}, sealmlofe I (*L*)
propositionem	foresetenisse A, forsetenesse B, foresetynysse C, foregesetenesse E^{3}, forgesettenysse F, forsetennesse ł race G*, foresetnesse J, race DHK, ingehygdnessa ł foresetnysse I*
meam	mine ABDFGHIK, min C, minre E^{3}J

ED: Inclinabo (C)] I[m]clinabo *Wildhagen.* mine (G) (*2nd*)] min[ ] *Rosier.*

OE: Ic Onhilde (E$^{3/x}$)] Ic *added by corr.* forsetennesse ł race (G)] *added in diff.* (?) *hand.* ingehygdnessa ł foresetnysse (I)] *final* e *formed from another letter.*

LTg: Inclinabo] H: *initial letter faint but visible,* C: *orig.* Imclinabo: *left leg of* m *eras. to form* n. psalterio] L: *letter eras. after* l.

LTg: Inclinabo] INclinabo β. propositionem] propossitionem ϑ.

GAg: ad similitudinem] in parabolam FGHIJK.

GAu: ad similitudinem] in parabolam δεζϑιλμξοπϱστυφχψ.

6

Ut*	ǀ	tohwon *ABCD*F, Tohwon E$^{3/x}$*, la hwy I, forhwi K (*L*)
quid*	ǀ	
timebo		ondredu ic A, ondræde ic CIK, andræde ic DH, ic ondrede E^{3}, ic ondræde J, ic ondræde ic B, ic me ondræde *G,* adræde F
in	ǀ	in A, on BCDE^{3}FGHJK, dæge I
die	ǀ	dege AE$^{3/x}$*, dæge BFGHJ, dęge D, dæg K, yflum C, on I
mala	ǀ	ðæm yflan A, ðam yflan B, yfelæn E^{3}*, yfelu FG, yfel J, yuelum H, yfelum I, yfelum cwist þu *D**, dæge *C* (*KLM*)
⟨num⟩		(*LM*)
iniquitas		unrehtwisnis A, unryhtwisnes B, unrihtwisnys C, unryhtwisness D, unrihtwisnys F, unrihtwisnes GHIK, unrihtwisnesse E$^{3/x}$*J
calcanei		helspuran ABJ, hellspuran C, spuran DE^{3}*HK,* [ ]ran G, hos FI*
mei		minre A, minne B, mine CE^{3}*FGJ*K,* mines DHI

circumdedit* — ymbseleþ A*, ymbseleð B, ymbsylyð *C,* ymbsylþ F, ymbsyleþ J, ymbsealde DG, ymbseælde E^{3}, ymbesealdan K, ymb H, ymbhwyrfð ł embtrymð I*
me — me ABCE^{3}FHIJK (*G*)

ED: [ ]r (G)] *Cur Rosier.* [ ]ur (H)] Cur *Campbell.* tohwon (ABD)] to hwon *Kuhn, Brenner, Roeder.* tim[ ]bo (G)] *tim*ebo *Rosier.* mala (D)] malo *Roeder.* yfelum cwist þu (D)] yfelum cwistþu *Roeder.* calcánei (H)] calcanei *Campbell.* circundedit (C)] circu[m]dedit *Wildhagen.* circúndabit (H)] circundabit *Campbell.* circúmdabit (I)] circumdabit *Lindelöf.*

OE: Tohwon ($E^{3/x}$)] hwon *on eras. by corr.* dege ($E^{3/x}$)] ge *on eras. by corr.* yfelæn (E^{3})] *retraced by corr.* yfelum cwist þu (D)] *see LTg note to* mala. unrihtwisnesse ($E^{3/x}$)] wisnesse *on eras. by corr.* hos (I)] *gloss eras. before word.* mine (E^{3})] *gloss eras. before word.* ymbseleþ (A)] þ *possibly altered from another letter.* ymbhwyrfð ł embtrymð (I)] ł embtrymð *written after following* me *and extending into right margin.*

LTg: Ut] Vt ABCD; V́t L. timebo] tim[ ]bo G. mala] K: *no room for gloss,* D: *orig.* malo: o *altered to* a, *eras.* (*5 letters?*) *after word;* malo C: *cf. Weber MSS* αη; malo num M: num *added interl.;* malo núm L. calcanei] K: *orig.* calcaneum: *right leg of* u *and all of* m *eras., small eras. after* e; calcánei H. mei] K: *orig.* meum: *right leg of* u *and all of* m *eras.* circumdedit] circundedit C: *orig.* circumdedit: *left leg of* m *eras. to form* n. me] *lost* G.

LTu: mala] οπ: *orig.* malo: o *altered to* a; malo β; malo num ν.

GAg: Ut quid] Cur FIJ; cur K: *orig.* Quur: Q *deleted by 4 surrounding dots, 2nd* u *eras.,* c *added after* Q *by corr.;* [ ]r G; [ ]ur H: *outline of initial* C *visible.* circumdedit] circumdabit FGJK; circúmdabit I; circúndabit H: *eras. after* n.

GAu: Ut quid] Cur δεζϑιλμξοπϱστυφχψ. circumdedit] circumdabit δζλμξπϱυχψ; circundabit ειφ; circūdabit ϑοστ.

7
Qui — ða ðe AB, þa þe CGHIJK, þa ðe DF, ðæ þe $E^{3/x}$*
confidunt — getreowað ABH, getrywað CD, getrywaþ F, getriwæð E^{3}, getriwaþ J, getreowiað GI, truwiaþ K
in — in A, on BCDE^{3}FGHIJK
uirtute — megne A, mægene BDH, mægyne C, megene E^{3}, mægne J, mæg K, mægne ł mihte I, mihte FG
sua — heara A, hira *B,* hyra C, heora D$E^{3/x}$*HIJK, his F, he[ ] G
⟨et⟩ — ⁊ *B*
quique* — ⁊ ða AD, ða B, þa þe C, ⁊ FJK, witoþlice E^{3}
in — in A, on BCDE^{3}FIJK (*G*)

abundantia* genyhtsumnisse A, genyhtsumnesse *B,* genihtsumnysse *C,* genihsumunga *D,* genihtsummunga ł fulsumnesse E$^{3/x}$*, mænifealdnysse F, mænigfealdnesse IJ, mycelnesse K (*LM*)

diuitiarum weolena A, welena BDFGHIJ, welyna C, welenæ *E^{3},* welan K

suarum heara A, hira B, hyra C, heora DFGHIJK, hiræ E^{3}

gloriabuntur* bioð gewuldrade A, beoð gewuldrade B, beoð gewuldrude C, hy beoð gewuldrude D, hi beoð gewuldrode F, bioð wuldriende E^{3}, ⁊ hig wuldriaþ I, hi wuldriaþ J, h[ ] wuldr[ ] G, wuldriað K

ED: þa þe (G)] :a þe *Rosier.* mihte (G)] mihte he *Rosier.* sua (G)] swa *Rosier.* he[ ] (G)] *no gloss Rosier.* abundantia (C)] [h]abundantia *Wildhagen.* h[ ] wuldr[ ] (G)] hy wuldri[ ] *Rosier.*

OE: ðæ þe (E$^{3/x}$)] þe *added by corr.* heora (E^{3})] eo *on eras. by corr.* genihtsummunga ł fulsumnesse (E$^{3/x}$)] unga ł fulsu *by corr.*, mnesse *on eras.*

LTg: sua] sua et B: *cf. Weber MS* η2. in (*2nd*)] *lost* G. abundantia] C: *eras. before word;* habundantia BDLM. diuitiarum] diuiciarum E.

LTu: uirtute sua] uirtute & sua μ: s *added by main hand* (*orig.* ?uirtut&ua = uirtute tua). abundantia] habundantia βv. abundantia diuitiarum] habundantiarum ς.

GAg: quique] et FHIJK; *lost* G. abundantia] multitudine HIJK, F: n *on eras.* (?); [ ]tudine G. gloriabuntur] gloriantur FHIJK; gloria[ ] G.

GAu: quique] et δεζϑιλμξοπρστυφχψ. abundantia] multitudine δεζϑιλμξοπρστυφχψ. gloriabuntur] gloriantur δεζϑιλμξοπρστυφχψ.

8

Frater broður AD, broþur *H,* broðor BCE^{3}F*G*I, broþor J, broþer K

non | ne ABCE^{3}FGI*, na DHJ, nalyseð K

redemit* | aleseð A, alieseð B, alysyð C, alýseþ ł F*, aliseð J, alysede D, ælisede E$^{3/x}$*, alesde I*, onlysde GH (*M*)

redemit* aleseð A, alieseð B, alysyð C, alyseþ F, alyseð K, alesð I, aliseþ J*, he alysde DGH, ælisede E$^{3/x}$* (*LM*)

homo mon ABE^{3}*, mann CDG, man F*H*IJK

non | ne ABCDE^{3}FGHJ, he ne I, na K

dabit | seleð ABE^{3}, sylyð C, sileþ J, selð DHI, sylþ F, sylð G, gif K

deo gode ABCDE^{3}FGHIJK

placationem geðinge AB, geþinge C, gecwemnisse DH, gecwemnysse F, gecwemnesse GJK, gecwemnesse ł licungæ E$^{3/x}$*, gecwemnesse ł gladunge I*

suam his ABDE^{3}FGHIJK, hyra C (*L*)

ED: rédimit (H)] redimit *Campbell*. alýseþ ł (F)] alýseþ *Kimmens*. rédimet (H)] redimet *Campbell*. non (H)] Non *Campbell*.

OE: ne (I)] *eras. (of gloss?) before word.* alýseþ ł (F)] ł *added in light brown ink by corr., followed by eras.* ælisede (E[3/x]) (*1st*)] *orig.* æliseð: ð *altered to* d *by corr.*, e *added, gloss retraced.* alesde (I)] *eras. (of gloss?) after word.* aliseþ (J)] ⁊ *eras. after word (note preceding* redim&). ælisede (E[3/x]) (*2nd*)] *orig.* æliseð: ð *altered to* d *by corr.*, e *added, gloss retraced.* mon (E[3])] se *eras. before word.* gecwemnesse ł licungæ (E[3/x])] gecwemnesse ł *added by corr.* gecwemnesse ł gladunge (I)] ł gladunge *written in right margin.*

LTg: Frater] H: *initial letter faint but visible;* [ ]rater G: *fragment of initial letter visible.* redemit (*1st*)] M: *small eras. after* i, *perhaps orig.* i *altered to* e *and then back to* i. redemit (*2nd*)] M: *small eras. after* i, *perhaps orig.* i *altered to* e *and then back to* i; rédimet L. homo] H: *small eras. after word, perhaps of punct.* suam] L: *eras. after word.*

LTu: Frater] rater τ: *initial letter wanting.* redemit (*1st*)] redemet β. redemit (*2nd*)] redemet β; redimet ς.

GAg: redemit (*1st*)] redimit J, F: *1st* i *on eras.*, K: *1st* i *on eras. by corr.;* rédimit H: *2nd* i *on eras.*, I: *1st* i *altered from another letter.* redemit (*2nd*)] redimet FGIJK; rédimet H: *orig.* redimit: *2nd* i *altered to* e.

GAu: redemit (*1st*)] redimit ζιπτφχ, ξϱ: *orig.* redemit: *2nd* e *deleted,* i *interl.;* redimet ϑλσχ; redemet μψ; redimi ν. redemit (*2nd*)] redimet εζϑιλξοπϱστυφψ; redemet μ.

9

nec*	ne ABCDE[3], ⁊ FGIJK
pretium	weorð *A*BDFHI, wiorþ *E[3]*, wyrð *C*K, wurð *G*, wurh J (*LM*)
redemptionis	alesnisse *A*, aliesnesse B, alysnysse *C*, alisnesse E[3], alisnes J, alysednisse D, alysednysse FH, alysednes G, alesednesse I, alysednesse K
animae	sawle *ABCDFGIJK*, saule *H*, saul *E[3]* (*L*)
suae	his *ABDE[3]FGHIJK*, hyre *C* (*L*)
et	⁊ ABCE[3]*FGIJK
laborauit	won ABJ, wann *C*, he swang *DGH*, swanc *F*, he swinceð *I*, he swanc *K*, sceal swinccan *E[x]** (*LM*)
in	in A, on BCDE[3]FGHIJK
aeternum	ecnisse A*D*, ecnesse *BE[3]GHIJK*, ecnysse *CF* (*L*)

ED: Et (I)] et *Lindelöf.* redemptionis (C)] redemtionis *Wildhagen.* suę (E)] suae *Harsley.* sue (I)] suae *Lindelöf.* æternum (D)] aeternum *Roeder.* ęternum (E)] aeternum *Harsley.*

OE: ꝥ (E^{3})] *retraced by corr.* sceal swinccan (E^{3})] *on eras. by corr.*

LTg: pretium] A: *letter eras. after* r, C: r *interl.*, M: *orig.* praetium: a *deleted by dot in bowl;* prętium GL; precium E. redemptionis] A: mp *written by corr.*, C: *orig.* redemtionis: p *added outside left grid by corr.* animae] animæ B; animę CDGHIKL; anime EFJ. suae] suæ BKL; suę CDEFGH; sue J, I: *orig.* suae: a *eras.* laborauit] laborabit CDEFIKL, G: *orig.* laborauit: u *altered to* b, H: *2nd* b *altered from another letter,* M: *orig.* laborauit: u *deleted by subscript dot,* b *interl.* aeternum] æternum BDK; eternum CJL; ęternum EFGH.

LTu: pretium] praetium βμ; precium ιτ*τφ, ϱ: *orig.* pretium: t *deleted,* c *interl.* animae] animę ειλμνξσφ; animæ ϑ; anime πϛτ*τ. suae] suę ειλνξσφ; suæ ϑχ; sue ϛτ*τ. laborauit] laborabit δεζϑιλμνξοπϱφ. aeternum] ęternum ειλξφ; æternum ϑ; eternum σϛτ*τ.

GAg: nec] Et FGHIJK.

GAu: nec] Et δεζϑιλμξοπστυχψ.

10

et	ꝥ ABCE^{3}FGHIJK
uiuet	leofað *A*BFK, leofaþ J, he leofað DGHI, lyfað C, lifæþ E^{3}
(adhuc)*	nu gyt FI*, nu git J, gyt K
in	in A, on BCDE^{3}FGHIJK
finem	ende ABCDE^{3}FGHIJK

ED: nu git (J)] nugit *Brenner.*

OE: nu gyt (I)] *letter eras. after* t.

LTg: uiuet] A: *orig.* uiuit: *2nd* i *altered to* e.

LTu: uiuet] uiuit β.

GAg: uiuet] uiuet adhuc FGHJK, I: *eras. after* adhuc.

GAu: uiuet] uiuet adhuc δεζϑιλμξοπϱστυφχψ.

11

Quoniam*		forðon AB, forþon C, forðæn E^{3}
non	ǀ	ne ABCE^{3}*GJ,* na D*FHK,* he ne *I*
uidebit	ǀ	gesið A, gesihð B*CI*, gesihþ E^{3}, gesyhð K, he gesyhð D, he gesihð FH, he ne gesyhð G, sihþ J
interitum		forwyrd ABDG*HIK,* forwird E^{3}*, on forwyrd C, on forwird J, on ecnysse F*
cum		ðonne A, þonne BGI, þonne CDE^{x}FHJ, þænne K
uiderit		he gesið A, he gesihð BFH, he gesyhð DGK, he gesihþ E$^{3/x}$**I,* gesihð CJ

sapientes	snotre ABC, snotere J, wise ł snitro E[3/x]*, wise DFGHK, þa wisan ł ða snoteren I
morientes	sweltende ABDE[3]FGHIK, sweltynde C, swiltende J
simul	somud A, somod BD, samod CFGHI*JK, somed E[3]*
insipiens	se unwisa A*B*CJ, unwis DGH, unwise K, unwis ł snitro E[3/x]*, na wis F, se unsnotera ł se dysega I
et	⁊ ABDE[3]FGHIJK, ⁊ ⁊ C*
stultus	se ðygsa A, se dysega B, se disiga J, dysig CD*G, disig E[3]*FH, dysige K, se stunta I
peribunt	forweorðað ABG, forwurðað C, forweorþað DH, forwiorðæþ E[3], forweorðaþ I, forwurþeð J, forwyrðan K, losað ł forweorð F
Et	⁊ ABCDE[3]F*G*HIJ*K*
relinquent	forletað A, forlætað BC, forlæteþ J, hy forlætað DGH, hi forletæþ E[3/x]*, hi forlæteð F, hi forlætaþ IK
alienis	fremðum A, fremdum BJ, fremdum C, fremedum DH, fremedum G, fremdæn E[3]*, fremdan K, ælfremdum F, ælfremedum *I** (*M*)
diuitias	weolan A, welan BCDFGHIJK, welæn E[3]
suas	heara A, hira B, heora DFGHIJK, heræ E[3]*, hys C

ED: forðon (A)] for ðon *Kuhn.* forðæn (E)] Forðæn *Harsley.* uíderit (I)] uiderit *Lindelöf.* [ ]t (G)] Et *Rosier.* aliénis (I)] alienis *Lindelöf.*

OE: forwird (E[3])] *eras. (1–2 letters) before word.* on ecnysse (F)] ecnysse *eras. but visible.* he gesihþ (E[3/x])] he *on eras. by corr.* wise ł snitro (E[3/x])] wise ł *added by corr.* samod (I)] a *altered from* o. somed (E[3])] o *and left leg of* m *on eras. by corr.* unwis ł snitro (E[3/x])] *orig.* un/snitro: wis ł *added by corr.* ⁊ ⁊ (C)] *1st* ⁊ *on fol. 82r, 2nd on fol. 82v.* dysig (D)] rihtlice *written in left margin in 11th-c. hand as gloss on* iure *in marginal commentary:* Stultus iure discendus qui christum uenientem recipere noluit. disig (E[3])] *letter eras. after word.* hi forletæþ (E[3/x])] hi *added by corr.* fremdæn (E[3])] *eras. before word,* fr *retraced by corr., macron by corr., eras. after* ē. ælfremedum (I)] *2nd* e *interl.* heræ (E[3])] *orig.* hiræ: i *altered to* e *by corr.*

LTg: non] Non FGHIJK. uidebit] C: ui *interl.* interitum] HK: *small eras. after word, perhaps of punct.* uiderit] uíderit I. morientes] morięntes G. insipiens] insipientes B. Et] K: t *on eras. by main hand;* [ ]t G: *outline of initial* E *visible.* alienis] aliénis I; álienis M.

LTu: non] Non δεζϑιλμξοπϱστυφχψ. sapientes] sapientem ς: *cf. Weber MS* ε.

GAg: Quoniam] *om.* FGHIJK.

GAu: Quoniam] *om.* δεζϑιλμξοπϱστυφχψ.

12

et	⁊ ABCE^{3}FGHIJ*K*
sepulchra	byrgenne AB, byrgenna BD*GHI*, byrgynna C, birigene E^{3}*, birgena J, byrigene K, byrgen F
eorum	heara A, hira B, hyra C, heora DFGHIJK, heræ E^{3}*
domus	hus AB*C*DE^{3}HIK, husis G*, huses FJ
eorum*	heara A, hira B, hyra C, heora DFGIJ, heor(a) K*, heræ E^{3}*
in	in A, on BCDE^{3}FGHIJK
aeternum	ecnisse A*DH*, ecnesse *BE^{3}GIJK*, ecnysse *C*, écnysse *F* (*L*)
Tabernacula	geteld ABCDFGHJ*K*, Eærdungæ ł geteld E$^{3/x}$*, eardungstowa I*
eorum	heara A, hira B, hyra C, heora DFGHIJK, hioræ E^{3}
in	in *A*, on BCDE^{3}FGHIJ*K*
generatione*	cneorisse A*BDGHJ, cneorysse *C*, cneowrisse ł on cynrene E$^{3/x}$*, cynrine F, cynrene I
et	⁊ ABCDE^{3}*FGHIJ (*K*)
progenie	cynne *AB*CJ, forecynrene D*H*, forcynrene G, on mægþe *F*, cneorisse ł mægþe I, forecneowrisse *E^{3}** (*L*)
inuocabunt*	gecegað AB, gecigað C, gecigæþ E^{3}, hy gecigað D, hi gecigaþ J, hi cygað K, hi gecegdon F, hi gecigdon G, hi gecygdon I
nomina	noman AB, nomæn E^{3}, naman CDFGHIK, nama J
eorum*	heara A, hira B, hyra C, heora FGI, hiræ E^{3}, his J (*M*)
in	in A, on BCDE^{3}FGHIJK
terris	eorðum ADE^{x}*G, eorðum BJ, eorþum H, eorðan CF, eorþan K, eorðan ł landum I*
ipsorum*	heara A, hira B, hyra C, heora DFGI, hiræ E^{3}, his JK

ED: heor(a) (K) (*2nd*)] heora *Sisam*. æternum (D)] aeternum *Roeder*. ęternum (E)] aeternum *Harsley*. progenię (E)] progeniae *Harsley*.

OE: byrgenna (D)] a *eras. after 2nd* n *and written on other side of ascender of* l *in* sepulchra *below*. byrgenna (I)] s. sunt : ⁊ synt *written in left margin*. birigene (E^{3})] *final* e *added by corr*. heræ (E^{3}) (*1st*)] *orig*. hiræ: i *altered to* e *by corr*. husis (G)] *orig*. husus: *right leg of 2nd* u *eras. to form* i. heor(a) (K) (*2nd*)] a *partly lost*. heræ (E^{3}) (*2nd*)] *orig*. hiræ: i *altered to* e *by corr*. Eærdungæ ł geteld (E$^{3/x}$)] ł geteld *added by corr*. eardungstowa (I)] s. manet : wuniaþ *written in left margin*. cneorisse (A)] n *interl*. cneowrisse ł on cynrene (E$^{3/x}$)] ł on cynrene *added by corr*., ł *on eras*. ⁊ (E^{3}) (*2nd*)] *eras. before word*. forecneowrisse (E^{3})] *final* e *on eras. by corr*. eorðum (E^{x})] *on eras*. eorðan ł landum (I)] ł landum *written in right margin*.

LTg: et (*1st*)] K (*as* e÷t:): e *altered by main hand from* E. domus] domos C. aeternum] æternum BDKL; ęternum CEFGHI. Tabernacula] K: T *on eras. by main* *hand.* in (*2nd*)] A: *eras.* (*3–4 letters*) *after word;* i[ ] K: *letter lost due to excision of initial from fol. 51r.* et (*2nd*)] K: *written in left margin.* progenie] A: *letter eras. after* i, F: *eras.* (?) *after word,* H: *eras. below final* e, *perhaps of cauda;* progenię BE, L: *eras. after word.* eorum (*4th*)] M: *on eras.*

LTu: sepulchra] ς: h *interl.;* sepuchra ν. aeternum] ęternum εινξφ; æternum ϑ; eternum σςτ*τ. progenie] progeniae βυ; progenię π; progeniem μ.

GAg: eorum (*2nd*)] illorum FGHIJK. generatione] progenie FIJ, H: *eras. below final* e, *perhaps of cauda;* progenię G, K: *lost due to excision of initial from fol. 51r, gloss lost.* inuocabunt] uocauerunt FGHIJK. eorum (*4th*)] sua FGHIJ; su[ ] K: *letter lost due to excision of initial from fol. 51r, gloss lost, fragment of ascender visible.* ipsorum] suis FGHIJK.

GAu: eorum (*2nd*)] illorum δεζϑιλμξοπρστυφχψ. generatione] progenie δεζϑιλμξορτφχψ; progenię πυ; progenies σ. inuocabunt] uocauerunt δεζϑιλμξοπρστυφχψ. eorum (*4th*)] sua δεζϑιλμξοπρστυφχψ. ipsorum] suis δεζϑιλμξοπρστυφχψ.

13

Et — ⁊ ABCE^{3}FG*K* (*J*)
homo — mon ABE^{3}, mann CDF, man GHI*J*K
cum — mid ðy AB, mid þi J, mid þy þe C, mid E^{3}, þonne DFH, þonne G, þonne K, þa þa I*
in | he on ABCJ, on DFGHI*K
honore — are ABCJ, arweorþunge DH, arweorðunge G, arwurþunge F, wiorðmynde E^{3}*, weorðmynte I*, wyrðmynte K
esset | wes A, wæs BC, wes E^{3}, he wæs DGHI, wesan F*, bið J, byð K
non | ne ABE^{3}G*I,* na DFHJ*K,* he ne C
intellexit | onget he AB, ongiet E^{3}, he ongit J, ongæt C, ongyt K, he aget DH, he ageatt F, he ageat *G,* undergeat I
conparatus — efenameten *A,* efnmeten *B,* efenmete *J,* efyngemetyn *C,* efenameten ł wiðmeten *E^{x}**, wiðmeten D*FHI***K,* wiðmen *G* (*L*)
est — he is ABDHIJ, he ys C, is E^{3}FGJ*K*
iumentis — neatum AC, neatum B, netenum D, nietenum E^{3}, nytenum I, nytenum J, nitenu F, nytenu G, nyten H, nyte[ ] *K**
insipientibus — ðæm unwisum A, unwisum BCHI, unwisum DJ, on unwisum FG, unwisan K, unwisum ł unsnytrum E$^{3/x}$*
et — ⁊ ABCDE^{3}FGHIJK
similis — gelic ABCE^{3}FGHI*JK, gelic D*
factus — geworden ABDE^{3}FGHIJ, gewordyn C, gedon K

est	is ABE^{3}FGJ, he ys C*, he is DHI (*K*)
illis	him ABCE^{3}FGH, him DJ, heom I (*K*)

ED: mid þy þe (C)] midþy þe *Wildhagen.* þa þa (I)] þaþa *Lindelöf.* comparatus (C)] co[n]paratus *Wildhagen.*

OE: þa þa (I)] *on eras.* (?). on (I)] *on eras.* (?). wiorðmynde (E^3)] y *altered from another letter* (i?) *by corr.* weorðmynte (I)] *on eras.* (?). wesan (F)] an *eras. but visible.* efenameten ł wiðmeten (E^x)] efenameten *on eras.*, ł wiðmeten *added.* wiðmeten (I)] *on eras.* (?). nyte[ ] (K)] *letters lost due to excision of initial from fol. 51r.* unwisum ł unsnytrum (E$^{3/x}$)] unwisum ł *added by corr.* gelic (I)] *eras. after word.* gelic (D)] [ ](n)licnesse, *with left leg of* n *cropped, written in left margin in 11th-c. hand as gloss on* imaginem dei *in marginal commentary:* qui intellegit se habere imaginem dei debet facere ea que dei sunt. he ys (C)] he *interl.*

LTg: Et] E÷t: K: *see v. 12; om.* J. homo] Homo J. non] I: *eras. above word;* no[ ] K: *final letter lost due to excision of initial from fol. 51r.* intellexit] intellex[ ] G. conparatus] comparatus ABEFGHIJKL; comparatus C: *letter eras. after* o, *macron added by corr.* est (*1st*)] ést K. iumentis] iu[ ] K: *letters lost due to excision of initial from fol. 51r.* est (*2nd*)] K: *lost due to excision of initial from fol. 51r.* illis] K: *lost due to excision of initial from fol. 51r.*

LTu: Et] *om.* ϑσ. homo] Homo ϑσ. conparatus] comparatus δζϑιμνξοπϱςτ*τυχ; cōparatus λσφ.

14

Haec	ðes A*BE^3*, þes *CDFGH*I**JK* (*L*)
uia	weg ABCDE$^{3/x}$*FGHI*JK
eorum*	heara A, hira B, hyra C, heora DFGIJK, hioræ E^3
scandalum	eswic A, æswic BCDGHK, ǽswic biþ F, æswicung I, æswic ł wroht E^x*, æswic ł wroht biþ J
ipsis	him ABCDE^{3}FG, him JK, hym H, him sylfa I
et	⁊ ABCDE^{3}FGHIJK
postea	efter ðon A, æfter ðon B, æftyr þon C, æfter þon J, efter þæm E^3, syþðan D, syþþan F, syððan GI, siþþan H, syþan K (*L*)
in	in A, on BCDE^{3}FGI*JK, o H
ore	muþe A*IJ, muðe BCDE^{3}FGH, mvðe K
suo	heara A, hira B, hyra C, heora IJK, hiræ E^3, his DFGH
benedicent*	bledsiað AC, bletsiað B, bletsiæþ E^3, hy bletsiað D, hi bletsiað F*, hi bletsiaþ J, hig geliciað G*, hi beoð gecwemde ł hig geliciaþ I

ED: Hæc (D)] Haec *Roeder.* Hęc (E)] Haec *Harsley.* him sylfa (I)] him sylfa *Lindelöf.* postea (A)] post ea *Kuhn.* æftyr þon (C)] æftyrþon *Wildhagen.*

OE: þes (I)] s. est : is *written in left margin.* weg ($E^{3/x}$)] g *added by corr.* weg (I)] *eras. after word.* æswic ł wroht (E^{x})] æswic *on eras.*, ł wroht *added.* on (I)] *eras. before word.* muþe (A)] þ *altered from* n. hi bletsiað (F)] bletsiað *eras. but visible.* hig geliciað (G)] *3rd* i *interl.*

LTg: Haec] Hæc BDKL; Hęc EFH; [ ]aec G. postea] póstea L.

LTu: Haec] Hęc ειξφ; Hec ϑσςτ*τ.

GAg: eorum] illorum FGHIJK. benedicent] conplacebunt F; complacebunt GHIJK.

GAu: eorum] illorum δεζϑιλμξοπρστυφχψ. benedicent] conplacebunt δεζϑμχψ; complacebunt ιλξοπρστυ; cōplacebunt φ.

15

Sicut	swe swe A, swa swa BCDFGHIJ, swæ swæ $E^{3/x}$*, swa K
oues	scep ABCE^{3}, sceap DFGHIJK
in	in A, on BCDE^{3}FGHIJK
inferno	helle ABCDE^{3}FGJ, hello H, hele K, hellebrogan I
positi	gesette *A*BCD$E^{3/x}$*FGHI**J*K (*M*)
sunt	sind A, sint B, synd CFGJK, sindon E^{3}, hi syndon I
et*	⁊ ABCE^{3}
mors	deað ABCFGH, deaþ DI*JK, deæþ E^{3}
depascet	misfoedeð *A*B, misfedeþ J, fedyð C, fedeþ F, afedeþ I, misfedeþ ł fritt $E^{3/x}$*, fritt *D*H, frytt G, fryt K (*M*)
eos	hie AB, hi *CK*, hy DGH, híí E^{3}, hig FIJ
Et	⁊ A*B*CE^{3}FGIJK
obtinebunt*	bigetað AB, begytað *C*, begitæþ E^{3}, oferswiþað D, oferswiþaþ F*, oferswiðaþ J, oferswiðaþ J, oferswiþæð K, gewyldað G, geanwealdiaþ ł gewyldaþ I
eos*	hie AB, hi CK, hy D, híí E^{3}, heora FGIJ
iusti	ða rehtwisan A, rihtwisan I*, ryhtwise BD, rihtwise CFGHK, rihtwisnes J, soðfeste E^{3}
in	in A, on BCDFGIJK, ðe on E^{3}
matutino	margentid A, morgentid B, morgyntide C, morgentid ł un uhtontid J, glæterunga D, uhttide ł in morgentid $E^{3/x}$*, uhttide F, uhtanning G, dægrede I, dægred K
et	⁊ ABCDE^{3}FGHIJK
auxilium	fultum ABCE^{3}FGIJ, fultum DH, fyltum K
eorum	heora ADFG*H*IJK, hira B, hyra C, hiræ E^{3}
ueterescet	aldað *A*, ealdað B*C*, eældæþ *E^{3}*, ealdaþ J, ealdiaþ *K*, forrotað D*GH*, forrotaþ ł ealdað *F**, forealdaþ *I**
in	in AJ, on BCDE^{x}FGHIK

inferno	helle ACDE[x]FG*H*IK, on helle BJ
et*	⁊ ABCE[3]
a	from A, fram BD*GHJ*K, fram *E*[3]FI, of C (*M*)
gloria	wuldre ABCDFGIJ, wuldra HK, wuldor E[3]
sua*	his AC*, hira B, heora DFGHIJK, hiræ E[3]
expulsi*	onweg adrifene AE[x]*, onweg adrifyne C, aweg adrifene B, anydde D
sunt*	sind A, sint BE[3], synd C, hy synt D

ED: swa swa (GIJ) swaswa *Rosier, Lindelöf, Oess.* depascet (D)] depascit *Roeder.* híí (E) (*1st*)] hii *Harsley.* híí (E) (*2nd*)] hii *Harsley.* et (D) (*3rd*) *no gloss*] ⁊ *Roeder.* á (E)] a *Harsley.* onweg adrifene (A)] on weg adrifene *Kuhn.* onweg adrifyne (C)] onwegadrifyne *Wildhagen.*

OE: swæ swæ (E[3/x])] *2nd* swæ *added by corr.* gesette (E[3/x])] ge *retraced,* sette *on eras. by corr.* gesette (I)] ge *on eras.* (?). deaþ (I)] *eras.* (?) *after word.* misfedeþ ł fritt (E[3/x])] mis *and* ł fritt *added by corr.* oferswiþaþ (F)] *eras. but visible.* rihtwisan (I)] *orig.* rihtwisen: e *altered to* a, n *in same darker ink.* uhttide ł in morgentid (E[3/x])] uht *retraced by corr.,* tide *on eras.,* ł in morgentid *added.* forrotaþ ł ealdað (F)] rotaþ *eras. but visible.* forealdaþ (I)] *eras. after* r. his (C)] i *interl.* onweg adrifene (E[x])] *on eras.*

LTg: positi] A: *final* i *on eras. by corr.,* M: *orig.* positae: ae *deleted by subscript dots,* i *interl.;* possiti J. depascet] A: *2nd* e *on eras. by corr.,* DM: *orig.* depascit: i *altered to* e. eos (*1st*)] eós K. Et] et B. obtinebunt] C: *1st* b *altered from another letter* (p?). eorum] H: *added interl. by glossator.* ueterescet] A: *4th* e *on eras. by corr.;* ueterascet EG, CFI: *orig.* ueterescet: *3rd* e *deleted by subscript dot,* a *interl.,* H: *orig.* ueterescet: *3rd* e *altered to* a, K: a *on eras. by corr.* inferno (*2nd*)] H: *small eras. after word.* a] H: *small eras. after word;* á EM; ac G.

LTu: positi] possiti ϑ; posita ς. depascet] depacet ψ; depascit ς: *cf. Weber MSS* MSγε. matutino] matutina ς. ueterescet] ueterascet ι, ϱ: *orig.* ueterescet: *3rd* e *deleted,* a *interl.;* ueterescent ς: *cf. Weber MSS* moz[x]. a] ac ιλφ, ϱσ: *orig.* a: c *interl.; om.* ς: *cf. Weber MSS* α*ζ[2]η* moz[c].

GAg: et (*1st*)] *om.* FGHIJK. obtinebunt] dominabuntur FGHIJK. eos] eorum FGHIJK. et (*3rd*)] *om.* FGHIJK. sua] eorum FGHIJK. expulsi sunt] *om.* FGHIJK.

GAu: et (*1st*)] *om.* δεζϑιλμξοπϱστυφχψ. obtinebunt] dominabuntur δεζϑιλμξοπϱστυφχψ. eos] eorum δεζϑιλμξοπϱστυφχψ. et (*3rd*)] *om.* δεζϑιλμξοπϱστυφχψ. sua] eorum δεζιλμξοπϱστυφχψ. expulsi sunt] *om.* δεζϑιλμξοπϱστυφχψ.

16

Uerumtamen	hweðre soðlice A, hwæðre soðlice *B*, hwæþere soþlice *J*, soðlice þehhwæðere *C*, þeahhwæþre *DI*, þeahhweþre *E*$^{3/x}$*, ðeahhwæðere *F*, þeahhwæðere *G*, þeahhwæþere *H**, witodlice *K** (*LM*)
deus	god ABCE^{3}FGIJK
liberauit*	gefreað *A*, gefreoð C, gefriolsæþ *E*^{3}, alieseð B, alyseð FG, aleseð I, aliseþ J, alyseð K, alysde *D* (*LM*)
animam	sawle ABCDE^{3}FGHIJK
meam	mine ABCDE^{3}FHIJK (*G*)
de	of ABCDE^{3}F*G*HIJK
manu	honda AB, handa DFGHIJK, hænde E^{3}, hand C
inferi	helle ABC*DE*^{x}*FJK, on helle GH, hellebrogan I (*M*)
dum*	ðonne AK, þonne BFI, þonne CDJ, midþi E^{3}*
acceperit	onfoeð A, he onfoehð B, he onfehð *C*E$^{3/x}$*I*, he onfeh(ð) *G**, he anfehð DHK, he afecð F, hig onfoþ J (*M*)
me	mec A, me BCE^{3}FHIJK (*G*)

ED: Verumtamen (BD)] Verum tamen *Brenner;* Uerumtamen *Roeder.* Veruntamen (C)] Veru[m]tamen *Wildhagen.* [ ]erumptamen (G)] Verumptamen *Rosier.* þeahhwæþre (DI)] þeah hwæþre *Roeder, Lindelöf.* þeahhweþre (E)] þeah hweþre *Harsley.* þeahhwæðere (G)] þeah hwæðere *Rosier.* þeahhwæþere (H)] þeah hwæþere *Campbell.* liberabit (D)] libera[u]it *Roeder.* [ ]e (G)] *de Rosier.* of (G)] [ ]f *Rosier.* acceperi[ ] (G)] accepe*rit Rosier.* he onfeh(ð) (G)] he onfen[ ] *Rosier.*

OE: þeahhweþre (E$^{3/x}$)] þeah *on eras. by corr.* þeahhwæþere (H)] *descender of 2nd* þ *partly lost due to eras. in Lat. line below.* witodlice (K)] *1st* i *partly effaced from eras. in Lat. line above.* helle (E^{x})] *on eras.* midþi (E^{3})] *final* i *retouched* (?). he onfehð (E$^{3/x}$)] he *added by corr.* he onfehð (I)] *eras. before* he. he onfeh(ð) (G)] *cross-stroke of* ð *not visible.*

LTg: Uerumtamen] Verumtamen BDEIL; Veruntamen C: *eras. after* u, H: *eras. after 1st* n; Uerumptamen FJ; Verumptamen K; [ ]erumptamen G. liberauit] liberabit EL, A: *2nd* b *on eras. by corr.*, DM: *2nd* b *on eras.* meam] *lost* G. de] [ ]e G. inferi] inferni DM: *cf. Weber MSS* αγη* moz. acceperit] M: *orig.* acciperit: *1st* i *altered to* e; aceperit C; acceperi[ ] G. me] *lost* G.

LTu: Uerumtamen] Ueruntamen βεζλτ*τχ; Veruntamen ισφ; Verumptamen ξς; Verumtamen ο; Uerumptamen υ. liberauit] liberabit τ*. inferi] inferni ϑ: *cf. Weber MSS* αγη* moz. acceperit] acciperit β.

GAg: liberauit] redimet FGHIJK. dum] cum FGHIJ, K: *small eras.* (?) *before* c.

GAu: liberauit] redimet δεζϑιλμξοπϱστυφχψ. dum] cum δεζϑιλμξοπϱστυφχψ.

17

Ne	ne ABCDFHIJ, Ne E^{3}, na K (*G*)
timueris	ondred ðu A, ondræd ðu B, ondræd þu *C*K, andræd þu D*H*, adræd ðu F, [ ]ræd þu *G*, ondred þu þe E^{3}, ondræd þu þe na I*, ondræd þu þe J
cum	ðonne A, þonne BFIK, þonne CDE^{x}*HJ, þonne G
diues	weolig A, welig BCDGHIJ, welyg E$^{3/x}$*, weli K, weligan F
factus	geworðen A, geworden BDE^{3}*F*GHIJ, gewordyn C, gedon K
fuerit	bið ABCDGHIK, biþ FJ, bieð E^{3}
homo	mon ABE^{3}, mann CD, man FHIJK, [ ]ann *G*
et	⁊ ABCE^{3}FGHIJK
cum	ðonne AK, þonne BFGI, þonne CDE^{x}*J, þonn[ ] H*
multiplicata	gemonigfaldad A, gemonigfaldod B, gemonifalded E$^{3/x}$*, gemænigfealdod J, gemænigfyld DFI*, gemænigfylled G, gemeenifyld H, gemanifæld K*, gemonig C (*L*)
fuerit	bið ABCDE^{3}GH*K*, biþ FI*J
gloria	wuldur ACDH, wuldor BE^{3}FGIJK
domus	huses ABDFGHJK, hus CE^{3}, husrædenne I
eius	his ABCE^{3}FHIJ*K*

ED: [ ]mueris (G)] *tim*ueris *Rosier.* timúeris (H)] timueris *Campbell.* [ ]ræd þu (G)] [ ]ræd *Rosier.* geworden (F)] geworgden *Kimmens.* þonn[ ] (H)] þonne *Campbell.*

OE: ondræd þu þe na (I)] [ ]rædst *written in left margin.* þonne (E^{x}) (*1st*)] *on eras.* welyg (E$^{3/x}$)] we *retraced,* lyg *on eras. by corr., eras. after gloss.* geworden (E^{3})] geword *retraced.* geworden (F)] g *eras. after* r. þonne (E^{x}) (*2nd*)] *on eras.* þonn[ ] (H)] *final letter fragmentary, only tip visible.* gemonifalded (E$^{3/x}$)] ed *added by corr.* gemænigfyld (I)] ld *on eras., eras. after word.* gemanifæld (K)] bið *eras. after word.* biþ (I)] *on eras.*

LTg: Ne] *lost* G. timueris] timúeris CH; [ ]mueris G. homo] [ ]omo G. multiplicata] L: *on eras.* (?), *written slightly above line.* fuerit] K: *on eras. by corr.* eius] eíus K.

LTu: factus] π: *interl. by corr.* multiplicata] mul/multiplicata β.

18

Quoniam	forðon ABJ, forþon C, forðæn E^{3}*, forðon þe I, forþam þe *G*
non*	nales AB, nalys C, na DE^{x}*
cum	ðonne *A*, þonne BFGI, þonne *C*DE^{x}*J (*L*)
morietur*	he swilteð AB, he swylteð E^{x}*, swylt D, he swylt FJ, gemænigfealdud C, he forwyrð GI* (*L*)
(non)*	| ne FJ, he ne GI, na K

accipiet*	onfoð A, onfoehð B, onfehð C, onfehþ E^{3}, anfehð D, underfehð GI*, hym he ⁊ F, nimþ ⁊ J*, beo ⁊ K*
haec*	ðas A*B*, þas *CD*, ðæs *E*^{3} (*L*)
omnia	all A, ealle BCDGIK, eallæ E^{3}, ealla H, ealle his þyngc F, ealle his þing J (*L*)
neque	ne A*BCE^{3}, na J, ⁊ na DGHK, ⁊ ne F, ne na I
simul*	somud AC, somod BD, semed E^{3}
descendit*	astigeð AB, astigyð *C*, adune astag D, adune astah FH, adunnestah G, adune astige J, dun astah K, astæh adune *E*$^{3/x}$*, niðerastigeþ I (*LM*)
cum	mid ABCDE^{3}FGHIJK
eo*	hine A, him BCE^{3}FGHI, hi<u>m</u> DJK
gloria	wuldur ACDH, wuldor BE^{3}FGIJK
domus*	huses ABD, hus CE^{3}
eius	his ABCDE^{3}FGHIJ*K*

ED: Quoniam (B)] quoniam *Brenner.* [ ]uoniam (G)] Quoniam *Rosier.* forðon (A)] for ðon *Kuhn.* forðæn (E)] Forðæn *Harsley.* cvm (D)] cum *Roeder.* interíerit (H)] interierit *Campbell.* hæc (D)] haec *Roeder.* hęc (E)] haec *Harsley.* adunnestah (G)] adun ne stah *Rosier.* astæh adune (E)] astǽh adúne *Harsley.*

OE: forðæn (E^{3})] n *retouched.* na (E^{x})] *on eras.* þon<u>ne</u> (E^{x})] *on eras.* he swylteð (E^{x})] *on eras.* he forwyrð (I)] *eras.* (bið?) *after* he. underfehð (I)] *partly on eras.* (?). nimþ ⁊ (J)] ⁊ *crossed through in lighter ink* (*note* sum&). beo ⁊ (K)] *lemma misread as* sum et. ne (A)] *gloss* (*7 letters?*) *eras. before word.* astæh adune (E$^{3/x}$)] adune *added by corr., transposition marks* (astæ̋h adűne > adűne astæ̋h) *eras.*

LTg: Quoniam] [ ]uoniam G: *letter fragments visible in initial position.* cum (*1st*)] A: u *on eras. by corr.;* cvm D. cum morietur] commorietur L. haec] hæc BDL; hęc CE. neque] nequę G. descendit] E: i *on eras.*, t *retraced in darker ink;* descendet CL; discendet M: *orig.* discendit: *2nd* i *altered to* e: *see Weber MSS* PQRUαδη moz med, *see GAg.* eius] eíus K.

LTu: non cum] cum non τ*. haec] hęc ν; hec τ*. descendit] descendet ν: *see GAu.*

GAg: non] *om.* FGHIJK. morietur] interierit non FGIJK; interíerit non H. accipiet] sumet FGJK, H: *eras. after* u, met *interl. by corr.*, I: et (&) *on eras.* haec] *om.* FGHIJK. simul] *om.* FGHIJK. descendit] descendet FGIJK, H: *orig.* descendit: i *altered to* e, CL: *see LTg.* domus] *om.* FGHIJK.

GAu: non] *om.* δεζϑιλμξοπϱστυφχψ. morietur] interierit non δεζϑιλμξοπϱστυφχψ. accipiet] sumet δεζϑιλμξοπϱστυφχψ. haec] *om.* δεζϑιλμξοπϱστυφχψ. simul] *om.* δεζϑιλμξοπϱστυφχψ. descendit] descendet δεζϑιλμξοπϱστυφχψ, ν: *see LTu.* eo] eo pone ϑ: *cf. Weber MS* η* (*Ga. sub ast.*). domus] *om.* δεζιλμξοπϱστυφχψ.

19

Quoniam*	forðon ABFJ, forþon C, Forðan E^{x}*, forþā K, forþon þe I, forþy G
anima	sawul A, sawl BCDGH, sæwl E^{3}, sawla F, sawle IJ, sawel K
eius	his A*B*CDE^{3}FGHIJ*K*
in	in A, on BCDE^{3}FGHIJK
uita	life ABCDE^{3}GHIJK, lyfe F
ipsius	his ABCDE^{3}GHIJ*K*, hys F
benedicetur	bið gebledsad *A*, bið gebledsod C*, bið gebletsod BD*GHIK, bið gebletsad $E^{3/x}$*, biþ gebletsod J, biþ geblesod F
et*	⁊ ABCE^{3}
confitebitur	we ondettað A, we andyttað C, ondetteð B, bið geandet DGHK, bið geandette $E^{3/x}$*, bið geandetteþ F*, he andet I, ic andetta J
tibi	ðe ABF, þe CDGHIJK
dum*	ðonne AF, þonne BHIK, þonne CDE^{x}*J, þonne G
benefeceris	ðu bledsas A, ðu wel dest BE$^{3/x}$*, þu wel dest CDF*GI*JK, hu wel dest H
ei	him ABC*E^{3}FG, him DIJK (*H*)

ED: forðon (A)] for ðon *Kuhn*. bið gebledsod (C)] bið gebletsod *Wildhagen*. ðu wel dest (E)] ðu weldest *Harsley*. þu wel dest (F)] þu wealdest *Kimmens*.

OE: Forðan (E^{x})] For *on eras*. bið gebledsod (C)] *orig*. bið gebletsod: t *altered to* d. bið gebletsod (D)] [ ]ehirea *written in left margin in 11th-c. hand to left of marginal gloss* cum diripiunt, *minim visible before 1st* e; *Roeder* (*p. xv*) *suggests* [þonn]e hi rea[fiað] (Mali tunc deum benedicunt quando temporalia bona precipiunt ⁊ cum diripiunt pauperes dicunt [*etc.*]). bið gebletsad ($E^{3/x}$)] bið *added by corr*. bið geandette ($E^{3/x}$)] bið ge *on eras. by corr*. bið geandetteþ (F)] teþ *eras. but visible*. þonne (E^{x})] *on eras*. ðu wel dest ($E^{3/x}$)] de *on eras. by corr*. þu wel dest (F)] *orig*. þu wealdest: a *eras*. þu wel dest (I)] *written as* þu dest: *eras*. (*3–4 letters?*) *after* þu, *with* wel *written in right margin as gloss on* bene, *also in right margin*. him (C)] m *partly obscured by show-through*.

LTg: eius] B: *on eras.;* eíus K. ipsius] ípsius K. benedicetur] A: *orig*. benedicitur: *2nd* i *altered to* e. ei] H: *orig*. ęi: *cauda eras*.

LTu: Quoniam] uoniam τ*: *initial letter wanting*. et] *interl*. β. ei] illi ι.

GAg: Quoniam] Quia FGHIJK. et] *om*. FGHIJK. dum] cum FGHIJK.

GAu: Quoniam] Quia δεζθιλμξοπϱστυφχψ. et] *om*. δεζθιλμξοπϱστυφχψ. dum] cum δεζθιλμξοπϱστυφχψ.

20

Et*	⁊ ABCE³
introibit	ingaeð A, ingæð BC, ingeð E³/ˣ*, he ingæð D*GH*, he ingæþ *IJK*, he infærð *F*
usque	oð ABC*G*HK, oþ DI*, oðþe E³*, oðþæt F, oðþæt J
in	in A, on BCDE³FGH
progeniem*	cyn AB, cynn C, cyn forecirreþ J, forecynred D, forekinred E³, forecyrred H, cynrynes F, cynrene G, cynren K, cneorisse I
patrum	feddra A, fædra BC, fædera DFJK, fæder GH, fedræ E³, fæderena I
suorum	his ABD, heora CFGIJK, hioræ E³
et*	⁊ ABCDE³ (*K*)
usque	oð ABC*FGHI*, oþ K, oððet E³, oþðæt J
in	in A, on BCDE³FGHJK
aeternum	ecnisse A*D*, ecnesse *BGH*IJ*K*, ecnysse *C*, eccnesse *E³*, écnysse *F* (*L*)
non	| ne ABCE³GJ, na DFHK, he ne I
uidebit	| gesið A, gesihð BCHI, gesihð D, gesioþ E³, gesyhð *G*, gesihþ J, gesyh he F, geseah K
lumen	leht A, leoht BCDFGHIJK, lioht E³

ED: oðþæt (F)] oð þæt *Kimmens.* oðþæt (J)] oð þæt *Oess.* cyn forecirreþ (J)] cyn fore cirreþ *Oess.* oþðæt (J)] oþ ðæt *Oess.* æternum (D)] aeternum *Roeder.* ęternum (E)] aeternum *Harsley.*

OE: ingeð (E³/ˣ)] ge *on eras. by corr.* oþ (I)] *eras.* (?) *after word.* oðþe (E³)] *letter eras. after* e. oð (C) (*2nd*)] *orig.* on: n *altered to* ð. oð (I)] *eras. after word.*

LTg: introibit] Introibit FGHIJK. usque (*1st*)] usquę G. .et] K: *added interl. by corr.* aeternum] æternum BD; eternum C; ęternum EFGHKL. uidebit] uideb[ ] G.

LTu: introibit] introiuit β; Introibit δεζϑιλξπρστυφχψ. aeternum] ęternum ειξφ; æternum ϑ; eternum σςτ*τ.

GAg: Et] *om.* FGHIJK. progeniem] progenies FGHIJK. et] *om.* FGHIJ.

GAu: Et] *om.* δεζϑιλμξοπρστυφχψ. progeniem] progenies δεζϑιλμξοπρστυφχψ. et] *om.* δεζιμξοπρσυχψ.

21

Et*	⁊ ABCE³ (M*)
homo	monn A, mon B, mann *CFG*, man DE³/ˣ**HI*JK*
cum	ða ðe A, þa ða B, þa þe C, þa þa FGIJ, þa DEˣ*H, þonne K

in	I	he in AC, he on BDE^{x}*FGHIJ, on K
honore		are ABC, hare J, weorþscipe D, wurðscype F, weorðscipe ł are E^{x}*, woruldscipe G, woruldscype H, arweorþunge I, wyrþmynte K
esset		wes AE^{x}*, wæs BCDFGHI*J, biþ K
non	I	ne ABCE^{3}I, na FK, he ne DGH, ⁊ na J
intellexit	I	onget he AB, ongęt he C, ongiet he E^{3}, he ongeat F, ongyt K, anget D, ageat GH, ongeat I, ongiteþ J
conparatus	I	efenmeten *A,* efenmeten *B,* efynmetyn *C,* he wæs wiðmeten D*GH,* wiðmeten *J,* þæt he wiðmeten *K,* he wæs togeteald *F,* gemætfæsted *I,* gemetfest ł efenmeten *E^{3}** (*LM*)
est	I	wes A, wæs BJ, he wæs I, ys C, is DE^{3}G*K*
iumentis		neatum AC, neatum B, nytenum DJ, nytenum FGHI, nutenan K, nietenum E^{3}
insipientibus		unwisum ABCDGH, unwisum J, unwissum K, on unwisum F*, unsnytrum ł unwise E$^{3/x}$*, unsnoterum ł dysegum I
et		⁊ ABCE^{3}*F**GHIJK
similis		gelic ABCE^{3}FGHIJK
factus		geworden ABE^{3}FGHIJ, gewordyn C, gedon K
est		is ABE^{3}FJ*K,* ys C, he is GHI
illis		his AE^{3}*, him BCFGHJ, him K, heom I

ED: þa þa (IJ)] þaþa *Lindelöf, Oess.* wurðscype (F)] worðscype *Kimmens.* woruldscype (H)] woruldscipe *Campbell.* comparatus (C)] co[n]paratus *Wildhagen.* on unwisum (F)] on unwinsum *Kimmens.*

OE: M: *written in right margin as gloss to entire verse:* þa þa se man on wurþmynte wæs he hyt ne under-stód ac wæs wiþmeten stuntum nytenum. ⁊ him gelíc geworden. man (E$^{3/x}$)] *orig.* mon: o *altered to* a *by corr.* man (I)] *eras. before word.* þa (E^{x})] *on eras.* he on (E^{x})] *on eras.* weorðscipe ł are (E^{x})] *on eras.* wes (E^{x})] *on eras.* wæs (I)] *eras. after word.* gemetfest ł efenmeten (E^{3})] g *and 1st* m *retouched.* on unwisum (F)] *orig.* on unwinsum: n *eras.* unsnytrum ł unwise (E$^{3/x}$)] ł unwise *added by corr.* ⁊ (F)] *added by corr.* his (E^{3})] s *altered from another letter, eras. after word.*

LTg: homo] Homo FGHIJK. conparatus] M: n *altered from another letter;* comparatus ABFGHIJKL, E: com *on eras.;* comparatus C: *eras. after* o, *macron added by corr.* est (*1st*)] ést K. et] F: *added by corr.* est (*2nd*)] ést K.

LTu: homo] Homo δεζϑιλμξοπϱστυφχψ. conparatus] comparatus εϑιμνξοπϱςτ*τφχ, β: *orig.* conparatus: n *crossed through,* m *interl.;* cōparatus ζλσυ.

GAg: Et] *om.* FGHIJK.

GAu: Et] *om.* δεζϑιλμξοπϱστυφχψ.

PSALM 49

1

Deus		god *ACF**GIJ, God *E^{x}* (*BDHKM*)
deorum		goda AB*C*DE^{x}GHIJ, ealra goda F
dominus		drihten E^{x}FI, drihtyn C, dryht̄ AB, drih́t G, driht̄ H, drih́ J
locutus	|	spreocende A, sprecende BE^{3}*FIJ, sprecynde C, spræcende G, spræc D*H,* spæc K
est	|	wes A, wæs F, is BE^{x}GJ, ys C, wæs ł spræc I (*K*)
et		⁊ ABCE^{3}FGHIJK
uocauit		cede A, cegde B, gecigde CJ, gecegde F, he gecygde I, chigð ł cleopede E$^{3/x}$*, cleopude D, cleopode GH*, clypede K*
terram		eorðan ABCFH*I, eorðæn E^{3}, eorþan K, on eorðan G, eorðam J
A		from AE^{3}, from̲ C, fram I, fram̲ J, of DFG*H*K (*B*)
solis		sunnan ACDGHIJK, sunnæn E^{3}, sunan F, from̲ sunnan B
ortu		upcyme A, upgonge B, upgange E^{3}J, upryne C, upspringe̲ D, upspringe I, upsprince F, oppringe G, upspinge K
usque		oð ABCFGHJ, oþ DK, oððe E^{3}, oþþe I
ad		(*G*)
occasum		setgong *A,* setlgong B, setlgang DJ, setlgange E^{x}*IK, setlgan H, setlgan ł oð setlunge G, setellung F, iestdæl C

ED: A (H)] *A Campbell.* from (E)] From *Harsley.*

OE: god (F)] *written in bowl of* D *in* DS̄. sprecende (E^{3})] *possibly by corr.* chigð ł cleopede (E$^{3/x}$)] ł cleopede *added by corr.* cleopode (H)] *1st* e *partly obscured.* clypede (K)] cy *eras. before word.* eorðan (H)] *otiose* (?) *stroke above* a. setlgange (E^{x})] *on eras.*

LTg: Deus] DS̄ ABDHKM, F: S *written within bowl of* D; DEVS C; DEUS E. deorum] DEORVM C. locutus] loqutus H: *orig.* locutus: c *altered to* q. est] ést K. A] H: *lost, outline visible only; om.* B. ad] et G. occasum] A: *eras.* (*5–6 letters*) *after word, initial* e *visible.*

LTu: Deus] DEVS ις; DEUS τ*τφ; DS̄ βλμνϱχψ. deorum] Deorum β; DEORUM λμνψ; DEORVM ϱ. dominus] DN̄S λμϱψ. locutus] LOCUTUS λϱ. est] EST λ.

2

ex	of *A*BCE^{3}FGJ
sion	sione *ABCE^{3},* seonne G, sion FJ (I**M*)
species	hiow A, hyow E^{3}, hiw BCGHIK, hyw D, hiwes J, hyhtes F*

decoris | wlites ABDGHJK, wlitys C, wlitan F, his E^{3}I
eius | his ABCFGHJ, wlites E^3*I

ED: syon (C)] sion *Wildhagen.* sion (IK)] sione *Lindelöf;* Sion *Sisam.*

OE: sion (I, *Lat.*)] est : is *written in left margin.* hyhtes (F)] *obscured by eras. but visible.* wlites (E^3)] s *added by corr.* (?).

LTg: ex] A: *added by corr. in left margin.* sion] A: *added by corr. in left margin;* syon E, C: *orig.* sion: i *deleted by subscript dot,* y *interl.;* sîon M.

LTu: ex sion] ξπ: s *interl.;* exion δσςυ; ex syon ειτ*τφ.

3
Deus god *A*BCE^{3}F*G*JK
manifestus* sweotullice *A,* sweotollice *B,* swutollice *C,* swutelice I, switolloce J, eawunga *D*FGH, openliche *E*^{x}*, openlice K (*LM*)
ueniet cymeð AGH, cymyð C, cimeþ E^3, cymeþ DFJ, cymð BK, cymþ I
deus god A*B*CE^{3}FGIJK
noster ur A, ure *BC*E^{3}FGIJK (*M*)
et ⁊ ACDE^{3}FGHIJ (*K*)
non | ne ACE^{3}I*, na K, he na DFGH
silebit | swigað ACDGK, swigaþ H, swigoð E$^{3/x}$*, swigeð F, swugaþ I

Ignis fyr ABCDE^{3}FGHIJK
in in A, on BCDE^{3}FGHIJK
conspectu gesihðe ABCG, gesyhþe D, gesihþe E^{3}HJ, gesyhðe FI, ansyne K
eius his ABCDE^{3}FGIJ (*K*)
ardebit* beorneð A, byrnð BDFGIK, bærnyð C, birnþ E^3, birneþ J
et ⁊ ABCDE^{3}FGHIJK
in | in A, on BCDFGHJK, bið on I
circuitu | ymbhwyrfte ABCDFGJ, ymbhwirfte *H,* ymbegænge E^3, embehwyrfte K, his I
eius | his ABCDE^{3}FGHJ*K,* ymbhwyrfe I
tempestas d storm A*, storm BCE^x*J, hreoh DGH, hreohnys F, reohnys I, hreohnes K
ualida strong AB, strang CDFGHJ, stang E^x*, swyðlic *I,* swyðe K

ED: fyr (E)] Fyr *Harsley.* uálida (I)] ualida *Lindelöf.* stang (E)] st[r]ang *Harsley.*

OE: openliche (E^x)] *on eras.* ne (I)] n *on eras.* swigoð (E$^{3/x}$)] *cross-stroke of* ð *by corr., letter eras. after word.* d storm (A)] *Kuhn notes 'Ascender too long for* d; *false start on some word in* ð.' storm (E^x)] *on eras.* stang (E^x)] *on eras.*

LTg: Deus] DS̄ A; [ ]eus G. manifestus] manifeste ABCDEL, M: *final* e *altered from another letter, perhaps left minim of* u, *and followed by eras.*: *cf. Weber MSS* γδεζηχ moz med, *see GAg.* deus] B: *eras. below shoulder of* s, *perhaps altered from* n. noster] B: n *eras. below left leg of* n, *perhaps altered from* s, C: *eras. after word* (t?), M: est *added after word and toward right margin.* et (*1st*)] *interl.* K. eius (*1st*)] eíus K. circuitu] circumitu H: *macron by corr.* (?). eius (*2nd*)] eíus K. ualida] uálida I: s. erit *written in left margin.*

LTu: Deus] deus ζ. manifestus] manifeste νς: *cf. Weber MSS* γδεζηχ moz med, *see GAu.*

GAg: manifestus] manifeste FGHIJK, ABCDLM: *see LTg.* ardebit] exardescet FGHIJK.

GAu: manifestus] manifeste δεζϑιλμξοπϱστυφχψ, νς: *see LTu.* ardebit] exardescet δεζιλμξοπϱστυφχψ.

4

Aduocauit	togeceð A, togecegð B, gecigyð C, to he gecygde D, to he gecegde F, to he gecigde *G,* to he gecigde *H,* to he gechigde E³, he gecygð *I,* ⁊ togeciged ł genemnod J, toclypude *K* (*LM*)
caelum	heofen A*G,* heofon *BDFHJ,* hefyn *C,* hefon *E³,* heofonan I, heouenas *K* (*L*)
sursum*	up ABE³, upp C, uppe DFGH, uppon J, of ufan IK
et	⁊ ABC*E³*FGIJK
terram	eorðan ABCDFGHI, eorðæn *E³,* eorþan K, eorþe J
ut*	ðæt A, þæt B, þæt CD (*E*)
discerneret*	he toscade AB, he tosceade C, he toscéde D, he tosceod K, þæt he tosceade F, þæt he toscade J, tosceadon GH, toscadan I, ðet he sceæwie *E³*
populum	folc ABCDE³FGHIJK
suum	his ABCDE³FGHIJK

ED: togecegð (B)] to gecegð *Brenner.* cælum (D)] caelum *Roeder.* cęlum (E)] caelum *Harsley.*

LTg: Aduocauit] HK: *2nd* u *on eras.*, M: *orig.* uocauit: Ad *added before 1st* u; Aduocabit I; Et uocauit GL: *cf. Weber MS* K. caelum] cælum BDK; cęlum CEFGHJ; celum L. et] E: *retraced in darker ink.* terram] E *retraced in darker ink.* ut] *om.* E. discerneret] E: *retraced in darker ink.*

LTu: Aduocauit] Aduocabit σψ; Et uocauit βς: *cf. Weber MS* K. caelum] cęlum ειμνζςφ; cælum ϑ; celum στ*τ. ut] *interl.* β; *om.* τ*. discerneret] discernere τ*: *see GAu.*

GAg: sursum] desursum FGHIJK. ut discerneret] discernere FGHIJK.

GAu: sursum] desursum δεζϑιλμξοπϱστυφχψ. ut discerneret] discernere δεζιλμξοπϱστυφχψ, ϑ: re *written below line,* τ*: *see LTu.*

5

Congregate	gesomniað ABCK, gesomniað D, gesomniæð E^3, gesamniað H, gesomniaþ J, [ ]esamniað *G*, gegaderiað *F*, gegaderiaþ ł gesomnigað I*
illi	ðider *A*, ðær *B*, þidyr C*, hredlice *E^3*, him DFK, him H, h[ ] G, to him I, þar J (*M*)
sanctos	halge AB, halige C*F*J, hælige E^3, halig H, halie K, halgan GI
eius	his ABCE^3FGHIJ*K*
qui	ða AB, þa CDFHK, ðæ E^3, þe G, þa þe I
ordinauerunt*	geendebyrdun A, geendebyrddon B, geendebyrdan $E^{3/x}$*, geendebyrde C, endebyrdenc F, endebyrden DH, endebyrdon K, endebyrdiaþ I*, endeb(y)[ ]d[ ] G*
testamentum	cyðnisse A, cyðnesse BGH, cyðnysse C, cyþnisse D, cyþnesse E^3K, gecyþnysse F, gecyðnesse I, cyþnessa J
eius	his ABCDE^3FGHIJK
super	ofer ABE^3FGIJK, ofyr C
sacrificia	onsegdnisse A, onsægdnessa BI, onsægdnysse C, onsægednessa J, offrungæ ł æsegdnessæ $E^{3/x}$*, ofrunga DFK, offrunga GH

ED: Co[ ]egate (G)] *Congr*egate *Rosier.* ordin[ ] (G)] ord*inant Rosier.* endebyrdenc (F)] endebyrdent *Kimmens.* endeb(y)[ ]d[ ] (G)] endeby:d[ ] *Rosier.*

OE: gegaderiaþ ł gesomnigað (I)] gega *written in left margin.* þidyr (C)] d *altered from another letter* (n?). geendebyrdan ($E^{3/x}$)] eendebyrdan *on eras. by corr.* endebyrdiaþ (I)] iaþ *in darker ink on eras., another* diaþ *faintly written in right margin.* endeb(y)[ ]d[ ] (G)] *stem of* y *not visible,* an (?) *written after 2nd* d. offrungæ ł æsegdnessæ ($E^{3/x}$)] offrungæ ł *added by corr.*

LTg: Congregate] F: *orig.* Congregati: i *altered to* e; Co[ ]egate G. illi] illic ABEM: *cf. Weber MSS* KT. sanctos] F: *final* s *added by corr.* eius] eíus K.

LTu: ordinauerunt] β: *orig.* ordiuerunt: na *written in left margin.* super] supra ϑ: *cf. Weber MS* η.

GAg: ordinauerunt] ordinant FHIK; ordin[ ] G.

GAu: ordinauerunt] ordinant δεζϑιλμξοπϱστυφχψ.

6

(Et)*	⁊ *ABE*^{x}*FGIJK (*DM*)
Adnuntiauerunt*	secgað *AC*, secgeað *B*, cyþað *D*K, Cyþað *$E^{3/x}$**, cýðaþ F, cyðaþ I, cyþ H, bododon ł sædon G, sædon ł bododon J (*M*)
caeli	heofenas A, heofonas *BDF*I*J*, hefynas *C*, hefonæs *E^3*, heofenes *G*, heofones *H*, heofenas *K* (*L*)

iustitiam rehtwisnisse A, ryhtwisnesse BD, rihtwisnysse *C*F, rihtwisnesse HJ, rihtwis[ ]esse *G**, rihtwisnessa I, rihwisnesse K, rihtwisnes E^{x}*
eius his ABCE^{3}GHIJ*K*, hys F
quoniam forðon ABCHJ, forðæn E^{3}, forðan K, forðan ðe F, forðon þe I, forþam þe G
deus god ABCE^{3}FGHIJK
iudex doema AB, dema CDFGHIJK, demæ E^{3}
est is ABE^{3}FGIJ*K*, ys C

ED: Anuntiauerunt (C)] A[d]nuntiauerunt C. secgað (C)] seçgað *Wildhagen.* cęli (E)] caeli *Harsley.* iusticiam (C)] iusti[t]iam *Wildhagen.* rihtwis[ ]esse (G)] rihtwisnesse *Rosier.* forðon (A)] for ðon *Kuhn.*

OE: ꝛ (E^{x})] *on eras.* Cyþað (E$^{3/x}$)] það *on eras. by corr.* rihtwis[ ]esse (G)] *letter after 1st* s *blotted and obscured by patch.* rihtwisnes (E^{x})] *on eras.*

LTg: Adnuntiauerunt] Anuntiauerunt C: *letter eras. after* A; Et adnuntiabunt A: *eras. (2 letters) after 2nd* a, b *on eras. by corr.,* B: b *on eras.,* D: d *on eras., 1st* a *added,* E: *1st* t, *1st and 2nd* a *retraced,* bunt *on eras. by corr.,* M: *orig.* Adnuntiau[er]unt: Et *added before word, 2nd* u *altered to* b, *eras.* (2 *letters*) *after* b; *another hand then added* ł *interl. before* b *and* ł ue (> ue[r]?) *above* b: *cf. Weber MS* αγδεηS moz^{c} med, *see GAg.* caeli] cæli BK; cęli CDEFHJL; celi G. iustitiam] iusticiam C: *orig.* iustitiam: *2nd* t *altered to* c; iustitia[ ] G. eius] eíus K. est] ést K.

LTu: Adnuntiauerunt] Et annuntiauerunt β: *orig.* Et adnuntiauerunt: d *deleted,* n *interl.;* Et adnuntiabunt τ*: *see GAu.* caeli] cęli ειμξοσςφ; cæli ϑ; ccli τ*τ. iustitiam] β: *initial* i *interl.;* iusticiam τ*τφ, ϱ: *orig.* iustitiam: *2nd* t *deleted,* c *interl.*

GAg: Adnuntiauerunt] Et annuntiabunt I, F: *orig.* Et adnuntiabunt: d *deleted by subscript dot,* n *interl. by corr.,* H: *initial* E *partly lost, 1st* n *on eras.,* K: *1st* n *on eras.;* [ ]t adnuntiabunt G; Et adnuntiabunt J, ABDEM: *see LTg.*

GAu: Adnuntiauerunt] Et adnuntiabunt δϑμψ, τ*; Et annuntiabunt εζιλξπστυχ, o: *orig.* Et adnuntiabunt: d *deleted,* n *interl.;* Et annunciabunt φ, ϱ: *orig.* Et annuntiabunt: *1st* t *deleted,* c *interl.*

7
Audi geher AB, Geher E^{3}*, gehyr CFG*H*IK, g̱ehyr D, gehir J
populus | folc ABCDE^{3}FJK, folcc GH, min I
meus | min ABCDE^{3}FGHJK, folc I
et ꝛ ABCE^{3}FGHIJK
loquar* sprecu A, sprece E^{3}, ic sprece B*C*DFGH*I*J, ic spece K
israhel to israhela folce ABG, to israela folce C, to isrła folce *J,* to isræhele *E$^{3/x}$**, to israhele F (*HIKM*)

et ⁊ ABCDE^{3}FGHIJK
testificabor ic cyðu A, ic cyðe BCE^{3}FG, ic cyþe DHJK, ic gesweotelige ł ic geseðe I
tibi ðe ABE^{3}F, þe CGHIJK
quoniam* ðætte A, þætte B, ðætt E^{x}*, forþon C, forðon D
deus god ABCE^{3}FGHIJ
deus god ABCE^{3}GIJ
tuus ðin ABF, þin CE^{3}GHIJK
ego ic ABCDE^{3}FGHIJK
sum eam A, eom BCDE^{3}FGHJK, eam I

ED: isrł (EHIJK)] israhel *Campbell, Oess;* israel *Harsley, Lindelöf;* Israhel *Sisam.* to isrła folce (J)] to isr*ae*la folce *Oess.*

OE: Geher (E^{3})] *orig.* Gehir: i *altered to* e, *letter* (e?) *eras. after word.* to isræhele (E$^{3/x}$)] to *added by corr.* ðætt (E^{x})] *on eras.*

LTg: Audi] [ ]udi H: *outline only of initial* A *visible.* loquar] C: *small eras. above malformed* o, I: *small eras. after word.* israhel] isrł EHJKM, I: *gloss eras.*

LTu: ϱ: *v. 7–end wanting.* israhel] isrł διλξοπστ*τυφχ; israel εϛ. testificabor] testificor ϑ. tibi] ν: *remainder of psalm wanting.*

GAg: quoniam] *om.* FGHIJK.

GAu: loquar] loquar tibi ϑ: *cf. Weber MS* η. quoniam] *om.* δζϑιλμξοπστυφχψ.

8
Non | nales AB, nalys C, nalæs J, na DFHK, Na E$^{3/x}$*, ne G
super* ofer BDE^{3}, ofyr C, on GHJK
sacrificia* onsegdnisse A, onsægdnessa *B,* onsægdnyssa C, onsægednyssa F, æsegðnessæ E^{3}, onsægdnessum I, ofrunga DJK, offrungum GH
tua* ðine AB, þine J, þina CDK, þin E^{3}, ðinum F, þinum G, þinum H, on þinum I
arguam | ic dregu A, ic ðreage B, ic þreage DFG*HJ*K, ic þrea C, ic þræwie E^{3}, ic ne þreage I*
te ðe A*B,* þe CE^{3}FGIJK (*L*)
holocausta onsegdnisse A, onsægdnessa B, onsægdnyssa C, onsegdnissa D, onsægednyssa F, onsæigdnessa G, onsægednessa J, onsægd H, ofrungæ ł onsegdnisse E$^{3/x}$*, offrunga I, lac K
autem soð A, soðlice BCFGI, soþlice HJ, eællengæ E^{3}, witodlice K
tua ðine ABE$^{3/x}$*, þine CGIJ, þina DH, ðina F, þin K
in in A, on BCDE^{3}FGHIJK
conspectu gesihðe ABCFGI, gesyhðe D, gesiehðe E^{3}, gesihþe HJ, ansyne K

meo — minre ABCDE^{3}FGIJ
sunt — sind *A*, sint BE^{3}, synd CFGHJ, synt D, syndon I
semper — aa *A*, áa B, symle CDI, simle E^{3}, simble F, symble H, æfre G, sind J

OE: Na ($E^{3/x}$)] a *on eras. by corr.* ic ne þreage (I)] ne *interl.* ofrungæ ł onsegdnisse ($E^{3/x}$)] ł onsegdnisse *added by corr.* ðine ($E^{3/x}$)] e *added by corr.*

LTg: sacrificia] B: *2nd* i *on eras., bowl of final* a *partly on eras.* arguam] H: *eras. after 2nd* a; arguamp J. te] té BL. sunt] A: u *on eras.*, nt *added by corr.* semper] A: *orig.* semper: *crossbar through* p *eras.*, er *added by corr.*

LTu: tua] *om.* μ.

GAg: super] in FGHIJK. sacrificia] sacrificiis FGHIJK. tua] tuis FGHIJK.

GAu: super] in δεζϑιλμξοπστυφχψ. sacrificia] sacrificiis δεζιλμξοπστυφχψ; sacrificis ϑ. tua] tuis δεζϑιλξοστυφψ; *om.* μ.

9
Non — | ic ne ABCI, Ic ne E^{x}*, ne F*G*, na JK
accipiam — | onfoo A, onfo BCFJ, onfó E^{x}*, ic afo DGHK, ic onfo J, underfo I*
de — of ABCDE^{3}FGHIJK
domo — huse ABCDE^{3}FGHIJK (*M*)
tua — ðinum AB, þinum *CD*J, þinum E^{3}GHI, ðinum F, þinan K
uitulos — calferu A, cealfru DHI, ceælfru $E^{3/x}$*, cealf BJ, cealfas CK, calfas F, ccalfra G
neque — ne ABCE^{3}I, ⁊ na D*G*HJK, ne ne F
de — of ABCDE^{3}FGHIJK
gregibus — eowdum ABCFH, ewedum E^{3}G, ewedum J, eowedum I, efodum D, heorde K
tuis — ðinum AE^{3}F, ðinum B, þinum CDHJ, þinum GI, þinre K
hircos — buccan ABC*DFGHIJK*, buccæn *$E^{3/x}$** (*L*)

OE: Ic ne (E^{x})] *on eras.* onfó (E^{x})] *on eras.* underfo (I)] erfo *on eras. in darker ink, another* ic ne underfo *barely visible in left margin.* ceælfru ($E^{3/x}$)] ru *added by corr.* buccæn (E^{3})] n *added by corr.*

LTg: Non] G: N *partly lost.* domo] domv M: *orig.* domo: *final* o *deleted by supra- and subscript dots,* v *interl.* tua] tuo CD. neque] nequę G. hircos] hyrcos DEHIJKL; yrcos FG.

LTu: tua] tuo ς. hircos] hyrcos ειλξοςτ*τυφψ; yrcos ζ, π: *orig.* hyrcos: h *eras.*

10

Quoniam	forðon AB, forþon J, forþan CK, Forðæn E^{3}, forþæn G, forþon ðe F, forðon þe I
meae	min A*K*, mine *BCDE^{3}FGHIJ* (*L*)
sunt	sind A, sint BE^{3}, synd CFGHJK, synt D, syndon I
omnes	all A, ealle B*C*DFGHIJK, eælle E^{3}
ferae	wildeor A*CDFGHJK,* wilddeor *B,* wildedeor *E^{x}*I* (*LM*)
siluarum	wuda ABCDFGHI*J, on wudæ E$^{3/x}$*, wudan K
iumenta	neat AB, nytyn C, nytenu DFGHIK, nietenæ E^{3}, nytena J
in	in A, on BCDE^{3}FGHIJK
montibus	muntum ABCFGH, muntum DJ, muntan K, dunum E^{3}I
et	⁊ ABCDE^{3}FGHIJK
boues	oexen A, oxan BCDFGHIJ, oxæn E^{3}, oxsan K

ED: forðon (A)] for ðon *Kuhn*. meæ (D)] meae *Roeder.* meę (E)] meae *Harsley.* mee (I)] meae *Lindelöf.*

OE: wildedeor (E^{x})] *on eras.* wuda (I)] a *on eras.* (?). on wudæ (E$^{3/x}$)] on *on eras. by corr.*

LTg: meae] meæ BD; meę EFGHKL, C: *orig.* męę: *cauda below 1st* e *eras.;* mee J, I: *orig.* meae: a *eras.* omnes] C: *eras. after* n. ferae] feræ B; fere CEIJ; ferę DFGKLM, H: f *altered from another letter and followed by eras., cauda added by corr.* (*cf. v. 12* terrę *and Ps 50.14* lętitiam, *Ps 50.20* ędificentur).

LTu: meae] meę ειμξςυφ; meæ ϑ; mee στ*τχ. ferae] ferę ελμοπφ; fere ζιξσςτ*τυψ; feræ ϑ; uere β.

11

Cognoui	ic oncneow ABCFGIJ, Ic oncneow E^{3}, ic ancneow DHK (*M*)
omnia	all A, ealle BCDFGHIJK, eælle E^{3}
uolatilia	ða flegendan A, þa fleogyndan C, fleogende fuglas B, fleogende fugelas J, ða flegende ł fugulæs E$^{3/x}$*, fugelas DFGHIK
caeli	heofenes A*G,* heofones *BD,* hefynys *C,* hefonæs *E^{3},* heofonas F*HI,* heofanas *J,* heofenan *K* (*L*)
et	⁊ ABCE^{3}FGIJK
species*	hiow A, hiw BCDE^{3}, fægernys F, fægernes GJK, fægerness I
agri	londes AB, landys C, landes DE$^{3/x}$*FGHJ, æceres I, felda K
mecum	mid mec A*, mid me BCE^{3}FGHIJ, mine K
est	is ABDE^{3}FGHIJ, ys C, synd *K*

ED: cęli (E)] caeli *Harsley*. celi (I)] caeli *Lindelöf*.

OE: ða flegende ł fugulæs (E$^{3/x}$)] ða flegende ł *added by corr.* landes (E$^{3/x}$)] *orig.* londes: o *altered to* a *by corr.* mid mec (A)] c *altered from another letter.*

LTg: Cognoui] M: *2nd* o *on eras.*, ui *interl.* caeli] cæli BK; cęli CDEGHL; celi J, I: *orig.* caeli: a *eras.* est] ést K.

LTu: caeli] cęli βειξοφ; cæli ϑ; celi σςτ*τ.

GAg: species] pulchritudo FGHIJK.

GAu: species] pulchritudo δεζϑιλμξοπστυφχψ.

12

Si	gif ABCDE^{3}FGHIJK
esuriero	ic hyngriu A, ic hyngre B, ic gehingrie C, ic hingrie E^{3}, ic hingrige J*K, hyngrige ic D, hingrie ic *H*, hyngrie F, hingrige G, me hingraþ *I*
non	| ne ABCGJ, na DFHK, ic ne E^{3}I
dicam	| cweoðu ic A, cweðe ic BCJ, cweþe I, ic secge DFH, segge E^{x}*, secge G, sege ic K
tibi	to ðe AB, to þe C*J, þe DE^{3}GHIK, ðe F
meus	min ABCDE^{3}FGHIJK
est	is ABE^{3}FGIJ*K*, ys C
enim	soðlice ABCF*H*I, soþlicȩ D, soþlice J, soðliche E^{x}*, soð G, witodlice K
orbis	ymbhwerft A, ymbhwyrft BCDFGH*IJ, ymbhwirft E^{3}, embehwyrft K
terrae	eorðan *ABCDFGIK*, eorðæn *E^{3}*, eorþan *HJ* (*L*)
et	⁊ ABCE^{3}FGIJK
plenitudo	fylnis A, fylnes BJ, fylnys C, filnes E^{3}, fulnis DH, fullnys F, fullnis G, fulnes K, gefyllednys I
eius	his ABCDE^{3}FGHJ*K*, hire I

ED: esuríero (HI)] esuriero *Campbell, Lindelöf.* terrę (E)] terrae *Harsley.* terre (I)] terrae *Lindelöf.*

OE: ic hingrige (J)] h *eras. before* ic. segge (E^{x})] *on eras.* to þe (C)] to *interl.* soðliche (E^{x})] *on eras.* ymbhwyrft (H)] h *interl.*

LTg: esuriero] esuríero HI. est] ést K. enim] H: *macron written above* n *rather than* i. terrae] terræ BL; terrę CDEFGK, H: *cauda added by corr.* (*cf. v. 10* ferę *and Ps 50.14* lętitiam, *Ps 50.20* ędificentur); terre J, I: *orig.* terrae: a *eras.* eius] eíus K.

LTu: esuriero] essuriero ϑ. terrae] terre βσ́ςτ*τ; terrę ειξοφ; terræ ϑ.

13

Numquid	ah A*B*, ac la *G*, cwysþu *C*, cwistu *H*, cwyst þu J, cwyþst þu K, cwyst þu la F, cweðst þu la I, swist þu D, Is ðes wén ðet *E*^{3}
manducabo	ic eotu A, ic ete BCE^{3}FG, ete ic DHIK, hlaf ic ete J
carnes	flęsc A, flæsc BCFGJ, flesc E^3, flæscu D, flascu H, flæs K, flæscmettas I
taurorum	ferra A, fearra BCDFGHI, fearras J, feærræ E^3, ramma K
aut	oððe ABCFGH, oþðe D*K**, oþþe E^{3}I, soþlice J
sanguinem	blod ABCDE^3*FGHIJK
hircorum	buccena *A*B*IJ*, buccyna C, buccuna *D*, buccænæ *E*^{3}*, buccana *GH*, buccan *FK* (*L*)
potabo	ic drinco A*, ic drince BCE^{3}J, drince ic D*G*HI, drýnge ic F, drinc K

ED: Nunquid (C)] Nu[m]quid *Wildhagen*. swist þu (D)] swistþu *Roeder*. hyrcorum (I)] hircorum *Lindelöf*.

OE: oþðe (K)] ⁊ *eras. before word*. blod (E^3)] *eras. after word*. buccænæ (E^3)] *retraced*. ic drinco (A)] n *interl*.

LTg: Numquid] B: quid *on eras.;* Nunquid E, C: *orig*. Numquid: *left leg of* m *eras. to form* n, G: *orig*. Numquid: *right leg of* m *eras. to form* n, H: *eras. after* n. aut] K: a *altered from* u *by main hand*. hircorum] A: *orig*. hyrcorum: *right arm of* y *eras.;* hyrcorum DEFHIJKL; yrcorum G. potabo] G: *orig*. putabo: u *altered to* o.

LTu: Numquid] Nunquid ειλτ*τφ; Numquit ζ. hircorum] hyrcorum δειλξσςτ*τυφψ; yrcorum ζ, π: *orig*. hyrcorum: h *eras*.

14

Immola	ageld A, agild BJ, agyld *C*, ofra DK, offra E^x*F*G*HI
deo	gode ABCDE^{3}FGIJK, goda H
sacrificium	onsegdnisse A, onsægdnisse BD*, onsægnysse C, onsegdnesse E^3, onsægednyssa F, onsægdnesse G, onsægdnisse H, onsægdnessa I, onsægednessa J, onsægenesse K
laudis	lofes ABDE^{3}FGIJK, lofys C, leofes H
et	⁊ ABCE^{3}FGHIJK
redde	geld A, gild B, gyld CF, ic gild E^3*, agyld DHI, agild JK, agy[ ] G
altissimo	ðæm hestan A, þæm hehstan BI, þon hiehstan C, þam hehstan D, ðæm hihstæn E^3, þam hyhstan GH, þam hyhstan K, þam hihstan J, þam ehstan F

uota	gehat ABCE^{3}, gehac J, behat FI, gewilnunga DGH, behæse K
tua	ðin A, ðine BF, þin CE^{3}, þina DH, þinra G, þine IJK

ED: lofes (G) lofe *Rosier.*

OE: offra (E^{x})] *eras. after word.* onsægdnisse (D)] ofruncg *written in bottom right margin as gloss on* uictimę *in commentary:* Nullo modo te liberabunt tuę uictimę. si fidem dei stabilem non tenes. ic gild (E^{3})] *letter eras. after* d.

LTg: Immola] C: *2nd* m *malformed* (?): *cf. v. 19* dolum; [ ]mmola G.

LTu: laudis] ς: u *interl.*

15

(Et)*	⁊ FGIJK
Inuoca	gece A, geceg B, gecig *CGHJK,* gecyg D*I,* Gechige E$^{3/x}$*, ic gecege *F*
me	mec A, me BCE^{3}FGIJK
in	in A, on BCDE^{3}FGHIJK
die	dege A, dæge BCDFGHIJ, dæg K, dei E^{3}*
tribulationis	geswinces ABDGHJ, geswnces K, geswencydnysse C, geswencednesse I, geswinkes ł eærfoðnesse E$^{3/x}$*, gedrefednysse F
tuae*	ðines *AB,* þines *D,* þinys þæt *C,* þín *E^{3}* (*L*)
⟨ut⟩	ðæt *A,* þætte *B,* þet *E^{3}* (*D*)
(et)*	⁊ FGIJK
eripiam*	ic gcncrgc ABCK, ic generige DGIJ, ic generie E^{3}F
te	ðec A, ðe *B*DE^{3}, þe CFGIJK
et	⁊ ABCE^{3}FGIJK (*H*)
magnificabis*	ðu miclas A, þu miclast B, þu gemiclast CDF, ðu gemiclæst E^{3}, þu gemyclast K, þu arwurþast G, þu arweorðast I*, na J
me	mec A, me *B*CDE^{3}FGIJK

ED: ínuoca (I)] inuoca *Lindelöf.* tuæ (BD)] tua *Brenner;* tuae *Roeder.* tuę (E)] tuae *Harsley.*

OE: Gechige (E$^{3/x}$)] Ge *on eras. by corr.* dei (E^{3})] i *has form of* j. geswinkes ł eærfoðnesse (E$^{3/x}$)] geswinkes ł *added by corr.,* swin *on eras.* þu arweorðast (I)] *eras.* (?) *after* u.

LTg: Inuoca] inuoca FGJK; ínuoca HI. tuae] tuę CL; tuae ut A; tuæ ut B: æ *cropped due to excision of initial from fol. 53v,* D: u *on eras.;* tuę ut E: ut *on eras. by corr.* te] té B. et] H: *added by corr.* me (*2nd*)] B: *lost due to excision of initial from fol. 53v, letter fragment visible.*

LTu: Inuoca] INuoca β; inuoca δεζθιλμξοπστυφχψ. tuae] tue ϛ; tue ut τ*. eripiam] et eripiam β.

GAg: Inuoca] Et inuoca FGJK; Et ínuoca HI. tuae] *om.* FGHIJK. eripiam] et eruam FHIK; et ęruam G; et eruamp J. magnificabis] honorificabis FGHIJK.

GAu: Inuoca] Et inuoca δεζθιλμξοπστυφχψ. tuae] *om.* δεθιλμξοπστυφχψ. eripiam] et eruam δεζθιλμξοπστυφχψ. magnificabis] honorificabis δεζθιλμξοπστυφχψ.

16

Peccatori	to ðæm synfullan AB, To þam senfullæn $E^{3/x}$*, to þam sinfullan J, þan synfullan C, þam synfullan D*G*H, þæm synfullan I, þa synfullum F, synfulle K
autem	soðlice ABC$E^{3/x}$*GI, soþlice FJ, witodlice K
dixit	cweð AE^{3}, cwæð BF, cwæþ JK, sæde CGI
deus	god ABCE^{3}FGIJK
quare	forhwon A*B*C*J, forwæn E^{3}, hwy D, hwi HK, forhwy FI, forþam þe G (*L*)
tu	ðu A, þu CE^{3}FGIJK (*B*)
enarras	asagas A, asagast *C*, asegst *G*J, segst E^{3}, cyþest DFHIK (*B*)
iustitias	rehtwisnisse A, ryhtwisnessa BD, rihtwisnysse *C*F, rihtwisnesse $E^{3/x}$*GJK, rihtwisnessa HI*
meas	mine ACE^{3}FGIJK, mina BD, mea H
et	⁊ ABCE^{3}FGHIJK
adsumis	genimes *A*, genimst *B*, genymyst *C*, genimest DE^{x}*GHJ*, genymest *F*, þu underfehst *I* (*K*)
testamentum	cyðnisse A, cyðnysse C, cyþnisse D, cyðnesse E^{3}*G*H*, cyþnessa J, cyþnesse K, cyðness[ ] *B**, gecyðnysse F, gecyðnesse I
meum	mine ACDFGHIJK, min E^{3} (*B*)
per	ðorh A, ðurh BE^{3}K, þurh CDFGHIJ
os	mud *A*, muð *BCDE*^{3}*G*I*K, muþ FHJ (*LM*)
tuum	ðinne ABE^{3}F, þinne CDGHIJK

ED: Peccatori (B)] peccatori *Brenner.* forhwon (A)] for hwon *Kuhn.* tú (E)] tu *Harsley.* ęnarras (G)] enarras *Rosier.* iusticias (C)] iusti[t]ias *Wildhagen.* assumis (C)] a[d]sumis *Wildhagen.* testam[ ]ntum (H)] testamentum *Campbell.* ðurh (B)] þurh *Brenner.* ós (AEI)] os *Kuhn, Harsley, Lindelöf.* muþ (H)] muð *Campbell.*

OE: To þam senfullæn ($E^{3/x}$)] To þam sen *on eras. by corr.*, f *retraced.* soðlice ($E^{3/x}$)] lice *by corr.* forhwon (C)] r *interl.* rihtwisnesse ($E^{3/x}$)] rihtwis *on eras. by corr.* rihtwisnessa (I)] *orig.* rihtwisnesse: *final* e *altered to* a. genimest (E^{x})] *on eras., eras. before and after* ge. cyðness[ ] (B)] B: *partly lost due to excision of initial from fol. 53v.*

LTg: Peccatori] G: *partly lost.* quare] quáre L; quar[ ] B: *partly lost due to excision of initial from fol. 53v.* tu] B: *lost due to excision of initial from fol. 53v;* tú E. enarras] B: *lost due to excision of initial from fol. 53v;* ęnarras CG. iustitias] iusticias C: *orig.* iustitias: *2nd* t *altered to* c. adsumis] E: a *retouched,* d *on eras.,* su *added by corr.;* adsumes A; assumes B; assumis FIJ, CH: *1st* s *on eras. by corr.,* K: *eras. after* a, *1st* s *interl. by main hand;* asumis G: *orig.* adsumis: d *crossed through,* s *added on the line.* testamentum] test[ ] B: *partly lost due to excision of initial from fol. 53v;* testam[ ]ntum H: *letter lost due to hole in leaf.* meum] B: *lost due to excision of initial from fol. 53v.* os] ós ABEILM.

LTu: Peccatori] Pecatori βϑ. iustitias] iusticias τ*τφ. adsumis] assumis δεζιλξοπστ*τυφχ.

17

Tu	ðu ABCE^{3}F, þu _G_IJK
uero	soðlice ABCE^{3}FGI, soþlice DH*J, witodlice K
odisti	ðu fiodes A, feodes B*, fiodes E^{3}, þu feodyst C, hatudest DF_H_, hatodest IJ_K_, þu hatudest G
disciplinam	ðeodscipe AB, þeodscype C, þeodscipe J, þiodscipe ł lare E^{3}*, lare DFGHK, steore I
et	⁊ ABCE^{3}FGHIJK
proiecisti	ðu awurpe AF, þu awurpe BCD_HI_*, þu awirpe E^{3}, awurpe J, þu awurfe G, forwurpe K
sermones	word ABCJ, spræce ł word E^{x}*, spræca DFH, spræce I, spæce K, spr[ ] G
meos	min AJ, mine BCDE^{3}FGHIK
post*	efter AE^{3}, æfter B, æftyr _C_, beæftan _D_, bæfta þe H, bæfta[ ] þe G*, underbæc FJ, on bæclingc ł underbæc I, on bæc K
te*	ðe AB*E^{x}*, þe C_D_

ED: proieci(s)[ ]i (H)] proiecisti *Campbell.* post (C)] pos *Wildhagen.* retrorsum (G)] retro*r*sum *Rosier.* bæfta þe (H)] bafta þe *Campbell.* underbæc (F)] under bæc *Kimmens.* on bæclingc ł underbæc (I)] on bæclingc ł under bæc *Lindelöf.*

OE: soþlice (H)] *eras. after word.* feodes (B)] þ *and perhaps* i *eras. before word.* þiodscipe ł lare (E^{3})] ł lare *added by corr.* þu awurpe (I)] a *on eras.* (?): *cf. v. 22* ahwanne. spræce ł word (E^{x})] spræce *on eras.* bæfta[ ] þe (G)] *not certain final letter after* a *ever existed.* ðe (B)] *faint but visible.* ðe (E^{x})] *on eras.*

LTg: Tu] [ ]u G. odisti] H: o *interl.,* K: o *interl. by main hand.* proiecisti] proieci(s)[ ]i H: *top of* s *and following letter lost due to hole in leaf.* post te] C: *1st* t *interl. by corr.;* poste D.

LTu: odisti] hodisti ς.

GAg: post te] retrorsum FGHIJK.

GAu: post te] retrorsum δεζϑιλμξοπστυφχψ.

18

Si — gif ABCDGHIJK, Gif E[3]*, gyf F

uidebas — ðu gesege A, þu gesege K, ðu gesage E[3/x]*, ðu gesawe BDI, þu gesawe FHJ, þu gesaw[ ] *G*, þu geseo C

furem — ðeof A, þeof BCDFGHIJ, ðiof E[3/x]*, þeofas K

simul* — somud A, somod BD, samod C, samed E[3]*

currebas — ðu urne A, þu urne BCDE[3]FGHIJK

cum — mid ABCDE[3]FGHIJK

eo — hine AB, him CE[3]FGHI, him DJ, heom K

et — ⁊ ABCE[3]FGHJK

cum — mid ABCE[3]FGIJK

adulteris — unrehthæmderum A, unryhthæmerum B, unrihthæmdum C, unryhthæmrum D, unrihthæmerum FJ, unrihthemeðe E[3], u[ ]æmrum G*, unriht H, forligerum ł mid unrihthæmerum I, æwswican K

portionem | ðæl A, dæl BCE[x]*J, byrþenne D, byrðene GK, byrþene H, byrðene dæl F*, þinne I

tuam | ðinne AF, þine CE[3]GH, ðine K, ðin B, þin J, dæl I

ponebas — ðu settes A, þu settes B, þu settest DGHJ*K*, þu setest E[3], þu gesettyst C, þu gesettest F, ⁊ þu gesettest I*

ED: (u)ideba[ ] (G)] uidebas *Rosier.*

OE: Gif (E[3])] *retraced by corr.* ðu gesage (E[3/x])] s *retraced,* age *on eras. by corr.* ðiof (E[3/x])] ð *by corr.,* i *retraced.* samed (E[3])] *orig.* somed: o *altered to* a *by corr.* u[ ]æmrum (G)] *1st* m *shows 4 minims.* dæl (E[x])] *gloss eras. before word.* byrðene dæl (F)] rðene dæl *obscured by eras. but visible.* ⁊ þu gesettest (I)] ge *interl.*

LTg: uidebas] (u)ideba[ ] G: *left leg of* u *visible.* ponebas] K: bas *orig. at end of next line after* malitia (*v. 19*), *but eras. and written after* pone (*same hand as fol. 50v* eius *and* iacob).

LTu: Si] SI β.

GAg: simul] *om.* FGHIJK.

GAu: simul] *om.* δζϑλμξοπστυφχψ.

19

Os — muð *AB*CH, muþ *DFGIJK,* Muð E[3] (*LM*)

tuum — ðin ABDE[3], þin CF*GHI*JK

abundauit — genyhtsumað A*B,* genihtsumað *C,* genihtsumaþ *J,* genihsumude *D*, genihtsumæde *E^{3}**, genihtsumode *F*, genihtsumade *G*, genihtsumude H, genihtsumede I*K* (*LM*)

nequitia* — mid niðe AB, mid niþe *C*, of niðe D, of hete ł niþæ *$E^{3/x}$**, of yfele F, on yfelnesse IK, wean G, wirigunga J

et — ⁊ ABCE^{3}FGHJK (*I*)

lingua — tunge ABCDE^{3}FGHI*JK

tua — ðin AB, þin CE^{3}FGIJK, þine H

concinnauit* — hleoðrade A*, hleoðrode BC, hleoþrade J, sang DFGHK, sang ł leoðrade E^{x}*, gealchatte ł gereonode I

dolum* — facen AD, facn BFGH*J*K, facyn *C*, facnu I, facen ł sær $E^{3/x}$*

ED: Ós (AB)] Os *Kuhn, Brenner.* [ ]s (G)] Os *Rosier.* abundauit (C)] [h]abundauit *Wildhagen.*

OE: þin (F)] *orig.* þinne: ne *eras.* þin (I)] *eras. after word.* genihtsumæde (E^{3})] d *on eras.* of hete ł niþæ ($E^{3/x}$)] of, ł, *and* æ *by corr.*, ł *on eras.* tunge (I)] ⁊ *eras. before word.* hleoðrade (A)] *glossator possibly confused* concinnare/concinere (?): *see also* BCEJ. sang ł leoðrade (E^{x})] sang ł *on eras.* facen ł sær ($E^{3/x}$)] facen ł *added by corr.*

LTg: Os] Ós ABDKLM; [ ]s G. abundauit] C: *letter eras. before word,* E: uit *retraced;* habundauit BDFGJKLM. nequitia] E: equitia *on eras.* nęquitia C. et] I: *eras. after word* (?). dolum] C: m *malformed* (?): *cf. v. 14* Immola; dolus J.

LTu: abundauit] habundauit βζϑξσςτ*υ. nequitia] nequitiam ς: u *interl.: cf. Weber MSS* Sε moz^{x}.

GAg: nequitia] malitia FGHIJ, K: *eras. after word: see v. 18* ponebas. concinnauit] concinnabat FGHIJK. dolum] dolos FGIK, H: *2nd* o *altered from another letter;* dolus J.

GAu: nequitia] malitia δεζϑλμξοπσυχ; malicia ιτφψ. concinnauit] concinnabat δεζϑιλμξοπστυφχψ. dolum] dolos δεζϑιλμξοπστυφχψ.

20

Sedens — sittende ABGHIJK, sittynde C, sittendȩ D, Sittende E^{3}, þu sæte F

aduersus — wið ABC, wiþ E^{3}*J, angean D, togeanes FI, ongean GH*K*

fratrem — broeðer A, broðor BCE^{3}G, broður D, broþor IJ, broþur H, broþra K, boþor F

tuum — ðinum A, ðinne B, þinne CDFGHIJ, þine E^{3}K

detrahebas* — ðu teldes A, ðu tældes B, þu tældyst C, þu tældest D, þu tildest $E^{3/x}$*, þu spræce F, þu spæce K, þu spræce ł þu wære sprecende I, sprecende G

et — ⁊ ABCDE^{3}FGHIJK

aduersus — wið ABCE^{3}, wiþ J, agean D, angean H, ongean I, ongen K, togeanes F

filium	suna A, suno B, sunu CDE^{3}*FGHJK, bearn I
matris	moeder A, modor BCE^{3}FGHIJK, modur D
tuae	ðinre *AB,* þinre *CDE^{3}GHIK,* ðine *F,* þin *J* (*LM*)
ponebas	ðu settes A, þu setes B, þu settyst C, þu settest DE^{x}*FGHJ, þu setest K*, þu gesettest I*
scandalum	eswic *A,* æswic BCDGHJK, ǽswicunge F, æswicunge I, geswic ł flit E$^{3/x}$*

ED: ⁊ (G)] *no gloss Rosier.* tuæ (D)] tuae *Roeder.* tuę (E)] tuae *Harsley.* ǽswicunge (F)] æswicunge *Kimmens.*

OE: wiþ (E^{3})] *eras. before word.* þu tildest (E$^{3/x}$)] *eras. after* þu, dest *on eras. by corr.* sunu (E^{3})] *descender extends from right minim of final* u. þu settest (E^{x})] *on eras.* þu setest (K)] *obscured by stain but visible.* þu gesettest (I)] ge *written in left margin.* geswic ł flit (E$^{3/x}$)] ł flit *added by corr.*

LTg: aduersus] áduersus K. tuae] tuę ACEFGHKLM; tuæ BD; tue J. scandalum] A: n *interl. by corr.,* m *added.*

LTu: tuae] tuę ειμξου; tuæ ϑ; tue σς.

GAg: detrahebas] loquebaris FGHIJK.

GAu: detrahebas] loquebaris δεζϑιλμξοπστυφχψ.

21

Haec	ðas A*B,* þas *CDGHJK,* þæs *E^{3},* ðis *F,* þas þing *I* (*L*)
fecisti	ðu dydes AB, þu dydyst C, þu dydest DGH, ðu didest E^{3}*J, ðu dydest FIK
et	⁊ ABCE^{3}FGHIK
tacui	ic swigade AF, ic swigode BCDGHK, ic swigude E^{3}, ic swygode I
existimasti	ðu gewoendes A, þu gewendes BE^{3}, þu wendyst C, þu wendest D*FGHIJK*
iniquitatem*	on unrehtwisnisse *A,* on unrihwisnysse C, unryhtwisnesse BD, unrihtwisnesse K, unrihtnessæ E^{3}, unrihtwis F, unrihtwise GJ, unrihtlice I*
quod	ðæt A, þæt BFGI, þæt CDHJK, þet E^{3}
ero	ic were A, ic wære BCJK, ic beo D*FHI, ic bio E^{3}, ic beo ł wære *G**
tibi*	ðe ABE^{3}, þe CDJ, þin FGIK
similis	gelic ABCE^{3}FGHIJ, gelíc D, gelica K
arguam	ic ðreu *A,* ic þrea *C*I, ic ðreage *B*F, ic þreage *D*GHJ, Ic þræge *E$^{3/x}$*,* ic þræge (*LM*)

te	ðec A, ðe *BF*, þe CDE^{3}GHIJK
et	⁊ ABCDE^{3}FGHIJK
statuam	ic setto A, ic sette BCDFGHIJK, ic gesette E^3
illa*	ða AB, þa *C*DE^x*
contra	ongegn AB, ongen CE^x*K, ongean DFGHIJ
faciem	onsiene AE^3*, onsine B, ansyne CDFGHJK, ansene I
tuam	ðinre *A*, þinre IJ*K*, ðine BF, þine CDGH, þin E^3

ED: Hæc (D)] Haec *Roeder.* Hęc (E)] Haec *Harsley.* haec (I)] Haec *Lindelöf.*

OE: ðu didest (E^3)] t *added by corr.* unrihtlice (I)] o inique : eala þu unrihtwisa *written in left margin.* ic beo (D)] þe *eras. after gloss and rewritten above following* tibi. ic beo ł wære (G)] ł wære *added in diff.* (?) *hand above following* þin. Ic þræge (E$^{3/x}$)] *eras. before* þræge, ge *on eras. by corr.* þa (E^x)] *on eras.* ongen (E^x)] *on eras.* onsiene (E^3)] *final* e *added by corr.*

LTg: Haec] Hæc BD; Hęc EL; hęc FGHJK; haec I. existimasti] Existimasti FGHIJK. iniquitatem] A: *eras. above* e (*macron?*), m *added by corr.* ero] ęro G. arguam] Arguam ABCDEL; Argûam M. te] té B. illa] illam C. tuam] A: m *added by corr.*, K: *small eras. after word.*

LTu: Haec] Hec τ*; haec δζοπυ; hęc ειλμξφχ; hæc ϑ; hec στ. fecisti] fęcisti ι. tacui] tacuę β. existimasti] Existimasti δεζϑιλμξοπστυφχ; Exaestimasti ψ. arguam] ARguam β; Arguam ϛτ*.

GAg: iniquitatem] inique FGHIJK. tibi] tui FGHIJK. illa] *om.* FGHIJK.

GAu: iniquitatem] inique δεζλμξστυφχ; iniquię ιπ; iniquae ψ. tibi] tui δεζιλμξοπστυφχψ. illa] *om.* δεζϑιλμξοπστυφχψ.

22

Intellegite*	ongeotað A, ongitað *BH*, ongytað *CDG*, ongytaþ *I*, ongitæð *E^3*, ongyteþ *F*, ongiteþ *J*, ongita *K* (*LM*)
haec	ðas A*B*, þas *CDFGHJK*, ðæs *E^3*, þas þing I (*L*)
omnes*	alle A, ealle BCD, eælle E^3
qui	ða A, þa E^x*, ða ðe B, þa þe C, þa ðe FK, þa þe̲ J, þe DGH, ge þe I
obliuiscimini	ofergeoteliað A, ofergitiliað B, ofyrgytuliað C, ofergitelieð E$^{3/x}$*, ofergiteliað J, ofergytað DG, ofergitað FH, forgytað I, forgitað K
dominum*	dryhtnes *D*, drihten E^3, drihtten K, dryht AB, drıhꞇ C, god FIJ, go[ ] G* (*L*)
nequando	ne hwonne AE^x*, þylæs hwonne B, þylæs hwænne D*G, þilæs hwænne HJ, þelæs he hwonne C, þelæs hwænne F, ahwanne I*, þalæs K

rapiat	gereafie A, gereafige BJ, gereafie $E^{3/x}$*, reafige CDGK, reafie FH, hreafige I*
et	⁊ ABCE^{3}FGHIJK
non	ne ABCE^{3}FGIJ, na DHK
sit	sie ABE^{3}H, sy CDFGIJ, beo K
qui	se AE^{3}*, se ðe B, se þe IJ, þe CDF, þe þe GH, þa K
eṛipiat	generge AB, generige CDIJ, genyrie F, nerige *G*H, alise ł anerige $E^{3/x}$*, alyse K

ED: intellígite (H)] INtelligite *Campbell.* hæc (D)] haec *Roeder.* hęc (E)] haec *Harsley.* dominum (D)] domini *Roeder.* go[ ] (G)] g[ ] *Rosier.* nequando (BCDEFJK)] ne quando *Brenner, Wildhagen, Roeder, Harsley, Kimmens, Oess, Sisam.* þylæs hwonne (B)] þy læs hwonne *Brenner.*

OE: þa (E^{x})] *on eras.* ofergitelieð ($E^{3/x}$)] *retraced,* lieð *on eras. by corr.* go[ ] (G)] *top of ascender visible after* o. ne hwonne (E^{x})] *on eras.* þylæs hwænne (D)] hwænne *written below* nequando (*last word on folio*). ahwanne (I)] *initial* a *on eras.* (?): *cf. v. 17* þu awurpe. gereafie ($E^{3/x}$)] eafie *on eras. by corr.* hreafige (I)] ne rapiat : þæt he ne gelæcce *written in left margin.* se (E^{3})] *eras. after word.* alise ł anerige ($E^{3/x}$)] ł anerige *added by corr.*

LTg: Intellegite] Intelligite FIJ, GK: *orig.* Intellegite: *2nd* e *altered to* i; intellígite H: í *altered from another letter;* intellegite BDLM, E: *initial* i *on eras. by corr., orig. red initial* I; intelligite C. haec] hæc BDKL; hęc CEFGJ; hec H. dominum] D: *orig.* domini: *final* i *altered to* m *by corr.* (> dominum); domini L. eripiat] ęripiat G.

LTu: Intellegite] intellegite βς; Intelligite εζιλξοπστ*τυφχ. haec] hęc ειξφ; hæc ϑ; hec στ; ħ τ*. obliuiscimini] obliuiscemini β. dominum] deum ς: *cf. Weber MSS* η* med, *see GAu.* eripiat] eripiet β: *orig.* eripiat: a *deleted,* e *interl.*

GAg: omnes] *om.* FGHIJK. dominum] deum FGHIJK.

GAu: Intellegite] Intellegite nunc ϑ: *cf. Weber MSS* η* moz[c]. omnes] *om.* δεζϑιλμξοπστυφχψ. dominum] deum δεζιλμξοπστυφχψ, ς: *see LTu.*

23

Sacrificium	onsegdnis A, onsægdnes B, onsægdnys C, onsægdnis DH, Æsegdnessæ E^{3}, onsægednys F, onsægnys G, onsægdnesse I, onsægednesse J, onsægnesse K
laudis	lofes ABD$E^{3/x}$*FGIJK, lofys C, leofes H
honorificauit*	gearað *A*B, he arað *C,* araþ J, arweorþað *D,* arweorðað H, arweorðaþ I, arwurðað FG, arwyrðiað K, wiorðæð ł áreð *$E^{3/x}$* (LM)*
me	mec A, me BCDE^{3}FGHIJK
et	⁊ *A*BCFGHI*JK, ond E^{3}

illic	|	ðer A, þer E^{3}, ðær BFK, þær CDGH, þar J, is þær I
iter		siðfet AE^{3}, siðfæt BGIK, siþfæt DH, syþfæt J, weg C, se weg F
est*	|	is ABDE^{3}, ys C
in*		on DE^{3} (*ΛBM*)
quo*		ðider AB, þæt C, þam D, ðæm E^{3}, þæt *F,* mid þam *I,* þan *K* (*GHJ*)
ostendam		ic oteawu A, ic æteawe B, ic æteowe CG, ic æteowie I*, ic ettiewe E^{3}*, ic ætywe J, ic ætywe K, ic oþeowe D, ic oðeowe FH
illi		him AE^{3}FGIJ, him BK (*CD*)
salutare		haelu A, hælo BDFGHIJ, hæle CK, helo E^{3}
dei		godes AB*D**E^{3}FGJK, godys C, godes ł þone halwendan godes I*

ED: dei (D)] meum *Roeder* (*see note, p. 92*): *see OE and LTg.*

OE: lofes (E$^{3/x}$)] es *added by corr.* (?). wiorðæð ł áreð (E$^{3/x}$)] ł áreð *added by corr.* ⁊ (I)] s. est : is *written in right margin.* ic æteowie (I)] *on eras.* (?). ic ettiewe (E^{3})] ti *and stem of* w *retraced.* godes (D)] *added by corr.: see LTg.* godes ł þone halwendan godes (I)] ł þone halwendan godes *written in right margin.*

LTg: honorificauit] honorificabit CDELM, A: b *on eras.: cf. Weber MSS* η moz^{x}, *see GAg.* et] A: *rest of verse in diff. hand: verse eras. from fol. 51v and rewritten here on fol. 51r as 23rd line of normally 22-line text.* in] A: *interl.,* M: *added in right margin; om.* B. quo] F: *eras. after word and between lemma and gloss,* GH: *letter eras. after word,* I: *letter eras. after word, eras. above word,* J: o *altered from another letter,* K: *small eras. after word.* illi] *om.* CD. dei] D: *orig.* meum: *crossed through and* dei *added by corr. along with gloss.*

LTu: honorificauit] honorificabit τ*: *see GAu.*

GAg: honorificauit] honorificabit FIJK, H: *orig.* honorificauit: u *altered to* b, ADEL: *see LTg.* est in] *om.* FGHIJK.

GAu: honorificauit] honorificabit εθιλμξοπστυφχψ, τ*: *see LTu.* est in] *om.* δεζθιλμξοπστυφχ. quo] quod δθμυψ.

PSALM 50

3

Miserere	mildsa *AJK**, (m)iltsa *B**, miltsa G, myldsa *C,* gemiltsa D*E*^{x}***F*I, gemildsa *H* (*M*)
mei	min AB*CF*I, me DE^{x}*GHJ, me me K
deus	god ABCDE^{x}**F**GH*I*JK

secundum — efter AE^{3}, æfter B*F*GHI, æftyr C, æfter DJ, neh *K*
magnam — | ðere miclan A, þære miclan BC, micelan I, micclan J, þere micelre E$^{3/x}$*, micelre D*G*H, mycelre F, þinre K
misericordiam — | mildheortnisse A*D, mildheortnysse CF, mildheortnesse E^{3}GHIJ, [ ]ildheortnesse *B**, myclan K
tuam — | ðinre ABE$^{3/x}$*, þinre CDFGIJ, þ[ ]nre L*, þin H, mildheortnesse K

Et — ⁊ ABCDF*G*HIJK, Ond E^{3}
secundum — efter AE^{3}, æftyr C, æfter DJ, æfter FGHIK, æf[ ] *B**
multitudinem — mengu A, mengo B, mænigeo CG, mænigo DHJ, mængo K, micelnesse ł manege E$^{3/x}$*, manigfealdre F, manifealdnesse ł I*
miserationum — mildsa AJ, miltsa B, myldsa C, miltsunga DF*G*, mildsunga E$^{3/x}$*HI, mildsynga K
tuarum — ðinra ABF, þinra CDGHIJ, þinræ E^{3}, þinre K
dele — adilga ABDFHJ, adylga CGI, adilgæ E^{3}, adylega K
iniquitatem — unrehtwisnisse A*, unryhtwisnesse BD, unrihtwisnysse CF, unrihtwisnesse E$^{3/x}$*GHIJK
meam — mine ABCDFGHIJK, minre E^{3}

ED: Miserere (G)] Misere *Rosier.* [ ]iserere (H)] MISERERE *Campbell.* (m)isericordiam (B)] ..isericordiam *Brenner.* þ[ ]nre (L)] *no gloss Lindelöf*^{2}. [ ]t (G)] Et *Rosier.* Et (I)] et *Lindelöf.* secun[ ]um (B)] secundum *Brenner.*

OE: mildsa (K)] *psalm title partly glossed:* Psalmus iste quinque membre… : sealm þes fif andgyt. (m)iltsa (B)] *left leg of* m *lost due to excision of psalm initial.* gemiltsa (E^{x})] *on eras.*, t *on eras. by another corr.* me (E^{x})] *on eras.* god (E^{x})] *on eras.* god (F)] *letter* (o?) *eras. before word.* god (I)] o *written before word.* þere micelre (E$^{3/x}$)] *2nd* re *added by corr.* mildheortnisse (A)] *2nd* i *written below line.* [ ]ildheortnesse (B)] *initial letter lost due to excision of psalm initial.* ðinre (E$^{3/x}$)] re *added by corr.* þ[ ]nre (L)] *eras. but partly visible.* æft[ ] (B)] *letters lost due to excision of psalm initial, descender of* r *visible.* micelnesse ł manege (E$^{3/x}$)] ł manege *added by corr.* manifealdnesse ł (I)] *gloss eras. after* ł. mildsunga (E$^{3/x}$)] sunga *on eras. by corr.* unrehtwisnisse (A)] *1st* i *written below line.* unrihtwisnesse (E$^{3/x}$)] wisnesse *on eras. by corr.*, iht *retraced.*

LTg: Miserere] MIserere AKM; MISERERE CEF; [ ]erere B: *initial letters excised;* [ ]iserere H: *initial letter lost, outline visible.* mei] MEI CF. deus] H: u *on eras.;* DEUS F. secundum (*1st*)] K: *eras. after* n, dum *on next line;* SECUNDUM F. magnam] magna[ ] G. misericordiam] (m)isericordiam B: *left leg of initial* m *lost due to excision of psalm initial.* Et] [ ]t G: *outline of initial* E *visible.* secundum (*2nd*)] secun[ ]um B: *only lower portion of bowl visible after* n. miserationum] miseratio[ ] G.

LTu: ν: *psalm wanting*, ϱ: *vv 3–11 wanting*. Miserere] MISErere βς; MISERERE ιλμτ*τφχψ; Misserere ϑ. mei] MEI λμψ. deus] DS̄ λμψ. secundum (*1st*)] SECUNDUM λ. magnam] MAgnam λ. misericordiam] missericordiam ϑ. Et] et ϑ. miserationum] misserationum ϑ.

4

Amplius — mae A, má B, ma DFGHK, Ma E[3]*, iet ma C, git ma J, swyþor ł swiðlice I

laua — aðuaeh A, aðweh B, aþweh CK, aþweah FJ, aðweah I, þweah DH, þweach E[x], þwean G

me — mec A, me BCDE[3]FGHIJK

ab — from AE[3], from BC, fram FJK, fram GI, of D

iniustitia* — unrehtwisnisse A, unryhtwisnesse B, unrihtwisnysse *C*F, unrihtwisnesse DE[x]*GIJ, unrihtwisnes K

mea — minre AB*C*DE[3]FGHIJK

et — ⁊ ABCE[3]FGIJKL*

a — from AE[3], from BC, fram GI, fram J, of DFK (*M*)

delicto* — scylde ABCD, scilde J, egyltum ł scylde E[3/x]*, gylte I, synnum FG, synnan K

meo — minre ABCE[3], minum DJ, minum FGHI, minan K, [ ]re L*

munda — geclasna A, geclænsa BC*J*, clænsa DG*H*K, clensæ E[3], clansa F, geclænsa ł afeorma I

me — mec A, me BCE[3]FGHIJK

ED: iniusticia (C)] iniusti[t]ia *Wildhagen*. ⁊ (L)] *no gloss Lindelöf*[2]. [ ]re (L)] *no gloss Lindelöf*[2].

OE: Ma (E[3])] *eras. after word.* unrihtwisnesse (E[x])] *on eras.* ⁊ (L)] *eras. but visible.* egyltum ł scylde (E[3/x])] ł scylde *added by corr.* [ ]re (L)] *eras. but partly visible.* clænsa (G)] *otiose mark above* æ. clænsa (H)] *eras. before word.*

LTg: iniustitia] iniusticia C: *orig.* iniustitia: *2nd* t *altered to* c. mea] C: *eras. after word.* a] á M. munda] J: n *interl.*

LTu: iniustitia] iniusticia τ*.

GAg: iniustitia] iniquitate FGHIJK. delicto] peccato FGHIJK.

GAu: iniustitia] iniquitate δεζϑιλμξοπστυφχψ. delicto] peccato δεζϑιλμξοπστυφχψ.

5

Quoniam — forðon A*BJ, forþon C, Forðæn E[3], forðan F, forðam G, forþon þe I

iniquitatem — unrehtwisnisse A, unryhtwisnesse B, unrihtwisnysse CF, unrihtwisnesse E[3/x]*GIJK

meam	mine AB*C*IJK, minre E^{3}FG
ego	ic ABCDE^{3}FGHIJKL*
agnosco*	oncnawu A, oncnawe BFGHIJ, oncnæwe C, ancnawe D, ongite ł ancnáwa E$^{3/x}$*, gecnawe K
et	⁊ ABCE^{3}*FGIJKL*
delictum*	scyld ABCD, egylt ł scyld E$^{3/x}$*, synne FK, synna G, scyld ł synn I
meum	min ABCDE^{3}*I, mine FGK
coram*	biforan A, beforan BCDIK, beforæn E^{3}, ongean FG
me	me ABCDE^{3}FGIK
est	is ABDE^{3}FGIK, ys C
semper	aa A, simle BE^{3}, symle CD, symble FHIK, symble ł æfre G, æfre K (*L*)

ED: forðon (A)] for ðon *Kuhn.* ic (L)] *no gloss Lindelöf*^{2}. ⁊ (L)] *no gloss Lindelöf*^{2}. pe[ ]catum (H)] peccatum *Campbell.*

OE: forðon (A)] *1st* o *interl.* unrihtwisnesse (E$^{3/x}$)] wisnesse *on eras. by corr.* ic (L)] *eras. but visible.* ongite ł ancnáwa (E$^{3/x}$)] ł ancnáwa *added by corr.* ⁊ (E^{3})] *eras. after word.* ⁊ (L)] *eras. but visible.* egylt ł scyld (E$^{3/x}$)] ł scyld *added by corr.,* ł *on eras.* min (E^{3})] m *on eras.* (*by corr.?*).

LTg: meam] C: *final* m *on eras.* semper] L: s *altered from* p.

GAg: agnosco] cognosco FGHIJK. delictum] peccatum FGIJK; pe[ ]catum H: *letter lost due to hole in leaf, fragment visible.* coram] contra FGHIJK.

GAu: agnosco] cognosco δεζθιλμξοπστυφχψ. delictum] peccatum δεζθιλμξοπστυφχψ. coram] contra δεζθιλμξοπστυφχψ.

6

Tibi	ðe A*BE^{3}F, þe CD*G*HIJK (*L*)
soli	anum ABDHJ, anum CE^{3}FGI, anan K
peccaui	ic synngade A, ic syngode DFGK, ic sinegode E$^{3/x}$*, ic singode H, ic gesyngode BI, ic gesyngode C, asingode J
et	⁊ ABCDE^{3}FGIJKL*
malum	yfel ABDE^{3}FGHIJKL*, yfyl C
coram	biforan A, beforan BCDFG*HJ*K, beforæn E^{3}, toforan I (*L*)
te	ðe ABDF, þe CE^{3}GHIJK (*L*)
feci	ðyde A*, ic dyde BDE$^{3/x}$*FGHIK, ic dide J, ic gedyde C (*L*)
ut	ðæt A, þæt B, þæt CDFGHIJK, þet E^{3}
iustificeris	ðu sie gerehtwisad A, ðu sie geryhtwisod B, þu sy gerihtwisod C, þu sy gerihtwisod I, þu beo geryhtwisad D,

	þu beo gerihtwisad E^{x}*, þu beo gerihtwisod FGH, þu beo gerihtwisode J, du beo gerihtwisod K
in	in A, on BCDE^{3}FGHIJK
sermonibus	worðum A, wordum B, wordum CE^{3}, spræcum D, spræcum FGHJ, spæcum I, spæce K
tuis	ðinum ABF, þinum CD*H**J, þinum E^{3}GI, þinre K
et	⁊ ABCDE^{3}FGHIJK
uincas	ðu wrices A, þu wricest B, þu wyrcst C, ðu oferswiðe D, þu oferswyþe F, þu oferswiðe GHK, þu oferswyðe I*, þu oferswiþe J, oferswiðe ðu E^{3}
dum*	ðonne A, þonne BCGIKL, þonne DHJ, þone F*, midþi E^{3}
iudicaris	ðu ðoemes A*, ðu doemest B, þu demest L, þu demed eart DHJ, ðu demed eart E$^{3/x}$*, þu dend eart F, ðu demend eart G*, ðu dæmed eart K, þu demende bist I, þu wyrcst C

ED: ic gesyngode (C)] ic gesyngode *Wildhagen.* ⁊ (L)] *no gloss Lindelöf*^{2}*.* yfel (L)] *no gloss Lindelöf*^{2}*.* yfel (G)] yfe[ ] *Rosier.* beforan (H)] beforam *Campbell.* feci (J)] feei *Oess.* ðyde (A)] dyde *Kuhn: see OE.* þu beo gerihtwisod (G)] þu beo gerihtwisode *Rosier: final* e *seems to be* d *of* hatudest *on fol. 55r.* sermonibus (G)] sermonibus *Rosier.* ðinum (B)] dinum *Brenner.* þinum (G)] þinu[ ] *Rosier.*

OE: ðe (A) (*1st*)] e *malformed, perhaps altered from another letter.* ic sinegode (E$^{3/x}$)] ic *by corr., eras. before* s, sinego *on eras. by corr.* ⁊ (L)] *eras. but visible.* yfel (L)] *eras. but visible.* ðyde (A)] d *malformed; Kuhn notes '...d from* b.' ic dyde (E$^{3/x}$)] ic *added by corr.* þu beo gerihtwisad (E^{x})] eo gerihtwisad *on eras. by corr.* þinum (H)] *otiose stroke (partly eras.?) after word.* þu oferswyðe (I)] *on eras.* þone (F)] *false start on another letter (minim showing) beneath* þ. ðu ðoemes (A)] *1st* e *and left leg of* m *obscured by stain but visible.* ðu demed eart (E$^{3/x}$)] ðu *by corr., 2nd* d *on eras.,* eart *by corr.* ðu demend eart (G)] *bowl of 1st* d *obscured by small hole.*

LTg: Tibi] L: *single letter of gloss eras. above word;* [ ]ibi G. coram] H: *eras. after word,* L: *gloss eras. above word;* coramp J. te] L: *gloss eras. above word.* feci] L: *gloss eras. above word.* tuis] H: *small eras. after word.*

LTu: iudicaris] iudicaberis ϑ.

GAg: dum] cum FGHIJK.

GAu: dum] cum εζιλμξοπσφχ.

7

Ecce	sehðe AB, on gesihðe D, on gesihðe GHJ, gesehðe L, efne nu C, efne FIK, Eællengæ E^{3}
enim	soð A, soðlice BCHIL, soþlice D, soþlice FGJK, witoðlice E^{3} (*M*)

in	in A, on BCDE^{x}*FG*H*IJKL
iniquitatibus	unrehtwisnissum A, unryhtwisnessum B, unrihtwisnessum I*L*, unrehtwisnysse CF, unryhtwisnesse D, unrihtwisnesse E^{x}*GHJK
conceptus	geecnad A, geeacnad B, geeacnod CDFGHIJKL*, geeæcnod E^{3}
sum	ic eam AI, ic eom BCDE^{x}FGHJKL
et	⁊ ABCE^{3}FGIJKL
in	in A, on BCDE^{3}FGIJKL
delictis*	scyldum AC, scyldum D, leahtrum B, leahtrum L, egyltum E^{3}, synnum FI, synne G, synnan K
peperit*	cende ABCD$E^{3/x}$*L, gecende G, geeacnode I, afeng K (*F*)
me	mec A, me *B*CE^{3}FGIKL
mater	modur *A*, modor BCDFGHIJL, moder E^{3}K
mea	min ABCDE^{3}FGHIJ*K*L

ED: on gesihðe (H)] ongesihðe *Campbell*. efne nu (C)] efnenu *Wildhagen*. me (D) *no gloss*] me *Roeder*.

OE: on (E^{x})] *on eras*. unrihtwisnesse (E^{x})] *on eras*. geeacnod (L)] *deleting dot below blotted* c, c *interl*. cende ($E^{3/x}$)] ce *on eras. by corr.*, nd *retraced*. concepit (F)] *gloss eras*.

LTg: enim] enm M. in (*1st*)] *interl*. H. iniquitatibus] L: *eras. after 2nd* i. me] B: *interl. by glossator*. mater] A: e *slightly obscured by show-through from fol. 52r* (u *of* sacrificium, *l. 16*). mea] K: *followed by a paragraphus, used typically to indicate that a word (or more) from a following psalm-verse is written after it, here, however, followed by eras.: see note to v. 8* incerta.

LTu: iniquitatibus] ξ: *lost due to damage*. conceptus] concoeptus π.

GAg: delictis] peccatis FGIJK; pectis H. peperit] concepit GHIJK, F: *gloss eras*.

GAu: delictis] peccatis δεζϑιλμξοπστυφχψ. peperit] concepit δεζϑιλμξοπστυφχψ.

8

Ecce	sehðe AB, efne nu C, efne FGIJK, Eællenga E^{3}, on gesihþe J, gesehþe L
enim	soð A, soðlice BCGI, soþlice FJK, witodlice L, witoþlice E^{3}
ueritatem	soðfestnisse A, soðfæstnesse BGI, soðfæstnysse CL, soþfæstnisse D, soðfestnesse E^{3}, soþfæstnysse F, soðfæstnisse H, soþfæstnesse J, soþfæstnes K
dilexisti	ðu lufades A, ðu lufodes BE^{3}, þu lufodes L, þu lufudyst C, þu lufudest DFHJ, þu lufodest GI, þu lufedest K
incerta	ða uncuðan AB, þa uncuðan CL, ungewissu DGHJ, ungewissa E^{x}, ungewise *K*, ongewissu F, on ungewisse þingc I*

et	ꝛ ABCE^{3}FGHIJKL
occulta	ða deglan A, ða dieglan *B,* þa diglan C, þa dieglan L, ðæ dihlu $E^{3/x}$*, dihlu DGHJ, diglu F, dygelnyssa I*, digole K
sapientiae	syntru A, snyttru *C,* snyttro *B,* wisdomes *DFGHIJKL,* wisdomes ł snitro *$E^{3/x}$**
tuae	ðinre A*B,* þinre *C,* þines D*GH*I**JKL,* þínes *$E^{3/x}$**, ðines *F*
manifestasti	ðu gesweotuladcs A*, þu gesweotolodes B, þu geswutulodyst C, þu gesweotolodest I, þu geswutelodest J*, þu gesweotoledest L, þu swutoludest DH, þu swutelodest FG, þu swutolodest K, þu gecyþdes E^{3}
mihi	me AB*CDE*^{3}FGHJ*K*L

ED: efne nu (C)] efnenu *Wildhagen.* ðu lufodes (B)] du lufodes *Brenner.* sapientiæ (D)] sapientiae *Roeder.* sapientię (E)] sapientiae *Harsley.* tuæ (D)] tuae *Roeder.* tuę (E)] tuae *Harsley.*

OE: on ungewisse þingc (I)] þingc *extends into right margin,* þ *overlaps final* e *of* ungewisse. ðæ dihlu ($E^{3/x}$)] hlu *on eras. by corr.* dygelnyssa (I)] lnyss *on eras.* wisdomes ł snitro ($E^{3/x}$)] wisdomes ł *added by corr.* þines (I)] es *on eras.* þínes ($E^{3/x}$)] es *added by corr.* ðu gesweotulades (A)] tu *interl.* þu geswutelodest (J)] *orig.* þu geswutolodest: *1st* o *altered to* e.

LTg: incerta] K: mihi *eras. after word: see note to v. 7* mea. occulta] B: st *written in red in right margin: cf. v. 10* humiliata. sapientiae] sapientiæ BDL; sapientię CEFGHIJK. tuae] tuæ BD; tuę CEFGHJKL. mihi] K: *added later by main hand;* michi E, C: *orig.* mihi: c *interl. by corr.*

LTu: sapientiae] sapientię ειξοπςυφ; sapientiæ ϑ; sapientie στ*τ. tuae] tuę ειξοφ; tuæ ϑμυ; tue σςτ*τ. mihi] michi ισςτ*τφ, π: c *interl.;* m[1] ξυ.

9

Asparges	ðu onstrigdes A, þu onstregdes B, þu onstregdst L, ðu astregdest *$E^{3/x}$*,* ðu tostredyst C, þu onscridest *J,* þu stredest *DGM^{2},* ðu stredest *FH,* þu stred *K,* þu besprengc ł geand[ ]ædst *I**
me	mec A, me B*CE*^{3}FGI*JKL** (*H*)
⟨domine⟩	drihт̄ *C,* drih̃ *J* (*L*)
hysopo	mid ysopan ABL, mid isopon *CJ,* mid hysopon *F,* myd ysopo *E^{x}*,* mid ysopon G, issopu<u>m</u> K, hlenorteare I* (*H*)
et	ꝛ ABCE^{3}FGHIJKL
mundabor	ic biom geclasnad A, ic beo geclæsnod BL, ic beo geclænsod CFGJK, ic beo geclensod $E^{3/x}$*, ic beo<u>m</u> clænsod D, ic beo clænsod H, ic beo geclænsod ł ꝛ ic beo afeormod I
lauabis	ðu ðwes A, þu þwehst B, ðu þwehst L, þu þwyhst C, þu

	þweæhst E$^{3/x}$*, þu ðwehst I, þu þreahst J, þu aþwihst D, þu aðwihst H, ðu aþweahst F, þu ahwyhst G, ðu wæxst K
me	mec A, me BCE^{3}FGHIJKL
et	⁊ ABCE^{3}FGHIJKL
super	ofer ABDE^{3}FGHIJKL, ofyr C
niuem	snaw ABDFGHJKL, snawe CI, snæw E^{3}
dealbabor	ic biom gehwitad *A,* ic beo<u>m</u> gehwitod C, ic bio gehwitad E^{3}*, ic beo ablæced *B,* ic béo ablicen D, ic beo ablicen FGHKM^{2}, ⁊ ic beo gehwited I, ic bea ahwitod J, ic beo ablæced ⁊ ahwitod L

ED: þu onscridest (J)] þu onstridest *Oess.* ðu stredest (H)] þu stredest *Campbell.* þu besprengc ł geand[ ]ædst (I)] þu besprengc ł geandbædst (?) *Lindelöf, p. 83:* 'unsicher ob der anfangskonsonant der letzten silbe wirklich "b" ist.' hysópo (H)] hysopo *Campbell.* ic bea ahwitod (J)] ic beo ahwitod *Oess.*

OE: ðu astregdest (E$^{3/x}$)] *eras. after* ðu, g *on eras., final* t *added, 2nd* e *altered from another letter* (?). þu besprengc ł geand[ ]ædst (I)] ł geand[ ]ædst *written in left margin, letter after 1st* d *lost due to tight binding.* me (L)] s. o d<u>omi</u>ne : driht̄ *interl. after* me. myd ysopo (E^{x})] *on eras.* hlenorteare (I)] *eras. before word.* ic beo geclensod (E$^{3/x}$)] ic beo *added by corr., letter eras. after* d. þu þweæhst (E$^{3/x}$)] st *added by corr.* ic bio gehwitad (E^{3})] ad *by corr.*

LTg: Asparges] Asperges DEFGHIJ, M: *orig.* Asparges: a *deleted by subscript dot,* e *interl.;* Assperges K: *cf. Weber MSS* med. me] H: *word eras. after;* me domine CJ, L: *see OE note to* me: *cf. Weber MSS* Vabc. hysopo] hýsopo C; ysopo EJ, F: *letter eras. before word;* hysópo H. dealbabor] dealuabor AB.

LTu: Asparges] Aspargis β; Asperges δζιλξοςτ*τυφχψ: *cf. Weber MSS* med. hysopo] hisopo δϑ; ysopo ειμξστ*τφ, π: *orig.* hysopo: h *eras.*

10

Auditui	gehernisse A, gehiernesse BE^{3}, g̲ehyrnysse C, gehyrnisse D*H*M^{2}, gehyrnysse F, gehyrnesse GKL, gehernesse I, gehirnesse J
meo	minre ABCDFHIKLM^{2}, min E^{3}, mine G, mire J
dabis	ðu seles AB, þu sylyst C, þu sylst FGK, þu selst DHI, þu selest E^{3}L, þu silest J
gaudium	gefian A, gefean BDFHIJL, gefeæn E^{3}, gefean ł blisse G, blisse CK
et	⁊ ABCFGHIJKL, ond E^{3}
laetitiam	blisse A*BDE^{3}FGHIJL,* gefean *CK*
et	⁊ ABCE^{3}FGIJKL

exultabunt	gefiað A, gefeoð BC, gefeogað DGHL, gefeogaþ IJ, hihtæþ ł gefeogað E$^{3/x}$*, hi hyhtað F, gegladiaþ K
ossa	ban ABCDFGHIJKL, bæn E^{3}
humiliata	ða geeðmodedan A, ða geeaðmeddan *B,* þa geeadmododan *C,* þa geeadmedan J, þa geæaðmeddan L, geeaðmeddu DFGH, eædmodæn E^{3}*, eadmode K

ED: Audítui (H)] Auditui *Campbell.* leticiam (C)] leti[t]iam *Wildhagen.* lætitiam (D)] laetitiam *Roeder.* lętitiam (E)] laetitiam *Harsley.*

OE: hihtæþ ł gefeogað (E$^{3/x}$)] ł gefeogað *added by corr.* eædmodæn (E^{3})] *eras. before word.*

LTg: Auditui] Audítui H. laetitiam] leticiam C: *orig.* letitiam: *2nd* t *altered to* c; lætitiam BD; lętitiam EFGHIL; letitiam JK. humiliata] B: st *written in red in right margin: cf. v. 8* occulta, C: li *interl.*

LTu: laetitiam] lętitiam ει; letitiam ϑλξσςυ; leticiam τ*τ; lęticiam φ. exultabunt] exsultabunt ψ.

11

Auerte	acer AB, acyrr CD, acyr GHK, Ahwirf ł acer E$^{3/x}$*, awend F, awend ł acer I, acir ł awænd J, acier ⁊ awend L
faciem	onsiene ABE^{3}, onsine L, ansyne CDFGK, ansiene H, ansene I, ansyn J
tuam	ðine AE$^{3/x}$*, þine BCFGHIJKL
a	fro A, from B, from E^{3}L, fram CDFHJK, fram GI
peccatis	synnum AE^{3}FGIL, synnum BCDH, sinnum J, synnan K
meis	minum AFGI, minum BCDHJL, mine E^{x}, minan K
et	⁊ ABCE^{3}FGHIJKL
omnes	alle A, ealle BCDFGHIJKL, eælle E^{3} (*M*)
iniquitates	unrehtwisnisse A, unryhtwisnessa BD, unrihtwisnysse C, unrihtwisnessæ E$^{3/x}$*, unrihtwisnyssa F, unrihtwisnesse GJL, unrihtwisnessa HI*, unrihtwisnes K
meas	mine AE^{3}FGIJKL, mina BDH, mune C
dele	adilga ABIJL, adylga C, adilgæ E^{3}, dilga DF*H**, dylga G, dilega K

ED: á (E)] a *Harsley.*

OE: Ahwirf ł acer (E$^{3/x}$)] Ah *on eras. by corr., eras. after* f, ł acer *added by corr.* ðine (E$^{3/x}$)] e *added by corr.* unrihtwisnessæ (E$^{3/x}$)] un *retraced,* riht *by corr.,* t *on eras., eras. after 1st* s. unrihtwisnessa (I)] *orig.* unrihtwisnesse: *final* e *altered to* a. dilga (H)] i *slightly obscured by eras. from lemma.*

LTg: a] á E. omnes] M: *orig.* omes: *macron added by corr.* dele] H: *final* e *on eras.*

LTu: ς: *vv 11–end wanting.*

12

Cor	heortan A*BCDFHIJKL, heorte E^{3}G (*M*)
mundum	clæne ABCDFGHIKL, clene E^3, læne J
crea	gecwica ABCJL, scype DE^{3}GKM^2, scipe FH, scyp I
in	in A, on BCDE^{3}FGHIJKL
me	me ABCDE^{3}FGHIJKL
deus	god ABCE^{3}FGHI*JKL
et	⁊ *A*BCDE^{3}FGHIJ*K*L
spiritum	gast ABCDFGHIJ*K**L, gæst E^3
rectum	rehtne A, ryhtne B, rihtne CE^{3}FJL, riht I*, ryhtwisne D, rihtwisne GH
innoua	geniowa A, geniwa BCDFG*H*JL, geníwa M^2, geniwæ E^3, geedneowa *I*
in	on BCDE^{3}FGHIJL
uisceribus	innoðum ABCGIJ, innoðum D, innoþum HL, innoðe E^3, hinoðe F
meis	minum AE^{3}FGHI, minum BCDJL

ED: ínnoua (HI)] innoua *Campbell, Lindelöf.*

OE: heortan (A)] *eras.* (*3 letters:* cle?) *after word.* god (I)] o *written before word.* gast (K)] *psalm breaks off here and recommences at Ps 53.3* (*wanting 2 fols*). riht (I)] *eras. after word.*

LTg: Cor] Cór M. et] A: *interl.*, K: *inserted by corr. on eras.* spiritum] K: *psalm breaks off here and recommences at Ps 53.3* (*wanting 2 fols*). innoua] ínnoua H, I: *2nd* n *on eras.*

LTu: et] *interl.* λ; *eras.* π.

13

Ne	ne ABCDFGHIJL, Ne E^3
proicias	aweorp ðu AB, awerp þu C, æwiorp ðu E^3, awyrp þu I, aweorp ðu L, awyrp ł ascyhh DG, awurp ł ascyhh H, wyrp ðu F, afir þu J
me	mec A, me BCDE^{3}FGHIJL
a	from AL, from E^{x}*, fram BC*J*, fram FI, of DGH (*M*)
facie	onsiene AB, onsine E^3, ansyne *C*DFGH, ansene I, ansine *JL*
tua	ðin A, ðinre BE^3, þinre CFGHIL, þine J
et	⁊ ABCE^{3}FGHIJL

spiritum	gast ABCDGHIJL, gæst E[3], gaste F
sanctum	haligne ABDFGHJL, hæligne E[3], halgan CI
tuum	ðinne A, þinne BCDE[3]FGHIJL
ne	ne ABCDE[3]FGHJL, ⁊ ne I*
auferas	afir ðu AB, afyr þu C, afir þu L, fir ðu J, afyrre ðu D, æfyrre þu E[3/x]*, afyrre GH, afyrse þu F, ætbred þu ł ne afyrsa þu I*
a	from A*E*[3]L, fro<u>m</u> B, fram CGI, fra<u>m</u> FHJ (*M*)
me	me ABCE[3]FGHIJL

ED: afyrre ðu (D) awyrpe ðu *Roeder.* á (E)] a *Harsley.*

OE: fro<u>m</u> (E[x])] *on eras.* ⁊ ne (I)] *written in left margin.* æfyrre þu (E[3/x])] þu *added by corr.* ætbred þu ł ne afyrsa þu (I)] ætbred þu *written in left margin.*

LTg: a (*1st*)] á M. a facie] C: i *on eras.;* a facię L; affacie J. a (*2nd*)] á EM.

LTu: facie] facię ε. a (*2nd*)] *interl.* ο.

14

Redde	agef A, agif BJL, agyf C, agyld DFGH, AGild E[3]*, ageld ł forgyf I
mihi	me ABCD*E*[3]FGHIJL
laetitiam	blisse A*BCDE*[3]*FGHIJL*
salutaris	haelu A, hælo BDFGHJ, helo E[3], hæle CL, halwendan I
tui	ðinre A, þinre BCDGHL, ðine E[3]F, þine J, þines I
et	⁊ ABCE[3]FGHIJL
spiritu	mid gaste AB, gaste CGL, of gaste DH, of gæste E[3], gast F, gasta J, mid ealdorlicum I*
principali	alderlice A, aldorlice BC, aldorlicu<u>m</u> D, aldorlicum H, eældordomlican E[3], ealdorlicum GL, ealdormannes F, gaste I
confirma	getrime AE[3], getryme BCDL, getrima J, getrym FGI, getry H
me	me ABCE[3]FGHIJL

ED: AGild (E)] Agild *Harsley.* leticiam (C)] leti[t]iam *Wildhagen.* lętitiam (E)] laetitiam *Harsley.* aldorlice (C)] aldorliche *Wildhagen.*

OE: AGild (E[3])] A *added* (?). mid ealdorlicum (I)] *eras. before* mid, *with another* mid *written in left margin in diff. hand.*

LTg: mihi] michi E. laetitiam] lætitiam B; leticiam C: *orig.* letitiam: *2nd* t *altered to* c; letitiam DJL; lętitiam EFG, H: *cauda, perhaps by corr., same as that of Pss 49.10* ferę, *49.12* terrę, *and 50.20* ędificentur.

LTu: mihi] michi ιλξτ*τ, πϱ: c *interl.;* m[1] σφ. laetitiam] lętitiam ειλξ; lætitiam ϑ; laeticiam ϱ: *orig.* laetitiam: *2nd* t *deleted,* c *interl.;* letitiam συ; leticiam τ*τ; lęticiam φ. et] *interl.* β.

15

Doceam*	ic lęru A, ic lære B*CD*GHIJ*L*, Ic lere *E^3*, ic tæce F (*M*)
iniquos	ða urehtwisan A, ða unryhtwisan B, þa unrihtwisan C*J*L, ðæ unrihtwisan E$^{3/x}$*, þam unrihtwisan I*, unryhtwise D, unrihtwise FGH
uias	wegas ABCDFGHIJL, wegæs E^3
tuas	ðine ABL, þine CDE^{3}FGHIJ
et	⁊ ABCE^{3}FGHIJL
impii	ða arleasan A, þa arleasan BCI, þa arleæsæ *E$^{3/x}$**, arlease DGHJL, arleasum F
ad	to ABCDE^{3}FGHIJL
te	ðe ABDG, þe CE^{3}HIJL, ðe F
conuertentur	bioð gecerde A, beoð gecirde B, beoð gecyrryde C, beoð gecirrede E$^{3/x}$*, beoð gecyrred D, beoð gecyrred FGH, gecyrrað I*, sin gecirrede J, sien gecyrrede L (*M*)

ED: impíí (E)] impii *Harsley.*

OE: ðæ unrihtwisan (E$^{3/x}$)] wisan *on eras. by corr.* þam unrihtwisan (I)] an *in darker ink.* þa arleæsæ (E$^{3/x}$)] þa *on eras. by corr.* beoð gecirrede (E$^{3/x}$)] beoð *added by corr.* gecyrrað (I)] að *on eras.*

LTg: Doceam] M: ā *on eras.*, ł docebo *written in left margin;* Docebo CDEL: *cf. Weber MSS* εη med, *see GAg.* iniquos] iniquo J. impii] impíí E. conuertentur] conuertêntur M.

LTu: Doceam] Docebo τ*: *see GAu.* et] υ: *remainder of psalm wanting.*

GAg: Doceam] Docebo FHIJ, CDEL: *see LTg;* [ ]ocebo G; *for* M *see LTg.*

GAu: Doceam] Docebo δεζϑιλμξοπϱστυφχψ, τ*: *see LTu.*

16

Libera	gefrea A, gefreo C, Gefriolsæ E^3, alies BL, alys DFGHJ, ales I
me	mec A, me BCDE^{3}FGHIJL (*M*)
de	of ABCDE^{3}FGHIJL
sanguinibus	blodum ABCE^{3}FGHL, blodum DJ, blodgeotendum I
deus	god ABCE^{3}FGI*JL
deus	god ABCE^{3}FGIJL
salutis	hælu A, hælo BFJL, helo E^3, hæle CDGH, hæl I*
meae	minre A*C*D*FI*L*, mynre *J*, mine *E^{3}G*, inre *B* (*H*)
et	⁊ A*BCDE^{3}FGHIJL
exultauit*	gefið *A*, gefihð *B*, gefihþ *L*, uppahefð *C*, upahefð *D*GHI, upahefþ F, upahefþ J, winsumæð *E^3* (*M*)

lingua	tunge ABCDGIJL, tungæ E[3], tunga F, tuncge H
mea	min ABCDE[3]FGHIJL
iustitiam	rehtwisnisse A, ryhtwisnesse BD, rihtwisnysse *C*F, rihtwisnesse E[x]*GHIJL
tuam	ðine ABE[3], þine CDFGHIJ, þinre L

ED: god god (C)] god *Wildhagen.* hæle (G)] hælo *Rosier.* meæ (D)] meae *Roeder.* meę (E)] meae *Harsley.* inre (B)] minre *Brenner.* upahefþ̄] upahefþ *Oess.*

OE: god (I) (*1st*)] o *written before word.* hæl (I)] *eras. after word.* minre (C)] r *interl.* ⁊ (A)] *gloss eras.* (*ca 8 letters*) *after word.* rihtwisnesse (E[x])] rihtwis *on eras.*

LTg: me] mé M. meae] meæ BD; meę CEGL; męę H; mee J. exultauit] exultabit BE, A: b *on eras. by corr.;* exaltabit CELM, D: *orig.* exultabit: u *deleted by subscript dot, 1st* a *interl.: cf. Weber MSS* δ med, *see GAg.* iustitiam] iusticiam C: *orig.* iustitiam: *2nd* t *altered to* c.

LTu: δ: *rest of psalm wanting.* meae] meę ειξφ; meæ ϑ; mee στ*τ. exultauit] exaltabit τ*: *see GAu.* iustitiam] iusticiam τ*τφ, ϱ: *orig.* iustitiam: *2nd* t *deleted,* c *interl.*

GAg: exultauit] exaltabit FGI, CDELM: *see LTg,* H: *orig.* exultabit: u *altered to* a; exaltauit J; exultabit G, ABE: *see LTg.*

GAu: exultauit] exultabit δεζιλμξοπστψ; exaltabit ϑφχ, ϱ: *orig.* exultabit: u *deleted, 1st* a *interl.,* τ*: *see LTu.*

17

Domine	dryhten A, drihten FGI, drihtæn E[3]*, dryht̄ B, driht̄ CL, drih̄ J (*H*)
labia	weolere A, weleras BDGHIJL, welyras C, weleræs E[3], welerum F
mea	mine ABCDE[3]FGHIJL
aperies	ontyn ðu *A*BL, ontyn þu C, þu antyn DH, ðu untyn E[3]*, þu untýn F, þu untyn G, þu antynst I, untine J
et	⁊ ABCE[3]FGHIJL
os	muð ABC*D*E[3]FGHL, muþ IJ (*M*)
meum	min ABCDE[3]*I, minne FGJL
adnuntiabit	segeð *A*, sægyð *C*, bodað BG*H*, bodaþ D*F*, segeð ł bodaþ ł cyþeð E[3/x]*, ⁊ cyþ ł bodaþ *I*, to bodigenne J, ⁊ bodað L
laudem	lof ABCDE[3]FGHIJL
tuam	ðin ABF, þin CDE[3]GHIJL

ED: [ ]omine (H)] Domine *Campbell.* annuntiabit (C)] a[d]nuntiabit *Wildhagen.*

OE: drihtæn (E[3])] d *retouched.* ðu untyn (E[3])] *eras. after word.* min (E[3])] *eras. after word.* segeð ł bodaþ ł cyþeð (E[3/x])] segeð ł bodaþ ł *added by corr.*

LTg: Domine] [ ]omine H: *outline only of initial letter visible.* aperies] A: s *added by corr.* (?). os] ós DM. adnuntiabit] A: b *on eras. by corr.*; annuntiabit FI, CH: *1st* n *on eras. by corr.*

LTu: adnuntiabit] annuntiabit εζιλξπστ*τχ; annunciabit φ, ϱ: *orig.* annuntiabit: t *deleted,* c *interl.*; adnunciabit ψ.

18

Quoniam	forðon ABJL, forþon CG, forðæn E^3, forþon þe I
si	gif ABCDE^3GHIJL, gyf F
uoluisses	ðu walde A, ðu wolde BD, þu wolde H, þu woldyst C, ðu woldest $E^{3/x}$*I, þu woldest FGJ, þu woldes L
sacrificium	onsegdnisse A, onsægdnisse BDH, onsægdnysse CL, onsegdnesse E^3, onsægednysse F, onsægdnesse GI, onsægednesse J
dedissem	ic salde A, ic sealde B*C*DFG*H*IL, ic seælde E^3, ic sealde þe J
utique	gewislice ABC, witodlice D*E*^{3}*FGH*I*JL
holocaustis	onsegdnisse A, onsægdnysse *C,* on onsægdnyssum I, on bærningum *B,* ofrungum *D,* ofrungum *F*H, offrungum *G,* offrungum *J,* offrengæ *E*^{3}, bærningum ⁊ offrungum *L* (*M*)
⟨autem⟩	soðlice *BCE*^{3}*GL* (*DM*)
non	ðu ne A, þu ne BIL, na CDGH, ne E^3F
delectaberis	gelustfullas *A,* gelustfullast BIL, þu gelustfullast CDFGH, þu gelustfulledest J, gelustfullæst þu E^3

ED: forðon (A)] for ðon *Kuhn.* forðæn (E)] Forðæn *Harsley.* onsægdnysse (L)] onsægdnvsse *Lindelöf*[2]. utiquę (E)] utiquae *Harsley.*

OE: ðu woldest ($E^{3/x}$)] st *added by corr.* witodlice (E^3)] d *on eras. by corr.*

LTg: dedissem] C: *2nd* s *interl. by corr.,* H: *small eras. after* m. utique] I: *eras. after word;* utiquę EG. holocaustis] F: *eras. after word* (*5 letters*); holochaustis J; holocaustis autem BCDEGL, M: autem *interl.*: *cf. Weber MSS* KT*εη[2]. delectaberis] A: b *on eras. by corr.*

LTu: uoluisses] uoluises ϑ. dedissem] dedisem ϑ. holocaustis] holochaustis ϑ; holocaustis autem τ*: *cf. Weber MSS* KT*εη[2]. delectaberis] delectaueris β.

19

Sacrificium	onsegdnis *A,* onsægdnes BI*L, onsægdniss C, onsægdnis DH, onsægdnes *G,* onsegdnesse $E^{3/x}$*, onsægednysse F, onsægednesse J
deo	gode ABCE^3FGIJL
spiritus	gast A*BCDFGHIJL, gæst E^3

contribulatus	geswenced ABL, geswænced J, geswincys C, geswenced ł geunrotsod D, geswenced ł geunrotsod E^x*G, geswenced geunrotsod H, geunrotsad ł gedrefed I, gedrefed F
cor	heorte ABCE^x*FJL, heortan DGHI (*M*)
contritum	forðrested A, forþræst CJ, geðræste B, þræst L, forgnidene DE^x*F*G*H, forgnídene M², þa tobryttan I
et	⁊ ABCE³FGHJL
humiliatum	geeaðmodad A*, geeaðmedde BDFGH, geadmedd C, geeadmed J, geeaðmed L, ðæ eæðmodæ E³*
deus	god ABCE³FGI*JL
non	ne ABCFGIJL, na DF (*E*)
spernit*	forhogad AG, forhogað BCL, forhogaþ J, forhygeð D, ne forhogad E^{3/x}*, beheold F, forhyge þu ł þu ne forsihst I (*M*)

ED: onsegdnesse (E)] Onsegdnesse *Harsley.* gast (A)] gas *Kuhn: see OE.* contribulatus (B)] contristatus *Brenner.* heortan (G)] [ ]rtan *Rosier.* con[ ]itum (G)] contritum *Rosier.* forhogad (G)] forh::[ ] *Rosier.*

OE: onsægdnes (I)] *eras. after word.* onsegdnesse (E^{3/x})] ons *on eras. by corr.,* egd *retraced.* gast (A)] *drypoint* t *incised after* s. geswenced ł geunrotsod (E^x)] ł geunrotsod *on eras.* heorte (E^x)] *on eras.* forgnidene (E^x)] *on eras.* geeaðmodad (A)] *letter eras. after final* d. ðæ eæðmodæ (E³)] *letter eras. after final* æ. god (I)] s. o *written before word.* ne forhogad (E^{3/x})] *on eras.*

LTg: Sacrificium] A: u *obscured by show-through from fol. 51v* (e *of* mater, *l. 15*), G: S *partly lost.* cor] cór M. contritum] con[ ]itum G. non] *om.* E. spernit] M: *remainder of psalm wanting.*

LTu: contribulatus] o: *remainder of psalm wanting.*

GAg: spernit] despicies GHI, F: *orig.* despicias: a *underlined to signal deletion,* e *interl.,* J: *2nd* e *on eras.*

GAu: spernit] despicies εζιλμξπϱστφχψ.

20

Benigne	freamsumlice A, fremsumlice BL, fremsumlice CJ, medomlice DH, medem[ ]ice G, Estelice E³, ealwerlic F, wellwillendlice I
fac	doa A, dó B*CDL, do E³FGHJ, do drihten I*
domine	drihten E³L, dryhṫ AB, drihṫ C, driħt FG, driħ J (*I*)
in	in A, on BCDE³FGHIJL
bona	godum ABD*FGH,* godum J, godan CIL, góde E³
uoluntate	willan ABCDFGHIJL, willæn E³
tua	ðinum AB, þinum CI, þinum DFGHJL, þines E³

sion	sion *CE*^{3}GJL
ut*	ðæt A, þæt D, þætte BL, þætte C, þett E$^{3/x}$*, ⁊ GI, ⁊ þæt FH, ⁊ þæt þe J
aedificentur	sien getimbred A, sien getimbred *D,* sien getimbrede *BL,* syn getimbryde *C,* sien getymbrede *E$^{3/x}$*,* sýn getymbrod *F,* sien getymbred *H,* syn getimbrode G, beoð getimbrede *I,* firn getimbrode *J*
muri	wallas A, weallas BCDFG*H**IJL, weællæs E^{3}
hierusalem	hierusalemys *C,* hierusælem E^{3}, hierusalem L, ierussał G, on hierłm I, ierłm *J* (*H*)

ED: medem[ ]ice (G)] me[ ] *Rosier.* fac (I)] fac domine *Lindelöf* (*but see note, p. 83*). ædificentur (D)] aedificentur *Roeder.* ędificentur (E)] aedificentur *Harsley.* ierusalem (C)] [h]ierusalem *Wildhagen.* hierłm (J)] hierusalem *Oess.* on hierłm (I)] on hier*usalem* *Lindelöf.* ierłm (J)] ier*usalem* *Oess.*

OE: dó (B)] *accent faint but visible.* do drihten (I)] s. o *written before* drihten. þett (E$^{3/x}$)] *final* t *altered from another letter and on eras.* sien getymbrede (E$^{3/x}$)] ien *on eras. by corr.* weallas (H)] *eras. after word from Lat. line below.*

LTg: domine] I: *eras.,* e *partly visible.* bona] F: *orig.* bone: e *altered to* a, H: a *altered from another letter.* sion] syon E, C: *orig.* sion: i *deleted by subscript dot,* y *interl. by corr.* aedificentur] ædificentur BD; edificentur CJ; ędificentur EFL, H: *cauda, perhaps by corr., same as Pss 49.10* ferę, *49.12* terrę, *and 50.14* lętitiam; aedificæntur I. muri] H: *eras. after word.* hierusalem] ierusalem H, C: *orig.* hierusalem: h *eras.;* hierłm J.

LTu: Benigne] β: i *interl.* domine] σ: *interl., but before* fac. sion] syon εζιξστ*τφ. aedificentur] edificentur βλξστ*τ; ędificentur ειφ; ædificentur ϑ. hierusalem] ierusalem εζιλσφ, π: *orig.* hierusalem: h *eras.;* ierłm τ*τ.

GAg: ut] et FGHI.

GAu: ut] et εζϑιλμξπϱτφχψ.

21

Tunc	ðonne AE^{3}, þonne BGIL, þonne CDFHJ
acceptabis	ðu onfoest A, þu onfehst BCE^{3}FIJL, ðu anfehst D, þu anfehst H, þu ahefst G
sacrificium	onsegdnisse A, onsægdnesse BI*, onsægdnysse CL, onsægednysse F, onsægednes J, offrunge ł onsegdnesse E$^{3/x}$*, ofrunge D, offrunge GH
iustitiae	rehtwisnisse A, ryhtwisnesse *B,* rihtwisnysse *CFL,* rihtwisnesse *IJ,* of rihtwisnesse *E^{x}*,* ryhtwise *D,* rihtwise *GH*
oblationes	oflatan ABL, ofletan J, oblatan C, bringas DGH, bringas ł oflaten E^{x}, ofrunga F, freolaca I

et ⁊ ABCFGHIJL, ond E^{3}
holocausta onsegdnisse A, onsægdnysse C, offrunga BGIL, ofrunge D, offrunge E^{3}, ofrunga H*J*, bringað F*
tunc ðonne AE^{3}, þonne BCGIL, þonne DFHJ
inponam* onsettað *AC*, onsetteð *E*^{x}*, gesettað *B*, gesittað *L*, hy asettað *D*GH, hi asettað F, hi asсttaþ J
super ofer *A*BDE^{3}FG*H*IJL, ofyr C
altare wibed *A*B, wigbed CD, wigbede I, þibed GH, wifod $E^{3/x}$*, weofod FJL
tuum ðin AE^{3}F, þin ḄCDGHJ, þinum I, þinum L
uitulos calfur A, cealfur B, cealfas C, calfas F, cealfru DHI*, ceælfre $E^{3/x}$*, cealfra G, cealf J, celfru L

ED: iusticię (C)] iusti[t]ię *Wildhagen.* iustitiæ (D)] iustitiae *Roeder.* iustitię (E)] iustitiae *Harsley.* iustitie (I)] iustitiae *Lindelöf.* oblationes (F)] Oblationes *Kimmens.*

OE: onsægdnesse (I)] *eras. before 1st* s. offrunge ł onsegdnesse ($E^{3/x}$)] offrunge ł *added by corr.* of rihtwisnesse (E^{x})] *on eras.* bringað (F)] ringað *obscured by eras. but visible.* onsetteð (E^{x})] on *on eras.* wifod ($E^{3/x}$)] f *on eras. by corr.* cealfru (I)] *eras. between gloss and lemma.* ceælfre ($E^{3/x}$)] re *added by corr.*

LTg: iustitiae] iustitiæ BDL; iusticię C: *orig.* iustitię: *2nd* t *altered to* c; iustitię EHJ; iustitie G, I: *orig.* iustitiae: a *eras., eras. after word.* holocausta] holochausta J. inponam] imponent C: *orig.* inponent: i (*blotted*) *added initially, orig.* i *and 1st* n *linked to form* m: *see GAg;* inponent BDL, A: ent *on eras. by corr.,* E: inp *on eras. by corr.: cf. Weber MSS* αγδεζη moz med, *see GAg.* super] A: *orig.* super: *cross-stroke through descender of* p *eras.,* er *added by corr.,* H: *eras. before word.* altare] A: *eras. (2 letters) after word.*

LTu: iustitiae] iustitiæ ϑ; iustitię ιξ; iustitie σ; iusticie τ*τ; iusticię φ. oblationes] oblationis β; obla[ ] φ: *remainder of verse wanting.* holocausta] holochausta ϑ. inponam] imponent t*: *see GAu.*

GAg: inponam] imponent H: *orig.* inponent: *middle leg added to 1st* n *to form* m, C: *see LTg;* inponent FGJ, I: *gloss eras.,* ABDEL: *see LTg.*

GAu: inponam] imponent ειλξπσ; inponent ζϑμϱτχψ, τ*: *see LTu.*

Note: *The following doxology is given in C immediately after v. 21:*

wuldyr fædyr ⁊ suna ⁊ halgum gaste swa swa wæs on fruman ⁊ nu ⁊
Gloria patri et filio et spiritui sancto sicut erat in principio et nunc et
symle ⁊ on woruld worulde sy swa
semper et in secula seculorum amen

ED: worulde] woruld *Wildhagen.*

synopsis of arrangement and features

text of Roman version, to be read down page

italic siglum = Latin (LT) note — asterisk = Old English (OE) note

Laetabor — **ic blisige *B*D, ic blissige F***

MS sigla

aequitatem* — asterisk after lemma = Gallican variant

(sedes) — parentheses around lemma = Gallican addition

qui |
iudicas | — vertical bars call attention to order of OE gloss

⟨meam⟩ — angled brackets around lemma = reading not within standard Roman or Gallican version

Regnabit }
dominus } — curly braces = altered word order in Gallican version but same lemmata

ED: readings by various editors
OE: notes on Old English glosses
LTg: notes on Latin texts of glossed psalters
LTu: notes on Latin texts of unglossed psalters
GAg: Gallican readings of glossed psalters
GAu: Gallican readings of unglossed psalters

list of manuscript sigla

MSS of Psalms with Old English Glosses

A London, BL, Cotton Vespasian A. 1 (Vespasian Psalter)
B Oxford, Bodleian Library, Junius 27 (5139) (Junius Psalter)
C Cambridge University Library, Ff. 1. 23 (Cambridge Psalter)
D London, BL, Royal 2 B. v (Regius Psalter)
E Cambridge, Trinity College, R. 17. 1 (987) (Eadwine Psalter)
F London, BL, Stowe 2 (Stowe Psalter)
G London, BL, Cotton Vitellius E. xviii (Vitellius Psalter)
H London, BL, Cotton Tiberius C. vi (Tiberius Psalter)
I London, Lambeth Palace 427 (Lambeth Psalter)
J London, BL, Arundel 60 (Arundel Psalter)
K Salisbury, Cathedral Library, 150 (Salisbury Psalter)
L London, BL, Additional 37517 (Bosworth Psalter)
M New York, Pierpont Morgan Library, M. 776 (Blickling Psalter)
N^a Sondershausen, Schloßmuseum, Hs. Br. 1. (Sondershäuser Psalter)
N^b Cambridge, Pembroke College, 312, C. nos 1 and 2 (Cambridge Fragments)
N^c Haarlem, Stadsbibliotheek, s.n. (Haarlem Fragments)
O Paris, BN, lat. 8846

Additional MSS of the Psalms

α Basel, Universitätsbibliothek N. I. 2
β Berlin, Staatsbibliothek Preussischer Kulturbesitz, Hamilton 353
γ Cambridge University Library, Ff. 5. 27
δ Cambridge, Corpus Christi College, 272
ε Cambridge, Corpus Christi College, 391
ζ Cambridge, Corpus Christi College, 411
η Cambridge, Magdalene College, Pepys 2981 (3)
ϑ Cambridge, St. John's College, 59 (C. 9) (Southampton Psalter)
ι Cambridge, Trinity College, R. 17. 1 (Gallican version)
ϰ Durham, Dean and Chapter Muniments, Misc. Charter 5670
λ London, BL, Arundel 155 (Eadui Psalter)
μ London, BL, Cotton Galba A. xviii (Athelstan Psalter)
ν London, BL, Harley 603 (Harley Psalter)
ξ London, BL, Harley 863
ο London, BL, Harley 2904 (Ramsey Psalter)
π London, BL, Royal 1. E. viii
ϱ Oxford, Bodleian Library, Douce 296 (21870) (Crowland Psalter)
σ Oxford, Bodleian Library, Laud lat. 81 (768)
ς Paris, BN, lat. 8824
τ* Paris, BN, lat. 8846 (Roman version)
τ Paris, BN, lat. 8846 (Gallican version)
υ Rome, Vatican City, Bibliotheca Apostolica Vaticana, Reg. lat. 12 (Bury Psalter)
φ Rouen, Bibliothèque Municipale, 231 (A. 44)
χ Salisbury, Cathedral Library, 180
ψ Utrecht, Universiteitsbibliotheek, 32 (Script. eccl. 484). (Utrecht Psalter)
ω Worcester, Cathedral Library, F. 173, fol. 1*